## The Oxford-Hachette Language Programme

The Oxford-Hachette Language Programme is the result of a unique partnership between two of the world's foremost reference publishers. Its inauguration marked the start of a new age of bilingual dictionaries. The Programme has produced the only French dictionaries to be written using the evidence of scores of millions of words of English and French, drawn from every type of written and spoken language. Each dictionary provides a more accurate, up-to-date, and complete picture of _real_ language than has ever been possible before.

### ● The Bank of French

Capturing current French as it is truly used is the primary aim of The Bank of French, a unique 13-million-word database of current French. The Bank shapes every dictionary entry and translation to meet the needs of today's users, highlighting important constructions, illustrating difficult meanings, and focusing attention on common usage.

### ● The richest choice of words

Combining a comprehensive vocabulary with the full variety of idiomatic and colloquial French is a distinctive element of the Oxford–Hachette Language Programme. The Programme covers standard, regional, and world French. In addition, variant pronunciations and the register of words, from formal right through to taboo, are signalled throughout.

### ● The library of French Literature

From Racine and Balzac to Gide and Camus, a library of the works of the greatest of France's playwrights, poets, and novelists has been included in the Bank of French, enabling the editors of the Programme to analyse and describe the vocabulary and usage of literary French – historical and contemporary – to assist readers and students of French literature.

### ● The British National Corpus

Each English entry ⋯⋯⋯⋯⋯⋯⋯⋯⋯⋯⋯⋯⋯⋯⋯ itish National Corpus, an unrivall⋯⋯⋯⋯⋯⋯⋯⋯⋯⋯⋯ ⋯ds of text representing every kin⋯

# Total Language Accessibility

Oxford's unparalleled reputation in the field of dictionary publishing is founded on more than 150 years of experience. Each dictionary in the range bears the Oxford hallmarks of integrity and authority. The Oxford-Hachette French dictionaries are an integral part of this tradition and offer an unequalled range of carefully-designed benefits to ensure maximum language accessibility.

## ● Rapid Access Design

Oxford's new quick-access page designs and typography have been specially created to ensure exceptional clarity and accessibility. Entries are written in clear, jargon-free language without confusing abbreviations.

## ● Unrivalled practical help

Extended treatment of the core vocabulary offers the user step-by-step guidance on how to translate a given word correctly. Unrivalled practical grammatical help has been built into every dictionary within the range. Thousands of examples are carefully chosen to illustrate the many different nuances of meaning and context. A clear, efficient system of translation signposting guides the user to the most appropriate translation.

## ● Supplementary Information

All the dictionaries in the Oxford-Hachette range offer valuable additional help and information, including verb tables, thematic vocabulary boxes, political and cultural information, guides to effective communication (how to write letters, CVs, book holidays, or take minutes), pronunciation guidance, and colour texts for easy access.

## ● Business, technical, and computing vocabulary

The editors of The Oxford-Hachette Language Programme have provided the widest and most accurate representation of the language of every important specialist field. All translations are checked by a skilled team of specialist translators before being included.

# The Oxford
# **Quick Reference**
# **French**
# Dictionary

FRENCH–ENGLISH
ENGLISH–FRENCH

FRANÇAIS–ANGLAIS
ANGLAIS–FRANÇAIS

*Edited by*
*Edwin Carpenter*
*Dora Carpenter*

French in Context
*prepared by*
*Natalie Pomier*

OXFORD UNIVERSITY PRESS
1998

Oxford University Press, Great Clarendon Street, Oxford OX2 6DP

Oxford  New York

Athens  Auckland  Bangkok  Bogota  Bombay
Buenos Aires  Calcutta  Cape Town  Dar es Salaam
Delhi  Florence  Hong Kong  Istanbul  Karachi
Kuala Lumpur  Madras  Madrid  Melbourne
Mexico City  Nairobi  Paris  Singapore
Taipei  Tokyo  Toronto  Warsaw

and associated companies in
Berlin  Ibadan

Oxford is a trade mark of Oxford University Press
© Oxford University Press 1998

This edition first published 1998

Based on The Oxford French Minidictionary
© Oxford University Press, 1993

British Library Cataloguing in Publication Data
Data available

Library of Congress Cataloging-in-Publication Data
The Oxford quick reference French dictionary / edited by Edwin Carpenter
[and] Dora Carpenter.  1. French language—Dictionaries—English.  2. English
language—Dictionaries—French.  I. Carpenter, Edwin.  II. Carpenter, Dora.
PC2640.086 1998  443'.21—dc21  97–40951

ISBN 0-19-860187-5

10 9 8 7 6 5 4 3 2 1

Printed in Great Britain by
Mackays of Chatham plc
Chatham, Kent

# Contents

............................................................

# Preface

*The Oxford Quick Reference French Dictionary* is the latest addition to the Oxford French Dictionary range. It is specifically designed for beginners of French as an affordable, accessible dictionary with valuable additional help provided by the unique *French in Context* supplement in the middle of the book. *French in Context* is designed to help you build your knowledge of grammar and vocabulary, and provides essential practice in dealing with everyday situations and conversations.

.........................................................

# Pronunciation of French

### Phonetic symbols
### Vowels

| | | | | | | | |
|---|---|---|---|---|---|---|---|
| i | vie | ɑ | bas | y | vêtu | ɛ̃ | matin |
| e | pré | ɔ | mort | ø | peu | ɑ̃ | sans |
| ɛ | lait | o | mot | œ | peur | ɔ̃ | bon |
| a | plat | u | genou | ə | de | œ̃ | lundi |

### Consonants and semi-consonants

| | | | | | | | |
|---|---|---|---|---|---|---|---|
| p | payer | f | feu | m | main | j | yeux |
| b | bon | v | vous | n | nous | w | oui |
| t | terre | s | sale | l | long | ɥ | huile |
| d | dans | z | zero | r | rue | | |
| k | cou | ʃ | chat | ɲ | agneau | | |
| g | gant | ʒ | je | ŋ | camping | | |

*Notes:* ' before the pronunciation of a word beginning with *h* indicates no liaison or elision.

An asterisk immediately following an apostrophe in some words like **qu'\*** shows that this form of the word is used before a vowel or mute 'h'.

.........................................................

# Proprietary terms

This dictionary includes some words which are, or are asserted to be, proprietary terms or trade marks. The presence or absence of such assertions should not be regarded as affecting the legal status of any proprietary name or trade mark.

# Abbreviations / Abréviations

| | | |
|---|---|---|
| abbreviation | *abbr., abrév.* | abréviation |
| adjective(s) | *a. (adjs.)* | adjectif(s) |
| adverb(s) | *adv(s).* | adverbe(s) |
| American | *Amer.* | américain |
| anatomy | *anat.* | anatomie |
| approximately | *approx.* | approximativement |
| archaeology | *archaeol., archéol.* | archéologie |
| architecture | *archit.* | architecture |
| motoring | *auto.* | automobile |
| auxiliary | *aux.* | auxiliaire |
| aviation | *aviat.* | aviation |
| botany | *bot.* | botanique |
| computing | *comput.* | informatique |
| commerce | *comm.* | commerce |
| conjunction(s) | *conj(s).* | conjonction(s) |
| cookery | *culin.* | culinaire |
| electricity | *electr., électr.* | électricité |
| feminine | *f.* | féminin |
| familiar | *fam.* | familier |
| figurative | *fig.* | figuré |
| geography | *geog., géog.* | géographie |
| geology | *geol., géol.* | géologie |
| grammar | *gram.* | grammaire |
| humorous | *hum.* | humoristique |
| interjection(s) | *int(s).* | interjection(s) |
| invariable | *invar.* | invariable |
| legal, law | *jurid.* | juridique |
| language | *lang.* | langue |
| masculine | *m.* | masculin |
| medicine | *med., méd.* | médecine |
| military | *mil.* | militaire |
| music | *mus.* | musique |
| noun(s) | *n(s).* | nom(s) |
| nautical | *naut.* | nautique |
| oneself | *o.s.* | se, soi-même |

| proprietary term | *P.* | marque déposée |
|---|---|---|
| pejorative | *pej., péj.* | péjoratif |
| philosophy | *phil.* | philosophie |
| photography | *photo.* | photographie |
| plural | *pl.* | pluriel |
| politics | *pol.* | politique |
| possessive | *poss.* | possessif |
| past participle | *p.p.* | participe passé |
| prefix | *pref., préf.* | préfixe |
| preposition(s) | *prep(s)., prép(s).* | préposition(s) |
| present participle | *pres. p.* | participe présent |
| pronoun | *pron.* | pronom |
| relative pronoun | *pron. rel.* | pronom relatif |
| psychology | *psych.* | psychologie |
| past tense | *p.t.* | passé |
| something | *qch.* | quelque chose |
| someone | *qn.* | quelqu'un |
| railway | *rail.* | chemin de fer |
| religion | *relig.* | religion |
| relative pronoun | *rel. pron.* | pronom relatif |
| school, scholastic | *schol., scol.* | scolaire |
| singular | *sing.* | singulier |
| slang | *sl.* | argot |
| someone | *s.o.* | quelqu'un |
| something | *sth.* | quelque chose |
| technical | *techn.* | technique |
| television | *TV* | télévision |
| university | *univ.* | université |
| auxiliary verb | *v. aux.* | verb auxiliaire |
| intransitive verb | *v.i.* | verbe intransitif |
| pronominal verb | *v. pr.* | verbe pronominal |
| transitive verb | *v.t.* | verbe transitif |

**a** /a/ *voir* **avoir**.

**à** /a/ *prép.* (*à* + *le* = **au**, *à* + *les* = **aux**) in, at; (*direction*) to; (*temps*) at; (*jusqu'à*) to, till; (*date*) on; (*époque*) in; (*moyen*) by, on; (*prix*) for; (*appartenance*) of; (*mesure*) by. **donner**/*etc.* **à qn.,** give/*etc.* to s.o. **apprendre**/*etc.* **à faire,** learn/*etc.* to do. **l'homme à la barbe,** the man with the beard. **à la radio,** on the radio. **c'est à moi,** it is mine. **dix km à l'heure,** ten km. per hour.

**abaisser** /abese/ *v.t.* lower; (*levier*) pull *ou* push down; (*fig.*) humiliate. **s'∼** *v. pr.* go down, drop; (*fig.*) humiliate o.s. **s'∼ à,** stoop to.

**abandon** /abɑ̃dɔ̃/ *n.m.* abandonment; desertion; (*sport*) withdrawal; (*naturel*) abandon. **à l'∼,** in a state of neglect. **∼ner** /-ɔne/ *v.t.* abandon, desert; (*renoncer à*) give up, abandon.

**abat-jour** /abaʒur/ *n.m. invar.* lampshade.

**abats** /aba/ *n.m. pl.* offal.

**abattement** /abatmɑ̃/ *n.m.* (*comm.*) allowance.

**abattoir** /abatwar/ *n.m.* abattoir.

**abattre** /abatr/ *v.t.* knock down; (*arbre*) cut down; (*animal*) slaughter; (*avion*) shoot down; (*affaiblir*) weaken; (*démoraliser*) dishearten. **s'∼** *v. pr.* come down, fall (down). **se laisser ∼,** let things get one down.

**abbaye** /abei/ *n.f.* abbey.

**abbé** /abe/ *n.m.* priest.

**abcès** /apsɛ/ *n.m.* abscess.

**abdi|quer** /abdike/ *v.t./i.* abdicate. **∼cation** *n.f.* abdication.

**abdom|en** /abdɔmɛn/ *n.m.* abdomen. **∼inal** (*m. pl.* **∼inaux**) *a.* abdominal.

**abeille** /abɛj/ *n.f.* bee.

**aberrant,** **∼e** /abɛrɑ̃, -t/ *a.* absurd.

**abîmer** /abime/ *v.t.* damage, spoil. **s'∼** *v. pr.* get damaged *ou* spoilt.

**abject** /abʒɛkt/ *a.* abject.

**aboiement** /abwamɑ̃/ *n.m.* bark (ing). **∼s,** barking.

**abol|ir** /abɔlir/ *v.t.* abolish. **∼ition** *n.f.* abolition.

**abominable** /abɔminabl/ *a.* abominable.

**abond|ant,** **∼ante** /abɔ̃dɑ̃, -t/ *a.* abundant, plentiful. **∼amment** *adv.* abundantly. **∼ance** *n.f.* abundance; (*prospérité*) affluence.

**abonn|er (s')** /(s)abɔne/ *v. pr.* subscribe (**à,** to). **∼é, ∼ée** *n.m., f.* subscriber; season-ticket holder. **∼ement** *n.m.* (*à un journal*) subscription; (*de bus, théâtre, etc.*) season-ticket.

**abord** /abɔr/ *n.m.* access. **∼s,** surroundings. **d'∼,** first.

**abordable** /abɔrdabl/ *a.* (*prix*) reasonable; (*personne*) approachable.

**abordage** /abɔrdaʒ/ *n.m.* (*accident: naut.*) collision.

**aborder** /abɔrde/ *v.t.* approach; (*lieu*) reach; (*problème etc.*) tackle. ● *v.i.* reach land.

**aboutir** /abutir/ *v.i.* succeed, achieve a result. **∼ à,** end (up) in, lead to. **n'∼ à rien,** come to nothing.

**aboyer** /abwaje/ *v.i.* bark.

**abrasi|f, ∼ve** /abrazif, -v/ *a. & n.m.*

**abréger** /abreʒe/ *v.t.* (*texte*) shorten, abridge; (*mot*) abbreviate, shorten; (*visite*) cut short.

**abreuv|er** /abrœve/ *v.t.* water; (*fig.*) overwhelm (**de,** with). **s'∼er** *v. pr.* drink.

**abréviation** /abrevjɑsjɔ̃/ *n.f.* abbreviation.

**abri** /abri/ *n.m.* shelter. **à l'∼,** under cover. **à l'∼ de** sheltered from.

**abricot** /abriko/ *n.m.* apricot.

**abriter** /abrite/ *v.t.* shelter; (*recevoir*) house. **s'∼** *v. pr.* (take) shelter.

**abrupt** /abrypt/ *a.* steep, sheer; (*fig.*) abrupt.

**abruti, ∼e** /abryti/ *n.m., f.* (*fam.*) idiot.

**absence** /apsɑ̃s/ *n.f.* absence.

**absent, ∼e** /apsɑ̃, -t/ *a.* absent, away; (*chose*) missing. ● *n.m., f.* absentee.

**absenter (s')** /(s)apsɑ̃te/ *v. pr.* go out *ou* be away; (*sortir*) go out, leave.

**absolu** /apsɔly/ *a.* absolute. **∼ment** *adv.* absolutely.

**absor|ber** /apsɔrbe/ *v.t.* absorb; (*temps etc.*) take up. **∼bant, ∼bante** *a.* (*travail etc.*) absorbing; (*matière*) absorbent. **∼ption** *n.f.* absorption.

**absten|ir (s')** /(s)apstənir/ *v. pr.* abstain. **s'∼ir de,** refrain from.

**abstr|aire** /apstrer/ *v.t.* abstract. **∼action** *n.f.* abstraction. **∼ait, ∼aite** *a. & n.m.* abstract.

**absurd|e** /apsyrd/ *a.* absurd. **∼ité** *n.f.* absurdity.

**abus** /aby/ *n.m.* abuse, misuse; (*injustice*) abuse. **∼ de confiance,** breach of trust.

**abuser** /abyze/ *v.t.* deceive. ● *v.i.* go too far. **∼ de,** abuse, misuse; (*profiter de*) take advantage of; (*alcool etc.*) over-indulge in.

**académ|ie** /akademi/ *n.f.* academy; (*circonscription*) educational district. **A∼ie,** Academy. **∼ique** *a.* academic.

**acajou** /akaʒu/ *n.m.* mahogany.

**accablement** /akɑbləmɑ̃/ *n.m.* despondency.

**accabl|er** /akɑble/ *v.t.* overwhelm. ~**ant,** ~**ante** *a.* (*chaleur*) oppressive.

**accaparer** /akapare/ *v.t.* monopolize; (*fig.*) take up all the time of.

**accéder** /aksede/ *v.i.* ~ **à,** reach; (*pouvoir, requête, trône, etc.*) accede to.

**accélér|er** /akselere/ *v.i./i.* (*auto.*)accelerate. ● *v.t.,* **s'**~**er** *v. pr.* speed up. ~**ateur** *n.m.* accelerator. ~**ation** *n.f.* acceleration; speeding up.

**accent** /aksɑ̃/ *n.m.* accent; (*sur une syllabe*) stress, accent; (*ton*) tone. **mettre l'**~ **sur,** stress.

**accent|uer** /aksɑ̃tɥe/ *v.t.* (*lettre, syllabe*) accent; (*fig.*) emphasize, accentuate. **s'**~**uer** *v. pr.* become more pronounced, increase.

**accept|er** /aksɛpte/ *v.t.* accept. ~**er de,** agree to. ~**able** *a.* acceptable. ~**ation** *n.f.* acceptance.

**accès** /aksɛ/ *n.m.* access; (*porte*) entrance; (*de fièvre*) attack; (*de colère*) fit; (*de joie*) (out)burst. **les** ~ **de,** (*voies*) the approaches to. **facile d'**~, easy to get to.

**accessible** /aksesibl/ *a.* accessible; (*personne*) approachable.

**accession** /aksesjɔ̃/ *n.f.* ~ **à,** accession to.

**accessoire** /akseswar/ *a.* secondary. ● *n.m.* accessory; (*théâtre*) prop.

**accident** /aksidɑ̃/ *n.m.* accident. ~ **de train/d'avion,** train/ plane crash. **par** ~, by accident. ~**é** /-te/ *a.* damaged *ou* hurt (in an accident); (*terrain*) uneven, hilly.

**accidentel,** ~**le** /aksidɑ̃tɛl/ *a.* accidental.

**acclam|er** /aklame/ *v.t.* cheer, acclaim. ~**ations** *n.f. pl.* cheers.

**accommodant,** ~**e** /akɔmɔdɑ̃, -t/ *a.* accommodating.

**accommoder** /akɔmɔde/ *v.t.* adapt (**à,** to); (*cuisiner*) prepare; (*assaisonner*) flavour. **s'**~**er de,** be happy with.

**accompagn|er** /akɔ̃paɲe/ *v.t.* accompany. **s'**~**er de,** be accompanied by. ~**ateur,** ~**atrice** *n.m., f.* (*mus.*) accompanist; (*guide*) guide. ~**ement** *n.m.* (*mus.*) accompaniment.

**accompli** /akɔ̃pli/ *a.* accomplished.

**accompl|ir** /akɔ̃plir/ *v.t.* carry out, fulfil. ~**issement** *n.m.* fulfilment.

**accord** /akɔr/ *n.m.* agreement; (*harmonie*) harmony; (*mus.*) chord. **être d'**~, agree (**pour,** to). **se mettre d'**~, come to an agreement, agree. **d'**~**!,** all right!

**accordéon** /akɔrdeɔ̃/ *n.m.* accordion.

**accord|er** /akɔrde/ *v.t.* grant; (*couleurs etc.*) match; (*mus.*) tune. **s'**~**er** *v. pr.* agree. **s'**~**er avec,** (*s'entendre avec*) get on with.

**accotement** /akɔtmɑ̃/ *n.m.* roadside, verge; (*Amer.*) shoulder.

**accouch|er** /akuʃe/ *v.i.* give birth (**de,** to); (*être en travail*) be in labour. ● *v.t.* deliver. ~**ement** *n.m.* childbirth; (*travail*) labour.

**accoud|er (s')** /(s)akude/ *v. pr.* lean (one's elbows) on. ~**oir** *n.m.* armrest.

**accoutumance** /akutymɑ̃s/ *n.f.* habituation; (*méd.*) addiction.

**accro** /akro/ *n.m./f.* (*drogué*) addict; (*amateur*) fan.

**accroc** /akro/ *n.m.* tear, rip; (*fig.*) hitch.

**accroch|er** /akrɔʃe/ *v.t.* (*suspendre*) hang up; (*attacher*) hook, hitch; (*déchirer*) catch; (*heurter*) hit; (*attirer*) attract. **s'**~**er** *v. pr.* cling, hang on; (*se disputer*) clash. ~**age** *n.m.* hanging; hooking; (*auto.*) collision; (*dispute*) clash; (*mil.*) encounter.

**accroissement** /akrwasmɑ̃/ *n.m.* increase (**de,** in).

**accroître** /akrwatr/ *v.t.,* **s'**~ *v. pr.* increase.

**accroup|ir (s')** /(s)akrupir/ *v. pr.* squat. ~**i** *a.* squatting.

**accru** /akry/ *a.* increased, greater.

**accueil** /akœj/ *n.m.* reception, welcome.

**accueill|ir** /akœjir/ *v.t.* receive, welcome; (*aller chercher*) meet. ~**ant,** ~**ante** *a.* friendly.

**accumul|er** /akymyle/ *v.t.,* **s'**~**er** *v. pr.* accumulate, pile up. ~**ateur** *n.m.* accumulator. ~**ation** *n.f.* accumulation.

**accusation** /akyzasjɔ̃/ *n.f.* accusation; (*jurid.*) charge. **l'**~, (*magistrat*) the prosecution.

**accus|er** /akyze/ *v.t.* accuse (**de,** of); (*blâmer*) blame (**de,** for); (*jurid.*) charge (**de,** with); (*fig.*) show, emphasize. ~**é,** ~**ée** *a.* marked; *n.m., f.* accused.

**acharn|é** /aʃarne/ *a.* relentless, ferocious. ~**ement** *n.m.* relentlessness.

**acharner (s')** /(s)aʃarne/ *v. pr.* **s'**~ **sur,** set upon; (*poursuivre*) hound.

**achat** /aʃa/ *n.m.* purchase. ~**s,** shopping. **faire l'**~ **de,** buy.

**achet|er** /aʃte/ *v.t.* buy ~**er à,** buy from; (*pour*) buy for. ~**eur,** ~**euse** *n.m., f.* buyer; (*client de magasin*) shopper.

**achèvement** /aʃɛvmɑ̃/ *n.m.* completion.

**achever** /aʃve/ *v.t.* finish (off). **s'**~ *v. pr.* end.

**acid|e** /asid/ *a.* acid, sharp. ● *n.m.* acid. ~**ité** *n.f.* acidity.

**acier** /asje/ *n.m.* steel. **aciérie** *n.f.* steelworks.

**acné** /akne/ *n.f.* acne.

**acompte** /akɔ̃t/ *n.m.* deposit, part-payment.

**acqu|érir** /akerir/ *v.t.* acquire, gain; (*biens*) purchase, acquire. ~**éreur** *n.m.* purchaser. ~**isition** *n.f.* acquisition; purchase.

**acquiescer** /akjese/ *v.i.* acquiesce, agree.

**acquis,** ~**e** /aki, -z/ *n.m.* experience. ● *a.* acquired; (*fait*) established; (*faveurs*) secured. ~ **à,** (*projet*) in favour of.

**acquit** /aki/ *n.m.* receipt. **par** ~ **de conscience,** for peace of mind.

**acquitt|er** /akite/ *v.t.* acquit; (*dette*) settle. **s'~er de,** (*promesse, devoir*) carry out. **s'~er envers,** repay. **~ement** *n.m.* acquittal; settlement.

**acrobate** /akrɔbat/ *n.m./f.* acrobat.

**acrobatie** /akrɔbasi/ *n.f.* acrobatics. **acrobatique** /-tik/ *a.* acrobatic.

**acte** /akt/ *n.m.* act, action, deed; (*théâtre*) act; (*de naissance, mariage*) certificate.

**acteur** /aktœr/ *n.m.* actor.

**acti|f, ~ve** /aktif, -v/ *a.* active. ● *n.m.* (*comm.*) assets. **~vement** *adv.* actively.

**action** /aksjɔ̃/ *n.f.* action; (*comm.*) share; (*jurid.*) action. **~naire** /-jɔnɛr/ *n.m./f.* shareholder.

**actionner** /aksjɔne/ *v.t.* work, activate.

**activer** /aktive/ *v.t.* speed up; (*feu*) boost. **s'~** *v. pr.* hurry, rush.

**activité** /aktivite/ *n.f.* activity.

**actrice** /aktris/ *n.f.* actress.

**actualiser** /aktɥalize/ *v.t.* update.

**actualité** /aktɥalite/ *n.f.* topicality. **l'~,** current events. **les ~s,** news. **d'~,** topical.

**actuel, ~le** /aktɥɛl/ *a.* present; (*d'actualité*) topical. **~lement** *adv.* at the present time.

**acupunct|ure** /akypɔ̃ktyr/ *n.f.* acupuncture.

**adapt|er** /adapte/ *v.t.* adapt; (*fixer*) fit. **s'~er** *v. pr.* adapt (o.s.); (*techn.*) fit, **~ateur** *n.m.* (*électr.*) adapter. **~ation** *n.f.* adaptation.

**additif** /aditif/ *n.m.* (*note*) rider; (*substance*) additive.

**addition** /adisjɔ̃/ *n.f.* addition; (*au café etc.*) bill. **~ner** /-jɔne/ *v.t.* add; (*totaliser*) add (up).

**adepte** /adɛpt/ *n.m./f.* follower.

**adéquat, ~e** /adekwa, -t/ *a.* suitable.

**adhérent, ~e** /aderɑ̃, -t/ *n.m./f.* member.

**adhé|rer** /adere/ *v.i.* adhere, stick (à, to). **~rer à,** (*club etc.*) be a member of; (*s'inscrire à*) join. **~sif, ~sive** *a.* & *n.m.* adhesive. **~sion** *n.f.* membership; (*accord*) adherence.

**adieu** (*pl.* **~x**) /adjø/ *int.* & *n.m.* goodbye, farewell.

**adjacent, ~e** /adʒasɑ̃, -t/ *a.* adjacent.

**adjectif** /adʒɛktif/ *n.m.* adjective.

**adjoint, ~e** /adʒwɛ̃, -t/ *n.m., f.* & *a.* assistant. **~ au maire,** deputy mayor.

**admettre** /admɛtr/ *v.t.* let in, admit; (*tolérer*) allow; (*reconnaître*) admit; (*candidat*) pass.

**administrati|f, ~ve** /administratif, -v/ *a.* administrative.

**administr|er** /administre/ *v.t.* run, manage. **~ateur, ~atrice** *n.m., f.* administrator, director. **~ation** *n.f.* administration. **A~ation,** Civil Service.

**admirable** /admirabl/ *a.* admirable.

**admirati|f, ~ve** /admiratif, -v/ *a.* admiring.

**admir|er** /admire/ *v.t.* admire. **~ateur, ~atrice** *n.m., f.* admirer. **~ation** *n.f.* admiration.

**admissible** /admisibl/ *a.* admissible; (*candidat*) eligible.

**admission** /admisjɔ̃/ *n.f.* admission.

**adolescen|t, ~te** /adɔlesɑ̃, -t/ *n.m., f.* adolescent. **~ce** *n.f.* adolescence.

**adopt|er** /adɔpte/ *v.t.* adopt. **~ion** /-psjɔ̃/ *n.f.* adoption.

**adopti|f, ~ve** /adɔptif, -v/ *a.* (*enfant*) adopted; (*parents*) adoptive.

**adorable** /adɔrabl/ *a.* delightful, adorable.

**ador|er** /adɔre/ *v.t.* adore; (*relig.*) worship, adore.

**adouci|r** /adusir/ *v.t.* soften. **s'~r** *v. pr.* soften; mellow; ease; (*temps*) become milder. **~ssant** *n.m.* (fabric) softener.

**adresse** /adrɛs/ *n.f.* address; (*habileté*) skill.

**adresser** /adrese/ *v.t.* send; (*écrire l'adresse sur*) address; (*remarque etc.*) address. **~ la parole à,** speak to. **s'~ à,** address; (*aller voir*) go and ask ou see; (*bureau*) enquire at; (*viser, intéresser*) be directed at.

**adroit, ~e** /adrwa, -t/ *a.* skilful, clever. **~ement** /-tmɑ̃/ *adv.* skilfully, cleverly.

**adulte** /adylt/ *n.m./f.* adult. ● *a.* adult.

**adultère** /adyltɛr/ *a.* adulterous. ● *n.m.* adultery.

**adverbe** /advɛrb/ *n.m.* adverb.

**adversaire** /advɛrsɛr/ *n.m.* opponent, adversary.

**adverse** /advɛrs/ *a.* opposing.

**aér|er** /aere/ *v.t.* air; (*texte*) lighten. **s'~er** *v. pr.* get some air. **~ation** *n.f.* ventilation. **~é** *a.* airy.

**aérien, ~ne** /aerjɛ̃, -jɛn/ *a.* air; (*photo*) aerial; (*câble*) overhead; (*fig.*) airy.

**aérobic** /aerɔbik/ *m.* aerobics.

**aérodrome** /aerɔdrom/ *n.m.* aerodrome.

**aérodynamique** /aerɔdinamik/ *a.* streamlined, aerodynamic.

**aérogare** /aerɔgar/ *n.f.* air terminal.

**aéroglisseur** /aerɔglisœr/ *n.m.* hovercraft.

**aérogramme** /aerɔgram/ *n.m.* airmail letter; (*Amer.*) aerogram.

**aéronautique** /aerɔnotik/ *a.* aeronautical. ● *n.f.* aeronautics.

**aéronavale** /aerɔnaval/ *n.f.* Fleet Air Arm; (*Amer.*) Naval Air Force.

**aéroport** /aerɔpɔr/ *n.m.* airport.

**aérosol** /aerɔsɔl/ *n.m.* aerosol.

**affaibl|ir** /afeblir/ *v.t.* **s'~ir** *v. pr.* weaken. **~issement** *n.m.* weakening.

**affaire** /afɛr/ *n.f.* matter, affair; (*histoire*) affair; (*transaction*) deal; (*occasion*) bargain; (*firme*) business; (*jurid.*) case. **~s,** affairs; (*comm.*) business; (*effets*) belongings. **avoir ~**

**à,** (have to) deal with. **ce sont mes ~s,** that is my business. **faire l'~,** do the job. **tirer qn. d'~,** help s.o. out.

**affairé** /afere/ *a.* busy.

**affaissement** /afɛsmã/ *n.m.* subsidence.

**affaler (s')** /(s)afale/ *v. pr.* slump (down), collapse.

**affamé** /afame/ *a.* starving.

**affect|é** /afɛkte/ *a.* affected. **~ation**[1] *n.f.* affectation.

**affect|er** /afɛkte/ *v.t.* (*feindre, émouvoir*) affect; (*destiner*) assign; (*nommer*) appoint, post. **~ation** *n.f.* assignment; appointment, posting.

**affecti|f, ~ve** /afɛktif, -v/ *a.* emotional.

**affection** /afɛksjɔ̃/ *n.f.* affection; (*maladie*) ailment. **~ner** /-jɔne/ *v.t.* be fond of.

**affectueu|x, ~se** /afɛktɥø, -z/ *a.* affectionate.

**affiche** /afiʃ/ *n.f.* (public) notice; (*publicité*) poster; (*théâtre*) bill.

**affich|er** /afiʃe/ *v.t.* (*announce*) put up; (*événement*) announce; (*sentiment etc., comput.*) display. **~age** *n.m.* billposting; (*électronique*) display.

**affiner** /afine/ *v.t.* refine.

**affirmati|f, ~ve** /afirmatif, -v/ *a.* affirmative. ● *n.f.* affirmative.

**affirm|er** /afirme/ *v.t.* assert. **~ation** *n.f.* assertion.

**affligé** /afliʒe/ *a.* distressed.

**affluence** /aflyãs/ *n.f.* crowd(s).

**affluent** /aflyã/ *n.m.* tributary.

**afflux** /afly/ *n.m.* influx, flood; (*du sang*) rush.

**affol|er (s')** /(s)afole/ *v. pr.* panic. **~ant, ~ante** *a.* alarming. **~ement** *n.m.* panic.

**affranch|ir** /afrãʃir/ *v.t.* stamp; (*à la machine*) frank; (*fig.*) free. **~issement** *n.m.* (*tarif*) postage.

**affréter** /afrete/ *v.t.* charter.

**affreu|x, ~se** /afrø, -z/ *a.* (*laid*) hideous; (*mauvais*) awful. **~sement** *adv.* awfully, hideously.

**affront** /afrɔ̃/ *n.m.* affront.

**affront|er** /afrɔ̃te/ *v.t.* confront. **s'~er** *v. pr.* confront each other.

**afin** /afɛ̃/ *prép. & conj.* **~ de/que,** in order to/that.

**africain, ~e** /afrikɛ̃, -ɛn/ *a. & n.m., f.* African.

**Afrique** /afrik/ *n.f.* Africa. **~ du Sud,** South Africa.

**agacer** /agase/ *v.t.* irritate, annoy.

**âge** /aʒ/ *n.m.* age. **quel ~ avez-vous?,** how old are you?

**âgé** /aʒe/ *a.* elderly. **~ de cinq ans**/*etc.*, five years/*etc.* old.

**agence** /aʒãs/ *n.f.* agency, bureau, office; (*succursale*) branch. **~ d'interim,** employment agency. **~ de voyages,** travel agency.

**agenc|er** /aʒãse/ *v.t.* organize, arrange. **~ement** *n.m.* organization.

**agenda** /aʒɛ̃da/ *n.m.* diary.

**agenouiller (s')** /(s)aʒnuje/ *v. pr.* kneel (down).

**agent** /aʒã/ *n.m.* **~ (de police),** policeman. **~ de change,** stockbroker.

**agglomération** /aglɔmerasjɔ̃/ *n.f.* built-up area, town.

**aggloméré** /aglɔmere/ *n.m.* (*bois*) chipboard.

**agglomérer** /aglɔmere/ *v.t.*, **s'~** *v. pr.* pile up.

**agglutiner** /aglytine/ *v.t.*, **s'~** *v. pr.* stick together.

**aggraver** /agrave/ *v.t.*, **s'~** *v. pr.* worsen.

**agil|e** /aʒil/ *a.* agile, nimble. **~ité** *n.f.* agility.

**agir** /aʒir/ *v.i.* act. **il s'agit de faire,** it is a matter of doing; (*il faut*) it is necessary to do. **dans ce livre il s'agit de,** this book is about. **dont il s'agit,** in question.

**agité** /aʒite/ *a.* restless, fidgety; (*troublé*) agitated; (*mer*) rough.

**agit|er** /aʒite/ *v.t.* (*bras etc.*) wave; (*liquide*) shake. **s'~er** *v. pr.* bustle about; (*enfant*) fidget; (*foule, pensées*) stir. **~ateur, ~atrice** *n.m.,f.* agitator. **~ation** *n.f.* bustle; (*trouble*) agitation.

**agneau** (*pl.* **~x**) /aɲo/ *n.m.* lamb.

**agraf|e** /agraf/ *n.f.* hook; (*pour papiers*) staple. **~er** *v.t.* hook (up); staple. **~euse** *n.f.* stapler.

**agrand|ir** /agrãdir/ *v.t.* enlarge. **s'~ir** *v. pr.* expand, grow. **~issement** *n.m.* extension; (*de photo*) enlargement.

**agréable** /agreabl/ *a.* pleasant. **~ment** /-əmã/ *adv.* pleasantly.

**agré|er** /agree/ *v.t.* accept. **~é à** *a.* authorized.

**agress|er** /agrese/ *v.t.* attack. **~eur** /-ɛsœr/ *n.m.* attacker; (*mil.*) aggressor. **~ion** /-ɛsjɔ̃/ *n.f.* attack; (*mil.*) aggression.

**agressi|f, ~ve** /agresif, -v/ *a.* aggressive. **~vité** *n.f.* aggressiveness.

**agricole** /agrikɔl/ *a.* agricultural; (*ouvrier etc.*) farm.

**agriculteur** /agrikyltœr/ *n.m.* farmer.

**agriculture** /agrikyltyr/ *n.f.* agriculture, farming.

**agripper** /agripe/ *v.t.*, **s'~ à,** grab, clutch.

**agroalimentaire** /agrɔalimãter/ *n.m.* food industry.

**agrumes** /agrym/ *n.m. pl.* citrus fruit(s).

**ah** /a/ *int.* ah, oh.

**ahur|ir** /ayrir/ *v.t.* dumbfound. **~issement** *n.m.* stupefaction.

**ai** /e/ *voir* **avoir.**

**aide** /ɛd/ *n.f.* help, assistance, aid. ● *n.m./f.* assistant. **à l'~ de**, with the help of. **~ mémoire** *n.m. invar.* handbook of facts. **venir en ~ à**, help.

**aider** /ede/ *v.t./i.* help, assist. **~ à faire**, help to do. **s'~ de**, use.

**aïe** /aj/ *int.* ouch, ow.

**aigle** /ɛgl/ *n.m.* eagle.

**aigr|e** /ɛgr/ *a.* sour, sharp; (*fig.*) sharp. **~eurs d'estomac**, heartburn.

**aigrir** /egrir/ *v.t.* embitter; (*caractère*) sour. **être aigre**, be embittered.

**aigu, ~ë** /egy/ *a.* acute; (*objet*) sharp; (*voix*) shrill. (*mus.*) **les ~s**, the high notes.

**aiguillage** /eguijaʒ/ *n.m.* (*rail.*) points; (*rail., Amer.*) switches.

**aiguille** /eguij/ *n.f.* needle; (*de montre*) hand; (*de balance*) pointer.

**aiguill|er** /eguije/ *v.t.* shunt; (*fig.*) steer. **~eur** *n.m.* pointsman. **~eur du ciel**, air traffic controller.

**aiguiser** /eg(ɥ)ize/ *v.t.* sharpen; (*fig.*) stimulate.

**ail** (*pl.* **~s**) /aj/ *n.m.* garlic.

**aile** /ɛl/ *n.f.* wing.

**ailé** /ele/ *a.* winged.

**aille** /aj/ *voir* **aller¹**.

**ailleurs** /ajœr/ *adv.* elsewhere. **d'~**, besides, moreover. **par ~**, moreover, furthermore. **partout ~**, everywhere else.

**ailloli** /ajɔli/ *n.m.* garlic mayonnaise.

**aimable** /ɛmabl/ *a.* kind. **~ment** /-əmɑ̃/ *adv.* kindly.

**aimant¹** /ɛmɑ̃/ *n.m.* magnet. **~er** /-te/ *v.t.* magnetize.

**aimant², ~e** /ɛmɑ̃, -t/ *a.* loving.

**aimer** /eme/ *v.t.* like; (*d'amour*) love. **j'aimerais faire**, I'd like to do. **~ bien**, quite like. **~ mieux** *ou* **autant**, prefer.

**aine** /ɛn/ *n.f.* groin.

**aîné, ~e** /ene/ *a.* eldest; (*entre deux*) elder. ● *n.m., f.* eldest (child); elder (child).

**ainsi** /ɛ̃si/ *adv.* thus; (*donc*) so. **~ que**, as well as; (*comme*) as. **et ~ de suite**, and so on. **pour ~ dire**, so to speak, as it were.

**air** /ɛr/ *n.m.* air; (*mine*) look, air; (*mélodie*) tune. **~s** *n.m. pl.* airs. **avoir l'~ de**, look like. **avoir l'~ de faire**, appear to be doing. **en l'~**, (up) in the air; (*promesses etc.*) empty.

**aire** /ɛr/ *n.f.* area. **~ d'atterrissage**, landing-strip.

**aisance** /ɛzɑ̃s/ *n.f.* ease; (*richesse*) affluence.

**aise** /ɛz/ *n.f.* joy. ● *a.* **à l'~, (sur un siège)** comfortable; (*pas gêné*) at ease; (*fortuné*) comfortably off. **mal à l'~**, uncomfortable; ill at ease. **se mettre à l'~**, make o.s. comfortable.

**aisé** /eze/ *a.* easy; (*fortuné*) well-off. **~ment** *adv.* easily.

**aisselle** /ɛsɛl/ *n.f.* armpit.

**ait** /ɛ/ *voir* **avoir**.

**ajourn|er** /aʒurne/ *v.t.* postpone; (*assemblée*) adjourn. **~ement** *n.m.* postponement; adjournment.

**ajout** /aʒu/ *n.m.* addition.

**ajouter** /aʒute/ *v.t.* **s'~** *v. pr.* add (à, to). **~ foi à**, lend credence to.

**ajust|er** /aʒyste/ **s'~er** *v. pr.* fit. **~é** *a.* close-fitting. **~ement** *n.m.* adjustment. **~eur** *n.m.* fitter.

**alarme** /alarm/ *n.f.* alarm. **donner l'~,** sound the alarm.

**alarmer** /alarme/ *v.t.* alarm. **s'~** *v. pr.* become alarmed (**de**, at).

**alarmiste** /alarmist/ *a. & n.m.* alarmist.

**albatros** /albatros/ *n.m.* albatross.

**album** /albɔm/ *n.m.* album.

**albumine** /albymin/ *n.f.* albumin.

**alcool** /alkɔl/ *n.m.* alcohol; (*eau de vie*) brandy. **~ à brûler**, methylated spirit. **~ique** *a. & n.m./f.* alcoholic. **~isé** *a.* (*boisson*) alcoholic. **~isme** *n.m.* alcoholism.

**alcootest** /alkɔtɛst/ *n.m.* (P.) breath test; (*appareil*) breathalyser.

**alcôve** /alkov/ *n.f.* alcove.

**alentour** /alɑ̃tur/ *adv.* around. **~s** *n.m. pl.* surroundings. **aux ~s de**, round about.

**alerte** /alɛrt/ *n.f.* alert. **~ à la bombe**, bomb scare.

**alerter** /alɛrte/ *v.t.* alert.

**alg|èbre** /alʒɛbr/ *n.f.* algebra. **~ébrique** *a.* algebraic.

**Alger** /alʒe/ *n.m./f.* Algiers.

**Algérie** /alʒeri/ *n.f.* Algeria.

**algérien, ~ne** /alʒerjɛ̃, -jɛn/ *a. & n.m., f.* Algerian.

**algue** /alg/ *n.f.* seaweed. **les ~s**, (*bot.*) algae.

**alias** /aljɑs/ *adv.* alias.

**alibi** /alibi/ *n.m.* alibi.

**aligner** /aliɲe/ *v.t.* (*objets*) line up, make lines of; (*chiffres*) string together. **s'~** *v. pr.* line up. **s'~ sur**, align o.s. on. **alignement** /-əmɑ̃/ *n.m.* alignment.

**aliment** /alimɑ̃/ *n.m.* food. **~aire** /-tɛr/ *a.* food; (*fig.*) bread-and-butter.

**aliment|er** /alimɑ̃te/ *v.t.* feed; (*fournir*) supply; (*fig.*) sustain. **~ation** *n.f.* feeding; supply(ing); (*régime*) diet.

**allaiter** /alete/ *v.t.* feed. **~ au biberon**, bottle-feed. **~ au sein**, breast-feed; (*Amer.*) nurse.

**allée** /ale/ *n.f.* path, lane; (*menant à une maison*) drive(way). **~s et venues,** comings and goings.

**allégation** /alegɑsjɔ̃/ *n.f.* allegation.

**allég|er** /aleʒe/ *v.t.* make lighter; (*poids*) lighten; (*fig.*) alleviate. **~é** *a.* (*diététique*) light.

**Allemagne** /almaɲ/ *n.f.* Germany.

**allemand,** ~**e** /almɑ̃, -d/ a. & n.m., f. German. ● n.m. (lang.) German.

**aller**[1] /ale/ (aux. être) go. **s'en** ~ v. pr. go away. ~ **à,** (convenir à) suit; (s'adapter à) fit. ~ **faire,** be going to do. **comment allez-vous?, (comment) ça va?,** how are you? **ça va!,** all right! **il va bien,** he is well. **il va mieux,** he's better. **allez-y!,** go on! **allez!,** come on! **allons-y!,** let's go!

**aller**[2] /ale/ n.m. outward journey; ~ **(simple),** single (ticket); (Amer.) one-way (ticket). ~ **(et) retour,** return journey; (Amer.) round trip; (billet) return (ticket); (Amer.) round trip (ticket).

**allerg|ie** /alɛrʒi/ n.f. allergy. ~**ique** a. allergic.

**alliance** /aljɑ̃s/ n.f. alliance; (bague) wedding-ring.

**allié,** ~**e** /alje/ n.m., f. ally.

**alligator** /aligatɔr/ n.m. alligator.

**allô** /alo/ int. hallo, hello.

**allocation** /alɔkasjɔ̃/ n.f. allowance. ~ **(de) chômage,** unemployment benefit. ~**s familiales,** family allowance.

**allongé** /alɔ̃ʒe/ a. elongated.

**allongement** /alɔ̃ʒmɑ̃/ n.m. lengthening.

**allonger** /alɔ̃ʒe/ v.t. lengthen; (bras, jambe) stretch (out). **s'**~ v. pr. get longer; (s'étendre) stretch (o.s.) out.

**allum|er** /alyme/ v.t. light; (radio, lampe, etc.) turn on; (pièce) switch the light(s) on in. **s'**~**er** v. pr. (lumière) come on. ~**age** n.m. lighting; (auto.) ignition. ~**e-gaz** n.m. invar. gas lighter.

**allumette** /alymɛt/ n.f. match.

**allure** /alyr/ n.f. speed, pace; (démarche) walk; (prestance) bearing; (air) look. **à toute** ~**,** at full speed. **avoir de l'**~**,** have style.

**allusion** /alyzjɔ̃/ n.f. allusion (**à,** to); (implicite) hint (**à,** at). **faire** ~ **à,** allude to; hint at.

**alors** /alɔr/ adv. then. ● conj. so, then. ~ **que,** when, while; (tandis que) whereas. **ça** ~**l,** well! **et** ~**?,** so what?

**alouette** /alwɛt/ n.f. lark.

**alourdir** /alurdir/ v.t. weigh down.

**aloyau** (pl. ~**x**) /alwajo/ n.m. sirloin.

**Alpes** /alp/ n.f. pl. **les** ~**,** the Alps.

**alpestre** /alpɛstr/ a. alpine.

**alphab|et** /alfabɛ/ n.m. alphabet. ~**étique** a. alphabetical.

**alpinis|te** /alpinist/ n.m./f. mountaineer. ~**me** n.m. mountaineering.

**altér|er** /altere/ v.t. falsify; (abîmer) spoil. **s'**~**er** v. pr. deteriorate.

**alternati|f,** ~**ve** /altɛrnatif, -v/ a. alternating. ● n.f. alternative. ~**vement** adv. alternately.

**altern|er** /altɛrne/ v.t./i. alternate. ~**ance** n.f. alternation. **en** ~**ance,** alternately.

**altitude** /altityd/ n.f. altitude, height.

**aluminium** /alyminjɔm/ n.m. aluminium.

**amabilité** /amabilite/ n.f. kindness.

**amaigr|ir** /amegrir/ v.t. make thin(ner). ~**issant,** ~**issante** a. (régime) slimming.

**amalgam|e** /amalgam/ n.m. combination. ~**er** v.t. combine, amalgamate.

**amande** /amɑ̃d/ n.f. almond; (d'un fruit à noyau) kernel.

**amant** /amɑ̃/ n.m. lover.

**amarr|e** /amar/ n.f. (mooring) rope. ~**es,** moorings. ~**er** v.t. moor.

**amas** /amɑ/ n.m. heap, pile.

**amasser** /amase/ v.t. amass, gather; (empiler) pile up.

**amateur** /amatœr/ n.m. amateur. ~ **de,** lover of. **d'**~**,** amateur; (péj.) amateurish.

**Amazonie** /amazɔni/ n.f. Amazonia.

**ambassade** /ɑ̃basad/ n.f. embassy.

**ambassa|deur** /ɑ̃basadœr, -dris/ n.m., f. ambassador.

**ambiance** /ɑ̃bjɑ̃s/ n.f. atmosphere.

**ambigu,** ~**ë** /ɑ̃bigy/ a. ambiguous. ~**ïté** /-ɥite/ n.f. ambiguity.

**ambitieu|x,** ~**se** /ɑ̃bisjø, -z/ a. ambitious.

**ambition** /ɑ̃bisjɔ̃/ n.f. ambition.

**ambre** /ɑ̃br/ n.m. amber.

**ambulanc|e** /ɑ̃bylɑ̃s/ n.f. ambulance. ~**ier,** ~**ière** n.m., f. ambulance driver.

**ambulant,** ~**e** /ɑ̃bylɑ̃, -t/ a. itinerant.

**âme** /ɑm/ n.f. soul.

**améior|er** /ameljɔre/ v.t., **s'**~**er** v. pr. improve. ~**ation** n.f. improvement.

**aménag|er** /amenaʒe/ v.t. (arranger) fit out; (transformer) convert; (installer) fit up; (territoire) develop. ~**ement** n.m. fitting out; conversion; fitting up; development; (modification) adjustment.

**amende** /amɑ̃d/ n.f. fine.

**amendement** /amɑ̃dmɑ̃/ n.m. (de texte) amendment.

**amener** /amne/ v.t. bring; (causer) bring about. ~ **qn. à faire,** cause sb. to do. **s'**~ v. pr. (fam.) come along.

**amer, amère** /amɛr/ a. bitter.

**américain,** ~**e** /amerikɛ̃, -ɛn/ a. & n.m., f. American.

**Amérique** /amerik/ n.f. America. ~ **centrale/latine,** Central/ Latin America. ~ **du Nord/Sud,** North/South America.

**amertume** /amɛrtym/ n.f. bitterness.

**ami,** ~**e** /ami/ n.m., f. friend; (de la nature, des livres, etc.) lover. ● a. friendly.

**amiable** /amjabl/ a. amicable. **à l'**~ adv. amicably; a. amicable.

**amiante** /amjɑ̃t/ n.m. asbestos.

**amic|al** (m. pl. ~**aux**) /amikal, -o/ a. friendly. ~**alement** adv. in a friendly manner.

**amicale** /amikal/ n.f. association.

**amidon** /amidɔ̃/ *n.m.* starch.

**amincir** /amɛ̃sir/ *v.t.* make thinner. **s'~** *v. pr.* get thinner.

**amir|al** (*pl.* **~aux**) /amiral,-o/ *n.m.* admiral.

**amitié** /amitje/ *n.f.* friendship. **~s,** kind regards.

**ammoniac** /amɔnjak/ *n.m.* (*gaz*) ammonia.

**ammoniaque** /amɔnjak/ *n.f.* (*eau*) ammonia.

**amnésie** /amnezi/ *n.f.* amnesia.

**amnistie** /amnisti/ *n.f.* amnesty.

**amoindrir** /amwɛ̃drir/ *v.t.* diminish.

**amonceler** /amɔ̃sle/ *v.t.*, **s'~** *v.pr.* pile up.

**amont (en)** /(ɑ̃n)amɔ̃/ *adv.* upstream.

**amorc|e** /amɔrs/ *n.f.* bait; (*début*) start. **~er** *v.t.* start; (*hameçon*) bait; (*pompe*) prime.

**amortir** /amɔrtir/ *v.t.* (*choc*) cushion; (*bruit*) deaden; (*dette*) pay off; (*objet acheté*) make pay for itself.

**amortisseur** /amɔrtisœr/ *n.m.* shock absorber.

**amour** /amur/ *n.m.* love. **~-propre** *n.m.* self-respect.

**amoureu|x, ~se** /amurø, -z/ *a.* (*ardent*) amorous; (*vie*) love. ● *n.m., f.* lover. **~x de qn.,** in love with s.o.

**amovible** /amɔvibl/ *a.* removable.

**ampère** /ɑ̃pɛr/ *n.m.* amp(ere).

**amphithéâtre** /ɑ̃fiteatr/ *n.m.* amphitheatre; (*d'université*) lecture hall.

**ample** /ɑ̃pl/ *a.* ample; (*mouvement*) broad. **~ment** /-əmɑ̃/ *adv.* amply.

**ampleur** /ɑ̃plœr/ *n.f.* extent, size; (*de vêtement*) fullness.

**ampli** /ɑ̃pli/ *n.m.* amplifier.

**amplif|ier** /ɑ̃plifje/ *v.t.* amplify; (*fig.*) expand, develop. **s'~ier** *v.pr.* expand, develop. **~icateur** *n.m.* amplifier.

**ampoule** /ɑ̃pul/ *n.f.* (*électrique*) bulb; (*sur la peau*) blister; (*de médicament*) phial.

**amput|er** /ɑ̃pyte/ *v.t.* amputate; (*fig.*) reduce. **~ation** *n.f.* amputation; (*fig.*) reduction.

**amuse-gueule** /amyzɡœl/ *n.m. invar.* appetizer.

**amus|er** /amyze/ *v.t.* amuse. **s'~er** *v. pr.* enjoy o.s.; (*jouer*) play. **~ant, ~ante** *a.* funny.

**amygdale** /amidal/ *n.f.* tonsil.

**an** /ɑ̃/ *n.m.* year. **avoir dix**/*etc.* **ans,** be ten/*etc.* years old.

**analgésique** /analʒezik/ *a.* & *n.m.* analgesic.

**analog|ie** /analɔʒi/ *n.f.* analogy. **~ique** *a.* analogical, (*comput.*) analogue.

**analogue** /analɔɡ/ *a.* similar.

**analphabète** /analfabɛt/ *a.* & *n.m./f.* illiterate.

**analy|se** /analiz/ *n.f.* analysis; (*de sang*) test. **~ser** *v.t.* analyse. **~ste** *n.m./f.* analyst. **~tique** *a.* analytical.

**ananas** /anana(s)/ *n.m.* pineapple.

**anarch|ie** /anarʃi/ *n.f.* anarchy. **~ique** *a.* anarchic.

**anatom|ie** /anatɔmi/ *n.f.* anatomy. **~ique** *a.* anatomical.

**ancêtre** /ɑ̃sɛtr/ *n.m.* ancestor.

**anchois** /ɑ̃ʃwa/ *n.m.* anchovy.

**ancien, ~ne** /ɑ̃sjɛ̃, -jɛn/ *a.* old; (*de jadis*) ancient; (*meuble*) antique; (*précédent*) former, ex-, old; (*dans une fonction*) senior. ● *n.m., f.* senior; (*par l'âge*) elder.

**ancre** /ɑ̃kr/ *n.f.* anchor.

**âne** /ɑn/ *n.m.* donkey, ass; (*imbécile*) ass.

**anéantir** /aneɑ̃tir/ *v.t.* destroy; (*accabler*) overwhelm.

**aném|ie** /anemi/ *n.f.* anaemia. **~ié, ~ique** *adjs.* anaemic.

**anesthés|ie** /anɛstezi/ *n.f.* (*opération*) anaesthetic. **~ique** *a.* & *n.m.* (*substance*) anaesthetic.

**ange** /ɑ̃ʒ/ *n.m.* angel.

**angine** /ɑ̃ʒin/ *n.f.* throat infection.

**anglais, ~e** /ɑ̃ɡlɛ, -z/ *a.* English. ● *n.m., f.* Englishman, Englishwoman. ● *n.m.* (*lang.*) English.

**angle** /ɑ̃ɡl/ *n.m.* angle; (*coin*) corner.

**Angleterre** /ɑ̃ɡlətɛr/ *n.f.* England.

**anglicisme** /ɑ̃ɡlisism/ *n.m.* anglicism.

**anglo-** /ɑ̃ɡlɔ/ *préf.* Anglo-.

**anglophone** /ɑ̃ɡlɔfɔn/ *a.* English-speaking. ● *n.m./f.* English speaker.

**angoiss|e** /ɑ̃ɡwas/ *n.f.* anxiety. **~ant, ~ante** *a.* harrowing. **~é** *a.* anxious. **~er** *v.t.* make anxious.

**anguleux, ~se** /ɑ̃ɡylø, -z/ *a.* (*traits*) angular.

**anim|al** (*pl.* **~aux**) /animal, -o/ *n.m.* animal. ● *a.* (*m. pl.* **~aux**) animal.

**anima|teur, ~trice** /animatœr, -tris/ *n.m., f.* organizer, leader; (*TV*) host, hostess.

**animé** /anime/ *a.* lively; (*affairé*) busy.

**animer** /anime/ *v.t.* liven up; (*mener*) lead; (*mouvoir, pousser*) drive; (*encourager*) spur on. **s'~** *v. pr.* liven up.

**anis** /anis/ *n.m.* (*parfum, boisson*) aniseed.

**anneau** (*pl.* **~x**) /ano/ *n.m.* ring; (*de chaîne*) link.

**année** /ane/ *n.f.* year.

**annexe** /anɛks/ *a.* attached; (*question*) related. (*bâtiment*) adjoining. ● *n.f.* annexe; (*Amer.*) annex.

**annexer** /anɛkse/ *v.t.* annex; (*document*) attach.

**anniversaire** /anivɛrsɛr/ *n.m.* birthday; (*d'un événement*) anniversary. ● *a.* anniversary.

**annonc|e** /anɔ̃s/ *n.f.* announcement; (*publicitaire*) advertisement; (*indice*) sign. **~er** *v.t.* announce; (*dénoter*) indicate.

**annuaire** /anɥɛr/ *n.m.* year-book. ∼ **(téléphonique),** (telephone) directory.

**annuel, ∼le** /anɥɛl/ *a.* annual, yearly. ∼**lement** *adv.* annually, yearly.

**annul|er** /anyle/ *v.t.* cancel. ∼**ation** *n.f.* cancellation.

**anodin, ∼e** /anɔdɛ̃, -in/ *a.* insignificant; (*blessure*) harmless.

**anomalie** /anɔmali/ *n.f.* anomaly.

**anonyme** /anɔnim/ *a.* anonymous.

**anorak** /anɔrak/ *n.m.* anorak.

**anorexie** /anɔreksi/ *n.f.* anorexia.

**anorm|al** (*m. pl.* ∼**aux**) /anɔrmal, -o/ *a.* abnormal.

**antagonis|me** /ɑ̃tagɔnism/ *n.m.* antagonism. ∼**te** *n.m./f.* antagonist; *a.* antagonistic.

**antarctique** /ɑ̃tarktik/ *a. & n.m.* Antarctic.

**antenne** /ɑ̃tɛn/ *n.f.* aerial; (*Amer.*) antenna; (*d'insecte*) antenna; (*succursale*) agency.

**antérieur** /ɑ̃terjœr/ *a.* previous, earlier; (*placé devant*) front. ∼ **à,** prior to.

**anthologie** /ɑ̃tɔlɔʒi/ *n.f.* anthology.

**anthropolo|gie** /ɑ̃trɔpɔlɔʒi/ *n.f.* anthropology. ∼**gue** *n.m./f.* anthropologist.

**anti-** /ɑ̃ti/ *préf.* anti-.

**antiadhési|f, ∼ve** /ɑ̃tiadezif, -v/ *a.* nonstick.

**antibiotique** /ɑ̃tibjɔtik/ *n.m.* antibiotic.

**anticonceptionnel, ∼le** /ɑ̃tikɔ̃sɛpsjɔnɛl/ *a.* contraceptive.

**anticorps** /ɑ̃tikɔr/ *n.m.* antibody.

**anticyclone** /ɑ̃tisyklon/ *n.m.* anticyclone.

**antidote** /ɑ̃tidɔt/ *n.m.* antidote.

**antigel** /ɑ̃tiʒɛl/ *n.m.* antifreeze.

**antihistaminique** /ɑ̃tiistaminik/ *a. & n.m.* antihistamine.

**antillais, ∼e** /ɑ̃tijɛ, -z/ *a. & n.m., f.* West Indian.

**Antilles** /ɑ̃tij/ *n.f. pl.* **les ∼,** the West Indies.

**antilope** /ɑ̃tilɔp/ *n.f.* antelope.

**antipath|ie** /ɑ̃tipati/ *n.f.* antipathy. ∼**ique** *a.* unpleasant.

**antiquaire** /ɑ̃tikɛr/ *n.m./f.* antique dealer.

**antiqu|e** /ɑ̃tik/ *a.* ancient. ∼**ité** *n.f.* antiquity; (*objet*) antique.

**antiseptique** /ɑ̃tisɛptik/ *a. & n.m.* antiseptic.

**antivol** /ɑ̃tivɔl/ *n.m.* anti-theft lock or device.

**anus** /anys/ *n.m.* anus.

**anxiété** /ɑ̃ksjete/ *n.f.* anxiety.

**anxieu|x, ∼se** /ɑ̃ksjø, -z/ *a.* anxious. ● *n.m., f.* worrier.

**août** /u(t)/ *n.m.* August.

**apaiser** /apeze/ *v.t.* calm down, (*douleur, colère*) soothe (*faim*) appease.

**apath|ie** /apati/ *n.f.* apathy. ∼**ique** *a.* apathetic.

**apercevoir** /apɛrsəvwar/ *v.t.* see. **s'∼ de,** notice. **s'∼ que,** notice *ou* realize that.

**apéritif** /aperitif/ *n.m.* aperitif.

**à-peu-près** /apøprɛ/ *n.m. invar.* approximation.

**apeuré** /apœre/ *a.* scared.

**aphte** /aft/ *n.m.* mouth ulcer.

**apit|oyer** /apitwaje/ *v.t.* move (to pity). **s'∼oyer sur,** feel pity for. ∼**oiement** *n.m.* pity.

**aplatir** /aplatir/ *v.t.* flatten (out). **s'∼** *v. pr.* (*s'allonger*) lie flat; (*s'humilier*) grovel; (*tomber: fam.*) fall flat on one's face.

**aplomb** /aplɔ̃/ *n.m.* balance; (*fig.*) self-possession.

**apparaître?** /aparɛtr/ *v.i.* appear.

**appareil** /aparɛj/ *n.m.* apparatus; (*électrique*) appliance; (*anat.*) system; (*téléphonique*) phone; (*dentaire*) brace; (*auditif*) hearing-aid; (*avion*) plane; (*culin.*) mixture. **l'∼ du parti,** the party machinery. **c'est Gabriel à l'∼,** it's Gabriel on the phone. ∼**(-photo),** camera. ∼ **électroménager,** household electrical appliance.

**appareiller** /apareje/ *v.i.* (*navire*) cast off, put to sea.

**apparemment** /aparamɑ̃/ *adv.* apparently.

**apparence** /aparɑ̃s/ *n.f.* appearance.

**apparent, ∼e** /aparɑ̃, -t/ *a.* apparent; (*visible*) conspicuous.

**appariteur** /aparitœr/ *n.m.* (*univ.*) attendant, porter.

**apparition** /aparisjɔ̃/ *n.f.* appearance; (*spectre*) apparition.

**appartement** /apartəmɑ̃/ *n.m.* flat; (*Amer.*) apartment.

**appartenance** /apartənɑ̃s/ *n.f.* membership (**à,** of), belonging (**à,** to).

**appartenir** /apartənir/ *v.i.* belong (**à,** to) **il lui/vous/***etc.* **appartient de,** it is up to him/you/*etc.* to.

**appât** /apɑ/ *n.m.* bait; (*fig.*) lure. ∼**er** /-te/ *v.t.* lure.

**appauvrir** /apovrir/ *v.t.* impoverish. **s'∼** *v. pr.* grow impoverished.

**appel** /apɛl/ *n.m.* call; (*jurid.*) appeal; (*mil.*) call-up. **faire ∼,** appeal. **faire ∼ à,** (*recourir à*) call on; (*invoquer*) appeal to; (*évoquer*) call up; (*exiger*) call for. ∼ **d'offres,** (*comm.*) invitation to tender. **faire un ∼ de phares,** flash one's headlights.

**appel|er** /aple/ *v.t.* call; (*nécessiter*) call for. **s'∼er** *v. pr.* be called. **il s'appelle,** his name is. ∼**lation** /apelasjɔ̃/ *n.f.* designation.

**appendic|e** /apɛ̃dis/ *n.m.* appendix. ∼**ite** *n.f.* appendicitis.

**appétissant, ∼e** /apetisɑ̃, -t/ *a.* appetizing.

**appétit** /apeti/ *n.m.* appetite.

**applaud|ir** /aplodir/ *v.t./i.* applaud. ∼**ir à,** applaud. ∼**issements** *n.m. pl.* applause.

**appliquer** /aplike/ *v.t.* apply; (*loi*) enforce. **s'~** *v. pr.* apply o.s. (**à**, to). **s'~ à,** (*concerner*) apply to.

**appoint** /apwɛ̃/ *n.m.* contribution. **d'~,** extra. **faire l'~,** give the correct money.

**apport** /apɔr/ *n.m.* contribution.

**apporter** /apɔrte/ *v.t.* bring.

**apposer** /apoze/ *v.t.* affix.

**appréciable** /apresjabl/ *a.* appreciable.

**appréc|ier** /apresje/ *v.t.* appreciate; (*évaluer*) appraise. **~iation** *n.f.* appreciation; appraisal.

**appréhension** /apreɑ̃sjɔ̃/ *n.f.* apprehension.

**apprendre** /aprɑ̃dr/ *v.t./i.* learn; (*être informé de*) hear of. **~ qch. à qn.,** teach s.o. sth.; (*informer*) tell s.o. sth. **~ à faire,** learn to do. **~ à qn. à faire,** teach s.o. to do. **~ que,** learn that; (*être informé*) hear that.

**apprentissage** /aprɑ̃tisaʒ/ *n.m.* apprenticeship; (*d'un sujet*) learning.

**apprivoiser** /aprivwaze/ *v.t.* tame.

**approba|teur, ~trice** /aprɔbatœr, -tris/ *a.* approving.

**approbation** /aprɔbasjɔ̃/ *n.f.* approval.

**approchant, ~e** /aprɔʃɑ̃, -t/ *a.* close, similar.

**approcher** /aprɔʃe/ *v.t.* (*objet*) move near(er) (**de,** to); (*personne*) approach. **● ~ (de),** approach. **s'~ de,** approach, move near(er) to.

**approfond|ir** /aprɔfɔ̃dir/ *v.t.* deepen; (*fig.*) go into thoroughly. **~i** *a.* thorough.

**approprié** /aprɔprije/ *a.* appropriate.

**approuver** /apruve/ *v.t.* approve; (*trouver louable*) approve of; (*soutenir*) agree with.

**approvisionn|er** /aprɔvizjɔne/ *v.t.* supply. **s'~er** *v. pr.* stock up. **~ement** *n.m.* supply.

**approximati|f, ~ve** /aprɔksimatif, -v/ *a.* approximate. **~vement** *adv.* approximately.

**appui** /apɥi/ *n.m.* support; (*de fenêtre*) sill; (*pour objet*) rest.

**appuyer** /apɥije/ *v.t.* lean, rest; (*presser*) press; (*soutenir*) support, back. **● *v.i.* ~ sur,** press (on); (*fig.*) stress. **s'~ sur,** lean on; (*compter sur*) rely on.

**après** /apre/ *prép.* after; (*au-delà de*) beyond. **● *adv.* after(wards); (*plus tard*) later. **~ avoir fait,** after doing. **~ qu'il est parti,** after he left. **~ coup,** after the event. **~ tout,** after all. **d'~,** (*selon*) according to. **~demain** *adv.* the day after tomorrow. **~midi** *n.m./f. invar.* afternoon. **~rasage** *n.m.* aftershave.

**aquarelle** /akwarɛl/ *n.f.* water-colour, aquarelle.

**aquarium** /akwarjɔm/ *n.m.* aquarium.

**aquatique** /akwatik/ *a.* aquatic.

**aqueduc** /akdyk/ *n.m.* aqueduct.

**arabe** /arab/ *a.* Arab; (*lang.*) Arabic; (*désert*) Arabian. **●** *n.m./f.* Arab. **●** *n.m.* (*lang.*) Arabic.

**Arabie** /arabi/ *n.f.* **~ Séoudite,** Saudi Arabia.

**arachide** /araʃid/ *n.f.* peanut.

**araignée** /areɲe/ *n.f.* spider.

**arbitraire** /arbitrɛr/ *a.* arbitrary.

**arbitr|e** /arbitr/ *n.m.* referee; (*cricket, tennis*) umpire; (*maître*) arbiter; (*jurid.*) arbitrator. **~age** *n.m.* arbitration; (*sport*) refereeing. **~er** *v.t.* (*match*) referee; (*jurid.*) arbitrate.

**arbre** /arbr/ *n.m.* tree; (*techn.*) shaft.

**arbuste** /arbyst/ *n.m.* bush.

**arc** /ark/ *n.m.* (*arme*) bow; (*voûte*) arch. **~ de cercle,** arc of a circle.

**arcade** /arkad/ *n.f.* arch. **~s,** arcade, arches.

**arc-en-ciel** (*pl.* **arcs-en-ciel**) /arkɑ̃sjɛl/ *n.m.* rainbow.

**archéolo|gie** /arkeɔlɔʒi/ *n.f.* archaeology. **~gique** *a.* archaeological. **~gue** *n.m./f.* archaeologist.

**archet** /arʃɛ/ *n.m.* (*mus.*) bow.

**archevêque** /arʃəvɛk/ *n.m.* archbishop.

**archi-** /arʃi/ *préf.* (*fam.*) tremendously.

**architecte** /arʃitɛkt/ *n.m.* architect.

**architecture** /arʃitɛktyr/ *n.f.* architecture.

**arctique** /arktik/ *a. & n.m.* Arctic.

**ardoise** /ardwaz/ *n.f.* slate.

**are** /ar/ *n.m.* are (= 100 *square metres*).

**arène** /arɛn/ *n.f.* arena. **~(s),** (*pour courses de taureaux*) bullring.

**arête** /arɛt/ *n.f.* (*de poisson*) bone; (*bord*) ridge.

**argent** /arʒɑ̃/ *n.m.* money; (*métal*) silver. **~ comptant,** cash. **~ de poche,** pocket money.

**argenté** /arʒɑ̃te/ *a.* silver(y); (*métal*) (silver-) plated.

**argenterie** /arʒɑ̃tri/ *n.f.* silverware.

**argentin, ~e** /arʒɑ̃tɛ̃, -in/ *a. & n.m., f.* Argentinian, Argentine.

**Argentine** /arʒɑ̃tin/ *n.f.* Argentina.

**argile** /arʒil/ *n.f.* clay.

**argot** /argo/ *n.m.* slang.

**argument** /argymɑ̃/ *n.m.* argument. **~er** /-te/ *v.i.* argue.

**aride** /arid/ *a.* arid, barren.

**aristocrate** /aristɔkrat/ *n.m./f.* aristocrat.

**aristocrat|ie** /aristɔkrasi/ *n.f.* aristocracy. **~ique** /-atik/ *a.* aristocratic.

**arithmétique** /aritmetik/ *n.f.* arithmetic. **●** *a.* arithmetical.

**arme** /arm/ *n.f.* arm, weapon.

**armée** /arme/ *n.f.* army. **~ de l'air,** Air Force. **~ de terre,** Army.

**armement** /arməmɑ̃/ *n.m.* arms.

**armer** /arme/ *v.t.* arm; (*fusil*) cock; (*photo.*) wind on. **s'~ de,** arm o.s. with.

**armoire** /armwar/ *n.f.* cupboard; (*penderie*) wardrobe; (*Amer.*) closet.

**aromatisé** /arɔmatize/ *a.* flavoured.

**arôme** /arom/ *n.m.* aroma.

**arracher** /araʃe/ *v.t.* pull out *ou* off; (*plante*) pull *ou* dig up; (*page*) tear *ou* pull out. ∼ **à**, (*enlever à*) snatch from; (*fig.*) force *ou* wrest from.

**arrangement** /arãʒmã/ *n.m.* arrangement.

**arranger** /arãʒe/ *v.t.* arrange, fix up; (*réparer*) put right; (*régler*) sort out; (*convenir à*) suit. **s'**∼ *v. pr.* (*se mettre d'accord*) come to an arrangement; (*se débrouiller*) manage (**pour,** to).

**arrestation** /arɛstasjɔ̃/ *n.f.* arrest.

**arrêt** /arɛ/ *n.m.* stopping (**de,** of); (*lieu*) stop; (*pause*) pause; (*jurid.*) decree. **à l'**∼, stationary. **sans** ∼, without stopping. ∼ **maladie,** sick leave. ∼ **de travail,** (*grève*) stoppage; (*méd.*) sick leave.

**arrêté** /arete/ *n.m.* order.

**arrêter** /arete/ *v.t./i.* stop; (*date, regard*) fix; (*appareil*) turn off; (*appréhender*) arrest. **s'**∼ *v. pr.* stop. **(s')**∼ **de faire,** stop doing.

**arrhes** /ar/ *n.f. pl.* deposit.

**arrière** /arjɛr/ *n.m.* back, rear; (*football*) back. ● *a. invar.* back, rear. **à l'**∼, in *ou* at the back. **en** ∼, behind; (*marcher*) backwards. **en** ∼ **de,** behind. ∼**-goût** *n.m.* after-taste. ∼**-pays** *n.m.* backcountry. ∼**-pensée** *n.f.* ulterior motive. ∼**-plan** *n.m.* background.

**arriéré** /arjere/ *a.* backward. ● *n.m.* arrears.

**arrivage** /arivaʒ/ *n.m.* consignment.

**arrivée** /arive/ *n.f.* arrival; (*sport*) finish.

**arriver** /arive/ *v.i.* (*aux. être*) arrive, come; (*réussir*) succeed; (*se produire*) happen. ∼ **à,** (*atteindre*) reach. ∼ **à faire,** manage to do. **en** ∼ **à faire,** get to the stage of doing. **il arrive que,** it happens that. **il lui arrive de faire,** he (sometimes) does.

**arrogan|t,** ∼**te** /arɔgã, -t/ *a.* arrogant. ∼**ce** *n.f.* arrogance.

**arrondir** /arɔ̃dir/ *v.t.* (make) round; (*somme*) round off.

**arrondissement** /arɔ̃dismã/ *n.m.* district.

**arros|er** /aroze/ *v.t.* water; (*repas*) wash down; (*rôti*) baste; (*victoire*) celebrate with a drink. ∼**oir** *n.m.* watering-can.

**arsen|al** (*pl.* ∼**aux**) /arsənal, -o/ *n.m.* arsenal; (*naut.*) dockyard.

**art** /ar/ *n.m.* art. ∼**s et métiers,** arts and crafts.

**artère** /artɛr/ *n.f.* artery. **(grande)** ∼, main road.

**arthrite** /artrit/ *n.f.* arthritis.

**arthrose** /artroz/ *n.f.* osteoarthritis.

**artichaut** /artiʃo/ *n.m.* artichoke.

**article** /artikl/ *n.m.* article; (*comm.*) item, article.

**articul|er** /artikyle/ *v.t.* articulate. ∼**ation** *n.f.* articulation; (*anat.*) joint.

**artificiel, ∼le** /artifisjɛl/ *a.* artificial. ∼**lement** *adv.* artificially.

**artisan** /artizã/ *n.m.* artisan, craftsman. ∼**al** (*m. pl.* ∼**aux**) /-anal, -o/ *a.* of *ou* by craftsmen, craft; (*amateur*) home-made. ∼**at** /-ana/ *n.m.* craft; (*classe*) artisans.

**artist|e** /artist/ *n.m./f.* artist. ∼**ique** *a.* artistic.

**as¹** /a/ *voir* **avoir**.

**as²** /ɑs/ *n.m.* ace.

**ascendant** /asãdã/ *n.m.* influence. ∼**s,** ancestors.

**ascenseur** /asãsœr/ *n.m.* lift; (*Amer.*) elevator.

**aseptis|er** /asɛptize/ *v.t.* disinfect; (*stériliser*) sterilize. ∼**é** (*péj.*) sanitized.

**asiatique** /azjatik/ *a. & n.m./f.* Asian

**Asie** /azi/ *n.f.* Asia.

**asile** /azil/ *n.m.* refuge; (*pol.*) asylum; (*pour malades, vieillards*) home.

**aspect** /aspɛ/ *n.m.* appearance; (*fig.*) aspect. **à l'**∼ **de,** at the sight of.

**asperge** /aspɛrʒ/ *n.f.* asparagus.

**asperger** /aspɛrʒe/ *v.t.* spray.

**asphalte** /asfalt/ *n.m.* asphalt.

**asphyxie** /asfiksi/ *n.f.* suffocation.

**asphyxier** /asfiksje/ *v.t.,* **s'**∼ *v. pr.* suffocate, asphyxiate; (*fig.*) stifle.

**aspirateur** /aspiratœr/ *n.m.* vacuum cleaner.

**aspir|er** /aspire/ *v.t.* inhale; (*liquide*) suck up.

**aspirine** /aspirin/ *n.f.* aspirin.

**assaillir** /asajir/ *v.t.* assail.

**assainir** /asenir/ *v.t.* clean up.

**assaisonn|er** /asɛzɔne/ *v.t.* season. ∼**ement** *n.m.* seasoning.

**assassin** /asasɛ̃/ *n.m.* murderer; (*pol.*) assassin.

**assassin|er** /asasine/ *v.t.* murder; (*pol.*) assassinate. ∼**at** *n.m.* murder; (*pol.*) assassination.

**assaut** /aso/ *n.m.* assault, onslaught.

**assemblée** /asãble/ *n.f.* meeting; (*gens réunis*) gathering; (*pol.*) assembly.

**assembl|er** /asãble/ *v.t.* assemble, put together; (*réunir*) gather. **s'**∼**er** *v. pr.* gather, assemble. ∼**age** *n.m.* assembly; (*combinaison*) collection; (*techn.*) joint.

**asseoir** /aswar/ *v.t.* sit (down), seat; (*affermir*) establish; (*baser*) base. **s'**∼ *v. pr.* sit (down).

**assez** /ase/ *adv.* enough; (*plutôt*) quite, fairly. ∼ **grand/rapide** *etc.,* big/fast/*etc.* enough (**pour,** to). ∼ **de,** enough. **j'en ai** ∼ **(de),** I've had enough (of).

**assid|u** /asidy/ *a.* (*zèle*) assiduous; (*régulier*) regular. ∼**u auprès de,** attentive to. ∼**uité** /-ɥite/ *n.f.* assiduousness; regularity. ∼**ûment** *adv.* assiduously.

**assiéger** /asjeʒe/ *v.t.* besiege.

**assiette** /asjɛt/ *n.f.* plate; (*équilibre*) seat. ~ **anglaise**, assorted cold meats. ~ **creuse/ plate**, soup-/dinner-plate.

**assimil|er** /asimile/ *v.t.*, **s'~er** *v. pr.* assimilate. ~**er à**, liken to; (*classer*) class as. ~**ation** *n.f.* assimilation; likening; classification.

**assis, ~e** /asi, -z/ *voir* **asseoir**. ● *a.* sitting (down), seated.

**assistance** /asistɑ̃s/ *n.f.* audience; (*aide*) assistance. **l'A~ (publique)**, government child care service.

**assistant, ~e** /asistɑ̃, -t/ *n.m., f.* assistant; (*univ.*) assistant lecturer. ~**s**, (*spectateurs*) members of the audience. ~ **social, ~e sociale**, social worker.

**assist|er** /asiste/ *v.t.* assist. ● *v.i.* ~**er à**, attend, be (present) at; (*scène*) witness. ~**é par ordinateur**, computer-assisted.

**association** /asɔsjasjɔ̃/ *n.f.* association.

**associé, ~e** /asɔsje/ *n.m., f.* partner, associate. ● *a.* associate.

**associer** /asɔsje/ *v.t.* associate; (*mêler*) combine (**à, with**). ~ **qn. à**, (*projet*) involve s.o. in; (*bénéfices*) give s.o. a share of. **s'~ à**, (*projet*) take part in.

**assoiffé** /aswafe/ *a.* thirsty.

**assommer** /asɔme/ *v.t.* knock out; (*tuer*) kill; (*animal*) stun; (*fig.*) overwhelm; (*ennuyer: fam.*) bore.

**assorti** /asɔrti/ *a.* matching; (*objets variés*) assorted.

**assort|ir** /asɔrtir/ *v.t.* match (**à, with, to**). ~**iment** *n.m.* assortment.

**assoupir (s')** /(s)asupir/ *v. pr.* doze off.

**assouplir** /asuplir/ *v.t.* make supple; (*fig.*) make flexible.

**assourdir** /asurdir/ *v.t.* (*personne*) deafen; (*bruit*) deaden.

**assumer** /asyme/ *v.t.* assume.

**assurance** /asyrɑ̃s/ *n.f.* (self-)assurance; (*garantie*) assurance; (*contrat*) insurance. ~ **maladie** *n.f.* health insurance. ~**s sociales**, National Insurance. ~**vie** *n.f.* life assurance.

**assuré, ~e** /asyre/ *a.* certain, assured; (*sûr de soi*) (self-)confident, assured. ● *n.m., f.* insured.

**assur|er** /asyre/ *v.t.* ensure; (*fournir*) provide; (*exécuter*) carry out; (*comm.*) insure; (*stabiliser*) steady. ~ **à qn. que**, assure s.o. that. ~ **la gestion de**, manage. **s'~ de/que**, make sure of/that. ~**eur** /-œr/ *n.m.* insurer.

**asthm|e** /asm/ *n.m.* asthma. ~**atique** *a. & n.m., f.* asthmatic.

**asticot** /astiko/ *n.m.* maggot.

**astiquer** /astike/ *v.t.* polish.

**astringent, ~e** /astrɛ̃ʒɑ̃, -t/ *a.* astringent.

**astrolo|gie** /astrɔlɔʒi/ *n.f.* astrology. ~**gue** *n.m./f.* astrologer.

**astronaute** /astrɔnot/ *n.m./f.* astronaut.

**astronom|ie** /astrɔnɔmi/ *n.f.* astronomy. ~**e** *n.m./f.* astronomer. ~**ique** *a.* astronomical.

**astuce** /astys/ *n.f.* smartness; (*truc*) trick.

**astucieu|x, ~se** /astysjø, -z/ *a.* smart, clever.

**atelier** /atəlje/ *n.m.* workshop; (*de peintre*) studio.

**athé|e** /ate/ *n.m./f.* atheist. ● *a.* atheistic. ~**isme** *n.m.* atheism .

**athl|ète** /atlɛt/ *n.m./f.* athlete. ~**étique** *a.* athletic. ~**étisme** *n.m.* athletics.

**atlantique** /atlɑ̃tik/ *a.* Atlantic. ● *n.m.* **A~**, Atlantic (Ocean).

**atlas** /atlɑs/ *n.m.* atlas.

**atmosph|ère** /atmosfɛr/ *n.f.* atmosphere. ~**érique** *a.* atmospheric.

**atome** /atom/ *n.m.* atom.

**atomique** /atɔmik/ *a.* atomic.

**atomiseur** /atɔmizœr/ *n.m.* spray.

**atout** /atu/ *n.m.* trump (card); (*avantage*) great asset.

**atroc|e** /atrɔs/ *a.* atrocious. ~**ité** *n.f.* atrocity.

**attabler (s')** /(s)atable/ *v. pr.* sit down at table.

**attachant, ~e** /ataʃɑ̃, -t/ *a.* likeable.

**attache** /ataʃ/ *n.f.* (*agrafe*) fastener; (*lien*) tie.

**attaché** /ataʃe/ *a.* **être ~ à**, (*aimer*) be attached to. ● *n.m., f.* (*pol.*) attaché. ~-**case** *n.m.* attaché case.

**attacher** /ataʃe/ *v.t.* tie (up); (*ceinture, robe, etc.*) fasten; (*étiquette*) attach. ~ **à**, (*attribuer à*) attach to. ● *v.i.* (*culin.*) stick. **s'~ à**, (*se lier à*) become attached to; (*se consacrer à*) apply o.s. to.

**attaque** /atak/ *n.f.* attack. ~ **(cérébrale)**, stroke. **il va en faire une ~**, he'll have a fit. ~ **à main armée**, armed attack.

**attaquer** /atake/ *v.t./i.*, **s'~ à**, attack; (*problème, sujet*) tackle.

**attarder (s')** /(s)atarde/ *v. pr.* linger.

**atteindre** /atɛ̃dr/ *v.t.* reach; (*blesser*) hit; (*affecter*) affect.

**atteint, ~e** /atɛ̃, -t/ *a.* ~ **de**, suffering from.

**atteinte** /atɛ̃t/ *n.f.* attack (**à, on**). **porter ~ à**, make an attack on.

**attelle** /atɛl/ *n.f.* splint.

**attendant (en)** /(ɑ̃n)atɑ̃dɑ̃/ *adv.* meanwhile.

**attendre** /atɑ̃dr/ *v.t.* wait for; (*bébé*) expect; (*être le sort de*) await; (*escompter*) expect. ● *v.i.* wait. ~ **que qn. fasse**, wait for s.o. to do. **s'~ à**, expect.

**attendr|ir** /atɑ̃drir/ *v.t.* move (to pity). **s'~ir** *v. pr.* be moved to pity. ~**issant, ~issante** *a.* moving.

**attendu** /atɑ̃dy/ *a.* (*escompté*) expected; (*espéré*) long-awaited. **~ que,** considering that.

**attentat** /atɑ̃ta/ *n.m.* murder attempt. **~ (à la bombe),** (bomb) attack.

**attente** /atɑ̃t/ *n.f.* wait(ing); (*espoir*) expectation.

**attenter** /atɑ̃te/ *v.i.* **~ à,** make an attempt on; (*fig.*) violate.

**attenti|f, ~ve** /atɑ̃tif, -v/ *a.* attentive; (*scrupuleux*) careful. **~f à,** mindful of; (*soucieux*) careful of. **~vement** *adv.* attentively.

**attention** /atɑ̃sjɔ̃/ *n.f.* attention; (*soin*) care. **~ (à)!,** watch out (for)! **faire ~ à,** (*professeur*) pay attention to; (*marche*) mind. **faire ~ à faire,** be careful to do.

**atténuer** /atenɥe/ *v.t.* (*violence*) tone down; (*douleur*) ease; (*faute*) mitigate. **s'~** *v. pr.* subside.

**atterr|ir** /aterir/ *v.i.* land. **~issage** *n.m.* landing.

**attestation** /atɛstasjɔ̃/ *n.f.* certificate.

**attester** /atɛste/ *v.t.* testify to. **~ que,** testify that.

**attirail** /atiraj/ *n.m.* (*fam.*) gear.

**attirance** /atirɑ̃s/ *n.f.* attraction.

**attirant, ~e** /atirɑ̃, -t/ *a.* attractive.

**attirer** /atire/ *v.t.* draw, attract; (*causer*) bring. **s'~** *v. pr.* bring upon o.s.; (*amis*) win.

**attitude** /atityd/ *n.f.* attitude; (*maintien*) bearing.

**attrait** /atrɛ/ *n.m.* attraction.

**attraper** /atrape/ *v.t.* catch; (*habitude, style*) pick up; (*duper*) take in; (*gronder: fam.*) tell off.

**attrayant, ~e** /atrɛjɑ̃, -t/ *a.* attractive.

**attrib|uer** /atribɥe/ *v.t.* award; (*donner*) assign; (*imputer*) attribute. **~utions** *n.f. pl.* attributions.

**attrister** /atriste/ *v.t.* sadden.

**attroup|er (s')** /(s)atrupe/ *v. pr.* gather. **~ement** *n.m.* crowd.

**au** /o/ *voir* **à.**

**aubaine** /obɛn/ *n.f.* (stroke of) good fortune.

**aube** /ob/ *n.f.* dawn, daybreak.

**aubépine** /obepin/ *n.f.* hawthorn.

**auberg|e** /obɛrʒ/ *n.f.* inn. **~e de jeunesse,** youth hostel. **~iste** *n.m./f.* innkeeper.

**aubergine** /obɛrʒin/ *n.f.* aubergine; (*Amer.*) egg-plant.

**aucun, ~e** /okœ̃, okyn/ *a.* no, not any; (*positif*) any. ● *pron.* none, not any; (*positif*) any. **~ des deux,** neither of the two.

**audace** /odas/ *n.f.* daring; (*impudence*) audacity.

**audacieu|x, ~se** /odasjø, -z/ *a.* daring.

**au-delà** /odla/ *adv.,* **~ de** *prép.* beyond.

**au-dessous** /odsu/ *adv.,* **~ de** *prép.* below; (*couvert par*) under.

**au-dessus** /odsy/ *adv.,* **~ de** *prép.* above.

**au-devant (de)** /odvɑ̃(də)/ *prép.* **aller ~ de qn.,** go to meet s.o.

**audience** /odjɑ̃s/ *n.f.* audience; (*d'un tribunal*) hearing; (*intérêt*) attention.

**audio-visuel, ~le** /odjovizɥɛl/ *a.* audio-visual.

**audi|teur, ~trice** /oditœr, -tris/ *n.m., f.* listener.

**audition** /odisjɔ̃/ *n.f.* hearing; (*théâtre, mus.*) audition.

**auditoire** /oditwar/ *n.m.* audience.

**auditorium** /oditɔrjɔm/ *n.m.* (*mus., radio*) recording studio.

**augment|er** /ogmɑ̃te/ *v.t./i.* increase; (*employé*) increase the pay of. **~ation** *n.f.* increase. **~ation (de salaire),** (pay) rise; (*Amer.*) raise.

**augure** /ogyr/ *n.m.* (*devin*) oracle. **être de bon/mauvais ~,** be a good/bad sign.

**aujourd'hui** /oʒurdɥi/ *adv.* today.

**aumône** /omon/ *n.f.* alms.

**auparavant** /oparavɑ̃/ *adv.* before(hand).

**auprès (de)** /oprɛ(də)/ *prép.* by, next to; (*comparé à*) compared with; (*s'adressant à*) to.

**auquel, ~le** /okɛl/ *voir* **lequel.**

**aura, aurait** /ora, orɛ/ *voir* **avoir.**

**auréole** /oreɔl/ *n.f.* halo.

**aurore** /orɔr/ *n.f.* dawn.

**ausculter** /ɔskylte/ *v.t.* examine with a stethoscope.

**aussi** /osi/ *adv.* too, also; (*comparaison*) as; (*tellement*) so. ● *conj.* (*donc*) therefore. **~ bien que,** as well as.

**aussitôt** /osito/ *adv.* immediately. **~ que,** as soon as. **~ arrivé/levé/** *etc.,* as soon as one has arrived/got up/*etc.*

**aust|ère** /ostɛr/ *a.* austere. **~érité** *n.f.* austerity.

**Australie** /ɔstrali/ *n.f.* Australia.

**australien, ~ne** /ɔstraljɛ̃, -jɛn/ *a. & n.m., f.* Australian.

**autant** /otɑ̃/ *adv.* (*travailler, manger, etc.*) as much (**que,** as). **~ de, (de),** (*quantité*) as much (**que,** as); (*nombre*) as many (**que,** as); (*tant*) so much; so many. **~ faire,** one had better do. **d'~ plus que,** all the more since. **en faire ~,** do the same. **pour ~,** for all that.

**auteur** /otœr/ *n.m.* author. **l'~ du crime,** the person who committed the crime.

**authentifier** /otɑ̃tifje/ *v.t.* authenticate.

**authenti|que** /otɑ̃tik/ *a.* authentic. **~cité** *n.f.* authenticity.

**auto** /oto/ *n.f.* car. **~s tamponneuses,** dodgems, bumper cars.

**auto-** /oto/ *préf.* self-, auto-.

**autobiographie** /otobjɔgrafi/ *n.f.* autobiography.

**autobus** /otɔbys/ *n.m.* bus.

**autocar** /otɔkar/ *n.m.* coach.

**autocuiseur** /otɔkyizœr/ *n.* pressure cooker.

**autodéfense** /otɔdefãs/ *n.f.* self-defence.

**autodidacte** /otɔdidakt/ *a. & n.m./f.* self-taught (person).

**auto-école** /otɔekɔl/ *n.f.* driving school.

**automatique** /otɔmatik/ *a.* automatic. ∼ment *adv.* automatically.

**automne** /otɔn/ *n.m.* autumn; (*Amer.*) fall.

**automobil|e** /otɔmɔbil/ *a.* motor, car. ● *n.f.* (motor) car. **l'∼e**, (*sport*) motoring. ∼iste *n.m./f.* motorist.

**autonom|e** /otɔnɔm/ *a.* autonomous. ∼ie *n.f.* autonomy.

**autopsie** /otɔpsi/ *n.f.* post-mortem, autopsy.

**autoradio** /otɔradjo/ *n.m.* car radio.

**autorisation** /otɔrizasjõ/ *n.f.* permission, authorization; (*permis*) permit.

**autoriser** /otɔrize/ *v.t.* authorize, permit; (*rendre possible*) allow (of).

**autoritaire** /otɔritɛr/ *a.* authoritarian.

**autorité** /otɔrite/ *n.f.* authority.

**autoroute** /otɔrut/ *n.f.* motorway; (*Amer.*) highway.

**auto-stop** /otɔstɔp/ *n.m.* hitch-hiking. **faire de l'∼,** hitch-hike. **prendre en ∼,** give a lift to. ∼peur, ∼peuse *n.m., f.* hitch-hiker.

**autour** /otur/ *adv.,* ∼ **de** *prép.* around. **tout ∼,** all around.

**autre** /otr/ *a.* other. **un ∼ jour**/*etc.,* another day/*etc.* ● *pron.* **un ∼, une ∼,** another (one). **l'∼,** the other (one). **les autres,** the others; (*autrui*) others. **d'∼s,** (some) others. **l'un l'∼,** each other. **l'un et l'∼,** both of them. ∼ **chose/part,** sth./somewhere else. **qn./rien d'∼,** s.o./nothing else. **quoi d'∼?,** what else? **d'∼ part,** on the other hand. **vous ∼s Anglais,** you English. **d'un jour**/*etc.* **à l'∼,** (*bientôt*) any day/*etc.* now. **entre ∼s,** among other things.

**autrefois** /otrəfwa/ *adv.* in the past.

**autrement** /otrəmã/ *adv.* differently; (*sinon*) otherwise; (*plus*) far more. ∼ **dit,** in other words.

**Autriche** /otriʃ/ *n.f.* Austria.

**autrichien, ∼ne** /otriʃjɛ̃, -jɛn/ *a. & n.m.,f.* Austrian.

**autruche** /otryʃ/ *n.f.* ostrich.

**aux** /o/ *voir* **à.**

**auxquel|s, ∼les** /okɛl/ *voir* **lequel.**

**aval (en)** /(ɑ̃n)aval/ *adv.* downstream.

**avalanche** /avalɑ̃ʃ/ *n.f.* avalanche.

**avaler** /avale/ *v.t.* swallow.

**avance** /avɑ̃s/ *n.f.* advance; (*sur un concurrent*) lead. ∼ **(de fonds),** advance. **à l'∼, d'∼,** in advance. **en ∼,** early; (*montre*) fast. **en ∼ (sur),** (*menant*) ahead (of).

**avancement** /avɑ̃smɑ̃/ *n.m.* promotion.

**avanc|er** /avɑ̃se/ *v.i.* move forward, advance; (*travail*) make progress; (*montre*) be fast; (*faire saillie*) jut out. ● *v.t.* (*argent*) advance; (*montre*) put forward. **s'∼er** *v. pr.* move forward, advance; (*se hasarder*) commit o.s. ∼é, ∼ée *a.* advanced; *n.f.* projection.

**avant** /avɑ̃/ *prép & adv.* before. ● *a. invar.* front. ● *n.m.* front; (*football*) forward. ∼ **de faire,** before doing. ∼ **qu'il (ne) fasse,** before he does. **en ∼,** (*mouvement*) forward. **en ∼ (de),** (*position, temps*) in front (of). ∼ **peu,** before long. ∼ **tout,** above all. **bien ∼ dans,** very deep(ly) *ou* far into. **s'∼er** *v. pr.* move forward, advance; (*se hasarder*) **dernier, ∼dernière** *a. & n.m.,f.* last but one. **∼-guerre** *n.m.* pre-war period. **∼-hier** /-tjɛr/ *adv.* the day before yesterday. **∼-veille** *n.f.* two days before.

**avantag|e** /avɑ̃taʒ/ *n.m.* advantage; (*comm.*) benefit. **∼er** *v.t.* favour; (*embellir*) show off to advantage.

**avantageu|x, ∼se** /avɑ̃taʒø, -z/ *a.* attractive.

**avar|e** /avar/ *a.* miserly. ● *n.m./f.* miser. **∼ice** *n.f.* avarice.

**avec** /avɛk/ *prép.* with; (*envers*) towards. ● *adv.* (*fam.*) with it *ou* them.

**avènement** /avɛnmɑ̃/ *n.m.* advent; (*d'un roi*) accession.

**avenir** /avnir/ *n.m.* future. **à l'∼,** in future. **d'∼,** with (future) prospects.

**aventur|e** /avɑ̃tyr/ *n.f.* adventure; (*sentimentale*) affair. **∼eux, ∼euse** *a.* adventurous; (*hasardeux*) risky. **∼ier, ∼ière** *n.m.,f.* adventurer.

**aventurer (s')** /(s)avɑ̃tyre/ *v. pr.* venture.

**avenue** /avny/ *n.f.* avenue.

**averse** /avɛrs/ *n.f.* shower.

**avert|ir** /avɛrtir/ *v.t.* inform; (*mettre en garde, menacer*) warn. **∼i** *a.* informed. **∼issement** *n.m.* warning.

**avertisseur** /avɛrtisœr/ *n.m.* (*auto.*) horn.

**aveu** (*pl.* ∼x) /avø/ *n.m.* confession. **de l'∼ de,** by the admission of.

**aveugl|e** /avœgl/ *a.* blind. ● *n.m./f.* blind man, blind woman. **∼er** *v.t.* blind.

**aviation** /avjasjõ/ *n.f.* (*industrie*) aviation; (*mil.*) air force.

**avid|e** /avid/ *a.* greedy (**de,** for); (*anxieux*) eager (**de,** for). **∼e de faire,** eager to do. **∼ité** *n.f.* greed; eagerness.

**avion** /avjõ/ *n.m.* plane, aeroplane, aircraft; (*Amer.*) airplane.

**aviron** /avirõ/ *n.m.* oar. **l'∼,** (*sport*) rowing.

**avis** /avi/ *n.m.* opinion; (*renseignement*) notification; (*comm.*) advice. **à mon ∼,** in my opinion. **changer d'∼,** change one's mind.

**avocat¹, ∼e** /avɔka, -t/ *n.m., f.* barrister; (*Amer.*) attorney; (*fig.*) advocate.

**avocat²** /avɔka/ *n.m.* (*fruit*) avocado (pear).

**avoine** /avwan/ *n.f.* oats.

**avoir** /avwar/ v. aux. have. ● v.t. have; (obtenir) get; (duper: fam.) take in. ● n.m. assets. **je n'ai pas de café,** I haven't (got) any coffee; (Amer.) I don't have any coffee. **est-ce que tu as du café?,** have you (got) any coffee?; (Amer.) do you have any coffee? ∼ **à faire,** have to do. **tu n'as qu'à l'appeler,** all you have to do is call her. ∼ **chaud/faim**/etc., be hot/hungry/etc. ∼ **dix**/etc. **ans,** be ten/etc. years old. ∼ **lieu,** take place. **en** ∼ **assez,** have had enough. **en** ∼ **pour une minute**/etc., be busy for a minute/etc. **il en a pour cent francs,** it will cost him one hundred francs. **qu'est-ce que vous avez?,** what is the matter with you? **on m'a eu!,** I've been had.

**avort|er** /avɔrte/ v.i. (projet etc.) miscarry. **(se faire)** ∼**er,** have an abortion. ∼**é** a. abortive. ∼**ement** n.m. (méd.) abortion.

**avouer** /avwe/ v.t. confess (to). ● v.i. confess.

**avril** /avril/ n.m. April.

**axe** /aks/ n.m. axis; (essieu) axle. ∼**(routier),** main road.

**ayant** /ɛjɑ̃/ voir **avoir.**

**azote** /azɔt/ n.m. nitrogen.

# Bb

**baba** /baba/ n.m. ∼ **(au rhum),** rum baba.

**babiole** /babjɔl/ n.f. knick-knack.

**bâbord** /bɑbɔr/ n.m. port (side).

**baby-foot** /babifut/ n.m. invar. table football.

**baby-sitt|er** /bebisitœr/ n.m./f. baby-sitter. ∼**ing** n.m. **faire du** ∼**ing,** babysit.

**bac¹** /bak/ n.m. = **baccalauréat.**

**bac²** /bak/ n.m. (bateau) ferry; (récipient) tub; (plus petit) tray.

**baccalauréat** /bakalɔrea/ n.m. school leaving certificate.

**bâch|e** /bɑʃ/ n.f. tarpaulin. ∼**er** v.t. cover (with a tarpaulin).

**bachel|ier, ∼ière** /baʃəlje, -jɛr/ n.m., f. holder of the baccalauréat.

**bachot** /baʃo/ n.m. (fam.) = **baccalauréat.**

**bâcler** /bɑkle/ v.t. botch (up).

**bactérie** /bakteri/ n.f. bacterium.

**badiner** /badine/ v.i. joke (sur, avec, about).

**badminton** /badmintɔn/ n.m. badminton.

**baffe** /baf/ n.f. (fam.) slap.

**baffle** /bafl/ n.m. speaker.

**bafouer** /bafwe/ v.t. scoff at.

**bafouiller** /bafuje/ v.t./i. stammer.

**bagage** /bagaʒ/ n.m. bag; (fig.) (store of) knowledge. ∼**s,** luggage, baggage. ∼**s à main,** hand luggage.

**bagarr|e** /bagar/ n.f. fight. ∼**er** v.i., **se** ∼**er** v. pr. fight.

**bagnard** /baɲar/ n.m. convict.

**bagnole** /baɲɔl/ n.f. (fam.) car.

**bagu|e** /bag/ n.f. (anneau) ring. ∼**er** v.t. ring.

**baguette** /bagɛt/ n.f. stick; (de chef d'orchestre) baton; (chinoise) chopstick; (magique) wand; (pain) stick of bread. ∼ **de tambour,** drumstick.

**baie** /bɛ/ n.f. (géog.) bay; (fruit) berry. ∼ **(vitrée),** picture window.

**baign|er** /beɲe/ v.t. bathe; (enfant) bath. ● v.i. ∼**er dans,** soak in; (être enveloppé dans) be steeped in. **se** ∼**er** v. pr. go swimming (ou) bathing. ∼**é de,** bathed in; (sang) soaked in. ∼**ade** /beɲad/ n.f. bathing, swimming. ∼**eur, ∼euse** /beɲœr, -øz/ n.m., f. bather.

**baignoire** /beɲwar/ n.f. bath(-tub).

**bail** (pl. **baux**) /baj, bo/ n.m. lease.

**bâill|er** /bɑje/ v.i. yawn. ∼**ement** n.m. yawn.

**bailleur** /bɑjœr/ n.m. ∼ **de fonds,** (comm.) backer.

**bain** /bɛ̃/ n.m. bath; (de mer) bathe. ∼**(s) de soleil,** sunbathing. ∼**-marie** (pl. ∼**s-marie**) n.m. double boiler. ∼ **de bouche,** mouthwash. **mettre qn. dans le** ∼, (au courant) put s.o. in the picture.

**baiser** /beze/ n.m. kiss. ● v.t. (main) kiss; (fam.) screw.

**baisse** /bɛs/ n.f. fall, drop. **en** ∼, falling.

**baisser** /bese/ v.t. lower; (radio, lampe, etc.) turn down. ● v.i. go down, fall; (santé, forces) fail. **se** ∼ v. pr. bend down.

**bal** (pl. ∼**s**) /bal/ n.m. dance; (habillé) ball.

**balad|e** /balad/ n.f. stroll; (en auto) drive. ∼**er** v.t. take for a stroll. **se** ∼**er** v. pr. (go for a) stroll. **se** ∼**er (en auto),** go for a drive.

**baladeur** /baladœr/ n.m. personal stereo.

**balai** /balɛ/ n.m. broom.

**balance** /balɑ̃s/ n.f. scales. **la B∼,** Libra.

**balancer** /balɑ̃se/ v.t. swing; (doucement) sway; (lancer: fam.) chuck; (se débarrasser de: fam.) chuck out. ● v.i., **se** ∼ v. pr. swing; sway.

**balancier** /balɑ̃sje/ n.m. (d'horloge) pendulum.

**balançoire** /balɑ̃swar/ n.f. swing; (bascule) see-saw.

**balay|er** /baleje/ v.t. sweep (up); (chasser) sweep away; (se débarrasser de) sweep aside. ∼**age** n.m. sweeping; (cheveux) highlights. ∼**eur, ∼euse** n.m., f. road sweeper.

**balcon** /balkɔ̃/ n.m. balcony; (théâtre) dress circle.

**baleine** /balɛn/ n.f. whale.

**balis|e** /baliz/ n.f. beacon; (bouée) buoy; (auto.) (road) sign. ∼**er** v.t. mark out (with beacons); (route) signpost.

**balistique** /balistik/ a. ballistic.

**ballast** /balast/ n.m. ballast.

**balle** /bal/ *n.f.* ( *projectile* ) bullet; ( *sport* ) ball; ( *paquet* ) bale.

**ballet** /balɛ/ *n.m.* ballet.

**ballon** /balɔ̃/ *n.m.* balloon; ( *sport* ) ball. ~ **de football,** football.

**ballottage** /balɔtaʒ/ *n.m.* second ballot ( *due to indecisive result* ).

**balnéaire** /balneɛr/ *a.* seaside.

**balustrade** /balystrad/ *n.f.* railing(s).

**bambou** /bãbu/ *n.m.* bamboo.

**ban** /bã/ *n.m.* round of applause. ~**s,** ( *de mariage* ) banns.

**banal** ( *m. pl.* ~**s** ) /banal/ *a.* commonplace, banal. ~**ité** *n.f.* banality.

**banane** /banan/ *n.f.* banana.

**banc** /bã/ *n.m.* bench; ( *de poissons* ) shoal. ~ **des accusés,** dock.

**bancaire** /bãkɛr/ *a.* banking; ( *chèque* ) bank.

**bancal** ( *m. pl.* ~**s** ) /bãkal/ *a.* wobbly; ( *raisonnement* ) shaky.

**bandage** /bãdaʒ/ *n.m.* bandage.

**bande**[1] /bãd/ *n.f.* ( *de papier etc.* ) strip; ( *rayure* ) stripe; ( *de film* ) reel; ( *radio* ) band; ( *pansement* ) bandage. ~ **(magnétique),** tape. ~ **dessinée,** comic strip. ~ **sonore,** sound-track.

**bande**[2] /bãd/ *n.f.* ( *groupe* ) bunch, band, gang.

**bandeau** ( *pl.* ~**x** ) /bãdo/ *n.m.* headband; ( *sur les yeux* ) blindfold.

**bander** /bãde/ *v.t.* ( *plaie* ) bandage. ~ **les yeux à,** blindfold.

**bandit** /bãdi/ *n.m.* bandit. ~**isme** /-tism/ *n.m.* crime.

**bandoulière (en)** /(ã)bãduljɛr/ *adv.* across one's shoulder.

**banlieu|e** /bãljø/ *n.f.* suburbs. **de** ~**e,** suburban. ~**sard,** ~**sarde** /-zar, -zard/ *n.m.,* *f.* (suburban) commuter.

**bannière** /banjɛr/ *n.f.* banner.

**bannir** /banir/ *v.t.* banish.

**banque** /bãk/ *n.f.* bank; ( *activité* ) banking. ~ **d'affaires,** merchant bank.

**banqueroute** /bãkrut/ *n.f.* (fraudulent) bankruptcy.

**banquet** /bãkɛ/ *n.m.* dinner; ( *fastueux* ) banquet.

**banquette** /bãkɛt/ *n.f.* seat.

**banquier** /bãkje/ *n.m.* banker.

**bapt|ême** /batɛm/ *n.m.* baptism; christening. ~**iser** *v.t.* baptize, christen; ( *appeler* ) christen.

**bar** /bar/ *n.m.* ( *lieu* ) bar.

**baraque** /barak/ *n.f.* hut, shed; ( *boutique* ) stall; ( *maison: fam.* ) house. ~**ments** *n.m. pl.* huts.

**baratin** /baratɛ̃/ *n.m.* ( *fam.* ) sweet *ou* smooth talk.

**barbar|e** /barbar/ *a.* barbaric.

**barbe** /barb/ *n.f.* beard. ~ **à papa,** candy-floss; ( *Amer.* ) cotton candy.

**barbecue** /barbəkju/ *n.m.* barbecue.

**barbelé** /barbəle/ *a.* **fil** ~, barbed wire.

**barbiche** /barbiʃ/ *n.f.* goatee.

**barbiturique** /barbityrik/ *n.m.* barbiturate.

**barboter** /barbɔte/ *v.i.* paddle, splash.

**barbouill|er** /barbuje/ *v.t.* ( *souiller* ) smear; ( *griffonner* ) scribble. **avoir l'estomac** ~**é** *ou* **se sentir** ~**é** feel liverish.

**barbu** /barby/ *a.* bearded.

**barème** /barɛm/ *n.m.* list, table; ( *échelle* ) scale.

**bariolé** /barjɔle/ *a.* motley.

**barman** /barman/ *n.m.* barman; ( *Amer.* ) bartender.

**baromètre** /barɔmɛtr/ *n.m.* barometer.

**baroque** /barɔk/ *a.* baroque.

**barque** /bark/ *n.f.* (small) boat.

**barrage** /baraʒ/ *n.m.* dam; ( *sur route* ) roadblock.

**barre** /bar/ *n.f.* bar; ( *trait* ) line, stroke; ( *naut.* ) helm.

**barreau** ( *pl.* ~**x** ) /baro/ *n.m.* ( *d'échelle* ) rung. **le** ~, ( *jurid.* ) the bar.

**barrer** /bare/ *v.t.* block; ( *porte* ) bar; ( *rayer* ) cross out; ( *naut.* ) steer. **se** ~ *v. pr.* ( *fam.* ) hop it.

**barrette** /barɛt/ *n.f.* (hair-)slide.

**barricad|e** /barikad/ *n.f.* barricade. ~**er** *v.t.* barricade. **se** ~**er** *v. pr.* barricade o.s.

**barrière** /barjɛr/ *n.f.* ( *porte* ) gate; ( *clôture* ) fence; ( *obstacle* ) barrier.

**baryton** /baritɔ̃/ *n.m.* baritone.

**bas, basse** /ba, bas/ *a.* low; ( *action* ) base. ● *n.m.* bottom; ( *chaussette* ) stocking. ● *n.f.* ( *mus.* ) bass. ● *adv.* low. **à** ~, down with. **en** ~, down below; ( *dans une maison* ) downstairs. **en** ~ **âge,** young. **en** ~ **de,** at the bottom of. **plus** ~, further *ou* lower down. ~**-côté** *n.m.* ( *de route* ) verge; ( *Amer.* ) shoulder. ~ **de casse** *n.m. invar.* lower case.

**bascule** /baskyl/ *n.f.* ( *balance* ) scales. **cheval/fauteuil à** ~, rocking-horse/-chair.

**basculer** /baskyle/ *v.t./i.* topple over; ( *benne* ) tip up.

**base** /baz/ *n.f.* base; ( *fondement* ) basis; ( *pol.* ) rank and file. **de** ~, basic.

**baser** /baze/ *v.t.* base. **se** ~ **sur,** base o.s. on.

**basilic** /bazilik/ *n.m.* basil.

**basilique** /bazilik/ *n.f.* basilica.

**basket(-ball)** /baskɛt(bol)/ *n.m.* basketball.

**basque** /bask/ *a. & n.m./f.* Basque.

**basse** /bas/ *voir* **bas.**

**basse-cour** ( *pl.* **basses-cours** ) /baskur/ *n.f.* farmyard.

**bassesse** /basɛs/ *n.f.* baseness; ( *action* ) base act.

**bassin** /basɛ̃/ *n.m.* bowl; (*pièce d'eau*) pond; (*rade*) dock; (*géog.*) basin; (*anat.*) pelvis. ~ **houiller,** coalfield.

**bat** /ba/ *voir* **battre**.

**batail|le** /bataj/ *n.f.* battle; (*fig.*) fight. ~**er** *v.i.* fight.

**bataillon** /batajɔ̃/ *n.m.* battalion.

**bateau** (*pl.* ~**x**) /bato/ *n.m.* boat. ~**-mouche** (*pl.* ~**x-mouches**) *n.m.* sightseeing boat.

**bâti** /bɑti/ *a.* **bien** ~, well-built.

**bâtiment** /bɑtimɑ̃/ *n.m.* building; (*navire*) vessel; (*industrie*) building trade.

**bâtir** /bɑtir/ *v.t.* build.

**bâtisse** /bɑtis/ *n.f.* (*péj.*) building.

**bâton** /bɑtɔ̃/ *n.m.* stick.

**battant** /batɑ̃/ *n.m.* (*vantail*) flap. **porte à deux** ~**s,** double door.

**battement** /batmɑ̃/ *n.m.* (*de cœur*) beat(-ing); (*temps*) interval.

**batterie** /batri/ *n.f.* (*mil.*, *électr.*) battery; (*mus.*) drums. ~ **de cuisine,** pots and pans.

**batteur** /batœr/ *n.m.* (*mus.*) drummer; (*culin.*) whisk.

**battre** /batr/ *v.t./i.* beat; (*cartes*) shuffle; (*faire du bruit*) bang. **se** ~ *v. pr.* fight. ~ **des ailes,** flap its wings. ~ **des mains,** clap. ~ **pavillon britannique**/*etc.*, fly the British/ *etc.* flag. ~ **son plein,** be in full swing.

**battue** /baty/ *n.f.* (*chasse*) beat; (*de police*) search.

**bavard,** ~**e** /bavar,-d/ *a.* talkative. ● *n.m.*, *f.* chatterbox.

**bavard|er** /bavarde/ *v.i.* chat; (*jacasser*) chatter, gossip. ~**age** *n.m.* chatter, gossip.

**bav|e** /bav/ *n.f.* dribble, slobber; (*de limace*) slime. ~**er** *v.i.* dribble, slobber.

**bav|ette** /bavɛt/ *n.f.*, ~**oir** *n.m.* bib.

**bazar** /bazar/ *n.m.* bazaar; (*objets: fam.*) clutter.

**BCBG** *abrév.* (*bon chic bon genre*) posh.

**BD** *abrév.* (*bande dessinée*) comic strip.

**béant,** ~**e** /beɑ̃, -t/ *a.* gaping.

**beau** *ou* **bel\*, belle** (*m. pl.* ~**x**) /bo, bɛl/ *a.* fine, beautiful; (*femme*) beautiful; (*homme*) handsome; (*grand*) big. ● *n.f.* beauty; (*sport*) deciding game. **au** ~ **milieu,** right in the middle. **bel et bien,** well and truly. **on a** ~ **essayer/insister**/*etc.*, however much one tries/insists/*etc.*, it is no use trying/ insisting/*etc.* ~**x-arts** *n.m. pl.* fine arts. ~**frère** (*pl.* ~**x-frères**) *n.m.* brother-in-law. ~**père** (*pl.* ~**x-pères**) *n.m.* father-in-law; stepfather. ~**x-parents** *n.m. pl.* parents-in-law.

**beaucoup** /boku/ *adv.* a lot, very much. ● *pron.* many (people). ~ **de,** (*nombre*) many; (*quantité*) a lot of. ~ **plus**/*etc.*, much more/ *etc.* ~ **trop,** much too much. **de** ~, by far.

**beauté** /bote/ *n.f.* beauty.

**bébé** /bebe/ *n.m.* baby. ~**-éprouvette,** test-tube baby.

**bec** /bɛk/ *n.m.* beak; (*de bouilloire*) spout; (*bouche: fam.*) mouth.

**bécane** /bekan/ *n.f.* (*fam.*) bike.

**bécasse** /bekas/ *n.f.* woodcock.

**bêche** /bɛʃ/ *n.f.* spade.

**bêcher** /beʃe/ *v.t.* dig.

**bécoter** /bekɔte/ *v.t.*, **se** ~ *v. pr.* (*fam.*) kiss.

**becquée** /beke/ *n.f.* **donner la** ~ **à,** (*oiseau*) feed; (*fig.*) spoonfeed.

**bedonnant,** ~**e** /bədɔnɑ̃, -t/ *a.* paunchy.

**beffroi** /befrwa/ *n.m.* belfry.

**bégayer** /begeje/ *v.t./i.* stammer.

**bègue** /bɛg/ *n.m./f.* stammerer. **être** ~, stammer.

**béguin** /begɛ̃/ *n.m.* **avoir le** ~ **pour,** (*fam.*) have a crush on.

**beige** /bɛʒ/ *a. & n.m.* beige.

**beignet** /bɛɲɛ/ *n.m.* fritter.

**bel** /bɛl/ *voir* **beau**.

**bêler** /bele/ *v.i.* bleat.

**belette** /bəlɛt/ *n.f.* weasel.

**belge** /bɛlʒ/ *a. & n.m./f.* Belgian.

**Belgique** /bɛlʒik/ *n.f.* Belgium.

**bélier** /belje/ *n.m.* ram. **le B**~, Aries.

**belle** /bɛl/ *voir* **beau**.

**belle|-fille** (*pl.* ~**s-filles**) /bɛlfij/ *n.f.* daughter-in-law; (*remariage*) stepdaughter. ~**-mère** (*pl.* ~**s-mères**) *n.f.* mother-in-law; stepmother. ~**-sœur** (*pl.* ~**-sœurs**) *n.f.* sister-in-law.

**bémol** /bemɔl/ *n.m.* (*mus.*) flat.

**bénédiction** /benediksjɔ̃/ *n.f.* blessing.

**bénéfice** /benefis/ *n.m.* (*gain*) profit; (*avantage*) benefit.

**bénéficiaire** /benefisjɛr/ *n.m./f.* beneficiary.

**bénéficier** /benefisje/ *v.i.* ~ **de,** benefit from.

**bénéfique** /benefik/ *a.* beneficial.

**Bénélux** /benelyks/ *n.m.* Benelux.

**bénévole** /benevɔl/ *a.* voluntary.

**bén|in,** ~**igne** /benɛ̃, -iɲ/ *a.* mild, slight; (*tumeur*) benign.

**bénir** /benir/ *v.t.* bless.

**bénitier** /benitje/ *n.m.* stoup.

**benne** /bɛn/ *n.f.* (*de grue*) scoop; (*amovible*) skip. ~ **(basculante),** dump truck.

**béquille** /bekij/ *n.f.* crutch; (*de moto*) stand.

**berceau** (*pl.* ~**x**) /bɛrso/ *n.m.* cradle.

**bercer** /bɛrse/ *v.t.* (*balancer*) rock.

**berceuse** /bɛrsøz/ *n.f.* lullaby.

**béret** /berɛ/ *n.m.* beret.

**berge** /bɛrʒ/ *n.f.* (*bord*) bank.

**berg|er,** ~**ère** /bɛrʒe, -ɛr/ *n.m.*, *f.* shepherd, shepherdess.

**berlingot** /bɛrlɛ̃go/ *n.m.* boiled sweet; (*emballage*) carton.

**berne (en)** /(ɑ̃)bɛrn/ *adv.* at half-mast.

**besogne** /bəzɔɲ/ *n.f.* task, job, chore.

**besoin** /bəzwɛ̃/ *n.m.* need. **avoir ∼ de,** need. **au ∼,** if need be.

**bestiole** /bɛstjɔl/ *n.f.* creepy-crawly.

**bétail** /betaj/ *n.m.* farm animals.

**bête¹** /bɛt/ *n.f.* animal. **∼ noire,** pet hate, pet peeve.

**bête²** /bɛt/ *a.* stupid. **∼ment** *adv.* stupidly.

**bêtise** /betiz/ *n.f.* stupidity; (*action*) stupid thing.

**béton** /betɔ̃/ *n.m.* concrete. **∼ armé,** reinforced concrete.

**betterave** /bɛtrav/ *n.f.* beetroot. **∼ su-crière,** sugar-beet.

**beur** /bœr/ *n.m./f. & a.* (*fam.*) young French North African.

**beurr|e** /bœr/ *n.m.* butter. **∼er** *v.t.* butter. **∼ier** *n.m.* butter-dish. **∼é,** *a.* buttered; (*fam.*) drunk.

**bévue** /bevy/ *n.f.* blunder.

**biais** /bjɛ/ *n.m.* **de ∼, en ∼,** at an angle. **de ∼,** (*fig.*) indirectly.

**bibelot** /biblo/ *n.m.* curio.

**biberon** /bibrɔ̃/ *n.m.* (feeding-)bottle. **nourrir au ∼,** bottle-feed.

**bible** /bibl/ *n.f.* bible. **la B∼,** the Bible.

**bibliographie** /biblijɔgrafi/ *n.f.* bibliography.

**bibliophile** /biblijɔfil/ *n.m./f.* book-lover.

**biblioth|èque** /biblijɔtɛk/ *n.f.* library; (*meuble*) bookcase; **∼écaire** *n.m./f.* librarian.

**biblique** /biblik/ *a.* biblical.

**bic** /bik/ *n.m.* (P.) biro (P.).

**bicarbonate** /bikarbɔnat/ *n.m.* **∼ (de soude),** bicarbonate (of soda).

**biceps** /bisɛps/ *n.m.* biceps.

**biche** /biʃ/ *n.f.* doe.

**bicyclette** /bisiklɛt/ *n.f.* bicycle.

**bidet** /bidɛ/ *n.m.* bidet.

**bidon** /bidɔ̃/ *n.m.* can. ● *a.* invar. (*fam.*) phoney.

**bidonville** /bidɔ̃vil/ *n.f.* shanty town.

**bidule** /bidyl/ *n.m.* (*fam.*) thing.

**bielle** /bjɛl/ *n.f.* connecting rod.

**bien** /bjɛ̃/ *adv.* well; (*très*) quite, very. ● *n.m.* good; (*patrimoine*) possession. ● *a. invar.* good; (*passable*) all right; (*en forme*) well; (*à l'aise*) comfortable; (*beau*) attractive; (*respectable*) nice, respectable. ● *conj.* **∼ que,** (al)though. **∼ que ce soit/que ça ait,** although it is/it has. **∼ du,** (*quantité*) a lot of, much. **ce n'est pas ∼ de,** it is not right to. **∼ sûr,** of course. **∼s de consommation,** consumer goods. **bien-être** *n.m.* well being.

**bienfaisance** /bjɛ̃fəzɑ̃s/ *n.f.* **fête de ∼,** fête.

**bienfait** /bjɛ̃fɛ/ *n.m.* (kind) favour; (*avantage*) benefit.

**bienfai|teur, ∼trice** /bjɛ̃fɛtœr, -tris/ *n.m., f.* benefactor.

**bientôt** /bjɛ̃to/ *adv.* soon. **à ∼,** see you soon.

**bienveillan|t, ∼te** /bjɛ̃vɛjɑ̃, -t/ *a.* kind(ly). **∼ce** *n.f.* kind(li)ness.

**bienvenu, ∼e** /bjɛ̃vny/ *a.* welcome. ● *n.f.* welcome. ● *n.m., f.* être le ∼, être la ∼e, be welcome. **souhaiter la ∼e à,** welcome.

**bière** /bjɛr/ *n.f.* beer; (*cercueil*) coffin. **∼ blonde,** lager. **∼ brune,** stout, brown ale. **∼ pression,** draught beer.

**bifteck** /biftɛk/ *n.m.* steak.

**bifur|quer** /bifyrke/ *v.i.* branch off, fork. **∼cation** *n.f.* fork, junction.

**bigot, ∼e** /bigo, -ɔt/ *n.m., f.* religious fanatic. ● *a.* over-pious.

**bijou** (*pl.* **∼x**) /biʒu/ *n.m.* jewel. **∼terie** *n.f.* (*boutique*) jeweller's shop; (*comm.*) jewellery. **∼tier, ∼tière** *n.m., f.* jeweller.

**bikini** /bikini/ *n.m.* bikini.

**bilan** /bilɑ̃/ *n.m.* outcome; (*d'une catastrophe*) (casualty) toll; (*comm.*) balance sheet. **faire le ∼ de,** assess. **∼ de santé,** check-up.

**bile** /bil/ *n.f.* bile. **se faire de la ∼,** (*fam.*) worry.

**bilingue** /bilɛ̃g/ *a.* bilingual.

**billard** /bijar/ *n.m.* billiards; (*table*) billiard-table.

**bille** /bij/ *n.f.* (*d'enfant*) marble.

**billet** /bijɛ/ *n.m.* ticket; (*lettre*) note; (*article*) column. **∼ (de banque),** (bank)note. **∼ d'aller et retour,** return ticket. **∼ aller simple,** single ticket.

**billetterie** /bijɛtri/ *n.f.* cash dispenser.

**bimensuel, ∼le** /bimɑ̃sɥɛl/ *a.* fortnightly, bimonthly.

**biochimie** /bjoʃimi/ *n.f.* biochemistry.

**biodégradable** /bjodegradabl/ *a.* biodegradable.

**biograph|ie** /bjografi/ *n.f.* biography. **∼e** *n.m./f.* biographer.

**biolog|ie** /bjolɔʒi/ *n.f.* biology. **∼ique** *a.* biological. **∼iste** *n.m./f.* biologist.

**bis** /bis/ *a. invar.* (*numéro*) A, a. ● *n.m. & int.* encore.

**biscotte** /biskɔt/ *n.f.* rusk.

**biscuit** /biskɥi/ *n.m.* (*salé*) biscuit; (*Amer.*) cracker; (*sucré*) biscuit; (*Amer.*) cookie.

**bise¹** /biz/ *n.f.* (*fam.*) kiss.

**bise²** /biz/ *n.f.* (*vent*) north wind.

**bison** /bizɔ̃/ *n.m.* (American) buffalo, bison.

**bisou** /bizu/ *n.m.* (*fam.*) kiss.

**bistouri** /bisturi/ *n.m.* lancet.

**bistro(t)** /bistro/ *n.m.* café, bar.

**bit** /bit/ *n.m.* (*comput.*) bit.

**bitume** /bitym/ *n.m.* asphalt.

**bizarre** /bizar/ *a.* odd, peculiar. **∼ment** *adv.* oddly. **∼rie** *n.f.* peculiarity.

**blafard, ∼e** /blafar, -d/ *a.* pale.

**blagu|e** /blag/ *n.f.* joke. **∼er** *v.i.* joke; *v.t.* tease.

**blaireau** (*pl.* ~**x**) /blɛro/ *n.m.* shaving-brush; (*animal*) badger.

**blâm|e** /blɑm/ *n.m.* rebuke, blame. ~**er** *v.t.* rebuke, blame.

**blanc, blanche** /blɑ̃, blɑ̃ʃ/ *a.* white; (*papier, page*) blank. ● *n.m.* white; (*espace*) blank. ● *n.m., f.* white man, white woman. ● *n.f.* (*mus.*) minim. ~ (**de poulet**), breast. **le** ~, (*linge*) whites. **laisser en** ~, leave blank.

**blancheur** /blɑ̃ʃœr/ *n.f.* whiteness.

**blanch|ir** /blɑ̃ʃir/ *v.t.* whiten; (*linge*) launder; (*personne: fig.*) clear; (*culin.*) blanch. ~**ir (à la chaux)**, whitewash. ● *v.i.* turn white. ~**issage** *n.m.* laundering. ~**isserie** *n.f.* laundry.

**blasé** /blaze/ *a.* blasé.

**blasphème** /blasfɛm/ *n.m.* blasphemy.

**blatte** /blat/ *n.f.* cockroach.

**blazer** /blezœr/ *n.m.* blazer.

**blé** /ble/ *n.m.* wheat.

**bled** /blɛd/ *n.m.* (*fam.*) dump, hole.

**blême** /blɛm/ *a.* (sickly) pale.

**bless|er** /blese/ *v.t.* injure, hurt; (*par balle*) wound; (*offenser*) hurt, wound. **se** ~**er** *v. pr.* injure *ou* hurt o.s. ~**é, ~ée** *n.m., f.* casualty, injured person.

**blessure** /blesyr/ *n.f.* wound.

**bleu** /blø/ *a.* blue; (*culin.*) very rare. ~ **marine**, navy blue. ● *n.m.* blue; (*contusion*) bruise. ~**(s)**, (*vêtement*) overalls.

**bleuet** /bløɛ/ *n.m.* cornflower.

**blindé** /blɛ̃de/ *a.* armoured; (*fig.*) immune (**contre**, to); *n.m.* armoured car, tank.

**bloc** /blɔk/ *n.m.* block; (*de papier*) pad; (*système*) unit; (*pol.*) bloc. ~-**notes** (*pl.* ~**s-notes**) *n.m.* note-pad.

**blocage** /blɔkaʒ/ *n.m.* (*des prix*) freeze, freezing; (*des roues*) locking; (*psych.*) block.

**blocus** /blɔkys/ *n.m.* blockade.

**blond, ~e** /blɔ̃, -d/ *a.* fair, blond. ● *n.m., f.* fair-haired *ou* blond man *ou* woman. ~**eur** /-dœr/ *n.f.* fairness.

**bloquer** /blɔke/ *v.t.* block; (*porte, machine*) jam; (*freins*) slam on; (*roues*) lock; (*prix, crédits*) freeze. **se** ~ *v. pr.* jam; (*roues*) lock.

**blottir (se)** /(sə)blɔtir/ *v. pr.* snuggle, huddle.

**blouse** /bluz/ *n.f.* smock.

**blouson** /bluzɔ̃/ *n.m.* lumber-jacket; (*Amer.*) windbreaker.

**blue-jean** /bludʒin/ *n.m.* jeans.

**bluff** /blœf/ *n.m.* bluff. ~**er** *v.t./i.* bluff.

**blush** /bløʃ/ *n.m.* blusher.

**boa** /bɔa/ *n.m.* boa.

**bobine** /bɔbin/ *n.f.* reel; (*sur machine*) spool; (*électr.*) coil.

**bobo** /bɔbo/ *n.m.* (*fam.*) sore, cut. **avoir** ~, have a pain.

**boc|al** (*pl.* ~**aux**) /bɔkal, -o/ *n.m.* jar.

**body** /bɔdi/ *n.m.* leotard.

**bœuf** (*pl.* ~**s**) /bœf, bø/ *n.m.* ox; (*viande*) beef. ~**s**, oxen.

**bogue** /bɔg/ *n.m.* (*comput.*) bug.

**boire†** /bwar/ *v.t./i.* drink; (*absorber*) soak up.

**bois**[1] /bwa/ *voir* **boire**.

**bois**[2] /bwa/ *n.m.* (*matériau, forêt*) wood. **de** ~, **en** ~, wooden.

**boisé** /bwaze/ *a.* wooded.

**boisson** /bwasɔ̃/ *n.f.* drink.

**boit** /bwa/ *voir* **boire**.

**boîte** /bwat/ *n.f.* box; (*de conserves*) tin, can; (*firme: fam.*) firm. ~ **à gants**, glove compartment. ~ **aux lettres**, letter-box. ~ **de nuit**, night-club. ~ **postale**, post-office box. ~ **de vitesses**, gear box.

**boiter** /bwate/ *v.i.* limp; (*meuble*) wobble.

**boiteu|x, ~se** /bwatø, -z/ *a.* lame; (*meuble*) wobbly; (*raisonnement*) shaky.

**boîtier** /bwatje/ *n.m.* case.

**bol** /bɔl/ *n.m.* bowl. **avoir du** ~, (*fam.*) be lucky.

**Bolivie** /bɔlivi/ *n.f.* Bolivia.

**bolivien, ~ne** /bɔlivjɛ̃, -jɛn/ *a. & n.m., f.* Bolivian.

**bombard|er** /bɔ̃barde/ *v.t.* bomb; (*par obus*) shell. ~**ement** *n.m.* bombing; shelling.

**bombe** /bɔ̃b/ *n.f.* bomb; (*atomiseur*) spray, aerosol.

**bombé** /bɔ̃be/ *a.* rounded; (*route*) cambered.

**bon, bonne** /bɔ̃, bɔn/ *a.* good; (*qui convient*) right; (*prudent*) wise. ~ **à/pour**, (*approprié*) fit to/for. **tenir** ~, stand firm. ● *n.m.* (*billet*) voucher, coupon; (*comm.*) bond. **du** ~, some good. **pour de** ~, for good. **à quoi** ~?, what's the good *ou* point? **bonne année**, happy New Year. ~ **anniversaire**, happy birthday. ~ **appétit/voyage**, enjoy your meal/ trip. **bonne chance/nuit**, good luck/night. **bonne femme**, (*péj.*) woman. ~ **sens**, common sense. ~ **vivant**, bon viveur. **de bonne heure**, early.

**bonbon** /bɔ̃bɔ̃/ *n.m.* sweet; (*Amer.*) candy.

**bonbonne** /bɔ̃bɔn/ *n.f.* demijohn; (*de gaz*) canister.

**bond** /bɔ̃/ *n.m.* leap. **faire un** ~, leap in the air; (*de surprise*) jump.

**bonde** /bɔ̃d/ *n.f.* plug; (*trou*) plughole.

**bondé** /bɔ̃de/ *a.* packed.

**bondir** /bɔ̃dir/ *v.i.* leap; (*de surprise*) jump.

**bonheur** /bɔnœr/ *n.m.* happiness. **par** ~, luckily.

**bonhomme** (*pl.* **bonshommes**) /bɔnɔm, bɔ̃zɔm/ *n.m.* fellow. ~ **de neige**, snowman.

**bonjour** /bɔ̃ʒur/ *n.m. & int.* hallo, hello, good morning *ou* afternoon.

**bon marché** /bɔ̃marʃe/ *a. invar.* cheap. ● *adv.* cheap(ly).

**bonne**[1] /bɔn/ *a.f. voir* **bon**.

**bonne**[^2] /bɔn/ *n.f.* (*domestique*) maid. ~ **d'enfants**, nanny.

**bonnet** /bɔnɛ/ *n.m.* hat; (*de soutien-gorge*) cup. ~ **de bain**, swimming cap.

**bonneterie** /bɔnɛtri/ *n.f.* hosiery.

**bonsoir** /bɔswar/ *n.m. & int.* good evening; (*en se couchant*) good night.

**bonté** /bɔte/ *n.f.* kindness.

**bonus** /bɔnys/ *n.m.* (*auto.*) no claims bonus.

**bord** /bɔr/ *n.m.* edge; (*rive*) bank. **à ~ (de)**, on board. **au ~ de la mer**, at the seaside. **au ~ des larmes**, on the verge of tears. **~ de la route**, roadside.

**bordeaux** /bɔrdo/ *n.m. invar.* Bordeaux (wine), claret. ● *a. invar.* maroon.

**border** /bɔrde/ *v.t.* line, border; (*personne, lit*) tuck in.

**bordereau** (*pl.* ~**x**) /bɔrdəro/ *n.m.* (*liste*) note, slip; (*facture*) invoice.

**bordure** /bɔrdyr/ *n.f.* border. **en ~ de**, on the edge of.

**borne** /bɔrn/ *n.f.* boundary marker. ~ **(kilométrique)**, (*approx.*) milestone. ~**s**, limits.

**borner** /bɔrne/ *v.t.* confine. **se ~** *v. pr.* confine o.s. (**à**, to).

**bosquet** /bɔskɛ/ *n.m.* grove.

**bosse** /bɔs/ *n.f.* bump; (*de chameau*) hump.

**bosser** /bɔse/ *v.i.* (*fam.*) work (hard). ● *v.t.* (*fam.*) work (hard) at.

**bossu, ~e** /bɔsy/ *n.m., f.* hunch-back.

**botanique** /bɔtanik/ *n.f.* botany. ● *a.* botanical.

**botte** /bɔt/ *n.f.* boot; (*de fleurs, légumes*) bunch; (*de paille*) bundle, bale. ~ **s de caoutchouc**, wellingtons.

**Bottin** /bɔtɛ̃/ *n.m.* (P.) phone book.

**bouc** /buk/ *n.m.* (billy-)goat; (*barbe*) goatee. ~ **émissaire**, scapegoat.

**boucan** /bukɑ̃/ *n.m.* (*fam.*) din.

**bouche** /buʃ/ *n.f.* mouth. ~ **bée**, open-mouthed. ~ **d'égout**, manhole. ~ **d'incendie**, (fire) hydrant. ~ **de métro**, entrance to the underground *ou* subway (*Amer.*). ~-**à-bouche** *n.m.* mouth-to-mouth resuscitation.

**bouché** /buʃe/ *a.* **c'est ~**, (*profession, avenir*) it's a dead end.

**bouchée** /buʃe/ *n.f.* mouthful.

**boucher**[^1] /buʃe/ *v.t.* block; (*bouteille*) cork. **se ~** *v. pr.* get blocked. **se ~ le nez**, hold one's nose.

**bouch|er**[^2], ~**ère** /buʃe, -ɛr/ *n.m., f.* butcher. ~**erie** *n.f.* butcher's (shop); (*carnage*) butchery.

**bouchon** /buʃɔ̃/ *n.m.* stopper; (*en liège*) cork; (*de bidon, tube*) cap; (*de pêcheur*) float; (*de circulation: fig.*) hold-up.

**boucle** /bukl/ *n.f.* (*de ceinture*) buckle; (*forme*) loop; (*de cheveux*) curl. ~ **d'oreille**, ear-ring.

**boucl|er** /bukle/ *v.t.* fasten; (*terminer*) finish off; (*enfermer: fam.*) shut up; (*encercler*) seal off; (*budget*) balance. ● *v.i.* curl. ~**é** *a.* (*cheveux*) curly.

**bouclier** /buklije/ *n.m.* shield.

**bouddhiste** /budist/ *a. & n.m./f.* Buddhist.

**bouder** /bude/ *v.i.* sulk. ● *v.t.* steer clear of.

**boudin** /budɛ̃/ *n.m.* black pudding.

**boue** /bu/ *n.f.* mud.

**bouée** /bwe/ *n.f.* buoy. ~ **de sauvetage**, lifebuoy.

**boueu|x, ~se** /bwø, -z/ *a.* muddy.

**bouff|e** /buf/ *n.f.* (*fam.*) food, grub. ~**er** *v.t./i.* (*fam.*) eat.

**bouffée** /bufe/ *n.f.* puff, whiff; (*méd.*) flush; (*d'orgueil*) fit.

**bouffi** /bufi/ *a.* bloated.

**bouffon, ~ne** /bufɔ̃, -ɔn/ *a.* farcical. ● *n.m.* buffoon.

**bougeoir** /buʒwar/ *n.m.* candlestick.

**bougeotte** /buʒɔt/ *n.f.* **la ~**, (*fam.*) the fidgets.

**bouger** /buʒe/ *v.t./i.* move; (*agir*) stir. **se ~** *v. pr.* (*fam.*) move.

**bougie** /buʒi/ *n.f.* candle; (*auto.*) spark(ing)-plug.

**bouillie** /buji/ *n.f.* (*pour bébé*) baby food; (*péj.*) mush.

**bouill|ir**[^†] /bujir/ *v.i.* boil. ● *v.t.* (**faire**) ~**ir**, boil. ~**ant, ~ante** *a.* boiling; (*très chaud*) boiling hot.

**bouilloire** /bujwar/ *n.f.* kettle.

**bouillon** /bujɔ̃/ *n.m.* (*aliment*) stock. ~ **cube**, stock cube.

**bouillote** /bujɔt/ *n.f.* hot-water bottle.

**boulang|er, ~ère** /bulɑ̃ʒe, -ɛr/ *n.m., f.* baker. ~**erie** *n.f.* bakery.

**boule** /bul/ *n.f.* ball; (*de machine à écrire*) golf ball. ~**s**, (*jeu*) bowls. **jouer aux ~s**, play bowls. ~ **de neige**, snowball.

**bouleau** (*pl.* ~**x**) /bulo/ *n.m.* (silver) birch.

**boulet** /bulɛ/ *n.m.* (*de canon*) cannon-ball; (*de forçat: fig.*) ball and chain.

**boulette** /bulɛt/ *n.f.* (*de papier*) pellet; (*aliment*) meat ball.

**boulevard** /bulvar/ *n.m.* boulevard.

**boulevers|er** /bulvɛrse/ *v.t.* turn upside down; (*pays, plans*) disrupt; (*émouvoir*) distress, upset. ~**ant, ante** *a.* deeply moving. ~**ement** *n.m.* upheaval.

**boulimie** /bulimi/ *n.f.* compulsive eating; (*méd.*) bulimia.

**boulon** /bulɔ̃/ *n.m.* bolt.

**boulot**[^1] /bulo/ *n.m.* (*travail: fam.*) work.

**boulot**[^2], ~**te** /bulo, -ɔt/ *a.* (*rond: fam.*) dumpy.

**boum** /bum/ *n.m. & int.* bang.

**bouquet** /bukɛ/ *n.m.* (*de fleurs*) bunch, bouquet; (*d'arbres*) clump.

**bouquin** /bukɛ̃/ *n.m.* (*fam.*) book.

**bourdon** /burdɔ̃/ n.m. bumble-bee.

**bourdonn|er** /burdɔne/ v.i. buzz. ~**ement** n.m. buzzing.

**bourgeois**, ~**e** /burʒwa, -z/ a. & n.m., f. middle-class (person); (péj.) bourgeois. ~**ie** /-zi/ n.f. middle class(es).

**bourgeon** /burʒɔ̃/ n.m. bud. ~**ner** /-ɔne/ v.i. bud.

**bourgogne** /burgɔɲ/ n.m. burgundy. ● n.f. la B~, Burgundy.

**bourrade** /burad/ n.f. prod.

**bourrasque** /burask/ n.f. squall.

**bourrati|f**, ~**ve** /buratif, -v/ a. filling, stodgy.

**bourreau** (pl. ~**x**) /buro/ n.m. executioner. ~ **de travail**, workaholic.

**bourrer** /bure/ v.t. cram (**de**, with). ~ **de coups**, thrash.

**bours|e** /burs/ n.f. purse; (subvention) grant. **la B~e**, the Stock Exchange. ~**ier**, ~**ière** a. Stock Exchange; n.m., f. holder of a grant.

**bousculer** /buskyle/ v.t. (pousser) jostle; (presser) rush.

**bouse** /buz/ n.f. (cow) dung.

**bousiller** /buzije/ v.t. (fam.) mess up.

**boussole** /busɔl/ n.f. compass.

**bout** /bu/ n.m. end; (de langue, bâton) tip; (morceau) bit. **à** ~, exhausted. **à** ~ **de souffle**, out of breath. **au** ~ **de**, (après) after. ~ **filtre**, filter-tip.

**bouteille** /butɛj/ n.f. bottle.

**boutique** /butik/ n.f. shop; (de mode) boutique.

**bouton** /butɔ̃/ n.m. button; (pustule) pimple; (pousse) bud; (de porte, radio, etc.) knob. ~ **de manchette**, cuff-link. ~**ner** /-ɔne/ v.t. button (up). ~**nière** /-ɔnjɛr/ n.f. buttonhole. ~-**pression** (pl. ~**s-pression**) n.m. press-stud; (Amer.) snap.

**bouture** /butyr/ n.f. (plante) cutting.

**bovin**, ~**e** /bɔvɛ̃, -in/ a. bovine. ~**s** n.m. pl. cattle.

**bowling** /boliŋ/ n.m. bowling; (salle) bowling-alley.

**box** (pl. ~ ou **boxes**) /bɔks/ n.m. (jurid.) dock.

**box|e** /bɔks/ n.f. boxing. ~**er** v.t./i. box. ~**eur** n.m. boxer.

**boyau** (pl. ~**x**) /bwajo/ n.m. gut; (corde) catgut; (galerie) gallery; (de bicyclette) tyre.

**boycott|er** /bɔjkɔte/ v.t. boycott. ~**age** n.m. boycott.

**BP** abrév. (boîte postale) PO Box.

**bracelet** /braslɛ/ n.m. bracelet; (de montre) strap.

**brad|er** /brade/ v.t. sell off. ~**erie** n.f. open-air sale.

**braguette** /bragɛt/ n.f. fly.

**braille** /braj/ n.m. & a. Braille.

**braire** /brɛr/ v.i. bray.

**braiser** /breze/ v.t. braise.

**brancard** /brɑ̃kar/ n.m. stretcher; (bras) shaft.

**branche** /brɑ̃ʃ/ n.f. branch.

**branché** /brɑ̃ʃe/ a. (fam.) trendy.

**branch|er** /brɑ̃ʃe/ v.t. connect; (électr.) plug in. ~**ement** n.m. connection.

**branchies** /brɑ̃ʃi/ n.f. pl. gills.

**brandir** /brɑ̃dir/ v.t. brandish.

**braquer** /brake/ v.t. aim; (regard) fix; (roue) turn; (banque: fam.) hold up. ● v.i. (auto.) turn (the wheel). ● v. pr. **se** ~, dig one's heels in.

**bras** /bra/ n.m. arm. ● n.m. pl. (fig.) labour, hands. ~ **dessus bras dessous**, arm in arm. ~ **droit**, (fig.) right-hand man.

**brassard** /brasar/ n.m. arm-band.

**brasse** /bras/ n.f. (breast-)stroke.

**brass|er** /brase/ v.t. mix; (bière) brew; (affaires) handle a lot of. ~**erie** n.f. brewery; (café) brasserie.

**brassière** /brasjɛr/ n.f. (baby's) vest.

**brave** /brav/ a. brave; (bon) good. ~**ment** adv. bravely.

**braver** /brave/ v.t. defy.

**bravo** /bravo/ int. bravo. ● n.m. cheer.

**bravoure** /bravur/ n.f. bravery.

**break** /brɛk/ n.m. estate car.

**brebis** /brəbi/ n.f. ewe. ~ **galeuse**, black sheep.

**bredouiller** /brəduje/ v.t./i. mumble.

**bref**, **brève** /brɛf, -v/ a. short, brief. ● adv. in short. **en** ~, in short.

**Brésil** /brezil/ n.m. Brazil.

**brésilien**, ~**ne** /breziljɛ̃, -jɛn/ a. & n.m., f. Brazilian.

**Bretagne** /brətaɲ/ n.f. Brittany.

**bretelle** /brətɛl/ n.f. (shoulder-)strap; (d'autoroute) access road. ~**s**, (pour pantalon) braces.

**breton**, ~**ne** /brətɔ̃, -ɔn/ a. & n.m., f. Breton.

**brève** /brɛv/ voir **bref**.

**brevet** /brəvɛ/ n.m. diploma. ~ (**d'invention**), patent.

**brevet|er** /brəvte/ v.t. patent. ~**é** a. patented.

**bribes** /brib/ n.f. pl. scraps.

**bric-à-brac** /brikabrak/ n.m. invar. bric-à-brac.

**bricole** /brikɔl/ n.f. trifle.

**bricol|er** /brikɔle/ v.i. do odd (do-it-yourself) jobs. ● v.t. fix (up). ~**age** n.m. do-it-yourself (jobs).

**bride** /brid/ n.f. bridle.

**bridé** /bride/ a. **yeux** ~**s**, slit eyes.

**bridge** /bridʒ/ n.m. (cartes) bridge.

**brière|ment** /brijɛvmɑ̃/ adv. briefly. ~**té** n.f. brevity.

**brigad|e** /brigad/ *n.f.* (*de police*) squad; (*mil.*) brigade; (*fig.*) team. **~ier** *n.m.* (*de police*) sergeant.

**brill|ant, ~ante** /brijã, -t/ *a.* (*couleur*) bright; (*luisant*) shiny; (*remarquable*) brilliant. ● *n.m.* (*éclat*) shine; (*diamant*) diamond. **~amment** *adv.* brilliantly.

**briller** /brije/ *v.i.* shine.

**brimer** /brime/ *v.t.* bully, harass. **se sentir brimé**, feel put down.

**brin** /brɛ̃/ *n.m.* **~ d'herbe**, blade of grass. **un ~ de**, a bit of.

**brindille** /brɛ̃dij/ *n.f.* twig.

**brioche** /brijɔʃ/ *n.f.* brioche (*small round sweet cake*); (*ventre: fam.*) paunch.

**brique** /brik/ *n.f.* brick.

**briquer** /brike/ *v.t.* polish.

**briquet** /brikɛ/ *n.m.* (cigarette-)lighter.

**brise** /briz/ *n.f.* breeze.

**briser** /brize/ *v.t.* break. **se ~er** *v. pr.* break.

**britannique** /britanik/ *a.* British. ● *n.m./f.* Briton. **les B~s**, the British.

**broc** /bro/ *n.m.* pitcher.

**brocant|e** /brɔkãt/ *n.f.* second-hand goods. **~eur, ~euse** *n.m., f.* second-hand goods dealer.

**broche** /brɔʃ/ *n.f.* brooch; (*culin.*) spit. **à la ~**, spit-roasted.

**brochet** /brɔʃɛ/ *n.m.* (*poisson*) pike.

**brochette** /brɔʃɛt/ *n.f.* skewer.

**brochure** /brɔʃyr/ *n.f.* brochure, booklet.

**brod|er** /brɔde/ *v.t.* embroider. **~erie** *n.f.* embroidery.

**broncher** /brɔ̃ʃe/ *v.i.* **sans ~**, without turning a hair.

**bronch|es** /brɔ̃ʃ/ *n.f. pl.* bronchial tubes. **~ite** *n.f.* bronchitis.

**bronze** /brɔ̃z/ *n.m.* bronze.

**bronz|er** /brɔ̃ze/ *v.i.*, **se ~er** *v. pr.* get a (sun-)tan. **~age** *n.m.* (sun-)tan. **~é** *a.* (sun-)tanned.

**brosse** /brɔs/ *n.f.* brush. **~ à dents**, toothbrush. **~ à habits**, clothes-brush.

**brosser** /brɔse/ *v.t.* brush; (*fig.*) paint. **se ~ les dents/les cheveux**, brush one's teeth/hair.

**brouette** /bruɛt/ *n.f.* wheelbarrow.

**brouhaha** /bruaa/ *n.m.* hubbub.

**brouillard** /brujar/ *n.m.* fog.

**brouille** /bruj/ *n.f.* quarrel.

**brouiller** /bruje/ *v.t.* mix up; (*vue*) blur; (*œufs*) scramble; (*radio*) jam; (*amis*) set at odds. **se ~** *v. pr.* (*amis*) fall out.

**brouillon** /brujɔ̃/ *n.m.* (rough) draft.

**broussailles** /brusaj/ *n.f. pl.* undergrowth.

**brousse** /brus/ *n.f.* **la ~**, the bush.

**brouter** /brute/ *v.t./i.* graze.

**broyer** /brwaje/ *v.t.* crush; (*moudre*) grind.

**bru** /bry/ *n.f.* daughter-in-law.

**bruit** /brɥi/ *n.m.* noise; (*fig.*) rumour.

**bruitage** /brɥitaʒ/ *n.m.* sound effects.

**brûlant, ~e** /brylã, -t/ *a.* burning (hot); (*sujet*) red-hot.

**brûl|er** /bryle/ *v.t./i.* burn; (*essence*) use (up); (*signal*) go through *ou* past (without stopping). **se ~er** *v. pr.* burn o.s. **~eur** *n.m.* burner.

**brûlure** /brylyr/ *n.f.* burn. **~s d'estomac**, heartburn.

**brum|e** /brym/ *n.f.* mist. **~eux, ~euse** *a.* misty; (*idées*) hazy.

**brun, ~e** /brœ̃, bryn/ *a.* brown, dark. ● *n.m.* brown. ● *n.m., f.* dark-haired person. **~ir** /brynir/ *v.i.* turn brown; (*se bronzer*) get a tan.

**brunch** /brœnʃ/ *n.m.* brunch.

**brushing** /brœʃiŋ/ *n.m.* blow-dry.

**brusque** /brysk/ *a.* abrupt. **~ment** /-əmã/ *adv.* suddenly, abruptly.

**brusquer** /bryske/ *v.t.* rush.

**brut** /bryt/ *a.* (*pétrole*) crude; (*comm.*) gross.

**brut|al** (*m. pl. ~aux*) /brytal, -o/ *a.* brutal. **~alité** *n.f.* brutality.

**brute** /bryt/ *n.f.* brute.

**Bruxelles** /brysɛl/ *n.m./f.* Brussels.

**bruy|ant, ~ante** /brɥijã, -t/ *a.* noisy. **~amment** *adv.* noisily.

**bruyère** /bryjɛr/ *n.f.* heather.

**bu** /by/ *voir* **boire**.

**bûche** /byʃ/ *n.f.* log. **~ de Noël**, Christmas log.

**bûcheron** /byʃrɔ̃/ *n.m.* woodcutter.

**budg|et** /bydʒɛ/ *n.m.* budget. **~étaire** *a.* budgetary.

**buée** /bye/ *n.f.* mist, condensation.

**buffet** /byfɛ/ *n.m.* sideboard; (*réception, restaurant*) buffet.

**buffle** /byfl/ *n.m.* buffalo.

**buisson** /bɥisɔ̃/ *n.m.* bush.

**bulbe** /bylb/ *n.m.* bulb.

**bulgare** /bylgar/ *a. & n.m./f.* Bulgarian.

**Bulgarie** /bylgari/ *n.f.* Bulgaria.

**bulldozer** /byldozɛr/ *n.m.* bulldozer.

**bulle** /byl/ *n.f.* bubble.

**bulletin** /byltɛ̃/ *n.m.* bulletin, report. **~ d'information**, news bulletin. **~ météorologique**, weather report. **~ (de vote)**, ballot-paper. **~ de salaire**, pay-slip.

**buraliste** /byralist/ *n.m./f.* tobacconist; (*à la poste*) clerk.

**bureau** (*pl. ~x*) /byro/ *n.m.* office; (*meuble*) desk; (*comité*) board. **~ de location**, booking-office; (*théâtre*) box-office. **~ de poste**, post office. **~ de tabac**, tobacconist's (shop). **~ de vote**, polling station.

**bureaucratie** /byrokrasi/ *n.f.* bureaucracy.

**burlesque** /byrlɛsk/ *a.* ludicrous; (*théâtre*) burlesque.

**bus** /bys/ *n.m.* bus.

**buste** /byst/ n.m. bust.

**but** /by(t)/ n.m. target; (*dessein*) aim, goal; (*football*) goal. **avoir pour ~ de,** aim to. **dans le ~ de,** with the intention of.

**butane** /bytan/ n.f. butane, Calor gas (P.).

**buté** /byte/ a. obstinate.

**buter** /byte/ v.i. ~ **contre,** knock against; (*problème*) come up against. ● v.t. antagonize. **se ~** v. pr. (*s'entêter*) become obstinate.

**butin** /bytɛ̃/ n.m. booty, loot.

**butiner** /bytine/ v.i. gather nectar.

**butte** /byt/ n.f. mound.

**buvard** /byvar/ n.m. blotting-paper.

**buvette** /byvɛt/ n.f. (refreshment) bar.

**buveu|r, ~se** /byvœr, -øz/ n.m., f. drinker.

●●●●●●●●●●●●●●●●●●●●●●●●●●●●●●●●

# Cc

●●●●●●●●●●●●●●●●●●●●●●●●●●●●●●●●

**c'** /s/ *voir* ce¹.

**ça** /sa/ pron. it, that; (*pour désigner*) that; (*plus près*) this. **ça va?,** (*fam.*) how's it going? **ça va!,** (*fam.*) all right! **où ça?,** (*fam.*) where? **quand ça?,** (*fam.*) when? **c'est ça,** that's right.

**çà** /sa/ adv. **çà et là,** here and there.

**cabane** /kaban/ n.f. hut; (*à outils*) shed.

**cabaret** /kabarɛ/ n.m. night-club.

**cabas** /kabɑ/ n.m. shopping bag.

**cabillaud** /kabijo/ n.m. cod.

**cabine** /kabin/ n.f. (*à la piscine*) cubicle; (*à la plage*) (beach) hut; (*de bateau*) cabin; (*de pilotage*) cockpit. ~ **(téléphonique),** phone-booth, phone-box.

**cabinet** /kabinɛ/ n.m. (*de médecin*) surgery; (*d'avocat*) office; (*clientèle*) practice; (*pol.*) Cabinet; (*pièce*) room. **~s,** (*toilettes*) toilet. ~ **de toilette,** toilet.

**câble** /kɑbl/ n.m. cable; (*corde*) rope.

**cabot|age** /kabotaʒ/ n.m. coastal navigation. **~eur** n.m. coaster.

**cabrer (se)** /kabre/ v.t., **se ~** v. pr. (*cheval*) rear up. **se ~ contre,** rebel against.

**cabriole** /kabrijol/ n.f. (*culbute*) somersault.

**cacahuète** /kakaɥɛt/ n.f. peanut.

**cacao** /kakao/ n.m. cocoa.

**cachalot** /kaʃalo/ n.m. sperm whale.

**cache** /kaʃ/ n.m. mask; (*photo.*) lens cover.

**cachemire** /kaʃmir/ n.m. cashmere.

**cach|er** /kaʃe/ v.t. hide, conceal (**à,** from). **se ~er** v. pr. hide; (*se trouver caché*) be hidden. **~e-cache** n.m. invar. hide-and-seek.

**cachet** /kaʃɛ/ n.m. seal; (*de la poste*) postmark; (*comprimé*) tablet; (*d'artiste*) fee; (*fig.*) style.

**cacheter** /kaʃte/ v.t. seal.

**cachette** /kaʃɛt/ n.f. hiding-place. **en ~,** in secret.

**cachot** /kaʃo/ n.m. dungeon.

**cactus** /kaktys/ n.m. cactus.

**cadavre** /kadavr/ n.m. corpse.

**caddie** /kadi/ n.m. trolley.

**cadeau** (pl. **~x**) /kado/ n.m. present, gift. **faire un ~ à qn.,** give s.o. a present.

**cadenas** /kadna/ n.m. padlock.

**cadet, ~te** /kadɛ, -t/ a. youngest; (*entre deux*) younger. ● n.m., f. youngest (child); younger (child).

**cadran** /kadrɑ̃/ n.m. dial. ~ **solaire,** sundial.

**cadre** /kadr/ n.m. frame; (*milieu*) surroundings; (*limites*) scope; (*contexte*) framework. ● n.m./f. (*personne: comm.*) executive. **les ~s,** (*comm.*) the managerial staff.

**cadrer** /kadre/ v.t. (*photo*) centre.

**cafard** /kafar/ n.m. (*insecte*) cockroach. **avoir le ~,** (*fam.*) be feeling low.

**caf|é** /kafe/ n.m. coffee; (*bar*) café. ~**é au lait,** white coffee. ~**etière** n.f. coffee-pot.

**caféine** /kafein/ n.f. caffeine.

**cage** /kaʒ/ n.f. cage; (*d'escalier*) well; (*d'ascenseur*) shaft.

**cageot** /kaʒo/ n.m. crate.

**cagoule** /kagul/ n.f. hood.

**cahier** /kaje/ n.m. notebook; (*scol.*) exercise-book.

**caille** /kaj/ n.f. quail.

**caillot** /kajo/ n.m. (blood) clot.

**caillou** (pl. **~x**) /kaju/ n.m. stone; (*galet*) pebble. **~teux, ~teuse** a. stony.

**caisse** /kɛs/ n.f. crate, case; (*tiroir, machine*) till; (*guichet*) pay-desk; (*bureau*) office; (*mus.*) drum. ~ **d'épargne,** savings bank. ~ **de retraite,** pension fund.

**caiss|ier, ~ière** /kesje, -jɛr/ n.m., f. cashier.

**cake** /kɛk/ n.m. fruit-cake.

**calamité** /kalamite/ n.f. calamity.

**calcaire** /kalkɛr/ a. (*sol*) chalky; (*eau*) hard.

**calciné** /kalsine/ a. charred.

**calcium** /kalsjɔm/ n.m. calcium.

**calcul** /kalkyl/ n.m. calculation; (*scol.*) arithmetic; (*différentiel*) calculus. ~ **biliaire,** gallstone.

**calcul|er** /kalkyle/ v.t. calculate. **~ateur** n.m. (*ordinateur*) computer, calculator. **~atrice** n.f. (*ordinateur*) calculator. **~ette** n.f. (pocket) calculator.

**calé** /kale/ a. (*fam.*) clever.

**caleçon** /kalsɔ̃/ n.m. underpants; (*de femme*) leggings.

**calendrier** /kalɑ̃drije/ n.m. calendar; (fig.) timetable.

**calepin** /kalpɛ̃/ n.m. notebook.

**caler** /kale/ v.t. wedge; (moteur) stall. ● v.i. stall.

**calfeutrer** /kalføtre/ v.t. stop up the cracks of.

**calibr|e** /kalibr/ n.m. calibre; (d'un œuf, fruit) grade.

**câlin, ~e** /kɑlɛ̃, -in/ a. endearing, cuddly. **~er** /-ine/ v.t. cuddle.

**calmant** /kalmɑ̃/ n.m. sedative.

**calm|e** /kalm/ a. calm ● n.m. calm(ness). **du ~e!**, calm down! **~er** v.t., **se ~er** v. pr. (personne) calm (down); (diminuer) ease.

**calomn|ie** /kalɔmni/ n.f. slander; (écrite) libel. **~ier** v.t. slander; libel.

**calorie** /kalɔri/ n.f. calorie.

**calqu|e** /kalk/ n.m. tracing; (fig.) exact copy. **~er** v.t. trace; (fig.) copy. **~er sur,** model on.

**calvaire** /kalvɛr/ n.m. (croix) calvary; (fig.) suffering.

**calvitie** /kalvisi/ n.f. baldness.

**camarade** /kamarad/ n.m./f. friend; (pol.) comrade. **~rie** n.f. good companionship.

**cambiste** /kɑ̃bist/ n.m./f. foreign exchange dealer.

**cambouis** /kɑ̃bwi/ n.m. (engine) oil.

**cambrer** /kɑ̃bre/ v.t. arch. **se ~** v. pr. arch one's back.

**cambriol|er** /kɑ̃brijɔle/ v.t. burgle. **~age** n.m. burglary. **~eur, ~euse** n.m., f. burglar.

**camembert** /kamɑ̃bɛr/ n.m. Camembert (cheese).

**caméra** /kamera/ n.f. (cinéma, télévision) camera.

**caméra|man** (pl. **~men**) /kameraman, -mɛn/ n.m. cameraman.

**camion** /kamjɔ̃/ n.m. lorry, truck. **~citerne** n.m. tanker. **~nage** /-jɔnaʒ/ n.m. haulage. **~nette** /-jɔnɛt/ n.f. van. **~neur** /-jɔnœr/ n.m. lorry ou truck driver.

**camoufl|er** /kamufle/ v.t. camouflage. **~age** n.m. camouflage.

**camp** /kɑ̃/ n.m. camp; (sport) side.

**campagn|e** /kɑ̃paɲ/ n.f. country (side); (mil., pol.) campaign.

**camp|er** /kɑ̃pe/ v.i. camp. **~ement** n.m. encampment. **~eur, ~euse** n.m., f. camper.

**camphre** /kɑ̃fr/ n.m. camphor.

**camping** /kɑ̃piŋ/ n.m. camping. **faire du ~,** go camping. **~-car** n.m. camper-van. **~-gaz** n.m. invar. (P.) camping-gaz. **(terrain de) ~,** campsite.

**campus** /kɑ̃pys/ n.m. campus.

**Canada** /kanada/ n.m. Canada.

**canadien, ~ne** /kanadjɛ̃, -jɛn/ a. & n.m., f. Canadian.

**can|al** (pl. **~aux**) /kanal, -o/ n.m. (artificiel) canal; (bras de mer) channel; (techn., TV) channel. **par le ~al de,** through.

**canalisation** /kanalizasjɔ̃/ n.f. (tuyaux) main(s).

**canapé** /kanape/ n.m. sofa.

**canard** /kanar/ n.m. duck; (journal: fam.) rag.

**canari** /kanari/ n.m. canary.

**cancans** /kɑ̃kɑ̃/ n.m. pl. malicious gossip.

**canc|er** /kɑ̃sɛr/ n.m. cancer. **le C~er,** Cancer. **~éreux, ~éreuse** a. cancerous. **~érigène** a. carcinogenic.

**cancre** /kɑ̃kr/ n.m. dunce.

**candeur** /kɑ̃dœr/ n.f. naïvety.

**candidat, ~e** /kɑ̃dida, -t/ n.m., f. candidate; (à un poste) applicant, candidate (à, for). **~ure** /-tyr/ n.f. application; (pol.) candidacy. **poser sa ~ pour,** apply for.

**candide** /kɑ̃did/ a. naïve.

**cane** /kan/ n.f. (female) duck. **~ton** n.m. duckling.

**canette** /kanɛt/ n.f. (de bière) bottle.

**caniche** /kaniʃ/ n.m. poodle.

**canicule** /kanikyl/ n.f. hot summer days.

**canif** /kanif/ n.m. penknife.

**caniveau** (pl. **~x**) /kanivo/ n.m. gutter.

**cannabis** /kanabis/ n.m. cannabis.

**canne** /kan/ n.f. (walking-)stick. **~ à pêche,** fishing-rod. **~ à sucre,** sugar-cane.

**cannelle** /kanɛl/ n.f. cinnamon.

**canoë** /kanɔe/ n.m. canoe; (sport) canoeing.

**canon** /kanɔ̃/ n.m. (big) gun; (d'une arme) barrel.

**canot** /kano/ n.m. boat. **~ de sauvetage,** lifeboat. **~ pneumatique,** rubber dinghy.

**cantate** /kɑ̃tat/ n.f. cantata.

**cantatrice** /kɑ̃tatris/ n.f. opera singer.

**cantine** /kɑ̃tin/ n.f. canteen.

**cantique** /kɑ̃tik/ n.m. hymn.

**canton** /kɑ̃tɔ̃/ n.m. (en France) district; (en Suisse) canton.

**canular** /kanylar/ n.m. hoax.

**caoutchou|c** /kautʃu/ n.m. rubber; (élastique) rubber band.

**cap** /kap/ n.m. cape, headland; (direction) course.

**capable** /kapabl/ a. able, capable. **~ de qch.,** capable of sth. **~ de faire,** able to do, capable of doing.

**capacité** /kapasite/ n.f. ability; (contenance) capacity.

**cape** /kap/ n.f. cape.

**capillaire** /kapilɛr/ a. (lotion, soins) hair. **(vaisseau) ~,** capillary.

**capitaine** /kapitɛn/ n.m. captain.

**capit|al**, ~**ale** (*m. pl.* ~**aux**) /kapital,-o/ *a.* major, fundamental; (*peine, lettre*) capital. ●*n.m.* (*pl.* ~**aux**) (*comm.*) capital; (*fig.*) stock. ~**aux**, (*comm.*) capital. ●*n.f.* (*ville, lettre*) capital.

**capitalis|te** /kapitalist/ *a.* & *n.m./f.* capitalist. ~**me** *n.m.* capitalism.

**capitonné** /kapitone/ *a.* padded.

**capitul|er** /kapityle/ *v.i.* capitulate. ~**ation** *n.f.* capitulation.

**capor|al** (*pl.* ~**aux**) /kaporal, -o/ *n.m.* corporal.

**capot** /kapo/ *n.m.* (*auto.*) bonnet; (*auto., Amer.*) hood.

**capote** /kapɔt/ *n.f.* (*auto.*) hood; (*auto., Amer.*) (*convertible*) top; (*fam.*) condom.

**câpre** /kɑpr/ *n.f.* (*culin.*) caper.

**capric|e** /kapris/ *n.m.* whim, caprice. ~**ieux**, ~**ieuse** *a.* capricious; (*appareil*) temperamental.

**Capricorne** /kaprikɔrn/ *n.m.* le ~, Capricorn.

**capsule** /kapsyl/ *n.f.* capsule; (*de bouteille*) cap.

**capter** /kapte/ *v.t.* (*émission*) pick up.

**capti|f**, ~**ve** /kaptif,-v/ *a.* & *n.m., f.* captive.

**captiver** /kaptive/ *v.t.* captivate.

**captivité** /kaptivite/ *n.f.* captivity.

**captur|e** /kaptyr/ *n.f.* capture. ~**er** *v.t.* capture.

**capuche|e** /kapyʃ/ *n.f.* hood. ~ **on** *n.m.* hood; (*de stylo*) cap.

**car**[1] /kar/ *conj.* because, for.

**car**[2] /kar/ *n.m.* coach; (*Amer.*) bus.

**carabine** /karabin/ *n.f.* rifle.

**caractère** /karakter/ *n.m.* (*nature, lettre*) character. ~ **d'imprimerie**, block letters.

**caractéristique** /karakteristik/ *a.* & *n.f.* characteristic.

**carafe** /karaf/ *n.f.* carafe; (*pour le vin*) decanter.

**caraïbe** /karaib/ *a.* Caribbean. **les C**~**s**, the Caribbean.

**caramel** /karamɛl/ *n.m.* caramel. ~**iser** *v.t./i.* caramelize.

**carapace** /karapas/ *n.f.* shell.

**caravane** /karavan/ *n.f.* (*auto.*) caravan. (*convoi*) caravan.

**carbone** /karbon/ *n.m.* carbon.

**carboniser** /karbonize/ *v.t.* burn (to ashes).

**carburant** /karbyrɑ̃/ *n.m.* (motor) fuel.

**carburateur** /karbyratœr/ *n.m.* carburettor; (*Amer.*) carburetor.

**carcasse** /karkas/ *n.f.* carcass; (*d'immeuble, de voiture*) frame.

**cardiaque** /kardjak/ *a.* heart. ●*n.m./f.* heart patient.

**cardigan** /kardigɑ̃/ *n.m.* cardigan.

**cardin|al** (*m. pl.* ~**aux**) /kardinal, -o/ *a.* cardinal. ●*n.m.* (*pl.* ~**aux**) cardinal.

**Carême** /karɛm/ *n.m.* Lent.

**carence** /karɑ̃s/ *n.f.* inadequacy; (*manque*) deficiency.

**caress|e** /karɛs/ *n.f.* caress. ~**er** /-ese/ *v.t.* caress, stroke; (*espoir*) cherish.

**cargaison** /kargɛzɔ̃/ *n.f.* cargo.

**cargo** /kargo/ *n.m.* cargo boat.

**caricature** /karikatyr/ *n.f.* caricature.

**car|ie** /kari/ *n.f.* cavity. ~**ié** *a.* (*dent*) decayed.

**carillon** /karijɔ̃/ *n.m.* chimes.

**caritati|f**, ~**ve** /karitatif, -v/ *a.* **association** ~**ve,** charity.

**carlingue** /karlɛ̃g/ *n.f.* (*d'avion*) cabin.

**carnaval** (*pl.* ~**s**) /karnaval/ *n.m.* carnival.

**carnet** /karnɛ/ *n.m.* notebook; (*de tickets etc.*) book. ~ **de chèques**, cheque-book. ~ **de notes**, school report.

**carotte** /karɔt/ *n.f.* carrot.

**carpe** /karp/ *n.f.* carp.

**carpette** /karpɛt/ *n.f.* rug.

**carré** /kare/ *a.* (*forme, mesure*) square; (*fig.*) straightforward. ●*n.m.* square; (*de terrain*) patch.

**carreau** (*pl.* ~**x**) /karo/ *n.m.* (window) pane; (*par terre, au mur*) tile; (*dessin*) check; (*cartes*) diamonds. **à** ~**x**, check(ed).

**carrefour** /karfur/ *n.m.* crossroads.

**carrel|er** /karle/ *v.t.* tile. ~**age** *n.m.* tiling; (*sol*) tiles.

**carrelet** /karlɛ/ *n.m.* (*poisson*) plaice.

**carrément** /karemɑ̃/ *adv.* straight; (*dire*) straight out.

**carrière** /karjɛr/ *n.f.* career; (*terrain*) quarry.

**carrosse** /karɔs/ *n.m.* (horse-drawn) coach.

**carrosserie** /karɔsri/ *n.f.* (*auto.*) body (-work).

**carrure** /karyr/ *n.f.* build; (*fig.*) calibre.

**cartable** /kartabl/ *n.m.* satchel.

**carte** /kart/ *n.f.* card; (*géog.*) map; (*naut.*) chart; (*au restaurant*) menu. ~**s**, (*jeu*) cards. **à la** ~, (*manger*) à la carte. ~ **de crédit**, credit card. ~ **des vins**, wine list. ~ **de visite**, (business) card. ~ **grise**, (car) registration card. ~ **postale**, postcard.

**cartilage** /kartilaʒ/ *n.m.* cartilage.

**carton** /kartɔ̃/ *n.m.* cardboard; (*boîte*) (cardboard) box. ~ **à dessin**, portfolio.

**cartonné** /kartone/ *a.* (*livre*) hardback.

**cartouche** /kartuʃ/ *n.f.* cartridge; (*de cigarettes*) carton.

**cas** /ka/ *n.m.* case. **au** ~ **où**, in case. ~ **urgent**, emergency. **en aucun** ~, on no account. **en** ~ **de**, in the event of, in case of. **en tout** ~, in any case.

**casan|ier**, ~**ière** /kazanje, -jɛr/ *a.* home-loving.

**casaque** /kazak/ *n.f.* (*de jockey*) shirt.

**cascade** /kaskad/ *n.f.* waterfall.

**case** /kɑz/ *n.f.* hut; (*compartiment*) pigeon-hole; (*sur papier*) square.

**caserne** /kazɛrn/ *n.f.* barracks.

**cash** /kaʃ/ *adv.* **payer ~,** pay (in) cash.

**casier** /kazje/ *n.m.* pigeon-hole, compartment; (*meuble*) cabinet; (*à bouteilles*) rack. **~ judiciaire,** criminal record.

**casino** /kazino/ *n.m.* casino.

**casque** /kask/ *n.m.* helmet.

**casquette** /kaskɛt/ *n.f.* cap.

**cassation** /kasastjɔ̃/ *n.f.* **cour de ~,** appeal court.

**casse** /kɑs/ *n.f.* (*objets*) breakages. **mettre à la ~,** scrap.

**cass|er** /kɑse/ *v.t./i.* break; (*annuler*) annul. **se ~er** *v. pr.* break. **~e-croûte** *n.m. invar.* snack. **~e-noisettes** *ou* **~e-noix** *n.m. invar.* nutcrackers. **~e-tête** *n.m. invar.* (*problème*) headache; (*jeu*) brain teaser.

**casserole** /kasrɔl/ *n.f.* saucepan.

**cassette** /kasɛt/ *n.f.* casket; (*de magnéto-phone*) cassette; (*de video*) video tape.

**cassis**[1] /kasis/ *n.m.* black currant.

**cassis**[2] /kasi/ *n.m.* (*auto.*) dip.

**cassoulet** /kasulɛ/ *n.m.* stew (of beans and meat).

**cassure** /kɑsyr/ *n.f.* break.

**caste** /kast/ *n.f.* caste.

**castor** /kastɔr/ *n.m.* beaver.

**catalogue** /katalɔg/ *n.m.* catalogue.

**catalyseur** /katalizœr/ *n.m.* catalyst.

**cataracte** /katarakt/ *n.f.* cataract.

**catastroph|e** /katastrɔf/ *n.f.* disaster, catastrophe. **~ique** *a.* catastrophic.

**catch** /katʃ/ *n.m.* (all-in) wrestling. **~eur, ~euse** *n.m., f.* (all-in) wrestler.

**catégorie** /kategɔri/ *n.f.* category.

**catégorique** /kategɔrik/ *a.* categorical.

**cathédrale** /katedral/ *n.f.* cathedral.

**catholi|que** /katɔlik/ *a.* Catholic. **~cisme** *n.m.* Catholicism. **pas très ~que,** a bit fishy.

**cauchemar** /koʃmar/ *n.m.* nightmare.

**cause** /koz/ *n.f.* cause; (*jurid.*) case. **à ~ de,** because of.

**causer** /koze/ *v.t.* cause. ● *v.i.* chat.

**caustique** /kostik/ *a.* caustic.

**caution** /kosjɔ̃/ *n.f.* surety; (*jurid.*) bail; (*appui*) backing; (*garantie*) deposit. **sous ~,** on bail.

**cautionner** /kosjɔne/ *v.t.* guarantee; (*soutenir*) back.

**caval|ier, ~ière** /kavalje, -jɛr/ *n.m., f.* rider; (*pour danser*) partner. ● *n.m.* (*échecs*) knight.

**cave** /kav/ *n.f.* cellar.

**caveau** (*pl.* **~x**) /kavo/ *n.m.* vault.

**caverne** /kavɛrn/ *n.f.* cave.

**caviar** /kavjar/ *n.m.* caviare.

**CD** (*abrév.*) (*compact disc*) CD.

**ce**[1], **c'**[*] /sə, s/ *pron.* it, that. **c'est,** it *ou* that is. **ce sont,** they are. **c'est moi,** it's me. **c'est un chanteur/une chanteuse**/*etc.*, he/she is a singer/*etc.* **ce qui, ce que,** what. **ce que c'est bon**/*etc.*!, how good/*etc.* it is! **tout ce qui, tout ce que,** everything that.

**ce**[2] *ou* **cet**[*], **cette** (*pl.* **ces**) /sə, sɛt, se /*a.* that; (*proximité*) this. **ces,** those; (*proximité*) these.

**CE** *abrév.* (*Communauté Européenne*) EC.

**ceci** /səsi/ *pron.* this.

**céder** /sede/ *v.t.* give up. ● *v.i.* (*se rompre*) give way; (*se soumettre*) give in.

**cèdre** /sɛdr/ *n.m.* cedar.

**CEE** *abrév.* (*Communauté économique euro-péenne*) EEC.

**ceinture** /sɛ̃tyr/ *n.f.* belt; (*taille*) waist. **~ de sauvetage,** lifebelt. **~ de sécurité,** seat-belt.

**cela** /səla/ *pron.* it, that; (*pour désigner*) that.

**célèbre** /selɛbr/ *a.* famous.

**célébr|er** /selebre/ *v.t.* celebrate. **~ation** *n.f.* celebration (**de,** of).

**célébrité** /selebrite/ *n.f.* fame; (*personne*) celebrity.

**céleri** /sɛlri/ *n.m.* (*en branches*) celery. **~ (-rave),** celeriac.

**célibataire** /selibatɛr/ *a.* unmarried. ● *n.m.* bachelor. ● *n.f.* unmarried woman.

**celle, celles** /sɛl/ *voir* **celui.**

**cellophane** /selɔfan/ *n.f.* (P.) Cellophane (P.).

**cellule** /selyl/ *n.f.* cell.

**celui, celle** (*pl.* **ceux, celles**) /səlɥi, sɛl, sø/ *pron.* the one. **~ de mon ami,** my friend's. **~-ci,** this (one). **~-là,** that (one). **ceux-ci,** these (ones). **ceux-là,** those (ones).

**cendre** /sɑ̃dr/ *n.f.* ash.

**cendrier** /sɑ̃drije/ *n.m.* ashtray.

**censé** /sɑ̃se/ *a.* **être ~ faire,** be supposed to do.

**censur|e** /sɑ̃syr/ *n.f.* censorship. **~er** *v.t.* censor; (*critiquer*) censure.

**cent** (*pl.* **~s**) /sɑ̃/ (*generally* /sɑ̃t/ *pl.* /sɑ̃z/ *before vowel*) *a. & n.m.* (a) hundred. **~ un** /sɑ̃œ̃ / a hundred and one.

**centaine** /sɑ̃tɛn/ *n.f.* hundred. **une ~ (de),** (about) a hundred.

**centième** /sɑ̃tjɛm/ *a. & n.m./f.* hundredth.

**centigrade** /sɑ̃tigrad/ *a.* centigrade.

**centilitre** /sɑ̃tilitr/ *n.m.* centilitre.

**centime** /sɑ̃tim/ *n.m.* centime.

**centimètre** /sɑ̃timɛtr/ *n.m.* centimetre; (*ruban*) tape-measure.

**centr|al, ~ale** (*m. pl.* **~aux**) /sɑ̃tral, -o / *a.* central. ● *n.m.* (*pl.* **~aux**). **~al (téléphonique),** (telephone) exchange. ● *n.f.* power-station.

**centr|e** /sɑ̃tr/ *n.m.* centre. **~e-ville** *n.m.* town centre. **~er** *v.t.* centre.

**cépage** /sepaʒ/ *n.m.* (variety of) vine.

**cèpe** /sɛp/ *n.m.* (edible) boletus.

**cependant** /səpãdã/ *adv.* however.

**céramique** /seramik/ *n.f.* ceramic.

**cercle** /sɛrkl/ *n.m.* circle.~**vicieux,** vicious circle.

**cercueil** /sɛrkœj/ *n.m.* coffin.

**céréale** /sereal/ *n.f.* cereal.

**cérébr|al** (*m. pl.* ~**aux**) /serebral, -o/ *a.* cerebral.

**cérémonial** (*pl.* ~**s**) /seremɔnjal/ *n.m.* ceremonial.

**cérémonie** /seremɔni/ *n.f.* ceremony. ~(**s**), (*façons*) fuss.

**cerf** /sɛr/ *n.m.* stag.

**cerfeuil** /sɛrfœj/ *n.m.* chervil.

**cerf-volant** (*pl.* **cerfs-volants**) /sɛrvɔlã/ *n.m.* kite.

**ceris|e** /sriz/ *n.f.* cherry. ~**ier** *n.m.* cherry tree.

**certain,** ~**e** /sɛrtɛ̃, -ɛn/ *a.* certain; (*sûr*) certain, sure (**de,** of; **que,** that). ● *pron.* ~**s,** certain people. **un** ~ **temps,** some time.

**certainement** /sɛrtɛnmã/ *adv.* certainly.

**certificat** /sɛrtifika/ *n.m.* certificate.

**certif|ier** /sɛrtifje/ *v.t.* certify. ~**ier qch. à qn.,** assure s.o. of sth. ~**ié** *a.* (*professeur*) qualified.

**certitude** /sɛrtityd/ *n.f.* certainty.

**cerveau** (*pl.* ~**x**) /sɛrvo/ *n.m.* brain.

**cervelas** /sɛrvəla/ *n.m.* saveloy.

**cervelle** /sɛrvɛl/ *n.f.* (*anat.*) brain; (*culin.*) brains.

**ces** /se/ *voir* **ce².**

**césarienne** /sezarjɛn/ *n.f.* Caesarean (section).

**cessation** /sɛsasjɔ̃/ *n.f.* suspension.

**cesse** /sɛs/ *n.f.* **sans** ~**,** incessantly.

**cesser** /sese/ *v.t./i.* stop. ~ **de faire,** stop doing.

**cessez-le-feu** /seselfø/ *n.m. invar.* ceasefire.

**c'est-à-dire** /setadir/ *conj.* that is (to say).

**cet, cette** /sɛt/ *voir* **ce².**

**ceux** /sø/ *voir* **celui.**

**chacal** (*pl.* ~**s**) /ʃakal/ *n.m.* jackal.

**chacun,** ~**e** /ʃakœ̃, -yn/ *pron.* each (one), every one; (*tout le monde*) everyone.

**chagrin** /ʃagrɛ̃/ *n.m.* sorrow. **avoir du** ~**,** be distressed.

**chahut** /ʃay/ *n.m.* row, din.

**chaîne** /ʃɛn/ *n.f.* chain; (*de télévision*) channel. ~ **de montagnes,** mountain range. ~ **de montage/fabrication,** assembly/production line. ~ **hi-fi,** hi-fi system.

**chair** /ʃɛr/ *n.f.* flesh.

**chaire** /ʃɛr/ *n.f.* (*d'église*) pulpit; (*univ.*) chair.

**chaise** /ʃɛz/ *n.f.* chair. ~ **longue,** deckchair.

**châle** /ʃal/ *n.m.* shawl.

**chalet** /ʃalɛ/ *n.m.* chalet.

**chaleur** /ʃalœr/ *n.f.* heat; (*moins intense*) warmth; (*d'un accueil, d'une couleur*) warmth. ~**eux,** ~**euse** *a.* warm.

**challenge** /ʃalãʒ/ *n.m.* contest.

**chalumeau** (*pl.* ~**x**) /ʃalymo/ *n.m.* blowlamp.

**chamailler (se)** /(sə)ʃamaje/ *v. pr.* squabble.

**chambre** /ʃãbr/ *n.f.* (bed)room; (*pol., jurid.*) chamber. ~ **à air,** inner tube. ~ **d'amis,** spare *ou* guest room. ~ **à coucher,** bedroom. ~ **à un lit/deux lits,** single/double room.

**chambrer** /ʃãbre/ *v.t.* (*vin*) bring to room temperature.

**chameau** (*pl.* ~**x**) /ʃamo/ *n.m.* camel.

**chamois** /ʃamwa/ *n.m.* chamois.

**champ** /ʃã/ *n.m.* field. ~ **de courses,** racecourse.

**champagne** /ʃãpaɲ/ *n.m.* champagne.

**champignon** /ʃãpiɲɔ̃/ *n.m.* mushroom; (*moisissure*) fungus. ~ **de Paris,** button mushroom.

**champion,** ~**ne** /ʃãpjɔ̃, -jɔn/ *n.m., f.* champion. ~**nat** /-jɔna/ *n.m.* championship.

**chance** /ʃãs/ *n.f.* (good) luck; (*possibilité*) chance. **avoir de la** ~**,** be lucky. **quelle** ~**l,** what luck!

**chancelier** /ʃãsəlje/ *n.m.* chancellor.

**chanceu|x,** ~**se** /ʃãsø, -z/ *a.* lucky.

**chandail** /ʃãdaj/ *n.m.* sweater.

**chandelier** /ʃãdəlje/ *n.m.* candlestick.

**chandelle** /ʃãdɛl/ *n.f.* candle. **dîner aux** ~**s,** candlelight dinner.

**change** /ʃãʒ/ *n.m.* (foreign) exchange.

**changeant,** ~**e** /ʃãʒã, -t/ *a.* changeable.

**changement** /ʃãʒmã/ *n.m.* change. ~ **de vitesses** (*dispositif*) gears.

**changer** /ʃãʒe/ *v.t./i.* change. **se** ~ *v. pr.* change (one's clothes). ~ **de nom,** change one's name. ~ **de train,** change trains. ~ **d'avis** change one's mind. ~ **de vitesses,** change gear.

**changeur** /ʃãʒœr/ *n.m.* ~ **automatique,** (money) change machine.

**chanson** /ʃãsɔ̃/ *n.f.* song.

**chant** /ʃã/ *n.m.* singing; (*chanson*) song; (*religieux*) hymn.

**chant|er** /ʃãte/ *v.t./i.* sing. ~**eur,** ~**euse** *n.m., f.* singer.

**chantier** /ʃãtje/ *n.m.* building site. ~ **naval,** shipyard.

**chantonner** /ʃãtɔne/ *v.t./i.* hum.

**chanvre** /ʃãvr/ *n.m.* hemp.

**chapeau** (*pl.* ~**x**) /ʃapo/ *n.m.* hat. ~**l,** well done!

**chapelet** /ʃaplɛ/ *n.m.* rosary.

**chapelle** /ʃapɛl/ *n.f.* chapel.

**chapelure** /ʃaplyr/ *n.f.* breadcrumbs.

**chapiteau** (pl. ~x) /ʃapito/ n.m. (de cirque) big top; (de colonne) capital.

**chapitre** /ʃapitr/ n.m. chapter; (fig.) subject.

**chaque** /ʃak/ a. every, each.

**char** /ʃar/ n.m. (mil.) tank; (de carnaval) float; (charrette) cart; (dans l'antiquité) chariot.

**charbon** /ʃarbɔ̃/ n.m. coal. ~ de bois, charcoal. ~nages /-ɔnaʒ/ n.m.pl. coal-mines.

**charcuterie** /ʃarkytri/ n.f. pork-butcher's shop; (aliments) (cooked) pork meats.

**chardon** /ʃardɔ̃/ n.m. thistle.

**charge** /ʃarʒ/ n.f. load, burden; (mil., électr., jurid.) charge; (mission) responsibility. ~s, expenses; (de locataire) service charges. ~s sociales, social security contributions.

**chargé** /ʃarʒe/ a. (journée) busy; (langue) coated.

**charg|er** /ʃarʒe/ v.t. load; (attaquer) charge; (batterie) charge. ● v.i. (attaquer) charge. se ~ de, take charge ou care of. ~ qn. de, weigh. s.o. down with; (tâche) entrust s.o. with. ~ement /-əmɑ̃/ n.m. loading; (objets) load.

**chariot** /ʃarjo/ n.m. (à roulettes) trolley; (charrette) cart.

**charitable** /ʃaritabl/ a. charitable.

**charité** /ʃarite/ n.f. charity.

**charmant, ~e** /ʃarmɑ̃, -t/ a. charming.

**charm|e** /ʃarm/ n.m. charm. ~er v.t. charm.

**charnier** /ʃarnje/ n.m. mass grave.

**charnière** /ʃarnjɛr/ n.f. hinge.

**charpente** /ʃarpɑ̃t/ n.f. framework; (carrure) build.

**charpentier** /ʃarpɑ̃tje/ n.m. carpenter.

**charrette** /ʃarɛt/ n.f. cart.

**charrier** /ʃarje/ v.t. carry.

**charrue** /ʃary/ n.f. plough.

**charte** /ʃart/ n.f. charter.

**charter** /ʃartɛr/ n.m. charter flight.

**chasse** /ʃas/ n.f. hunting; (au fusil) shooting; (poursuite) chase; (recherche) hunt. ~ (d'eau), (toilet) flush.

**châsse** /ʃɑs/ n.f. shrine, reliquary.

**chass|er** /ʃase/ v.t./i. hunt; (faire partir) chase away; (odeur, employé) get rid of. ~e-neige n.m. invar. snow-plough. ~eur, ~euse n.m., f. hunter.

**châssis** /ʃɑsi/ n.m. frame; (auto.) chassis.

**chaste** /ʃast/ a. chaste.

**chat, ~te** /ʃa, ʃat/ n.m., f. cat.

**châtaigne** /ʃatɛɲ/ n.f. chestnut.

**châtaignier** /ʃatɛɲe/ n.m. chestnut tree.

**châtain** /ʃatɛ̃/ a. invar. chestnut (brown).

**château** (pl. ~x) /ʃato/ n.m. castle. ~ d'eau, water-tower. ~ fort, fortifed castle.

**châtiment** /ʃatimɑ̃/ n.m. punishment.

**chaton** /ʃatɔ̃/ n.m. (chat) kitten.

**chatouill|er** /ʃatuje/ v.t. tickle. ~ement n.m. tickling.

**chatouilleu|x, ~se** /ʃatujø, -z/ a. ticklish; (susceptible) touchy.

**chatte** /ʃat/ voir chat.

**chaud, ~e** /ʃo, ʃod/ a. warm; (brûlant) hot; (vif: fig.) warm. ● n.m. heat. au ~, in the warm(th). avoir ~, be warm; be hot. il fait ~, it is warm; it is hot.

**chaudière** /ʃodjɛr/ n.f. boiler.

**chauffage** /ʃofaʒ/ n.m. heating. ~ central, central heating.

**chauff|er** /ʃofe/ v.t./i. heat (up). se ~er v. pr. warm o.s. (up). ~e-eau n.m. invar. water-heater.

**chauffeur** /ʃofœr/ n.m. driver; (aux gages de qn.) chauffeur.

**chaum|e** /ʃom/ n.m. (de toit) thatch.

**chaussée** /ʃose/ n.f. road(way).

**chausser** /ʃose/ v.t. (chaussures) put on. ~ du 35/etc., take a size 35/etc. shoe.

**chaussette** /ʃosɛt/ n.f. sock.

**chausson** /ʃosɔ̃/ n.m. slipper; (de bébé) bootee. ~ (aux pommes), (apple) turnover.

**chaussure** /ʃosyr/ n.f. shoe. ~s de ski, ski boots. ~s de marche, hiking boots.

**chauve** /ʃov/ a. bald.

**chauve-souris** (pl. chauves-souris) /ʃov suri/ n.f. bat.

**chaux** /ʃo/ n.f. lime.

**chef** /ʃɛf/ n.m. leader, head; (culin.) chef; (de tribu) chief. ~ d'État, head of State. ~ de gare, station-master. ~ d'orchestre, conductor. ~ de service, department head. ~ lieu (pl. ~s-lieux) n.m. county town.

**chef-d'œuvre** (pl. chefs-d'œuvre) /ʃɛ dœvr/ n.m. masterpiece.

**chemin** /ʃmɛ̃/ n.m. path, road; (direction, trajet) way. beaucoup de ~ à faire, a long way to go. ~ de fer, railway.

**cheminée** /ʃmine/ n.f. chimney; (intérieure) fireplace; (encadrement) mantelpiece; (de bateau) funnel.

**chemise** /ʃmiz/ n.f. shirt; (dossier) folder; (de livre) jacket. ~ de nuit, night-dress.

**chemisier** /ʃmizje/ n.m. blouse.

**chêne** /ʃɛn/ n.m. oak.

**chenil** /ʃni(l)/ n.m. kennels.

**chenille** /ʃnij/ n.f. caterpillar.

**chèque** /ʃɛk/ n.m. cheque. ~ de voyage, traveller's cheque.

**chéquier** /ʃekje/ n.m. cheque-book.

**cher, chère** /ʃɛr/ a. (coûteux) dear, expensive; (aimé) dear. ● adv. (coûter, payer) a lot (of money). ● n.m., f. mon ~, ma chère, my dear.

**chercher** /ʃɛrʃe/ v.t. look for; (aide, paix, gloire) seek. aller ~, go and get ou fetch, go for.

**chéri, ~e** /ʃeri/ a. beloved. ● n.m., f. darling.

**chérir** /ʃerir/ v.t. cherish.

**chev|al** (pl. ~aux) /ʃval, -o/ n.m. horse. ~al (vapeur), horsepower. **faire du** ~al, ride (a horse).

**chevalet** /ʃvalɛ/ n.m. easel.

**chevalier** /ʃvalje/ n.m. knight.

**chevelu** /ʃəvly/ a. hairy.

**chevelure** /ʃəvlyr/ n.f. hair.

**cheveu** (pl. ~x) /ʃvø/ n.m. (poil) hair. ~x, (chevelure) hair. **avoir les** ~x **longs**, have long hair.

**cheville** /ʃvij/ n.f. ankle; (fiche) peg, pin; (pour mur) (wall) plug.

**chèvre** /ʃɛvr/ n.f. goat.

**chevreau** (pl. ~x) /ʃəvro/ n.m. kid.

**chevreuil** /ʃəvrœj/ n.m. roe(-deer); (culin.) venison.

**chevron** /ʃəvrɔ̃/ n.m. (poutre) rafter. **à** ~s, herring-bone.

**chevronné** /ʃəvrɔne/ a. experienced, seasoned.

**chewing-gum** /ʃwiŋɡɔm/ n.m. chewing-gum.

**chez** /ʃe/ prép. at ou to the house of; (parmi) among; (dans le caractère ou l'œuvre de) in. ~ **le boucher/**etc., at the butcher's/ etc. ~ **soi**, at home; (avec direction) home. ~-**soi** n.m. invar. home.

**chic** /ʃik/ a. invar. smart; (gentil) kind. **sois** ~, do me a favour.

**chichis** /ʃiʃi/ n.m. pl. (fam.) fuss.

**chicorée** /ʃikore/ n.f. (frisée) endive; (à café) chicory.

**chien,** ~**ne** /ʃjɛ̃, ʃjɛn/ n.m. dog. ● n.f. dog, bitch. ~ **de garde**, watch-dog. ~**loup** n.m. (pl. ~**s-loups**) wolfhound.

**chiffon** /ʃifɔ̃/ n.m. rag.

**chiffre** /ʃifr/ n.m. figure; (code) code. ~**s arabes/romains**, Arabic/Roman numerals. ~ **d'affaires**, turnover.

**chignon** /ʃiɲɔ̃/ n.m. bun, chignon.

**Chili** /ʃili/ n.m. Chile.

**chilien,** ~**ne** /ʃiljɛ̃, -jɛn/ a. & n.m., f. Chilean.

**chim|ie** /ʃimi/ n.f. chemistry. ~**ique** a. chemical. ~**iste** n.m./f. chemist.

**chimpanzé** /ʃɛ̃pɑ̃ze/ n.m. chimpanzee.

**Chine** /ʃin/ n.f. China.

**chinois,** ~**e** /ʃinwa,-z/ a. & n.m., f. Chinese. ● n.m. (lang.) Chinese.

**chiot** /ʃjo/ n.m. pup(py).

**chips** /ʃips/ n.m. pl. crisps; (Amer.) chips.

**chirurgic|al** (m. pl. ~**aux**) /ʃiryrʒikal,-o/ a. surgical.

**chirurg|ie** /ʃiryrʒi/ n.f. surgery. ~**ie esthétique**, plastic surgery. ~**ien** n.m. surgeon.

**chlore** /klɔr/ n.m. chlorine.

**choc** /ʃɔk/ n.m. (heurt) impact, shock; (émotion) shock; (collision) crash; (affrontement) clash; (méd.) shock.

**chocolat** /ʃɔkɔla/ n.m. chocolate; (à boire) drinking chocolate. ~ **au lait**, milk chocolate. ~ **chaud**, hot chocolat.

**chœur** /kœr/ n.m. (antique) chorus; (chanteurs, nef) choir.

**chois|ir** /ʃwazir/ v.t. choose, select.

**choix** /ʃwa/ n.m. choice, selection. **au** ~, according to preference. **de premier** ~, top quality.

**choléra** /kɔlera/ n.m. cholera.

**chômage** /ʃomaʒ/ n.m. unemployment. **en** ~, unemployed.

**chômeur,** ~**euse** /ʃomœr, -øz/ n.m., f. unemployed person. **les** ~**s**, the unemployed.

**chope** /ʃɔp/ n.f. tankard.

**choquer** /ʃɔke/ v.t. shock.

**choral** /kɔral/ n.f. choir, choral society.

**chorégraph|ie** /kɔregrafi/ n.f. choreography. ~**e** n.m./f. choreographer.

**choriste** /kɔrist/ n.m./f. (à l'église) chorister; (opéra, etc.) member of the chorus ou choir.

**chose** /ʃoz/ n.f. thing.

**chou** (pl. ~x) /ʃu/ n.m. cabbage. ~ (**à la crème**), cream puff. ~x **de Bruxelles**, Brussels sprouts.

**chouchou,** ~**te** /ʃuʃu, -t/ n.m., f. pet, darling. **le** ~ **du prof.**, the teacher's pet.

**choucroute** /ʃukrut/ n.f. sauerkraut.

**chouette¹** /ʃwɛt/ n.f. owl.

**chouette²** /ʃwɛt/ a. (fam.) super.

**chou-fleur** (pl. **choux-fleurs**) /ʃuflœr/ n.m. cauliflower.

**chrétien,** ~**ne** /kretjɛ̃, -jɛn/ a. & n.m., f. Christian.

**Christ** /krist/ n.m. **le** ~, Christ.

**christianisme** /kristjanism/ n.m. Christianity.

**chrom|e** /krom/ n.m. chromium, chrome. ~**é** a. chromium-plated.

**chromosome** /krɔmozom/ n.m. chromosome.

**chronique** /krɔnik/ a. chronic. ● n.f. (rubrique) column; (nouvelles) news; (annales) chronicle.

**chronolog|ie** /krɔnɔlɔʒi/ n.f. chronology. ~**ique** a. chronological.

**chronom|ètre** /krɔnɔmɛtr/ n.m. stopwatch. ~**étrer** v.t. time.

**chrysanthème** /krizɑ̃tɛm/ n.m. chrysanthemum.

**chuchot|er** /ʃyʃɔte/ v.t./i. whisper. ~**ement** n.m. whisper(ing).

**chut** /ʃyt/ int. shush.

**chute** /ʃyt/ n.f. fall. ~ (**d'eau**), waterfall. ~ **de pluie**, rainfall. **la** ~ **des cheveux**, hair loss.

**Chypre** /ʃipr/ n.f. Cyprus.

**-ci** /si/ adv. (après un nom précédé de ce, cette, etc.) **cet homme-ci**, this man. **ces maisons-ci**, these houses.

**ci-** /si/ adv. here. **ci-après**, hereafter. **ci-contre**, opposite. **ci-dessous**, below. **ci-dessus**, above. **ci-inclus**, **ci-incluse**, **ci-joint**, **ci-jointe**, enclosed.

**cible** /sibl/ n.f. target.

**ciboul|e** /sibul/ n.f., **~ette** n.f. chive(s).

**cicatrice** /sikatris/ n.f. scar.

**cicatriser** /sikatrize/ v.t., **se ~** v. pr. heal (up).

**cidre** /sidr/ n.m. cider.

**ciel** (pl. **cieux**, **ciels**) /sjɛl, sjø/ n.m. sky; (relig.) heaven.

**cierge** /sjɛrʒ/ n.m. candle.

**cigale** /sigal/ n.f. cicada.

**cigare** /sigar/ n.m. cigar.

**cigarette** /sigarɛt/ n.f. cigarette.

**cigogne** /sigɔɲ/ n.f. stork.

**cil** /sil/ n.m. (eye)lash.

**ciment** /simɑ̃/ n.m. cement. **~er** /-te/ v.t. cement.

**cimetière** /simtjɛr/ n.m. cemetery.

**cinéaste** /sineast/ n.m./f. film-maker.

**cinéma** /sinema/ n.m. cinema.

**cinémathèque** /sinematɛk/ n.f. film library; (salle) film theatre.

**cinglé** /sɛ̃gle/ a. (fam.) crazy.

**cinq** /sɛ̃k/ a. & n.m. five. **~ième** a. & n.m./f. fifth.

**cinquantaine** /sɛ̃kɑ̃tɛn/ n.f. une ~ (de), about fifty.

**cinquant|e** /sɛ̃kɑ̃t/ a. & n.m. fifty. **~ième** a. & n.m./f. fiftieth.

**cintre** /sɛ̃tr/ n.m. coat-hanger; (archit.) curve.

**cintré** /sɛ̃tre/ a. (chemise) fitted.

**cirage** /siraʒ/ n.m. (wax) polish.

**circonférence** /sirkɔ̃ferɑ̃s/ n.f. circumference.

**circonflexe** /sirkɔ̃flɛks/ a. circumflex.

**circonscription** /sirkɔ̃skripsjɔ̃/ n.f. district. ~ **(électorale)**, constituency.

**circonstance** /sirkɔ̃stɑ̃s/ n.f. circumstance; (occasion) occasion.

**circuit** /sirkɥi/ n.m. circuit; (trajet) tour, trip.

**circulaire** /sirkylɛr/ a. & n.f. circular.

**circul|er** /sirkyle/ v.i. circulate; (train, automobile, etc.) travel; (piéton) walk. **faire ~er**, (badauds) move on. **~ation** n.f. circulation; (de véhicules) traffic.

**cire** /sir/ n.f. wax.

**ciré** /sire/ n.m. oilskin; waterproof.

**cir|er** /sire/ v.t. polish, wax.

**cirque** /sirk/ n.m. circus; (arène) amphitheatre.

**cirrhose** /siroz/ n.f. cirrhosis.

**ciseau** (pl. **~x**) /sizo/ n.m. chisel. **~x**, scissors.

**citadelle** /sitadɛl/ n.f. citadel.

**citadin**, **~e** /sitadɛ̃, -in/ n.m., f. city dweller. ● a. city.

**cité** /site/ n.f. city. ~ **ouvrière**, (workers') housing estate. ~ **universitaire**, (university) halls of residence.

**cit|er** /site/ v.t. quote, cite. **~ation** n.f. quotation.

**citerne** /sitɛrn/ n.f. tank.

**citoyen**, **~ne** /sitwajɛ̃, -jɛn/ n.m., f. citizen. **~neté** /-jɛnte/ n.f. citizenship.

**citron** /sitrɔ̃/ n.m. lemon. ~ **vert**, lime. **~nade** /-ɔnad/ n.f. lemon squash ou drink, (still) lemonade.

**citrouille** /sitruj/ n.f. pumpkin.

**civet** /sive/ n.m. stew. ~ **de lièvre/ lapin**, jugged hare/rabbit.

**civière** /sivjɛr/ n.f. stretcher.

**civil** /sivil/ n.m. civilian. **dans le ~**, in civilian life. **en ~**, in plain clothes.

**civilisation** /sivilizasjɔ̃/ n.f. civilization.

**civi|que** /sivik/ a. civic. **~sme** n.m. civic sense.

**clair** /klɛr/ a. clear; (éclairé) light, bright; (couleur) light; (liquide) thin. ● adv. clearly. ● n.m. ~ **de lune**, moonlight. **le plus ~ de**, most of. **~ement** adv. clearly.

**clairon** /klɛrɔ̃/ n.m. bugle.

**clan** /klɑ̃/ n.m. clan.

**clandestin**, **~e** /klɑ̃dɛstɛ̃, -in/ a. secret; (journal) underground. **passager ~**, stowaway.

**clapier** /klapje/ n.m. (rabbit) hutch.

**clapot|er** /klapɔte/ v.i. lap.

**claque** /klak/ n.f. slap.

**claqu|er** /klake/ v.i. bang; (porte) slam, bang; (fouet) snap, crack; (mourir: fam.) snuff it. ● v.t. (porte) slam, bang; (dépenser: fam.) blow; (fatiguer: fam.) tire out. **~ement** n.m. bang(ing); slam(ming); snap(ping).

**clarinette** /klarinɛt/ n.f. clarinet.

**clarté** /klarte/ n.f. light, brightness; (netteté) clarity.

**classe** /klɑs/ n.f. class; (salle: scol.) class (-room). **aller en ~**, go to school. ~ **ouvrière/ moyenne**, working/middle class.

**class|er** /klɑse/ v.t. classify; (par mérite) grade; (papiers) file; (affaire) close. **se ~er premier/ dernier**, come first/last. **~ement** n.m. classification; grading; filing; (rang) place, grade; (de coureur) placing.

**classeur** /klɑsœr/ n.m. filing cabinet; (chemise) file.

**classif|ier** /klasifje/ v.t. classify. **~ication** n.f. classification.

**classique** /klasik/ a. classical; (de qualité) classic(al); (habituel) classic. ● n.m. classic; (auteur) classical author.

**clause** /kloz/ n.f. clause.

**claustrophobie** /klostrɔfɔbi/ n.f. claustrophobia.

**clavecin** /klavsɛ̃/ n.m. harpsichord.

**clavicule** /klavikyl/ n.f. collar-bone.

**clavier** /klavje/ n.m. keyboard.

**claviste** /klavist/ n.m./f. keyboarder.

**clé, clef** /kle/ n.f. key; (outil) spanner; (mus.) clef. ● a. invar. key. ~ **anglaise**, (monkey-)wrench. ~ **de contact**, ignition key.

**clémentine** /klemãtin/ n.f. clementine.

**clergé** /klɛrʒe/ n.m. clergy.

**cliché** /kliʃe/ n.m. cliché; (photo.) negative.

**client, ~e** /klijã, -t/ n.m., f. customer; (d'un avocat) client; (d'un médecin) patient; (d'hôtel) guest.

**cligner** /kliɲe/ v.i. ~ **des yeux**, blink. ~ **de l'œil**, wink.

**clignot|er** /kliɲɔte/ v.i. blink; (lumière) flicker; (comme signal) flash. ~**ant** n.m. (auto.) indicator.

**climat** /klima/ n.m. climate. ~**ique** /-tik/ a. climatic.

**climatis|ation** /klimatizasjɔ̃/ n.f. air-conditioning. ~**é** a. air-conditioned.

**clin d'œil** /klɛ̃dœj/ n.m. wink. **en un ~**, in a flash.

**clinique** /klinik/ a. clinical. ● n.f. (private) clinic.

**clinquant, ~e** /klɛ̃kã, -t/ a. showy.

**clip** /klip/ n.m. video.

**clitoris** /klitɔris/ n.m. clitoris.

**clochard, ~e** /klɔʃar, -d/ n.m., f. tramp.

**cloch|e** /klɔʃ/ n.f. bell; (fam.) idiot. ~ **à fromage**, cheese-cover. ~**ette** n.f. bell.

**clocher**[1] /klɔʃe/ n.m. bell-tower; (pointu) steeple. **de ~**, parochial.

**clocher**[2] /klɔʃe/ v.i. (fam.) be wrong.

**cloison** /klwazɔ̃/ n.f. partition; (fig.) barrier.

**cloître** /klwatr/ n.m. cloister.

**cloîtrer (se)** /(sə)klwatre/ v. pr. shut o.s. away.

**cloque** /klɔk/ n.f. blister.

**clore** /klɔr/ v.t. close.

**clos, ~e** /klo, -z/ a. closed.

**clôtur|e** /klotyr/ n.f. fence; (fermeture) closure. ~**er** v.t. enclose; (festival, séance, etc.) close.

**clou** /klu/ n.m. nail; (furoncle) boil; (de spectacle) star attraction. ~ **de girofle**, clove. **les ~s**, (passage) zebra ou pedestrian crossing. ~**er** v.t. nail down.

**clouté** /klute/ a. studded.

**clown** /klun/ n.m. clown.

**club** /klœb/ n.m. club.

**coaguler** /kɔagyle/ v.t./i., **se ~** v. pr. coagulate.

**coalition** /kɔalisjɔ̃/ n.f. coalition.

**coasser** /kɔase/ v.i. croak.

**cobaye** /kɔbaj/ n.m. guinea-pig.

**coca** /kɔka/ n.m. (P.) Coke.

**cocaïne** /kɔkain/ n.f. cocaine.

**cocasse** /kɔkas/ a. comical.

**coccinelle** /kɔksinɛl/ n.f. ladybird; (voiture) beetle.

**cocher** /kɔʃe/ v.t. tick (off), check.

**cochon, ~ne** /kɔʃɔ̃, -ɔn/ n.m. pig. ● n.m., f. (personne: fam.) pig. ● a. (fam.) filthy. ~**nerie** /-ɔnri/ n.f. (saleté: fam.) filth; (marchandise: fam.) rubbish.

**cocktail** /kɔktɛl/ n.m. cocktail; (réunion) cocktail party.

**cocon** /kɔkɔ̃/ n.m. cocoon.

**cocorico** /kɔkɔriko/ n.m. cock-a-doodle-doo.

**cocotier** /kɔkɔtje/ n.m. coconut palm.

**cocotte** /kɔkɔt/ n.f. (marmite) casserole. ~ **minute**, (P.) pressure-cooker.

**cocu** /kɔky/ n.m. (fam.) cuckold.

**code** /kɔd/ n.m. code. ~**s, phares ~**, dipped headlights. ~ **de la route**, Highway Code. **se mettre en ~**, dip one's headlights.

**coder** /kɔde/ v.t. code.

**codifier** /kɔdifje/ v.t. codify.

**coéquip|ier, ~ière** /kɔekipje, -jɛr/ n.m., f. team-mate.

**cœur** /kœr/ n.m. heart; (cartes) hearts. ~ **d'artichaut**, artichoke heart. ~ **de palmier**, heart of palm. **avoir mal au ~**, feel sick.

**coexist|er** /kɔɛgziste/ v.i. coexist. ~**ence** n.f. coexistence.

**coffre** /kɔfr/ n.m. chest; (pour argent) safe; (auto.) boot. ~**-fort** (pl. ~**s-forts**) n.m. safe.

**coffret** /kɔfrɛ/ n.m. casket, box.

**cognac** /kɔɲak/ n.m. cognac.

**cogner** /kɔɲe/ v.t./i. knock. **se ~** v. pr. knock o.s.

**cohérent, ~e** /kɔerã, -t/ a. coherent.

**cohésion** /kɔezjɔ̃/ n.f. cohesion.

**cohue** /kɔy/ n.f. crowd.

**coiff|er** /kwafe/ v.t. do the hair of; (surmonter) cap. **se ~er** v. pr. do one's hair. ~**é de**, wearing. **bien/mal ~é**, with tidy/untidy hair. ~**eur**, ~**euse** n.m., f. hairdresser; n.f. dressing-table.

**coiffure** /kwafyr/ n.f. hairstyle; (chapeau) hat; (métier) hairdressing.

**coin** /kwɛ̃/ n.m. corner; (endroit) spot; (cale) wedge. **au ~ du feu**, by the fireside. **dans le ~**, locally. **du ~**, local.

**coincer** /kwɛ̃se/ v.t. jam; (caler) wedge; (attraper: fam.) catch. **se ~** v. pr. get jammed.

**coïncid|er** /kɔɛ̃side/ v.i. coincide. ~**ence** n.f. coincidence.

**coing** /kwɛ̃/ n.m. quince.

**coït** /kɔit/ n.m. intercourse.

**coke** /kɔk/ n.m. coke.

**col** /kɔl/ n.m. collar; (de bouteille) neck; (de montagne) pass. ~ roulé, polo-neck. ~ de l'utérus, cervix.

**coléoptère** /kɔleɔptɛr/ n.m. beetle.

**colère** /kɔlɛr/ n.f. anger; (accès) fit of anger. en ~, angry. se mettre en ~, lose one's temper.

**colér|eux**, **~euse** /kɔlerø, -z/, **~ique** adjs. quick-tempered.

**colibri** /kɔlibri/ n.m. humming-bird.

**colin** /kɔlɛ̃/ n.m. (poisson) hake.

**colique** /kɔlik/ n.f. diarrhoea; (méd.) colic.

**colis** /kɔli/ n.m. parcel.

**collabor|er** /kɔlabɔre/ v.i. collaborate (à, on). ~er à, (journal) contribute to. ~ateur, ~atrice n.m., f. collaborator; contributor. ~ation n.f. collaboration (à, on); contribution (à, to).

**collant**, **~e** /kɔlɑ̃, -t/ a. skin-tight; (poisseux) sticky. ● n.m. (bas) tights; (de danseur) leotard.

**colle** /kɔl/ n.f. glue; (en pâte) paste.

**collect|e** /kɔlɛkt/ n.f. collection. ~er v.t. collect.

**collecteur** /kɔlɛktœr/ n.m. (égout) main sewer.

**collecti|f**, **~ve** /kɔlɛktif, -v/ a. collective; (billet, voyage) group. ~vement adv. collectively.

**collection** /kɔlɛksjɔ̃/ n.f. collection.

**collectionn|er** /kɔlɛksjɔne/ v.t. collect. ~eur, ~euse n.m., f. collector.

**collectivité** /kɔlɛktivite/ n.f. community.

**collège** /kɔlɛʒ/ n.m. (secondary) school; (assemblée) college.

**collègue** /kɔlɛg/ n.m./f. colleague.

**coller** /kɔle/ v.t. stick; (avec colle liquide) glue; (affiche) stick up. ● v.i. stick (à, to); (être collant) be sticky.

**collier** /kɔlje/ n.m. necklace; (de chien) collar.

**colline** /kɔlin/ n.f. hill.

**collision** /kɔlizjɔ̃/ n.f. (choc) collision; (lutte) clash.

**colloque** /kɔlɔk/ n.m. symposium.

**collyre** /kɔlir/ n.m. eye drops.

**colmater** /kɔlmate/ v.t. seal; (trou) fill in.

**colombe** /kɔlɔ̃b/ n.f. dove.

**Colombie** /kɔlɔ̃bi/ n.f. Colombia.

**colon** /kɔlɔ̃/ n.m. settler.

**colonel** /kɔlɔnɛl/ n.m. colonel.

**colonie** /kɔlɔni/ n.f. colony. ~ de vacances, children's holiday camp.

**coloniser** /kɔlɔnize/ v.t. colonize.

**colonne** /kɔlɔn/ n.f. column. ~ vertébrale, spine.

**color|er** /kɔlɔre/ v.t. colour; (bois) stain. ~ant n.m. colouring.

**colorier** /kɔlɔrje/ v.t. colour (in).

**coloris** /kɔlɔri/ n.m. colour.

**colosse** /kɔlɔs/ n.m. giant.

**colza** /kɔlza/ n.m. rape(-seed).

**coma** /kɔma/ n.m. coma. dans le ~, in a coma.

**combat** /kɔ̃ba/ n.m. fight; (sport) match. ~s, fighting.

**combati|f**, **~ve** /kɔ̃batif, -v/ a. eager to fight; (esprit) fighting.

**combatt|re†** /kɔ̃batr/ v.t./i. fight. ~ant, ~ante n.m., f. fighter; (mil.) combatant.

**combien** /kɔ̃bjɛ̃/ adv. ~ (de), (quantité) how much; (nombre) how many; (temps) how long. ~ il a changé!, (comme) how he has changed!

**combinaison** /kɔ̃binɛzɔ̃/ n.f. combination; (manigance) scheme; (de femme) slip; (bleu de travail) boiler suit; (de plongée) wetsuit.

**combiné** /kɔ̃bine/ n.m. (de téléphone) receiver.

**combiner** /kɔ̃bine/ v.t. (réunir) combine; (calculer) devise.

**comble¹** /kɔ̃bl/ a. packed.

**comble²** /kɔ̃bl/ n.m. c'est le ~!, that's the (absolute) limit!

**combler** /kɔ̃ble/ v.t. fill; (perte, déficit) make good; (désir) fulfil; (personne) gratify.

**combustible** /kɔ̃bystibl/ n.m. fuel.

**combustion** /kɔ̃bystjɔ̃/ n.f. combustion.

**comédie** /kɔmedi/ n.f. comedy. ~ musicale, musical. jouer la ~, put on an act.

**comédien**, **~ne** /kɔmedjɛ̃, -jɛn/ n.m., f. actor, actress.

**comestible** /kɔmɛstibl/ a. edible. ~s n.m. pl. foodstuffs.

**comète** /kɔmɛt/ n.f. comet.

**comique** /kɔmik/ a. comical; (genre) comic. ● n.m. (acteur) comic; (comédie) comedy; (côté drôle) comical aspect.

**comité** /kɔmite/ n.m. committee.

**commandant** /kɔmɑ̃dɑ̃/ n.m. commander; (armée de terre) major. ~ (de bord), captain.

**commande** /kɔmɑ̃d/ n.f. (comm.) order. ~s, (d'avion etc.) controls.

**commander** /kɔmɑ̃de/ v.t. command; (acheter) order. ● v.i. be in command. ~ à qn. de, command s.o. to.

**comme** /kɔm/ conj. as. ● prép. like. ● adv. (exclamation) how. ~ ci comme ça, so-so. ~ d'habitude, as usual. ~ il faut, proper(ly). ~ c'est bon!, it's so good! ~ il est mignon! isn't he sweet!

**commémor|er** /kɔmemɔre/ v.t. commemorate. ~ation n.f. commemoration.

**commenc|er** /kɔmɑ̃se/ v.t. begin, start. ~er à faire, begin ou start to do. ~ement n.m. beginning, start.

**comment** /kɔmɑ̃/ *adv.* how. **~?**, (*répétition*) pardon?; (*surprise*) what? **~ est-il?**, what is he like?

**commentaire** /kɔmɑ̃tɛr/ *n.m.* comment; (*d'un texte*) commentary.

**commenter** /kɔmɑ̃te/ *v.t.* comment on.

**commerçant, ~e** /kɔmɛrsɑ̃, -t/ *a.* (*rue*) shopping. ● *n.m., f.* shopkeeper.

**commerce** /kɔmɛrs/ *n.m.* trade, commerce; (*magasin*) business. **faire du ~**, trade.

**commerc|ial** (*m. pl.* **~iaux**) /kɔmɛrsjal, -jo/ *a.* commercial.

**commettre** /kɔmɛtr/ *v.t.* commit.

**commissaire** /kɔmisɛr/ *n.m.* **~ (de police)**, (police) superintendent.

**commissariat** /kɔmisarja/ *n.m.* **~ (de police)**, police station.

**commission** /kɔmisjɔ̃/ *n.f.* commission; (*course*) errand; (*message*) message. **~s**, shopping.

**commode** /kɔmɔd/ *a.* handy; (*facile*) easy. ● *n.f.* chest (of drawers).

**commun, ~e** /kɔmœ̃, -yn/ *a.* common; (*effort, action*) joint; (*frais, pièce*) shared. ● *n.f.* (*circonscription*) commune. **~al** (*m. pl.* **~aux**) /-ynal, -o/ *a.* of the commune, local.

**communauté** /kɔmynote/ *n.f.* community. **~ des biens** (*entre époux*) shared estate.

**commune** /kɔmyn/ *voir* commun.

**communicati|f, ~ve** /kɔmynikatif, -v/ *a.* communicative.

**communication** /kɔmynikɑsjɔ̃/ *n.f.* communication; (*téléphonique*) call. **~ interurbaine**, long-distance call.

**commun|ier** /kɔmynje/ *v.i.* (*relig.*) receive communion; (*fig.*) commune. **~ion** *n.f.* communion.

**communiqué** /kɔmynike/ *n.m.* communiqué.

**communiquer** /kɔmynike/ *v.t.* pass on, communicate. ● *v.i.* communicate.

**communis|te** /kɔmynist/ *a. & n.m./f.* communist. **~me** *n.m.* communism.

**commutateur** /kɔmytatœr/ *n.m.* (*électr.*) switch.

**compact** /kɔ̃pakt/ *a.* dense; (*voiture*) compact.

**compact disc** /kɔ̃paktdisk/ *n.m.* (P.) compact disc.

**compagne** /kɔ̃paɲ/ *n.f.* companion.

**compagnie** /kɔ̃paɲi/ *n.f.* company. **tenir ~ à**, keep company.

**compagnon** /kɔ̃paɲɔ̃/ *n.m.* companion. **~ de jeu**, playmate.

**comparaître** /kɔ̃parɛtr/ *v.i.* (*jurid.*) appear (**devant**, before).

**compar|er** /kɔ̃pare/ *v.t.* compare. **~er qch./qn. à** *ou* **et** compare sth./s.o. with *ou* and. **~able** *a.* comparable. **~aison** *n.f.* comparison.

**compartiment** /kɔ̃partimɑ̃/ *n.m.* compartment.

**compas** /kɔ̃pa/ *n.m.* (pair of) compasses.

**compassion** /kɔ̃pasjɔ̃/ *n.f.* compassion.

**compatible** /kɔ̃patibl/ *a.* compatible.

**compatir** /kɔ̃patir/ *v.i.* sympathize. **~ à**, share in.

**compatriote** /kɔ̃patrijɔt/ *n.m./f.* compatriot.

**compens|er** /kɔ̃pɑ̃se/ *v.t.* compensate for, make up for. **~ation** *n.f.* compensation.

**compéten|t, ~te** /kɔpetɑ̃, -t/ *a.* competent. **~ce** *n.f.* competence.

**compétiti|f, ~ve** /kɔpetitif, -v/ *a.* competitive.

**compétition** /kɔpetisjɔ̃/ *n.f.* competition; (*sportive*) event.

**complainte** /kɔplɛ̃t/ *n.f.* lament.

**complément** /kɔplemɑ̃/ *n.m.* complement; (*reste*) rest. **~ (d'objet)**, (*gram.*) object. **~aire** /-tɛr/ *a.* complementary; (*renseignements*) supplementary.

**compl|et¹, ~ète** /kɔplɛ, -t/ *a.* complete; (*train, hôtel, etc.*) full. **~ètement** *adv.* completely.

**complet²** /kɔplɛ/ *n.m.* suit.

**compléter** /kɔplete/ *v.t.* complete; (*agrémenter*) complement. **se ~** *v. pr.* complement each other.

**complex|e¹** /kɔplɛks/ *a.* complex. **~ité** *n.f.* complexity.

**complex|e²** /kɔplɛks/ *n.m.* (*sentiment, bâtiments*) complex. **~é** *a.* hung up.

**complication** /kɔplikɑsjɔ̃/ *n.f.* complication; (*complexité*) complexity.

**complic|e** /kɔplis/ *n.m.* accomplice. **~ité** *n.f.* complicity.

**compliment** /kɔplimɑ̃/ *n.m.* compliment. **~s**, (*félicitations*) congratulations. **~er** /-te/ *v.t.* compliment.

**compliqu|er** /kɔplike/ *v.t.* complicate. **se ~er** *v. pr.* become complicated. **~é** *a.* complicated.

**complot** /kɔplo/ *n.m.* plot. **~er** /-ɔte/ *v.t./i.* plot.

**comporter¹** /kɔ̃pɔrte/ *v.t.* contain; (*impliquer*) involve.

**comport|er² (se)** /(sə)kɔ̃pɔrte/ *v. pr.* behave. **~ement** *n.m.* behaviour.

**composé** /kɔ̃poze/ *n.m., a.* compound.

**composer** /kɔ̃poze/ *v.t.* make up, compose; (*chanson, visage*) compose; (*numéro*) dial. **se ~ de**, be made up *ou* composed of.

**composi|teur, ~trice** /kɔ̃pozitœr, -tris/ *n.m., f.* (*mus.*) composer.

**composition** /kɔ̃pozisjɔ̃/ *n.f.* composition; (*examen*) test, exam.

**composter** /kɔ̃pɔste/ *v.t.* (*billet*) punch.

**compote** /kɔ̃pɔt/ *n.f.* stewed fruit. **~e de pommes**, stewed apples.

**compréhensible** /kɔ̃preɑ̃sibl/ *a.* understandable.

**compréhensi|f, ~ve** /kɔ̃preɑ̃sif, -v/ *a.* understanding.

**compréhension** /kɔ̃preɑ̃sjɔ̃/ *n.f.* understanding, comprehension.

**comprendre†** /kɔ̃prɑ̃dr/ *v.t.* understand; (*comporter*) comprise.

**compresse** /kɔ̃prɛs/ *n.f.* compress.

**compression** /kɔ̃presjɔ̃/ *n.f.* (*physique*) compression, (*réduction*) reduction. **~ de personnel,** staff cuts.

**comprimé** /kɔ̃prime/ *n.m.* tablet.

**comprimer** /kɔ̃prime/ *v.t.* compress; (*réduire*) reduce.

**compris, ~e** /kɔ̃pri, -z/ *a.* included; (*d'accord*) agreed. **service (non) ~,** service (not) included, (not) including service. **tout ~,** (all) inclusive. **y ~,** including.

**compromettre** /kɔ̃prɔmɛtr/ *v.t.* compromise.

**compromis** /kɔ̃prɔmi/ *n.m.* compromise.

**comptab|le** /kɔ̃tabl/ *a.* accounting. ● *n.m.* accountant. **~ilité** *n.f.* accountancy; (*comptes*) accounts; (*service*) accounts department.

**comptant** /kɔ̃tɑ̃/ *adv.* (*payer*) (in) cash; (*acheter*) for cash.

**compte** /kɔ̃t/ *n.m.* count; (*facture, à la banque, comptabilité*) account; (*nombre exact*) right number. **demander/rendre des ~s,** ask for/give an explanation. **à bon ~,** cheaply. **à son ~,** (*travailler*) for o.s., on one's own. **faire le ~ de,** count. **sur le ~ de,** about. **~ rendu,** report; (*de film, livre*) review.

**compter** /kɔ̃te/ *v.t.* count; (*prévoir*) reckon; (*facturer*) charge for; (*classer*) consider. ● *v.i.* (*calculer, importer*) count. **~ sur,** rely on.

**compteur** /kɔ̃tœr/ *n.m.* meter.

**comptoir** /kɔ̃twar/ *n.m.* counter; (*de café*) bar.

**comt|e, ~esse** /kɔ̃t, -ɛs/ *n.m., f.* count, countess.

**comté** /kɔ̃te/ *n.m.* county.

**concave** /kɔ̃kav/ *a.* concave.

**concentr|er** /kɔ̃sɑ̃tre/ *v.t., se ~er v. pr.* concentrate. **~ation** *n.f.* concentration. **~é é a.** concentrated; (*lait*) condensed; (*personne*) absorbed; *n.m.* concentrate.

**concept** /kɔ̃sɛpt/ *n.m.* concept.

**conception** /kɔ̃sɛpsjɔ̃/ *n.f.* conception.

**concerner** /kɔ̃sɛrne/ *v.t.* concern. **en ce qui me concerne,** as far as I am concerned.

**concert** /kɔ̃sɛr/ *n.m.* concert.

**concerter** /kɔ̃sɛrte/ **se ~** *v. pr.* confer.

**concerto** /kɔ̃sɛrto/ *n.m.* concerto.

**concession** /kɔ̃sesjɔ̃/ *n.f.* concession; (*terrain*) plot.

**concessionnaire** /kɔ̃sesjɔnɛr/ *n.m./f.* (authorized) dealer.

**concevoir†** /kɔ̃svwar/ *v.t.* (*imaginer, engendrer*) conceive; (*comprendre*) understand.

**concierge** /kɔ̃sjɛrʒ/ *n.m./f.* caretaker.

**concil|ier** /kɔ̃silje/ *v.t.* reconcile. **~iation** *n.f.* conciliation.

**concis, ~e** /kɔ̃si, -z/ *a.* concise.

**concitoyen, ~ne** /kɔ̃sitwajɛ̃, -jɛn/ *n.m., f.* fellow citizen.

**concl|ure†** /kɔ̃klyr/ *v.t./i.* conclude. **~usion** *n.f.* conclusion.

**concombre** /kɔ̃kɔ̃br/ *n.m.* cucumber.

**concorder** /kɔ̃kɔrde/ *v.i.* agree.

**concourir** /kɔ̃kurir/ *v.i.* compete. **~ à,** contribute towards.

**concours** /kɔ̃kur/ *n.m.* competition; (*examen*) competitive examination; (*aide*) aid; (*de circonstances*) combination.

**concr|et, ~ète** /kɔ̃krɛ, -t/ *a.* concrete. **~ètement** *adv.* in concrete terms.

**concrétiser** /kɔ̃kretize/ *v.t.* give concrete form to. **se ~** *v. pr.* materialize.

**conçu** /kɔ̃sy/ *a.* **bien/mal ~,** (*appartement etc.*) well/badly planned.

**concurrenc|e** /kɔ̃kyrɑ̃s/ *n.f.* competition. **~er** *v.t.* compete with.

**concurrent, ~e** /kɔ̃kyrɑ̃, -t/ *n.m., f.* competitor; (*scol.*) candidate. ● *a.* competing.

**condamn|er** /kɔ̃dɑne/ *v.t.* (*censurer, obliger*) condemn; (*jurid.*) sentence; (*porte*) block up. **~ation** *n.f.* condemnation; (*peine*) sentence.

**condens|er** /kɔ̃dɑse/ *v.t., se ~er v. pr.* condense. **~ation** *n.f.* condensation.

**condiment** /kɔ̃dimɑ̃/ *n.m.* condiment.

**condition** /kɔ̃disjɔ̃/ *n.f.* condition. **~s,** (*prix*) terms. **à ~ de ou que,** provided (that). **~nel** *n.m.* conditional (tense).

**conditionnement** /kɔ̃disjɔnmɑ̃/ *n.m.* conditioning; (*emballage*) packaging.

**condoléances** /kɔ̃dɔleɑ̃s/ *n.f. pl.* condolences.

**conduc|teur, ~trice** /kɔ̃dyktœr, -tris/ *n.m., f.* driver.

**conduire†** /kɔ̃dɥir/ *v.t.* lead; (*auto.*) drive; (*affaire*) conduct. ● *v.i.* drive. **se ~** *v. pr.* behave.

**conduite** /kɔ̃dɥit/ *n.f.* conduct; (*auto.*) driving; (*tuyau*) main. **~ à droite,** (*place*) right-hand drive.

**cône** /kon/ *n.m.* cone.

**confection** /kɔ̃fɛksjɔ̃/ *n.f.* making. **de ~,** ready-made. **la ~,** the clothing industry.

**confédération** /kɔ̃federasjɔ̃/ *n.f.* confederation.

**conférenc|e** /kɔ̃ferɑ̃s/ *n.f.* conference; (*exposé*) lecture.

**conférer** /kɔ̃fere/ *v.t.* give; (*décerner*) confer.

**confess|er** /kɔ̃fese/ v.t., **se ~er** v. pr. confess. **~ion** n.f. confession; (*religion*) denomination.

**confiance** /kɔ̃fjɑ̃s/ n.f. trust. **avoir ~ en,** trust.

**confiant, ~e** /kɔ̃fjɑ̃, -t/ a. (*assuré*) confident; (*sans défiance*) trusting.

**confiden|t, ~te** /kɔ̃fidɑ̃, -t/ n.m., f. confidant, confidante. **~ce** n.f. confidence.

**confidentiel, ~le** /kɔ̃fidɑ̃sjɛl/ a. confidential.

**confier** /kɔ̃fje/ v.t. **~ à qn.,** entrust s.o. with; (*secret*) confide to s.o. **se ~ à,** confide in.

**confirm|er** /kɔ̃firme/ v.t. confirm. **~ation** n.f. confirmation.

**confiserie** /kɔ̃fizri/ n.f. sweet shop. **~s,** confectionery.

**confis|quer** /kɔ̃fiske/ v.t. confiscate. **~cation** n.f. confiscation.

**confit, ~e** /kɔ̃fi, -t/ a. (*culin.*) candied. **fruits ~s,** crystallized fruits. ●n.m. **~ d'oie,** goose liver conserve.

**confiture** /kɔ̃fityr/ n.f. jam.

**conflit** /kɔ̃fli/ n.m. conflict.

**confondre** /kɔ̃fɔ̃dr/ v.t. confuse, mix up; (*consterner, étonner*) confound.

**conforme** /kɔ̃fɔrm/ a. **~ à,** in accordance with.

**conformément** /kɔ̃fɔrmemɑ̃/ adv. **~ à,** in accordance with.

**conform|er** /kɔ̃fɔrme/ v.t. adapt. **se ~er à,** conform to. **~ité** n.f. conformity.

**confort** /kɔ̃fɔr/ n.m. comfort. **tout ~** with all mod cons. **~able** /-tabl/ a. comfortable.

**confrère** /kɔ̃frɛr/ n.m. colleague.

**confront|er** /kɔ̃frɔ̃te/ v.t. confront; (*textes*) compare. **~ation** n.f. confrontation.

**confus, ~e** /kɔ̃fy, -z/ a. confused; (*gêné*) embarrassed.

**congé** /kɔ̃ʒe/ n.m. holiday; (*arrêt momentané*) time off. **~ de maladie,** sick-leave. **~ de maternité,** maternity leave. **jour de ~,** day off.

**cong|eler** /kɔ̃ʒle/ v.t. freeze. **les ~elés,** frozen food. **~élateur** n.m. freezer.

**congénit|al** (m. pl. **~aux**) /kɔ̃ʒenital, -o/ a. congenital.

**congère** /kɔ̃ʒɛr/ n.f. snow-drift.

**congestion** /kɔ̃ʒɛstjɔ̃/ n.f. congestion.

**congrégation** /kɔ̃gregasjɔ̃/ n.f. congregation.

**congrès** /kɔ̃grɛ/ n.m. congress.

**conifère** /kɔnifɛr/ n.m. conifer.

**conique** /kɔnik/ a. conic(al).

**conjecture** /kɔ̃ʒɛktyr/ n.f. conjecture.

**conjoint, ~e¹** /kɔ̃ʒwɛ̃, -t/ n.m., f. spouse.

**conjoint, ~e²** /kɔ̃ʒwɛ̃, -t/ a. joint. **~ement** /-tmɑ̃/ adv. jointly.

**conjonction** /kɔ̃ʒɔ̃ksjɔ̃/ n.f. conjunction.

**conjonctivite** /kɔ̃ʒɔ̃ktivit/ n.f. conjunctivitis.

**conjoncture** /kɔ̃ʒɔ̃ktyr/ n.f. circumstances; (*économique*) economic climate.

**conjugaison** /kɔ̃ʒygɛzɔ̃/ n.f. conjugation.

**conjug|al** (m. pl. **~aux**) /kɔ̃ʒygal, -o/ a. conjugal.

**conjuguer** /kɔ̃ʒyge/ v.t. (*gram.*) conjugate; (*efforts*) combine.

**connaissance** /kɔnɛsɑ̃s/ n.f. knowledge; (*personne*) acquaintance. **~s,** (*science*) knowledge. **faire la ~ de,** meet. **perdre ~,** lose consciousness.

**connaisseur** /kɔnɛsœr/ n.m. connoisseur.

**connaître†** /kɔnɛtr/ v.t. know; (*avoir*) have. **se ~** v. pr. (*se rencontrer*) meet.

**conne|cter** /kɔnɛkte/ v.t. connect. **~xion** n.f. connection.

**connu** /kɔny/ a. well-known.

**conquér|ir** /kɔ̃kerir/ v.t. conquer. **~ant, ~ante** n.m., f. conqueror.

**conquête** /kɔ̃kɛt/ n.f. conquest.

**consacrer** /kɔ̃sakre/ v.t. devote. **se ~** v. pr. devote o.s. (**à,** to).

**consciemment** /kɔ̃sjamɑ̃/ adv. consciously.

**conscience** /kɔ̃sjɑ̃s/ n.f. conscience; (*perception*) consciousness. **perdre ~,** lose consciousness. **avoir bonne/mauvaise ~,** have a clear/guilty conscience.

**consciencieu|x, ~se** /kɔ̃sjɑ̃sjø, -z/ a. conscientious.

**conscient, ~e** /kɔ̃sjɑ̃, -t/ a. conscious. **~ de,** aware ou conscious of.

**consécration** /kɔ̃sekrasjɔ̃/ n.f. consecration.

**consécuti|f, ~ve** /kɔ̃sekytif, -v/ a. consecutive.

**conseil** /kɔ̃sɛj/ n.m. (piece of) advice; (*assemblée*) council, committee; (*séance*) meeting; (*personne*) consultant. **~ d'administration,** board of directors. **~ des ministres,** Cabinet. **~ municipal,** town council.

**conseiller¹** /kɔ̃seje/ v.t. advise. **~ à qn. de,** advise s.o. to. **~ qch. à qn.,** recommend sth. to s.o.

**conseill|er², ~ère** /kɔ̃seje, -ɛjɛr/ n.m., f. adviser, counsellor. **~er municipal,** town councillor.

**consent|ir** /kɔ̃sɑ̃tir/ v.i. agree (**à,** to). **~ement** n.m. consent.

**conséquence** /kɔ̃sekɑ̃s/ n.f. consequence. **en ~,** consequently.

**conséquent** /kɔ̃sekɑ̃/ a. **par ~,** consequently.

**conserva|teur, ~trice** /kɔ̃sɛrvatœr, -tris/ a. conservative. ●n.m., f. (*pol.*) conservative.

**conservatoire** /kɔ̃sɛrvatwar/ n.m. academy.

**conserve** /kɔ̃sɛrv/ *n.f.* tinned *ou* canned food. **en ~,** tinned, canned.

**conserver** /kɔ̃sɛrve/ *v.t.* keep; (*en bon état*) preserve. **se ~** *v. pr.* (*culin.*) keep.

**considérable** /kɔ̃siderabl/ *a.* considerable.

**considération** /kɔ̃siderɑsjɔ̃/ *n.f.* consideration; (*respect*) regard. **prendre en ~,** take into consideration.

**considérer** /kɔ̃sidere/ *v.t.* consider; (*respecter*) esteem. **~ comme,** consider to be.

**consigne** /kɔ̃siɲ/ *n.f.* (*de gare*) left luggage (office); (*ordres*) orders. **~ automatique,** (left-luggage) lockers; (*Amer.*) (baggage) lockers.

**consistan|t, ~te** /kɔ̃sistɑ̃, -t/ *a.* solid; (*épais*) thick. **~ce** *n.f.* consistency; (*fig.*) solidity.

**consister** /kɔ̃siste/ *v.i.* **~ en/dans,** consist of/in. **~ à faire,** consist in doing.

**consœur** /kɔ̃sœr/ *n.f.* colleague; fellow member.

**consoler** /kɔ̃sɔle/ *v.t.* console. **se ~** *v. pr.* be consoled (**de,** for).

**consolider** /kɔ̃sɔlide/ *v.t.* strengthen; (*fig.*) consolidate.

**consomma|teur, ~trice** /kɔ̃sɔmatœr, -tris/ *n.m., f.* (*comm.*) consumer; (*dans un café*) customer.

**consommé** /kɔ̃sɔme/ *n.m.* (*bouillon*) consommé.

**consomm|er** /kɔ̃sɔme/ *v.t.* consume. ● *v.i.* drink. **~ation** *n.f.* consumption; consummation; (*boisson*) drink. **de ~ation,** (*comm.*) consumer.

**consonne** /kɔ̃sɔn/ *n.f.* consonant.

**const|ant, ~ante** /kɔ̃stɑ̃, -t/ *a.* constant. ● *n.f.* constant. **~amment** /-amɑ̃/ *adv.* constantly. **~ance** *n.f.* constancy.

**constat** /kɔ̃sta/ *n.m.* (official) report.

**constat|er** /kɔ̃state/ *v.t.* note; (*certifier*) certify. **~ation** *n.f.* observation, statement of fact.

**constellation** /kɔ̃stelɑsjɔ̃/ *n.f.* constellation.

**constip|é** /kɔ̃stipe/ *a.* constipated; (*fig.*) stilted. **~ation** *n.f.* constipation.

**constitu|er** /kɔ̃stitɥe/ *v.t.* make up, constitute; (*organiser*) form; (*être*) constitute. **~é de,** made up of.

**constitution** /kɔ̃stitysjɔ̃/ *n.f.* formation; (*d'une équipe*) composition; (*pol., méd.*) constitution. **~nel, ~nelle** /-jɔnɛl/ *a.* constitutional.

**constructeur** /kɔ̃stryktœr/ *n.m.* manufacturer.

**constructi|f, ~ve** /kɔ̃stryktif, -v/ *a.* constructive.

**constr|uire**† /kɔ̃strɥir/ *v.t.* build; (*système, phrase, etc.*) construct. **~uction** *n.f.* building; (*structure*) construction.

**consul** /kɔ̃syl/ *n.m.* consul. **~aire** *a.* consular. **~at** *n.m.* consulate.

**consult|er** /kɔ̃sylte/ *v.t.* consult. **se ~er** *v. pr.* confer. **~ation** *n.f.* consultation; (*réception: méd.*) surgery.

**contact** /kɔ̃takt/ *n.m.* contact; (*toucher*) touch. **mettre/ couper le ~,** (*auto.*) switch on/off the ignition. **~er** *v.t.* contact.

**contag|ieux, ~ieuse** /kɔ̃taʒjø, -z/ *a.* contagious. **~ion** *n.f.* contagion.

**contamin|er** /kɔ̃tamine/ *v.t.* contaminate. **~ation** *n.f.* contamination.

**conte** /kɔ̃t/ *n.m.* tale. **~ de fées,** fairy tale.

**contempl|er** /kɔ̃tɑ̃ple/ *v.t.* contemplate. **~ation** *n.f.* contemplation.

**contemporain, ~e** /kɔ̃tɑ̃pɔrɛ̃, -ɛn/ *a.* & *n.m., f.* contemporary.

**contenance** /kɔ̃tnɑ̃s/ *n.f.* (*contenu*) capacity

**conteneur** /kɔ̃tnœr/ *n.m.* container.

**contenir**† /kɔ̃tnir/ *v.t.* contain; (*avoir une capacité de*) hold.

**content, ~e** /kɔ̃tɑ̃, -t/ *a.* pleased (**de,** with).

**contenter** /kɔ̃tɑ̃te/ *v.t.* satisfy. **se ~ de,** content o.s. with.

**contenu** /kɔ̃tny/ *n.m.* contents.

**contestataire** /kɔ̃tɛstatɛr/ *n.m./f.* protester.

**contest|er** /kɔ̃tɛste/ *v.t.* dispute; (*s'opposer*) protest against. ● *v.i.* protest. **~able** *a.* debatable. **~ation** *n.f.* dispute; (*opposition*) protest.

**contexte** /kɔ̃tɛkst/ *n.m.* context.

**continent** /kɔ̃tinɑ̃/ *n.m.* continent. **~al** (*m. pl.* **~aux**) /-tal, -to/ *a.* continental.

**continu** /kɔ̃tiny/ *a.* continuous.

**continuel, ~le** /kɔ̃tinɥɛl/ *a.* continual. **~lement** *adv.* continually.

**continuer** /kɔ̃tinɥe/ *v.t.* continue. ● *v.i.* continue, go on. **~ à ou de faire,** carry on *ou* go on *ou* continue doing.

**continuité** /kɔ̃tinɥite/ *n.f.* continuity.

**contour** /kɔ̃tur/ *n.m.* outline, contour.

**contourner** /kɔ̃turne/ *v.t.* go round; (*difficulté*) get round.

**contracepti|f, ~ve** /kɔ̃trasɛptif, -v/ *a.* & *n.m.* contraceptive.

**contraception** /kɔ̃trasɛpsjɔ̃/ *n.f.* contraception.

**contract|er** /kɔ̃trakte/ *v.t.* (*maladie, dette*) contract; (*muscle*) tense, contract; (*assurance*) take out. **se ~er** *v. pr.* contract. **~é** *a.* tense. **~ion** /-ksjɔ̃/ *n.f.* contraction.

**contractuel, ~le** /kɔ̃traktɥɛl/ *n.m., f.* (*agent*) traffic warden.

**contradiction** /kɔ̃tradiksjɔ̃/ *n.f.* contradiction.

**contradictoire** /kɔ̃tradiktwar/ *a.* contradictory; (*débat*) open.

**contraignant,** ~e /kɔ̃trɛɲɑ̃, -t/ *a.* restricting.

**contraire** /kɔ̃trɛr/ *a. & n.m.* opposite. ~ à, contrary to. au ~, on the contrary. ~ment *adv.* ~ment à, contrary to.

**contralto** /kɔ̃tralto/ *n.m.* contralto.

**contrar|ier** /kɔ̃trarje/ *v.t.* annoy; (*action*) frustrate. ~iété *n.f.* annoyance.

**contrast|e** /kɔ̃trast/ *n.m.* contrast.

**contrat** /kɔ̃tra/ *n.m.* contract.

**contravention** /kɔ̃travɑ̃sjɔ̃/ *n.f.* (parking-) ticket.

**contre** /kɔ̃tr(ə)/ *prép.* against; (*en échange de*) for. par ~, on the other hand. ~indiqué *a.* (*méd.*) contra-indicated; (*déconseillé*) not recommended. ~plaqué *n.m.* plywood.

**contreband|e** /kɔ̃trəbɑ̃d/ *n.f.* contraband. faire la ~e de, passer en ~e, smuggle. ~ier *n.m.* smuggler.

**contrebasse** /kɔ̃trəbas/ *n.f.* double-bass.

**contredire**† /kɔ̃trədir/ *v.t.* contradict. se ~ *v. pr.* contradict o.s.

**contrefaçon** /kɔ̃trəfasɔ̃/ *n.f.* (*objet imité, action*) forgery.

**contrefaire** /kɔ̃trəfɛr/ *v.t.* (*falsifier*) forge; (*parodier*) mimic.

**contremaître** /kɔ̃trəmɛtr/ *n.m.* foreman.

**contrepartie** /kɔ̃trəparti/ *n.f.* compensation. en ~, in exchange, in return.

**contrer** /kɔ̃tre/ *v.t.* counter.

**contresens** /kɔ̃trəsɑ̃s/ *n.m.* misinterpretation.

**contresigner** /kɔ̃trəsiɲe/ *v.t.* countersign.

**contretemps** /kɔ̃trətɑ̃/ *n.m.* hitch.

**contribuable** /kɔ̃tribɥabl/ *n.m./f.* taxpayer.

**contribuer** /kɔ̃tribɥe/ *v.t.* contribute (à, to, towards).

**contribution** /kɔ̃tribɥsjɔ̃/ *n.f.* contribution. ~s, (*impôts*) taxes; (*administration*) tax office.

**contrôl|e** /kɔ̃trol/ *n.m.* check; (*des prix, d'un véhicule*) control; (*poinçon*) hallmark; (*scol.*) test. ~e continu, continuous assessment. ~e des changes, exchange control. ~e des naissances birth-control. ~er *v.t.* check; (*surveiller, maîtriser*) control. se ~er *v. pr.* control o.s.

**contrôleu|r,** ~se /kɔ̃troloer, -øz/ *n.m., f.* (bus) conductor *ou* conductress; (*de train*) (ticket) inspector.

**controvers|e** /kɔ̃trɔvɛrs/ *n.f.* controversy. ~é *a.* controversial.

**contusion** /kɔ̃tyzjɔ̃/ *n.f.* bruise.

**convaincre**† /kɔ̃vɛ̃kr/ *v.t.* convince. ~ qn. de faire, persuade s.o. to do.

**convalescen|t,** ~te /kɔ̃valesɑ̃, -t/ *a. & n.m., f.* convalescent. ~ce *n.f.* convalescence.

**convenable** /kɔ̃vnabl/ *a.* (*correct*) decent, proper; (*approprié*) suitable.

**convenance** /kɔ̃vnɑ̃s/ *n.f.* à sa ~, to one's satisfaction. les ~s, the proprieties.

**convenir**† /kɔ̃vnir/ *v.i.* be suitable. ~ à suit. ~ de qch., (*s'accorder sur*) agree on sth. ~ de faire, agree to do.

**convention** /kɔ̃vɑ̃sjɔ̃/ *n.f.* convention. ~s, (*convenances*) convention. ~né *a.* (*prix*) official; (*médecin*) health service (*not private*). ~nel, ~nelle /-jɔnɛl/ *a.* conventional.

**convenu** /kɔ̃vny/ *a.* agreed.

**converger** /kɔ̃vɛrʒe/ *v.i.* converge.

**convers|er** /kɔ̃vɛrse/ *v.i.* converse. ~ation *n.f.* conversation.

**conver|tir** /kɔ̃vɛrtir/ *v.t.* convert (à, to; en, into). ~tible *a.* convertible.

**convexe** /kɔ̃vɛks/ *a.* convex.

**conviction** /kɔ̃viksjɔ̃/ *n.f.* conviction.

**convier** /kɔ̃vje/ *v.t.* invite.

**convocation** /kɔ̃vɔkasjɔ̃/ *n.f.* (*document*) notification to attend.

**convoi** /kɔ̃vwa/ *n.m.* convoy; (*train*) train. ~ (funèbre), funeral procession.

**convoiter** /kɔ̃vwate/ *v.t.* desire, covet, envy.

**convoquer** /kɔ̃vɔke/ *v.t.* (*assemblée*) convene; (*personne*) summon.

**convulsion** /kɔ̃vylsjɔ̃/ *n.f.* convulsion.

**coopérati|f,** ~ve /kɔɔperatif, -v/ *a.* co-operative. ● *n.f.* co-operative (society).

**coopér|er** /kɔɔpere/ *v.i.* co-operate (à, in). ~ation *n.f.* co-operation.

**coordination** /kɔɔrdinasjɔ̃/ *n.f.* coordination.

**coordonn|er** /kɔɔrdɔne/ *v.t.* coordinate. ~ées *n.f. pl.* (*adresse: fam.*) particulars.

**copain** /kɔpɛ̃/ *n.m.* (*fam.*) pal; (*petit ami*) boyfriend.

**copeau** (*pl.* ~x) /kɔpo/ *n.m.* (*lamelle de bois*) shaving.

**cop|ie** /kɔpi/ *n.f.* copy; (*scol.*) paper. ~ier *v.t./i.* copy.

**copieu|x,** ~se /kɔpjø, -z/ *a.* copious.

**copine** /kɔpin/ *n.f.* (*fam.*) pal; (*petite amie*) girlfriend.

**coproduction** /kɔprɔdyksjɔ̃/ *n.f.* co-production.

**copropriété** /kɔprɔprijete/ *n.f.* co-ownership.

**coq** /kɔk/ *n.m.* cock.

**coque** /kɔk/ *n.f.* shell; (*de bateau*) hull.

**coquelicot** /kɔkliko/ *n.m.* poppy.

**coqueluche** /kɔklyʃ/ *n.f.* whooping cough.

**coquet,** ~te /kɔkɛ, -t/ *a.* (*élégant*) pretty; (*somme: fam.*) tidy.

**coquetier** /kɔktje/ *n.m.* egg-cup.

**coquillage** /kɔkijaʒ/ *n.m.* shellfish; (*coquille*) shell.

**coquille** /kɔkij/ *n.f.* shell; (*faute*) misprint. ~ Saint-Jacques, scallop.

**coquin,** ~e /kɔkɛ̃, -in/ *a.* naughty.

**cor** /kɔr/ n.m. (mus.) horn; (au pied) corn.

**cor|ail** (pl. ∼aux) /kɔraj, -o/ n.m. coral.

**Coran** /kɔrɑ̃/ n.m. Koran.

**corbeau** (pl. ∼x) /kɔrbo/ n.m. (oiseau) crow.

**corbeille** /kɔrbɛj/ n.f. basket. ∼ **à papier,** waste-paper basket.

**corbillard** /kɔrbijar/ n.m. hearse.

**corde** /kɔrd/ n.f. rope; (d'arc, de violon, etc.) string. ∼ **à linge,** washing line. ∼s **vocales,** vocal cords.

**cordée** /kɔrde/ n.f. roped party.

**cordon** /kɔrdɔ̃/ n.m. string, cord. ∼-**bleu** (pl. ∼s-bleus) n.m. first-rate cook.

**cordonnier** /kɔrdɔnje/ n.m. shoe mender.

**Corée** /kɔre/ n.f. Korea.

**coriace** /kɔrjas/ a. (aliment) tough.

**corne** /kɔrn/ n.f. horn.

**cornée** /kɔrne/ n.f. cornea.

**corneille** /kɔrnɛj/ n.f. crow.

**cornemuse** /kɔrnəmyz/ n.f. bagpipes.

**corner**[1] /kɔrne/ v.t. (page) make dog-eared. ● v.i. (auto.) hoot; (auto., Amer.) honk.

**corner**[2] /kɔrnɛr/ n.m. (football) corner.

**cornet** /kɔrnɛ/ n.m. (paper) cone; (crème glacée) cornet, cone.

**corniche** /kɔrniʃ/ n.f. cornice; (route) cliff road.

**cornichon** /kɔrniʃɔ̃/ n.m. gherkin.

**corporation** /kɔrpɔrasjɔ̃/ n.f. professional body.

**corps** /kɔr/ n.m. body; (mil., pol.) corps.

**correct** /kɔrɛkt/ a. proper, correct; (exact) correct; (tenue) decent. ∼**ement** adv. properly; correctly; decently.

**correc|teur, ∼trice** /kɔrɛktœr, -tris/ n.m., f. proof-reader.

**correction** /kɔrɛksjɔ̃/ n.f. correction; (punition) beating.

**corrélation** /kɔrelasjɔ̃/ n.f. correlation.

**correspondan|t, ∼te** /kɔrɛspɔ̃dɑ̃, -t/ a. corresponding. ● n.m., f. correspondent; (au téléphone) caller. ∼**ce** n.f. correspondence; (de train, d'autobus) connection. **vente par ∼ce,** mail order.

**correspondre** /kɔrɛspɔ̃dr/ v.i. (s'accorder, écrire) correspond; (chambres) communicate.

**corrida** /kɔrida/ n.f. bullfight.

**corridor** /kɔridɔr/ n.m. corridor.

**corriger** /kɔriʒe/ v.t. correct; (devoir) mark, correct; (punir) beat; (guérir) cure.

**corrosi|f, ∼ve** /kɔrozif, -v/ a. corrosive.

**corruption** /kɔrypsjɔ̃/ n.f. corruption.

**corsage** /kɔrsaʒ/ n.m. bodice; (chemisier) blouse.

**Corse** /kɔrs/ n.f. Corsica.

**corse** /kɔrs/ a. & n.m./f. Corsican.

**corsé** /kɔrse/ a. (vin) full-bodied; (scabreux) spicy.

**cortège** /kɔrtɛʒ/ n.m. procession.

**cortisone** /kɔrtizɔn/ n.f. cortisone.

**corvée** /kɔrve/ n.f. chore.

**cosmétique** /kɔsmetik/ n.m. cosmetic.

**cosmique** /kɔsmik/ a. cosmic.

**cosmonaute** /kɔsmɔnot/ n.m./f. cosmonaut.

**cosmopolite** /kɔsmɔpɔlit/ a. cosmopolitan.

**cosmos** /kɔsmɔs/ n.m. (espace) (outer) space; (univers) cosmos.

**cosse** /kɔs/ n.f. (de pois) pod.

**costaud, ∼e** /kɔsto, -d/ a. (fam.) strong. ● n.m. (fam.) strong man.

**costume** /kɔstym/ n.m. suit; (théâtre) costume.

**cote** /kɔt/ n.f. (classification) mark; (en Bourse) quotation; (de cheval) odds (de, on).

**côte** /kot/ n.f. (littoral) coast; (pente) hill; (anat.) rib; (de porc) chop. ∼ **à côte,** side by side. **la C∼ d'Azur,** the (French) Riviera.

**côté** /kote/ n.m. side; (direction) way. **à ∼,** nearby; (voisin) nextdoor. **à ∼ de,** next to; (comparé à) compared to; (cible) wide of. **aux ∼s de,** by the side of. **de ∼,** aside; (regarder) sideways. **mettre de ∼,** put aside. **de ce ∼,** this way. **de chaque ∼,** on each side. **de tous les ∼s,** on every side; (partout) everywhere. **du ∼ de,** towards; (proximité) near; (provenance) from.

**coteau** (pl. ∼x) /kɔto/ n.m. hill.

**côtelette** /kotlɛt/ n.f. chop.

**coter** /kɔte/ v.t. (comm.) quote; (apprécier, noter) rate.

**côt|ier, ∼ière** /kotje, -jɛr/ a. coastal.

**cotis|er** /kɔtize/ v.i. pay one's contributions (à, to). **se ∼er** v. pr. club together. ∼**ation** n.f. contribution(s); subscription.

**coton** /kɔtɔ̃/ n.m. cotton. ∼ **hydrophile,** cotton wool.

**cou** /ku/ n.m. neck.

**couchant** /kuʃɑ̃/ n.m. sunset.

**couche** /kuʃ/ n.f. layer; (de peinture) coat; (de bébé) nappy.

**coucher** /kuʃe/ n.m. ∼ **(du soleil),** sunset. ● v.t. put to bed. ● v.i. sleep. **se ∼** v. pr. go to bed; (s'étendre) lie down; (soleil) set. **couché** a. in bed; (étendu) lying down.

**couchette** /kuʃɛt/ n.f. (rail.) couchette; (naut.) bunk.

**coucou** /kuku/ n.m. cuckoo.

**coude** /kud/ n.m. elbow.

**coudre**† /kudr/ v.t./i. sew.

**couette** /kwɛt/ n.f. duvet, continental quilt.

**couffin** /kufɛ̃/ n.m. Moses basket.

**coulant, ∼e** /kulɑ̃, -t/ a. (indulgent) easygoing; (fromage) runny.

**couler**[1] /kule/ *v.i.* flow, run; (*fromage, nez*) run; (*fuir*) leak.

**couler**[2] /kule/ *v.t./i.* (*bateau*) sink.

**couleur** /kulœr/ *n.f.* colour. **en ~s**, (*télévision, film*) colour.

**couleuvre** /kulœvr/ *n.f.* (grass *ou* smooth) snake.

**coulis** /kuli/ *n.m.* (*culin.*) coulis.

**couliss|e** /kulis/ *n.f.* runner. **~es**, (*théâtre*) wings. **~er** *v.i.* slide.

**couloir** /kulwar/ *n.m.* corridor; (*de bus*) gangway; (*sport*) lane.

**coup** /ku/ *n.m.* blow; (*choc*) knock; (*sport*) stroke; (*de crayon, chance, cloche*) stroke; (*de fusil, pistolet*) shot; (*fois*) time; (*aux échecs*) move. **à ~ sûr**, definitely. **après ~**, after the event. **boire un ~**, have a drink. **~ de couteau**, stab. **~ d'état** (*pol.*) coup. **~ de feu**, shot. **~ de fil**, phone call. **~ de frein**, sudden braking. **~ de main**, helping hand. **avoir le ~ de main**, have the knack. **~ d'œil**, glance. **~ de pied**, kick. **~ de poing**, punch. **~ de soleil**, sunburn. **~ de sonnette**, ring (on a bell). **~ de téléphone**, (tele)phone call. **~ de tête**, wild impulse. **~ de tonnerre**, thunderclap. **~ franc**, free kick. **d'un seul ~**, in one go. **du premier ~**, first go. **tenir le coup**, take it.

**coupable** /kupabl/ *a.* guilty. ● *n.m./f.* culprit.

**coupe**[1] /kup/ *n.f.* cup; (*de champagne*) goblet; (*à fruits*) dish.

**coupe**[2] /kup/ *n.f.* (*de vêtement etc.*) cut; (*dessin*) section. **~ de cheveux**, haircut.

**coup|er** /kupe/ *v.t./i.* cut; (*arbre*) cut down; (*arrêter*) cut off; (*voyage*) break; (*appétit*) take away; (*vin*) water down. **~er par**, take a short cut via. **se ~er** *v. pr.* cut o.s.; (*routes*) intersect. **~er la parole à**, cut short. **~e-papier** *n.m. invar.* paper-knife.

**couple** /kupl/ *n.m.* couple.

**couplet** /kuplɛ/ *n.m.* verse.

**coupole** /kupɔl/ *n.f.* dome.

**coupon** /kupɔ̃/ *n.m.* (*étoffe*) remnant; (*billet, titre*) coupon.

**coupure** /kupyr/ *n.f.* cut; (*billet de banque*) note; (*de presse*) cutting. **~ (de courant)**, power cut.

**cour** /kur/ *n.f.* (court)yard; (*de roi*) court; (*tribunal*) court. **~ (de récréation)**, playground. **~ martiale**, court martial. **faire la ~ à**, court.

**courag|e** /kuraʒ/ *n.m.* courage. **~eux, ~euse** *a.* courageous.

**couramment** /kuramã/ *adv.* frequently; (*parler*) fluently.

**courant**[1], **~e** /kurã, -t/ *a.* standard, ordinary.

**courant**[2] /kurã/ *n.m.* current; (*de mode, d'idées*) trend. **~ d'air**, draught. **être/mettre au ~ de**, know/tell about.

**courbature** /kurbatyr/ *n.f.* ache.

**courbe** /kurb/ *n.f.* curve. ● *a.* curved.

**courber** /kurbe/ *v.t./i.*, **se ~** *v. pr.* bend.

**coureu|r, ~se** /kurœr, -øz/ *n.m., f.* (*sport*) runner. ● *n.m.* womanizer.

**courge** /kurʒ/ *n.f.* marrow.

**courgette** /kurʒɛt/ *n.f.* courgette.

**courir**† /kurir/ *v.i.* run; (*se hâter*) rush. ● *v.t.* (*risque*) run; (*danger*) face; (*épreuve sportive*) run *ou* compete in; (*fréquenter*) do the rounds of; (*files*) chase.

**couronne** /kurɔn/ *n.f.* crown; (*de fleurs*) wreath.

**couronner** /kurɔne/ *v.t.* crown.

**courrier** /kurje/ *n.m.* post, mail; (*à écrire*) letters; (*de journal*) column.

**courroie** /kurwa/ *n.f.* strap; (*techn.*) belt.

**cours** /kur/ *n.m.* (*leçon*) class; (*série de leçons*) course; (*prix*) price; (*cote*) rate; (*déroulement, d'une rivière*) course. **au ~ de**, in the course of. **~ d'eau**, river, stream. **~ du soir**, evening class. **en ~**, current; (*travail*) in progress. **en ~ de route**, on the way.

**course** /kurs/ *n.f.* run(ning); (*épreuve de vitesse*) race; (*commission*) errand. **~s**, (*achats*) shopping; (*de chevaux*) races.

**court**[1], **~e** /kur, -t/ *a.* short. **~-circuit** (*pl.* **~s-circuits**) *n.m.* short circuit.

**court**[2] /kur/ *n.m.* **~ (de tennis)**, (tennis) court.

**court|ier, ~ière** /kurtje, -jɛr/ *n.m., f.* broker.

**courtois, ~e** /kurtwa, -z/ *a.* courteous. **~ie** /-zi/ *n.f.* courtesy.

**cousin, ~e** /kuzɛ̃, -in/ *n.m., f.* cousin. **~ germain**, first cousin.

**coussin** /kusɛ̃/ *n.m.* cushion.

**coût** /ku/ *n.m.* cost.

**couteau** (*pl.* **~x**) /kuto/ *n.m.* knife.

**coûter** /kute/ *v.t./i.* cost.

**coutume** /kutym/ *n.f.* custom.

**coutur|e** /kutyr/ *n.f.* sewing; (*métier*) dressmaking; (*points*) seam. **~ier** *n.m.* fashion designer. **~ière** *n.f.* dressmaker.

**couvent** /kuvã/ *n.m.* convent.

**couver** /kuve/ *v.t.* (*œufs*) hatch; (*personne*) pamper.

**couvercle** /kuvɛrkl/ *n.m.* (*de marmite, boîte*) lid; (*d'objet allongé*) top.

**couvert**[1], **~e** /kuvɛr, -t/ *a.* covered (**de**, with); (*habillé*) covered up; (*ciel*) overcast.

**couvert**[2] /kuvɛr/ *n.m.* (*à table*) place-setting; (*prix*) cover charge. **~s**, (*couteaux etc.*) cutlery. **mettre le ~**, lay the table.

**couverture** /kuvɛrtyr/ *n.f.* cover; (*de lit*) blanket.

**couvr|ir**† /kuvrir/ *v.t.* cover. **se ~ir** *v. pr.* (*s'habiller*) cover up; (*ciel*) become overcast. **~e-feu** (*pl.* **~e-feux**) *n.m.* curfew. **~e-lit** *n.m.* bedspread.

**cow-boy** /kɔbɔj/ *n.m.* cowboy.

**crabe** /krab/ *n.m.* crab.

**cracher** /kraʃe/ *v.t. i.* spit (out).

**craie** /krɛ/ *n.f.* chalk.

**craindre**† /krɛ̃dr/ *v.t.* be afraid of, fear; (*être sensible à*) be easily damaged by.

**crainte** /krɛ̃t/ *n.f.* fear. **de ∼ de/que,** for fear of/that.

**crainti|f, ∼ve** /krɛ̃tif, -v/ *a.* timid.

**crampe** /krɑ̃p/ *n.f.* cramp.

**crampon** /krɑ̃pɔ̃/ *n.m.* (*de chaussure*) stud.

**cramponner (se)** /(sə)krɑ̃pɔne/ *v. pr.* **se ∼ à,** cling to.

**cran** /krɑ̃/ *n.m.* (*entaille*) notch; (*trou*) hole; (*courage: fam.*) pluck.

**crâne** /krɑn/ *n.m.* skull.

**crapaud** /krapo/ *n.m.* toad.

**crapule** /krapyl/ *n.f.* villain.

**craqu|er** /krake/ *v.i.* crack, snap; (*plancher*) creak; (*couture*) split; (*fig.*) break down; (*céder*) give in. **∼ement** *n.m.* crack(ing), snap(ping); creak(ing); striking.

**crass|e** /kras/ *n.f.* grime. **∼eux, ∼euse** *a.* grimy.

**cratère** /kratɛr/ *n.m.* crater.

**cravache** /kravaʃ/ *n.f.* horsewhip.

**cravate** /kravat/ *n.f.* tie.

**crawl** /krol/ *n.m.* (*nage*) crawl.

**crayon** /krɛjɔ̃/ *n.m.* pencil. **∼ (de couleur),** crayon. **∼ à bille,** ball-point pen. **∼ optique,** light pen.

**créanc|ier, ∼ière** /kreɑ̃sje, -jɛr/ *n.m., f.* creditor.

**créa|teur, ∼trice** /kreatœr, -tris/ *n.m., f.* creator.

**création** /kreɑsjɔ̃/ *n.f.* creation; (*comm.*) product.

**créature** /kreatyr/ *n.f.* creature.

**crèche** /krɛʃ/ *n.f.* day nursery; (*relig.*) crib.

**crédibilité** /kredibilite/ *n.f.* credibility.

**crédit** /kredi/ *n.m.* credit; (*banque*) bank. **∼s,** funds. **à ∼,** on credit. **faire ∼ (à,** to). **∼er** /-te/ *v.t.* credit. **∼eur, ∼euse** /-tœr, -tøz/ *a.* in credit.

**crédule** /kredyl/ *a.* credulous.

**créer** /kree/ *v.t.* create.

**crème** /krɛm/ *n.f.* cream; (*dessert*) cream dessert. ● *a. invar.* cream. ● *n.m.* (*café*) **∼,** white coffee. **∼ anglaise,** fresh custard. **∼ à raser,** shaving-cream.

**crémeu|x, ∼se** /kremø, -z/ *a.* creamy.

**créole** /kreɔl/ *n.m./f.* Creole.

**crêpe**[1] /krɛp/ *n.f.* (*galette*) pancake. **∼rie** *n.f.* pancake shop.

**crêpe**[2] /krɛp/ *n.m.* (*tissu*) crêpe; (*matière*) crêpe (rubber).

**crépu** /krepy/ *a.* frizzy.

**crépuscule** /krepyskyl/ *n.m.* twilight, dusk.

**crescendo** /kreʃɛndo/ *adv. & n.m. invar.* crescendo.

**cresson** /kresɔ̃/ *n.m.* (water)cress.

**crête** /krɛt/ *n.f.* crest; (*de coq*) comb.

**crétin, ∼e** /kretɛ̃, -in/ *n.m., f.* cretin.

**creuser** /krøze/ *v.t.* dig; (*évider*) hollow out; (*fig.*) go deeply into.

**creu|x, ∼se** /krø, -z/ *a.* hollow; (*heures*) off-peak. ● *n.m.* hollow; (*de l'estomac*) pit.

**crevaison** /krəvɛzɔ̃/ *n.f.* puncture.

**crevasse** /krəvas/ *n.f.* crack; (*de glacier*) crevasse; (*de la peau*) chap.

**crevé** /krəve/ *a.* (*fam.*) worn out.

**crever** /krəve/ *v.t./i.* burst; (*pneu*) puncture, burst; (*exténuer: fam.*) exhaust; (*mourir: fam.*) die; (*œil*) put out.

**crevette** /krəvɛt/ *n.f.* **∼ (grise),** shrimp. **∼ (rose),** prawn.

**cri** /kri/ *n.m.* cry; (*de douleur*) scream, cry.

**cric** /krik/ *n.m.* (*auto.*) jack.

**crier** /krije/ *v.i.* (*fort*) shout, cry (out); (*de douleur*) scream; (*grincer*) creak. ● *v.t.* (*ordre*) shout (out).

**crim|e** /krim/ *n.m.* crime; (*meurtre*) murder. **∼inel, ∼inelle** *a.* criminal; *n.m., f.* criminal; (*assassin*) murderer.

**crin** /krɛ̃/ *n.m.* horsehair.

**crinière** /krinjɛr/ *n.f.* mane.

**crique** /krik/ *n.f.* creek.

**criquet** /krikɛ/ *n.m.* locust.

**crise** /kriz/ *n.f.* crisis; (*méd.*) attack; (*de colère*) fit. **∼ cardiaque,** heart attack. **∼ de foie,** bilious attack.

**crisp|er** /krispe/ *v.t.,* **se ∼er** *v. pr.* tense; (*poings*) clench. **∼é** *a.* tense.

**crist|al** (*pl.* **∼aux**) /kristal, -o/ *n.m.* crystal.

**critère** /kritɛr/ *n.m.* criterion.

**critique** /kritik/ *a.* critical. ● *n.f.* criticism; (*article*) review.

**critiquer** /kritike/ *v.t.* criticize.

**croasser** /krɔase/ *v.i.* caw.

**croc** /kro/ *n.m.* (*dent*) fang.

**croche** /krɔʃ/ *n.f.* quaver. **double ∼,** semiquaver.

**crochet** /krɔʃɛ/ *n.m.* hook; (*détour*) detour; (*signe*) (square) bracket; (*tricot*) crochet. **faire au ∼,** crochet.

**crochu** /krɔʃy/ *a.* hooked.

**crocodile** /krɔkɔdil/ *n.m.* crocodile.

**crocus** /krɔkys/ *n.m.* crocus.

**croire**† /krwar/ *v.t./i.* believe (**à, en,** in); (*estimer*) think, believe (**que,** that).

**croisade** /krwazad/ *n.f.* crusade.

**croisé** /krwaze/ *a.* (*veston*) double-breasted. ● *n.m.* crusader.

**crois|er¹** /krwaze/ v.t., **se ∼er** v. pr. cross; ( passant, véhicule ) pass (each other). **(se) ∼er les bras,** fold one's arms. **(se) ∼er les jambes,** cross one's legs. **∼ement** n.m. crossing; passing; ( carrefour ) crossroads.

**crois|er²** /krwaze/ v.i. ( bateau ) cruise. **∼ière** n.f. cruise.

**croissan|t¹,** **∼te** /krwasã, -t/ a. growing. **∼ce** n.f. growth.

**croissant¹** /krwasã/ n.m. crescent; ( pâtisserie ) croissant.

**croix** /krwa/ n.f. cross. **C∼-Rouge,** Red Cross.

**croque-monsieur** /krɔkməsjø/ n.m. invar. toasted ham and cheese sandwich.

**croquer** /krɔke/ v.t./i. crunch; ( dessiner ) sketch.

**croquette** /krɔkɛt/ n.f. croquette.

**croquis** /krɔki/ n.m. sketch.

**crosse** /krɔs/ n.f. ( de fusil ) butt.

**crotte** /krɔt/ n.f. droppings.

**crotté** /krɔte/ a. muddy.

**crottin** /krɔtɛ̃/ n.m. (horse) dung.

**croupier** /krupje/ n.m. croupier.

**croustill|er** /krustije/ v.i. be crusty. **∼ant,** **∼ante** a. crusty; ( fig. ) spicy.

**croûte** /krut/ n.f. crust; ( de fromage ) rind; ( de plaie ) scab.

**croûton** /krutɔ̃/ n.m. ( bout de pain ) crust; ( avec potage ) croûton.

**croyable** /krwajabl/ a. credible.

**croyan|t,** **∼te** /krwajã, -t/ n.m., f. believer. **∼ce** n.f. belief.

**CRS** abrév. ( Compagnies républicaines de sécurité ) French state security police.

**cru¹** /kry/ voir **croire.**

**cru²** /kry/ a. raw; ( lumière ) harsh; ( propos ) crude. ● n.m. vineyard; ( vin ) wine.

**crû** /kry/ voir **croître.**

**cruauté** /kryote/ n.f. cruelty.

**cruche** /kryʃ/ n.f. pitcher.

**crudités** /krydite/ n.f. pl. ( culin. ) raw vegetables.

**crue** /kry/ n.f. rise in water level. **en ∼,** in spate.

**cruel,** **∼le** /kryɛl/ a. cruel.

**crustacés** /krystase/ n.m. pl. shellfish.

**crypte** /kript/ n.f. crypt.

**Cuba** /kyba/ n.m. Cuba.

**cubain,** **∼e** /kybɛ̃, -ɛn/ a. & n.m., f. Cuban.

**cub|e** /kyb/ n.m. cube. ● a. ( mètre etc. ) cubic. **∼ique** a. cubic.

**cueill|ir†** /kœjir/ v.t. pick, gather; ( personne: fam. ) pick up. **∼ette** n.f. picking, gathering.

**cuill|er,** **∼ère** /kɥijɛr/ n.f. spoon. **∼er à soupe,** soup-spoon; ( mesure ) tablespoonful. **∼erée** n.f. spoonful.

**cuir** /kɥir/ n.m. leather. **∼ chevelu,** scalp.

**cuire** /kɥir/ v.t./i. cook. **∼ (au four),** bake. **faire ∼,** cook.

**cuisine** /kɥizin/ n.f. kitchen; ( art ) cookery, cooking; ( aliments ) cooking. **faire la ∼,** cook.

**cuisin|er** /kɥizine/ v.t./i. cook. **∼ier,** **∼ière** n.m., f. cook; n.f. ( appareil ) cooker, stove.

**cuisse** /kɥis/ n.f. thigh; ( de poulet, mouton ) leg.

**cuisson** /kɥisɔ̃/ n.m. cooking.

**cuit,** **∼e** /kɥi, -t/ a. cooked. **bien ∼,** well done ou cooked. **trop ∼,** overdone.

**cuivr|e** /kɥivr/ n.m. copper. **∼e (jaune),** brass. **∼es,** ( mus. ) brass. **∼é** a. coppery.

**cul** /ky/ n.m. ( derrière: fam. ) backside, bum.

**culasse** /kylas/ n.f. ( auto. ) cylinder head; ( arme ) breech.

**culbute** /kylbyt/ n.f. somersault; ( chute ) tumble.

**cul-de-sac** ( pl. **culs-de-sac** ) /kydsak/ n.m. cul-de-sac.

**culinaire** /kyliner/ a. culinary; ( recette ) cooking.

**culot** /kylo/ n.m. ( audace: fam. ) nerve, cheek.

**culotte** /kylɔt/ n.f. ( de femme ) knickers.

**culpabilité** /kylpabilite/ n.f. guilt.

**culte** /kylt/ n.m. cult, worship; ( religion ) religion; ( protestant ) service.

**cultivé** /kyltive/ a. cultured.

**cultiv|er** /kyltive/ v.t. cultivate; ( plantes ) grow. **∼ateur,** **∼atrice** n.m., f. farmer.

**culture** /kyltyr/ n.f. cultivation; ( de plantes ) growing; ( agriculture ) farming; ( éducation ) culture.

**culturel,** **∼le** /kyltyrɛl/ a. cultural.

**cupide** /kypid/ a. grasping.

**cure** /kyr/ n.f. (course of) treatment, cure.

**curé** /kyre/ n.m. (parish) priest.

**cur|er** /kyre/ v.t. clean. **se ∼er les dents/ongles,** clean one's teeth/nails. **∼e-dent** n.m. toothpick. **∼e-pipe** n.m. pipe-cleaner.

**curieu|x,** **∼se** /kyrjø, -z/ a. curious.

**curiosité** /kyrjozite/ n.f. curiosity.

**curriculum vitae** /kyrikylɔm vite/ n.m. invar. curriculum vitae.

**curseur** /kyrsœr/ n.m. cursor.

**cutané** /kytane/ a. skin.

**cuve** /kyv/ n.f. tank.

**cuvée** /kyve/ n.f. ( de vin ) vintage.

**cuvette** /kyvet/ n.f. bowl; ( de lavabo ) (wash-)basin; ( des cabinets ) pan, bowl.

**CV** /seve/ n.m. CV.

**cycl|e** /sikl/ n.m. cycle. **∼ique** a. cyclic(al).

**cyclis|te** /siklist/ n.m./f. cyclist. ● a. cycle. **∼me** n.m. cycling.

**cyclomoteur** /syklɔmɔtœr/ n.m. moped.

**cyclone** /syklon/ n.m. cyclone.

**cygne** /siɲ/ n.m. swan.

**cylindr|e** /silɛ̃dr/ *n.m.* cylinder. **~ique** *a.* cylindrical.

**cymbale** /sɛ̃bal/ *n.f.* cymbal.

**cystite** /sistit/ *n.f.* cystitis.

**cyni|que** /sinik/ *a.* cynical. ● *n.m.* cynic. **~sme** *n.m.* cynicism.

**cyprès** /siprɛ/ *n.m.* cypress.

**cypriote** /siprijɔt/ *a. & n.m./f.* Cypriot.

•••••••••••••••••••••••••••

# Dd

•••••••••••••••••••••••••••

**d'** /d/ *voir* de.

**d'abord** /dabɔr/ *adv.* first; (*au début*) at first.

**dactylo** /daktilo/ *n.f.* typist. **~(graphie)** *n.f.* typing. **~graphier** *v.t.* type.

**dada** /dada/ *n.m.* hobby-horse.

**dahlia** /dalja/ *n.f.* dahlia.

**daim** /dɛ̃/ *n.m.* (fallow) deer; (*cuir*) suede.

**dall|e** /dal/ *n.f.* paving stone, slab. **~age** *n.m.* paving.

**daltonien, ~ne** /daltɔnjɛ̃, -jɛn/ *a.* colour-blind.

**dame** /dam/ *n.f.* lady; (*cartes, échecs*) queen. **~s,** (*jeu*) draughts; (*jeu: Amer.*) checkers.

**damier** /damje/ *n.m.* draught-board.

**dancing** /dɑ̃siŋ/ *n.m.* dance-hall.

**Danemark** /danmark/ *n.m.* Denmark.

**danger** /dɑ̃ʒe/ *n.m.* danger. **en ~,** in danger. **mettre en ~,** endanger.

**dangereu|x, ~se** /dɑ̃ʒrø, -z/ *a.* dangerous.

**danois, ~e** /danwa, -z/ *a.* Danish. ● *n.m., f.* Dane. ● *n.m.* (*lang.*) Danish.

**dans** /dɑ̃/ *prép.* in; (*mouvement*) into; (*à l'intérieur de*) inside, in; (*approximation*) about. **~ dix jours,** in ten days' time.

**dans|e** /dɑ̃s/ *n.f.* dance; (*art*) dancing. **~er** *v.t./i.* dance. **~eur, ~euse** *n.m., f.* dancer.

**darne** /darn/ *n.f.* steak (*of fish*).

**date** /dat/ *n.f.* date. **~ limite,** deadline; **~ limite de vente,** sell-by date; **~ de péremption,** expiry date.

**datt|e** /dat/ *n.f.* (*fruit*) date. **~ier** *n.m.* date-palm.

**daube** /dob/ *n.f.* casserole.

**dauphin** /dofɛ̃/ *n.m.* (*animal*) dolphin.

**davantage** /davɑ̃taʒ/ *adv.* more; (*plus longtemps*) longer. **~ de,** more. **~ que,** more than; longer than.

**de, d'*** /də, d/ *prép.* (*de + le = du, de + les = des*) of; (*provenance*) from; (*moyen, manière*) with; (*agent*) by. ● *article* some; (*interrogation*) any. some. **le livre de mon ami,** my friend's book. **un pont de fer,** an iron bridge. **dix**

**mètres de haut,** ten metres high. **du pain,** (some) bread; **une tranche de pain,** a slice of bread. **des fleurs,** (some) flowers.

**dé** /de/ *n.m.* (*à jouer*) dice; (*à coudre*) thimble. **dés,** (*jeu*) dice.

**déballer** /debale/ *v.t.* unpack.

**débarbouiller** /debarbuje/ *v.t.* wash the face of. **se ~** *v. pr.* wash one's face.

**débarcadère** /debarkadɛr/ *n.m.* landing-stage.

**débardeur** /debardœr/ *n.m.* docker; (*vêtement*) tank top.

**débarqu|er** /debarke/ *v.t./i.* disembark, land; (*arriver: fam.*) turn up.

**débarras** /debara/ *n.m.* junk room. **bon ~!,** good riddance!

**débarrasser** /debarase/ *v.t.* clear (**de,** of). **~ qn. de,** take from s.o.; (*défaut, ennemi*) rid s.o. of. **se ~ de,** get rid of, rid o.s. of.

**débat** /deba/ *n.m.* debate.

**débattre†¹** /debatr/ *v.t.* debate. ● *v.i.* **~ de,** discuss.

**débattre† (se)** /(sə)debatr/ *v. pr.* struggle (to get free).

**débit** /debi/ *n.m.* **~ de tabac,** tobacconist's shop; **~ de boissons,** licensed premises.

**débi|ter** /debite/ *v.t.* cut up; (*fournir*) produce; (*vendre*) sell; (*dire: péj.*) spout; (*compte*) debit. **~teur, ~trice** *n.m., f.* debtor. *a.* (*compte*) in debit.

**déblayer** /debleje/ *v.t.* clear.

**débloquer** /deblɔke/ *v.t.* (*prix, salaires*) free.

**débord|er** /debɔrde/ *v.i.* overflow. ● *v.t.* (*dépasser*) extend beyond. **~é** *a.* snowed under (**de,** with).

**débouché** /debuʃe/ *n.m.* opening; (*carrière*) prospect; (*comm.*) outlet; (*sortie*) end, exit.

**déboucher** /debuʃe/ *v.t.* (*bouteille*) uncork; (*évier*) unblock.

**debout** /dəbu/ *adv.* standing; (*levé, éveillé*) up. **être ~, se tenir ~,** be standing, stand. **se mettre ~,** stand up.

**déboutonner** /debutɔne/ *v.t.* unbutton.

**débraillé** /debraje/ *a.* slovenly.

**débrancher** /debrɑ̃ʃe/ *v.t.* unplug, disconnect.

**débray|er** /debreje/ *v.i.* (*auto.*) declutch; (*faire grève*) stop work. **~age** /debrɛjaʒ/ *n.m.* (*pédale*) clutch; (*grève*) stoppage.

**débris** /debri/ *n.m. pl.* fragments; (*détritus*) rubbish, debris.

**débrouill|er** /debruje/ *v.t.* disentangle; (*problème*) sort out. **se ~er** *v. pr.* manage. **~ard, ~arde** *a.* (*fam.*) resourceful.

**début** /deby/ *n.m.* beginning.

**débu|ter** /debyte/ *v.i.* begin; (*dans un métier etc.*) start out. **~ant, ~ante** *n.m., f.* beginner.

**déca** /deka/ *n.m.* decaffeinated coffee.

**décafeiné** /dekafeine/ a. decaffeinated. ● n.m. du ∼, decaffeinated coffee.

**deçà (en)** /(ã)dəsa/ adv. this side. ● prép. en ∼ de, this side of.

**décacheter** /dekaʃte/ v.t. open.

**décall|er** /dekale/ v.t. shift. ∼age n.m. (écart) gap. ∼age horaire, time difference.

**décanter** /dekãte/ v.t. allow to settle. se ∼ v. pr. settle.

**décap|er** /dekape/ v.t. scrape down; (surface peinte) strip. ∼ant n.m. chemical agent; (pour peinture) paint stripper.

**décapotable** /dekapɔtabl/ a. convertible.

**décapsul|er** /dekapsyle/ v.t. take the cap off. ∼eur n.m. bottle-opener.

**décéd|er** /desede/ v.i. die. ∼é a. deceased.

**décembre** /desãbr/ n.m. December.

**décennie** /deseni/ n.f. decade.

**déc|ent, ∼ente** /desã, -t/ a. decent. ∼emment /-amã/ adv. decently. ∼ence n.f. decency.

**décentralis|er** /desãtralize/ v.t. decentralize. ∼ation n.f. decentralization.

**déception** /desɛpsjɔ̃/ n.f. disappointment.

**décerner** /desɛrne/ v.t. award.

**décès** /desɛ/ n.m. death.

**décev|oir**† /desvwar/ v.t. disappoint. ∼ant, e a. disappointing.

**déchaîner** /deʃene/ v.t. (violence etc.) unleash; (enthousiasme) arouse a good deal of. se ∼ v. pr. erupt.

**décharge** /deʃarʒ/ n.f. ∼ (électrique), electrical discharge. ∼ (publique), rubbish tip.

**décharg|er** /deʃarʒe/ v.t. unload; (arme, accusé) discharge. ∼er de, release from. se ∼er v. pr. (batterie, pile) go flat. ∼ement n.m. unloading.

**déchausser (se)** /(sə)deʃose/ v.pr. take off one's shoes; (dent) work loose.

**déchet** /deʃɛ/ n.m. (reste) scrap; (perte) waste. ∼s, (ordures) refuse.

**déchiffrer** /deʃifre/ v.t. decipher.

**déchiqueter** /deʃikte/ v.t. tear to shreds.

**déchirant, ∼ante** /deʃirã, -t/ a. heartbreaking.

**déchir|er** /deʃire/ v.t. tear; (diviser) tear apart. se ∼er v. pr. tear. ∼ure n.f. tear.

**décid|er** /deside/ v.t. decide on. ∼er que/de, decide that/to. ● v.i. decide. ∼er de qch., decide on sth. se ∼er v.pr. make up one's mind (à, to). ∼é a. (résolu) determined; (fixé, marqué) decided. ∼ément adv. really.

**décim|al, ∼ale** /m. pl. ∼aux) /desimal,-o/ a. & n.f. decimal.

**décimètre** /desimɛtr/ n.m. decimetre.

**décision** /desizjɔ̃/ n.f. decision.

**déclar|er** /deklare/ v.t. declare; (naissance) register. ∼ation n.f. declaration; (commentaire politique) statement. ∼ation d'impôts, tax return.

**déclench|er** /deklãʃe/ v.t. (techn.) release, set off; (lancer) launch; (provoquer) trigger off. se ∼er v. pr. (techn.) go off. ∼eur n.m. (photo.) trigger.

**déclic** /deklik/ n.m. click; (techn.) trigger mechanism.

**déclin** /deklɛ̃/ n.m. decline.

**déclinaison** /deklinɛzɔ̃/ n.f. (lang.) declension.

**décoder** /dekɔde/ v.t. decode.

**décoiffer** /dekwafe/ v.t. (ébouriffer) disarrange the hair of.

**décoincer** /dekwɛ̃se/ v.t. free.

**décoll|er**¹ /dekɔle/ v.i. (avion) take off. ∼age n.m. take-off.

**décoller**² /dekɔle/ v.t. unstick.

**décolleté** /dekɔlte/ a. low-cut. ● n.m. low neckline.

**décolorer** /dekɔlɔre/ v.t. fade; (cheveux) bleach.

**décombres** /dekɔ̃br/ n.m. pl. rubble.

**décommander** /dekɔmãde/ v.t. cancel.

**décompos|er** /dekɔ̃poze/ v.t. break up; (substance) decompose. se ∼er v. pr. (pourrir) decompose. ∼ition n.f. decomposition.

**décompte** /dekɔ̃t/ n.m. deduction; (détail) breakdown.

**décongel|er** /dekɔ̃ʒle/ v.t. thaw. ∼ation n.f. thawing.

**déconseill|er** /dekɔ̃seje/ v.t. ∼er qch. à qn., advise s.o. against sth. ∼é a. not advisable, inadvisable.

**décontract|er** /dekɔ̃trakte/ v.t., se ∼v.pr. relax. ∼é a. relaxed.

**décor** /dekɔr/ n.m. (paysage, théâtre) scenery; (cinéma) set; (cadre) setting; (de maison) décor.

**décor|er** /dekɔre/ v.t. decorate. ∼ateur, ∼atrice n.m., f. (interior) decorator. ∼ation n.f. decoration.

**découdre (se)** /(sə)dekudr/ v. pr. come unstitched.

**découp|er** /dekupe/ v.t. cut up; (viande) carve; (détacher) cut out. ∼age n.m. (image) cut-out.

**décourag|er** /dekuraʒe/ v.t. discourage. se ∼er v. pr. become discouraged. ∼ement n.m. discouragement. ∼é a. discouraged.

**décousu** /dekuzy/ a. (vêtement) falling apart; (idées etc.) disjointed.

**découvert, ∼e** /dekuver, -t/ a. (tête etc.) bare; (terrain) open. ● n.m. (de compte) overdraft. ● n.f. discovery.

**découvrir**† /dekuvrir/ v.t. discover; (enlever ce qui couvre) uncover; (voir) see; (montrer) reveal.

**décret** /dekrɛ/ n.m. decree. ~**er** /-ete/ v.t. decree.

**décrire†** /dekrir/ v.t. describe.

**décrisper (se)** /(sə)dekrispe/ v.pr. become less tense.

**décroch|er** /dekrɔʃe/ v.t. unhook; (obtenir: fam.) get. ● v.i. (abandonner: fam.) give up. ~**er (le téléphone)**, pick up the phone. ~**é** a. (téléphone) off the hook.

**décroître** /dekrwatr/ v.i. decrease.

**décrue** /dekry/ n.f. going down (of river water).

**déçu** /desy/ a. disappointed.

**dédain** /dedɛ̃/ n.m. scorn.

**dédale** /dedal/ n.m. maze.

**dedans** /dədɑ̃/ adv. & n.m. inside. **au ~ (de)**, inside. **en ~**, on the inside.

**dédicac|e** /dedikas/ n.f. dedication, inscription. ~**er** v.t. dedicate, inscribe.

**dédier** /dedje/ v.t. dedicate.

**dédommag|er** /dedɔmaʒe/ v.t. compensate (**de**, for). ~**ement** n.m. compensation.

**dédouaner** /dedwane/ v.t. clear through customs.

**déd|uire†** /dedɥir/ v.t. deduct; (conclure) deduce. ~**uction** n.f. deduction; ~**uction d'impôts** tax deduction.

**déesse** /deɛs/ n.f. goddess.

**défaillance** /defajɑ̃s/ n.f. weakness; (évanouissement) black-out; (panne) failure.

**défaire†** /defɛr/ v.t. undo; (valise) unpack; (démonter) take down; (débarrasser) rid. **se ~** v. pr. come undone. **se ~ de**, rid o.s. of.

**défaite** /defɛt/ n.f. defeat.

**défaut** /defo/ n.m. fault, defect; (d'un verre, diamant, etc.) flaw; (carence) lack; (pénurie) shortage.

**défav|eur** /defavœr/ n.f. disfavour. ~**orable** a. unfavourable.

**défavoriser** /defavɔrize/ v.t. put at a disadvantage.

**défect|ueux, ~ueuse** /defɛktɥø, -z/ a. faulty, defective.

**défendre** /defɑ̃dr/ v.t. defend; (interdire) forbid. ~ **à qn. de**, forbid s.o. to. **se ~** v. pr. defend o.s.; (se débrouiller) manage; (se protéger) protect o.s.

**défense** /defɑ̃s/ n.f. defence; (d'éléphant) tusk. ~ **de fumer**/ etc., no smoking/etc.

**défenseur** /defɑ̃sœr/ n.m. defender.

**défensi|f, ~ve** /defɑ̃sif, -v/ a. & n.f. defensive.

**déferler** /defɛrle/ v.i. (vagues) break; (violence etc.) erupt.

**dé†** /defi/ n.m. challenge; (refus) defiance. **mettre au ~**, challenge.

**déficeler** /defisle/ v.t. untie.

**déficience** /defisjɑ̃s/ n.f. deficiency.

**déficient** /defisjɑ̃/ a. deficient.

**déficit** /defisit/ n.m. deficit. ~**aire** a. in deficit.

**défier** /defje/ v.t. challenge; (braver) defy. **se ~ de**, mistrust.

**défilé** /defile/ n.m. procession; (mil.) parade; (fig.) (continual) stream. ~ **de mode**, fashion parade.

**défiler** /defile/ v.i. march (past); (visiteurs) stream; (images) flash by. **se ~** v. pr. (fam.) sneak off.

**défini** /defini/ a. definite.

**définir** /definir/ v.t. define.

**définissable** /definisabl/ a. definable.

**définiti|f, ~ve** /definitif, -v/ a. final; (permanent) definitive. ~**vement** adv. definitively, permanently.

**définition** /definisjɔ̃/ n.f. definition; (de mots croisés) clue.

**déflagration** /deflagrasjɔ̃/ n.f. explosion.

**déflation** /deflɑsjɔ̃/ n.f. deflation. ~**niste** /-jɔnist/ a. deflationary.

**défoncer** /defɔ̃se/ v.t. (porte etc.) break down.

**déform|er** /defɔrme/ v.t. put out of shape; (membre) deform; (faits, pensée) distort. ~**ation** n.f. loss of shape; deformation; distortion.

**défouler (se)** /(sə)defule/ v.pr. let off steam.

**défricher** /defriʃe/ v.t. clear (for cultivation).

**défroisser** /defrwase/ v.t. smooth out.

**défunt, ~e** /defœ̃, -t/ a. (mort) late. ● n.m., f. deceased.

**dégagé** /degaʒe/ a. clear.

**dégager** /degaʒe/ v.t. (exhaler) give off; (désencombrer) clear; (délivrer) free; (faire ressortir) bring out. **se ~** v. pr. free o.s.; (ciel, rue) clear; (odeur etc.) emanate.

**dégarnir** /degarnir/ **se ~** v.pr. clear, empty; (crâne) go bald.

**dégâts** /dega/ n.m. pl. damage.

**dégel** /deʒɛl/ n.m. thaw. ~**er** /deʒle/ v.t./i. thaw (out). **(faire) ~er**, (culin.) thaw.

**dégénér|er** /deʒenere/ v.i. degenerate. ~**é**, ~**ée** a. & n.m., f. degenerate.

**dégivrer** /deʒivre/ v.t. (auto.) de-ice; (frigo) defrost.

**déglacer** /deglase/ v.t. (culin.) deglaze.

**déglingu|er** /deglɛ̃ge/ (fam.) v.t. knock about. **se ~er** v. pr. fall to bits. ~**é** adj. falling to bits.

**dégonfl|er** /degɔ̃fle/ v.t. let down, deflate. **se ~er** v. pr. (fam.) get cold feet. ~**é** a. (pneu) flat; (lâche: fam.) yellow.

**dégouliner** /deguline/ v.i. trickle.

**dégourdi** /degurdi/ a. smart.

**dégourdir** /degurdir/ **se ~ les jambes**, stretch one's legs.

**dégoût** /degu/ n.m. disgust.

**dégoût|er** /degute/ v.t. disgust. **~er qn. de qch.**, put s.o. off sth. **~ant**, **~ante** a. disgusting. **~é** a. disgusted. **~é de**, sick of.

**dégradant** /degradã/ a. degrading.

**dégrader** /degrade/ **se ~** v. pr. (se détériorer) deteriorate.

**dégrafer** /degrafe/ v.t. unhook.

**degré** /dǝgre/ n.m. degree.

**dégressi|f, ~ve** /degresif, -v/ a. gradually lower.

**dégrèvement** /degrɛvmã/ n.m. **~fiscal ou d'impôts**, tax reduction.

**dégrever** /degrǝve/ v.t. reduce the tax on.

**dégringoler** /degrɛ̃gɔle/ v.i. tumble (down). ● v.t. rush down.

**dégueulasse** /degœlas/ a. (argot) disgusting, lousy.

**déguis|er** /degize/ v.t. disguise. **se ~er** v. pr. disguise o.s.; (au carnaval etc.) dress up. **~ement** n.m. disguise; (de carnaval etc.) fancy dress.

**dégust|er** /degyste/ v.t. taste, sample; (savourer) enjoy. **~ation** n.f. tasting, sampling.

**dehors** /dǝɔr/ adv. & n.m. outside. **en ~ de**, (hormis) apart from. **jeter/mettre/etc. ~**, throw/put/etc. out.

**déjà** /deʒa/ adv. already; (avant) before, already.

**déjà-vu** /deʒavy/ n.m. inv. déjà vu.

**déjeuner** /deʒœne/ v.i. (have) lunch; (le matin) (have) breakfast. ● n.m. lunch. **(petit) ~**, breakfast.

**delà** /dǝla/ adv. & prép. **au ~ (de)**, **en ~ (de)**, **par ~**, beyond.

**délai** /delɛ/ n.m. time-limit; (attente) wait; (sursis) extension (of time).

**délation** /delasjɔ̃/ n.f. informing.

**délavé** /delave/ a. faded.

**délayer** /deleje/ v.t. mix (with liquid); (idée) drag out.

**delco** /dɛlko/ n.m. (P., auto.) distributor.

**délégation** /delegasjɔ̃/ n.f. delegation.

**délégu|er** /delege/ v.t. delegate. **~é, ~ée** n.m., f. delegate.

**délibéré** /delibere/ a. deliberate; (résolu) determined. **~ment** adv. deliberately.

**délibér|er** /delibere/ v.i. deliberate. **~ation** n.f. deliberation.

**délicat, ~e** /delika, -t/ a. delicate; (plein de tact) tactful; (exigeant) particular. **~ement** /-tmã/ adv. delicately; tactfully. **~esse** /-tɛs/ n.f. delicacy; tact.

**délice** /delis/ n.m. delight.

**délicieu|x, ~se** /delisjø, -z/ a. (au goût) delicious.

**délimiter** /delimite/ v.t. determine, demarcate.

**délinquan|t, ~te** /delɛ̃kã, -t/ a. & n.m., f. delinquent. **~ce** n.f. delinquency.

**délire** /delir/ n.m. delirium; (fig.) frenzy.

**délirer** /delire/ v.i. be delirious (**de**, with); (déraisonner) rave.

**délit** /deli/ n.m. offence, crime.

**délivr|er** /delivre/ v.t. free, release; (pays) deliver; (remettre) issue.

**déloger** /delɔʒe/ v.t. force out.

**déloy|al** (m. pl. **~aux**) /delwajal, -jo/ a. disloyal; (procédé) unfair.

**delta** /dɛlta/ n.m. delta.

**deltaplane** /dɛltaplan/ n.m. hang-glider.

**déluge** /delyʒ/ n.m. flood; (pluie) downpour.

**demain** /dǝmɛ̃/ adv. tomorrow.

**demande** /dǝmãd/ n.f. request; (d'emploi) application; (exigence) demand.

**demandé** /dǝmãde/ a. in demand.

**demander** /dǝmãde/ v.t. ask for; (chemin, heure) ask; (emploi) apply for; (nécessiter) require. **~ que/si**, ask that/if. **~ qch. à qn.**, ask s.o. for sth. **~ à qn. de**, ask s.o. to. **se ~ si/où/etc.**, wonder if/where/etc.

**demandeu|r, ~se** /dǝmãdœr, -øz/ n.m., f. **les ~rs d'emploi** job seekers.

**démang|er** /demãʒe/ v.t./i. itch. **~eaison** n.f. itch(ing).

**démaquill|er (se)** /(sǝ)demakije/ v. pr. remove one's make-up. **~ant** n.m. make-up remover.

**démarcation** /demarkasjɔ̃/ n.f. demarcation.

**démarche** /demarʃ/ n.f. walk, gait; (procédé) step. **faire des ~s auprès de**, make approaches to.

**démarr|er** /demare/ v.i. (moteur) start (up); (partir) move off; (fig.) get moving. ● v.t. (fam.) get moving. **~age** n.m. start. **~eur** n.m. starter.

**démasquer** /demaske/ v.t. unmask.

**démêlant** /demelã/ n.m. conditioner.

**démêler** /demele/ v.t. disentangle.

**déménag|er** /demenaʒe/ v.i. move (house). ● v.t. (meubles) remove. **~ement** n.m. move; (de meubles) removal. **~eur** n.m. removal man; (Amer.) furniture mover.

**démener (se)** /(sǝ)demne/ v. pr. move about wildly; (fig.) exert o.s.

**démen|t, ~te** /demã, -t/ a. insane. ● n.m., f. lunatic. **~ce** n.f. insanity.

**démenti** /demãti/ n.m. denial.

**démentir** /demãtir/ v.t. refute; (ne pas être conforme à) belie.

**demeure** /dǝmœr/ n.f. residence.

**demeurer** /dǝmœre/ v.i. live; (rester) remain.

**demi, ~e** /dmi/ a. half(-). ● n.m., f. half. ● n.m. (bière) (half-pint) glass of beer. ● adv. à ~, half; (ouvrir, fermer) half-way. **à la ~e**, at half-past. **une heure et ~e**, an hour and a half; (à l'horloge) half past one. **une ~journée/-livre/etc.**, half a day/pound/etc., a half-day/-pound/*etc*. ~-**cercle** *n.m.* semi-circle. ~-**finale** *n.f.* semifinal. ~-**frère** *n.m.* stepbrother. ~-**heure** *n.f.* half-hour, half an hour. ~-**sel** *a. invar.* slightly salted. ~-**sœur** *n.f.* stepsister. ~-**tarif** *n.m.* half-fare. ~-**tour** *n.m.* about turn; (*auto.*) U-turn. **faire** ~-**tour,** turn back.

**démis,** ~e /demi, -z/ *a.* dislocated.

**démission** /demisjɔ̃/ *n.f.* resignation. ~**ner** /-jɔne/ *v.i.* resign.

**démobiliser** /demɔbilize/ *v.t.* demobilize.

**démocrate** /demɔkrat/ *n.m./f.* democrat. ● *a.* democratic.

**démocrat|ie** /demɔkrasi/ *n.f.* democracy. ~**ique** /-atik/ *a.* democratic.

**démodé** /demɔde/ *a.* old-fashioned.

**démographi|e** /demɔgrafi/ *n.f.* demography. ~**que** *a.* demographic.

**demoiselle** /dəmwazɛl/ *n.f.* young lady.

**démol|ir** /demɔlir/ *v.t.* demolish. ~**ition** *n.f.* demolition.

**démon** /demɔ̃/ *n.m.* demon.

**démonstration** /demɔ̃strasjɔ̃/ *n.f.* demonstration; (*de force*) show.

**démonter** /demɔ̃te/ *v.t.* take apart, dismantle; (*installation*) take down.

**démontrer** /demɔ̃tre/ *v.t.* show, demonstrate.

**démoraliser** /demɔralize/ *v.t.* demoralize.

**démystifier** /demistifje/ *v.t.* enlighten.

**dénigrer** /denigre/ *v.t.* denigrate.

**dénivellation** /denivɛlasjɔ̃/ *n.f.* (*pente*) slope.

**dénombrer** /denɔ̃bre/ *v.t.* count; (*énumérer*) enumerate.

**dénomination** /denɔminasjɔ̃/ *n.f.* designation.

**dénommé,** ~e /denɔme/ *n. m., f.* **le** ~ **X,** the said X.

**dénoncer** /denɔ̃se/ *v.t.* denounce; (*scol.*) tell on. **se** ~**er** *v. pr.* give o.s. up.

**dénoter** /denɔte/ *v.t.* denote.

**dénouement** /denumɑ̃/ *n.m.* outcome; (*théâtre*) dénouement.

**dénouer** /denwe/ *v.t.* unknot, undo. **se** ~ *v. pr.* (*nœud*) come undone.

**dénoyauter** /denwajote/ *v.t.* stone.

**denrée** /dɑ̃re/ *n.f.* foodstuff.

**dens|e** /dɑ̃s/ *a.* dense. ~**ité** *n.f.* density.

**dent** /dɑ̃/ *n.f.* tooth; (*de roue*) cog.

**dentelle** /dɑ̃tɛl/ *n.f.* lace.

**dentier** /dɑ̃tje/ *n.m.* denture.

**dentifrice** /dɑ̃tifris/ *n.m.* toothpaste.

**dentiste** /dɑ̃tist/ *n.m./f.* dentist.

**dentition** /dɑ̃tisjɔ̃/ *n.f.* teeth.

**dénué** /denɥe/ *a.* ~ **de,** devoid of.

**dénuement** /denɥmɑ̃/ *n.m.* destitution.

**déodorant** /deɔdɔrɑ̃/ *a.m. & n.m.* (**produit**) ~, deodorant.

**déontologi|e** /deɔ̃tɔlɔʒi/ *n.f.* code of practice. ~**que** *a.* ethical.

**dépann|er** /depane/ *v.t.* repair; (*fig.*) help out. ~**age** *n.m.* repair. **de** ~**age,** (*service etc.*) breakdown. ~**euse** *n.f.* breakdown lorry; (*Amer.*) wrecker.

**départ** /depar/ *n.m.* departure; (*sport*) start. **au** ~, at the outset.

**département** /departəmɑ̃/ *n.m.* department.

**dépassé** /depase/ *a.* outdated.

**dépass|er** /depase/ *v.t.* go past, pass; (*véhicule*) overtake; (*excéder*) exceed; (*rival*) surpass; (*dérouter: fam.*) be beyond. ● *v.i.* stick out; (*véhicule*) overtake. ~**ement** *n.m.* overtaking.

**dépays|er** /depeize/ *v.t.* disorientate, disorient. ~**ant,** ~e *a.* disorientating. ~**ement** *n.m.* disorientation; (*changement*) change of scenery.

**dépêcher (se)** /(sə)depeʃe/ *v. pr.* hurry (up).

**dépendre** /depɑ̃dr/ *v.i.* depend (**de,** on).

**dépens (aux)** /(o)depɑ̃/ *prép.* **aux** ~ **de,** at the expense of.

**dépens|e** /depɑ̃s/ *n.f.* expense; expenditure. ~**er** *v.t./i.* spend; (*énergie etc.*) expend. **se** ~**er** *v. pr.* exert o.s.

**dépens|ier,** ~**ière** /depɑ̃sje, -jɛr/ *a.* **être** ~**ier,** be a spendthrift.

**dépilatoire** /depilatwar/ *a. & n.m.* depilatory.

**dépist|er** /depiste/ *v.t.* detect. ~**age** *n.m.* detection.

**dépit** /depi/ *n.m.* resentment. **en** ~ **de,** despite. **en** ~ **du bon sens,** against all common sense.

**déplacé** /deplase/ *a.* out of place.

**déplac|er** /deplase/ *v.t.* move. **se** ~**er** *v. pr.* move; (*voyager*) travel. ~**ement** *n.m.* moving; travel(ling).

**déplaire** /deplɛr/ *v.i.* ~ **à,** (*irriter*) displease. **ça me déplaît,** I dislike that.

**déplaisant,** ~e /deplɛzɑ̃, -t/ *a.* unpleasant, disagreeable.

**dépliant** /deplijɑ̃/ *n.m.* leaflet.

**déplier** /deplije/ *v.t.* unfold.

**déplor|er** /deplore/ *v.t.* (*trouver regrettable*) deplore; (*mort*) lament. ~**able** *a.* deplorable.

**déporter** /deporte/ *v.t.* (*exiler*) deport; (*dévier*) carry off course.

**déposer** /depoze/ *v.t.* put down; (*laisser*) leave; (*passager*) drop; (*argent*) deposit; (*plainte*) lodge. **se** ~ *v. pr.* settle.

**déposition** /depozisjɔ̃/ *n.f.* (*jurid.*) statement.

**dépôt** /depo/ *n.m.* (*garantie, lie*) deposit; (*entrepôt*) warehouse; (*d'autobus*) depot; (*d'ordures*) dump.

**dépouiller** /depuje/ *v.t.* go through; (*votes*) count.

**dépourvu** /depurvy/ a. ~ **de,** devoid of.

**dépr|imer** /deprime/ v.t. depress. ~**ession** n.f. depression. ~**ession nerveuse,** nervous breakdown.

**depuis** /dəpɥi/ prép. since; (durée) for; (à partir de) from. ● adv. (ever) since. ~ **que,** since. ~ **quand attendez-vous?,** how long have you been waiting?

**député,** ~**e** /depyte/ n.m., f. Member of Parliament.

**déraciné,** ~**e** /derasine/ a. & n.m., f. rootless (person).

**déraill|er** /deraje/ v.i. be derailed; (fig., fam.) be talking nonsense. ~**eur** n.m. (de vélo) gear mechanism, dérailleur.

**dérang|er** /deraʒe/ v.t. (gêner) bother, disturb. **se** ~**er** v. pr. put o.s. out. **ça vous** ~**e si ...?,** do you mind if ...? **en** ~**ement,** out of order.

**dérap|er** /derape/ v.i. skid; (fig.) get out of control. ~**age** n.m. skid.

**déréglé** /deregle/ a. (vie) dissolute; (estomac) upset; (pendule) (that is) not running properly.

**dérégler** /deregle/ v.t. put out of order. **se** ~ v. pr. go wrong.

**dériv|e** /deriv/ n.f. **aller à la** ~**e,** drift. ~**er** v.i. (bateau) drift; v.t. (détourner) divert.

**dermatolo|gie** /dɛrmatɔlɔʒi/ n.f. dermatology. ~**gue** /-g/ n.m./f. dermatologist.

**dern|ier,** ~**ière** /dɛrnje, -jɛr/ a. last; (nouvelles, mode) latest; (étage) top. ● n.m., f. last (one). **ce** ~**ier,** the latter. **en** ~**ier,** last.

**dernièrement** /dɛrnjɛrmɑ̃/ adv. recently.

**dérogation** /derɔgasjɔ̃/ n.f. exemption.

**dérouler** /derule/ v.t. (fil etc.) unwind. **se** ~ v. pr. unwind; (avoir lieu) take place.

**déroute** /derut/ n.f. (mil.) rout.

**derrière** /dɛrjɛr/ prép. & adv. behind. ● n.m. back, rear; (postérieur) behind. **de** ~, back, rear; (pattes) hind. **par** ~, (from) behind, at the back ou rear.

**des** /de/ voir **de.**

**dès** /dɛ/ prép. (right) from, from the time of. ~ **que,** as soon as.

**désaccord** /dezakɔr/ n.m. disagreement. ~**é** /-de/ a. out of tune.

**désaffecté** /dezafɛkte/ a. disused.

**désagréable** /dezagreabl/ a. unpleasant.

**désagrément** /dezagremɑ̃/ n.m. annoyance.

**désaltérant** /dezalterɑ̃/ a. thirst-quenching, refreshing.

**désamorcer** /dezamɔrse/ v.t. (situation, obus) defuse.

**désappr|ouver** /dezapruve/ v.t. disapprove of. ~**obation** n.f. disapproval.

**désarçonner** /dezarsɔne/ v.t. disconcert, throw.

**désarmant** /dezarmɑ̃/ a. disarming.

**désarm|er** /dezarme/ v.t./i. disarm. ~**ement** n.m. (pol.) disarmament.

**désarroi** /dezarwa/ n.m. confusion.

**désastr|e** /dezastr/ n.m. disaster. ~**eux,** ~**euse** a. disastrous.

**désavantag|e** /dezavɑ̃taʒ/ n.m. disadvantage. ~**er** v.t. put at a disadvantage. ~**eux,** ~**euse** a. disadvantageous.

**désaxé,** ~**e** /dezakse/ a. & n.m., f. unbalanced (person).

**descendan|t,** ~**te** /desɑ̃dɑ̃, -t/ n.m., f. descendant. ~**ce** n.f. descent; (enfants) descendants.

**descendre** /desɑ̃dr/ v.i. (aux. être) go down; (venir) come down; (passager) get off ou out; (nuit) fall. ~ **de,** (être issu de) be descended from. ~ **à l'hôtel,** go to a hotel. ● v.t. (aux. avoir) (escalier etc.) go ou come down; (objet) take down.

**descente** /desɑ̃t/ n.f. descent; (pente) (downward) slope; (raid) raid. ~ **de lit,** bedside rug.

**description** /dɛskripsjɔ̃/ n.f. description.

**désemplir** /dezɑ̃plir/ v.i. **ne pas** ~, be always crowded.

**désendettement** /dezɑ̃dɛtmɑ̃/ n.m. getting out of debt.

**désenfler** /dezɑ̃fle/ v.i. go down.

**déséquilibre** /dezekilibr/ n.m. imbalance. **en** ~, unsteady.

**déséquilibr|er** /dezekilibre/ v.t. throw off balance. ~**é,** ~**ée** a. & n.m., f. unbalanced (person).

**désert¹** ~**e** /dezɛr, -t/ a. deserted.

**désert²** /dezɛr/ n.m. desert. ~**ique** /-tik/ a. desert.

**désert|er** /dezɛrte/ v.t./i. desert. ~**eur** n.m. deserter. ~**ion** /-ɛrsjɔ̃/ n.f. desertion.

**désespér|er** /dezɛspere/ v.i., **se** ~**er** v. pr. despair. ~**er de,** despair of. ~**é** a. in despair; (état, cas) hopeless; (effort) desperate.

**désespoir** /dezɛspwar/ n.m. despair. **au** ~, in despair.

**déshabill|er** /dezabije/ v.t. **se** ~**er** v. pr. undress, get undressed. ~**é** a. undressed; n. m. négligée.

**désherb|er** /dezɛrbe/ v.t. weed. ~**ant** n.m. weed-killer.

**déshérit|er** /dezerite/ v.t. disinherit. ~**é** a. (région) deprived. **les** ~**és** n.m. pl. the underprivileged.

**déshonneur** /dezɔnœr/ n.m. dishonour.

**déshonor|er** /dezɔnɔre/ v.t. dishonour. ~**ant,** ~**ante** a. dishonourable.

**déshydrater** /dezidrate/ v.t., **se** ~ v. pr. dehydrate.

**désigner** /dezine/ v.t. (montrer) point to ou out; (élire) appoint.

**désincrust|er** /dezɛ̃kryste/ v. pr. (chaudière) descale; (peau) exfoliate. ~**ant** a. **produit** ~**ant,** (skin) scrub.

**désinfect|er** /dezɛ̃fɛkte/ *v.t.* disinfect. **~ant** *n.m.* disinfectant.

**désintégrer** /dezɛ̃tegre/ *v.t.*, **se ~** *v. pr.* disintegrate.

**désintéressé** /dezɛ̃terese/ *a.* disinterested.

**désintoxication** /dezɛ̃tɔksikasjɔ̃/ *n.f.* detoxification. **cure de ~**, detoxification course.

**désintoxiquer** /dezɛ̃tɔksike/ *v.t.* cure of an addiction; (*régime*) purify.

**désir** /dezir/ *n.m.* wish, desire; (*convoitise*) desire.

**désirer** /dezire/ *v.t.* want; (*convoiter*) desire. **~ faire,** want *ou* wish to do.

**désireu|x**, **~se** /dezirø, -z/ *a.* **~x de,** anxious to.

**désobéir** /dezɔbeir/ *v.i.* **~ (à)**, disobey.

**désobéissan|t**, **~te** /dezɔbeisã, -t/ *a.* disobedient. **~ce** *n.f.* disobedience.

**désodé** /desɔde/ *a.* sodium-free.

**désodorisant** /dezɔdɔrizã/ *n.m.* air freshener.

**désol|er** /dezɔle/ *v.t.* distress. **être ~é,** (*regretter*) be sorry.

**désordonné** /dezɔrdɔne/ *a.* untidy; (*mouvements*) uncoordinated.

**désordre** /dezɔrdr/ *n.m.* disorder; untidiness.

**désorganiser** /dezɔrganize/ *v.t.* disorganize.

**désormais** /dezɔrmɛ/ *adv.* from now on.

**désosser** /dezɔse/ *v.t.* bone.

**desquels, desquelles** /dekɛl/ *voir* **lequel**.

**dessécher** /desefe/ *v.t.*, **se ~** *v. pr.* dry out *ou* up.

**desserrer** /desere/ *v.t.* loosen. **se ~** *v. pr.* come loose.

**dessert** /desɛr/ *n.m.* dessert.

**desservir** /desɛrvir/ *v.t./i.* clear away; (*autobus*) provide a service to, serve.

**dessin** /desɛ̃/ *n.m.* drawing; (*motif*) design; (*contour*) outline. **~ animé,** (*cinéma*) cartoon. **~ humoristique,** cartoon.

**dessin|er** /desine/ *v.t./i.* draw; (*fig.*) outline. **~ateur, ~atrice** *n.m.*, *f.* artist; (*industriel*) draughtsman.

**dessous** /dsu/ *adv.* underneath. ● *n.m.* under-side, underneath. ● *n.m. pl.* underclothes. **du ~,** bottom; (*voisins*) downstairs. **en ~, par ~,** underneath.

**dessus** /dsy/ *adv.* on top (of it), on it. ● *n.m.* top. **du ~,** top; (*voisins*) upstairs. **en ~,** above. **par ~,** over (it). **~-de-lit** *n.m. invar.* bedspread.

**destin** /dɛstɛ̃/ *n.m.* (*sort*) fate; (*avenir*) destiny.

**destinataire** /dɛstinatɛr/ *n.m./f.* addressee.

**destination** /dɛstinasjɔ̃/ *n.f.* destination; (*emploi*) purpose. **à ~ de,** (going) to.

**destinée** /dɛstine/ *n.f.* (*sort*) fate; (*avenir*) destiny.

**destiner** /dɛstine/ *v.t.* **~ à,** intend for; (*vouer*) destine for; (*affecter*) earmark for.

**destituer** /dɛstitɥe/ *v.t.* dismiss (from office).

**destruc|teur, ~trice** /dɛstryktœr, -tris/ *a.* destructive.

**destruction** /dɛstryksjɔ̃/ *n.f.* destruction.

**désunir** /dezynir/ *v.t.* divide.

**détachant** /detaʃɑ̃/ *n.m.* stain-remover.

**détach|é** /detaʃe/ *a.* detached. **~ement** *n.m.* detachment.

**détacher** /detaʃe/ *v.t.* untie; (*ôter*) remove, detach; (*déléguer*) send (on assignment *ou* secondment). **se ~** *v. pr.* come off, break away.

**détail** /detaj/ *n.m.* detail; (*de compte*) breakdown; (*comm.*) retail. **au ~,** (*vendre etc.*) retail. **de ~,** (*prix etc.*) retail. **en ~,** in detail.

**détaillé** /detaje/ *a.* detailed.

**détaill|er** /detaje/ *v.t.* (*articles*) sell in small quantities, split up. **~ant, ~ante** *n.m.*, *f.* retailer.

**détartrant** /detartrã/ *n.m.* descaler.

**détaxer** /detakse/ *v.t.* reduce the tax on.

**détecter** /detɛkte/ *v.t.* detect.

**détective** /detɛktiv/ *n.m.* detective.

**déteindre** /detɛ̃dr/ *v.i.* (*couleur*) run (**sur,** on to).

**détend|re** /detɑ̃dr/ *v.t.* slacken; (*ressort*) release; (*personne*) relax. **se ~re** *v. pr.* become slack, slacken; be released; relax. **~u** *a.* (*calme*) relaxed.

**détenir†** /detnir/ *v.t.* hold; (*secret, fortune*) possess.

**détente** /detɑ̃t/ *n.f.* relaxation; (*pol.*) détente; (*saut*) spring; (*gâchette*) trigger.

**détention** /detɑ̃sjɔ̃/ *n.f.* **~ préventive,** custody.

**détenu, ~e** /detny/ *n.m.*, *f.* prisoner.

**détergent** /detɛrʒɑ̃/ *n.m.* detergent.

**détérior|er** /deterjɔre/ *v.t.* damage. **se ~er** *v. pr.* deteriorate. **~ation** *n.f.* damaging; deterioration.

**détermin|er** /detɛrmine/ *v.t.* determine. **~ation** *n.f.* determination. **~é** *a.* (*résolu*) determined; (*précis*) definite.

**déterrer** /detere/ *v.t.* dig up.

**détester** /detɛste/ *v.t.* hate.

**déton|er** /detɔne/ *v.i.* explode, detonate. **~ateur** *n.m.* detonator. **~ation** *n.f.* explosion, detonation.

**détour** /detur/ *n.m.* bend; (*crochet*) detour; (*fig.*) roundabout means.

**détourné** /deturne/ *a.* roundabout.

**détourn|er** /deturne/ v.t. divert; (tête, yeux) turn away; (avion) hijack; (argent) embezzle. **~ement** n.m. hijack(ing); embezzlement.

**détraquer** /detrake/ v.t. break, put out of order; (estomac) upset. **se ~** v. pr. (machine) go wrong.

**détresse** /detrɛs/ n.f. distress.

**détritus** /detritys/ n.m. pl. rubbish.

**détroit** /detrwa/ n.m. strait.

**détruire**† /detrɥir/ v.t. destroy.

**dette** /dɛt/ n.f. debt.

**deuil** /dœj/ n.m. mourning; (perte) bereavement.

**deux** /dø/ a. & n.m. two. **~ fois,** twice. **tous (les) ~,** both. **~-pièces** n.m. invar. (vêtement) two-piece; (logement) two-room flat or apartment. **~-points** n.m. invar. (gram.) colon. **~-roues** n.m. invar. two-wheeled vehicle.

**deuxième** /døzjɛm/ a. & n.m./f. second. **~ment** adv. secondly.

**dévaloriser** /devalɔrize/ v.t., **se ~** v. pr. reduce in value.

**déval|uer** /devalɥe/ v.t., **se ~uer** v. pr. devalue. **~uation** n.f. devaluation.

**devancer** /dəvɑ̃se/ v.t. be ou go ahead of; (arriver) arrive ahead of; (prévenir) anticipate.

**devant** /dəvɑ̃/ prép. in front of; (distance) ahead of; (avec mouvement) past; (en présence de) before; (face à) in the face of. ● adv. in front; (à distance) ahead. ● n.m. front. **de ~,** front. **par ~,** at ou from the front, in front.

**devanture** /dəvɑ̃tyr/ n.f. shop front; (étalage) shop-window.

**développ|er** /devlɔpe/ v.t., **se ~er** v. pr. develop. **~ement** n.m. development; (de photos) developing.

**devenir**† /dəvnir/ v.i. (aux. être) become. **qu'est-il devenu?,** what has become of him?

**déviation** /devjasjɔ̃/ n.f. diversion.

**dévier** /devje/ v.t. divert; (coup) deflect.

**deviner** /dvine/ v.t. guess; (apercevoir) distinguish.

**devinette** /dvinɛt/ n.f. riddle.

**devis** /dvi/ n.m. estimate.

**dévisager** /devizaʒe/ v.t. stare at.

**devise** /dviz/ n.f. motto. **~s,** (monnaie) (foreign) currency.

**dévisser** /devise/ v.t. unscrew.

**dévitaliser** /devitalize/ v.t. (dent) kill the nerve in.

**dévoiler** /devwale/ v.t. reveal.

**devoir**[1] /dvwar/ n.m. duty; (scol.) homework; (fait en classe) exercise.

**devoir**†[2] /dvwar/ v.t. owe. ● v. aux. **~ faire,** (nécessité) must do, have (got) to do; (intention) be due to do. **~ être,** (probabilité) must be. **vous devriez,** you should. **il aurait dû,** he should have.

**dévorer** /devɔre/ v.t. devour.

**dévou|er (se)** /(sə)devwe/ v. pr. devote o.s. (à, to); (se sacrifier) sacrifice o.s. **~é** a. devoted. **~ement** /-vumɑ̃/ n.m. devotion.

**diab|ète** /djabɛt/ n.m. diabetes. **~étique** a. & n.m./f. diabetic.

**diab|le** /djabl/ n.m. devil. **~olique** a. diabolical.

**diagnosti|c** /djagnɔstik/ n.m. diagnosis. **~quer** v.t. diagnose.

**diagon|al, ~ale** (m. pl. ~aux) /djagɔnal, -o/ a. & n.f. diagonal. **en ~ale,** diagonally.

**dialecte** /djalɛkt/ n.m. dialect.

**dialogu|e** /djalɔg/ n.m. dialogue. **~er** v.i. (pol.) have a dialogue.

**diamant** /djamɑ̃/ n.m. diamond.

**diamètre** /djamɛtr/ n.m. diameter.

**diaphragme** /djafragm/ n.m. diaphragm.

**diapo** /djapo/ n.f. (colour) slide.

**diapositive** /djapozitiv/ n.f. (colour) slide.

**diarrhée** /djare/ n.f. diarrhoea.

**dictat|eur** /diktatœr/ n.m. dictator. **~ure** n.f. dictatorship.

**dict|er** /dikte/ v.t. dictate. **~ée** n.f. dictation.

**dictionnaire** /diksjɔnɛr/ n.m. dictionary.

**dièse** /djɛz/ n.m. (mus.) sharp.

**diesel** /djezɛl/ n.m. & a. invar. diesel.

**diététicien, ~ne** /djetetisjɛ̃, -jɛn/ n.m., f. dietician.

**diététique** /djetetik/ n.f. dietetics. ● a. **produit** ou **aliment ~,** dietary product.

**dieu** (pl. ~x) /djø/ n.m. god. **D~,** God.

**diffamatoire** /difamatwar/ a. defamatory.

**diffam|er** /difame/ v.t. slander; (par écrit) libel. **~ation** n.f. slander; libel.

**différé (en)** /(ɑ̃)difere/ adv. (émission) recorded.

**différemment** /diferamɑ̃/ adv. differently.

**différence** /diferɑ̃s/ n.f. difference.

**différent, ~e** /diferɑ̃, -t/ a. different (**de,** from).

**différer** /difere/ v.i. differ (**de,** from).

**difficile** /difisil/ a. difficult. **~ment** adv. with difficulty.

**difficulté** /difikylte/ n.f. difficulty.

**difform|e** /difɔrm/ a. deformed. **~ité** n.f. deformity.

**diffus|er** /difyze/ v.t. broadcast; (lumière, chaleur) diffuse. **~ion** n.f. broadcasting; diffusion.

**dig|érer** /diʒere/ v.t. digest; (endurer: fam.) stomach. **~este, ~estible** adjs. digestible. **~estion** n.f. digestion.

**digesti|f, ~ve** /diʒɛstif, -v/ a. digestive. ● n.m. after-dinner liqueur.

**digit|al** (m. pl. ~aux) /diʒital, -o/ a. digital.

**digne** /diɲ/ a. (noble) dignified; (honnête) worthy. **~ de,** worthy of. **~ de foi,** trustworthy.

**dignité** /diɲite/ n.f. dignity.

**digue** /dig/ n.f. dike.

**dilapider** /dilapide/ v.t. squander.

**dilater** /dilate/ v.t., **se** ~er v. pr. dilate.

**dilemme** /dilɛm/ n.m. dilemma.

**diluant** /dilɥɑ̃/ n.m. thinner.

**diluer** /dilɥe/ v.t. dilute.

**dimanche** /dimɑ̃ʃ/ n.m. Sunday.

**dimension** /dimɑ̃sjɔ̃/ n.f. (*taille*) size; (*mesure*) dimension.

**dimin|uer** /diminɥe/ v.t. reduce, decrease. ● v.i. decrease. ~**ution** n.f. decrease (**de**, in).

**diminutif** /diminytif/ n.m. diminutive; (*surnom*) pet name *ou* form.

**dinde** /dɛ̃d/ n.f. turkey.

**dindon** /dɛ̃dɔ̃/ n.m. turkey.

**dîn|er** /dine/ n.m. dinner. ● v.i. have dinner.

**dingue** /dɛ̃g/ a. (*fam.*) crazy.

**dinosaure** /dinozɔr/ n.m. dinosaur.

**diocèse** /djɔsɛz/ n.m. diocese.

**diphtérie** /difteri/ n.f. diphtheria.

**diphtongue** /diftɔ̃g/ n.f. diphthong.

**diplomate** /diplɔmat/ n.m. diplomat. ● a. diplomatic.

**diplomat|ie** /diplɔmasi/ n.f. diplomacy. ~**ique** /-atik/ a. diplomatic.

**diplôm|e** /diplom/ n.m. certificate, diploma; (*univ.*) degree. ~**é** a. qualified.

**dire**† /dir/ v.t. say; (*secret, vérité, heure*) tell; (*penser*) think. ~**que**, say that. ~ **à qn. que/de**, tell s.o. that/to. **ça me/vous**/*etc.* **dit de faire, I**/you/*etc.* feel like doing. **on dirait que**, it would seem that, it seems that. **dis**/**dites donc!**, hey!

**direct** /dirɛkt/ a. direct. **en** ~, (*émission*) live. ~**ement** adv. directly.

**direc|teur**, ~**trice** /dirɛktœr, -tris/ n.m., f. director; (*chef de service*) manager, manageress; (*d'école*) headmaster, headmistress.

**direction** /dirɛksjɔ̃/ n.f. (*sens*) direction; (*de société etc.*) management; (*auto.*) steering. **en** ~ **de**, (going) to.

**dirigeant**, ~**e** /diriʒɑ̃, -t/ n.m., f. (*pol.*) leader; (*comm.*) manager.

**diriger** /diriʒe/ v.t. run, manage, direct; (*véhicule*) steer; (*orchestre*) conduct; (*braquer*) aim; (*tourner*) turn. **se** ~ v. pr. guide o.s. **se** ~ **vers**, make one's way to.

**dis** /di/ voir **dire**.

**disciple** /disipl/ n.m. disciple.

**discipline** /disiplin/ n.f. discipline.

**discontinu** /diskɔ̃tiny/ a. intermittent.

**discothèque** /diskɔtɛk/ n.f. record library; (*club*) disco(thèque).

**discount** /diskunt/ n.m. discount.

**discours** /diskur/ n.m. speech.

**discréditer** /diskredite/ v.t. discredit.

**discr|et**, ~**ète** /diskrɛ, -t/ a. discreet. ~**ètement** adv. discreetly.

**discrétion** /diskresjɔ̃/ n.f. discretion. **à** ~, as much as one desires.

**discrimination** /diskriminasjɔ̃/ n.f. discrimination.

**discriminatoire** /diskriminatwar/ a. discriminatory.

**discussion** /diskysjɔ̃/ n.f. discussion; (*querelle*) argument.

**discuté** /diskyte/ a. controversial.

**discuter** /diskyte/ v.t. discuss; (*contester*) question. ● v.i. (*parler*) talk; (*répliquer*) argue. ~ **de**, discuss.

**disgrâce** /disgrɑs/ n.f. disgrace.

**disjoindre** /disʒwɛ̃dr/ v.t. take apart. **se** ~ v. pr. come apart.

**dislo|quer** /dislɔke/ v.t. (*membre*) dislocate; (*machine etc.*) break (apart). **se** ~**quer** v. pr. (*parti, cortège*) break up; (*meuble*) come apart.

**dispar|aître**† /disparɛtr/ v.i. disappear; (*mourir*) die. **faire** ~**aître**, get rid of. ~**ition** n.f. disappearance; (*mort*) death. ~**u**, ~**ue** a. (*soldat etc.*) missing; n.m., f. missing person; (*mort*) dead person.

**dispensaire** /dispɑ̃sɛr/ n.m. clinic.

**dispense** /dispɑ̃s/ n.f. exemption.

**dispenser** /dispɑ̃se/ v.t. exempt (**de**, from).

**disponib|le** /dispɔnibl/ a. available. ~**ilité** n.f. availability.

**dispos**, ~**e** /dispo, -z/ a. **frais et** ~, fresh and alert.

**disposé** /dispoze/ a. **bien/mal** ~, in a good/ bad mood. ~ **à**, prepared to.

**disposer** /dispoze/ v.t. arrange. ~ **à**, (*engager à*) incline to. ● v.i. ~ **de**, have at one's disposal.

**dispositif** /dispozitif/ n.m. device; (*plan*) plan of action.

**disposition** /dispozisjɔ̃/ n.f. arrangement; (*humeur*) mood. **à la** ~ **de**, at the disposal of.

**disproportionné** /disprɔpɔrsjɔne/ a. disproportionate.

**dispute** /dispyt/ n.f. quarrel.

**disputer** /dispyte/ v.t. (*match*) play; (*course*) run in; (*prix*) fight for. **se** ~ v. pr. quarrel; (*match*) be played.

**disquaire** /diskɛr/ n.m./f. record dealer.

**disqualif|ier** /diskalifje/ v.t. disqualify. ~**ication** n.f. disqualification.

**disque** /disk/ n.m. (*mus.*) record; (*sport*) discus; (*cercle*) disc, disk. ~ **dur**, hard disk.

**disquette** /diskɛt/ n.f. (*floppy*) disk.

**dissection** /disɛksjɔ̃/ n.f. dissection.

**disséquer** /diseke/ v.t. dissect.

**dissertation** /disɛrtasjɔ̃/ n.f. (*scol.*) essay.

**dissiden|t**, ~**te** /disidɑ̃, -t/ a. & n.m., f. dissident. ~**ce** n.f. dissidence.

**dissimuler** /disimyle/ v.t. conceal (**à**, from).

**dissolvant** /disɔlvɑ̃/ *n.m.* solvent; (*pour ongles*) nail polish remover.

**dissonant, ~e** /disɔnɑ̃, -t/ *a.* discordant.

**dissoudre†** /disudr/ *v.t.,* se ~ *v. pr.* dissolve.

**dissua|der** /disɥade/ *v.t.* dissuade (**de**, from). **~sion** /-ɥazjɔ̃/ *n.f.* dissuasion. **force de ~sion**, deterrent force.

**dissuasi|f, ~ve** /disɥazif, -v/ *a.* dissuasive.

**distance** /distɑ̃s/ *n.f.* distance; (*écart*) gap. **à ~**, at *ou* from a distance.

**distant, ~e** /distɑ̃, -t/ *a.* distant.

**distill|er** /distile/ *v.t.* distil. **~ation** *n.f.* distillation.

**distillerie** /distilri/ *n.f.* distillery.

**distinct, ~e** /distɛ̃(kt), -ɛkt/ *a.* distinct. **~ement** /-ɛktəmɑ̃/ *adv.* distinctly.

**distinction** /distɛ̃ksjɔ̃/ *n.f.* distinction.

**distingué** /distɛ̃ge/ *a.* distinguished.

**distinguer** /distɛ̃ge/ *v.t.* distinguish.

**distraction** /distraksjɔ̃/ *n.f.* absent-mindedness; (*oubli*) lapse; (*passe-temps*) distraction.

**distraire†** /distrɛr/ *v.t.* amuse; (*rendre inattentif*) distract. **se ~** *v. pr.* amuse o.s.

**distrait, ~e** /distrɛ, -t/ *a.* absent-minded.

**distrayant, ~e** /distrɛjɑ̃, -t/ *a.* entertaining.

**distrib|uer** /distribɥe/ *v.t.* hand out, distribute; (*répartir, amener*) distribute; (*courrier*) deliver. **~uteur** *n.m.* (*auto., comm.*) distributor. **~uteur (automatique)**, vending-machine; (*de billets*) (cash) dispenser.

**district** /distrikt/ *n.m.* district.

**dit, dites** /di, dit/ *voir* **dire**.

**diurétique** /djyretik/ *a. & n.m.* diuretic.

**divan** /divɑ̃/ *n.m.* divan.

**divergen|t, ~te** /divɛrʒɑ̃, -t/ *a.* divergent. **~ce** *n.f.* divergence.

**diverger** /divɛrʒe/ *v.i.* diverge.

**divers, ~e** /divɛr, -s/ *a.* (*varié*) diverse; (*différent*) various.

**diversifier** /divɛrsifje/ *v.t.* diversify.

**diversité** /divɛrsite/ *n.f.* diversity.

**divert|ir** /divɛrtir/ *v.t.* amuse. **se ~ir** *v. pr.* amuse o.s. **~issement** *n.m.* amusement.

**dividende** /dividɑ̃d/ *n.m.* dividend.

**divis|er** /divize/ *v.t.,* se ~er *v. pr.* divide. **~ion** *n.f.* division.

**divorc|e** /divɔrs/ *n.m.* divorce. **~é** *a.* **~ée** *a.* divorced; *n.m.,* f. divorcee. **~er** *v.i.* **~er (d'avec)**, divorce.

**dix** /dis/ (/di/ *before consonant,* /diz/ *before vowel*) *a. & n.m.* ten. **~ième** /dizjɛm/ *a. & n.m./f.* tenth.

**dix-huit** /dizɥit/ *a. & n.m.* eighteen. **~ième** *a. & n.m./f.* eighteenth.

**dix-neu|f** /dizncœf/ *a. & n.m.* nineteen. **~vième** *a. & n.m./f.* nineteenth.

**dix-sept** /disɛt/ *a. & n.m.* seventeen. **~ième** *a. & n.m./f.* seventeenth.

**dizaine** /dizɛn/ *n.f.* (about) ten.

**docile** /dɔsil/ *a.* docile.

**docilité** /dɔsilite/ *n.f.* docility.

**dock** /dɔk/ *n.m.* dock.

**docker** /dɔkɛr/ *n.m.* docker.

**doct|eur** /dɔktœr/ *n.m.* doctor. **~oresse** *n.f.* (*fam.*) lady doctor.

**doctorat** /dɔktɔra/ *n.m.* doctorate.

**doctrine** /dɔktrin/ *n.f.* doctrine.

**document** /dɔkymɑ̃/ *n.m.* document. **~aire** /-tɛr/ *a. & n.m.* documentary.

**documentaliste** /dɔkymɑ̃talist/ *n.m./f.* information officer.

**document|er** /dɔkymɑ̃te/ **se ~er** *v. pr.* collect information. **~ation** *n.f.* information, literature. **~é** *a.* well-documented.

**dodo** /dodo/ *n.m.* **faire ~,** (*langage enfantin*) go to byebyes.

**dodu** /dody/ *a.* plump.

**doigt** /dwa/ *n.m.* finger. **un ~ de**, a drop of. **~ de pied,** toe.

**dois, doit** /dwa/ *voir* **devoir**[1].

**Dolby** /dɔlbi/ *n.m. & a.* (P.) Dolby (P.).

**dollar** /dɔlar/ *n.m.* dollar.

**domaine** /dɔmɛn/ *n.m.* estate, domain; (*fig.*) domain.

**dôme** /dom/ *n.m.* dome.

**domestique** /dɔmɛstik/ *a.* domestic. ● *n.m./f.* servant.

**domicile** /dɔmisil/ *n.m.* home. **à ~,** (*livrer*) to the home.

**domicilié** /dɔmisilje/ *a.* resident.

**dominer** /dɔmine/ *v.t./i.* dominate; (*surplomber*) tower over, dominate; (*équipe*) dictate the game (to).

**dommage** /dɔmaʒ/ *n.m.* (*tort*) harm. **~(s)**, (*dégâts*) damage. **c'est ~**, it's a pity. **quel ~**, what a shame. **~s-intérêts** *n.m. pl.* (*jurid.*) damages.

**don** /dɔ̃/ *n.m.* (*cadeau, aptitude*) gift.

**donation** /dɔnasjɔ̃/ *n.f.* donation.

**donc** /dɔ̃(k)/ *conj.* so, then; (*par conséquent*) so, therefore.

**donjon** /dɔ̃ʒɔ̃/ *n.m.* (*tour*) keep.

**donné** /dɔne/ *a.* (*fixé*) given; (*pas cher: fam.*) dirt cheap.

**données** /dɔne/ *n.f. pl.* (*de science*) data; (*de problème*) facts.

**donner** /dɔne/ *v.t.* give; (*vieilles affaires*) give away; (*distribuer*) give out; (*récolte etc.*) produce; (*film*) show; (*pièce*) put on. ● *v.i.* **~ sur,** look out on to. **~ à réparer/**etc., take to be repaired/*etc.* **se ~ du mal,** go to a lot of trouble (**pour faire,** to do).

**donneu|r, ~se** /dɔnœr, -øz/ *n.m., f.* (*de sang*) donor.

**dont** /dɔ̃/ *pron. rel.* (*chose*) whose, of which; (*personne*) whose; (*partie d'un tout*) of whom; (*chose*) of which; (*provenance*) from which; (*manière*) in which. **le père ~ la fille,** the father whose daughter. **ce ~,** what. **~ il a besoin,** which he needs.

**dopage** /dɔpaʒ/ *n.m.* doping.

**doré** /dɔre/ *a.* (*couleur d'or*) golden; (*avec dorure*) gold. **la bourgeoisie ~e** the affluent middle class.

**dorénavant** /dɔrenavɑ̃/ *adv.* henceforth.

**dormir**† /dɔrmir/ *v.i.* sleep; (*être endormi*) be asleep. **il dort debout,** he can't keep awake.

**dortoir** /dɔrtwar/ *n.m.* dormitory.

**dos** /do/ *n.m.* back; (*de livre*) spine. **de ~,** from behind.

**dos|e** /doz/ *n.f.* dose. **~age** *n.m.* (*mélange*) mixture. **~er** *v.t.* measure out; (*équilibrer*) balance.

**dossier** /dɔsje/ *n.m.* (*documents*) file; (*de chaise*) back.

**dot** /dɔt/ *n.f.* dowry.

**doter** /dɔte/ *v.t.* **~ de,** equip with.

**douan|e** /dwan/ *n.f.* customs. **~ier, ~ière** *a.* customs; *n.m., f.* customs officer.

**double** /dubl/ *a. & adv.* double. ● *n.m.* (*copie*) duplicate; (*sosie*) double. **le ~ (de),** twice as much *ou* as many (as). **~ décimètre,** ruler.

**doubl|er** /duble/ *v.t./i.* double; (*dépasser*) overtake; (*vêtement*) line; (*film*) dub; (*classe*) repeat; (*cap*) round. **~ure** *n.f.* (*étoffe*) lining.

**douce** /dus/ *voir* **doux.**

**doucement** /dusmɑ̃/ *adv.* gently.

**douceur** /dusœr/ *n.f.* (*mollesse*) softness; (*de climat*) mildness; (*de personne*) gentleness.

**douch|e** /duʃ/ *n.f.* shower. **~er** *v.t.* give a shower to. **se ~er** *v. pr.* have *ou* take a shower.

**doudoune** /dudun/ *n.f.* (*fam.*) anorak.

**doué** /dwe/ *a.* gifted.

**douille** /duj/ *n.f.* (*électr.*) socket.

**douillet, ~te** /duje, -t/ *a.* cosy, comfortable; (*personne: péj.*) soft.

**doul|eur** /dulœr/ *n.f.* pain; (*chagrin*) grief. **~oureux, ~oureuse** *a.* painful. **la ~oureuse** *n.f.* the bill.

**doute** /dut/ *n.m.* doubt. **sans ~,** no doubt.

**douter** /dute/ *v.i.* **~ de,** doubt. **se ~ de,** suspect.

**douteu|x, ~se** /dutø, -z/ *a.* doubtful.

**Douvres** /duvr/ *n.m./f.* Dover.

**doux, douce** /du, dus/ *a.* (*moelleux*) soft; (*sucré*) sweet; (*clément, pas fort*) mild; (*pas brusque, bienveillant*) gentle.

**douzaine** /duzɛn/ *n.f.* about twelve; (*douze*) dozen. **une ~ d'œufs**/*etc.,* a dozen eggs/*etc.*

**douz|e** /duz/ *a. & n.m.* twelve. **~ième** *a. & n.m./f.* twelfth.

**doyen, ~ne** /dwajɛ̃, -jɛn/ *n.m., f.* dean; (*en âge*) most senior person.

**dragée** /draʒe/ *n.f.* sugared almond.

**dragon** /dragɔ̃/ *n.m.* dragon.

**drain** /drɛ̃/ *n.m.* drain.

**drainer** /drene/ *v.t.* drain.

**dramatique** /dramatik/ *a.* dramatic; (*tragique*) tragic. ● *n.f.* (television) drama.

**drame** /dram/ *n.m.* drama.

**drap** /dra/ *n.m.* sheet. **~-housse** /draus/ *n.m.* fitted sheet.

**drapeau** (*pl.* **~x**) /drapo/ *n.m.* flag.

**dresser** /drese/ *v.t.* put up, erect; (*tête*) raise; (*animal*) train; (*liste*) draw up. **se ~** *v. pr.* (*bâtiment etc.*) stand; (*personne*) draw o.s. up.

**drive** /drajv/ *n.m.* (*comput.*) drive.

**drogue** /drɔg/ *n.f.* drug. **la ~,** drugs.

**drogu|er** /drɔge/ **se ~er** *v. pr.* take drugs. **~é, ~ée** *n.m., f.* drug addict.

**droguerie** /drɔgri/ *n.f.* hardware and chemist's shop.

**droit¹, ~e** /drwa, -t/ *a.* (*non courbe*) straight; (*loyal*) upright; (*angle*) right. ● *adv.* straight. ● *n.f.* straight line.

**droit²~e** /drwa, -t/ *a.* (*contraire de gauche*) right. **à ~e,** on the right; (*direction*) to the right. **la ~e,** the right (side); (*pol.*) the right (wing). **~ier, ~ière** /-tje, -tjɛr/ *a. & n.m., f.* right-handed (person).

**droit³** /drwa/ *n.m.* right. **~(s),** (*taxe*) duty; (*d'inscription*) fee(s). **le ~,** (*jurid.*) law. **avoir ~ à,** be entitled to. **avoir le ~ de,** be allowed to. **~s d'auteur,** royalties.

**drôle** /drol/ *a.* funny. **~ment** *adv.* (*extrêmement: fam.*) dreadfully.

**dromadaire** /drɔmadɛr/ *n.m.* dromedary.

**drugstore** /drœgstɔr/ *n.m.* drugstore.

**du** /dy/ *voir* **de.**

**dû, due** /dy/ *voir* **devoir¹.** ● *a.* due. ● *n.m.* due; (*argent*) dues. **du à,** due to.

**duc, duchesse** /dyk, dyʃɛs/ *n.m., f.* duke, duchess.

**duel** /dɥɛl/ *n.m.* duel.

**dune** /dyn/ *n.f.* dune.

**duo** /dɥo/ *n.m.* (*mus.*) duet.

**duplex** /dyplɛks/ *n.m.* split-level apartment; (*émission*) link-up.

**duquel** /dykɛl/ *voir* **lequel.**

**dur** /dyr/ *a.* hard; (*sévère*) harsh, hard; (*viande*) tough, hard; (*col, brosse*) stiff. ● *adv.* hard.

**durable** /dyrabl/ *a.* lasting.

**durant** /dyrɑ̃/ *prép.* during; (*mesure de temps*) for.

**durc|ir** /dyrsir/ *v.t./i.,* **se ~ir** *v. pr.* harden. **~issement** *n.m.* hardening.

**durée** /dyre/ *n.f.* length; (*période*) duration.

**durement** /dyrmɑ̃/ *adv.* harshly.

**durer** /dyre/ *v.i.* last.

**dureté** /dyrte/ *n.f.* hardness; (*sévérité*) harshness.

**duvet** /dyvɛ/ *n.m.* down; (*sac*) (down-filled) sleeping-bag.

**dynami|que** /dinamik/ *a.* dynamic. ~sme *n.m.* dynamism.

**dynamit|e** /dinamit/ *n.f.* dynamite. ~er *v.t.* dynamite.

**dynamo** /dinamo/ *n.f.* dynamo.

**dynastie** /dinasti/ *n.f.* dynasty.

**dysenterie** /disɑ̃tri/ *n.f.* dysentery.

# Ee

**eau** (*pl.* ~x) /o/ *n.f.* water. ~ **courante/ dormante**, running/still water. ~ **de Cologne**, eau-de-Cologne. ~ **de toilette**, toilet water. ~**-de-vie** (*pl.* ~**x-de-vie**) *n.f.* brandy. ~ **douce/ salée**, fresh/salt water. ~ **potable**, drinking water. ~ **de Javel**, bleach. ~ **minérale**, mineral water. ~ **gazeuse**, fizzy water. ~ **plate**, still water.

**ébène** /ebɛn/ *n.f.* ebony.

**ébéniste** /ebenist/ *n.m.* cabinet-maker.

**éblouir** /ebluir/ *v.t.* dazzle.

**éboueur** /ebwœr/ *n.m.* dustman.

**ébouillanter** /ebujɑ̃te/ *v.t.* scald.

**éboulement** /ebulmɑ̃/ *n.m.* landslide.

**ébriété** /ebrijete/ *n.f.* intoxication.

**ébullition** /ebylisjɔ̃/ *n.f.* boiling. **en ~**, boiling.

**écaille** /ekaj/ *n.f.* (*de poisson*) scale; (*matière*) tortoiseshell.

**écailler** /ekaje/ *v.t.* (*poisson*) scale.

**écarlate** /ekarlat/ *a. & n.f.* scarlet.

**écarquiller** /ekarkije/ *v.t.* ~ **les yeux**, open one's eyes wide.

**écart** /ekar/ *n.m.* gap; (*de prix etc.*) difference; (*embardée*) swerve; (*de conduite*) lapse (**de**, in). **à l'~**, out of the way.

**écarté** /ekarte/ *a.* (*lieu*) remote. **les jambes ~es**, (with) legs apart. **les bras ~s**, with one's arms out.

**écartement** /ekartəmɑ̃/ *n.m.* gap.

**écarter** /ekarte/ *v.t.* (*objets*) move apart; (*ouvrir*) open; (*éliminer*) dismiss. ~ **qch. de**, move sth. away from. ~ **qn. de**, keep s.o. away from. **s'~** *v. pr.* (*s'éloigner*) move away. **s'~ de**, stray from.

**ecclésiastique** /eklezjastik/ *a.* ecclesiastical. ● *n.m.* clergyman.

**échafaud|age** /eʃafodaʒ/ *n.m.* scaffolding; (*amas*) heap. ~er *v.t.* (*projets*) construct.

**échalote** /eʃalɔt/ *n.f.* shallot.

**échang|e** /eʃɑ̃ʒ/ *n.m.* exchange. **en ~e (de)**, in exchange (for). ~er *v.t.* exchange (**contre**, for).

**échangeur** /eʃɑ̃ʒœr/ *n.m.* (*auto.*) interchange.

**échantillon** /eʃɑ̃tijɔ̃/ *n.m.* sample.

**échappement** /eʃapmɑ̃/ *n.m.* exhaust.

**échapper** /eʃape/ *v.i.* ~ **à**, escape; (*en fuyant*) escape (from). **s'~** *v. pr.* escape.

**écharde** /eʃard/ *n.f.* splinter.

**écharpe** /eʃarp/ *n.f.* scarf; (*de maire*) sash. **en ~**, (*bras*) in a sling.

**échasse** /eʃas/ *n.f.* stilt.

**échassier** /eʃasje/ *n.m.* wader.

**échéance** /eʃeɑ̃s/ *n.f.* due date (for payment); (*délai*) deadline; (*obligation*) (financial) commitment.

**échéant (le cas)** /(ləkaz)eʃeɑ̃/ *adv.* if the occasion arises, possibly.

**échec** /eʃɛk/ *n.m.* failure. ~**s**, (*jeu*) chess. ~ **et mat**, checkmate.

**échelle** /eʃɛl/ *n.f.* ladder; (*dimension*) scale.

**échelon** /eʃlɔ̃/ *n.m.* rung; (*de fonctionnaire*) grade; (*niveau*) level.

**échelonner** /eʃlɔne/ *v.t.* spread out, space out.

**échiquier** /eʃikje/ *n.m.* chessboard.

**écho** /eko/ *n.m.* echo.

**échographie** /ekɔɡrafi/ *n.f.* ultrasound (scan).

**échouer**[1] /eʃwe/ *v.i.* fail.

**échouer**[2] /eʃwe/ *v.t.* (*bateau*) ground. ● *v.i.*, **s'~** *v. pr.* run aground.

**éclabouss|er** /eklabuse/ *v.t.* splash. ~ure *n.f.* splash.

**éclair** /eklɛr/ *n.m.* (flash of) lightning; (*gâteau*) éclair.

**éclairage** /eklɛraʒ/ *n.m.* lighting.

**éclaircie** /eklɛrsi/ *n.f.* sunny interval.

**éclaircir** /eklɛrsir/ *v.t.* make lighter; (*mystère*) clear up.

**éclairer** /eklere/ *v.t.* light (up); (*personne*) give some light to.

**éclaireu|r, ~se** /eklɛrœr, -øz/ *n.m., f.* (boy) scout, (girl) guide.

**éclat** /ekla/ *n.m.* fragment; (*de lumière*) brightness; (*de rire*) (out)burst; (*splendeur*) brilliance.

**éclatant, ~e** /eklatɑ̃, -t/ *a.* brilliant.

**éclater** /eklate/ *v.i.* burst; (*exploser*) go off; (*verre*) shatter; (*guerre*) break out; (*groupe*) split up. ~ **de rire**, burst out laughing.

**éclipse** /eklips/ *n.f.* eclipse.

**éclipser** /eklipse/ *v.t.* eclipse. **s'~** *v. pr.* slip away.

**écl|ore** /eklɔr/ *v.i.* (*œuf*) hatch; (*fleur*) open. ~osion *n.f.* hatching; opening.

**écluse** /eklyz/ *n.f.* (*de canal*) lock.

**écœurant, ~e** /ekœrɑ̃, -t/ *a.* (*gâteau*) sickly; (*fig.*) disgusting.

**école** /ekɔl/ *n.f.* school. ∼ **maternelle /
primaire / secondaire,** nursery / primary /
secondary school.

**écol|ier,** ∼**ière** /ekɔlje, -jɛr/ *n.m., f.*
schoolboy, schoolgirl.

**écolo** /ekɔlɔ/ *a. & n.m./f.* green.

**ecolog|ie** /ekɔlɔʒi/ *n.f.* ecology. ∼**ique** *a.*
ecological, green.

**écologiste** /ekɔlɔʒist/ *n.m./f.* ecologist.

**économat** /ekɔnɔma/ *n.m.* bursary.

**économe** /ekɔnɔm/ *a.* thrifty. ● *n.m./f.*
bursar.

**econom|ie** /ekɔnɔmi/ *n.f.* economy. ∼**ies,**
(*argent*) savings. **une** ∼**ie de,** (*gain*) a saving
of. ∼**ique** *a.* (*pol.*) economic; (*bon marché*)
economical. ∼**iser** *v.t./i.* save. ∼**iste** *n.m./f.*
economist.

**écorce** /ekɔrs/ *n.f.* bark; (*de fruit*) peel.

**écorch|er** /ekɔrʃe/ **s'**∼**er** *v. pr.* graze o.s.
∼**ure** *n.f.* graze.

**écossais,** ∼**e** /ekɔsɛ,-z/ *a.* Scottish. ● *n.m.,
f.* Scot.

**Écosse** /ekɔs/ *n.f.* Scotland.

**écosser** /ekɔse/ *v.t.* shell.

**écouler**¹ /ekule/ *v.t.* dispose of, sell.

**écoul|er²(s')** /(s)ekule/ *v. pr.* flow (out), run
(off); (*temps*) pass. ∼**ement** *n.m.* flow.

**écourter** /ekurte/ *v.t.* shorten.

**écoute** /ekut/ *n.f.* listening. **à l'**∼ **(de),**
listening in (to). **heures de grande** ∼**,** peak
time.

**écout|er** /ekute/ *v.t.* listen to; (*radio*) listen
(in) to. ● *v.i.* listen. ∼**eur** *n.m.* earphones;
(*de téléphone*) receiver.

**écran** /ekrã/ *n.m.* screen. ∼ **total,** sun-block.

**écrasant,** ∼**e** /ekrazã,-t/ *a.* overwhelming.

**écraser** /ekraze/ *v.t.* crush; (*piéton*) run
over. **s'**∼ *v. pr.* crash (**contre,** into).

**écrémé** /ekreme/ *a.* **lait** ∼**,** skimmed milk.
**lait demi-**∼**,** semi-skimmed milk.

**écrevisse** /ekrəvis/ *n.f.* crayfish.

**écrin** /ekrɛ̃/ *n.m.* case.

**écrire†** /ekrir/ *v.t./i.* write; (*orthographier*)
spell.

**écrit** /ekri/ *n.m.* document; (*examen*) written
paper. **par** ∼**,** in writing.

**écriteau** (*pl.* ∼**x**) /ekrito/ *n.m.* notice.

**écriture** /ekrityr/ *n.f.* writing.

**écrivain** /ekrivɛ̃/ *n.m.* writer.

**écrou** /ekru/ *n.m.* nut.

**écrouer** /ekrue/ *v.t.* imprison.

**écrouler (s')** /(s)ekrule/ *v. pr.* collapse.

**écru** /ekry/ *a.* (*couleur*) natural; (*tissu*) raw.

**Écu** /eky/ *n.m. invar.* ecu.

**écueil** /ekœj/ *n.m.* reef; (*fig.*) danger.

**écume** /ekym/ *n.f.* foam.

**écureuil** /ekyrœj/ *n.m.* squirrel.

**écurie** /ekyri/ *n.f.* stable.

**écuy|er,** ∼**ère** /ekɥije, -jɛr/ *n.m., f.* (horse)
rider.

**eczéma** /ɛgzema/ *n.m.* eczema.

**édifice** /edifis/ *n.m.* building.

**édi|ter** /edite/ *v.t.* publish; (*annoter*) edit.
∼**teur,** ∼**trice** *n.m., f.* publisher; editor.

**édition** /edisjɔ̃/ *n.f.* edition; (*industrie*)
publishing.

**édredon** /edrədɔ̃/ *n.m.* eiderdown.

**éducateur,** ∼**trice** /edykatœr, -tris/
*n.m., f.* teacher.

**éducati|f,** ∼**ve** /edykatif, -v/ *a.* educa-
tional.

**éducation** /edykasjɔ̃/ *n.f.* education; (*dans
la famille*) upbringing; (*manières*) manners.
∼ **physique,** physical education.

**édulcorant** /edylkɔrã/ *n.m. & a.* **(produit)**
∼**,** sweetener.

**éduquer** /edyke/ *v.t.* educate; (*à la maison*)
bring up.

**effacer** /efase/ *v.t.* (*gommer*) rub out; (*par
lavage*) wash out; (*souvenir etc.*) erase. **s'**∼
*v. pr.* fade; (*s'écarter*) step aside.

**effecti|f,** ∼**ve** /efɛktif, -v/ *a.* effective.
∼**vement** *adv.* effectively; (*en effet*) indeed.

**effectuer** /efɛktɥe/ *v.t.* carry out, make.

**effervescen|t,** ∼**te** /efɛrvesã, -t/ *a.*
**comprimé** ∼**t,** effervescent tablet. ∼**ce**
*n.f.* excitement.

**effet** /efɛ/ *n.m.* effect; (*impression*) impression. **en** ∼**,** indeed. **faire bon/mauvais** ∼**,**
make a good/bad impression.

**efficac|e** /efikas/ *a.* effective; (*personne*)
efficient. ∼**ité** *n.f.* effectiveness; efficiency.

**effleurer** /eflœre/ *v.t.* touch lightly; (*sujet*)
touch on.

**effluves** /eflyv/ *n.m. pl.* exhalations.

**effondr|er (s')** /(s)efɔ̃dre/ *v. pr.* collapse.
∼**ement** *n.m.* collapse.

**efforcer (s')** /(s)efɔrse/ *v.pr.* try (hard) (**de,**
to).

**effort** /efɔr/ *n.m.* effort.

**effraction** /efraksjɔ̃/ *n.f.* **entrer par** ∼**,**
break in.

**effray|er** /efreje/ *v.t.* frighten. ∼**ant,** ∼**ante**
*a.* frightening; (*fig.*) frightful.

**effriter (s')** /(s)efrite/ *v. pr.* crumble.

**effroi** /efrwa/ *n.m.* dread.

**effronté** /efrɔ̃te/ *a.* impudent.

**effroyable** /efrwajabl/ *a.* dreadful.

**ég|al,** ∼**ale** (*m. pl.* ∼**aux**) /egal,-o/ *a.* equal;
(*surface, vitesse*) even. ● *n.m., f.* equal. **ça
m'est/lui est** ∼**al,** it is all the same to me/
him. **sans égal,** matchless. **d'**∼ **à égal,**
between equals.

**également** /egalmã/ *adv.* equally; (*aussi*)
as well.

**égaler** /egale/ *v.t.* equal.

**égaliser** /egalize/ *v.t.* (*cheveux*) trim.

**égalité** /egalite/ n.f. equality; (*de surface, d'humeur*) evenness.

**égard** /egar/ n.m. regard. ~s, consideration.

**égarer** /egare/ s'~v.pr. get lost; (*se tromper*) go astray.

**égayer** /egeje/ v.t. (*personne*) cheer up; (*pièce*) brighten up.

**églantier** /eglɑ̃tje/ n.m. wild rose (-bush).

**églefin** /egləfɛ̃/ n.m. haddock.

**église** /egliz/ n.f. church.

**égoïs|te** /egoist/ a. selfish. ● n.m./f. egoist. ~me n.m. selfishness, egoism.

**égorger** /egɔrʒe/ v.t. slit the throat of.

**égout** /egu/ n.m. sewer.

**égout|er** /egute/ v.t./i., s'~er v. pr. (*vaisselle*) drain. ~oir n.m. draining-board; (*panier*) dish drainer.

**égratign|er** /egratiɲe/ v.t. scratch. ~ure n.f. scratch.

**Égypte** /eʒipt/ n.f. Egypt.

**égyptien, ~ne** /eʒipsjɛ̃, -jɛn/ a. & n.m., f. Egyptian.

**eh** /e/ int. hey. **eh bien,** well.

**éjecter** /eʒɛkte/ v.t. eject.

**élaborer** /elabɔre/ v.t. elaborate.

**élaguer** /elage/ v.t. prune.

**élan**[1] /elɑ̃/ n.m. (*sport*) run-up; (*vitesse*) momentum; (*fig.*) surge.

**élan**[2] /elɑ̃/ n.m. (*animal*) moose.

**élancé** /elɑ̃se/ a. slender.

**élancement** /elɑ̃smɑ̃/ n.m. twinge.

**élancer (s')** /(s)elɑ̃se/ v. pr. leap forward, dash; (*se dresser*) soar.

**élargir** /elarʒir/ v.t., s'~ v. pr. widen.

**élasti|que** /elastik/ a. elastic. ● n.m. elastic band; (*tissu*) elastic. ~cité n.f. elasticity.

**élec|teur, ~trice** /elɛktœr, -tris/ n.m., f. voter, elector.

**élection** /elɛksjɔ̃/ n.f. election.

**élector|al** (m. pl. ~aux) /elɛktɔral, -o/ a. (*réunion etc.*) election; (*collège*) electoral.

**électorat** /elɛktɔra/ n.m. electorate, voters.

**électricien** /elɛktrisjɛ̃/ n.m. electrician.

**électricité** /elɛktrisite/ n.f. electricity.

**électrique** /elɛktrik/ a. electric (al).

**électroménager** /elɛktrɔmenaʒe/ n.m. l'~, household appliances.

**électron** /elɛktrɔ̃/ n.m. electron.

**électronique** /elɛktrɔnik/ a. electronic. ● n.f. electronics.

**électrophone** /elɛktrɔfɔn/ n.m. record-player.

**élég|ant, ~ante** /elegɑ̃, -t/ a. elegant. ~ance n.f. elegance.

**élément** /elemɑ̃/ n.m. element; (*meuble*) unit. ~aire /-tɛr/ a. elementary.

**éléphant** /elefɑ̃/ n.m. elephant.

**élevage** /ɛlvaʒ/ n.m. (stock-)breeding.

**élève** /elɛv/ n.m./f. pupil.

**élevé** /ɛlve/ a. high; (*noble*) elevated. **bien ~,** well-mannered.

**élever** /ɛlve/ v.t. raise; (*enfants*) bring up, raise; (*animal*) breed. s'~ à, amount to.

**éleveu|r, ~se** /ɛlvœr, -øz/ n.m., f. (stock-) breeder.

**élimin|er** /elimine/ v.t. eliminate. ~ation n.f. elimination.

**élire**† /elir/ v.t. elect.

**elle** /ɛl/ pron. she; (*complément*) her; (*chose*) it. ~-même pron. herself; itself.

**elles** /ɛl/ pron. they; (*complément*) them. ~-mêmes pron. themselves.

**ellipse** /elips/ n.f. ellipse.

**élocution** /elɔkysjɔ̃/ n.f. diction.

**éloge** /elɔʒ/ n.m. praise. **faire l'~ de,** praise.

**éloigné** /elwaɲe/ a. distant. ~ de, far away from. **parent ~,** distant relative.

**éloigner** /elwaɲe/ v.t. take away ou remove (**de**, from). s'~ v. pr. go ou move away (**de,** from).

**élongation** /elɔ̃gasjɔ̃/ n.f. strained muscle.

**éloquen|t, ~te** /elɔkɑ̃, -t/ a. eloquent. ~ce n.f. eloquence.

**élu, ~e** /ely/ a. elected. ● n.m., f. (*pol.*) elected representative.

**ém|ail** (pl. ~aux) /emaj, -o/ n.m. enamel.

**émaillé** /emaje/ a. enamelled.

**emballer** /ɑ̃bale/ v.t. pack, wrap; (*personne: fam.*) enthuse. s'~er v. pr. (*personne*) get carried away. ~age n.m. package, wrapping.

**embarcadère** /ɑ̃barkader/ n.m. landing-stage.

**embarcation** /ɑ̃barkasjɔ̃/ n.f. boat.

**embarqu|er** /ɑ̃barke/ v.t. embark; (*charger*) load; (*emporter: fam.*) cart off. ● v.i., s'~er v. pr. board, embark. ~ement n.m. embarkation; loading.

**embarras** /ɑ̃bara/ n.m. (*gêne*) embarrassment; (*difficulté*) difficulty.

**embarrasser** /ɑ̃barase/ v.t. (*fig.*) embarrass.

**embauch|e** /ɑ̃boʃ/ n.f. hiring; (*emploi*) employment. ~er v.t. hire, take on.

**embauchoir** /ɑ̃boʃwar/ n.m. shoe tree.

**embaumer** /ɑ̃bome/ v.t./i. (make) smell fragrant.

**embellir** /ɑ̃belir/ v.t. brighten up; (*récit*) embellish.

**embêt|er** /ɑ̃bete/ v.t. (*fam.*) annoy. s'~er v. pr. (*fam.*) get bored. ~ant, ~ante a. (*fam.*) annoying. ~ement /ɑ̃bɛtmɑ̃/ n.m. (*fam.*) annoyance.

**emboîter** /ɑ̃bwate/ v.t., s'~ v. pr. fit together.

**embouchure** /ɑ̃buʃyr/ n.f. (*de fleuve*) mouth.

**embourber (s')** /(s)ɑ̃burbe/ v. pr. get bogged down.

**embout** /ɑ̃bu/ n.m. tip.

**embouteillage | encaustique**

**embouteillage** /ãbutɛjaʒ/ n.m. traffic jam.

**emboutir** /ãbutir/ v.t. ( *heurter* ) crash into.

**embranchement** /ãbrãʃmã/ n.m. ( *de routes* ) junction.

**embrasser** /ãbrase/ v.t. kiss; ( *adopter, contenir* ) embrace. **s'~** v. pr. kiss.

**embray|er** /ãbreje/ v.i. let in the clutch. **~age** /ãbrɛjaʒ/ n.m. clutch.

**embrouiller** /ãbruje/ v.t. mix up; ( *fils* ) tangle. **s'~** v. pr. get mixed up.

**embryon** /ãbrijɔ̃/ n.m. embryo. **~naire** /-jɔnɛr/ a. embryonic.

**embûches** /ãbyʃ/ n.f. pl. traps.

**éméché** /emeʃe/ a. tipsy.

**émeraude** /ɛmrod/ n.f. emerald.

**émerg|er** /emɛrʒe/ v.i. emerge; ( *fig.* ) stand out.

**émerveill|er** /emɛrveje/ v.t. amaze. **s'~er de,** marvel at, be amazed at. **~ement** /-vɛjmã/ n.m. amazement, wonder.

**émett|re**† /emɛtr/ v.t. give out; ( *message* ) transmit; ( *timbre, billet* ) issue; ( *opinion* ) express. **~eur** n.m. transmitter.

**émeute** /emøt/ n.f. riot.

**émietter** /emjete/ v.t., **s'~** v. pr. crumble.

**émigrant, ~e** /emigrã,-t/ n.m., f. emigrant.

**émigr|er** /emigre/ v.i. emigrate. **~ation** n.f. emigration.

**émincer** /emɛ̃se/ v.t. cut into thin slices.

**émin|ent, ~ente** /eminã, -t/ a. eminent. **~emment** /-amã/ adv. eminently.

**émissaire** /emisɛr/ n.m. emissary.

**émission** /emisjɔ̃/ n.f. emission; ( *de message* ) transmission; ( *de timbre* ) issue; ( *programme* ) bro adcast.

**emmanchure** /ãmãʃyr/ n.f. armhole.

**emmêler** /ãmele/ v.t. tangle. **s'~** v. pr. get mixed up.

**emménager** /ãmenaʒe/ v.i. move in. **~ dans,** move into.

**emmener** /ãmne/ v.t. take; ( *comme prisonnier* ) take away.

**emmerder** /ãmɛrde/ v.t. ( *argot* ) bother. **s'~** v. pr. ( *argot* ) get bored.

**emmitoufler** /ãmitufle/ v.t., **s'~** v. pr. wrap up (warmly).

**émonder** /emɔ̃de/ v.t. prune.

**émoti|f, ~ve** /emɔtif, -v/ a. emotional.

**émotion** /emosjɔ̃/ n.f. emotion; ( *peur* ) fright.

**émouv|oir** /emuvwar/ v.t. move. **~ant, ~ante** a. moving.

**empailler** /ãpaje/ v.t. stuff.

**empaqueter** /ãpakte/ v.t. package.

**emparer (s')** /(s)ãpare/ v. pr. **s'~ de,** seize.

**empêchement** /ãpɛʃmã/ n.m. hitch, difficulty.

**empêcher** /ãpeʃe/ v.t. prevent. **~ de faire,** prevent *ou* stop (from) doing.

**empereur** /ãprœr/ n.m. emperor.

**empester** /ãpɛste/ v.i. stink.

**empêtrer (s')** /(s)ãpetre/ v. pr. become entangled.

**emphase** /ãfaz/ n.f. pomposity.

**empiler** /ãpile/ v.t., **s'~** v. pr. pile (up).

**empire** /ãpir/ n.m. empire; ( *fig.* ) control.

**empirer** /ãpire/ v.i. worsen.

**emplacement** /ãplasmã/ n.m. site.

**emplâtre** /ãplɑtr/ n.m. ( *méd.* ) plaster.

**emplir** /ãplir/ v.t., **s'~** v. pr. fill.

**emploi** /ãplwa/ n.m. use; ( *travail* ) job. **~ du temps,** timetable. **l'~,** ( *pol.* ) employment.

**employ|er** /ãplwaje/ v.t. use; ( *personne* ) employ. **~é, ~ée** n.m., f. employee. **~eur, ~euse** n.m., f. employer.

**empocher** /ãpɔʃe/ v.t. pocket.

**empoisonn|er** /ãpwazone/ v.t. poison ( *embêter: fam.* ) annoy. **~ement** n.m. poisoning.

**emport|é** /ãpɔrte/ a. quicktempered. **~ement** n.m. anger.

**emporter** /ãpɔrte/ v.t. take (away); ( *entraîner* ) carry away; ( *prix* ) carry off; ( *arracher* ) tear off. **s'~** v. pr. lose one's temper. **plat à ~,** take-away.

**empreinte** /ãprɛ̃t/ n.f. mark. **~ (digitale),** fingerprint.

**empress|er (s')** /(s)ãprese/ v. pr. **s'~er auprès de,** be attentive to. **s'~er de,** hasten to. **~é a.** eager, attentive. **~ement** /ãprɛsmã/ n.m. eagerness.

**emprise** /ãpriz/ n.f. influence.

**emprisonn|er** /ãprizone/ v.t. imprison. **~ement** n.m. imprisonment.

**emprunt** /ãprœ̃/ n.m. loan. **faire un ~,** take out a loan.

**emprunter** /ãprœ̃te/ v.t. borrow (**à,** from); ( *route* ) use; ( *fig.* ) assume.

**ému** /emy/ a. moved; ( *apeuré* ) nervous; ( *joyeux* ) excited.

**émulsion** /emylsjɔ̃/ n.f. emulsion.

**en¹** /ã/ prép. in; ( *avec direction* ) to; ( *manière, état* ) in, on; ( *moyen de transport* ) by; ( *composition* ) made of.

**en²** /ã/ pron. of it, of them; ( *moyen* ) with it; ( *cause* ) from it; ( *lieu* ) from there. **en avoir/vouloir/***etc.***,** have/want/*etc.* some. **ne pas en avoir/vouloir/***etc.***,** not have/want/*etc.* any. **j'en ai assez,** I've had enough. **en êtes-vous sûr?,** are you sure?

**encadr|er** /ãkadre/ v.t. frame; ( *entourer d'un trait* ) circle; ( *entourer* ) surround. **~ement** n.m. framing; ( *de porte* ) frame.

**encaisser** /ãkese/ v.t. ( *argent* ) collect; ( *chèque* ) cash.

**encastré** /ãkastre/ a. built-in.

**encaustiqu|e** /ãkɔstik/ n.f. wax polish. **~er** v.t. wax.

**enceinte**[1] /ãsɛ̃t/ *a.f.* pregnant. ∼ **de 3 mois,** 3 months pregnant.

**enceinte**[2] /ãsɛ̃t/ *n.f.* enclosure. ∼ **(acoustique),** loudspeaker.

**encens** /ãsã/ *n.m.* incense.

**encercler** /ãsɛrkle/ *v.t.* surround.

**enchaîner** /ãʃene/ *v.t.* chain (up); (*coordonner*) link (up).

**enchant|er** /ãʃãte/ *v.t.* delight; (*ensorceler*) enchant. ∼**é** *a.* (*ravi*) delighted.

**enchère** /ãʃɛr/ *n.f.* bid. **mettre** *ou* **vendre aux** ∼**s,** sell by auction.

**enclave** /ãklav/ *n.f.* enclave.

**enclencher** /ãklãʃe/ *v.t.* engage.

**enclore** /ãklɔr/ *v.t.* enclose.

**enclos** /ãklo/ *n.m.* enclosure.

**enclume** /ãklym/ *n.f.* anvil.

**encoche** /ãkɔʃ/ *n.f.* notch.

**encoignure** /ãkɔɲyr/ *n.f.* corner.

**encolure** /ãkɔlyr/ *n.f.* neck.

**encombr|er** /ãkɔ̃bre/ *v.t.* clutter (up); (*gêner*) hamper. **s'**∼**er de,** burden o.s. with. ∼**ant,** ∼**ante** *a.* cumbersome. ∼**ement** *n.m.* (*auto.*) traffic jam.

**encore** /ãkɔr/ *adv.* (*toujours*) still; (*de nouveau*) again; (*de plus*) more; (*aussi*) also. ∼ **mieux/ plus grand/**etc., even better/ larger/etc. ∼ **une heure/un café/**etc., another hour/coffee/ etc. **pas** ∼, not yet.

**encourag|er** /ãkuraʒe/ *v.t.* encourage. ∼**ement** *n.m.* encouragement.

**encr|e** /ãkr/ *n.f.* ink. ∼**er** *v.t.* ink.

**encrier** /ãkrije/ *n.m.* ink-well.

**encyclopéd|ie** /ãsiklɔpedi/ *n.f.* encyclopaedia. ∼**ique** *a.* encyclopaedic.

**endetter** /ãdete/ *v.t.,* **s'**∼ *v.pr.* get into debt.

**endive** /ãdiv/ *n.f.* chicory.

**endocrinolo|gie** /ãdɔkrinɔlɔʒi/ *n.f.* endocrinology. ∼**gue** *n.m./f.* endocrinologist.

**endommager** /ãdɔmaʒe/ *v.t.* damage.

**endorm|ir** /ãdɔrmir/ *v.t.* send to sleep; (*atténuer*) allay. **s'**∼**ir** *v.pr.* fall asleep. ∼**i** *a.* asleep.

**endosser** /ãdose/ *v.t.* (*vêtement*) put on; (*assumer*) assume; (*comm.*) endorse.

**endroit** /ãdrwa/ *n.m.* place; (*de tissu*) right side. **à l'**∼, the right way round, right side out.

**end|uire** /ãdɥir/ *v.t.* coat. ∼**uit** *n.m.* coating.

**endurance** /ãdyrãs/ *n.f.* endurance.

**endurcir** /ãdyrsir/ *v.t.* harden. **s'**∼ *v.pr.* become hard(ened).

**énerg|ie** /enɛrʒi/ *n.f.* energy; (*techn.*) power. ∼**étique** *a.* energy. ∼**ique** *a.* energetic.

**énervant,** ∼**e** /enɛrvã, -t/ *a.* irritating, annoying.

**énerver** /enɛrve/ *v.t.* irritate. **s'**∼ *v.pr.* get worked up.

**enfance** /ãfãs/ *n.f.* childhood.

**enfant** /ãfã/ *n.m./f.* child. ∼**in,** ∼**ine** /-tɛ̃, -tin/ *a.* childlike; (*puéril*) childish; (*jeu, langage*) children's.

**enfer** /ãfɛr/ *n.m.* hell.

**enfermer** /ãfɛrme/ *v.t.* shut up. **s'**∼ *v.pr.* shut o.s. up.

**enfilade** /ãfilad/ *n.f.* string, row.

**enfiler** /ãfile/ *v.t.* (*aiguille*) thread; (*vêtement*) slip on.

**enfin** /ãfɛ̃/ *adv.* at last, finally; (*en dernier lieu*) finally; (*somme toute*) after all; (*résignation, conclusion*) well.

**enflammer** /ãflame/ *v.t.* set fire to; (*méd.*) inflame. **s'**∼ *v.pr.* catch fire.

**enfl|er** /ãfle/ *v.t./i.,* **s'**∼**er** *v.pr.* swell. ∼**é** *a.* swollen.

**enfoncer** /ãfɔ̃se/ *v.t.* (*épingle etc.*) push *ou* drive in; (*chapeau*) push down; (*porte*) break down; (*mettre*) thrust, put. ● *v.i.,* **s'**∼ *v.pr.* sink (**dans,** into).

**enfouir** /ãfwir/ *v.t.* bury.

**enfourcher** /ãfurʃe/ *v.t.* mount.

**enfourner** /ãfurne/ *v.t.* put in the oven.

**enfreindre** /ãfrɛ̃dr/ *v.t.* infringe.

**enfuir†** (**s'**) /(s)ãfɥir/ *v.pr.* run off.

**engagé** /ãgaʒe/ *a.* committed.

**engageant,** ∼**e** /ãgaʒã, -t/ *a.* attractive.

**engager** /ãgaʒe/ *v.t.* (*lier*) bind, commit; (*embaucher*) take on; (*commencer*) start; (*introduire*) insert; (*investir*) invest. **s'**∼ *v.pr.* (*promettre*) commit o.s.; (*concurrent*) enter. **s'**∼ **à faire,** undertake to do. **s'**∼ **dans,** (*voie*) enter.

**engelure** /ãʒlyr/ *n.f.* chilblain.

**engendrer** /ãʒãdre/ *v.t.* beget; (*causer*) generate.

**engin** /ãʒɛ̃/ *n.m.* machine; (*outil*) instrument; (*projectile*) missile. ∼ **explosif,** explosive device.

**englober** /ãglɔbe/ *v.t.* include.

**engloutir** /ãglutir/ *v.t.* swallow (up).

**engouffrer** /ãgufre/ *v.t.* devour. **s'**∼ **dans,** rush into (with force).

**engourd|ir** /ãgurdir/ *v.t.* numb. **s'**∼**ir** *v.pr.* go numb. ∼**i** *a.* numb.

**engrais** /ãgrɛ/ *n.m.* manure; (*chimique*) fertilizer.

**engraisser** /ãgrese/ *v.t.* fatten. **s'**∼ *v.pr.* get fat.

**engrenage** /ãgrənaʒ/ *n.m.* gears; (*fig.*) chain (of events).

**énième** /ɛnjɛm/ *a.* (*fam.*) umpteenth.

**énigm|e** /enigm/ *n.f.* riddle, enigma. ∼**atique** *a.* enigmatic.

**enivrer** /ãnivre/ *v.t.* intoxicate. **s'**∼ *v.pr.* get drunk.

**enjamb|er** /ãʒãbe/ *v.t.* step over; (*pont*) span. ∼**ée** *n.f.* stride.

**enjeu** (*pl.* ∼**x**) /ãʒø/ *n.m.* stake(s).

**enjoliveur** /ãʒɔliværr/ *n.m.* hub-cap.

**enlacer** /ɑ̃lase/ *v.t.* entwine.

**enlaidir** /ɑ̃ledir/ *v.t.* make ugly. ● *v.i.* grow ugly.

**enlèvement** /ɑ̃lɛvmɑ̃/ *n.m.* removal; (*rapt*) kidnapping.

**enlever** /ɑ̃lve/ *v.t.* (*emporter*) take (away), remove (**à,** from); (*vêtement*) take off, remove; (*tache, organe*) take out, remove; (*kidnapper*) kidnap.

**enliser (s')** /(s)ɑ̃lize/ *v. pr.* get bogged down.

**enluminure** /ɑ̃lyminyr/ *n.f.* illumination.

**enneig|é** /ɑ̃neʒe/ *a.* snow-covered. **~ement** /ɑ̃nɛʒmɑ̃/ *n.m.* snow conditions.

**ennemi** /ɛnmi/ *n.m. & a.* enemy.

**ennui** /ɑ̃nɥi/ *n.m.* boredom; (*tracas*) trouble, worry.

**ennuyer** /ɑ̃nɥije/ *v.t.* bore; (*irriter*) annoy; (*préoccuper*) worry. **s'~** *v. pr.* get bored.

**ennuyeu|x, ~se** /ɑ̃nɥijø, -z/ *a.* boring; (*fâcheux*) annoying.

**énoncé** /enɔ̃se/ *n.m.* wording, text; (*gram.*) utterance.

**énoncer** /enɔ̃se/ *v.t.* express, state.

**énorm|e** /enɔrm/ *a.* enormous. **~ément** *adv.* enormously. **~ément de,** an enormous amount of.

**enquêt|e** /ɑ̃kɛt/ *n.f.* investigation; (*jurid.*) inquiry; (*sondage*) survey. **~er** /-ete/ *v.i.* **~er (sur),** investigate.

**enraciné** /ɑ̃rasine/ *a.* deep-rooted.

**enrag|er** /ɑ̃raʒe/ *v.i.* be furious. **faire ~er,** annoy. **~é** *a.* furious; (*chien*) mad; (*fig.*) fanatical.

**enregistr|er** /ɑ̃rʒistre/ *v.t.* note, record; (*mus.*) record. **(faire) ~er,** (*bagages*) register, check in. **~ement** *n.m.* recording; (*des bagages*) registration.

**enrhumer (s')** /(s)ɑ̃ryme/ *v.pr.* catch a cold.

**enrich|ir** /ɑ̃riʃir/ *v.t.* enrich. **s'~ir** *v.pr.* grow rich(er). **~issement** *n.m.* enrichment.

**enrou|er (s')** /(s)ɑ̃rwe/ *v.pr.* become hoarse. **~é** *a.* hoarse.

**enrouler** /ɑ̃rule/ *v.t.,* **s'~** *v. pr.* wind. **s'~ dans une couverture,** roll o.s. up in a blanket.

**enseignant, ~e** /ɑ̃sɛɲɑ̃, -t/ *n.m., f.* teacher. ● *a.* teaching.

**enseigne** /ɑ̃sɛɲ/ *n.f.* sign.

**enseignement** /ɑ̃sɛɲmɑ̃/ *n.m.* teaching; (*instruction*) education.

**enseigner** /ɑ̃seɲe/ *v.t./i.* teach. **~ qch. à qn.,** teach s.o. sth.

**ensemble** /ɑ̃sɑ̃bl/ *adv.* together. ● *n.m.* unity; (*d'objets*) set; (*mus.*) ensemble; (*vêtements*) outfit. **dans l'~,** on the whole. **d'~,** (*idée etc.*) general. **l'~ de,** (*totalité*) all of, the whole of.

**ensoleill|é** /ɑ̃sɔleje/ *a.* sunny. **~ement** /ɑ̃sɔlɛjmɑ̃/ *n.m.* (period of) sunshine.

**ensommeillé** /ɑ̃sɔmeje/ *a.* sleepy.

**ensuite** /ɑ̃sɥit/ *adv.* next, then; (*plus tard*) later.

**ensuivre (s')** /(s)ɑ̃sɥivr/ *v. pr.* follow. **et tout ce qui s'ensuit,** and so on.

**entaill|e** /ɑ̃taj/ *n.f.* notch; (*blessure*) gash. **~er** *v.t.* notch; gash.

**entamer** /ɑ̃tame/ *v.t.* start; (*inciser*) cut into.

**entasser** /ɑ̃tase/ *v.t.,* **s'~** *v. pr.* pile up. **(s')~ dans,** cram (together) into.

**entendre** /ɑ̃tɑ̃dr/ *v.t.* hear; (*comprendre*) understand; (*vouloir*) intend, mean; (*vouloir dire*) mean. **s'~** *v. pr.* (*être d'accord*) agree. **~ dire que,** hear that. **~ parler de,** hear of. **s'~ (bien),** get on (**avec,** with).

**entendu** /ɑ̃tɑ̃dy/ *a.* (*convenu*) agreed; (*sourire, air*) knowing. **bien ~,** of course. **(c'est) ~!,** all right!

**entente** /ɑ̃tɑ̃t/ *n.f.* understanding. **à double ~,** with a double meaning.

**entériner** /ɑ̃terine/ *v.t.* ratify.

**enterr|er** /ɑ̃tere/ *v.t.* bury. **~ement** /ɑ̃tɛrmɑ̃/ *n.m.* burial, funeral.

**en-tête** /ɑ̃tɛt/ *n.m.* heading. **à ~,** headed.

**entêt|é** /ɑ̃tete/ *a.* stubborn. **~ement** /ɑ̃tɛtmɑ̃/ *n.m.* stubbornness.

**entêter (s')** /(s)ɑ̃tete/ *v.pr.* persist (**à, dans,** in).

**enthousias|me** /ɑ̃tuzjasm/ *n.m.* enthusiasm. **~mer** *v.t.* enthuse. **s'~mer pour,** enthuse over. **~te** *a.* enthusiastic.

**ent|ier, ~ière** /ɑ̃tje, -jɛr/ *a.* whole; (*absolu*) absolute; (*entêté*) unyielding. ● *n.m.* whole. **en ~ier,** entirely. **~ièrement** *adv.* entirely.

**entonnoir** /ɑ̃tɔnwar/ *n.m.* funnel.

**entorse** /ɑ̃tɔrs/ *n.f.* sprain. **~ à,** (*loi*) infringement of.

**entortiller** /ɑ̃tɔrtije/ *v.t.* wrap (up); (*enrouler*) wind, wrap.

**entourage** /ɑ̃turaʒ/ *n.m.* circle of family and friends.

**entourer** /ɑ̃ture/ *v.t.* surround (**de,** with). **~ de,** wrap round.

**entracte** /ɑ̃trakt/ *n.m.* interval.

**entraide** /ɑ̃trɛd/ *n.f.* mutual aid.

**entraider (s')** /(s)ɑ̃trede/ *v. pr.* help each other.

**entrain** /ɑ̃trɛ̃/ *n.m.* zest, spirit.

**entraînant, ~e** /ɑ̃trɛnɑ̃, -t/ *a.* rousing.

**entraînement** /ɑ̃trɛnmɑ̃/ *n.m.* (*sport*) training.

**entraîn|er** /ɑ̃trene/ *v.t.* carry away *ou* along; (*emmener, influencer*) lead; (*impliquer*) entail; (*sport*) train; (*roue*) drive. **~eur** /ɑ̃trœnœr/ *n.m.* trainer.

**entre** /ɑ̃tr(ə)/ *prép.* between; (*parmi*) among(st). **l'un d'~ nous/vous/eux,** one of us/you/ them.

**entrebâillé** /ɑ̃trəbɑje/ *a.* ajar.

**entrechoquer (s')** /(s)ɑ̃trəʃɔke/ *v.pr.* knock against each other.

**entrecôte** /ătrəkot/ *n.f.* rib steak.

**entrecroiser (s')** /(s)ătrəkrwaze/ *v. pr.* (*routes*) intersect.

**entrée** /ătre/ *n.f.* entrance; (*accès*) admission, entry; (*billet*) ticket; (*culin.*) first course; (*de données: techn.*) input. ∼ **interdite**, no entry.

**entrefilet** /ătrəfilɛ/ *n.m.* paragraph.

**entrejambe** /ătrəʒãb/ *n.m.* crotch.

**entremets** /ătrəmɛ/ *n.m.* dessert.

**entremetteu|r, ∼se** /ătrəmɛtœr, -øz/ *n.m., f.* (*péj.*) go-between.

**entre|mettre (s')** /(s)ătrəmɛtr/ *v. pr.* intervene. ∼**mise** *n.f.* intervention. **par l'∼mise de**, through.

**entreposer** /ătrəpoze/ *v.t.* store.

**entrepôt** /ătrəpo/ *n.m.* warehouse.

**entreprendre†** /ătrəprădr/ *v.t.* ∼ **de faire**, undertake to do.

**entrepreneur** /ătrəprɔnœr/ *n.m.* ∼ **(de bâtiments)**, (building) contractor.

**entreprise** /ătrəpriz/ *n.f.* undertaking; (*société*) firm.

**entrer** /ătre/ *v.i.* (*aux. être*) go in, enter; (*venir*) come in, enter. **faire ∼**, (*personne*) show in.

**entresol** /ătrəsɔl/ *n.m.* mezzanine.

**entre-temps** /ătrətã/ *adv.* meanwhile.

**entretenir†** /ătrətnir/ *v.t.* maintain; (*faire durer*) keep alive. **s'∼** *v. pr.* speak (**de**, about; **avec**, to).

**entretien** /ătrətjɛ̃/ *n.m.* maintenance; (*discussion*) talk; (*audience pour un emploi*) interview.

**entrevue** /ătrəvy/ *n.f.* interview.

**entrouvrir†** /ătruvrir/ *v.t.* half-open.

**énumér|er** /enymere/ *v.t.* enumerate. ∼**ation** *n.f.* enumeration.

**envah|ir** /ăvair/ *v.t.* invade, overrun; (*douleur, peur*) overcome. ∼**isseur** *n.m.* invader.

**enveloppe** /ăvlɔp/ *n.f.* envelope; (*emballage*) covering; (*techn.*) casing.

**envelopper** /ăvlɔpe/ *v.t.* wrap (up); (*fig.*) envelop.

**envers** /ăvɛr/ *prép.* toward(s), to. ● *n.m.* (*de tissu*) wrong side. **à l'∼**, upside down; (*pantalon*) back to front; (*chaussette*) inside out.

**envie** /ăvi/ *n.f.* desire, wish; (*jalousie*) envy. **avoir ∼ de**, want, feel like. **avoir ∼ de faire**, want to do, feel like doing.

**envier** /ăvje/ *v.t.* envy.

**envieu|x, ∼se** /ăvjø, -z/ *a. & n.m., f.* envious (person).

**environ** /ăvirɔ̃/ *adv.* (round) about. ∼**s** *n.m. pl.* surroundings. **aux ∼s de**, round about.

**environnement** /ăvirɔnmã/ *n.m.* environment.

**envoi** /ăvwa/ *n.m.* dispatch; (*paquet*) consignment.

**envoler (s')** /(s)ăvɔle/ *v. pr.* fly away; (*avion*) take off; (*papiers*) blow away.

**envoyer†** /ăvwaje/ *v.t.* send; (*lancer*) throw.

**enzyme** /ăzim/ *n.m.* enzyme.

**épagneul, ∼e** /epaɲœl/ *n.m., f.* spaniel.

**épais, ∼se** /epɛ, -s/ *a.* thick. ∼**seur** /-sœr/ *n.f.* thickness.

**épaissir** /epesir/ *v.t./i.*, **s'∼** *v. pr.* thicken.

**épanoui** /epanwi/ *a.* (*joyeux*) beaming, radiant.

**épanouir (s')** /(s)epanwir/ *v. pr.* (*fleur*) open out; (*visage*) beam; (*personne*) blossom.

**épargne** /eparɲ/ *n.f.* saving; (*somme*) savings. **caisse d'∼**, savings bank.

**épargn|er** /eparɲe/ *v.t./i.* save; (*ne pas tuer*) spare. ∼**ant, ∼ante** *n.m., f.* saver.

**épat|er** /epate/ *v.t.* (*fam.*) amaze. ∼**ant, ∼ante** *a.* (*fam.*) amazing.

**épaule** /epol/ *n.f.* shoulder.

**épauler** /epole/ *v.t.* (*arme*) raise; (*aider*) support.

**épave** /epav/ *n.f.* wreck.

**épée** /epe/ *n.f.* sword.

**épeler** /ɛple/ *v.t.* spell.

**éperon** /eprɔ̃/ *n.m.* spur.

**épervier** /epɛrvje/ *n.m.* sparrow-hawk.

**éphémère** /efemɛr/ *a.* ephemeral.

**épi** /epi/ *n.m.* (*de blé*) ear. ∼ **de cheveux**, tuft of hair.

**épic|e** /epis/ *n.f.* spice. ∼**é** *a.* spicy. ∼**er** *v.t.* spice.

**épic|ier, ∼ière** /episje, -jɛr/ *n.m., f.* grocer. ∼**erie** *n.f.* grocery shop; (*produits*) groceries.

**épidémie** /epidemi/ *n.f.* epidemic.

**épiderme** /epidɛrm/ *n.m.* skin.

**épier** /epje/ *v.t.* spy on.

**épilep|sie** /epilɛpsi/ *n.f.* epilepsy. ∼**tique** *a. & n.m./f.* epileptic.

**épiler** /epile/ *v.t.* remove unwanted hair from; (*sourcils*) pluck.

**épilogue** /epilɔg/ *n.m.* epilogue; (*fig.*) outcome.

**épinard** /epinar/ *n.m.* (*plante*) spinach. ∼**s**, (*nourriture*) spinach.

**épine** /epin/ *n.f.* thorn, prickle.

**épingl|e** /epɛ̃gl/ *n.f.* pin. ∼**e de nourrice**, ∼**e de sûreté**, safety-pin.

**épisode** /epizɔd/ *n.m.* episode.

**épithète** /epitɛt/ *n.f.* epithet.

**épluche-légumes** /eplyʃlegym/ *n.m. invar.* (potato) peeler.

**épluch|er** /eplyʃe/ *v.t.* peel; (*examiner: fig.*) scrutinize. ∼**ures** *n.f. pl.* peelings.

**épong|e** /epɔ̃ʒ/ *n.f.* sponge. ∼**er** *v.t.* (*liquide*) sponge up; (*surface*) sponge (down); (*front*) mop.

**époque** /epɔk/ *n.f.* time, period. **à l'~**, at the time. **d'~**, period.

**épouse** /epuz/ *n.f.* wife.

**épouser** /epuze/ *v.t.* marry.

**épouvantable** /epuvɑ̃tabl/ *a.* appalling.

**épouvantail** /epuvɑ̃taj/ *n.m.* scarecrow.

**épouvant|e** /epuvɑ̃t/ *n.f.* terror. **~er** *v.t.* terrify.

**époux** /epu/ *n.m.* husband. **les ~**, the married couple.

**épreuve** /eprœv/ *n.f.* test; (*sport*) event; (*malheur*) ordeal; (*photo.*) print; (*d'imprimerie*) proof. **mettre à l'~**, put to the test.

**éprouv|er** /epruve/ *v.t.* test; (*ressentir*) experience; (*affliger*) distress. **~ant, ~ante** *a.* testing.

**éprouvette** /epruvɛt/ *n.f.* test-tube. **bébé-~**, test-tube baby.

**épuis|er** /epɥize/ *v.t.* (*fatiguer, user*) exhaust. **s'~er** *v. pr.* become exhausted. **~é** *a.* exhausted; (*livre*) out of print. **~ement** *n.m.* exhaustion.

**épuisette** /epɥizɛt/ *n.f.* fishing-net.

**équateur** /ekwatœr/ *n.m.* equator.

**équation** /ekwɑsjɔ̃/ *n.f.* equation.

**équerre** /ekɛr/ *n.f.* (set) square.

**équilibr|e** /ekilibr/ *n.m.* balance. **être** *ou* **se tenir en ~e**, (*personne*) balance; (*objet*) be balanced. **~é** *a.* well-balanced. **~er** *v.t.* balance.

**équinoxe** /ekinɔks/ *n.m.* equinox.

**équipage** /ekipaʒ/ *n.m.* crew.

**équipe** /ekip/ *n.f.* team. **~ de nuit/jour**, night/day shift.

**équipé** /ekipe/ *a.* **bien/mal ~**, well/poorly equipped.

**équipement** /ekipmɑ̃/ *n.m.* equipment. **~s**, (*installations*) amenities, facilities.

**équiper** /ekipe/ *v.t.* equip (**de**, with). **s'~** *v. pr.* equip o.s.

**équip|ier, ~ière** /ekipje, -jɛr/ *n.m., f.* team member.

**équitation** /ekitɑsjɔ̃/ *n.f.* (horse-)riding.

**équivalen|t, ~te** /ekivalɑ̃, -t/ *a.* equivalent. **~ce** *n.f.* equivalence.

**érable** /erabl/ *n.m.* maple.

**érafl|er** /erafle/ *v.t.* scratch. **~ure** *n.f.* scratch.

**ère** /ɛr/ *n.f.* era.

**érection** /erɛksjɔ̃/ *n.f.* erection.

**ermite** /ɛrmit/ *n.m.* hermit.

**érosion** /erozjɔ̃/ *n.f.* erosion.

**éroti|que** /erotik/ *a.* erotic. **~sme** *n.m.* eroticism.

**errer** /ɛre/ *v.i.* wander.

**erreur** /erœr/ *n.f.* mistake, error. **dans l'~**, mistaken. **par ~**, by mistake. **~ judiciaire**, miscarriage of justice.

**erroné** /ɛrɔne/ *a.* erroneous.

**érudit, ~e** /erydi, -t/ *a.* scholarly. ● *n.m., f.* scholar.

**éruption** /erypsjɔ̃/ *n.f.* eruption; (*méd.*) rash.

**es** /ɛ/ *voir* **être.**

**escabeau** (*pl.* **~x**) /ɛskabo/ *n.m.* stepladder; (*tabouret*) stool.

**escadron** /ɛskadrɔ̃/ *n.m.* (*mil.*) squadron.

**escalad|e** /ɛskalad/ *n.f.* climbing; (*pol., comm.*) escalation. **~er** *v.t.* climb.

**escalator** /ɛskalatɔr/ *n.m.* (P.) escalator.

**escale** /ɛskal/ *n.f.* (*d'avion*) stopover; (*port*) port of call. **faire ~ à**, (*avion, passager*) stop over at; (*navire, passager*) put in at.

**escalier** /ɛskalije/ *n.m.* stairs. **~ méca-nique** *ou* **roulant**, escalator.

**escalope** /ɛskalɔp/ *n.f.* escalope.

**escamotable** /ɛskamɔtabl/ *a.* (*techn.*) retractable.

**escargot** /ɛskargo/ *n.m.* snail.

**escarpé** /ɛskarpe/ *a.* steep.

**escarpin** /ɛskarpɛ̃/ *n.m.* pump.

**esclav|e** /ɛsklav/ *n.m./f.* slave. **~age** *n.m.* slavery.

**escompte** /ɛskɔ̃t/ *n.m.* discount.

**escompter** /ɛskɔ̃te/ *v.t.* expect; (*comm.*) discount.

**escort|e** /ɛskɔrt/ *n.f.* escort. **~er** *v.t.* escort.

**escrime** /ɛskrim/ *n.f.* fencing.

**escroc** /ɛskro/ *n.m.* swindler.

**escroqu|er** /ɛskrɔke/ *v.t.* swindle. **~er qch. à qn.**, swindle s.o. out of sth. **~erie** *n.f.* swindle.

**espace** /ɛspas/ *n.m.* space. **~s verts**, gardens, parks.

**espacer** /ɛspase/ *v.t.* space out. **s'~** *v. pr.* become less frequent.

**espadrille** /ɛspadrij/ *n.f.* rope sandals.

**Espagne** /ɛspaɲ/ *n.f.* Spain.

**espagnol, ~e** /ɛspaɲɔl/ *a.* Spanish. ● *n.m., f.* Spaniard. ● *n.m.* (*lang.*) Spanish.

**espèce** /ɛspɛs/ *n.f.* kind, sort; (*race*) species. **~s**, (*argent*) cash.

**espérance** /ɛsperɑ̃s/ *n.f.* hope.

**espérer** /ɛspere/ *v.t.* hope for. **~ faire/que**, hope to do/that. ● *v.i.* hope. **~ en**, have faith in.

**espiègle** /ɛspjɛgl/ *a.* mischievous.

**espion, ~ne** /ɛspjɔ̃, -jɔn/ *n.m., f.* spy.

**espionn|er** /ɛspjɔne/ *v.t./i.* spy (on). **~age** *n.m.* espionage, spying.

**espoir** /ɛspwar/ *n.m.* hope.

**esprit** /ɛspri/ *n.m.* spirit; (*intellect*) mind; (*humour*) wit. **perdre l'~**, lose one's mind.

**Esquimau, ~de** (*m. pl.* **~x**) /ɛskimo, -d/ *n.m., f.* Eskimo.

**esquisse** /ɛskis/ *n.f.* sketch.

**essai** /esɛ/ *n.m.* testing; (*épreuve*) test, trial; (*tentative*) try; (*article*) essay. **à l'~**, on trial.

**essaim** /esɛ̃/ n.m. swarm.

**essayage** /esɛjaʒ/ n.m. (devêtement)fitting. **salon d'~,** fitting room.

**essayer** /eseje/ v.t./i. try; (vêtement) try (on); (voiture etc.) try (out). **~ de faire,** try to do.

**essence**[1] /esɑ̃s/ n.f. (carburant) petrol; (Amer.) gas.

**essence**[2] /esɑ̃s/ n.f. (nature, extrait) essence.

**essentiel, ~le** /esɑ̃sjɛl/ a. essential. ● n.m. **l'~,** the main thing; (quantité) the main part. **~lement** adv. essentially.

**essieu** (pl. ~x) /esjø/ n.m. axle.

**essor** /esɔr/ n.m. expansion.

**essor|er** /esɔre/ v.t. (linge) spin-dry; (en tordant) wring. **~euse** n.f. spin-drier.

**essouffler (s')** /(s)esufle/ v.pr. get out of breath.

**ess|uyer** /esɥije/ v.t. wipe. **s'~uyer** v. pr. dry ou wipe o.s. **~uie-glace** n.m. invar. windscreen wiper.

**est**[1] /ɛ/ voir **être.**

**est**[2] /ɛst/ n.m. east. ● a. invar. east; (partie) eastern; (direction) easterly.

**estampe** /ɛstɑ̃p/ n.f. print.

**esthéticienne** /ɛstetisjɛn/ n.f. beautician.

**estimable** /ɛstimabl/ a. worthy.

**estimation** /ɛstimasjɔ̃/ n.f. valuation.

**estime** /ɛstim/ n.f. esteem.

**estimer** /ɛstime/ v.t. (objet) value; (calculer)estimate; (respecter) esteem; (considérer) consider.

**estiv|al** (m. pl. ~aux) /ɛstival, -o/ a. summer. **~ant, ~ante** n.m., f. summer visitor, holiday-maker.

**estomac** /ɛstɔma/ n.m. stomach.

**estrade** /ɛstrad/ n.f. platform.

**estragon** /ɛstragɔ̃/ n.m. tarragon.

**estuaire** /ɛstɥɛr/ n.m. estuary.

**esturgeon** /ɛstyrʒɔ̃/ n.m. sturgeon.

**et** /e/ conj. and. **et moi/lui/etc.?,** what about me/him/etc.?

**étable** /etabl/ n.f. cow-shed.

**établi**[1] /etabli/ a. established. **un fait bien ~,** a well-established fact.

**établi**[2] /etabli/ n.m. work-bench.

**établir** /etablir/ v.t. establish; (liste, facture) draw up; (personne, camp, record) set up. **s'~ à son compte,** set up on one's own.

**établissement** /etablismɑ̃/ n.m. (bâtiment, institution) establishment.

**étage** /etaʒ/ n.m. floor, storey; (de fusée) stage. **à l'~,** upstairs. **au premier ~,** on the first floor.

**étagère** /etaʒɛr/ n.f. shelf; (meuble) shelving unit.

**étain** /etɛ̃/ n.m. pewter.

**étais, était** /etɛ/ voir **être.**

**étal** (pl. ~s) /etal/ n.m. stall.

**étalage** /etalaʒ/ n.m. display; (vitrine)shop-window.

**étaler** /etale/ v.t. spread; (journal) spread (out); (vacances) stagger; (exposer) display. **s'~ sur,** (paiement) be spread over.

**étalon** /etalɔ̃/ n.m. (cheval) stallion; (modèle) standard.

**étanche** /etɑ̃ʃ/ a. watertight; (montre) waterproof.

**étang** /etɑ̃/ n.m. pond.

**étant** /etɑ̃/ voir **être.**

**étape** /etap/ n.f. stage; (lieu d'arrêt) stopover.

**état** /eta/ n.m. state; (liste) statement; (métier) profession; (nation) State. **en bon/mauvais ~,** in good/bad condition. **en ~ de,** in a position to. **~ civil,** civil status. **~ des lieux,** inventory.

**étatisé** /etatize/ a. State-controlled.

**États-Unis** /etazyni/ n.m. pl. **~ (d'Amérique),** United States (of America).

**étau** (pl. ~x) /eto/ n.m. vice.

**été**[1] /ete/ voir **être.**

**été**[2] /ete/ n.m. summer.

**étein|dre**† /etɛ̃dr/ v.t. put out, extinguish; (lumière, radio) turn off. **s'~dre** v. pr. (feu) go out; (mourir) die. **~t, ~te** /etɛ̃, -t/ a. (feu) out; (volcan) extinct.

**étendard** /etɑ̃dar/ n.m. standard.

**étendre** /etɑ̃dr/ v.t.spread; (journal, nappe) spread out; (bras, jambes) stretch (out); (linge)hang out. **s'~** v.pr. (s'allonger) stretch out.

**étendu, ~e** /etɑ̃dy/ a. extensive. ● n.f. area; (d'eau) stretch; (importance) extent.

**éternel, ~le** /etɛrnɛl/ a. eternal. **~lement** adv. eternally.

**éternité** /etɛrnite/ n.f. eternity.

**étern|uer** /etɛrnɥe/ v.i. sneeze. **~uement** /-ymɑ̃/ n.m. sneeze.

**êtes** /ɛt/ voir **être.**

**éthique** /etik/ a. ethical. ● n.f. ethics.

**ethn|ie** /ɛtni/ n.f. ethnic group. **~ique** a. ethnic.

**éthylisme** /etilism/ n.m. alcoholism.

**étinceler** /etɛ̃sle/ v.i. sparkle.

**étincelle** /etɛ̃sɛl/ n.f. spark.

**étiquette** /etikɛt/ n.f. label; (protocole) etiquette.

**étirer** /etire/ v.t., **s'~** v. pr. stretch.

**étoffe** /etɔf/ n.f. fabric.

**étoil|e** /etwal/ n.f. star. **à la belle ~e,** in the open. **~e de mer,** starfish. **~é** a. starry.

**étonn|er** /etone/ v.t. amaze. **s'~er** v. pr. be amazed (**de,** at). **~ant, ~ante** a. amazing. **~ement** n.m. amazement.

**étouffée** /etufe/ n.f. **cuire à l'~,** braise.

**étouff|er** /etufe/ *v.t./i.* suffocate; (*sentiment, révolte*) stifle; (*feu*) smother; (*bruit*) muffle. **on ~e,** it is stifling. **s'~er** *v. pr.* suffocate; (*en mangeant*) choke. **~ant, ~ante** *a.* stifling.

**étourd|i, ~ie** /eturdi/ *a.* unthinking, scatter-brained. ● *n.m., f.* scatter-brain. **~erie** *n.f.* thoughtlessness; (*acte*) thoughtless act.

**étrange** /etrɑ̃ʒ/ *a.* strange.

**étrang|er, ~ère** /etrɑ̃ʒe, -ɛr/ *a.* strange, unfamiliar; (*d'un autre pays*) foreign. ● *n.m., f.* foreigner; (*inconnu*) stranger. **à l'~er,** abroad. **de l'~er,** from abroad.

**étrangler** /etrɑ̃gle/ *v.t.* strangle; (*col*) stifle. **s'~** *v. pr.* choke.

**être**† /ɛtr/ *v.i.* be. ● *v. aux.* (*avec aller, sortir, etc.*) have. **~ donné/fait par,** (*passif*) be given/done by. ● *n.m.* (*personne, créature*) being. **~ humain,** human being **~ médecin/ tailleur/***etc.*, be a doctor/a tailor/*etc.* **~ à qn.,** be s.o.'s. **c'est à faire,** it needs to be *ou* should be done. **est-ce qu'il travaille?,** is he working?, does he work? **vous travaillez, n'est-ce pas?,** you are working, aren't you?, you work, don't you? **il est deux heures/***etc.*, it is two o'clock/*etc.* **nous sommes le six mai,** it is the sixth of May.

**étrier** /etrije/ *n.m.* stirrup.

**étriqué** /etrike/ *a.* tight; (*fig.*) small-minded.

**étroit, ~e** /etrwa, -t/ *a.* narrow; (*vêtement*) tight; (*liens, surveillance*) close. **à l'~,** cramped.

**étude** /etyd/ *n.f.* study; (*bureau*) office. **(salle d')~,** (*scol.*) prep room. **faire des ~s (de),** study.

**étudiant, ~e** /etydjɑ̃, -t/ *n.m., f.* student.

**étudier** /etydje/ *v.t./i.* study.

**étui** /etɥi/ *n.m.* case.

**étuve** /etyv/ *n.f.* steamroom. **quelle étuve!,** it's like a hothouse in here.

**étuvée** /etyve/ *n.f.* **cuire à l'~,** braise.

**etymologie** /etimɔlɔʒi/ *n.f.* etymology.

**eu, eue** /y/ *voir* avoir.

**eucalyptus** /økaliptys/ *n.m.* eucalyptus.

**Europe** /ørɔp/ *n.f.* Europe.

**européen, ~ne** /ørɔpeɛ̃, -eɛn/ *a. & n.m., f.* European.

**eux** /ø/ *pron.* they; (*complément*) them. **~ mêmes** *pron.* themselves.

**évac|uer** /evakɥe/ *v.t.* evacuate. **~uation** *n.f.* evacuation.

**évad|er (s')** /(s)evade/ *v. pr.* escape. **~é, ~ée** *a.* escaped; *n.m., f.* escaped prisoner.

**éval|uer** /evalɥe/ *v.t.* assess. **~uation** *n.f.* assessment.

**évang|ile** /evɑ̃ʒil/ *n.m.* gospel. **l'Évangile,** the Gospel.

**évan|ouir (s')** /(s)evanwir/ *v. pr.* faint; (*disparaître*) vanish. **~ouissement** *n.m.* (*syncope*) fainting fit.

**évapor|er** /evapɔre/ *v.t.*, **s'~er** *v. pr.* evaporate. **~ation** *n.f.* evaporation.

**évasion** /evaziɔ̃/ *n.f.* escape.

**éveil** /evɛj/ *n.m.* awakening.

**éveill|er** /eveje/ *v.t.* awake(n); (*susciter*) arouse. **s'~er** *v. pr.* awake(n); be aroused. **~é** *a.* awake; (*intelligent*) alert.

**événement** /evɛnmɑ̃/ *n.m.* event.

**éventail** /evɑ̃taj/ *n.m.* fan; (*gamme*) range.

**éventaire** /evɑ̃tɛr/ *n.m.* stall, stand.

**éventé** /evɑ̃te/ *a.* (*gâté*) stale.

**éventualité** /evɑ̃tɥalite/ *n.f.* possibility.

**éventuel, ~le** /evɑ̃tɥɛl/ *a.* possible. **~lement** *adv.* possibly.

**évêque** /evɛk/ *n.m.* bishop.

**évidemment** /evidamɑ̃/ *adv.* obviously; (*bien sûr*) of course.

**évidence** /evidɑ̃s/ *n.f.* obviousness; (*fait*) obvious fact. **être en ~,** be conspicuous. **mettre en ~,** (*fait*) highlight.

**évident, ~e** /evidɑ̃, -t/ *a.* obvious, evident.

**évider** /evide/ *v.t.* hollow out.

**évier** /evje/ *n.m.* sink.

**éviter** /evite/ *v.t.* avoid (**de faire,** doing). **~ à qn.,** (*dérangement etc.*) spare s.o.

**évolué** /evolɥe/ *a.* highly developed.

**évol|uer** /evolɥe/ *v.i.* develop. **~ution** *n.f.* development; (*d'une espèce*) evolution.

**évoquer** /evɔke/ *v.t.* call to mind, evoke.

**ex-** /ɛks/ *préf.* ex-.

**exact, ~e** /ɛgza(kt), -akt/ *a.* exact, accurate; (*correct*) correct; (*personne*) punctual. **~e-ment** /-ktɔmɑ̃/ *adv.* exactly.

**ex aequo** /ɛgzeko/ *adv.* (*classer*) equal. **être ~,** be equally placed.

**exagéré** /ɛgzaʒere/ *a.* excessive.

**exagér|er** /ɛgzaʒere/ *v.t./i.* exaggerate; (*abuser*) go too far. **~ation** *n.f.* exaggeration.

**examen** /ɛgzamɛ̃/ *n.m.* examination; (*scol.*) exam(ination).

**examin|er** /ɛgzamine/ *v.t.* examine. **~a-teur, ~atrice** *n.m., f.* examiner.

**exaspér|er** /ɛgzaspere/ *v.t.* exasperate. **~ation** *n.f.* exasperation.

**exaucer** /ɛgzose/ *v.t.* grant; (*personne*) grant the wish(es) of.

**excavateur** /ɛkskavatœr/ *n.m.* digger.

**excavation** /ɛkskavasjɔ̃/ *n.f.* excavation.

**excédent** /ɛksedɑ̃/ *n.m.* surplus. **~ de bagages,** excess luggage. **~ de la balance commerciale,** trade surplus. **~aire** /-tɛr/ *a.* excess, surplus.

**excéder** /ɛksede/ *v.t.* (*dépasser*) exceed.

**excellen|t, ~te** /ɛksɛlɑ̃, -t/ *a.* excellent. **~ce** *n.f.* excellence.

**excentrique** /ɛksɑ̃trik/ *a. & n.m./f.* eccentric.

**excepté** /ɛksɛpte/ *a. & prép.* except.

**exception** /ɛksɛpsjɔ̃/ *n.f.* exception. **à l'~ de,** except for. **~nel,** **~nelle** /-jɔnɛl/ *a.* exceptional. **~nellement** /-jɔnɛlmɑ̃/ *adv.* exceptionally.

**excès** /ɛksɛ/ *n.m.* excess. **~ de vitesse,** speeding.

**excessi|f,** **~ve** /ɛksesif, -v/ *a.* excessive. **~vement** *adv.* excessively.

**excitant** /ɛksitɑ̃/ *n.m.* stimulant.

**excit|er** /ɛksite/ *v.t.* excite; (*encourager*) exhort (**à,** to); (*irriter: fam.*) annoy. **~ation** *n.f.* excitement.

**exclam|er (s')** /(s)ɛksklame/ *v.pr.* exclaim. **~ation** *n.f.* exclamation.

**exclu|re†** /ɛksklyr/ *v.t.* exclude; (*expulser*) expel; (*empêcher*) preclude. **~sion** *n.f.* exclusion.

**exclusi|f,** **~ve** /ɛksklyzif, -v/ *a.* exclusive. **~vement** *adv.* exclusively. **~vité** *n.f.* (*comm.*) exclusive rights. **en ~vité à,** (*film*) (showing) exclusively at.

**excursion** /ɛkskyrsjɔ̃/ *n.f.* excursion; (*à pied*) hike.

**excuse** /ɛkskyz/ *n.f.* excuse. **~s,** apology. **faire des ~s,** apologize.

**excuser** /ɛkskyze/ *v.t.* excuse. **s'~** *v.pr.* apologize (**de,** for). **je m'excuse,** (*fam.*) excuse me.

**exécrable** /ɛgzekrabl/ *a.* abominable.

**exécuter** /ɛgzekyte/ *v.t.* carry out, execute; (*mus.*) perform; (*tuer*) execute.

**exécuti|f,** **~ve** /ɛgzekytif, -v/ *a.* & *n.m.* (*pol.*) executive.

**exemplaire** /ɛgzɑ̃plɛr/ *a.* exemplary. ● *n.m.* copy.

**exemple** /ɛgzɑ̃pl/ *n.m.* example. **par ~,** for example. **donner l'~,** set an example.

**exempt,** **~e** /ɛgzɑ̃, -t/ *a.* **~ de,** exempt from.

**exempt|er** /ɛgzɑ̃te/ *v.t.* exempt (**de,** from). **~ion** /-psjɔ̃/ *n.f.* exemption.

**exercer** /ɛgzɛrse/ *v.t.* exercise; (*influence, contrôle*) exert; (*métier*) work at; (*former*) train, exercise. **s'~ (à),** practise.

**exercice** /ɛgzɛrsis/ *n.m.* exercise; (*mil.*) drill; (*de métier*) practice. **en ~,** in office; (*médecin*) in practice.

**exigence** /ɛgziʒɑ̃s/ *n.f.* demand.

**exig|er** /ɛgziʒe/ *v.t.* demand. **~eant,** **~eante** *a.* demanding.

**exigu,** **~ê** /ɛgzigy/ *a.* tiny.

**exil** /ɛgzil/ *n.m.* exile. **~é,** **~ée** *n.m., f.* exile. **~er** *v.t.* exile. **s'~er** *v.pr.* go into exile.

**existence** /ɛgzistɑ̃s/ *n.f.* existence.

**exist|er** /ɛgziste/ *v.i.* exist. **~ant,** **~ante** *a.* existing.

**exode** /ɛgzɔd/ *n.m.* exodus.

**exonér|er** /ɛgzɔnere/ *v.t.* exempt (**de,** from). **~ation** *n.f.* exemption.

**exorbitant,** **~e** /ɛgzɔrbitɑ̃, -t/ *a.* exorbitant.

**exotique** /ɛgzɔtik/ *a.* exotic.

**expansion** /ɛkspɑ̃sjɔ̃/ *n.f.* expansion.

**expatr|ier (s')** /(s)ɛkspatrije/ *v. pr.* leave one's country. **~ié,** **~iée** *n.m., f.* expatriate.

**expéd|ier** /ɛkspedje/ *v.t.* send, dispatch; (*tâche: péj.*) dispatch. **~iteur,** **~itrice** *n.m., f.* sender. **~ition** *n.f.* dispatch; (*voyage*) expedition.

**expérience** /ɛksperjɑ̃s/ *n.f.* experience; (*scientifique*) experiment.

**expérimenté** /ɛksperimɑ̃te/ *a.* experienced.

**expériment|er** /ɛksperimɑ̃te/ *v.t.* test, experiment with. **~al** (*m. pl.* **~aux**) *a.* experimental.

**expert,** **~e** /ɛkspɛr, -t/ *a.* expert. ● *n.m.* expert; (*d'assurances*) valuer. **~-comptable** (*pl.* **~s-comptables**) *n.m.* accountant.

**expertis|e** /ɛkspɛrtiz/ *n.f.* expert appraisal. **~er** *v.t.* appraise.

**expir|er** /ɛkspire/ *v.i.* breathe out; (*finir, mourir*) expire. **~ation** *n.f.* expiry.

**explicati|f,** **~ve** /ɛksplikatif, -v/ *a.* explanatory.

**explication** /ɛksplikɑsjɔ̃/ *n.f.* explanation; (*fig.*) discussion; (*scol.*) commentary.

**explicite** /ɛksplisit/ *a.* explicit.

**expliquer** /ɛksplike/ *v.t.* explain. **s'~** *v. pr.* explain o.s.; (*discuter*) discuss things; (*être compréhensible*) be understandable.

**exploit** /ɛksplwa/ *n.m.* exploit.

**exploitant** /ɛksplwatɑ̃/ *n.m.* **~ (agricole),** farmer.

**exploit|er** /ɛksplwate/ *v.t.* (*personne*) exploit; (*ferme*) run; (*champs*) work. **~ation** *n.f.* exploitation; running; working; (*affaire*) concern.

**explor|er** /ɛksplɔre/ *v.t.* explore. **~ateur,** **~atrice** *n.m., f.* explorer. **~ation** *n.f.* exploration.

**explos|er** /ɛksploze/ *v.i.* explode. **faire ~er,** explode; (*bâtiment*) blow up. **~ion** *n.f.* explosion.

**explosi|f,** **~ve** /ɛksplozif, -v/ *a.* & *n.m.* explosive.

**export|er** /ɛkspɔrte/ *v.t.* export. **~ateur,** **~atrice** *n.m., f.* exporter; *a.* exporting. **~ation** *n.f.* export.

**exposant,** **~e** /ɛkspozɑ̃, -t/ *n.m., f.* exhibitor.

**exposé** /ɛkspoze/ *n.m.* talk (**sur,** on); (*d'une action*) account.

**expos|er** /ɛkspoze/ *v.t.* display, show. **~é au nord**/etc., facing north/etc.

**exposition** /ɛkspozisjɔ̃/ *n.f.* display; (*salon*) exhibition.

**exprès¹** /ɛksprɛ/ *adv.* specially; (*délibérément*) on purpose.

**expr|ès²,** **~esse** /ɛksprɛs/ *a.* express.

**exprès³** /ɛksprɛs/ *a. invar.* & *n.m.* **lettre ~,** express letter. **(par) ~,** sent special delivery.

**express** /ɛksprɛs/ *a. & n.m. invar.* (**café**) **∼**, espresso. (**train**) **∼**, fast train.

**expression** /ɛkspresjɔ̃/ *n.f.* expression.

**exprimer** /ɛksprime/ *v.t.* express. **s'∼** *v. pr.* express o.s.

**expuls|er** /ɛkspylse/ *v.t.* expel; (*locataire*) evict. **∼ion** *n.f.* expulsion; eviction.

**extasier (s')** /(s)ɛkstazje/ *v. pr.* **s'∼ sur**, be ecstatic about.

**extensible** /ɛkstɑ̃sibl/ *a.* expandable, extendible. **tissu ∼**, stretch fabric.

**extension** /ɛkstɑ̃sjɔ̃/ *n.f.* extension; (*expansion*) expansion.

**extérieur** /ɛksterjœr/ *a.* outside; (*signe, gaieté*) outward; (*politique*) foreign. ● *n.m.* outside, exterior; (*de personne*) exterior. **à l'∼ (de)**, outside. **∼ement** *adv.* outwardly.

**exterminer** /ɛkstɛrmine/ *v.t.* exterminate.

**externe** /ɛkstɛrn/ *a.* external. ● *n.m./f.* (*scol.*) day pupil.

**extincteur** /ɛkstɛ̃ktœr/ *n.m.* fire extinguisher.

**extinction** /ɛkstɛ̃ksjɔ̃/ *n.f.* extinction. **∼ de voix**, loss of voice.

**extorquer** /ɛkstɔrke/ *v.t.* extort.

**extra** /ɛkstra/ *a. invar.* first-rate.

**extra-** /ɛkstra/ *préf.* extra-.

**extrader** /ɛkstrade/ *v.t.* extradite.

**extr|aire†** /ɛkstrɛr/ *v.t.* extract. **∼action** *n.f.* extraction.

**extrait** /ɛkstrɛ/ *n.m.* extract.

**extraordinaire** /ɛkstraɔrdinɛr/ *a.* extraordinary.

**extravagan|t, ∼te** /ɛkstravagɑ̃, -t/ *a.* extravagant. **∼ce** *n.f.* extravagance.

**extrême** /ɛkstrɛm/ *a. & n.m.* extreme. **E∼-Orient** *n.m.* Far East. **∼ment** *adv.* extremely.

**extrémiste** /ɛkstremist/ *n.m., f.* extremist.

**extrémité** /ɛkstremite/ *n.f.* extremity, end.

**exubéran|t, ∼te** /ɛgzyberɑ̃, -t/ *a.* exuberant. **∼ce** *n.f.* exuberance.

· · · · · · · · · · · · · · · · · · · · · · · · · · · · · · · ·

# Ff

· · · · · · · · · · · · · · · · · · · · · · · · · · · · · · · ·

**F** *abrév.* (*franc, francs*) franc, francs.

**fabrique** /fabrik/ *n.f.* factory.

**fabri|quer** /fabrike/ *v.t.* make; (*industriellement*) manufacture; (*fig.*) make up. **∼cant, ∼cante** *n.m., f.* manufacturer. **∼cation** *n.f.* making; manufacture.

**fabuleu|x, ∼se** /fabylø, -z/ *a.* fabulous.

**fac** /fak/ *n.f.* (*fam.*) university.

**façade** /fasad/ *n.f.* front; (*fig.*) façade.

**face** /fas/ *n.f.* face; (*d'un objet*) side. **en ∼ (de), d'en ∼**, opposite. **en ∼ de**, (*fig.*) faced with. **∼ à**, facing; (*fig.*) faced with. **faire ∼ à**, face.

**fâch|er** /faʃe/ *v.t.* anger. **se ∼er** *v. pr.* get angry; (*se brouiller*) fall out. **∼é** *a.* angry.

**facile** /fasil/ *a.* easy; (*caractère*) easygoing. **∼ement** *adv.* easily. **∼ité** *n.f.* easiness. **∼ités de paiement**, easy terms.

**faciliter** /fasilite/ *v.t.* facilitate.

**façon** /fasɔ̃/ *n.f.* way; (*de vêtement*) cut. **∼s**, (*chichis*) fuss. **de toute ∼**, anyway.

**façonner** /fasɔne/ *v.t.* shape; (*faire*) make.

**facteur¹** /faktœr/ *n.m.* postman.

**facteur²** /faktœr/ *n.m.* (*élément*) factor.

**factice** /faktis/ *a.* artificial.

**factur|e** /faktyr/ *n.f.* bill; (*comm.*) invoice. **∼er** *v.t.* invoice.

**facultati|f, ∼ve** /fakyltatif, -v/ *a.* optional.

**faculté** /fakylte/ *n.f.* faculty; (*possibilité*) power; (*univ.*) faculty.

**fade** /fad/ *a.* insipid.

**faibl|e** /fɛbl/ *a.* weak; (*espoir, quantité, écart*) slight; (*revenu, intensité*) low. ● *n.m.* weakling; (*penchant, défaut*) weakness. **∼esse** *n.f.* weakness.

**faïence** /fajɑ̃s/ *n.f.* earthenware.

**faille** /faj/ *n.f.* (*géog.*) fault.

**faillir** /fajir/ *v.i.* **j'ai failli acheter**/*etc.*, I almost bought/*etc.*

**faillite** /fajit/ *n.f.* bankruptcy.

**faim** /fɛ̃/ *n.f.* hunger. **avoir ∼**, be hungry.

**faire†** /fɛr/ *v.t.* make; (*activité*) do; (*rêve, chute, etc.*) have; (*dire*) say. **ça fait 20 F**, that's 20 F. **ça fait 3 ans**, it's been 3 years. ● *v.i.* do; (*paraître*) look. **se ∼**, *v. pr.* (*petit etc.*) make o.s.; (*amis, argent*) make; (*illusions*) have; (*devenir*) become. **∼ du rugby/du violon/** *etc.*, play rugby/the violin/*etc.* **∼ construire/punir**/*etc.*, have *ou* get built/punished/*etc.*, **pleurer/tomber**/ *etc.*, make cry/fall/*etc.* **se ∼ tuer**/*etc.*, get killed/*etc.* **se ∼ couper les cheveux**, have one's hair cut. **il fait beau/chaud**/*etc.*, it is fine/hot/*etc.* **∼ l'idiot**, play the fool. **ça ne fait rien**, it doesn't matter. **ça se fait**, that is done. **∼-part** *n.m. invar.* announcement.

**fais, fait¹** /fɛ/ *voir* faire.

**faisable** /fəzabl/ *a.* feasible.

**faisan** /fəzɑ̃/ *n.m.* pheasant.

**fait², ∼e** /fɛ, fɛt/ *a.* done; (*fromage*) ripe. **∼ pour**, made for. **c'est bien ∼ pour toi**, it serves you right.

**fait³** /fɛ/ *n.m.* fact; (*événement*) event. **∼ divers**, (*trivial*) news item.

**faites** /fɛt/ *voir* faire.

**faitout** /fɛtu/ *n.m.* stew-pot.

**falaise** /falɛz/ *n.f.* cliff.

**falloir**† /falwar/ v.i. **il faut qch./qn.**, we, you, etc. need sth./so. **il faut du pain**, he needs bread. **il faut rester**, we, you, etc. have to ou must stay. **il faut que j'y aille**, I have to ou must go. **il faudrait que tu partes**, you should leave. **il aurait fallu le faire**, we, you, etc. should have done it. **comme il faut**, properly; a. proper.

**falsifier** /falsifje/ v.t. falsify.

**fameu|x, ~se** /famø, -z/ a. famous; (excellent: fam.) first-rate.

**famil|ial** (m. pl. **~iaux**) /familjal, -jo/ a. family.

**familiar|iser** /familjarize/ v.t. familiarize (avec, with). **se ~iser** v. pr. familiarize o.s. **~isé** a. familiar. **~ité** n.f. familiarity.

**famil|ier, ~ière** /familje, -jɛr/ a. familiar; (amical) informal. ● n.m. regular visitor.

**famille** /famij/ n.f. family. **en ~**, with one's family.

**famine** /famin/ n.f. famine.

**fanati|que** /fanatik/ a. fanatical. ● n.m./f. fanatic. **~sme** n.m. fanaticism.

**faner (se)** /(sə)fane/ v. pr. fade.

**fanfare** /fɑ̃far/ n.f. brass band; (musique) fanfare.

**fantaisie** /fɑ̃tezi/ n.f. imagination, fantasy; (caprice) whim. **(de) ~**, (boutons etc.) fancy.

**fantasme** /fɑ̃tasm/ n.m. fantasy.

**fantastique** /fɑ̃tastik/ a. fantastic.

**fantôme** /fɑ̃tom/ n.m. ghost. ● a. (péj.) bogus.

**faon** /fɑ̃/ n.m. fawn.

**farc|e¹** /fars/ n.f. (practical) joke; (théâtre) farce. **~eur, ~euse** n.m., f. joker.

**farc|e²** /fars/ n.f. (hachis) stuffing. **~ir** v.t. stuff.

**fard** /far/ n.m. make-up. **piquer un ~**, blush. **~er** /-de/ v.t., **se ~er** v. pr. make up.

**fardeau** (pl. **~x**) /fardo/ n.m. burden.

**farfelu, ~e** /farfəly/ a. & n.m., f. eccentric.

**farine** /farin/ n.f. flour.

**farouche** /faruʃ/ a. shy; (peu sociable) unsociable; (violent) fierce. **~ment** adv. fiercely.

**fascicule** /fasikyl/ n.m. volume.

**fascin|er** /fasine/ v.t. fascinate. **~ation** n.f. fascination.

**fasci|ste** /faʃist/ a. & n.m./f. fascist. **~me** n.m. fascism.

**fasse** /fas/ voir **faire**.

**faste** /fast/ n.m. splendour.

**fast-food** /fastfud/ n.m. fast-food place.

**fastidieu|x, ~se** /fastidjø, -z/ a. tedious.

**fat|al** (m. pl. **~als**) /fatal/ a. inevitable; (mortel) fatal. **~alité** n.f. (destin) fate.

**fatidique** /fatidik/ a. fateful.

**fatigant, ~e** /fatigɑ̃, -t/ a. tiring; (ennuyeux) tiresome.

**fatigue** /fatig/ n.f. fatigue, tiredness.

**fatigu|er** /fatige/ v.t. tire; (yeux, moteur) strain. ● v.i. (moteur) labour. **se ~er** v. pr. get tired, tire (**de**, of). **~é** a. tired.

**faubourg** /fobur/ n.m. suburb.

**fauché** /foʃe/ a. (fam.) broke.

**faucille** /fosij/ n.f. sickle.

**faucon** /fokɔ̃/ n.m. falcon, hawk.

**faudra, faudrait** /fodra, fodrɛ/ voir **falloir**.

**faufiler (se)** /(sə)fofile/ v. pr. edge one's way.

**faune** /fon/ n.f. wildlife, fauna.

**faussaire** /fosɛr/ n.m. forger.

**fausse** /fos/ voir **faux²**.

**faussement** /fosmɑ̃/ adv. falsely, wrongly.

**faut** /fo/ voir **falloir**.

**faute** /fot/ n.f. mistake; (responsabilité) fault; (délit) offence. **sans faute**, without fail.

**fauteuil** /fotœj/ n.m. armchair; (de président) chair; (théâtre) seat. **~ roulant**, wheelchair.

**fauve** /fov/ a. (couleur) fawn. ● n.m. wild cat.

**faux¹** /fo/ n.f. scythe.

**faux², fausse** /fo, fos/ a. false; (falsifié) fake, forged; (numéro, calcul) wrong; (voix) out of tune. **c'est ~!**, that is wrong! **~ témoignage**, perjury. ● adv. (chanter) out of tune. ● n.f. forgery. **fausse alerte**, false alarm. **fausse couche**, miscarriage. **~filet** n.m. sirloin.

**faveur** /favœr/ n.f. favour.

**favorable** /favɔrabl/ a. favourable.

**favori, ~te** /favɔri, -t/ a. & n.m., f. favourite.

**favoriser** /favɔrize/ v.t. favour.

**fax** /faks/ n.m. fax. **~er** v.t. fax.

**fébrile** /febril/ a. feverish.

**fécond, ~e** /fekɔ̃, -d/ a. fertile. **~er** /-de/ v.t. fertilize. **~ité** /-dite/ n.f. fertility.

**fédér|al** (m. pl. **~aux**) /federal, -o/ a. federal.

**fédération** /federasjɔ̃/ n.f. federation.

**fée** /fe/ n.f. fairy.

**fêler** /fele/ v.t., **se ~** v. pr. crack.

**félicit|er** /felisite/ v.t. congratulate (**de**, on). **~ations** n.f. pl. congratulations (**pour**, on).

**félin, ~e** /felɛ̃, -in/ a. & n.m. feline.

**femelle** /fəmɛl/ a. & n.f. female.

**fémin|in, ~ine** /feminɛ̃, -in/ a. feminine; (sexe) female; (mode, équipe) women's. ● n.m. feminine. **~ité** n.f. femininity.

**féministe** /feminist/ n.m./f. feminist.

**femme** /fam/ n.f. woman; (épouse) wife. **~ au foyer**, housewife. **~ de chambre**, chambermaid. **~ de ménage**, cleaning lady.

**fémur** /femyr/ n.m. thigh-bone.

**fendre** /fɑ̃dr/ v.t. (couper) split; (fissurer) crack; (foule) push through. **se ~** v. pr. crack.

**fenêtre** /fənɛtr/ n.f. window.

**fenouil** /fənuj/ n.m. fennel.

**fente** /fɑ̃t/ n.f. (ouverture) slit, slot; (fissure) crack.

**fer** /fɛr/ n.m. iron. ~ **(à repasser),** iron. ~ **forgé,** wrought iron.

**fera, ferait** /fəra, fərɛ/ voir **faire**.

**férié** /ferje/ a. **jour** ~, public holiday.

**ferme**[1] /fɛrm/ a. firm.

**ferme**[2] /fɛrm/ n.f. farm; (maison) farm (house).

**fermé** /fɛrme/ a. closed; (gaz, radio, etc.) off.

**fermer** /fɛrme/ v.t./i. close, shut; (cesser d'exploiter) close ou shut down; (gaz, robinet) turn off. **se** ~ v. pr. close, shut.

**fermeté** /fɛrməte/ n.f. firmness.

**fermeture** /fɛrmətyr/ n.f. closing; (dispositif) catch. ~ **annuelle,** annual closure. ~ **éclair,** (P.) zip(-fastener); (Amer.) zipper.

**ferm|ier, ~ière** /fɛrmje, -jɛr/ n.m. farmer. ● n.f. farmer's wife. ● a. farm.

**féroc|e** /feros/ a. ferocious. ~**ité** n.f. ferocity.

**ferroviaire** /fɛrovjɛr/ a. rail(way).

**ferry(-boat)** /fɛri(bot)/ n.m. ferry.

**fertil|e** /fɛrtil/ a. fertile. ~**e en,** (fig.) rich in. ~**iser** v.t. fertilize. ~**ité** n.f. fertility.

**fesse** /fɛs/ n.f. buttock.

**fessée** /fese/ n.f. spanking.

**festin** /fɛstɛ̃/ n.m. feast.

**festival** (pl. ~s) /fɛstival/ n.m. festival.

**festivités** /fɛstivite/ n.f. pl. festivities.

**fête** /fɛt/ n.f. holiday; (religieuse) feast; (du nom) name-day; (réception) party; (en famille) celebration; (foire) fair; (folklorique) festival. ~ **foraine,** fun-fair. **les ~s (de fin d'année),** the Christmas season.

**fêter** /fete/ v.t. celebrate.

**fétiche** /fetiʃ/ n.m. fetish; (fig.) mascot.

**feu** (pl. ~**x**) /fø/ n.m. fire; (lumière) light; (de réchaud) burner. ~**x(rouges),** (traffic)lights. **à** ~**doux/vif,** on a low/high heat. **du** ~, (pour cigarette) a light. **au** ~!, fire! ~ **d'artifice,** firework display. ~ **rouge/ vert/orange, red/green/amber.** ~ **de position,** sidelight. **mettre le** ~ **à,** set fire to. **prendre** ~, catch fire.

**feuille** /fœj/ n.f. leaf; (de papier, bois, etc.) sheet; (formulaire) form.

**feuillet** /fœjɛ/ n.m. leaf.

**feuilleter** /fœjte/ v.t. leaf through.

**feuilleton** /fœjtɔ̃/ n.m. (à suivre) serial; (histoire complète) series.

**feutre** /føtr/ n.m. felt; (chapeau) felt hat; (crayon) felt-tip (pen).

**fève** /fɛv/ n.f. broad bean.

**février** /fevrije/ n.m. February.

**fiançailles** /fjɑ̃saj/ n.f. pl. engagement.

**fianc|er (se)** /(sə)fjɑ̃se/ v. pr. become engaged (**avec,** to). ~**é,** ~**ée** a. engaged; n.m. fiancé; n.f. fiancée.

**fiasco** /fjasko/ n.m. fiasco.

**fibre** /fibr/ n.f. fibre. ~ **de verre,** fibreglass.

**ficeler** /fisle/ v.t. tie up.

**ficelle** /fisɛl/ n.f. string.

**fiche** /fiʃ/ n.f. (index) card; (formulaire) form, slip; (électr.) plug.

**ficher**[1] /fiʃe/ v.t. (faire: fam.) do; (donner: fam.) give; (mettre: fam.) put. **se** ~ **de,** (fam.) make fun of. ~ **le camp,** (fam.) clear off. **il s'en fiche,** (fam.) he couldn't care less.

**fichier** /fiʃje/ n.m. file.

**fichu** /fiʃy/ a. (mauvais: fam.) rotten; (raté: fam.) done for. **mal** ~, (fam.) terrible.

**ficti|f, ~ve** /fiktif, -v/ a. fictitious.

**fiction** /fiksjɔ̃/ n.f. fiction.

**fidèle** /fidɛl/ a. faithful. ● n.m./f. (client) regular; (relig.) believer.

**fidélité** /fidelite/ n.f. fidelity.

**fier, fière** /fjɛr/ a. proud (**de,** of). **fièrement** adv. proudly. ~**té** n.f. pride.

**fièvre** /fjɛvr/ n.f. fever.

**fiévreu|x, ~se** /fjevrø, -z/ a. feverish.

**figu|e** /fig/ n.f. fig. ~**ier** n.m. fig-tree.

**figurant, ~e** /figyrɑ̃, -t/ n.m., f. (cinéma) extra.

**figure** /figyr/ n.f. face.

**figuré** /figyre/ a. (sens) figurative. **au** ~, figuratively.

**fil** /fil/ n.m. thread; (métallique, électrique) wire; (de couteau) edge; (à coudre) cotton. ~ **de fer,** wire. **au bout du** ~, on the phone.

**filament** /filamɑ̃/ n.m. filament.

**filature** /filatyr/ n.f. (textile) mill; (surveillance) shadowing.

**file** /fil/ n.f. line; (voie: auto.) lane. ~ **(d'attente),** queue.

**filer** /file/ v.t. spin; (suivre) shadow. ~ **qch. à qn.,** (fam.) slip s.o. sth. ● v.i. (bas) ladder, run; (liquide) run; (aller vite: fam.) speed along, fly by; (partir: fam.) dash off.

**filet** /filɛ/ n.m. net; (d'eau) trickle; (de viande) fillet. ~ **(à bagages),** (luggage) rack. ~ **à provisions,** string bag (for shopping).

**fil|ial, ~iale** (m. pl. ~**iaux**) /filjal, -jo/ a. filial. ● n.f. subsidiary (company).

**filière** /filjɛr/ n.f. (official) channels; (de trafiquants) network.

**fille** /fij/ n.f. girl; (opposé à fils) daughter.

**fillette** /fijɛt/ n.f. little girl.

**filleul** /fijœl/ n.m. godson. ~**e** n.f. god-daughter.

**film** /film/ n.m. film. ~ **d'épouvante / muet / parlant,** horror/silent/talking film. ~**er** v.t. film.

**fils** /fis/ n.m. son.

**filtr|e** /filtr/ n.m. filter. ~**er** v.t./i. filter; (personne) screen.

**fin**[1] /fɛ̃/ n.f. end. **à la** ~, finally. **en** ~ **de compte,** all things considered. ~ **de semaine,** weekend. **mettre** ~ **à,** put an end to. **prendre** ~, come to an end.

**fin²,fine** /fɛ̃,fin/ a. fine;(*tranche,couche*)thin; (*taille*) slim; (*plat*) exquisite; (*esprit, vue*) sharp. ● adv. (*couper*) finely. **~es herbes,** herbs.

**fin|al, ~ale** (*m. pl.* **~aux** *ou* **~als**)/final,-o/ a. final. ● n.f. (*sport*) final; (*gram.*) final syllable. ● n.m. (*pl.* **~aux** *ou* **~als**) (*mus.*) finale. **~alement** adv. finally; (*somme toute*) after all.

**finaliste** /finalist/ n.m./f. finalist.

**financ|e** /finɑ̃s/ n.f. finance. **~er** v.t. finance. **~ier, ~ière** a. financial; n.m. financier.

**finesse** /fines/ n.f. fineness; (*de taille*) slimness;(*acuité*)sharpness. **~s,** (*de langue*) niceties.

**fini** /fini/ a. finished.

**finir** /finir/ v.t./i. finish, end; (*arrêter*) stop; (*manger*) finish (up).

**finlandais, ~e** /fɛ̃lɑ̃de, -z/ a. Finnish. ● n.m., f. Finn.

**Finlande** /fɛ̃lɑ̃d/ n.f. Finland.

**finnois, ~e** /finwa, -z/ a. Finnish. ● n.m. (*lang.*) Finnish.

**firme** /firm/ n.f. firm.

**fisc** /fisk/ n.m. tax authorities. **~al** (*m. pl.* **~aux**) a. tax, fiscal. **~alité** n.f. tax system.

**fission** /fisjɔ̃/ n.f. fission.

**fissur|e** /fisyr/ n.f. crack. **~er** v.t., **se ~er** v. pr. crack.

**fixation** /fiksɑsjɔ̃/ n.f. fixing; (*complexe*) fixation.

**fixe** /fiks/ a. fixed;(*stable*)steady.**à heure ~,** at a set time. **menu à prix ~,** set menu.

**fixer** /fikse/ v.t. fix.

**flacon** /flakɔ̃/ n.m. bottle.

**flageolet** /flaʒɔle/ n.m. (*haricot*) (dwarf) kidney bean.

**flagrant, ~e** /flagrɑ̃, -t/ a. flagrant. **en ~ délit,** in the act.

**flair** /flɛr/ n.m. (sense of) smell; (*fig.*) intuition.

**flamand, ~e** /flamɑ̃, -d/ a. Flemish. ● n.m. (*lang.*) Flemish. **~, ~e** n.m., f. Fleming.

**flamant** /flamɑ̃/ n.m. flamingo.

**flambé, ~e** /flɑ̃be/ a. (*culin.*) flambé.

**flambeau** (*pl.* **~x**) /flɑ̃bo/ n.m. torch.

**flamme** /flam/ n.f. flame; (*fig.*) ardour. **en ~s,** ablaze.

**flan** /flɑ̃/ n.m. custard-pie.

**flanc** /flɑ̃/ n.m. side; (*d'animal, d'armée*) flank.

**Flandre(s)** /flɑ̃dr/ n.f. (*pl.*) Flanders.

**flanelle** /flanɛl/ n.f. flannel.

**flân|er** /flɑne/ v.i. stroll. **~erie** n.f. stroll.

**flanquer** /flɑ̃ke/ v.t. flank; (*jeter*: fam.) chuck;(*donner*: fam.)give. **~ à la porte,** kick out.

**flaque** /flak/ n.f. (*d'eau*) puddle; (*de sang*) pool.

**flash** (*pl.* **~es**) /flaʃ/ n.m. (*photo.*) flash; (*information*) news flash.

**flatter** /flate/ v.t. flatter.

**flèche** /flɛʃ/ n.f. arrow; (*de clocher*) spire. **monter en ~,** spiral.

**fléchette** /fleʃet/ n.f. dart.

**flegmatique** /flɛgmatik/ a. phlegmatic.

**flemm|e** /flɛm/ n.f. (*fam.*) laziness. **j'ai la ~e de faire,** I can't be bothered doing. **~ard, ~arde** a. (*fam.*) lazy; n.m., f. (*fam.*) lazy-bones.

**flétrir** /fletrir/ v.t., **se ~** v. pr. wither.

**fleur** /flœr/ n.f. flower. **à ~s,** flowery. **en ~s,** in flower.

**fleur|ir** /flœrir/ v.i. flower; (*arbre*) blossom; (*fig.*) flourish. ● v.t. adorn with flowers. **~i** a. flowery.

**fleuriste** /flœrist/ n.m./f. florist.

**fleuve** /flœv/ n.m. river.

**flexible** /flɛksibl/ a. flexible.

**flexion** /flɛksjɔ̃/ n.f. (*anat.*) flexing.

**flic** /flik/ n.m. (*fam.*) cop.

**flipper** /flipœr/ n.m. pinball (machine).

**flirter** /flœrte/ v.i. flirt.

**flocon** /flɔkɔ̃/ n.m. flake.

**flore** /flɔr/ n.f. flora.

**florissant, ~e** /flɔrisɑ̃, -t/ a. flourishing.

**flot** /flo/ n.m. flood, stream.

**flottant, ~e** /flɔtɑ̃, -t/ a. (*vêtement*) loose; (*indécis*) indecisive.

**flotte** /flɔt/ n.f. fleet;(*pluie: fam.*)rain;(*eau: fam.*) water.

**flott|er** /flɔte/ v.i. float; (*drapeau*) flutter; (*nuage, parfum, pensées*) drift; (*pleuvoir: fam.*) rain. **~eur** n.m. float.

**flou** /flu/ a. out of focus; (*fig.*) vague.

**fluct|uer** /flyktɥe/ v.i. fluctuate. **~uation** n.f. fluctuation.

**fluide** /flɥid/ a. & n.m. fluid.

**fluor** /flyɔr/ n.m. (*pour les dents*) fluoride.

**fluorescent, ~e** /flyɔresɑ̃, -t/ a. fluor-escent.

**flût|e** /flyt/ n.f. flute; (*verre*) champagne glass. **~iste** n.m./f. flautist.

**fluv|ial** (*m. pl.* **~iaux**) /flyvjal, -jo/ a. river.

**flux** /fly/ n.m. flow.

**FM** /ɛfɛm/ abrév. f. FM.

**foc** /fɔk/ n.m. jib.

**foi** /fwa/ n.f. faith. **être de bonne/mauvaise ~,** be acting in good/bad faith.

**foie** /fwa/ n.m. liver. **~ gras,** foie gras.

**foin** /fwɛ̃/ n.m. hay.

**foire** /fwar/ n.f. fair.

**fois** /fwa/ n.f. time. **une ~,** once. **deux ~,** twice. **à la ~,** at the same time. **des ~,** (*parfois*) sometimes. **une ~ pour toutes,** once and for all.

**fol** /fɔl/ *voir* **fou.**

**folie** /fɔli/ *n.f.* madness; (*bêtise*) foolish thing, folly.

**folklor|e** /fɔlklɔr/ *n.m.* folklore. **~ique** *a.* folk.

**folle** /fɔl/ *voir* **fou**.

**follement** /fɔlmã/ *adv.* madly.

**fonc|er**[1] /fɔ̃se/ *v.t./i.* darken. **~é** *a.* dark.

**foncer**[2] /fɔ̃se/ *v.i.* (*fam.*) dash along. **~ sur**, (*fam.*) charge at.

**fonc|ier, ~ière** /fɔ̃sje, -jɛr/ *a.* fundamental; (*comm.*) real estate.

**fonction** /fɔ̃ksjɔ̃/ *n.f.* function; (*emploi*) position. **en ~ de**, according to.

**fonctionnaire** /fɔ̃ksjɔnɛr/ *n.m./f.* civil servant.

**fonctionnel, ~le** /fɔ̃ksjɔnɛl/ *a.* functional.

**fonctionn|er** /fɔ̃ksjɔne/ *v.i.* work. **faire ~er**, work. **~ement** *n.m.* working.

**fond** /fɔ̃/ *n.m.* bottom; (*de salle, magasin, etc.*) back; (*essentiel*) basis; (*plan*) background. **à ~**, thoroughly. **au ~**, basically. **au** *ou* **dans le ~**, really.

**fondament|al** (*m. pl.* **~aux**) /fɔ̃damãtal, -o/ *a.* fundamental.

**fondation** /fɔ̃dasjɔ̃/ *n.f.* foundation.

**fond|er** /fɔ̃de/ *v.t.* found; (*baser*) base (**sur**, on). **se ~er sur**, be guided by, place one's reliance on. **~ateur, ~atrice** *n.m., f.* founder.

**fonderie** /fɔ̃dri/ *n.f.* foundry.

**fondre** /fɔ̃dr/ *v.t./i.* melt; (*dans l'eau*) dissolve; (*mélanger*) merge. **faire ~**, melt; dissolve. **~ en larmes**, burst into tears.

**fondrière** /fɔ̃drijɛr/ *n.f.* pot-hole.

**fonds** /fɔ̃/ *n.m.* fund. ● *n.m. pl.* (*capitaux*) funds. **~ de commerce**, business.

**fondu** /fɔ̃dy/ *a.* melted.

**font** /fɔ̃/ *voir* **faire**.

**fontaine** /fɔ̃tɛn/ *n.f.* fountain; (*source*) spring.

**fonte** /fɔ̃t/ *n.f.* melting; (*fer*) cast iron. **~ des neiges**, thaw.

**foot** /fut/ *n.m.* (*fam.*) football.

**football** /futbol/ *n.m.* football. **~eur** *n.m.* footballer.

**footing** /futiŋ/ *n.m.* fast walking.

**forage** /fɔraʒ/ *n.m.* drilling.

**force** /fɔrs/ *n.f.* force; (*physique*) strength; (*hydraulique etc.*) power. **~s**, (*physiques*) strength. **à ~ de**, by sheer force of. **de ~, par la ~**, by force. **~s de l'ordre**, police (force).

**forcé** /fɔrse/ *a.* forced; (*inévitable*) inevitable.

**forcément** /fɔrsemã/ *adv.* necessarily; (*évidemment*) obviously.

**forceps** /fɔrsɛps/ *n.m.* forceps.

**forcer** /fɔrse/ *v.t.* force (**à faire**, to do). **se ~** *v. pr.* force o.s.

**forer** /fɔre/ *v.t.* drill.

**forest|ier, ~ière** /fɔrɛstje, -jɛr/ *a.* forest.

**forêt** /fɔrɛ/ *n.f.* forest.

**forfait** /fɔrfɛ/ *n.m.* (*comm.*) inclusive price. **~aire** /-tɛr/ *a.* (*prix*) inclusive.

**forge** /fɔrʒ/ *n.f.* forge.

**forgeron** /fɔrʒərɔ̃/ *n.m.* blacksmith.

**formalité** /fɔrmalite/ *n.f.* formality.

**format** /fɔrma/ *n.m.* format.

**formater** /fɔrmate/ *v.t.* (*comput.*) format.

**formation** /fɔrmasjɔ̃/ *n.f.* formation; (*de médecin etc.*) training; (*culture*) education. **~ professionnelle**, professional training.

**forme** /fɔrm/ *n.f.* form; (*contour*) shape, form. **en ~**, (*sport*) in good shape, on form. **en ~ de**, in the shape of.

**formel, ~le** /fɔrmɛl/ *a.* formal; (*catégorique*) positive.

**former** /fɔrme/ *v.t.* form; (*instruire*) train. **se ~** *v. pr.* form.

**formidable** /fɔrmidabl/ *a.* fantastic.

**formulaire** /fɔrmylɛr/ *n.m.* form.

**formule** /fɔrmyl/ *n.f.* formula; (*expression*) expression. **~ de politesse**, polite phrase, letter ending.

**fort**[1], **~e** /fɔr, -t/ *a.* strong; (*grand*) big; (*pluie*) heavy; (*bruit*) loud; (*pente*) steep; (*élève*) clever. ● *adv.* (*frapper*) hard; (*parler*) loud; (*très*) very; (*beaucoup*) very much.

**fort**[2] /fɔr/ *n.m.* (*mil.*) fort.

**forteresse** /fɔrtərɛs/ *n.f.* fortress.

**fortifiant** /fɔrtifjã/ *n.m.* tonic.

**fortune** /fɔrtyn/ *n.f.* fortune. **de ~**, (*improvisé*) makeshift. **faire ~**, make one's fortune.

**fortuné** /fɔrtyne/ *a.* wealthy.

**fosse** /fos/ *n.f.* pit; (*tombe*) grave. **~ d'orchestre**, orchestral pit. **~ septique**, septic tank.

**fossé** /fose/ *n.m.* ditch; (*fig.*) gulf.

**fossette** /fosɛt/ *n.f.* dimple.

**fossile** /fosil/ *n.m.* fossil.

**fou** *ou* **fol***, **folle** /fu, fɔl/ *a.* mad; (*course, regard*) wild; (*énorme: fam.*) tremendous. **~ de**, crazy about. ● *n.m.* madman; (*bouffon*) jester. ● *n.f.* madwoman; (*fam.*) gay. **le ~ rire**, the giggles.

**foudre** /fudr/ *n.f.* lightning.

**foudroyer** /fudrwaje/ *v.t.* strike by lightning; (*maladie etc.*) strike down; (*atterrer*) stagger.

**fouet** /fwɛ/ *n.m.* whip; (*culin.*) whisk.

**fouetter** /fwete/ *v.t.* whip; (*crème etc.*) whisk.

**fougère** /fuʒɛr/ *n.f.* fern.

**fouill|e** /fuj/ *n.f.* search; (*archéol.*) excavation. **~er** *v.t./i.* search; (*creuser*) dig. **~er dans**, (*tiroir*) rummage through.

**fouillis** /fuji/ *n.m.* jumble.

**fouine** /fwin/ *n.f.* beech-marten.

**foulard** /fular/ *n.m.* scarf.

**foule** /ful/ *n.f.* crowd. **une ~ de**, (*fig.*) a mass of.

**fouler** /fule/ v.t. press; (sol) tread. **se ~ le poignet/le pied** sprain one's wrist/foot.

**foulure** /fulyr/ n.f. sprain.

**four** /fur/ n.m. oven;(de potier)kiln;(théâtre) flop. **~ à micro-ondes,** microwave oven.

**fourbe** /furb/ a. deceitful.

**fourche** /furʃ/ n.f. fork; (à foin) pitchfork.

**fourchette** /furʃɛt/ n.f. fork; (comm.) margin.

**fourgon** /furgɔ̃/ n.m. van;(wagon)wagon.**~ mortuaire,** hearse.

**fourgonnette** /furgɔnɛt/ n.f. (small) van.

**fourmi** /furmi/ n.f. ant. **avoir des ~s,** have pins and needles.

**fourneau** (pl. **~x**) /furno/ n.m. stove.

**fournée** /furne/ n.f. batch.

**fourni** /furni/ a. (épais) thick.

**fourn|ir** /furnir/ v.t. supply, provide;(client) supply; (effort) put in. **~ir à qn.,** supply s.o. with. **se ~ir chez,** shop at. **~isseur** n.m. supplier. **~iture** n.f. supply.

**fourrage** /furaʒ/ n.m. fodder.

**fourré** /fure/ a. (vêtement) fur-lined;(gâteau etc.) filled (with jam, cream, etc.).

**fourr|er** /fure/ v.t. (mettre: fam.) stick. **~e-tout** n.m. invar. (sac) holdall.

**fourreur** /furœr/ n.m. furrier.

**fourrière** /furjɛr/ n.f. (lieu) pound.

**fourrure** /furyr/ n.f. fur.

**foutre** /futr/ v.t. (argot) = **ficher²**.

**foutu, ~e** /futy/ a. (argot) = **fichu**.

**foyer** /fwaje/ n.m. home;(âtre)hearth;(club) club; (d'étudiants) hostel; (théâtre) foyer; (photo.) focus;(centre) centre.

**fracas** /fraka/ n.m. din; (de train) roar; (d'objet qui tombe) crash.

**fracasser** /frakase/ v.t., **se ~** v. pr. smash.

**fraction** /fraksjɔ̃/ n.f.fraction.**~ner** /-jɔne/ v.t., **se ~ner** v. pr. split (up).

**fractur|e** /fraktyr/ n.f. fracture. **~er** v.t. (os) fracture; (porte etc.) break open.

**fragil|e** /fraʒil/ a. fragile. **~ité** n.f. fragility.

**fragment** /fragmã/ n.m. bit, fragment.

**fraîche** /frɛʃ/ voir **frais¹**.

**fraîcheur** /frɛʃœr/ n.f. coolness; (nouveauté) freshness.

**fraîchir** /freʃir/ v.i. freshen.

**frais¹, fraîche** /frɛ, -ʃ/ a. fresh; (temps, accueil)cool;(peinture)wet. ● n.m.**mettre au ~,** put in a cool place. **il fait ~,** it is cool.

**frais²** /frɛ/ n.m. pl. expenses;(droits)fees. **~ généraux,** (comm.) overheads, running expenses. **~ de scolarité,** school fees.

**fraise** /frɛz/ n.f. strawberry.

**framboise** /frɑ̃bwaz/ n.f. raspberry.

**fran|c¹, ~che** /frã, -ʃ/ a. frank; (regard) open; (net) clear.

**franc²** /frã/ n.m. franc.

**français, ~e** /frɑ̃sɛ, -z/ a. French. ● n.m., f. Frenchman, Frenchwoman. ● n.m. (lang.) French.

**France** /frɑ̃s/ n.f. France.

**franche** /frɑ̃ʃ/ voir **franc¹**.

**franchement** /frɑ̃ʃmã/ adv. frankly; (tout à fait) really.

**franchir** /frɑ̃ʃir/ v.t. (obstacle) get over; (traverser) cross; (distance) cover; (limite) exceed.

**franchise** /frɑ̃ʃiz/ n.f. frankness; (douanière) exemption (from duties).

**franco** /frɑ̃ko/ adv. postage paid.

**franco-** /frɑ̃ko/ préf. Franco-.

**francophone** /frɑ̃kɔfɔn/ a. French-speaking. ● n.m./f. French speaker.

**frange** /frɑ̃ʒ/ n.f. fringe.

**frappe** /frap/ n.f. (de courrier etc.) typing; (de dactylo) touch.

**frappé, ~e** /frape/ a. chilled.

**frapper** /frape/ v.t./i. strike; (battre) hit, strike; (monnaie) mint; (à la porte) knock, bang.

**fratern|el, ~elle** /fratɛrnɛl/ a. brotherly.

**fraude** /frod/ n.f. fraud; (à un examen) cheating.

**frauder** /frode/ v.t./i. cheat.

**frauduleu|x, ~se** /frodylø, -z/ a. fraudulent.

**fredonner** /frədɔne/ v.t. hum.

**free-lance** /frilɑ̃s/ a. & n.m./f. freelance.

**freezer** /frizœr/ n.m. freezer.

**frégate** /fregat/ n.f. frigate.

**frein** /frɛ̃/ n.m. brake. **~ à main,** hand brake.

**frein|er** /frene/ v.t. slow down; (modérer, enrayer) curb. ● v.i. (auto.) brake. **~age** /frenaʒ/ n.m. braking.

**frêle** /frɛl/ a. frail.

**frelon** /frəlɔ̃/ n.m. hornet.

**frémir** /fremir/ v.i. shudder, shake; (feuille, eau) quiver.

**frêne** /frɛn/ n.m. ash.

**fréné|sie** /frenezi/ n.f. frenzy. **~tique** a. frenzied.

**fréqu|ent, ~ente** /frekã, -t/ a. frequent. **~emment** /-amã/ adv. frequently. **~ence** n.f. frequency.

**fréquenté** /frekãte/ a. crowded.

**fréquent|er** /frekãte/ v.t. frequent; (école) attend; (personne) see. **~ations** n.f. pl. acquaintances.

**frère** /frɛr/ n.m. brother.

**fresque** /frɛsk/ n.f. fresco.

**fret** /frɛ/ n.m. freight.

**friable** /frijabl/ a. crumbly.

**friand, ~e** /frijã, -d/ a. **~ de,** fond of.

**friandise** /frijãdiz/ n.f.sweet;(gâteau)cake.

**fric** /frik/ n.m. (fam.) money.

**fricassée** /frikase/ n.f. casserole.

**friction** /friksjɔ̃/ *n.f.* friction; (*massage*) rub-down. ~**ner** /-jone/ *v.t.* rub (down).

**frigidaire** /friʒidɛr/ *n.m.* (P.) refrigerator.

**frigo** /frigo/ *n.m.* (*fam.*) fridge.

**frileu|x**, ~**se** /frilø, -z/ *a.* sensitive to cold.

**fringale** /frɛ̃gal/ *n.f.* (*fam.*) ravenous appetite.

**friper** /fripe/ *v.t.*, **se** ~ *v. pr.* crumple.

**fripouille** /fripuj/ *n.f.* rogue.

**frire** /frir/ *v.t./i.* fry. **faire** ~, fry.

**frise** /friz/ *n.f.* frieze.

**fris|er** /frize/ *v.t./i.* (*cheveux*) curl; (*personne*) curl the hair of. ~**é** *a.* curly.

**frisquet** /friskɛ/ *a.m.* (*fam.*) chilly.

**frisson** /frisɔ̃/ *n.m.* (*de froid*) shiver; (*de peur*) shudder. ~**ner** /-ɔne/ *v.i.* shiver; shudder.

**frit**, ~**e** /fri, -t/ *a.* fried. ● *n.f.* chip. **avoir la** ~**e**, (*fam.*) feel good.

**friteuse** /fritøz/ *n.f.* (deep)fryer.

**friture** /frityr/ *n.f.* fried fish; (*huile*) (frying) oil *ou* fat.

**frivol|e** /frivɔl/ *a.* frivolous. ~**ité** *n.f.* frivolity.

**froid**, ~**e** /frwa, -d/ *a. & n.m.* cold. **avoir/prendre** ~, be/catch cold. **il fait** ~, it is cold.

**froisser** /frwase/ *v.t.* crumple; (*fig.*) offend. **se** ~ *v. pr.* crumple; (*fig.*) take offence. **se** ~ **un muscle**, strain a muscle.

**frôler** /frole/ *v.t.* brush against, skim; (*fig.*) come close to.

**fromage** /frɔmaʒ/ *n.m.* cheese.

**froment** /frɔmɑ̃/ *n.m.* wheat.

**froncer** /frɔ̃se/ *v.t.* gather. ~ **les sourcils**, frown.

**front** /frɔ̃/ *n.m.* forehead; (*mil., pol.*) front.

**frontali|er**, **ère** /frɔ̃talje, -ɛr/ *a.* border. (**travailleur**) ~**er**, commuter from across the border.

**frontière** /frɔ̃tjɛr/ *n.f.* border, frontier.

**frott|er** /frɔte/ *v.t./i.* rub; (*allumette*) strike. ~**ement** *n.m.* rubbing.

**frottis** /frɔti/ *n.m.* ~ **vaginal**, smear test.

**frouss|e** /frus/ *n.f.* (*fam.*) fear. **avoir la** ~**e**, (*fam.*) be scared. ~**ard**, ~**arde** *n.m.*, *f.* (*fam.*) coward.

**fructifier** /fryktifje/ *v.i.* **faire** ~, put to work.

**fructueu|x**, ~**se** /fryktyø, -z/ *a.* fruitful.

**fruit** /frɥi/ *n.m.* fruit. **des** ~**s**, (some) fruit. ~**s de mer**, seafood.

**frustr|er** /frystre/ *v.t.* frustrate. ~**ant**, ~**ante** *a.* frustrating. ~**ation** *n.f.* frustration.

**fuel** /fjul/ *n.m.* fuel oil.

**fugue** /fyg/ *n.f.* (*mus.*) fugue. **faire une** ~, run away.

**fuir**† /fɥir/ *v.i.* flee, run away; (*eau, robinet, etc.*) leak. ● *v.t.* (*éviter*) shun.

**fuite** /fɥit/ *n.f.* flight; (*de liquide, d'une nouvelle*) leak. **prendre la** ~, take (to) flight.

**fumée** /fyme/ *n.f.* smoke; (*vapeur*) steam.

**fum|er** /fyme/ *v.t./i.* smoke. ~**e-cigarette** *n.m. invar.* cigarette-holder. ~**é** *a.* (*poisson, verre*) smoked. ~**eur**, ~**euse** *n.m.*, *f.* smoker.

**fumet** /fymɛ/ *n.m.* aroma.

**fumier** /fymje/ *n.m.* manure.

**funambule** /fynɑ̃byl/ *n.m./f.* tightrope walker.

**funèbre** /fynɛbr/ *a.* funeral; (*fig.*) gloomy.

**funérailles** /fynerɑj/ *n.f. pl.* funeral.

**funéraire** /fynerɛr/ *a.* funeral.

**funiculaire** /fynikylɛr/ *n.m.* funicular.

**fur** /fyr/ *n.m.* **au** ~ **et à mesure**, as one goes along, progressively. **au** ~ **et à mesure que**, as.

**furet** /fyrɛ/ *n.m.* ferret.

**fureur** /fyrœr/ *n.f.* fury; (*passion*) passion.

**furie** /fyri/ *n.f.* fury; (*femme*) shrew.

**furieu|x**, ~**se** /fyrjø, -z/ *a.* furious.

**furoncle** /fyrɔ̃kl/ *n.m.* boil.

**fusain** /fyzɛ̃/ *n.m.* (*crayon*) charcoal; (*arbre*) spindle-tree.

**fuseau** (*pl.* ~**x**) /fyzo/ *n.m.* ski trousers; (*pour filer*) spindle. ~ **horaire**, time zone.

**fusée** /fyze/ *n.f.* rocket.

**fuselage** /fyzlaʒ/ *n.m.* fuselage.

**fusible** /fyzibl/ *n.m.* fuse.

**fusil** /fyzi/ *n.m.* rifle, gun; (*de chasse*) shotgun.

**fusill|er** /fyzije/ *v.t.* shoot. ~**ade** *n.f.* shooting.

**fusion** /fyzjɔ̃/ *n.f.* fusion; (*comm.*) merger. ~**ner** /-jone/ *v.t./i.* merge.

**fut** /fy/ *voir* **être**.

**fût** /fy/ *n.m.* (*tonneau*) barrel.

**futé** /fyte/ *a.* cunning.

**futil|e** /fytil/ *a.* futile. ~**ité** *n.f.* futility.

**futur** /fytyr/ *a. & n.m.* future. ~**e femme/maman**, wife-/mother-to-be.

**fuyard**, ~**e** /fɥijar, -d/ *n.m.*, *f.* runaway.

# Gg

**gabardine** /gabardin/ *n.f.* gabardine; rain-coat.

**gabarit** /gabari/ *n.m.* dimension; (*patron*) template; (*fig.*) calibre.

**gâcher** /gaʃe/ *v.t.* (*gâter*) spoil; (*gaspiller*) waste.

**gâchette** /gaʃɛt/ *n.f.* trigger.

**gâchis** /gaʃi/ *n.m.* waste.

**gaff|e** /gaf/ *n.f.* blunder. **faire** ~**e**, (*fam.*) be careful (**à**, of). ~**er** *v.i.* blunder.

**gag** /gag/ *n.m.* gag.

**gagn|er** /gaɲe/ v.t. (*match, prix, etc.*) win; (*argent, pain*) earn; (*temps, terrain*) gain. ● v.i. win; (*fig.*) gain. ~**er sa vie,** earn one's living. ~**ant,** ~**ante,** a. winning; n.m., f. winner. ~**e-pain** n.m. invar. job.

**gai** /ɡe/ a. cheerful; (*ivre*) merry. ~**ement** adv. cheerfully.

**gaillard** /ɡajar/ n.m. (*type: fam.*) fellow.

**gain** /ɡɛ̃/ n.m. (*salaire*) earnings; (*avantage*) gain; (*économie*) saving. ~**s,** (*comm.*) profits; (*au jeu*) winnings.

**gala** /ɡala/ n.m. gala.

**galant,** ~**e** /ɡalɑ̃, -t/ a. courteous; (*scène, humeur*) romantic.

**galb|e** /ɡalb/ n.m. curve. ~**é** a. shapely.

**galère** /ɡalɛr/ n.f. (*navire*) galley. **c'est la** ~**!,** (*fam.*) what an ordeal!

**galérer** /ɡalere/ v.i. (*fam.*) have a hard time.

**galerie** /ɡalri/ n.f. gallery; (*théâtre*) circle; (*de voiture*) roof-rack.

**galet** /ɡalɛ/ n.m. pebble.

**galette** /ɡalɛt/ n.f. flat cake.

**Galles** /ɡal/ n.f. pl. **le pays de** ~, Wales.

**gallois,** ~**e** /ɡalwa, -z/ a. Welsh. ● n.m., f. Welshman, Welshwoman. ● n.m. (*lang.*) Welsh.

**galon** /ɡalɔ̃/ n.m. braid; (*mil.*) stripe. **prendre du** ~, be promoted.

**galop** /ɡalo/ n.m. gallop. ~**er** v.i. (*cheval*) gallop; (*personne*) run.

**galopade** /ɡalopad/ n.f. wild rush.

**gamelle** /ɡamɛl/ n.f. (*de soldat*) mess bowl *ou* tin; (*d'ouvrier*) food-box.

**gamin,** ~**e** /ɡamɛ̃, -in/ a. playful. ● n.m., f. (*fam.*) kid.

**gamme** /ɡam/ n.f. (*mus.*) scale; (*série*) range. **haut de** ~, up-market, top of the range. **bas de** ~, down-market, bottom of the range.

**ganglion** /ɡɑ̃ɡlijɔ̃/ n.m. swelling.

**gangster** /ɡɑ̃ɡstɛr/ n.m. gangster; (*escroc*) crook.

**gant** /ɡɑ̃/ n.m. glove. ~ **de toilette,** face-flannel, face-cloth.

**garag|e** /ɡaraʒ/ n.m. garage. ~**iste** n.m. garage owner; (*employé*) garage mechanic.

**garant|ie** /ɡarɑ̃ti/ n.f. guarantee; (*protection*) safeguard. ~**ies,** (*de police d'assurance*) cover. ~**ir** v.t. guarantee; (*protéger*) protect (**de,** from).

**garçon** /ɡarsɔ̃/ n.m. boy; (*célibataire*) bachelor. ~ **(de café),** waiter. ~ **d'honneur,** best man.

**garde¹** /ɡard/ n.f. guard; (*d'enfants, de bagages*) care; (*service*) guard (duty). **de** ~, on duty. **mettre en** ~, warn. **prendre** ~, be careful (**à,** of). **(droit de)** ~, custody (**de,** of).

**garde²** /ɡard/ n.m. (*personne*) guard; (*de propriété*) warden.

**gard|er** /ɡarde/ v.t. (*conserver, maintenir*) keep; (*vêtement*) keep on; (*surveiller*) look after; (*défendre*) guard. **se** ~**er** v. pr. (*denrée*) keep. ~**er le lit,** stay in bed. ~**e-boue** n.m. invar. mudguard. ~**e-manger** n.m. invar. (*food*) safe; (*placard*) larder. ~**e-robe** n.f. wardrobe.

**garderie** /ɡardəri/ n.f. crèche.

**gardien,** ~**ne** /ɡardjɛ̃, -jɛn/ n.m., f. (*de prison, réserve*) warden; (*d'immeuble*) caretaker; (*de musée*) attendant; (*garde*) guard. ~ **de but,** goalkeeper. ~ **de la paix,** policeman. ~**ne d'enfants,** child-minder.

**gare¹** /ɡar/ n.f. (*rail.*) station. ~ **routière,** coach station.

**gare²** /ɡar/ int. ~ **(à toi),** watch out!

**garer** /ɡare/ v.t., **se** ~ v. pr. park.

**gargarisme** /ɡarɡarism/ n.m. gargle.

**gargouille** /ɡarɡuj/ n.f. (water-)spout; (*sculptée*) gargoyle.

**garn|ir** /ɡarnir/ v.t. fill; (*décorer*) decorate; (*culin.*) garnish. ~**i** a. (*plat*) served with vegetables.

**garniture** /ɡarnityr/ n.f. (*légumes*) vegetables; (*ornement*) trimming.

**garrot** /ɡaro/ n.m. (*méd.*) tourniquet.

**gars** /ɡa/ n.m. (*fam.*) fellow.

**gas-oil** /ɡazɔjl/ n.m. diesel oil.

**gaspill|er** /ɡaspije/ v.t. waste. ~**age** n.m. waste.

**gastrique** /ɡastrik/ a. gastric.

**gastronom|e** /ɡastronom/ n.m./f. gourmet. ~**ie** n.f. gastronomy.

**gâteau** (pl. ~**x**) /ɡato/ n.m. cake. ~ **sec,** biscuit.

**gâter** /ɡate/ v.t. spoil. **se** ~ v. pr. (*temps*) get worse.

**gâterie** /ɡatri/ n.f. little treat.

**gauch|e¹** /ɡoʃ/ a. left. **à** ~**e,** on the left; (*direction*) (to the) left. **la** ~**e,** the left (side); (*pol.*) the left (wing). ~**er,** ~**ère** a. & n.m., f. left-handed (person). ~**iste** a. & n.m./f. (*pol.*) leftist.

**gauche²** /ɡoʃ/ a. (*maladroit*) awkward.

**gaufre** /ɡofr/ n.f. waffle.

**gaufrette** /ɡofrɛt/ n.f. wafer.

**gaulois,** ~**e** /ɡolwa, -z/ a. Gallic; (*fig.*) bawdy. ● n.m., f. Gaul.

**gaz** /ɡaz/ n.m. invar. gas.

**gaze** /ɡaz/ n.f. gauze.

**gazelle** /ɡazɛl/ n.f. gazelle.

**gazeu|x,** ~**se** /ɡazø, -z/ a. (*boisson*) fizzy.

**gazoduc** /ɡazɔdyk/ n.m. gas pipeline.

**gazomètre** /ɡazɔmɛtr/ n.m. gasometer.

**gazon** /ɡazɔ̃/ n.m. lawn, grass.

**geai** /ʒɛ/ n.m. jay.

**géant,** ~**e** /ʒeɑ̃, -t/ a. & n.m., f. giant.

**gel** /ʒɛl/ n.m. frost; (*pâte*) gel.

**gélatine** /ʒelatin/ n.f. gelatine.

**gel|er** /ʒəle/ *v.t./i.* freeze. **on gèle,** it's freezing. **~é** *a.* frozen; (*membre abîmé*) frostbitten. **~ée** *n.f.* frost; (*culin.*) jelly.

**gélule** /ʒelyl/ *n.f.* (*méd.*) capsule.

**Gémeaux** /ʒemo/ *n.m. pl.* Gemini.

**gém|ir** /ʒemir/ *v.i.* groan. **~issement** *n.m.* groan(ing).

**gênant, ~e** /ʒenɑ̃, -t/ *a.* embarrassing; (*irritant*) annoying.

**gencive** /ʒɑ̃siv/ *n.f.* gum.

**gendarme** /ʒɑ̃darm/ *n.m.* policeman, gendarme. **~rie** /-əri/ *n.f.* police force; (*local*) police station.

**gendre** /ʒɑ̃dr/ *n.m.* son-in-law.

**gène** /ʒɛn/ *n.m.* gene.

**gêne** /ʒɛn/ *n.f.* discomfort; (*confusion*) embarrassment.

**gên|er** /ʒene/ *v.t.* bother, disturb; (*troubler*) embarrass; (*encombrer*) hamper; (*bloquer*) block. **~é** *a.* embarrassed.

**génér|al** (*m. pl.* **~aux**) /ʒeneral, -o/ *a.* general. ● *n.m.* (*pl.* **~aux**) general. **en ~al,** in general. **~alement** *adv.* generally.

**généralis|er** /ʒeneralize/ *v.t./i.* generalize.

**généraliste** /ʒeneralist/ *n.m./f.* general practitioner, GP.

**génération** /ʒenerɑsjɔ̃/ *n.f.* generation.

**généreu|x, ~se** /ʒenerø, -z/ *a.* generous. **~sement** *adv.* generously.

**générosité** /ʒenerozite/ *n.f.* generosity.

**genêt** /ʒənɛ/ *n.m.* (*plante*) broom.

**génétique** /ʒenetik/ *a.* genetic. ● *n.f.* genetics.

**Genève** /ʒənɛv/ *n.m./f.* Geneva.

**gén|ial** (*m. pl.* **~iaux**) /ʒenjal, -jo/ *a.* brilliant; (*fam.*) fantastic.

**génie** /ʒeni/ *n.m.* genius. **~ civil,** civil engineering.

**genièvre** /ʒənjɛvr/ *n.m.* juniper.

**génit|al** (*m. pl.* **~aux**) /ʒenital, -o/ *a.* genital.

**génoise** /ʒenwaz/ *n.f.* sponge (cake).

**genou** (*pl.* **~x**) /ʒnu/ *n.m.* knee. **à ~x,** kneeling.

**genre** /ʒɑ̃r/ *n.m.* sort, kind; (*gram.*) gender.

**gens** /ʒɑ̃/ *n.m./f. pl.* people.

**genti|l, ~lle** /ʒɑ̃ti, -j/ *a.* kind, nice; (*agréable*) nice; (*sage*) good. **~llesse** /-jɛs/ *n.f.* kindness. **~ment** *adv.* kindly.

**géograph|ie** /ʒeɔɡrafi/ *n.f.* geography. **~e** *n.m./f.* geographer. **~ique** *a.* geographical.

**géolo|gie** /ʒeɔlɔʒi/ *n.f.* geology. **~gique** *a.* geological.

**géométr|ie** /ʒeɔmetri/ *n.f.* geometry. **~ique** *a.* geometric.

**géranium** /ʒeranjɔm/ *n.m.* geranium.

**géran|t, ~te** /ʒerɑ̃, -t/ *n.m., f.* manager, manageress.

**gercé** /ʒɛrse/ *a.* chapped.

**gérer** /ʒere/ *v.t.* manage.

**germain, ~e** /ʒɛrmɛ̃, -ɛn/ *a.* **cousin ~,** first cousin.

**germanique** /ʒɛrmanik/ *a.* Germanic.

**germ|e** /ʒɛrm/ *n.m.* germ. **~er** *v.i.* germinate.

**gésier** /ʒezje/ *n.m.* gizzard.

**geste** /ʒɛst/ *n.m.* gesture.

**gesticul|er** /ʒɛstikyle/ *v.i.* gesticulate. **~ation** *n.f.* gesticulation.

**gestion** /ʒɛstjɔ̃/ *n.f.* management.

**geyser** /ʒɛzɛr/ *n.m.* geyser.

**gibier** /ʒibje/ *n.m.* game.

**giboulée** /ʒibule/ *n.f.* shower.

**gifl|e** /ʒifl/ *n.f.* slap (in the face). **~er** *v.t.* slap.

**gigantesque** /ʒiɡɑ̃tɛsk/ *a.* gigantic.

**gigot** /ʒiɡo/ *n.m.* leg (of lamb).

**gilet** /ʒilɛ/ *n.m.* waistcoat; (*cardigan*) cardigan. **~ de sauvetage,** life-jacket.

**gin** /dʒin/ *n.m.* gin.

**gingembre** /ʒɛ̃ʒɑ̃br/ *n.m.* ginger.

**gingivite** /ʒɛ̃ʒivit/ *n.f.* gum infection.

**girafe** /ʒiraf/ *n.f.* giraffe.

**giratoire** /ʒiratwar/ *a.* **sens ~,** roundabout.

**giroflée** /ʒirɔfle/ *n.f.* wallflower.

**girouette** /ʒirwɛt/ *n.f.* weathercock, weather-vane.

**gisement** /ʒizmɑ̃/ *n.m.* deposit.

**gitan, ~e** /ʒitɑ̃, -an/ *n.m., f.* gypsy.

**gîte** /ʒit/ *n.m.* (*maison*) home; (*abri*) shelter. **~ rural,** holiday cottage.

**givre** /ʒivr/ *n.m.* (hoar-)frost.

**glace** /ɡlas/ *n.f.* ice; (*crème*) ice-cream. (*miroir*) mirror.

**glac|er** /ɡlase/ *v.t.* (*gâteau, boisson*) ice; (*papier*) glaze; (*pétrifier*) chill. **~é** *a.* (*vent, accueil*) icy.

**glac|ial** (*m. pl.* **~iaux**) /ɡlasjal, -jo/ *a.* icy.

**glacier** /ɡlasje/ *n.m.* (*géog.*) glacier; (*vendeur*) ice-cream man.

**glacière** /ɡlasjɛr/ *n.f.* icebox.

**glaçon** /ɡlasɔ̃/ *n.m.* ice-cube.

**glaïeul** /ɡlajœl/ *n.m.* gladiolus.

**glaise** /ɡlɛz/ *n.f.* clay.

**gland** /ɡlɑ̃/ *n.m.* acorn; (*ornement*) tassel.

**glande** /ɡlɑ̃d/ *n.f.* gland.

**glissant, ~e** /ɡlisɑ̃, -t/ *a.* slippery.

**gliss|er** /ɡlise/ *v.i.* slide; (*sur l'eau*) glide; (*déraper*) slip; (*véhicule*) skid. **~ement de terrain,** landslide.

**glissière** /ɡlisjɛr/ *n.f.* groove. **à ~,** (*porte, système*) sliding.

**glob|al** (*m. pl.* **~aux**) /ɡlɔbal, -o/ *a.* (*entier, général*) overall. **~alement** *adv.* as a whole.

**globe** /ɡlɔb/ *n.m.* globe. **~ oculaire,** eyeball. **~ terrestre,** globe.

**globule** /ɡlɔbyl/ *n.m.* (*du sang*) corpuscle.

**gloire** /ɡlwar/ *n.f.* glory.

**glorieu|x**, **~se** /glɔrjø, -z/ *a.* glorious.
**~sement** *adv.* gloriously.

**glossaire** /glɔsɛr/ *n.m.* glossary.

**glouton**, **~ne** /glutɔ̃, -ɔn/ *a.* gluttonous.
● *n.m.*, *f.* glutton.

**gluant**, **~e** /glyã, -t/ *a.* sticky.

**glucose** /glykoz/ *n.m.* glucose.

**glycérine** /gliserin/ *n.f.* glycerine.

**glycine** /glisin/ *n.f.* wisteria.

**gnome** /gnom/ *n.m.* gnome.

**GO** (*abrév.* **grandes ondes**) long wave.

**goal** /gol/ *n.m.* goalkeeper.

**gobelet** /gɔblɛ/ *n.m.* tumbler, mug.

**goéland** /gɔelã/ *n.m.* (sea)gull.

**goélette** /gɔelɛt/ *n.f.* schooner.

**gogo (à)** /(a)gogo/ *adv.* (*fam.*) galore, in
abundance.

**goinfr|e** /gwɛ̃fr/ *n.m.* (*glouton: fam.*) pig. **se
~er** *v. pr.* (*fam.*) stuff o.s. like a pig (**de**, with).

**golf** /gɔlf/ *n.m.* golf; golf course.

**golfe** /gɔlf/ *n.m.* gulf.

**gomm|e** /gom/ *n.f.* rubber; (*Amer.*) eraser;
(*résine*) gum. **~er** *v.t.* rub out.

**gond** /gɔ̃/ *n.m.* hinge. **sortir de ses ~s**, go
mad.

**gondole** /gɔ̃dɔl/ *n.f.* gondola.

**gonfl|er** /gɔ̃fle/ *v.t./i.* swell; (*ballon, pneu*)
pump up, blow up; (*exagérer*) inflate. **se ~er**
*v. pr.* swell. **~é** *a.* swollen. **~ement** *n.m.*
swelling.

**gorge** /gɔrʒ/ *n.f.* throat; (*poitrine*) breast;
(*vallée*) gorge.

**gorgée** /gɔrʒe/ *n.f.* sip, gulp.

**gorille** /gɔrij/ *n.m.* gorilla; (*garde: fam.*)
bodyguard.

**gosier** /gozje/ *n.m.* throat.

**gosse** /gɔs/ *n.m./f.* (*fam.*) kid.

**gothique** /gɔtik/ *a.* Gothic.

**goudron** /gudrɔ̃/ *n.m.* tar. **à faible teneur
en ~**, low tar.

**gouffre** /gufr/ *n.m.* gulf, abyss.

**goulot** /gulo/ *n.m.* neck.

**goulu**, **~e** /guly/ *a.* gluttonous. ● *n.m.*, *f.*
glutton.

**gourde** /gurd/ *n.f.* (*à eau*) flask.

**gourdin** /gurdɛ̃/ *n.m.* club, cudgel.

**gourmand**, **~e** /gurmã, -d/ *a.* greedy.
● *n.m.*, *f.* glutton. **~ise** /-diz/ *n.f.* greed;
(*mets*) delicacy.

**gourmet** /gurmɛ/ *n.m.* gourmet.

**gourmette** /gurmɛt/ *n.f.* chain bracelet.

**gousse** /gus/ *n.f.* **~ d'ail**, clove of garlic.

**goût** /gu/ *n.m.* taste.

**goûter** /gute/ *v.t.* taste; (*apprécier*) enjoy.
● *v.i.* have tea. ● *n.m.* tea, snack. **~ à** *ou* **de**,
taste.

**goutt|e** /gut/ *n.f.* drop; (*méd.*) gout.

**gouttière** /gutjɛr/ *n.f.* gutter.

**gouvernail** /guvɛrnaj/ *n.m.* rudder; (*barre*)
helm.

**gouvernante** /guvɛrnãt/ *n.f.* governess.

**gouvernement** /guvɛrnəmã/ *n.m.* government.

**gouvern|er** /guvɛrne/ *v.t./i.* govern. **~eur**
*n.m.* governor.

**grâce** /grɑs/ *n.f.* (*charme*) grace; (*jurid.*)
pardon. **~ à**, thanks to.

**gracieu|x**, **~se** /grasjø, -z/ *a.* graceful;
(*gratuit*) free. **~sement** *adv.* gracefully; free
(of charge).

**grade** /grad/ *n.m.* rank.

**gradé** /grade/ *n.m.* non-commissioned
officer.

**gradin** /gradɛ̃/ *n.m.* tier, step.

**gradué** /gradye/ *a.* graded, graduated.

**graffiti** /grafiti/ *n.m. pl.* graffiti.

**grain** /grɛ̃/ *n.m.* grain; (*naut.*) squall; (*de
café*) bean; (*de poivre*) pepper corn. **~ de
beauté**, beauty spot. **~ de raisin**, grape.

**graine** /grɛn/ *n.f.* seed.

**graiss|e** /grɛs/ *n.f.* fat; (*lubrifiant*) grease.
**~er** *v.t.* grease.

**gramm|aire** /gramɛr/ *n.f.* grammar. **~a-
tical** (*m. pl.* **~aticaux**) *a.* grammatical.

**gramme** /gram/ *n.m.* gram.

**grand**, **~e** /grã, -d/ *a.* big, large; (*haut*) tall;
(*mérite, distance, ami*) great; (*bruit*) loud;
(*plusâgé*) big. ● *adv.* (*ouvrir*) wide. **~ouvert**,
wide open. **voir ~**, think big. ● *n.m.*, *f.* (*adulte*)
grown-up; (*enfant*) older child. **au ~ air**, in the
open air. **en ~e partie**, largely. **~angle**, *n.m.*
wide angle. **~e banlieue**, outer suburbs.
**G~e-Bretagne** *n.f.* Great Britain. **pas ~-
chose**, not much. **~es lignes**, (*rail.*) main
lines. **~ magasin**, department store. **~-mère**
(*pl.* **~s-mères**) *n.f.* grandmother. **~s-
parents** *n.m. pl.* grandparents. **~-père** (*pl.*
**~s-pères**) *n.m.* grandfather. **~e personne**,
grown-up. **~e surface**, hypermarket. **~es
vacances**, summer holidays.

**grandiose** /grãdjoz/ *a.* grandiose.

**grandir** /grãdir/ *v.i.* grow; (*bruit*) grow
louder. ● *v.t.* make taller.

**grange** /grãʒ/ *n.f.* barn.

**granit** /granit/ *n.m.* granite.

**granulé** /granyle/ *n.m.* granule.

**graphique** /grafik/ *a.* graphic. ● *n.m.* graph.

**grappe** /grap/ *n.f.* cluster. **~ de raisin**,
bunch of grapes.

**gras**, **~se** /grɑ, -s/ *a.* fat; (*aliment*) fatty;
(*surface*) greasy; (*épais*) thick; (*caractères*)
bold. ● *n.m.* (*culin.*) fat.

**gratification** /gratifikasjɔ̃/ *n.f.* bonus,
satisfaction.

**gratifiant ~ante** /gratifjeã, -t/ *a.* reward-
ing.

**gratin** /gratɛ̃/ *n.m.* baked dish with cheese
topping; (*élite: fam.*) upper crust.

**gratis** /gratis/ *adv.* free.

**gratitude** /gratityd/ *n.f.* gratitude.

**gratter** /grate/ *v.t./i.* scratch; (*avec un outil*) scrape. **se ~** *v. pr.* scratch o.s. **ça me gratte,** (*fam.*) it itches.

**gratuit, ~e** /gratɥi, -t/ *a.* free; (*acte*) gratuitous. **~ement** /-tmã/ *adv.* free (of charge).

**grave** /grav/ *a.* serious; (*solennel*) grave; (*voix*) deep; (*accent*) grave. **~ment** *adv.* seriously; gravely.

**grav|er** /grave/ *v.t.* engrave; (*sur bois*) carve. **~eur** *n.m.* engraver.

**gravier** /gravje/ *n.m.* gravel.

**gravure** /gravyr/ *n.f.* engraving; (*de tableau, photo*) print, plate.

**gré** /gre/ *n.m.* **bon ~ mal gré,** like it or not.

**grec, ~que** /grɛk/ *a. & n.m., f.* Greek. ● *n.m.* (*lang.*) Greek.

**Grèce** /grɛs/ *n.f.* Greece.

**greff|e** /grɛf/ *n.f.* graft; (*d'organe*) transplant. **~er** /grefe/ *v.t.* graft; transplant.

**grêle**[1] /grɛl/ *a.* (*maigre*) spindly; (*voix*) shrill.

**grêl|e**[2] /grɛl/ *n.f.* hail. **~er** /grele/ *v.i.* hail. **~on** *n.m.* hailstone.

**grelot** /grəlo/ *n.m.* (little) bell.

**grelotter** /grələte/ *v.i.* shiver.

**grenade**[1] /grənad/ *n.f.* (*fruit*) pomegranate.

**grenade**[2] /grənad/ *n.f.* (*explosif*) grenade.

**grenat** /grəna/ *a. invar.* dark red.

**grenier** /grənje/ *n.m.* attic.

**grenouille** /grənuj/ *n.f.* frog.

**grès** /grɛ/ *n.m.* sandstone; (*poterie*) stoneware.

**grève**[1] /grɛv/ *n.f.* strike.

**grève**[2] /grɛv/ *n.f.* (*rivage*) shore.

**gréviste** /grevist/ *n.m./f.* striker.

**gribouill|er** /gribuje/ *v.t./i.* scribble. **~is** /-ji/ *n.m.* scribble.

**grièvement** /grijɛvmã/ *adv.* seriously.

**griff|e** /grif/ *n.f.* claw; (*de couturier*) label. **~er** *v.t.* scratch, claw.

**griffonner** /grifɔne/ *v.t./i.* scrawl.

**grignoter** /griɲɔte/ *v.t./i.* nibble.

**gril** /gril/ *n.m.* grill, grid(iron).

**grillade** /grijad/ *n.f.* (*viande*) grill.

**grillage** /grijaʒ/ *n.m.* wire netting.

**grille** /grij/ *n.f.* railings; (*portail*) (metal) gate; (*de fenêtre*) bars; (*de cheminée*) grate; (*fig.*) grid.

**grill|er** /grije/ *v.t./i.* burn; (*ampoule*) blow; (*feu rouge*) go through. **(faire) ~er,** (*pain*) toast; (*viande*) grill; (*café*) roast. **~e-pain** *n.m. invar.* toaster.

**grillon** /grijɔ̃/ *n.m.* cricket.

**grimace** /grimas/ *n.f.* (funny) face; (*de douleur, dégoût*) grimace.

**grimper** /grɛ̃pe/ *v.t./i.* climb.

**grinc|er** /grɛ̃se/ *v.i.* creak. **~ement** *n.m.* creak(ing).

**gripp|e** /grip/ *n.f.* influenza, flu. **être ~é,** have (the) flu; (*mécanisme*) be seized up *ou* jammed.

**gris, ~e** /gri, -z/ *a.* grey.

**grive** /griv/ *n.f.* (*oiseau*) thrush.

**grog** /grɔg/ *n.m.* grog.

**grogn|er** /grɔɲe/ *v.i.* growl; (*fig.*) grumble. **~ement** *n.m.* growl; grumble.

**grognon, ~ne** /grɔɲɔ̃, -ɔn/ *a.* grumpy.

**grond|er** /grɔ̃de/ *v.i.* rumble; (*chien*) growl; (*conflit etc.*) be brewing. ● *v.t.* scold. **~ement** *n.m.* rumbling; growling.

**groom** /grum/ *n.m.* page(-boy).

**gros, ~se** /gro, -s/ *a.* big, large; (*gras*) fat; (*épais*) thick. ● *n.m., f.* fat man, fat woman. ● *n.m.* **de ~,** (*comm.*) wholesale. **en ~,** roughly; (*comm.*) wholesale. **~ mot,** rude word. **~ plan,** close-up.

**groseille** /grozɛj/ *n.f.* (red *ou* white) currant. **~ à maquereau,** gooseberry.

**grosse** /gros/ *voir* **gros.**

**grossesse** /grosɛs/ *n.f.* pregnancy.

**grosseur** /grosœr/ *n.f.* (*volume*) size; (*enflure*) lump.

**gross|ier, ~ière** /grosje, -jɛr/ *a.* coarse, rough; (*imitation, instrument*) crude; (*vulgaire*) coarse; (*insolent*) rude; (*erreur*) gross. **~ièreté** *n.f.* rudeness; (*mot*) rude word.

**grossir** /grosir/ *v.t./i.* swell; (*personne*) put on weight; (*au microscope*) magnify; (*augmenter*) grow; (*exagérer*) magnify.

**grossiste** /grosist/ *n.m./f.* wholesaler.

**grotesque** /grotɛsk/ *a.* grotesque; (*ridicule*) ludicrous.

**grotte** /grɔt/ *n.f.* cave, grotto.

**groupe** /grup/ *n.m.* group; (*mus.*) band. **~ électrogène,** generating set.

**group|er** /grupe/ *v.t.*, **se ~er** *v. pr.* group (together). **~ement** *n.m.* grouping.

**grue** /gry/ *n.f.* crane.

**grumeau** (*pl.* **~x**) /grymo/ *n.m.* lump.

**gruyère** /gryjɛr/ *n.m.* gruyère (cheese).

**guenon** /gənɔ̃/ *n.f.* female monkey.

**guépard** /gepar/ *n.m.* cheetah.

**guêp|e** /gɛp/ *n.f.* wasp. **~ier** /gepje/ *n.m.* wasp's nest; (*fig.*) trap.

**guère** /gɛr/ *adv.* **(ne) ~,** hardly. **il n'y a ~ d'espoir,** there is no hope.

**guéridon** /geridɔ̃/ *n.m.* pedestal table.

**guér|ir** /gerir/ *v.t.* (*personne, maladie, mal*) cure (**de,** of); (*plaie, membre*) heal. ● *v.i.* get better; (*blessure*) heal.

**guerre** /gɛr/ *n.f.* war.

**guerr|ier, ~ière** /gɛrje, -jɛr/ *a.* warlike. ● *n.m., f.* warrior.

**guetter** /gete/ *v.t.* watch; (*attendre*) watch out for.

**gueule** /gœl/ n.f. mouth; (figure: fam.) face. **ta ~!**, (fam.) shut up!

**gueuler** /gœle/ v.i. (fam.) bawl.

**gueuleton** /gœltɔ̃/ n.m. (repas: fam.) blow-out, slap-up meal.

**gui** /gi/ n.m. mistletoe.

**guichet** /giʃɛ/ n.m. window, counter; (de gare) ticket-office (window); (de théâtre) box-office (window).

**guide** /gid/ n.m. guide. ● n.f. (fille scout) girl guide. **~s** n.f. pl. (rênes) reins.

**guider** /gide/ v.t. guide.

**guidon** /gidɔ̃/ n.m. handlebars.

**guignol** /giɲɔl/ n.m. puppet; (personne) clown; (spectacle) puppet-show.

**guillemets** /gijmɛ/ n.m. pl. quotation marks, inverted commas. **entre ~**, in inverted commas.

**guimauve** /gimov/ n.f. marshmallow.

**guirlande** /girlɑ̃d/ n.f. garland.

**guitar|e** /gitar/ n.f. guitar. **~iste** n.m./f. guitarist.

**gym** /ʒim/ n.f. gym.

**gymnas|e** /ʒimnɑz/ n.m. gym (nasium). **~tique** /-astik/ n.f. gymnastics.

**gynécolo|gie** /ʒinekɔlɔʒi/ n.f. gynae-cology. **~gue** n.m./f. gynaecologist.

**gypse** /ʒips/ n.m. gypsum.

# Hh

**habile** /abil/ a. skilful, clever. **~té** n.f. skill.

**habilité** /abilite/ a. **~ à faire**, entitled to do.

**habill|er** /abije/ v.t. dress (de, in). **s'~er** v. pr. dress (o.s.), get dressed. **~é** a. (costume) dressy. **~ement** n.m. clothing.

**habit** /abi/ n.m. dress, outfit; (de cérémonie) tails. **~s**, clothes.

**habitant**, **~e** /abitɑ̃, -t/ n.m., f. (de maison) occupant; (de pays) inhabitant.

**habitation** /abitasjɔ̃/ n.f. living; (logement) house.

**habit|er** /abite/ v.i. live. ● v.t. live in; (planète, zone) inhabit. **~é** a. (terre) inhabited.

**habitude** /abityd/ n.f. habit. **avoir l'~ de faire**, be used to doing. **d'~**, usually. **comme d'~**, as usual.

**habitué**, **~e** /abitɥe/ n.m., f. regular visitor; (client) regular.

**habituel**, **~le** /abitɥɛl/ a. usual. **~lement** adv. usually.

**habituer** /abitɥe/ v.t. **~ à**, accustom to. **s'~ à**, get used to.

**hache** /ˈaʃ/ n.f. axe.

**haché** /ˈaʃe/ a. (viande) minced.

**hacher** /ˈaʃe/ v.t. mince; (au couteau) chop.

**hachis** /ˈaʃi/ n.m. minced meat.

**haie** /ˈɛ/ n.f. hedge; (rangée) row. **course de ~s**, hurdle race.

**haillon** /ˈajɔ̃/ n.m. rag.

**hain|e** /ˈɛn/ n.f. hatred. **~eux**, **~euse** a. full of hatred.

**haïr** /ˈair/ v.t. hate.

**hâl|e** /ˈɑl/ n.m. (sun-)tan. **~é** a. (sun-)tanned.

**haleine** /alɛn/ n.f. breath. **hors d'~**, out of breath.

**hal|er** /ˈale/ v.t. tow. **~age** n.m. towing.

**hall** /ˈol/ n.m. hall; (de gare) concourse.

**halle** /ˈal/ n.f. (covered) market. **~s**, (main) food market.

**halte** /ˈalt/ n.f. stop; (repos) break; (escale) stopping place. ● int. stop; (mil.) halt. **faire ~**, stop.

**hamac** /ˈamak/ n.m. hammock.

**hamburger** /ˈɑ̃burgœr/ n.m. hamburger.

**hameau** (pl. **~x**) /ˈamo/ n.m. hamlet.

**hameçon** /amsɔ̃/ n.m. (fish-)hook.

**hanche** /ˈɑ̃ʃ/ n.f. hip.

**hand-ball** /ˈɑ̃dbal/ n.m. handball.

**handicap** /ˈɑ̃dikap/ n.m. handicap. **~é**, **~ée** a. & n.m., f. handicapped (person). **~er** v.t. handicap.

**hangar** /ˈɑ̃gar/ n.m. shed; (pour avions) hangar.

**hanneton** /ˈantɔ̃/ n.m. May-bug.

**hanter** /ˈɑ̃te/ v.t. haunt.

**haras** /ˈarɑ/ n.m. stud-farm.

**harcèlement** /arsɛlmɑ̃/ n.m. **~ sexuel**, sexual harassment.

**harceler** /ˈarsəle/ v.t. harass.

**hareng** /ˈarɑ̃/ n.m. herring.

**haricot** /ˈariko/ n.m. bean. **~ vert**, French ou string bean.

**harmonica** /armɔnika/ n.m. harmonica.

**harmon|ie** /armɔni/ n.f. harmony. **~ieux**, **~ieuse** a. harmonious.

**harnais** /ˈarnɛ/ n.m. harness.

**harp|e** /ˈarp/ n.f. harp. **~iste** n.m./f. harpist.

**hasard** /ˈazar/ n.m. chance; (coïncidence) coincidence. **~s**, (risques) hazards. **au ~**, (choisir etc.) at random; (flâner) aimlessly. **~eux**, **~euse** /-dø, -z/ a. risky.

**hâte** /ˈɑt/ n.f. haste. **à la ~**, **en ~**, hurriedly. **avoir ~ de**, be eager to.

**hâter** /ˈɑte/ v.t. hasten. **se ~** v. pr. hurry (de, to).

**hauss|e** /ˈos/ n.f. rise (de, in). **~e des prix**, price rises. **en ~e**, rising. **~er** v.t. raise; (épaules) shrug.

**haut**, **~e** /ˈo, ˈot/ a. high; (de taille) tall. ● adv. high; (parler) loud(ly); (lire) aloud. ● n.m. top. **à ~e voix**, aloud. **des ~s et des bas**, ups and downs. **en ~**, (regarder, jeter) up;

(*dans une maison*) upstairs. **en ~ (de),** at the top (of). **plus ~,** further up, higher up; (*dans un texte*) above. **~parleur** *n.m.* loudspeaker.

**hautain,** **~e** /'otɛ̃, -ɛn/ *a.* haughty.

**hautbois** /'obwɑ/ *n.m.* oboe.

**hautement** /'otmɑ̃/ *adv.* highly.

**hauteur** /'otœr/ *n.f.* height; (*colline*) hill; (*arrogance*) haughtiness. **à la ~,** (*fam.*) up to it.

**Haye (La)** /(la)'ɛ/ *n.f.* The Hague.

**hayon** /'ɛjɔ̃/ *n.m.* (*auto.*) rear opening, tailgate.

**hebdo** /ɛbdo/ *n.m.* (*fam.*) weekly.

**hebdomadaire** /ɛbdɔmadɛr/ *a. & n.m.* weekly.

**héberg|er** /ebɛrʒe/ *v.t.* accommodate, take in. **~ement** *n.m.* accommodation.

**hébraïque** /ebraik/ *a.* Hebrew.

**hébreu** (*pl.* **~x**) /ebrø/ *a.m.* Hebrew. ● *n.m.* (*lang.*) Hebrew.

**hectare** /ɛktar/ *n.m.* hectare(= *10,000 square metres*).

**hein** /'ɛ̃/ *int.* (*fam.*) eh.

**hélas** /'elas/ *int.* alas. ● *adv.* sadly.

**hélice** /elis/ *n.f.* propeller.

**hélicoptère** /elikɔptɛr/ *n.m.* helicopter.

**helvétique** /ɛlvetik/ *a.* Swiss.

**hématome** /ematom/ *n.m.* bruise.

**hémisphère** /emisfɛr/ *n.m.* hemisphere.

**hémorragie** /emɔraʒi/ *n.f.* haemorrhage.

**hémorroïdes** /emɔrɔid/ *n.f. pl.* piles, haemorrhoids.

**hépatite** /epatit/ *n.f.* hepatitis.

**herbe** /ɛrb/ *n.f.* grass; (*méd., culin.*) herb.

**herbicide** /ɛrbisid/ *n.m.* weed-killer.

**hérédit|é** /eredite/ *n.f.* heredity. **~aire** *a.* hereditary.

**héré|sie** /erezi/ *n.f.* heresy. **~tique** *a.* heretical; *n.m./f.* heretic.

**hérisson** /'erisɔ̃/ *n.m.* hedgehog.

**héritage** /eritaʒ/ *n.m.* inheritance; (*spirituel etc.*) heritage.

**hérit|er** /erite/ *v.t./i.* inherit (**de,** from). **~er de qch.,** inherit sth. **~ier,** **~ière** *n.m., f.* heir, heiress.

**hermétique** /ɛrmetik/ *a.* airtight.

**hermine** /ɛrmin/ *n.f.* ermine.

**hernie** /'ɛrni/ *n.f.* hernia.

**héroïne** /erɔin/ *n.f.* (*femme*) heroine.

**héroï|que** /erɔik/ *a.* heroic. **~sme** *n.m.* heroism.

**héron** /'erɔ̃/ *n.m.* heron.

**héros** /'ero/ *n.m.* hero.

**hésit|er** /ezite/ *v.i.* hesitate (**à,** to). **en ~ant,** hesitantly. **~ant,** **~ante** *a.* hesitant. **~ation** *n.f.* hesitation.

**hétérosexuel,** **~le** /eterɔseksyɛl/ *n.m., f. & a.* heterosexual.

**hêtre** /'ɛtr/ *n.m.* beech.

**heure** /œr/ *n.f.* time; (*mesure de durée*) hour; (*scol.*) period. **quelle ~ est-il?,** what time is it? **il est dix**/*etc.* **~s,** it is ten/*etc.* o'clock. **à l'~,** (*venir, être*) on time. **~ d'affluence,** **~ de pointe,** rush-hour.

**heureusement** /œrøzmɑ̃/ *adv.* fortunately, luckily.

**heureu|x,** **~se** /œrø, -z/ *a.* happy; (*chanceux*) lucky, fortunate.

**heurter** /'œrte/ *v.t.* (*cogner*) hit; (*mur etc.*) bump into, hit. **se ~ à,** bump into, hit.

**hexagone** /ɛgzagɔn/ *n.m.* hexagon. **l'~,** France.

**hibou** (*pl.* **~x**) /'ibu/ *n.m.* owl.

**hier** /jɛr/ *adv.* yesterday. **~ soir,** last night, yesterday evening.

**hiérarch|ie** /jerarʃi/ *n.f.* hierarchy. **~ique** *a.* hierarchical.

**hi-fi** /'ifi/ *a. invar. & n.f.* (*fam.*) hi-fi.

**hindou,** **~e** /ɛ̃du/ *a. & n.m., f.* Hindu.

**hippi|que** /ipik/ *a.* horse, equestrian. **~sme** *n.m.* horse-riding.

**hippodrome** /ipɔdrom/ *n.m.* racecourse.

**hippopotame** /ipɔpɔtam/ *n.m.* hippopotamus.

**hirondelle** /irɔdɛl/ *n.f.* swallow.

**hisser** /'ise/ *v.t.* hoist, haul.

**histoire** /istwar/ *n.f.* (*récit, mensonge*) story; (*étude*) history; (*affaire*) business. **~(s),** (*chichis*) fuss. **~s,** (*ennuis*) trouble.

**historique** /istɔrik/ *a.* historical.

**hiver** /ivɛr/ *n.m.* winter. **~nal** (*m.pl.* **~naux**) *a.* winter; (*glacial*) wintry. **~ner** *v.i.* winter.

**H.L.M.** /'aʃɛlɛm/ *n.m./f.* (= *habitation à loyer modéré*) block of council flats.

**hocher** /'ɔʃe/ *v.t.* **~ la tête,** (*pour dire oui*) nod; (*pour dire non*) shake one's head.

**hochet** /'ɔʃɛ/ *n.m.* rattle.

**hockey** /'ɔkɛ/ *n.m.* hockey.

**hollandais,** **~e** /'ɔlɑ̃dɛ,-z/ *a.* Dutch. ● *n.m., f.* Dutchman, Dutchwoman. ● *n.m.* (*lang.*) Dutch.

**Hollande** /'ɔlɑ̃d/ *n.f.* Holland.

**hologramme** /ɔlɔgram/ *n.m.* hologram.

**homard** /'ɔmar/ *n.m.* lobster.

**homéopathie** /ɔmeopati/ *n.f.* homoeopathy.

**homicide** /ɔmisid/ *n.m.* homicide.

**hommage** /ɔmaʒ/ *n.m.* tribute. **~s,** (*salutations*) respects.

**homme** /ɔm/ *n.m.* man; (*espèce*) man(kind). **~ d'affaires,** businessman.

**homologue** /ɔmɔlɔg/ *n.m./f.* counterpart.

**homologué** /ɔmɔlɔge/ *a.* (*record*) officially recognized; (*tarif*) official.

**homonyme** /ɔmɔnim/ *n.m.* (*personne*) namesake.

**homosex|uel,** **~uelle** /ɔmɔsɛksyɛl/ *a. & n.m., f.* homosexual. **~ualité** *n.f.* homosexuality.

**Hongrie** /'ɔ̃gri/ *n.f.* Hungary.

**hongrois**, **~e** /'ɔ̃grwa, -z/ *a. & n.m.*, *f.* Hungarian.

**honnête** /ɔnɛt/ *a.* honest; (*satisfaisant*) fair. **~ment** *adv.* honestly; fairly. **~té** *n.f.* honesty.

**honneur** /ɔnœr/ *n.m.* honour; (*mérite*) credit. **d'~**, (*invité*, *place*) of honour; (*membre*) honorary. **en l'~ de**, in honour of.

**honorable** /ɔnɔrabl/ *a.* honourable; (*convenable*) respectable.

**honoraire** /ɔnɔrɛr/ *a.* honorary. **~s** *n.m. pl.* fees.

**honorer** /ɔnɔre/ *v.t.* honour; (*faire honneur à*) do credit to.

**hont|e** /'ɔ̃t/ *n.f.* shame. **avoir ~e**, be ashamed (**de**, of). **~eux, ~euse** *a.* (*personne*) ashamed (**de**, of); (*action*) shameful.

**hôpit|al** (*pl.* **~aux**) /ɔpital, -o/ *n.m.* hospital.

**hoquet** /'ɔkɛ/ *n.m.* hiccup. **le ~**, (the) hiccups.

**horaire** /ɔrɛr/ *a.* hourly. ● *n.m.* timetable. **~ flexible**, flexitime.

**horizon** /ɔrizɔ̃/ *n.m.* horizon.

**horizont|al** (*m. pl.* **~aux**) /ɔrizɔ̃tal, -o/ *a.* horizontal.

**horloge** /ɔrlɔʒ/ *n.f.* clock.

**horlog|er**, **~ère** /ɔrlɔʒe, -ɛr/ *n.m.*, *f.* watchmaker.

**hormon|al** (*m. pl.* **~aux**) /ɔrmɔnal, -no/ *a.* hormonal, hormone.

**hormone** /ɔrmɔn/ *n.f.* hormone.

**horoscope** /ɔrɔskɔp/ *n.m.* horoscope.

**horreur** /ɔrœr/ *n.f.* horror. **avoir ~ de**, detest.

**horrible** /ɔribl/ *a.* horrible.

**hors** /'ɔr/ *prép.* **~ de**, out of; (*à l'extérieur de*) outside. **~-bord** *n.m. invar.* speedboat. **~-d'œuvre** *n.m. invar.* hors-d'œuvre. **~ de prix**, exorbitant. **~-taxe** *a. invar.* duty-free.

**hortensia** /ɔrtɑ̃sja/ *n.m.* hydrangea.

**horticulture** /ɔrtikyltyr/ *n.f.* horticulture.

**hospice** /ɔspis/ *n.m.* home.

**hospital|ier**, **~ière**[1] /ɔspitalje, -jɛr/ *a.* hospitable. **~ité** *n.f.* hospitality.

**hospital|ier**, **~ière**[2] /ɔspitalje, -jɛr/ *a.* (*méd.*) hospital.

**hostie** /ɔsti/ *n.f.* (*relig.*) host.

**hostil|e** /ɔstil/ *a.* hostile. **~ité** *n.f.* hostility.

**hôte** /'ot/ *n.m.* (*maître*) host; (*invité*) guest.

**hôtel** /otɛl/ *n.m.* hotel. **~ (particulier)**, (private) mansion. **~ de ville**, town hall. **~ier**, **~ière** /otalje, -jɛr/ *a.* hotel; *n.m.*, *f.* hotelier. **~lerie** *n.f.* hotel business; (*auberge*) country hotel.

**hôtesse** /otɛs/ *n.f.* hostess. **~ de l'air**, air hostess.

**hotte** /'ɔt/ *n.f.* basket; (*de cuisinière*) hood.

**houblon** /'ublɔ̃/ *n.m.* **le ~**, hops.

**houille** /'uj/ *n.f.* coal.

**hourra** /'ura/ *n.m. & int.* hurrah.

**housse** /'us/ *n.f.* dust-cover.

**houx** /'u/ *n.m.* holly.

**hublot** /'yblo/ *n.m.* porthole.

**huer** /'ɥe/ *v.t.* boo. **huées** *n.f. pl.* boos.

**huile** /ɥil/ *n.f.* oil.

**huissier** /ɥisje/ *n.m.* (*appariteur*) usher; (*jurid.*) bailiff.

**huit** /'ɥi(t)/ *a.* eight. ● *n.m.* eight. **~ jours**, a week. **lundi en ~**, a week on Monday. **~ième** /'ɥitjɛm/ *a. & n.m./f.* eighth.

**huître** /ɥitr/ *n.f.* oyster.

**humain**, **~e** /ymɛ̃, ymɛn/ *a.* human; (*compatissant*) humane.

**humanitaire** /ymanitɛr/ *a.* humanitarian.

**humanité** /ymanite/ *n.f.* humanity.

**humble** /œ̃bl/ *a.* humble.

**humeur** /ymœr/ *n.f.* mood; (*tempérament*) temper. **de bonne/mauvaise ~**, in a good/bad mood.

**humid|e** /ymid/ *a.* damp; (*chaleur*, *climat*) humid; (*lèvres*, *yeux*) moist. **~ité** *n.f.* humidity.

**humili|er** /ymilje/ *v.t.* humiliate. **~ation** *n.f.* humiliation.

**humilité** /ymilite/ *n.f.* humility.

**humorist|e** /ymɔrist/ *n.m./f.* humorist. **~ique** *a.* humorous.

**humour** /ymur/ *n.m.* humour; (*sens*) sense of humour.

**hurl|er** /'yrle/ *v.t./i.* howl. **~ement** *n.m.* howl(ing).

**hydratant**, **~e** /idratɑ̃, -t/ *a.* (*lotion*) moisturizing.

**hydrate** /idrat/ *n.m.* **~ de carbone**, carbohydrate.

**hydraulique** /idrolik/ *a.* hydraulic.

**hydravion** /idravjɔ̃/ *n.m.* seaplane.

**hydro-electrique** /idroelɛktrik/ *a.* hydro-electric.

**hydrogène** /idrɔʒɛn/ *n.m.* hydrogen.

**hyène** /jɛn/ *n.f.* hyena.

**hygiène** /iʒjɛn/ *n.f.* hygiene.

**hymne** /imn/ *n.m.* hymn. **~ national**, national anthem.

**hyper-** /ipɛr/ *préf.* hyper-.

**hypermarché** /ipɛrmarʃe/ *n.m.* (*supermarché*) hypermarket.

**hypermétrope** /ipɛrmetrɔp/ *a.* long-sighted.

**hypertension** /ipɛrtɑ̃sjɔ̃/ *n.f.* high blood-pressure.

**hypnose** /ipnoz/ *n.f.* hypnosis.

**hypocrisie** /ipɔkrizi/ *n.f.* hypocrisy.

**hypocrite** /ipɔkrit/ *a.* hypocritical. ● *n.m.*/ *f.* hypocrite.

**hypoth|èque** /ipotɛk/ *n.f.* mortgage. **~équer** *v.t.* mortgage.

**hypoth|èse** /ipotɛz/ *n.f.* hypothesis. **~étique** *a.* hypothetical.

**iceberg** /isbɛrg/ n.m. iceberg.

**ici** /isi/ adv. (espace) here; (temps) now. **d'~ peu**, shortly.

**icône** /ikon/ n.f. icon.

**idé|al** (m. pl. ~aux) /ideal, -o/ a. ideal. ● n.m. (pl. ~aux) ideal.

**idéaliste** /idealist/ a. idealistic. ● n.m./f. idealist.

**idée** /ide/ n.f. idea; (esprit) mind.

**identif|ier** /idɑ̃tifje/ v.t., **s'~ier** v. pr. identify (à, with). ~**ication** n.f. identification.

**identique** /idɑ̃tik/ a. identical.

**identité** /idɑ̃tite/ n.f. identity.

**idéolog|ie** /ideolɔʒi/ n.f. ideology. ~**ique** a. ideological.

**idiom|e** /idjom/ n.m. idiom. ~**atique** /idjɔmatik/ a. idiomatic.

**idiot, ~e** /idjo, idjɔt/ a. idiotic. ● n.m., f. idiot. ~**ie** /idjɔsi/ n.f. idiocy; (acte, parole) idiotic thing.

**idole** /idɔl/ n.f. idol.

**if** /if/ n.m. (arbre) yew.

**igloo** /iglu/ n.m. igloo.

**ignifugé** /iɲifyʒe/ a. fireproof.

**ignoble** /iɲɔbl/ a. vile.

**ignoran|t, ~te** /iɲɔrɑ̃, -t/ a. ignorant. ● n.m., f. ignoramus. ~**ce** n.f. ignorance.

**ignorer** /iɲɔre/ v.t. not know; (personne) ignore.

**il** /il/ pron. he; (chose) it. **il neige/pleut**/etc., it is snowing/raining/etc. **il y a**, there is; (pluriel) there are; (temps) ago; (durée) for. **il y a 2 ans**, 2 years ago. **il y a plus d'une heure que j'attends**, I've been waiting for over an hour.

**île** /il/ n.f. island. ~ **déserte**, desert island. ~ **anglo-normandes**, Channel Islands. ~**s Britanniques**, British Isles.

**illég|al** (m. pl. ~aux) /ilegal, -o/ a. illegal. ~**alité** n.f. illegality.

**illicite** /ilisit/ a. illicit.

**illisible** /ilizibl/ a. illegible; (livre) unreadable.

**illogique** /ilɔʒik/ a. illogical.

**illumin|er** /ilymine/ v.t., **s'~er** v. pr. light up. ~**ation** n.f. illumination. ~**é** a. (monument) floodlit.

**illusion** /ilyzjɔ̃/ n.f. illusion.

**illustre** /ilystr/ a. illustrious.

**illustr|er** /ilystre/ v.t. illustrate. ~**ation** n.f. illustration. ~**é** a. illustrated; n.m. illustrated magazine.

**ils** /il/ pron. they.

**imag|e** /imaʒ/ n.f. picture; (métaphore) image; (reflet) reflection. ~**éa**. full of imagery.

**imaginaire** /imaʒinɛr/ a. imaginary.

**imagin|er** /imaʒine/ v.t. imagine; (inventer) think up. **s'~er** v. pr. imagine (**que**, that). ~**ation** n.f. imagination.

**imbattable** /ɛ̃batabl/ a. unbeatable.

**imbécile** /ɛ̃besil/ a. idiotic. ● n.m./f. idiot.

**imbuvable** /ɛ̃byvabl/ a. undrinkable; (personne: fam.) insufferable.

**imit|er** /imite/ v.t. imitate; (personnage) impersonate; (faire comme) do the same as; (document) copy. ~**ateur, ~atrice** n.m., f. imitator; impersonator. ~**ation** n.f. imitation; impersonation.

**immaculé** /imakyle/ a. spotless.

**immangeable** /ɛ̃mɑ̃ʒabl/ a. inedible.

**immatricul|er** /imatrikyle/ v.t. register. **(se) faire ~er**, register. ~**ation** n.f. registration.

**immature** /imatyr/ a. immature.

**immédiat, ~e** /imedja, -t/ a. immediate. ● n.m. **dans l'~**, for the moment. ~**ement** /-tmɑ̃/ adv. immediately.

**immens|e** /imɑ̃s/ a. immense. ~**ément** adv. immensely.

**immeuble** /imœbl/ n.m. block of flats, building. ~ **(de bureaux)**, (office) building ou block.

**immigr|er** /imigre/ v.i. immigrate. ~**ant, ~ante** a. & n.m., f. immigrant. ~**ation** n.f. immigration. ~**é, ~ée** a. & n.m., f. immigrant.

**imminen|t, ~te** /iminɑ̃, -t/ a. imminent. ~**ce** n.f. imminence.

**immobil|e** /imɔbil/ a. still, motionless. ~**ité** n.f. stillness; (inaction) immobility.

**immobil|ier, ~ière** /imɔbilje, -jɛr/ a. property. **agence ~ière**, estate agent's office **agent ~ier**, estate agent. **l'~ier**, property.

**immobilis|er** /imɔbilize/ v.t. immobilize; (stopper) stop. **s'~er** v. pr. stop. ~**ation** n.f. immobilization.

**immonde** /imɔ̃d/ a. filthy.

**immondices** /imɔ̃dis/ n.f. pl. refuse.

**immor|al** (m. pl. ~aux) /imɔral, -o/ a. immoral. ~**alité** n.f. immorality.

**immort|el, ~elle** /imɔrtɛl/ a. immortal. ~**alité** n.f. immortality.

**immunis|er** /imynize/ v.t. immunize. ~**é contre**, (à l'abri de) immune to.

**immunité** /imynite/ n.f. immunity.

**impact** /ɛ̃pakt/ n.m. impact.

**impair** /ɛ̃pɛr/ a. (numéro) odd.

**impardonnable** /ɛ̃pardɔnabl/ a. unforgivable.

**imparfait, ~e** /ɛ̃parfɛ, -t/ a. & n.m. imperfect.

**impartial** (m. pl. ~iaux) /ɛ̃parsjal, -jo/ a. impartial.

**impasse** /ɛ̃pɑs/ n.f. (rue) dead end; (situation) deadlock.

**impat|ient,** ~**iente** /ɛ̃pasjɑ̃, -t/ a. impatient. ~**iemment** /-jamã/ adv. impatiently. ~**ience** n.f. impatience.

**impatienter** /ɛ̃pasjɑ̃te/ v.t. annoy. **s'**~ v.pr. lose patience (**contre,** with).

**impayé** /ɛ̃peje/ a. unpaid.

**impeccable** /ɛ̃pekabl/ a. impeccable.

**impensable** /ɛ̃pɑ̃sabl/ a. unthinkable.

**impérati|f,** ~**ve** /ɛ̃peratif, -v/ a. imperative. ● n.m. requirement; (gram.) imperative.

**impératrice** /ɛ̃peratris/ n.f. empress.

**imperceptible** /ɛ̃persɛptibl/ a. imperceptible.

**imperfection** /ɛ̃pɛrfɛksjɔ̃/ n.f. imperfection.

**impér|ial** (m. pl. ~**iaux**) /ɛ̃perjal, -jo/ a. imperial. ~**ialisme** n.m. imperialism.

**impériale** /ɛ̃perjal/ n.f. upper deck.

**imperméable** /ɛ̃pɛrmeabl/ a. impervious (**à,** to); (manteau, tissu) waterproof. ● n.m. raincoat.

**impertinen|t,** ~**te** /ɛ̃pɛrtinɑ̃, -t/ a. impertinent. ~**ce** n.f. impertinence.

**imperturbable** /ɛ̃pɛrtyrbabl/ a. unshakeable.

**impitoyable** /ɛ̃pitwajabl/ a. merciless.

**implacable** /ɛ̃plakabl/ a. implacable.

**implant|er** /ɛ̃plɑ̃te/ v.t. establish. **s'**~er v.pr. become established.

**implication** /ɛ̃plikɑsjɔ̃/ n.f. implication.

**impliquer** /ɛ̃plike/ v.t. imply (**que,** that). ~ **dans,** implicate in.

**impoli** /ɛ̃poli/ a. impolite. ~**tesse** n.f. impoliteness; (remarque) impolite remark.

**impopulaire** /ɛ̃pɔpylɛr/ a. unpopular.

**importance** /ɛ̃pɔrtɑ̃s/ n.f. importance; (taille) size; (ampleur) extent. **sans** ~, unimportant.

**important,** ~**e** /ɛ̃pɔrtɑ̃, -t/ a. important; (en quantité) considerable, sizeable, big. ● n.m. **l'**~, the important thing.

**import|er**[1] /ɛ̃pɔrte/ v.t. (comm.) import. ~**ateur,** ~**atrice** n.m., f. importer; a. importing. ~**ation** n.f. import.

**import|er**[2] /ɛ̃pɔrte/ v.i. matter, be important (**à,** to). **n'**~**e où,** anywhere. **n'**~**e qui,** anybody. **n'**~**e quoi,** anything.

**imposant,** ~**e** /ɛ̃pozɑ̃, -t/ a. imposing.

**imposer** /ɛ̃poze/ v.t. impose (**à,** on); (taxer) tax.

**imposition** /ɛ̃pozisjɔ̃/ n.f. taxation.

**impossibilité** /ɛ̃pɔsibilite/ n.f. impossibility. **dans l'**~ **de,** unable to.

**impossible** /ɛ̃pɔsibl/ a. & n.m. impossible. **faire l'**~, do the impossible.

**impost|eur** /ɛ̃pɔstœr/ n.m. impostor. ~**ure** n.f. imposture.

**impôt** /ɛ̃po/ n.m. tax. ~**s,** (contributions) tax(ation), taxes. ~ **sur le revenu,** income tax.

**impraticable** /ɛ̃pratikabl/ a. (route) impassable.

**imprécis,** ~**e** /ɛ̃presi, -z/ a. imprecise. ~**ion** /-zjɔ̃/ n.f. imprecision.

**impression** /ɛ̃presjɔ̃/ n.f. impression; (de livre) printing.

**impressionn|er** /ɛ̃presjone/ v.t. impress. ~**ant,** ~**ante** a. impressive.

**imprévisible** /ɛ̃previzibl/ a. unpredictable.

**imprévoyant,** ~**e** /ɛ̃prevwajɑ̃, -t/ a. improvident.

**imprévu** /ɛ̃prevy/ a. unexpected. ● n.m. unexpected incident.

**imprim|er** /ɛ̃prime/ v.t. print; (marquer) imprint; (transmettre) impart. ~**ante** n.f. (d'un ordinateur) printer. ~**é** a. printed; n.m. (formulaire) printed form. ~**erie** n.f. printing works. ~**eur** n.m. printer.

**improbable** /ɛ̃prɔbabl/ a. unlikely, improbable.

**impropre** /ɛ̃prɔpr/ a. incorrect.

**improvis|er** /ɛ̃prɔvize/ v.t./i. improvise. ~**ation** n.f. improvisation.

**improviste (à l')** /(al)ɛ̃prɔvist/ adv. unexpectedly.

**imprud|ent,** ~**ente** /ɛ̃prydɑ̃, -t/ a. careless. **il est** ~**ent de,** it is unwise to. ~**emment** /-amã/ adv. carelessly. ~**ence** n.f. carelessness; (acte) careless action.

**impuissan|t,** ~**te** /ɛ̃pɥisɑ̃, -t/ a. helpless; (méd.) impotent. ~**t à,** powerless to. ~**ce** n.f. helplessness; (méd.) impotence.

**impulsi|f,** ~**ve** /ɛ̃pylsif, -v/ a. impulsive.

**impunément** /ɛ̃pynemã/ adv. with impunity.

**impur** /ɛ̃pyr/ a. impure. ~**eté** n.f. impurity.

**inabordable** /inabɔrdabl/ a. (prix) prohibitive.

**inacceptable** /inaksɛptabl/ a. unacceptable; (scandaleux) outrageous.

**inaccessible** /inaksesibl/ a. inaccessible.

**inachevé** /inaʃve/ a. unfinished.

**inacti|f,** ~**ve** /inaktif, -v/ a. inactive.

**inaction** /inaksjɔ̃/ n.f. inactivity.

**inadapté,** ~**e** /inadapte/ n.m., f. (psych.) maladjusted person.

**inadmissible** /inadmisibl/ a. unacceptable.

**inaltérable** /inalterabl/ a. stable, that does not deteriorate.

**inanimé** /inanime/ a. (évanoui) unconscious; (mort) lifeless.

**inaperçu** /inapɛrsy/ a. unnoticed.

**inappréciable** /inapresjabl/ a. invaluable.

**inapte** /inapt/ a. unsuited (**à,** to).

**inattendu** /inatɑ̃dy/ a. unexpected.

**inattenti|f,** ~**ve** /inatɑ̃tif, -v/ a. inattentive (**à,** to).

**inattention** /inatɑ̃sjɔ̃/ *n.f.* inattention.

**inaugur|er** /inɔgyre/ *v.t.* inaugurate. ∼a-tion *n.f.* inauguration.

**inaugur|al** (*m. pl.* ∼**aux**) /inɔgyral, -o/ *a.* inaugural.

**incalculable** /ɛ̃kalkylabl/ *a.* incalculable.

**incapable** /ɛ̃kapabl/ *a.* incapable (**de qch.,** of sth.). ∼ **de faire,** unable to do, incapable of doing. ● *n.m./f.* incompetent.

**incapacité** /ɛ̃kapasite/ *n.f.* incapacity. **dans l'** ∼ **de,** unable to.

**incarcérer** /ɛ̃karsere/ *v.t.* incarcerate.

**incarn|er** /ɛ̃karne/ *v.t.* embody. ∼é *a.* (*ongle*) ingrowing.

**incassable** /ɛ̃kɑsabl/ *a.* unbreakable.

**incend|ie** /ɛ̃sɑ̃di/ *n.m.* fire. ∼**ie criminel,** arson. ∼**ier** *v.t.* set fire to.

**incert|ain,** ∼**aine** /ɛ̃sɛrtɛ̃, -ɛn/ *a.* uncertain; (*contour*) vague. ∼**itude** *n.f.* uncertainty.

**incessamment** /ɛ̃sesamɑ̃/ *adv.* shortly.

**incessant,** ∼**e** /ɛ̃sesɑ̃, -t/ *a.* incessant.

**inchangé** /ɛ̃ʃɑ̃ʒe/ *a.* unchanged.

**incidence** /ɛ̃sidɑ̃s/ *n.f.* effect.

**incident** /ɛ̃sidɑ̃/ *n.m.* incident. ∼ **technique,** technical hitch.

**incinér|er** /ɛ̃sinere/ *v.t.* incinerate; (*mort*) cremate. ∼**ateur** *n.m.* incinerator.

**inciser** /ɛ̃size/ *v.t.* (*abcès etc.*) lance.

**incit|er** /ɛ̃site/ *v.t.* incite (**à,** to). ∼**ation** *n.f.* incitement.

**inclinaison** /ɛ̃klinɛzɔ̃/ *n.f.* incline; (*de la tête*) tilt.

**incliner** /ɛ̃kline/ *v.t.* tilt, lean; (*courber*) bend. ∼ **la tête,** (*approuver*) nod; (*révérence*) bow.

**incl|ure** /ɛ̃klyr/ *v.t.* include; (*enfermer*) enclose. **jusqu'au lundi** ∼**us,** up to and including Monday.

**incohéren|t,** ∼**te** /ɛ̃kɔerɑ̃, -t/ *a.* incoherent. ∼**ce** *n.f.* incoherence.

**incollable** /ɛ̃kɔlabl/ *a.* **il est** ∼, he can't be stumped.

**incolore** /ɛ̃kɔlɔr/ *a.* colourless; (*crème, verre*) clear.

**incombustible** /ɛ̃kɔ̃bystibl/ *a.* incombustible.

**incomparable** /ɛ̃kɔ̃parabl/ *a.* incomparable.

**incompatib|le** /ɛ̃kɔ̃patibl/ *a.* incompatible. ∼**ilité** *n.f.* incompatibility.

**incompéten|t,** ∼**te** /ɛ̃kɔ̃petɑ̃, -t/ *a.* incompetent. ∼**ce** *n.f.* incompetence.

**incompl|et,** ∼**ète** /ɛ̃kɔ̃plɛ, -t/ *a.* incomplete.

**incompréhensible** /ɛ̃kɔ̃preɑ̃sibl/ *a.* incomprehensible.

**incompréhension** /ɛ̃kɔ̃preɑ̃sjɔ̃/ *n.f.* lack of understanding.

**inconcevable** /ɛ̃kɔ̃svabl/ *a.* inconceivable.

**inconditionnel,** ∼**le** /ɛ̃kɔ̃disjɔnɛl/ *a.* unconditional.

**inconduite** /ɛ̃kɔ̃dɥit/ *n.f.* loose behaviour.

**inconfort** /ɛ̃kɔ̃fɔr/ *n.m.* discomfort. ∼**able** /-tabl/ *a.* uncomfortable.

**inconnu,** ∼**e** /ɛ̃kɔny/ *a.* unknown (**à,** to). ● *n.m., f.* stranger. ● *n.m.* **l'**∼, the unknown. ● *n.f.* unknown (quantity).

**inconsc|ient,** ∼**iente** /ɛ̃kɔ̃sjɑ̃, -t/ *a.* unconscious (**de,** of); (*fou*) mad. ● *n.m.* (*psych.*) subconscious.

**inconsolable** /ɛ̃kɔ̃sɔlabl/ *a.* inconsolable.

**incontest|able** /ɛ̃kɔ̃tɛstabl/ *a.* indisputable. ∼é *a.* undisputed.

**incontinen|t,** ∼**te** /ɛ̃kɔ̃tinɑ̃, -t/ *a.* incontinent. ∼**ce** *n.f.* incontinence.

**incontrôlable** /ɛ̃kɔ̃trolabl/ *a.* unverifiable.

**inconvenan|t,** ∼**te** /ɛ̃kɔ̃vnɑ̃, -t/ *a.* improper. ∼**ce** *n.f.* impropriety.

**inconvénient** /ɛ̃kɔ̃venjɑ̃/ *n.m.* disadvantage; (*risque*) risk; (*objection*) objection.

**incorpor|er** /ɛ̃kɔrpɔre/ *v.t.* incorporate; (*mil.*) enlist.

**incorrect** /ɛ̃kɔrɛkt/ *a.* (*faux*) incorrect; (*malséant*) improper; (*impoli*) impolite.

**incorrigible** /ɛ̃kɔriʒibl/ *a.* incorrigible.

**increvable** /ɛ̃krəvabl/ *a.* (*fam.*) tireless.

**incriminer** /ɛ̃krimine/ *v.t.* incriminate.

**incroyable** /ɛ̃krwajabl/ *a.* incredible.

**incrust|er** /ɛ̃kryste/ *v.t.* (*décorer*) inlay (**de,** with). **s'**∼**er** (*invité: péj.*) take root. ∼**ation** *n.f.* inlay.

**incubateur** /ɛ̃kybatœr/ *n.m.* incubator.

**inculp|er** /ɛ̃kylpe/ *v.t.* charge (**de,** with). ∼**ation** *n.f.* charge. ∼é, ∼ée *n.m., f.* accused.

**inculquer** /ɛ̃kylke/ *v.t.* instil (**à,** into).

**inculte** /ɛ̃kylt/ *a.* uncultivated; (*personne*) uneducated.

**incurable** /ɛ̃kyrabl/ *a.* incurable.

**Inde** /ɛ̃d/ *n.f.* India.

**indécen|t,** ∼**te** /ɛ̃desɑ̃, -t/ *a.* indecent. ∼**ce** *n.f.* indecency.

**indéchiffrable** /ɛ̃deʃifrabl/ *a.* indecipherable.

**indécis,** ∼**e** /ɛ̃desi, -z/ *a.* indecisive; (*qui n'a pas encore pris de décision*) undecided. ∼**ion** /-izjɔ̃/ *n.f.* indecision.

**indéfini** /ɛ̃defini/ *a.* indefinite; (*vague*) undefined. ∼**ment** *adv.* indefinitely.

**indélébile** /ɛ̃delebil/ *a.* indelible.

**indemne** /ɛ̃dɛmn/ *a.* unharmed.

**indemniser** /ɛ̃dɛmnize/ *v.t.* compensate (**de,** for).

**indemnité** /ɛ̃dɛmnite/ *n.f.* indemnity; (*allocation*) allowance.

**indéniable** /ɛ̃denjabl/ *a.* undeniable.

**indépend|ant, ~ante** /ɛ̃depɑ̃dɑ̃, -t/ *a.* independent. **~amment** *adv.* independently. **~amment de,** apart from. **~ance** *n.f.* independence.

**indescriptible** /ɛ̃dɛskriptibl/ *a.* indescribable.

**indestructible** /ɛ̃dɛstryktibl/ *a.* indestructible.

**indéterminé** /ɛ̃detɛrmine/ *a.* unspecified.

**index** /ɛ̃dɛks/ *n.m.* forefinger; (*liste*) index. **~er** *v.t.* index.

**indicateur** /ɛ̃dikatœr/ *n.m.* (*livre*) guide; (*techn.*) indicator. **~ des chemins de fer,** railway timetable. **~ des rues,** street directory.

**indicatif** /ɛ̃dikatif/ *n.m.* (*radio*) signature tune; (*téléphonique*) dialling code; (*gram.*) indicative.

**indication** /ɛ̃dikasjɔ̃/ *n.f.* indication; (*renseignement*) information; (*directive*) instruction.

**indice** /ɛ̃dis/ *n.m.* sign; (*dans une enquête*) clue; (*des prix*) index; (*de salaire*) rating.

**indien, ~ne** /ɛ̃djɛ̃, -jɛn/ *a. & n.m., f.* Indian.

**indifféremment** /ɛ̃diferamɑ̃/ *adv.* equally.

**indifféren|t, ~te** /ɛ̃diferɑ̃, -t/ *a.* indifferent (à, to). **~ce** *n.f.* indifference.

**indigène** /ɛ̃diʒɛn/ *a. & n.m./f.* native.

**indigest|e** /ɛ̃diʒɛst/ *a.* indigestible. **~ion** *n.f.* indigestion.

**indignation** /ɛ̃diɲasjɔ̃/ *n.f.* indignation.

**indigne** /ɛ̃diɲ/ *a.* unworthy (de, of); (*acte*) vile.

**indigner** /ɛ̃diɲe/ **s'~** *v.pr.* become indignant (de, at).

**indiquer** /ɛ̃dike/ *v.t.* show, indicate; (*renseigner sur*) point out, tell; (*déterminer*) give, state, appoint. **~ du doigt,** point to *ou* out *ou* at.

**indirect** /ɛ̃dirɛkt/ *a.* indirect.

**indiscipliné** /ɛ̃disipline/ *a.* unruly.

**indiscr|et, ~ète** /ɛ̃diskrɛ, -t/ *a.* inquisitive. **~étion** *n.f.* indiscretion; inquisitiveness.

**indiscutable** /ɛ̃diskytabl/ *a.* unquestionable.

**indispensable** /ɛ̃dispɑ̃sabl/ *a.* indispensable.

**individu** /ɛ̃dividy/ *n.m.* individual. **~ualiste** *n.m./f.* individualist.

**individuel, ~le** /ɛ̃dividɥɛl/ *a.* individual; (*opinion*) personal. **chambre ~le,** single room.

**indivisible** /ɛ̃divizibl/ *a.* indivisible.

**indolore** /ɛ̃dɔlɔr/ *a.* painless.

**Indonésie** /ɛ̃dɔnezi/ *n.f.* Indonesia.

**Indonésien, ~ne** /ɛ̃dɔnezjɛ̃, -jɛn/ *a. & n.m., f.* Indonesian.

**indu, ~e** /ɛ̃dy/ *a.* **à une heure ~e,** at some ungodly hour.

**induire** /ɛ̃dɥir/ *v.t.* infer (de, from). **~ en erreur,** mislead.

**indulgen|t, ~te** /ɛ̃dylʒɑ̃, -t/ *a.* indulgent; (*clément*) lenient. **~ce** *n.f.* indulgence; leniency.

**industr|ie** /ɛ̃dystri/ *n.f.* industry. **~ialisé** *a.* industrialized.

**industriel, ~le** /ɛ̃dystrijɛl/ *a.* industrial. ● *n.m.* industrialist. **~lement** *adv.* industrially.

**inébranlable** /inebrɑ̃labl/ *a.* unshakeable.

**inédit, ~e** /inedi, -t/ *a.* unpublished; (*fig.*) original.

**inefficace** /inefikas/ *a.* ineffective.

**inég|al** (*m. pl.* **~aux**) /inegal, -o/ *a.* unequal; (*irrégulier*) uneven. **~alité** *n.f.* (*injustice*) inequality; (*différence*) difference (de, between).

**inéluctable** /inelyktabl/ *a.* inescapable.

**inépuisable** /inepɥizabl/ *a.* inexhaustible.

**inespéré** /inɛspere/ *a.* unhoped for.

**inestimable** /inɛstimabl/ *a.* priceless.

**inévitable** /inevitabl/ *a.* inevitable.

**inexact, ~e** /inɛgza(kt), -akt/ *a.* (*imprécis*) inaccurate; (*incorrect*) incorrect.

**inexcusable** /inɛkskyzabl/ *a.* unforgivable.

**inexistant, ~e** /inɛgzistɑ̃, -t/ *a.* non-existent.

**inexpérience** /inɛksperjɑ̃s/ *n.f.* inexperience.

**inexpli|cable** /inɛksplikabl/ *a.* inexplicable. **~qué** *a.* unexplained.

**infaillible** /ɛ̃fajibl/ *a.* infallible.

**infantile** /ɛ̃fɑ̃til/ *a.* infantile.

**infarctus** /ɛ̃farktys/ *n.m.* coronary (thrombosis).

**infatigable** /ɛ̃fatigabl/ *a.* tireless.

**infect** /ɛ̃fɛkt/ *a.* revolting.

**infect|er** /ɛ̃fɛkte/ *v.t.* infect. **s'~er** *v. pr.* become infected. **~ion** /-ksjɔ̃/ *n.f.* infection.

**infectieu|x, ~se** /ɛ̃fɛksjø, -z/ *a.* infectious.

**inférieur, ~e** /ɛ̃ferjœr/ *a.* (*plus bas*) lower; (*moins bon*) inferior (à, to). ● *n.m., f.* inferior. **~ à,** (*plus petit que*) smaller than.

**infériorité** /ɛ̃ferjorite/ *n.f.* inferiority.

**infern|al** (*m. pl.* **~aux**) /ɛ̃fɛrnal, -o/ *a.* infernal.

**infid|èle** /ɛ̃fidɛl/ *a.* unfaithful. **~élité** *n.f.* unfaithfulness; (*acte*) infidelity.

**infiltr|er (s')** /(s)ɛ̃filtre/ *v.pr.* **s'~er (dans),** (*personnes, idées, etc.*) infiltrate; (*liquide*) percolate. **~ation** *n.f.* infiltration.

**infime** /ɛ̃fim/ *a.* tiny, minute.

**infini** /ɛ̃fini/ *a.* infinite. ● *n.m.* infinity. **à l'~,** endlessly. **~ment** *adv.* infinitely.

**infinité** /ɛ̃finite/ *n.f.* **une ~ de,** an infinite amount of.

**infinitif** /ɛ̃finitif/ *n.m.* infinitive.

**infirm|e** /ɛ̃firm/ a. & n.m./f. disabled (person). ∼ité n.f. disability.

**infirm|erie** /ɛ̃firməri/ n.f. sickbay, infirmary. ∼ier n.m. (male) nurse. ∼ière n.f. nurse.

**inflammable** /ɛ̃flamabl/ a. (in)flammable.

**inflammation** /ɛ̃flamasjɔ̃/ n.f. inflammation.

**inflation** /ɛ̃flɑsjɔ̃/ n.f. inflation.

**influen|ce** /ɛ̃flyɑ̃s/ n.f. influence. ∼çable a. easily influenced. ∼cer v.t. influence.

**influent, ∼e** /ɛ̃flyɑ̃, -t/ a. influential.

**info** /ɛ̃fo/ n.f. (some) news. les ∼s, the news.

**informaticien, ∼ne** /ɛ̃fɔrmatisjɛ̃, -jɛn/ n.m., f. computer scientist.

**information** /ɛ̃fɔrmɑsjɔ̃/ n.f. information; (jurid.) inquiry. une ∼, (some) information; (nouvelle) (some) news. les ∼s, the news.

**informatique** /ɛ̃fɔrmatik/ n.f. computer science; (techniques) data processing.

**informer** /ɛ̃fɔrme/ v.t. inform (de, about, of). s'∼ v. pr. enquire (de, about).

**infraction** /ɛ̃fraksjɔ̃/ n.f. offence. ∼ à, breach of.

**infranchissable** /ɛ̃frɑ̃ʃisabl/ a. impassable; (fig.) insuperable.

**infrarouge** /ɛ̃fraruʒ/ a. infra-red.

**infrastructure** /ɛ̃frastryktyr/ n.f. infrastructure.

**infus|er** /ɛ̃fyze/ v.t./i. infuse, brew. ∼ion n.f. herb-tea, infusion.

**ingénieur** /ɛ̃ʒenjœr/ n.m. engineer.

**ingén|ieux, ∼ieuse** /ɛ̃ʒenjø, -z/ a. ingenious. ∼iosité n.f. ingenuity.

**ingér|er (s')** /(s)ɛ̃ʒere/ v. pr. s'∼er dans, interfere in. ∼ence n.f. interference.

**ingrat, ∼e** /ɛ̃gra, -t/ a. ungrateful; (pénible) thankless; (disgracieux) unattractive. ∼itude /-tityd/ n.f. ingratitude.

**ingrédient** /ɛ̃gredjɑ̃/ n.m. ingredient.

**inhabité** /inabite/ a. uninhabited.

**inhabituel, ∼le** /inabityɛl/ a. unusual.

**inhalation** /inalasjɔ̃/ n.f. inhaling.

**inhospital|ier, ∼ière** /inɔspitalje, -jɛr/ a. inhospitable.

**inhumain, ∼e** /inymɛ̃, -ɛn/ a. inhuman.

**inhum|er** /inyme/ v.t. bury. ∼ation n.f. burial.

**inimaginable** /inimaʒinabl/ a. unimaginable.

**ininterrompu** /inɛ̃terɔ̃py/ a. continuous, uninterrupted.

**initiale** /inisjal/ n.f. initial.

**initialis|er** /inisjalize/ (comput.) format. ∼ation n.f. formatting.

**initiative** /inisjativ/ n.f. initiative.

**initier** /inisje/ v.t. initiate (à, into). s'∼ v. pr. become initiated (à, into).

**inject|er** /ɛ̃ʒɛkte/ v.t. inject. ∼ion /-ksjɔ̃/ n.f. injection.

**injur|e** /ɛ̃ʒyr/ n.f. insult. ∼ier v.t. insult.

**injust|e** /ɛ̃ʒyst/ a. unjust, unfair. ∼ice n.f. injustice.

**innocen|t, ∼te** /inɔsɑ̃, -t/ a. & n.m., f. innocent. ∼ce n.f. innocence.

**innombrable** /inɔ̃brabl/ a. countless.

**inoccupé** /inɔkype/ a. unoccupied.

**inoculer** /inɔkyle/ v.t. inoculate.

**inodore** /inɔdɔr/ a. odourless.

**inoffensi|f, ∼ve** /inɔfɑ̃sif, -v/ a. harmless.

**inond|er** /inɔ̃de/ v.t. flood; (mouiller) soak; (envahir) inundate (de, with). ∼ation n.f. flood; (action) flooding.

**inoubliable** /inublijabl/ a. unforgettable.

**inouï** /inwi/ a. incredible.

**inox** /inɔks/ n.m. (P.) stainless steel.

**inoxydable** /inɔksidabl/ a. **acier ∼,** stainless steel.

**inqu|iet, ∼iète** /ɛ̃kjɛ, -ɛkjɛt/ a. worried. ● n.m., f. worrier.

**inquiét|er** /ɛ̃kjete/ v.t. worry. s'∼er worry (de, about). ∼ant, ∼ante a. worrying.

**inquiétude** /ɛ̃kjetyd/ n.f. anxiety, worry.

**insalubre** /ɛ̃salybr/ a. unhealthy.

**insatiable** /ɛ̃sasjabl/ a. insatiable.

**insatisfaisant, ∼e** /ɛ̃satisfəzɑ̃, -t/ a. unsatisfactory.

**insatisfait, ∼e** /ɛ̃satisfɛ, -t/ a. (mécontent) dissatisfied; (frustré) unfulfilled.

**inscription** /ɛ̃skripsjɔ̃/ n.f. inscription; (immatriculation) enrolment.

**inscrire†** /ɛ̃skrir/ v.t. write (down); (graver, tracer) inscribe; (personne) enrol; (sur une liste) put down. s'∼ v. pr. put one's name down. s'∼ à, (école) enrol at; (club, parti) join; (examen) enter for.

**insecte** /ɛ̃sɛkt/ n.m. insect.

**insecticide** /ɛ̃sɛktisid/ n.m. insecticide.

**insécurité** /ɛ̃sekyrite/ n.f. insecurity.

**insensé** /ɛ̃sɑ̃se/ a. mad.

**insensib|le** /ɛ̃sɑ̃sibl/ a. insensitive (à, to); (graduel) imperceptible.

**inséparable** /ɛ̃separabl/ a. inseparable.

**insérer** /ɛ̃sere/ v.t. insert.

**insigne** /ɛ̃siɲ/ n.m. badge.

**insignifian|t, ∼te** /ɛ̃siɲifjɑ̃, -t/ a. insignificant. ∼ce n.f. insignificance.

**insinuer** /ɛ̃sinɥe/ v.t. insinuate.

**insipide** /ɛ̃sipid/ a. insipid.

**insistan|t, ∼te** /ɛ̃sistɑ̃, -t/ a. insistent. ∼ce n.f. insistence.

**insister** /ɛ̃siste/ v.i. insist (**pour faire,** on doing). ∼ sur, stress.

**insolation** /ɛ̃sɔlɑsjɔ̃/ n.f. (méd.) sunstroke.

**insolen|t, ∼te** /ɛ̃sɔlɑ̃, -t/ a. insolent. ∼ce n.f. insolence.

**insolite** /ɛ̃sɔlit/ a. unusual.

**insomnie** /ɛ̃sɔmni/ n.f. insomnia.

**insonoriser** /ɛ̃sɔnɔrize/ v.t. soundproof.

**insoucian|t,** ~**te** /ɛ̃susjɑ̃, -t/ a. carefree.
~**ce** n.f. unconcern.

**insoutenable** /ɛ̃sutnabl/ a. unbearable;
(argument) untenable.

**inspec|ter** /ɛ̃spɛkte/ v.t. inspect. ~**teur,**
~**trice** n.m., f. inspector. ~**tion** /-ksjɔ̃/ n.f.
inspection.

**inspir|er** /ɛ̃spire/ v.t. inspire. ● v.i. breathe
in. ~**ation** n.f. inspiration; (respiration)
breath.

**instable** /ɛ̃stabl/ a. unstable; (temps)
unsettled; (meuble, équilibre) unsteady.

**install|er** /ɛ̃stale/ v.t. install; (gaz, meuble)
put in; (étagère) put up; (équiper) fit out. **s'**~**er**
v. pr. settle (down); (emménager) settle in.
~**ation** n.f. installation; (de local) fitting out;
(de locataire) settling in. ~**ations** n.f. pl.
(appareils) fittings.

**instant** /ɛ̃stɑ̃/ n.m. moment, instant. **à l'**~,
this instant.

**instantané** /ɛ̃stɑ̃tane/ a. instantaneous;
(café) instant.

**instinct** /ɛ̃stɛ̃/ n.m. instinct. **d'**~, instinctively.

**instincti|f,** ~**ve** /ɛ̃stɛ̃ktif, -v/ a. instinctive.
~**vement** adv. instinctively.

**instit** /ɛ̃stit/ n.m./f. (fam.) teacher.

**instituer** /ɛ̃stitɥe/ v.t. establish.

**institut** /ɛ̃stity/ n.m. institute. ~**de beauté,**
beauty parlour.

**institu|teur,** ~**trice** /ɛ̃stitytœr, -tris/
n.m., f. primary-school teacher.

**institution** /ɛ̃stitysjɔ̃/ n.f. institution;
(école) private school.

**instructi|f,** ~**ve** /ɛ̃stryktif, -v/ a. instruct-
ive.

**instruction** /ɛ̃stryksjɔ̃/ n.f. education;
(document) directive. ~**s,** (ordres, mode
d'emploi) instructions.

**instruire**† /ɛ̃strɥir/ v.t. teach, educate. ~**de,**
inform of. **s'**~ v. pr. educate o.s.

**instruit,** ~**e** /ɛ̃strɥi, -t/ a. educated.

**instrument** /ɛ̃strymɑ̃/ n.m. instrument;
(outil) implement.

**insuffisan|t,** ~**te** /ɛ̃syfizɑ̃, -t/ a. inade-
quate; (en nombre) insufficient. ~**ce** n.f.
inadequacy.

**insulaire** /ɛ̃sylɛr/ a. island. ● n.m./f.
islander.

**insuline** /ɛ̃sylin/ n.f. insulin.

**insult|e** /ɛ̃sylt/ n.f. insult. ~**er** v.t. insult.

**insupportable** /ɛ̃syportabl/ a. unbearable.

**insurmontable** /ɛ̃syrmɔ̃tabl/ a. insurmountable.

**insurrection** /ɛ̃syrɛksjɔ̃/ n.f. insurrection.

**intact** /ɛ̃takt/ a. intact.

**intégr|al** (m. pl. ~**aux**) /ɛ̃tegral, -o/ a.
complete; (édition) unabridged. ~**alement**
adv. in full.

**intègre** /ɛ̃tɛgr/ a. upright.

**intégrer** /ɛ̃tegre/ v.t., **s'**~ v. pr. integrate.

**intégri|ste** /ɛ̃tegrist/ a. fundamentalist.
~**sme** /-sm/ n.m. fundamentalism.

**intégrité** /ɛ̃tegrite/ n.f. integrity.

**intellect** /ɛ̃telɛkt/ n.m. intellect. ~**uel,**
~**uelle** a. & n.m., f. intellectual.

**intelligence** /ɛ̃teliʒɑ̃s/ n.f. intelligence;
(compréhension) understanding; (complicité)
complicity.

**intellig|ent,** ~**ente** /ɛ̃teliʒɑ̃, -t/ a.
intelligent. ~**emment** /-amɑ̃/ adv. intelli-
gently.

**intelligible** /ɛ̃teliʒibl/ a. intelligible.

**intempéries** /ɛ̃tɑ̃peri/ n.f. pl. severe
weather.

**intenable** /ɛ̃tnabl/ a. unbearable; (enfant)
impossible.

**intens|e** /ɛ̃tɑ̃s/ a. intense; (circulation)
heavy. ~**ément** adv. intensely. ~**ité** n.f.
intensity.

**intensi|f,** ~**ve** /ɛ̃tɑ̃sif, -v/ a. intensive.

**intenter** /ɛ̃tɑ̃te/ v.t. ~ **un procès** ou **une
action,** institute proceedings (**à, contre,**
against).

**intention** /ɛ̃tɑ̃sjɔ̃/ n.f. intention (**de faire,** of
doing). **à l'**~ **de qn.,** for s.o. ~**né** /-jone/ a.
**bien/mal** ~**né,** well-/ill-intentioned.

**inter-** /ɛ̃tɛr/ préf. inter-.

**intercaler** /ɛ̃tɛrkale/ v.t. insert.

**intercéder** /ɛ̃tɛrsede/ v.i. intercede (**en
faveur de,** on behalf of).

**intercepter** /ɛ̃tɛrsɛpte/ v.t. intercept.

**interchangeable** /ɛ̃tɛrʃɑ̃ʒabl/ a. interchangeable.

**interdiction** /ɛ̃tɛrdiksjɔ̃/ n.f. ban. ~ **de
fumer,** no smoking.

**interdire**† /ɛ̃tɛrdir/ v.t. forbid; (officiellement) ban, prohibit. ~ **à qn. de faire,** forbid
s.o. to do.

**intéressant,** ~**e** /ɛ̃teresɑ̃, -t/ a. interest-
ing; (avantageux) attractive.

**intéressé,** ~**e** /ɛ̃terese/ a. (en cause)
concerned; (pour profiter) self-interested.
● n.m., f. person concerned.

**intéresser** /ɛ̃terese/ v.t. interest; (concerner) concern. **s'**~ **à,** be interested in.

**intérêt** /ɛ̃terɛ/ n.m. interest; (égoïsme) self-
interest. ~**(s),** (comm.) interest. **vous avez
**~ **à,** it is in your interest to.

**interférence** /ɛ̃tɛrferɑ̃s/ n.f. interference.

**intérieur** /ɛ̃terjœr/ a. inner, inside; (vol,
politique) domestic; (vie, calme) inner. ● n.m.
interior; (de boîte, tiroir) inside. **à l'**~ **(de),**
inside; (fig.) within.

**intérim** /ɛ̃terim/ n.m. interim. **faire de l'**~,
temp. ~**aire** a. temporary, interim.

**interjection** /ɛ̃tɛrʒɛksjɔ̃/ n.f. interjection.

**interlocu|teur,** ~**trice** /ɛ̃tɛrlɔkytœr,
-tris/ n.m., f. **son** ~**teur,** the person one
is speaking to.

**intermédiaire** /ɛ̃tɛrmedjɛr/ a. intermediate. ● n.m./f. intermediary.

**interminable** /ɛ̃tɛrminabl/ a. endless.

**internat** /ɛ̃tɛrna/ n.m. boarding-school.

**internation|al** (m.pl. **~aux**)/ɛ̃tɛrnasjɔnal, -o/ a. international.

**interne** /ɛ̃tɛrn/ a. internal. ● n.m./f. (scol.) boarder.

**interner** /ɛ̃tɛrne/ v.t. (pol.) intern; (méd.) confine.

**interpeller** /ɛ̃tɛrpəle/ v.t. shout to; (apostropher) shout at; (interroger) question.

**interphone** /ɛ̃tɛrfɔn/ n.m. intercom.

**interposer (s')** /(s)ɛ̃tɛrpoze/ v. pr. intervene.

**interprète** /ɛ̃tɛrprɛt/ n.m./f. interpreter; (artiste) performer.

**interprét|er** /ɛ̃tɛrprete/ v.t. interpret; (jouer) play; (chanter) sing. **~ation** n.f. interpretation; (d'artiste) performance.

**interrogati|f, ~ve** /ɛ̃tɛrɔgatif, -v/ a. interrogative.

**interrogatoire** /ɛ̃tɛrɔgatwar/ n.m. interrogation.

**interro|ger** /ɛ̃tɛrɔʒe/ v.t. question; (élève) test. **~gation** n.f. question; (action) questioning; (épreuve) test.

**interr|ompre†** /ɛ̃tɛrɔ̃pr/ v.t. break off, interrupt. **~upteur** n.m. switch. **~uption** n.f. interruption; (arrêt) break.

**intersection** /ɛ̃tɛrsɛksjɔ̃/ n.f. intersection.

**intervalle** /ɛ̃tɛrval/ n.m. space; (temps) interval.

**interven|ir†** /ɛ̃tɛrvənir/ v.i. intervene; (survenir) occur; (méd.) operate. **~tion** /-vɑ̃sjɔ̃/ n.f. intervention; (méd.) operation.

**interview** /ɛ̃tɛrvju/ n.f. interview. **~er** /-ve/ v.t. interview.

**intestin** /ɛ̃tɛstɛ̃/ n.m. intestine.

**intim|e** /ɛ̃tim/ a. intimate; (fête, vie) private; (dîner) quiet. ● n.m./f. intimate friend. **~ement** adv. intimately. **~ité** n.f. intimacy; (vie privée) privacy.

**intolérable** /ɛ̃tɔlerabl/ a. intolerable.

**intoléran|t, ~te** /ɛ̃tɔlerɑ̃, -t/ a. intolerant. **~ce** n.f. intolerance.

**intonation** /ɛ̃tɔnasjɔ̃/ n.f. intonation.

**intoxi|quer** /ɛ̃tɔksike/ v.t. poison. **~cation** n.f. poisoning.

**intraduisible** /ɛ̃tradɥizibl/ a. untranslatable.

**intransigean|t, ~te** /ɛ̃trɑ̃sizɑ̃, -t/ a. intransigent. **~ce** n.f. intransigence.

**intransiti|f, ~ve** /ɛ̃trɑ̃zitif, -v/ a. intransitive.

**intraveineu|x, ~se** /ɛ̃travenø, -z/ a. intravenous.

**intrigu|e** /ɛ̃trig/ n.f. intrigue; (théâtre) plot. **~er** v.t./i. intrigue.

**introduction** /ɛ̃trɔdyksjɔ̃/ n.f. introduction.

**introduire†** /ɛ̃trɔdɥir/ v.t. introduce, bring in; (insérer) put in, insert. **~ qn.**, show s.o. in. **s'~ dans**, get into, enter.

**introuvable** /ɛ̃truvabl/ a. that cannot be found.

**intrus, ~e** /ɛ̃try, -z/ n.m., f. intruder. **~ion** /-zjɔ̃/ n.f. intrusion.

**intuition** /ɛ̃tɥisjɔ̃/ n.f. intuition.

**inusable** /inyzabl/ a. hard-wearing.

**inutil|e** /inytil/ a. useless; (vain) needless. **~ement** adv. needlessly. **~ité** n.f. uselessness.

**inutilisable** /inytilizabl/ a. unusable.

**invalide** /ɛ̃valid/ a. & n.m./f. disabled (person).

**invariable** /ɛ̃varjabl/ a. invariable.

**invasion** /ɛ̃vazjɔ̃/ n.f. invasion.

**inventaire** /ɛ̃vɑ̃tɛr/ n.m. inventory. **faire l'~ de**, take stock of.

**invent|er** /ɛ̃vɑ̃te/ v.t. invent. **~eur** n.m. inventor. **~ion** /ɛ̃vɑ̃sjɔ̃/ n.f. invention.

**inverse** /ɛ̃vɛrs/ a. opposite; (ordre) reverse. ● n.m. reverse. **~ment** /-əmɑ̃/ adv. conversely.

**invers|er** /ɛ̃vɛrse/ v.t. reverse, invert. **~ion** n.f. inversion.

**invest|ir** /ɛ̃vɛstir/ v.t. invest. **~issement** n.m. (comm.) investment.

**investiture** /ɛ̃vɛstityr/ n.f. nomination.

**invincible** /ɛ̃vɛ̃sibl/ a. invincible.

**invisible** /ɛ̃vizibl/ a. invisible.

**invit|er** /ɛ̃vite/ v.t. invite (à, to). **~ation** n.f. invitation. **~é, ~ée** n.m., f. guest.

**involontaire** /ɛ̃vɔlɔ̃tɛr/ a. involuntary.

**invraisembl|able** /ɛ̃vrɛsɑ̃blabl/ a. improbable; (incroyable) incredible.

**iode** /jɔd/ n.m. iodine.

**ion** /jɔ̃/ n.m. ion.

**ira, irait** /ira, irɛ/ voir aller¹.

**Irak** /irak/ n.m. Iraq. **~ien, ~ienne** a. & n. m., f. Iraqi.

**Iran** /irɑ̃/ n.m. Iran. **~ien, ~ienne** /iranjɛ̃, -jɛn/ a. & n.m., f. Iranian.

**iris** /iris/ n.m. iris.

**irlandais, ~e** /irlɑ̃dɛ, -z/ a. Irish. ● n.m., f. Irishman, Irishwoman.

**Irlande** /irlɑ̃d/ n.f. Ireland.

**iron|ie** /irɔni/ n.f. irony. **~ique** a. ironic(al).

**irrationnel, ~le** /irasjɔnɛl/ a. irrational.

**irréalisable** /irealizabl/ a. (projet) unworkable.

**irrégul|ier, ~ière** /iregylje, -jɛr/ a. irregular. **~arité** n.f. irregularity.

**irremplaçable** /irɑ̃plasabl/ a. irreplaceable.

**irréparable** /ireparabl/ a. beyond repair.

**irréprochable** /ireprɔʃabl/ a. flawless.

**irrésistible** /irezistibl/ a. irresistible; (*drôle*) hilarious.

**irrespirable** /irɛspirabl/ a. stifling.

**irresponsable** /irɛspɔ̃sabl/ a. irresponsible.

**irréversible** /irevɛrsibl/ a. irreversible.

**irrigation** /irigɑsjɔ̃/ n.f. irrigation.

**irriguer** /irige/ v.t. irrigate.

**irrit|er** /irite/ v.t. irritate. **s'~er de**, be annoyed at. **~able** a. irritable. **~ation** n.f. irritation.

**Islam** /islam/ n.m. Islam.

**islamique** /islamik/ a. Islamic.

**islandais, ~e** /islɑ̃dɛ, -z/ a. Icelandic. ● n.m., f. Icelander. ● n.m. (*lang.*) Icelandic.

**Islande** /islɑ̃d/ n.f. Iceland.

**isolé** /izɔle/ a. isolated.

**isol|er** /izɔle/ v.t. isolate; (*électr.*) insulate. **s'~er** v. pr. isolate o.s. **~ant** n.m. insulating material. **~ation** n.f. insulation. **~ement** n.m. isolation.

**isotope** /izɔtɔp/ n.m. isotope.

**Israël** /israɛl/ n.m. Israel.

**israélien, ~ne** /israeljɛ̃, -jɛn/ a. & n.m., f. Israeli.

**israélite** /israelit/ a. Jewish. ● n.m./f. Jew, Jewess.

**issue** /isy/ n.f. exit; (*résultat*) outcome; (*fig.*) solution. **rue** *ou* **voie sans ~**, dead end.

**Italie** /itali/ n.f. Italy.

**italien, ~ne** /italjɛ̃, -jɛn/ a. & n.m., f. Italian. ● n.m. (*lang.*) Italian.

**italique** /italik/ n.m. italics.

**itinéraire** /itinerɛr/ n.m. itinerary, route.

**I.U.T.** /iyte/ n.m. (*abrév.*) polytechnic.

**I.V.G.** /iveʒe/ n.f. (*abrév.*) abortion.

**ivoire** /ivwar/ n.m. ivory.

**ivr|e** /ivr/ a. drunk. **~esse** n.f. drunkenness. **~ogne** n.m. drunk(ard).

---

# Jj

---

**j'** /ʒ/ *voir* je.

**jacinthe** /ʒasɛ̃t/ n.f. hyacinth.

**jade** /ʒad/ n.m. jade.

**jaillir** /ʒajir/ v.i. (*liquide*) spurt (out); (*lumière*) stream out; (*apparaître, fuser*) burst forth.

**jalou|x, ~se** /ʒalu, -z/ a. jealous. **~sie** n.f. jealousy.

**jamais** /ʒamɛ/ adv. ever. **(ne) ~**, never.

**jambe** /ʒɑ̃b/ n.f. leg.

**jambon** /ʒɑ̃bɔ̃/ n.m. ham.

**jante** /ʒɑ̃t/ n.f. rim.

**janvier** /ʒɑ̃vje/ n.m. January.

**Japon** /ʒapɔ̃/ n.m. Japan.

**japonais, ~e** /japɔnɛ, -z/ a. & n.m., f. Japanese. ● n.m. (*lang.*) Japanese.

**jaquette** /ʒakɛt/ n.f. (*de livre, femme*) jacket; (*d'homme*) morning coat.

**jardin** /ʒardɛ̃/ n.m. garden. **~ d'enfants**, nursery (school). **~ public**, public park.

**jardin|er** /ʒardine/ v.i. garden. **~age** n.m. gardening. **~ier, ~ière** n.m., f. gardener; n.f. (*meuble*) plant-stand. **~ière de légumes**, mixed vegetables.

**jarret** /ʒarɛ/ n.m. back of the knee.

**jasmin** /ʒasmɛ̃/ n.m. jasmine.

**jatte** /ʒat/ n.f. bowl.

**jauge** /ʒoʒ/ n.f. gauge.

**jaun|e** /ʒon/ a. & n.m. yellow; (*péj.*) scab. **~e d'œuf**, (egg) yolk. **~ir** v.t./i. turn yellow.

**jaunisse** /ʒonis/ n.f. jaundice.

**javelot** /ʒavlo/ n.m. javelin.

**jazz** /dʒaz/ n.m. jazz.

**J.C.** /ʒezykri/ n.m. (*abrév.*) **500 avant/après ~**, 500 B.C./A.D.

**je, j'** * /ʒə, ʒ/ pron. I.

**jean** /dʒin/ n.m. jeans.

**jeep** /(d)ʒip/ n.f. jeep.

**jerrycan** /(d)ʒerikan/ n.m. jerrycan.

**jersey** /ʒɛrze/ n.m. jersey.

**Jersey** /ʒɛrze/ n.f. Jersey.

**Jésus** /ʒezy/ n.m. Jesus.

**jet¹** /ʒɛ/ n.m. throw; (*de liquide, vapeur*) jet. **~ d'eau**, fountain.

**jet²** /dʒɛt/ n.m. (*avion*) jet.

**jetable** /ʒətabl/ a. disposable.

**jetée** /ʒte/ n.f. pier.

**jeter** /ʒte/ v.t. throw; (*au rebut*) throw away; (*regard, ancre, lumière*) cast; (*cri*) utter; (*bases*) lay. **~ un coup d'œil**, have *ou* take a look (**à**, at). **se ~ contre**, (*heurter*) bash into. **se ~ sur**, (*se ruer sur*) rush at.

**jeu** (*pl.* **~x**) /ʒø/ n.m. game; (*amusement*) play; (*au casino etc.*) gambling; (*théâtre*) acting; (*série*) set; (*de lumière, ressort*) play. **~ de cartes**, (*paquet*) pack of cards. **~ d'échecs**, (*boîte*) chess set.

**jeudi** /ʒødi/ n.m. Thursday.

**jeun (à)** /(a)ʒœ̃/ adv. **être/rester à ~**, be/stay without food.

**jeune** /ʒœn/ a. young. ● n.m./f. young person. **~ fille**, girl. **~s mariés**, newlyweds. **les ~s**, young people.

**jeunesse** /ʒœnɛs/ n.f. youth; (*apparence*) youthfulness. **la ~**, (*jeunes*) the young.

**joaill|ier, ~ière** /ʒɔaje, -jɛr/ n.m., f. jeweller.

**job** /dʒɔb/ n.m. (*fam.*) job.

**jockey** /ʒɔkɛ/ n.m. jockey.

**joie** /ʒwa/ n.f. joy.

**joindre**† /ʒwɛ̃dr/ *v.t.* join (**à**, to); (*contacter*) contact; (*dans une enveloppe*) enclose.

**joint, ∼e** /ʒwɛ̃, -t/ *a.* (*efforts*) joint; (*pieds*) together. ● *n.m.* joint; (*ligne*) join; (*de robinet*) washer.

**joker** /ʒɔkɛr/ *n.m.* (*carte*) joker.

**joli** /ʒɔli/ *a.* pretty, nice; (*somme, profit*) nice. **c'est du ∼!**, (*ironique*) charming!

**jonc** /ʒɔ̃/ *n.m.* (bul)rush.

**jonction** /ʒɔ̃ksjɔ̃/ *n.f.* junction.

**jongl|er** /ʒɔ̃gle/ *v.i.* juggle. **∼eur, ∼euse** *n.m., f.* juggler.

**jonquille** /ʒɔ̃kij/ *n.f.* daffodil.

**Jordanie** /ʒɔrdani/ *n.f.* Jordan.

**joue** /ʒu/ *n.f.* cheek.

**jou|er** /ʒwe/ *v.t./i.* play; (*théâtre*) act; (*au casino etc.*) gamble. **∼er à**, play. **∼er la comédie**, put on an act. **bien ∼él**, well done!

**jouet** /ʒwɛ/ *n.m.* toy.

**joueu|r, ∼se** /ʒwœr, -øz/ *n.m., f.* player; (*parieur*) gambler.

**joufflu** /ʒufly/ *a.* chubby-cheeked; (*visage*) chubby.

**jouir** /ʒwir/ *v.i.* (*sexe*) come.

**joujou** (*pl.* ∼x) /ʒuʒu/ *n.m.* (*fam.*) toy.

**jour** /ʒur/ *n.m.* day; (*opposé à nuit* die (time); (*lumière*) daylight. **de nos ∼s**, nowadays. **du ∼ au lendemain**, overnight. **il fait ∼**, it is (day)light. **∼ chômé** *ou* **férié**, public holiday. **∼ de fête**, holiday. **∼ ouvrable**, **∼ de travail**, working day.

**journ|al** (*pl.* ∼aux) /ʒurnal, -o/ *n.m.* (news)paper; (*spécialisé*) journal; (*intime*) diary; (*radio*) news. **∼al de bord**, log-book.

**journalis|te** /ʒurnalist/ *n.m./f.* journalist. **∼me** *n.m.* journalism.

**journée** /ʒurne/ *n.f.* day.

**joyeu|x, ∼se** /ʒwajø, -z/ *a.* merry, joyful. **∼x anniversaire**, happy birthday.

**judiciaire** /ʒydisjɛr/ *a.* judicial.

**judicieu|x, ∼se** /ʒydisjø, -z/ *a.* judicious.

**judo** /ʒydo/ *n.m.* judo.

**juge** /ʒyʒ/ *n.m.* judge; (*arbitre*) referee. **∼ de paix**, Justice of the Peace. **∼ de touche**, linesman.

**jugement** /ʒyʒmɑ̃/ *n.m.* judgement; (*criminel*) sentence.

**juger** /ʒyʒe/ *v.t./i.* judge; (*estimer*) consider (**que**, that). **∼ de**, judge.

**jui|f, ∼ve** /ʒyif, -v/ *a.* Jewish. ● *n.m., f.* Jew, Jewess.

**juillet** /ʒyijɛ/ *n.m.* July.

**juin** /ʒɥɛ̃/ *n.m.* June.

**jules** /ʒyl/ *n.m.* (*fam.*) guy.

**jum|eau, ∼elle** (*m. pl.* ∼eaux) /ʒymo, -ɛl/ *a. & n.m., f.* twin. **∼elage** *n.m.* twinning. **∼eler** *v.t.* (*villes*) twin.

**jumelles** /ʒymɛl/ *n.f. pl.* binoculars.

**jument** /ʒymɑ̃/ *n.f.* mare.

**jungle** /ʒœ̃gl/ *n.f.* jungle.

**junior** /ʒynjɔr/ *n.m./f. & a.* junior.

**jupe** /ʒyp/ *n.f.* skirt.

**jupon** /ʒypɔ̃/ *n.m.* slip, petticoat.

**juré, ∼e** /ʒyre/ *n.m., f.* juror.

**jurer** /ʒyre/ *v.t.* swear (**que**, that). ● *v.i.* (*pester*) swear.

**juridiction** /ʒyridiksjɔ̃/ *n.f.* jurisdiction; (*tribunal*) court of law.

**juridique** /ʒyridik/ *a.* legal.

**juriste** /ʒyrist/ *n.m./f.* legal expert.

**juron** /ʒyrɔ̃/ *n.m.* swear-word.

**jury** /ʒyri/ *n.m.* jury.

**jus** /ʒy/ *n.m.* juice; (*de viande*) gravy. **∼ de fruit**, fruit juice.

**jusque** /ʒysk(ə)/ *prép.* **jusqu'à**, (up) to, as far as; (*temps*) until, till; (*limite*) up to; (*y compris*) even. **jusqu'à ce que**, until. **jusqu'à présent**, until now. **jusqu'en**, until. **jusqu'ou?**, how far?

**juste** /ʒyst/ *a.* fair, just; (*légitime*) just; (*correct, exact*) right; (*vrai*) true; (*vêtement*) tight; (*quantité*) on the short side. **le ∼ milieu**, the happy medium. ● *adv.* rightly, correctly; (*chanter*) in tune; (*seulement, exactement*) just. **(un peu) ∼**, (*calculer, mesurer*) a bit fine *ou* close.

**justement** /ʒystəmɑ̃/ *adv.* just; (*avec justice ou justesse*) justly.

**justice** /ʒystis/ *n.f.* justice; (*autorités*) law; (*tribunal*) court.

**justif|ier** /ʒystifje/ *v.t.* justify. ● *v.i.* **∼ier de**, prove. **se ∼ier** *v. pr.* justify o.s.

**juteu|x, ∼se** /ʒytø, -z/ *a.* juicy.

**kaki** /kaki/ *a. invar. & n.m.* khaki.

**kangourou** /kɑ̃guru/ *n.m.* kangaroo.

**karaté** /karate/ *n.m.* karate.

**kascher** /kaʃɛr/ *a. invar.* kosher.

**képi** /kepi/ *n.m.* kepi.

**kermesse** /kɛrmɛs/ *n.f.* fair; (*de charité*) fête.

**kérosène** /kerozɛn/ *n.m.* kerosene, aviation fuel.

**kidnapper** /kidnape/ *v.t.* kidnap.

**kilo** /kilo/ *n.m.* kilo.

**kilogramme** /kilɔgram/ *n.m.* kilogram.

**kilohertz** /kilɔɛrts/ *n.m.* kilohertz.

**kilom|ètre** /kilɔmɛtr/ *n.m.* kilometre. **∼étrage** *n.m.* (*approx.*) mileage.

**kilowatt** /kilɔwat/ *n.m.* kilowatt.

**kinésithérapie** /kineziterapi/ *n.f.* physiotherapy.

**kiosque** /kjɔsk/ *n.m.* kiosk. ~ **à musique,** bandstand.

**kit** /kit/ *n.m.* **meubles en ~,** flat-pack furniture.

**kiwi** /kiwi/ *n.m.* kiwi (*fruit, bird*).

**klaxon** /klaksɔn/ *n.m.* (P.) (*auto.*) horn. ~**ner** /-e/ *v.i.* sound one's horn.

**ko** /kao/ *n.m.* (*comput.*) k.

**K.O.** /kao/ *a. invar.* (knocked) out.

**kyste** /kist/ *n.m.* cyst.

**l', la** /l, la/ *voir* **le.**

**là** /la/ *adv.* there; (*ici*) here; (*chez soi*) in; (*temps*) then. **c'est là que,** this is where. **là où,** where. **là-bas** *adv.* over there. **là-dedans** *adv.* inside, in there. **là-dessous** *adv.* underneath, under there. **là-dessus** *adv.* on there. **là-haut** *adv.* up there; (*à l'étage*) upstairs.

**-là** /la/ *adv.* (*après un nom précédé de ce, cette, etc.*) **cet homme-là,** that man. **ces maisons-là,** those houses.

**laboratoire** /laboratwar/ *n.m.* laboratory.

**labour** /labur/ *n.m.* ploughing. ~**er** *v.t./i.* plough.

**labyrinthe** /labirɛ̃t/ *n.m.* maze.

**lac** /lak/ *n.m.* lake.

**lacer** /lase/ *v.t.* lace up.

**lacérer** /lasere/ *v.t.* tear (up).

**lacet** /lasɛ/ *n.m.* (shoe-)lace; (*de route*) sharp bend, zigzag.

**lâche** /laʃ/ *a.* cowardly; (*détendu*) loose. ● *n.m./f.* coward.

**lâcher** /laʃe/ *v.t.* let go of; (*abandonner*) give up; (*laisser*) leave; (*libérer*) release; (*parole*) utter; (*desserrer*) loosen. ● *v.i.* give way. ~ **prise,** let go.

**lâcheté** /laʃte/ *n.f.* cowardice.

**lacrymogène** /lakrimɔʒɛn/ *a.* **gaz ~,** tear gas. **grenade ~,** tear gas grenade.

**lacté** /lakte/ *a.* milk.

**laid,** ~**e** /lɛ, lɛd/ *a.* ugly; (*action*) vile. ~**eur** /lɛdœr/ *n.f.* ugliness.

**lain|e** /lɛn/ *n.f.* wool. **de ~e,** woollen. ~**age** *n.m.* woollen garment.

**laïque** /laik/ *a.* secular; (*habit, personne*) lay.

**laisse** /lɛs/ *n.f.* lead, leash.

**laisser** /lese/ *v.t.* leave. ~ **qn. faire,** let s.o. do. ~ **qch. à qn.,** let s.o. have sth., leave s.o. sth. ~ **tomber,** drop. **laissez-passer** *n.m. invar.* pass.

**lait** /lɛ/ *n.m.* milk. ~**age** /lɛtaʒ/ *n.m.* milk product.

**lait|ier,** ~**ière** /letje, letjɛr/ *a.* dairy. ● *n.m.* (*livreur*) milkman. ~**erie** /lɛtri/ *n.f.* dairy.

**laiton** /lɛtɔ̃/ *n.m.* brass.

**laitue** /lety/ *n.f.* lettuce.

**lama** /lama/ *n.m.* llama.

**lambeau** (*pl.* ~**x**) /lãbo/ *n.m.* shred. **en ~x,** in shreds.

**lambris** /lãbri/ *n.m.* panelling.

**lame** /lam/ *n.f.* blade; (*lamelle*) strip; (*vague*) wave.

**lamelle** /lamɛl/ *n.f.* (thin) strip.

**lamentable** /lamãtabl/ *a.* deplorable.

**lamenter (se)** /(sə)lamãte/ *v. pr.* moan.

**lampadaire** /lãpadɛr/ *n.m.* standard lamp; (*de rue*) street lamp.

**lampe** /lãp/ *n.f.* lamp. ~ **(de poche),** torch. ~ **de chevet,** bedside lamp.

**lance** /lãs/ *n.f.* spear; (*de tournoi*) lance; (*tuyau*) hose. ~ **d'incendie,** fire hose.

**lanc|er** /lãse/ *v.t.* throw; (*avec force*) hurl; (*navire, idée, personne*) launch. **se ~er dans,** launch into. ● *n.m.* throw; (*action*) throwing. ~**ement** *n.m.* throwing; (*de navire*) launching.

**landau** /lãdo/ *n.m.* pram; (*Amer.*) baby carriage.

**lande** /lãd/ *n.f.* heath, moor.

**langage** /lãgaʒ/ *n.m.* language.

**langoust|e** /lãgust/ *n.f.* (spiny) lobster. ~**ine** *n.f.* (Norway) lobster.

**langue** /lãg/ *n.f.* tongue; (*idiome*) language. **de ~ anglaise/française,** English-/French-speaking. ~ **maternelle,** mother tongue.

**languette** /lãgɛt/ *n.f.* tongue.

**lanière** /lanjɛr/ *n.f.* strap.

**lanterne** /lãtɛrn/ *n.f.* lantern; (*électrique*) lamp.

**laper** /lape/ *v.t./i.* lap.

**lapin** /lapɛ̃/ *n.m.* rabbit. **poser un ~ à qn.,** stand s.o. up.

**laqu|e** /lak/ *n.f.* lacquer. ~**er** *v.t.* lacquer.

**laquelle** /lakɛl/ *voir* **lequel.**

**lard** /lar/ *n.m.* (pig's) fat; (*viande*) bacon.

**large** /larʒ/ *a.* wide, broad; (*grand*) large; (*non borné*) broad; (*généreux*) generous. ● *n.m.* **de ~,** (*mesure*) wide. **au ~ de,** (*en face de: naut.*) off. ~ **d'esprit,** broad-minded. ~**ment** /-əmã/ *adv.* widely; (*ouvrir*) wide; (*amplement*) amply; (*généreusement*) generously; (*au moins*) easily.

**largeur** /larʒœr/ *n.f.* width, breadth; (*fig.*) breadth.

**larguer** /large/ *v.t.* drop. ~ **les amarres,** cast off.

**larme** /larm/ *n.f.* tear.

**larve** /larv/ *n.f.* larva.

**laryngite** /larɛ̃ʒit/ *n.f.* laryngitis.

**larynx** /larɛ̃ks/ *n.m.* larynx.

**las,** ~**se** /la, las/ *a.* weary.

**lasagnes** /lazaɲ/ *n.f. pl.* lasagne.

**laser** /lazɛr/ *n.m.* laser.

**lasse** /lɑs/ *voir* **las.**

**lasser** /lɑse/ *v.t.* weary. **se ~** *v. pr.* weary (**de,** of).

**lassitude** /lɑsityd/ *n.f.* weariness.

**latent, ~e** /latɑ̃, -t/ *a.* latent.

**latér|al** (*m. pl.* **~aux**) /lateral, -o/ *a.* lateral.

**latex** /latɛks/ *n.m.* latex.

**latin, ~e** /latɛ̃, -in/ *a. & n.m., f.* Latin. ● *n.m.* (*lang.*) Latin.

**latitude** /latityd/ *n.f.* latitude.

**latte** /lat/ *n.f.* lath; (*de plancher*) board.

**lauréat, ~e** /lɔrea, -t/ *a.* prize-winning. ● *n.m., f.* prize-winner.

**laurier** /lɔrje/ *n.m.* laurel; (*culin.*) bay-leaves.

**lavable** /lavabl/ *a.* washable.

**lavabo** /lavabo/ *n.m.* wash-basin. **~s,** toilet(s).

**lavage** /lavaʒ/ *n.m.* washing. **~ de cerveau,** brainwashing.

**lavande** /lavɑ̃d/ *n.f.* lavender.

**lave** /lav/ *n.f.* lava.

**lav|er** /lave/ *v.t.* wash; (*injure etc.*) avenge. **se ~er** *v. pr.* wash (o.s.). **~e-vaisselle** *n.m. invar.* dishwasher.

**laverie** /lavri/ *n.f.* **~ (automatique),** launderette.

**laxati|f, ~ve** /laksatif, -v/ *a. & n.m.* laxative.

**layette** /lɛjɛt/ *n.f.* baby clothes.

**le** *ou* **l'*, **la** *ou* **l'*** (*pl.* **les**) /lə, l, la, le/ *article* the; (*mesure*) a, per. ● *pron.* (*homme*) him; (*femme*) her; (*chose, animal*) it. **les** *pron.* them. **aimer le thé/la France,** like tea/France. **le matin,** in the morning. **il sort le mardi,** he goes out on Tuesdays. **levez le bras,** raise your arm.

**lécher** /leʃe/ *v.t.* lick.

**lèche-vitrines** /lɛʃvitrin/ *n.m.* **faire du ~,** go window-shopping.

**leçon** /ləsɔ̃/ *n.f.* lesson.

**lec|teur, ~trice** /lɛktœr, -tris/ *n.m., f.* reader; (*univ.*) foreign language assistant. **~teur de cassettes,** cassette player. **~teur de disquettes,** (disk) drive.

**lecture** /lɛktyr/ *n.f.* reading.

**lég|al** (*m. pl.* **~aux**) /legal, -o/ *a.* legal. **~alement** *adv.* legally. **~aliser** *v.t.* legalize. **~alité** *n.f.* legality; (*loi*) law.

**légende** /leʒɑ̃d/ *n.f.* legend.

**lég|er, ~ère** /leʒe, -ɛr/ *a.* light; (*bruit, faute, maladie*) slight; (*café, argument*) weak. **~èrement** /-ɛrmɑ̃/ *adv.* lightly; (*un peu*) slightly. **~èreté** /-ɛrte/ *n.f.* lightness; thoughtlessness.

**législati|f, ~ve** /leʒislatif, -v/ *a.* legislative.

**législation** /leʒislasjɔ̃/ *n.f.* legislation.

**législature** /leʒislatyr/ *n.f.* term of office.

**légitim|e** /leʒitim/ *a.* legitimate. **en état de ~e défense,** acting in self-defence. **~ité** *n.f.* legitimacy.

**léguer** /lege/ *v.t.* bequeath.

**légume** /legym/ *n.m.* vegetable.

**lendemain** /lɑ̃dmɛ̃/ *n.m.* **le ~,** the next day, the day after; (*fig.*) the future. **le ~ de,** the day after. **le ~ matin/soir,** the next morning/evening.

**lent, ~e** /lɑ̃, lɑ̃t/ *a.* slow. **~ement** /lɑ̃tmɑ̃/ *adv.* slowly. **~eur** /lɑ̃tœr/ *n.f.* slowness.

**lentille**[1] /lɑ̃tij/ *n.f.* (*plante*) lentil.

**lentille**[2] /lɑ̃tij/ *n.f.* (*verre*) lens; **~s de contact,** (contact) lenses.

**léopard** /leɔpar/ *n.m.* leopard.

**lequel, laquelle** (*pl.* **lequel(le)s**) /ləkɛl, lakɛl, lekɛl/ *pron.* (*à* + *lequel* = *auquel*, *à* + *lesquel(le)s* = *auxquel(le)s*; *de* + *lequel* = *duquel*, *de* + *lesquel(le)s* = *desquel(le)s*) which; (*interrogatif*) which (one); (*personne*) who; (*complément indirect*) whom.

**les** /le/ *voir* **le.**

**lésiner** /lezine/ *v.i.* **ne pas ~ sur,** not stint on.

**lésion** /lezjɔ̃/ *n.f.* lesion.

**lesquels, lesquelles** /lekɛl/ *voir* **lequel.**

**lessive** /lesiv/ *n.f.* washing-powder; (*linge, action*) washing.

**lettre** /lɛtr/ *n.f.* letter. **~ exprès,** express letter. **les ~s,** (*univ.*) (the) arts.

**leucémie** /løsemi/ *n.f.* leukaemia.

**leur** /lœr/ *a.* (*f. invar.*) their. ● *pron.* (to) them. **le ~, la ~, les ~s,** theirs.

**levain** /ləvɛ̃/ *n.m.* leaven.

**levé** /ləve/ *a.* (*debout*) up.

**levée** /ləve/ *n.f.* (*de courrier*) collection.

**lever** /ləve/ *v.t.* lift (up), raise; (*interdiction*) lift; (*séance*) close; (*armée, impôts*) levy. ● *v.i.* (*pâte*) rise. **se ~** *v. pr.* get up; (*soleil, rideau*) rise; (*jour*) break. ● *n.m.,* **~ du rideau,** (*théâtre*) curtain (up). **~ du soleil,** sunrise.

**levier** /ləvje/ *n.m.* lever.

**lèvre** /lɛvr/ *n.f.* lip.

**lévrier** /levrije/ *n.m.* greyhound.

**levure** /ləvyr/ *n.f.* yeast. **~ alsacienne** *ou* **chimique,** baking powder.

**lexicographie** /lɛksikɔgrafi/ *n.f.* lexicography.

**lexique** /lɛksik/ *n.m.* vocabulary; (*glossaire*) lexicon.

**lézard** /lezar/ *n.m.* lizard.

**liaison** /ljɛzɔ̃/ *n.f.* connection; (*transport*) link; (*gram., mil.*) liaison; (*amoureuse*) affair.

**liane** /ljan/ *n.f.* creeper.

**liasse** /ljas/ *n.f.* bundle, wad.

**Liban** /libɑ̃/ *n.m.* Lebanon.

**libanais, ~e** /libanɛ, -z/ *a. & n.m., f.* Lebanese.

**libell|er** /libele/ *v.t.* (*cheque*) write; (*lettre*) draw up. **~é à l'ordre de,** made out to.

**libellule** /libelyl/ *n.f.* dragonfly.

**libér|al** (*m. pl.* ~**aux**) /liberal, -o/ *a.* liberal. **les professions** ~**ales** the professions.

**libér|er** /libere/ *v.t.* (*personne*) free, release; (*pays*) liberate, free. **se** ~**er** *v. pr.* free o.s. ~**ateur**, ~**atrice** *a.* liberating; *n.m.*, *f.* liberator. ~**ation** *n.f.* release; (*de pays*) liberation.

**liberté** /liberte/ *n.f.* freedom, liberty; (*loisir*) free time. **être/mettre en** ~, be/set free.

**librair|e** /librer/ *n.m./f.* bookseller. ~**ie** /-eri/ *n.f.* bookshop.

**libre** /libr/ *a.* free; (*place, pièce*) vacant, free; (*passage*) clear. ~ **de faire,** free to do. ~**échange** *n.m.* free trade. ~**ment** /-əmɑ̃/ *adv.* freely. ~**service** (*pl.* ~**s-services**) *n.m.* self-service.

**Libye** /libi/ *n.f.* Libya.

**libyen,** ~**ne** /libjɛ̃, -jɛn/ *a. & n.m.*, *f.* Libyan.

**licence** /lisɑ̃s/ *n.f.* licence; (*univ.*) degree.

**licencié,** ~**e** /lisɑ̃sje/ *n.m.*, *f.* ~**ès lettres/sciences,** Bachelor of Arts/Science.

**licenc|ier** /lisɑ̃sje/ *v.t.* make redundant, (*pour faute*) dismiss. ~**iements** *n.m. pl.* redundancies.

**lichen** /likɛn/ *n.m.* lichen.

**licite** /lisit/ *a.* lawful.

**licorne** /likɔrn/ *n.f.* unicorn.

**liège** /liɛʒ/ *n.m.* cork.

**lien** /ljɛ̃/ *n.m.* (*rapport*) link; (*attache*) bond, tie; (*corde*) rope.

**lier** /lje/ *v.t.* tie (up), bind; (*relier*) link; (*engager, unir*) bind. **ils sont très liés,** they are very close.

**lierre** /ljɛr/ *n.m.* ivy.

**lieu** (*pl.* ~**x**) /ljø/ *n.m.* place. ~**x,** (*locaux*) premises; (*d'un accident*) scene. **au** ~ **de,** instead of.

**lieutenant** /ljøtnɑ̃/ *n.m.* lieutenant.

**lièvre** /ljɛvr/ *n.m.* hare.

**ligament** /ligamɑ̃/ *n.m.* ligament.

**ligne** /liɲ/ *n.f.* line; (*trajet*) route; (*formes*) lines; (*de femme*) figure. **en** ~, (*personne au téléphone*) on the phone.

**ligue** /lig/ *n.f.* league.

**lilas** /lila/ *n.m. & a. invar.* lilac.

**limace** /limas/ *n.f.* slug.

**limande** /limɑ̃d/ *n.f.* (*poisson*) dab.

**lim|e** /lim/ *n.f.* file. ~**e à ongles,** nail file. ~**er** *v.t.* file.

**limitation** /limitasjɔ̃/ *n.f.* limitation. ~ **de vitesse,** speed limit.

**limit|e** /limit/ *n.f.* limit; (*de jardin, champ*) boundary. ● *a.* (*vitesse, âge*) maximum. **date** ~**e,** deadline. ~**er** *v.t.* limit; (*délimiter*) form the border of.

**limon** /limɔ̃/ *n.m.* stilt.

**limonade** /limɔnad/ *n.f.* lemonade.

**limpide** /lɛ̃pid/ *a.* limpid, clear.

**lin** /lɛ̃/ *n.m.* (*tissu*) linen.

**linceul** /lɛ̃sœl/ *n.m.* shroud.

**linéaire** /lineɛr/ *a.* linear.

**linge** /lɛ̃ʒ/ *n.m.* linen; (*lessive*) washing; (*torchon*) cloth. ~**rie** *n.f.* underwear.

**linguiste** /lɛ̃gɥist/ *n.m./f.* linguist.

**linguistique** /lɛ̃gɥistik/ *a.* linguistic. ● *n.f.* linguistics.

**lion,** ~**ne** /ljɔ̃, ljɔn/ *n.m.*, *f.* lion, lioness. **le L**~**,** leo.

**lionceau** (*pl.* ~**x**) /ljɔ̃so/ *n.m.* lion cub.

**liqueur** /likœr/ *n.f.* liqueur.

**liquide** /likid/ *a. & n.m.* liquid. **(argent)** ~, ready money. **payer en** ~, pay cash.

**liquid|er** /likide/ *v.t.* liquidate; (*vendre*) sell. ~**ation** *n.f.* liquidation; (*vente*) (clearance) sale.

**lire¹†** /lir/ *v.t./i.* read.

**lire²** /lir/ *n.f.* lira.

**lis¹** /li/ *voir* **lire¹**.

**lis²** /lis/ *n.m.* (*fleur*) lily.

**lisible** /lizibl/ *a.* legible; (*roman etc.*) readable.

**lisse** /lis/ *a.* smooth.

**liste** /list/ *n.f.* list. ~ **électorale,** register of voters.

**listing** /listiŋ/ *n.m.* printout.

**lit¹** /li/ *voir* **lire¹**.

**lit²** /li/ *n.m.* (*de personne, fleuve*) bed. **se mettre au** ~, get into bed. ~ **de camp,** camp-bed. ~ **d'enfant,** cot.

**litchi** /litʃi/ *n.m.* litchi.

**literie** /litri/ *n.f.* bedding.

**litige** /litiʒ/ *n.m.* dispute.

**litre** /litr/ *n.m.* litre.

**littéraire** /literɛr/ *a.* literary.

**littérature** /literatyr/ *n.f.* literature.

**littor|al** (*pl.* ~**aux**) /litɔral, -o/ *n.m.* coast.

**liturgie** /lityrʒi/ *n.f.* liturgy.

**livraison** /livrɛzɔ̃/ *n.f.* delivery.

**livre¹** /livr/ *n.m.* book. ~ **de bord,** log-book. ~ **de compte,** books. ~ **de poche,** paperback.

**livre²** /livr/ *n.f.* (*monnaie, poids*) pound.

**livrer** /livre/ *v.t.* deliver; (*abandonner*) give over (**à,** to); (*secret*) give away.

**livret** /livrɛ/ *n.m.* book; (*mus.*) libretto. ~ **scolaire,** school report (book).

**livreu|r,** ~**se** /livrœr, -øz/ *n.m.*, *f.* delivery boy *ou* girl.

**lobe** /lɔb/ *n.m.* lobe.

**loc|al¹** (*m. pl.* ~**aux**) /lɔkal, -o/ *a.* local. ~**alement** *adv.* locally.

**loc|al²** (*pl.* ~**aux**) /lɔkal, -o/ *n.m.* premises. ~**aux,** premises.

**localisé** /lɔkalize/ *a.* localized.

**localité** /lɔkalite/ *n.f.* locality.

**locataire** /lɔkatɛr/ *n.m./f.* tenant; (*de chambre, d'hôtel*) lodger.

**location** /lɔkasjɔ̃/ *n.f. (de maison)* renting; *(de voiture)* hiring, renting; *(de place)* booking, reservation; *(guichet)* booking office; *(théâtre)* box office; *(par propriétaire)* renting out; hiring out. **en ~,** *(voiture)* on hire, rented.

**locomotion** /lɔkɔmosjɔ̃/ *n.f.* locomotion.

**locomotive** /lɔkɔmɔtiv/ *n.f.* engine, locomotive.

**loge** /lɔʒ/ *n.f. (de concierge)* lodge; *(d'acteur)* dressing-room; *(de spectateur)* box.

**logement** /lɔʒmɑ̃/ *n.m.* accommodation; *(appartement)* flat; *(habitat)* housing.

**log|er** /lɔʒe/ *v.t.* accommodate. ● *v.i.,* **se ~er** *v. pr.* live. **trouver à se ~er,** find accommodation. **être ~é,** live.

**logeu|r, ~se** /lɔʒœr, -øz/ *n.m., f.* landlord, landlady.

**logiciel** /lɔʒisjɛl/ *n.m.* software.

**logique** /lɔʒik/ *a.* logical. ● *n.f.* logic. **~ment** *adv.* logically.

**logistique** /lɔʒistik/ *n.f.* logistics.

**logo** /lɔgo/ *n.m.* logo.

**loi** /lwa/ *n.f.* law.

**loin** /lwɛ̃/ *adv.* far (away). **au ~,** far away. **de ~,** from far away; *(de beaucoup)* by far. **~ de là,** far from it. **plus ~,** further. **il revient de ~,** *(fig.)* he had a close shave.

**lointain, ~e** /lwɛ̃tɛ̃, -ɛn/ *a.* distant. ● *n.m.* distance.

**loir** /lwar/ *n.m.* dormouse.

**loisir** /lwazir/ *n.m.* (spare) time. **~s,** spare time; *(distractions)* spare time activities.

**londonien, ~ne** /lɔ̃dɔnjɛ̃, -jɛn/ *a.* London. ● *n.m., f.* Londoner.

**Londres** /lɔ̃dr/ *n.m./f.* London.

**long, ~ue** /lɔ̃, lɔ̃g/ *a.* long. ● *n.m.* **de ~,** *(mesure)* long. **(tout) le ~ de,** (all) along.

**longer** /lɔ̃ʒe/ *v.t.* go along.

**longitude** /lɔ̃ʒityd/ *n.f.* longitude.

**longtemps** /lɔ̃tɑ̃/ *adv.* a long time. **avant ~,** before long. **trop ~,** too long. **ça prendra ~,** it will take a long time.

**longue** /lɔ̃g/ *voir* **long.**

**longuement** /lɔ̃gmɑ̃/ *adv.* at length.

**longueur** /lɔ̃gœr/ *n.f.* length. **~ d'onde,** wavelength.

**longue-vue** /lɔ̃gvy/ *n.f.* telescope.

**look** /luk/ *n.m. (fam.)* look, image.

**lopin** /lɔpɛ̃/ *n.m.* **~ de terre,** patch of land.

**loquet** /lɔkɛ/ *n.m.* latch.

**lors de** /lɔrdə/ *prép.* at the time of.

**lorsque** /lɔrsk(ə)/ *conj.* when.

**losange** /lɔzɑ̃ʒ/ *n.m.* diamond.

**lot** /lo/ *n.m.* prize; *(portion, destin)* lot.

**loterie** /lɔtri/ *n.f.* lottery.

**lotion** /losjɔ̃/ *n.f.* lotion.

**lotissement** /lɔtismɑ̃/ *n.m. (à construire)* building plot; *(construit)* (housing) development.

**louange** /lwɑ̃ʒ/ *n.f.* praise.

**louche** /luʃ/ *a.* shady, dubious.

**loucher** /luʃe/ *v.i.* squint.

**louer** /lwe/ *v.t. (maison)* rent; *(voiture)* hire, rent; *(place)* book, reserve; *(propriétaire)* rent out; hire out. **à ~,** to let.

**loup** /lu/ *n.m.* wolf.

**loupe** /lup/ *n.f.* magnifying glass.

**lourd, ~e** /lur, -d/ *a.* heavy; *(chaleur)* close; *(faute)* gross.

**loutre** /lutr/ *n.f.* otter.

**louve** /luv/ *n.f.* she-wolf.

**louveteau** *(pl.* **~x)** /luvto/ *n.m.* wolf cub; *(scout)* Cub (Scout).

**louvoyer** /luvwaje/ *v.i. (fig.)* sidestep the issue; *(naut.)* tack.

**loy|al** *(m. pl.* **~aux)** /lwajal, -o/ *a.* loyal; *(honnête)* fair. **~alement** *adv.* loyally; fairly. **~auté** *n.f.* loyalty; fairness.

**loyer** /lwaje/ *n.m.* rent.

**lu** /ly/ *voir* **lire¹**.

**lubrif|ier** /lybrifje/ *v.t.* lubricate. **~iant** *n.m.* lubricant.

**lucarne** /lykarn/ *n.f.* skylight.

**lucid|e** /lysid/ *a.* lucid. **~ité** *n.f.* lucidity.

**lucrati|f, ~ve** /lykratif, -v/ *a.* lucrative. **à but non ~f,** non-profit-making.

**lueur** /lɥœr/ *n.f.* (faint) light, glimmer; *(fig.)* glimmer, gleam.

**luge** /lyʒ/ *n.f.* toboggan.

**lugubre** /lygybr/ *a.* gloomy.

**lui** /lɥi/ *pron.* him; *(sujet)* he; *(chose)* it; *(objet indirect)* (to) him; *(femme)* (to) her; *(chose)* (to) it. **~-même** *pron.* himself; itself.

**lumbago** /lɔ̃bago/ *n.m.* lumbago.

**lumière** /lymjɛr/ *n.f.* light.

**luminaire** /lyminɛr/ *n.m.* lamp.

**lumineu|x, ~se** /lyminø, -z/ *a.* luminous; *(éclairé)* illuminated; *(source, rayon)* (of) light; *(vif)* bright.

**lunaire** /lynɛr/ *a.* lunar.

**lunatique** /lynatik/ *a.* temperamental.

**lunch** /lœntʃ/ *n.m.* buffet lunch.

**lundi** /lœdi/ *n.m.* Monday.

**lune** /lyn/ *n.f.* moon. **~ de miel,** honeymoon.

**lunette** /lynɛt/ *n.f.* **~s,** glasses; *(de protection)* goggles. **~ arrière,** *(auto.)* rear window. **~s de soleil,** sun-glasses.

**lustre** /lystr/ *n.m. (éclat)* lustre; *(objet)* chandelier.

**luth** /lyt/ *n.m.* lute.

**lutin** /lytɛ̃/ *n.m.* goblin.

**lutt|e** /lyt/ *n.f.* fight, struggle; *(sport)* wrestling. **~er** *v.i.* fight, struggle; *(sport)* wrestle.

**luxe** /lyks/ *n.m.* luxury. **de ~,** luxury; (*produit*) de luxe.

**Luxembourg** /lyksãbur/ *n.m.* Luxemburg.

**lux|er** /lykse/ *v.t.* **se ~er le genou,** dislocate one's knee. **~ation** *n.f.* dislocation.

**luxueu|x, ~se** /lyksɥø, -z/ *a.* luxurious.

**luzerne** /lyzɛrn/ *n.f.* (*plante*) lucerne, alfalfa.

**lycée** /lise/ *n.m.* (secondary) school. **~n, ~nne** /-ɛ̃, -ɛn/ *n.m., f.* pupil (at secondary school).

**lynx** /lɛ̃ks/ *n.m.* lynx.

**lyophilis|er** /ljofilize/ *v.t.* freeze-dry. **~é** *a.* freeze-dried.

**lyre** /lir/ *n.f.* lyre.

**lyri|que** /lirik/ *a.* (*poésie*) lyric; (*passionné*) lyrical. **artiste/ théâtre ~que,** opera singer/ -house. **~sme** *n.m.* lyricism.

**lys** /lis/ *n.m.* lily.

• • • • • • • • • • • • • • • • • • • • • • • • • • • • • •

# Mm

• • • • • • • • • • • • • • • • • • • • • • • • • • • • • •

**m'** /m/ *voir* me.

**ma** /ma/ *voir* mon.

**maboul** /mabul/ *a.* (*fam.*) mad.

**macabre** /makabr/ *a.* gruesome, macabre.

**macadam** /makadam/ *n.m.* (*goudronné*) Tarmac (P.).

**macaron** /makarɔ̃/ *n.m.* (*gâteau*) macaroon; (*insigne*) badge.

**macaronis** /makarɔni/ *n.m. pl.* macaroni.

**macédoine** /masedwan/ *n.f.* mixed vegetables. **~ de fruits,** fruit salad.

**macérer** /masere/ *v.t./i.* soak; (*dans du vinaigre*) pickle.

**mâcher** /mɑʃe/ *v.t.* chew.

**machin** /maʃɛ̃/ *n.m.* (*chose: fam.*) thing; (*personne: fam.*) what's-his-name.

**machin|al** (*m. pl. ~aux*) /maʃinal, -o/ *a.* automatic. **~alement** *adv.* automatically.

**machine** /maʃin/ *n.f.* machine; (*d'un train, navire*) engine. **~ à écrire,** typewriter. **~ à laver/ coudre,** washing-/sewing-machine. **~ à sous,** fruit machine.

**machiniste** /maʃinist/ *n.m.* (*théâtre*) stage-hand; (*conducteur*) driver.

**mâchoire** /mɑʃwar/ *n.f.* jaw.

**maçon** /masɔ̃/ *n.m.* builder; (*poseur de briques*) bricklayer.

**macrobiotique** /makrɔbjɔtik/ *a.* macrobiotic.

**Madagascar** /madagaskar/ *n.f.* Madagascar.

**madame** (*pl.* **mesdames**) /madam, medam/ *n.f.* madam. **M~ ou Mme Dupont,** Mrs Dupont. **bonsoir, mesdames,** good evening, ladies.

**madeleine** /madlɛn/ *n.f.* madeleine (*small shell-shaped sponge-cake*).

**mademoiselle** (*pl.* **mesdemoiselles**) /madmwazɛl, medmwazɛl/ *n.f.* miss. **M~ ou Mlle Dupont,** Miss Dupont. **bonsoir, mesdemoiselles,** good evening, ladies.

**madère** /madɛr/ *n.m.* (*vin*) Madeira.

**maf(f)ia** /mafja/ *n.f.* Mafia.

**magasin** /magazɛ̃/ *n.m.* shop, store; (*entrepôt*) warehouse.

**magazine** /magazin/ *n.m.* magazine; (*émission*) programme.

**Maghreb** /magrɛb/ *n.m.* North Africa. **~in, ~ine** *a. & n.m., f.* North African.

**magicien, ~ne** /maʒisjɛ̃, -jɛn/ *n.m., f.* magician.

**magie** /maʒi/ *n.f.* magic.

**magique** /maʒik/ *a.* magic; (*mystérieux*) magical.

**magistr|al** (*m. pl. ~aux*) /maʒistral, -o/ *a.* masterly; (*grand: hum.*) colossal.

**magistrat** /maʒistra/ *n.m.* magistrate.

**magistrature** /maʒistratyr/ *n.f.* judiciary.

**magnésie** /maɲezi/ *n.f.* magnesia.

**magnéti|que** /maɲetik/ *a.* magnetic. **~ser** *v.t.* magnetize. **~sme** *n.m.* magnetism.

**magnétophone** /maɲetɔfɔn/ *n.m.* tape recorder. **~ à cassettes,** cassette recorder.

**magnétoscope** /maɲetɔskɔp/ *n.m.* video-recorder.

**magnifique** /maɲifik/ *a.* magnificent.

**magnolia** /maɲɔlja/ *n.m.* magnolia.

**magret** /magrɛ/ *n.m.* **~ de canard,** steaklet of duck.

**mai** /mɛ/ *n.m.* May.

**maigr|e** /mɛgr/ *a.* thin; (*viande*) lean; (*yaourt*) low-fat; (*fig.*) poor, meagre. **~eur** *n.f.* thinness; leanness.

**maigrir** /megrir/ *v.i.* get thin(ner); (*en suivant un régime*) slim.

**maille** /mɑj/ *n.f.* stitch; (*de filet*) mesh. **~ filée,** ladder, run.

**maillet** /majɛ/ *n.m.* mallet.

**maillon** /majɔ̃/ *n.m.* link.

**maillot** /majo/ *n.m.* (*de sport*) jersey. **~ (de corps),** vest. **~ (de bain),** (swimming) costume.

**main** /mɛ̃/ *n.f.* hand. **donner la ~ à qn.,** hold s.o.'s hand. **en ~s propres,** in person. **en bonnes ~s,** in good hands. **~-d'œuvre** *n.f.* labour; (*ensemble d'ouvriers*) labour force.

**maintenant** /mɛ̃tnɑ̃/ *adv.* now; (*de nos jours*) nowadays.

**maintenir†** /mɛ̃tnir/ v.t. keep, maintain; (*soutenir*) hold up; (*affirmer*) maintain. **se ~** v. pr. (*continuer*) persist; (*rester*) remain.

**maintien** /mɛ̃tjɛ̃/ n.m. (*attitude*) bearing; (*conservation*) maintenance.

**maire** /mɛr/ n.m. mayor.

**mairie** /meri/ n.f. town hall; (*administration*) town council.

**mais** /mɛ/ conj. but. **~ oui, ~ si,** of course. **~ non,** definitely not.

**maïs** /mais/ n.m. (*à cultiver*) maize; (*culin.*) sweet corn.

**maison** /mɛzɔ̃/ n.f. house; (*foyer*) home; (*immeuble*) building. **~ (de commerce),** firm. ● a. invar. (*culin.*) home-made. **à la ~,** at home. **rentrer** ou **aller à la ~,** go home. **~ des jeunes,** youth centre. **~ de retraite,** old people's home. **~ mère,** parent company.

**maître** /mɛtr/ n.m. master. **~ (d'école),** schoolmaster. **~ de,** in control of. **~ d'hôtel,** head waiter. **~ nageur,** swimming instructor.

**maîtresse** /mɛtrɛs/ n.f. mistress. **~ (d'école),** schoolmistress. **~ de,** in control of.

**maîtris|e** /metriz/ n.f. mastery; (*univ.*) master's degree. **~ (de soi),** self-control. **~er** v.t. master; (*incendie*) control; (*personne*) subdue. **se ~er** v. pr. control o.s.

**maïzena** /maizena/ n.f. (P.) cornflour.

**majesté** /maʒɛste/ n.f. majesty.

**majestueu|x, ~se** /maʒɛstɥø, -z/ a. majestic. **~sement** adv. majestically.

**majeur** /maʒœr/ a. major; (*jurid.*) of age. ● n.m. middle finger. **en ~e partie,** mostly. **la ~e partie de,** most of.

**major|er** /maʒɔre/ v.t. increase. **~ation** n.f. increase (**de,** in).

**majorit|é** /maʒɔrite/ n.f. majority. **en ~é,** chiefly. **~aire** a. majority. **être ~aire,** be in the majority.

**Majorque** /maʒɔrk/ n.f. Majorca.

**majuscule** /maʒyskyl/ a. capital. ● n.f. capital letter.

**mal¹** /mal/ adv. badly; (*incorrectement*) wrong(ly). **~ (à l'aise),** uncomfortable. **aller ~,** (*malade*) be bad. **c'est ~ de,** it is wrong ou bad to. **~ entendre/comprendre,** not hear/ understand properly. **pas ~,** not bad; quite a lot.

**mal²** (pl. **maux**) /mal,mo/ n.m. evil; (*douleur*) pain, ache; (*effort*) trouble; (*dommage*) harm. **avoir~à la tête/aux dents/à la gorge,** have a headache/a toothache/a sore throat. **avoir le ~ de mer/du pays,** be seasick/homesick. **faire du~à,** hurt, harm. **se donner du~pour faire qch.,** go to a lot of trouble to do sth.

**malade** /malad/ a. sick, ill; (*bras, gorge*) bad. ● n.m./f. sick person; (*d'un médecin*) patient.

**maladie** /maladi/ n.f. illness, disease.

**maladresse†** /maladrɛs/ n.f. clumsiness; (*erreur*) blunder.

**maladroit, ~e** /maladrwa, -t/ a. & n.m., f. clumsy (person).

**malais, ~e¹** /malɛ, -z/ a. & n.m., f. Malay.

**malaise²** /malɛz/ n.m. feeling of faintness ou dizziness; (*fig.*) uneasiness, malaise.

**malaria** /malarja/ n.f. malaria.

**Malaysia** /malɛzja/ n.f. Malaysia.

**malaxer** /malakse/ v.t. (*pétrir*) knead; (*mêler*) mix.

**malchanc|e** /malʃɑ̃s/ n.f. misfortune. **~eux, ~euse** a. unlucky.

**mâle** /mɑl/ a. male; (*viril*) manly. ● n.m. male.

**malédiction** /malediksjɔ̃/ n.f. curse.

**malencontreu|x, ~se** /malɑ̃kɔ̃trø, -z/ a. unfortunate.

**malentendant, ~e** a. & n.m., f. hard of hearing.

**malentendu** /malɑ̃tɑ̃dy/ n.m. misunderstanding.

**malfaçon** /malfasɔ̃/ n.f. fault.

**malfaiteur** /malfɛtœr/ n.m. criminal.

**malformation** /malfɔrmasjɔ̃/ n.f. malformation.

**malgache** /malgaʃ/ a. & n.m./f. Malagasy.

**malgré** /malgre/ prép. in spite of, despite. **~ tout,** after all.

**malheur** /malœr/ n.m. misfortune; (*accident*) accident. **faire un ~,** be a big hit.

**malheureu|x, ~se** /malœrø, -z/ a. unhappy; (*regrettable*) unfortunate; (*sans succès*) unlucky; (*insignifiant*) wretched. ● n.m., f. (poor) wretch. **~sement** adv. unfortunately.

**malhonnête** /malɔnɛt/ a. dishonest. **~té** n.f. dishonesty; (*action*) dishonest action.

**mal|in, ~igne** /malɛ̃, -iɲ/ a. clever, smart; (*méchant*) malicious; (*tumeur*) malignant; (*difficile*: *fam.*) difficult.

**malle** /mal/ n.f. (*valise*) trunk; (*auto.*) boot.

**mallette** /malɛt/ n.f. (small) suitcase.

**malmener** /malmǝne/ v.t. manhandle, handle roughly.

**malnutrition** /malnytrisjɔ̃/ n.f. malnutrition.

**malodorant, ~e** /malɔdɔrɑ̃, -t/ a. smelly, foul-smelling.

**malpoli** /malpɔli/ a. impolite.

**malpropre** /malprɔpr/ a. dirty. **~té** /-ǝte/ n.f. dirtiness.

**malsain, ~e** /malsɛ̃, -ɛn/ a. unhealthy.

**malt** /malt/ n.m. malt.

**maltais, ~e** /maltɛ, -z/ a. & n.m., f. Maltese.

**Malte** /malt/ n.f. Malta.

**maltraiter** /maltrete/ v.t. ill-treat.

**maman** /mamɑ̃/ n.f. mum(my), mother.

**mamelle** /mamɛl/ n.f. teat.

**mamie** /mami/ n.f. (*fam.*) granny.

**mammifère** /mamifɛr/ n.m. mammal.

**mammouth** /mamut/ *n.m.* mammoth.

**manche**[1] /mãʃ/ *n.f.* sleeve; (*sport, pol.*) round. **la M~,** the Channel.

**manche**[2] /mãʃ/ *n.m.* (*d'un instrument*) handle.

**manchette** /mãʃɛt/ *n.f.* cuff; (*de journal*) headline.

**manchot** /mãʃo/ *n.m.* (*oiseau*) penguin.

**mandarin** /mãdarɛ̃/ *n.m.* (*fonctionnaire*) mandarin.

**mandarine** /mãdarin/ *n.f.* tangerine, mandarin (orange).

**mandat** /mãda/ *n.m.* (*postal*) money order; (*pol.*) mandate; (*procuration*) proxy; (*de police*) warrant.

**manège** /manɛʒ/ *n.m.* riding-school; (*à la foire*) merry-go-round; (*manœuvre*) wiles, ploy.

**manette** /manɛt/ *n.f.* lever; (*comput.*) joystick.

**mangeable** /mãʒabl/ *a.* edible.

**mang|er** /mãʒe/ *v.t./i.* eat; (*fortune*) go through; (*ronger*) eat into. ● *n.m.* food. **donner à ~er à,** feed. **~eur, ~euse** *n.m., f.* eater.

**mangue** /mãg/ *n.f.* mango.

**maniable** /manjabl/ *a.* easy to handle.

**maniaque** /manjak/ *a.* fussy. ● *n.m./f.* fusspot; (*fou*) maniac.

**manie** /mani/ *n.f.* habit; obsession.

**man|ier** /manje/ *v.t.* handle. **~iement** *n.m.* handling.

**manière** /manjɛr/ *n.f.* way, manner. **~s,** (*politesse*) manners; (*chichis*) fuss. **de cette ~,** in this way. **de ~ à,** so as to. **de toute ~,** anyway, in any case.

**maniéré** /manjere/ *a.* affected.

**manifestant, ~e** /manifɛstã, -t/ *n.m., f.* demonstrator.

**manifester**[1] /manifɛste/ *v.t.* show, manifest. **se ~** *v. pr.* (*sentiment*) show itself; (*apparaître*) appear.

**manifest|er**[2] /manifɛste/ *v.i.* (*pol.*) demonstrate. **~ation** *n.f.* (*pol.*) demonstration; (*événement*) event.

**manipul|er** /manipyle/ *v.t.* handle; (*péj.*) manipulate. **~ation** *n.f.* handling; (*péj.*) manipulation.

**manivelle** /manivɛl/ *n.f.* crank.

**mannequin** /mankɛ̃/ *n.m.* (*personne*) model; (*statue*) dummy.

**manœuvr|e**[1] /manœvr/ *n.f.* manœuvre. **~er** *v.t./i.* manœuvre; (*machine*) operate.

**manœuvre**[2] /manœvr/ *n.m.* (*ouvrier*) labourer.

**manoir** /manwar/ *n.m.* manor.

**manque** /mãk/ *n.m.* lack (**de,** of); (*vide*) gap. **~s,** (*défauts*) faults.

**manqué** /mãke/ *a.* (*écrivain etc.*) failed. **garçon ~,** tomboy.

**manquer** /mãke/ *v.t.* miss; (*gâcher*) spoil; (*examen*) fail. ● *v.i.* be short *ou* lacking; (*absent*) be absent; (*en moins, disparu*) be missing; (*échouer*) fail. **~ à,** (*devoir*) fail in. **~ de,** be short of, lack. **il/ça lui manque,** he misses him/it.

**manteau** (*pl.* **~x**) /mãto/ *n.m.* coat.

**manucur|e** /manykyr/ *n.m./f.* manicurist. **~er** *v.t.* manicure.

**manuel, ~le** /manɥɛl/ *a.* manual. ● *n.m.* (*livre*) manual.

**manufactur|e** /manyfaktyr/ *n.f.* factory. **~é** *a.* manufactured.

**manuscrit, ~e** /manyskri, -t/ *a.* handwritten. ● *n.m.* manuscript.

**manutention** /manytãsjõ/ *n.f.* handling.

**maquereau** (*pl.* **~x**) /makro/ *n.m.* (*poisson*) mackerel.

**maquette** /makɛt/ *n.f.* (scale) model; (*mise en page*) paste-up.

**maquill|er** /makije/ *v.t.* make up; (*truquer*) fake. **se ~er** *v. pr.* make (o.s.) up. **~age** *n.m.* make-up.

**maraîch|er, ~ère** /mareʃe, -ɛʃer/ *n.m., f.* market gardener. **cultures ~ères,** market gardening.

**marais** /marɛ/ *n.m.* marsh.

**marbre** /marbr/ *n.m.* marble.

**marc** /mar/ *n.m.* (*eau-de-vie*) marc.

**marchand, ~e** /marʃã, -d/ *n.m., f.* trader; (*de charbon, vins*) merchant. ● *a.* (*valeur*) market. **~ de journaux,** newsagent. **~ de légumes,** greengrocer. **~ de poissons,** fishmonger.

**marchander** /marʃãde/ *v.t.* haggle over. ● *v.i.* haggle.

**marchandise** /marʃãdiz/ *n.f.* goods.

**marche** /marʃ/ *n.f.* (*démarche, trajet*) walk; (*rythme*) pace; (*mil., mus.*) march; (*d'escalier*) step; (*sport*) walking; (*de machine*) working; (*de véhicule*) running. **en ~,** (*train etc.*) moving. **faire ~ arrière,** (*véhicule*) reverse. **mettre en ~,** start (up).

**marché** /marʃe/ *n.m.* market; (*contrat*) deal. **faire son ~,** do one's shopping. **~ aux puces,** flea market. **M~ commun,** Common Market. **~ noir,** black market.

**march|er** /marʃe/ *v.i.* walk; (*aller*) go; (*fonctionner*) work, run; (*prospérer*) go well. **~eur, ~euse** *n.m., f.* walker.

**mardi** /mardi/ *n.m.* Tuesday. **M~ gras,** Shrove Tuesday.

**mare** /mar/ *n.f.* (*étang*) pond; (*flaque*) pool.

**marécag|e** /mareka ʒ/ *n.m.* marsh. **~eux, ~euse** *a.* marshy.

**marée** /mare/ *n.f.* tide; (*poissons*) fresh fish. **~ haute/basse,** high/low tide. **~ noire,** oil-slick.

**margarine** /margarin/ *n.f.* margarine.

**marge** /marʒ/ *n.f.* margin. **~ bénéficiaire,** profit margin.

**margin|al, ~ale** (m. pl. ~aux) /marʒinal, -o/ a. marginal. ● n.m., f. drop-out.

**marguerite** /margərit/ n.f. daisy.

**mari** /mari/ n.m. husband.

**mariage** /marjaʒ/ n.m. marriage; (cérémonie) wedding.

**marié, ~e** /marje/ a. married. ● n.m. (bride)groom. ● n.f. bride. **les ~s,** the bride and groom.

**marier** /marje/ v.t. marry. **se ~,** marry, get married (**avec,** to).

**marin, ~e** /marɛ̃, -in/ a. sea. ● n.m. sailor. ● n.f. navy.

**mariner** /marine/ v.t./i. marinate.

**marionnette** /marjɔnɛt/ n.f. puppet; (à fils) marionette.

**maritime** /maritim/ a. maritime, coastal; (droit, agent) shipping.

**mark** /mark/ n.m. mark.

**marmelade** /marməlad/ n.f. ~ (d'oranges), marmelade.

**marmite** /marmit/ n.f. (cooking-)pot.

**marmonner** /marmone/ v.t./i. mumble.

**Maroc** /marɔk/ n.m. Morocco.

**marocain, ~e** /marɔkɛ̃, -ɛn/ a. & n.m., f. Moroccan.

**maroquinerie** /marɔkinri/ n.f. (magasin) leather goods shop.

**marquant, ~e** /markɑ̃, -t/ a. (remarquable) outstanding; (qu'on n'oublie pas) significant.

**marque** /mark/ n.f. mark; (de produits) brand, make. **de ~,** (comm.) brand-name; (fig.) important. ~ **déposée,** registered trade mark.

**marquer** /marke/ v.t. mark; (indiquer) show; (écrire) note down; (point, but) score. ● v.i. (trace) leave a mark; (événement) stand out.

**marraine** /marɛn/ n.f. godmother.

**marrant, ~e** /marɑ̃, -t/ a. (fam.) funny.

**marre** /mar/ adv. **en avoir ~,** (fam.) be fed up (**de,** with).

**marrer (se)** /(sə)mare/ v. pr. (fam.) laugh, have a (good) laugh.

**marron** /marɔ̃/ n.m. chestnut; (couleur) brown ● a. invar. brown.

**mars** /mars/ n.m. March.

**marsouin** /marswɛ̃/ n.m. porpoise.

**marteau** (pl. ~x) /marto/ n.m. hammer. ~ **piqueur** pneumatic drill.

**martien, ~ne** /marsjɛ̃, -jɛn/ a. & n.m., f. Martian.

**martyr, ~e** /martir/ n.m., f. martyr. ● a. martyred. ~**iser** v.t. martyr; (fig.) batter.

**marxis|te** /marksist/ a. & n.m./f. Marxist. ~**me** n.m. Marxism.

**mascara** /maskara/ n.m. mascara.

**masculin, ~e** /maskylɛ̃, -in/ a. masculine; (sexe) male; (mode, équipe) men's. ● n.m. masculine. ~**ité** /-inite/ n.f. masculinity.

**masochis|te** /mazɔʃist/ n.m./f. masochist. ● a. masochistic. ~**me** n.m. masochism.

**masqu|e** /mask/ n.m. mask. ~**er** v.t. (cacher) hide, conceal (à, from); (lumière) block (off).

**massacr|e** /masakr/ n.m. massacre. ~**er** v.t. massacre; (abîmer: fam.) spoil.

**massage** /masaʒ/ n.m. massage.

**masse** /mas/ n.f. (volume) mass; (gros morceau) lump, mass; (outil) sledge-hammer. **en ~,** (vendre) in bulk; (venir) in force; (production) mass. **la ~,** (foule) the masses. **une ~ de,** (fam.) masses of.

**mass|er** /mase/ v.t. (pétrir) massage. ~**eur, ~euse** n.m., f. masseur, masseuse.

**massi|f, ~ve** /masif, -v/ a. massive; (or, argent) solid. ● n.m. (de fleurs) clump; (géog.) massif.

**massue** /masy/ n.f. club, bludgeon.

**mastiquer** /mastike/ v.t. (mâcher) chew.

**mat** /mat/ a. (couleur) matt; (bruit) dull. **être ~,** (aux échecs) be checkmate.

**mât** /mɑ/ n.m. mast; (pylône) pole.

**match** /matʃ/ n.m. match; (Amer.) game. **(faire) ~ nul,** tie, draw. ~ **aller,** first leg. ~ **retour,** return match.

**matelas** /matla/ n.m. mattress. ~ **pneumatique,** air mattress.

**matelassé** /matlase/ a. padded; (tissu) quilted.

**matelot** /matlo/ n.m. sailor.

**matérialiste** /materjalist/ a. materialistic. ● n.m./f. materialist.

**matériaux** /materjo/ n.m. pl. materials.

**matériel, ~le** /materjɛl/ a. material.

**maternel, ~le** /matɛrnɛl/ a. motherly, maternal; (rapport de parenté) maternal. ● n.f. nursery school.

**maternité** /matɛrnite/ n.f. maternity hospital; (état de mère) motherhood.

**mathémati|que** /matematik/ a. mathematical. ● n.f. pl. mathematics. ~**cien, ~cienne** n.m., f. mathematician.

**maths** /mat/ n.f. pl. (fam.) maths.

**matière** /matjer/ n.f. matter; (produit) material; (sujet) subject. ~ **plastique,** plastic. ~**s grasses,** fat. **à 0% de ~s grasses,** fat free. ~**s premières,** raw materials.

**matin** /matɛ̃/ n.m. morning. **de bon ~,** early in the morning.

**matin|al** (m. pl. ~aux) /matinal, -o/ a. morning; (de bonne heure) early. **être ~,** be up early.

**matinée** /matine/ n.f. morning; (spectacle) matinée.

**matrimon|ial** (*m. pl.* ~**iaux**) /matrimɔnjal, -jo/ *a.* matrimonial.

**maturité** /matyrite/ *n.f.* maturity.

**maudit, ~e** /modi, -t/ *a.* (*fam.*) damned.

**maussade** /mosad/ *a.* gloomy.

**mauvais, ~e** /mɔvɛ, -z/ *a.* bad; (*erroné*) wrong; (*malveillant*) evil; (*désagréable*) nasty, bad; (*mer*) rough. ●*n.m.* **il fait ~,** the weather is bad. **le ~ moment,** the wrong time.

**mauve** /mov/ *a. & n.m.* mauve.

**maux** /mo/ *voir* **mal¹.**

**maxim|al** (*m. pl.* ~**aux**) /maksimal, -o/ *a.* maximum.

**maximum** /maksimɔm/ *a. & n.m.* maximum. **au ~,** as much as possible; (*tout au plus*) at most.

**mayonnaise** /majɔnɛz/ *n.f.* mayonnaise.

**mazout** /mazut/ *n.m.* (fuel) oil.

**me, m'¹*** /mə, m/ *pron.* me; (*indirect*) (to) me; (*réfléchi*) myself.

**mec** /mɛk/ *n.m.* (*fam.*) bloke, guy.

**mécanicien** /mekanisjɛ̃/ *n.m.* mechanic; (*rail.*) train driver.

**mécanique** /mekanik/ *a.* mechanical; (*jouet*) clockwork. **problème ~,** engine trouble. ●*n.f.* mechanics; (*mécanisme*) mechanism.

**mécanisme** /mekanism/ *n.m.* mechanism.

**méch|ant, ~ante** /meʃɑ̃, -t/ *a.* (*cruel*) wicked; (*désagréable*) nasty; (*enfant*) naughty; (*chien*) vicious; (*sensationnel: fam.*) terrific. ●*n.m., f.* (*enfant*) naughty child. ~**amment** *adv.* wickedly. ~**anceté** *n.f.* wickedness; (*action*) wicked action.

**mèche** /mɛʃ/ *n.f.* (*de cheveux*) lock; (*de bougie*) wick; (*d'explosif*) fuse.

**méconnu** /mekɔny/ *a.* unrecognized.

**mécontent, ~e** /mekɔ̃tɑ̃, -t/ *a.* dissatisfied (**de,** with); (*irrité*) annoyed (**de,** at, with). ~**ement** /-tmɑ̃/ *n.m.* dissatisfaction; annoyance.

**médaill|e** /medaj/ *n.f.* medal; (*insigne*) badge; (*bijou*) medallion.

**médaillon** /medajɔ̃/ *n.m.* medallion; (*bijou*) locket.

**médecin** /mɛdsɛ̃/ *n.m.* doctor.

**médecine** /mɛdsin/ *n.f.* medicine.

**média** /medja/ *n.m.* medium. **les ~s,** the media.

**média|teur, ~trice** /medjatœr, -tris/ *n.m., f.* mediator.

**médiation** /medjasjɔ̃/ *n.f.* mediation.

**médiatique** /medjatik/ *a.* **événement/ personnalité ~,** media event/personality.

**médic|al** (*m. pl.* ~**aux**) /medikal, -o/ *a.* medical.

**médicament** /medikamɑ̃/ *n.m.* medicine.

**médiév|al** (*m. pl.* ~**aux**) /medjeval, -o/ *a.* medieval.

**médiocr|e** /medjɔkr/ *a.* mediocre, poor. ~**ement** *adv.* (*peu*) not very; (*mal*) in a mediocre way. ~**ité** *n.f.* mediocrity.

**Méditerranée** /mediterane/ *n.f.* **la ~,** the Mediterranean.

**méditerranéen, ~ne** /mediteraneɛ̃, -ɛn/ *a.* Mediterranean.

**médium** /medjɔm/ *n.m.* (*personne*) medium.

**méduse** /medyz/ *n.f.* jellyfish.

**meeting** /mitiŋ/ *n.m.* meeting.

**méfait** /mefɛ/ *n.m.* misdeed.

**méfian|t, ~te** /mefjɑ̃, -t/ *a.* distrustful. ~**ce** *n.f.* distrust.

**méfier (se)** /(sə)mefje/ *v. pr.* be wary *ou* careful. **se ~ de,** distrust, be wary of.

**mégarde (par)** /(par)megard/ *adv.* by accident, accidentally.

**mégot** /mego/ *n.m.* (*fam.*) cigarette-end.

**meilleur, ~e** /mɛjœr/ *a. & adv.* better (**que,** than). **le ~ livre**/*etc.*, the best book/*etc.* **mon ~ ami**/*etc.*, my best friend/*etc.* ~ **marché,** cheaper. ●*n.m., f.* **le ~/la ~e,** the best (one).

**mélancol|ie** /melɑ̃kɔli/ *n.f.* melancholy. ~**ique** *a.* melancholy.

**mélang|e** /melɑ̃ʒ/ *n.m.* mixture, blend. ~**er** *v.t.*, **se ~er** *v. pr.* mix, blend; (*embrouiller*) mix up.

**mêler** /mele/ *v.t.* mix (**à,** with). **se ~ à,** (*se joindre à*) join. **se ~ de,** meddle in. **mêle-toi de ce qui te regarde,** mind your own business.

**mélo** /melo/ (*fam.*) *n.m.* melodrama. ●*a. invar.* melodramatic.

**mélod|ie** /melɔdi/ *n.f.* melody. ~**ieux, ~ieuse** *a.* melodious. ~**ique** *a.* melodic.

**mélodrame** /melɔdram/ *n.m.* melodrama.

**mélomane** /melɔman/ *n.m./f.* music lover.

**melon** /mlɔ̃/ *n.m.* melon.

**membrane** /mɑ̃bran/ *n.f.* membrane.

**membre¹** /mɑ̃br/ *n.m.* limb.

**membre²** /mɑ̃br/ *n.m.* member.

**même** /mɛm/ *a.* same. ●*pron.* **le ~/la ~,** the same (one). **de ~,** (*aussi*) too; (*de la même façon*) likewise. **de ~ que,** just as. **en ~ temps,** at the same time.

**mémé** /meme/ *n.f.* (*fam.*) granny.

**mémoire** /memwar/ *n.f.* memory. ●*n.m.* (*requête*) memorandum; (*univ.*) dissertation. ~**s,** (*souvenirs écrits*) memoirs. **à la ~ de,** to the memory of. **de ~,** from memory. ~ **morte/vive,** (*comput.*) ROM/RAM.

**menac|e** /mənas/ *n.f.* threat. ~**er** *v.t.* threaten (**de faire,** to do).

**ménage** /menaʒ/ *n.m.* (married) couple; (*travail*) housework. **se mettre en ~,** set up house. **scène de ~,** scene. **dépenses du ~,** household expenditure.

**ménagement** /menaʒmɑ̃/ *n.m.* care and consideration.

**ménag|er¹**, **~ère** /menaʒe, -ɛr/ a. household, domestic. **travaux ~ers**, housework.

**ménager²** /menaʒe/ v.t. treat with tact; (*utiliser*) be sparing in the use of.

**mendiant**, **~e** /mãdjã, -t/ n.m., f. beggar.

**mendier** /mãdje/ v.t. beg for. ● v.i. beg.

**mener** /məne/ v.t. lead; (*entreprise, pays*) run. ● v.i. lead. **~ à**, (*accompagner à*) take to.

**méningite** /menẽʒit/ n.f. meningitis.

**ménopause** /menɔpoz/ n.f. menopause.

**mensonge** /mãsɔ̃ʒ/ n.m. lie.

**menstruation** /mãstryasjɔ̃/ n.f. menstruation.

**mensualité** /mãsɥalite/ n.f. monthly payment.

**mensuel**, **~le** /mãsɥel/ a. & n.m. monthly. **~lement** adv. monthly.

**mensurations** /mãsyrasjɔ̃/ n.f. pl. measurements.

**ment|al** (m. pl. **~aux**) /mãtal, -o/ a. mental.

**mentalité** /mãtalite/ n.f. mentality.

**menteu|r**, **~se** /mãtœr, -øz/ n.m., f. liar. ● a. untruthful.

**menthe** /mãt/ n.f. mint.

**mention** /mãsjɔ̃/ n.f. mention; (*annotation*) note; (*scol.*) grade. **~ner** /-jɔne/ v.t. mention.

**mentir†** /mãtir/ v.i. lie.

**menton** /mãtɔ̃/ n.m. chin.

**menu¹** /məny/ n.m. (*carte*) menu; (*repas*) meal.

**menu²** /məny/ a. (*petit*) tiny; (*fin*) fine; (*insignifiant*) minor. ● adv. (*couper*) fine.

**menuis|ier** /mənɥizje/ n.m. carpenter, joiner. **~erie** n.f. carpentry, joinery.

**mépris** /mepri/ n.m. contempt, scorn (**de**, for).

**méprisable** /meprizabl/ a. despicable.

**mépris|er** /meprize/ v.t. scorn, despise. **~ant**, **~ante** a. scornful.

**mer** /mɛr/ n.f. sea; (*marée*) tide.

**merci** /mɛrsi/ int. thank you, thanks (**de**, **pour**, for). ● n.f.mercy.**~ beaucoup**, **~ bien**, thank you very much.

**mercredi** /mɛrkrədi/ n.m. Wednesday.

**mercure** /mɛrkyr/ n.m. mercury.

**merde** /mɛrd/ n.f. (*fam.*) shit. **être dans la ~**, be in a mess.

**mère** /mɛr/ n.f. mother. **~ de famille**, mother.

**méridien** /meridjẽ/ n.m. meridian.

**méridion|al**, **~ale** (m. pl. **~aux**) /meridjɔnal, -o/ a. southern. ● n.m., f. southerner.

**meringue** /mərẽg/ n.f. meringue.

**mérite** /merit/ n.m. merit.

**mériter** /merite/ v.t. deserve.

**merlan** /mɛrlã/ n.m. whiting.

**merle** /mɛrl/ n.m. blackbird.

**merveille** /mɛrvɛj/ n.f. wonder, marvel. **à ~**, wonderfully.

**merveilleu|x**, **~se** /mɛrvɛjø, -z/ a. wonderful, marvellous.

**mes** /me/ voir **mon**.

**mésange** /mezãʒ/ n.f. tit(mouse).

**mésaventure** /mezavãtyr/ n.f. misadventure.

**mesdames** /medam/ voir **madame**.

**mesdemoiselles** /medmwazɛl/ voir **mademoiselle**.

**mésentente** /mezãtãt/ n.f. disagreement.

**mesquin**, **~e** /mɛskẽ, -in/ a. mean.

**messag|e** /mesaʒ/ n.m. message. **~er**, **~ère** n.m., f. messenger.

**messe** /mɛs/ n.f. (*relig.*) mass.

**Messie** /mesi/ n.m. Messiah.

**messieurs** /mesjø/ voir **monsieur**.

**mesure** /məzyr/ n.f. measurement; (*quantité, étalon*) measure; (*disposition*) measure, step; (*cadence*) time; (*modération*) moderation. **dans la ~ où**, in so far as.

**mesurer** /məzyre/ v.t. measure; (*argent, temps*) ration.

**met** /mɛ/ voir **mettre**.

**métabolisme** /metabɔlism/ n.m. metabolism.

**mét|al** (pl. **~aux**) /metal, -o/ n.m. metal. **~allique**a. (*objet*)metal;(*éclatetc.*)metallic.

**métallurg|ie** /metalyrʒi/ n.f. (*industrie*) steel ou metal industry. **~iste** n.m. steel ou metal worker.

**métamorphos|e** /metamɔrfoz/ n.f. metamorphosis. **~er** v.t., **se ~er** v. pr. transform.

**météo** /meteo/ n.f. (*bulletin*) weather forecast.

**météore** /meteɔr/ n.m. meteor.

**météorolog|ie** /meteɔrɔlɔʒi/ n.f. meteorology; (*service*) weather bureau. **~ique** a. weather; (*études etc.*) meteorological.

**méthod|e** /metɔd/ n.f. method; (*ouvrage*) course, manual. **~ique** a. methodical.

**méticuleu|x**, **~se** /metikylø, -z/ a. meticulous.

**métier** /metje/ n.m. job; (*manuel*) trade; (*intellectuel*) profession; (*expérience*) skill. **~ (à tisser)**, loom.

**métrage** /metraʒ/ n.m. length. **court ~**, short film. **long ~**, full-length film.

**mètre** /mɛtr/ n.m. metre; (*règle*) rule. **~ ruban**, tape-measure.

**métrique** /metrik/ a. metric.

**métro** /metro/ n.m. underground; (*à Paris*) Métro.

**métropole** /metrɔpɔl/ n.f. metropolis; (*pays*) mother country.

**mets¹** /mɛ/ n.m. dish.

**mets²** /mɛ/ voir **mettre**.

**mettable** /metabl/ a. wearable.

**metteur** /mɛtœr/ *n.m.* ~ **en scène**, (*théâtre*) producer; (*cinéma*) director.

**mettre†** /mɛtr/ *v.t.* put; (*vêtement*) put on; (*radio, chauffage, etc.*) put *ou* switch on; (*table*) lay; (*temps*) take; (*installer*) put in. se ~ *v. pr.* put o.s.; (*objet*) go; (*porter*) wear. ~ en colère, make angry. se ~ à faire, start doing. se ~ à l'aise, make o.s. comfortable. se ~ à table, sit down at the table. se ~ au travail, set to work. se ~ dans tous ses états, get into a state.

**meuble** /mœbl/ *n.m.* piece of furniture. ~s, furniture.

**meublé** /møble/ *n.m.* furnished flatlet.

**meubler** /møble/ *v.t.* furnish; (*fig.*) fill. se ~ *v. pr.* buy furniture.

**meule** /møl/ *n.f.* (*de foin*) haystack; (*à moudre*) millstone.

**meurs, meurt** /mœr/ *voir* **mourir**.

**meurtr|e** /mœrtr/ *n.m.* murder. ~ier, ~ière *a.* deadly; *n.m.* murderer; *n.f.* murderess.

**mexicain, ~e** /mɛksikɛ̃, -ɛn/ *a. & n.m., f.* Mexican.

**Mexique** /mɛksik/ *n.m.* Mexico.

**mi-** /mi/ *préf.* mid-, half-. à mi-chemin, half-way. la mi-juin/*etc.*, mid-June/*etc.*

**miaou** /mjau/ *n.m.* mew.

**miauler** /mjole/ *v.i.* mew.

**miche** /miʃ/ *n.f.* round loaf.

**micro** /mikro/ *n.m.* microphone, mike; (*comput.*) micro.

**micro-** /mikro/ *préf.* micro-.

**microbe** /mikrɔb/ *n.m.* germ.

**micro-onde** /mikroɔ̃d/ *n.f.* microwave. un (four à) ~s, microwave (oven).

**microphone** /mikrɔfɔn/ *n.m.* microphone.

**microprocesseur** /mikroprɔsɛsœr/ *n.m.* microprocessor.

**microscop|e** /mikroskɔp/ *n.m.* microscope. ~ique *a.* microscopic.

**midi** /midi/ *n.m.* twelve o'clock, midday, noon; (*déjeuner*) lunch-time; (*sud*) south. le M~, the South of France.

**mie** /mi/ *n.f.* soft part (of the loaf). un pain de ~, a sandwich loaf.

**miel** /mjɛl/ *n.m.* honey.

**mien, ~ne** /mjɛ̃, mjɛn/ *pron.* le ~, la ~ne, les ~(ne)s, mine.

**miette** /mjɛt/ *n.f.* crumb.

**mieux** /mjø/ *adv. & a. invar.* better (que, than). le ou la ou les ~, (the) best. ● *n.m.* best; (*progrès*) improvement. faire de son ~, do one's best. tu ferais ~ de faire, you would be better off doing.

**mignon, ~ne** /miɲɔ̃, -ɔn/ *a.* pretty.

**migraine** /migrɛn/ *n.f.* headache.

**migration** /migrasjɔ̃/ *n.f.* migration.

**mijoter** /miʒote/ *v.t./i.* simmer.

**milieu** (*pl.* ~x) /miljø/ *n.m.* middle; (*environnement*) environment; (*groupe*) cir-cle. au ~ de, in the middle of.

**militaire** /militɛr/ *a.* military. ● *n.m.* soldier.

**milk-shake** /milkʃɛk/ *n.m.* milk shake.

**mille**[1] /mil/ *a. & n.m. invar.* a thousand. deux ~, two thousand. dans le ~, bang on target.

**mille**[2] /mil/ *n.m.* ~ (marin), (nautical) mile.

**millénaire** /milenɛr/ *n.m.* millennium.

**mille-pattes** /milpat/ *n.m. invar.* centi-pede.

**millésime** /milezim/ *n.m.* year.

**millésimé** /milezime/ *a.* vin ~, vintage wine.

**milliard** /miljar/ *n.m.* thousand million, billion. ~aire /-dɛr/ *n.m./f.* multimillion-aire.

**millier** /milje/ *n.m.* thousand. un ~ (de), about a thousand.

**millimètre** /milimɛtr/ *n.m.* millimetre.

**million** /miljɔ̃/ *n.m.* million. deux ~s (de), two million. ~naire /-jɔnɛr/ *n.m./f.* million-aire.

**mimosa** /mimoza/ *n.m.* mimosa.

**minable** /minabl/ *a.* shabby.

**minaret** /minarɛ/ *n.m.* minaret.

**minc|e** /mɛ̃s/ *a.* (*svelte, insignifiant*) slim. ● *int.* dash (it). ~ir *v.i.* get slimmer. ça te ~it, it makes you look slimmer. ~eur *n.f.* thinness; slimness.

**mine**[1] /min/ *n.f.* expression; (*allure*) appearance. avoir bonne ~, look well.

**mine**[2] /min/ *n.f.* (*exploitation, explosif*) mine; (*de crayon*) lead.

**minerai** /minrɛ/ *n.m.* ore.

**minér|al** (*m. pl.* ~aux) /mineral, -o/ *a.* mineral. ● *n.m.* (*pl.* ~aux) mineral.

**minéralogique** /mineralɔʒik/ *a.* plaque ~, number/license (*Amer.*) plate.

**mineur**[1], ~e /minœr/ *n.m.* minor; (*jurid.*) under age. ● *n.m., f.* (*jurid.*) minor.

**mineur**[2] /minœr/ *n.m.* (*ouvrier*) miner.

**mini-** /mini/ *préf.* mini-.

**miniature** /minjatyr/ *n.f. & a.* miniature.

**minibus** /minibys/ *n.m.* minibus.

**minim|al** (*m. pl.* ~aux) /minimal, -o/ *a.* minimum.

**minimum** /minimɔm/ *a. & n.m.* minimum. au ~, (*pour le moins*) at the very least.

**mini-ordinateur** /miniɔrdinatœr/ *n.m.* minicomputer.

**minist|ère** /ministɛr/ *n.m.* ministry; (*gou-vernement*) government. ~ère de l'Inté-rieur, Home Office. ~ériel, ~érielle *a.* ministerial, government.

**ministre** /ministr/ *n.m.* minister. ~ de l'Intérieur, Home Secretary.

**Minitel** /minitɛl/ *n.m.* (P.) Minitel (*telephone videotext system*).

**minorit|é** /minɔrite/ *n.f.* minority. **être** ~**aire**, be in the minority.

**minuit** /minɥi/ *n.m.* midnight.

**minuscule** /minyskyl/ *a.* minute. ● *n.f.* **(lettre)** ~, small letter.

**minute** /minyt/ *n.f.* minute.

**minuterie** /minytri/ *n.f.* time-switch.

**minutieu|x**, ~**se** /minysjø, -z/ *a.* meticulous. ~**sement** *adv.* meticulously.

**mirabelle** /mirabɛl/ *n.f.* (mirabelle) plum.

**miracle** /mirakl/ *n.m.* miracle.

**miraculeu|x**, ~**se** /mirakylø, -z/ *a.* miraculous.

**mirage** /miraʒ/ *n.m.* mirage.

**mire** /mir/ *n.f.* (*fig.*) centre of attraction; (TV) test card.

**miroir** /mirwar/ *n.m.* mirror.

**mis**, ~**e**[1] /mi, miz/ *voir* **mettre**. ● *a.* **bien** ~, well-dressed.

**mise**[2] /miz/ *n.f.* (*argent*) stake; (*tenue*) attire. ~ **au point**, adjustment; (*fig.*) clarification. ~ **en scène**, (*théâtre*) production; (*cinéma*) direction.

**miser** /mize/ *v.t.* (*argent*) bet, stake (**sur**, on).

**misérable** /mizerabl/ *a.* miserable, wretched; (*indigent*) poverty-stricken; (*minable*) seedy. ● *n.m./f.* wretch.

**misère** /mizɛr/ *n.f.* (grinding) poverty; (*malheur*) misery.

**miséricorde** /mizerikɔrd/ *n.f.* mercy.

**missel** /misɛl/ *n.m.* missal.

**missile** /misil/ *n.m.* missile.

**mission** /misjɔ̃/ *n.m.* mission.

**mistral** /mistral/ *n.m. invar.* (*vent*) mistral.

**mite** /mit/ *n.f.* (clothes-)moth.

**mi-temps** /mitɑ̃/ *n.f. invar.* (*repos: sport*) half-time; (*période: sport*) half. **à** ~, part time.

**mitonner** /mitɔne/ *v.t.* cook slowly with care; (*fig.*) cook up.

**mitoyen**, ~**ne** /mitwajɛ̃, -ɛn/ *a.* **mur** ~, party wall.

**mitraill|ette** /mitrajɛt/ *n.f.* sub-machine-gun. ~**euse** *n.f.* machine-gun.

**mixeur** /miksœr/ *n.m.* liquidizer, blender.

**mixte** /mikst/ *a.* mixed; (*usage*) dual; (*tribunal*) joint; (*école*) co-educational.

**mobile** /mɔbil/ *a.* mobile; (*pièce*) moving; (*feuillet*) loose. ● *n.m.* (*art*) mobile.

**mobilier** /mɔbilje/ *n.m.* furniture.

**mobilis|er** /mɔbilize/ *v.t.* mobilize. ~**ation** *n.f.* mobilization.

**mobilité** /mɔbilite/ *n.f.* mobility.

**mobylette** /mɔbilɛt/ *n.f.* (P.) moped.

**mocassin** /mɔkasɛ̃/ *n.m.* moccasin.

**moche** /mɔʃ/ *a.* (*laid: fam.*) ugly; (*mauvais: fam.*) lousy.

**modalité** /mɔdalite/ *n.f.* mode.

**mode**[1] /mɔd/ *n.f.* fashion; (*coutume*) custom. **à la** ~, fashionable.

**mode**[2] /mɔd/ *n.m.* method, mode; (*genre*) way. ~ **d'emploi**, directions (for use).

**modèle** /mɔdɛl/ *n.m.* & *a.* model.

**modem** /mɔdɛm/ *n.m.* modem.

**modéré**, ~**e** /mɔdere/ *a.* & *n.m.*, *f.* moderate. ~**ment** *adv.* moderately.

**modér|er** /mɔdere/ *v.t.* moderate. ~**ation** *n.f.* moderation.

**modern|e** /mɔdɛrn/ *a.* modern. ● *n.m.* modern style. ~**iser** *v.t.* modernize.

**modest|e** /mɔdɛst/ *a.* modest. ~**ement** *adv.* modestly. ~**ie** *n.f.* modesty.

**modif|ier** /mɔdifje/ *v.t.* modify. **se** ~**ier** *v. pr.* alter. ~**ication** *n.f.* modification.

**moelle** /mwal/ *n.f.* marrow. ~ **épinière**, spinal cord.

**moelleu|x**, ~**se** /mwalø, -z/ *a.* soft; (*onctueux*) smooth.

**mœurs** /mœr(s)/ *n.f. pl.* (*morale*) morals; (*habitudes*) customs; (*manières*) ways.

**moi** /mwa/ *pron.* me; (*indirect*) (to) me; (*sujet*) I. ● *n.m.* self. ~**même** *pron.* myself.

**moindre** /mwɛ̃dr/ *a.* (*moins grand*) less(er). **le ou la** ~, **les** ~**s**, the slightest, the least.

**moine** /mwan/ *n.m.* monk.

**moineau** (*pl.* ~**x**) /mwano/ *n.m.* sparrow.

**moins** /mwɛ̃/ *adv.* less (**que**, than). ● *prép.* (*soustraction*) minus. ~ **de**, (*quantité*) less, not so much (**que**, as); (*objets, personnes*) fewer, not so many (**que**, as); ~ **de dix francs/d'une livre**/*etc.*, less than ten francs/one pound/ *etc.* **le ou la ou les** ~, the least. **le** ~ **grand/haut**, the smallest/lowest. **au** ~, **du** ~, at least. **de** ~, less. **en** ~, less; (*manquant*) missing. **une heure** ~ **dix**, ten to one. **à** ~ **que**, unless. **de** ~ **en moins**, less and less.

**mois** /mwa/ *n.m.* month.

**moïse** /mɔiz/ *n.m.* moses basket.

**mois|i** /mwazi/ *a.* mouldy. ● *n.m.* mould. **de** ~**i**, (*odeur, goût*) musty. ~**ir** *v.i.* go mouldy. ~**issure** *n.f.* mould.

**moisson** /mwasɔ̃/ *n.f.* harvest.

**moissonn|er** /mwasɔne/ *v.t.* harvest, reap. ~**euse-batteuse** (*pl.* ~**euses-batteuses**) *n.f.* combine harvester.

**moit|e** /mwat/ *a.* sticky, clammy. ~**eur** *n.f.* stickiness.

**moitié** /mwatje/ *n.f.* half; (*milieu*) half-way mark. **à** ~, half-way. **à** ~ **vide/fermé**/*etc.*, half empty/ closed/*etc.* **à** ~ **prix**, (at) half-price. **la** ~ **de**, half (of). ~ **moitié**, half-and-half.

**moka** /mɔka/ *n.m.* (*gâteau*) coffee cream cake.

**mol** /mɔl/ *voir* **mou**.

**molaire** /mɔlɛr/ *n.f.* molar.

**molécule** /mɔlekyl/ *n.f.* molecule.

**molle** /mɔl/ *voir* **mou**.

**mollement** /mɔlmɑ̃/ *adv.* softly; (*faiblement*) feebly.

**mollet** /mɔlɛ/ *n.m.* (*de jambe*) calf.

**molletonné** /mɔltɔne/ *a.* (fleece-)lined.

**mollusque** /mɔlysk/ *n.m.* mollusc.

**môme** /mom/ *n.m./f.* (*fam.*) kid.

**moment** /mɔmɑ̃/ *n.m.* moment; (*période*) time. **(petit) ~,** short while. **au ~ où,** when. **en ce ~,** at the moment.

**momentané** /mɔmɑ̃tane/ *a.* momentary. **~ment** *adv.* momentarily; (*en ce moment*) at present.

**mon, ma** *ou* **mon*** (*pl.* **mes**) /mɔ̃, ma, mɔ̃, me/ *a.* my.

**Monaco** /mɔnako/ *n.f.* Monaco.

**monarchie** /mɔnarʃi/ *n.f.* monarchy.

**monastère** /mɔnastɛr/ *n.m.* monastery.

**mondain, ~e** /mɔ̃dɛ̃, -ɛn/ *a.* society, social.

**monde** /mɔ̃d/ *n.m.* world. **du ~,** (a lot of) people; (*quelqu'un*) somebody.

**mond|ial** (*m. pl.* **~iaux**) /mɔ̃djal, -jo/ *a.* world; (*influence*) worldwide. **~ialement** *adv.* the world over.

**monégasque** /mɔnegask/ *a.* & *n.m./f.* Monegasque.

**monétaire** /mɔnetɛr/ *a.* monetary.

**moni|teur, ~trice** /mɔnitœr, -tris/ *n.m., f.* instructor, instructress; (*de colonie de vacances*) supervisor; (*Amer.*) (camp) counselor.

**monnaie** /mɔnɛ/ *n.f.* currency; (*pièce*) coin; (*appoint*) change. **faire la ~ de,** get change for. **faire à qn. la ~ de,** give s.o. change for. **menue** *ou* **petite ~,** small change.

**mono** /mɔno/ *a. invar.* mono.

**monopol|e** /mɔnɔpɔl/ *n.m.* monopoly. **~iser** *v.t.* monopolize.

**monoton|e** /mɔnɔtɔn/ *a.* monotonous. **~ie** *n.f.* monotony.

**monseigneur** /mɔ̃sɛɲœr/ *n.m.* Your *ou* His Grace.

**monsieur** (*pl.* **messieurs**) /məsjø, mesjø/ *n.m.* gentleman. **M~** *ou* **M. Dupont,** Mr Dupont. **Messieurs** *ou* **MM. Dupont,** Messrs Dupont. **oui ~,** yes; (*avec déférence*) yes, sir.

**monstre** /mɔ̃str/ *n.m.* monster. ● *a.* (*fam.*) colossal.

**monstr|ueux, ~ueuse** /mɔ̃stryø, -z/ *a.* monstrous.

**mont** /mɔ̃/ *n.m.* mount.

**montage** /mɔ̃taʒ/ *n.m.* (*assemblage*) assembly; (*cinéma*) editing.

**montagn|e** /mɔ̃taɲ/ *n.f.* mountain; (*région*) mountains. **~es russes,** roller-coaster. **~ard, ~arde** *n.m., f.* mountain dweller. **~eux, ~euse** *a.* mountainous.

**montant**[1]**, ~e** /mɔ̃tɑ̃, -t/ *a.* rising; (*col*) high-necked.

**montant**[2] /mɔ̃tɑ̃/ *n.m.* amount; (*pièce de bois*) upright.

**monte-charge** /mɔ̃tʃarʒ/ *n.m. invar.* service lift.

**montée** /mɔ̃te/ *n.f.* ascent, climb; (*de prix*) rise; (*côte*) hill.

**monter** /mɔ̃te/ *v.i.* (*aux. être*) go *ou* come up; (*grimper*) climb; (*prix, mer*) rise. **~ à,** (*cheval*) mount. **~ dans,** (*train, avion*) get on to; (*voiture*) get into. **~ sur,** (*colline*) climb up; (*trône*) ascend. ● *v.t.* (*aux. avoir*) go *ou* come up; (*objet*) take *ou* bring up; (*cheval, garde*) mount; (*société*) start up. **~ à cheval,** (*sport*) ride.

**monteu|r, ~se** /mɔ̃tœr, -øz/ *n.m., f.* (*techn.*) fitter; (*cinéma*) editor.

**montre** /mɔ̃tr/ *n.f.* watch.

**montrer** /mɔ̃tre/ *v.t.* show (**à,** to). **~ du doigt,** point to.

**monture** /mɔ̃tyr/ *n.f.* (*cheval*) mount; (*de lunettes*) frame.

**monument** /mɔnymɑ̃/ *n.m.* monument. **~ aux morts,** war memorial.

**moqu|er (se)** /(sə)mɔke/ *v. pr.* **se ~er de,** make fun of.

**moquette** /mɔkɛt/ *n.f.* fitted carpet.

**mor|al, ~ale** (*m. pl.* **~aux**) /mɔral, -o/ *a.* moral. ● *n.m.* (*pl.* **~aux**) morale. ● *n.f.* moral code; (*mœurs*) morals; (*de fable*) moral. **avoir le ~al,** be on form.

**morceau** (*pl.* **~x**) /mɔrso/ *n.m.* piece, bit; (*de sucre*) lump; (*de viande*) cut; (*passage*) passage. **manger un ~,** have a bite to eat.

**mordre** /mɔrdr/ *v.t./i.* bite. **~ sur,** overlap into. **~ à l'hameçon,** bite.

**morgue** /mɔrg/ *n.f.* morgue, mortuary.

**morne** /mɔrn/ *a.* dull.

**morose** /mɔroz/ *a.* morose.

**morphine** /mɔrfin/ *n.f.* morphine.

**mors** /mɔr/ *n.m.* (*de cheval*) bit.

**morse**[1] /mɔrs/ *n.m.* walrus.

**morse**[2] /mɔrs/ *n.m.* (*code*) Morse code.

**morsure** /mɔrsyr/ *n.f.* bite.

**mort**[1] /mɔr/ *n.f.* death.

**mort**[2]**, ~e** /mɔr, -t/ *a.* dead. ● *n.m., f.* dead man, dead woman. **les ~s,** the dead. **~ de fatigue,** dead tired. **~-né** *a.* stillborn.

**mortadelle** /mɔrtadɛl/ *n.f.* mortadella.

**mortalité** /mɔrtalite/ *n.f.* death rate.

**mortel, ~le** /mɔrtɛl/ *a.* mortal; (*accident*) fatal; (*poison, silence*) deadly. ● *n.m., f.* mortal.

**mortier** /mɔrtje/ *n.m.* mortar.

**morue** /mɔry/ *n.f.* cod.

**mosaïque** /mɔzaik/ *n.f.* mosaic.

**Moscou** /mɔsku/ *n.m./f.* Moscow.

**mosquée** /mɔske/ *n.f.* mosque.

**mot** /mo/ *n.m.* word; (*lettre, message*) line, note. **~s croisés,** crossword (puzzle).

**motard** /mɔtar/ *n.m.* biker; (*policier*) police motorcyclist.

**motel** /mɔtɛl/ *n.m.* motel.

**moteur**[1] /mɔtœr/ *n.m.* engine, motor. **barque à ~,** motor launch.

**mo|teur²**, **~trice** /mɔtœr, -tris/ *a.* (*nerf*) motor; (*force*) driving. **à 4 roues motrices**, 4-wheel drive.

**motif** /mɔtif/ *n.m.* reason; (*jurid.*) motive; (*dessin*) pattern.

**motiv|er** /mɔtive/ *v.t.* motivate; (*justifier*) justify. **~ation** *n.f.* motivation.

**moto** /mɔto/ *n.f.* motor cycle. **~cycliste** *n.m./f.* motorcyclist.

**motorisé** /mɔtɔrize/ *a.* motorized.

**motrice** /mɔtris/ *voir* **moteur¹**.

**motte** /mɔt/ *n.f.* lump; (*de beurre*) slab; (*de terre*) clod.

**mou** *ou* **mol\***, **molle** /mu, mɔl/ *a.* soft; (*péj.*) flabby; (*faible, indolent*) feeble.

**mouche** /muʃ/ *n.f.* fly.

**moucher (se)** /(sə)muʃe/ *v. pr.* blow one's nose.

**moucheron** /muʃrɔ̃/ *n.m.* midge.

**mouchoir** /muʃwar/ *n.m.* hanky; handkerchief; (*en papier*) tissue.

**moudre** /mudr/ *v.t.* grind.

**moue** /mu/ *n.f.* long face. **faire la ~,** pull a long face.

**mouette** /mwɛt/ *n.f.* (sea)gull.

**moufle** /mufl/ *n.f.* (*gant*) mitten.

**mouill|er** /muje/ *v.t.* wet, make wet. **se ~er** *v. pr.* get (o.s.) wet. **~er (l'ancre),** anchor.

**moulage** /mulaʒ/ *n.m.* cast.

**moul|e¹** /mul/ *n.m.* mould. **~er** *v.t.* mould; (*statue*) cast. **~e à gâteau,** cake tin. **~e à tarte,** flan dish.

**moule²** /mul/ *n.f.* (*coquillage*) mussel.

**moulin** /mulɛ̃/ *n.m.* mill. **~ à vent,** windmill.

**moulinet** /mulinɛ/ *n.m.* (*de canne à pêche*) reel.

**mourir†** /murir/ *v.i.* (*aux. être*) die. **~ d'envie de,** be dying to. **~ de faim,** be starving. **~ d'ennui,** be dead bored.

**mousquetaire** /muskətɛr/ *n.m.* musketeer.

**mousse** /mus/ *n.f.* moss; (*écume*) froth, foam; (*de savon*) lather; (*dessert*) mousse. **~ à raser,** shaving cream.

**mousseline** /muslin/ *n.f.* muslin; (*de soie*) chiffon.

**mousser** /muse/ *v.i.* froth, foam; (*savon*) lather.

**mousseu|x, ~se** /musø, -z/ *a.* frothy. ● *n.m.* sparkling wine.

**moustach|e** /mustaʃ/ *n.f.* moustache. **~es,** (*d'animal*) whiskers. **~u** *a.* wearing a moustache.

**moustiquaire** /mustikɛr/ *n.f.* mosquito-net.

**moustique** /mustik/ *n.m.* mosquito.

**moutarde** /mutard/ *n.f.* mustard.

**mouton** /mutɔ̃/ *n.m.* sheep; (*peau*) sheepskin; (*viande*) mutton.

**mouvement** /muvmɑ̃/ *n.m.* movement; (*agitation*) bustle; (*en gymnastique*) exercise. **en ~,** in motion.

**mouvementé** /muvmɑ̃te/ *a.* eventful.

**moyen¹**, **~ne** /mwajɛ̃, -jɛn/ *a.* average; (*médiocre*) poor. ● *n.f.* average; (*scol.*) passmark. **de taille ~ne,** medium-sized. **~ âge,** Middle Ages. **M~Orient** *n.m.* Middle East.

**moyen²** /mwajɛ̃/ *n.m.* means, way. **~s,** means; (*dons*) abilities. **il n'y a pas ~ de,** it is not possible to.

**moyeu** (*pl.* **~x**) /mwajø/ *n.m.* hub.

**mucoviscidose** /mykɔvisidoz/ *n.f.* cystic fibrosis.

**mue** /my/ *n.f.* moulting; (*de voix*) breaking of the voice.

**muer** /mye/ *v.i.* moult; (*voix*) break. **se ~ en,** change into.

**muesli** /mysli/ *n.m.* muesli.

**muet**, **~te** /mɥɛ, -t/ *a.* (*personne*) dumb; (*fig.*) speechless (**de,** with); (*silencieux*) silent. ● *n.m.*, *f.* dumb person.

**mufle** /myfl/ *n.m.* nose, muzzle.

**muguet** /mygɛ/ *n.m.* lily of the valley.

**mule** /myl/ *n.f.* (she-)mule; (*pantoufle*) mule.

**mulet** /mylɛ/ *n.m.* (he-)mule.

**multi-** /mylti/ *préf.* multi-.

**multicolore** /myltikɔlɔr/ *a.* multicoloured.

**multination|al**, **~ale** (*m. pl.* **~aux**) /myltinasjɔnal, -o/ *a.* & *n.f.* multinational.

**multiple** /myltipl/ *a.* & *n.m.* multiple.

**multipl|ier** /myltiplije/ *v.t.*, **se ~ier** *v. pr.* multiply. **~ication** *n.f.* multiplication.

**municip|al** (*m. pl.* **~aux**) /mynisipal, -o/ *a.* municipal; (*conseil*) town. **~alité** *n.f.* (*ville*) municipality; (*conseil*) town council.

**munir** /mynir/ *v.t.* **~ de,** provide with. **se ~ de,** provide o.s. with.

**mur** /myr/ *n.m.* wall.

**mûr** /myr/ *a.* ripe; (*personne*) mature.

**muraille** /myraj/ *n.f.* (high) wall.

**mûre** /myr/ *n.f.* blackberry.

**mûrir** /myrir/ *v.t./i.* ripen; (*personne, projet*) mature.

**murmur|e** /myrmyr/ *n.m.* murmur. **~er** *v.t./i.* murmur.

**muscade** /myskad/ *n.f.* **noix (de) ~,** nutmeg.

**muscl|e** /myskl/ *n.m.* muscle. **~é** *a.* muscular, brawny.

**muscul|aire** /myskylɛr/ *a.* muscular. **~ature** *n.f.* muscles.

**museau** (*pl.* **~x**) /myzo/ *n.m.* muzzle; (*de porc*) snout.

**musée** /myze/ *n.m.* museum; (*de peinture*) art gallery.

**museler** /myzle/ *v.t.* muzzle.

**muselière** /myzəljɛr/ *n.f.* muzzle.

**muséum** /myzeɔm/ *n.m.* (natural history) museum.

**music|al** (*m. pl.* ∼**aux**) /myzikal, -o/ *a.* musical.

**music-hall** /myzikol/ *n.m.* variety theatre.

**musicien, ∼ne** /myzisjɛ̃, -jɛn/ *a.* musical. ● *n.m., f.* musician.

**musique** /myzik/ *n.f.* music; (*orchestre*) band.

**musulman, ∼e** /myzylmɑ̃,-an/ *a. & n.m., f.* Muslim.

**mutation** /mytɑsjɔ̃/ *n.f.* change; (*biologique*) mutation.

**muter** /myte/ *v.t.* transfer.

**mutuel, ∼le** /mytɥɛl/ *a.* mutual. ● *n.f.* Friendly Society; (*Amer.*) benefit society. **∼lement** *adv.* mutually; (*l'un l'autre*) each other.

**myop|e** /mjɔp/ *a.* short-sighted. **∼ie** *n.f.* short-sightedness.

**myosotis** /mjozotis/ *n.m.* forget-me-not.

**myrtille** /mirtij/ *n.f.* bilberry.

**mystère** /mistɛr/ *n.m.* mystery.

**mystérieu|x, ∼se** /misterjø, -z/ *a.* mysterious.

**mystif|ier** /mistifje/ *v.t.* deceive, hoax. **∼ication** *n.f.* hoax.

**mystique** /mistik/ *a.* mystic(al). ● *n.m./f.* mystic.

**mythe** /mit/ *n.m.* myth.

**mytholog|ie** /mitɔlɔʒi/ *n.f.* mythology. **∼ique** *a.* mythological.

# Nn

**n'** /n/ *voir* **ne**.

**nacr|e** /nakr/ *n.f.* mother-of-pearl. **∼é** *a.* pearly.

**nage** /naʒ/ *n.f.* swimming; (*manière*) (swimming) stroke. **à la ∼,** by swimming. **traverser à la ∼,** swim across. **en ∼,** sweating.

**nageoire** /naʒwar/ *n.f.* fin.

**nag|er** /naʒe/ *v.t./i.* swim. **∼eur, ∼euse** *n.m., f.* swimmer.

**naï|f, ∼ve** /naif, -v/ *a.* naïve.

**nain, ∼e** /nɛ̃, nɛn/ *n.m., f. & a.* dwarf.

**naissance** /nesɑ̃s/ *n.f.* birth.

**naître†** /nɛtr/ *v.i.* be born; (*résulter*) arise (**de**, from). **faire ∼,** (*susciter*) give rise to.

**naïveté** /naivte/ *n.f.* naïvety.

**nana** /nana/ *n.f.* (*fam.*) girl.

**naphtaline** /naftalin/ *n.f.* mothballs.

**nappe** /nap/ *n.f.* table-cloth; (*de pétrole, gaz*) layer.

**napperon** /naprɔ̃/ *n.m.* (cloth) table-mat.

**narcotique** /narkɔtik/ *a. & n.m.* narcotic.

**narine** /narin/ *n.f.* nostril.

**naseau** (*pl.* ∼**x**) /nazo/ *n.m.* nostril.

**nat|al** (*m. pl.* ∼**als**) /natal/ *a.* native.

**natalité** /natalite/ *n.f.* birth rate.

**natation** /natɑsjɔ̃/ *n.f.* swimming.

**nati|f, ∼ve** /natif, -v/ *a.* native.

**nation** /nɑsjɔ̃/ *n.f.* nation.

**nation|al, ∼ale** (*m. pl.* ∼**aux**) /nasjɔnal, -o/ *a.* national. ● *n.f.* A road. **∼aliser** *v.t.* nationalize. **∼alisme** *n.m.* nationalism.

**nationalité** /nasjɔnalite/ *n.f.* nationality.

**Nativité** /nativite/ *n.f.* **la ∼,** the Nativity.

**natte** /nat/ *n.f.* (*de cheveux*) plait; (*tapis de paille*) mat.

**naturaliser** /natyralize/ *v.t.* naturalize.

**nature** /natyr/ *n.f.* nature. ● *a. invar.* (*eau, omelette, etc.*) plain.

**naturel, ∼le** /natyrɛl/ *a.* natural. ● *n.m.* nature; (*simplicité*) naturalness. **∼lement** *adv.* naturally.

**naufrage** /nofraʒ/ *n.m.* (ship)-wreck. **faire ∼,** be shipwrecked; (*bateau*) be wrecked.

**nausée** /noze/ *n.f.* nausea.

**nautique** /notik/ *a.* nautical; (*sports*) aquatic.

**naval** (*m. pl.* ∼**s**) /naval/ *a.* naval.

**navet** /navɛ/ *n.m.* turnip; (*film, tableau*) dud.

**navette** /navɛt/ *n.f.* shuttle.

**navigable** /navigabl/ *a.* navigable.

**navig|uer** /navige/ *v.i.* sail; (*piloter*) navigate. **∼ateur** *n.m.* seafarer; (*d'avion*) navigator. **∼ation** *n.f.* navigation; (*trafic*) shipping.

**navire** /navir/ *n.m.* ship.

**navré** /navre/ *a.* sorry (**de,** to).

**ne, n'** /nə, n/ *adv.* **ne pas,** not. **ne jamais,** never. **ne plus,** (*temps*) no longer, not any more. **ne que,** only.

**né, née** /ne/ *voir* **naître**. ● *a. & n.m., f.* born. **il est né,** he was born.

**néanmoins** /neɑ̃mwɛ̃/ *adv.* nevertheless.

**néant** /neɑ̃/ *n.m.* nothingness; (*aucun*) none.

**nécessaire** /nesesɛr/ *a.* necessary. ● *n.m.* (*sac*) bag; (*trousse*) kit. **le ∼,** (*l'indispensable*) the necessities. **faire le ∼,** do what is necessary.

**nécessiter** /nesesite/ *v.t.* necessitate.

**néerlandais, ∼e** /neɛrlɑ̃dɛ, -z/ *a.* Dutch. ● *n.m., f.* Dutchman, Dutchwoman. ● *n.m.* (*lang.*) Dutch.

**nef** /nɛf/ *n.f.* nave.

**négati|f, ∼ve** /negatif, -v/ *a. & n.m., f.* negative.

**négation** /negɑsjɔ̃/ *n.f.* negation.

**négligeable** /negliʒabl/ *a.* negligible, insignificant.

**négligen|t, ∼te** /negliʒɑ̃, -t/ *a.* careless, negligent. **∼ce** *n.f.* carelessness, negligence; (*erreur*) omission.

**négliger** /neglize/ v.t. neglect; (ne pas tenir compte de) disregard. **se ~** v. pr. neglect o.s.

**négoc|e** /negos/ n.m. business. **~iant, ~iante** n.m., f. merchant.

**négoc|ier** /negosje/ v.t./i. negotiate. **~iable** a. negotiable. **~iateur, ~iatrice** n.m., f. negotiator. **~iation** n.f. negotiation.

**nègre** /negr/ a. Negro.

**neig|e** /nɛʒ/ n.f. snow. **~eux, ~euse** a. snowy.

**neiger** /neʒe/ v.i. snow.

**nénuphar** /nenyfar/ n.m. waterlily.

**néon** /neõ/ n.m. neon.

**néo-zélandais, ~e** /neozelãdɛ, -z/ a. New Zealand. ● n.m., f. New Zealander.

**nerf** /nɛr/ n.m. nerve.

**nerv|eux, ~euse** /nɛrvø, -z/ a. nervous; (irritable) nervy; (centre, cellule) nerve-; (voiture) responsive. **~osité** n.f. (irritabilité) touchiness.

**net, ~te** /nɛt/ a. (clair, distinct) clear; (propre) clean; (soigné) neat; (prix, poids) net. ● adv. (s'arrêter) dead; (refuser) flatly.

**nettoy|er** /netwaje/ v.t. clean. **~age** n.m. cleaning. **~age à sec,** dry-cleaning.

**neuf¹** /nœf/ (/nœv/ before heures, ans) a. & n.m. nine.

**neu|f², ~ve** /nœf, -v/ a. & n.m. new.

**neutr|e** /nøtr/ a. neutral; (gram.) neuter. ● n.m. (gram.) neuter. **~alité** n.f. neutrality.

**neutron** /nøtrõ/ n.m. neutron.

**neuve** /nœv/ voir **neuf².**

**neuvième** /nœvjɛm/ a. & n.m./f. ninth.

**neveu** (pl. **~x**) /nəvø/ n.m. nephew.

**nez** /ne/ n.m. nose.

**ni** /ni/ conj. neither, nor. **ni grand ni petit,** neither big nor small. **ni l'un ni l'autre ne fument,** neither (one nor the other) smokes.

**niche** /niʃ/ n.f. (de chien) kennel; (cavité) niche; (farce) trick.

**nicher** /niʃe/ v.i. nest. **se ~** v. pr. nest; (se cacher) hide.

**nickel** /nikɛl/ n.m. nickel.

**nicotine** /nikɔtin/ n.f. nicotine.

**nid** /ni/ n.m. nest.

**nièce** /njɛs/ n.f. niece.

**nier** /nje/ v.t. deny.

**nippon, ~e** /nipõ, -ɔn/ a. & n.m., f. Japanese.

**niveau** (pl. **~x**) /nivo/ n.m. level; (compétence) standard. **~ de vie,** standard of living.

**nivel|er** /nivle/ v.t. level. **~lement** /-ɛlmã/ n.m. levelling.

**noble** /nɔbl/ a. noble. ● n.m./f. nobleman, noblewoman.

**noblesse** /nɔblɛs/ n.f. nobility.

**noce** /nɔs/ n.f. wedding. **faire la ~,** (fam.) make merry.

**noci|f, ~ve** /nɔsif, -v/ a. harmful.

**noctambule** /nɔktãbyl/ n.m./f. night-owl, late-night reveller.

**nocturne** /nɔktyrn/ a. nocturnal.

**Noël** /nɔel/ n.m. Christmas.

**nœud¹** /nø/ n.m. knot; (ornemental) bow. **~s,** (fig.) ties. **~ papillon,** bow-tie.

**nœud²** /nø/ n.m. (naut.) knot.

**noir, ~e** /nwar/ a. black; (obscur, sombre) dark; (triste) gloomy. ● n.m. black; (obscurité) dark. **travail au ~,** moonlighting. ● n.m., f. (personne) Black. ● n.f. (mus.) crotchet.

**noix** /nwa/ n.f. nut; (du noyer) walnut; (de beurre) knob. **~ de cajou,** cashew nut. **~ de coco,** coconut. **à la ~,** (fam.) useless.

**nom** /nõ/ n.m. name; (gram.) noun. **au ~ de,** on behalf of. **~ de famille,** surname. **~ de jeune fille,** maiden name. **~ propre,** proper noun.

**nomade** /nɔmad/ a. nomadic. ● n.m./f. nomad.

**nombre** /nõbr/ n.m. number. **en (grand) ~,** in large numbers.

**nombreu|x, ~se** /nõbrø, -z/ a. numerous; (important) large.

**nombril** /nõbri/ n.m. navel.

**nomination** /nɔminasjõ/ n.f. appointment.

**nommer** /nɔme/ v.t. name; (élire) appoint. **se ~** v. pr. (s'appeler) be called.

**non** /nõ/ adv. no; (pas) not. ● n.m. invar. no. **moi ~ plus,** neither am, do, can, etc. I.

**non-** /nõ/ préf. non-. **~fumeur,** non-smoker.

**nonante** /nɔnãt/ a. & n.m. ninety.

**non-sens** /nõsãs/ n.m. absurdity.

**nord** /nɔr/ n.m. north. ● a. invar. north; (partie) northern; (direction) northerly. **au ~ de,** to the north of. **~-africain, ~-africaine** a. & n.m., f. North African. **~-est** n.m. northeast. **~-ouest** n.m. north-west.

**nordique** /nɔrdik/ a. & n.m./f. Scandinavian.

**norm|al, ~ale** (m. pl. **~aux**) /nɔrmal, -o/ a. normal. ● n.f. normality; (norme) norm; (moyenne) average. **~alement** adv. normally.

**normand, ~e** /nɔrmã, -d/ a. & n.m., f. Norman.

**Normandie** /nɔrmãdi/ n.f. Normandy.

**norme** /nɔrm/ n.f. norm; (de production) standard.

**Norvège** /nɔrvɛʒ/ n.f. Norway.

**norvégien, ~ne** /nɔrveʒjɛ̃, -jɛn/ a. & n.m., f. Norwegian.

**nos** /no/ voir **notre.**

**nostalgie** /nɔstalʒi/ n.f. nostalgia.

**notaire** /nɔtɛr/ n.m. notary.

**notamment** /nɔtamã/ adv. notably.

**note** /nɔt/ n.f. (remarque) note; (chiffrée) mark; (facture) bill; (mus.) note.

**noter** /nɔte/ v.t. note, notice; (écrire) note (down); (devoir) mark.

**notice** /nɔtis/ n.f. note; (mode d'emploi) directions.

**notion** /nɔsjɔ̃/ n.f. notion.

**notoire** /nɔtwar/ a. well-known; (criminel) notorious.

**notre** (pl. **nos**) /nɔtr, no/ a. our.

**nôtre** /nɔtr/ pron. **le** ou **la** ∼, **les** ∼**s**, ours.

**nouer** /nwe/ v.t. tie, knot; (relations) strike up.

**nougat** /nuga/ n.m. nougat.

**nouilles** /nuj/ n.f. pl. noodles.

**nounours** /nunurs/ n.m. teddy bear.

**nourri** /nuri/ a. (fig.) intense. **logé** ∼, bed and board.

**nourrice** /nuris/ n.f. child-minder.

**nourr|ir** /nurir/ v.t. feed. **se** ∼**ir** v. pr. eat. ∼**issant**, ∼**issante** a. nourishing.

**nourrisson** /nurisɔ̃/ n.m. infant.

**nourriture** /nurityr/ n.f. food.

**nous** /nu/ pron. we; (complément) us; (indirect) (to) us; (réfléchi) ourselves; (l'un l'autre) each other. ∼-**mêmes** pron. ourselves.

**nouveau** ou **nouvel***, **nouvelle**[1] (m. pl. ∼**x**) /nuvo, nuvɛl/ a. & n.m. new. ● n.m., f. (élève) new boy, new girl. **de** ∼, **à** ∼, again. **du** ∼, (fait nouveau) some new development. **nouvel an**, new year. ∼**x mariés**, newlyweds. ∼**né**, ∼**née** a. new-born; n.m., f. newborn baby. **Nouvelle Zélande**, New Zealand.

**nouveauté** /nuvote/ n.f. novelty; (chose) new thing.

**nouvelle**[2] /nuvɛl/ n.f. (piece of) news; (récit) short story. ∼**s**, news.

**novembre** /nɔvɑ̃br/ n.m. November.

**noyade** /nwajad/ n.f. drowning.

**noyau** (pl. ∼**x**) /nwajo/ n.m. (de fruit) stone; (de cellule) nucleus; (groupe) group; (centre; fig.) core.

**noyer**[1] /nwaje/ v.t. drown; (inonder) flood. **se** ∼ v. pr. drown; (volontairement) drown o.s.

**noyer**[2] /nwaje/ n.m. (arbre) walnut-tree.

**nu** /ny/ a. naked; (mains, mur, fil) bare. ● n.m. nude. **nu-pieds** adv. barefoot. **nu-tête** adv. bareheaded. **à l'oeil nu**, to the naked eye.

**nuag|e** /nɥaʒ/ n.m. cloud. ∼**eux**, ∼**euse** a. cloudy.

**nuance** /nɥɑ̃s/ n.f. shade; (de sens) nuance; (différence) difference.

**nuancer** /nɥɑ̃se/ v.t. (opinion) qualify.

**nucléaire** /nykleɛr/ a. nuclear.

**nudis|te** /nydist/ n.m./f. nudist. ∼**me** n.m. nudism.

**nudité** /nydite/ n.f. (de personne) nudity; (de chambre etc.) bareness.

**nuire**† /nɥir/ v.i. ∼ **à**, harm.

**nuisible** /nɥizibl/ a. harmful.

**nuit** /nɥi/ n.f. night. **cette** ∼, tonight; (hier) last night. **il fait** ∼, it is dark. ∼ **blanche**, sleepless night. **la** ∼, **de** ∼, at night. ∼ **de noces**, wedding night.

**nul**, ∼**le** /nyl/ a. (aucun) no; (zéro) nil; (qui ne vaut rien) useless; (non valable) null. **match** ∼, draw. ∼ **en**, no good at.

**numérique** /nymerik/ a. numerical; (montre, horloge) digital.

**numéro** /nymero/ n.m. number; (de journal) issue; (spectacle) act. ∼**ter** /-ɔte/ v.t. number.

**nuque** /nyk/ n.f. nape (of the neck).

**nurse** /nœrs/ n.f. (children's) nurse.

**nutriti|f**, ∼**ve** /nytritif, -v/ a. nutritious; (valeur) nutritional.

**nutrition** /nytrisjɔ̃/ n.f. nutrition.

**nylon** /nilɔ̃/ n.m. nylon.

**oasis** /ɔazis/ n.f. oasis.

**obéir** /ɔbeir/ v.i. obey. ∼ **à**, obey.

**obéissan|t**, ∼**te** /ɔbeisɑ̃, -t/ a. obedient. ∼**ce** n.f. obedience.

**obèse** /ɔbɛz/ a. obese.

**obésité** /ɔbezite/ n.f. obesity.

**object|er** /ɔbʒɛkte/ v.t. put forward (as an excuse). ∼**er que**, object that. ∼**ion** /-ksjɔ̃/ n.f. objection.

**objecti|f**, ∼**ve** /ɔbʒɛktif, -v/ a. objective. ● n.m. objective; (photo.) lens. ∼**vement** adv. objectively. ∼**vité** n.f. objectivity.

**objet** /ɔbʒɛ/ n.m. object; (sujet) subject. ∼ **d'art**, objet d'art. ∼**s trouvés**, lost property.

**obligation** /ɔbligasjɔ̃/ n.f. obligation; (comm.) bond. **être dans l'**∼ **de**, be under obligation to.

**obligatoire** /ɔbligatwar/ a. compulsory. ∼**ment** adv. of necessity; (fam.) inevitably.

**oblig|er** /ɔbliʒe/ v.t. compel, oblige (**à faire**, to do); (aider) oblige. **être** ∼**é de**, have to.

**oblique** /ɔblik/ a. oblique.

**obliquer** /ɔblike/ v.i. turn off (**vers**, towards).

**oblitérer** /ɔblitere/ v.t. (timbre) cancel.

**obsc|ène** /ɔpsɛn/ a. obscene. ∼**énité** n.f. obscenity.

**obscur** /ɔpskyr/ a. dark; (confus, humble) obscure.

**obscurité** /ɔpskyrite/ n.f. dark(-ness); (passage, situation) obscurity.

**obséd|er** /ɔpsede/ v.t. obsess. ∼**ant**, ∼**ante** a. obsessive. ∼**é**, ∼**ée** n.m., f. maniac.

**obsèques** /ɔpsɛk/ n.f. pl. funeral.

**observation** /ɔpsɛrvasjɔ̃/ *n.f.* observation; (*reproche*) criticism; (*obéissance*) observance. **en ~,** under observation.

**observatoire** /ɔpsɛrvatwar/ *n.m.* observatory.

**observ|er** /ɔpsɛrve/ *v.t.* observe; (*surveiller*) watch, observe. **faire ~er qch.,** point sth. out (**à,** to). **~ateur, ~atrice** *a.* observant; *n.m., f.* observer.

**obsession** /ɔpsesjɔ̃/ *n.f.* obsession.

**obstacle** /ɔpstakl/ *n.m.* obstacle; (*cheval*) jump; (*athlète*) hurdle. **faire ~ à,** stand in the way of.

**obstin|é** /ɔpstine/ *a.* obstinate. **~ation** *n.f.* obstinacy.

**obstiner (s')** /(s)ɔpstine/ *v. pr.* persist (**à,** in).

**obstruction** /ɔpstryksjɔ̃/ *n.f.* obstruction.

**obtenir†** /ɔptənir/ *v.t.* get, obtain.

**obturateur** /ɔptyratœr/ *n.m.* (*photo.*) shutter.

**obus** /ɔby/ *n.m.* shell.

**occasion** /ɔkazjɔ̃/ *n.f.* opportunity (**de faire,** of doing); (*circonstance*) occasion; (*achat*) bargain; (*article non neuf*) second-hand buy. **d'~,** second-hand.

**occasionner** /ɔkazjone/ *v.t.* cause.

**occident** /ɔksidɑ̃/ *n.m.* west. **~al, ~ale** (*m. pl. ~aux*) /-tal, -to/ *a.* western. ● *n.m., f.* westerner.

**occupant, ~e** /ɔkypɑ̃, -t/ *n.m., f.* occupant. ● *n.m.* (*mil.*) forces of occupation.

**occupation** /ɔkypasjɔ̃/ *n.f.* occupation.

**occupé** /ɔkype/ *a.* busy; (*place, pays*) occupied; (*téléphone*) engaged.

**occuper** /ɔkype/ *v.t.* occupy; (*poste*) hold. **s'~ de,** (*personne, problème*) take care of; (*bureau, firme*) be in charge of.

**océan** /ɔseɑ̃/ *n.m.* ocean.

**ocre** /ɔkr/ *a. invar.* ochre.

**octante** /ɔktɑ̃t/ *a.* (*régional*) eighty.

**octave** /ɔktav/ *n.f.* (*mus.*) octave.

**octet** /ɔktɛ/ *n.m.* byte.

**octobre** /ɔktɔbr/ *n.m.* October.

**octogone** /ɔktɔgon/ *n.m.* octagon.

**octroyer** /ɔktrwaje/ *v.t.* grant.

**oculiste** /ɔkylist/ *n.m./f.* eye-specialist.

**odeur** /ɔdœr/ *n.f.* smell.

**odieu|x, ~se** /ɔdjø, -z/ *a.* odious.

**odorat** /ɔdora/ *n.m.* (sense of) smell.

**œcuménique** /ekymenik/ *a.* ecumenical.

**œil** (*pl.* **yeux**) /œj, jø/ *n.m.* eye. **à l'~,** (*fam.*) free. **à mes yeux,** in my view. **ouvrir l'~,** keep one's eye open. **fermer l'~,** shut one's eyes.

**œillet** /œjɛ/ *n.m.* (*plante*) carnation; (*trou*) eyelet.

**œuf** (*pl. ~s*) /œf, ø/ *n.m.* egg. **~ à la coque/ dur/sur le plat,** boiled/hard-boiled/fried egg.

**œuvre** /œvr/ *n.f.* (*ouvrage, travail*) work. **~ d'art,** work of art. **~ (de bienfaisance),** charity.

**offense** /ɔfɑ̃s/ *n.f.* insult.

**offenser** /ɔfɑ̃se/ *v.t.* offend.

**offert, ~e** /ɔfɛr, -t/ *voir* **offrir**.

**office** /ɔfis/ *n.m.* office; (*relig.*) service; (*de cuisine*) pantry. **d'~,** automatically.

**officiel, ~le** /ɔfisjɛl/ *a. & n.m.* official. **~lement** *adv.* officially.

**officier** /ɔfisje/ *n.m.* officer.

**officieu|x, ~se** /ɔfisjø, -z/ *a.* unofficial. **~sement** *adv.* unofficially.

**offrant** /ɔfrɑ̃/ *n.m.* **au plus ~,** to the highest bidder.

**offre** /ɔfr/ *n.f.* offer; (*aux enchères*) bid. **l'~ et la demande,** supply and demand. **~s d'emploi,** jobs advertised, (*rubrique*) situations vacant.

**offrir†** /ɔfrir/ *v.t.* offer (**de faire,** to do); (*cadeau*) give; (*acheter*) buy. **s'~** *v. pr.* offer o.s. (**comme,** as); (*spectacle*) present itself; (*s'acheter*) treat o.s. to. **~ à boire à,** (*chez soi*) give a drink to; (*au café*) buy a drink for.

**oh** /o/ *int.* oh.

**oie** /wa/ *n.f.* goose.

**oignon** /ɔɲɔ̃/ *n.m.* (*légume*) onion; (*de tulipe etc.*) bulb.

**oiseau** (*pl. ~x*) /wazo/ *n.m.* bird.

**O.K.** /ɔke/ *int.* O.K.

**oléoduc** /ɔleɔdyk/ *n.m.* oil pipeline.

**oliv|e** /ɔliv/ *n.f. & a. invar.* olive. **~ier** *n.m.* olive-tree.

**olympique** /ɔlɛ̃pik/ *a.* Olympic.

**ombre** /ɔ̃br/ *n.f.* (*pénombre*) shade; (*contour*) shadow; (*soupçon: fig.*) hint, shadow.

**omelette** /ɔmlɛt/ *n.f.* omelette.

**omettre†** /ɔmɛtr/ *v.t.* omit.

**omission** /ɔmisjɔ̃/ *n.f.* omission.

**omnibus** /ɔmnibys/ *n.m.* stopping train.

**omoplate** /ɔmoplat/ *n.f.* shoulder-blade.

**on** /ɔ̃/ *pron.* we, you, one; (*les gens*) people, they; (*quelqu'un*) someone. **on dit,** people say, they say, it is said (**que,** that).

**once** /ɔ̃s/ *n.f.* ounce.

**oncle** /ɔ̃kl/ *n.m.* uncle.

**onctueu|x, ~se** /ɔ̃ktɥø, -z/ *a.* smooth.

**onde** /ɔ̃d/ *n.f.* wave. **~s courtes/longues,** short/longwave. **sur les ~s,** on the radio.

**ondul|er** /ɔ̃dyle/ *v.i.* undulate; (*cheveux*) be wavy. **~é a.** (*chevelure*) wavy.

**ongle** /ɔ̃gl/ *n.m.* (finger-)nail.

**ont** /ɔ̃/ *voir* **avoir**.

**ONU** *abrév.* (*Organisation des nations unies*) UN.

**onz|e** /ɔ̃z/ *a. & n.m.* eleven. **~ième** *a. & n.m./ f.* eleventh.

**opale** /ɔpal/ *n.f.* opal.

**open** /ɔpɛn/ *n.m.* open (champion-ship).

**opéra** /ɔpera/ *n.m.* opera; (*édifice*) opera-house. **~-comique** (*pl.* **~s-comiques**) *n.m.* light opera.

**opérateur** /ɔperatœr/ *n.m.* (*caméraman*) cameraman.

**opération** /ɔperasjɔ̃/ *n.f.* operation; (*comm.*) deal.

**opérationnel, ~le** /ɔperasjɔnɛl/ *a.* operational.

**opératoire** /ɔperatwar/ *a.* (*méd.*) surgical. **bloc ~,** operating suite.

**opérer** /ɔpere/ *v.t.* (*personne*) operate on; (*kyste etc.*) remove. **se faire ~,** have an operation. ● *v.i.* (*méd.*) operate.

**opérette** /ɔperɛt/ *n.f.* operetta.

**opinion** /ɔpinjɔ̃/ *n.f.* opinion.

**opium** /ɔpjɔm/ *n.m.* opium.

**opportun, ~e** /ɔpɔrtœ̃, -yn/ *a.* opportune. **~ité** /-ynite/ *n.f.* opportuneness.

**opposant, ~e** /ɔpozɑ̃, -t/ *n.m., f.* opponent.

**opposé** /ɔpoze/ *a.* (*sens, angle, etc.*) opposite; (*factions*) opposing; (*intérêts*) conflicting. ● *n.m.* opposite. **être ~ à,** be opposed to.

**opposer** /ɔpoze/ *v.t.* (*personnes*) oppose; (*contraster*) contrast; (*résistance, argument*) put up. **s'~** *v. pr.* (*personnes*) confront each other; (*styles*) contrast. **s'~ à,** oppose.

**opposition** /ɔpozisjɔ̃/ *n.f.* opposition. **faire ~ à un chèque,** stop a cheque.

**opticien, ~ne** /ɔptisjɛ̃, -jɛn/ *n.m., f.* optician.

**optimis|te** /ɔptimist/ *n.m./f.* optimist. ● *a.* optimistic. **~me** *n.m.* optimism.

**option** /ɔpsjɔ̃/ *n.f.* option.

**optique** /ɔptik/ *a.* (*verre*) optical. ● *n.f.* (*perspective*) perspective.

**or¹** /ɔr/ *n.m.* gold. **d'~,** golden. **en or,** gold; (*occasion*) golden.

**or²** /ɔr/ *conj.* now, well.

**orag|e** /ɔraʒ/ *n.m.* (thunder)storm. **~eux, ~euse** *a.* stormy.

**or|al** (*m.pl.* **~aux**) /ɔral, -o/ *a.* oral. ● *n.m.* (*pl.* **~aux**) oral.

**orang|e** /ɔrɑ̃ʒ/ *n.f. & a. invar.* orange. **~é** *a.* orange-coloured. **~er** *n.m.* orange-tree.

**orangeade** /ɔrɑ̃ʒad/ *n.f.* orangeade.

**orateur** /ɔratœr/ *n.m.* speaker.

**orchestr|e** /ɔrkɛstr/ *n.m.* orchestra; (*de jazz*) band; (*parterre*) stalls. **~er** *v.t.* orchestrate.

**orchidée** /ɔrkide/ *n.f.* orchid.

**ordinaire** /ɔrdinɛr/ *a.* ordinary; (*habituel*) usual; (*qualité*) standard. ● *n.m.* **l'~,** the ordinary; (*nourriture*) the standard fare. **d'~, à l'~,** usually.

**ordinateur** /ɔrdinatœr/ *n.m.* computer.

**ordonnance** /ɔrdɔnɑ̃s/ *n.f.* (*de médecin*) prescription.

**ordonné** /ɔrdɔne/ *a.* tidy.

**ordonner** /ɔrdɔne/ *v.t.* order (**à qn. de,** s.o. to); (*agencer*) arrange; (*méd.*) prescribe; (*prêtre*) ordain.

**ordre** /ɔrdr/ *n.m.* order; (*propreté*) tidiness. **de premier ~,** first-rate. **mettre en ~,** tidy (up). **de premier ~,** first-rate. **jusqu'à nouvel ~,** until further notice.

**ordure** /ɔrdyr/ *n.f.* filth. **~s,** (*détritus*) rubbish. **~s ménagères,** household refuse.

**oreille** /ɔrɛj/ *n.f.* ear.

**oreiller** /ɔreje/ *n.m.* pillow.

**oreillons** /ɔrɛjɔ̃/ *n.m. pl.* mumps.

**orfèvr|e** /ɔrfɛvr/ *n.m.* goldsmith, silversmith. **~erie** *n.f.* goldsmith's *ou* silversmith's trade.

**organe** /ɔrgan/ *n.m.* organ.

**organigramme** /ɔrganigram/ *n.m.* flow chart.

**organique** /ɔrganik/ *a.* organic.

**organisation** /ɔrganizasjɔ̃/ *n.f.* organization.

**organis|er** /ɔrganize/ *v.t.* organize. **s'~er** *v. pr.* organize o.s. **~ateur, ~atrice** *n.m., f.* organizer.

**organisme** /ɔrganism/ *n.m.* body, organism.

**organiste** /ɔrganist/ *n.m./f.* organist.

**orge** /ɔrʒ/ *n.f.* barley.

**orgelet** /ɔrʒəlɛ/ *n.m.* (*furoncle*) sty.

**orgue** /ɔrg/ *n.m.* organ. **~s** *n.f. pl.* organ.

**orgueil** /ɔrgœj/ *n.m.* pride.

**orgueilleu|x, ~se** /ɔrgœjø, -z/ *a.* proud.

**Orient** /ɔrjɑ̃/ *n.m.* **l'~,** the Orient.

**orientable** /ɔrjɑ̃tabl/ *a.* adjustable.

**orient|al, ~ale** (*m.pl.* **~aux**) /ɔrjɑ̃tal, -o/ *a.* eastern; (*de l'Orient*) oriental. ● *n.m., f.* Oriental.

**orientation** /ɔrjɑ̃tasjɔ̃/ *n.f.* direction; (*de maison*) aspect.

**orienter** /ɔrjɑ̃te/ *v.t.* position; (*personne*) direct. **s'~** *v. pr.* (*se repérer*) find one's bearings. **s'~ vers,** turn towards.

**orifice** /ɔrifis/ *n.m.* orifice.

**origan** /ɔrigɑ̃/ *n.m.* oregano.

**originaire** /ɔriʒinɛr/ *a.* **être ~ de,** be a native of.

**origin|al, ~ale** (*m. pl.* **~aux**) /ɔriʒinal, -o/ *a.* original; (*curieux*) eccentric. ● *n.m.* original. ● *n.m., f.* eccentric. **~alité** *n.f.* originality; eccentricity.

**origine** /ɔriʒin/ *n.f.* origin. **à l'~,** originally. **d'~,** (*pièce, pneu*) original.

**orme** /ɔrm/ *n.m.* elm.

**ornement** /ɔrnəmɑ̃/ *n.m.* ornament.

**orner** /ɔrne/ *v.t.* decorate.

**ornière** /ɔrnjɛr/ *n.f.* rut.

**orphelin, ~e** /ɔrfəlɛ̃, -in/ *n.m., f.* orphan. ● *a.* orphaned. **~at** /-ina/ *n.m.* orphanage.

**orteil** /ɔrtɛj/ *n.m.* toe.

**orthodox|e** /ɔrtɔdɔks/ *a.* orthodox.
**orthograph|e** /ɔrtɔgraf/ *n.f.* spelling. **~ier** *v.t.* spell.
**orthopédique** /ɔrtɔpedik/ *a.* orthopaedic.
**ortie** /ɔrti/ *n.f.* nettle.
**os** (*pl.* **os**) /ɔs, o/ *n.m.* bone.
**OS** *abrév. voir* **ouvrier spécialisé.**
**oscar** /ɔskar/ *n.m.* award; (*au cinéma*) oscar.
**oseille** /ozɛj/ *n.f.* (*plante*) sorrel.
**os|er** /oze/ *v.t./i.* dare. **~é** *a.* daring.
**osier** /ozje/ *n.m.* wicker.
**ostéopathe** /ɔsteɔpat/ *n.m./f.* osteopath.
**otage** /ɔtaʒ/ *n.m.* hostage.
**otarie** /ɔtari/ *n.f.* sea-lion.
**ôter** /ote/ *v.t.* remove (**à qn.,** from s.o.); (*déduire*) take away.
**otite** /ɔtit/ *n.f.* ear infection.
**ou** /u/ *conj.* or. **ou bien,** or else. **vous ou moi,** either you or me.
**où** /u/ *adv. & pron.* where; (*dans lequel*) in which; (*sur lequel*) on which; (*auquel*) at which. **d'où,** from which; (*pour cette raison*) hence. **d'où?,** from where? **par où,** through which. **par où?,** which way? **au prix où c'est,** at those prices. **le jour où,** the day when.
**ouate** /wat/ *n.f.* cotton wool.
**oubli** /ubli/ *n.m.* forgetfulness; (*trou de mémoire*) lapse of memory; (*négligence*) oversight.
**oublier** /ublije/ *v.t.* forget.
**ouest** /wɛst/ *n.m.* west. **●** *a. invar.* west; (*partie*) western; (*direction*) westerly.
**ouf** /uf/ *int.* phew.
**oui** /wi/ *adv.* yes.
**ouïe** /wi/ *n.f.* hearing.
**ouïes** /wi/ *n.f. pl.* gills.
**ouille** /uj/ *int.* ouch.
**ouragan** /uragɑ̃/ *n.m.* hurricane.
**ourlet** /urlɛ/ *n.m.* hem.
**ours** /urs/ *n.m.* bear. **~ en peluche,** teddy bear.
**ouste** /ust/ *int.* (*fam.*) scram.
**outil** /uti/ *n.m.* tool.
**outillage** /utijaʒ/ *n.m.* tools; (*d'une usine*) equipment.
**outre** /utr/ *prép.* besides. **en ~,** besides. **~-mer** *adv.* overseas.
**outsider** /awtsajdœr/ *n.m.* outsider.
**ouvert, ~e** /uvɛr, -t/ *voir* **ouvrir.** **●** *a.* open; (*gaz, radio, etc.*) on. **~ement** /-təmɑ̃/ *adv.* openly.
**ouverture** /uvɛrtyr/ *n.f.* opening; (*mus.*) overture; (*photo.*) aperture. **~s,** (*offres*) overtures. **~ d'esprit,** open-mindedness.
**ouvrable** /uvrabl/ *a.* **jour ~,** working day.
**ouvrag|e** /uvraʒ/ *n.m.* (*travail, livre*) work; (*couture*) needlework. **~é** *a.* finely worked.
**ouvreuse** /uvrøz/ *n.f.* usherette.

**ouvr|ier, ~ière** /uvrije, -jɛr/ *n.m., f.* worker. **●** *a.* working-class; (*conflit*) industrial; (*syndicat*) workers'.
**ouvr|ir**† /uvrir/ *v.t.* open (up); (*gaz, robinet, etc.*) turn *ou* switch on. **●** *v.i.* open (up). **s'~ir** *v. pr.* open (up). **~e-boîte(s)** *n.m.* tin-opener. **~e-bouteille(s)** *n.m.* bottle-opener.
**ovaire** /ɔvɛr/ *n.m.* ovary.
**ovale** /ɔval/ *a. & n.m.* oval.
**ovule** /ɔvyl/ *n.f.* (*à féconder*) egg; (*gynécologique*) pessary.
**oxyder (s')** /(s)ɔkside/ *v. pr.* become oxidized.
**oxygène** /ɔksiʒɛn/ *n.m.* oxygen.
**ozone** /ozon/ *n.f.* ozone. **la couche d'~,** the ozone layer.

• • • • • • • • • • • • • • • • • • • • • • • • • • •

# Pp

• • • • • • • • • • • • • • • • • • • • • • • • • • •

**pacemaker** /pesmɛkœr/ *n.m.* pacemaker.
**pacifique** /pasifik/ *a.* peaceful; (*personne*) peaceable; (*géog.*) Pacific.
**pacotille** /pakɔtij/ *n.f.* trash.
**pacte** /pakt/ *n.m.* pact.
**pagaille** /pagaj/ *n.f.* mess, shambles.
**page** /paʒ/ *n.f.* page.
**paie** /pɛ/ *n.f.* pay.
**paiement** /pɛmɑ̃/ *n.m.* payment.
**paillasson** /pajasɔ̃/ *n.m.* doormat.
**paille** /pɑj/ *n.f.* straw.
**paillette** /pajɛt/ *n.f.* (*sur robe*) sequin; (*de savon*) flake.
**pain** /pɛ̃/ *n.m.* bread; (*unité*) loaf (of bread); (*de savon etc.*) bar. **~ d'épice,** gingerbread. **~ grillé,** toast.
**pair**¹ /pɛr/ *a.* (*nombre*) even.
**pair**² /pɛr/ *n.m.* (*personne*) peer. **au ~,** (*jeune fille etc.*) au pair.
**paire** /pɛr/ *n.f.* pair.
**paisible** /pezibl/ *a.* peaceful.
**paître** /pɛtr/ *v.i.* (*brouter*) graze.
**paix** /pɛ/ *n.f.* peace; (*papier*) peace treaty.
**Pakistan** /pakistɑ̃/ *n.m.* Pakistan.
**pakistanais, ~e** /pakistanɛ, -z/ *a. & n.m., f.* Pakistani.
**palace** /palas/ *n.m.* luxury hotel.
**palais**¹ /palɛ/ *n.m.* palace. **P~ de Justice,** Law Courts. **~ des sports,** sports stadium.
**palais**² /palɛ/ *n.m.* (*anat.*) palate.
**pâle** /pɑl/ *a.* pale.
**Palestine** /palɛstin/ *n.f.* Palestine.
**palestinien, ~ne** /palɛstinjɛ̃, -jɛn/ *a. & n.m., f.* Palestinian.
**palet** /palɛ/ *n.m.* (*hockey*) puck.

**palette** /palɛt/ *n.f.* palette.
**pâleur** /pɑlœr/ *n.f.* paleness.
**palier** /palje/ *n.m.* (*d'escalier*) landing; (*étape*) stage.
**pâlir** /pɑlir/ *v.t./i.* (turn) pale.
**palissade** /palisad/ *n.f.* fence.
**palmarès** /palmarɛs/ *n.m.* list of prize-winners.
**palm|e** /palm/ *n.f.* palm leaf; (*symbole*) palm; (*de nageur*) flipper. **~ier** *n.m.* palm(-tree).
**pâlot, ~te** /pɑlo, -ɔt/ *a.* pale.
**palourde** /palurd/ *n.f.* clam.
**palper** /palpe/ *v.t.* feel.
**palpit|er** /palpite/ *v.i.* (*battre*) pound, palpitate; (*frémir*) quiver. **~ations** *n.f. pl.* palpitations.
**paludisme** /palydism/ *n.m.* malaria.
**pamplemousse** /pɑ̃pləmus/ *n.m.* grapefruit.
**pan** /pɑ̃/ *int.* bang.
**panaché** /panaʃe/ *a.* (*bariolé, mélangé*) motley. **glace ~e,** mixed-flavour ice cream. ● *n.m.* shandy. **bière ~e, demi ~,** shandy.
**pancarte** /pɑ̃kart/ *n.f.* sign; (*de manifestant*) placard.
**pancréas** /pɑ̃kreas/ *n.m.* pancreas.
**pané** /pane/ *a.* breaded.
**panier** /panje/ *n.m.* basket. **~ à provisions,** shopping basket.
**paniqu|e** /panik/ *n.f.* panic. (*fam.*) **~er** *v.i.* panic.
**panne** /pan/ *n.f.* breakdown. **être en ~,** have broken down. **être en ~ sèche,** have run out of petrol. **~ d'électricité** *ou* **de courant,** power failure.
**panneau** (*pl.* **~x**) /pano/ *n.m.* sign; (*publicitaire*) hoarding; (*de porte etc.*) panel. **~ (d'affichage),** notice-board. **~ (de signalisation),** road sign.
**pans|er** /pɑ̃se/ *v.t.* (*plaie*) dress. **~ement** *n.m.* dressing. **~ement adhésif,** sticking-plaster.
**pantalon** /pɑ̃talɔ̃/ *n.m.* (pair of) trousers. **~s,** trousers.
**panthère** /pɑ̃tɛr/ *n.f.* panther.
**pantin** /pɑ̃tɛ̃/ *n.m.* puppet.
**pantomime** /pɑ̃tɔmim/ *n.f.* mime; (*spectacle*) mime show.
**pantoufle** /pɑ̃tufl/ *n.f.* slipper.
**paon** /pɑ̃/ *n.m.* peacock.
**papa** /papa/ *n.m.* dad(dy).
**pape** /pap/ *n.m.* pope.
**paperass|e** /papras/ *n.f.* **~e(s),** (*péj.*) papers. **~erie** *n.f.* (*péj.*) papers; (*tracasserie*) red tape.
**papeterie** /papetri/ *n.f.* (*magasin*) stationer's shop.
**papier** /papje/ *n.m.* paper; (*formulaire*) form. **~s (d'identité),** (identity) papers. **~ à lettres,** writing-paper. **~ aluminium,** tin

foil. **~ de verre,** sandpaper. **~ hygiénique,** toilet-paper. **~ journal,** newspaper. **~ peint,** wallpaper.
**papillon** /papijɔ̃/ *n.m.* butterfly; (*contravention*) parking-ticket. **~ (de nuit),** moth.
**paprika** /paprika/ *n.m.* paprika.
**Pâque** /pɑk/ *n.f.* Passover.
**paquebot** /pakbo/ *n.m.* liner.
**pâquerette** /pɑkrɛt/ *n.f.* daisy.
**Pâques** /pɑk/ *n.f. pl.* & *n.m.* Easter.
**paquet** /pakɛ/ *n.m.* packet; (*de cartes*) pack; (*colis*) parcel.
**par** /par/ *prép.* by; (*à travers*) through; (*motif*) out of, from; (*provenance*) from. **commencer/ finir ~ qch.,** begin/end with sth. **commencer/finir ~ faire,** begin by/end up (by) doing. **~ an/mois/***etc.*, a *ou* per year/month/*etc.* **~ avion,** (*lettre*) (by) airmail. **~ contre,** on the other hand. **~ hasard,** by chance. **~ ici/là,** this/that way. **~ l'intermédiaire de,** through. **~ jour,** a day. **~ moments,** at times. **~ opposition à,** as opposed to. **~ personne,** each, per person.
**paracétamol** /parasetamɔl/ *n.m.* paracetamol.
**parachut|e** /paraʃyt/ *n.m.* parachute. **~er** *v.t.* parachute. **~iste** *n.m./f.* parachutist; (*mil.*) paratrooper.
**parade** /parad/ *n.f.* parade.
**paradis** /paradi/ *n.m.* paradise. **~fiscal,** tax haven.
**paraffine** /parafin/ *n.f.* paraffin wax.
**paragraphe** /paragraf/ *n.m.* paragraph.
**paraître†** /parɛtr/ *v.i.* appear; (*sembler*) seem, appear; (*ouvrage*) be published, come out. **faire ~,** (*ouvrage*) bring out.
**parallèle** /paralɛl/ *a.* parallel. ● *n.m.* parallel. **faire le ~,** make a connection. ● *n.f.* parallel (line). **~ment** *adv.* parallel (**à,** to).
**paraly|ser** /paralize/ *v.t.* paralyse. **~sie** *n.f.* paralysis.
**paramètre** /parametr/ *n.m.* parameter.
**parapet** /parapɛ/ *n.m.* parapet.
**parapluie** /paraplɥi/ *n.m.* umbrella.
**parasite** /parazit/ *n.m.* parasite. **~s,** (*radio*) interference.
**parasol** /parasɔl/ *n.m.* sunshade.
**paratonnerre** /paratɔner/ *n.m.* lightning-conductor *ou* -rod.
**paravent** /paravɑ̃/ *n.m.* screen.
**parc** /park/ *n.m.* park; (*de bébé*) play-pen. **~ de stationnement,** car-park.
**parcelle** /parsɛl/ *n.f.* fragment; (*de terre*) plot.
**parce que** /parsk(ə)/ *conj.* because.
**parcmètre** /parkmetr/ *n.m.* parking-meter.
**parcourir†** /parkurir/ *v.t.* travel *ou* go through; (*distance*) travel; (*des yeux*) glance at *ou* over.

**parcours** /parkur/ *n.m.* route; (*voyage*) journey.

**par-delà** /pardəla/ *prép. & adv.* beyond.

**par-derrière** /pardɛrjɛr/ *prép. & adv.* behind, at the back *ou* rear (of).

**par-dessous** /pardsu/ *prép. & adv.* under (-neath).

**pardessus** /pardəsy/ *n.m.* overcoat.

**par-dessus** /pardsy/ *prép. & adv.* over. ~ **bord**, overboard. ~ **le marché**, into the bargain.

**par-devant** /pardvã/ *adv.* at *ou* from the front, in front.

**pardon** /pardɔ̃/ *n.m.* forgiveness. **(je vous demande)** ~**l,** (I am) sorry!; (*pour demander qch.*) excuse me!

**pardonn|er** /pardɔne/ *v.t.* forgive. ~**er qch. à qn.,** forgive s.o. for sth. ~**able** *a.* forgivable.

**pare-brise** /parbriz/ *n.m. invar.* windscreen; (*Amer.*) windshield.

**pare-chocs** /parʃɔk/ *n.m. invar.* bumper.

**pareil,** ~**le** /parɛj/ *a.* similar (**à** to); (*tel*) such (a). ● *n.m., f.* equal. ● *adv.* (*fam.*) the same. **c'est** ~, it is the same.

**parent,** ~**e** /parã, -t/ *a.* related (**de,** to). ● *n.m., f.* relative, relation. ~**s** (*père et mère*) *n.m. pl.* parents. ~ **seul,** single parent.

**parenthèse** /parãtɛz/ *n.f.* bracket, parenthesis; (*fig.*) digression.

**paress|e** /parɛs/ *n.f.* laziness. ~**er** /-ese/ *v.i.* laze (about). ~**eux,** ~**euse** *a.* lazy; *n.m., f.* lazybones.

**parfait,** ~**e** /parfɛ, -t/ *a.* perfect. ~**ement** /-tmã/ *adv.* perfectly; (*bien sûr*) certainly.

**parfois** /parfwa/ *adv.* sometimes.

**parfum** /parfœ̃/ *n.m.* scent; (*substance*) perfume, scent; (*goût*) flavour.

**parfum|er** /parfyme/ *v.t.* perfume; (*gâteau*) flavour. **se** ~**er** *v. pr.* put on one's perfume. ~**é** *a.* fragrant; (*savon*) scented. ~**erie** *n. f.* (*produits*) perfumes; (*boutique*) perfume shop.

**pari** /pari/ *n.m.* bet.

**par|ier** /parje/ *v.t.* bet. ~**ieur,** ~**ieuse** *n.m., f.* punter, better.

**Paris** /pari/ *n.m./f.* Paris.

**parisien,** ~**ne** /parizjɛ̃, -jɛn/ *a.* Paris, Parisian. ● *n.m., f.* Parisian.

**parit|é** /parite/ *n.f.* parity. ~**aire** *a.* (*commission*) joint.

**parking** /parkiŋ/ *n.m.* car-park; (*stationnement*) parking.

**parlement** /parləmã/ *n.m.* parliament.

**parl|er** /parle/ *v.i.* talk, speak (**à,** to). ● *v.t.* (*langue*) speak; (*politique, affaires, etc.*) talk. **se** ~**er** *v. pr.* (*langue*) be spoken. ● *n.m.* speech; (*dialecte*) dialect.

**parmi** /parmi/ *prép.* among(st).

**paroi** /parwa/ *n.f.* wall; (*cloison*) partition (wall). ~ **rocheuse,** rock face.

**paroisse** /parwas/ *n.f.* parish.

**parole** /parɔl/ *n.f.* (*mot, promesse*) word; (*langage*) speech. **demander la** ~, ask to speak. **prendre la** ~, (begin to) speak.

**paroxysme** /parɔksism/ *n.m.* height, highest point.

**parquer** /parke/ *v.t.,* **se** ~ *v. pr.* (*auto.*) park.

**parquet** /parkɛ/ *n.m.* floor; (*jurid.*) public prosecutor's department.

**parrain** /parɛ̃/ *n.m.* godfather; (*fig.*) sponsor. ~**er** /-ene/ *v.t.* sponsor.

**pars, part¹** /par/ *voir* **partir**.

**part²** /par/ *n.f.* share, part. **à** ~, (*decôté*) aside; (*séparément*) apart; (*excepté*) apart from. **d'autre** ~, on the other hand; (*de plus*) moreover. **de la** ~ **de,** from. **d'une** ~, on the one hand. **prendre** ~ **à,** take part in; (*joie, douleur*) share.

**partag|e** /partaʒ/ *n.m.* dividing; sharing out; (*part*) share. ~**er** *v.t.* divide; (*distribuer*) share out; (*avoir en commun*) share. **se** ~**er qch.,** share sth.

**partance (en)** /(ã)partãs/ *adv.* about to depart.

**partant** /partã/ *n.m.* (*sport*) starter.

**partenaire** /partənɛr/ *n.m./f.* partner.

**parterre** /partɛr/ *n.m.* flower-bed; (*théâtre*) stalls.

**parti** /parti/ *n.m.* (*pol.*) party; (*en mariage*) match; (*décision*) decision. ~ **pris,** prejudice. **prendre** ~ **pour,** side with.

**part|ial** (*m. pl.* ~**iaux**) /parsjal, -jo/ *a.* biased. ~**ialité** *n.f.* bias.

**participe** /partisip/ *n.m.* (*gram.*) participle.

**particip|er** /partisipe/ *v.i.* ~**er à,** take part in, participate in; (*profits, frais*) share; (*spectacle*) appear in. ~**ant,** ~**ante** *n.m., f.* participant (**à,** in); (*à un concours*) entrant. ~**ation** *n.f.* participation; sharing; (*comm.*) interest.

**particularité** /partikylarite/ *n.f.* particularity.

**particule** /partikyl/ *n.f.* particle.

**particul|ier,** ~**ière** /partikylje, -jɛr/ *a.* (*spécifique*) particular; (*bizarre*) peculiar; (*privé*) private. ● *n.m.* private individual. **en** ~**ier,** in particular; (*en privé*) in private. ~**ièrement** *adv.* particularly.

**partie** /parti/ *n.f.* part; (*cartes, sport*) game; (*jurid.*) party; (*sortie*) outing, party. **une** ~ **de pêche,** a fishing trip. **en** ~, partly. **faire** ~ **de,** be part of; (*adhérer à*) belong to. **en grande** ~, largely.

**partir†** /partir/ *v.i.* (*aux. être*) go; (*quitter un lieu*) leave, go; (*tache*) come out; (*bouton*) come off. **à** ~ **de,** from.

**partisan,** ~**e** /partizã, -an/ *n.m., f.* supporter. ● *n.m.* (*mil.*) partisan. **être** ~ **de,** be in favour of.

**partition** /partisjɔ̃/ *n.f.* (*mus.*) score.

**partout** /partu/ *adv.* everywhere. ~ **où,** wherever.

**paru** /pary/ *voir* paraître.

**parure** /paryr/ *n.f.* adornment; (*bijoux*) jewellery; (*de draps*) set.

**parution** /parysjɔ̃/ *n.f.* publication.

**parvenir**† /parvənir/ *v.i.* (*aux. être*) ~ **à,** reach; (*résultat*) achieve. ~ **à faire,** manage to do. **faire** ~, send.

**parvis** /parvi/ *n.m.* (*place*) square.

**pas**[1] /pa/ *adv.* not. (ne) ~, not. **je ne sais** ~, I do not know. ~ **de sucre/livres/etc.,** no sugar/ books/*etc.* ~ **du tout,** not at all. ~ **encore,** not yet. ~ **mal,** not bad; (*beaucoup*) quite a lot (**de,** of). ~ **vrai?,** (*fam.*) isn't that so?

**pas**[2] /pa/ *n.m.* step; (*bruit*) footstep; (*trace*) footprint; (*vitesse*) pace; (*de vis*) thread. **à deux** ~ (**de**), close by. **au** ~, at a walking pace; (*véhicule*) very slowly.

**passable** /pasabl/ *a.* tolerable.

**passage** /pasaʒ/ *n.m.* passing, passage; (*traversée*) crossing; (*visite*) visit; (*chemin*) way, passage; (*d'une œuvre*) passage. **de** ~, (*voyageur*) visiting; (*amant*) casual. ~ **à niveau,** level crossing. ~ **clouté,** pedestrian crossing. ~ **interdit,** (*panneau*) no thoroughfare. ~ **souterrain,** subway.

**passag|er,** ~**ère** /pasaʒe, -ɛr/ *a.* temporary. ● *n.m.,* *f.* passenger.

**passant,** ~**e** /pasã, -t/ *a.* (*rue*) busy. ● *n.m.,* *f.* passer-by.

**passe** /pas/ *n.f.* pass. ~-**partout** *n.m. invar.* master-key; *a. invar.* for all occasions. ~ **temps** *n.m. invar.* pastime.

**passé** /pase/ *a.* (*révolu*) past; (*dernier*) last; (*fini*) over; (*fané*) faded. ● *prép.* after. ● *n.m.* past. ~ **de mode,** out of fashion.

**passeport** /paspɔr/ *n.m.* passport.

**passer** /pase/ *v.i.* (*aux. être ou avoir*) pass; (*aller*) go; (*venir*) come; (*temps*) pass (by), go by; (*film*) be shown; (*couleur*) fade. ● *v.t.* (*aux. avoir*) pass, cross; (*donner*) pass, hand; (*mettre*) put; (*oublier*) overlook; (*enfiler*) slip on; (*dépasser*) go beyond; (*temps*) spend, pass; (*film*) show; (*examen*) take; (*commande*) place; (*soupe*) strain. **se** ~ *v. pr.* happen, take place. **laisser** ~, let through; (*occasion*) miss. ~ **devant,** (*édifice*) go past. ~ **par,** go through. ~ **pour,** (*riche etc.*) be taken to be. ~ **sur,** (*détail*) pass over. ~ **l'aspirateur,** hoover, vacuum. ~ **un coup de fil à qn.,** give s.o. a ring. **je vous passe Mme X,** (*par le standard*) I'm putting you through to Mrs X; (*en donnant l'appareil*) I'll hand you over to Mrs X. **se** ~ **de,** go *ou* do without.

**passerelle** /pasrɛl/ *n.f.* footbridge; (*pour accéder à un avion, à un navire*) gangway.

**passible** /pasibl/ *a.* ~ **de,** liable to.

**passi|f,** ~**ve** /pasif, -v/ *a.* passive. ● *n.m.* (*comm.*) liabilities. ~**vité** *n.f.* passiveness.

**passion** /pasjɔ̃/ *n.f.* passion.

**passionn|er** /pasjɔne/ *v.t.* fascinate. ~**é** *a.* passionate. **être** ~**é de,** have a passion for. ~**ément** *adv.* passionately.

**passoire** /paswar/ *n.f.* (*à thé*) strainer; (*à légumes*) colander.

**pastel** /pastɛl/ *n.m.* & *a. invar.* pastel.

**pastèque** /pastɛk/ *n.f.* watermelon.

**pasteur** /pastœr/ *n.m.* (*relig.*) minister.

**pasteurisé** /pastœrize/ *a.* pasteurized.

**pastille** /pastij/ *n.f.* (*bonbon*) pastille, lozenge.

**pastis** /pastis/ *n.m.* aniseed liqueur.

**patate** /patat/ *n.f.* (*fam.*) potato. ~ (**douce**), sweet potato.

**patauger** /patoʒe/ *v.i.* splash about.

**pâte** /pat/ *n.f.* paste; (*farine*) dough; (*à tarte*) pastry; (*à frire*) batter. ~**s (alimentaires),** pasta. ~ **à modeler,** Plasticine (P.). ~ **dentifrice,** toothpaste.

**pâté** /pate/ *n.m.* (*culin.*) pâté; (*d'encre*) ink-blot. ~ **de maisons,** block of houses; (*de sable*) sand-pie. ~ **en croûte,** meat pie.

**pâtée** /pate/ *n.f.* feed, mash.

**patelin** /patlɛ̃/ *n.m.* (*fam.*) village.

**patent|e** /patãt/ *n.f.* trade licence. ~**é** *a.* licensed.

**patern|el,** ~**elle** /patɛrnɛl/ *a.* paternal. ~**ité** *n.f.* paternity.

**pâteu|x,** ~**se** /patø, -z/ *a.* pasty.

**pathétique** /patetik/ *a.* moving.

**patholog|ie** /patɔlɔʒi/ *n.f.* pathology. ~**ique** *a.* pathological.

**pat|ient,** ~**iente** /pasjã, -t/ *a.* & *n.m., f.* patient. ~**iemment** /-jamã/ *adv.* patiently. ~**ience** *n.f.* patience.

**patienter** /pasjãte/ *v.i.* wait.

**patin** /patɛ̃/ *n.m.* skate. ~ **à roulettes,** roller-skate.

**patin|er** /patine/ *v.i.* skate; (*voiture*) spin. ~**age** *n.m.* skating. ~**eur,** ~**euse** *n.m., f.* skater.

**patinoire** /patinwar/ *n.f.* skating-rink.

**pâtiss|ier,** ~**ière** /patisje, -jɛr/ *n.m., f.* pastry-cook. ~**erie** *n.f.* cake shop; (*gâteau*) pastry.

**patois** /patwa/ *n.m.* patois.

**patrie** /patri/ *n.f.* homeland.

**patrimoine** /patrimwan/ *n.m.* heritage.

**patron**[1]**,** ~**ne** /patrɔ̃, -ɔn/ *n.m., f.* employer, boss; (*propriétaire*) owner, boss; (*saint*) patron saint. ~**al** (*m. pl.* ~**aux**) /-ɔnal, -o/ *a.* employers'. ~**at** /-ɔna/ *n.m.* employers.

**patron**[2] /patrɔ̃/ *n.m.* (*couture*) pattern.

**patrouill|e** /patruj/ *n.f.* patrol. ~**er** *v.i.* patrol.

**patte** /pat/ *n.f.* leg; (*pied*) foot; (*de chat*) paw.

**pâturage** /patyraʒ/ *n.m.* pasture.

**paume** /pom/ *n.f.* (*de main*) palm.

**paupière** /popjɛr/ *n.f.* eyelid.

**pause** /poz/ *n.f.* pause; (*halte*) break.

**pauvre** /povr/ *a.* poor. ● *n.m./f.* poor man, poor woman. ~**ment** /-əmã/ *adv.* poorly. ~**té** /-əte/ *n.f.* poverty.

**pavé** /pave/ *n.m.* paving-stone; cobble (-stone).

**pavillon**¹ /pavijõ/ *n.m.* house.

**pavillon**² /pavijõ/ *n.m.* (*drapeau*) flag.

**payant,** ~**e** /pejã, -t/ *a.* (*billet*) for which a charge is made; (*spectateur*) (fee-)paying; (*rentable*) profitable.

**payer** /peje/ *v.t./i.* pay; (*service, travail, etc.*) pay for; (*acheter*) buy (**à,** for). **se** ~ *v. pr.* (*s'acheter*) buy o.s. **faire** ~ **à qn.,** (*cent francs etc.*) charge s.o. (**pour,** for).

**pays** /pei/ *n.m.* country; (*région*) region; (*village*) village. **du** ~, local. **les P**~**-Bas,** the Netherlands. **le** ~ **de Galles,** Wales.

**paysage** /peizaʒ/ *n.m.* landscape.

**paysan,** ~**ne** /peizã, -an/ *n.m., f.* farmer, country person; (*péj.*) peasant. ● *a.* (*agricole*) farming; (*rural*) country.

**PCV (en)** /(ã)peseve/ *adv.* **appeler** *ou* **téléphoner en** ~, reverse the charges.

**PDG** *abrév. voir* **président directeur général.**

**péage** /peaʒ/ *n.m.* toll; (*lieu*) toll-gate.

**peau** (*pl.* ~**x**) /po/ *n.f.* skin; (*cuir*) hide. **être bien/mal dans sa** ~, be/not be at ease with oneself.

**pêche**¹ /pɛʃ/ *n.f.* peach.

**pêche**² /pɛʃ/ *n.f.* (*activité*) fishing; (*poissons*) catch. ~ **à la ligne,** angling.

**péché** /peʃe/ *n.m.* sin.

**pêch|er** /peʃe/ *v.t.* (*poisson*) catch; (*dénicher: fam.*) dig up. ● *v.i.* fish. ~**eur** *n.m.* fisherman; (*à la ligne*) angler.

**pédago|gie** /pedagɔʒi/ *n.f.* education. ~**gique** *a.* educational.

**pédal|e** /pedal/ *n.f.* pedal. ~**er** *v.i.* pedal.

**pédalo** /pedalo/ *n.m.* pedal boat.

**pédant,** ~**e** /pedã, -t/ *a.* pedantic.

**pédestre** /pedɛstr/ *a.* **faire de la randonnée** ~, go walking *ou* hiking.

**pédiatre** /pedjatr/ *n.m./f.* paediatrician.

**pédicure** /pedikyr/ *n.m./f.* chiropodist.

**pedigree** /pedigri/ *n.m.* pedigree.

**peign|e** /pɛɲ/ *n.m.* comb. ~**er** /peɲe/ *v.t.* comb; (*personne*) comb the hair of. **se** ~**er** *v. pr.* comb one's hair.

**peignoir** /peɲwar/ *n.m.* dressing-gown.

**peindre†** /pɛ̃dr/ *v.t.* paint.

**peine** /pɛn/ *n.f.* sadness, sorrow; (*effort, difficulté*) trouble; (*punition*) punishment; (*jurid.*) sentence. **avoir de la** ~, feel sad. **faire de la** ~ **à,** hurt. **ce n'est pas la** ~ **de faire,** it is not worth (while) doing.

**peine (à)** /(a)pɛn/ *adv.* hardly.

**peintre** /pɛ̃tr/ *n.m.* painter. ~ **en bâtiment,** house painter.

**peinture** /pɛ̃tyr/ *n.f.* painting; (*matière*) paint. ~ **à l'huile,** oil-painting.

**péjorati|f,** ~**ve** /peʒɔratif, -v/ *a.* pejorative.

**pelage** /pəlaʒ/ *n.m.* coat, fur.

**peler** /pəle/ *v.t./i.* peel.

**pèlerin** /pɛlrɛ̃/ *n.m.* pilgrim. ~**age** /-inaʒ/ *n.m.* pilgrimage.

**pélican** /pelikã/ *n.m.* pelican.

**pelle** /pɛl/ *n.f.* shovel; (*d'enfant*) spade. ~**tée** *n.f.* shovelful.

**pellicule** /pelikyl/ *n.f.* film. ~**s,** (*cheveux*) dandruff.

**pelote** /pəlɔt/ *n.f.* ball; (*d'épingles*) pincushion.

**peloton** /plɔtõ/ *n.m.* troop, squad; (*sport*) pack.

**pelouse** /pluz/ *n.f.* lawn.

**peluche** /plyʃ/ *n.f.* (*tissu*) plush; (*jouet*) cuddly toy. **en** ~, (*lapin, chien*) fluffy, furry.

**pén|al** (*m. pl.* ~**aux**) /penal, -o/ *a.* penal. ~**aliser** *v.t.* penalize. ~**alité** *n.f.* penalty.

**penalt|y** (*pl.* ~**ies**) /penalti/ *n.m.* penalty (kick).

**penchant** /pãʃã/ *n.m.* inclination; (*goût*) liking (**pour,** for).

**pencher** /pãʃe/ *v.t.* tilt. ● *v.i.* lean (over), tilt. **se** ~ *v. pr.* lean (forward).

**pendant** /pãdã/ *prép.* (*au cours de*) during; (*durée*) for. ~ **que,** while.

**pendentif** /pãdãtif/ *n.m.* pendant.

**penderie** /pãdri/ *n.f.* wardrobe.

**pend|re** /pãdr/ *v.t./i.* hang. **se** ~**re** *v. pr.* hang (**à,** from); (*se tuer*) hang o.s. ~**re la crémaillère,** have a house-warming. ~**u,** ~**ue** *a.* hanging (**à,** from); *n.m., f.* hanged man, hanged woman.

**pendul|e** /pãdyl/ *n.f.* clock. ● *n.m.* pendulum. ~**ette** *n.f.* (travelling) clock.

**pénétr|er** /penetre/ *v.i.* ~**er (dans),** enter. ● *v.t.* penetrate.

**pénible** /penibl/ *a.* difficult; (*douloureux*) painful; (*fatigant*) tiresome. ~**ment** /-əmã/ *adv.* with difficulty; (*cruellement*) painfully.

**péniche** /peniʃ/ *n.f.* barge.

**pénicilline** /penisilin/ *n.f.* penicillin.

**péninsule** /penɛ̃syl/ *n.f.* peninsula.

**pénis** /penis/ *n.m.* penis.

**pensée**¹ /pãse/ *n.f.* thought.

**pensée**² /pãse/ *n.f.* (*fleur*) pansy.

**pens|er** /pãse/ *v.t./i.* think. ~**er à,** (*réfléchir à*) think about; (*se souvenir de, prévoir*) think of. ~**er faire,** think of doing. **faire** ~**er à,** remind one of.

**pensi|f,** ~**ve** /pãsif, -v/ *a.* pensive.

**pension** /pãsjõ/ *n.f.* (*scol.*) boarding-school; (*repas, somme*) board; (*allocation*) pension. ~ **(de famille),** guest-house. ~ **alimentaire,** (*jurid.*) alimony. ~**naire** /-jɔner/ *n.m./f.* boarder; (*d'hôtel*) guest. ~**nat** /-jɔna/ *n.m.* boarding-school.

**pente** /pãt/ n.f. slope. **en ~,** sloping.

**Pentecôte** /pãtkot/ n.f. **la ~,** Whitsun.

**pénurie** /penyri/ n.f. shortage.

**pépin** /pepɛ̃/ n.m. (graine) pip; (ennui: fam.) hitch; (parapluie: fam.) brolly.

**perce-neige** /pɛrsənɛʒ/ n.m./f. invar. snowdrop.

**percepteur** /pɛrsɛptœr/ n.m. tax-collector.

**perceptible** /pɛrsɛptibl/ a. perceptible.

**perception** /pɛrsɛpsjɔ̃/ n.f. perception; (d'impôts) collection.

**percer** /pɛrse/ v.t. pierce; (avec perceuse) drill.

**perceuse** /pɛrsøz/ n.f. drill.

**percevoir**† /pɛrsəvwar/ v.t. perceive; (impôt) collect.

**perche** /pɛrʃ/ n.f. (bâton) pole.

**perch|er** /pɛrʃe/ v.t., **se ~er** v. pr. perch. **~oir** n.m. perch.

**percolateur** /pɛrkɔlatœr/ n.m. percolator.

**percussion** /pɛrkysjɔ̃/ n.f. percussion.

**percuter** /pɛrkyte/ v.t. strike; (véhicule) crash into.

**perd|re** /pɛrdr/ v.t./i. lose; (gaspiller) waste; (ruiner) ruin. **se ~re** v. pr. get lost; (rester inutilisé) go to waste. **~ant, ~ante** a. losing; n.m., f. loser. **~u** a. (endroit) isolated; (moments) spare.

**perdreau** (pl. **~x**) /pɛrdro/ n.m. (young) partridge.

**perdrix** /pɛrdri/ n.f. partridge.

**père** /pɛr/ n.m. father. **~ de famille,** father, family man. **le ~ Noël,** Father Christmas, Santa Claus.

**perfection** /pɛrfɛksjɔ̃/ n.f. perfection.

**perfectionn|er** /pɛrfɛksjɔne/ v.t. improve. **se ~er en anglais**/etc., improve one's English/etc. **~é** a. sophisticated. **~ement** n.m. improvement.

**perfectionniste** /pɛrfɛksjɔnist/ n.m./f. perfectionist.

**perforer** /pɛrfɔre/ v.t. perforate; (billet, bande) punch.

**performance** /pɛrfɔrmãs/ n.f. performance.

**perfusion** /pɛrfysjɔ̃/ n.f. drip. **mettre qn. sous ~,** put s.o. on a drip.

**péridural** /peridyral/ a. **(anesthésie) ~e,** epidural.

**péril** /peril/ n.m. peril.

**périlleu|x, ~se** /perijø, -z/ a. perilous.

**périmé** /perime/ a. expired; (désuet) outdated.

**périmètre** /perimetr/ n.m. perimeter.

**périod|e** /perjɔd/ n.f. period. **~ique** a. periodic(al); n.m. (journal) periodical.

**périphér|ie** /periferi/ n.f. periphery; (banlieue) outskirts. **~ique** a. peripheral; n.m. (boulevard) **~ique,** ring road.

**perle** /pɛrl/ n.f. (bijou) pearl; (boule, de sueur) bead.

**permanence** /pɛrmanãs/ n.f. permanence; (bureau) duty office. **en ~,** permanently. **assurer une ~,** keep the office open.

**permanent, ~e** /pɛrmanã, -t/ a. permanent; (spectacle) continuous; (comité) standing. ● n.f. (coiffure) perm.

**perméable** /pɛrmeabl/ a. permeable.

**permettre**† /pɛrmɛtr/ v.t. allow, permit. **~ à qn. de,** allow ou permit s.o. to.

**permis, ~e** /pɛrmi, -z/ a. allowed. ● n.m. licence, permit. **~ (de conduire),** driving-licence.

**permission** /pɛrmisjɔ̃/ n.f. permission. **en ~,** (mil.) on leave.

**Pérou** /peru/ n.m. Peru.

**perpendiculaire** /pɛrpãdikylɛr/ a. & n.f. perpendicular.

**perpétuel, ~le** /pɛrpetɥɛl/ a. perpetual.

**perpétuité (à)** /(a)pɛrpetɥite/ adv. for life.

**perron** /pɛrɔ̃/ n.m. (front) steps.

**perroquet** /pɛrɔkɛ/ n.m. parrot.

**perruche** /pɛryʃ/ n.f. budgerigar.

**perruque** /pɛryk/ n.f. wig.

**persan, ~e** /pɛrsã, -an/ a. & n.m. (lang.) Persian.

**persécut|er** /pɛrsekyte/ v.t. persecute. **~ion** /-ysjɔ̃/ n.f. persecution.

**persévér|er** /pɛrsevere/ v.i. persevere. **~ance** n.f. perseverance.

**persienne** /pɛrsjɛn/ n.f. (outside) shutter.

**persil** /pɛrsi/ n.m. parsley.

**persister** /pɛrsiste/ v.i. persist (**à faire,** in doing).

**personnage** /pɛrsɔnaʒ/ n.m. character; (important) personality.

**personnalité** /pɛrsɔnalite/ n.f. personality.

**personne** /pɛrsɔn/ n.f. person. **~s,** people. ● pron. (quelqu'un) anybody. **(ne) ~,** nobody.

**personnel, ~le** /pɛrsɔnɛl/ a. personal; (égoïste) selfish. ● n.m. staff. **~lement** adv. personally.

**perspective** /pɛrspɛktiv/ n.f. (art) perspective; (vue) view; (possibilité) prospect; (point de vue) viewpoint, perspective.

**persuader** /pɛrsɥade/ v.t. persuade (**de faire,** to do).

**perte** /pɛrt/ n.f. loss; (ruine) ruin. **~ de,** (temps, argent) waste of. **~s,** (méd.) discharge.

**perturber** /pɛrtyrbe/ v.t. disrupt; (personne) perturb.

**pervenche** /pɛrvãʃ/ n.f. periwinkle; (fam.) traffic warden.

**pervers, ~e** /pɛrvɛr, -s/ a. perverse; (dépravé) perverted.

**pes|ant, ~ante** /pəzã, -t/ a. heavy. **la ~anteur,** gravity.

**pèse-personne** /pɛzpɛrsɔn/ n.m. (bathroom) scales.

**peser** /pəze/ v.t./i. weigh.

**peseta** /pezeta/ n.f. peseta.

**pessimis|te** /pesimist/ a. pessimistic. ● n.m. pessimist. ∼me n.m. pessimism.

**peste** /pɛst/ n.f. plague; (personne) pest.

**pester** /pɛste/ v.i. ∼ (contre), curse.

**pétale** /petal/ n.m. petal.

**pétanque** /petɑ̃k/ n.f. bowls.

**pétard** /petar/ n.m. banger.

**péter** /pete/ v.i. fart; (fam.) go bang; (casser: fam.) snap.

**pétill|er** /petije/ v.i. (feu) crackle; (champagne, yeux) sparkle. ∼ant, ∼ante a. (gazeux) fizzy.

**petit, ∼e** /pti, -t/ a. small; (avec nuance affective) little; (jeune) young, small; (faible) slight; (mesquin) petty. ● n.m., f. little child. ∼ ami, boy-friend. ∼e amie, girl-friend. ∼ à petit, little by little. ∼es annonces, small ads. ∼e cuiller, teaspoon. ∼ déjeuner, breakfast. le ∼ écran, the small screen, television. ∼-enfant (pl. ∼s-enfants) n.m. grandchild. ∼e-fille (pl. ∼es-filles) n.f. granddaughter. ∼-fils (pl. ∼s-fils) n.m. grandson. ∼ pain, roll. ∼-pois (pl. ∼s-pois) n.m. garden pea.

**pétition** /petisjɔ̃/ n.f. petition.

**pétrir** /petrir/ v.t. knead.

**pétrol|e** /petrɔl/ n.m. (brut) oil; (pour lampe etc.) paraffin. lampe à ∼e, oil lamp. ∼ier, ∼ière a. oil; n.m. (navire) oil-tanker.

**peu** /pø/ adv. ∼ (de), (quantité) little, not much; (nombre) few, not many. ∼ intéressant/etc., not very interesting/etc. ● pron. few. ● n.m. little. un ∼ (de), a little. à ∼ près, more or less. ∼ après/avant, shortly after/before. ∼ de chose, not much. ∼ nombreux, few. ∼ souvent, seldom.

**peuple** /pœpl/ n.m. people.

**peupler** /pœple/ v.t. populate.

**peuplier** /pøplije/ n.m. poplar.

**peur** /pœr/ n.f. fear. avoir ∼, be afraid (de, of). de ∼ de, for fear of. faire ∼ à, frighten. ∼eux, ∼euse a. fearful, timid.

**peut** /pø/ voir **pouvoir**[1].

**peut-être** /pøtɛtr/ adv. perhaps, maybe. ∼ que, perhaps, maybe.

**peux** /pø/ voir **pouvoir**[1].

**phare** /far/ n.m. (tour) lighthouse; (de véhicule) headlight. ∼ antibrouillard, fog lamp.

**pharmaceutique** /farmasøtik/ a. pharmaceutical.

**pharmac|ie** /farmasi/ n.f. (magasin) chemist's (shop); (armoire) medicine cabinet. ∼ien, ∼ienne n.m., f. chemist, pharmacist.

**pharyngite** /farɛ̃ʒit/ n.f. pharyngitis.

**phénomène** /fenɔmɛn/ n.m. phenomenon; (original: fam.) eccentric.

**Philippines** /filipin/ n.f. pl. **les** ∼, the Philippines.

**philosoph|e** /filozɔf/ n.m./f. philosopher. ● a. philosophical. ∼ie n.f. philosophy. ∼ique a. philosophical.

**phonétique** /fɔnetik/ a. phonetic.

**phoque** /fɔk/ n.m. (animal) seal.

**phosphate** /fɔsfat/ n.m. phosphate.

**phosphore** /fɔsfɔr/ n.m. phosphorus.

**photo** /fɔto/ n.f. photo; (art) photography. **prendre en** ∼, take a photo of. ∼ d'identité, passport photograph.

**photocop|ie** /fɔtɔkɔpi/ n.f. photocopy. ∼ier v.t. photocopy. ∼ieuse n.f. photocopier.

**photograph|e** /fɔtɔgraf/ n.m./f. photographer. ∼ie n.f. photograph. ∼ier v.t. take a photo of.

**phrase** /frɑz/ n.f. sentence.

**physicien, ∼ne** /fizisjɛ̃, -jɛn/ n.m., f. physicist.

**physiologie** /fizjɔlɔʒi/ n.f. physiology.

**physique**[1] /fizik/ a. physical. ● n.m. physique. **au** ∼, physically. ∼ment adv. physically.

**physique**[2] /fizik/ n.f. physics.

**pian|o** /pjano/ n.m. piano. ∼iste n.m./f. pianist.

**pic** /pik/ n.m. (outil) pickaxe; (sommet) peak; (oiseau) woodpecker. à ∼, (verticalement) sheer; (couler) straight to the bottom; (arriver) just at the right time.

**pichet** /piʃɛ/ n.m. jug.

**pickpocket** /pikpɔkɛt/ n.m. pickpocket.

**pick-up** /pikœp/ n.m. invar. record-player.

**picot|er** /pikɔte/ v.t. prick; (yeux) make smart. ∼ement n.m. pricking; smarting.

**pie** /pi/ n.f. magpie.

**pièce** /pjɛs/ n.f. piece; (chambre) room; (écrit) document. ∼ (de monnaie), coin. ∼ (de théâtre), play. **dix francs/etc. (la)** ∼, ten francs/etc. each. ∼ de rechange, spare part. ∼ détachée, part. ∼ d'identité, identity paper. ∼s justificatives, supporting documents. **deux/trois** etc. ∼s, two-/three-/etc. room flat.

**pied** /pje/ n.m. foot; (de meuble) leg; (de lampe) base; (de salade) plant. à ∼, on foot. **avoir** ∼, have a footing. **mettre les** ∼s **dans le plat**, put one's foot in it. **c'est le** ∼**!**, (fam.) it's great!

**piège** /pjɛʒ/ n.m. trap.

**piég|er** /pjeʒe/ v.t. trap; (avec explosifs) booby-trap. **lettre/ voiture** ∼ée, letter-/carbomb.

**pierre** /pjɛr/ n.f. stone.

**piétiner** /pjetine/ v.i. stamp one's feet; (ne pas avancer: fig.) mark time. ● v.t. trample (on).

**piéton** /pjetɔ̃/ n.m. pedestrian. ∼nier, ∼nière /-ɔnje, -jɛr/ a. pedestrian.

**pieuvre** /pjœvr/ *n.f.* octopus.

**pif** /pif/ *n.m.* (*fam.*) nose.

**pigeon** /piʒɔ̃/ *n.m.* pigeon.

**piger** /piʒe/ *v.t./i.* (*fam.*) understand, get (it).

**pigment** /pigmã/ *n.m.* pigment.

**pile** /pil/ *n.f.* (*tas, pilier*) pile; (*électr.*) battery; (*atomique*) pile. ● *adv.* (*s'arrêter: fam.*) dead. **à dix heures ~,** (*fam.*) at ten on the dot. **~ ou face?,** heads or tails?

**pilier** /pilje/ *n.m.* pillar.

**pilot|e** /pilot/ *n.m.* pilot; (*auto.*) driver. ● *a.* pilot. **~er** *v.t* (*aviat., naut.*) pilot; (*auto.*) drive.

**pilule** /pilyl/ *n.f.* pill. **la ~,** the pill.

**piment** /pimã/ *n.m.* pepper, pimento; (*fig.*) spice. **~é** /-te/ *a.* spicy.

**pin** /pɛ̃/ *n.m.* pine.

**pinard** /pinar/ *n.m.* (*vin: fam.*) plonk, cheap wine.

**pince** /pɛ̃s/ *n.f.* (*outil*) pliers; (*levier*) crowbar; (*de crabe*) pincer. **~ (à épiler),** tweezers. **~ (à linge),** (clothes)-peg.

**pinceau** (*pl.* **~x**) /pɛ̃so/ *n.m.* paintbrush.

**pinc|er** /pɛ̃se/ *v.t.* pinch. **se ~er le doigt,** catch one's finger. **~ée** *n.f.* pinch (**de,** of).

**pinède** /pinɛd/ *n.f.* pine forest.

**pingouin** /pɛ̃gwɛ̃/ *n.m.* penguin.

**ping-pong** /piŋpɔ̃g/ *n.m.* table tennis, ping-pong.

**pingre** /pɛ̃gr/ *a.* miserly.

**pinson** /pɛ̃sɔ̃/ *n.m.* chaffinch.

**pintade** /pɛ̃tad/ *n.f.* guinea-fowl.

**pioche** /pjɔʃ/ *n.f.* pick(axe).

**pion** /pjɔ̃/ *n.m.* (*de jeu*) piece; (*échecs*) pawn; (*scol., fam.*) supervisor.

**pionnier** /pjɔnje/ *n.m.* pioneer.

**pipe** /pip/ *n.f.* pipe.

**pipe-line** /piplin/ *n.m.* pipeline.

**piquant, ~e** /pikã, -t/ *a.* (*barbe etc.*) prickly; (*goût*) pungent; (*détail etc.*) spicy. ● *n.m.* prickle; (*de hérisson*) spine, prickle.

**pique** /pik/ *n.m.* (*cartes*) spades.

**pique-niqu|e** /piknik/ *n.m.* picnic. **~er** *v.i.* picnic.

**piquer** /pike/ *v.t.* prick; (*langue*) burn, sting; (*abeille etc.*) sting; (*serpent etc.*) bite; (*enfoncer*) stick; (*coudre*) (machine-)stitch; (*curiosité*) excite; (*crise*) have; (*voler: fam.*) pinch. ● *v.i.* (*avion*) dive; (*goût*) be hot.

**piquet** /pikɛ/ *n.m.* stake; (*de tente*) peg. **au ~,** (*scol.*) in the corner.

**piqûre** /pikyr/ *n.f.* prick; (*d'abeille etc.*) sting; (*de serpent etc.*) bite; (*point*) stitch; (*méd.*) injection.

**pirate** /pirat/ *n.m.* pirate. **~ de l'air,** hijacker. **~rie** *n.f.* piracy.

**pire** /pir/ *a.* worse (**que,** than). **le ~ livre/etc.,** the worst book/etc. ● *n.m.* **le ~,** the worst (thing). **au ~,** at worst.

**pis**[1] /pi/ *n.m.* (*de vache*) udder.

**pis**[2] /pi/ *a. invar. & adv.* worse. **aller de mal en ~,** go from bad to worse.

**piscine** /pisin/ *n.f.* swimming-pool. **~ couverte,** indoor swimming-pool.

**pissenlit** /pisãli/ *n.m.* dandelion.

**pistache** /pistaʃ/ *n.f.* pistachio.

**piste** /pist/ *n.f.* track; (*de personne, d'animal*) track, trail; (*aviat.*) runway; (*de cirque*) ring; (*de ski*) run; (*de patinage*) rink; (*de danse*) floor; (*sport*) race-track. **~ cyclable,** cycle-track; (*Amer.*) bicycle path.

**pistolet** /pistolɛ/ *n.m.* gun, pistol.

**piston** /pistɔ̃/ *n.m.* (*techn.*) piston.

**pitié** /pitje/ *n.f.* pity. **il me fait ~, j'ai ~ de lui,** I pity him.

**piton** /pitɔ̃/ *n.m.* (*à crochet*) hook; (*sommet pointu*) peak.

**pitoyable** /pitwajabl/ *a.* pitiful.

**pitre** /pitr/ *n.m.* clown. **faire le ~,** clown around.

**pittoresque** /pitɔrɛsk/ *a.* picturesque.

**pivot** /pivo/ *n.m.* pivot.

**pizza** /pidza/ *n.f.* pizza.

**placard** /plakar/ *n.m.* cupboard; (*affiche*) poster. **~er** /-de/ *v.t.* (*affiche*) post up; (*mur*) cover with posters.

**place** /plas/ *n.f.* place; (*espace libre*) room, space; (*siège*) seat, place; (*prix d'un trajet*) fare; (*esplanade*) square; (*emploi*) position; (*de parking*) space. **à la ~ de,** instead of. **en ~, à sa ~,** in its place. **sur ~,** on the spot. **ça prend de la ~,** it takes up a lot of room. **se mettre à la ~ de qn.** put oneself in s.o.'s shoes *ou* place.

**plac|er** /plase/ *v.t.* place; (*invité, spectateur*) seat; (*argent*) invest. **se ~er** *v. pr.* (*personne*) take up a position; (*troisième etc.: sport*) come (in); (*à un endroit*) to go and stand (**à,** in). **~é a.** (*sport*) placed. **bien ~é pour,** in a position to. **~ement** *n.m.* (*d'argent*) investment.

**placide** /plasid/ *a.* placid.

**plafond** /plafɔ̃/ *n.m.* ceiling.

**plage** /plaʒ/ *n.f.* beach; (*station*) (seaside) resort; (*aire*) area.

**plaider** /plede/ *v.t./i.* plead.

**plaie** /plɛ/ *n.f.* wound; (*personne: fam.*) nuisance.

**plaignant, ~e** /plɛɲã, -t/ *n.m., f.* plaintiff.

**plaindre†** /plɛ̃dr/ *v.t.* pity. **se ~** *v. pr.* complain (**de,** about). **se ~ de,** (*souffrir de*) complain of.

**plaine** /plɛn/ *n.f.* plain.

**plaint|e** /plɛ̃t/ *n.f.* complaint; (*gémissement*) groan. **~if, ~ive** *a.* plaintive.

**plaire†** /plɛr/ *v.i.* **~ à,** please. **ça lui plaît,** he likes it. **elle lui plaît,** he likes her. **s'il vous plaît,** please.

**plaisance** /plɛzãs/ *n.f.* **la (navigation de) ~,** yachting.

**plaisant, ~e** /plɛzã, -t/ *a.* pleasant; (*drôle*) amusing.

**plaisant|er** /plɛzɑ̃te/ *v.i.* joke. **~erie** *n.f.* joke. **~in** *n.m.* joker.

**plaisir** /plezir/ *n.m.* pleasure. **faire ~ à,** please. **pour le ~,** for fun *ou* pleasure.

**plan** /plɑ̃/ *n.m.* plan; (*de ville*) map; (*surface, niveau*) plane.

**planche** /plɑ̃ʃ/ *n.f.* board, plank. **~ à repasser,** ironing-board. **~ à voile,** sail-board; (*sport*) windsurfing.

**plancher** /plɑ̃ʃe/ *n.m.* floor.

**plan|er** /plane/ *v.i.* glide. **~eur** *n.m.* (*avion*) glider.

**planète** /planɛt/ *n.f.* planet.

**planif|ier** /planifje/ *v.t.* plan. **~ication** *n.f.* planning.

**plante** /plɑ̃t/ *n.f.* plant. **~ des pieds,** sole (of the foot).

**plant|er** /plɑ̃te/ *v.t.* (*plante etc.*) plant; (*enfoncer*) drive in. **~ation** *n.f.* planting; (*de tabac etc.*) plantation.

**plaque** /plak/ *n.f.* plate; (*de marbre*) slab; (*insigne*) badge; (*commémorative*) plaque. **~ chauffante,** hotplate. **~ minéralogique,** number-plate.

**plaquer** /plake/ *v.t.* (*bois*) veneer; (*aplatir*) flatten; (*rugby*) tackle; (*abandonner: fam.*) ditch.

**plasma** /plasma/ *n.m.* plasma.

**plastique** /plastik/ *a. & n.m.* plastic. **en ~,** plastic.

**plat¹, ~e** /pla, -t/ *a.* flat. ● *n.m.* (*de la main*) flat. **à ~** *adv.* (*poser*) flat; *a.* (*batterie, pneu*) flat. **à ~ ventre,** flat on one's face.

**plat²** /pla/ *n.m.* (*culin.*) dish; (*partie de repas*) course.

**platane** /platan/ *n.m.* plane(-tree).

**plateau** (*pl.* **~x**) /plato/ *n.m.* tray; (*d'électrophone*) turntable, deck; (*de balance*) pan; (*géog.*) plateau. **~ de fromages,** cheeseboard.

**plateau-repas** (*pl.* **plateaux-repas**) *n.m.* tray meal.

**plate-bande** (*pl.* **plates-bandes**) /platbɑ̃d/ *n.f.* flower-bed.

**plate-forme** (*pl.* **plates-formes**) /platfɔrm/ *n.f.* platform.

**platine¹** /platin/ *n.m.* platinum.

**platine²** /platin/ *n.f.* (*de tourne-disque*) turntable.

**plâtr|e** /plɑtr/ *n.m.* plaster; (*méd.*) (plaster) cast. **~er** *v.t.* plaster; (*membre*) put in plaster.

**plein, ~e** /plɛ̃, plɛn/ *a.* full (**de**, of); (*total*) complete. ● *n.m.* **faire le ~ (d'essence),** fill up (the tank). **à ~,** to the full. **à ~ temps,** full-time. **en ~ air,** in the open air. **en ~ milieu/visage,** right in the middle/the face. **en ~e nuit/etc.,** in the middle of the night/*etc.*

**pleurer** /plœre/ *v.i.* cry, weep (**sur,** over); (*yeux*) water. ● *v.t.* mourn.

**pleurésie** /plœrezi/ *n.f.* pleurisy.

**pleurs (en)** /(ɑ̃)plœr/ *adv.* in tears.

**pleuvoir†** /pløvwar/ *v.i.* rain. **il pleut,** it is raining.

**pli** /pli/ *n.m.* fold; (*de jupe*) pleat; (*de pantalon*) crease; (*enveloppe*) cover; (*habitude*) habit. **(faux) ~,** crease.

**pliant, ~e** /plijɑ̃, -t/ *a.* folding; (*parapluie*) telescopic. ● *n.m.* folding stool, camp-stool.

**plier** /plije/ *v.t.* fold; (*courber*) bend. ● *v.i.* bend. **se ~** *v. pr.* fold.

**plomb** /plɔ̃/ *n.m.* lead; (*fusible*) fuse. **~s,** (*de chasse*) lead shot. **de ou en ~,** lead. **de ~,** (*ciel*) leaden.

**plomb|er** /plɔ̃be/ *v.t.* (*dent*) fill. **~age** *n.m.* filling.

**plomb|ier** /plɔ̃bje/ *n.m.* plumber. **~erie** *n.f.* plumbing.

**plongeant, ~e** /plɔ̃ʒɑ̃, -t/ *a.* (*vue*) from above; (*décolleté*) plunging.

**plongeoir** /plɔ̃ʒwar/ *n.m.* diving-board.

**plongeon** /plɔ̃ʒɔ̃/ *n.m.* dive.

**plong|er** /plɔ̃ʒe/ *v.i.* dive; (*route*) plunge. ● *v.t.* plunge. **se ~er** *v. pr.* plunge (**dans,** into). **~é dans,** (*lecture*) immersed in. **~ée** *n.f.* diving. **en ~ée** (*sous-marin*) submerged.

**plouf** /pluf/ *n.m. & int.* splash.

**plu** /ply/ *voir* **plaire, pleuvoir.**

**pluie** /plɥi/ *n.f.* rain; (*averse*) shower.

**plume** /plym/ *n.f.* feather; (*stylo*) pen; (*pointe*) nib.

**plupart** /plypar/ *n.f.* most. **la ~ des,** (*gens, cas, etc.*) most. **la ~ du temps,** most of the time.

**pluriel, ~le** /plyrjɛl/ *a. & n.m.* plural. **au ~,** (*nom*) plural.

**plus¹** /ply/ *adv. de négation.* **(ne) ~,** (*temps*) no longer, not any more. **(ne) ~ de,** (*quantité*) no more. **je n'y vais ~,** I do not go there any longer *ou* any more. **(il n'y a) ~ de pain,** (there is) no more bread.

**plus²** /ply/ (/plyz/ *before vowel,* /plys/ *in final position*) *adv.* more (**que,** than). **~ âgé/tard/etc.,** older/later/*etc.* **~ beau/etc.,** more beautiful/*etc.* **le ~,** the most. **le ~ beau/etc.,** the most beautiful; (*de deux*) the more beautiful. **le ~ de,** (*gens etc.*) most. **~ de,** (*pain etc.*) more; (*dix jours etc.*) more than. **il est ~ de huit heures/etc.** it is after eight/*etc.* o'clock. **de ~,** more (**que,** than); (*en outre*) moreover. **(âgés) de ~ de** (*huit ans etc.*) over, more than. **de ~ en plus,** more and more. **en ~,** extra. **en ~ de,** in addition to. **~ ou moins,** more or less.

**plus³** /plys/ *conj.* plus.

**plusieurs** /plyzjœr/ *a. & pron.* several.

**plus-value** /plyvaly/ *n.f.* (*bénéfice*) profit.

**plutôt** /plyto/ *adv.* rather (**que,** than).

**pluvieu|x, ~se** /plyvjø, -z/ *a.* rainy.

**pneu** (*pl.* **~s**) /pnø/ *n.m.* tyre; (*lettre*) express letter. **~matique** *a.* inflatable.

**pneumonie** /pnømɔni/ *n.f.* pneumonia.

**poche** /pɔʃ/ *n.f.* pocket; (*sac*) bag. **~s,** (*sous les yeux*) bags.

**pocher** /pɔʃe/ v.t. (œuf) poach.

**pochette** /pɔʃɛt/ n.f. pack(et), envelope; (sac) bag, pouch; (d'allumettes) book; (de disque) sleeve; (mouchoir) pocket handkerchief. ~ **surprise,** lucky bag.

**podium** /pɔdjɔm/ n.m. rostrum.

**poêle**[1] /pwal/ n.f. ~ **(à frire),** frying-pan.

**poêle**[2] /pwal/ n.m. stove.

**poème** /pɔɛm/ n.m. poem.

**poésie** /pɔezi/ n.f. poetry; (poème) poem.

**poète** /pɔɛt/ n.m. poet.

**poétique** /pɔetik/ a. poetic.

**poids** /pwa/ n.m. weight. ~ **lourd,** (camion) lorry, juggernaut.

**poignard** /pwaɲar/ n.m. dagger.

**poignée** /pwaɲe/ n.f. handle; (quantité) handful. ~ **de main,** handshake.

**poignet** /pwaɲɛ/ n.m. wrist; (de chemise) cuff.

**poil** /pwal/ n.m. hair; (pelage) fur; (de brosse) bristle. ~**s,** (de tapis) pile. **à** ~, (fam.) naked. ~**u** a. hairy.

**poinçon** /pwɛ̃sɔ̃/ n.m. awl; (marque) hallmark. ~**ner** /-ɔne/ v.t. (billet) punch.

**poing** /pwɛ̃/ n.m. fist.

**point**[1] /pwɛ̃/ n.m. point; (note: scol.) mark; (tache) spot, dot; (de couture) stitch. ~ **(final),** full stop, period. **à** ~, (culin.) medium; (arriver) at the right time. **mettre au** ~, (photo.) focus. **deux** ~**s,** colon. ~**s de suspension,** suspension points. ~ **de suture,** (méd.) stitch. ~ **de vente,** retail outlet. ~ **de vue,** point of view. ~ **d'interrogation / d'exclamation,** question/exclamation mark. ~ **mort,** (auto.) neutral. ~ **virgule,** semicolon.

**point**[2] /pwɛ̃/ adv. **(ne)** ~, not.

**pointe** /pwɛ̃t/ n.f. point, tip; (clou) tack; (de grille) spike; (fig.) touch (**de,** of). **de** ~, (industrie) highly advanced. **en** ~, pointed. **heure de** ~, peak hour. **sur la** ~ **des pieds,** on tiptoe.

**pointillé** /pwɛ̃tije/ n.m. dotted line. ● a. dotted.

**pointu** /pwɛ̃ty/ a. pointed; (aiguisé) sharp.

**pointure** /pwɛ̃tyr/ n.f. size.

**poire** /pwar/ n.f. pear.

**poireau** (pl. ~**x**) /pwaro/ n.m. leek.

**poirier** /pwarje/ n.m. pear-tree.

**pois** /pwa/ n.m. pea; (dessin) dot.

**poison** /pwazɔ̃/ n.m. poison.

**poisseu|x,** ~**se** /pwasø, -z/ a. sticky.

**poisson** /pwasɔ̃/ n.m. fish. ~ **rouge,** goldfish. ~ **d'avril,** April fool. **les P** ~**s,** Pisces.

**poissonn|ier,** ~**ière** /pwasɔnje, -jɛr/ n.m., f. fishmonger. ~**erie** n.f. fish shop.

**poitrine** /pwatrin/ n.f. chest; (seins) bosom; (culin.) breast.

**poivr|e** /pwavr/ n.m. pepper. ~**é** a. peppery. ~**ière** n.f. pepper-pot.

**poivron** /pwavrɔ̃/ n.m. pepper, capsicum.

**poker** /pɔkɛr/ n.m. poker.

**polaire** /pɔlɛr/ a. polar.

**polaroïd** /pɔlarɔid/ n.m. (P.) Polaroid (P.).

**pôle** /pol/ n.m. pole.

**polémique** /pɔlemik/ n.f. argument. ● a. controversial.

**poli** /pɔli/ a. (personne) polite. ~**ment** adv. politely.

**polic|e**[1] /pɔlis/ n.f. police; (discipline) (law and) order. ~**ier,** ~**ière** a. police; (roman) detective; n.m. policeman.

**police**[2] /pɔlis/ n.f. (d'assurance) policy.

**polio(myélite)** /pɔljo(mjelit)/ n.f. polio(myelitis).

**polir** /pɔlir/ v.t. polish.

**politesse** /pɔlitɛs/ n.f. politeness.

**politique** /pɔlitik/ a. political. ● n.f. politics.

**pollen** /pɔlɛn/ n.m. pollen.

**poll|uer** /pɔlɥe/ v.t. pollute. ~**ution** n.f. pollution.

**polo** /pɔlo/ n.m. polo; (vêtement) sports shirt, tennis shirt.

**Pologne** /pɔlɔɲ/ n.f. Poland.

**polonais,** ~**e** /pɔlɔnɛ, -z/ a. Polish. ● n.m., f. Pole. ● n.m. (lang.) Polish.

**polycopier** /pɔlikɔpje/ v.t. duplicate, stencil.

**polyglotte** /pɔliɡlɔt/ n.m./f. polyglot.

**pommade** /pɔmad/ n.f. ointment.

**pomme** /pɔm/ n.f. apple; (d'arrosoir) rose. ~ **d'Adam,** Adam's apple. ~ **de pin,** pine cone. ~ **de terre,** potato. ~**s frites,** chips.

**pommier** /pɔmje/ n.m. apple-tree.

**pompe** /pɔ̃p/ n.f. pump; (splendeur) pomp. ~ **à incendie,** fire-engine. ~**s funèbres,** undertaker's.

**pomper** /pɔ̃pe/ v.t. pump.

**pompier** /pɔ̃pje/ n.m. fireman.

**pompiste** /pɔ̃pist/ n.m./f. petrol pump attendant.

**poncer** /pɔ̃se/ v.t. rub down.

**ponctuation** /pɔ̃ktɥasjɔ̃/ n.f. punctuation.

**ponct|uel,** ~**uelle** /pɔ̃ktɥɛl/ a. punctual. ~**ualité** n.f. punctuality.

**ponctuer** /pɔ̃ktɥe/ v.t. punctuate.

**pondre** /pɔ̃dr/ v.t./i. lay.

**poney** /pɔnɛ/ n.m. pony.

**pont** /pɔ̃/ n.m. bridge; (de navire) deck; (de graissage) ramp. **faire le** ~, take the extra day('s) off (between holidays). ~ **aérien,** airlift.

**pop** /pɔp/ n.m. & a. invar. (mus.) pop.

**popul|aire** /pɔpylɛr/ a. popular; (expression) colloquial; (quartier, origine) working-class. ~**arité** n.f. popularity.

**population** /pɔpylasjɔ̃/ n.f. population.

**porc** /pɔr/ n.m. pig; (viande) pork.

**porcelaine** /pɔrsəlɛn/ n.f. china, porcelain.

**porc-épic** (pl. **porcs-épics**) /pɔrkepik/ n.m. porcupine.

**porche** /pɔrʃ/ n.m. porch.

**porcherie** /pɔrʃari/ n.f. pigsty.

**por|e** /pɔr/ n.m. pore. **~eux, ~euse** a. porous.

**pornograph|ie** /pɔrnɔgrafi/ n.f. pornography. **~ique** a. pornographic.

**port¹** /pɔr/ n.m. port, harbour. **à bon ~,** safely. **~ maritime,** seaport.

**port²** /pɔr/ n.m. (transport) carriage; (d'armes) carrying.

**portail** /pɔrtaj/ n.m. portal.

**portant, ~e** /pɔrtɑ̃, -t/ a. **bien/mal ~,** in good/bad health.

**portati|f, ~ve** /pɔrtatif, -v/ a. portable.

**porte** /pɔrt/ n.f. door; (passage) doorway; (de jardin, d'embarquement) gate. **mettre à la ~,** throw out. **~ d'entrée,** front door.

**portée** /pɔrte/ n.f. (d'animaux) litter; (impact) significance; (mus.) stave. **à ~ de,** within reach of. **à ~ de (la) main,** within (arm's) reach. **à la ~ de qn.** at s.o.'s level.

**portefeuille** /pɔrtəfœj/ n.m. wallet; (de ministre) portfolio.

**portemanteau** (pl. **~x**) /pɔrtmɑ̃to/ n.m. coat ou hat stand.

**port|er** /pɔrte/ v.t. carry; (vêtement, bague) wear; (fruits, responsabilité, nom) bear; (coup) strike; (amener) bring. ● v.i. (bruit) carry; (coup) hit home. **se ~er bien,** be ou feel well. **~e-bagages** n.m. invar. luggage rack. **~e-bonheur** n.m. invar. (objet) charm. **~e-clefs** n.m. invar. key-ring. **~e-documents** n.m. invar. attaché case, document wallet. **~e-monnaie** n.m. invar. purse.

**porteu|r, ~se** /pɔrtœr, -øz/ n.m., f. (méd.) carrier. ● n.m. (rail.) porter.

**portier** /pɔrtje/ n.m. door-man.

**portière** /pɔrtjɛr/ n.f. door.

**portillon** /pɔrtijɔ̃/ n.m. gate.

**portion** /pɔrsjɔ̃/ n.f. portion.

**porto** /pɔrto/ n.m. port (wine).

**portrait** /pɔrtrɛ/ n.m. portrait. **~-robot** (pl. **~s-robots**) n.m. identikit, photofit.

**portuaire** /pɔrtɥɛr/ a. port.

**portugais, ~e** /pɔrtygɛ, -z/ a. & n.m., f. Portuguese. ● n.m. (lang.) Portuguese.

**Portugal** /pɔrtygal/ n.m. Portugal.

**pose** /poz/ n.f. installation; (attitude) pose; (photo.) exposure.

**poser** /poze/ v.t. put (down); (installer) install, put in; (fondations) lay; (question) ask; (problème) pose. ● v.i. (modèle) pose. **se ~** v. pr. (avion, oiseau) land; (regard) alight.

**positi|f, ~ve** /pozitif, -v/ a. positive.

**position** /pozisjɔ̃/ n.f. position; (banque) balance (of account).

**posologie** /pozɔlɔʒi/ n.f. directions for use.

**poss|éder** /posede/ v.t. possess; (propriété) own, possess. **~esseur** n.m. possessor; owner.

**possession** /posesjɔ̃/ n.f. possession.

**possibilité** /posibilite/ n.f. possibility.

**possible** /posibl/ a. possible. **dès que ~,** as soon as possible. **faire son ~,** do one's utmost. **le plus tard/etc. ~,** as late/etc. as possible. **pas ~,** impossible; (int.) really!

**post-** /post/ préf. post-.

**post|al** (m. pl. **~aux**) /postal, -o/ a. postal.

**poste¹** /post/ n.f. (service) post; (bureau) post office. **~ aérienne,** airmail. **mettre à la ~,** post. **~ restante,** poste restante.

**poste²** /post/ n.m. (lieu, emploi) post; (de radio, télévision) set; (téléphone) extension (number). **~ d'essence,** petrol station. **~ d'incendie,** fire point. **~ de police,** police station. **~ de secours,** first-aid post.

**poster¹** /poste/ v.t. (lettre, personne) post.

**poster²** /postɛr/ n.m. poster.

**postérieur** /posterjœr/ a. later; (partie) back. **~ à,** after.

**postiche** /postiʃ/ a. false.

**post|ier, ~ière** /postje, -jɛr/ n.m., f. postal worker.

**post-scriptum** /postskriptɔm/ n.m. invar. postscript.

**postuler** /postyle/ v.t./i. apply (à ou pour, for).

**posture** /postyr/ n.f. posture.

**pot** /po/ n.m. pot; (en carton) carton; (en verre) jar; (chance: fam.) luck; (boisson: fam.) drink. **~-au-feu** /potofø/ n.m. invar. (plat) stew. **~ d'échappement,** exhaust-pipe.

**potable** /potabl/ a. drinkable. **eau ~,** drinking water.

**potage** /potaʒ/ n.m. soup.

**potag|er, ~ère** /potaʒe, -ɛr/ a. vegetable. ● n.m. vegetable garden.

**poteau** (pl. **~x**) /poto/ n.m. post; (télégraphique) pole. **~ indicateur,** signpost.

**pot|erie** /potri/ n.f. pottery; (objet) piece of pottery. **~ier** n.m. potter.

**potiron** /potirɔ̃/ n.m. pumpkin.

**pou** (pl. **~x**) /pu/ n.m. louse.

**poubelle** /pubɛl/ n.f. dustbin.

**pouce** /pus/ n.m. thumb; (de pied) big toe; (mesure) inch.

**poudr|e** /pudr/ n.f. powder. **en ~e,** (lait) powdered; (chocolat) drinking. **~er** v.t. powder.

**poudrier** /pudrije/ n.m. (powder) compact.

**pouf** /puf/ n.m. pouffe.

**poulailler** /pulaje/ n.m. (hen-)coop.

**poulain** /pulɛ̃/ n.m. foal; (protégé) protégé.

**poule** /pul/ n.f. hen; (culin.) fowl.

**poulet** /pulɛ/ n.m. chicken.

**pouliche** /puliʃ/ n.f. filly.

**poulie** /puli/ n.f. pulley.

**pouls** /pu/ *n.m.* pulse.

**poumon** /pumɔ̃/ *n.m.* lung.

**poupée** /pupe/ *n.f.* doll.

**poupon** /pupɔ̃/ *n.m.* baby. **~nière** /-ɔnjɛr/ *n.f.* crèche, day nursery.

**pour** /pur/ *prép.* for; (*envers*) to; (*à la place de*) on behalf of; (*comme*) as. **~ cela**, for that reason. **~ cent**, per cent. **~ de bon**, for good. **~ faire**, (in order) to do. **~ que**, so that. **le ~ et le contre**, the pros and cons.

**pourboire** /purbwar/ *n.m.* tip.

**pourcentage** /pursɑ̃taʒ/ *n.m.* percentage.

**pourchasser** /purʃase/ *v.t.* pursue.

**pourpre** /purpr/ *a. & n.m.* crimson; (*violet*) purple.

**pourquoi** /purkwa/ *conj. & adv.* why. ● *n.m. invar.* reason.

**pourra, pourrait** /pura, purɛ/ *voir* **pouvoir¹**.

**pourr|ir** /purir/ *v.t./i.* rot. **~i** *a.* rotten. **~iture** *n.f.* rot.

**poursuite** /pursɥit/ *n.f.* pursuit (**de**, of). **~s**, (*jurid.*) legal action.

**poursuiv|re†** /pursɥivr/ *v.t.* pursue; (*continuer*) continue (with). **~re (en justice)**, (*au criminel*) prosecute; (*au civil*) sue. ● *v.i.*, **se ~re** *v. pr.* continue. **~ant, ~ante** *n.m., f.* pursuer.

**pourtant** /purtɑ̃/ *adv.* yet.

**pourvu que** /purvyk(ə)/ *conj.* (*condition*) provided (that); (*souhait*) let us hope (that). **pourvu qu'il ne soit rien arrivé**, I hope nothing's happened.

**pousse** /pus/ *n.f.* growth; (*bourgeon*) shoot.

**poussé** /puse/ *a.* (*études*) advanced.

**pousser** /puse/ *v.t.* push; (*du coude*) nudge; (*cri*) let out; (*soupir*) heave; (*continuer*) continue; (*exhorter*) urge (**à**, to); (*forcer*) drive (**à**, to); (*amener*) bring (**à**, to). ● *v.i.* push; (*grandir*) grow. **faire ~** (*cheveux*) let grow; (*plante*) grow. **se ~** *v. pr.* move over *ou* up.

**poussette** /pusɛt/ *n.f.* push-chair.

**pouss|ière** /pusjɛr/ *n.f.* dust. **~iéreux, ~iéreuse** *a.* dusty.

**poussin** /pusɛ̃/ *n.m.* chick.

**poutre** /putr/ *n.f.* beam.

**pouvoir¹†** /puvwar/ *v. aux.* (*possibilité*) can, be able; (*permission, éventualité*) may, can. **il peut/pouvait/pourrait venir**, he can/could/might come. **je n'ai pas pu**, I could not. **j'ai pu faire**, (*réussi à*) I managed to do. **je n'en peux plus**, I am exhausted.

**pouvoir²** /puvwar/ *n.m.* power; (*gouvernement*) government.

**prairie** /preri/ *n.f.* meadow.

**praline** /pralin/ *n.f.* sugared almond.

**praticable** /pratikabl/ *a.* practicable.

**praticien, ~ne** /pratisjɛ̃, -jɛn/ *n.m., f.* practitioner.

**pratique** /pratik/ *a.* practical. ● *n.f.* practice; (*expérience*) experience. **la ~ du cheval**, riding. **~ment** *adv.* in practice; (*presque*) practically.

**pratiquer** /pratike/ *v.t./i.* practise; (*sport*) play; (*faire*) make.

**pré** /pre/ *n.m.* meadow.

**pré-** /pre/ *préf.* pre-.

**préalable** /prealabl/ **au ~**, first.

**préavis** /preavi/ *n.m.* (advance) notice.

**précaution** /prekosjɔ̃/ *n.f.* (*mesure*) precaution; (*prudence*) caution.

**précéd|ent, ~ente** /presedɑ̃, -t/ *a.* previous. ● *n.m.* precedent.

**précéder** /presede/ *v.t./i.* precede.

**précepte** /presɛpt/ *n.m.* precept.

**précep|teur, ~trice** /preseptœr, -tris/ *n.m., f.* tutor.

**prêcher** /preʃe/ *v.t./i.* preach.

**précieu|x, ~se** /presjø, -z/ *a.* precious.

**précipice** /presipis/ *n.m.* abyss, chasm.

**précipité** /presipite/ *a.* hasty.

**précipiter** /presipite/ *v.t.* throw, precipitate; (*hâter*) hasten. **se ~** *v. pr.* rush (**sur**, at on to); (*se jeter*) throw o.s.; (*s'accélérer*) speed up.

**précis, ~e** /presi, -z/ *a.* precise; (*mécanisme*) accurate. **dix heures ~es**, ten o'clock sharp.

**préciser** /presize/ *v.t./i.* specify; (*pensée*) be more specific about.

**précision** /presizjɔ̃/ *n.f.* precision; (*détail*) detail.

**précoce** /prekɔs/ *a.* early; (*enfant*) precocious.

**prédécesseur** /predesesœr/ *n.m.* predecessor.

**prédire†** /predir/ *v.t.* predict.

**préfabriqué** /prefabrike/ *a.* prefabricated.

**préface** /prefas/ *n.f.* preface.

**préfecture** /prefɛktyr/ *n.f.* prefecture. **~ de police**, police headquarters.

**préférence** /preferɑ̃s/ *n.f.* preference. **de ~**, preferably.

**préférentiel, ~le** /preferɑ̃sjɛl/ *a.* preferential.

**préfér|er** /prefere/ *v.t.* prefer (**à**, to). **je ne préfère pas**, I'd rather not. **~er faire**, prefer to do. **~é, ~ée** *a. & n.m., f.* favourite.

**préfet** /prefɛ/ *n.m.* prefect. **~ de police**, prefect *ou* chief of police.

**préfixe** /prefiks/ *n.m.* prefix.

**préhistorique** /preistɔrik/ *a.* prehistoric.

**préjudic|e** /preʒydis/ *n.m.* harm, prejudice. **porter ~e à**, harm.

**préjugé** /preʒyʒe/ *n.m.* prejudice. **avoir un ~ contre**, be prejudiced against. **sans ~s**, without prejudices.

**prél|ever** /prelve/ *v.t.* deduct (**sur**, from); (*sang*) take. **~èvement** *n.m.* deduction. **~èvement de sang**, blood sample.

**préliminaire** /preliminɛr/ a. & n.m. preliminary. ~s, (sexuels) foreplay.

**prélude** /prelyd/ n.m. prelude.

**prématuré** /prematyre/ a. premature. ● n.m. premature baby.

**prémédit|er** /premedite/ v.t. premeditate. ~ation n.f. premeditation.

**prem|ier, ~ière** /prəmje, -jɛr/ a. first; (rang) front, first; (nécessité, souci) prime; (qualité) top, prime; (état) original. ● n.m., f. first (one). ● n.m. (date) first; (étage) first floor. ● n.f. (rail.) first class; (exploit jamais vu) first; (cinéma, théâtre) première. de ~ier ordre, first-rate. en ~ier, first. ~ier ministre, Prime Minister.

**premièrement** /prəmjɛrmɑ̃/ adv. firstly.

**prémunir** /premynir/ v.t. protect (contre, against).

**prénatal** (m. pl. ~s) /prenatal/ a. antenatal.

**prendre†** /prɑ̃dr/ v.t. take; (attraper) catch, get; (acheter) get; (repas) have; (engager, adopter) take on; (poids) put on; (chercher) pick up. ● v.i. (liquide) set; (feu) catch; (vaccin) take. se ~ pour, think one is. s'y ~, set about (it).

**prénom** /prenɔ̃/ n.m. first name. ~mer /-ɔme/ v.t. call. se ~mer v. pr. be called.

**préoccup|er** /preɔkype/ v.t. worry; (absorber) preoccupy. ~ation n.f. worry.

**préparatifs** /preparatif/ n.m. pl. preparations.

**préparatoire** /preparatwar/ a. preparatory.

**prépar|er** /prepare/ v.t. prepare; (repas, café) make. se ~er v. pr. prepare o.s.; (être proche) be brewing. ~er à qn., (surprise) have (got) in store for s.o. ~ation n.f. preparation.

**préposé, ~ée** /prepoze/ n.m., f. employee; (des postes) postman, postwoman.

**préposition** /prepozisjɔ̃/ n.f. preposition.

**près** /prɛ/ adv. near, close. ~ de, near (to), close to; (presque) nearly. de ~, closely.

**presbyte** /prɛsbit/ a. long-sighted, far-sighted.

**presbytère** /prɛsbitɛr/ n.m. presbytery.

**prescr|ire†** /prɛskrir/ v.t. prescribe. ~iption n.f. prescription.

**présence** /prezɑ̃s/ n.f. presence; (scol.) attendance.

**présent, ~e** /prezɑ̃, -t/ a. present. ● n.m. (temps, cadeau) present. à ~, now.

**présent|er** /prezɑ̃te/ v.t. present; (personne) introduce (à, to); (montrer) show. se ~er v. pr. introduce o.s. (à, to); (aller) go; (apparaître) appear; (candidat) come forward; (occasion etc.) arise. se ~er à, (examen) sit for; (élection) stand for. ~able a. presentable. ~ateur, ~atrice n.m., f. presenter. ~ation n.f. presentation; introduction.

**préservatif** /prezɛrvatif/ n.m. condom.

**présiden|t, ~te** /prezidɑ̃, -t/ n.m., f. president; (de firme, comité) chairman, chairwoman. ~t directeur général, managing director.

**présidentiel, ~le** /prezidɑ̃sjɛl/ a. presidential.

**presque** /prɛsk(ə)/ adv. almost, nearly. ~ jamais, hardly ever. ~ rien, hardly anything. ~ pas (de), hardly any.

**presqu'île** /prɛskil/ n.f. peninsula.

**presse** /prɛs/ n.f. (journaux, appareil) press.

**pressent|ir** /presɑ̃tir/ v.t. sense. ~iment n.m. presentiment.

**press|er** /prese/ v.t. squeeze, press; (appuyer sur, harceler) press; (hâter) hasten; (inciter) urge (de, to). ● v.i. (temps) press; (affaire) be pressing. se ~er v. pr. (se hâter) hurry; (se grouper) crowd. ~é a. in a hurry; (orange, citron) freshly squeezed. ~e-papiers n.m. invar. paperweight.

**pressing** /presiŋ/ n.m. (magasin) dry-cleaner's.

**pression** /presjɔ̃/ n.f. pressure. ● n.m./f. (bouton) press-stud.

**prestation** /prɛstasjɔ̃/ n.f. allowance; (d'artiste etc.) performance.

**prestig|e** /prɛstiʒ/ n.m. prestige. ~ieux, ~ieuse a. prestigious.

**présumer** /prezyme/ v.t. presume.

**prêt¹, ~e** /prɛ, -t/ a. ready (à qch., for sth., à faire, to do). ~-à-porter /prɛ(t)apɔrte/ n.m. invar. ready-to-wear clothes.

**prêt²** /prɛ/ n.m. loan.

**prétend|re** /pretɑ̃dr/ v.t. claim (que, that); (vouloir) intend. ~re qn. riche/etc., claim that s.o. is rich/etc. ~u a. so-called.

**prétentieux, ~ieuse** /pretɑ̃sjø, -z/ a. pretentious.

**prêter** /prete/ v.t. lend (à, to); (attribuer) attribute. ● v.i. ~er à, lead to. ~er attention, pay attention.

**prétext|e** /pretɛkst/ n.m. pretext, excuse. ~er v.t. plead.

**prêtre** /prɛtr/ n.m. priest.

**preuve** /prœv/ n.f. proof.

**prévaloir** /prevalwar/ v.i. prevail.

**prévenant, ~e** /prevnɑ̃, -t/ a. thoughtful.

**prévenir†** /prevnir/ v.t. (menacer) warn; (informer) tell.

**préventi|f, ~ve** /prevɑ̃tif, -v/ a. preventive.

**prévention** /prevɑ̃sjɔ̃/ n.f. prevention; (préjuge) prejudice. ~ routière, road safety.

**prévenu, ~e** /prevny/ n.m., f. defendant.

**prév|oir†** /prevwar/ v.t. foresee; (temps) forecast; (organiser) plan (for), provide for; (envisager) allow (for). ~u pour, (jouet etc.) designed for. ~isible a. foreseeable. ~ision n.f. prediction; (météorologique) forecast.

**prévoyant, ~e** /prevwajã, -t/ *a.* showing foresight.

**prier** /prije/ *v.i.* pray. ● *v.t.* pray to; (*implorer*) beg (**de,** to); (*demander à*) ask (**de,** to). **je vous en prie,** please; (*il n'y a pas de quoi*) don't mention it.

**prière** /prijɛr/ *n.f.* prayer; (*demande*) request. **~ de,** (*vous êtes prié de*) will you please.

**primaire** /primɛr/ *a.* primary.

**prime** /prim/ *n.f.* free gift; (*d'employé*)bonus; (*subvention*) subsidy; (*d'assurance*) premium.

**primé** /prime/ *a.* prize-winning.

**primeurs** /primœr/ *n.f. pl.* early fruit and vegetables.

**primevère** /primvɛr/ *n.f.* primrose.

**primiti|f, ~ve** /primitif, -v/ *a.* primitive; (*originel*) original.

**primord|ial** (*m. pl.* **~iaux**) /primɔrdjal, -jo/ *a.* essential.

**princ|e** /prɛ̃s/ *n.m.* prince. **~esse** *n.f.* princess.

**princip|al** (*m. pl.* **~aux**) /prɛ̃sipal, -o/ *a.* main, principal. ● *n.m.* (*pl.* **~aux**) headmaster; (*chose*) main thing. **~alement** *adv.* mainly.

**principauté** /prɛ̃sipote/ *n.f.* principality.

**principe** /prɛ̃sip/ *n.m.* principle. **en ~,** theoretically; (*d'habitude*) as a rule.

**printemps** /prɛ̃tã/ *n.m.* spring.

**priorit|é** /prijorite/ *n.f.* priority; (*auto.*) right of way. **~aire** *a.* priority. **être ~aire,** have priority.

**pris, ~e¹** /pri, -z/ *voir* **prendre.** ● *a.* (*place*) taken; (*personne, journée*) busy; (*gorge*) infected.

**prise²** /priz/ *n.f.* hold, grip; (*animal etc. attrapé*) catch; (*mil.*) capture. **~** (**de courant**), (*mâle*) plug; (*femelle*) socket. **~ de sang,** blood test.

**prison** /prizɔ̃/ *n.f.* prison, gaol, jail; (*réclusion*) imprisonment. **~nier, ~nière** /-onje, -jɛr/ *n.m., f.* prisoner.

**privé** /prive/ *a.* private. ● *n.m.* (*comm.*) private sector. **en ~, dans le ~,** in private.

**priv|er** /prive/ *v.t.* **~er de,**deprive of. **se ~er de,** go without.

**privil|ège** /privilɛʒ/ *n.m.* privilege. **~égié, ~égiée** *a. & n.m., f.* privileged (person).

**prix** /pri/ *n.m.* price; (*récompense*) prize. **à tout ~,** at all costs. **~ coûtant, ~ de revient,** cost price. **à ~ fixe,** set price.

**pro-** /pro/ *préf.* pro-.

**probab|le** /prɔbabl/ *a.* probable, likely. **~ilité** *n.f.* probability. **~lement** *adv.* probably.

**problème** /prɔblɛm/ *n.m.* problem.

**procédure** /prɔsedyr/ *n.f.* procedure.

**procès** /prɔsɛ/ *n.m.* (*criminel*) trial; (*civil*) lawsuit, proceedings. **~-verbal** (*pl.* **~verbaux**) *n.m.* report; (*contravention*) ticket.

**procession** /prɔsesjɔ̃/ *n.f.* procession.

**processus** /prɔsesys/ *n.m.* process.

**prochain, ~e** /prɔʃɛ̃, -ɛn/ *a.* (*suivant*)next; (*proche*) imminent; (*avenir*) near. **je descends à la ~e,** I'm getting off at the next stop. ● *n.m.* fellow. **~ement** /-ɛnmã/ *adv.* soon.

**proche** /prɔʃ/ *a.* near, close; (*avoisinant*) neighbouring; (*parent, ami*) close. **~ de,** close *ou* near to. **être ~,** (*imminent*) be approaching. **~s** *n.m. pl.* close relations. **P~-Orient** *n.m.* Near East.

**proclam|er** /prɔklame/ *v.t.* declare, proclaim. **~ation** *n.f.* declaration, proclamation.

**procuration** /prɔkyrasjɔ̃/ *n.f.* proxy.

**procurer** /prɔkyre/ *v.t.* bring (**à,** to). **se ~** *v. pr.* obtain.

**procureur** /prɔkyrœr/ *n.m.* public prosecutor.

**prodige** /prɔdiʒ/ *n.m.* marvel; (*personne*) prodigy.

**producti|f, ~ve** /prɔdyktif, -v/ *a.* productive. **~vité** *n.f.* productivity.

**prod|uire†** /prɔdɥir/ *v.t.* produce. **se ~uire** *v. pr.* (*survenir*) happen; (*acteur*) perform. **~ucteur, ~uctrice** *a.* producing; *n.m., f.* producer. **~uction** *n.f.* production; (*produit*) product.

**produit** /prɔdɥi/ *n.m.* product. **~s,** (*de la terre*) produce. **~ chimique,** chemical. **~s alimentaires,** foodstuffs. **~ de consommation,** consumer goods. **~ national brut,** gross national product.

**prof** /prɔf/ *n.m.* (*fam.*) teacher.

**professeur** /prɔfesœr/ *n.m.* teacher; (*univ.*) lecturer; (*avec chaire*) professor.

**profession** /prɔfesjɔ̃/ *n.f.* occupation; (*intellectuelle*) profession. **~nel, ~nelle** /-jɔnɛl/ *a.* professional; (*école*) vocational; *n.m., f.* professional.

**profil** /prɔfil/ *n.m.* profile.

**profit** /prɔfi/ *n.m.* profit. **au ~ de,** in aid of. **~able** /-tabl/ *a.* profitable.

**profiter** /prɔfite/ *v.i.* **~ à,** benefit. **~ de,** take advantage of.

**profond, ~e** /prɔfɔ̃, -d/ *a.* deep; (*sentiment, intérêt*) profound; (*causes*) underlying. **~ément** /-demã/ *adv.* deeply; (*différent, triste*) profoundly; (*dormir*) soundly. **~eur** /-dœr/ *n.f.* depth.

**programmation** /prɔgramasjɔ̃/ *n.f.* programming.

**programm|e** /prɔgram/ *n.m.* programme; (*matières: scol.*) syllabus; (*informatique*) program. **~e (d'études),** curriculum. **~er** *v.t.* (*ordinateur, appareil*) program; (*émission*) schedule. **~eur, ~euse** *n.m., f.* computer programmer.

**progrès** /prɔgrɛ/ *n.m. & n.m. pl.* progress. **faire des ~**, make progress.

**progress|er** /prɔgrese/ *v.i.* progress. **~ion** /-ɛsjɔ̃/ *n.f.* progression.

**progressi|f, ~ve** /prɔgresif, -v/ *a.* progressive. **~vement** *adv.* progressively.

**prohib|er** /prɔibe/ *v.t.* prohibit. **~ition** *n.f.* prohibition.

**prohibiti|f, ~ve** /prɔibitif, -v/ *a.* prohibitive.

**projecteur** /prɔʒɛktœr/ *n.m.* floodlight; (*cinéma*) projector.

**projection** /prɔʒɛksjɔ̃/ *n.f.* projection; (*séance*) show.

**projet** /prɔʒɛ/ *n.m.* plan; (*ébauche*) draft. **~ de loi**, bill.

**projeter** /prɔʒte/ *v.t.* plan (**de**, to); (*film*) project, show; (*jeter*) hurl, project.

**prologue** /prɔlɔg/ *n.m.* prologue.

**prolongation** /prɔlɔ̃gasjɔ̃/ *n.f.* extension. **~s**, (*football*) extra time.

**prolong|er** /prɔlɔ̃ʒe/ *v.t.* prolong. **se ~er** *v. pr.* continue, extend. **~é** *a.* prolonged. **~ement** *n.m.* extension.

**promenade** /prɔmnad/ *n.f.* walk; (*à bicyclette, à cheval*) ride; (*en auto*) drive, ride. **faire une ~**, go for a walk.

**promen|er** /prɔmne/ *v.t.* take for a walk. **se ~er** *v. pr.* walk. **(aller) se ~er**, go for a walk. **~eur, ~euse** *n.m., f.* walker.

**promesse** /prɔmɛs/ *n.f.* promise.

**promett|re†** /prɔmɛtr/ *v.t./i.* promise. **~eur, ~euse** *a.* promising.

**promoteur** /prɔmɔtœr/ *n.m.* (*immobilier*) property developer.

**prom|ouvoir** /prɔmuvwar/ *v.t.* promote. **être ~u**, be promoted. **~otion** *n.f.* promotion; (*comm.*) special offer.

**pronom** /prɔnɔ̃/ *n.m.* pronoun. **~inal** (*m. pl. ~inaux*) /-ɔminal, -o/ *a.* pronominal.

**prononc|er** /prɔnɔ̃se/ *v.t.* pronounce; (*discours*) make. **se ~er** *v. pr.* (*mot*) be pronounced. **~iation** *n.f.* pronunciation.

**pronosti|c** /prɔnɔstik/ *n.m.* forecast; (*méd.*) prognosis.

**propagande** /prɔpagɑ̃d/ *n.f.* propaganda.

**propager** /prɔpaʒe/ *v.t.*, **se ~er** *v. pr.* spread.

**prophète** /prɔfɛt/ *n.m.* prophet.

**proportion** /prɔpɔrsjɔ̃/ *n.f.* proportion; (*en mathématiques*) ratio. **~né** /-jɔne/ *a.* proportionate (**à**, to). **~nel, ~nelle** /-jɔnɛl/ *a.* proportional. **~ner** /-jɔne/ *v.t.* proportion.

**propos** /prɔpo/ *n.m.* intention; (*sujet*) subject. ● *n.m. pl.* (*paroles*) remarks. **à ~**, at the right time; (*dans un dialogue*) by the way. **à ~ de**, about. **à tout ~**, at every possible occasion.

**propos|er** /prɔpoze/ *v.t.* propose; (*offrir*) offer. **se ~er** *v. pr.* volunteer (**pour**, to); (*but*) set o.s. **~ition** *n.f.* proposal; (*affirmation*) proposition; (*gram.*) clause.

**propre¹** /prɔpr/ *a.* clean; (*soigné*) neat; (*honnête*) decent. **mettre au ~**, write out again neatly. **c'est du ~!** (*ironique*) well done!

**propre²** /prɔpr/ *a.* (*à soi*) own; (*sens*) literal. **~ à**, (*qui convient*) suited to; (*spécifique*) peculiar to.

**propreté** /prɔprəte/ *n.f.* cleanliness; (*netteté*) neatness.

**propriétaire** /prɔprijetɛr/ *n.m./f.* owner; (*comm.*) proprietor; (*qui loue*) landlord, landlady.

**propriété** /prɔprijete/ *n.f.* property; (*droit*) ownership.

**proroger** /prɔrɔʒe/ *v.t.* (*contrat*) defer; (*passeport*) extend.

**proscr|ire** /prɔskrir/ *v.t.* proscribe. **~it, ~ite** *a.* proscribed; *n.m., f.* (*exilé*) exile.

**prose** /proz/ *n.f.* prose.

**prospec|ter** /prɔspɛkte/ *v.t.* prospect. **~teur, ~trice** *n.m., f.* prospector. **~tion** /-ksjɔ̃/ *n.f.* prospecting.

**prospectus** /prɔspɛktys/ *n.m.* leaflet.

**prosp|ère** /prɔspɛr/ *a.* flourishing, thriving. **~érer** *v.i.* thrive, prosper. **~érité** *n.f.* prosperity.

**prostit|uée** /prɔstitɥe/ *n.f.* prostitute. **~ution** *n.f.* prostitution.

**protec|teur, ~trice** /prɔtɛktœr, -tris/ *n.m., f.* protector. ● *a.* protective.

**protection** /prɔtɛksjɔ̃/ *n.f.* protection; (*fig.*) patronage.

**protég|er** /prɔteʒe/ *v.t.* protect; (*fig.*) patronize. **se ~er** *v. pr.* protect o.s.

**protéine** /prɔtein/ *n.f.* protein.

**protestant, ~e** /prɔtɛstɑ̃, -t/ *a. & n.m., f.* Protestant.

**protest|er** /prɔtɛste/ *v.t./i.* protest. **~ation** *n.f.* protest.

**prouver** /pruve/ *v.t.* prove.

**provenance** /prɔvnɑ̃s/ *n.f.* origin. **en ~ de**, from.

**provenç|al, ~ale** (*m. pl. ~aux*) /prɔvɑ̃sal, -o/ *a. & n.m., f.* Provençal.

**Provence** /prɔvɑ̃s/ *n.f.* Provence.

**provenir†** /prɔvnir/ *v.i.* **~ de**, come from.

**proverbe** /prɔvɛrb/ *n.m.* proverb.

**providence** /prɔvidɑ̃s/ *n.f.* providence.

**provinc|e** /prɔvɛ̃s/ *n.f.* province. **de ~e**, provincial. **la ~e**, the provinces. **~ial, ~iale** (*m. pl. ~iaux*) *a. & n.m., f.* provincial.

**proviseur** /prɔvizœr/ *n.m.* headmaster, principal.

**provision** /prɔvizjɔ̃/ *n.f.* supply, store; (*dans un compte*) funds; (*acompte*) deposit. **~s**, (*vivres*) provisions.

**provisoire** /prɔvizwar/ a. temporary. ∼**ment** adv. temporarily.

**provo|quer** /prɔvoke/ v.t. cause; (exciter) arouse; (défier) provoke. ∼**cation** n.f. provocation.

**proximité** /prɔksimite/ n.f. proximity. **à** ∼ **de,** close to.

**prud|ent, ∼ente** /prydã, -t/ a. cautious; (sage) wise. **soyez ∼ent,** be careful. ∼**emment** /-amã/ adv. cautiously; wisely. ∼**ence** n.f. caution; wisdom.

**prune** /pryn/ n.f. plum.

**pruneau** (pl. ∼**x**) /pryno/ n.m. prune.

**pseudo-** /psødo/ préf. pseudo-

**pseudonyme** /psødɔnim/ n.m. pseudonym.

**psychanalys|e** /psikanaliz/ n.f. psychoanalysis. ∼**er** v.t. psychoanalyse. ∼**te** /-st/ n.m./f. psychoanalyst.

**psychiatre** /psikjatr/ n.m./f. psychiatrist.

**psychique** /psiʃik/ a. mental, psychological.

**psycholo|gie** /psikɔlɔʒi/ n.f. psychology. ∼**gique** a. psychological. ∼**gue** n.m./f. psychologist.

**PTT** abrév. (Postes, Télécommunications et Télédiffusion) Post Office.

**pu** /py/ voir **pouvoir**[1].

**puant, ∼e** /pɥã, -t/ a. stinking.

**pub** /pyb/ n.f. **la** ∼, advertising. **une** ∼, an advert.

**publi|c, ∼que** /pyblik/ a. public. ● n.m. public; (assistance) audience. **en ∼c,** in public.

**publicit|é** /pyblisite/ n.f. publicity, advertising; (annonce) advertisement. ∼**aire** a. publicity.

**publ|ier** /pyblije/ v.t. publish. ∼**ication** n.f. publication.

**publiquement** /pyblikmã/ adv. publicly.

**puce**[1] /pys/ n.f. flea. **marché aux ∼s,** flea market.

**puce**[2] /pys/ n.f. (électronique) chip.

**pud|eur** /pydœr/ n.f. modesty. ∼**ique** a. modest.

**puer** /pɥe/ v.i. stink. ● v.t. stink of.

**puis** /pɥi/ adv. then.

**puisque** /pɥisk(ə)/ conj. since, as.

**puissance** /pɥisãs/ n.f. power.

**puiss|ant, ∼ante** /pɥisã, -t/ a.powerful. ∼**amment** adv. powerfully.

**puits** /pɥi/ n.m. well; (de mine) shaft.

**pull(-over)** /pyl(ɔvɛr)/ n.m. pullover, jumper.

**pulpe** /pylp/ n.f. pulp.

**pulsation** /pylsasjɔ̃/ n.f. (heart-)beat.

**pulvéris|er** /pylverize/ v.t. pulverize; (liquide) spray. ∼**ateur** n.m. spray.

**punaise** /pynɛz/ n.f. (insecte) bug; (clou) drawing-pin.

**punch** /pɔ̃ʃ/ n.m. punch.

**pun|ir** /pynir/ v.t. punish. ∼**ition** n.f. punishment.

**punk** /pœnk/ a. invar. punk.

**pupille** /pypij/ n.f. (de l'œil) pupil.

**pur** /pyr/ a. pure; (whisky) neat. ∼**ement** adv. purely. ∼**eté** n.f. purity. ∼**-sang** n.m. invar. (cheval) thoroughbred.

**purée** /pyre/ n.f. purée; (de pommes de terre) mashed potatoes.

**purif|ier** /pyrifje/ v.t. purify. ∼**ication** n.f. purification.

**puritain, ∼e** /pyritɛ̃, -ɛn/ n.m., f. puritan. ● a. puritanical.

**pus** /py/ n.m. pus.

**putain** /pytɛ̃/ n.f. (fam.) whore.

**putsch** /putʃ/ n.m. putsch.

**puzzle** /pœzl/ n.m. jigsaw (puzzle).

**P-V** abrév. (procès-verbal) ticket, traffic fine.

**pyjama** /piʒama/ n.m. pyjamas. **un** ∼**,** a pair of pyjamas.

**pylône** /pilon/ n.m. pylon.

**pyramide** /piramid/ n.f. pyramid.

**Pyrénées** /pirene/ n.f. pl. **les** ∼**,** the Pyrenees.

**Qq**

**QG** abrév. (quartier général) HQ.

**QI** abrév. (quotient intellectuel) IQ.

**qu'** /k/ voir **que.**

**quadrupl|e** /kadrypl/ a. & n.m. quadruple. ∼**er** v.t./i. quadruple.

**quai** /ke/ n.m. (de gare) platform; (de port) quay; (de rivière) embankment.

**qualificatif** /kalifikatif/ n.m. (épithète) term.

**qualif|ier** /kalifje/ v.t. qualify; (décrire) describe (de, as). **se ∼ier** v. pr. qualify (pour, for).

**qualité** /kalite/ n.f. quality; (titre) occupation.

**quand** /kã/ conj. & adv. when. ∼ **même,** all the same. ∼ **(bien) même,** even if.

**quant (à)** /kãt(a)/ prép. as for.

**quantité** /kãtite/ n.f. quantity. **une** ∼ **de,** a lot of. **des** ∼**s,** masses.

**quarantaine** /karãtɛn/ n.f. (méd.) quarantine. **une** ∼ **(de),** about forty.

**quarant|e** /karãt/ a. & n.m. forty. ∼**ième** a. & n.m./f. fortieth.

**quart** /kar/ n.m. quarter; (naut.) watch. ∼ **(de litre),** quarter litre. ∼ **de finale,** quarterfinal. ∼ **d'heure,** quarter of an hour.

**quartier** /kartje/ n.m. neighbourhood, district; (*de lune, bœuf*) quarter; (*de fruit*) segment. **de ~, du ~,** local.

**quasi-** /kazi/ préf. quasi-.

**quatorz|e** /katɔrz/ a. & n.m. fourteen. **~ième** a. & n.m./f. fourteenth.

**quatre** /katr(ə)/ a. & n.m. four. **~-vingt(s)** a. & n.m. eighty. **~-vingt-dix** a. & n.m. ninety.

**quatrième** /katrijɛm/ a. & n.m./f. fourth. **~ment** adv. fourthly.

**quatuor** /kwatyɔr/ n.m. quartet.

**que, qu'** */kə, k/ conj.* that; (*comparaison*) than. **qu'il vienne,** let him come. **qu'il vienne ou non,** whether he comes or not. **ne faire ~ demander**/etc., only ask/etc. ● adv. (**ce**)**~tu es bête, qu'est-ce ~ tu es bête,** how silly you are. **~ de,** what a lot of. ● pron. rel. (*personne*) that, whom; (*chose*) that, which; (*temps, moment*) when; (*interrogatif*) what. **un jour**/etc. **~,** one day/etc. when. **~ faites-vous?, qu'est-ce ~ vous faites?,** what are you doing?

**Québec** /kebɛk/ n.m. Quebec.

**quel, ~le** /kɛl/ a. what; (*interrogatif*) which, what; (*qui*) who. ● pron. which. **~ dommage,** what a pity. **~ qu'il soit,** (*chose*) whatever *ou* whichever it may be; (*personne*) whoever he may be.

**quelconque** /kɛlkɔ̃k/ a. (*banal*) ordinary; (*médiocre*) poor.

**quelque** /kɛlkə/ a. some. **~s,** a few, some. ● adv. (*environ*) some. **et ~,** (*fam.*) and a bit. **~ chose,** something; (*interrogation*) anything. **~ part,** somewhere. **~ peu,** somewhat.

**quelquefois** /kɛlkəfwa/ adv. sometimes.

**quelques|-uns, ~-unes** /kɛlkəzœ̃, -yn/ pron. some, a few.

**quelqu'un** /kɛlkœ̃/ pron. someone, somebody; (*interrogation*) anyone, anybody.

**quereller (se)** /(sə)kərele/ v. pr. quarrel.

**question** /kɛstjɔ̃/ n.f. question; (*affaire*) matter, question. **en ~,** in question; (*enjeu*) at stake. **il est ~ de,** (*cela concerne*) it is about; (*on parle de*) there is talk of. **il n'en est pas ~,** it is out of the question. **~ner** /-jɔne/ v.t. question.

**questionnaire** /kɛstjɔnɛr/ n.m. questionnaire.

**quête** /kɛt/ n.f. (*relig.*) collection.

**quetsche** /kwɛtʃ/ n.f. (sort of dark red) plum.

**queue** /kø/ n.f. tail; (*de poêle*) handle; (*file*) queue; (*de train*) rear. **faire la ~,** queue (up). **~ de cheval,** pony-tail.

**qui** /ki/ pron. rel. (*personne*) who; (*chose*) which, that; (*interrogatif*) who; (*après prép.*) whom; (*quiconque*) whoever. **à ~ est ce stylo**/etc.?, whose pen/etc. is this? **qu'est-ce ~?,** what? **~ est-ce qui?,** who?

**quiche** /kiʃ/ n.f. quiche.

**quiconque** /kikɔ̃k/ pron. whoever; (*n'importe qui*) anyone.

**quint|al** (*pl. ~aux*) /kɛ̃tal, -o/ n.m. quintal (= 100 kg.).

**quinte** /kɛ̃t/ n.f. **~ de toux,** coughing fit.

**quintette** /kɛ̃tɛt/ n.m. quintet.

**quintupl|e** /kɛ̃typl/ a. fivefold. ● n.m. quintuple. **~er** v.t./i. increase fivefold.

**quinzaine** /kɛ̃zɛn/ n.f. **une ~ (de),** about fifteen.

**quinz|e** /kɛ̃z/ a. & n.m. fifteen. **~e jours,** two weeks. **~ième** a. & n.m./f. fifteenth.

**quiproquo** /kiprɔko/ n.m. misunderstanding.

**quittance** /kitãs/ n.f. receipt.

**quitte** /kit/ a. quits (**envers,** with).

**quitter** /kite/ v.t. leave; (*vêtement*) take off. **se ~** v. pr. part.

**quoi** /kwa/ pron. what; (*après prép.*) which. **de ~ vivre/ manger**/etc., (*assez*) enough to live on/to eat/etc. **de ~ écrire,** sth. to write with, what is necessary to write with. **~ que,** whatever. **~ que ce soit,** anything.

**quoique** /kwak(ə)/ conj. (al)though.

**quota** /kɔta/ n.m. quota.

**quotidien, ~ne** /kɔtidjɛ̃, -jɛn/ a. daily; (*banal*) everyday. ● n.m. daily (paper). **~nement** /-jɛnmã/ adv. daily.

# Rr

**rabais** /rabɛ/ n.m. (price) reduction.

**rabaisser** /rabese/ v.t. (*déprécier*) belittle; (*réduire*) reduce.

**rabat** /raba/ n.m. flap. **~-joie** n.m. invar. killjoy.

**rabattre** /rabatr/ v.t. pull *ou* put down; (*déduire*) take off. **se ~** v. pr. (*se refermer*) close; (*véhicule*) cut in, turn sharply.

**rabbin** /rabɛ̃/ n.m. rabbi.

**rabot** /rabo/ n.m. plane. **~er** /-ɔte/ v.t. plane.

**raccommoder** /rakɔmɔde/ v.t. mend; (*personnes: fam.*) reconcile.

**raccompagner** /rakɔ̃paɲe/ v.t. see *ou* take back (home).

**raccord** /rakɔr/ n.m. link; (*de papier peint*) join. **~ (de peinture),** touch-up.

**raccord|er** /rakɔrde/ v.t. connect, join. **~ement** n.m. connection.

**raccourci** /rakursi/ n.m. short cut. **en ~,** in brief.

**raccourcir** /rakursir/ v.t. shorten. ● v.i. get shorter.

**raccrocher** /rakrɔʃe/ v.t. hang back up; (*personne*) grab hold of; (*relier*) connect. ~ **(le récepteur),** hang up.

**rac|e** /ras/ n.f. race; (*animale*) breed. **de ~e,** pure-bred. **~ial** (*m. pl.* **~iaux**) a. racial.

**rachat** /raʃa/ n.m. buying (back).

**racheter** /raʃte/ v.t. buy (back); (*davantage*) buy more; (*nouvel objet*) buy another.

**racine** /rasin/ n.f. root. ~ **carrée/cubique,** square/cube root.

**racis|te** /rasist/ a. & n.m./f. racist. **~me** n.m. racism.

**racler** /rakle/ v.t. scrape. **se ~ la gorge,** clear one's throat.

**raconter** /rakɔ̃te/ v.t. (*histoire*) tell, relate; (*vacances etc.*) tell about. ~ **à qn. que,** tell s.o. that, say to s.o. that.

**radar** /radar/ n.m. radar.

**rade** /rad/ n.f. harbour.

**radeau** (*pl.* **~x**) /rado/ n.m. raft.

**radiateur** /radjatœr/ n.m. radiator; (*électrique*) heater.

**radiation** /radjɑsjɔ̃/ n.f. (*énergie*) radiation.

**radic|al** (*m. pl.* **~aux**) /radikal, -o/ a. radical. ● n.m. (*pl.* **~aux**) radical.

**radin,** ~e /radɛ̃, -in/ a. (*fam.*) stingy.

**radio** /radjo/ n.f. radio; (*radiographie*) X-ray.

**radioacti|f,** ~ve /radjoaktif, -v/ a. radioactive. ~vité n.f. radioactivity.

**radiocassette** /radjokaset/ n.f. radiocassette-player.

**radiograph|ie** /radjografi/ n.f. (*photographie*) X-ray. ~ier v.t. X-ray. ~ique a. X-ray.

**radiologue** /radjolɔg/ n.m./f. radiographer.

**radiophonique** /radjofɔnik/ a. radio.

**radis** /radi/ n.m. radish.

**radoucir (se)** /(sə)radusir/ v. pr. calm down; (*temps*) become milder.

**rafale** /rafal/ n.f. (*de vent*) gust; (*tir*) burst of gunfire.

**raffiné** /rafine/ a. refined.

**raffin|er** /rafine/ v.t. refine. ~age n.m. refining. ~erie n.f. refinery.

**raffoler** /rafɔle/ v.i. ~ **de,** be extremely fond of.

**rafle** /rɑfl/ n.f. (police) raid.

**rafraîch|ir** /rafreʃir/ v.t. cool (down); (*raviver*) brighten up; (*personne, mémoire*) refresh. **se ~ir** v. pr. (*se laver*) freshen up; (*boire*) refresh o.s.; (*temps*) get cooler. **~issant, ~issante** a. refreshing.

**rafraîchissement** /rafreʃismɑ̃/ n.m. (*boisson*) cold drink. ~s, (*fruits etc.*) refreshments.

**rage** /raʒ/ n.f. rage; (*maladie*) rabies. **faire ~,** rage. ~ **de dents,** raging toothache.

**ragot(s)** /rago/ n.m. (*pl.*) (*fam.*) gossip.

**ragoût** /ragu/ n.m. stew.

**raide** /rɛd/ a. stiff; (*côte*) steep; (*corde*) tight; (*cheveux*) straight. ● adv. (*en pente*) steeply.

**raie**[1] /rɛ/ n.f. line; (*bande*) strip; (*de cheveux*) parting.

**raie**[2] /rɛ/ n.f. (*poisson*) skate.

**raifort** /rɛfɔr/ n.m. horse-radish.

**rail** /rɑj/ n.m. (*barre*) rail. **le ~,** (*transport*) rail.

**rainure** /renyr/ n.f. groove.

**raisin** /rezɛ̃/ n.m. ~(s), grapes. ~ **sec,** raisin.

**raison** /rezɔ̃/ n.f. reason. **avec ~,** rightly. **avoir ~,** be right (**de faire,** to do). **donner ~ à,** prove right. **en ~ de,** (*cause*) because of. ~ **de plus,** all the more reason. **perdre la ~,** lose one's mind.

**raisonnable** /rezɔnabl/ a. reasonable, sensible.

**raisonn|er** /rezɔne/ v.i. reason. ● v.t. (*personne*) reason with. ~ement n.m. reasoning; (*propositions*) argument.

**rajeunir** /raʒœnir/ v.t. make (look) younger.

**rajout** /raʒu/ n.m. addition. ~er /-te/ v.t. add.

**ralent|ir** /ralɑ̃tir/ v.t./i., **se ~ir** v. pr. slow down. ~i a. slow; n.m. (*cinéma*) slow motion. **être** ou **tourner au ~i,** tick over, idle.

**rall|ier** /ralje/ v.t. rally; (*rejoindre*) rejoin. **se ~ier** v. pr. rally.

**rallonge** /ralɔ̃ʒ/ n.f. (*de table*) extension.

**rallonger** /ralɔ̃ʒe/ v.t. lengthen.

**rallumer** /ralyme/ v.t. light (up) again; (*lampe*) switch on again; (*ranimer*: *fig.*) revive.

**rallye** /rali/ n.m. rally.

**ramadan** /ramadɑ̃/ n.m. Ramadan.

**ramass|er** /ramɑse/ v.t. pick up; (*récolter*) gather; (*recueillir*) collect. ~age n.m. (*cueillette*) gathering. ~age scolaire, school bus service.

**rambarde** /rɑ̃bard/ n.f. guardrail.

**rame** /ram/ n.f. (*aviron*) oar; (*train*) train; (*perche*) stake.

**rameau** (*pl.* **~x**) /ramo/ n.m. branch.

**ramener** /ramne/ v.t. bring back.

**ram|er** /rame/ v.i. row. ~eur, ~euse n.m., f. rower.

**ramollir** /ramɔlir/ v.t., **se ~** v. pr. soften.

**ramon|er** /ramɔne/ v.t. sweep. ~eur n.m. (chimney-)sweep.

**rampe** /rɑ̃p/ n.f. banisters; (*pente*) ramp.

**ramper** /rɑ̃pe/ v.i. crawl.

**ranc|e** /rɑ̃s/ a. rancid.

**rançon** /rɑ̃sɔ̃/ n.f. ransom.

**rancun|e** /rɑ̃kyn/ n.f. grudge. **sans ~!,** no hard feelings. ~ier, ~ière a. vindictive.

**randonnée** /rɑ̃dɔne/ n.f. walk; (*en auto, vélo*) ride.

**rang** /rã/ *n.m.* row; (*hiérarchie, condition*) rank. **se mettre en ~,** line up. **au premier ~,** in the first row; (*fig.*) at the forefront. **de second ~,** (*péj.*) second-rate.

**rangée** /rãʒe/ *n.f.* row.

**rang|er** /rãʒe/ *v.t.* put away; (*chambre etc.*) tidy (up); (*disposer*) place; (*véhicule*) park. **~ement** *n.m.* (*de chambre*) tidying (up); (*espace*) storage space.

**ranimer** /ranime/ *v.t./i.,* **se ~** *v. pr.* revive.

**rapace** /rapas/ *n.m.* bird of prey.

**rapatr|ier** /rapatrije/ *v.t.* repatriate. **~iement** *n.m.* repatriation.

**râp|e** /rɑp/ *n.f.* (*culin.*) grater; (*lime*) rasp. **~er** *v.t.* grate; (*bois*) rasp.

**rapid|e** /rapid/ *a.* fast, rapid. ● *n.m.* (*train*) express (train); (*cours d'eau*) rapids *pl.* **~ement** *adv.* fast, rapidly. **~ité** *n.f.* speed.

**rappel** /rapɛl/ *n.m.* recall; (*deuxième avis*) reminder; (*de salaire*) back pay; (*méd.*) booster.

**rappeler** /raple/ *v.t.* call back; (*diplomate, réserviste*) recall; (*évoquer*) remind, recall. **~ qch. à qn.,** (*redire*) remind s.o. of sth. **se ~** *v. pr.* remember, recall.

**rapport** /rapɔr/ *n.m.* connection; (*compte rendu*) report; (*profit*) yield. **~s,** (*relations*) relations. **par ~ à,** in relation to. **~s (sexuels),** intercourse.

**rapport|er** /rapɔrte/ *v.t.* bring back; (*profit*) bring in; (*dire, répéter*) report. ● *v.i.* (*comm.*) bring in a good return; (*mouchard: fam.*) tell. **se ~er à,** relate to. **~eur, ~euse** *n.m., f.* tell-tale.

**rapprocher** /raprɔʃe/ *v.t.* bring closer (**de,** to); (*réconcilier*) bring together; (*comparer*) compare. **se ~** *v. pr.* get ou come closer (**de,** to); (*personnes, pays*) come together; (*s'approcher de,* renter*) be close (**de,** to).

**rapt** /rapt/ *n.m.* abduction.

**raquette** /rakɛt/ *n.f.* (*de tennis*) racket; (*de ping-pong*) bat.

**rare** /rar/ *a.* rare; (*insuffisant*) scarce. **~ment** *adv.* rarely, seldom.

**ras, ~e** /rɑ, rɑz/ *a.* (*herbe, poil*) short. **à ~ de,** very close to. **pull ~ du cou,** round-neck pull-over. **en avoir ~ le bol,** be fed-up.

**ras|er** /rɑze/ *v.t.* shave; (*cheveux, barbe*) shave off; (*frôler*) skim; (*abattre*) raze; (*ennuyer: fam.*) bore. **se ~er** *v. pr.* shave.

**rasoir** /rɑzwar/ *n.m.* razor.

**rassembl|er** /rasãble/ *v.t.* gather; (*courage*) muster. **se ~er** *v. pr.* gather. **~ement** *n.m.* gathering.

**rasseoir (se)** /(sə)raswar/ *v. pr.* sit down again.

**rass|is, ~ise** *ou* **~ie** /rasi, -z/ *a.* (*pain*) stale.

**rassurer** /rasyre/ *v.t.* reassure.

**rat** /ra/ *n.m.* rat.

**rate** /rat/ *n.f.* spleen.

**râteau** (*pl.* **~x**) /rɑto/ *n.m.* rake.

**râtelier** /rɑtəlje/ *n.m.;* (*fam.*) dentures.

**rat|er** /rate/ *v.t./i.* miss; (*gâcher*) spoil; (*échouer*) fail. **c'est ~é,** that's right out. **~é, ~ée** *n.m., f.* (*personne*) failure. **avoir des ~és,** (*auto.*) backfire.

**ratio** /rasjo/ *n.m.* ratio.

**ration** /rasjɔ̃/ *n.f.* ration.

**rationnel, ~le** /rasjɔnɛl/ *a.* rational.

**rattacher** /rataʃe/ *v.t.* tie up again; (*relier*) link; (*incorporer*) join.

**rattraper** /ratrape/ *v.t.* catch; (*rejoindre*) catch up with; (*retard, erreur*) make up for. **se ~** *v. pr.* catch up; (*se dédommager*) make up for it. **se ~ à,** catch hold of.

**rauque** /rok/ *a.* raucous, harsh.

**ravi** /ravi/ *a.* delighted (**que,** that).

**ravier** /ravje/ *n.m.* hors-d'œuvre dish.

**ravin** /ravɛ̃/ *n.m.* ravine.

**ravioli** /ravjɔli/ *n.m. pl.* ravioli.

**ravissant, ~e** /ravisã, -t/ *a.* beautiful.

**ravisseu|r, ~se** /ravisœr, -øz/ *n.m., f.* kidnapper.

**ravitaill|er** /ravitaje/ *v.t.* provide with supplies; (*avion*) refuel. **se ~er** *v. pr.* stock up. **~ement** *n.m.* provision of supplies (**de,** to), refuelling; (*denrées*) supplies.

**rayé** /reje/ *a.* striped.

**rayer** /reje/ *v.t.* scratch; (*biffer*) cross out.

**rayon** /rɛjɔ̃/ *n.m.* ray; (*planche*) shelf; (*de magasin*) department; (*de roue*) spoke; (*de cercle*) radius.

**rayonner** /rɛjɔne/ *v.i.* radiate; (*de joie*) beam; (*se déplacer*) tour around (*from a central point*).

**rayure** /rejyr/ *n.f.* scratch; (*dessin*) stripe. **à ~s,** striped.

**raz-de-marée** /rɑdmare/ *n.m. invar.* tidal wave.

**re-** /rə/ *préf.* re-.

**ré-** /re/ *préf.* re-.

**réacteur** /reaktœr/ *n.m.* jet engine; (*nucléaire*) reactor.

**réaction** /reaksjɔ̃/ *n.f.* reaction. **~naire** /-jɔnɛr/ *a. & n.m./f.* reactionary.

**réaffirmer** /reafirme/ *v.t.* reaffirm.

**réagir** /reaʒir/ *v.i.* react.

**réalis|er** /realize/ *v.t.* carry out; (*rêve*) fulfil; (*film*) produce, direct; (*se rendre compte de*) realize. **se ~er** *v. pr.* materialize. **~ateur, ~atrice** *n.m., f.* (*cinéma*) director; (*TV*) producer. **~ation** *n.f.* realization; (*œuvre*) achievement.

**réalis|te** /realist/ *a.* realistic. ● *n.m./f.* realist. **~me** *n.m.* realism.

**réalité** /realite/ *n.f.* reality.

**réanim|er** /reanime/ *v.t.* resuscitate. **~ation** *n.f.* resuscitation. **service de ~ation,** intensive care.

**réapparaître** /reaparɛtr/ *v.i.* reappear.

**rebelle** /rəbɛl/ a. rebellious; (*soldat*) rebel.
● *n.m./f.* rebel.

**rebeller (se)** /(sə)rəbele/ *v. pr.* rebel, hit
back defiantly.

**rébellion** /rebeljɔ̃/ *n.f.* rebellion.

**rebond** /rəbɔ̃/ *n.m.* bounce; (*par ricochet*)
rebound. ∼**ir** /-dir/ *v.i.* bounce; rebound.

**rebondissement** /rəbɔ̃dismɑ̃/ *n.m.* (new)
development.

**rebord** /rəbɔr/ *n.m.* edge. ∼ **de la fenêtre,**
window-ledge.

**rebours (à)** /(a)rəbur/ *adv.* the wrong way.

**rebrousser** /rəbruse/ *v.t.* ∼ **chemin,** turn
back.

**rébus** /rebys/ *n.m.* rebus.

**rebut|er** /rəbyte/ *v.t.* put off. ∼**ant,** ∼**ante**
*a.* off-putting.

**récalcitrant,** ∼**e** /rekalsitrɑ̃, -t/ *a.* stubborn.

**récapitul|er** /rekapityle/ *v.t./i.* recapitu-
late. ∼**ation** *n.f.* recapitulation.

**récemment** /resamɑ̃/ *adv.* recently.

**récent,** ∼**e** /resɑ̃, -t/ *a.* recent.

**récépissé** /resepise/ *n.m.* receipt.

**récepteur** /reseptœr/ *n.m.* receiver.

**réception** /resɛpsjɔ̃/ *n.f.* reception. ∼ **de,**
(*lettre etc.*)receipt of. ∼**niste** /-jɔnist/ *n.m./f.*
receptionist.

**récession** /resesjɔ̃/ *n.f.* recession.

**recette** /rəsɛt/ *n.f.* (*culin.*) recipe; (*argent*)
takings. ∼**s,** (*comm.*) receipts.

**receveu|r,** ∼**se** /rəsvœr, -øz/ *n.m., f.* (*des
impôts*) tax collector.

**recevoir**† /rəsvwar/ *v.t.* receive; (*client,
malade*) see; (*obtenir*) get, receive. **être reçu
(à),** pass. ● *v.i.* (*médecin*) receive patients. **se
∼** *v. pr.* (*tomber*) land.

**rechange (de)** /(də)rəʃɑ̃ʒ/ *a.* (*roue,
vêtements, etc.*) spare.

**recharg|e** /rəʃarʒ/ *n.f.* (*de stylo*) refill. ∼**er**
*v.t.* refill; (*batterie*) recharge.

**réchaud** /reʃo/ *n.m.* stove.

**réchauff|er** /reʃofe/ *v.t.* warm up. **se ∼er**
*v. pr.* warm o.s. up; (*temps*) get warmer.

**rêche** /rɛʃ/ *a.* rough.

**recherche** /rəʃɛrʃ/ *n.f.* search (**de,** for);
(*raffinement*) elegance. ∼**s,** (*enquête*) in-
vestigations.

**recherch|er** /rəʃɛrʃe/ *v.t.* search for. ∼**é**
*a.* in great demand; (*élégant*) elegant.

**rechut|e** /rəʃyt/ *n.f.* (*méd.*) relapse. ∼**er** *v.i.*
relapse.

**récif** /resif/ *n.m.* reef.

**récipient** /resipjɑ̃/ *n.m.* container.

**réciproque** /resiprɔk/ *a.* mutual, reciprocal. ∼**ment** *adv.* each other; (*inversement*)
conversely.

**récit** /resi/ *n.m.* (*compte rendu*) account,
story; (*histoire*) story.

**récital** (*pl.* ∼**s**) /resital/ *n.m.* recital.

**récit|er** /resite/ *v.t.* recite. ∼**ation** *n.f.*
recitation.

**réclame** /reklam/ *n.f.* **faire de la ∼,**
advertise. **en ∼,** on offer.

**réclam|er** /reklame/ *v.t.* call for, demand;
(*revendiquer*) claim. ● *v.i.* complain. ∼**ation**
*n.f.* complaint.

**récolt|e** /rekɔlt/ *n.f.* (*action*) harvest;
(*produits*) crop, harvest; (*fig.*) crop. ∼**er**
*v.t.* harvest, gather; (*fig.*) collect.

**recommand|er** /rəkɔmɑ̃de/ *v.t.* recom-
mend; (*lettre*) register. **envoyer en ∼é,** send
registered. ∼**ation** *n.f.* recommendation.

**recommenc|er** /rəkɔmɑ̃se/ *v.t./i.* (*re-
prendre*) begin *ou* start again; (*refaire*)
repeat. **ne ∼ pas,** don't do it again.

**récompens|e** /rekɔ̃pɑ̃s/ *n.f.* reward; (*prix*)
award. ∼**er** *v.t.* reward (**de,** for).

**réconcil|ier** /rekɔ̃silje/ *v.t.* reconcile. **se
∼ier** *v. pr.* become reconciled (**avec,** with).
∼**iation** *n.f.* reconciliation.

**reconduire**† /rəkɔ̃dɥir/ *v.t.* see home; (*à la
porte*) show out; (*renouveler*) renew.

**réconfort** /rekɔ̃fɔr/ *n.m.* comfort. ∼**er** /-te/
*v.t.* comfort.

**reconnaissable** /rəkɔnɛsabl/ *a.* recogniz-
able.

**reconnaissan|t,** ∼**te** /rəkɔnɛsɑ̃, -t/ *a.*
grateful (**de,** for). ∼**ce** *n.f.* gratitude.

**reconnaître**† /rəkɔnɛtr/ *v.t.* recognize;
(*admettre*) admit (**que,** that); (*enfant, tort*)
acknowledge.

**reconstituant** /rəkɔ̃stitɥɑ̃/ *n.m.* tonic.

**reconstituer** /rəkɔ̃stitɥe/ *v.t.* reconstitute;
(*crime*) reconstruct.

**reconstr|uire**† /rəkɔ̃strɥir/ *v.t.* rebuild.
∼**uction** *n.f.* rebuilding.

**reconversion** /rəkɔ̃vɛrsjɔ̃/ *n.f.* (*de main-
d'œuvre*) redeployment.

**recopier** /rəkɔpje/ *v.t.* copy out.

**record** /rəkɔr/ *n.m. & a. invar.* record.

**recours** /rəkur/ *n.m.* resort. **avoir ∼ à,** have
recourse to, resort to.

**recouvrer** /rəkuvre/ *v.t.* recover.

**recouvrir**† /rəkuvrir/ *v.t.* cover.

**récréation** /rekreasjɔ̃/ *n.f.* recreation;
(*scol.*) playtime.

**récrimination** /rekriminasjɔ̃/ *n.f.* recrimination.

**recrut|er** /rəkryte/ *v.t.* recruit. ∼**ement**
*n.m.* recruitment.

**rectang|le** /rɛktɑ̃gl/ *n.m.* rectangle. ∼**u-
laire** *a.* rectangular.

**rectif|ier** /rɛktifje/ *v.t.* correct, rectify.
∼**ication** *n.f.* correction.

**recto** /rɛkto/ *n.m.* front of the page.

**reçu** /rəsy/ *voir* **recevoir.** ● *n.m.* receipt.

**recueil** /rəkœj/ *n.m.* collection.

**recueill|ir**† /rəkœjir/ *v.t.* collect; (*prendre
chez soi*) take in.

**recul** /rəkyl/ *n.m.* retreat; (*éloignement*) distance; (*déclin*) decline.

**reculé** /rəkyle/ *a.* (*région*) remote.

**reculer** /rəkyle/ *v.t./i.* move back; (*véhicule*) reverse; (*diminuer*) decline; (*différer*) postpone. ~ **devant**, (*fig.*) shrink from.

**reculons (à)** /(ə)rəkylɔ̃/ *adv.* backwards.

**récupér|er** /rekypere/ *v.t./i.* recover; (*vieux objets*) salvage. ~**ation** *n.f.* recovery; salvage.

**récurer** /rekyre/ *v.t.* scour. **poudre à ~**, scouring powder.

**recycl|er** /rəsikle/ *v.t.* (*personne*) retrain; (*chose*) recycle. se ~**er** *v. pr.* retrain. ~**age** *n.m.* retraining; recycling.

**rédac|teur, ~trice** /redaktœr, -tris/ *n.m., f.* writer, editor. le ~**teur en chef**, the editor (in chief).

**rédaction** /redaksjɔ̃/ *n.f.* writing; (*scol.*) composition; (*personnel*) editorial staff.

**redemander** /rədmɑ̃de/ *v.t.* ask again for; ask for more of.

**redevance** /rədvɑ̃s/ *n.f.* (*de télévision*) licence fee.

**rédiger** /rediʒe/ *v.t.* write; (*contrat*) draw up.

**redire**† /rədir/ *v.t.* repeat.

**redonner** /rədɔne/ *v.t.* give back; (*davantage*) give more.

**redoubler** /rəduble/ *v.t./i.* increase; (*classe*: *scol.*) repeat.

**redout|er** /rədute/ *v.t.* dread. ~**able** *a.* formidable.

**redoux** /rədu/ *n.m.* milder weather.

**redress|er** /rədrese/ *v.t.* straighten (out *ou* up); (*situation*) right, redress. se ~**er** *v. pr.* (*personne*) straighten (o.s.) up; (*se remettre debout*) stand up; (*pays, économie*) recover. ~**ement** /rədrɛsmɑ̃/ *n.m.* (*relèvement*) recovery.

**réduction** /redyksjɔ̃/ *n.f.* reduction.

**réduire**† /reduir/ *v.t.* reduce (**à**, to). se ~ **à**, (*revenir à*) come down to.

**réduit, ~e** /redui, -t/ *a.* (*objet*) small-scale; (*limité*) limited.

**réel, ~le** /reɛl/ *a.* real. ● *n.m.* reality. ~**lement** *adv.* really.

**réexpédier** /reɛkspedje/ *v.t.* forward; (*retourner*) send back.

**refaire**† /rəfɛr/ *v.t.* do again; (*erreur, voyage*) make again; (*réparer*) do up, redo.

**réfectoire** /refɛktwar/ *n.m.* refectory.

**référence** /referɑ̃s/ *n.f.* reference.

**référendum** /referɛ̃dɔm/ *n.m.* referendum.

**référer** /refere/ *v.i.* **en ~ à**, refer the matter to. se ~ **à**, refer to.

**refermer** /rəfɛrme/ *v.t.*, se ~, *v. pr.* close (again).

**réfléch|ir** /refleʃir/ *v.i.* think (**à**, about). ● *v.t.* reflect. se ~**ir** *v. pr.* be reflected

**refl|et** /rəflɛ/ *n.m.* reflection; (*lumière*) light. ~**éter** /-ete/ *v.t.* reflect. se ~**éter** *v. pr.* be reflected.

**réflexe** /reflɛks/ *a. & n.m.* reflex.

**réflexion** /reflɛksjɔ̃/ *n.f.* reflection; (*pensée*) thought, reflection.

**reflux** /rəfly/ *n.m.* (*de marée*) ebb.

**réforme** /reform/ *n.f.* reform.

**refouler** /rəfule/ *v.t.* (*larmes*) force back; (*désir*) repress.

**refrain** /rəfrɛ̃/ *n.m.* chorus. **le même ~**, the same old story.

**réfrigér|er** /refriʒere/ *v.t.* refrigerate. ~**ateur** *n.m.* refrigerator.

**refroid|ir** /rəfrwadir/ *v.t./i.* cool (down). se ~**ir** *v. pr.* (*personne, temps*) get cold; (*ardeur*) cool (off). ~**issement** *n.m.* cooling; (*rhume*) chill.

**refuge** /rəfyʒ/ *n.m.* refuge; (*chalet*) mountain hut.

**réfug|ier (se)** /(sə)refyʒje/ *v. pr.* take refuge. ~**ié, ~iée** *n.m., f.* refugee.

**refus** /rəfy/ *n.m.* refusal. **ce n'est pas de ~**, I wouldn't say no. ~/-ze/ *v.t.* refuse (**de**, to); (*recaler*) fail. se ~**er à**, (*évidence etc.*) reject.

**régal** (*pl.* ~**s**) /regal/ *n.m.* treat. ~**er** *v.t.* treat (**de**, to). se ~**er** *v. pr.* treat o.s. (**de**, to).

**regard** /rəgar/ *n.m.* (*expression, coup d'œil*) look; (*fixe*) stare.

**regarder** /rəgarde/ *v.t.* look at; (*observer*) watch; (*considérer*) consider; (*concerner*) concern. ~ (**fixement**), stare at. ● *v.i.* look. se ~ *v. pr.* (*personnes*) look at each other.

**régates** /regat/ *n.f. pl.* regatta.

**régen|t, ~te** /reʒɑ̃, -t/ *n.m., f.* regent. ~**ce** *n.f.* regency.

**régie** /reʒi/ *n.f.* (*entreprise*) public corporation; (*radio, TV*) control room; (*cinéma, théâtre*) production.

**régime** /reʒim/ *n.m.* (*pol.*) regime; (*méd.*) diet; (*de moteur*) speed; (*de bananes*) bunch. **se mettre au ~**, go on a diet.

**régiment** /reʒimɑ̃/ *n.m.* regiment.

**région** /reʒjɔ̃/ *n.f.* region. ~**al** (*m. pl.* ~**aux**) /-jɔnal, -o/ *a.* regional.

**registre** /rəʒistr/ *n.m.* register.

**réglage** /reglaʒ/ *n.m.* adjustment.

**règle** /rɛgl/ *n.f.* rule; (*instrument*) ruler. ~**s**, (*de femme*) period. **en ~**, in order.

**réglé** /regle/ *a.* (*vie*) ordered; (*arrangé*) settled.

**règlement** /rɛgləmɑ̃/ *n.m.* regulation; (*règles*) regulations; (*solution, paiement*) settlement.

**réglement|er** /rɛgləmɑ̃te/ *v.t.* regulate. ~**ation** *n.f.* regulation.

**régler** /regle/ *v.t.* settle; (*machine*) adjust; (*programmer*) set; (*facture*) settle; (*personne*) settle up with; (*papier*) rule.

**réglisse** /reglis/ *n.f.* liquorice.

**règne** /rɛɲ/ n.m. reign; (végétal, animal, minéral) kingdom.

**régner** /reɲe/ v.i. reign.

**regret** /rəgrɛ/ n.m. regret.

**regrett|er** /rəgrete/ v.t. regret; (personne) miss. ~able a. regrettable.

**regrouper** /rəgrupe/ v.t., group together. se ~ v. pr. gather (together).

**régulariser** /regylarize/ v.t. regularize.

**régulation** /regylasjɔ̃/ n.f. regulation.

**régul|ier, ~ière** /regylje, -jɛr/ a. regular; (qualité, vitesse) steady, even; (ligne, paysage) even; (légal) legal; (honnête) honest. ~ièrement adv. regularly; (d'ordinaire) normally.

**rein** /rɛ̃/ n.m. kidney. ~s, (dos) back.

**reine** /rɛn/ n.f. queen. ~-claude n.f. greengage.

**réintégrer** /reɛ̃tegre/ v.t. (lieu) return to; (jurid.) reinstate.

**rejet** /rəʒɛ/ n.m. rejection.

**rejeter** /rəʒte/ v.t. throw back; (refuser) reject; (vomir) bring up; (déverser) discharge.

**rejoindre†** /rəʒwɛ̃dr/ v.t. go back to, rejoin; (rattraper) catch up with; (rencontrer) join, meet. se ~ v. pr. (personnes) meet; (routes) join, meet.

**réjoui** /reʒwi/ a. joyful.

**réjou|ir** /reʒwir/ v.t. delight. se ~ir v. pr. be delighted (de qch., at sth.). ~issances n.f. pl. festivities.

**relâche** /rəlɑʃ/ n.m. (repos) respite. faire ~, (théâtre) close.

**relâch|er** /rəlɑʃe/ v.t. slacken; (personne) release; (discipline) relax. se ~er v. pr. slacken. ~ement n.m. slackening.

**relais** /rəlɛ/ n.m. relay. ~(routier), roadside café.

**relanc|e** /rəlɑ̃s/ n.f. boost. ~er v.t. boost, revive; (renvoyer) throw back.

**relati|f, ~ve** /rəlatif, -v/ a. relative.

**relation** /rəlasjɔ̃/ n.f. relation(ship); (ami) acquaintance. ~s, relation.

**relativement** /rəlativmɑ̃/ adv. relatively. ~ à, in relation to.

**relax|er (se)** /(sə)rəlakse/ v. pr. relax. ~ation n.f. relaxation. ~e a. (fam.) laid-back.

**relevé** /rəlve/ n.m. list; (de compte) statement; (de compteur) reading. ● a. spicy.

**relever** /rəlve/ v.t. pick up; (personne tombée) help up; (remonter) raise; (col) turn up; (manches) roll up; (sauce) season; (goût) bring out; (compteur) read; (défi) accept; (relayer) relieve; (remarquer, noter) note; (rebâtir) rebuild.

**relief** /rəljɛf/ n.m. relief. mettre en ~, highlight.

**relier** /rəlje/ v.t. link (à, to); (ensemble) link together; (livre) bind.

**religieu|x, ~se** /rəliʒjø, -z/ a. religious. ● n.m. monk. ● n.f. nun; (culin.) choux bun.

**religion** /rəliʒjɔ̃/ n.f. religion.

**relique** /rəlik/ n.f. relic.

**reliure** /rəljyr/ n.f. binding.

**reman|ier** /rəmanje/ v.t. revise; (ministère) reshuffle. ~iement n.m. revision; reshuffle.

**remarier (se)** /(sə)rəmarje/ v. pr. remarry.

**remarquable** /rəmarkabl/ a. remarkable.

**remarque** /rəmark/ n.f. remark; (par écrit) note.

**remarquer** /rəmarke/ v.t. notice; (dire) say. faire ~, point out (à, to). se faire ~, attract attention. remarque(z), mind you.

**rembours|er** /rɑ̃burse/ v.t. repay; (billet, frais) refund. ~ement n.m. repayment; refund.

**remède** /rəmɛd/ n.m. remedy; (médicament) medicine.

**remerc|ier** /rəmɛrsje/ v.t. thank (de, for); (licencier) dismiss. ~iements n.m. pl. thanks.

**remettre†** /rəmɛtr/ v.t. put back; (vêtement) put back on; (donner) hand (over); (devoir, démission) hand in; (restituer) give back; (différer) put off; (ajouter) add. se ~ à, go back to. se ~ à faire, start doing again.

**remise¹** /rəmiz/ n.f. (abri) shed.

**remise²** /rəmiz/ n.f. (rabais) discount; (livraison) delivery; (ajournement) postponement.

**rémission** /remisjɔ̃/ n.f. remission.

**remontant** /rəmɔ̃tɑ̃/ n.m. tonic.

**remontée** /rəmɔ̃te/ n.f. ~ mécanique, ski-lift.

**remont|er** /rəmɔ̃te/ v.i. go ou come (back) up; (prix, niveau) rise (again); (revenir) go back. ● v.t. (rue etc.) go ou come (back) up; (relever) raise; (montre) wind up; (objet démonté) put together again; (personne) buck up. ~e-pente n.m. ski-lift.

**remords** /rəmɔr/ n.m. remorse.

**remorqu|e** /rəmɔrk/ n.f. (véhicule) trailer. ~er v.t. tow.

**remorqueur** /rəmɔrkœr/ n.m. tug.

**rempart** /rɑ̃par/ n.m. rampart.

**remplaçant, ~e** /rɑ̃plasɑ̃, -t/ n.m., f. replacement; (joueur) reserve.

**remplac|er** /rɑ̃plase/ v.t. replace. ~ement n.m. replacement.

**rempli** /rɑ̃pli/ a. full (de, of).

**remplir** /rɑ̃plir/ v.t. fill (up); (formulaire) fill (in ou out); se ~ v. pr. fill (up).

**remporter** /rɑ̃pɔrte/ v.t. take back; (victoire) win.

**remuer** /rəmɥe/ v.t./i. move; (thé, café) stir; (gigoter) fidget.

**rémunér|er** /remynere/ v.t. pay. ~ation n.f. payment.

**renaître** /rənɛtr/ v.i. be reborn; (sentiment) be revived.

**renard** /rənar/ n.m. fox.

**rencontr|e** /rᾱkɔ̃tr/ *n.f.* meeting; (*de routes*) junction; (*match*) match. **~er** *v.t.* meet; (*heurter*) strike; (*trouver*) find. **se ~er** *v. pr.* meet.

**rendement** /rᾱdmᾱ/ *n.m.* yield; (*travail*) output.

**rendez-vous** /rᾱdevu/ *n.m.* appointment; (*d'amoureux*) date; (*lieu*) meeting-place. **prendre ~ (avec),** make an appointment (with).

**rendormir (se)** /(sə)rᾱdɔrmir/ *v. pr.* go back to sleep.

**rendre** /rᾱdr/ *v.t.* give back, return; (*donner en retour*) return; (*monnaie*) give; (*hommage*) pay. **~ heureux/possible/***etc.*, make happy/possible/*etc.* ● *v.i.* (*terres*) yield; (*vomir*) vomit. **se ~** *v. pr.* (*capituler*) surrender; (*aller*) go (à, to); (*ridicule, utile, etc.*) make o.s. **~ service (à),** help. **~ visite à,** visit. **se ~ compte de,** realize.

**rêne** /rɛn/ *n.f.* rein.

**renfermer** /rᾱfɛrme/ *v.t.* contain.

**renfl|é** /rᾱfle/ *a.* bulging. **~ement** *n.m.* bulge.

**renforcer** /rᾱfɔrse/ *v.t.* reinforce.

**renfort** /rᾱfɔr/ *n.m.* reinforcement. **à grand ~ de,** with a great deal of.

**renier** /rənje/ *v.t.* (*personne, pays*) disown, deny; (*foi*) renounce.

**renifler** /rənifle/ *v.t./i.* sniff.

**renne** /rɛn/ *n.m.* reindeer.

**renom** /rənɔ̃/ *n.m.* renown; (*réputation*) reputation. **~mé** /-ɔme/ *a.* famous. **~mée** /-ɔme/ *n.f.* fame; reputation.

**renoncer** /rənɔ̃se/ *v.i.* **~ à,** (*habitude, ami, etc.*) give up, renounce. **~ à faire,** give up (all thought of) doing.

**renouer** /rənwe/ *v.t.* tie up (again); (*reprendre*) renew. ● *v.i.* **~ avec,** start up again with.

**renouveler** /rənuvle/ *v.t.* renew; (*réitérer*) repeat. **se ~** *v. pr.* be renewed; be repeated.

**rénov|er** /renɔve/ *v.t.* (*édifice*) renovate; (*institution*) reform. **~ation** *n.f.* renovation; reform.

**renseignement** /rᾱsɛɲmᾱ/ *n.m.* **~(s),** information. **(bureau des) ~s,** information desk.

**renseigner** /rᾱseɲe/ *v.t.* inform, give information to. **se ~** *v. pr.* enquire, make enquiries, find out.

**rentab|le** /rᾱtabl/ *a.* profitable. **~ilité** *n.f.* profitability.

**rent|e** /rᾱt/ *n.f.* (private) income; (*pension*) pension, annuity.

**rentrée** /rᾱtre/ *n.f.* return; **la ~ parlementaire,** the reopening of Parliament; (*scol.*) start of the new year.

**rentrer** /rᾱtre/ (*aux. être*) *v.i.* go *ou* come back home, return home; (*entrer*) go *ou* come in; (*entrer à nouveau*) go *ou* come back in;

(*revenu*) come in; (*élèves*) go back. **~ dans,** (*heurter*) smash into. ● *v.t.* (*aux. avoir*) bring in.

**renverser** /rᾱvɛrse/ *v.t.* knock over *ou* down; (*piéton*) knock down; (*liquide*) upset, spill; (*mettre à l'envers*) turn upside down; (*gouvernement*) overturn; (*inverser*) reverse. **se ~** *v. pr.* (*véhicule*) overturn; (*verre, vase*) fall over.

**renv|oi** /rᾱvwa/ *n.m.* return; dismissal; expulsion; postponement; reference; (*rot*) belch. **~oyer†** *v.t.* send back, return; (*employé*) dismiss; (*élève*) expel; (*ajourner*) postpone; (*référer*) refer; (*réfléchir*) reflect.

**réorganiser** /reɔrganize/ *v.t.* reorganize.

**réouverture** /reuvɛrtyr/ *n.f.* reopening.

**repaire** /rəpɛr/ *n.m.* den.

**répandre** /repᾱdr/ *v.t.* (*liquide*) spill; (*étendre, diffuser*) spread; (*lumière, sang*) shed; (*odeur*) give off. **se ~** *v. pr.* spread; (*liquide*) spill.

**répandu** /repᾱdy/ *a.* (*courant*) widespread.

**réparer** /repare/ *v.t.* repair, mend.

**repartir†** /rəpartir/ *v.i.* start (up) again; (*voyageur*) set off again; (*s'en retourner*) go back.

**répart|ir** /repartir/ *v.t.* distribute; (*partager*) share out; (*étaler*) spread. **~ition** *n.f.* distribution.

**repas** /rəpɑ/ *n.m.* meal.

**repass|er** /rəpɑse/ *v.i.* come *ou* go back. ● *v.t.* (*linge*) iron; (*film*) show again. **~age** *n.m.* ironing.

**repère** /rəpɛr/ *n.m.* mark; (*jalon*) marker; (*fig.*) landmark.

**repérer** /rəpere/ *v.t.* locate, spot. **se ~** *v. pr.* find one's bearings.

**répert|oire** /repɛrtwar/ *n.m.* index; (*artistique*) repertoire. **~orier** *v.t.* index.

**répéter** /repete/ *v.t.* repeat. ● *v.t./i.* (*théâtre*) rehearse. **se ~** *v. pr.* be repeated; (*personne*) repeat o.s.

**répétition** /repetisjɔ̃/ *n.f.* repetition; (*théâtre*) rehearsal.

**replacer** /rəplase/ *v.t.* replace.

**repl|i** /rəpli/ *n.m.* fold; (*retrait*) withdrawal. **~ier** *v.t.* fold (up); (*ailes, jambes*) tuck in. **se ~ier** *v. pr.* withdraw (**sur soi-même,** into o.s.).

**répliqu|e** /replik/ *n.f.* reply; (*riposte*) retort; (*discussion*) objection; (*théâtre*) line(s); (*copie*) replica. **~er** *v.t./i.* reply; (*riposter*) retort; (*objecter*) answer back.

**répondeur** /repɔ̃dœr/ *n.m.* answering machine.

**répondre** /repɔ̃dr/ *v.t..* **~ que,** answer *ou* reply that. ● *v.i.* answer, reply. **~ à,** answer. **~ de,** answer for.

**réponse** /repɔ̃s/ *n.f.* answer, reply; (*fig.*) response.

**report** /rəpɔr/ *n.m.* (*transcription*) transfer; (*renvoi*) postponement.

**reportage** /rəpɔrtaʒ/ *n.m.* report; (*en direct*) commentary, (*par écrit*) article.

**reporter** /rəpɔrte/ *v.t.* take back; (*ajourner*) put off; (*transcrire*) transfer. **se ~ à,** refer to.

**repos** /rəpo/ *n.m.* rest; (*paix*) peace; (*tranquillité*) peace and quiet; (*moral*) peace of mind.

**repos|er** /rəpoze/ *v.t.* put down again; (*délasser*) rest. ● *v.i.* rest (**sur,** on). **se ~er** *v. pr.* rest. **~ant, ~ante** *a.* restful. **laisser ~er,** (*pâte*) leave to stand.

**repousser** /rəpuse/ *v.t.* push back; (*écarter*) push away; (*dégoûter*) repel; (*décliner*) reject; (*ajourner*) put back. ● *v.i.* grow again.

**reprendre†** /rəprɑ̃dr/ *v.t.* take back; (*retrouver*) regain; (*souffle*) get back; (*recommencer*) resume; (*redire*) repeat. **~ du pain**/*etc.*, take some more bread/*etc.* ● *v.i.* (*recommencer*) resume; (*affaires*) pick up.

**représent|er** /rəprezɑ̃te/ *v.t.* represent; (*théâtre*) perform. **~ant, ~ante** *n.m.*, *f.* representative. **~ation** *n.f.* representation; (*théâtre*) performance.

**réprimand|e** /reprimɑ̃d/ *n.f.* reprimand. **~er** *v.t.* reprimand.

**répr|imer** /reprime/ *v.t.* (*peuple*) repress; (*sentiment*) suppress. **~ession** *n.f.* repression.

**reprise** /rəpriz/ *n.f.* resumption; (*théâtre*) revival; (*télévision*) repeat; (*de tissu*) darn, mend; (*essor*) recovery; (*comm.*) part-exchange, trade-in. **à plusieurs ~s,** on several occasions.

**reproch|e** /rəprɔʃ/ *n.m.* reproach, blame. **~er** *v.t.* **~er qch. à qn.,** reproach *ou* blame s.o. for sth.

**reproduire†** /rəprɔdɥir/ *v.t.* reproduce. **se ~** *v. pr.* reproduce; (*arriver*) recur.

**reptile** /rɛptil/ *n.m.* reptile.

**république** /repyblik/ *n.f.* republic.

**réputation** /repytasjɔ̃/ *n.f.* reputation.

**réputé** /repyte/ *a.* renowned (**pour,** for). **~ pour être,** reputed to be.

**requérir** /rəkerir/ *v.t.* require, demand.

**requête** /rəkɛt/ *n.f.* request; (*jurid.*) petition.

**requin** /rəkɛ̃/ *n.m.* shark.

**requis, ~e** /rəki, -z/ *a.* required.

**rescapé, ~e** /rɛskape/ *n.m.*, *f.* survivor. ● *a.* surviving.

**réseau** (*pl.* **~x**) /rezo/ *n.m.* network.

**réservation** /rezɛrvasjɔ̃/ *n.f.* reservation. **bureau de ~,** booking office.

**réserve** /rezɛrv/ *n.f.* reserve; (*restriction*) reservation, reserve; (*indienne*) reservation; (*entrepôt*) store-room. **en ~,** in reserve.

**réserv|er** /rezɛrve/ *v.t.* reserve; (*place*) book, reserve. **~é** *a.* (*personne, place*) reserved.

**réservoir** /rezɛrvwar/ *n.m.* tank; (*lac*) reservoir.

**résidence** /rezidɑ̃s/ *n.f.* residence.

**résident, ~e** /rezidɑ̃, -t/ *n.m.*, *f.* resident foreigner. **~iel, ~ielle** /-sjɛl/ *a.* residential.

**résider** /rezide/ *v.i.* reside.

**résidu** /rezidy/ *n.m.* residue.

**résigner (se)** /(sə)reziɲe/ *v. pr.* **se ~ à faire,** resign o.s. to doing.

**résilier** /rezilje/ *v.t.* terminate.

**résine** /rezin/ *n.f.* resin.

**résistance** /rezistɑ̃s/ *n.f.* resistance; (*fil électrique*) element.

**résistant, ~e** /rezistɑ̃, -t/ *a.* tough.

**résister** /reziste/ *v.i.* resist. **~ à,** resist; (*examen, chaleur*) stand up to.

**résolution** /rezɔlysjɔ̃/ *n.f.* (*fermeté*) resolution; (*d'un problème*) solving.

**résonance** /rezɔnɑ̃s/ *n.f.* resonance.

**résonner** /rezɔne/ *v.i.* resound.

**résoudre†** /rezudr/ *v.t.* solve; (*décider*) decide on.

**respect** /rɛspɛ/ *n.m.* respect.

**respectab|le** /rɛspɛktabl/ *a.* respectable. **~ilité** *n.f.* respectability.

**respecter** /rɛspɛkte/ *v.t.* respect. **faire ~,** (*loi, décision*) enforce.

**respecti|f, ~ve** /rɛspɛktif, -v/ *a.* respective. **~vement** *adv.* respectively.

**respectueu|x, ~se** /rɛspɛktɥø, -z/ *a.* respectful.

**respir|er** /rɛspire/ *v.i.* breathe; (*se reposer*) get one's breath. ● *v.t.* put. pr. smile alike; (*exprimer*) radiate. **~ation** *n.f.* breathing; (*haleine*) breath. **~atoire** *a.* breathing.

**resplend|ir** /rɛsplɑ̃dir/ *v.i.* shine (**de,** with). **~issant, ~issante** *a.* radiant.

**responsabilité** /rɛspɔ̃sabilite/ *n.f.* responsibility; (*légale*) liability.

**responsable** /rɛspɔ̃sabl/ *a.* responsible (**de,** for). **~ de,** (*chargé de*) in charge of. ● *n.m.*/*f.* person in charge; (*coupable*) person responsible.

**ressembl|er** /rəsɑ̃ble/ *v.i.* **~er à,** resemble, look like. **se ~** *v. pr.* look alike. **~ance** *n.f.* resemblance. **~ant, ~ante** (*portrait*) true to life; (*pareil*) alike.

**ressemeler** /rəsəmle/ *v.t.* sole.

**ressentir†** /rəsɑ̃tir/ *v.t.* feel.

**resserre** /rəsɛr/ *n.f.* shed.

**resserrer** /rəsere/ *v.t.* tighten; (*contracter*) contract. **se ~** *v. pr.* tighten; contract; (*route etc.*) narrow.

**resservir** /rəsɛrvir/ *v.i.* come in useful (again).

**ressort** /rəsɔr/ *n.m.* (*objet*) spring; (*fig.*) energy.

**ressortir†** /rəsɔrtir/ *v.i.* go *ou* come back out; (*se voir*) stand out. **faire ~,** bring out.

**ressortissant, ~e** /rəsɔrtisɑ̃, -t/ *n.m.*, *f.* national.

**ressource** /rəsurs/ *n.f.* resource.

**ressusciter** /resysite/ *v.i.* come back to life.

**restant, ~e** /rɛstɑ̃, -t/ *a.* remaining. ● *n.m.* remainder.

**restaur|ant** /rɛstɔrɑ̃/ *n.m.* restaurant. **~ateur, ~atrice** *n.m., f.* restaurant owner.

**restaur|er** /rɛstɔre/ *v.t.* restore. **se ~er** *v. pr.* eat. **~ation** *n.f.* restoration; (*hôtellerie*) catering.

**reste** /rɛst/ *n.m.* rest; (*d'une soustraction*) remainder. **~s,** remains (de, of); (*nourriture*) leftovers.

**rest|er** /rɛste/ *v.i.* (*aux. être*) stay, remain; (*subsister*) be left, remain. **il ~e du pain**/*etc.,* there is some bread/*etc.* left (over).

**restit|uer** /rɛstitɥe/ *v.t.* (*rendre*) return, restore; (*son*) reproduce. **~ution** *n.f.* return.

**restreindre†** /rɛstrɛ̃dr/ *v.t.* restrict. **se ~** *v. pr.* (*dans les dépenses*) cut down.

**restricti|f, ~ve** /rɛstriktif, -v/ *a.* restrictive.

**restriction** /rɛstriksjɔ̃/ *n.f.* restriction.

**résultat** /rezylta/ *n.m.* result.

**résulter** /rezylte/ *v.i.* **~ de,** result from.

**résum|er** /rezyme/ *v.t.,* **se ~er** *v. pr.* summarize. **~é** *n.m.* summary. **en ~é,** in short.

**rétabl|ir** /retablir/ *v.t.* restore; (*personne*) restore to health. **se ~ir** *v. pr.* be restored; (*guérir*) recover. **~issement** *n.m.* restoring; (*méd.*) recovery.

**retaper** /rətape/ *v.t.* (*maison etc.*) do up.

**retard** /rətar/ *n.m.* lateness; (*sur un programme*) delay. **avoir du ~,** be late; (*montre*) be slow. **en~,** late. **en~sur,** behind. **rattraper** *ou* **combler son ~,** catch up.

**retardataire** /rətardatɛr/ *n.m./f.* latecomer. ● *a.* (*arrivant*) late.

**retardement (à)** /(a)rətardəmɑ̃/ *a.* (*bombe etc.*) delayed-action.

**retarder** /rətarde/ *v.t.* delay; (*sur un programme*) set back; (*montre*) put back. ● *v.i.* (*montre*) be slow.

**retenir†** /rətnir/ *v.t.* hold back; (*souffle, attention, prisonnier*) hold; (*eau, chaleur*) retain, hold; (*larmes*) hold back; (*garder*) keep; (*retarder*) detain; (*réserver*) book; (*se rappeler*) remember; (*déduire*) deduct.

**rétention** /retɑ̃sjɔ̃/ *n.f.* retention.

**retenue** /rətny/ *n.f.* restraint; (*somme*) deduction; (*scol.*) detention.

**rétine** /retin/ *n.f.* retina.

**retiré** /rətire/ *a.* (*vie*) secluded; (*lieu*) remote.

**retirer** /rətire/ *v.t.* (*ôter*) take off; (*argent*) withdraw. **~ à qn.,** take away from s.o. **se ~** *v. pr.* withdraw, retire.

**retomber** /rətɔ̃be/ *v.i.* fall; (*à nouveau*) fall again. **~ dans,** (*erreur etc.*) fall back into.

**retour** /rətur/ *n.m.* return. **être de ~,** be back (de, from). **par ~ du courrier,** by return of post. **en ~,** in return.

**retourner** /rəturne/ *v.t.* (*aux. avoir*) turn over; (*lettre*) return. ● *v.i.* (*aux. être*) go back, return. **se ~** *v. pr.* turn round; (*dans son lit*) twist and turn.

**retrait** /rətrɛ/ *n.m.* withdrawal.

**retraite** /rətrɛt/ *n.f.* retirement; (*pension*) (retirement) pension. **prendre sa ~,** retire.

**retraité, ~e** /rətrete/ *a.* retired. ● *n.m., f.* (old-age) pensioner, senior citizen.

**retransm|ettre** /rətrɑ̃smɛtr/ *v.t.* broadcast. **~ission** *n.f.* broadcast.

**rétrécir** /retresir/ *v.t.* narrow; (*vêtement*) take in. ● *v.i.* (*tissu*) shrink. **se ~,** (*rue*) narrow.

**rétroacti|f, ~ve** /retrɔaktif, -v/ *a.* retrospective.

**rétrospectivement** /retrɔspɛktivmɑ̃/ *adv.* in retrospect.

**retrousser** /rətruse/ *v.t.* pull up.

**retrouvailles** /rətruvɑj/ *n.f. pl.* reunion.

**retrouver** /rətruve/ *v.t.* find (again); (*rejoindre*) meet (again); (*forces, calme*) regain; (*se rappeler*) remember. **se ~** *v. pr.* find o.s. (back); (*se réunir*) meet (again). **s'y ~,** (*s'orienter, comprendre*) find one's way.

**rétroviseur** /retrɔvizœr/ *n.m.* (*auto.*) (rearview) mirror.

**réunion** /reynjɔ̃/ *n.f.* meeting.

**réunir** /reynir/ *v.t.* gather, collect; (*rapprocher*) bring together; (*convoquer*) call together; (*raccorder*) join; (*qualités*) combine. **se ~** *v. pr.* meet.

**réussi** /reysi/ *a.* successful.

**réussir** /reysir/ *v.i.* succeed, be successful (à faire, in doing). ● *v.t.* make a success of.

**réussite** /reysit/ *n.f.* success; (*jeu*) patience.

**revanche** /rəvɑ̃ʃ/ *n.f.* revenge; (*sport*) return *ou* revenge match. **en ~,** on the other hand.

**rêve** /rɛv/ *n.m.* dream. **faire un ~,** have a dream.

**réveil** /revɛj/ *n.m.* waking up, (*pendule*) alarm-clock.

**réveill|er** /reveje/ *v.t.,* **se ~er** *v. pr.* wake (up); (*fig.*) awaken. **~é** *a.* awake. **~e-matin** *n.m. invar.* alarm-clock.

**réveillon** /revɛjɔ̃/ *n.m.* (*Noël*) Christmas Eve; (*nouvel an*) New Year's Eve. **~ner** /-jone/ *v.i.* celebrate the *réveillon.*

**révéler** /revele/ *v.t.* reveal.

**revendi|quer** /rəvɑ̃dike/ *v.t.* claim. **~cation** *n.f.* claim; (*action*) claiming.

**revend|re** /rəvɑ̃dr/ *v.t.* sell (again). **~eur, ~euse** *n.m., f.* dealer.

**revenir†** /rəvnir/ *v.i.* (*aux. être*) come back, return (à, to). **~ à,** (*coûter*) cost. **faire ~,** (*culin.*) brown. **ça me revient,** it comes back to me.

**revente** /rəvɑ̃t/ *n.f.* resale.

**revenu** /rəvny/ *n.m.* income; (*d'un état*) revenue.

**rêver** /reve/ v.t./i. dream (**à** ou **de,** of).

**réverbération** /reverberasjɔ̃/ n.f. reflection, reverberation.

**réverbère** /reverber/ n.m. street lamp.

**révérence** /reverɑ̃s/ n.f. reverence; (*salut d'homme*) bow; (*salut de femme*) curtsy.

**revers** /rəver/ n.m. (*d'étoffe*) wrong side; (*de veste*) lapel; (*tennis*) backhand; (*fig.*) set-back.

**réversible** /reversibl/ a. reversible.

**revêtement** /rəvɛtmɑ̃/ n.m. covering; (*de route*) surface.

**rêveu|r,** **~se** /rɛvœr, -øz/ a. dreamy. ●n.m., f. dreamer.

**révis|er** /revize/ v.t. revise; (*véhicule*) overhaul. **~ion** n.f. revision; overhaul.

**revivre†** /rəvivr/ v.i. live again. ●v.t. relive. **faire ~,** revive.

**revoir†** /rəvwar/ v.t. see (again); (*réviser*) revise. **au ~,** goodbye.

**révolte** /revɔlt/ n.f. revolt.

**révolter** /revɔlte/ v.t., **se ~er** v. pr. revolt.

**révolution** /revɔlysjɔ̃/ n.f. revolution. **~ner** /-jɔne/ v.t. revolutionize.

**revolver** /revɔlver/ n.m. revolver, gun.

**revue** /rəvy/ n.f. (*examen, défilé*) review; (*magazine*) magazine; (*spectacle*) variety show.

**rez-de-chaussée** /redʃose/ n.m. invar. ground floor.

**RF** abrév. (*République Française*) French Republic.

**rhabiller (se)** /(sə)rabije/ v. pr. get dressed (again), dress (again).

**rhinocéros** /rinɔserɔs/ n.m. rhinoceros.

**rhubarbe** /rybarb/ n.f. rhubarb.

**rhum** /rɔm/ n.m. rum.

**rhumatisme** /rymatism/ n.m. rheumatism.

**rhume** /rym/ n.m. cold. **~ des foins,** hay fever.

**ri** /ri/ voir **rire.**

**riche** /riʃ/ a. rich (**en,** in). ●n.m./f. rich person. **~ment** adv. richly.

**richesse** /riʃɛs/ n.f. wealth; (*de sol, décor*) richness. **~s,** wealth.

**ride** /rid/ n.f. wrinkle.

**rideau** (*pl.* **~x**) /rido/ n.m. curtain; (*métallique*) shutter.

**ridicule** /ridikyl/ a. ridiculous. ●n.m. absurdity. **le ~,** ridicule.

**rien** /rjɛ̃/ pron. (**ne**) **~,** nothing. ●n.m. trifle. **de ~!,** don't mention it! **~ d'autre/de plus,** nothing else/more. **~ du tout,** nothing at all. **trois fois ~,** next to nothing. **il n'y est pour ~,** he has nothing to do with it. **~ à faire,** it's no good!

**rigid|e** /riʒid/ a. rigid; (*muscle*) stiff. **~ité** n.f. rigidity; stiffness.

**rigol|er** /rigɔle/ v.i. laugh; (*s'amuser*) have some fun; (*plaisanter*) joke. **~ade** n.f. fun.

**rigolo,** **~te** /rigɔlo, -ɔt/ a. (*fam.*) funny. ●n.m., f. (*fam.*) joker.

**rigoureu|x,** **~se** /rigurø, -z/ a. rigorous; (*hiver*) harsh. **~sement** adv. rigorously.

**rigueur** /rigœr/ n.f. rigour. **à la ~,** at a pinch.

**rim|e** /rim/ n.f. rhyme. **~er** v.i. rhyme (**avec,** with).

**rin|cer** /rɛ̃se/ v.t. rinse. **~çage** n.m. rinse; (*action*) rinsing.

**ring** /riŋ/ n.m. boxing ring.

**rire†** /rir/ v.i. laugh (**de,** at); (*plaisanter*) joke; (*s'amuser*) have fun. **c'était pour ~,** it was a joke. ●n.m. laugh. **~s, le ~,** laughter.

**risible** /rizibl/ a. laughable.

**risqu|e** /risk/ n.m. risk. **~é** a. risky; (*osé*) daring. **~er** v.t. risk. **~er de faire,** stand a good chance of doing.

**rissoler** /risɔle/ v.t./i. brown. (**faire) ~,** brown.

**ristourne** /risturn/ n.f. discount.

**rivage** /rivaʒ/ n.m. shore.

**riv|al,** **~ale** (m. pl. **~aux**) /rival, -o/ n.m., f. rival. ●a. rival. **~aliser** v.i. compete (**avec,** with). **~alité** n.f. rivalry.

**rive** /riv/ n.f. (*de fleuve*) bank; (*de lac*) shore.

**riverain,** **~e** /rivrɛ̃, -ɛn/ a. riverside. ●n.m., f. riverside resident; (*d'une rue*) resident.

**rivière** /rivjɛr/ n.f. river.

**riz** /ri/ n.m. rice.

**robe** /rɔb/ n.f. (*de femme*) dress. **~ de chambre,** dressing-gown.

**robinet** /rɔbinɛ/ n.m. tap.

**robot** /rɔbo/ n.m. robot.

**robuste** /rɔbyst/ a. robust.

**roc** /rɔk/ n.m. rock.

**rocaill|e** /rɔkaj/ n.f. rocky ground; (*de jardin*) rockery. **~eux,** **~euse** a. (*terrain*) rocky.

**roch|e** /rɔʃ/ n.f. rock. **~eux,** **~euse** a. rocky.

**rocher** /rɔʃe/ n.m. rock.

**rock** /rɔk/ n.m. (*mus.*) rock.

**rod|er** /rɔde/ v.t. (*auto.*) run in. **être ~é,** (*personne*) be broken in. **~age** n.m. running in.

**rognon** /rɔɲɔ̃/ n.m. (*culin.*) kidney.

**roi** /rwa/ n.m. king. **les Rois mages,** the Magi. **la fête des Rois,** Twelfth Night.

**rôle** /rol/ n.m. role, part.

**romain,** **~e** /rɔmɛ̃, -ɛn/ a. & n.m., f. Roman. ●n.f. (*laitue*) cos.

**roman** /rɔmɑ̃/ n.m. novel.

**romanesque** /rɔmanɛsk/ a. romantic; (*fantastique*) fantastic.

**romanti|que** /rɔmɑ̃tik/ a. & n.m./f. romantic. **~sme** n.m. romanticism.

**rompre†** /rɔ̃pr/ v.t./i. break; (*relations*) break off; (*fiancés*) break it off. **se ~** v. pr. break.

**ronces** /rõs/ *n.f. pl.* brambles.

**rond, ~e**[1] /rõ, rõd/ *a.* round; (*gras*) plump; (*ivre*: *fam.*) tight. ● *n.m.* (*cercle*) ring; (*tranche*) slice. **il n'a pas un ~,** (*fam.*) he hasn't got a penny. **~-point** (*pl.* **~s-points**) *n.m.* roundabout.

**ronde**[2] /rõd/ *n.f.* round(s); (*de policier*) beat; (*mus.*) semibreve.

**rondelle** /rõdɛl/ *n.f.* (*techn.*) washer; (*tranche*) slice.

**ronfl|er** /rõfle/ *v.i.* snore; (*moteur*) hum. **~ement(s)** *n.m.* (*pl.*) snoring; humming.

**rong|er** /rõʒe/ *v.t.* gnaw (at); (*vers*) eat into. **se ~er les ongles,** bite one's nails. **~eur** *n. m.* rodent.

**ronronn|er** /rõrone/ *v.i.* purr. **~ement** *n. m.* purr(ing).

**rosace** /rozas/ *n.f.* (*d'église*) rose window.

**rosbif** /rosbif/ *n.m.* roast beef.

**rose** /roz/ *n.f.* rose. ● *a.* pink; (*situation, teint*) rosy. ● *n.m.* pink.

**rosé** /roze/ *a.* pinkish; (*vin*) rosé. ● *n.m.* rosé.

**roseau** (*pl.* **~x**) /rozo/ *n.m.* reed.

**rosée** /roze/ *n.f.* dew.

**rosier** /rozje/ *n.m.* rose-bush, rose tree.

**rossignol** /rosiɲol/ *n.m.* nightingale.

**rot** /ro/ *n.m.* (*fam.*) burp.

**rotation** /rotasjõ/ *n.f.* rotation.

**roter** /rote/ *v.i.* (*fam.*) burp.

**rotin** /rotɛ̃/ *n.m.* (*rattan*) cane.

**rôt|ir** /rotir/ *v.t./i.* roast. **~i** *n.m.* roasting meat; (*cuit*) roast. **~i de porc,** roast pork.

**rotule** /rotyl/ *n.f.* kneecap.

**rouage** /rwaʒ/ *n.m.* (*techn.*) (working) part.

**roue** /ru/ *n.f.* wheel. **~ (dentée),** cog(-wheel). **~ de secours,** spare wheel.

**rouge** /ruʒ/ *a.* red; (*fer*) red-hot. ● *n.m.* red. (*fard*) rouge. **~ (à lèvres),** lipstick. **~-gorge** (*pl.* **~s-gorges**) *n.m.* robin.

**rougeole** /ruʒol/ *n.f.* measles.

**rouget** /ruʒɛ/ *n.m.* red mullet.

**rougeur** /ruʒœr/ *n.f.* redness; (*tache*) red blotch; (*gêne, honte*) red face.

**rougir** /ruʒir/ *v.t./i.* turn red; (*de honte*) blush.

**rouill|e** /ruj/ *n.f.* rust. **~é** *a.* rusty.

**roulant, ~e** /rulã, -t/ *a.* (*meuble*) on wheels; (*escalier*) moving.

**rouleau** (*pl.* **~x**) /rulo/ *n.m.* roll; (*outil, vague*) roller. **~ à pâtisserie,** rolling-pin. **~ compresseur,** steamroller.

**roulement** /rulmã/ *n.m.* rotation; (*bruit*) rumble; (*succession de personnes*) turnover; (*de tambour*) roll. **~ à billes,** ball-bearing. **par ~,** in rotation.

**rouler** /rule/ *v.t./i.* roll; (*manches*) roll up; (*duper*: *fam.*) cheat; (*véhicule, train*) go, travel; (*conducteur*) drive.

**roulette** /rulɛt/ *n.f.* (*de meuble*) castor; (*de dentiste*) drill; (*jeu*) roulette. **comme sur des ~s,** very smoothly.

**roulis** /ruli/ *n.m.* rolling.

**roulotte** /rulot/ *n.f.* caravan.

**roumain, ~e** /rumɛ̃, -ɛn/ *a.* & *n.m.*, *f.* Romanian.

**Roumanie** /rumani/ *n.f.* Romania.

**rousse** /rus/ *voir* **roux.**

**roussir** /rusir/ *v.t.* scorch. ● *v.i.* turn brown.

**route** /rut/ *n.f.* road; (*naut., aviat.*) route; (*direction*) way; (*voyage*) journey. **en ~,** on the way. **en ~!,** let's go! **mettre en ~,** start. **~ nationale,** trunk road, main road. **se mettre en ~,** set out.

**routine** /rutin/ *n.f.* routine.

**rouvrir** /ruvrir/ *v.t.*, **se ~ir** *v. pr.* reopen, open again.

**rou|x, ~sse** /ru, rus/ *a.* red, reddish-brown; (*personne*) red-haired. ● *n.m., f.* redhead.

**roy|al** (*m. pl.* **~aux**) /rwajal, -jo/ *a.* royal; (*total*: *fam.*) thorough.

**royaume** /rwajom/ *n.m.* kingdom. **R~-Uni** *n.m.* United Kingdom.

**ruban** /rybã/ *n.m.* ribbon; (*de magnétophone*) tape; (*de chapeau*) band. **~ adhésif,** sticky tape.

**rubéole** /rybeol/ *n.f.* German measles.

**rubis** /rybi/ *n.m.* ruby; (*de montre*) jewel.

**rubrique** /rybrik/ *n.f.* heading; (*article*) column.

**ruche** /ryʃ/ *n.f.* beehive.

**rude** /ryd/ *a.* rough; (*pénible*) tough; (*grossier*) crude; (*fameux*: *fam.*) tremendous. **~ment** *adv.* (*frapper etc.*) hard; (*traiter*) harshly; (*très*: *fam.*) awfully.

**rue** /ry/ *n.f.* street.

**ruelle** /ryɛl/ *n.f.* alley.

**ruer** /rye/ *v.i.* (*cheval*) kick. **se ~ dans/ vers,** rush into/towards.

**rugby** /rygbi/ *n.m.* Rugby.

**rug|ir** /ryʒir/ *v.i.* roar. **~issement** *n.m.* roar.

**rugueu|x, ~se** /rygø, -z/ *a.* rough.

**ruin|e** /rɥin/ *n.f.* ruin. **en ~e(s),** in ruins. **~er** *v.t.* ruin.

**ruineu|x, ~se** /rɥinø, -z/ *a.* ruinous.

**ruisseau** (*pl.* **~x**) /rɥiso/ *n.m.* stream; (*rigole*) gutter.

**ruisseler** /rɥisle/ *v.i.* stream.

**rumeur** /rymœr/ *n.f.* rumour.

**ruminer** /rymine/ *v.t./i.* (*herbe*) ruminate; (*méditer*) meditate.

**rupture** /ryptyr/ *n.f.* break; (*action*) breaking; (*de contrat*) breach; (*de pourparlers*) breakdown.

**rur|al** (*m. pl.* **~aux**) /ryral, -o/ *a.* rural.

**rus|e** /ryz/ *n.f.* **une ~e,** a trick, a ruse. **~é** *a.* cunning.

**russe** /rys/ *a.* & *n.m./f.* Russian. ● *n.m.* (*lang.*) Russian.

**Russie** /rysi/ *n.f.* Russia.

**rustique** /rystik/ *a.* rustic.

**rythm|e** /ritm/ *n.m.* rhythm; (*vitesse*) rate; (*de la vie*) pace.

.........................................

# Ss

.........................................

**s'** /s/ *voir* se.

**sa** /sa/ *voir* son¹.

**SA** *abrév.* (*société anonyme*) PLC.

**sabbat** /saba/ *n.m.* sabbath.

**sabl|e** /sabl/ *n.m.* sand. **~es mouvants**, quicksands. **~er le champagne**, drink champagne.

**sablier** /sablije/ *n.m.* (*culin.*) eggtimer.

**sabot** /sabo/ *n.m.* (*de cheval etc.*) hoof; (*chaussure*) clog; (*de frein*) shoe. **~ de Denver**, (wheel) clamp.

**sabot|er** /sabɔte/ *v.t.* sabotage; (*bâcler*) botch. **~age** *n.m.* sabotage; (*acte*) act of sabotage.

**sabre** /sabr/ *n.m.* sabre.

**sac** /sak/ *n.m.* bag; (*grand, en toile*) sack. **~ à dos**, rucksack. **~ à main**, handbag. **~ de couchage**, sleeping-bag.

**saccager** /sakaʒe/ *v.t.* (*ville, pays*) sack; (*maison*) ransack; (*ravager*) wreck.

**saccharine** /sakarin/ *n.f.* saccharin.

**sachet** /saʃɛ/ *n.m.* (small) bag; (*de médicament etc.*) sachet. **~ de thé**, tea-bag.

**sacoche** /sakɔʃ/ *n.f.* bag; (*d'élève*) satchel; (*de moto*) saddle-bag.

**sacquer** /sake/ *v.t.* (*fam.*) sack.

**sacré** /sakre/ *a.* sacred; (*maudit: fam.*) damned.

**sacrifice** /sakrifis/ *n.m.* sacrifice.

**sacrifier** /sakrifje/ *v.t.* sacrifice. **~ à**, conform to. **se ~** *v. pr.* sacrifice o.s.

**sacrilège** /sakrilɛʒ/ *n.m.* sacrilege. ● *a.* sacrilegious.

**sacristie** /sakristi/ *n.f.* (*protestante*) vestry; (*catholique*) sacristy.

**sadi|que** /sadik/ *a.* sadistic. ● *n.m./f.* sadist. **~sme** *n.m.* sadism.

**safari** /safari/ *n.m.* safari.

**sage** /saʒ/ *a.* wise; (*docile*) good. ● *n.m.* wise man. **~-femme** (*pl.* **~s-femmes**) *n.f.* midwife. **~ment** *adv.* wisely; (*docilement*) quietly. **~sse** /-ɛs/ *n.f.* wisdom.

**Sagittaire** /saʒitɛr/ *n.m.* **le ~**, Sagittarius.

**Sahara** /saara/ *n.m.* **le ~**, the Sahara (desert).

**saignant, ~e** /sɛɲã, -t/ *a.* (*culin.*) rare.

**saign|er** /seɲe/ *v.t./i.* bleed. **~er du nez**, have a nosebleed. **~ement** *n.m.* bleeding.

**sain, ~e** /sɛ̃, sɛn/ *a.* healthy; (*moralement*) sane. **~ et sauf**, safe and sound. **~ement** /sɛnmã/ *adv.* healthily; (*juger*) sanely.

**saindoux** /sɛ̃du/ *n.m.* lard.

**saint, ~e** /sɛ̃, sɛ̃t/ *a.* holy; (*bon*) saintly. ● *n.m., f.* saint. **S~-Esprit** *n.m.* Holy Spirit. **S~-Sylvestre** *n.f.* New Year's Eve. **S~e Vierge**, Blessed Virgin.

**sais** /sɛ/ *voir* savoir.

**saisie** /sezi/ *n.f.* (*jurid.*) seizure; (*comput.*) keyboarding. **~ de données**, data capture.

**sais|ir** /sezir/ *v.t.* grab (hold of), seize; (*occasion, biens*) seize; (*comprendre*) grasp; (*comput.*) keyboard, capture.

**saison** /sɛzɔ̃/ *n.f.* season. **la morte ~**, the off season. **~nier, ~nière** /-ɔnje, -jɛr/ *a.* seasonal.

**sait** /sɛ/ *voir* savoir.

**salad|e** /salad/ *n.f.* salad; (*laitue*) lettuce; (*désordre: fam.*) mess. **~ier** *n.m.* salad bowl.

**salaire** /salɛr/ *n.m.* wages, salary.

**salami** /salami/ *n.m.* salami.

**salarié, ~e** /salarje/ *a.* wage-earning. ● *n.m., f.* wage-earner.

**salaud** /salo/ *n.m.* (*argot*) bastard.

**sale** /sal/ *a.* dirty, filthy; (*mauvais*) nasty.

**sal|er** /sale/ *v.t.* salt. **~é** *a.* (*goût*) salty; (*plat*) salted; (*viande, poisson*) salt; (*grivois: fam.*) spicy.

**saleté** /salte/ *n.f.* (*crasse*) dirt; (*action*) dirty trick. **~s**, (*détritus*) mess.

**salière** /saljɛr/ *n.f.* salt-cellar.

**sal|ir** /salir/ *v.t.* (make) dirty; (*réputation*) tarnish. **se ~ir** *v. pr.* get dirty. **~issant, ~issante** *a.* dirty; (*étoffe*) easily dirtied.

**salive** /saliv/ *n.f.* saliva.

**salle** /sal/ *n.f.* room; (*grande, publique*) hall; (*d'hôpital*) ward; (*théâtre, cinéma*) auditorium. **~ à manger**, dining-room. **~ d'attente**, waiting-room. **~ de bains**, bathroom. **~ de séjour**, living-room. **~ de classe**, classroom. **~ d'embarquement**, departure lounge. **~ d'opération**, operating theatre. **~ des ventes**, saleroom.

**salon** /salɔ̃/ *n.m.* lounge; (*de coiffure, beauté*) salon; (*exposition*) show. **~ de thé**, tea-room.

**salope** /salɔp/ *n.f.* (*argot*) bitch.

**saloperie** /salɔpri/ *n.f.* (*fam.*) (*action*) dirty trick; (*chose de mauvaise qualité*) rubbish.

**salopette** /salɔpɛt/ *n.f.* dungarees; (*d'ouvrier*) overalls.

**salsifis** /salsifi/ *n.m.* salsify.

**saluer** /salɥe/ *v.t.* greet; (*en partant*) take one's leave of; (*de la tête*) nod to; (*de la main*) wave to.

**salut** /saly/ *n.m.* greeting; (*de la tête*) nod; (*de la main*) wave; (*mil.*) salute; (*sauvegarde, rachat*) salvation. ● *int.* (*bonjour: fam.*) hallo; (*au revoir: fam.*) bye-bye.

**salutation** /salytɑsjɔ̃/ *n.f.* greeting. **veuillez agréer, Monsieur, mes ∼s distingués,** yours faithfully.

**samedi** /samdi/ *n.m.* Saturday.

**sanction** /sɑ̃ksjɔ̃/ *n.f.* sanction.

**sandale** /sɑ̃dal/ *n.f.* sandal.

**sandwich** /sɑ̃dwitʃ/ *n.m.* sandwich.

**sang** /sɑ̃/ *n.m.* blood. **∼-froid** *n.m. invar.* calm, self-control.

**sangl|e** /sɑ̃gl/ *n.f.* strap. **∼er** *v.t.* strap.

**sanglier** /sɑ̃glije/ *n.m.* wild boar.

**sanglot** /sɑ̃glo/ *n.m.* sob.

**sangsue** /sɑ̃sy/ *n.f.* leech.

**sanguin,** **∼e** /sɑ̃gɛ̃, -in/ *a.* (*groupe etc.*) blood; (*caractère*) fiery.

**sanitaire** /saniter/ *a.* health; (*conditions*) sanitary; (*appareils, installations*) bathroom, sanitary. **∼s** *n.m. pl.* bathroom.

**sans** /sɑ̃/ *prép.* without. **∼ que vous le sachiez,** without your knowing. **∼-abri** /sɑ̃zabri/ *n.m./f. invar.* homeless person. **∼ ça, ∼ quoi,** otherwise. **∼ arrêt,** nonstop. **∼ encombre/faute/ tarder,** without incident/fail/ delay. **∼-fin/goût/limite,** endless/tasteless/limitless. **∼-gêne** *a. invar.* inconsiderate, thoughtless; *n.m. invar.* thoughtlessness. **∼ importance / pareil / précédent / travail,** unimportant / unparalleled / unprecedented / unemployed.

**santé** /sɑ̃te/ *n.f.* health. **à ta** *ou* **votre santé,** cheers!

**saoul,** **∼e** /su, sul/ *voir* **soûl.**

**sapeur** /sapœr/ *n.m.* (*mil.*) sapper. **∼-pompier** (*pl.* **∼s-pompiers**) *n.m.* fireman.

**saphir** /safir/ *n.m.* sapphire.

**sapin** /sapɛ̃/ *n.m.* fir(-tree). **∼ de Noël,** Christmas tree.

**sardine** /sardin/ *n.f.* sardine.

**satellite** /satelit/ *n.m.* satellite.

**satin** /satɛ̃/ *n.m.* satin.

**satir|e** /satir/ *n.f.* satire. **∼ique** *a.* satirical.

**satisfaction** /satisfaksjɔ̃/ *n.f.* satisfaction.

**satis|faire†** /satisfer/ *v.t.* satisfy. ● *v.i.* **∼faire à,** satisfy. **∼faisant,** **∼faisante** *a.* (*acceptable*) satisfactory. **∼fait,** **∼faite** *a.* satisfied (**de,** with).

**sauc|e** /sos/ *n.f.* sauce; (*jus de viande*) gravy. **∼er** *v.t.* (*plat*) wipe. **∼e tartare,** tartar sauce. **∼ière** *n.f.* sauce-boat.

**saucisse** /sosis/ *n.f.* sausage.

**saucisson** /sosisɔ̃/ *n.m.* (slicing) sausage.

**sauf¹** /sof/ *prép.* except. **∼ erreur/imprévu,** barring error/ the unforeseen.

**sau|f²,** **∼ve** /sof, sov/ *a.* safe, unharmed.

**sauge** /soʒ/ *n.f.* (*culin.*) sage.

**saule** /sol/ *n.m.* willow. **∼ pleureur,** weeping willow.

**saumon** /somɔ̃/ *n.m.* salmon. ● *a. invar.* salmon-pink.

**saumure** /somyr/ *n.f.* brine.

**sauna** /sona/ *n.m.* sauna.

**saupoudrer** /sopudre/ *v.t.* sprinkle (**de,** with).

**saut** /so/ *n.m.* jump, leap. **faire un ∼ chez qn.,** pop round to s.o.'s (place). **le ∼,** (*sport*) jumping. **∼ en hauteur/longueur,** high/long jump.

**sauté** /sote/ *a. & n.m.* (*culin.*) sauté.

**sauter** /sote/ *v.i.* jump, leap; (*exploser*) blow up; (*fusible*) blow; (*se détacher*) come off. ● *v.t.* jump (over); (*page, classe*) skip. **faire ∼,** (*détruire*) blow up; (*fusible*) blow; (*casser*) break; (*culin.*) sauté. **∼ à la corde,** skip. **∼ sur une occasion,** jump at an opportunity.

**sauterelle** /sotrɛl/ *n.f.* grasshopper.

**sautiller** /sotije/ *v.i.* hop.

**sauvage** /sovaʒ/ *a.* wild; (*primitif, cruel*) savage; (*farouche*) unsociable; (*illégal*) unauthorized. ● *n.m./f.* unsociable person; (*brute*) savage.

**sauve** /sov/ *voir* **sauf¹.**

**sauvegard|e** /sovgard/ *n.f.* safeguard; (*comput.*) backup. **∼er** *v.t.* safeguard; (*comput.*) save.

**sauv|er** /sove/ *v.t.* save; (*d'un danger*) rescue, save; (*matériel*) salvage. **se ∼er** *v. pr.* (*fuir*) run away; (*partir: fam.*) be off. **∼etage** *n.m.* rescue; salvage. **∼eteur** *n.m.* rescuer.

**savan|t,** **∼e** /savɑ̃, -t/ *a.* learned; (*habile*) skilful. ● *n.m.* scientist.

**saveur** /savœr/ *n.f.* flavour; (*fig.*) savour.

**savoir†** /savwar/ *v.t.* know; (*apprendre*) hear. **elle sait conduire/nager,** she can drive/ swim. ● *n.m.* learning. **faire ∼ à qn. que,** inform s.o. to that.

**savon** /savɔ̃/ *n.m.* soap. **∼ner** /-ɔne/ *v.t.* soap. **∼nette** /-ɔnɛt/ *n.f.* bar of soap.

**savour|er** /savure/ *v.t.* savour. **∼eux,** **∼euse** *a.* tasty; (*fig.*) spicy.

**saxo(phone)** /saksɔ(fɔn)/ *n.m.* sax(o-phone).

**scandal|e** /skɑ̃dal/ *n.m.* scandal; (*tapage*) uproar; (*en public*) noisy scene. **faire ∼e,** shock people. **faire un ∼e,** make a scene. **∼eux,** **∼euse** *a.* scandalous.

**scandinave** /skɑ̃dinav/ *a. & n.m./f.* Scandinavian.

**Scandinavie** /skɑ̃dinavi/ *n.f.* Scandinavia.

**scarabée** /skarabe/ *n.m.* beetle.

**scarlatine** /skarlatin/ *n.f.* scarlet fever.

**scarole** /skarɔl/ *n.f.* endive.

**sceau** (*pl.* **∼x**) /so/ *n.m.* seal.

**scell|er** /sele/ *v.t.* seal; (*fixer*) cement. **∼és** *n.m. pl.* seals.

**scénario** /senarjo/ *n.m.* scenario.

**scène** /sen/ *n.f.* scene; (*estrade, art dramatique*) stage. **mettre en ∼,** (*pièce*) stage. **∼ de ménage,** domestic scene.

**scepti|que** /sɛptik/ *a.* sceptical. ● *n.m./f.* sceptic. **∼cisme** *n.m.* scepticism.

**schéma** /ʃema/ *n.m.* diagram.

**sciatique** /sjatik/ *n.f.* sciatica.

**scie** /si/ *n.f.* saw.

**scien|ce** /sjɑ̃s/ *n.f.* science; (*savoir*) knowledge. **~ce-fiction** *n.f.* science fiction. **~tifique** *a.* scientific; *n.m./f.* scientist.

**scier** /sje/ *v.t.* saw.

**scintiller** /sɛ̃tije/*v.i.*glitter;(*étoile*)twinkle.

**scission** /sisjɔ̃/ *n.f.* split.

**sciure** /sjyr/ *n.f.* sawdust.

**sclérose** /skleroz/ *n.f.* sclerosis. **~ en plaques,** multiple sclerosis.

**scol|aire** /skɔlɛr/ *a.* school. **~arisation** *n.f.*, **~arité** *n.f.* schooling.

**scorbut** /skɔrbyt/ *n.m.* scurvy.

**score** /skɔr/ *n.m.* score.

**scorpion** /skɔrpjɔ̃/ *n.m.* scorpion. **le S~,** Scorpio.

**scotch**[1] /skɔtʃ/ *n.m.* (*boisson*) Scotch (whisky).

**scotch**[2] /skɔtʃ/ *n.m.* (P.) Sellotape (P.); (*Amer.*) Scotch (tape) (P.).

**scout, ~e** /skut/ *n.m. & a.* scout.

**script** /skript/ *n.m.* (*cinéma*) script; (*écriture*) printing.

**scrupule** /skrypyl/ *n.m.* scruple.

**scrutin** /skrytɛ̃/ *n.m.* (*vote*) ballot; (*opération électorale*) poll.

**sculpt|er** /skylte/ *v.t.* sculpture; (*bois*) carve(**dans,**outof).**~eur***n.m.*sculptor.**~ure** *n.f.* sculpture.

**se, s'**[*] /sə,s/ *pron.* himself;(*femelle*)herself; (*indéfini*) oneself; (*non humain*) itself; (*pl.*) themselves; (*réciproque*) each other, one another. **se parler,** (*à soi-même*) talk to o.s.; (*réciproque*) talk to each other. **se faire,** (*passif*) be done. **se laver les mains,** (*possessif*) wash one's hands.

**séance** /seɑ̃s/ *n.f.* session; (*cinéma, théâtre*) show.

**seau** (*pl.* **~x**) /so/ *n.m.* bucket, pail.

**sec, sèche** /sɛk, sɛʃ/ *a.* dry; (*fruits*) dried; (*coup, bruit*) sharp; (*cœur*) hard; (*whisky*) neat. ● *n.m.* **à ~,** (*sans eau*) dry; (*sans argent*) broke.

**sécateur** /sekatœr/ *n.m.* (*pour les haies*) shears; (*petit*) secateurs.

**sèche** /sɛʃ/ *voir* **sec. ~ment** *adv.* drily.

**sèche-cheveux** /sɛʃʃəvø/ *n.m. invar.* hair-drier.

**sécher** /seʃe/*v.t./i.* dry. **se ~** *v. pr.* dry o.s.

**sécheresse** /seʃrɛs/ *n.f.* dryness; (*temps sec*) drought.

**séchoir** /seʃwar/ *n.m.* drier.

**second, ~e**[1] /sgɔ̃, -d/ *a. & n.m., f.* second. ● *n.m.* (*adjoint*) second in command; (*étage*) second floor. ● *n.f.* second class.

**seconde**[2] /sgɔ̃d/ *n.f.* (*instant*) second.

**secouer** /skwe/ *v.t.* shake; (*poussière, torpeur*)shake off. **se ~,** (*fam.*)(*se dépêcher*) get a move on; (*réagir*) shake o.s. up.

**secour|ir** /skurir/ *v.t.* assist, help. **~iste** *n.m./f.* first-aid worker.

**secours** /skur/ *n.m.* assistance, help. ● *n.m. pl.* (*méd.*) first aid. **au ~l,** help! **de ~,** emergency; (*équipe, opération*) rescue.

**secousse** /skus/ *n.f.* jolt, jerk; (*électrique*) shock; (*séisme*) tremor.

**secr|et, ~ète** /səkrɛ, -t/ *a.* secret. ● *n.m.* secret; (*discrétion*) secrecy. **en ~et,** in secret, secretly.

**secrétaire** /skretɛr/ *n.m./f.* secretary. ● *n.m.* (*meuble*) writing-desk. **~ d'État,** junior minister.

**secrétariat** /skretarja/ *n.m.* (*bureau*) secretary's office.

**secte** /sɛkt/ *n.f.* sect.

**secteur** /sɛktœr/ *n.m.* area; (*comm.*) sector; (*électr.*) mains.

**section** /sɛksjɔ̃/ *n.f.* section; (*transports publics*) fare stage.

**sécu** /seky/ *n.f.* (*fam.*) **la ~,** the social security services.

**sécuriser** /sekyrize/ *v.t.* reassure.

**sécurité** /sekyrite/ *n.f.* security; (*absence de danger*) safety. **en ~,** safe, secure. **S~ sociale,** social services, social security services.

**sédatif** /sedatif/ *n.m.* sedative.

**séd|uire**† /seɥir/ *v.t.* charm; (*plaire à*) appeal to; (*abuser de*) seduce. **~ucteur, ~uctrice** *a.* seductive; *n.m., f.* seducer. **~uisant, ~uisante** *a.* attractive.

**segment** /sɛgmɑ̃/ *n.m.* segment.

**ségrégation** /segregasjɔ̃/ *n.f.* segregation.

**seigle** /sɛgl/ *n.m.* rye.

**seigneur** /sɛɲœr/ *n.m.* lord. **le S~,** the Lord.

**sein** /sɛ̃/ *n.m.* breast; (*fig.*) bosom.

**Seine** /sɛn/ *n.f.* Seine.

**séisme** /seism/ *n.m.* earthquake.

**seiz|e** /sɛz/ *a. & n.m.* sixteen. **~ième** *a. & n.m./f.* sixteenth.

**séjour** /seʒur/ *n.m.* stay; (*pièce*) living-room. **~ner** *v.i.* stay.

**sel** /sɛl/ *n.m.* salt; (*piquant*) spice.

**sélection** /selɛksjɔ̃/ *n.f.* selection. **~ner** /-jɔne/ *v.t.* select.

**self(-service)** /sɛlf(sɛrvis)/ *n.m.* self-service.

**selle** /sɛl/ *n.f.* saddle.

**selon** /slɔ̃/ *prép.* according to (**que,** whether).

**semaine** /smɛn/ *n.f.* week. **en ~,** in the week.

**semblable** /sɑ̃blabl/ *a.* similar (**à,** to). ● *n.m.* fellow (creature).

**semblant** /sɑ̃blɑ̃/ *n.m.* **faire ~ de,** pretend to.

**sembl|er** /sɑ̃ble/ *v.i.* seem (**à**, to; **que**, that). **il me ~e que**, it seems to me that.

**semelle** /smɛl/ *n.f.* sole.

**sem|er** /sme/ *v.t.* sow; (*jeter, parsemer*) strew; (*répandre*) spread; (*personne: fam.*) lose.

**semestre** /sməstr/ *n.m.* half-year; (*univ.*) semester.

**semi-** /səmi/ *préf.* semi-.

**séminaire** /seminɛr/ *n.m.* (*relig.*) seminary; (*univ.*) seminar.

**semi-remorque** /səmirəmork/ *n.m.* articulated lorry; (*Amer.*) semi(-trailer).

**semoule** /smul/ *n.f.* semolina.

**sénat** /sena/ *n.m.* senate. **~eur** /-tœr/ *n.m.* senator.

**sénile** /senil/ *a.* senile.

**sens** /sɑ̃s/ *n.m.* sense; (*signification*) meaning, sense; (*direction*) direction. **à ~ unique**, (*rue etc.*) one-way. **ça n'a pas de ~**, that does not make sense. **~ giratoire**, roundabout. **~ interdit**, no entry; (*rue*) one-way street.

**sensation** /sɑ̃sɑsjɔ̃/ *n.f.* feeling, sensation.

**sensé** /sɑ̃se/ *a.* sensible.

**sensibiliser** /sɑ̃sibilize/ *v.t.* **~ à**, make sensitive to.

**sensib|le** /sɑ̃sibl/ *a.* sensitive (**à**, to); (*appréciable*) noticeable. **~ilité** *n.f.* sensitivity.

**sens|uel**, **~uelle** /sɑ̃sɥel/ *a.* sensuous; (*sexuel*) sensual. **~ualité** *n.f.* sensuousness; sensuality.

**senteur** /sɑ̃tœr/ *n.f.* scent.

**sentier** /sɑ̃tje/ *n.m.* path.

**sentiment** /sɑ̃timɑ̃/ *n.m.* feeling.

**sentiment|al** (*m. pl.* **~aux**) /sɑ̃timɑ̃tal, -o/ *a.* sentimental.

**sentinelle** /sɑ̃tinɛl/ *n.f.* sentry.

**sentir†** /sɑ̃tir/ *v.t.* feel; (*odeur*) smell; (*goût*) taste; (*pressentir*) sense. **~ la lavande**/*etc.*, smell of lavender/*etc.* **se ~ fier/mieux**/*etc.*, feel proud/better/*etc.*

**séparé** /separe/ *a.* separate; (*conjoints*) separated. **~ment** *adv.* separately.

**sépar|er** /separe/ *v.t.* separate; (*en deux*) split. **se ~er** *v. pr.* separate, part (**de**, from); (*se détacher*) split. **se ~er de**, (*se défaire de*) part with. **~ation** *n.f.* separation.

**sept** /sɛt/ *a. & n.m.* seven.

**septante** /sɛptɑ̃t/ *a. & n.m.* (*en Belgique, Suisse*) seventy.

**septembre** /sɛptɑ̃br/ *n.m.* September.

**septième** /sɛtjɛm/ *a. & n.m./f.* seventh.

**séquence** /sekɑ̃s/ *n.f.* sequence.

**sera, serait** /sra, srɛ/ *voir* **être**.

**serein**, **~e** /sərɛ̃, -ɛn/ *a.* serene.

**sérénité** /serenite/ *n.f.* serenity.

**sergent** /sɛrʒɑ̃/ *n.m.* sergeant.

**série** /seri/ *n.f.* series; (*d'objets*) set. **de ~**, (*véhicule etc.*) standard. **fabrication** *ou* **production en ~**, mass production.

**sérieu|x**, **~se** /serjø, -z/ *a.* serious; (*digne de foi*) reliable; (*chances, raison*) good. ● *n.m.* seriousness. **garder/perdre son ~x**, keep/ be unable to keep a straight face. **prendre au ~x**, take seriously. **~sement** *adv.* seriously.

**seringue** /srɛ̃g/ *n.f.* syringe.

**serment** /sɛrmɑ̃/ *n.m.* oath; (*promesse*) pledge.

**sermon** /sɛrmɔ̃/ *n.m.* sermon.

**séropositi|f**, **~ve** /seropozitif, -v/ *a.* HIV-positive.

**serpent** /sɛrpɑ̃/ *n.m.* snake.

**serpillière** /sɛrpijɛr/ *n.f.* floor-cloth.

**serre¹** /sɛr/ *n.f.* (*local*) greenhouse.

**serre²** /sɛr/ *n.f.* (*griffe*) claw.

**serré** /sere/ *a.* (*habit, nœud, programme*) tight; (*personnes*) packed, crowded; (*lutte, mailles*) close; (*cœur*) heavy.

**serrer** /sere/ *v.t.* (*saisir*) grip; (*presser*) squeeze; (*vis, corde, ceinture*) tighten; (*poing, dents*) clench; (*pieds*) pinch. **~ qn. dans ses bras**, hug. **~ qn.**, (*vêtement*) be tight on s.o. ● *v.i.* **~ à droite**, keep over to the right. **se ~** *v. pr.* (*se rapprocher*) squeeze (up) (**contre**, against). **~ la main à**, shake hands with.

**serrur|e** /seryr/ *n.f.* lock. **~ier** *n.m.* locksmith.

**sérum** /serom/ *n.m.* serum.

**servante** /sɛrvɑ̃t/ *n.f.* (maid)servant.

**serveu|r**, **~se** /sɛrvœr, -øz/ *n.m., f.* waiter, waitress; (*au bar*) barman, barmaid.

**serviable** /sɛrvjabl/ *a.* helpful.

**service** /sɛrvis/ *n.m.* service; (*fonction, temps de travail*) duty; (*pourboire*) service (charge). **~ (non) compris**, service (not) included. **être de ~**, be on duty. **rendre un ~ à qn.**, do s.o. a favour. **~ d'ordre**, (*policiers*) police. **~ après-vente**, after-sales service. **~ militaire**, military service.

**serviette** /sɛrvjɛt/ *n.f.* (*de toilette*) towel; (*sac*) briefcase. **~ (de table)**, serviette. **~ hygiénique**, sanitary towel.

**servir†** /sɛrvir/ *v.t./i.* serve; (*être utile*) be of use, serve. **~ qn.** (*à table*), wait on s.o. **ça sert à**, (*outil, récipient, etc.*) it is used for. **ça me sert à/de**, I use it for/as. **~ de**, serve as, be used as. **se ~** *v. pr.* (*à table*) help o.s. (**de**, to). **se ~ de**, use.

**serviteur** /sɛrvitœr/ *n.m.* servant.

**ses** /se/ *voir* **son¹**.

**session** /sesjɔ̃/ *n.f.* session.

**seuil** /sœj/ *n.m.* doorstep; (*entrée*) doorway; (*fig.*) threshold.

**seul**, **~e** /sœl/ *a.* alone, on one's own; (*unique*) only. **un ~ travail**/*etc.*, only one job/ *etc.* **pas un ~ ami**/*etc.*, not a single friend/*etc.* **parler tout ~**, talk to o.s. **faire qch. tout ~**, do sth. on one's own. ● *n.m.*, *f.* **le ~, la ~e,** the only one. **un ~, une ~e,** only one. **pas un ~,** not (a single) one.

**seulement** /sœlmɑ̃/ *adv.* only.

**sève** /sɛv/ *n.f.* sap.

**sévère** /sevɛr/ *a.* severe.

**sevrer** /səvre/ *v.t.* wean.

**sexe** /sɛks/ *n.m.* sex; (*organes*) sex organs.

**sex|uel, ~uelle** /sɛksɥɛl/ *a.* sexual. **~ualité** *n.f.* sexuality.

**seyant, ~e** /sejɑ̃, -t/ *a.* becoming.

**shampooing** /ʃɑ̃pwɛ̃/ *n.m.* shampoo.

**short** /ʃɔrt/ *n.m.* (pair of) shorts.

**si¹** (**s'** *before* **il, ils**) /si, s/ *conj.* if; (*interrogation indirecte*) if, whether. **si on partait?,** (*suggestion*) what about going? **s'il vous** *ou* **te plait,** please. **si oui,** if so.

**si²** /si/ *adv.* (*tellement*) so; (*oui*) yes. **un si bon repas,** such a good meal. **pas si riche que,** not as rich as.

**Sicile** /sisil/ *n.f.* Sicily.

**sida** /sida/ *n.m.* (*méd.*) AIDS.

**sidérurgie** /sideryrʒi/ *n.f.* iron and steel industry.

**siècle** /sjɛkl/ *n.m.* century; (*époque*) age.

**siège** /sjɛʒ/ *n.m.* seat. **~ social,** head office, headquarters.

**siéger** /sjeʒe/ *v.i.* (*assemblée*) sit.

**sien, ~ne** /sjɛ̃, sjɛn/ *pron.* **le ~, la ~ne, les ~(ne)s,** his; (*femme*) hers; (*chose*) its.

**sieste** /sjɛst/ *n.f.* nap. **faire la ~,** have an afternoon nap.

**siffl|er** /sifle/ *v.i.* whistle; (*avec un sifflet*) blow one's whistle; (*serpent, gaz*) hiss. ● *v.t.* (*air*) whistle; (*chien*) whistle to *ou* for.

**siffet** /sifle/ *n.m.* whistle.

**sigle** /sigl/ *n.m.* abbreviation, acronym.

**sign|al** (*pl.* **~aux**) /siɲal, -o/ *n.m.* signal.

**signaler** /siɲale/ *v.t.* indicate; (*par une sonnerie, un écriteau*) signal; (*dénoncer, mentionner*) report; (*faire remarquer*) point out.

**signalisation** /siɲalizasjɔ̃/ *n.f.* signalling, signposting; (*signaux*) signals.

**signature** /siɲatyr/ *n.f.* signature; (*action*) signing.

**signe** /siɲ/ *n.m.* sign; (*de ponctuation*) mark. **faire ~ à,** beckon (**de,** to); (*contacter*) contact.

**signer** /siɲe/ *v.t.* sign.

**signification** /siɲifikasjɔ̃/ *n.f.* meaning.

**signifier** /siɲifje/ *v.t.* mean, signify.

**silenc|e** /silɑ̃s/ *n.m.* silence; (*mus.*) rest. **~ieux, ~ieuse** *a.* silent.

**silhouette** /silwɛt/ *n.f.* outline, silhouette.

**silicium** /silisjɔm/ *n.m.* silicon.

**sillon** /sijɔ̃/ *n.m.* furrow; (*de disque*) groove.

**sillonner** /sijɔne/ *v.t.* criss-cross.

**silo** /silo/ *n.m.* silo.

**simil|aire** /similɛr/ *a.* similar. **~itude** *n.f.* similarity.

**simple** /sɛ̃pl/ *a.* simple; (*non double*) single. ● *n.m.* (*tennis*) singles. **~ment** /-əmɑ̃/ *adv.* simply.

**simplicité** /sɛ̃plisite/ *n.f.* simplicity; (*naïveté*) simpleness.

**simplif|ier** /sɛ̃plifje/ *v.t.* simplify. **~ication** *n.f.* simplification.

**simultané** /simyltane/ *a.* simultaneous. **~ment** *adv.* simultaneously.

**sinc|ère** /sɛ̃sɛr/ *a.* sincere. **~èrement** *adv.* sincerely. **~érité** *n.f.* sincerity.

**singe** /sɛ̃ʒ/ *n.m.* monkey, ape.

**singer** /sɛ̃ʒe/ *v.t.* mimic, ape.

**singul|ier, ~ière** /sɛ̃gylje, -jɛr/ *a.* peculiar, remarkable; (*gram.*) singular. ● *n.m.* (*gram.*) singular.

**sinistre¹** /sinistr/ *a.* sinister.

**sinistr|e²** /sinistr/ *n.m.* disaster; (*incendie*) blaze; (*dommages*) damage. **~é** *a.* disaster-stricken; *n.m.*, *f.* disaster victim.

**sinon** /sinɔ̃/ *conj.* (*autrement*) otherwise; (*sauf*) except (**que,** that); (*si ce n'est*) if not.

**sinus** /sinys/ *n.m.* (*anat.*) sinus.

**sionisme** /sjɔnism/ *n.m.* Zionism.

**siphon** /sifɔ̃/ *n.m.* siphon; (*de WC*) U-bend.

**sirène¹** /sirɛn/ *n.f.* (*appareil*) siren.

**sirène²** /sirɛn/ *n.f.* (*femme*) mermaid.

**sirop** /siro/ *n.m.* syrup; (*boisson*) cordial.

**site** /sit/ *n.m.* setting; (*pittoresque*) beauty spot; (*emplacement*) site; (*monument etc.*) place of interest.

**sitôt** /sito/ *adv.* **~ entré**/*etc.*, immediately after coming in/*etc.* **pas de ~,** not for a while.

**situation** /sitɥasjɔ̃/ *n.f.* situation, position. **~ de famille,** marital status.

**situ|er** /sitɥe/ *v.t.* situate, locate. **se ~er** *v. pr.* (*se trouver*) be situated. **~é** *a.* situated.

**six** /sis/ (/si/ *before consonant,* /siz/ *before vowel*) *a.* & *n.m.* six. **~ième** /sizjɛm/ *a.* & *n.m./f.* sixth.

**sketch** (*pl.* **~es**) /skɛtʃ/ *n.m.* (*théâtre*) sketch.

**ski** /ski/ *n.m.* (*patin*) ski; (*sport*) skiing. **faire du ~,** ski. **~ de fond,** cross-country skiing. **~ nautique,** water-skiing.

**sk|ier** /skje/ *v.i.* ski. **~ieur, ~ieuse** *n.m.*, *f.* skier.

**slalom** /slalɔm/ *n.m.* slalom.

**slave** /slav/ *a.* Slav; (*lang.*) Slavonic. ● *n.m./f.* Slav.

**slip** /slip/ *n.m.* (*d'homme*) (under)-pants; (*de femme*) knickers. **~ de bain,** (swimming) trunks. briefs.

**smoking** /smɔkiŋ/ *n.m.* evening *ou* dinner suit, dinner-jacket.

**snack(-bar)** /snak(bar)/ *n.m.* snack-bar.

**snob** /snɔb/ *n.m./f.* snob. ● *a.* snobbish. **~isme** *n.m.* snobbery.

**sociable** /sɔsjabl/ *a.* sociable.

**soc|ial** (*m. pl.* ∼**iaux**) /sɔsjal, -jo/ *a.* social. ∼**me** *n.m.* socialism.

**socialis|te** /sɔsjalist/ *n.m./f.* socialist.

**société** /sɔsjete/ *n.f.* society; (*compagnie, firme*) company.

**sociolo|gie** /sɔsjɔlɔʒi/ *n.f.* sociology. ∼**gique** *a.* sociological.

**socle** /sɔkl/ *n.m.* (*de colonne, statue*) plinth; (*de lampe*) base.

**socquette** /sɔkɛt/ *n.f.* ankle sock.

**soda** /sɔda/ *n.m.* (fizzy) drink.

**sodium** /sɔdjɔm/ *n.m.* sodium.

**sœur** /sœr/ *n.f.* sister.

**sofa** /sɔfa/ *n.m.* sofa.

**soi** /swa/ *pron.* oneself. ∼**-disant** *a. invar.* so-called. *adv.* supposedly.

**soie** /swa/ *n.f.* silk.

**soif** /swaf/ *n.f.* thirst. **avoir** ∼, be thirsty. **donner** ∼ **à**, make thirsty.

**soigné** /swaɲe/ *a.* tidy, neat; (*bien fait*) careful.

**soigner** /swaɲe/ *v.t.* look after, take care of; (*tenue, style*) take care over; (*maladie*) treat. **se** ∼ *v. pr.* look after o.s.

**soigneu|x, ∼se** /swaɲø, -z/ *a.* careful (**de**, about); (*ordonné*) tidy. ∼**sement** *adv.* carefully.

**soi-même** /swamɛm/ *pron.* oneself.

**soin** /swɛ̃/ *n.m.* care; (*ordre*) tidiness. ∼**s**, care; (*méd.*) treatment. **premiers** ∼**s**, first aid.

**soir** /swar/ *n.m.* evening.

**soirée** /sware/ *n.f.* evening; (*réception*) party. ∼ **dansante**, dance.

**soit** /swa/ *voir* **être.** ● *conj.* (*à savoir*) that is to say. ∼ **... soit,** either &ddd. or.

**soixantaine** /swasãtɛn/ *n.f.* **une** ∼ (**de**), about sixty.

**soixant|e** /swasãt/ *a.&n.m. invar.* sixty. ∼**e-dix** *a. & n.m.* seventy. ∼**e-dixième** *a. & n.m./f.* seventieth. ∼**ième** *a. & n.m./f.* sixtieth.

**soja** /sɔʒa/ *n.m.* (*graines*) soya beans; (*plante*) soya.

**sol** /sɔl/ *n.m.* ground; (*de maison*) floor; (*terrain agricole*) soil.

**solaire** /sɔlɛr/ *a.* solar; (*huile, filtre*) sun. **les rayons** ∼**s**, the sun's rays.

**soldat** /sɔlda/ *n.m.* soldier.

**solde** /sɔld/ *n.m.* (*comm.*) balance. ∼**s**, (*articles*) sale goods. **en** ∼, (*acheter etc.*) at sale price. **les** ∼**s**, the sales.

**solder** /sɔlde/ *v.t.* reduce; (*liquider*) sell off at sale price; (*compte*) settle.

**sole** /sɔl/ *n.f.* (*poisson*) sole.

**soleil** /sɔlɛj/ *n.m.* sun; (*chaleur*) sunshine. **il y a du** ∼, it is sunny.

**solex** /sɔlɛks/ *n.m.* (P.) moped.

**solfège** /sɔlfɛʒ/ *n.m.* elementary musical theory.

**solid|aire** /sɔlidɛr/ *a.* (*couple*) (mutually) supportive; (*ouvriers*) who show solidarity. ∼**arité** *n.f.* solidarity.

**solid|e** /sɔlid/ *a.* solid. ∼**ité** *n.f.* solidity.

**soliste** /sɔlist/ *n.m./f.* soloist.

**solitaire** /sɔlitɛr/ *a.* solitary. ● *n.m./f.* (*personne*) loner.

**solitude** /sɔlityd/ *n.f.* solitude.

**solliciter** /sɔlisite/ *v.t.* request.

**solo** /sɔlo/ *n.m. & a. invar.* (*mus.*) solo.

**solstice** /sɔlstis/ *n.m.* solstice.

**soluble** /sɔlybl/ *a.* soluble.

**solution** /sɔlysjɔ̃/ *n.f.* solution.

**solvable** /sɔlvabl/ *a.* solvent.

**solvant** /sɔlvã/ *n.m.* solvent.

**sombre** /sɔ̃br/ *a.* dark; (*triste*) sombre.

**sommaire** /sɔmɛr/ *a.* summary. ● *n.m.* summary.

**somme**[1] /sɔm/ *n.f.* sum. **en** ∼, ∼ **toute**, in short. **faire la** ∼ **de**, add (up), total (up).

**somme**[2] /sɔm/ *n.m.* (*sommeil*) nap.

**sommeil** /sɔmɛj/ *n.m.* sleep; (*besoin de dormir*) drowsiness. **avoir** ∼, be ou feel sleepy.

**sommelier** /sɔməlje/ *n.m.* wine waiter.

**sommes** /sɔm/ *voir* **être.**

**sommet** /sɔmɛ/ *n.m.* top; (*de montagne*) summit; (*de triangle*) apex; (*gloire*) height.

**sommier** /sɔmje/ *n.m.* base (of bed).

**somnambule** /sɔmnãbyl/ *n.m.* sleep-walker.

**somnifère** /sɔmnifɛr/ *n.m.* sleeping-pill.

**somnolen|t, ∼te** /sɔmnɔlã, -t/ *a.* drowsy. ∼**ce** *n.f.* drowsiness.

**somnoler** /sɔmnɔle/ *v.i.* doze.

**sompt|ueux, ∼ueuse** /sɔ̃ptɥø, -z/ *a.* sumptuous.

**son**[1], sa *ou* **son***\** (*pl.* **ses**) /sɔ̃, sa, sɔ̃, se/ *a.* his; (*femme*) her; (*chose*) its; (*indéfini*) one's.

**son**[2] /sɔ̃/ *n.m.* (*bruit*) sound.

**son**[3] /sɔ̃/ *n.m.* (*de blé*) bran.

**sonate** /sɔnat/ *n.f.* sonata.

**sonde** /sɔ̃d/ *n.f.* (*pour les forages*) drill; (*méd.*) probe.

**sond|er** /sɔ̃de/ *v.t.* sound; (*terrain*) drill; (*personne*) sound out. ∼**age** *n.m.* ∼ (**d'opinion**), (opinion) poll.

**song|e** /sɔ̃ʒ/ *n.m.* dream. ∼**er** *v.i.* dream; *v.t.* ∼**er que**, think that. ∼**er à**, think about. ∼**eur, ∼euse** *a.* pensive.

**sonnantes** /sɔnãt/ *a.f.pl.* **à six** /*etc.* **heures** ∼, on the stroke of six/*etc.*

**sonné** /sɔne/ *a.* (*fam.*) crazy; (*fatigué*) knocked out.

**sonn|er** /sɔne/ *v.t./i.* ring; (*clairon, glas*) sound; (*heure*) strike; (*domestique*) ring for. **midi** ∼**é**, well past noon. ∼**er de**, (*clairon etc.*) sound, blow.

**sonnerie** /sɔnri/ *n.f.* ringing; (*de clairon*) sound; (*mécanisme*) bell.

**sonnette** /sɔnɛt/ n.f. bell.

**sonor|e** /sɔnɔr/ a. resonant; (*onde, effets, etc.*) sound. **~ité** n.f. resonance; (*d'un instrument*) tone.

**sonoris|er** /sɔnɔrize/ v.t. (*salle*) wire for sound. **~ation** n.f. (*matériel*) sound equipment.

**sont** /sɔ̃/ *voir* **être**.

**sophistiqué** /sɔfistike/ a. sophisticated.

**sorbet** /sɔrbɛ/ n.m. sorbet.

**sorc|ier** /sɔrsje/ n.m. sorcerer. **~ière** n.f. witch.

**sordide** /sɔrdid/ a. sordid; (*lieu*) squalid.

**sort** /sɔr/ n.m. (*destin, hasard*) fate; (*condition*) lot; (*maléfice*) spell. **tirer (qch.) au ~,** draw lots (for sth.).

**sorte** /sɔrt/ n.f. sort, kind. **faire en ~ que,** see to it that.

**sortie** /sɔrti/ n.f. departure, exit; (*porte*) exit; (*promenade, dîner*) outing; (*invective*) outburst; (*parution*) appearance; (*de disque, gaz*) release; (*d'un ordinateur*) output. **~s,** (*argent*) outgoings.

**sortir†** /sɔrtir/ v.i. (*aux. être*) go out, leave; (*venir*) come out; (*aller au spectacle etc.*) go out; (*livre, film*) come out. **~ de,** (*pièce*) leave. ● v.t. (*aux. avoir*) take out; (*livre, modèle*) bring out; (*dire: fam.*) come out with. **(s')en ~,** get out of an awkward situation.

**sot,** **~te** /so, sɔt/ a. foolish.

**sottise** /sɔtiz/ n.f. foolishness; (*action, remarque*) foolish thing.

**sou** /su/ n.m. **~s,** money. **pas un ~,** not a penny.

**souche** /suʃ/ n.f. (*d'arbre*) stump; (*de famille, vigne*) stock; (*de carnet*) counterfoil.

**souci¹** /susi/ n.m. (*inquiétude*) worry; (*préoccupation*) concern. **se faire du ~,** worry.

**souci²** /susi/ n.m. (*plante*) marigold.

**soucieu|x,** **~se** /susjø, -z/ a. concerned (**de,** about).

**soucoupe** /sukup/ n.f. saucer. **~ volante,** flying saucer.

**soudain,** **~e** /sudɛ̃, -ɛn/ a. sudden. ● adv. suddenly.

**soude** /sud/ n.f. soda.

**souder** /sude/ v.t. solder; (*à la flamme*) weld.

**souffle** /sufl/ n.m. blow, puff; (*haleine*) breath; (*respiration*) breathing; (*explosion*) blast; (*vent*) breath of air.

**soufflé** /sufle/ n.m. (*culin.*) soufflé.

**souffl|er** /sufle/ v.i. blow; (*haleter*) puff. ● v.t. (*bougie*) blow out; (*poussière, fumée*) blow; (*par explosion*) destroy.

**souffrance** /sufrɑ̃s/ n.f. suffering.

**souffrir†** /sufrir/ v.i. suffer (**de,** from). ● v.t. (*endurer*) suffer.

**soufre** /sufr/ n.m. sulphur.

**souhait** /swɛ/ n.m. wish. **nos ~s de,** (*vœux*) good wishes for. **à vos ~s!,** bless you!

**souhait|er** /swete/ v.t. (*bonheur etc.*) wish for. **~er qch. à qn.,** wish s.o. sth. **~er que faire,** hope that/to do. **~able** /swetabl/ a. desirable.

**souiller** /suje/ v.t. soil.

**soûl,** **~e** /su, sul/ a. drunk.

**soulag|er** /sulaʒe/ v.t. relieve. **~ement** n.m. relief.

**soûler** /sule/ v.t. make drunk. **se ~** v. pr. get drunk.

**soulèvement** /sulɛvmɑ̃/ n.m. uprising.

**soulever** /sulve/ v.t. lift, raise. **se ~** v. pr. lift ou raise o.s. up; (*se révolter*) rise up.

**soulier** /sulje/ n.m. shoe.

**souligner** /suliɲe/ v.t. underline; (*taille, yeux*) emphasize.

**soumettre†** /sumɛtr/ v.t. (*dompter, assujettir*) subject (**à,** to); (*présenter*) submit (**à,** to). **se ~** v. pr. submit (**à,** to).

**soupape** /supap/ n.f. valve.

**soupçon** /supsɔ̃/ n.m. suspicion. **un ~ de,** (*fig.*) a touch of. **~ner** /-ɔne/ v.t. suspect. **~neux,** **~neuse** /-ɔnø, -z/ a. suspicious.

**soupe** /sup/ n.f. soup.

**souper** /supe/ n.m. supper. ● v.i. have supper.

**soupière** /supjɛr/ n.f. (soup) tureen.

**soupir** /supir/ n.m. sigh. **pousser un ~,** heave a sigh. **~er** /-e/ v.i. sigh.

**souple** /supl/ a. supple; (*règlement, caractère*) flexible. **~sse** /-ɛs/ n.f. suppleness; flexibility.

**source** /surs/ n.f. source; (*eau*) spring. **~ thermale,** hot springs.

**sourcil** /sursi/ n.m. eyebrow.

**sourd,** **~e** /sur, -d/ a. deaf; (*bruit, douleur*) dull; (*inquiétude, conflit*) silent, hidden. ● n.m., f. deaf person.

**sourire** /surir/ n.m. smile. ● v.i. smile (**à,** at).

**souris** /suri/ n.f. mouse.

**sournois,** **~e** /surnwa, -z/ a. sly, underhand.

**sous** /su/ prép. under, beneath. **~ la main,** handy. **~ la pluie,** in the rain. **~ peu,** shortly. **~ terre,** underground.

**sous-** /su/ préf. (*subordination*) sub-; (*insuffisance*) under-.

**souscr|ire** /suskrir/ v.i. **~ire à,** subscribe to. **~iption** n.f. subscription.

**sous-direct|eur,** **~rice** /sudirɛktœr, -ris/ n.m., f. assistant manager.

**sous-entend|re** /suzɑ̃tɑ̃dr/ v.t. imply. **~u** n.m. insinuation.

**sous-estimer** /suzɛstime/ v.t. underestimate.

**sous-jacent,** **~e** /suʒasɑ̃, -t/ a. underlying.

**sous-marin,** ~**e** /sumaʀɛ̃, -in/ *a.* underwater. ● *n.m.* submarine.

**sous-préfecture** /supʀefɛktyʀ/ *n.f.* subprefecture.

**sous-produit** /supʀɔdɥi/ *n.m.* by-product.

**soussigné,** ~**e** /susiɲe/ *a.* & *n.m.*, *f.* undersigned.

**sous-sol** /susɔl/ *n.m.* (*cave*) basement.

**sous-titr|e** /sutitʀ/ *n.m.* subtitle. ~**er** *v.t.* subtitle.

**soustrair|e**† /sustʀɛʀ/ *v.t.* remove; (*déduire*) subtract. ~**action** *n.f.* (*déduction*) subtraction.

**sous-trait|er** /sutʀete/ *v.t.* subcontract. ~**ant** *n.m.* subcontractor.

**sous-vêtement** /suvɛtmɑ̃/ *n.m.* undergarment. ~**s,** underwear.

**soute** /sut/ *n.f.* (*de bateau*) hold. ~ **à charbon,** coal-bunker.

**soutenir**† /sutniʀ/ *v.t.* support; (*fortifier, faire durer*) sustain; (*résister à*) withstand.

**souterrain,** ~**e** /suteʀɛ̃, -ɛn/ *a.* underground. ● *n.m.* underground passage, subway.

**soutien** /sutjɛ̃/ *n.m.* support. ~**-gorge** (*pl.* ~**s-gorge**) *n.m.* bra.

**soutirer** /sutiʀe/ *v.t.* ~ **à qn.,** extract from s.o.

**souvenir**[1] /suvniʀ/ *n.m.* memory, recollection; (*objet*) memento; (*cadeau*) souvenir. **en** ~ **de,** in memory of.

**souvenir**[2]† (**se**) /(sə)suvniʀ/ *v. pr.* **se** ~ **de,** remember. **se** ~ **que,** remember that.

**souvent** /suvɑ̃/ *adv.* often.

**souverain,** ~**e** /suvʀɛ̃, -ɛn/ ● *n.m.*, *f.* sovereign. ~**eté** /-ɛnte/ *n.f.* sovereignty.

**soviétique** /sɔvjetik/ *a.* Soviet. ● *n.m./f.* Soviet citizen.

**soyeu|x,** ~**se** /swajø, -z/ *a.* silky.

**spacieu|x,** ~**se** /spasjø, -z/ *a.* spacious.

**spaghetti** /spageti/ *n.m. pl.* spaghetti.

**sparadrap** /spaʀadʀa/ *n.m.* sticking-plaster.

**spat|ial** (*m. pl.* ~**iaux**) /spasjal, -jo/ *a.* space.

**spatule** /spatyl/ *n.f.* spatula.

**speaker,** ~**ine** /spikœʀ, -ʀin/ *n.m.*, *f.* announcer.

**spéc|ial** (*m. pl.* ~**iaux**) /spesjal, -jo/ *a.* special; (*singulier*) peculiar. ~**ialement** *adv.* especially; (*exprès*) specially.

**spécialis|er (se)** /(sə)spesjalize/ *v. pr.* specialize (**dans,** in). ~**ation** *n.f.* specialization.

**spécialiste** /spesjalist/ *n.m./f.* specialist.

**spécialité** /spesjalite/ *n.f.* speciality.

**spécif|ier** /spesifje/ *v.t.* specify. ~**ication** *n.f.* specification.

**spécifique** /spesifik/ *a.* specific.

**spécimen** /spesimɛn/ *n.m.* specimen.

**spectacle** /spɛktakl/ *n.m.* sight, spectacle; (*représentation*) show.

**spectaculaire** /spɛktakylɛʀ/ *a.* spectacular.

**specta|teur,** ~**trice** /spɛktatœʀ, -tʀis/ *n.m.*, *f.* onlooker; (*sport*) spectator. **les** ~**teurs,** (*théâtre*) the audience.

**spectre** /spɛktʀ/ *n.m.* (*revenant*) spectre; (*images*) spectrum.

**spécul|er** /spekyle/ *v.i.* speculate. ~**ateur,** ~**atrice** *n.m.*, *f.* speculator. ~**ation** *n.f.* speculation.

**spéléologie** /speleɔlɔʒi/ *n.f.* cave exploration, pot-holing.

**sperme** /spɛʀm/ *n.m.* sperm.

**sph|ère** /sfɛʀ/ *n.f.* sphere. ~**érique** *a.* spherical.

**sphinx** /sfɛ̃ks/ *n.m.* sphinx.

**spirale** /spiʀal/ *n.f.* spiral.

**spirituel,** ~**le** /spiʀitɥɛl/ *a.* spiritual; (*amusant*) witty.

**spiritueux** /spiʀitɥø/ *n.m.* (*alcool*) spirit.

**splend|ide** /splɑ̃did/ *a.* splendid. ~**eur** *n.f.* splendour.

**sponsor** /spɔ̃sɔʀ/ *n.m.* sponsor. ~**iser** *v.t.* sponsor.

**spontané** /spɔ̃tane/ *a.* spontaneous. ~**ité** *n.f.* spontaneity. ~**ment** *adv.* spontaneously.

**sport** /spɔʀ/ *n.m.* sport. ● *a. invar.* (*vêtements*) casual.

**sporti|f,** ~**ve** /spɔʀtif, -v/ *a.* sporting; (*physique*) athletic; (*résultats*) sports. ● *n.m.* sportsman. ● *n.f.* sportswoman.

**spot** /spɔt/ *n.m.* spotlight; (*publicitaire*) ad.

**spray** /spʀe/ *n.m.* spray; (*méd.*) inhaler.

**square** /skwaʀ/ *n.m.* (*public*) garden.

**squash** /skwaʃ/ *n.m.* squash.

**squelette** /skəlɛt/ *n.m.* skeleton.

**stabiliser** /stabilize/ *v.t.* stabilize.

**stab|le** /stabl/ *a.* stable. ~**ilité** *n.f.* stability.

**stade**[1] /stad/ *n.m.* (*sport*) stadium.

**stade**[2] /stad/ *n.m.* (*phase*) stage.

**stag|e** /staʒ/ *n.m.* course. ~**iaire** *a.* & *n.m./f.* course member; (*apprenti*) trainee.

**stand** /stɑ̃d/ *n.m.* stand, stall.

**standard**[1] /stɑ̃daʀ/ *n.m.* switchboard. ~**iste** /-dist/ *n.m./f.* switchboard operator.

**standard**[2] /stɑ̃daʀ/ *a. invar.* standard.

**standing** /stɑ̃diŋ/ *n.m.* status, standing. **de** ~, (*hôtel etc.*) luxury.

**star** /staʀ/ *n.f.* (*actrice*) star.

**starter** /staʀtɛʀ/ *n.m.* (*auto.*) choke.

**station** /stasjɔ̃/ *n.f.* station; (*halte*) stop. ~ **balnéaire,** seaside resort. ~ **de taxis,** taxi rank. ~**-service** (*pl.* ~**s-service**) *n.f.* service station. ~ **thermale,** spa.

**stationn|er** /stasjɔne/ *v.i.* park. ~**ement** *n.m.* parking.

**statistique** /statistik/ *n.f.* statistic; (*science*) statistics. ● *a.* statistical.

**statue** /staty/ *n.f.* statue.

**statut** /staty/ *n.m.* status. ~**s**, (*règles*) statutes.

**steak** /stɛk/ *n.m.* steak.

**sténo** /steno/ *n.f.* (*personne*) stenographer; (*sténographie*) shorthand.

**stéréo** /stereo/ *n.f. & a. invar.* stereo.

**stéril|e** /steril/ *a.* sterile. ~**ité** *n.f.* sterility.

**stérilet** /sterilɛ/ *n.m.* coil, IUD.

**stérilis|er** /sterilize/ *v.t.* sterilize. ~**ation** *n.f.* sterilization.

**stéroïde** /steroid/ *a. & n.m.* steroid.

**stimul|er** /stimyle/ *v.t.* stimulate. ~**ant** *n.m.* stimulus; (*médicament*) stimulant. ~**ateur cardiaque,** pacemaker.

**stock** /stɔk/ *n.m.* stock. ~**er** *v.t.* stock. ~**iste** *n.m.* stockist; (*Amer.*) dealer.

**stop** /stɔp/ *int.* stop. ● *n.m.* stop sign; (*feu arrière*) brake light. **faire du ~,** (*fam.*) hitchhike.

**stopper** /stɔpe/ *v.t./i.* stop.

**store** /stɔr/ *n.m.* blind.

**strapontin** /strapɔ̃tɛ̃/ *n.m.* folding seat, jump seat.

**stratég|ie** /strateʒi/ *n.f.* strategy. ~**ique** *a.* strategic.

**stress** /strɛs/ *n.* stress, ~**ant** *a.* stressful. ~**er** *v.t.* put under stress.

**strict** /strikt/ *a.* strict; (*tenue, vérité*) plain. **le ~ minimum,** the absolute minimum. ~**ement** *adv.* strictly.

**strip-tease** /striptiz/ *n.m.* strip-tease.

**strophe** /strɔf/ *n.f.* stanza, verse.

**structur|e** /stryktyr/ *n.f.* structure. ~**er** *v.t.* structure.

**studieu|x, ~se** /stydjø, -z/ *a.* studious.

**studio** /stydjo/ *n.m.* (*d'artiste, de télévision, etc.*) studio; (*logement*) studio flat, bed-sitter.

**stupéf|ait, ~aite** /stypefɛ, -t/ *a.* amazed. ~**action** *n.f.* amazement.

**stupid|e** /stypid/ *a.* stupid. ~**ité** *n.f.* stupidity.

**style** /stil/ *n.m.* style.

**styliste** /stilist/ *n.m./f.* fashion designer.

**stylo** /stilo/ *n.m.* pen. ~ **(à) bille,** ball-point pen. ~ **(à) encre,** fountain-pen.

**su** /sy/ *voir* **savoir.**

**subconscient, ~e** /sypkɔ̃sjɑ̃, -t/ *a. & n.m.* subconscious.

**subir** /sybir/ *v.t.* suffer; (*traitement, expériences*) undergo.

**subit, ~e** /sybi, -t/ *a.* sudden. ~**ement** /-tmɑ̃/ *adv.* suddenly.

**subjecti|f, ~ve** /sybʒɛktif, -v/ *a.* subjective. ~**vité** *n.f.* subjectivity.

**subjonctif** /sybʒɔ̃ktif/ *a. & n.m.* subjunctive.

**sublime** /syblim/ *a.* sublime.

**submerger** /sybmɛrʒe/ *v.t.* submerge; (*fig.*) overwhelm.

**subside** /sybzid/ *n.m.* grant.

**subsist|er** /sybziste/ *v.i.* subsist; (*durer, persister*) exist. ~**ance** *n.f.* subsistence.

**substance** /sypstɑ̃s/ *n.f.* substance.

**substantif** /sypstɑ̃tif/ *n.m.* noun.

**substit|uer** /sypstitye/ *v.t.* substitute (**à,** for). **se ~uer à,** (*remplacer*) substitute for; (*évincer*) take over from. ~**ution** *n.f.* substitution.

**subtil** /syptil/ *a.* subtle. ~**ité** *n.f.* subtlety.

**subvenir** /sybvənir/ *v.i.* ~ **à,** provide for.

**subvention** /sybvɑ̃sjɔ̃/ *n.f.* subsidy. ~**ner** /-jɔne/ *v.t.* subsidize.

**subversi|f, ~ve** /sybvɛrsif, -v/ *a.* subversive.

**subversion** /sybvɛrsjɔ̃/ *n.f.* subversion.

**succéder** /syksede/ *v.i.* ~ **à,** succeed. **se ~** *v. pr.* succeed one another.

**succès** /syksɛ/ *n.m.* success. **avoir du ~,** be a success.

**successeur** /syksesœr/ *n.m.* successor.

**successi|f, ~ve** /syksesif, -v/ *a.* successive. ~**vement** *adv.* successively.

**succession** /syksesjɔ̃/ *n.f.* succession; (*jurid.*) inheritance.

**succulent, ~e** /sykylɑ̃, -t/ *a.* succulent.

**succursale** /sykyrsal/ *n.f.* (*comm.*) branch.

**sucer** /syse/ *v.t.* suck.

**sucette** /sysɛt/ *n.f.* (*bonbon*) lollipop; (*tétine*) dummy.

**sucr|e** /sykr/ *n.m.* sugar. ~**ier** *n.m.* (*récipient*) sugar-bowl.

**sucr|er** /sykre/ *v.t.* sugar, sweeten. ~**é** *a.* sweet; (*additionné de sucre*) sweetened.

**sucreries** /sykrəri/ *n.f. pl.* sweets.

**sud** /syd/ *n.m.* south. ● *a. invar.* south; (*partie*) southern; (*direction*) southerly. ~ **africain, ~africaine** *a. & n.m., f.* South African. ~**est** *n.m.* south-east. ~**ouest** *n.m.* south-west.

**Suède** /sɥɛd/ *n.f.* Sweden.

**suédois, ~e** /sɥedwa, -z/ *a.* Swedish. ● *n.m., f.* Swede. ● *n.m.* (*lang.*) Swedish.

**sueur** /sɥœr/ *n.f.* sweat. **en ~,** sweating.

**suff|ire†** /syfir/ *v.i.* be enough (**à qn.,** for s.o.). **il ~it de faire,** one only has to do. ~**ire à,** (*besoin*) satisfy.

**suffis|ant, ~ante** /syfizɑ̃, -t/ *a.* sufficient; (*vaniteux*) conceited. ~**amment** *adv.* sufficiently. ~**amment de,** sufficient.

**suffixe** /syfiks/ *n.m.* suffix.

**suffoquer** /syfɔke/ *v.t./i.* choke, suffocate.

**suffrage** /syfraʒ/ *n.m.* (*voix: pol.*) vote; (*modalité*) suffrage.

**sugg|érer** /sygʒere/ *v.t.* suggest. ~**estion** /-ʒɛstjɔ̃/ *n.f.* suggestion.

**suicide** /sɥisid/ n.m. suicide.

**suicider (se)** //(sə)sɥiside/ v. pr. commit suicide.

**suis** /sɥi/ voir être, suivre.

**Suisse** /sɥis/ n.f. Switzerland.

**suisse** /sɥis/ a. & n.m. Swiss. ∼**sse** /-ɛs/ n.f. Swiss (woman).

**suite** /sɥit/ n.f. continuation, rest; (d'un film) sequel; (série) series; (appartement, escorte) suite; (résultat) consequence. ∼**s**, (de maladie) after-effects. **à la** ∼, **de** ∼, (successivement) in succession. **faire** ∼ (**à**), follow. **par la** ∼, afterwards. ∼ **à votre lettre du,** further to your letter of the.

**suivant'**, ∼**e** /sɥivã, -t/ a. following, next. ● n.m., f. following ou next person.

**suivant²** /sɥivã/ prép. (selon) according to.

**suivi** /sɥivi/ a. steady, sustained; (cohérent) consistent. **peu**/**très** ∼, (cours) poorly-/well-attended.

**suivre†** /sɥivr/ v.t./i. follow; (comprendre) keep up (with), follow. **se** ∼ v. pr. follow each other. **faire** ∼, (courrier etc.) forward.

**sujet** /syʒɛ/ n.m. (matière, individu) subject; (motif) cause; (gram.) subject. **au** ∼ **de,** about.

**sulfurique** /sylfyrik/ a. sulphuric.

**super** /sypɛr/ n.m. (essence) four-star. ● a. invar. (fam.) great. ● adv. (fam.) ultra, fantastically.

**superbe** /sypɛrb/ a. superb.

**supérette** /sypɛrɛt/ n.f. minimarket.

**superficie** /sypɛrfisi/ n.f. area.

**superficiel,** ∼**le** /sypɛrfisjɛl/ a. superficial.

**superflu** /sypɛrfly/ a. superfluous. ● n.m. (excédent) surplus.

**supérieur,** ∼**e** /syperjœr/ a. (plus haut) upper; (quantité, nombre) greater (**à,** than); (études, principe) higher (**à,** than); (meilleur, hautain) superior (**à,** to). ● n.m., f. superior.

**supériorité** /syperjorite/ n.f. superiority.

**supermarché** /sypɛrmarʃe/ n.m. supermarket.

**superposer** /sypɛrpoze/ v.t. superimpose.

**superproduction** /sypɛrprɔdyksjɔ̃/ n.f. (film) spectacular.

**superstit|ion** /sypɛrstisjɔ̃/ n.f. superstition. ∼**ieux,** ∼**ieuse** a. superstitious.

**superviser** /sypɛrvize/ v.t. supervise.

**suppléer** /syplee/ v.t. (remplacer) replace; (ajouter) supply. ● v.i. ∼ **à,** (compenser) make up for.

**supplément** /syplemã/ n.m. (argent) extra charge; (de frites, légumes) extra portion. **en** ∼, extra. **un** ∼ **de,** (travail etc.) extra. **payer pour un** ∼ **de bagages,** pay extra for excess luggage. ∼**aire** /-tɛr/ a. extra, additional.

**supplice** /syplis/ n.m. torture.

**supplier** /syplije/ v.t. beg, beseech (**de,** to).

**support** /sypɔr/ n.m. support.

**support|er'** /sypɔrte/ v.t. (endurer) bear; (subir) suffer; (soutenir) support; (résister à) withstand. ∼**able** a. bearable.

**supporter²** /sypɔrtɛr/ n.m. (sport) supporter.

**suppos|er** /sypoze/ v.t. suppose; (impliquer) imply. ∼**ition** n.f. supposition.

**suppositoire** /sypozitwar/ n.m. suppository.

**suppr|imer** /syprime/ v.t. get rid of, remove; (annuler) cancel; (mot) delete.

**suprême** /syprɛm/ a. supreme.

**sur** /syr/ prép. on, upon; (pardessus) over; (au sujet de) about, on; (proportion) out of; (mesure) by. **aller**/**tourner**/etc. ∼, go/turn/ etc. towards. **mettre**/**jeter**/etc. ∼, put/ throw/etc. on to. ∼**-le-champ** adv. immediately. ∼ **mesure,** made to measure. ∼ **place,** on the spot. ∼ **ce,** hereupon.

**sur-** /syr/ préf. over-.

**sûr** /syr/ a. certain, sure; (sans danger) safe; (digne de confiance) reliable; (main) steady; (jugement) sound.

**surcharge** /syrʃarʒ/ n.f. overloading; (poids) extra load.

**sureau** (pl. ∼**x**) /syro/ n.m. (arbre) elder.

**sûrement** /syrmã/ adv. certainly; (sans danger) safely.

**surestimer** /syrɛstime/ v.t. overestimate.

**sûreté** /syrte/ n.f. safety; (garantie) surety; (d'un geste) steadiness. **être en** ∼, be safe. **S**∼ **(nationale),** division of French Ministère de l'Intérieur in charge of police.

**surexcité** /syrɛksite/ a. very excited.

**surf** /syrf/ n.m. surfing.

**surface** /syrfas/ n.f. surface. **en** ∼, (fig.) superficially.

**surgelé** /syrʒəle/ a. (deep-)frozen. **(aliments)** ∼**s,** frozen food.

**surgir** /syrʒir/ v.i. appear (suddenly); (difficulté) arise.

**surlendemain** /syrlãdmɛ̃/ n.m. **le** ∼, two days later. **le** ∼ **de,** two days after.

**surligneur** /syrliɲœr/ n.m. highlighter (pen).

**surmen|er** /syrməne/ v.t., **se** ∼**er** v. pr. overwork. ∼**age** n.m. overworking; (méd.) overwork.

**surmonter** /syrmɔ̃te/ v.t. (vaincre) overcome, surmount; (être au-dessus de) surmount, top.

**surnager** /syrnaʒe/ v.i. float.

**surnaturel,** ∼**le** /syrnatyrɛl/ a. supernatural.

**surnom** /syrnɔ̃/ n.m. nickname.

**surplomb** /syrplɔ̃/ n.m. **en** ∼, overhanging. ∼**er** /-be/ v.t./i. overhang.

**surplus** /syrply/ n.m. surplus.

**surpr|endre**† /syrprãdr/ *v.t.* (*étonner*) surprise; (*prendre au dépourvu*) catch, surprise; (*entendre*) overhear. **~enant, ~enante** *a.* surprising. **~is, ~ise** *a.* surprised (**de**, at).

**surprise** /syrpriz/ *n.f.* surprise. **~-partie** (*pl.* **~s-parties**) *n.f.* party.

**surréalisme** /syrrealism/ *n.m.* surrealism.

**sursaut** /syrso/ *n.m.* start, jump. **~er** /-te/ *v.i.* start, jump.

**sursis** /syrsi/ *n.m.* reprieve. **deux ans (de prison) avec ~**, a two-year suspended sentence.

**surtaxe** /syrtaks/ *n.f.* surcharge.

**surtout** /syrtu/ *adv.* especially, mainly; (*avant tout*) above all. **~ pas**, certainly not.

**surveillant, ~e** /syrvɛjã, -t/ *n.m., f.* (*de prison*) warder; (*au lycée*) supervisor (in charge of discipline).

**surveill|er** /syrveje/ *v.t.* watch; (*travaux, élèves*) supervise. **~ance** *n.f.* watch; supervision; (*de la police*) surveillance.

**survenir** /syrvənir/ *v.i.* occur, come about; (*personne*) turn up; (*événement*) take place.

**survêtement** /syrvɛtmã/ *n.m.* (*sport*) track suit.

**surviv|re**† /syrvivr/ *v.i.* survive. **~re à**, (*conflit etc.*) survive; (*personne*) outlive. **~ant, ~ante** *a.* surviving; *n.m., f.* survivor.

**survoler** /syrvole/ *v.t.* fly over.

**susceptib|le** /sysɛptibl/ *a.* touchy. **~ilité** *n.f.* susceptibility.

**susciter** /sysite/ *v.t.* (*éveiller*) arouse; (*occasionner*) create.

**suspect, ~e** /syspɛ, -ɛkt/ *a.* (*témoignage*) suspect; (*individu*) suspicious. **~ de**, suspected of. ● *n.m., f.* suspect. **~er** /-ɛkte/ *v.t.* suspect.

**suspendre** /syspãdr/ *v.t.* (*arrêter*) suspend; (*accrocher*) hang (up).

**suspense** /syspãs/ *n.m.* suspense.

**suspicion** /syspisjɔ̃/ *n.f.* suspicion.

**suture** /sytyr/ *n.f.* **point de ~**, stitch.

**svelte** /svɛlt/ *a.* slender.

**S.V.P.** *abrév.* *voir* **s'il vous plaît**.

**sweat-shirt** /switʃœrt/ *n.m.* sweat-shirt.

**syllabe** /silab/ *n.f.* syllable.

**symbol|e** /sɛ̃bɔl/ *n.m.* symbol. **~ique** *a.* symbolic(al).

**symétr|ie** /simetri/ *n.f.* symmetry. **~ique** *a.* symmetrical.

**sympa** /sɛ̃pa/ *a. invar.* (*fam.*) nice. **sois ~**, be a pal.

**sympath|ie** /sɛ̃pati/ *n.f.* (*goût*) liking; (*affinité*) affinity; (*condoléances*) sympathy. **~ique** *a.* nice, pleasant.

**symphon|ie** /sɛ̃fɔni/ *n.f.* symphony. **~ique** *a.* symphonic; (*orchestre*) symphony.

**symptôme** /sɛ̃ptom/ *n.m.* symptom.

**synagogue** /sinagɔg/ *n.f.* synagogue.

**syncope** /sɛ̃kɔp/ *n.f.* (*méd.*) black-out.

**syndic** /sɛ̃dik/ *n.m.* **~ (d'immeuble)**, managing agent.

**syndic|at** /sɛ̃dika/ *n.m.* (trade) union. **~at d'initiative**, tourist office. **~al** (*m. pl.* **~aux**) *a.* (trade-)union. **~aliste** *n.m./f.* trade-unionist; *a.* (trade-)union.

**syndiqué, ~e** /sɛ̃dike/ *n.m., f.* (trade-)union member.

**synonyme** /sinɔnim/ *a.* synonymous. ● *n.m.* synonym.

**synthétique** /sɛ̃tetik/ *a.* synthetic.

**synthé(tiseur)** /sɛ̃te(tizœr)/ *n.m.* synthesizer.

**syphilis** /sifilis/ *n.f.* syphilis.

**Syrie** /siri/ *n.f.* Syria.

**syrien, ~ne** /sirjɛ̃, -jɛn/ *a. & n.m., f.* Syrian.

**systématique** /sistematik/ *a.* systematic.

**système** /sistɛm/ *n.m.* system.

••••••••••••••••••••••••••••••

# Tt

••••••••••••••••••••••••••••••

**t'** /t/ *voir* **te**.

**ta** /ta/ *voir* **ton**[1].

**tabac** /taba/ *n.m.* tobacco; (*magasin*) tobacconist's shop.

**table** /tabl/ *n.f.* table. **à ~!**, come and eat! **~ de nuit**, bedside table. **~ des matières**, table of contents. **~ roulante**, (tea-)trolley.

**tableau** (*pl.* **~x**) /tablo/ *n.m.* picture; (*peinture*) painting; (*panneau*) board; (*graphique*) chart; (*liste*) list. **~ (noir)**, blackboard. **~ d'affichage**, notice-board. **~ de bord**, dashboard.

**tablette** /tablɛt/ *n.f.* shelf. **~ de chocolat**, bar of chocolate.

**tablier** /tablije/ *n.m.* apron.

**tabouret** /taburɛ/ *n.m.* stool.

**tabulateur** /tabylatœr/ *n.m.* tabulator.

**tache** /taʃ/ *n.f.* mark, spot; (*salissure*) stain. **faire ~ d'huile**, spread. **~ de rousseur**, freckle.

**tâche** /taʃ/ *n.f.* task, job.

**tacher** /taʃe/ *v.t.* stain. **se ~** *v. pr.* (*personne*) get stains on one's clothes.

**tâcher** /taʃe/ *v.i.* **~ de faire**, try to do.

**tact** /takt/ *n.m.* tact.

**tactique** /taktik/ *a.* tactical. ● *n.f.* tactics. **une ~**, a tactic.

**taie** /tɛ/ *n.f.* **~ d'oreiller**, pillowcase.

**taille**[1] /taj/ *n.f.* (*milieu du corps*) waist; (*hauteur*) height; (*grandeur*) size. **de ~**, sizeable.

**taill|e²** /taj/ *n.f.* cutting; pruning; (*forme*) cut. **~er** *v.t.* cut; (*arbre*) prune; (*crayon*) sharpen; (*vêtement*) cut out. **~e-crayon(s)** *n.m. invar.* pencil-sharpener.

**tailleur** /tɑjœr/ *n.m.* tailor; (*costume*) lady's suit. **en ~,** cross-legged.

**taillis** /taji/ *n.m.* copse.

**taire†** /tɛr/ *v.t.* say nothing about. **se ~** *v. pr.* be silent *ou* quiet; (*devenir silencieux*) fall silent. **faire ~,** silence.

**talc** /talk/ *n.m.* talcum powder.

**talent** /talɑ̃/ *n.m.* talent.

**talon** /talɔ̃/ *n.m.* heel; (*de chèque*) stub.

**talus** /taly/ *n.m.* embankment.

**tambour** /tɑ̃bur/ *n.m.* drum; (*personne*) drummer; (*porte*) revolving door.

**tamis** /tami/ *n.m.* sieve. **~er** /-ze/ *v.t.* sieve.

**Tamise** /tamiz/ *n.f.* Thames.

**tampon** /tɑ̃pɔ̃/ *n.m.* (*pour boucher*) plug; (*ouate*) wad, pad; (*timbre*) stamp; (*de train*) buffer. **~ (hygiénique),** tampon.

**tamponner** /tɑ̃pɔne/ *v.t.* (*timbrer*) stamp; (*plaie*) dab.

**tandem** /tɑ̃dɛm/ *n.m.* (*bicyclette*) tandem; (*personnes: fig.*) duo.

**tandis que** /tɑ̃dik(ə)/ *conj.* while.

**tanguer** /tɑ̃ge/ *v.i.* pitch.

**tank** /tɑ̃k/ *n.m.* tank.

**tann|er** /tane/ *v.t.* tan. **~ée** *a.* (*visage*) tanned, weather-beaten.

**tant** /tɑ̃/ *adv.* (*travailler, manger, etc.*) so much. **~ (de),** (*quantité*) so much; (*nombre*) so many. **~ que,** as long as. **~ mieux!,** fine!, all the better! **~ pis!,** too bad!

**tante** /tɑ̃t/ *n.f.* aunt.

**tantôt** /tɑ̃to/ *adv.* sometimes; (*cet après-midi*) this afternoon.

**tapage** /tapaʒ/ *n.m.* din.

**tapant, ~e** /tapɑ̃, -t/ *a.* **à deux/trois/***etc.* **heures~es** at exactly two/three/*etc.* o'clock.

**tape** /tap/ *n.f.* slap.

**taper** /tape/ *v.t.* bang; (*enfant*) slap; (*emprunter: fam.*) touch for money. **~ (à la machine),** type. ● *v.i.* (*cogner*) bang; (*soleil*) beat down.

**tapis** /tapi/ *n.m.* carpet; (*petit*) rug; (*aux cartes*) baize. **~ de bain,** bath mat. **~ roulant,** (*pour objets*) conveyor belt.

**tapiss|er** /tapise/ *v.t.* (wall)paper; (*fig.*) cover (**de,** with). **~erie** *n.f.* tapestry; (*papier peint*) wallpaper.

**tapoter** /tapɔte/ *v.t.* tap, pat.

**taquin, ~e** /takɛ̃, -in/ *a.* fond of teasing. ● *n.m., f.* tease(r). **~er** /-ine/ *v.t.* tease.

**tard** /tar/ *adv.* late. **au plus ~,** at the latest. **plus ~,** later.

**tard|er** /tarde/ *v.i.* be a long time coming. **~er (à faire),** take a long time (doing), delay (doing). **sans (plus) ~er,** without (further) delay.

**tardi|f, ~ve** /tardif, -v/ *a.* late; (*regrets*) belated.

**tare** /tar/ *n.f.* (*défaut*) defect.

**targette** /tarʒɛt/ *n.f.* bolt.

**tarif** /tarif/ *n.m.* tariff; (*de train, taxi*) fare. **~s postaux,** postage *ou* postal rates. **~aire** *a.* tariff.

**tarir** /tarir/ *v.t./i.,* **se ~** *v. pr.* dry up.

**tartare** /tartar/ *a.* (*culin.*) tartar.

**tarte** /tart/ *n.f.* tart.

**tartin|e** /tartin/ *n.f.* slice of bread. **~e beurrée,** slice of bread and butter. **~er** *v.t.* spread.

**tartre** /tartr/ *n.m.* (*bouilloire*) fur, calcium deposit; (*dents*) tartar.

**tas** /ta/ *n.m.* pile, heap. **un** *ou* **des ~ de,** (*fam.*) lots of.

**tasse** /tas/ *n.f.* cup. **~ à thé,** teacup.

**tasser** /tase/ *v.t.* pack, squeeze; (*terre*) pack (down).

**tâter** /tate/ *v.t.* feel; (*fig.*) sound out. ● *v.i.* **~ de,** try out.

**tâtonn|er** /tatɔne/ *v.i.* grope about. **~ements** *n.m. pl.* (*essais*) trial and error.

**tâtons (à)** /(a)tatɔ̃/ *adv.* **avancer** *ou* **marcher à ~,** grope one's way along.

**tatou|er** /tatwe/ *v.t.* tattoo. **~age** *n.m.* (*dessin*) tattoo.

**taudis** /todi/ *n.m.* hovel.

**taule** /tol/ *n.f.* (*fam.*) prison.

**taupe** /top/ *n.f.* mole.

**taureau** (*pl.* **~x**) /tɔro/ *n.m.* bull. **le T~,** Taurus.

**taux** /to/ *n.m.* rate.

**taverne** /tavɛrn/ *n.f.* tavern.

**tax|e** /taks/ *n.f.* tax. **~e sur la valeur ajoutée,** value added tax. **~er** *v.t.* tax; (*produit*) fix the price of.

**taxi** /taksi/ *n.m.* taxi(-cab); (*personne: fam.*) taxi-driver.

**taxiphone** /taksifɔn/ *n.m.* pay phone.

**Tchécoslovaquie** /tʃekɔslɔvaki/ *n.f.* Czechoslovakia.

**tchèque** /tʃɛk/ *a. & n.m./f.* Czech.

**te, t'*** /tə, t/ *pron.* you; (*indirect*) (to) you; (*réfléchi*) yourself.

**technicien, ~ne** /tɛknisjɛ̃, -jɛn/ *n.m., f.* technician.

**technique** /tɛknik/ *a.* technical. ● *n.f.* technique. **~ment** *adv.* technically.

**technolog|ie** /tɛknɔlɔʒi/ *n.f.* technology. **~ique** *a.* technological.

**teck** /tɛk/ *n.m.* teak.

**tee-shirt** /tiʃœrt/ *n.m.* tee-shirt.

**teindre†** /tɛ̃dr/ *v.t.* dye. **se ~ les cheveux** *v. pr.* dye one's hair.

**teint** /tɛ̃/ *n.m.* complexion.

**teinte** /tɛ̃t/ *n.f.* shade, tint.

**teintur|e** /tɛtyr/ n.f. dyeing; (*produit*) dye. **~erie** n.f. (*boutique*) dry-cleaner's.

**tel, ~le** /tɛl/ a. such. **~ quel**, (just) as it is.

**télé** /tele/ n.f. (*fam.*) TV.

**télécommande** /telekɔmɑ̃d/ n.f. remote control.

**télécommunications** /telekɔmynika- sjɔ̃/ n.f. pl. telecommunications.

**télécopi|e** /telekɔpi/ n.f. tele(fax). **~eur** n.m. fax machine.

**téléfilm** /telefilm/ n.m. (tele)film.

**télégramme** /telegram/ n.m. telegram.

**télégraph|e** /telegraf/ n.m. telegraph. **~ier** v.t./i. **~ier (à)**, cable. **~ique** a. telegraphic; (*fil, poteau*) telegraph.

**téléguid|er** /telegide/ v.t. control by radio. **~é** a. radio-controlled.

**téléphérique** /teleferik/ n.m. cable-car.

**téléphon|e** /telefɔn/ n.m. (tele)phone. **~er** v.t./i. **~er (à)**, (tele)phone. **~ique** a. (tele)phone. **~iste** n.m./f. operator.

**télésiège** /telesjɛʒ/ n.m. chair-lift.

**téléski** /teleski/ n.m. ski tow.

**téléspecta|teur, ~trice** /telespɛkta- tœr, -tris/ n.m., f. (television) viewer.

**télévente** /televɑ̃t/ n.f. telesales.

**télévis|é** /televize/ a. **émission ~ée**, television programme. **~eur** n.m. television set.

**télévision** /televizjɔ̃/ n.f. television.

**télex** /telɛks/ n.m. telex.

**télexer** /telɛkse/ v.t. telex.

**telle** /tɛl/ voir **tel**.

**tellement** /tɛlmɑ̃/ adv. (*tant*) so much; (*si*) so. **~ de**, (*quantité*) so much; (*nombre*) so many.

**témoignage** /temwaɲaʒ/ n.m. testimony, evidence; (*récit*) account. **~ de**, (*sentiment*) token of.

**témoigner** /temwaɲe/ v.i. testify (**de**, to).

**témoin** /temwɛ̃/ n.m. witness.

**tempérament** /tɑ̃peramɑ̃/ n.m. temperament; (*physique*) constitution. **à ~,** (*acheter*) on hire-purchase.

**température** /tɑ̃peratyr/ n.f. temperature.

**tempête** /tɑ̃pɛt/ n.f. storm.

**temple** /tɑ̃pl/ n.m. temple; (*protestant*) church.

**temporaire** /tɑ̃pɔrɛr/ a. temporary. **~ment** adv. temporarily.

**temps**[1] /tɑ̃/ n.m. time; (*gram.*) tense; (*étape*) stage. **à ~ partiel/plein**, part-/full-time. **ces derniers ~**, lately. **dans quelque ~**, in a while. **de ~ en temps**, from time to time.

**temps**[2] /tɑ̃/ n.m. weather. **quel ~ fait-il?**, what's the weather like?

**tenace** /tanas/ a. stubborn.

**tendance** /tɑ̃dɑ̃s/ n.f. tendency; (*opinions*) leanings; (*évolution*) trend. **avoir ~ à**, have a tendency to, tend to.

**tendon** /tɑ̃dɔ̃/ n.m. tendon.

**tendre**[1] /tɑ̃dr/ v.t. stretch; (*piège*) set; (*bras*) stretch out; (*main*) hold out; (*cou*) crane; (*tapisserie*) hang. **~ à qn.,** hold out to s.o.

**tendre**[2] /tɑ̃dr/ a. tender; (*couleur, bois*) soft. **~ment** /-əmɑ̃/ adv. tenderly. **~sse** /-ɛs/ n.f. tenderness.

**tendu** /tɑ̃dy/ a. (*corde*) tight; (*personne, situation*) tense.

**teneur** /tənœr/ n.f. content.

**tenir**† /tənir/ v.t. hold; (*pari, promesse, hôtel*) keep; (*place*) take up; (*propos*) utter; (*rôle*) play. **~ propre/ chaud**/etc., keep clean/ warm/ etc. ● v.i. hold. **~ à**, be attached to. **~ à faire**, be anxious to do. **~ dans**, fit into. **se ~** v. pr. (*rester*) remain; (*debout*) stand; (*avoir lieu*) be held. **se ~ à**, hold on to. **se ~ bien**, behave o.s. **se ~ compte de**, take into account. **tiens!,** (*surprise*) hey!

**tennis** /tenis/ n.m. tennis; (*terrain*) tennis-court. ● n.m. pl. (*chaussures*) sneakers. **~ de table**, table tennis.

**ténor** /tenɔr/ n.m. tenor.

**tension** /tɑ̃sjɔ̃/ n.f. tension. **avoir de la ~,** have high blood-pressure.

**tentative** /tɑ̃tativ/ n.f. attempt.

**tente** /tɑ̃t/ n.f. tent.

**tenter**[1] /tɑ̃te/ v.t. try (**de faire**, to do).

**tent|er**[2] /tɑ̃te/ v.t. (*allécher*) tempt. **~é de**, tempted to. **~ation** n.f. temptation.

**tenture** /tɑ̃tyr/ n.f. (wall) hanging. **~s,** drapery.

**tenu** /təny/ voir **tenir**. ● a. **bien ~**, well-kept. **~ de**, obliged to.

**tenue** /təny/ n.f. (*habillement*) dress; (*de sport*) clothes; (*de maison*) upkeep; (*conduite*) (good) behaviour; (*maintien*) posture. **~ de soirée**, evening dress.

**ter** /tɛr/ a. invar. (*numéro*) B, b.

**terme** /tɛrm/ n.m. (*mot*) term; (*date limite*) time-limit; (*fin*) end; (*date de loyer*) term.

**termin|al, ~ale** (m. pl. **~aux**) /tɛrminal, -o/ a. terminal. (**classe**) **~ale**, sixth form.

**termin|er** /tɛrmine/ v.t./i. finish; (*soirée, débat*) end, finish. **se ~er** v. pr. end (**par**, with). **~aison** n.f. (*gram.*) ending.

**terminus** /tɛrminys/ n.m. terminus.

**terne** /tɛrn/ a. dull, drab.

**terrain** /tɛrɛ̃/ n.m. ground; (*parcelle*) piece of land; (*à bâtir*) plot. **~ de camping**, camp-site. **~ de golf**, golf-course. **~ de jeu**, play-ground. **~ vague**, waste ground.

**terrasse** /teras/ n.f. terrace; (*de café*) pavement area.

**terre** /tɛr/ n.f. (*planète, matière*) earth; (*étendue, pays*) land; (*sol*) ground; (*domaine*) estate. **à ~**, (*naut.*) ashore. **par ~**, (*tomber, jeter*) to the ground; (*s'asseoir, poser*) on the ground. **~ (cuite)**, terracotta.

**terreau** /tɛro/ n.m. invar. compost.

**terrestre** /tɛrɛstr/ *a.* land; (*de notre planète*) earth's; (*fig.*) earthly.

**terreur** /tɛrœr/ *n.f.* terror.

**terrible** /tɛribl/ *a.* terrible; (*formidable*: *fam.*) terrific.

**terrier** /tɛrje/ *n.m.* (*trou de lapin etc.*) burrow; (*chien*) terrier.

**terrifier** /tɛrifje/ *v.t.* terrify.

**terrine** /tɛrin/ *n.f.* (*culin.*) terrine.

**territoire** /tɛritwar/ *n.m.* territory.

**terroir** /tɛrwar/ *n.m.* (*sol*) soil; (*région*) region. **du ~,** country.

**terroriser** /tɛrɔrize/ *v.t.* terrorize.

**terroris|te** /tɛrɔrist/ *n.m./f.* terrorist. **~me** *n.m.* terrorism.

**tes** /te/ *voir* **ton**[1].

**test** /tɛst/ *n.m.* test. **~er** *v.t.* test.

**testament** /tɛstamɑ̃/ *n.m.* (*jurid.*) will; (*politique*, *artistique*) testament. **Ancien/ Nouveau T~,** Old/New Testament.

**testicule** /tɛstikyl/ *n.m.* testicle.

**tétanos** /tetanos/ *n.m.* tetanus.

**têtard** /tɛtar/ *n.m.* tadpole.

**tête** /tɛt/ *n.f.* head; (*figure*) face; (*cheveux*) hair; (*cerveau*) brain. **à la ~ de,** at the head of. **de ~,** (*calculer*) in one's head. **en ~,** (*sport*) in the lead. **faire la ~,** sulk. **tenir ~ à qn.,** stand up to s.o. **une forte ~,** a rebel. **de la ~ aux pieds,** from head to toe. **~-à-queue** *n.m. invar.* (*auto.*) spin. **en ~-à-tête,** in private.

**tétée** /tete/ *n.f.* feed.

**téter** /tete/ *v.t./i.* suck.

**tétine** /tetin/ *n.f.* (*de biberon*) teat; (*sucette*) dummy.

**têtu** /tety/ *a.* stubborn.

**texte** /tɛkst/ *n.m.* text; (*de leçon*) subject; (*morceau choisi*) passage.

**textile** /tɛkstil/ *n.m. & a.* textile.

**texture** /tɛkstyr/ *n.f.* texture.

**thaïlandais, ~e** /tailɑ̃dɛ, -z/ *a. & n.m., f.* Thai.

**Thaïlande** /tailɑ̃d/ *n.f.* Thailand.

**thé** /te/ *n.m.* tea.

**théâtr|al** (*m. pl.* **~aux**) /teatral, -o/ *a.* theatrical.

**théâtre** /teatr/ *n.m.* theatre; (*jeu forcé*) play-acting; (*d'un crime*) scene. **faire du ~,** act.

**théière** /tejɛr/ *n.f.* teapot.

**thème** /tɛm/ *n.m.* theme; (*traduction: scol.*) prose.

**théologie** /teɔlɔʒi/ *n.f.* theology.

**théorème** /teɔrɛm/ *n.m.* theorem.

**théorie** /teɔri/ *n.f.* theory.

**thérapie** /terapi/ *n.f.* therapy.

**thermique** /tɛrmik/ *a.* thermal.

**thermomètre** /tɛrmɔmɛtr/ *n.m.* thermometer.

**thermos** /tɛrmos/ *n.m./f.* (P.) Thermos (P.) (flask).

**thermostat** /tɛrmɔsta/ *n.m.* thermostat.

**thèse** /tɛz/ *n.f.* thesis.

**thon** /tɔ̃/ *n.m.* (*poisson*) tuna.

**thrombose** /trɔ̃boz/ *n.f.* thrombosis.

**thym** /tɛ̃/ *n.m.* thyme.

**thyroïde** /tiroid/ *n.f.* thyroid.

**tibia** /tibja/ *n.m.* shin-bone.

**tic** /tik/ *n.m.* (*contraction*) twitch; (*manie*) mannerism.

**ticket** /tikɛ/ *n.m.* ticket.

**tic-tac** /tiktak/ *n.m. invar.* (*de pendule*) ticking. **faire ~,** go tick tock.

**tiède** /tjɛd/ *a.* lukewarm.

**tien, ~ne** /tjɛ̃, tjɛn/ *pron.* **le ~, la ~ne, les ~(ne)s,** yours. **à la ~ nel,** cheers!

**tiens, tient** /tjɛ̃/ *voir* **tenir.**

**tiercé** /tjɛrse/ *n.m.* place-betting.

**tier|s, ~ce** /tjɛr, -s/ *a.* third. ● *n.m.* (*fraction*) third; (*personne*) third party. **T~s-Monde** *n.m.* Third World.

**tige** /tiʒ/ *n.f.* (*bot.*) stem, stalk; (*en métal*) shaft.

**tigre** /tigr/ *n.m.* tiger.

**tigré** /tigre/ *a.* (*rayé*) striped; (*chat*) tabby.

**tilleul** /tijœl/ *n.m.* lime(-tree), linden(-tree); (*infusion*) lime tea.

**timbale** /tɛ̃bal/ *n.f.* (*gobelet*) (metal) tumbler.

**timbr|e** /tɛ̃br/ *n.m.* stamp; (*sonnette*) bell; (*de voix*) tone. **~e-poste** (*pl.* **~es-poste**) *n.m.* postage stamp. **~er** *v.t.* stamp.

**timid|e** /timid/ *a.* timid. **~ité** *n.f.* timidity.

**tint|er** /tɛ̃te/ *v.i.* ring; (*clefs*) jingle. **~ement** *n.m.* ringing; jingling.

**tique** /tik/ *n.f.* (*insecte*) tick.

**tir** /tir/ *n.m.* (*sport*) shooting; (*action de tirer*) firing; (*feu, rafale*) fire.

**tirage** /tiraʒ/ *n.m.* (*de photo*) printing; (*de loterie*) draw. **~ au sort,** drawing lots.

**tire-bouchon** /tirbuʃɔ̃/ *n.m.* cork-screw.

**tire-lait** /tirlɛ/ *n.m.* breastpump.

**tirelire** /tirlir/ *n.f.* money-box.

**tirer** /tire/ *v.t.* pull; (*navire*) tow, tug; (*langue*) stick out; (*conclusion, trait, rideaux*) draw; (*coup de feu*) fire; (*gibier*) shoot; (*photo*) print. **~ de,** (*sortir*) take *ou* get out of; (*extraire*) extract from. ● *v.i.* shoot, fire (**sur,** at). **~ sur,** (*couleur*) verge on; (*corde*) pull at. **se ~** *v. pr.* (*fam.*) clear off. **se ~ de,** get out of. **s'en ~,** (*en réchapper*) pull through; (*réussir*: *fam.*) cope. **~ au sort,** draw lots (for).

**tiret** /tirɛ/ *n.m.* dash.

**tireur** /tirœr/ *n.m.* gunman.

**tiroir** /tirwar/ *n.m.* drawer. **~-caisse** (*pl.* **~s-caisses**) *n.m.* till.

**tisane** /tizan/ *n.f.* herb-tea.

**tisonnier** /tizɔnje/ *n.m.* poker.

**tisser** /tise/ *v.t.* weave.

**tissu** /tisy/ *n.m.* fabric, material; (*biologique*) tissue.

**titre** /titr/ *n.m.* title; (*diplôme*) qualification; (*comm.*) bond. ~**s,** (*droits*) claims. (**gros**) ~**s,** headlines. ~ **de propriété,** title-deed.

**titré** /titre/ *a.* titled.

**tituber** /titybe/ *v.i.* stagger.

**titulaire** /titylɛr/ *a.* **être** ~, have tenure. **être** ~ **de,** hold. ● *n.m./f.* (*de permis etc.*) holder.

**toast** /tost/ *n.m.* piece of toast; (*allocution*) toast.

**toboggan** /tɔbɔgã/ *n.m.* slide.

**toc** /tɔk/ *int.* ~ **toc!** knock knock!

**toi** /twa/ *pron.* you; (*réfléchi*) yourself. **lève-** ~, stand up.

**toile** /twal/ *n.f.* cloth; (*sac, tableau*) canvas; (*coton*) cotton. ~ **d'araignée,** (spider's) web; (*délabrée*) cobweb.

**toilette** /twalɛt/ *n.f.* washing; (*habillement*) clothes, dress. ~**s,** (*cabinets*) toilet(s). **de** ~, (*articles, savon, etc.*) toilet. **faire sa** ~, wash (and get ready).

**toi-même** /twamɛm/ *pron.* yourself.

**toison** /twazõ/ *n.f.* (*laine*) fleece.

**toit** /twa/ *n.m.* roof. ~ **ouvrant,** (*auto.*) sunroof.

**tôle** /tol/ *n.f.* (*plaque*) iron sheet. ~ **ondulée,** corrugated iron.

**toléran|t,** ~**te** /tɔlerã, -t/ *a.* tolerant. ~**ce** *n.f.* tolerance.

**tolérer** /tɔlere/ *v.t.* tolerate; (*importations: comm.*) allow.

**tomate** /tɔmat/ *n.f.* tomato.

**tombe** /tõb/ *n.f.* grave; (*avec monument*) tomb.

**tombeau** (*pl.* ~**x**) /tõbo/ *n.m.* tomb.

**tombée** /tõbe/ *n.f.* ~ **de la nuit,** nightfall.

**tomber** /tõbe/ *v.i.* (*aux. être*) fall; (*fièvre, vent*) drop; (*enthousiasme*) die down. **faire** ~, knock over; (*gouvernement*) bring down. **laisser** ~, drop; (*abandonner*) let down. **laisse** ~**!,** forget it! ~ **en panne,** break down. ~ **sur,** (*trouver*) run across.

**tombola** /tõbɔla/ *n.f.* tombola.

**tome** /tɔm/ *n.m.* volume.

**ton**[1], **ta** *ou* **ton*** (*pl.* **tes**) /tõ, ta, tõn, te/ *a.* your.

**ton**[2] /tõ/ *n.m.* tone; (*gamme: mus.*) key; (*hauteur de la voix*) pitch.

**tonalité** /tɔnalite/ *n.f.* tone; (*téléphone*) dialling tone.

**tond|re** /tõdr/ *v.t.* (*herbe*) mow; (*mouton*) shear; (*cheveux*) clip. ~**euse** *n.f.* shears, clippers. ~**euse (à gazon),** (lawn-)mower.

**tonifier** /tɔnifje/ *v.t.* tone up.

**tonique** /tɔnik/ *a.* & *n.m.* tonic.

**tonne** /tɔn/ *n.f.* ton(ne).

**tonneau** (*pl.* ~**x**) /tɔno/ *n.m.* (*récipient*) barrel; (*naut.*) ton; (*culbute*) somersault.

**tonnerre** /tɔnɛr/ *n.m.* thunder.

**tonton** /tõtõ/ *n.m.* (*fam.*) uncle.

**tonus** /tɔnys/ *n.m.* energy.

**top** /tɔp/ *n.m.* (*signal pour marquer un instant précis*) stroke.

**toque** /tɔk/ *n.f.* (fur) hat; (*de jockey*) cap; (*de cuisinier*) hat.

**torche** /tɔrʃ/ *n.f.* torch.

**torchon** /tɔrʃõ/ *n.m.* cloth, duster; (*pour la vaisselle*) tea-towel.

**tordre** /tɔrdr/ *v.t.* twist; (*linge*) wring. **se** ~ *v. pr.* twist, bend; (*de douleur*) writhe. **se** ~ **(de rire),** split one's sides.

**tordu** /tɔrdy/ *a.* twisted, bent; (*esprit*) warped.

**tornade** /tɔrnad/ *n.f.* tornado.

**torpeur** /tɔrpœr/ *n.f.* lethargy.

**torréfier** /tɔrefje/ *v.t.* roast.

**torrent** /tɔrã/ *n.m.* torrent.

**torride** /tɔrid/ *a.* torrid.

**torsade** /tɔrsad/ *n.f.* twist.

**torse** /tɔrs/ *n.m.* chest; (*sculpture*) torso.

**tort** /tɔr/ *n.m.* wrong. **à** ~, wrongly. **à** ~ **et à travers,** without thinking. **avoir** ~, be wrong (**de faire,** to do).

**torticolis** /tɔrtikɔli/ *n.m.* stiff neck.

**tortiller** /tɔrtije/ *v.t.* twist, twirl. **se** ~ *v. pr.* wriggle, wiggle.

**tortue** /tɔrty/ *n.f.* tortoise; (*de mer*) turtle.

**tortueu|x,** ~**se** /tɔrtɥø, -z/ *a.* (*explication*) tortuous; (*chemin*) twisting.

**tortur|e(s)** /tɔrtyr/ *n.f.* (*pl.*) torture. ~**er** *v.t.* torture.

**tôt** /to/ *adv.* early. **plus** ~, earlier. **au plus** ~, at the earliest. **le plus** ~ **possible,** as soon as possible. ~ **ou tard,** sooner or later.

**tot|al** (*m. pl.* ~**aux**) /tɔtal, -o/ *a.* /total, -o/ *a.* total. ● *n.m.* (*pl.* ~**aux**) total. ● *adv.* (*fam.*) to conclude, in short. **au** ~**al,** all in all. ~**alement** *adv.* totally. ~**aliser** *v.t.* total.

**totalitaire** /tɔtalitɛr/ *a.* totalitarian.

**totalité** /tɔtalite/ *n.f.* entirety. **la** ~ **de,** all of.

**toubib** /tubib/ *n.m.* (*fam.*) doctor.

**touchant,** ~**e** /tuʃã, -t/ *a.* (*émouvant*) touching.

**touche** /tuʃ/ *n.f.* (*de piano*) key; (*de peintre*) touch. (**ligne de**) ~, touch-line. **une** ~ **de,** a touch of.

**toucher** /tuʃe/ *v.t.* touch; (*émouvoir*) move, touch; (*contacter*) get in touch with; (*cible*) hit; (*argent*) draw; (*chèque*) cash; (*concerner*) affect. ● *v.i.* ~ **à,** touch; (*question*) touch on; (*fin, but*) approach. **je vais lui en** ~ **un mot,** I'll talk to him about it. **se** ~ *v. pr.* (*lignes*) touch.

**touffe** /tuf/ *n.f.* (*de poils, d'herbe*) tuft; (*de plantes*) clump.

**touffu** /tufy/ *a.* thick, bushy; (*fig.*) complex.

**toujours** /tuʒur/ *adv.* always; (*encore*) still; (*en tout cas*) anyhow. **pour** ~, for ever.

**toupet** /tupɛ/ *n.m.* (*culot: fam.*) cheek, nerve.

**toupie** /tupi/ *n.f.* (*jouet*) top.

**tour**[1] /tur/ *n.f.* tower; (*immeuble*) tower block; (*échecs*) rook.

**tour**[2] /tur/ *n.m.* (*mouvement, succession, tournure*) turn; (*excursion*) trip; (*à pied*) walk; (*en auto*) drive; (*artifice*) trick; (*circonférence*) circumference; (*techn.*) lathe. ∼ **(de piste)**, lap. **à** ∼ **de rôle**, in turn. **à mon**/*etc.* ∼, when it is my/*etc.* turn. **c'est mon**/*etc.* ∼ **de**, it is my/*etc.* turn to. **faire le** ∼ **de**, go round. ∼ **de contrôle**, control tower. ∼ **de taille**, waist measurement; (*ligne*) waistline.

**tourbe** /turb/ *n.f.* peat.

**tourbillon** /turbijɔ̃/ *n.m.* whirlwind; (*d'eau*) whirlpool; (*fig.*) whirl, swirl.

**tourelle** /turɛl/ *n.f.* turret.

**tourisme** /turism/ *n.m.* tourism. **faire du** ∼, do some sightseeing.

**tourist|e** /turist/ *n.m./f.* tourist. ∼**ique** *a.* tourist; (*route*) scenic.

**tourment** /turmã/ *n.m.* torment. ∼**er** /-te/ *v.t.* torment. **se** ∼**er** *v. pr.* worry.

**tournage** /turnaʒ/ *n.m.* (*cinéma*) shooting.

**tournant**[1], ∼**e** /turnã, -t/ *a.* (*qui pivote*) revolving.

**tournant**[2] /turnã/ *n.m.* bend; (*fig.*) turning-point.

**tourne-disque** /turnədisk/ *n.m.* record-player.

**tournée** /turne/ *n.f.* (*voyage, consommations*) round; (*théâtre*) tour. **je paye** *ou* **j'offre la** ∼, I'll buy this round.

**tourner** /turne/ *v.t.* turn; (*film*) shoot, make. ● *v.i.* turn; (*toupie, tête*) spin; (*moteur, usine*) run. **se** ∼ *v. pr.* turn. **autour de,** go round; (*personne, maison*) hang around; (*terre*) revolve round; (*question*) centre on. ∼ **en ridicule,** ridicule. ∼ **le dos à,** turn one's back on.

**tournesol** /turnəsɔl/ *n.m.* sunflower.

**tournevis** /turnəvis/ *n.m.* screwdriver.

**tourniquet** /turnikɛ/ *n.m.* (*barrière*) turnstile.

**tournoi** /turnwa/ *n.m.* tournament.

**tournoyer** /turnwaje/ *v.i.* whirl.

**tournure** /turnyr/ *n.f.* turn; (*locution*) turn of phrase.

**tourte** /turt/ *n.f.* pie.

**tourterelle** /turtərɛl/ *n.f.* turtle-dove.

**Toussaint** /tusɛ̃/ *n.f.* **la** ∼, All Saints' Day.

**tousser** /tuse/ *v.i.* cough.

**tout**[1], ∼**e** (*pl.* **tous, toutes** /tu, tut/ *a.* all; (*n'importe quel*) any; (*tout à fait*) entirely. ∼ **le pays**/*etc.*, the whole country/*etc.*, all the country/*etc.* ∼ **la nuit**/**journée,** the whole night/day. ∼ **un paquet,** a whole pack. **tous les jours**/**mois**/*etc.*, every day/month/*etc.* ● *pron.* everything, all. **tous** /tus/, **toutes,** all. **prendre** ∼, take everything, take it all. ∼

**ce que,** all that. ∼ **le monde,** everyone. **tous les deux, toutes les deux,** both of them. **tous les trois,** all three (of them). ● *adv.* (*très*) very; (*tout à fait*) quite. ∼ **au bout**/**début**/*etc.*, right at the end/beginning/ *etc.* **le** ∼ **premier,** the very first. ∼ **en chantant**/**marchant**/*etc.*, while singing/walking/*etc.* ∼ **à coup,** all of a sudden. ∼ **à fait,** quite, completely. ∼ **à l'heure,** in a moment; (*passé*) a moment ago. ∼ **au** *ou* **le long de,** throughout. ∼ **de même,** all the same. ∼ **de suite,** straight away. ∼ **entier,** whole. ∼ **neuf,** brand-new. ∼ **nu,** stark naked. ∼ **près,** nearby. ∼ **seul,** alone. ∼ **terrain** *a. invar.* all terrain.

**tout**[2] /tu/ *n.m.* (*ensemble*) whole. **en** ∼, in all. **pas du** ∼**!,** not at all!

**tout-à-l'égout** /tutalegu/ *n.m.* main drainage.

**toutefois** /tutfwa/ *adv.* however.

**toux** /tu/ *n.f.* cough.

**toxicomane** /tɔksikɔman/ *n.m./f.* drug addict.

**toxine** /tɔksin/ *n.f.* toxin.

**toxique** /tɔksik/ *a.* toxic.

**trac** /trak/ *n.m.* **le** ∼, nerves; (*théâtre*) stage fright.

**tracas** /traka/ *n.m.* worry.

**trace** /tras/ *n.f.* trace, mark; (*d'animal, de pneu*) tracks; (*vestige*) trace. ∼**s de pas,** footprints.

**tracé** /trase/ *n.m.* (*ligne*) line; (*plan*) layout.

**tracer** /trase/ *v.t.* draw, trace; (*écrire*) write; (*route*) mark out.

**trachée(-artère)** /traʃe(artɛr)/ *n.f.* windpipe.

**tracteur** /traktœr/ *n.m.* tractor.

**tradition** /tradisjɔ̃/ *n.f.* tradition. ∼**nel,** ∼**nelle** /-jɔnɛl/ *a.* traditional.

**trad|uire**† /tradɥir/ *v.t.* translate; (*sentiment*) express. ∼**uire en justice,** take to court. ∼**ucteur,** ∼**uctrice** *n.m.,* *f.* translator. ∼**uction** *n.f.* translation.

**trafic** /trafik/ *n.m.* (*commerce, circulation*) traffic.

**trafiqu|er** /trafike/ *v.i.* traffic. ● *v.t.* (*fam.*) (*vin*) doctor; (*moteur*) fiddle with. ∼**ant,** ∼**ante** *n.m.,* *f.* trafficker; (*d'armes, de drogues*) dealer.

**tragédie** /traʒedi/ *n.f.* tragedy.

**tragique** /traʒik/ *a.* tragic. ∼**ment** *adv.* tragically.

**trah|ir** /trair/ *v.t.* betray. ∼**ison** *n.f.* betrayal; (*crime*) treason.

**train** /trɛ̃/ *n.m.* (*rail.*) train; (*allure*) pace. **en** ∼ **de faire,** (busy) doing. ∼ **d'atterrissage,** undercarriage. ∼ **électrique,** (*jouet*) electric train set. ∼ **de vie,** lifestyle.

**traîneau** (*pl.* ∼**x**) /trɛno/ *n.m.* sledge.

**traînée** /trene/ *n.f.* (*trace*) trail; (*bande*) streak; (*femme: péj.*) slut.

**traîner** /trene/ v.t. drag (along); (véhicule) pull. ● v.i. (pendre) trail; (rester en arrière) trail behind; (flâner) hang about; (papiers, affaires) lie around. ~ **(en longueur)**, drag on.

**traire**† /trɛr/ v.t. milk.

**trait** /trɛ/ n.m. line; (en dessinant) stroke; (caractéristique) feature, trait. ~**s**, (du visage) features. ~ **d'union,** hyphen.

**traite** /trɛt/ n.f. (de vache) milking; (comm.) draft. **d'une (seule)** ~, in one go, at a stretch.

**traitement** /trɛtmɑ̃/ n.m. treatment; (salaire) salary. ~ **de données,** data processing. ~ **de texte,** word processing.

**traiter** /trete/ v.t. treat; (affaire) deal with; (données, produit) process. ~ **qn. de lâche** etc., call s.o. a coward/etc. ● v.i. deal (**avec**, with). ~ **de,** (sujet) deal with.

**traiteur** /trɛtœr/ n.m. caterer; (boutique) delicatessen.

**traître, ~sse** /trɛtr, -ɛs/ a. treacherous. ● n.m./f. traitor.

**trajectoire** /traʒɛktwar/ n.f. path.

**trajet** /traʒɛ/ n.m. (à parcourir) distance; (voyage) journey; (itinéraire) route.

**trame** /tram/ n.f. (de tissu) weft; (de récit etc.) framework.

**tramway** /tramwɛ/ n.m. tram.

**tranche** /trɑ̃ʃ/ n.f. (rondelle) slice; (partie) portion.

**tranch|er**¹ /trɑ̃ʃe/ v.t. cut; (question) decide. ● v.i. (décider) decide. ~**é** a. (net) clear-cut.

**trancher**² /trɑ̃ʃe/ v.i. (contraster) contrast (**sur**, with).

**tranquill|e** /trɑ̃kil/ a. quiet; (esprit) at rest; (conscience) clear. **être/laisser** ~**e,** be/leave in peace. ~**ement** adv. quietly.

**tranquillisant** /trɑ̃kilizɑ̃/ n.m. tranquillizer.

**tranquilliser** /trɑ̃kilize/ v.t. reassure.

**transaction** /trɑ̃zaksjɔ̃/ n.f. transaction.

**transat** /trɑ̃zat/ n.m. (fam.) deck-chair.

**transatlantique** /trɑ̃zatlɑ̃tik/ n.m. trans-atlantic liner.

**transcr|ire** /trɑ̃skrir/ v.t. transcribe. ~**ip-tion** n.f. transcription; (copie) transcript.

**transférer** /trɑ̃sfere/ v.t. transfer.

**transfert** /trɑ̃sfɛr/ n.m. transfer.

**transform|er** /trɑ̃sfɔrme/ v.t. change; (radicalement) transform; (vêtement) alter. **se** ~**er** v. pr. change; be transformed. **(se)** ~**er en,** turn into. ~**ateur** n.m. transformer. ~**ation** n.f. change; transformation.

**transfuge** /trɑ̃sfyʒ/ n.m. renegade.

**transfusion** /trɑ̃sfyzjɔ̃/ n.f. transfusion.

**transgresser** /trɑ̃sɡrese/ v.t. disobey.

**transistor** /trɑ̃zistɔr/ n.m. (dispositif, poste de radio) transistor.

**transit** /trɑ̃zit/ n.m. transit. ~**er** v.t./i. pass in transit.

**transiti|f, ~ve** /trɑ̃zitif, -v/ a. transitive.

**transition** /trɑ̃zisjɔ̃/ n.f. transition.

**transm|ettre**† /trɑ̃smɛtr/ v.t. pass on; (techn.) transmit; (radio) broadcast. ~**ission** n.f. transmission; (radio) broadcasting.

**transparen|t, ~te** /trɑ̃sparɑ̃, -t/ a. transparent. ~**ce** n.f. transparency.

**transpercer** /trɑ̃spɛrse/ v.t. pierce.

**transpir|er** /trɑ̃spire/ v.i. perspire. ~**ation** n.f. perspiration.

**transplant|er** /trɑ̃splɑ̃te/ v.t. (bot., méd.) transplant. ~**ation** n.f. (bot.) transplantation; (méd.) transplant.

**transport** /trɑ̃spɔr/ n.m. transport(ation). **les** ~**s en commun,** public transport.

**transport|er** /trɑ̃spɔrte/ v.t. transport; (à la main) carry.

**transposer** /trɑ̃spoze/ v.t. transpose.

**transvers|al** (m.pl. ~**aux**) /trɑ̃vɛrsal, -o/ a. cross, transverse.

**trappe** /trap/ n.f. trapdoor.

**trapu** /trapy/ a. stocky.

**traquer** /trake/ v.t. track down.

**traumatis|me** /tromatism/ n.m. trauma. ~**ant,** ~**ante** /-zɑ̃, -t/ a. traumatic.

**trav|ail** (pl. ~**aux**) /travaj, -o/ n.m. work; (emploi, poste) job; (façonnage) working. ~**aux,** work. **en** ~**ail,** (femme) in labour. ~**ail à la chaîne,** production line work. ~**ail au noir,** (fam.) moonlighting. ~**aux ménagers,** housework.

**travaill|er** /travaje/ v.i. work. ● v.t. (façonner) work; (étudier) work at ou on; (tourmenter) worry. ~**eur,** ~**euse** n.m., f. worker; a. hardworking.

**travailliste** /travajist/ a. Labour. ● n.m./f. Labour party member.

**travers** /travɛr/ n.m. **à** ~, through. **de** ~, (chapeau, nez) crooked; (mal) badly, the wrong way; (regarder) askance. **en** ~ **(de),** across.

**traversée** /travɛrse/ n.f. crossing.

**traverser** /travɛrse/ v.t. cross; (transpercer) go (right) through; (période, forêt) go ou pass through.

**traversin** /travɛrsɛ̃/ n.m. bolster.

**travesti** /travɛsti/ n.m. transvestite.

**trébucher** /trebyʃe/ v.i. stumble, trip (over). **faire** ~, trip (up).

**trèfle** /trɛfl/ n.m. (plante) clover; (cartes) clubs.

**treillis** /treji/ n.m. trellis; (en métal) wire mesh.

**treiz|e** /trɛz/ a. & n.m. thirteen. ~**ième** a. & n.m./f. thirteenth.

**tréma** /trema/ n.m. diaeresis.

**trembl|er** /trɑ̃ble/ v.i. shake, tremble; (lumière, voix) quiver. ~**ement** n.m. shaking; (frisson) shiver. ~**ement de terre,** earthquake.

**tremper** /trɑ̃pe/ *v.t./i.* soak; (*plonger*) dip; (*acier*) temper. **mettre à ~ ou faire ~,** soak. **se ~** *v. pr.* (*se baigner*) have a dip.

**trempette** /trɑ̃pɛt/ *n.f.* **faire ~,** have a little dip.

**tremplin** /trɑ̃plɛ̃/ *n.m.* springboard.

**trentaine** /trɑ̃tɛn/ *n.f.* **une ~ (de),** about thirty. **il a la ~,** he's about thirty.

**trent|e** /trɑ̃t/ *a. & n.m.* thirty. **~ième** *a. & n.m./f.* thirtieth.

**trépied** /trepje/ *n.m.* tripod.

**très** /trɛ/ (/trɛz/ *before vowel*) *adv.* very. **~ aimé/estimé,** much liked/esteemed.

**trésor** /trezɔr/ *n.m.* treasure; (*ressources: comm.*) finances. **le T~,** the revenue department.

**trésorerie** /trezɔrri/ *n.f.* (*bureaux*) accounts department; (*du Trésor*) revenue office; (*argent*) finances; (*gestion*) accounts.

**trésor|ier, ~ière** /trezɔrje, -jɛr/ *n.m., f.* treasurer.

**tressaillir** /tresajir/ *v.i.* shake, quiver; (*sursauter*) start.

**tressauter** /tresote/ *v.i.* (*sursauter*) start, jump.

**tresse** /trɛs/ *n.f.* braid, plait.

**tresser** /trese/ *v.t.* braid, plait.

**tréteau** (*pl.* **~x**) /treto/ *n.m.* trestle. **~x,** (*théâtre*) stage.

**treuil** /trœj/ *n.m.* winch.

**trêve** /trɛv/ *n.f.* truce; (*fig.*) respite. **~ de plaisanteries,** enough of this joking.

**tri** /tri/ *n.m.* (*classement*) sorting; (*sélection*) selection. **faire le ~ de,** sort; select.

**triang|le** /trijɑ̃gl/ *n.m.* triangle. **~ulaire** *a.* triangular.

**tribord** /tribɔr/ *n.m.* starboard.

**tribu** /triby/ *n.f.* tribe.

**tribun|al** (*m. pl.* **~aux**) /tribynal, -o/ *n.m.* court.

**tribune** /tribyn/ *n.f.* (*public*) gallery; (*dans un stade*) grandstand; (*d'orateur*) rostrum; (*débat*) forum.

**trich|er** /triʃe/ *v.i.* cheat. **~erie** *n.f.* cheating. **une ~erie,** piece of trickery. **~eur, ~euse** *n.m., f.* cheat.

**tricolore** /trikɔlɔr/ *a.* three-coloured; (*français*) red, white and blue; (*français: fig.*) French.

**tricot** /triko/ *n.m.* knitting; (*pull*) sweater. **en ~,** knitted. **~er** /-ɔte/ *v.t./i.* knit.

**trictrac** /triktrak/ *n.m.* backgammon.

**tricycle** /trisikl/ *n.m.* tricycle.

**trier** /trije/ *v.t.* (*classer*) sort; (*choisir*) select.

**trimestr|e** /trimɛstr/ *n.m.* quarter; (*scol.*) term. **~iel, ~ielle** *a.* quarterly; (*bulletin*) end-of-term.

**tringle** /trɛ̃gl/ *n.f.* rod.

**Trinité** /trinite/ *n.f.* **la ~,** (*dogme*) the Trinity; (*fête*) Trinity.

**trinquer** /trɛ̃ke/ *v.i.* clink glasses.

**trio** /trijo/ *n.m.* trio.

**triomph|e** /trijɔ̃f/ *n.m.* triumph. **~al** (*m. pl.* **~aux**) *a.* triumphant.

**triomph|er** /trijɔ̃fe/ *v.i.* triumph (**de,** over); (*jubiler*) be triumphant. **~ant, ~ante** *a.* triumphant.

**tripes** /trip/ *n.f. pl.* (*mets*) tripe.

**triple** /tripl/ *a.* triple, treble. ● *n.m.* **le ~,** three times as much (**de,** as).

**tripler** /triple/ *v.t./i.* triple, treble.

**trisomique** /trizɔmik/ *a.* **enfant ~,** Down's (syndrome) child.

**triste** /trist/ *a.* sad; (*rue, temps, couleur*) gloomy; (*lamentable*) wretched, dreadful. **~ment** /-əmɑ̃/ *adv.* sadly. **~sse** /-ɛs/ *n.f.* sadness; gloominess.

**triv|ial** (*m. pl.* **~iaux**) /trivjal, -jo/ *a.* coarse. **~ialité** *n.f.* coarseness.

**troc** /trɔk/ *n.m.* exchange; (*comm.*) barter.

**trognon** /trɔɲɔ̃/ *n.m.* core.

**trois** /trwɑ/ *a. & n.m.* three. **hôtel ~-étoiles,** three-star hotel. **~ième** /-zjɛm/ *a. & n.m./f.* third. **~ièmement** /-zjɛmmɑ̃/ *adv.* thirdly.

**trombe** /trɔ̃b/ *n.f.* **~ d'eau,** downpour.

**trombone** /trɔ̃bɔn/ *n.m.* (*mus.*) trombone; (*agrafe*) paper-clip.

**trompe** /trɔ̃p/ *n.f.* (*d'éléphant*) trunk; (*mus.*) horn.

**tromp|er** /trɔ̃pe/ *v.t.* deceive, mislead; (*déjouer*) elude. **se ~er** *v. pr.* be mistaken. **se ~er de route/train/**etc., take the wrong road/train/etc.

**trompette** /trɔ̃pɛt/ *n.f.* trumpet.

**tronc** /trɔ̃/ *n.m.* trunk; (*boîte*) collection box.

**tronçon** /trɔ̃sɔ̃/ *n.m.* section. **~ner** /-ɔne/ *v.t.* cut into sections.

**trône** /tron/ *n.m.* throne.

**tronquer** /trɔ̃ke/ *v.t.* truncate.

**trop** /tro/ *adv.* (*grand, loin, etc.*) too; (*boire, marcher,* etc.) too much. **~ (de),** (*quantité*) too much; (*nombre*) too many. **c'est ~ chauffé,** it's overheated. **de ~, en ~,** too much; too many.

**trophée** /trofe/ *n.m.* trophy.

**tropic|al** (*m. pl.* **~aux**) /trɔpikal, -o/ *a.* tropical.

**tropique** /trɔpik/ *n.m.* tropic. **~s,** tropics.

**troquer** /trɔke/ *v.t.* exchange; (*comm.*) barter (**contre,** for).

**trot** /tro/ *n.m.* trot.

**trotter** /trɔte/ *v.i.* trot.

**trotteuse** /trɔtøz/ *n.f.* (*aiguille de montre*) second hand.

**trottinette** /trɔtinɛt/ *n.f.* (*jouet*) scooter.

**trottoir** /trɔtwar/ *n.m.* pavement.

**trou** /tru/ *n.m.* hole; (*moment*) gap; (*lieu: péj.*) dump. **~ (de mémoire),** lapse (of memory). **~ de la serrure,** keyhole.

**trouble** /trubl/ *a.* (*eau*, *image*) unclear; (*louche*) shady. ● *n.m.* agitation. ~**s**, (*pol.*) disturbances; (*méd.*) trouble.

**troubl|er** /truble/ *v.t.* disturb; (*eau*) make cloudy; (*inquiéter*) trouble. ~**ant**, ~**ante** *a.* disturbing.

**trouer** /true/ *v.t.* make a hole *ou* holes in.

**trouille** /truj/ *n.f.* **avoir la ~,** (*fam.*) be scared.

**troupe** /trup/ *n.f.* troop; (*d'acteurs*) troupe. ~**s**, (*mil.*) troops.

**troupeau** (*pl.* ~**x**) /trupo/ *n.m.* herd; (*de moutons*) flock.

**trousse** /trus/ *n.f.* case, bag; (*de réparations*) kit. ~ **de toilette,** toilet bag.

**trousseau** (*pl.* ~**x**) /truso/ *n.m.* (*de clefs*) bunch; (*de mariée*) trousseau.

**trouver** /truve/ *v.t.* find; (*penser*) think. **se ~** *v. pr.* find o.s.; (*être*) be; (*se sentir*) feel.

**truc** /tryk/ *n.m.* (*moyen*) way; (*artifice*) trick; (*chose: fam.*) thing. ~**age** *n.m.* = **truquage.**

**truelle** /tryɛl/ *n.f.* trowel.

**truffe** /tryf/ *n.f.* (*champignon, chocolat*) truffle; (*nez*) nose.

**truffer** /tryfe/ *v.t.* (*fam.*) fill, pack (**de,** with).

**truie** /trɥi/ *n.f.* (*animal*) sow.

**truite** /trɥit/ *n.f.* trout.

**truqu|er** /tryke/ *v.t.* fix, rig; (*photo, texte*) fake. ~**age** *n.m.* fixing; faking; (*cinéma*) special effect.

**trust** /trœst/ *n.m.* (*comm.*) trust.

**tsigane** /tsigan/ *a. & n.m./f.* (Hungarian) gypsy.

**tu**[1] /ty/ *pron.* (*parent, ami, enfant, etc.*) you.

**tu**[2] /ty/ *voir* **taire.**

**tuba** /tyba/ *n.m.* (*mus.*) tuba; (*sport*) snorkel.

**tube** /tyb/ *n.m.* tube.

**tubercul|eux,** ~**euse** /tybɛrkylø, -z/ *a.* **être ~eux,** have tuberculosis. ~**ose** *n.f.* tuberculosis.

**tuer** /tɥe/ *v.t.* kill; (*d'une balle*) shoot, kill; (*épuiser*) exhaust. **se ~** *v. pr.* kill o.s.; (*accident*) be killed.

**tuile** /tɥil/ *n.f.* tile; (*malchance: fam.*) (stroke of) bad luck.

**tulipe** /tylip/ *n.f.* tulip.

**tumeur** /tymœr/ *n.f.* tumour.

**tumulte** /tymylt/ *n.m.* commotion; (*désordre*) turmoil.

**tunique** /tynik/ *n.f.* tunic.

**Tunisie** /tynizi/ *n.f.* Tunisia.

**tunisien,** ~**ne** /tynizjɛ̃, -jɛn/ *a. & n.m., f.* Tunisian.

**tunnel** /tynɛl/ *n.m.* tunnel.

**turban** /tyrbɑ̃/ *n.m.* turban.

**turbine** /tyrbin/ *n.f.* turbine.

**turbo** /tyrbo/ *n.f.* turbo. *n.f.* (*voiture*) turbo.

**turbulen|t,** ~**te** /tyrbylɑ̃, -t/ *a.* boisterous, turbulent. ~**ce** *n.f.* turbulence.

**tur|c,** ~**que** /tyrk/ *a.* Turkish. ● *n.m., f.* Turk. ● *n.m.* (*lang.*) Turkish.

**turf** /tyrf/ *n.m.* **le ~,** the turf. ~**iste** *n.m./f.* racegoer.

**Turquie** /tyrki/ *n.f.* Turkey.

**turquoise** /tyrkwaz/ *a. invar.* turquoise.

**tutelle** /tytɛl/ *n.f.* (*jurid.*) guardianship; (*fig.*) protection.

**tu|teur,** ~**trice** /tytœr, -tris/ *n.m., f.* (*jurid.*) guardian. ● *n.m.* (*bâton*) stake.

**tut|oyer** /tytwaje/ *v.t.* address familiarly (using *tu*). ~**oiement** *n.m.* use of (familiar) *tu*.

**tuyau** (*pl.* ~**x**) /tɥijo/ *n.m.* pipe; (*conseil: fam.*) tip. ~ **d'arrosage,** hose-pipe. ~**terie** *n.f.* piping.

**TVA** *abrév.* (*taxe sur la valeur ajoutée*) VAT.

**tympan** /tɛ̃pɑ̃/ *n.m.* ear-drum.

**type** /tip/ *n.m.* (*modèle*) type; (*traits*) features; (*individu: fam.*) bloke, guy. ● *a. invar.* typical.

**typhoïde** /tifɔid/ *n.f.* typhoid (fever).

**typhon** /tifɔ̃/ *n.m.* typhoon.

**typhus** /tifys/ *n.m.* typhus.

**typique** /tipik/ *a.* typical. ~**ment** *adv.* typically.

**tyran** /tirɑ̃/ *n.m.* tyrant.

**tyrann|ie** /tirani/ *n.f.* tyranny. ~**ique** *a.* tyrannical.

# Uu

**ulcère** /ylsɛr/ *n.m.* ulcer.

**ULM** *abrév. m.* (*ultraléger motorisé*) microlight.

**ultérieur** /ylterjœr/ *a.,* ~**ement** *adv.* later.

**ultimatum** /yltimatɔm/ *n.m.* ultimatum.

**ultra** /yltra/ *n.m./f.* hardliner.

**ultra-** /yltra/ *préf.* ultra-.

**un, une** /œ̃, yn/ *a.* one; (*indéfini*) a, an. **un enfant,** /œ̃ nɑ̃fɑ̃/ a child. ● *pron. & n.m., f.* one. **l'un,** one. **les uns,** some. **l'un et l'autre,** both. **l'un l'autre, les uns les autres,** each other. **l'un ou l'autre,** either. **la une,** (*de journal*) front page. **un autre,** another. **un par un,** one by one.

**unanim|e** /ynanim/ *a.* unanimous. ~**ité** *n.f.* unanimity. **à l'~ité,** unanimously.

**uni** /yni/ *a.* united; (*couple*) close; (*surface*) smooth; (*sans dessins*) plain.

**unième** /ynjɛm/ *a.* -first. **vingt et ~,** twenty-first. **cent ~,** one hundred and first.

**uniforme** /ynifɔrm/ *n.m.* uniform. ● *a.* uniform.

**unilatér|al** (*m. pl.* ~**aux**) /ynilateral, -o/ *a.* unilateral.

**union** /ynjɔ̃/ *n.f.* union. **l'U~ soviétique,** the Soviet Union.

**unique** /ynik/ *a.* (*seul*) only; (*prix,voie*) one; (*incomparable*) unique. **enfant ~,** only child. **sens ~,** one-way street. **~ment** *adv.* only, solely.

**unir** /ynir/ *v.t.,* **s'~** *v. pr.* unite, join.

**unité** /ynite/ *n.f.* unit; (*harmonie*) unity.

**univers** /yniver/ *n.m.* universe.

**universel, ~le** /yniversɛl/ *a.* universal.

**université** /yniversite/ *n.f.* university.

**uranium** /yranjɔm/ *n.m.* uranium.

**urbain, ~e** /yrbɛ̃, -ɛn/ *a.* urban.

**urgence** /yrʒɑ̃s/ *n.f.* (*cas*) emergency; (*de situation, tâche, etc.*) urgency. **d'~** *a.* emergency; *adv.* urgently.

**urgent, ~e** /yrʒɑ̃, -t/ *a.* urgent.

**urin|e** /yrin/ *n.f.* urine. **~er** *v.i.* urinate.

**urinoir** /yrinwar/ *n.m.* urinal.

**urne** /yrn/ *n.f.* (*électorale*) ballot-box; (*vase*) urn. **aller aux ~s,** go to the polls.

**urticaire** /yrtikɛr/ *n.f.* **une crise d'~,** nettle rash.

**usage** /yzaʒ/ *n.m.* use; (*coutume*) custom; (*de langage*) usage.

**usagé** /yzaʒe/ *a.* worn.

**usager** /yzaʒe/ *n.m.* user.

**usé** /yze/ *a.* worn (out).

**user** /yze/ *v.t.* wear (out); (*consommer*) use (up). ● *v.i.* **~ de,** use. **s'~** *v.pr.* (*tissu etc.*) wear (out).

**usine** /yzin/ *n.f.* factory; (*de métallurgie*) works.

**ustensile** /ystɑ̃sil/ *n.m.* utensil.

**usufruit** /yzyfrɥi/ *n.m.* usufruct.

**usure** /yzyr/ *n.f.* (*détérioration*) wear (and tear).

**utérus** /yterys/ *n.m.* womb, uterus.

**utile** /ytil/ *a.* useful. **~ment** *adv.* usefully.

**utilis|er** /ytilize/ *v.t.* use. **~able** *a.* usable. **~ation** *n.f.* use.

**utilitaire** /ytilitɛr/ *a.* utilitarian.

**utilité** /ytilite/ *n.f.* use(fulness).

**UV** *abrév. f.* (*unité de valeur*) (*scol.*) credit.

................................................

# Vv

................................................

**va** /va/ *voir* **aller**[1].

**vacanc|e** /vakɑ̃s/ *n.f.* (*poste*) vacancy. **~es,** holiday(s). **en ~es,** on holiday. **~ier, ~ière** *n.m., f.* holiday-maker.

**vacant, ~e** /vakɑ̃, -t/ *a.* vacant.

**vacarme** /vakarm/ *n.m.* uproar.

**vaccin** /vaksɛ̃/ *n.m.* vaccine; (*inoculation*) vaccination.

**vaccin|er** /vaksine/ *v.t.* vaccinate. **~ation** *n.f.* vaccination.

**vache** /vaʃ/ *n.f.* cow. ● *a.* (*méchant: fam.*) nasty. **~ment** *adv.* (*très: fam.*) damned; (*pleuvoir, manger, etc.: fam.*) a hell of a lot.

**va-et-vient** /vaevjɛ̃/ *n.m. invar.* to and fro (motion); (*de personnes*) comings and goings.

**vagabond, ~e** /vagabɔ̃, -d/ *n.m., f.* (*péj.*) vagrant, vagabond.

**vagin** /vaʒɛ̃/ *n.m.* vagina.

**vague**[1] /vag/ *a.* vague. ● *n.m.* vagueness. **~ment** *adv.* vaguely.

**vague**[2] /vag/ *n.f.* wave. **~ de froid,** cold spell. **~ de chaleur,** hot spell.

**vaille** /vaj/ *voir* **valoir**.

**vain, ~e** /vɛ̃, vɛn/ *a.* vain. **en ~,** in vain. **~ement** /vɛnmɑ̃/ *adv.* vainly.

**vain|cre†** /vɛ̃kr/ *v.t.* defeat; (*surmonter*) overcome. **~cu, ~cue** *n.m., f.* (*sport*) loser. **~queur** *n.m.* victor; (*sport*) winner.

**vais** /vɛ/ *voir* **aller**[1].

**vaisseau** (*pl.* **~x**) /vɛso/ *n.m.* ship; (*veine*) vessel. **~ spatial,** space-ship.

**vaisselle** /vɛsɛl/ *n.f.* crockery; (*à laver*) dishes. **faire la ~,** do the washing-up, wash the dishes. **produit pour la ~,** washing-up liquid.

**val** (*pl.* **~s** *ou* **vaux**) /val, vo/ *n.m.* valley.

**valable** /valabl/ *a.* valid; (*de qualité*) worthwhile.

**valet** /valɛ/ *n.m.* (*cartes*) jack.

**valeur** /valœr/ *n.f.* value; (*mérite*) worth, value. **~s,** (*comm.*) stocks and shares. **avoir de la ~,** be valuable.

**valid|e** /valid/ *a.* (*personne*) fit; (*billet*) valid. **~er** *v.t.* validate.

**valise** /valiz/ *n.f.* (suit)case. **faire ses ~s,** pack (one's bags).

**vallée** /vale/ *n.f.* valley.

**vallon** /valɔ̃/ *n.m.* (small) valley.

**valoir†** /valwar/ *v.i.* be worth; (*s'appliquer*) apply. **~ qch.,** be worth sth.; (*être aussi bon que*) be as good as sth. **se ~** *v. pr.* (*être équivalents*) be as good as each other. **~ la peine, ~ le coup,** be worth it. **ça ne vaut rien,** it is no good. **il vaudrait mieux faire,** we'd better do.

**vals|e** /vals/ *n.f.* waltz. **~er** *v.i.* waltz.

**valve** /valv/ *n.f.* valve.

**van** /vɑ̃/ *n.m.* van.

**vanille** /vanij/ *n.f.* vanilla.

**vanit|é** /vanite/ *n.f.* vanity. **~eux, ~euse** *a.* vain, conceited.

**vanne** /van/ *n.f.* (*d'écluse*) sluice(-gate); (*fam.*) joke.

**vantard, ~e** /vɑ̃tar, -d/ *a.* boastful; *n.m., f.* boaster.

**vanter** /vɑ̃te/ *v.t.* praise. **se ~** *v. pr.* boast (**de,** about).

**vapeur** /vapœr/ *n.f.* (*eau*) steam; (*brume, émanation*) vapour.

**vaporis|er** /vaporize/ *v.t.* spray. **~ateur** *n.m.* spray.

**varappe** /varap/ *n.f.* rock climbing.

**variable** /varjabl/ *a.* variable; (*temps*) changeable.

**variante** /varjãt/ *n.f.* variant.

**varicelle** /varisɛl/ *n.f.* chicken-pox.

**varices** /varis/ *n.f. pl.* varicose veins.

**var|ier** /varje/ *v.t./i.* vary. **~iation** *n.f.* variation. **~ié** *a.* (*non monotone, étendu*) varied; (*divers*) various.

**variété** /varjete/ *n.f.* variety. **~s,** (*spectacle*) variety.

**variole** /varjɔl/ *n.f.* smallpox.

**vase¹** /vaz/ *n.m.* vase.

**vase²** /vaz/ *n.f.* (*boue*) silt, mud.

**vaste** /vast/ *a.* vast, huge.

**vaudeville** /vodvil/ *n.m.* vaudeville, light comedy.

**vautour** /votur/ *n.m.* vulture.

**veau** (*pl.* **~x**) /vo/ *n.m.* calf; (*viande*) veal; (*cuir*) calfskin.

**vécu** /veky/ *voir* **vivre.** ● *a.* (*réel*) true, real.

**vedette¹** /vədɛt/ *n.f.* (*artiste*) star.

**vedette²** /vədɛt/ *n.f.* (*bateau*) launch.

**végét|al** (*m. pl.* **~aux**) /veʒetal, -o/ *a.* plant. ● *n.m.* (*pl.* **~aux**) plant.

**végétalien,** **~ne** /veʒetaljɛ̃, -jɛn/ *n.m., f. & a.* vegan.

**végétarien,** **~ne** /veʒetarjɛ̃, -jɛn/ *a. & n.m., f.* vegetarian.

**végétation** /veʒetasjɔ̃/ *n.f.* vegetation. **~s,** (*méd.*) adenoids.

**véhicule** /veikyl/ *n.m.* vehicle.

**veille¹** /vɛj/ *n.f.* **la ~ (de),** the day before. **la ~ de Noël,** Christmas Eve. **à la ~ de,** on the eve of.

**veille²** /vɛj/ *n.f.* (*état*) wakefulness.

**veillée** /veje/ *n.f.* evening (gathering); (*mortuaire*) vigil, wake.

**veiller** /veje/ *v.i.* stay up *ou* awake. **~ à,** attend to. **~ sur,** watch over. ● *v.t.* (*malade*) watch over.

**veilleur** /vɛjœr/ *n.m.* **~ de nuit,** night-watchman.

**veilleuse** /vɛjøz/ *n.f.* night-light; (*de véhicule*) sidelight; (*de réchaud*) pilot-light.

**veinard,** **~e** /vɛnar, -d/ *n.m., f.* (*fam.*) lucky devil.

**veine¹** /vɛn/ *n.f.* (*anat.*) vein; (*nervure, filon*) vein.

**veine²** /vɛn/ *n.f.* (*chance: fam.*) luck. **avoir de la ~,** (*fam.*) be lucky.

**velcro** /vɛlkro/ *n.m.* (P.) velcro.

**véliplanchiste** /veliplãʃist/ *n.m./f.* wind-surfer.

**vélo** /velo/ *n.m.* bicycle, bike; (*activité*) cycling.

**vélomoteur** /velomɔtœr/ *n.m.* moped.

**velours** /vlur/ *n.m.* velvet. **~ côtelé, ~ à côtes,** corduroy.

**velu** /vəly/ *a.* hairy.

**venaison** /vənɛzɔ̃/ *n.f.* venison.

**vendanges** /vãdãʒ/ *n.f. pl.* grape harvest.

**vendeu|r,** **~se** /vãdœr, -øz/ *n.m., f.* shop assistant; (*marchand*) salesman, sales-woman.

**vendre** /vãdr/ *v.t.,* **se ~** *v. pr.* sell. **à ~,** for sale.

**vendredi** /vãdrədi/ *n.m.* Friday. **V~ saint,** Good Friday.

**vénéneu|x,** **~se** /venenø, -z/ *a.* poisonous.

**vénérien,** **~ne** /venerjɛ̃, -jɛn/ *a.* venereal.

**vengeance** /vãʒãs/ *n.f.* revenge, ven-geance.

**venger** /vãʒe/ *v.t.* avenge. **se ~** *v. pr.* take (one's) revenge (**de,** for).

**ven|in** /vənɛ̃/ *n.m.* venom. **~imeux, ~imeuse** *a.* poisonous, venomous.

**venir†** /vənir/ *v.i.* (*aux. être*) come(**de,**from). **~ faire,** come to do. **~ de faire,** to have just done. **il vient/venait d'arriver,** he has/had just arrived. **faire ~,** send for.

**vent** /vã/ *n.m.* wind.

**vente** /vãt/ *n.f.* sale. **~ (aux enchères),** auction. **en ~,** on *ou* for sale. **~ de charité,** (charity) bazaar.

**ventil|er** /vãtile/ *v.t.* ventilate. **~ateur** *n.m.* fan, ventilator. **~ation** *n.f.* ventilation.

**ventouse** /vãtuz/ *n.f.* (*dispositif*) suction pad; (*pour déboucher l'évier etc.*) plunger.

**ventre** /vãtr/ *n.m.* belly, stomach; (*utérus*) womb.

**ventru** /vãtry/ *a.* pot-bellied.

**venu** /vəny/ *voir* **venir.**

**venue** /vəny/ *n.f.* coming.

**vêpres** /vɛpr/ *n.f. pl.* vespers.

**ver** /vɛr/ *n.m.* worm; (*des fruits, de la viande*) maggot; (*du bois*) woodworm. **~ à soie,** silkworm. **~ solitaire,** tapeworm. **~ de terre,** earthworm.

**véranda** /verãda/ *n.f.* veranda.

**verb|e** /vɛrb/ *n.m.* (*gram.*) verb. **~al** (*m. pl.* **~aux**) *a.* verbal.

**verdâtre** /vɛrdɑtr/ *a.* greenish.

**verdict** /vɛrdikt/ *n.m.* verdict.

**verdure** /vɛrdyr/ *n.f.* greenery.

**verger** /vɛrʒe/ *n.m.* orchard.

**vergla|s** /vɛrgla/ *n.m.* (black) ice. **~cé** *a.* icy.

**vérif|ier** /verifje/ *v.t.* check, verify; (*compte*) audit; (*confirmer*) confirm. **~ication** *n.f.* check(ing), verification.

**véritable** /veritabl/ *a.* true, real; (*authen-tique*) real. **~ment** /-əmã/ *adv.* really.

**vérité** /verite/ *n.f.* truth. **en ~,** in fact.

**vermicelle(s)** /vɛrmisɛl/ *n.m.* (*pl.*) vermicelli.

**vermouth** /vɛrmut/ *n.m.* (*apéritif*) vermouth.

**verni** /vɛrni/ *a.* (*fam.*) lucky. **chaussures ~es**, patent (leather) shoes.

**vernir** /vɛrnir/ *v.t.* varnish.

**vernis** /vɛrni/ *n.m.* varnish; (*de poterie*) glaze. **~ à ongles**, nail polish *ou* varnish.

**vernissage** /vɛrnisaʒ/ *n.m.* (*exposition*) preview.

**vernisser** /vɛrnise/ *v.t.* glaze.

**verra, verrait** /vɛra, vɛrɛ/ *voir* **voir**.

**verre** /vɛr/ *n.m.* glass. **prendre** *ou* **boire un ~**, have a drink. **~ de contact**, contact lens.

**verrou** /vɛru/ *n.m.* bolt.

**verrouiller** /vɛruje/ *v.t.* bolt.

**verrue** /vɛry/ *n.f.* wart.

**vers**[1] /vɛr/ *prép.* towards; (*temps*) about.

**vers**[2] /vɛr/ *n.m.* (*ligne*) line. **les ~**, (*poésie*) verse.

**versant** /vɛrsɑ̃/ *n.m.* slope, side.

**verse (à)** /(a)vɛrs/ *adv.* in torrents.

**Verseau** /vɛrso/ *n.m.* **le ~**, Aquarius.

**vers|er** /vɛrse/ *v.t./i.* pour; (*payer*) pay. **~ement** *n.m.* payment.

**verset** /vɛrsɛ/ *n.m.* (*relig.*) verse.

**version** /vɛrsjɔ̃/ *n.f.* version; (*traduction*) translation.

**verso** /vɛrso/ *n.m.* back (of the page).

**vert, ~e** /vɛr, -t/ *a.* green. • *n.m.* green.

**vertèbre** /vɛrtɛbr/ *n.f.* vertebra.

**vertic|al, ~ale** (*m. pl.* **~aux**) /vɛrtikal, -o/ *a. & n.f.* vertical. **~alement** *adv.* vertically.

**vertige** /vɛrtiʒ/ *n.m.* dizziness. **avoir le ~**, feel dizzy.

**vertu** /vɛrty/ *n.f.* virtue. **en ~ de**, by virtue of.

**verveine** /vɛrvɛn/ *n.f.* verbena.

**vésicule** /vezikyl/ *n.f.* **~ biliaire**, gallbladder.

**vessie** /vesi/ *n.f.* bladder.

**veste** /vɛst/ *n.f.* jacket.

**vestiaire** /vɛstjɛr/ *n.m.* cloakroom; (*sport*) changing-room.

**vestibule** /vɛstibyl/ *n.m.* hall.

**vestige** /vɛstiʒ/ *n.m.* (*objet*) relic; (*trace*) vestige.

**veston** /vɛstɔ̃/ *n.m.* jacket.

**vêtement** /vɛtmɑ̃/ *n.m.* article of clothing. **~s**, clothes.

**vétéran** /veterɑ̃/ *n.m.* veteran.

**vétérinaire** /veterinɛr/ *n.m./f.* vet, veterinary surgeon.

**vêt|ir** /vetir/ *v.t.*, **se ~ir** *v. pr.* dress. **~u** *a.* dressed (**de**, in).

**veto** /veto/ *n.m. invar.* veto.

**vétuste** /vetyst/ *a.* dilapidated.

**veu|f, ~ve** /vœf, -v/ *a.* widowed. • *n.m.* widower. • *n.f.* widow.

**veuille** /vœj/ *voir* **vouloir**.

**veut, veux** /vø/ *voir* **vouloir**.

**vex|er** /vɛkse/ *v.t.* upset, hurt. **se ~er** *v. pr.* be upset, be hurt. **~ant, ~ante** *a.* upsetting.

**via** /vja/ *prép.* via.

**viaduc** /vjadyk/ *n.m.* viaduct.

**viande** /vjɑ̃d/ *n.f.* meat.

**vibr|er** /vibre/ *v.i.* vibrate; (*être ému*) thrill. **~ation** *n.f.* vibration.

**vicaire** /vikɛr/ *n.m.* curate.

**vice** /vis/ *n.m.* (*moral*) vice; (*défectuosité*) defect.

**vice-** /vis/ *préf.* vice-.

**vice versa** /vis(e)vɛrsa/ *adv.* vice versa.

**vicieu|x, ~se** /visjø, -z/ *a.* depraved. • *n.m., f.* pervert.

**victime** /viktim/ *n.f.* victim; (*d'un accident*) casualty.

**vict|oire** /viktwar/ *n.f.* victory; (*sport*) win. **~orieux, ~orieuse** *a.* victorious; (*équipe*) winning.

**victuailles** /viktɥaj/ *n.f. pl.* provisions.

**vidang|e** /vidɑ̃ʒ/ *n.f.* emptying; (*auto.*) oil change; (*dispositif*) waste pipe. **~er** *v.t.* empty.

**vide** /vid/ *a.* empty. • *n.m.* emptiness, void; (*trou, manque*) gap; (*espace sans air*) vacuum.

**vidéo** /video/ *a. invar.* video. **jeu ~**, video game. **~cassette** *n.f.* video(tape). **~thèque** *n.f.* video library.

**vide-ordures** /vidɔrdyr/ *n.m. invar.* (rubbish) chute.

**vider** /vide/ *v.t.* empty; (*poisson*) gut; (*expulser: fam.*) throw out.

**videur** /vidœr/ *n.m.* bouncer.

**vie** /vi/ *n.f.* life; (*durée*) lifetime. **en ~**, alive.

**vieil** /vjɛj/ *voir* **vieux**.

**vieillard** /vjɛjar/ *n.m.* old man.

**vieille** /vjɛj/ *voir* **vieux**.

**vieillesse** /vjɛjɛs/ *n.f.* old age.

**vieill|ir** /vjɛjir/ *v.i.* grow old, age; (*mot, idée*) become old-fashioned. • *v.t.* age. **~issement** *n.m.* ageing.

**viens, vient** /vjɛ̃/ *voir* **venir**.

**vierge** /vjɛrʒ/ *n.f.* virgin. **la V~**, Virgo. • *a.* virgin; (*feuille, film*) blank.

**vieux** *ou* **vieil**\*, **vieille** (*m. pl.* **vieux**) /vjø, vjɛj/ *a.* old. • *n.m.* old man. • *n.f.* old woman. **mon ~**, (*fam.*) old man *ou* boy. **ma vieille**, (*fam.*) old girl, dear. **vieille fille**, (*péj.*) spinster. **~ garçon**, bachelor.

**vif, vive** /vif, viv/ *a.* lively; (*émotion, vent*) keen; (*froid*) biting; (*lumière*) bright; (*douleur, parole*) sharp; (*souvenir, style, teint*) vivid; (*succès, impatience*) great.

**vigilan|t, ~te** /viʒilɑ̃, -t/ *a.* vigilant. **~ce** *n.f.* vigilance.

**vigne** /viɲ/ *n.f.* (*plante*) vine; (*vignoble*) vineyard.

**vigneron, ~ne** /viɲrɔ̃, -ɔn/ *n.m., f.* winegrower.

**vignette** /viɲɛt/ *n.f.* (*étiquette*) label; (*auto.*) road tax sticker.

**vignoble** /viɲɔbl/ *n.m.* vineyard.

**vigoureu|x, ~se** /vigurø, -z/ *a.* vigorous, sturdy.

**vigueur** /vigœr/ *n.f.* vigour. **être/entrer en ~,** (*loi*) be/come into force. **en ~,** (*terme*) in use.

**VIH** *abrév.* (*virus d'immunodéficience humaine*) HIV.

**vilain, ~e** /vilɛ̃, -ɛn/ *a.* (*mauvais*) nasty; (*laid*) ugly.

**villa** /villa/ *n.f.* (detached) house.

**village** /vilaʒ/ *n.m.* village.

**villageois, ~e** /vilaʒwa, -z/ *a.* village. ● *n.m., f.* villager.

**ville** /vil/ *n.f.* town; (*importante*) city. **~ d'eaux,** spa.

**vin** /vɛ̃/ *n.m.* wine.

**vinaigre** /vinɛgr/ *n.m.* vinegar.

**vinaigrette** /vinɛgrɛt/ *n.f.* oil and vinegar dressing, vinaigrette.

**vindicati|f, ~ve** /vɛ̃dikatif, -v/ *a.* vindictive.

**vingt** /vɛ̃/ (/vɛ̃t/ *before vowel and in numbers 22-29*) *a.* & *n.m.* twenty. **~ième** *a.* & *n.m./f.* twentieth.

**vingtaine** /vɛ̃tɛn/ *n.f.* **une ~ (de),** about twenty.

**vinicole** /vinikɔl/ *a.* wine(-growing).

**vinyle** /vinil/ *n.m.* vinyl.

**viol** /vjɔl/ *n.m.* (*de femme*) rape; (*de lieu, loi*) violation.

**viol|ent, ~ente** /vjɔlɑ̃, -t/ *a.* violent. **~emment** /-amɑ̃/ *adv.* violently. **~ence** *n.f.* violence; (*acte*) act of violence.

**viol|er** /vjɔle/ *v.t.* rape; (*lieu, loi*) violate. **~ation** *n.f.* violation.

**violet, ~te** /vjɔlɛ, -t/ *a.* & *n.m.* purple. ● *n.f.* violet.

**violon** /vjɔlɔ̃/ *n.m.* violin. **~iste** /-ɔnist/ *n.m./f.* violinist. **~ d'Ingres,** hobby.

**violoncelle** /vjɔlɔ̃sɛl/ *n.m.* cello.

**vipère** /vipɛr/ *n.f.* viper, adder.

**virage** /viraʒ/ *n.m.* bend; (*de véhicule*) turn.

**vir|er** /vire/ *v.i.* turn. ● *v.t.* (*argent*) transfer; (*expulser: fam.*) throw out. **~ement** *n.m.* (*comm.*) (credit) transfer.

**virginité** /virʒinite/ *n.f.* virginity.

**virgule** /virgyl/ *n.f.* comma; (*dans un nombre*) (decimal) point.

**viril** /viril/ *a.* manly, virile.

**virus** /virys/ *n.m.* virus.

**vis¹** /vi/ *voir* **vivre, voir**.

**vis²** /vis/ *n.f.* screw.

**visa** /viza/ *n.m.* visa.

**visage** /vizaʒ/ *n.m.* face.

**vis-à-vis** /vizavi/ *adv.* face to face, opposite. **~ de,** opposite; (*à l'égard de*) with respect to.

**viscères** /visɛr/ *n.m. pl.* intestines.

**viser** /vize/ *v.t.* aim at; (*concerner*) be aimed at; (*timbrer*) stamp.

**visib|le** /vizibl/ *a.* visible. **~ilité** *n.f.* visibility.

**visière** /vizjɛr/ *n.f.* (*de casquette*) peak; (*de casque*) visor.

**vision** /vizjɔ̃/ *n.f.* vision.

**visionn|er** /vizjone/ *v.t.* view. **~euse** *n.f.* (*appareil*) viewer.

**visite** /vizit/ *n.f.* visit; (*examen*) examination; (*personne*) visitor. **heures de ~,** visiting hours. **~ guidée,** guided tour. **rendre ~ à,** visit.

**visit|er** /vizite/ *v.t.* visit. **~eur, ~euse** *n.m., f.* visitor.

**vison** /vizɔ̃/ *n.m.* mink.

**visqueu|x, ~se** /viskø, -z/ *a.* viscous.

**visser** /vise/ *v.t.* screw (on).

**visuel, ~le** /vizɥɛl/ *a.* visual.

**vit** /vi/ *voir* **vivre, voir**.

**vit|al** (*m. pl.* **~aux**) /vital, -o/ *a.* vital. **~alité** *n.f.* vitality.

**vitamine** /vitamin/ *n.f.* vitamin.

**vite** /vit/ *adv.* fast, quickly; (*tôt*) soon. **~!,** quick! **faire ~,** be quick.

**vitesse** /vites/ *n.f.* speed; (*régime: auto.*) gear. **à toute ~,** at top speed. **en ~,** in a hurry, quickly.

**vitic|ole** /vitikɔl/ *a.* wine. **~ulteur** *n.m.* wine-grower. **~ulture** *n.f.* wine-growing.

**vitrage** /vitraʒ/ *n.m.* (*vitres*) windows. **double-~,** double glazing.

**vitr|ail** (*pl.* **~aux**) /vitraj, -o/ *n.m.* stained-glass window.

**vitr|e** /vitr/ *n.f.* (window) pane; (*de véhicule*) window. **~é** *a.* glass, glazed. **~er** *v.t.* glaze.

**vitrine** /vitrin/ *n.f.* (shop) window.

**vivant, ~e** /vivɑ̃, -t/ *a.* (*doué de vie, en usage*) living; (*en vie*) alive, living; (*actif, vif*) lively. ● *n.m.* **un bon ~,** a bon viveur.

**vive¹** /viv/ *voir* **vif**.

**vive²** /viv/ *int.* **~ le roi/président/etc.!,** long live the king/president/etc.!

**vivier** /vivje/ *n.m.* fish-pond.

**vivisection** /viviseksjɔ̃/ *n.f.* vivisection.

**vivre†** /vivr/ *v.i.* live. **~ de,** (*nourriture*) live on. ● *v.t.* (*vie*) live; (*période, aventure*) live through. **~s** *n.m. pl.* supplies. **faire ~,** (*famille etc.*) support.

**vlan** /vlɑ̃/ *int.* bang.

**vocabulaire** /vɔkabylɛr/ *n.m.* vocabulary.

**vocation** /vɔkasjɔ̃/ *n.f.* vocation.

**vodka** /vɔdka/ *n.f.* vodka.

**vœu** (*pl.* **~x**) /vø/ *n.m.* (*souhait*) wish; (*promesse*) vow.

**voici** /vwasi/ *prép.* here is, this is; (*au pluriel*) here are, these are.

**voie** /vwa/ *n.f.* (*route*) road; (*chemin*) way; (*moyen*) means, way; (*partie de route*) lane; (*rails*) track; (*quai*) platform. **en ~ de,** in the process of. **en ~ de développement,** (*pays*) developing. **~ ferrée,** railway. **~ lactée,** Milky Way. **~ navigable,** waterway. **~ publique,** public highway. **~ sans issue,** cul-de-sac, dead end.

**voilà** /vwala/ *prép.* there is, that is; (*au pluriel*) there are, those are; (*voici*) here is; here are. **le ~,** there he is. **~!,** right!; (*en offrant qch.*) there you are!

**voilage** /vwalaʒ/ *n.m.* net curtain.

**voile**[1] /vwal/ *n.f.* (*de bateau*) sail; (*sport*) sailing.

**voile**[2] /vwal/ *n.m.* veil; (*tissu léger et fin*) net.

**voiler** /vwale/ *v.t.* veil. **~é** *a.* (*terme, femme*) veiled; (*flou*) hazy.

**voilier** /vwalje/ *n.m.* sailing-ship.

**voir**† /vwar/ *v.t./i.* see. **se ~** *v. pr.* (*être visible*) show; (*se produire*) be seen; (*se trouver*) find o.s.; (*se fréquenter*) see each other. **ça n'a rien à ~ avec,** that has nothing to do with. **faire ~, laisser ~,** show. **je ne peux pas le ~,** (*fam.*) I cannot stand him. **voyons!,** (*irritation*) come on!

**voirie** /vwari/ *n.f.* (*service*) highway maintenance. **travaux de ~,** road-works.

**voisin, ~e** /vwazɛ̃, -in/ *a.* (*proche*) neighbouring; (*adjacent*) next (**de,** to); (*semblable*) similar (**de,** to). ● *n.m., f.* neighbour. **le ~,** the man next door.

**voisinage** /vwazinaʒ/ *n.m.* neighbourhood; (*proximité*) proximity.

**voiture** /vwatyr/ *n.f.* (motor) car; (*wagon*) coach, carriage. **en ~!,** all aboard! **~ de course,** racing-car. **~ d'enfant,** pram. **~ de tourisme,** private car.

**voix** /vwa/ *n.f.* voice; (*suffrage*) vote.

**vol**[1] /vol/ *n.m.* (*d'avion, d'oiseau*) flight; (*groupe d'oiseaux etc.*) flock, flight.

**vol**[2] /vol/ *n.m.* (*délit*) theft; (*hold-up*) robbery.

**volaille** /volaj/ *n.f.* **la ~,** (*poules etc.*) poultry. **une ~,** a fowl.

**volant** /volã/ *n.m.* (steering-)wheel; (*de jupe*) flounce.

**volcan** /volkã/ *n.m.* volcano.

**volée** /vole/ *n.f.* flight; (*oiseaux*) flight, flock; (*de coups, d'obus*) volley.

**voler**[1] /vole/ *v.i.* (*oiseau etc.*) fly.

**vol|er**[2] /vole/ *v.t./i.* steal (**à,** from). **il ne l'a pas ~é,** he deserved it. **~er qn.,** rob s.o. **~eur, ~euse** *n.m., f.* thief; *a.* thieving.

**volet** /volɛ/ *n.m.* (*de fenêtre*) shutter; (*de document*) (folded *ou* tear-off) section.

**volontaire** /volõtɛr/ *a.* voluntary; (*personne*) determined. ● *n.m./f.* volunteer. **~ment** *adv.* voluntarily; (*exprès*) intentionally.

**volonté** /volõte/ *n.f.* (*faculté, intention*) will; (*souhait*) wish; (*énergie*) will-power. **à ~,** (*à son gré*) at will. **bonne ~,** goodwill. **mauvaise ~,** ill will.

**volontiers** /volõtje/ *adv.* (*de bon gré*) willingly, gladly.

**volt** /volt/ *n.m.* volt. **~age** *n.m.* voltage.

**volume** /volym/ *n.m.* volume.

**volumineu|x, ~se** /volyminø,-z/ *a.* bulky.

**vom|ir** /vomir/ *v.t./i.* vomit. **~i** *n.m.* vomit. **~issement(s)** *n.m.* (*pl.*) vomiting.

**vont** /võ/ *voir* **aller**[1].

**vorace** /voras/ *a.* voracious.

**vos** /vo/ *voir* **votre**.

**vote** /vot/ *n.m.* (*action*) voting; (*d'une loi*) passing; (*suffrage*) vote.

**voter** /vote/ *v.i.* vote. ● *v.t.* vote for; (*adopter*) pass; (*crédits*) vote.

**votre** (*pl.* **vos**) /votr, vo/ *a.* your.

**vôtre** /votr/ *pron.* **le** *ou* **la ~, les ~s,** yours.

**vouloir**† /vulwar/ *v.t.* want (**faire,** to do). **ça ne veut pas bouger** /*etc.*/, it will not move /*etc.* **je voudrais/voudrais bien venir** /*etc.*/, I should *ou* would like/really like to come /*etc.* **je veux bien venir** /*etc.*/, I am happy to come /*etc.* **voulez-vous attendre** /*etc.*/? will you wait /*etc.*? **veuillez attendre** /*etc.*/, kindly wait /*etc.* **~ absolument faire,** insist on doing. **comme** *ou* **si vous voulez,** if you like *ou* wish. **en ~ à qn.,** have a grudge against s.o.; (*être en colère contre*) be annoyed with s.o. **qu'est ce qu'il me veut?,** what does he want with me? **ne pas ~ de qch./qn.,** not want sth./s.o. **~ dire,** mean. **~ du bien à,** wish well.

**voulu** /vuly/ *a.* (*délibéré*) intentional; (*requis*) required.

**vous** /vu/ *pron.* (*sujet, complément*) you; (*indirect*) (to) you; (*réfléchi*) yourself; (*pl.*) yourselves; (*l'un l'autre*) each other. **~-même** *pron.* yourself. **~-mêmes** *pron.* yourselves.

**voûte** /vut/ *n.f.* (*plafond*) vault; (*porche*) archway.

**voûté** /vute/ *a.* bent, stooped.

**vouv|oyer** /vuvwaje/ *v.t.* address politely (using *vous*). **~oiement** *n.m.* use of (polite) *vous*.

**voyage** /vwajaʒ/ *n.m.* journey, trip; (*par mer*) voyage. **~(s),** (*action*) travelling. **~ d'affaires,** business trip. **~ de noces,** honeymoon. **~ organisé,** (package) tour.

**voyag|er** /vwajaʒe/ *v.i.* travel. **~eur, ~euse** *n.m., f.* traveller.

**voyant** /vwajã/ *n.m.* (*signal*) (warning) light.

**voyelle** /vwajɛl/ *n.f.* vowel.

**voyou** /vwaju/ *n.m.* hooligan.

**vrac (en)** /(ã)vrak/ *adv.* in disorder; (*sans emballage, au poids*) loose, in bulk.

**vrai** /vrɛ/ *a.* true; (*réel*) real.

**vraiment** /vrɛmã/ *adv.* really.

**vraisemblable** /vrɛsɑ̃blabl/ *a.* likely.
**VRP** *abrév. m.* (*voyageur représentant placier*) rep.
**vu** /vy/ *voir* voir. ~ **que,** seeing that.
**vue** /vy/ *n.f.* (*spectacle*) sight; (*sens*) (eye)-sight; (*panorama, idée*) view.
**vulg|aire** /vylgɛr/ *a.* (*grossier*) vulgar; (*ordinaire*) common. ~**arité** *n.f.* vulgarity.
**vulnérable** /vylnerabl/ *a.* vulnerable.
**vulve** /vylv/ *n.f.* vulva.

# Ww

**wagon** /vagɔ̃/ *n.m.* (*de voyageurs*) carriage; (*de marchandises*) wagon. ~**-lit** (*pl.* ~**s-lits**) *n.m.* sleeping-car, sleeper. ~**-restaurant** (*pl.* ~**s-restaurants**) *n.m.* dining-car.
**walkman** /wɔkman/ *n.m.* (P.) walkman.
**wallon,** ~**ne** /walɔ̃, -ɔn/ *a. & n.m., f.* Walloon.
**waters** /watɛr/ *n.m. pl.* toilet.
**watt** /wat/ *n.m.* watt.
**w.-c.** /(dubla)vese/ *n.m. pl.* toilet.
**week-end** /wikɛnd/ *n.m.* weekend.
**western** /wɛstɛrn/ *n.m.* western.
**whisk|y** (*pl.* ~**ies**) /wiski/ *n.m.* whisky.

# Xx

**xérès** /kseres/ *n.m.* sherry.
**xylophone** /ksilɔfɔn/ *n.m.* xylophone.

# Yy

**y** /i/ *adv. & pron.* there; (*dessus*) on it; (*pl.*) on them; (*dedans*) in it; (*pl.*) in them. **s'y habituer,** (*à cela*) get used to it. **s'y attendre,** expect it. **y penser,** think of it. **il y entra,** (*dans cela*) he entered it. **j'y vais,** I'm on my way. **ça y est,** that is it.
**yacht** /jɔt/ *n.m.* yacht.
**yaourt** /jaur(t)/ *n.m.* yoghurt.
**yeux** /jø/ *voir* œil.
**yiddish** /(j)idiʃ/ *n.m.* Yiddish.

**yoga** /jɔga/ *n.m.* yoga.
**yougoslave** /jugɔslav/ *a. & n.m./f.* Yugoslav.
**Yougoslavie** /jugɔslavi/ *n.f.* Yugoslavia.

# Zz

**zèbre** /zɛbr/ *n.m.* zebra.
**zèle** /zɛl/ *n.m.* zeal.
**zéro** /zero/ *n.m.* nought, zero; (*température*) zero; (*dans un numéro*) 0; (*football*) nil. **(re)partir de ~,** start from scratch.
**zeste** /zɛst/ *n.m.* peel. **un ~ de,** (*fig.*) a pinch of.
**zigzag** /zigzag/ *n.m.* zigzag.
**zinc** /zɛ̃g/ *n.m.* (*métal*) zinc; (*comptoir: fam.*) bar.
**zodiaque** /zɔdjak/ *n.m.* zodiac.
**zona** /zona/ *n.f.* (*méd.*) shingles.
**zone** /zon/ *n.f.* zone, area; (*faubourgs*) shanty town. ~ **bleue,** restricted parking zone.
**zoo** /zo(o)/ *n.m.* zoo.
**zoom** /zum/ *n.m.* zoom lens.
**zut** /zyt/ *int.* blast (it), (oh) hell.

# French in Context

## Contents

Jet Set

Making Tracks

Time Out

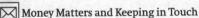Hotel Break

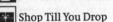Money Matters and Keeping in Touch

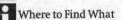Where to Find What

Shop Till You Drop

## Parlez-vous français?

Imagine you are in France or any other French-speaking country. Whether you want to travel around, spend a night out, or go shopping, you need to make yourself understood. With what you have learned so far in class or on your own, how well do you think you would cope?

Do you want to find out? The following section is a test-yourself conversation guide, which has been designed precisely to help you practise everyday language. It will help you build up your vocabulary in a fun and relaxed way through role play and model dialogues.

The section includes seven common situations as listed above. For each of them, you will find a variety of role play situations, a reminder of useful structures and vocabulary, and also a model dialogue.

# Jet Set

## Role Play

### Imagine . . .

1 You want to fly to Paris/Rome/etc.: buy a ticket.
2 You have missed your plane: ask if there is a later flight.
3 Your flight is delayed: ask why and when it will take off.
4 Your flight is cancelled: ask why, and try and find out how you can get to your destination.
5 You are to meet somebody at the airport. You know where they come from, but you don't know at what time exactly: ask at the information desk and find out where you have to wait for them.

### Useful vocabulary and structures

l'aéroport—*the airport*
l'aérogare—*the terminal*
le comptoir de vente
  —*the ticket office*
un billet (d'avion)—*a plane ticket*
un billet aller-retour
  —*a return ticket*
un aller simple—*a single ticket*
un passeport/une carte d'identité—*a passport/an identity card*
un visa—*a visa*
une hôtesse (d'accueil)
  —*an attendant (in the airport)*
une hôtesse de l'air/un steward
  —*a flight attendant*
un passager/une passagère
  —*a passenger*
l'enregistrement—*the check-in*
j'ai enregistré mes bagages
  —*I've checked my luggage in*
une carte d'embarquement
  —*a boarding card*

un chariot à bagages
  —*a luggage trolley*
un bagage à main
  —*a piece of hand luggage*
une salle d'attente
  —*a waiting lounge*
les boutiques hors taxes
  —*the duty-free shops*
les départs internationaux
  —*international departures*
un vol en provenance de
  Londres—*a flight from London*
un vol à destination de
  Bruxelles—*a flight to Brussels*
un vol en correspondance de
  Rio—*a connecting flight from Rio*
un vol sans escale—*a direct flight*
un vol qui fait escale à Los
  Angeles
  —*a flight which stops in L. A.*
le vol est annulé/retardé
  —*the flight is cancelled/delayed*

vous avez une place côté
   couloir/fenêtre
   *—you have an aisle/a window seat*
je prends/nous prenons l'avion
   pour . . .*—I'm/we are flying to . . .*
pour aller de l'aérogare 1 à
   l'aérogare 2, prenez la
   navette—*to get from terminal 1
   to terminal 2, take the shuttle*
il voyage toujours en classe

affaires/en classe économique
   *—he always travels business
   class/tourist class*
nous sommes passés à la douane
   *—we went through customs*
je n'ai rien à déclarer
   *—I've got nothing to declare*
embarquement porte 3
   *—boarding at gate 3*

## Model Dialogue

Trop tard, l'avion est parti!

   le passager = ●

   l'hôtesse = ○

● Excusez-moi, Mademoiselle, je devais prendre l'avion de 14h10 pour Berlin, mais j'ai été retardé par les embouteillages et je viens juste d'arriver. Je suppose que mon avion est déjà parti?

○ Oui, je regrette, Monsieur. Mais vous avez de la chance, il reste des places sur le vol de 15h30.

● C'est parfait, merci. À quelle heure arrive-t-il à Berlin?

○ 16h55. Puis-je avoir votre billet et votre passeport, s'il vous plaît?

● Oui, voilà.

○ Il ne reste que des places côté couloir, ça vous va?

● Oui, oui, très bien merci. Je dois absolument être à Berlin ce soir.

○ Vous avez des bagages à enregistrer?

● Je n'ai qu'un sac de voyage, je peux peut-être le garder comme bagage à main?

○ Oui, il n'est pas très grand, ça ne pose pas de problèmes. Voici votre billet et votre carte d'embarquement. L'embarquement est à 15 heures, porte 34. Je vous souhaite un bon voyage.

● Je ne connais pas bien l'aéroport, où se trouve la porte 34?

○ Montez au premier étage pour le contrôle des passeports. Après la douane, tournez à droite et longez les boutiques hors taxes. Vous arrivez ensuite dans le couloir des départs internationaux. La salle d'attente et la porte 34 sont tout au bout de ce couloir.

● Merci beaucoup, Mademoiselle.

# Making Tracks

## Role Play

### Imagine ...

1 You want to go to Lyon/Lille/etc.: buy a ticket and book your seat.
2 There is no direct train to where you want to go: find out what the best route is and the time of the connection(s).
3 Your train was delayed so you have missed the connecting train: find out when the next one is and get your ticket changed.
4 You are going on holiday and you want to take your bike with you: ask if you have to pay extra and what the procedure is.
5 You have just arrived at Nice station: go to the information desk and find out which coach/bus/train you must catch to go to Antibes, your final destination.

## Useful vocabulary and structures

la gare (SNCF)—*the (railway) station*
les départs—*Departures*
les arrivées—*Arrivals*
le guichet—*the ticket office*
le guichet automatique
  —*the ticket machine*
un billet de train—*a train ticket*
une carte vermeil®
  —*a senior citizen's railcard*
un carré jeune®
  —*a young person's railcard*
une carte Kiwi®—*a family railcard*
une réservation—*a booking*
je voudrais enregistrer un vélo
  en bagage accompagné
  —*I would like to book a bicycle
  to go in accompanied luggage*
le buffet de la gare
  —*the station buffet*

le marchand de journaux
  —*the newspaper kiosk*
la consigne—*left luggage*
la consigne automatique
  —*the left luggage lockers*
j'ai laissé mon sac à la consigne
  —*I've left my bag at left luggage*
le quai no 6—*platform number 6*
vous devez changer de quai
  —*you've got to change platforms*
le train en provenance de
  Grenoble entre en gare voie 6
  —*the train from Grenoble is
  arriving at platform 6*
un TGV—*a high-speed train*
un train rapide/omnibus/direct/
  de banlieue
  —*an express/a local/a direct/
  a suburban train*

je voyage toujours en première/
   seconde classe—*I always travel*
   *first/second class*
un wagon fumeur/non fumeur
   —*a smoking/non-smoking carriage*
un compartiment—*a compartment*
il voyage souvent en train
   couchette
   —*he often travels by sleeper*

réverver une couchette—
   *to reserve a sleeping compartment*
il a mangé au wagon restaurant
   —*he ate in the restaurant car*
est-ce qu'il y a un bar dans le
   train?
   —*is there a bar on this train?*

## Model Dialogue

Destination soleil

   le voyageur = ●

   le guichetier = O

● Bonjour! Je voudrais un aller simple pour Cannes, s'il vous plaît.

O Quand est-ce que vous voulez partir?

● Vendredi prochain, le matin si possible.

O Vendredi . . . on sera le 4 juillet . . . Le plus rapide, c'est de prendre le
   TGV jusqu'à Marseille, puis une correspondance pour Cannes.

● Il faut que je réserve ou je peux prendre n'importe quel train?

O Ah, la réservation est obligatoire sur les TGV, Monsieur. De Marseille à Cannes, par contre, ce n'est pas la peine de réserver, il
   devrait y avoir de la place. Vous voulez partir tôt?

● Vers neuf ou dix heures.

O Alors, il y a un TGV au départ de Paris - Gare de Lyon à 8h55. Arrivée
   à Marseille 13h12. Correspondance pour Cannes à 13h28.

● Ce serait parfait.

O Première classe ou seconde?

● Seconde.

O Fumeur ou non fumeur?

● Non fumeur, s'il vous plaît.

O Voilà, ça vous fait 480 francs.

● Voilà.

O Voici votre billet et votre reçu. Bon voyage!

● Merci, au revoir!

# Time Out

## Role Play

### Imagine ...

1 You are eating out in a restaurant: ask questions about the menu and order your meal.
2 The waiter has just brought your starter, but it's not what you ordered: call him back and ask for it to be changed.
3 You decide to go to the cinema but you don't know what's on: ring the cinema and ask which films are on and what time the programme starts.
4 Call the box office of a theatre to book tickets for a play.
5 The concert/play you bought tickets for has been cancelled: go to the ticket office and ask if you can get your money back, or if the concert/play is rescheduled for a later date, etc.

## Useful vocabulary and structures

un café (*place*)—*a cafe*
une brasserie—*a bar*
un restaurant—*a restaurant*
j'ai réservé une table pour deux
  —*I've reserved a table for two*
une entrée—*a starter*
un plat principal—*a main course*
un dessert—*a pudding, a sweet*
une bouteille/un pichet de vin
  —*a bottle/a jug of wine*
un demi/une bière
  —*a half of lager/a lager*
un café (*drink*)—*an espresso*
je voudrais un petit/grand crème
  —*a small/large espresso with milk*
je vais prendre le menu à 120
  francs
  —*I'll have the 120 francs menu*

commander un repas à la carte
  —*to order à la carte*
je pourrais avoir l'addition, s'il
  vous plaît
  —*could I have the bill, please*
Bon appétit!—*Enjoy your meal!*
un cinéma—*a cinema*
un multisalles—*a cinema complex*
un théâtre—*a theatre*
être assis au deuxième rang de
  l'orchestre/au premier balcon
  —*to have seats in the second row of
  the stalls/in the dress circle*
une salle de concert
  —*a concert hall*
on s'est retrouvé à l'entracte
  —*we met up during the interval*

est-ce qu'on peut acheter les billets à l'avance?
  —*is it possible to buy tickets in advance?*

qu'est-ce qui passe au cinéma?
  —*what's on at the cinema?*

je voudrais un billet étudiant
  —*I would like a student ticket*

je suis allé voir une pièce en matinée—*I went to see a matinee performance*

je suis allé au théâtre voir une pièce de Molière—*I went to the theatre to see a play by Molière*

j'aime l'opéra/le rock/le jazz
  —*I like opera/rock/jazz*

est-ce que tu veux sortir ce soir?
  —*do you want to go out this evening?*

est-ce que tu es libre samedi soir?
  —*are you free on Saturday night?*

à quelle heure est-ce que ça commence?
  —*what time does it start?*

on pourrait se retrouver devant le ciné/au café à 8 heures
  —*we could meet in front of the cinema/in the cafe at eight o'clock*

## Model dialogue

Bon appétit!

- ● = le serveur
- ○ = la cliente
- □ = le client

● Vous avez choisi?

○ Oui, je vais prendre une salade au chèvre chaud en entrée, suivie d'une sole meunière, s'il vous plaît.

● Monsieur?

□ Pour moi, une entrecôte-frites, s'il vous plaît.

● Quelle cuisson pour l'entrecôte?

○ À point.

● Vous ne prenez pas d'entrée?

□ Non, merci.

● Et pour le petit?

○ Vous avez un menu enfant?

● Oui, saucisses-frites ou jambon-purée.

○ Saucisses-frites, s'il vous plaît.

● Comme boissons, qu'est-ce que vous prendrez?

□ Un demi, un verre de vin blanc sec et un jus de pomme. On pourrait avoir une carafe d'eau aussi, s'il vous plaît?

● Pas de problème, je vous apporte tout ça.

# Hotel Break

## Role Play

### Imagine ...

1 Ring a hotel to book a single room with ensuite bathroom.
2 You've just arrived in a hotel. There is something wrong with the room you have been given: go to reception and complain.
3 After the first night, you want to change rooms: the one you have is too noisy and you haven't been able to get any sleep.
4 You arrive in a hotel to find out that your room has been double-booked. There are no more rooms available in the hotel: ask the receptionist to ring other hotels and find you a room for a similar price.
5 You are checking out but you haven't got anywhere to leave your luggage for the day while you go sightseeing before your evening flight: ask if you can leave it in the hotel.

## Useful vocabulary and structures

un hôtel deux étoiles/trois étoiles
—*a two/three star hotel*

la réception—*reception*

le réceptionniste
—*the receptionist*

une chambre d'hôtel
—*a hotel room*

une chambre pour deux personnes or double—*a double room*

une chambre avec des lits jumeaux—*a twin bedded room*

une chambre pour une personne or simple—*a single room*

une chambre avec douche/salle de bains—*a room with a shower/ bathroom*

une chambre avec vue sur la mer/sur le port/etc.

—*a room with a view over the sea/the port/etc.*

y a-t-il le téléphone/la télévision/ l'air conditionné dans la chambre?—*is there a telephone/a television/air conditioning in the room?*

j'ai réservé une chambre
—*I have reserved a room*

la chambre que j'ai réservée est trop petite/sombre/etc.
—*the room I have reserved is too small/dark/etc.*

une réservation—*a reservation*

il va passer cinq jours dans un hôtel en pension complète/en demi-pension—*he is going to spend five days in a hotel with full board/half board* arriver à l'hôtel—to arrive at the hotel, to check in

quitter l'hôtel—to check out of the hotel, to leave the hotel

prendre sa clé—to collect the keys

une serviette de toilette—a towel

il n'y a pas d'eau chaude/de chauffage—there is no hot water/ the heating is not working

la télévision ne marche pas —the television doesn't work

pouvez-vous me réveiller à sept heures demain matin? —could you give me an alarm call at 7 o'clock tomorrow morning?

petit déjeuner compris —breakfast included

à quelle heure est le petit déjeuner/le dîner? —what time is breakfast/supper?

les chambres doivent être libérées avant 11 heures —please vacate your room by 11 a.m.

## Model Dialogue

le client = ●

le réceptionniste = ○

● Excusez-moi, Monsieur. Je crois qu'il y a un problème. Ma femme et moi venons d'arriver et la chambre que votre collègue nous a donnée ne correspond pas du tout à ce que nous avons demandé.

○ Qu'est-ce qui ne va pas?

● Au téléphone, on nous avait assuré que nous aurions une chambre avec vue sur la mer. En plus, nous avions réservé une chambre pour deux avec salle de bains et il n'y a pas de salle de bains.

○ Quelle chambre vous a-t-on donnée?

● La 35.

○ Et vous êtes Monsieur . . .?

● Monsieur Mills.

○ Laissez-moi vérifier. . . Ah, oui, voilà, c'est une erreur, on aurait dû vous donner la 32. Je suis vraiment désolé, Monsieur. Je vais monter avec vous et vous aidez à porter vos bagages.

● {. . .}

○ Voilà, Monsieur. . . vue sur la mer et la salle de bains est ici.

● Ah, c'est mieux comme ça. La vue est superbe.

○ Je suis vraiment désolé de ce désagrément. Je vous laisse vous installer tranquillement. Ensuite, la maison vous offre l'apéritif.

# Money Matters and Keeping in Touch

## Role Play

### Imagine ...

1 You want to send a letter/a postcard to Australia: ask the cashier for the correct stamps.

2 You want to send a present to a friend: ask for a box from the Post Office.

3 You want to withdraw some cash: talk to the cashier and find out what you have to do.

4 You have lost your wallet and your credit card was in it: ring the emergency number to cancel it.

5 You want to exchange pounds/dollars/etc. for French Francs.

### Useful vocabulary and structures

la poste—*the Post Office*

un employé/une employée de la poste—*a post office employee*

une boîte à lettres—*a letter box*

un timbre—*a stamp*

un carnet de timbres
—*a book of stamps*

une enveloppe pré-timbrée
—*a pre-paid envelope*

une enveloppe matelassée/en papier Kraft
—*a padded envelope/a brown envelope*

un mandat postal—*a postal order*

vous devez remplir ce formulaire
—*you must fill this form in*

allez au guichet numéro 6
—*go to cashier number 6*

à quelle heure est la dernière levée?
—*what time is the last collection?*

je voudrais envoyer un télé-gramme en Irlande/une lettre au tarif lent
—*I would like to send a telegramme to Ireland/this letter second class*

posez votre paquet sur la balance
—*put your parcel on the scales*

est-ce que vous vendez des timbres de collection?
—*do you sell special issue stamps?*

je voudrais envoyer cette lettre en recommandé
—*I would like to send this letter by recorded delivery*

je voudrais faire suivre mon courrier à ma nouvelle adresse— *I would like my post to be redirected to my new address*

j'attends un mandat international
—*I am expecting an International Money Order*

je voudrais ouvrir un compte
  postal/bancaire
  —*I would like to open a post office
  account/ a bank account*
une banque—*a bank*
un employé/une employée de
  banque—*a bank clerk/ a cashier*
un bureau de change
  —*a bureau de change*
le taux de change
  —*the exchange rate*
des billets de banque—*banknotes*
des pièces (de monnaie)
  —*coins/ small change*
une carte bancaire—*a bank card*
une carte de retrait—*a cash card*
une carte de crédit—*a credit card*
un chéquier—*a cheque book*
des chèques de voyage
  —*travellers' cheques*

changer de l'argent
  —*to change money*
retirer de l'argent liquide
  —*to take some cash out*
poser *or* encaisser un chèque
  —*to cash a cheque*
verser des espèces sur un compte
  —*to pay money into an account*
vous devez signer au dos du
  chèque—*you must sign the cheque
  on the back*
un bordereau de remise de
  chèques—*a paying in slip*
y a-t-il un distributeur
  automatique?
  —*is there a cashpoint machine?*
je voudrais annuler ma carte
  bancaire
  —*I would like to cancel my bank
  card*

## Model Dialogue

Bureau de change

> l'employé du bureau de change = ●
>
> le client = ○

○ Bonjour, je voudrais changer 200 livres sterling en francs français,
  s'il vous plaît.

● Pas de problème.

○ Quel est le taux de change, aujourd'hui?

● La livre est à 10,06 Francs.

○ Et vous prenez une commission?

● Oui, il y a une commission de 15 francs pour toute transaction.

○ Très bien, voici mes deux cents livres.

● Ça vous fait 2 012 francs, moins la commission 1 997 francs.

○ Merci. Je reste ici plusieurs jours, alors il me faudra sans doute plus
  d'argent: votre bureau est ouvert tous les jours?

● Nous sommes ouverts du lundi au samedi de 9 heures à 20 heures.

○ Merci beaucoup. Au revoir.

● Au revoir, Monsieur, bon séjour!

# Where to Find What

## Role Play

### Imagine ...

1 You are organizing a holiday in the region of Saint-Malo/etc.: ring the Tourist Information Centre: ask about places to visit, sporting activities, nightlife, accommodation.

2 You want to rent a gîte in the Auvergne: write to Clermont-Ferrand's tourist information centre and ask them for a list of gîtes in their region, with details of prices/location/size/etc.

3 You arrive at Nîmes but you haven't booked any accommodation: go to the tourist information centre and find accommodation for the night.

4 You see a poster in the tourist information centre's window advertising a concert: go in and ask for more details, buy a ticket.

5 You want to go and visit a castle but you don't know where it is: ask for details and for a map.

## Useful vocabulary and structures

l'office de tourisme
 —*the tourist information centre*
une brochure—*a brochure*
une affiche—*a poster*
une carte routière—*a road map*
un plan—*a map*
il m'a indiqué la direction de la poste
 —*he showed me how to get to the post office*
prenez la première rue à gauche/ la troisième rue à droite
 —*take the first road on your left/the third road on your right*
au carrefour, tournez à droite
 —*at the crossroads, turn right*

un hôtel—*a hotel*
loger chez l'habitant
 —*to stay as a paying guest*
un gîte rural—*a rural gîte*
un camping—*a campsite*
faire du camping itinérant
 —*to go on a camping tour*
une location de vacances
 —*a rented holiday flat/home*
réserver une chambre
 —*to reserve a room*
j'ai loué un studio/un deux-pièces pour une semaine
 —*I've rented a bedsit/a one-bedroom flat for a week*

je vais en vacances à la mer/
à la montagne
 —*I'm going to the seaside/to the
 mountains for my holiday*
un musée—*a museum*
un son et lumière
 —*a son and lumière display*
une exposition—*an exhibition*

un tour guidé—*a guided tour*
des spécialités régionales
 —*regional specialities*
les activités sportives
 —*sporting activities*
faire du pédalo/de la barque sur
 un lac—*to go pedal-boating/
 rowing on a lake*

## Model Dialogue

En avant la musique!

   l'hôtesse d'accueil = ●

   la touriste = O

O  Bonjour, Mademoiselle! Je peux vous renseigner?

●  Oui, je viens de voir l'affiche des Eurockéennes et j'aurais voulu quelques renseignements? C'est un concert de rock?

O  Une série de concerts, plutôt: c'est un festival qui dure trois jours. C'est le plus grand festival de rock en France. Il a lieu ici, à Belfort, chaque année.

●  Est-ce que vous avez le programme?

O  Oui, voilà. Le festival commence ce soir avec deux concerts principaux: les Smashing Pumpkins et Noir Désir.

●  Noir Désir, c'est un groupe français?

O  Oui, ils ont beaucoup de succès. Il ne reste presque plus de billets.

●  Ça pourrait être intéressant de découvrir la musique française. Combien coûtent les billets?

O  Cent vingt francs.

●  Je vais en prendre deux, s'il vous plaît.

O  Voilà, j'espère que ça vous plaira. Si vous voulez aller à d'autres concerts pendant le festival, vous pouvez aussi louer des places par téléphone. Au revoir!

●  Merci, au revoir!

# Shop Till You Drop

## Role play

### Imagine ...

1 You are staying in France with some friends and you want to buy some shampoo, a pair of jeans and a few postcards: ask one of your friends where you have to go to buy these items.

2 You see a tee-shirt you like in a shop but it's not the right size and you would prefer it in another colour: ask the shop assistant for some help.

3 You work in a souvenir shop. A French tourist who doesn't speak English asks for your advice: he wants to buy a present for both his parents, a present for his younger sister and a present for a friend.

4 You are organizing a barbecue: you are in the market and you have to buy the things you need.

5 You have just bought some yoghurts from a supermarket and you notice that they are passed their sell-by date: go to customer services and explain that you want a fresh pack instead or a refund.

## Useful vocabulary and structure

un supermarché—*a supermarket*

une superette—*a mini-market*

un grand magasin
  —*a department store*

un centre commercial
  —*a shopping centre*

un magasin de vêtements/
  chaussures—*a clothes/shoe shop*

un magasin de sport
  —*a sports shop*

une librairie—*a bookshop*

une bijouterie—*a jewellers*

il a fait les magasins
  —*he went shopping*

elle a fait les courses

  —*she did the shopping*

je ferai du lèche-vitrines
  —*I'm going window-shopping*

je suis allé au marché
  —*I went to the market*

je voudrais un kilo de poires/une
  livre de prunes/300 grammes
  de viande hachée—*I would like a
  kilo of pears/a pound of plums/
  300 grams of mince*

est-ce que vous avez des tomates?
  —*have you got any tomatoes?*

combien est-ce que ça coûte?
  —*how much does that cost/
  how much is it?*

c'est trop petit/grand
—*it's too small/big*

est-ce que vous avez la taille
en-dessous/au-dessus?
—*have you got the next size
down/up?*

j'aime la couleur/la forme/etc.
—*I like the colour/the shape/etc.*

est-ce que ça existe dans d'autres
couleurs?—*does this come in
any other colours?*

ce n'est pas la bonne taille
—*it's not the right size*

est-ce que vous avez d'autres
modèles?
—*do you have any other styles?*

je voudrais faire un échange
—*I would like to change this for
something else*

est-ce que je peux me faire
rembourser?
—*can I get a refund?*

les articles en soldes ne sont ni
repris ni échangés—*sale items
are not exchanged or refunded*

## Model Dialogue

la vendeuse = ●

la cliente = ○

● Bonjour, Mademoiselle, je peux vous renseigner?

○ Oui, j'ai vu un tee-shirt dans la vitrine et j'aurais voulu savoir si vous
avez ma taille?

● Quelle taille faites-vous?

○ Je ne sais pas exactement. En Angleterre, je fais du 10 mais je ne sais
pas à quoi ça correspond.

● À mon avis, vous devez faire du 38. Je vais regarder s'il en reste. Ah,
oui, voilà un 38. Vous pouvez l'essayer. Il y a une cabine au fond du
magasin.

○ Merci.

● Ça va la taille?

○ Oui, c'est bon, je crois. La forme me plaît beaucoup, mais je trouve
que la couleur ne me va pas très bien. Est-ce qu'il y a d'autres
couleurs?

● Dans votre taille, il me reste un bleu clair, un rouge et un vert foncé.

○ Le bleu clair est très joli.

● Oui, c'est pratique le bleu, ça se marie facilement avec d'autres
couleurs.

○ Combien est-ce qu'il coûte?

● Il est en promotion à 80 francs.

○ Très bien, je vais prendre le bleu, alors.

# Aa

**a** *a.* ( *before vowel* **an** ) un(e). **I'm a painter,** je suis peintre. **ten pence a kilo,** dix pence le kilo. **once a year,** une fois par an.

**abandon** *v.t.* abandonner. ● *n.* désinvolture *f.* **~ed** *a.* ( *behaviour* ) débauché.

**abate** *v.i.* se calmer. ● *v.t.* diminuer. **~ment** *n.* diminution *f.*

**abattoir** *n.* abattoir *m.*

**abbey** *n.* abbaye *f.*

**abbot** *n.* abbé *m.*

**abbreviat|e** *v.t.* abréger. **~ion** *n.* abréviation *f.*

**abdicat|e** *v.t./i.* abdiquer. **~ion** *n.* abdication *f.*

**abdom|en** *n.* abdomen *m.* **~inal** *a.* abdominal.

**abduct** *v.t.* enlever. **~ion** *n.* rapt *m.* **~or** *n.* ravisseu|r, -se *m.*, *f.*

**aberration** *n.* aberration *f.*

**abet** *v.t.* ( *jurid.* ) encourager.

**abhor** *v.t.* ( *p.t.* **abhorred**) exécrer. **~rence** *n.* horreur *f.* **~rent** *a.* exécrable.

**ability** *n.* aptitude *f.* (**to do**, à faire); ( *talent* ) talent *m.*

**abject** *a.* abject.

**able** *a.* capable (**to**, de). **be ~,** pouvoir; ( *know how to* ) savoir.

**abnormal** *a.* anormal. **~ity** *n.* anomalie *f.*

**aboard** *adv.* à bord. ● *prep.* à bord de.

**aboli|sh** *v.t.* supprimer, abolir. **~tion** *n.* suppression *f.*, abolition *f.*

**abominable** *a.* abominable.

**aboriginal** *a.* & *n.* aborigène ( *m.* ).

**aborigines** *n. pl.* aborigènes *m. pl.*

**abort** *v.t.* faire avorter. ● *v.i.* avorter. **~ive** *a.* ( *attempt etc.* ) manqué.

**abortion** *n.* avortement *m.* **have an ~,** se faire avorter.

**about** *adv.* ( *approximately* ) environ; ( *here and there* ) çà et là; ( *all round* ) partout, autour; ( *nearby* ) dans les parages; ( *of rumour* ) en circulation. ● *prep.* au sujet de; ( *round* ) autour de; ( *somewhere in* ) dans. **~-face, ~-turn** *ns.* ( *fig.* ) volteface *f. invar.* **~ here,** par ici. **be ~ to do,** être sur le point de faire. **how** *or* **what ~ leaving,** si on partait. **what's the film ~?,** quel est le sujet du film? **talk ~,** parler de.

**above** *adv.* au-dessus; ( *on page* ) ci-dessus. ● *prep.* au-dessus de. **he is not ~ lying,** il n'est pas incapable de mentir. **~ all,** par-dessus tout. **~-mentioned** *a.* mentionné ci-dessus.

**abrasive** *a.* abrasif; ( *manner* ) brusque. ● *n.* abrasif *m.*

**abreast** *adv.* de front. **keep ~ of,** se tenir au courant de.

**abroad** *adv.* à l'étranger; ( *far and wide* ) de tous côtés.

**abrupt** *a.* ( *sudden*, *curt* ) brusque; ( *steep* ) abrupt. **~ly** *adv.* ( *suddenly* ) brusquement; ( *curtly*, *rudely* ) avec brusquerie. **~ness** *n.* brusquerie *f.*

**abscess** *n.* abcès *m.*

**abseil** *v.i.* descendre en rappel.

**absen|t¹** *a.* absent; ( *look etc.* ) distrait. **~ce** *n.* absence *f.*; ( *lack* ) manque *m.* **in the ~ce of,** à défaut de. **~tly** *adv.* distraitement. **~t-minded** *a.* distrait.

**absent²** *v. pr.* **~ o.s.,** s'absenter.

**absentee** *n.* absent(e) *m.* ( *f.* ). **~ism** *n.* absentéisme *m.*

**absolute** *a.* absolu; ( *coward etc.*: *fam.* ) véritable. **~ly** *adv.* absolument.

**absolution** *n.* absolution *f.*

**absor|b** *v.t.* absorber. **~ption** *n.* absorption *f.*

**absorbent** *a.* absorbant.

**abst|ain** *v.i.* s'abstenir (**from**, de). **~ention** *n.* abstention *f.*

**abstinence** *n.* abstinence *f.*

**abstract** *a.* abstrait. ● *n.* ( *quality* ) abstrait *m.*; ( *summary* ) résumé *m.*

**absurd** *a.* absurde. **~ity** *n.* absurdité *f.*

**abundan|t** *a.* abondant. **~ce** *n.* abondance *f.*

**abuse¹** *v.t.* ( *misuse* ) abuser de; ( *ill-treat* ) maltraiter; ( *insult* ) injurier.

**abus|e²** *n.* ( *misuse* ) abus *m.* ( **of**, de); ( *insults* ) injures *f. pl.* **~ive** *a.* injurieux. **get ~ive,** devenir grossier.

**abyss** *n.* abîme *m.*

**academic** *a.* universitaire; ( *scholarly* ) intellectuel; ( *pej.* ) théorique. ● *n.* universitaire *m./f.* **~ally** *adv.* intellectuellement.

**academy** *n.* ( *school* ) école *f.* **A~,** ( *society* ) Académie *f.*

**accelerat|e** *v.t.* accélérer. ● *v.i.* ( *speed up* ) s'accélérer; ( *auto.* ) accélérer. **~ion** *n.* accélération *f.*

**accelerator** *n.* accélérateur *m.*

**accent** *n.* accent *m.*

**accept** *v.t.* accepter. **~able** *a.* acceptable. **~ance** *n.* acceptation *f.*; ( *approval*, *favour* ) approbation *f.*

**access** *n.* accès *m.* (**to sth.**, à qch.; **to s.o.**, auprès de qn.). **~ible** *a.* accessible. **~ road,** route d'accès *f.*

**accession** *n.* accession *f.*; ( *thing added* ) nouvelle acquisition *f.*

**accessory** *a.* accessoire. ● *n.* accessoire *m.*; (*person: jurid.*) complice *m./f.*

**accident** *n.* accident *m.*; (*chance*) hasard *m.* **~al** *a.* accidentel, fortuit. **~ally** *adv.* involontairement.

**acclaim** *v.t.* acclamer. ● *n.* acclamation(s) *f.* (*pl.*).

**acclimatiz|e** *v.t./i.* (s')acclimater. **~ation** *n.* acclimatation *f.*

**accommodat|e** *v.t.* loger, avoir de la place pour; (*adapt*) adapter; (*supply*) fournir; (*oblige*) obliger. **~ing** *a.* obligeant. **~ion** *n.* (*living premises*) logement *m.*; (*rented rooms*) chambres *f. pl.*

**accompan|y** *v.t.* accompagner. **~iment** *n.* accompagnement *m.* **~ist** *n.* accompagna|teur, -trice *m., f.*

**accomplice** *n.* complice *m./f.*

**accomplish** *v.t.* (*perform*) accomplir; (*achieve*) réaliser. **~ed** *a.* accompli. **~ment** *n.* accomplissement *m.* **~ments** *n. pl.* (*abilities*) talents *m. pl.*

**accord** *v.i.* concorder. ● *v.t.* accorder. ● *n.* accord *m.* **of one's own ~,** de sa propre initiative. **~ance** *n.* **in ~ance with,** conformément à.

**according** *adv.* **~ to,** selon, suivant. **~ly** *adv.* en conséquence.

**accordion** *n.* accordéon *m.*

**account** *n.* (*comm.*) compte *m.*; (*description*) compte rendu *m.*; (*importance*) importance *f.* ● *v.t.* considérer. **~ for,** rendre compte de, expliquer. **on ~ of,** à cause de. **on no ~,** en aucun cas. **take into ~,** tenir compte de. **~able** *a.* responsable (**for,** de; **to,** envers). **~ability** *n.* responsabilité *f.*

**accountan|t** *n.* comptable *m./f.*, expert-comptable *m.* **~cy** *n.* comptabilité *f.*

**accredited** *a.* accrédité.

**accumulat|e** *v.t./i.* (s')accumuler. **~ion** *n.* accumulation *f.*

**accumulator** *n.* (*battery*) accumulateur *m.*

**accura|te** *a.* exact, précis. **~cy** *n.* exactitude *f.*, précision *f.* **~tely** *adv.* exactement, avec précision.

**accus|e** *v.t.* accuser. **the ~ed,** l'accusé(e) *m.(f.).* **~ation** *n.* accusation *f.*

**accustom** *v.t.* accoutumer. **~ed** *a.* **become ~ed to,** s'accoutumer à.

**ace** *n.* (*card, person*) as *m.*

**ache** *n.* douleur *f.*, mal *m.* ● *v.i.* faire mal. **my leg ~s,** ma jambe me fait mal.

**achieve** *v.t.* réaliser, accomplir; (*success*) obtenir. **~ment** *n.* réalisation *f.* (**of,** de); (*feat*) exploit *m.*, réussite *f.*

**acid** *a. & n.* acide (*m.*). **~ity** *n.* acidité *f.* **~ rain,** pluies acides *f. pl.*

**acknowledge** *v.t.* reconnaître. **~ment** *n.* reconnaissance *f.*; accusé de réception *m.*

**acne** *n.* acné *f.*

**acorn** *n.* (*bot.*) gland *m.*

**acoustic** *a.* acoustique. **~s** *n. pl.* acoustique *f.*

**acquaint** *v.t.* **~ s.o. with sth.,** mettre qn. au courant de qch. **be ~ed with,** (*person*) connaître; (*fact*) savoir. **~ance** *n.* connaissance *f.*

**acquiesce** *v.i.* consentir. **~nce** *n.* consentement *m.*

**acqui|re** *v.t.* acquérir; (*habit*) prendre. **~sition** *n.* acquisition *f.*

**acquit** *v.t.* acquitter. **~tal** *n.* acquittement *m.*

**acre** *n.* (*approx.*) demi-hectare *m.* **~age** *n.* superficie *f.*

**acrid** *a.* âcre.

**acrobat** *n.* acrobate *m./f.* **~ic** *a.* acrobatique. **~ics** *n. pl.* acrobatie *f.*

**acronym** *n.* sigle *m.*

**across** *adv. & prep.* (*side to side*) d'un côté à l'autre (de); (*on other side*) de l'autre côté (**from,** de); (*crosswise*) en travers (de), à travers. **go** *or* **walk ~,** traverser.

**acrylic** *a. & n.* acrylique (*m.*).

**act** *n.* (*deed, theatre*) acte *m.*; (*in variety show*) numéro *m.*; (*decree*) loi *f.* ● *v.i.* agir; (*theatre*) jouer; (*function*) marcher; (*pretend*) jouer la comédie. ● *v.t.* (*part, role*) jouer. **~ as,** servir de. **~ing** *a.* (*temporary*) intérimaire; *n.* (*theatre*) jeu *m.*

**action** *n.* action *f.*; (*mil.*) combat *m.* **out of ~,** hors de service. **take ~,** agir.

**activate** *v.t.* (*machine*) actionner; (*reaction*) activer.

**activ|e** *a.* actif; (*interest*) vif; (*volcano*) en activité. **~ism** *n.* activisme *m.* **~ist** *n.* activiste *m./f.* **~ity** *n.* activité *f.*

**ac|tor** *n.* acteur *m.* **~tress** *n.* actrice *f.*

**actual** *a.* réel; (*example*) concret. **the ~ pen which,** le stylo même que. **in the ~ house,** (*the house itself*) dans la maison elle-même. **no ~ promise,** pas de promesse en tant que telle. **~ly** *adv.* (*in fact*) en réalité, réellement.

**acumen** *n.* perspicacité *f.*

**acupunctur|e** *n.* acupuncture *f.* **~ist** *n.* acupuncteur *m.*

**acute** *a.* aigu; (*mind*) pénétrant; (*emotion*) intense, vif; (*shortage*) grave. **~ly** *adv.* vivement.

**ad** *n.* (*fam.*) annonce *f.*

**AD** *abbr.* après J.-C.

**adamant** *a.* inflexible.

**Adam's apple** /'ædəmz'æpl/ *n.* pomme d'Adam *f.*

**adapt** *v.t./i.* (s')adapter. **~ation** *n.* adaptation *f.* **~or** *n.* (*electr.*) adaptateur *m.*; (*for two plugs*) prise multiple *f.*

**adaptab|le** *a.* souple; (*techn.*) adaptable. **~ility** *n.* souplesse *f.*

**add** *v.t./i.* ajouter. **~ (up),** (*total*) additionner. **~ up to,** (*total*) s'élever à.

**adder** *n.* vipère *f.*

**addict** *n.* intoxiqué(e) *m.* (*f.*); (*fig.*) fanatique *m./f.*

**addict|ed** *a.* ~**ed to**, (*drink*) adonné à. **be** ~**ed to**, (*fig.*) être un fanatique de. ~**ion** *n.* (*med.*) dépendance *f.*; (*fig.*) manie *f.* ~**ive** *a.* (*drug etc.*) qui crée une dépendance.

**addition** *n.* addition *f.* **in** ~, en outre. ~**al** *a.* supplémentaire.

**additive** *n.* additif *m.*

**address** *n.* adresse *f.*; (*speech*) allocution *f.* ● *v.t.* adresser; (*speak to*) s'adresser à.

**adenoids** *n. pl.* végétations (adénoïdes) *f. pl.*

**adept** *a. & n.* expert (**at**, en) (*m.*).

**adequa|te** *a.* suffisant; (*satisfactory*) satisfaisant. ~**cy** *n.* quantité suffisante *f.*; (*of person*) compétence *f.* ~**tely** *adv.* suffisamment.

**adhere** *v.i.* adhérer (**to**, à). ~ **to**, (*fig.*) respecter. ~**nce** *n.* adhésion *f.*

**adhesion** *n.* (*grip*) adhérence *f.*; (*support: fig.*) adhésion *f.*

**adhesive** *a. & n.* adhésif (*m.*).

**adjacent** *a.* contigu (**to**, à).

**adjective** *n.* adjectif *m.*

**adjoin** *v.t.* être contigu à.

**adjourn** *v.t.* ajourner. ● *v.t./i.* ~ (**the meeting**), suspendre la séance.

**adjust** *v.t.* (*machine*) régler; (*prices*) (r)ajuster; (*arrange*) rajuster, arranger. ● *v.t./i.* ~ (**o.s.**) **to**, s'adapter à. ~**able** *a.* réglable. ~**ment** *n.* (*techn.*) réglage *m.*; (*of person*) adaptation *f.*

**administer** *v.t.* administrer.

**administration** *n.* administration *f.*

**administrative** *a.* administratif.

**administrator** *n.* administra|teur, -trice *m., f.*

**admirable** *a.* admirable.

**admiral** *n.* amiral *m.*

**admir|e** *v.t.* admirer. ~**ation** *n.* admiration *f.* ~**er** *n.* admira|teur, -trice *m., f.*

**admissible** *a.* admissible.

**admission** *n.* admission *f.*; (*to museum, theatre, etc.*) entrée *f.*; (*confession*) aveu *m.*

**admit** *v.t.* (*p.t.* **admitted**) laisser entrer; (*acknowledge*) reconnaître, admettre. ~ **to**, avouer. ~**tance** *n.* entrée *f.* ~**tedly** *adv.* il est vrai (que).

**admonish** *v.t.* réprimander.

**adolescen|t** *n. & a.* adolescent(e) (*m.* (*f.*)). ~**ce** *n.* adolescence *f.*

**adopt** *v.t.* adopter. ~**ed** *a.* (*child*) adoptif. ~**ion** *n.* adoption *f.*

**adoptive** *a.* adoptif.

**ador|e** *v.t.* adorer. ~**able** *a.* adorable. ~**ation** *n.* adoration *f.*

**adorn** *v.t.* orner.

**adult** *a. & n.* adulte (*m./f.*).

**adultery** *n.* adultère *m.*

**advance** *v.t.* avancer. ● *v.i.* (s')avancer; (*progress*) avancer. ● *n.* avance *f.* ● *a.* (*payment*) anticipé. **in** ~, à l'avance. ~**d** *a.* avancé; (*studies*) supérieur.

**advantage** *n.* avantage *m.* **take** ~ **of**, profiter de; (*person*) exploiter.

**Advent** *n.* Avent *m.*

**adventur|e** *n.* aventure *f.* ~**er** *n.* explora-|teur, -trice *m., f.*; (*pej.*) aventur|ier, -ière *m., f.* ~**ous** *a.* aventureux.

**adverb** *n.* adverbe *m.*

**adversary** *n.* adversaire *m./f.*

**advers|e** *a.* défavorable. ~**ity** *n.* adversité *f.*

**advert** *n.* (*fam.*) annonce *f.*; (*TV*) pub *f.*, publicité *f.* ~**isement** *n.* publicité *f.*; (*in paper etc.*) annonce *f.*

**advertis|e** *v.t./i.* faire de la publicité (pour); (*sell*) mettre une annonce (pour vendre). ~ **for**, (*seek*) chercher (par voie d'annonce). ~**ing** *n.* publicité *f.*

**advice** *n.* conseil(s) *m.* (*pl.*); (*comm.*) avis *m.* **some** ~, **a piece of** ~, un conseil.

**advis|e** *v.t.* conseiller; (*inform*) aviser. ~**able** *a.* conseillé, prudent (**to**, de). ~**er** *n.* conseill|er, -ère *m., f.*

**advocate**[1] *n.* (*jurid.*) avocat *m.* ~**s of**, les défenseurs de.

**advocate**[2] *v.t.* recommander.

**aerial** *a.* aérien. ● *n.* antenne *f.*

**aerobatics** *n. pl.* acrobatie aérienne *f.*

**aerobics** *n.* aérobic *m.*

**aerodynamic** *a.* aérodynamique.

**aeroplane** *n.* avion *m.*

**aerosol** *n.* atomiseur *m.*

**aesthetic** *a.* esthétique.

**afar** *adv.* **from** ~, de loin.

**affable** *a.* affable.

**affair** *n.* (*matter*) affaire *f.*; (*romance*) liaison *f.*

**affect** *v.t.* affecter. ~**ation** *n.* affectation *f.* ~**ed** *a.* affecté.

**affection** *n.* affection *f.*

**affectionate** *a.* affectueux.

**affirm** *v.t.* affirmer. ~**ation** *n.* affirmation *f.*

**affirmative** *a.* affirmatif. ● *n.* affirmative *f.*

**affix** *v.t.* apposer.

**afflict** *v.t.* affliger. ~**ion** *n.* affliction *f.*, détresse *f.*

**affluen|t** *a.* riche. ~**ce** *n.* richesse *f.*

**afford** *v.t.* avoir les moyens d'acheter; (*provide*) fournir. ~ **to do**, avoir les moyens de faire; (*be able*) se permettre de faire.

**affront** *n.* affront *m.* ● *v.t.* insulter.

**afloat** *adv.* à flot.

**afoot** *adv.* **sth. is** ~, il se trame *or* se prépare qch.

**afraid** *a.* **be** ~, avoir peur (**of, to**, de; **that**, que); (*be sorry*) regretter. **I am** ~ **that**, (*regret to say*) je regrette de dire que.

**afresh** adv. de nouveau.

**Africa** n. Afrique f. ~n a. & n. africaine(e) (m. (f.)).

**after** adv. & prep. après. ● conj. après que. ~ doing, après avoir fait. ~ all après tout. ~ effect n. suite f. ~sales service, service après-vente m.

**afternoon** n. après-midi m./f. invar.

**aftershave** n. lotion après-rasage f.

**afterwards** adv. après, par la suite.

**again** adv. de nouveau, encore une fois; (besides) en outre. do ~, see ~/etc., refaire, revoir/etc.

**against** prep. contre. ~ the law, illégal.

**age** n. âge m. ● v.t./i. (pres.p. ageing) vieillir. ~ group, tranche d'âge f. ~ limit, limite d'âge. for ~s, (fam.) une éternité. of ~, (jurid.) majeur.

**aged**[1] a. ~ six, âgé de six ans.

**aged**[2] a. âgé, vieux.

**agen|cy** n. agence f.; (means) entremise f. ~t n. agent m.

**agenda** /ə'dʒendə/ n. ordre du jour m.

**aggravate** v.t. (make worse) aggraver; (annoy: fam.) exaspérer.

**aggregate** a. & n. total (m.).

**aggress|ive** a. agressif. ~ion n. agression f. ~iveness f. agressivité f.

**aghast** /ə'gɑːst/ a. horrifié.

**agil|e** a. agile. ~ity n. agilité f.

**agitat|e** v.t. agiter. ~ion n. agitation f. ~or n. agita|teur, -trice m., f.

**agnostic** a. & n. agnostique (m./f.).

**ago** /ə'gəʊ/ adv. il y a. a month ~, il y a un mois. long ~, il y a longtemps. how long ~?, il y a combien de temps?

**agon|y** n. grande souffrance f.; (mental) angoisse f. ~izing a. angoissant.

**agree** v.i. être or se mettre d'accord (on, sur); (of figures) concorder. ● v.t. (date) convenir de. ~ that, reconnaître que. ~ to do, accepter de faire. ~ to sth., accepter qch. onions don't ~ with me, je ne digère pas les oignons. ~d a. (time, place) convenu. be ~d, être d'accord.

**agreeable** a. agréable.

**agreement** n. accord m. in ~, d'accord.

**agricultur|e** n. agriculture f. ~al a. agricole.

**aground** adv. run ~, (of ship) (s')échouer.

**ahead** adv. (in front) en avant, devant; (in advance) à l'avance. ~ of s.o., devant qn.; en avance sur qn. ~ of time, en avance. straight ~, tout droit.

**aid** v.t. aider. ● n. aide f. in ~ of, au profit de.

**AIDS** n. (med.) sida m.

**aim** v.t. diriger; (gun) braquer (at, sur); (remark) destiner. ● v.i. viser. ● n. but m. ~ at, viser. ~ to, avoir l'intention de. take ~, viser. ~less a., ~lessly adv. sans but.

**air** n. air m. ● v.t. aérer; (views) exposer librement. ● a. (base etc.) aérien. ~bed n. matelas pneumatique m. ~-conditioned a. climatisé. ~-conditioning n. climatisation f. ~ force/hostess, armée/hôtesse de l'air f. ~ letter, aérogramme m. ~mail, poste aérienne f. by ~mail, par avion. by ~, par avion. in the ~, (rumour) répandu; (plan) incertain. on the ~, sur l'antenne.

**aircraft** n. invar. avion m. ~-carrier n. porte-avions m. invar.

**airfield** n. terrain d'aviation m.

**airgun** n. carabine à air comprimé f.

**airlift** n. pont aérien m. ● v.t. transporter par pont aérien.

**airline** n. ligne aérienne f. ~r n. avion de ligne m.

**airman** n. aviateur m.

**airplane** n. (Amer.) avion m.

**airport** n. aéroport m.

**airsickness** n. mal de l'air m.

**airtight** a. hermétique.

**airways** n. pl. compagnie d'aviation f.

**airworthy** a. en état de navigation.

**airy** a. bien aéré.

**aisle** n. (of church) nef latérale f.; (gangway) couloir m.

**ajar** adv. & a. entr'ouvert.

**akin** a. ~ to, apparenté à.

**à la carte** adv. & a. (culin.) à la carte.

**alacrity** n. empressement m.

**alarm** n. alarme f. ● v.t. alarmer. ~-clock n. réveil m.

**albatross** n. albatros m.

**album** n. album m.

**alcohol** n. alcool m. ~ic a. alcoolique; (drink) alcoolisé; n. alcoolique m./f. ~ism n. alcoolisme m.

**alcove** n. alcôve f.

**ale** n. bière f.

**alert** a. (lively) vif; (watchful) vigilant. ● n. alerte f. ● v.t. alerter. ~ s.o. to, prévenir qn. de. on the ~, sur le qui-vive. ~ness n. vivacité f.; vigilance f.

**A-level** n. baccalauréat m.

**algebra** n. algèbre f.

**Algeria** /æl'dʒɪərɪə/ n. Algérie f. ~n a. & n. algérien(ne) (m. (f.)).

**algorithm** n. algorithme m.

**alibi** /'ælɪbaɪ/ n. (pl. -is) alibi m.

**alien** n. & a. étrang|er, -ère (m., f.) (to, à).

**alight**[1] v.i. (person) descendre; (bird) se poser.

**alight**[2] a. en feu, allumé.

**align** v.t. aligner. ~ment n. alignement m.

**alike** a. semblable. ● adv. de la même façon. look or be ~, se ressembler.

**alimony** n. pension alimentaire f.

**alive** a. vivant.

**alkali** n. (pl. **-is**) alcali m.

**all** a. tout(e), tous, toutes. ● pron. tous, toutes; (everything) tout. ● adv. tout. ~ **(the) men,** tous les hommes. ~ **of it,** (le) tout. ~ **of us,** nous tous. ~ **for sth.,** à fond pour qch. ~ **in,** (exhausted) épuisé. ~**in** a. tout compris. ~ **out,** à fond. ~**out** a. (effort) maximum. ~ **over,** partout (sur or dans); (finished) fini. ~ **right,** bien; (agreeing) bon! ~ **round,** dans tous les domaines; (for all) pour tous. ~ **round** a. général. ~ **the same,** tout de même.

**allegation** n. allégation f.

**allege** v.t. prétendre. ~**dly** adv. d'après ce qu'on dit.

**allergy** n. allergie f. ~**ic** a. allergique (**to,** à).

**alley** n. (street) ruelle f.

**alliance** n. alliance f.

**allied** a. allié.

**alligator** n. alligator m.

**allocate** v.t. (assign) attribuer; (share out) distribuer. ~**ion** n. allocation f.

**allot** v.t. attribuer. ~**ment** n. (land) parcelle de terre f.

**allow** v.t. permettre; (grant) accorder; (reckon on) prévoir; (agree) reconnaître. ~ **s.o. to,** permettre à qn. de. ~ **for,** tenir compte de.

**allowance** n. allocation f., indemnité f. **make** ~**s for,** être indulgent envers; (take into account) tenir compte de.

**alloy** n. alliage m.

**allude** v.i. ~ **to,** faire allusion à.

**allusion** n. allusion f.

**ally**[1] n. allié(e) m. (f.).

**ally**[2] v.t. allier. ~ **o.s. with,** s'allier à or avec.

**almond** n. amande f.

**almost** adv. presque.

**alone** a. & adv. seul.

**along** prep. le long de. ● adv. **come** ~, venir. **go** or **walk** ~, passer. **all** ~, (time) tout le temps, depuis le début. ~ **with,** avec.

**alongside** adv. (naut.) bord à bord. **come** ~, accoster. ● prep. le long de.

**aloof** adv. à l'écart. ● a. distant. ~**ness** n. réserve f.

**aloud** adv. à haute voix.

**alphabet** n. alphabet m. ~**ical** a. alphabétique.

**alpine** a. (landscape) alpestre; (climate) alpin.

**Alpine** a. des Alpes.

**Alps** n. pl. **the** ~, les Alpes f. pl.

**already** adv. déjà.

**alright** a. & adv. = **all right.**

**Alsatian** n. (dog) berger allemand m.

**also** adv. aussi.

**altar** n. autel m.

**alter** v.t./i. changer. ~**ation** n. changement m.; (to garment) retouche f.

**alternate**[1] a. alterné, alternatif; (Amer.) = **alternative. on** ~ **days**/etc., (first one then the other) tous les deux jours/etc. ~**ly** adv. tour à tour.

**alternate**[2] v.i. alterner. ● v.t. faire alterner.

**alternative** a. autre; (policy) de rechange. ● n. alternative f., choix m. ~**ly** adv. comme alternative. **or** ~**ly,** ou alors.

**alternator** n. alternateur m.

**although** conj. bien que.

**altitude** n. altitude f.

**altogether** adv. (completely) tout à fait; (on the whole) à tout prendre.

**aluminium** n. aluminium m.

**always** adv. toujours.

**a.m.** adv. du matin.

**amalgamate** v.t./i. (s')amalgamer; (comm.) fusionner.

**amass** v.t. amasser.

**amateur** n. amateur m. ● a. (musician etc.) amateur.

**amaze** v.t. étonner. ~**ed** a. étonné. ~**ement** n. étonnement m. ~**ingly** adv. étonnamment.

**ambassador** n. ambassadeur m.

**amber** n. ambre m.; (auto.) feu orange m.

**ambiguous** a. ambigu.

**ambition** n. ambition f. ~**ous** a. ambitieux.

**amble** v.i. marcher sans se presser, s'avancer lentement.

**ambulance** n. ambulance f.

**amend** v.t. modifier, corriger. ~**ment** n. (to rule) amendement m.

**amends** n. pl. **make** ~, réparer son erreur.

**amenities** n. pl. (pleasant features) attraits m. pl.; (facilities) aménagements m. pl.

**America** n. Amérique f. ~**n** a. & n. américain(e) (m. (f.)).

**amiable** a. aimable.

**amicable** a. amical.

**amid(st)** prep. au milieu de.

**amiss** a. & adv. mal. **sth.** ~, qch. qui ne va pas.

**ammonia** n. (gas) ammoniac m.; (water) ammoniaque f.

**ammunition** n. munitions f. pl.

**amnesia** n. amnésie f.

**amnesty** n. amnistie f.

**among(st)** prep. parmi, entre. ~ **the crowd,** (in the middle of) parmi la foule. ~ **the English**/etc., (race, group) chez les Anglais/etc. ~ **ourselves**/etc., entre nous/etc.

**amoral** a. amoral.

**amorphous** a. amorphe.

**amount** n. quantité f.; (total) montant m.; (sum of money) somme f. ● v.i. ~ **to,** (add up to) s'élever à; (be equivalent to) revenir à.

**amp** n. (fam.) ampère m.

**ample** a. (enough) (bien) assez de; (large, roomy) ample. ~**y** adv. amplement.

**amplif|y** *v.t.* amplifier. **~ier** *n.* amplificateur *m.*

**amputat|e** *v.t.* amputer. **~ion** *n.* amputation *f.*

**amuse** *v.t.* amuser. **~ment** *n.* amusement *m.*, divertissement *m.* **~ment arcade,** salle de jeux *f.*

**anachronism** *n.* anachronisme *m.*

**anaem|ia** *n.* anémie *f.* **~ic** *a.* anémique.

**anaesthetic** *n.* anesthésique *m.* **give an ~,** faire une anesthésie (**to,** à).

**analogue, analog** *a.* analogique.

**analogy** *n.* analogie *f.*

**analys|e** *v.t.* analyser. **~t** *n.* analyste *m./f.*

**analysis** *n.* analyse *f.*

**analytic(al)** *a.* analytique.

**anarch|y** *n.* anarchie *f.* **~ist** *n.* anarchiste *m./f.*

**anatom|y** *n.* anatomie *f.* **~ical** *a.* anatomique.

**ancestor** *n.* ancêtre *m.*

**anchor** *n.* ancre *f.* ● *v.t.* mettre à l'ancre. ● *v.i.* jeter l'ancre.

**anchovy** *n.* anchois *m.*

**ancient** *a.* ancien.

**ancillary** *a.* auxiliaire.

**and** *conj.* et. **go ~ see him,** allez le voir.

**anecdote** *n.* anecdote *f.*

**angel** *n.* ange *m.*

**anger** *n.* colère *f.* ● *v.t.* mettre en colère, fâcher.

**angle** *n.* angle *m.*

**angler** *n.* pêcheu|r, -se *m., f.*

**Anglican** *a.* & *n.* anglican(e) (*m.* (*f.*)).

**angr|y** *a.* fâché, en colère. **get ~y,** se fâcher, se mettre en colère (**with,** contre). **make s.o. ~y,** mettre qn. en colère. **~ily** *adv.* en colère.

**anguish** *n.* angoisse *f.*

**animal** *n.* & *a.* animal (*m.*).

**animat|e** *v.t.* animer. **~ion** *n.* animation *f.*

**animosity** *n.* animosité *f.*

**aniseed** *n.* anis *m.*

**ankle** *n.* cheville *f.* **~ sock,** socquette *f.*

**annexe** *n.* annexe *f.*

**annihilate** *v.t.* anéantir.

**anniversary** *n.* anniversaire *m.*

**announce** *v.t.* annoncer. **~ment** *n.* annonce *f.* **~r** *n.* (*radio, TV*) speaker(ine) *m.* (*f.*).

**annoy** *v.t.* agacer, ennuyer. **~ance** *n.* contrariété *f.* **~ed** *a.* fâché (**with,** contre). **get ~ed,** se fâcher. **~ing** *a.* ennuyeux.

**annual** *a.* annuel. ● *n.* publication annuelle *f.* **~ly** *adv.* annuellement.

**annul** *v.t.* annuler. **~ment** *n.* annulation *f.*

**anomal|y** *n.* anomalie *f.* **~ous** *a.* anormal.

**anonymous** *a.* anonyme.

**anorak** *n.* anorak *m.*

**another** *a.* & *pron.* un(e) autre. **~ coffee,** (*one more*) encore un café.

**answer** *n.* réponse *f.*; (*solution*) solution *f.* ● *v.t.* répondre à; (*prayer*) exaucer. ● *v.i.* répondre. **~ the door,** ouvrir la porte. **~ing machine,** répondeur *m.*

**ant** *n.* fourmi *f.*

**antagonism** *n.* antagonisme *m.*

**antagonize** *v.t.* provoquer l'hostilité de.

**Antarctic** *a.* & *n.* antarctique (*m.*).

**antelope** *n.* antilope *f.*

**antenatal** *a.* prénatal.

**antenna** /æn'tenə/ *n.* (*of insect*) antenne *f.*; (*aerial*) antenne *f.*

**anti-** *pref.* anti-. **~-aircraft** *a.* antiaérien.

**antibiotic** *n.* antibiotique *m.*

**antibody** *n.* anticorps *m.*

**anticipat|e** *v.t.* (*foresee, expect*) prévoir, s'attendre à; (*forestall*) devancer. **~ion** *n.* attente *f.*

**anticlimax** *n.* (*let-down*) déception *f.*

**anticlockwise** *adv.* & *a.* dans le sens inverse des aiguilles d'une montre.

**anticyclone** *n.* anticyclone *m.*

**antidote** *n.* antidote *m.*

**antifreeze** *n.* antigel *m.*

**antihistamine** *n.* antihistaminique *m.*

**antipathy** *n.* antipathie *f.*

**antique** *n.* objet ancien *m.*, antiquité *f.* **~ dealer,** antiquaire *m./f.* **~ shop,** magasin d'antiquités *m.*

**anti-Semiti|c** *a.* antisémite. **~sm** *n.* antisémitisme *m.*

**antiseptic** *a.* & *n.* antiseptique (*m.*).

**antisocial** *a.* asocial, antisocial; (*unsociable*) insociable.

**antlers** *n. pl.* bois *m. pl.*

**anus** *n.* anus *m.*

**anxiety** *n.* (*worry*) anxiété *f.*; (*eagerness*) impatience *f.*

**anxious** *a.* (*troubled*) anxieux; (*eager*) impatient (**to,** de). **~ly** *adv.* anxieusement; impatiemment.

**any** *a.* (*some*) du, de l', de la, des; (*after negative*) de, d'; (*every*) tout; (*no matter which*) n'importe quel. **at ~ moment,** à tout moment. **have you ~ water?,** avez-vous de l'eau? ● *pron.* (*no matter which one*) n'importe lequel; (*someone*) quelqu'un; (*any amount of it or them*) en. **I do not have ~,** je n'en ai pas. **did you see ~ of them?,** en avez-vous vu? ● *adv.* (*a little*) un peu. **do you have ~ more?,** en avez-vous encore? **not ~,** nullement. **I don't do it ~ more,** je ne le fais plus.

**anybody** *pron.* n'importe qui; (*somebody*) quelqu'un; (*after negative*) personne. **he did not see ~,** il n'a vu personne.

**anyhow** *adv.* de toute façon; (*badly*) n'importe comment.

**anyone** *pron.* = **anybody**.

**anything** *pron.* n'importe quoi; (*something*) quelque chose; (*after negative*) rien. **he did not see ~,** il n'a rien vu.

**anyway** *adv.* de toute façon.

**anywhere** *adv.* n'importe où; (*somewhere*) quelque part; (*after negative*) nulle part. **he does not go ~,** il ne va nulle part. **~ you go,** partout où tu vas, où que tu ailles.

**apart** *adv.* (*on or to one side*) à part; (*separated*) séparé; (*into pieces*) en pièces. **~ from,** à part, excepté. **ten metres ~,** (*distant*) à dix mètres l'un de l'autre.

**apartment** *n.* (*Amer.*) appartement *m.* **~s,** logement *m.*

**apath|y** *n.* apathie *f.* **~etic** *a.* apathique.

**ape** *n.* singe *m.* ● *v.t.* singer.

**aperitif** *n.* apéritif *m.*

**aperture** *n.* ouverture *f.*

**apex** *n.* sommet *m.*

**apiece** *adv.* chacun.

**apologetic** *a.* (*tone etc.*) d'excuse. **be ~,** s'excuser.

**apologize** *v.i.* s'excuser (**for,** de; **to,** auprès de).

**apology** *n.* excuses *f. pl.*

**Apostle** *n.* apôtre *m.*

**apostrophe** *n.* apostrophe *f.*

**appal** *v.t.* épouvanter. **~ling** *a.* épouvantable.

**apparatus** *n.* appareil *m.*

**apparent** *a.* apparent. **~ly** *adv.* apparemment.

**appeal** *n.* appel *m.*; (*attractiveness*) attrait *m.*, charme *m.* ● *v.i.* (*jurid.*) faire appel. **~ to s.o.,** (*beg*) faire appel à qn.; (*attract*) plaire à qn. **~ to s.o. for sth.,** demander qch. à qn. **~ing** *a.* (*attractive*) attirant.

**appear** *v.i.* apparaître; (*arrive*) se présenter; (*seem, be published*) paraître; (*theatre*) jouer. **~ance** *n.* apparition *f.*; (*aspect*) apparence *f.*

**appease** *v.t.* apaiser.

**appendicitis** *n.* appendicite *f.*

**appendix** *n.* appendice *m.*

**appetite** *n.* appétit *m.*

**appetizing** *a.* appétissant.

**applau|d** *v.t./i.* applaudir; (*decision*) applaudir à. **~se** *n.* applaudissements *m. pl.*

**apple** *n.* pomme *f.* **~-tree** *n.* pommier *m.*

**appliance** *n.* appareil *m.*

**applicable** *a.* applicable.

**applicant** *n.* candidat(e) *m.* (*f.*) (**for,** à).

**application** /æplɪ'keɪʃn/ *n.* application *f.*; (*request, form*) demande *f.*; (*for job*) candidature *f.*

**apply** *v.t.* appliquer. ● *v.i.* for, (*job*) postuler pour; (*grant*) demander. **applied** *a.* appliqué.

**appoint** *v.t.* (*to post*) nommer; (*fix*) désigner. **~ment** *n.* nomination *f.*; (*meeting*) rendez-vous *m. invar.*; (*job*) poste *m.* **make an ~ment,** prendre rendez-vous (**with,** avec).

**apprais|e** *v.t.* évaluer. **~al** *n.* évaluation *f.*

**appreciable** *a.* appréciable.

**appreciat|e** *v.t.* (*like*) apprécier; (*understand*) comprendre; (*be grateful for*). être reconnaissant de. ● *v.i.* prendre de la valeur. **~ion** *n.* appréciation *f.*; (*gratitude*) reconnaissance *f.*; (*rise*) augmentation *f.*

**apprehensive** *a.* inquiet.

**apprentice** *n.* apprenti *m.* **~ship** *n.* apprentissage *m.*

**approach** *v.t.* (s')approcher de; (*accost*) aborder; (*with request*) s'adresser à. ● *v.i.* (s')approcher. ● *n.* approche *f.* **an ~ to,** (*problem*) une façon d'aborder; (*person*) une démarche auprès de. **~able** *a.* accessible; (*person*) abordable.

**appropriate** *a.* approprié, propre. **~ly** *adv.* à propos.

**approval** *n.* approbation *f.* **on ~,** à or sous condition.

**approve** *v.t./i.* approuver. **~ of,** approuver.

**approximate** *a.* approximatif. **~ly** *adv.* approximativement.

**apricot** *n.* abricot *m.*

**April** *n.* avril *m.* **make an ~ fool of,** faire un poisson d'avril à.

**apron** *n.* tablier *m.*

**apt** *a.* (*suitable*) approprié; (*pupil*) doué. **be ~ to,** avoir tendance à. **~ly** *adv.* à propos.

**aptitude** *n.* aptitude *f.*

**aqualung** *n.* scaphandre autonome *m.*

**aquarium** *n.* aquarium *m.*

**Aquarius** *n.* le Verseau.

**Arab** *n. & a.* arabe (*m./f.*). **~ic** *a. & n.* (*lang.*) arabe (*m.*).

**Arabian** *a.* arabe.

**arbitrary** *a.* arbitraire.

**arbitrat|e** *v.i.* arbitrer. **~ion** /-'treɪʃn/ *n.* arbitrage *m.*

**arc** *n.* arc *m.*

**arcade** *n.* (*shops*) galerie *f.*; (*arches*) arcades *f. pl.*

**arch** *n.* arche *f.*; (*in church etc.*) arc *m.*; (*of foot*) voûte plantaire *f.* ● *v.t./i.* (s')arquer.

**archaeolog|y** *n.* archéologie *f.* **~ical** *a.* archéologique. **~ist** *n.* archéologue *m./f.*

**archaic** *a.* archaïque.

**archbishop** *n.* archevêque *m.*

**archer** *n.* archer *m.* **~y** *n.* tir à l'arc *m.*

**architect** *n.* architecte *m.*

**architecture** *n.* architecture *f.*

**archives** *n. pl.* archives *f. pl.* **~ist** *n.* archiviste *m./f.*

**archway** *n.* voûte *f.*

**Arctic** *a. & n.* arctique (*m.*). **arctic** *a.* glacial.

**ardent** *a.* ardent. **~ly** *adv.* ardemment.

**ardour** *n.* ardeur *f.*

**arduous** *a.* ardu.

**area** n. (*surface*) superficie f.; (*region*) région f.; (*district*) quartier m.; (*fig.*) domaine m. **parking/picnic ~**, aire de parking/de pique-nique f.

**arena** n. arène f.

**Argentin|a** n. Argentine f. **~e**, **~ian** a. & n. argentin(e) (m. (f.)).

**argu|e** v.i. (*quarrel*) se disputer; (*reason*) argumenter. ● v.t. (*debate*) discuter. **~e that**, alléguer que. **~ably** adv. selon certains.

**argument** n. dispute f.; (*reasoning*) argument m.; (*discussion*) débat m. **~ative** a. raisonneur, contrariant.

**arid** a. aride.

**Aries** n. le Bélier.

**arise** v.i. se présenter; (*old use*) se lever. **~ from**, résulter de.

**aristocracy** n. aristocratie f.

**aristocrat** n. aristocrate m./f. **~ic** a. aristocratique.

**arithmetic** n. arithmétique f.

**ark** n. (*relig.*) arche f.

**arm**[1] n. bras m. **~ in arm**, bras dessus bras dessous. **~-band** n. brassard m.

**arm**[2] v.t. armer. **~ed robbery**, vol à main armée m.

**armament** n. armement m.

**armchair** n. fauteuil m.

**armour** n. armure f.; (*on tanks etc.*) blindage m.

**armpit** n. aisselle f.

**arms** n. pl. (*weapons*) armes f. pl. **~ dealer**, trafiquant d'armes m.

**army** n. armée f.

**aroma** n. arôme m.

**around** adv. (tout) autour; (*here and there*) çà et là. ● prep. autour de. **~ here**, par ici.

**arouse** v.t. (*awaken, cause*) éveiller; (*excite*) exciter.

**arrange** v.t. arranger; (*time, date*) fixer. **~ to**, s'arranger pour. **~ment** n. arrangement m. **make ~ments**, prendre des dispositions.

**array** n. **an ~ of**, (*display*) un étalage impressionnant de.

**arrears** n. pl. arriéré m. **in ~**, (*rent*) arriéré. **he is in ~**, il a des paiements en retard.

**arrest** v.t. arrêter; (*attention*) retenir. ● n. arrestation f. **under ~**, en état d'arrestation.

**arrival** n. arrivée f. **new ~**, nouveau venu m., nouvelle venue f.

**arrive** v.i. arriver.

**arrogan|t** a. arrogant. **~ce** n. arrogance f. **~tly** adv. avec arrogance.

**arrow** n. flèche f.

**arson** n. incendie criminel m. **~ist** n. incendiaire m./f.

**art** n. art m.; (*fine arts*) beaux-arts m. pl. **~s**, (*univ.*) lettres f. pl. **~ gallery**, (*public*) musée (d'art) m.; (*private*) galerie (d'art) f.

**artefact** n. objet fabriqué m.

**artery** n. artère f.

**artful** a. astucieux, rusé. **~ness** n. astuce f.

**arthriti|s** n. arthrite f. **~c** /-ɪtɪk/ a. arthritique.

**artichoke** n. artichaut m.

**article** n. article m. **~ of clothing**, vêtement m.

**articulate** a. (*person*) capable de s'exprimer clairement; (*speech*) distinct.

**articulated lorry** semi-remorque m.

**artificial** a. artificiel.

**artillery** n. artillerie f.

**artisan** n. artisan m.

**artist** n. artiste m./f. **~ic** a. artistique.

**artwork** n. (*of book*) illustrations f. pl.

**as** adv. & conj. comme; (*while*) pendant que. **as you get older**, en vieillissant. **as she came in**, en entrant. **as a mother**, en tant que mère. **as a gift**, en cadeau. **as from Monday**, à partir de lundi. **as tall as**, aussi grand que. **~ for, as to**, quant à **~ if**, comme si. **you look as if you're tired**, vous avez l'air (d'être) fatigué. **as much, as many**, autant (as, que). **as soon as**, aussitôt que. **as well**, aussi (as, bien que). **as wide as possible**, aussi large que possible.

**asbestos** n. amiante f.

**ascend** v.t. gravir; (*throne*) monter sur. ● v.i. monter.

**ascent** n. (*climbing*) ascension f.

**ascertain** v.t. s'assurer de. **~ that**, s'assurer que.

**ash**[1] n. **~(-tree)**, frêne m.

**ash**[2] n. cendre f.

**ashamed** a. **be ~**, avoir honte (of, de).

**ashore** adv. à terre.

**ashtray** n. cendrier m.

**Asia** n. Asie f. **~n** a. & n. asiatique (m./f.). **the ~n community**, la communauté indo-pakistanaise.

**aside** adv. de côté. ● n. aparté m. **~ from**, à part.

**ask** v.t./i. demander; (*a question*) poser; (*invite*) inviter. **~ s.o. sth.**, demander qch. à qn. **~ s.o. to do**, demander à qn. de faire. **~ about**, (*thing*) se renseigner sur; (*person*) demander des nouvelles de. **~ for**, demander.

**askew** adv. & a. de travers.

**asleep** a. endormi; (*numb*) engourdi. ● adv. **fall ~**, s'endormir.

**asparagus** n. (*plant*) asperge f.; (*culin.*) asperges f. pl.

**aspect** n. aspect m.; (*direction*) orientation f.

**asphalt** n. asphalte m. ● v.t. asphalter.

**asphyxiat|e** v.t./i. (s')asphyxier. **~ion** n. asphyxie f.

**aspir|e** /əsˈpaɪə(r)/ v.i. **~e to**, aspirer à. **~ation** /æspəˈreɪʃn/ n. aspiration f.

**aspirin** n. aspirine f.

**ass** n. âne m.; (*person: fam.*) idiot(e) m. (f.).

**assail** v.t. assaillir. **~ant** n. agresseur m.

**assassin** n. assassin m.

**assassinat|e** v.t. assassiner. **~ion** n. assassinat m.

**assault** n. (mil.) assaut m.; (jurid.) agression f. ● v.t. (person: jurid.) agresser.

**assemble** v.t. (things) assembler; (people) rassembler. ● v.i. s'assembler, se rassembler.

**assembly** n. assemblée f. **~ line,** chaîne de montage f.

**assent** n. assentiment m. ● v.i. consentir.

**assert** v.t. affirmer; (one's rights) revendiquer. **~ion** n. affirmation f. **~ive** a. affirmatif, péremptoire.

**assess** v.t. évaluer; (payment) déterminer le montant de. **~ment** n. évaluation f. **~or** n. (valuer) expert m.

**asset** n. (advantage) atout m. **~s,** (comm.) actif m.

**assign** v.t. (allot) assigner. **~ s.o. to,** (appoint) affecter qn. à.

**assignment** n. (task) mission f., tâche f.; (schol.) rapport m.

**assimilat|e** v.t./i. (s')assimiler. **~ion** n. assimilation f.

**assist** v.t./i. aider. **~ance** n. aide f.

**assistant** n. aide m./f.; (in shop) vendeu|r, -se m., f. ● a. (manager etc.) adjoint.

**associat|e**[1] v.t. associer. ● v.i. **~e with,** fréquenter. **~ion** n. âssociation f.

**associate**[2] n. & a. associé(e) (m. ( f.)).

**assort|ed** a. divers; (foods) assortis. **~ment** n. assortiment m.

**assume** v.t. supposer, présumer; (power, attitude) prendre; (role, burden) assumer.

**assumption** n. (sth. supposed) supposition f.

**assurance** n. assurance f.

**assure** v.t. assurer. **~d** a. assuré.

**asterisk** n. astérisque m.

**asthma** n. asthme m. **~tic** a. & n. asthmatique (m./f.).

**astonish** v.t. étonner. **~ment** n. étonnement m.

**astound** v.t. stupéfier.

**astray** adv. & a. go **~,** s'égarer. lead **~,** égarer.

**astride** adv. & prep. à califourchon (sur).

**astrolog|y** n. astrologie f. **~er** n. astrologue m.

**astronaut** n. astronaute m./f.

**astronom|y** n. astronomie f. **~er** n. astronome m. **~ical** /æstrə'nɒmɪkl/ a. astronomique.

**astute** a. astucieux.

**asylum** n. asile m.

**at** prep. à. **at the doctor's**/etc., chez le médecin/etc. **not at all,** pas du tout. **no wind**/etc. **at all,** (of any kind) pas le moindre vent/

etc. **at night,** la nuit. **at once,** tout de suite; (simultaneously) à la fois. **at sea,** en mer. **at times,** parfois.

**atheis|t** n. athée m./f. **~m** n. athéisme m.

**athlet|e** n. athlète m./f. **~ic** a. athlétique. **~ics** n. pl. athlétisme m.

**Atlantic** a. atlantique. ● n. **~ (Ocean),** Atlantique m.

**atlas** n. atlas m.

**atmospher|e** n. atmosphère f. **~ic** a. atmosphérique.

**atoll** n. atoll m.

**atom** n. atome m. **~ic** a. atomique. **~(ic) bomb,** bombe atomique f.

**atrocious** a. atroce.

**atrocity** n. atrocité f.

**attach** v.t./i. (s')attacher; (letter) joindre (to, à). **~ed** a. **be ~ed to,** (like) être attaché à. **~ment** n. (accessory) accessoire m.; (affection) attachement m.

**attaché** n. (pol.) attaché(e) m. ( f.). **~ case,** mallette f.

**attack** n. attaque f.; (med.) crise f. ● v.t. attaquer. **~er** n. agresseur m., attaquant(e) m. ( f.).

**attain** v.t. atteindre (à); (gain) acquérir. **~able** a. accessible. **~ment** n. acquisition f. (of, de). **~ments,** réussites f. pl.

**attempt** v.t. tenter. ● n. tentative f. **an ~ on s.o.'s life,** un attentat contre qn.

**attend** v.t. assister à; (class) suivre; (school, church) aller à; (escort) accompagner. ● v.i. assister. **~ (to),** (look after) s'occuper de. **~ance** n. présence f.; (people) assistance f.

**attendant** n. employé(e) m. ( f.); (servant) serviteur m.

**attention** n. attention f. **pay ~,** faire or prêter attention (to, à).

**attentive** a. attentif; (considerate) attentionné.

**attic** n. grenier m.

**attitude** n. attitude f.

**attorney** n. mandataire m.; (Amer.) avocat m.

**attract** v.t. attirer. **~ion** n. attraction f.; (charm) attrait m.

**attractive** a. attrayant, séduisant. **~ly** adv. agréablement. **~ness** n. attrait m., beauté f.

**attribute**[1] v.t. **~ to,** attribuer à.

**attribute**[2] n. attribut m.

**aubergine** n. aubergine f.

**auburn** a. châtain roux invar.

**auction** n. vente aux enchères f. ● v.t. vendre aux enchères.

**audaci|ous** a. audacieux. **~ty** n. audace f.

**audible** a. audible.

**audience** n. auditoire m.; (theatre, radio) public m.; (interview) audience f.

**audio typist** n. audiotypiste m./f.

**audio-visual** a. audio-visuel.

**audit** n. vérification des comptes f. ● v.t. vérifier.

**audition** n. audition f. ● v.t./i. auditionner.

**auditor** n. commissaire aux comptes m.

**auditorium** n. (of theatre etc.) salle f.

**August** n. août m.

**aunt** n. tante f.

**au pair** n. jeune fille au pair f.

**auster|e** a. austère. **~ity** n. austérité f.

**Australia** n. Australie f. **~n** a. & n. australien(ne) (m. (.f.)).

**Austria** n. Autriche f. **~n** a. & n. autrichien(ne) (m. (.f.)).

**authentic** a. authentique. **~ity** n. authenticité f.

**author** n. auteur m.

**authoritarian** a. autoritaire.

**authority** n. autorité f.; (permission) autorisation f.

**authoriz|e** v.t. autoriser. **~ation** n. autorisation f.

**autistic** a. autistique.

**autobiography** n. autobiographie f.

**autograph** n. autographe m. ● v.t. signer, dédicacer.

**auto-immune** a. auto-immune.

**automat|e** v.t. automatiser. **~ion** n. automatisation f.

**automatic** a. automatique. ● n. (auto.) voiture automatique f. **~ally** adv. automatiquement.

**autonom|y** n. autonomie f. **~ous** a. autonome.

**autumn** n. automne m.

**auxiliary** a. & n. auxiliaire (m./f.)

**available** a. disponible. **~ility** n. disponibilité f.

**avalanche** n. avalanche f.

**avaric|e** n. avarice f. **~ious** a. avare.

**avenge** v.t. venger. **~ o.s.,** se venger (on, de).

**avenue** n. avenue f.

**average** n. moyenne f. ● a. moyen. on **~,** en moyenne.

**avers|e** a. be **~e to,** répugner à. **~ion** n. aversion f.

**avert** v.t. (turn away) détourner; (ward off) éviter.

**aviation** n. aviation f.

**avid** a. avide.

**avocado** n. avocat m.

**avoid** v.t. éviter. **~able** a. évitable.

**await** v.t. attendre.

**awake** v.t./i. (s')éveiller. ● a. be **~,** ne pas dormir, être (r)éveillé.

**awaken** v.t./i. (s')éveiller.

**award** v.t. attribuer. ● n. récompense f., prix m.; (scholarship) bourse f. pay **~,** augmentation (salariale) f.

**aware** a. averti. be **~ of,** (danger) être conscient de; (fact) savoir. **become ~ of,** prendre conscience de. **~ness** n. conscience f.

**awash** a. inondé (with, de).

**away** adv. (far) (au) loin; (absent) absent, parti; (persistently) sans arrêt; (entirely) complètement. **~ from,** loin de. **move ~,** s'écarter; (to new home) déménager. **six kilometres ~,** à six kilomètres (de distance). **take~,** emporter. ● a. & n. **~ (match),** match à l'extérieur m.

**awe** n. crainte (révérencielle) f. **~-inspiring, ~some** adjs. terrifiant; (sight) imposant.

**awful** a. affreux. **~ly** adv. (badly) affreusement; (very: fam.) rudement.

**awkward** a. difficile; (inconvenient) inopportun; (clumsy) maladroit; (embarrassing) gênant; (embarrassed) gêné. **~ly** adv. maladroitement; avec gêne. **~ness** n. maladresse f.

**awning** n. auvent m.; (of shop) store m.

**axe,** n. hache f. ● v.t. (pres. p. **axing**) réduire; (eliminate) supprimer; (employee) renvoyer.

**axis** n. axe m.

**axle** n. essieu m.

# Bb

**babble** v.i. babiller; (stream) gazouiller. ● n. babillage m.

**baboon** n. babouin m.

**baby** n. bébé m. **~-sitter** n. baby-sitter m./f.

**bachelor** n. célibataire m. **B~ of Arts/ Science,** licencié(e) ès lettres/sciences m. (f.).

**back** n. (of person, hand, page, etc.) dos m.; (of house) derrière m.; (of vehicle) arrière m.; (of room) fond m.; (of chair) dossier m.; (football) arrière m. ● a. de derrière, arrière invar.; (taxes) arriéré. ● adv. en arrière; (returned) de retour, rentré. ● v.t. (support) appuyer; (beton) miser sur; (vehicle) faire reculer. ● v.i. (of person, vehicle) reculer. **at the ~ of the book,** à la fin du livre. **come ~,** revenir. **give ~,** rendre. **take ~,** reprendre. **I want it ~,** je veux le récupérer. **~ down,** abandonner, se dégonfler. **~ out,** se dégager, se dégonfler; (auto.) sortir en reculant. **~ up,** (support) appuyer. **~-up** n. appui m.; (comput.) sauvegarde f.; a. de réserve; (comput.) de sauvegarde.

**backache** n. mal de reins m., mal aux reins m.

**backbone** n. colonne vertébrale f.

**backdate** v.t. antidater; (arrangement) rendre rétroactif.

**backer** n. partisan m.; (comm.) bailleur de fonds m.

**backfire** v.i. (auto.) pétarader; (fig.) mal tourner.

**backgammon** n. trictrac m.

**background** n. fond m., arrière-plan m.; (context) contexte m.; (environment) milieu m.; (experience) formation f. ● a. (music, noise) de fond.

**backhand** n. revers m. ~**ed** a. équivoque. ~**ed stroke**, revers m.

**backing** n. appui m.

**backlash** n. choc en retour m., répercussions f. pl.

**backlog** n. accumulation (de travail) f.

**backpack** n. sac à dos m.

**backside** n. (buttocks: fam.) derrière m.

**backstage** a. & adv. dans les coulisses.

**backstroke** n. dos crawlé m.

**backtrack** v.i. rebrousser chemin; (change one's opinion) faire marche arrière.

**backward** a. (step etc.) en arrière; (retarded) arriéré.

**backwards** adv. en arrière; (walk) à reculons; (read) à l'envers; (fall) à la renverse. **go** ~ **and forwards,** aller et venir.

**bacon** n. lard m.; (in rashers) bacon m.

**bacteria** n. pl. bactéries f. pl.

**bad** a. mauvais; (wicked) méchant; (ill) malade; (accident) grave; (food) gâté. **feel** ~, se sentir mal. **go** ~, se gâter. ~ **language,** gros mots m. pl. ~-**tempered** a. grincheux. ~**ly** adv. mal; (hurt) grièvement. **too** ~! tant pis; (I'm sorry) dommage!

**badge** n. insigne m.; (of identity) plaque f.

**badger** n. blaireau m. ● v.t. harceler.

**badminton** n. badminton m.

**baffle** v.t. déconcerter.

**bag** n. sac m. ~**s,** (luggage) bagages m.pl. ● v.t. mettre en sac; (take: fam.) s'adjuger.

**baggage** n. bagages m. pl. ~ **reclaim,** livraison des bagages f.

**baggy** a. trop grand.

**Bahamas** n. pl. the ~, les Bahamas f. pl.

**bail**[1] n. caution f. **on** ~, sous caution. ● v.t. mettre en liberté (provisoire) sous caution. ~ **out,** (fig.) sortir d'affaire.

**bail**[2] n. (cricket) bâtonnet m.

**bail**[3] v.t. (naut.) écoper.

**bailiff** n. huissier m.

**bait** n. appât m. ● v.t. appâter; (fig.) tourmenter.

**bake** v.t. (faire) cuire (au four). ● v.i. cuire (au four); (person) faire du pain or des gâteaux. ~**ed beans,** haricots blancs à la tomate m.pl. ~**ed potato,** pomme de terre en robe des champs f. ~**er** n. boulanger, -ère m., f. ~**ing** n. cuisson f. ~**ing-powder** n. levure f.

**bakery** n. boulangerie f.

**balance** n. équilibre m.; (scales) balance f.; (outstanding sum: comm.) solde m.; (of payments, of trade) balance f.; (remainder) reste m.; (money in account) position f. ● v.t. tenir en équilibre; (weigh up & comm.) balancer; (budget) équilibrer; (to compensate) contrebalancer. ● v. i. être en équilibre. ~**d** a. équilibré.

**balcony** n. balcon m.

**bald** a. chauve; (tyre) lisse; (fig.) simple. ~**ness** n. calvitie f.

**bale**[1] n. (of cotton) balle f.; (of straw) botte f.

**bale**[2] v.i. ~ **out,** sauter en parachute.

**ball**[1] n. (golf, tennis, etc.) balle f.; (football) ballon m.; (croquet, billiards, etc.) boule f.; (of wool) pelote f.; (sphere) boule f. ~-**bearing** n. roulement à billes m. ~-**cock** n. robinet à flotteur m. ~-**point** n. stylo à bille m.

**ball**[2] n. (dance) bal m.

**ballet** n. ballet m.

**balloon** n. ballon m.

**ballot** n. scrutin m. ~-**box** n. urne f. ● v.i. (p.t. **balloted**) (pol.) voter. ● v.t. (members) consulter par voie de scrutin.

**ballroom** n. salle de bal f.

**bamboo** n. bambou m.

**ban** v.t. interdire. ~ **from,** exclure de. ● n. interdiction f.

**banal** a. banal. ~**ity** n. banalité f.

**banana** n. banane f.

**band** n. (strip, group of people) bande f.; (mus.) orchestre m.; (pop group) groupe m. (mil.) fanfare f. ● v.i. ~ **together,** se liguer.

**bandage** n. pansement m. ● v.t. bander, panser.

**bandit** n. bandit m.

**bang** n. (blow, noise) coup (violent) m.; (explosion) détonation f.; (of door) claquement m. ● v.t./i. frapper; (door) claquer. ● int. vlan. ● adv. (fam.) exactement. ~ **one's head,** se cogner la tête. ~**s,** frange f.

**banger** n. (firework) pétard m.; (culin., sl.) saucisse f. **(old)** ~, (car: sl.) guimbarde f.

**bangle** n. bracelet m.

**banish** v.t. bannir.

**banisters** n. pl. rampe (d'escalier) f.

**banjo** n. banjo m.

**bank**[1] n. (of river) rive f.; (of earth) talus m.; (of sand) banc m. ● v.t. (earth) amonceler; (fire) couvrir. ● v.i. (aviat.) virer.

**bank**[2] n. banque f. ● v.t. mettre en banque. ● v.i. ~ **with,** avoir un compte à. ~ **account,** compte en banque m. ~ **card,** carte bancaire f. ~ **holiday,** jour férié m. ~ **on,** compter sur. ~ **statement,** relevé de compte m.

**bankrupt** a. **be** ~, être en faillite. **go** ~, faire faillite. ● n. failli(e) m. (f.). ● v.t. mettre en faillite. ~**cy** n. faillite f.

**banner** n. bannière f.

**banquet** n. banquet m.

**banter** n. plaisanterie f. ● v.i. plaisanter.

**bap** n. petit pain m.

**baptism** n. baptême m.

**Baptist** n. baptiste m./f.

**baptize** v.t. baptiser.

**bar** n. (of metal) barre f.; (on window & jurid.) barreau m.; (of chocolate) tablette f.; (pub) bar m.; (counter) comptoir m., bar m.; (division: mus.) mesure f.; (fig.) obstacle m. ● v.t. (obstruct) barrer; (prohibit) interdire; (exclude) exclure. ● prep. sauf. ~ code, codebarres m. invar. ~ of soap, savonnette f.

**barbarian** n. barbare m./f.

**barbaric** a. barbare.

**barbarous** a. barbare.

**barbecue** n. barbecue m. ● v.t. griller, rôtir (au barbecue).

**barbed** a. ~ wire, fil de fer barbelé m.

**barber** n. coiffeur m. (pour hommes).

**barbiturate** n. barbiturique m.

**bare** a. (not covered or adorned) nu; (cupboard) vide; (mere) simple. ● v.t. mettre à nu.

**barefaced** a. éhonté.

**barefoot** a. nu-pieds invar., pieds nus.

**barely** adv. à peine.

**bargain** n. (deal) marché m.; (cheap thing) occasion f. ● v.i. négocier; (haggle) marchander. not ~ for, ne pas s'attendre à.

**barge** n. chaland m. ● v.i. ~ in, interrompre; (into room) faire irruption.

**baritone** n. baryton m.

**bark**[1] n. (of tree) écorce f.

**bark**[2] n. (of dog) aboiement m. ● v.i. aboyer.

**barley** n. orge f. ~ sugar, sucre d'orge m.

**barmaid** n. serveuse f.

**barman** n. barman m.

**barn** n. grange f.

**barometer** n. baromètre m.

**baroque** a. & n. baroque (m.).

**barracks** n. pl. caserne f.

**barrage** n. (barrier) barrage m.; (mil.) tir de barrage m.; (of complaints) série f.

**barrel** n. tonneau m.; (of oil) baril m.; (of gun) canon m.

**barren** a. stérile.

**barricade** n. barricade f. ● v.t. barricader.

**barrier** n. barrière f.

**barring** prep. sauf.

**barrister** n. avocat m.

**barrow** n. charrette à bras f.; (wheelbarrow) brouette f.

**bartender** n. (Amer.) barman m.

**barter** n. troc m., échange m. ● v.t. troquer, échanger (for, contre).

**base** n. base f. ● v.t. baser (on, sur; in, à). ● a. bas, ignoble.

**baseball** n. base-ball m.

**basement** n. sous-sol m.

**bash** v.t. cogner. ● n. coup (violent) m. ~ed in, enfoncé.

**basic** a. fondamental, élémentaire. the ~s, les éléments de base m. pl. ~ally adv. au fond.

**basil** n. basilic m.

**basin** n. (for liquids) cuvette f.; (for food) bol m.; (for washing) lavabo m.; (of river) bassin m.

**basis** n. base f.

**bask** v.i. se chauffer.

**basket** n. corbeille f.; (with handle) panier m.

**basketball** n. basket(-ball) m.

**Basque** a. & n. basque (m./f.).

**bass**[1] a. (mus.) bas, grave. ● n. basse f.

**bass**[2] n. invar. (freshwater fish) perche f.; (sea) bar m.

**bassoon** n. basson m.

**baste**[1] v.t. (sew) bâtir.

**baste**[2] v.t. (culin.) arroser.

**bat**[1] n. (cricket etc.) batte f.; (table tennis) raquette f. ● v.t. (ball) frapper.

**bat**[2] n. (animal) chauve-souris f.

**batch** n. (of papers) paquet m.; (of goods) lot m.

**bath** n. bain m.; (tub) baignoire f. (swimming) ~s, piscine f. ● a. de bain. have a ~, prendre un bain.

**bathe** v.t. baigner. ● v.i. se baigner; (Amer.) prendre un bain. ● n. bain (de mer) m. ~r n. baigneu|r, -se m., f.

**bathing** n. baignade f. ~-costume n. maillot de bain m.

**bathroom** n. salle de bains f.

**baton** n. (mil.) bâton m.; (mus.) baguette f.

**battalion** n. bataillon m.

**batter** v.t. (strike) battre; (ill-treat) maltraiter. ● n. (culin.) pâte (à frire) f. ~ed a. (pan, car) cabossé; (face) meurtri.

**battery** n. (mil., auto.) batterie f.; (of torch, radio) pile f.

**battle** n. bataille f.; (fig.) lutte f. ● v.i. se battre.

**baulk** v.t./i. = balk.

**bawl** v.t./i. brailler.

**bay**[1] n. (bot.) laurier m. ~-leaf n. feuille de laurier f.

**bay**[2] n. (geog., archit.) baie f.; (area) aire f. ~ window, fenêtre en saillie f.

**bay**[3] n. (bark) aboiement m. ● v.i. aboyer. keep or hold at ~, tenir à distance.

**bayonet** n. baïonnette f.

**bazaar** n. (shop, market) bazar m.; (sale) vente f.

**BC** abbr. (before Christ) avant J.-C.

**be** v.i. être. be hot/right/etc., avoir chaud/ raison/etc. he is 30, (age) il a 30 ans. it is fine/ cold/etc., (weather) il fait beau/froid/etc. how are you?, (health) comment allez-vous? how much is it?, (cost) ça fait or c'est combien? **be reading/walking/**etc., (aux.) lire/marcher/etc. **have been to,** avoir été à, être allé à.

**beach** n. plage f.

**beacon** n. (lighthouse) phare m.; (marker) balise f.

**bead** n. perle f.

**beak** n. bec m.

**beaker** n. gobelet m.

**beam** n. (timber) poutre f.; (of light) rayon m.; (of torch) faisceau m. ● v.i. (radiate) rayonner. ● v.t. (broadcast) diffuser. ~**ing** a. radieux.

**bean** n. haricot m.; (of coffee) grain m.

**bear**[1] n. ours m.

**bear**[2] v.t. (carry, show, feel) porter; (endure, sustain) supporter; (child) mettre au monde. ● v.i. ~ **left/**etc., (go) prendre à gauche/etc. ~ **in mind,** tenir compte de. ~**able** a. supportable. ~**er** n. porteu|r, -se m., f.

**beard** n. barbe f.

**bearing** n. (behaviour) maintien m.; (relevance) rapport m. **get one's ~s,** s'orienter.

**beast** n. bête f.; (person) brute f.

**beastly** a. (fam.) détestable.

**beat** v.t./i. battre. ● n. (of drum, heart) battement m.; (mus.) mesure f.; (of policeman) ronde f. ~ **it!**, dégage! ~ **s.o. down,** faire baisser son prix à qn. ~ **up,** tabasser. **it ~s me,** (fam.) ça me dépasse. ~**ing** n. raclée f.

**beautician** n. esthéticien(ne) m. (f.).

**beautiful** a. beau. ~**ly** adv. merveilleusement.

**beauty** n. beauté f. ~ **spot,** grain de beauté m.; (fig.) site pittoresque m.

**beaver** n. castor m.

**because** conj. parce que. ~ **of,** à cause de.

**beckon** v.t./i. ~ **(to),** faire signe à.

**become** v.t./i. devenir.

**bed** n. lit m.; (layer) couche f.; (of sea) fond m.; (of flowers) parterre m. **go to ~,** (aller) se coucher.

**bedbug** n. punaise f.

**bedclothes** n. pl. couvertures f. pl. et draps m. pl.

**bedraggled** a. (untidy) débraillé.

**bedroom** n. chambre (à coucher) f.

**bedside** n. chevet m.

**bedsit, bedsitter** ns. (fam.) n. chambre meublée f., studio m.

**bedspread** n. dessus-de-lit m. invar.

**bedtime** n. heure du coucher f.

**bee** n. abeille f. **make a ~-line for,** aller tout droit vers.

**beech** n. hêtre m.

**beef** n. bœuf m.

**beefburger** n. hamburger m.

**beehive** n. ruche f.

**beer** n. bière f.

**beet** n. (plant) betterave f.

**beetle** n. scarabée m.

**beetroot** n. invar. (culin.) betterave f.

**before** prep. (time) avant; (place) devant. ● adv. avant; (already) déjà. ● conj. ~ **leaving,** avant de partir. ~ **he leaves,** avant qu'il(ne)parte. **the day ~,** la veille. **two days ~,** deux jours avant.

**beforehand** adv. à l'avance, avant.

**beg** v.t. (entreat) supplier (**to do,** de faire). ~ **(for),** (money, food) mendier; (request) solliciter, demander. ● v.i. ~ **(for alms),** mendier. **it is going ~ging,** personne n'en veut.

**beggar** n. mendiant(e) m. (f.); (sl.) individu m.

**begin** v.t./i. commencer (**to do,** à faire). ~**ner** n. débutant(e) m. (f.). ~**ning** n. commencement m., début m.

**begrudge** v.t. (envy) envier; (give unwillingly) donner à contrecœur. ~ **doing,** faire à contrecœur.

**behalf** /br'hɑ:f/ n. **on ~ of,** pour; (as representative) au nom de, pour (le compte de).

**behave** v.i. se conduire. ~ **(o.s.),** se conduire bien.

**behaviour** n. conduite f., comportement m.

**behind** prep. derrière; (in time) en retard sur. ● adv. derrière; (late) en retard. ● n. (buttocks) derrière m. **leave ~,** oublier.

**behold** v.t. (old use) voir.

**beige** a. & n. beige (m.).

**being** n. (person) être m. **bring into ~,** créer. **come into ~,** prendre naissance.

**belch** v.i. faire un renvoi. ● v.t. ~ **out,** (smoke) vomir. ~ n. renvoi m.

**Belgi|um** n. Belgique f. ~**an** a. & n. belge (m./f.).

**belief** n. croyance f.; (trust) confiance f.; (faith: relig.) foi f.

**believ|e** v.t./i. croire. ~**e in,** croire à; (deity) croire en. ~**able** a. croyable. ~**er** n. croyant(e) m. (f.).

**bell** n. cloche f.; (small) clochette f.; (on door) sonnette f.; (of phone) sonnerie f.

**bellow** v.t./i. beugler.

**belly** n. ventre m. ~**-ache** n. mal au ventre m.

**belong** v.i. ~ **to,** appartenir à; (club) être membre de.

**belongings** n. pl. affaires f. pl.

**below** prep. au-dessous de; (fig.) indigne de. ● adv. en dessous; (on page) ci-dessous.

**belt** n. ceinture f.; (techn.) courroie f.; (fig.) région f. ● v.t. (hit: sl.) rosser.

**beltway** n. (Amer.) périphérique m.

**bemused** a. (confused) stupéfié; (thoughtful) pensif.

**bench** n. banc m.; (working-table) établi m. **the ~,** (jurid.) la magistrature (assise).

**bend** *v.t./i.* (se) courber; (*arm, leg*) plier. ● *n.* courbe *f.*; (*in road*) virage *m.*; (*of arm, knee*) pli *m.* ~ **down** *or* **over**, se pencher.

**beneath** *prep.* sous, au-dessous de; (*fig.*) indigne de. ● *adv.* (au-)dessous.

**beneficial** *a.* avantageux, favorable.

**benefit** *n.* avantage *m.*; (*allowance*) allocation *f.* ● *v.t.* (*be useful to*) profiter à; (*do good to*) faire du bien à. ~ **from**, tirer profit de.

**benign** *a.* (*kindly*) bienveillant; (*med.*) bénin.

**bent** *n.* (*talent*) aptitude *f.*; (*inclination*) penchant *m.* ● *a.* tordu; (*sl.*) corrompu. ~ **on doing**, décidé à faire.

**bequeath** *v.t.* léguer.

**bequest** *n.* legs *m.*

**beret** *n.* béret *m.*

**Bermuda** *n.* Bermudes *f. pl.*

**berry** *n.* baie *f.*

**berserk** *a.* go ~, devenir fou furieux.

**berth** *n.* (*in train, ship*) couchette *f.*; (*anchorage*) mouillage *m.* ● *v.i.* mouiller.

**beseech** *v.t.* supplier.

**beside** *prep.* à côté de. ~ **o.s.**, hors de soi. ~ **the point**, sans rapport.

**besides** *prep.* en plus de; (*except*) excepté. ● *adv.* en plus.

**besiege** *v.t.* assiéger.

**best** *a.* meilleur. **the ~ book**/*etc.*, le meilleur livre/*etc.* ● *adv.* (the) ~, (*sing etc.*) le mieux. ● *n.* the ~ (one), le meilleur, la meilleure. ~ **man**, garçon d'honneur *m.* **the ~ part of**, la plus grande partie de.

**best-seller** *n.* best-seller *m.*, succès de librairie *m.*

**bet** *n.* pari *m.* ● *v.t./i.* parier.

**betray** *v.t.* trahir.

**better** *a.* meilleur. ● *adv.* mieux. ● *v.t.* (*improve*) améliorer; (*do better than*) surpasser. **be ~ off**, (*financially*) avoir plus d'argent. **he's ~ off at home**, il est mieux chez lui. **I had ~ go**, je ferais mieux de partir. **get ~**, s'améliorer; (*recover*) se remettre. **get the ~ of**, l'emporter sur. **so much the ~**, tant mieux.

**betting-shop** *n.* bureau de P.M.U. *m.*

**between** *prep.* entre. ● *adv.* **in ~**, au milieu.

**beware** *v.i.* prendre garde (**of**, à).

**bewilder** *v.t.* désorienter, embarrasser. ~**ment** *n.* désorientation *f.*

**beyond** *prep.* au-delà de; (*doubt, reach*) hors de; (*besides*) excepté. ● *adv.* au-delà. **it is ~ me**, ça me dépasse.

**bias** *n.* (*inclination*) penchant *m.* ~**ed** *a.* partial.

**bib** *n.* bavoir *m.*

**Bible** *n.* Bible *f.*

**biblical** *a.* biblique.

**bicarbonate** *n.* bicarbonate *m.*

**biceps** *n.* biceps *m.*

**bicker** *v.i.* se chamailler.

**bicycle** *n.* bicyclette *f.*

**bid** *n.* (*at auction*) offre *f.*, enchère *f.*; (*attempt*) tentative *f.* ● *v.t./i.* (*offer*) faire une offre *or* une enchère (de).

**biennial** *a.* biennal.

**bifocals** *n. pl.* lunettes bifocales *f. pl.*

**big** *a.* grand; (*in bulk*) gros; (*generous*: *sl.*) généreux. ● *adv.* (*fam.*) en grand; (*earn*: *fam.*) gros. ~**headed** *a.* prétentieux. ~ **shot**, (*sl.*) huile *f.* **think ~**, (*fam.*) voir grand.

**bigamy** *n.* bigamie *f.*

**bigot** *n.* fanatique *m./f.* ~**ed** *a.* fanatique.

**bike** *n.* (*fam.*) vélo *m.*

**bikini** *n.* bikini *m.*

**bilberry** *n.* myrtille *f.*

**bile** *n.* bile *f.*

**bill**[1] *n.* (*invoice*) facture *f.*; (*in hotel, for gas, etc.*) note *f.*; (*in restaurant*) addition *f.*; (*of sale*) acte *m.*; (*pol.*) projet de loi *m.*; (*banknote*: *Amer.*) billet de banque *m.* ● *v.t.* (*person*: *comm.*) envoyer la facture à. (*theatre*) **on the ~**, à l'affiche.

**bill**[2] *n.* (*of bird*) bec *m.*

**billboard** *n.* panneau d'affichage *m.*

**billfold** *n.* (*Amer.*) portefeuille *m.*

**billiards** *n.* billard *m.*

**billion** *n.* billion *m.*; (*Amer.*) milliard *m.*

**billy-goat** *n.* bouc *m.*

**bin** *n.* (*for rubbish, litter*) boîte (à ordures) *f.*, poubelle *f.*

**binary** *a.* binaire.

**bind** *v.t.* lier; (*book*) relier; (*jurid.*) obliger. ● *n.* (*bore*: *sl.*) plaie *f.*

**binge** *n.* **go on a ~**, (*spree*: *sl.*) faire la bringue.

**bingo** *n.* loto *m.*

**binoculars** *n. pl.* jumelles *f. pl.*

**biodegradable** *a.* biodégradable.

**biography** *n.* biographie *f.*

**biolog|y** *n.* biologie *f.* ~**ical** *a.* biologique.

**biorhythm** *n.* biorythme *m.*

**birch** *n.* (*tree*) bouleau *m.*; (*whip*) verge *f.*, fouet *m.*

**bird** *n.* oiseau *m.*; (*fam.*) individu *m.*; (*girl*: *sl.*) poule *f.*

**Biro** *n.* (P.) stylo à bille *m.*, Bic *m.* (P.).

**birth** *n.* naissance *f.* **give ~**, accoucher. ~**control** *n.* contrôle des naissances *m.*

**birthday** *n.* anniversaire *m.*

**birthmark** *n.* tache de vin *f.*

**biscuit** *n.* biscuit *m.*

**bishop** *n.* évêque *m.*

**bit**[1] *n.* morceau *m.*; (*of horse*) mors *m.*; (*of tool*) mèche *f.* **a ~**, (*a little*) un peu.

**bit**[2] *n.* (*comput.*) bit *m.*, élement binaire *m.*

**bitch** *n.* chienne *f.*; (*woman*: *fam.*) garce *f.* ● *v.i.* (*grumble*: *fam.*) râler. ~**y** *a.* (*fam.*) vache.

**bite** *v.t./i.* mordre. ● *n.* morsure *f.*; (*by insect*) piqûre *f.*; (*mouthful*) bouchée *f.* **have a ~,** manger un morceau.

**bitter** *a.* amer; (*weather*) glacial, âpre. ● *n.* bière anglaise *f.* **~ness** *n.* amertume *f.*

**bizarre** *a.* bizarre.

**blab** *v.i.* jaser.

**black** *a.* noir. ● *n.* (*colour*) noir *m.* **B~,** (*person*) Noir(e) *m.* (*f.*). ● *v.t.* noircir; (*goods*) boycotter. **~ eye,** œil poché *m.* **~ ice,** verglas *m.* **~list,** liste noire *f.* **~market,** marché noir *m.* **~ spot,** point noir *m.*

**blackberry** *n.* mûre *f.*

**blackbird** *n.* merle *m.*

**blackboard** *n.* tableau noir *m.*

**blackcurrant** *n.* cassis *m.*

**blacken** *v.t./i.* noircir.

**blackhead** *n.* point noir *m.*

**blackleg** *n.* jaune *m.*

**blacklist** *v.t.* mettre sur la liste noire *or* à l'index.

**blackmail** *n.* chantage *m.* ● *v.t.* faire chanter. **~er** *n.* maître-chanteur *m.*

**blackout** *n.* panne d'électricité *f.*; (*med.*) syncope *f.*

**bladder** *n.* vessie *f.*

**blade** *n.* (*of knife etc.*) lame *f.*; (*of propeller, oar*) pale *f.* **~ of grass,** brin d'herbe *m.*

**blame** *v.t.* accuser. ● *n.* faute *f.* **~ s.o. for sth.,** reprocher qch. à qn. **he is to ~,** il est responsable (**for,** de).

**bland** *a.* (*gentle*) doux; (*insipid*) fade.

**blank** *a.* blanc; (*look*) vide; (*cheque*) en blanc. ● *n.* blanc *m.* **~ (cartridge),** cartouche à blanc *f.*

**blanket** *n.* couverture *f.*; (*layer: fig.*) couche *f.*

**blare** *v.t./i.* beugler. ● *n.* vacarme *m.*, beuglement *m.*

**blasé** *a.* blasé.

**blast** *n.* explosion *f.*; (*wave of air*) souffle *m.*; (*of wind*) rafale *f.*; (*noise from siren etc.*) coup *m.* ● *v.t.* (*blow up*) faire sauter. **~ed** *a.* (*fam.*) maudit, fichu. **~ off,** être mis à feu. **~-off** *n.* mise à feu *f.*

**blatant** *a.* (*obvious*) flagrant; (*shameless*) éhonté.

**blaze** *n.* flamme *f.*; (*conflagration*) incendie *m.*; (*fig.*) éclat *m.* ● *v.i.* (*fire*) flamber; (*sky, eyes, etc.*) flamboyer.

**blazer** *n.* blazer *m.*

**bleach** *n.* décolorant *m.*; (*for domestic use*) eau de Javel *f.* ● *v.t./i.* blanchir; (*hair*) décolorer.

**bleak** *a.* morne.

**bleary** *a.* (*eyes*) voilé.

**bleat** *n.* bêlement *m.* ● *v.i.* bêler.

**bleed** *v.t./i.* saigner.

**bleep** *n.* bip *m.* **~er** *n.* bip *m.*

**blemish** *n.* tare *f.*, défaut *m.*; (*on reputation*) tache *f.* ● *v.t.* entacher.

**blend** *v.t./i.* (se) mélanger. ● *n.* mélange *m.* **~er** *n.* mixer *n.*

**bless** *v.t.* bénir. **~ing** *n.* bénédiction *f.*; (*benefit*) avantage *m.*; (*stroke of luck*) chance *f.*

**blight** *n.* (*disease:bot.*) rouille *f.*; (*fig.*) fléau *m.*

**blind** *a.* aveugle. ● *v.t.* aveugler. ● *n.* (*on window*) store *m.*; (*deception*) feinte *f.* **~ corner,** virage sans visibilité *m.* **~ man,** aveugle *m.* **~ spot,** (*auto.*) angle mort *m. pl.* **~ly** *adv.* aveuglément. **~ness** *n.* cécité *f.*

**blindfold** *a. & adv.* les yeux bandés. ● *n.* bandeau *m.* ● *v.t.* bander les yeux à.

**blink** *v.i.* cligner des yeux; (*of light*) clignoter.

**blinkers** *n. pl.* œillères *f. pl.*

**bliss** *n.* félicité *f.* **~ful** *a.* bienheureux.

**blister** *n.* ampoule *f.*; (*on paint*) cloque *f.* ● *v.i.* se couvrir d'ampoules; cloquer.

**blizzard** *n.* tempête de neige *f.*

**bloated** *a.* gonflé.

**bloater** *n.* hareng saur *m.*

**blob** *n.* (*drop*) (grosse) goutte *f.*; (*stain*) tache *f.*

**bloc** *n.* bloc *m.*

**block** *n.* bloc *m.*; (*buildings*) pâté de maisons *m.*; (*in pipe*) obstruction *f.* **~ (of flats),** immeuble *m.* ● *v.t.* bloquer. **~ letters,** majuscules *f. pl.* **~age** *n.* obstruction *f.*

**blockade** *n.* blocus *m.* ● *v.t.* bloquer.

**bloke** *n.* (*fam.*) type *m.*

**blond** *a. & n.* blond (*m.*).

**blonde** *a. & n.* blonde (*f.*).

**blood** *n.* sang *m.* ● *a.* (*donor, bath, etc.*) de sang; (*bank, poisoning, etc.*) du sang; (*group, vessel*) sanguin. **~-pressure** *n.* tension artérielle *f.* **~test,** prise de sang *f.*

**bloodhound** *n.* limier *m.*

**bloodshed** *n.* effusion de sang *f.*

**bloodstream** *n.* sang *m.*

**bloody** *a.* sanglant; (*sl.*) sacré. ● *adv.* (*sl.*) vachement.

**bloom** *n.* fleur *f.* ● *v.i.* fleurir; (*fig.*) s'épanouir.

**blossom** *n.* fleur(s) *f.* (*pl.*). ● *v.i.* fleurir; (*person: fig.*) s'épanouir.

**blot** *n.* tache *f.* ● *v.t.* tacher; (*dry*) sécher. **~ out,** effacer.

**blotch** *n.* tache *f.* **~y** *a.* couvert de taches.

**blouse** *n.* chemisier *m.*

**blow**[1] *v.t./i.* souffler; (*fuse*) (faire) sauter; (*squander: sl.*) claquer; (*opportunity*) rater. **~ one's nose,** se moucher. **~ a whistle,** siffler. **~ away** *or* **off,** emporter. **~-dry** *v.t.* sécher; *n.* brushing *m.* **~-out** *n.* (*of tyre*) éclatement *m.* **~ over,** passer. **~ up,** (faire) sauter; (*tyre*) gonfler; (*photo.*) aggrandir.

**blow**[2] *n.* coup *m.*

**blowlamp** *n.* chalumeau *m.*

**blue** *a.* bleu; (*film*) porno. ● *n.* bleu *m.* **come out of the ~,** être inattendu.

**bluebell** *n.* jacinthe des bois *f.*

**bluebottle** *n.* mouche à viande *f.*

**blueprint** *n.* plan *m.*

**bluff** *v.t./i.* bluffer. ● *n.* bluff *m.* **call. s.o.'s ~,** dire chiche à qn.

**blunder** *v.i.* faire une gaffe; (*move*) avancer à tâtons. ● *n.* gaffe *f.*

**blunt** *a.* (*knife*) émoussé; (*person*) brusque. ● *v.t.* émousser. **~ly** *adv.* carrément.

**blur** *n.* tache floue *f.* ● *v.t.* rendre flou.

**blurt** *v.t.* **~ out,** lâcher, dire.

**blush** *v.i.* rougir. ● *n.* rougeur *f.* **~er** *n.* blush *m.*

**bluster** *v.i.* (*wind*) faire rage; (*swagger*) fanfaronner. **~y** *a.* à bourrasques.

**boar** *n.* sanglier *m.*

**board** *n.* planche *f.*; (*for notices*) tableau *m.*; (*food*) pension *f.*; (*committee*) conseil *m.* ● *v.t./i.* (*bus, train*) monter dans; (*naut.*) monter à bord (de). **~ of directors,** conseil d'administration *m.* **go by the ~,** passer à l'as. **full ~,** pension complète *f.* **half ~,** demi-pension *f.* **on ~,** à bord. **~ing-house** *n.* pension (de famille) *f.* **~ing-school** *n.* pensionnat *m.*, pension *f.*

**boast** *v.i.* se vanter (**about,** de). ● *v.t.* s'enorgueillir de. ● *n.* vantardise *f.* **~ful** *a.* vantard.

**boat** *n.* bateau *m.*; (*small*) canot *m.*

**boatswain** *n.* maître d'équipage *m.*

**bob** *v.i.* **~ up and down,** monter et descendre.

**bobby** *n.* (*fam.*) flic *m.*

**bobsleigh** *n.* bob(-sleigh) *m.*

**body** *n.* corps *m.*; (*mass*) masse *f.*; (*organization*) organisme *m.* **~(work),** (*auto.*) carrosserie *f.*

**bodyguard** *n.* garde du corps *m.*

**bog** *n.* marécage *m.* ● *v.t.* **get ~ged down,** s'embourber.

**bogus** *a.* faux.

**boil**¹ *n.* furoncle *m.*

**boil**² *v.t./i.* (faire) bouillir. **bring to the ~,** porter à ébullition. **~ down to,** se ramener à. **~ed** *a.* (*egg*) à la coque; (*potatoes*) à l'eau.

**boiler** *n.* chaudière *f.*

**boisterous** *a.* tapageur.

**bold** *a.* hardi; (*cheeky*) effronté; (*type*) gras. **~ness** *n.* hardiesse *f.*

**Bolivia** *n.* Bolivie *f.* **~n** *a.* & *n.* bolivien(ne)(*m.* (*f.*)).

**bollard** *n.* (*on road*) borne *f.*

**bolster** *n.* traversin *m.* ● *v.t.* soutenir.

**bolt** *n.* verrou *m.*; (*for nut*) boulon *m.*; (*lightning*) éclair *m.* ● *v.t.* (*door etc.*) verrouiller; (*food*) engouffrer. ● *v.i.* se sauver.

**bomb** *n.* bombe *f.* ● *v.t.* bombarder. **~ scare,** alerte à la bombe *f.* **~er** *n.* (*aircraft*) bombardier *m.*; (*person*) plastiqueur *m.*

**bombard** *v.t.* bombarder.

**bombshell** *n.* **be a ~,** tomber comme une bombe.

**bond** *n.* (*agreement*) engagement *m.*; (*link*) lien *m.*; (*comm.*) obligation *f.*, bon *m.*

**bone** *n.* os *m.*; (*of fish*) arête *f.* ● *v.t.* désosser. **~-dry** *a.* tout à fait sec.

**bonfire** *n.* feu *m.*; (*for celebration*) feu de joie *m.*

**bonnet** *n.* (*hat*) bonnet *m.*; (*of vehicle*) capot *m.*

**bonus** *n.* prime *f.*

**bony** *a.* (*thin*) osseux; (*meat*) plein d'os; (*fish*) plein d'arêtes.

**boo** *int.* hou. ● *v.t./i.* huer.

**booby-trap** *n.* engin piégé *m.* ● *v.t.* piéger.

**book** *n.* livre *m.*; (*of tickets etc.*) carnet *m.* **~s,** (*comm.*) comptes *m. pl.* ● *v.t.* (*reserve*) réserver; (*driver*) faire un P.V. à; (*player*) prendre le nom de; (*write down*) inscrire. ● *v.i.* retenir des places. **~ing office,** guichet *m.*

**bookcase** *n.* bibliothèque *f.*

**bookkeeping** *n.* comptabilité *f.*

**booklet** *n.* brochure *f.*

**bookmaker** *n.* bookmaker *m.*

**bookseller** *n.* libraire *m./f.*

**bookshop** *n.* librairie *f.*

**boom** *v.i.* (*gun, wind, etc.*) gronder; (*trade*) prospérer. ● *n.* grondement *m.*; (*comm.*) boom *m.*

**boon** *n.* (*benefit*) aubaine *f.*

**boost** *v.t.* stimuler; (*morale*) remonter; (*price*) augmenter; (*publicize*) faire de la réclame pour. ● *n.* **give a ~ to,** = boost.

**boot** *n.* (*knee-length*); botte *f.*; (*ankle-length*) chaussure (montante) *f.*; (*for walking*) chaussure de marche *f.*; (*sport*) chaussure de sport *f.*; (*of vehicle*) coffre *m.* ● *v.t./i.* **~ up,** (*comput.*) démarrer, lancer (le programme).

**booth** *n.* (*for telephone*) cabine *f.*; (*at fair*) baraque *f.*

**booty** *n.* butin *m.*

**booze** *v.i.* (*fam.*) boire (beaucoup). ● *n.* (*fam.*) alcool *m.*

**border** *n.* (*edge*) bord *m.*; (*frontier*) frontière *f.*; (*in garden*) bordure *f.* ● *v.i.* **~ on,** être voisin de, avoisiner.

**borderline** *n.* ligne de démarcation *f.* **~ case,** cas limite *m.*

**bore** *v.t./i.* (*techn.*) forer.

**bore** *v.t.* ennuyer. ● *n.* raseu|r, -se *m.*, *f.*; (*thing*) ennui *m.* **be ~d,** s'ennuyer. **~dom** *n.* ennui *m.* **boring** *a.* ennuyeux.

**born** *a.* né. **be ~,** naître.

**borrow** *v.t.* emprunter (**from,** à). **~ing** *n.* emprunt *m.*

**bosom** n. sein m. ~ **friend**, ami(e) intime m. (f.).

**boss** n. (fam.) patron(ne) m. (f.) ● v.t. ~ **(about)**, (fam.) donner des ordres à, régenter.

**bossy** a. autoritaire.

**botan|y** n. botanique f. ~**ical** a. botanique.

**botch** v.t. bâcler, saboter.

**both** a. les deux. ● pron. tous or toutes (les) deux, l'un(e) et l'autre. ● adv. à la fois. ~ **the books**, les deux livres. **we ~ agree**, nous sommes tous les deux d'accord. **I bought ~ (of them)**, j'ai acheté les deux. **I saw ~ of you**, je vous ai vus tous les deux. ~ **Paul and Anne**, (et) Paul et Anne.

**bother** v.t. (annoy, worry) ennuyer; (disturb) déranger. ● v.i. se déranger. ● n. ennui m.; (effort) peine f. **don't ~ (calling)**, ce n'est pas la peine (d'appeler). **don't ~ about us**, ne t'inquiète pas pour nous. **I can't be ~ed**, j'ai la flemme.

**bottle** n. bouteille f.; (for baby) biberon m. ● v.t. mettre en bouteille(s). ~ **bank**, collecteur (de verre usagé) m. ~**opener** n. ouvre-bouteille(s) m.

**bottleneck** n. (traffic jam) bouchon m.

**bottom** n. fond m.; (of hill, page, etc.) bas m.; (buttocks) derrière m. ● a. inférieur, du bas.

**bough** n. rameau m.

**boulder** n. rocher m.

**boulevard** n. boulevard m.

**bounce** v.i. rebondir; (person) faire des bonds, bondir; (cheques: sl.) être refusé. ● v.t. faire rebondir. ● n. rebond m.

**bouncer** n. videur m.

**bound**[1] v.i. (leap) bondir. ● n. bond m.

**bound**[2] a. **be ~ for**, être en route pour, aller. vers. ~ **to**, (obliged) obligé de; (certain) sûr de.

**boundary** n. limite f.

**bound|s** n. pl. limites f. pl. **out of ~s**, interdit. ~**ed by**, limité par.

**bouquet** n. bouquet m.

**bout** n. période f.; (med.) accès m.; (boxing) combat m.

**bow**[1] n. (weapon) arc m.; (mus.) archet m.; (knot) nœud m. ~**tie** n. nœud papillon m.

**bow**[2] n. (with head) salut m.; (with body) révérence f. ● v.t./i. (s')incliner.

**bow**[3] n. (naut.) proue f.

**bowels** n. pl. intestins m. pl.

**bowl**[1] n. cuvette f.; (for food) bol m.; (for soup etc.) assiette creuse f.

**bowl**[2] n. (ball) boule f. ● v.t./i. (cricket) lancer. ~**ing** n. jeu de boules m.

**bowler**[1] n. (cricket) lanceur m.

**bowler**[2] n. ~ (**hat**), (chapeau) melon m.

**box**[1] n. boîte f.; (cardboard) carton m. ● v.t. mettre en boîte. **the ~**, (fam.) la télé. ~**office** n. bureau de location m. **Boxing Day**, le lendemain de Noël.

**box**[2] v.t./i. (sport) boxer. ~**ing** n. boxe f.; a. de boxe.

**boy** n. garçon m. ~**friend** n. (petit) ami m.

**boycott** v.t. boycotter. ● n. boycottage m.

**bra** n. soutien-gorge m.

**brace** n. (fastener) attache f.; (dental) appareil m.; (for bit) vilbrequin m. ~**s**, (for trousers) bretelles f. pl. ● v.t. soutenir. ~**o.s.**, rassembler ses forces.

**bracelet** n. bracelet m.

**bracken** n. fougère f.

**bracket** n. (for shelf etc.) tasseau m., support m.; (group) tranche f. **(round) ~**, (printing sign) parenthèse f.

**brag** v.i. se vanter.

**braid** n. (trimming) galon m.; (of hair) tresse f.

**Braille** n. braille m.

**brain** n. cerveau m. ~**s**, (fig.) intelligence f.

**brainwash** v.t. faire un lavage de cerveau à.

**brainwave** n. idée géniale f.

**brainy** a. intelligent.

**braise** v.t. braiser.

**brake** n. frein m. ● v.t./i. freiner. ~ **fluid**, liquide de frein m. ~ **light**, feu de stop m. ~ **lining**, garniture de frein f.

**bramble** n. ronce f.

**bran** n. (husks) son m.

**branch** n. branche f.; (of road) embranchement m.; (comm.) succursale f.; (of bank) agence f. ● v.i. ~ **(off)**, bifurquer.

**brand** n. marque f. ● v.t. ~ **s.o. as**, donner à qn. la réputation de. ~**new** a. tout neuf.

**brandish** v.t. brandir.

**brandy** n. cognac m.

**brash** a. effronté.

**brass** n. cuivre m. **the ~**, (mus.) les cuivres m. pl.

**brassière** n. soutien-gorge m.

**brat** n. (child: pej.) môme m./f.; (ill-behaved) garnement m.

**bravado** n. bravade f.

**brave** a. courageux, brave. ● v.t. braver. ~**ry** n. courage m.

**bravo** int. bravo.

**brawl** n. bagarre f. ● v.i. se bagarrer.

**bray** n. braiment m. ● v.i. braire.

**Brazil** n. Brésil m. ~**ian** a. & n. brésilien(ne) (m. (f.)).

**breach** n. violation f.; (of contract) rupture f.; (gap) brèche f. ● v.t. ouvrir une brèche dans.

**bread** n. pain m. ~ **and butter**, tartine f. ~ **bin**, (Amer.) ~**box** ns. boîte à pain f.

**breadcrumbs** n. pl. (culin.) chapelure f.

**breadth** n. largeur f.

**break** v.t. casser; (smash into pieces) briser; (vow, silence, rank, etc.) rompre; (law) violer; (a record) battre; (news) révéler; (journey) interrompre; (heart, strike, ice) briser. ● v.i. (se) casser; se briser. ● n. cassure f., rupture *f.*; (*in relationship, continuity*) rupture *f.*; (*interval*) interruption *f.*; (*at school*) récréation *f.*, récré *f.*; (*for coffee*) pause *f.*; (*luck: fam.*) chance *f.* ~ **one's arm,** se casser le bras. ~ **down** *v.i.* (*collapse*) s'effondrer; (*fail*) échouer; (*machine*) tomber en panne; *v.t.* (*door*) enfoncer; (*analyse*) analyser. ~**in** *n.* cambriolage *m.* ~ **into,** cambrioler. ~ **off,** (se) détacher; (*suspend*) rompre; (*stop talking*) s'interrompre. ~ **out,** (*fire, war, etc.*) éclater. ~ **up,** (*end*) (faire) cesser; (*couple*) rompre; (*marriage*) (se) briser; (*crowd*) (se) disperser; (*schools*) entrer en vacances. ~**able** *a.* cassable. ~**age** *n.* casse *f.*

**breakdown** *n.* (*techn.*) panne *f.*; (*med.*) dépression *f.*; (*of figures*) analyse *f.*

**breakfast** *n.* petit déjeuner *m.*

**breakthrough** *n.* percée *f.*

**breast** *n.* sein *m.*; (*chest*) poitrine *f.* ~**-feed** *v.t.* allaiter. ~**-stroke** *n.* brasse *f.*

**breath** *n.* souffle *m.*, haleine *f.* **out of** ~, essoufflé.

**breathalyser** *n.* alcootest *m.*

**breath|e** *v.t./i.* respirer. ~ **in,** inspirer. ~ **out,** expirer. ~**ing** *n.* respiration *f.*

**breather** *n.* moment de repos *m.*

**breathtaking** *a.* à vous couper le souffle.

**breed** *v.t.* élever; (*give rise to*) engendrer. ● *v.i.* se reproduire. ● *n.* race *f.*

**breez|e** *n.* brise *f.* ~**y** *a.* (*weather*) frais; (*cheerful*) jovial.

**Breton** *a. & n.* breton(ne) (*m.* (*f.*)).

**brew** *v.t.* (*beer*) brasser; (*tea*) faire infuser. ● *v.i.* fermenter; (*fig.*) se préparer. ● *n.* décoction *f.* ~**ery** *n.* brasserie *f.*

**bribe** *n.* pot-de-vin *m.* ● *v.t.* soudoyer. ~**ry** *n.* corruption *f.*

**brick** *n.* brique *f.*

**bricklayer** *n.* maçon *m.*

**bridal** *a.* nuptial.

**bride** *n.* mariée *f.*

**bridegroom** *n.* marié *m.*

**bridesmaid** *n.* demoiselle d'honneur *f.*

**bridge**¹ *n.* pont *m.*; (*naut.*) passerelle *f.*; (*of nose*) arête *f.*

**bridge**² *n.* (*cards*) bridge *m.*

**bridle** *n.* bride *f.* ● *v.t.* brider. ~**-path** *n.* allée cavalière *f.*

**brief**¹ *a.* bref. ~**ly** *adv.* brièvement.

**brief**² *n.* instructions *f. pl.*; (*jurid.*) dossier *m.* ● *v.t.* donner des instructions à. ~**ing** *n.* briefing *m.*

**briefcase** *n.* serviette *f.*

**briefs** *n. pl.* slip *m.*

**brigad|e** *n.* brigade *f.* ~**ier** *n.* général de brigade *m.*

**bright** *a.* brillant, vif; (*day, room*) clair; (*cheerful*) gai; (*clever*) intelligent. ~**ness** *n.* éclat *m.*

**brighten** *v.t.* égayer. ● *v.i.* (*weather*) s'éclaircir; (*of face*) s'éclairer.

**brilliant** *a.* brillant; (*light*) éclatant; (*very good: fam.*) super.

**brim** *n.* bord *m.*

**brine** *n.* saumure *f.*

**bring** *v.t.* (*thing*) apporter; (*person, vehicle*) amener. ~ **back,** rapporter; ramener. ~ **down,** faire tomber; (*shoot down, knock down*) abattre. ~**forward,** avancer. ~**off,** réussir. ~ **up,** élever; (*med.*) vomir; (*question*) soulever.

**brink** *n.* bord *m.*

**brisk** *a.* vif.

**bristle** *n.* poil *m.* ● *v.i.* se hérisser.

**Britain** *n.* Grande-Bretagne *f.*

**British** *a.* britannique. **the** ~, les Britanniques *m. pl.*

**Brittany** *n.* Bretagne *f.*

**brittle** *a.* fragile.

**broad** *a.* large; (*daylight, outline*) grand. ~ **bean,** fève *f.* ~**-minded** *a.* large d'esprit.

**broadcast** *v.t./i.* diffuser; (*person*) parler à la télévision *or* à la radio. ● *n.* émission *f.*

**broaden** *v.t./i.* (s')élargir.

**broccoli** *n. invar.* brocoli *m.*

**brochure** *n.* brochure *f.*

**broke** *a.* (*penniless: sl.*) fauché.

**broker** *n.* courtier *f.*

**bronchitis** *n.* bronchite *f.*

**bronze** *n.* bronze *m.*

**brooch** *n.* broche *f.*

**brood** *n.* nichée *f.*, couvée *f.* ● *v.i.* couver; (*fig.*) méditer tristement. ~**y** *a.* mélancolique.

**brook** *n.* ruisseau *m.*

**broom** *n.* balai *m.*

**broomstick** *n.* manche à balai *m.*

**broth** *n.* bouillon *m.*

**brothel** *n.* maison close *f.*

**brother** *n.* frère *m.* ~**-in-law** *n.* beau-frère *m.*

**brow** *n.* front *m.*; (*of hill*) sommet *m.*

**browbeat** *v.t.* intimider.

**brown** *a.* marron (*invar.*); (*cheveux*) brun. ● *n.* marron *m.*; brun *m.* ● *v.t./i.* brunir; (*culin.*) (faire) dorer. ~ **bread,** pain bis *m.* ~ **sugar,** cassonade *f.*

**Brownie** *n.* jeannette *f.*

**browse** *v.i.* feuilleter.

**bruise** *n.* bleu *m.* ● *v.t.* (*hurt*) faire un bleu à; (*fruit*) abîmer. ~**d** *a.* couvert de bleus.

**brunch** *n.* petit déjeuner copieux *m.* (*pris comme déjeuner*)

**brunette** *n.* brunette *f.*

**brunt** *n.* **the** ~ **of,** le plus fort de.

**brush** *n.* brosse *f.*; (*bushes*) broussailles *f. pl.* ● *v.t.* brosser. ~ **aside,** écarter. **give s.o. the** ~**off,** (*reject: fam.*) envoyer promener qn.

**Brussels** *n.* Bruxelles *m./f.* ~ **sprouts,** choux de Bruxelles *m. pl.*

**brutal** *a.* brutal. ~**ity** *n.* brutalité *f.*

**brute** *n.* brute *f.* **by ~ force,** par la force.

**bubble** *n.* bulle *f.* ● *v.i.* bouillonner. **~ bath,** bain moussant *m.*

**buck**[1] *n.* mâle *m.* ● *v.i.* ruer. **~ up,** (*sl.*) prendre courage; (*hurry: sl.*) se grouiller.

**buck**[2] *n.* (*Amer., sl.*) dollar *m.*

**buck**[3] *n.* **pass the ~,** rejeter la responsabilité (**to,** sur).

**bucket** *n.* seau *m.*

**buckle** *n.* boucle *f.* ● *v.t./i.* (*fasten*) (se) boucler; (*bend*) voiler.

**bud** *n.* bourgeon *m.* ● *v.i.* bourgeonner.

**Buddhis|t** *a. & n.* bouddhiste (*m./f.*) **~m** *n.* bouddhisme *m.*

**buddy** *n.* (*fam.*) copain *m.*

**budge** *v.t./i.* (faire) bouger.

**budgerigar** *n.* perruche *f.*

**budget** *n.* budget *m.* ● *v.i.* **~ for,** prévoir (dans son budget).

**buff** *n.* (*colour*) chamois *m.*; (*fam.*) fanatique *m./f.*

**buffalo** *n.* buffle *m.*; (*Amer.*) bison *m.*

**buffer** *n.* tampon *m.* **~ zone,** zone tampon *f.*

**buffet** *n.* (*meal, counter*) buffet *m.* **~ car,** buffet *m.*

**buffoon** *n.* bouffon *m.*

**bug** *n.* (*insect*) punaise *f.*; (*any small insect*) bestiole *f.*; (*germ: sl.*) microbe *m.*; (*device: sl.*) micro *m.*; (*defect: sl.*) défaut *m.* ● *v.t.* mettre des micros dans; (*Amer., sl.*) embêter.

**buggy** *n.* (*child's*) poussette *f.*

**bugle** *n.* clairon *m.*

**build** *v.t./i.* bâtir, construire. ● *n.* carrure *f.* **~ up,** (*increase*) augmenter, monter; (*accumulate*) (s')accumuler. **~up** *n.* accumulation *f.*; (*fig.*) publicité *f.* **~er** *n.* entrepreneur *m.*; (*workman*) ouvrier *m.*

**building** *n.* bâtiment *m.*; (*dwelling*) immeuble *m.*

**bulb** *n.* oignon *m.*; (*electr.*) ampoule *f.*

**bulg|e** *n.* renflement *m.* ● *v.i.* se renfler, être renflé. **be ~ing with,** être gonflé *or* bourré de.

**bulimia** *n.* boulimie *f.*

**bulk** *n.* grosseur *f.* **in ~,** en gros; (*loose*) en vrac. **~y** *a.* gros.

**bull** *n.* taureau *m.*

**bulldog** *n.* bouledogue *m.*

**bulldozer** *n.* bulldozer *m.*

**bullet** *n.* balle *f.* **~-proof** *a.* pare-balles *invar.*; (*vehicle*) blindé.

**bulletin** *n.* bulletin *m.*

**bullfight** *n.* corrida *f.* **~er** *n.* torero *m.*

**bullion** *n.* or *or* argent en lingots *m.*

**bullring** *n.* arène *f.*

**bully** *n.* brute *f.*; tyran *m.* ● *v.t.* (*treat badly*) brutaliser; (*persecute*) tyranniser; (*coerce*) forcer (**into,** à).

**bum**[1] *n.* (*sl.*) derrière *m.*

**bum**[2] *n.* (*Amer., sl.*) vagabond(e) *m.* (*f.*).

**bumble-bee** *n.* bourdon *m.*

**bump** *n.* choc *m.*; (*swelling*) bosse *f.* ● *v.t./i.* cogner, heurter. **~ into,** (*hit*) rentrer dans; (*meet*) tomber sur. **~y** *a.* cahoteux.

**bumper** *n.* pare-chocs *m. invar.* ● *a.* exceptionnel.

**bun** *n.* (*cake*) petit pain au lait *m.*; (*hair*) chignon *m.*

**bunch** *n.* (*of flowers*) bouquet *m.*; (*of keys*) trousseau *m.*; (*of people*) groupe *m.*; (*of bananas*) régime *m.* **~ of grapes,** grappe de raisin *f.*

**bundle** *n.* paquet *m.* ● *v.t.* mettre en paquet; (*push*) pousser.

**bung** *n.* bonde *f.* ● *v.t.* boucher; (*throw: sl.*) flanquer.

**bungalow** *n.* bungalow *m.*

**bungle** *v.t.* gâcher.

**bunion** *n.* (*med.*) oignon *m.*

**bunk** *n.* couchette *f.* **~-beds** *n. pl.* lits superposés *m. pl.*

**bunker** *n.* (*mil.*) bunker *m.*

**buoy** *n.* bouée *f.* ● *v.t.* **~ up,** (*hearten*) soutenir, encourager.

**burden** *n.* fardeau *m.* ● *v.t.* accabler.

**bureau** *n.* bureau *m.*

**bureaucracy** *n.* bureaucratie *f.*

**bureaucrat** *n.* bureaucrate *m./f.* **~ic** *a.* bureaucratique.

**burglar** *n.* cambrioleur *m.* **~ize** *v.t.* (*Amer.*) cambrioler. **~ alarm,** alarme *f.* **~y** *n.* cambriolage *m.*

**burgle** *v.t.* cambrioler.

**Burgundy** *n.* (*wine*) bourgogne *m.*

**burial** *n.* enterrement *m.*

**burly** *a.* costaud.

**Burm|a** *n.* Birmanie *f.* **~ese** *a. & n.* birman(e) (*m.* (*f.*)).

**burn** *v.t./i.* brûler. ● *n.* brûlure *f.* **~er** *n.* brûleur *m.* **~ing** *a.* (*fig.*) brûlant.

**burp** *n.* (*fam.*) rot *m.* ● *v.i.* (*fam.*) roter.

**burrow** *n.* terrier *m.* ● *v.t.* creuser.

**burst** *v.t./i.* crever, (faire) éclater. ● *n.* explosion *f.*; (*of laughter*) éclat *m.*; (*surge*) élan *m.* **be ~ing with,** déborder de. **~ into,** faire irruption dans.

**bury** *v.t.* (*person etc.*) enterrer; (*hide, cover*) enfouir; (*engross, thrust*) plonger.

**bus** *n.* (auto)bus *m.* **~-stop** *n.* arrêt d'autobus *m.*

**bush** *n.* buisson *m.*; (*land*) brousse *f.* **~y** *a.* broussailleux.

**business** *n.* (*task, concern*) affaire *f.*; (*commerce*) affaires *f. pl.*; (*line of work*) métier *m.*; (*shop*) commerce *m.* **that's none of your ~!,** ça ne vous regarde pas! **~man,** homme d'affaires *m.*

**businesslike** *a.* sérieux.

**busker** *n.* musicien(ne) des rues *m.* (*f.*).

**bust**[1] *n.* buste *m.*; (*bosom*) poitrine *f.*

**bust²** v.t./i. (burst: sl.) crever; (break: sl.) (se) casser. ● a. (broken, finished: sl.) fichu. **~up** n. (sl.) engueulade f.

**bustl|e** v.i. s'affairer. ● n. remue-ménage m. **~ing** a. (place) bruyant, animé.

**bus|y** a. occupé; (street) animé; (day) chargé. **~ily** adv. activement.

**but** conj. mais. ● prep. sauf. ● adv. (only) seulement.

**butane** n. butane m.

**butcher** n. boucher m. ● v.t. massacrer.

**butler** n. maître d'hôtel m.

**butt** n. (of gun) crosse f.; (of cigarette) mégot m.; (target) cible f.; (barrel) tonneau m.; (Amer., fam.) derrière m. ● v.i. **~ in**, interrompre.

**butter** n. beurre m. ● v.t. beurrer. **~bean** n. haricot blanc m.

**buttercup** n. bouton-d'or m.

**butterfly** n. papillon m.

**buttock** n. fesse f.

**button** n. bouton m.

**buttonhole** n. boutonnière f. ● v.t. accrocher.

**buy** v.t. acheter (from, à); (believe: sl.) croire, avaler. ● n. achat m. **~ sth for s.o.** acheter qch. à qn. **~er** n. acheteu|r, -se m., f.

**buzz** n. bourdonnement m. ● v.i. bourdonner. **~er** n. sonnerie f.

**by** prep. par, de; (near) à côté de; (before) avant; (means) en, à, par. **by bike**, à vélo. **by car**, en auto. **by day**, de jour. **by the kilo**, au kilo. **by running** /etc., en courant/etc. **by sea**, par mer. **by that time**, à ce moment-là. **~ the way**, à propos. ● adv. (near) tout près. **by-law** n. arrêté m.; (of club etc.) statut m. **by o.s.**, tout seul. **~product** n. sous-produit m.; (fig.) conséquence f.

**bye(-bye)** int. (fam.) au revoir.

**bypass** n. (auto.) route qui contourne f.; (med.) pontage m. ● v.t. contourner.

**bystander** n. specta|teur, -trice m., f.

**byte** n. octet m.

• • • • • • • • • • • • • • • • • • • • • • • • • • • • •

# Cc

• • • • • • • • • • • • • • • • • • • • • • • • • • • • •

**cab** n. taxi m.; (of lorry, train) cabine f.

**cabaret** n. spectacle (de cabaret) m.

**cabbage** n. chou m.

**cabin** n. (hut) cabane f.; (in ship, aircraft) cabine f.

**cabinet** n. (petite) armoire f.; (for filing) classeur m. **C~**, (pol.) cabinet m.

**cable** n. câble m. ● v.t. câbler. **~car** n. téléphérique m. **~ railway**, funiculaire m.

**cache** n. (place) cachette f. **a ~ of arms**, des armes cachées.

**cactus** n. cactus m.

**caddie** n. (golf) caddie m.

**caddy** n. boîte à thé f.

**cadet** n. élève officier m.

**cadge** v.t. se faire payer, écornifler. ● v.i. quémander. **~ money from**, taper. **~r** n. écornifleu|r, -se m., f.

**Caesarean** a. **~ (section)**, césarienne f.

**café** n. café(-restaurant) m.

**cafeteria** n. cafétéria f.

**caffeine** n. caféine f.

**cage** n. cage f.

**cagey** a. peu communicatif.

**cagoule** n. K-way n. (P.).

**cajole** v.t. **~ s.o. into doing**, faire l'enjôleur pour que qn. fasse.

**cake** n. gâteau m.

**calamity** n. calamité f.

**calcium** n. calcium m.

**calculat|e** v.t./i. calculer. **~ed** a. (action) délibéré. **~ion** n. calcul m. **~or** n. calculatrice f.

**calendar** n. calendrier m.

**calf¹** n. (young cow or bull) veau m.

**calf²** n. (of leg) mollet m.

**calibre** n. calibre m.

**calico** n. calicot m.

**call** v.t./i. appeler. **~ (in or round)**, (visit) passer. ● n. appel m.; (of bird) cri m.; visite f. **be ~ed**, (named) s'appeler. **~ back**, rappeler; (visit) repasser. **~box** n. cabine téléphonique f. **~ for**, (require) demander; (fetch) passer prendre. **~ off**, annuler. **~ on**, (visit) passer chez; (appeal to) faire appel à. **~er** n. visiteu|r, -se m., f.; (on phone) personne qui appelle f. **~ing** n. vocation f.

**callous** a., **~ly** adv. sans pitié.

**calm** a. calme. ● n. calme m. ● v.t./i. **~ (down)**, (se) calmer. **~ness** n. calme m.

**calorie** n. calorie f.

**camber** n. (of road) bombement m.

**camcorder** n. caméscope m.

**camel** n. chameau m.

**cameo** n. camée m.

**camera** n. appareil(-photo) m.; (for moving pictures) caméra f. **~man** n. caméraman m.

**camouflage** n. camouflage m. ● v.t. camoufler.

**camp** n. camp m. ● v.i. camper. **~bed** n. lit de camp m. **~er** n. campeu|r, -se m., f. **~er (-van)**, camping-car m. **~ing** n. camping m.

**campaign** n. campagne f. ● v.i. faire campagne.

**campsite** n. (for holiday-makers) camping m.

**campus** n. campus m.

**can**[1] *n.* bidon *m.*; (*sealed container for food*) boîte *f.* ● *v.t.* mettre en boîte. **~-opener** *n.* ouvre-boîte(s) *m.*

**can**[2] *v. aux.* (*be able to*) pouvoir; (*know how to*) savoir.

**Canad|a** *n.* Canada *m.* **~ian** *a.* & *n.* canadien(ne) (*m.* (*f.*)).

**canal** *n.* canal *m.*

**canary** *n.* canari *m.*

**cancel** *v.t./i.* (*call off, revoke*) annuler; (*cross out*) barrer. **~lation** *n.* annulation *f.*; oblitération *f.*

**cancer** *n.* cancer *m.*

**Cancer** *n.* le Cancer.

**candid** *a.* franc.

**candidate** *n.* candidat(e) *m.* (*f.*).

**candle** *n.* bougie *f.*, chandelle *f.*; (*in church*) cierge *m.*

**candlestick** *n.* chandelier *m.*

**candour** *n.* franchise *f.*

**candy** *n.* (*Amer.*) bonbon(s) *m.* (*pl.*) **~-floss** *n.* barbe à papa *f.*

**cane** *n.* canne *f.*; (*for baskets*) rotin *m.*; (*for punishment: schol.*) baguette *f.*, bâton *m.*

**canister** *n.* boîte *f.*

**cannabis** *n.* cannabis *m.*

**cannibal** *n.* cannibale *m./f.*

**cannon** *n.* canon *m.*

**canny** *a.* rusé, madré.

**canoe** *n.* (*sport*) canoë *m.*, kayak *m.* ● *v.i.* faire du canoë *or* du kayak. **~ist** *n.* canoéiste *m./f.*

**canon** *n.* (*clergyman*) chanoine *m.*; (*rule*) canon *m.*

**canopy** *n.* dais *m.*; (*over doorway*) marquise *f.*

**canteen** *n.* (*restaurant*) cantine *f.*; (*flask*) bidon *m.*

**canter** *n.* petit galop *m.* ● *v.i.* aller au petit galop.

**canvas** *n.* toile *f.*

**canvass** *v.t./i.* (*comm., pol.*) solliciter des commandes *or* des voix (de).

**canyon** *n.* cañon *m.*

**cap** *n.* (*hat*) casquette *f.*; (*of bottle, tube*) bouchon *m.*; (*of beer or milk bottle*) capsule *f.*; (*of pen*) capuchon *m.*; (*for toy gun*) amorce *f.*

**capab|le** *a.* (*person*) capable (**of,** de), compétent. **be ~le of,** (*of situation, text, etc.*) être susceptible de. **~ility** *n.* capacité *f.*

**capacity** *n.* capacité *f.*

**cape**[1] *n.* (*cloak*) cape *f.*

**cape**[2] *n.* (*geog.*) cap *m.*

**caper**[1] *v.i.* gambader. ● *n.* (*prank*) farce *f.*; (*activity: sl.*) affaire *f.*

**caper**[2] *n.* (*culin.*) câpre *f.*

**capital** *a.* capital. ● *n.* (*town*) capitale *f.*; (*money*) capital *m.* **~ (letter),** majuscule *f.*

**capitalis|t** *a.* & *n.* capitaliste (*m./f.*). **~m** *n.* capitalisme *m.*

**capitalize** *v.i.* **~ on,** tirer profit de.

**Capricorn** *n.* le Capricorne.

**capsize** *v.t./i.* (faire) chavirer.

**capsule** *n.* capsule *f.*

**captain** *n.* capitaine *m.*

**caption** *n.* (*for illustration*) légende *f.*; (*heading*) sous-titre *m.*

**captivate** *v.t.* captiver.

**captiv|e** *a.* & *n.* capti|f, -ve (*m., f.*). **~ity** *n.* captivité *f.*

**capture** *v.t.* (*person, animal*) prendre, capturer; (*attention*) retenir. ● *n.* capture *f.*

**car** *n.* voiture *f.* **~ ferry,** ferry *m.* **~-park** *n.* parking *m.* **~ phone,** téléphone de voiture *m.* **~-wash** *n.* station de lavage *f.*

**carafe** *n.* carafe *f.*

**caramel** *n.* caramel *m.*

**carat** *n.* carat *m.*

**caravan** *n.* caravane *f.*

**carbohydrate** *n.* hydrate de carbone *m.*

**carbon** *n.* carbone *m.* **~ copy, ~ paper,** carbone *m.*

**carburettor,** *n.* carburateur *m.*

**carcass** *n.* carcasse *f.*

**card** *n.* carte *f.*

**cardboard** *n.* carton *m.*

**cardiac** *a.* cardiaque.

**cardigan** *n.* cardigan *m.*

**cardinal** *a.* cardinal. ● *n.* (*relig.*) cardinal *m.*

**care** *n.* (*attention*) soin *m.*, attention *f.*; (*worry*) souci *m.*; (*protection*) garde *f.* ● *v.i.* **~ about,** s'intéresser à. **~ for,** s'occuper de; (*invalid*) soigner. **~ to** *or* **for,** aimer, vouloir. **I don't ~,** ça m'est égal. **take ~ of,** s'occuper de. **take ~ to do sth.,** faire bien attention à faire qch.

**career** *n.* carrière *f.*

**carefree** *a.* insouciant.

**careful** *a.* soigneux; (*cautious*) prudent. (**be) ~l,** (fais) attention! **~ly** *adv.* avec soin.

**careless** *a.* négligent; (*work*) peu soigné. **~ about,** peu soucieux de.

**caress** *n.* caresse *f.* ● *v.t.* caresser.

**caretaker** *n.* gardien(ne) *m.* (*f.*).

**cargo** *n.* cargaison *f.*

**Caribbean** *a.* caraïbe. ● *n.* **the ~,** (*sea*) la mer des Caraïbes; (*islands*) les Antilles *f. pl.*

**caring** *a.* (*mother, son, etc.*) aimant. ● *n.* affection *f.*

**carnation** *n.* œillet *m.*

**carnival** *n.* carnaval *m.*

**carol** *n.* chant (de Noël) *m.*

**carp**[1] *n. invar.* carpe *f.*

**carp**[2] *v.i.* **~ (at),** critiquer.

**carpent|er** *n.* charpentier *m.*; (*for light woodwork, furniture*) menuisier *m.* **~ry** *n.* charpenterie *f.*; menuiserie *f.*

**carpet** *n.* tapis *m.* ● *v.t.* recouvrir d'un tapis.

**carriage** n. (*rail & horse-drawn*) voiture f.; (*of goods*) transport m.; (*cost*) port m.

**carriageway** n. chaussée f.

**carrier** n. transporteur m.; (*med.*) porteu|r, -se m., f. ~ **(bag),** sac en plastique m.

**carrot** n. carotte f.

**carry** v.t./i. porter; (*goods*) transporter; (*involve*) comporter; (*motion*) voter. ~**cot** n. porte-bébé m. ~ **off,** enlever; (*prize*) remporter. ~ **on,** continuer; (*behave: fam.*) se conduire (mal). ~ **out,** (*an order, plan*) exécuter; (*duty*) accomplir; (*task*) effectuer.

**cart** n. charrette f. ● v.t. transporter; (*heavy object: sl.*) trimballer.

**cartilage** n. cartilage m.

**carton** n. (*box*) carton m.; (*of yoghurt, cream*) pot m.; (*of cigarettes*) cartouche f.

**cartoon** n. dessin (humoristique) m.; (*cinema*) dessin animé m.

**cartridge** n. cartouche f.

**carve** v.t. tailler; (*meat*) découper.

**cascade** n. cascade f. ● v.i. tomber en cascade.

**case**[1] n. cas m.; (*jurid.*) affaire f.; (*phil.*) arguments m. pl. **in ~ he comes,** au cas où il viendrait. **in that ~,** à ce moment-là.

**case**[2] n. (*crate*) caisse f.; (*for camera, cigarettes, spectacles, etc.*) étui m.; (*suitcase*) valise f.

**cash** n. argent m. ● a. (*price etc.*) (au) comptant. ● v.t. encaisser. ~ **a cheque,** (*person*) encaisser un chèque; (*bank*) payer un chèque. **pay ~,** payer comptant. **in ~,** en espèces. ~ **desk,** caisse f. ~ **dispenser,** distributeur de billets m.

**cashew** n. noix de cajou f.

**cashier** n. caiss|ier, -ière m., f.

**cashmere** n. cachemire m.

**casino** n. casino m.

**cask** n. tonneau m.

**casket** n. (*box*) coffret m.; (*coffin: Amer.*) cercueil m.

**casserole** n. (*utensil*) cocotte f.; (*stew*) daube f.

**cassette** n. cassette f.

**cast** v.t. (*throw*) jeter; (*glance, look*) jeter; (*shadow*) projeter; (*vote*) donner; (*metal*) couler. ● n. (*theatre*) distribution f.; (*of dice*) coup m.; (*mould*) moule m.; (*med.*) plâtre m. ~ **iron,** fonte f. ~**iron** a. de fonte; (*fig.*) solide.

**castle** n. château m.; (*chess*) tour f.

**castor** n. (*wheel*) roulette f. ~ **sugar,** sucre en poudre m.

**casual** a. (*remark*) fait au hasard; (*meeting*) fortuit; (*attitude*) désinvolte; (*work*) temporaire; (*clothes*) sport invar.

**casualty** n. (*dead*) mort(e) m. (f.); (*injured*) blessé(e) m. (f.); (*accident victim*) accidenté(e) m. (f.).

**cat** n. chat m. **C~'s-eyes** n. pl. (P.) catadioptres m. pl.

**catalogue** n. catalogue m. ● v.t. cataloguer.

**catalyst** n. catalyseur m.

**catapult** n. lance-pierres m. invar. ● v.t. catapulter.

**cataract** n. (*waterfall & med.*) cataracte f.

**catarrh** n. rhume m., catarrhe m.

**catastroph|e** n. catastrophe f. ~**ic** a. catastrophique.

**catch** v.t. attraper; (*grab*) prendre, saisir; (*catch unawares*) surprendre; (*jam, trap*) prendre; (*understand*) saisir. ● v.i. prendre; (*get stuck*) se prendre (**in,** dans). ● n. capture f., prise f.; (*on door*) loquet m.; (*fig.*) piège m. ~ **s.o.'s eye,** attirer l'attention de qn. ~ **up,** se rattraper. ~ **up (with),** rattraper.

**catching** a. contagieux.

**categorical** a. catégorique.

**category** n. catégorie f.

**cater** v.i. s'occuper de la nourriture. ~ **for,** (*pander to*) satisfaire; (*of magazine etc.*) s'adresser à. ~**er** n. traiteur m.

**caterpillar** n. chenille f.

**cathedral** n. cathédrale f.

**catholic** a. universel. **C~** a. & n. catholique (m./f.).

**cattle** n. pl. bétail m.

**cauliflower** n. chou-fleur m.

**cause** n. cause f.; (*reason*) raison f., motif m. ● v.t. causer. ~**sth. to grow/move/**etc., faire pousser/bouger/etc. qch.

**causeway** n. chaussée f.

**cauti|on** n. prudence f.; (*warning*) avertissement m. ● v.t. avertir. ~**ous** a. prudent.

**cavalry** n. cavalerie f.

**cave** n. caverne f., grotte f. ● v.i. ~ **in,** s'effondrer; (*agree*) céder.

**cavern** n. caverne f.

**caviare** n. caviar m.

**cavity** n. cavité f.

**CD** n. compact disc m.

**cease** v.t./i. cesser. ~**fire** n. cessez-le-feu m. invar.

**cedar** n. cèdre m.

**cede** v.t. céder.

**cedilla** n. cédille f.

**ceiling** n. plafond m.

**celebrate** v.t. (*perform, glorify*) célébrer. ~**ion** n. fête f.

**celebrity** n. célébrité f.

**celery** n. céleri m.

**cell** n. cellule f.; (*electr.*) élément m.

**cellar** n. cave f.

**cell|o** n. violoncelle m. ~**ist** n. violoncelliste m./f.

**Cellophane** n. (P.) cellophane f. (P.).

**Celt** n. Celte m./f. ~**ic** a. celtique, celte.

**cement** n. ciment m. **~-mixer** n. bétonnière f.

**cemetery** n. cimetière m.

**censor** n. censeur m. ● v.t. censurer.

**census** n. recensement m.

**cent** n. (coin) cent m.

**centenary** n. centenaire m.

**centigrade** a. centigrade.

**centilitre** n. centilitre m.

**centimetre** n. centimètre m.

**centipede** n. millepattes m. invar.

**central** a. central. **~ heating**, chauffage central m.

**centre** n. centre m.

**century** n. siècle m.

**ceramic** a. (art) céramique; (object) en céramique.

**cereal** n. céréale f.

**ceremonial** a. de cérémonie. ● n. cérémonial m.

**ceremony** n. cérémonie f.

**certain** a. certain. **for ~**, avec certitude. **make ~ of**, s'assurer de. **~ly** adv. certainement. **~ty** n. certitude f.

**certificate** n. certificat m.

**certify** v.t. certifier.

**cervical** a. cervical.

**cessation** n. cessation f.

**chafe** v.t. frotter (contre).

**chaffinch** n. pinson m.

**chain** n. chaîne f. ● v.t. enchaîner. **~ store**, magasin à succursales multiples m.

**chair** n. chaise f.; (armchair) fauteuil m.; (univ.) chaire f. ● v.t. (preside over) présider.

**chairman** n. président(e) m. (f.).

**chalet** n. chalet m.

**chalk** n. craie f.

**challenge** n. défi m.; (task) gageure f. ● v.t. (summon) défier (**to do**, de faire); (question truth of) contester. **~er** n. (sport) challenger m.

**chamber** n. (old use) chambre f. **~ music**, musique de chambre f.

**chambermaid** n. femme de chambre f.

**chamois** n. **~(-leather)**, peau de chamois f.

**champagne** n. champagne m.

**champion** n. champion(ne) m. (f.). ● v.t. défendre. **~ship** n. championnat m.

**chance** n. (luck) hasard m.; (opportunity) occasion f.; (likelihood) chances f. pl.; (risk) risque m. ● a. fortuit. ● v.t. **~ doing**, prendre le risque de faire. **~ it**, risquer le coup. **by ~**, par hasard. **by any ~**, par hasard. **~s are that**, il est probable que.

**change** v.t. (alter) changer; (exchange) échanger (**for**, contre); (money) changer. **~ trains/one's dress/etc.** (by substitution) changer de train/de robe/etc. ● v.i. changer; (change clothes) se changer. ● n. changement

m.; (money) monnaie f. **a ~ for the better**, une amélioration. **~ into**, se transformer en; (clothes) mettre. **a ~ of clothes**, des vêtements de rechange. **~ one's mind**, changer d'avis. **for a ~**, pour changer. **~-over** n. passage m. **~able** a. changeant; (weather) variable. **~ing** a. changeant. **~ing room**, (in shop) cabine d'essayage f.; (sport.) vestiaire m.

**channel** n. chenal m.; (TV) chaîne f.; (medium, agency) canal m.; (groove) rainure f. **the (English) C~**, la Manche. **the C~ Islands**, les îles anglo-normandes f. pl.

**chant** n. (relig.) psalmodie f.; (of demonstrators) chant (scandé) m. ● v.t./i. psalmodier; scander (des slogans).

**chaos** n. chaos m. **~tic** a. chaotique.

**chap** n. (man: fam.) type m.

**chapel** n. chapelle f.

**chaperon** n. chaperon m. ● v.t. chaperonner.

**chaplain** n. aumônier m.

**chapped** a. gercé.

**chapter** n. chapitre m.

**char¹** n. (fam.) femme de ménage f.

**char²** v.t. carboniser.

**character** n. caractère m.; (in novel, play) personnage m.

**characteristic** a. & n. caractéristique (f.).

**charade** n. charade f.

**charcoal** n. charbon (de bois) m.

**charge** n. prix m.; (mil.) charge f.; (jurid.) inculpation f., accusation f.; (task, custody) charge f. **~s**, frais m. pl. ● v.t. faire payer; (ask) demander (**for**, pour); (enemy, gun) charger; (jurid.) inculper, accuser (**with**, de). ● v.i. foncer, se précipiter. **~ card**, carte d'achat f. **in ~ of**, responsable de. **take ~ of**, se charger de. **~able to**, (comm.) aux frais de.

**charisma** n. magnétisme m. **~tic** a. charismatique.

**charity** n. charité f.; (society) fondation charitable f.

**charm** n. charme m.; (trinket) amulette f. ● v.t. charmer. **~ing** a. charmant.

**chart** n. (naut.) carte (marine) f.; (table) tableau m., graphique m.

**charter** n. charte f. **~ (flight)**, charter m. ● v.t. affréter. **~ed accountant**, expert-comptable m.

**chase** v.t. poursuivre. ● v.i. courir (**after**, après). ● n. chasse f. **~ away** or **off**, chasser.

**chasm** n. abîme m.

**chassis** n. châssis m.

**chastity** n. chasteté f.

**chat** n. causette f. ● v.i. bavarder. **have a ~**, bavarder. **~ show**, talk-show m. **~ up**, (fam.) draguer.

**chatter** n. bavardage m. ● v.i. bavarder.

**chauffeur** n. chauffeur (de particulier) m.

**chauvinis|t** *n.* chauvin(e) *m.* (*f.*). **male ~t**, (*pej.*) phallocrate *m.* **~m** *n.* chauvinisme *m.*

**cheap** *a.* bon marché *invar.*; (*fare, rate*) réduit; (*worthless*) sans valeur. **~er**, meilleur marché *invar.* **~(ly)** *adv.* à bon marché.

**cheat** *v.i.* tricher; (*by fraud*) frauder. ● *v.t.* (*defraud*) frauder; (*deceive*) tromper. ● *n.* escroc *m.*

**check**[1] *v.t./i.* vérifier; (*tickets*) contrôler; (*stop*) enrayer, arrêter; (*restrain*) contenir; (*rebuke*) réprimander; (*tick off: Amer.*) cocher. ● *n.* vérification *f.*; contrôle *m.*; (*curb*) frein *m.*; (*chess*) échec *m.*; (*bill: Amer.*) addition *f.*; (*cheque: Amer.*) chèque *m.* **~ in**, signer le registre; (*at airport*) passer à l'enregistrement. **~-in** *n.* enregistrement *m.* **~-out** *n.* caisse *f.* **~ up**, verifier. **~ up on**, (*detail*) vérifier; (*situation*) s'informer sur. **~-up** *n.* examen médical *m.*

**check**[2] *n.* (*pattern*) carreaux *m. pl.* **~ed** *a.* à carreaux.

**checkmate** *n.* échec et mat *m.*

**cheek** *n.* joue *f.*; (*impudence*) culot *m.* **~y** *a.* effronté.

**cheer** *n.* gaieté *f.* **~s**, acclamations *f. pl.*; (*when drinking*) à votre santé. ● *v.t.* acclamer, applaudir. **~ up**, prendre courage. **~ful** *a.* gai.

**cheese** *n.* fromage *m.*

**cheetah** *n.* guépard *m.*

**chef** *n.* (*cook*) chef *m.*

**chemical** *a.* chimique. ● *n.* produit chimique *m.*

**chemist** *n.* pharmacien(ne) *m.* (*f.*); (*scientist*) chimiste *m./f.* **~'s shop**, pharmacie *f.* **~ry** *n.* chimie *f.*

**cheque** *n.* chèque *m.* **~-book** *n.* chéquier *m.* **~ card**, carte bancaire *f.*

**cherish** *v.t.* chérir; (*hope*) nourrir, caresser.

**cherry** *n.* cerise *f.*

**chess** *n.* échecs *m. pl.* **~-board** *n.* échiquier *m.*

**chest** *n.* (*anat.*) poitrine *f.*; (*box*) coffre *m.*

**chestnut** *n.* châtaigne *f.*; (*edible*) marron *m.*, châtaigne *f.*

**chew** *v.t.* mâcher. **~ing-gum** *n.* chewing-gum *m.*

**chic** *a.* chic *invar.*

**chick** *n.* poussin *m.*

**chicken** *n.* poulet *m.* ● *a.* (*sl.*) froussard. **~-pox** *n.* varicelle *f.*

**chick-pea** *n.* pois chiche *m.*

**chicory** *n.* (*for salad*) endive *f.*; (*in coffee*) chicorée *f.*

**chief** *n.* chef *m.* ● *a.* principal.

**chilblain** *n.* engelure *f.*

**child** *n.* enfant *m./f.* **~hood** *n.* enfance *f.* **~ish** *a.* enfantin. **~minder** *n.* nourrice *f.*

**Chile** *n.* Chili *m.* **~an** *a.* & *n.* chilien(ne) (*m.* (*f.*)).

**chill** *n.* froid *m.*; (*med.*) refroidissement *m.* ● *a.* froid. ● *v.t.* (*wine*) rafraichir; (*food*) mettre au frais. **~y** *a.* froid; (*sensitive to cold*) frileux. **be** *or* **feel ~y**, avoir froid.

**chilli** *n.* piment *m.*

**chime** *n.* carillon *m.* ● *v.t./i.* carillonner.

**chimney** *n.* cheminée *f.*

**chimpanzee** *n.* chimpanzé *m.*

**chin** *n.* menton *m.*

**china** *n.* porcelaine *f.*

**Chin|a** *n.* Chine *f.* **~ese** *a.* & *n.* chinois(e) (*m.* (*f.*)).

**chink**[1] *n.* (*slit*) fente *f.*

**chink**[2] *n.* tintement *m.* ● *v.t./i.* (faire) tinter.

**chip** *n.* (*on plate etc.*) ébréchure *f.*; (*piece*) éclat *m.*; (*of wood*) copeau *m.*; (*culin.*) frite *f.*; (*microchip*) puce *f.* ● *v.t./i.* (s')ébrécher. (**potato**) **~s**, (*Amer.*) chips *m. pl.*

**chipboard** *n.* aggloméré *m.*

**chiropodist** *n.* pédicure *m./f.*

**chirp** *n.* pépiement *m.* ● *v.i.* pépier.

**chisel** *n.* ciseau *m.* ● *v.t.* ciseler.

**chit** *n.* note *f.*, mot *m.*

**chit-chat** *n.* bavardage *m.*

**chives** *n. pl.* ciboulette *f.*

**chlorine** *n.* chlore *m.*

**choc-ice** *n.* esquimau *m.*

**chocolate** *n.* chocolat *m.*

**choice** *n.* choix *m.* ● *a.* de choix.

**choir** *n.* chœur *m.*

**choirboy** *n.* jeune choriste *m.*

**choke** *v.t./i.* (s')étrangler. ● *n.* starter *m.*

**cholera** *n.* choléra *m.*

**cholesterol** *n.* cholestérol *m.*

**choose** *v.t./i.* choisir. **~ to do**, décider de faire.

**choosy** *a.* (*fam.*) exigeant.

**chop** *v.t./i.* (*wood*) couper (à la hache); (*food*) hacher. ● *n.* (*meat*) côtelette *f.* **~ down**, abattre.

**choppy** *a.* (*sea*) agité.

**chopstick** *n.* baguette *f.*

**choral** *a.* choral.

**chord** *n.* (*mus.*) accord *m.*

**chore** *n.* travail (routinier) *m.*; (*unpleasant task*) corvée *f.*

**chortle** *n.* gloussement *m.* ● *v.i.* glousser.

**chorus** *n.* chœur *m.*; (*of song*) refrain *m.*

**Christ** *n.* le Christ *m.*

**christen** *v.t.* baptiser. **~ing** *n.* baptême *m.*

**Christian** *a.* & *n.* chrétien(ne) (*m.* (*f.*)). **~ name**, prénom *m.* **~ity** *n.* christianisme *m.*

**Christmas** *n.* Noël *m.* ● *a.* (*card, tree, etc.*) de Noël.

**chrome** *n.* chrome *m.*

**chromium** *n.* chrome *m.*

**chromosome** *n.* chromosome *m.*

**chronic** a. (*situation, disease*) chronique; (*bad: fam.*) affreux.

**chronicle** n. chronique f.

**chronolog|y** n. chronologie f. **∼ical** a. chronologique.

**chrysanthemum** n. chrysanthème m.

**chubby** a. dodu, potelé.

**chuck** v.t. (*fam.*) lancer. **∼ away** or **out**, (*fam.*) balancer.

**chuckle** n. gloussement m. ● v.i. glousser, rire.

**chum** n. cop|ain, -ine m., f.

**chunk** n. (*gros*) morceau m.

**chunky** a. trapu.

**church** n. église f.

**churchyard** n. cimetière m.

**churn** n. baratte f.; (*milk-can*) bidon m. ● v.t. baratter. **∼ out**, produire (en série).

**chute** n. glissière f.; (*for rubbish*) vide-ordures m. invar.

**chutney** n. condiment (de fruits) m.

**cider** n. cidre m.

**cigar** n. cigare m.

**cigarette** n. cigarette f.

**cinder** n. cendre f.

**cine-camera** n. caméra f.

**cinema** n. cinéma m.

**cinnamon** n. cannelle f.

**cipher** n. (*numeral, code*) chiffre m.; (*person*) nullité f.

**circle** n. cercle m.; (*theatre*) balcon m. ● v.t. (*go round*) faire le tour de; (*word, error, etc.*) entourer d'un cercle. ● v.i. décrire des cercles.

**circuit** n. circuit m. **∼-breaker** n. disjoncteur m.

**circular** a. & n. circulaire (f.).

**circulate** v.t./i. (faire) circuler.

**circumference** n. circonférence f.

**circumflex** n. circonflexe m.

**circumstance** n. circonstance f. **∼s**, (*financial*) situation financière f.

**circus** n. cirque m.

**cistern** n. réservoir m.

**cit|e** v.t. citer. **∼ation** n. citation f.

**citizen** n. citoyen(ne) m. (f.); (*of town*) habitant(e) m. (f.).

**citrus** a. **∼ fruit(s)**, agrumes m. pl.

**city** n. (*grande*) ville f.

**civic** a. civique. **∼ centre**, centre administratif m.

**civil** a. civil; (*rights*) civique; (*defence*) passif. **∼ engineer**, ingénieur civil m. **C∼ Servant**, fonctionnaire m./f. **∼ war**, guerre civile f.

**civilian** a. & n. civil(e) (m. (f.)).

**civiliz|e** v.t. civiliser. **∼ation** n. civilisation f.

**clad** a. **∼ in**, vêtu de.

**claim** v.t. revendiquer, réclamer; (*assert*) prétendre. ● n. revendication f., prétention f.; (*assertion*) affirmation f.; (*for insurance*) réclamation f.; (*right*) droit m.

**claimant** n. (*of social benefits*) demandeur m.

**clairvoyant** n. voyant(e) m. (f.).

**clam** n. palourde f.

**clamber** v.i. grimper.

**clammy** a. moite.

**clamour** n. clameur f., cris m. pl. ● v.i. **∼ for**, demander à grands cris.

**clamp** n. agrafe f.; (*large*) crampon m.; (*for carpentry*) serre-joint(s) m.; (*for car*) sabot de Denver m. ● v.t. serrer; (*car*) mettre un sabot de Denver à. **∼ down on**, sévir contre.

**clan** n. clan m.

**clandestine** a. clandestin.

**clang** n. son métallique m.

**clap** v.t./i. applaudir. ● n. applaudissement m.

**claret** n. bordeaux rouge m.

**clarif|y** v.t./i. (se) clarifier. **∼ication** n. clarification f.

**clarinet** n. clarinette f.

**clarity** n. clarté f.

**clash** n. choc m.; (*fig.*) conflit m. ● v.i. (*metal objects*) s'entrechoquer; (*fig.*) se heurter.

**clasp** n. (*fastener*) fermoir m., agrafe f. ● v.t. serrer.

**class** n. classe f. ● v.t. classer.

**classic** a. & n. classique (m.). pl. **∼al** a. classique.

**classif|y** v.t. classifier. **∼ication** n. classification f. **∼ied** a. (*information etc.*) secret. **∼ied advertisement**, petite annonce f.

**classroom** n. salle de classe f.

**classy** a. (*sl.*) chic invar.

**clatter** n. cliquetis m. ● v.i. cliqueter.

**clause** n. clause f.; (*gram.*) proposition f.

**claustrophob|ia** n. claustrophobie f. **∼ic** a. & n. claustrophobe (m./f.).

**claw** n. (*of animal, small bird*) griffe f.; (*of bird of prey*) serre f.; (*of lobster*) pince f. ● v.t. griffer.

**clay** n. argile f.

**clean** a. propre; (*shape, stroke, etc.*) net. ● adv. complètement. ● v.t. nettoyer. ● v.i. **∼ up**, faire le nettoyage. **∼ one's teeth**, se brosser les dents. **∼er** n. (*at home*) femme de ménage f.; (*industrial*) agent de nettoyage m./f.; (*of clothes*) teintur|ier, -ière m., f.

**cleans|e** v.t. nettoyer; (*fig.*) purifier. **∼ing cream**, crème démaquillante f.

**clear** a. clair; (*glass*) transparent; (*road*) dégagé. ● adv. complètement. ● v.t. (*free*) dégager (**of**, de); (*table*) débarrasser; (*building*) évacuer; (*cheque*) encaisser; (*jump over*) franchir; (*debt*) liquider; (*jurid.*) disculper. ● v.i. (*fog*) se dissiper. **∼ off** or **out**, (*sl.*) décamper. **∼ out**, (*clean*) nettoyer. **∼ up**,

( *tidy* ) ranger; ( *mystery* ) éclaircir; ( *of weather* ) s'éclaircir. **make sth. ~,** être très clair sur qch. **~ly** *adv.* clairement.

**clearance** *n.* ( *permission* ) autorisation *f.*; ( *space* ) dégagement *m.*

**clearing** *n.* clairière *f.*

**clearway** *n.* route à stationnement interdit *f.*

**cleavage** *n.* clivage *m.*; ( *breasts* ) décolleté *m.*

**clef** *n.* ( *mus.* ) clé *f.*

**cleft** *n.* fissure *f.*

**clench** *v.t.* serrer.

**clergy** *n.* clergé *m.* **~man** *n.* ecclésiastique *m.*

**clerk** *n.* employé(e) de bureau *m.* (*f.*).

**clever** *a.* intelligent; ( *skilful* ) habile. **~ly** *adv.* intelligemment; habilement.

**cliché** *n.* cliché *m.*

**click** *n.* déclic *m.* ● *v.i.* faire un déclic; ( *people: sl.* ) s'entendre, se plaire. ● *v.t.* ( *heels, tongue* ) faire claquer.

**client** *n.* client(e) *m.* (*f.*).

**clientele** *n.* clientèle *f.*

**cliff** *n.* falaise *f.*

**climate** *n.* climat *m.*

**climax** *n.* point culminant *m.*

**climb** *v.t.* ( *stairs* ) monter; ( *tree, ladder* ) monter *or* grimper à; ( *mountain* ) faire l'ascension de. ● *v.i.* monter, grimper. ● *n.* montée *f.* **~down,** *n.* recul *m.* **~er** *n.* ( *sport* ) alpiniste *m./f.*

**clinch** *v.t.* ( *a deal* ) conclure.

**cling** *v.i.* ( *p.t.* **clung** ) se cramponner ( **to,** à); ( *stick* ) coller. **~film** *n.* (P.) film adhésif.

**clinic** *n.* centre médical *m.*

**clinical** *a.* clinique.

**clink** *n.* tintement *m.* ● *v.t./i.* (faire) tinter.

**clip¹** *n.* ( *for paper* ) trombone *m.*; ( *for hair* ) barrette *f.*; ( *for tube* ) collier *m.* ● *v.t.* attacher ( **to,** à).

**clip²** *v.t.* ( *cut* ) couper. ● *n.* coupe *f.*; ( *of film* ) extrait *m.*

**clippers** *n. pl.* tondeuse *f.*; ( *for nails* ) coupe-ongles *m.*

**cloak** *n.* (grande) cape *f.*

**cloakroom** *n.* vestiaire *m.*; ( *toilet* ) toilettes *f. pl.*

**clock** *n.* pendule *f.*; ( *large* ) horloge *f.* ● *v.i.* **~ in** *or* **out,** pointer.

**clockwise** *a. & adv.* dans le sens des aiguilles d'une montre.

**clockwork** *n.* mécanisme *m.* ● *a.* mécanique.

**clog** *n.* sabot *m.* ● *v.t./i.* (se) boucher.

**cloister** *n.* cloître *m.*

**close¹** *a.* ( *near* ) proche ( **to,** de); ( *link, collaboration* ) étroit; ( *examination* ) attentif; ( *friend* ) intime; ( *weather* ) lourd. **~ together,** ( *crowded* ) serrés. ● *adv.* close. ● *n.* ( *street* ) impasse *f.* **~ by,** tout près. **~up** *n.* gros plan *m.* **~ly** *adv.* ( *follow* ) de près.

**close²** *v.t.* fermer. ● *v.i.* se fermer; ( *of shop etc.* ) fermer; ( *end* ) (se) terminer. ● *n.* fin *f.*

**closet** *n.* ( *Amer.* ) placard *m.*

**closure** *n.* fermeture *f.*

**clot** *n.* ( *of blood* ) caillot *m.* ● *v.t./i.* (se) coaguler.

**cloth** *n.* tissu *m.*; ( *duster* ) linge *m.*; ( *tablecloth* ) nappe *f.*

**clothes** *n. pl.* vêtements *m. pl.*, habits *m. pl.* **~hanger** *n.* cintre *m.* **~line** *n.* corde à linge *f.*

**clothing** *n.* vêtements *m. pl.*

**cloud** *n.* nuage *m.* **~y** *a.* ( *sky* ) couvert; ( *liquid* ) trouble.

**clout** *n.* ( *blow* ) coup de poing *m.*; ( *power: fam.* ) pouvoir effectif *m.* ● *v.t.* frapper.

**clove** *n.* clou de girofle *m.* **~ of garlic,** gousse d'ail *f.*

**clover** *n.* trèfle *m.*

**clown** *n.* clown *m.* ● *v.i.* faire le clown.

**club** *n.* ( *group* ) club *m.*; ( *weapon* ) massue *f.* **~s,** ( *cards* ) trèfle *m.* ● *v.t./i.* matraquer. **(golf) ~,** club (de golf) *m.* **~ together,** ( *share costs* ) se cotiser.

**cluck** *v.i.* glousser.

**clue** *n.* indice *m.*; ( *in crossword* ) définition *f.*

**clump** *n.* massif *m.*

**clumsy** *a.* maladroit; ( *tool* ) peu commode.

**cluster** *n.* (petit) groupe *m.* ● *v.i.* se grouper.

**clutch** *v.t.* ( *hold* ) serrer fort; ( *grasp* ) saisir. ● *v.i.* **~ at,** ( *try to grasp* ) essayer de saisir. ● *n.* étreinte *f.*; ( *auto.* ) embrayage *m.*

**clutter** *n.* désordre *m.*, fouillis *m.* ● *v.t.* encombrer.

**coach** *n.* autocar *m.*; ( *of train* ) wagon *m.*; ( *horse-drawn* ) carrosse *m.*; ( *sport* ) entraîneur, -se *m.* ● *v.t.* donner des leçons (particulières) à; ( *sport* ) entraîner.

**coagulate** *v.t./i.* (se) coaguler.

**coal** *n.* charbon *m.*

**coalition** *n.* coalition *f.*

**coarse** *a.* grossier.

**coast** *n.* côte *f.* ● *v.i.* ( *car, bicycle* ) descendre en roue libre. **~al** *a.* côtier.

**coastguard** *n.* garde-côte *m.*

**coastline** *n.* littoral *m.*

**coat** *n.* manteau *m.*; ( *of animal* ) pelage *m.*; ( *of paint* ) couche *f.* ● *v.t.* enduire, couvrir; ( *with chocolate* ) enrober ( **with,** de). **~hanger** *n.* cintre *m.* **~ing** *n.* couche *f.*

**coax** *v.t.* amadouer.

**cob** *n.* ( *of corn* ) épi *m.*

**cobble** *n.* pavé *m.* **~stone** *n.* pavé *m.*

**cobweb** *n.* toile d'araignée *f.*

**cocaine** *n.* cocaïne *f.*

**cock** *n.* (oiseau) mâle *m.*; ( *rooster* ) coq *m.* ● *v.t.* ( *gun* ) armer; ( *ears* ) dresser. **~up** *n.* ( *sl.* ) pagaille *f.*

**cockerel** *n.* jeune coq *m.*

**cockle** *n.* ( *culin.* ) coque *f.*

**cockpit** *n.* poste de pilotage *m.*

**cockroach** *n.* cafard *m.*

**cocktail** *n.* cocktail *m.* ∼ **party,** cocktail *m.* fruit ∼, macédoine (de fruits) *f.*

**cocky** *a.* arrogant.

**cocoa** *n.* cacao *m.*

**coconut** *n.* noix de coco *f.*

**cocoon** *n.* cocon *m.*

**COD** *abbr.* (*cash on delivery*) paiement à la livraison *m.*

**cod** *n. invar.* morue *f.*

**code** *n.* code *m.* ● *v.t.* coder.

**coerc|e** *v.t.* contraindre. ∼**ion** *n.* contrainte *f.*

**coexist** *v.i.* coexister. ∼**ence** *n.* coexistence *f.*

**coffee** *n.* café *m.* ∼ **bar,** café *m.*, cafétéria *f.* ∼**pot** *n.* cafetière *f.*

**coffin** *n.* cercueil *m.*

**cog** *n.* dent *f.*; (*fig.*) rouage *m.*

**coherent** *a.* cohérent.

**coil** *v.t./i.* (s')enrouler. ● *n.* rouleau *m.*; (*one ring*) spire *f.*; (*contraceptive*) stérilet *m.*

**coin** *n.* pièce (de monnaie) *f.* ● *v.t.* (*word*) inventer. ∼**box** *n.* téléphone public *m.*

**coincide** *v.i.* coïncider.

**coinciden|ce** *n.* coïncidence *f.* ∼**tal** *a.* dû à une coïncidence.

**coke** *n.* coke *m.*

**colander** *n.* passoire *f.*

**cold** *a.* froid. **be** or **feel** ∼, avoir froid. **it is** ∼, il fait froid. ● *n.* froid *m.*; (*med.*) rhume *m.* ∼**cream,** crème de beauté *f.* ∼ **sore,** bouton de fièvre *m.* ∼**ness** *n.* froideur *f.*

**coleslaw** *n.* salade de chou cru *f.*

**colic** *n.* coliques *f. pl.*

**collaborat|e** *v.i.* collaborer. ∼**or** *n.* collabora|teur, -trice *m.*, *f.*

**collapse** *v.i.* s'effondrer; (*med.*) avoir un malaise. ● *n.* effondrement *m.*

**collapsible** *a.* pliant.

**collar** *n.* col *m.*; (*of dog*) collier *m.* ● *v.t.* (*take: sl.*) piquer. ∼**bone** *n.* clavicule *f.*

**collateral** *n.* nantissement *m.*

**colleague** *n.* collègue *m./f.*

**collect** *v.t.* rassembler; (*pick up*) ramasser; (*call for*) passer prendre; (*money, rent*) encaisser; (*taxes*) percevoir; (*as hobby*) collectionner. ● *adv.* **call** ∼, (*Amer.*) téléphoner en PCV. ∼**ion** *n.* collection *f.*; (*in church*) quête *f.*; (*of mail*) levée *f.* ∼**or** *n.* (*as hobby*) collectionneu|r, -se *m.*, *f.*

**collective** *a.* collectif.

**college** *n.* (*for higher education*) institut *m.*, école *f.*; (*within university*) collège *m.*

**collide** *v.i.* entrer en collision (**with,** avec).

**colliery** *n.* houillère *f.*

**collision** *n.* collision *f.*

**collusion** *n.* collusion *f.*

**colon** *n.* (*gram.*) deux-points *m. invar.*; (*anat.*) côlon *m.*

**colonel** *n.* colonel *m.*

**colonize** *v.t.* coloniser.

**colon|y** *n.* colonie *f.* ∼**ial** *a. & n.* colonial(e) (*m.* (*f.*)).

**colossal** *a.* colossal.

**colour** *n.* couleur *f.* ● *a.* (*photo etc.*) en couleur; (*TV set*) couleur *invar.* ● *v.t.* colorer; (*with crayon*) colorier. ∼**blind** *a.* daltonien. ∼**fast** *a.* grand teint. *invar.* ∼**ful** *a.* coloré; (*person*) haut en couleur. ∼**ing** *n.* (*of skin*) teint *m.*; (*in food*) colorant *m.*

**coloured** *a.* (*person, pencil*) de couleur. ● *n.* personne de couleur *f.*

**colt** *n.* poulain *m.*

**column** *n.* colonne *f.*

**coma** *n.* coma *m.*

**comb** *n.* peigne *m.* ● *v.t.* peigner; (*search*) ratisser.

**combat** *n.* combat *m.* ● *v.t.* combattre.

**combination** *n.* combinaison *f.*

**combine**[1] *v.t./i.* (se) combiner, (s')unir.

**combine**[2] *n.* (*comm.*) trust *m.*, cartel *m.* ∼ **harvester,** moissonneuse-batteuse *f.*

**combustion** *n.* combustion *f.*

**come** *v.i.* venir; (*occur*) arriver; (*sexually*) jouir. ∼ **across,** rencontrer *or* trouver par hasard. ∼ **back,** revenir. ∼ **by,** obtenir. ∼ **down,** descendre; (*price*) baisser. ∼ **from,** être de. ∼ **in,** entrer. ∼ **into,** (*money*) hériter de. ∼ **on,** (*actor*) entrer en scène; (*light*) s'allumer; (*improve*) faire des progrès. ∼ **on!,** allez! ∼ **out,** sortir. ∼ **through,** s'en tirer (indemne de). ∼ **to,** (*amount*) revenir à; (*decision, conclusion*) arriver à. ∼ **up,** monter; (*fig.*) se présenter. ∼ **up with,** (*find*) trouver; (*produce*) produire.

**comedian** *n.* comique *m.*

**comedy** *n.* comédie *f.*

**comet** *n.* comète *f.*

**comfort** *n.* confort *m.*; (*consolation*) réconfort *m.* ● *v.t.* consoler. ∼**able** *a.* (*chair, car, etc.*) confortable; (*person*) à l'aise, bien; (*wealthy*) aisé.

**comfy** *a.* (*fam.*) = **comfortable.**

**comic** *a.* comique. ● *n.* (*person*) comique *m.*; (*periodical*) comic *m.* ∼**strip,** bande dessinée *f.*

**coming** *n.* arrivée *f.* ● *a.* à venir. ∼**s and goings,** allées et venues *f. pl.*

**comma** *n.* virgule *f.*

**command** *n.* (*authority*) commandement *m.*; (*order*) ordre *m.*; (*mastery*) maîtrise *f.* ● *v.t.* commander (**s.o. to,** à qn. de); (*be able to use*) disposer de; (*require*) nécessiter; (*respect*) inspirer. ∼**er** *n.* commandant *m.* ∼**ing** *a.* imposant.

**commandeer** *v.t.* réquisitionner.

**commandment** *n.* commandement *m.*

**commando** n. commando m.

**commemorat|e** v.t. commémorer. ∼**ion** n. commémoration f.

**commence** v.t./i. commencer. ∼**ment** n. commencement m.

**commend** v.t. (praise) louer; (entrust) confier.

**comment** n. commentaire m. ● v.i. faire des commentaires. ∼ **on,** commenter.

**commentary** n. commentaire m.; (radio, TV) reportage m.

**commentat|e** v.i. faire un reportage. ∼**or** n. commenta|teur, -trice m., f.

**commerce** n. commerce m.

**commercial** a. commercial; (traveller) de commerce. ● n. publicité f.

**commiserate** v.i. compatir (with, avec).

**commission** n. commission f.; (order for work) commande f. ● v.t. (order) commander; (mil.) nommer officier. ∼ **to do,** charger de faire. **out of** ∼, hors service. ∼**er** n. préfet (de police) m.; (in E.C.) commissaire m.

**commissionaire** n. commissionnaire m.

**commit** v.t. commettre; (entrust) confier. ∼ **o.s.,** s'engager. ∼ **suicide,** se suicider. ∼**ment** n. engagement m.

**committee** n. comité m.

**commodity** n. produit m.

**common** a. (shared by all) commun; (usual) courant, commun; (vulgar) vulgaire, commun. ● n. terrain communal m. **C**∼ **Market,** Marché Commun m. ∼ **sense,** bon sens m. **in** ∼, en commun.

**commotion** n. agitation f.

**communal** a. (shared) commun; (life) collectif.

**commune** n. (group) communauté f.

**communicat|e** v.t./i. communiquer. ∼**ion** n. communication f.

**communion** n. communion f.

**communiqué** n. communiqué m.

**Communis|t** a. & n. communiste (m./f.) ∼**m** n. communisme m.

**community** n. communauté f.

**commuter** n. banlieusard(e) m. (f.).

**compact**[1] a. compact. ∼ **disc,** (disque) compact m.

**compact**[2] n. (lady's case) poudrier m.

**companion** n. comp|agnon, -agne m., f.

**company** n. (companionship, firm) compagnie f.; (guests) invité(e)s m. (f.) pl.

**comparable** a. comparable.

**compar|e** v.t. comparer (**with, to,** à). ∼**ed with** or **to,** en comparaison de. ● v.i. être comparable. ∼**ative** a. (study, form) comparatif; (comfort etc.) relatif. ∼**atively** adv. relativement.

**comparison** n. comparaison f.

**compartment** n. compartiment m.

**compass** n. (for direction) boussole f.; (scope) portée f. ∼**(es),** (for drawing) compas m.

**compassion** n. compassion f.

**compatib|le** a. compatible. ∼**ility** n. compatibilité f.

**compatriot** n. compatriote m./f.

**compel** v.t. contraindre.

**compensat|e** v.t./i. (financially) dédommager (**for,** de). ∼**e for sth.,** compenser qch. ∼**ion** n. compensation f.; (financial) dédommagement m.

**compete** v.i. concourir. ∼ **with,** rivaliser avec.

**competen|t** a. compétent. ∼**ce** n. compétence f.

**competition** n. (contest) concours m.; (sport) compétition f.; (comm.) concurrence f.

**competitive** a. (prices) concurrentiel, compétitif.

**competitor** n. concurrent(e) m. (f.).

**compile** v.t. (list) dresser; (book) rédiger. ∼**r** n. rédac|teur, -trice m., f.

**complacen|t** a. content de soi. ∼**cy** contentement de soi m.

**complain** v.i. se plaindre (**about, of,** de).

**complaint** n. plainte f.; (in shop etc.) réclamation f.; (illness) maladie f.

**complement** n. complément m. ● v.t. compléter. ∼**ary** a. complémentaire.

**complet|e** a. complet; (finished) achevé; (downright) parfait. ● v.t. achever; (a form) remplir. ∼**ely** adv. complètement. ∼**ion** n. achèvement m.

**complex** a. complexe. ● n. (psych., archit.) complexe m. ∼**ity** n. complexité f.

**complexion** n. (of face) teint m.

**compliance** n. (agreement) conformité f.

**complicat|e** v.t. compliquer. ∼**ed** a. compliqué. ∼**ion** n. complication f.

**complicity** n. complicité f.

**compliment** n. compliment m. ● v.t. complimenter.

**complimentary** a. (offert) à titre gracieux; (praising) flatteur.

**comply** v.i. ∼ **with,** se conformer à, obéir à.

**component** n. (of machine etc.) pièce f.; (chemical substance) composant m.; (element: fig.) composante f. ● a. constituant.

**compose** v.t. composer. ∼ **o.s.,** se calmer. ∼**r** n. (mus.) compositeur m.

**composition** n. composition f.

**compost** n. compost m.

**composure** n. calme m.

**compound** n. (substance, word) composé m.; (enclosure) enclos m. ● a. composé.

**comprehen|d** v.t. comprendre. ∼**sion** n. compréhension f.

**comprehensive** a. étendu, complet; (*insurance*) tous-risques *invar*. ~ **school,** collège d'enseignement secondaire m.

**compress** v.t. comprimer. ~**ion** n. compression f.

**comprise** v.t. comprendre.

**compromise** n. compromis m. ● v.t. compromettre. ● v.i. transiger, trouver un compromis. **not** ~ **on,** ne pas transiger sur.

**compulsion** n. contrainte f.

**compulsive** a. (*psych.*) compulsif; (*liar, smoker*) invétéré.

**compulsory** a. obligatoire.

**computer** n. ordinateur m. ~ **science,** informatique f. ~**ize** v.t. informatiser.

**comrade** n. camarade m./f.

**con**[1] v.t. (*sl.*) rouler, escroquer (**out of,** de). ● n. (*sl.*) escroquerie f. ~ **s.o. into doing,** arnaquer qn. en lui faisant faire. ~ **man,** (*sl.*) escroc m.

**con**[2] *see* pro.

**concave** a. concave.

**conceal** v.t. dissimuler.

**concede** v.t. concéder.

**conceited** a. suffisant.

**conceivable** a. concevable.

**conceive** v.t./i. concevoir. ~ **of,** concevoir.

**concentrat|e** v.t./i. (se) concentrer. ~**ion** n. concentration f.

**concept** n. concept m.

**conception** n. conception f.

**concern** n. (*interest, business*) affaire f.; (*worry*) inquiétude f.; (*firm: comm.*) affaire f. ● v.t. concerner. **be** ~**ed with,** s'occuper de. ~**ing** prep. en ce qui concerne.

**concerned** a. inquiet.

**concert** n. concert m.

**concertina** n. concertina m.

**concerto** n. concerto m.

**concession** n. concession f.

**conciliation** n. conciliation f.

**concise** a. concis. ~**ly** adv. avec concision.

**conclu|de** v.t. conclure. ● v.i. se terminer. ~**sion** n. conclusion f.

**conclusive** a. concluant. ~**ly** adv. de manière concluante.

**concoct** v.t. confectionner; (*invent: fig.*) fabriquer. ~**ion** n. mélange m.

**concourse** n. (*rail.*) hall m.

**concrete** n. béton m. ● a. concret. ● v.t. bétonner. ~**-mixer** n. bétonnière f.

**concur** v.i. être d'accord.

**concussion** n. commotion (cérébrale) f.

**condemn** v.t. condamner. ~**ation** n. condamnation f.

**condens|e** v.t./i. (se) condenser. ~**ation** n. condensation f.; (*mist*) buée f.

**condescend** v.i. condescendre.

**condiment** n. condiment m.

**condition** n. condition f. **on** ~ **that,** à condition que. ~**al** a. conditionnel. ~**er** n. après-shampooing m.

**condom** n. préservatif m.

**condone** v.t. pardonner, fermer les yeux sur.

**conduct**[1] v.t. conduire; (*orchestra*) diriger.

**conduct**[2] n. conduite f.

**conductor** n. chef d'orchestre m.; (*of bus*) receveur m.; (*on train: Amer.*) chef de train m.; (*electr.*) conducteur m.

**cone** n. cône m.; (*of ice-cream*) cornet m.

**confectioner** n. confiserie f.

**confederation** n. confédération f.

**confer** v.t./i. conférer.

**conference** n. conférence f.

**confess** v.t./i. avouer; (*relig.*)(se) confesser. ~**ion** n. confession f.; (*of crime*) aveu m.

**confide** v.t. confier. ● v.i. ~ **in,** se confier à.

**confiden|t** a. sûr. ~**ce** n. (*trust*) confiance f.; (*boldness*) confiance en soi f.; (*secret*) confidence f.

**confidential** a. confidentiel.

**configure** v.t. (*comput.*) configurer.

**confine** v.t. enfermer; (*limit*) limiter. ~**d space,** espace réduit. ~**d to,** limité à.

**confines** n. pl. confins m. pl.

**confirm** v.t. confirmer. ~**ation** n. confirmation f.

**confiscate** v.t. confisquer.

**conflict**[1] n. conflit m.

**conflict**[2] v.i. (*statements, views*) être en contradiction (**with,** avec); (*appointments*) tomber en même temps (**with,** que). ~**ing** a. contradictoire.

**conform** v.t./i. (se) conformer.

**confound** v.t. confondre.

**confront** v.t. affronter. ~ **with,** confronter avec. ~**ation** n. confrontation f.

**confus|e** v.t. embrouiller; (*mistake, confound*) confondre. **become** ~**ed,** s'embrouiller. ~**ing** a. déroutant. ~**ion** n. confusion f.

**congeal** v.t./i. (se) figer.

**congenial** a. sympathique.

**congenital** a. congénital.

**congest|ed** a. encombré; (*med.*) congestionné. ~**ion** n. (*traffic*) encombrement(s) m. (*pl.*); (*med.*) congestion f.

**conglomerate** n. (*comm.*) conglomérat m.

**congratulat|e** v.t. féliciter (**on,** de). ~**ions** n. pl. félicitations f. pl.

**congregation** n. assemblée f.

**congress** n. congrès m. **C**~**,** (*Amer.*) le Congrès.

**conic(al)** a. conique.

**conifer** n. conifère m.

**conjecture** n. conjecture f. ● v.t./i. conjecturer.

**conjugat|e** v.t. conjuguer. ~**ion** n. conjugaison f.

**conjunction** *n.* conjonction *f.* **in ~ with,** conjointement avec.

**conjunctivitis** *n.* conjonctivite *f.*

**conjur|e** *v.t.* **~e up,** faire apparaître. **~or** *n.* prestidigita|teur, -trice *m., f.*

**conk** *v.i.* **~ out,** (*sl.*) tomber en panne.

**connect** *v.t./i.* (se) relier; (*in mind*) faire le rapport entre; (*install, wire up to mains*) brancher. **~ed** *a.* lié.

**connection** *n.* rapport *m.*; (*rail.*) correspondance *f.*; (*phone call*) communication *f.*; (*electr.*) contact *m.*; (*joining piece*) raccord *m.* **~s,** (*comm.*) relations *f. pl.*

**connive** *v.i.* **~e at,** se faire le complice de.

**connoisseur** *n.* connaisseur *m.*

**connotation** *n.* connotation *f.*

**conquer** *v.t.* vaincre; (*country*) conquérir. **~or** *n.* conquérant *m.*

**conquest** *n.* conquête *f.*

**conscience** *n.* conscience *f.*

**conscientious** *a.* consciencieux.

**conscious** *a.* conscient; (*deliberate*) voulu. **~ly** *adv.* consciemment. **~ness** *n.* conscience *f.*; (*med.*) connaissance *f.*

**conscript**[1] *v.t.* recruter par conscription. **~ion** *n.* conscription *f.*

**conscript**[2] *n.* conscrit *m.*

**consecrate** *v.t.* consacrer.

**consecutive** *a.* consécutif. **~ly** *adv.* consécutivement.

**consensus** *n.* consensus *m.*

**consent** *v.i.* consentir (**to,** à). ● *n.* consentement *m.*

**consequence** *n.* conséquence *f.*

**consequent** *a.* résultant. **~ly** *adv.* par conséquent.

**conservation** *n.* préservation *f.* **~ area,** zone classée *f.*

**conservationist** *n.* défenseur de l'environnement *m.*

**conservative** *a.* conservateur; (*estimate*) modeste. **C~** *a. & n.* conserva|teur, -trice (*m. (f.)*).

**conservatory** *n.* (*greenhouse*) serre *f.*; (*room*) véranda *f.*

**conserve** *v.t.* conserver; (*energy*) économiser.

**consider** *v.t.* considérer; (*allow for*) tenir compte de; (*possibility*) envisager (**doing,** de faire). **~ation** *n.* considération *f.*; (*respect*) égard(s) *m.* (*pl.*). **~ing** *prep.* compte tenu de.

**considerabl|e** *a.* considérable; (*much*) beaucoup de. **~y** *adv.* beaucoup, considérablement.

**considerate** *a.* attentionné.

**consist** *v.i.* consister (**of,** en; **in doing,** à faire).

**consistent** *a.* cohérent.

**consol|e** *v.t.* consoler. **~ation** *n.* consolation *f.*

**consolidat|e** *v.t./i.* (se) consolider. **~ion** *n.* consolidation *f.*

**consonant** *n.* consonne *f.*

**conspicuous** *a.* (*easily seen*) en évidence; (*showy*) voyant.

**conspiracy** *n.* conspiration *f.*

**conspire** *v.i.* (*person*) comploter (**to do,** de faire).

**constable** *n.* agent de police *m.*

**constant** *a.* incessant; (*unchanging*) constant. **~ly** *adv.* constamment.

**constellation** *n.* constellation *f.*

**consternation** *n.* consternation *f.*

**constipation** *n.* constipation *f.*

**constitut|e** *v.t.* constituer. **~ion** *n.* constitution *f.*

**constraint** *n.* contrainte *f.*

**constrict** *v.t.* resserrer; (*movement*) gêner. **~ion** *n.* resserrement *m.*

**construct** *v.t.* construire. **~ion** *n.* construction *f.*

**constructive** *a.* constructif.

**consul** *n.* consul *m.* **~ar** *a.* consulaire.

**consulate** *n.* consulat *m.*

**consult** *v.t.* consulter. ● *v.i.* **~ with,** conférer avec. **~ation** *n.* consultation *f.*

**consultant** *n.* conseill|er, -ère *m., f.*; (*med.*) spécialiste *m./f.*

**consume** *v.t.* consommer; (*destroy*) consumer. **~r** *n.* consomma|teur, -trice *m., f.*

**consumption** *n.* consommation *f.*; (*med.*) phtisie *f.*

**contact** *n.* contact *m.*; (*person*) relation *f.* ● *v.t.* contacter. **~ lenses,** lentilles (de contact) *f. pl.*

**contagious** *a.* contagieux.

**contain** *v.t.* contenir. **~ o.s.,** se contenir. **~er** *n.* récipient *m.*; (*for transport*) container *m.*

**contaminat|e** *v.t.* contaminer. **~ion** *n.* contamination *f.*

**contemplat|e** *v.t.* (*gaze at*) contempler; (*think about*) envisager. **~ion** *n.* contemplation *f.*

**contemporary** *a. & n.* contemporain(e) (*m. (f.)*).

**contempt** *n.* mépris *m.* **~ible** *a.* méprisable.

**contend** *v.t.* soutenir. ● *v.i.* **~ with,** (*compete*) rivaliser avec; (*face*) faire face à. **~er** *n.* adversaire *m./f.*

**content**[1] *a.* satisfait. ● *v.t.* contenter. **~ed** *a.* satisfait.

**content**[2] *n.* (*of letter*) contenu *m.*; (*amount*) teneur *f.* **~s,** contenu *m.*

**contention** *n.* dispute *f.*; (*claim*) affirmation *f.*

**contest**[1] *n.* (*competition*) concours *m.*; (*fight*) combat *m.*

**contest**[2] *v.t.* contester; (*compete for or in*) disputer. **~ant** *n.* concurrent(e) *m. (f.)*.

**context** *n.* contexte *m.*

**continent** n. continent m. ~**al** a. continental. ~**al quilt**, couette f.

**continual** a. continuel. ~**ly** adv. continuellement.

**continu|e** v.t./i. continuer; (resume) reprendre. ~**ation** n. continuation f. ~**ed** a. continu.

**continuous** a. continu. ~ **stationery**, papier continu m. ~**ly** adv. sans interruption.

**contort** v.t. tordre. ~ **o.s.**, se contorsionner. ~**ion** n. torsion f.; contorsion f.

**contour** n. contour m.

**contraband** n. contrebande f.

**contraception** n. contraception f.

**contraceptive** a. & n. contraceptif (m.).

**contract**[1] n. contrat m.

**contract**[2] v.t./i. (se) contracter. ~**ion** n. contraction f.

**contractor** n. entrepreneur m.

**contradict** v.t. contredire. ~**ion** n. contradiction f.

**contralto** n. contralto m.

**contraption** n. (fam.) engin m.

**contrary** a. contraire (**to**, à). **on the ~**, au contraire.

**contrast**[1] n. contraste m.

**contrast**[2] v.t./i. contraster. ~**ing** a. contrasté.

**contravene** v.t. enfreindre.

**contribut|e** v.t. donner. ● v.i. ~**e to**, contribuer à; (take part) participer à; (newspaper) collaborer à. ~**ion** n. contribution f. ~**or** n. collabora|teur, -trice m., f.

**contrive** v.t. imaginer. ~ **to do**, trouver moyen de faire. ~**d** a. tortueux.

**control** v.t. (a firm etc.) diriger; (check) contrôler; (restrain) maîtriser. ● n. contrôle m.; (mastery) maîtrise f. ~**s**, commandes f. pl.; (knobs) boutons m. pl. **have under ~**, (event) avoir en main. **in ~ of**, maître de.

**controversial** a. discutable, discuté.

**controversy** n. controverse f.

**convalesce** v.i. être en convalescence. ~**nce** n. convalescence f.

**convector** n. radiateur à convection m.

**convene** v.t. convoquer. ● v.i. se réunir.

**convenience** n. commodité f. ~**s**, toilettes f. pl. ~ **foods**, plats tout préparés m. pl.

**convenient** a. commode, pratique; (time) bien choisi. **be ~ for**, convenir à. ~**ly** adv. (arrive) à propos. ~**ly situated**, bien situé.

**convent** /'kɒnvənt/ n. couvent m.

**convention** n. (assembly, agreement) convention f.; (custom) usage m. ~**al** a. conventionnel.

**converge** v.i. converger.

**conversation** n. conversation f.

**converse**[1] v.i. s'entretenir, converser (**with**, avec).

**converse**[2] a. & n. inverse (m.). ~**ly** adv. inversement.

**conver|t**[1] v.t. convertir; (house) aménager. ● v.i. ~**t into**, se transformer en. ~**sion** n. conversion f. ~**tible** a. convertible. ● n. (car) décapotable f.

**convert**[2] n. converti(e) m. (f.).

**convex** a. convexe.

**convey** v.t. (wishes, order) transmettre; (goods, people) transporter; (idea, feeling) communiquer. ~**or belt**, tapis roulant m.

**convict**[1] v.t. déclarer coupable. ~**ion** n. condamnation f.; (opinion) conviction f.

**convict**[2] n. prisonni|er, ère m., f.

**convinc|e** v.t. convaincre. ~**ing** a. convaincant.

**convoy** n. convoi m.

**convulsion** n. convulsion f.

**coo** v.i. roucouler.

**cook** v.t./i. (faire) cuire; (of person) faire la cuisine. ● n. cuisin|ier, -ière m., f. ~**up**, (fam.) fabriquer. ~**ing** n. cuisine f.; a. de cuisine.

**cooker** n. (stove) cuisinière f.; (apple) pomme à cuire f.

**cookery** n. cuisine f. ~**book**, livre de cuisine m.

**cookie** n. (Amer.) biscuit m.

**cool** a. frais; (calm) calme; (unfriendly) froid. ● n. fraîcheur f.; (calmness: sl.) sang-froid m. ● v.t./i. rafraîchir. **in the ~**, au frais. ~ **box**, glacière f. ~**er** n. (for food) glacière f.; ~**ly** adv. calmement; froidement . ~**ness** n. fraîcheur f.; froideur f.

**coop** n. poulailler m. ● v.t. ~ **up**, enfermer.

**co-operat|e** v.i. coopérer. ~**ion** n. coopération f.

**co-operative** a. coopératif. ● n. coopérative f.

**co-ordinat|e** v.t. coordonner. ~**ion** n. coordination f.

**cop** v.t. (sl.) piquer. ● n. (policeman: sl.) flic m. ~ **out**, (sl.) se dérober. ~**out** n. (sl.) dérobade f.

**cope** v.i. assurer. ~ **with**, s'en sortir avec.

**copious** a. copieux.

**copper**[1] n. cuivre m.; (coin) sou m. ● a. de cuivre.

**copper**[2] n. (sl.) flic m.

**coppice, copse** ns. taillis m.

**copy** n. copie f.; (of book, newspaper) exemplaire m.; (print. photo.) épreuve f. ● v.t./i. copier.

**copyright** n. copyright m.

**coral** n. corail m.

**cord** n. (petite) corde f.; (of curtain, pyjamas, etc.) cordon m.; (electr.) cordon électrique m.; (fabric) velours côtelé m.

**cordial** a. cordial. ● n. (fruit-flavoured drink) sirop m.

**cordon** n. cordon m. ● v.t. ~ **off,** mettre un cordon autour de.

**corduroy** n. velours côtelé m.

**core** n. (of apple) trognon m.; (of problem) cœur m.; (techn.) noyau m. ● v.t. vider.

**cork** n. liège m.; (for bottle) bouchon m. ● v.t. boucher.

**corkscrew** n. tire-bouchon m.

**corn**¹ n. blé m.; (maize: Amer.) maïs m.; (seed) grain m. ~**cob** n. épi de maïs m.

**corn**² n. (hard skin) cor m.

**cornea** n. cornée f.

**corned** a. ~ **beef,** corned-beef m.

**corner** n. coin m.; (bend in road) virage m.; (football) corner m. ● v.t. coincer, acculer; (market) accaparer. ● v.i. prendre un virage.

**cornet** n. cornet m.

**cornflakes** n. pl. corn flakes m. pl.

**cornflour** n. farine de maïs f.

**Corn|wall** n. Cornouailles f. ~**ish** a. de Cornouailles.

**corny** a. (trite: fam.) rebattu; (mawkish: fam.) à l'eau de rose.

**corollary** n. corollaire m.

**coronary** n. infarctus m.

**coronation** n. couronnement m.

**coroner** n. coroner m.

**corporal**¹ n. caporal m.

**corporal**² a. ~ **punishment,** châtiment corporel m.

**corporate** a. en commun; (body) constitué.

**corporation** n. (comm.) société f.; (of town) municipalité f.

**corps** n. corps m.

**corpse** n. cadavre m.

**corpuscle** n. globule m.

**correct** a. (right) exact, juste, correct; (proper) correct. **you are** ~, vous avez raison. ● v.t. corriger. ~**ion** n. correction f.

**correlat|e** v.t./i. (faire) correspondre. ~**ion** n. corrélation f.

**correspond** v.i. correspondre. ~**ence** n. correspondance f. ~**ent** n. correspondant(e) m. (f.).

**corridor** n. couloir m.

**corroborate** v.t. corroborer.

**corro|de** v.t./i. (se) corroder. ~**sion** n. corrosion f.

**corrugated** a. ondulé. ~ **iron,** tôle ondulée f.

**corrupt** a. corrompu. ● v.t. corrompre. ~**ion** n. corruption f.

**corset** n. (boned) corset m.; (elasticated) gaine f.

**Corsica** n. Corse f.

**cortisone** n. cortisone f.

**cosh** n. matraque f. ● v.t. matraquer.

**cosmetic** n. produit de beauté m.

**cosmic** a. cosmique.

**cosmonaut** n. cosmonaute m./f.

**cosmopolitan** a. & n. cosmopolite (m./f.).

**cosmos** n. cosmos m.

**cosset** v.t. dorloter.

**cost** v.t. (be price of) coûter; (ask price of) établir le prix de. ● n. coût m. ~**s,** (jurid.) dépens m. pl. **at all** ~**s,** à tout prix. ~ **effective** a. rentable. ~**effectiveness** n. rentabilité f. ~ **of living,** coût de la vie.

**co-star** n. partenaire m./f.

**costly** a. coûteux; (valuable) précieux.

**costume** n. costume m.; (for swimming) maillot m. ~ **jewellery,** bijoux de fantaisie m. pl.

**cosy** a. confortable, intime. ● n. couvre-théière m.

**cot** n. lit d'enfant m.; (camp-bed: Amer.) lit de camp m.

**cottage** n. petite maison de campagne f.; (thatched) chaumière f. ~ **cheese,** fromage blanc (maigre) m.

**cotton** n. coton m.; (for sewing) fil (à coudre) m. ● v.i. ~ **on,** (sl.) piger. ~ **wool,** coton hydrophile m.

**couch** n. divan m.

**couchette** n. couchette f.

**cough** v.i. tousser. ● n. toux f. ~ **up,** (sl.) cracher, payer.

**council** n. conseil m. ~ **house,** (approx.) H.L.M. m./f.

**councillor** n. conseill|er, -ère municipal(e) m., f.

**counsel** n. conseil m. ● n. invar. (jurid.) avocat(e) m. (f.). ~**lor** n. conseill|er, -ère m., f.

**count**¹ v.t./i. compter. ● n. compte m. ~ **on,** compter sur.

**count**² n. (nobleman) comte m.

**countdown** n. compte à rebours m.

**countenance** n. mine f. ● v.t. admettre, approuver.

**counter**¹ n. comptoir m.; (in bank etc.) guichet m.; (token) jeton m.

**counter**² adv. ~ **to,** à l'encontre de. ● a. opposé. ● v.t. opposer; (blow) parer. ● v.i. riposter.

**counter-** pref. contre-.

**counteract** v.t. neutraliser.

**counter-attack** n. contre-attaque f. ● v.t./i. contre-attaquer.

**counterbalance** n. contrepoids m. ● v.t. contre-balancer.

**counter-clockwise** a. & adv. (Amer.) dans le sens inverse des aiguilles d'une montre.

**counterfeit** a. & n. faux (m.). ● v.t. contrefaire.

**counterfoil** n. souche f.

**countermand** v.t. annuler.

**counterpart** n. équivalent m.; (person) homologue m./f.

**counter-productive** a. (*measure*) qui produit l'effet contraire.

**counter-tenor** n. haute-contre m.

**countess** n. comtesse f.

**countless** a. innombrable.

**country** n. (*land, region*) pays m.; (*homeland*) patrie f.; (*countryside*) campagne f.

**countryman** n. campagnard m.; (*fellow citizen*) compatriote m.

**countryside** n. campagne f.

**county** n. comté m.

**coup** n. (*achievement*) joli coup m.; (*pol.*) coup d'état m.

**couple** n. (*people, animals*) couple m. **a ~ (of),** (*two or three*) deux ou trois.

**coupon** n. coupon m.; (*for shopping*) bon or coupon de réduction m.

**courage** n. courage m. **~ous** a. courageux.

**courgette** n. courgette f.

**courier** n. messager, -ère m., f.; (*for tourists*) guide m.

**course** n. cours m.; (*for training*) stage m.; (*series*) série f.; (*culin.*) plat m.; (*for golf*) terrain m.; (*at sea*) itinéraire m. **change ~,** changer de cap. **~ (of action),** façon de faire f. **of ~,** bien sûr.

**court** n. cour f.; (*tennis*) court m. ● v.t. faire la cour à; (*danger*) rechercher. **~-house** n. (*Amer.*) palais de justice m. **~-shoe,** escarpin m. **go to ~,** aller devant les tribunaux.

**courteous** a. courtois.

**courtesy** n. courtoisie f. **by ~ of,** avec la permission de.

**courtroom** n. salle de tribunal f.

**courtyard** n. cour f.

**cousin** n. cousin(e) m. (f.).

**cove** n. anse f., crique f.

**covenant** n. convention f.

**cover** v.t. couvrir. ● n. (*for bed, book, etc.*) couverture f.; (*lid*) couvercle m.; (*for furniture*) housse f.; (*shelter*) abri m. **~ charge,** couvert m. **~ up,** cacher; (*crime*) couvrir. **~-up** n. tentative pour cacher la vérité f. **~ing letter,** lettre f. (*jointe à un document*).

**coverage** n. reportage m.

**covert** a. (*activity*) secret; (*threat*) voilé (*look*) dérobé.

**covet** v.t. convoiter.

**cow** n. vache f.

**coward** n. lâche m./f. **~ly** a. lâche.

**cowardice** n. lâcheté f.

**cowboy** n. cow-boy m.

**cower** v.i. se recroqueviller (sous l'effet de la peur).

**cox** n. barreur m. ● v.t. barrer.

**coy** a. (faussement) timide.

**crab** n. crabe m. **~-apple** n. pomme sauvage f.

**crack** n. fente f.; (*in glass*) fêlure f.; (*noise*) craquement m.; (*joke: sl.*) plaisanterie f. ● a. (*fam.*) d'élite, ● v.t./i. (*break partially*) (se) fêler; (*split*) (se) fendre; (*nut*) casser; (*joke*) raconter; (*problem*) résoudre. **~ down on,** (*fam.*) sévir contre. **~ up,** (*fam.*) craquer. **get ~ing,** (*fam.*) s'y mettre.

**cracker** n. pétard m.; (*culin.*) biscuit (salé) m.

**crackers** a. (*sl.*) cinglé.

**crackle** v.i. crépiter. ● n. crépitement m.

**cradle** n. berceau m. ● v.t. bercer.

**craft**[1] n. métier artisanal m.; (*technique*) art m.; (*cunning*) ruse f.

**craft**[2] n. invar. (*boat*) bateau m.

**craftsman** n. artisan m. **~ship** n. art m.

**crafty** a. rusé.

**crag** n. rocher à pic m. **~gy** a. à pic; (*face*) rude.

**cram** v.t./i. **~ into,** (*pack*) (s')entasser dans. **~ with,** (*fill*) bourrer de.

**cramp** n. crampe f.

**cramped** a. à l'étroit.

**cranberry** n. canneberge f.

**crane** n. grue f. ● v.t. (*neck*) tendre.

**crank**[1] n. (*techn.*) manivelle f.

**crank**[2] n. excentrique m./f. **~y** a. excentrique; (*Amer.*) grincheux.

**cranny** n. fissure f.

**crash** n. accident m.; (*noise*) fracas m.; (*of thunder*) coup m.; (*of firm*) faillite f. ● v.t./i. avoir un accident (avec); (*of plane*) s'écraser; (*two vehicles*) se percuter. ● a. (*course*) intensif. **~-helmet** n. casque (anti-choc) m. **~ into,** rentrer dans.

**crass** a. grossier.

**crate** n. cageot m.

**crater** n. cratère m.

**cravat** n. foulard m.

**crav|e** v.t./i. **~e (for),** désirer ardemment. **~ing** n. envie irrésistible f.

**crawl** v.i. ramper; (*vehicle*) se traîner. ● n. (*pace*) pas m.; (*swimming*) crawl m. **be ~ing with,** grouiller de.

**crayfish** n. invar. écrevisse f.

**crayon** n. crayon m.

**craze** n. engouement m.

**crazy** a. fou. **~ about,** (*person*) fou de.

**creak** n. grincement m. ● v.i. grincer. **~y** a. grinçant.

**cream** n. crème f. ● a. crème invar. ● v.t. écrémer. **~ cheese,** fromage frais m. **~y** a. crémeux.

**crease** n. pli m. ● v.t./i. (se) froisser.

**creat|e** v.t. créer. **~ion** n. création f. **~ive** a. créateur. **~or** n. créa|teur, -trice m., f.

**creature** n. créature f.

**crèche** n. garderie f.

**credence** n. **give ~ to,** ajouter foi à.

**credentials** n. pl. (*identity*) pièces d'identité f. pl.; (*competence*) références f. pl.

**credib|le** a. (*excuse etc.*) croyable. **~ility** n. crédibilité f.

**credit** n. crédit m.; (*honour*) honneur m. **in ~,** créditeur. **~s,** (*cinema*) générique m. ● a. (*balance*) créditeur. ● v.t. croire; (*comm.*) créditer. **~ card,** carte de crédit f. **~ note,** avoir m. **~ s.o. with,** attribuer à qn. **~worthy** a. solvable. **~or** n. créanc|ier, -ière m., f.

**creditable** a. honorable.

**credulous** a. crédule.

**creed** n. credo m.

**creek** n. crique f.; (*Amer.*) ruisseau m.

**creep** v.i. ramper; (*fig.*) se glisser. ● n. (*person*: sl.) pauvre type m. **~er** n. liane f. **~y** a. qui fait frissonner.

**Creole** n. créole m./f.

**crêpe** n. crêpe m. **~ paper,** papier crêpon m.

**crescendo** n. crescendo m.

**crescent** n. croissant m.; (*fig.*) rue en demi-lune f.

**cress** n. cresson m.

**crest** n. crête f.; (*coat of arms*) armoiries f. pl.

**Crete** n. Crète f.

**cretin** n. crétin(e) m. (f.).

**crevasse** n. crevasse f.

**crevice** n. fente f.

**crew** n. équipage m.; (*gang*) équipe f. **~ cut,** coupe en brosse f. **~ neck,** (col) ras du cou m.

**crib**[1] n. lit d'enfant m.

**crib**[2] v.t./i. copier. ● n. (*schol., fam.*) traduction f., aide-mémoire m. invar.

**crick** n. (*in neck*) torticolis m.

**cricket**[1] n. (*sport*) cricket m. **~er** n. joueur de cricket m.

**cricket**[2] n. (*insect*) grillon m.

**crime** n. crime m.; (*minor*) délit m.; (*acts*) criminalité f.

**criminal** a. & n. criminel(le) (m. (f.)).

**crimp** v.t. (*hair*) friser.

**crimson** a. & n. cramoisi (m.).

**cring|e** v.i. reculer; (*fig.*) s'humilier. **~ing** a. servile.

**crinkle** v.t./i. (se) froisser. ● n. pli m.

**cripple** n. infirme m./f. ● v.t. estropier; (*fig.*) paralyser.

**crisis** n. crise f.

**crisp** a. (*culin.*) croquant; (*air, reply*) vif. **~s** n. pl. chips m. pl.

**criss-cross** a. entrecroisé. ● v.t./i. (s')entrecroiser.

**criterion** n. critère m.

**critic** n. critique m. **~al** a. critique. **~ally** adv. d'une manière critique; (*ill*) gravement.

**criticism** n. critique f.

**criticize** v.t./i. critiquer.

**croak** n. (*bird*) croassement; (*frog*) coassement m. ● v.i. croasser; coasser.

**crochet** n. crochet m. ● v.t. faire au crochet.

**crockery** n. vaisselle f.

**crocodile** n. crocodile m.

**crocus** n. crocus m.

**crook** n. (*criminal*: fam.) escroc m.; (*stick*) houlette f.

**crooked** a. tordu; (*winding*) tortueux; (*askew*) de travers; (*dishonest*: fig.) malhonnête.

**croon** v.t./i. chantonner.

**crop** n. récolte f.; (*fig.*) quantité f. ● v.i. **~ up,** se présenter.

**croquet** n. croquet m.

**croquette** n. croquette f.

**cross** n. croix f.; (*hybrid*) hybride m. ● v.t./i. traverser; (*legs, animals*) croiser; (*cheque*) barrer; (*paths*) se croiser. ● a. en colère, fâché (**with,** contre). **~-check** v.t. vérifier (pour confirmer). **~-country (running),** cross m. **~ off** or **out,** rayer. **~ s.o.'s mind,** venir à l'esprit de qn.

**crossbar** n. barre transversale f.

**cross-examine** v.t. faire subir un examen contradictoire à.

**cross-eyed** a. be **~,** loucher.

**crossfire** n. feux croisés m. pl.

**crossing** n. (*by boat*) traversée f.; (*on road*) passage clouté m.

**cross-reference** n. renvoi m.

**crossroads** n. carrefour m.

**cross-section** n. coupe transversale f.; (*sample*: fig.) échantillon m.

**crosswise** adv. en travers.

**crossword** n. mots croisés m. pl.

**crotch** n. (*of garment*) entre-jambes m. invar.

**crotchet** n. (*mus.*) noire f.

**crouch** v.i. s'accroupir.

**crow** n. corbeau m. ● v.i. (*of cock*) chanter; (*fig.*) jubiler. **~'s feet,** pattes d'oie f. pl.

**crowbar** n. pied-de-biche m.

**crowd** n. foule f. ● v.i. affluer. ● v.t. remplir. **~ into,** (s')entasser dans. **~ed** a. plein.

**crown** n. couronne f.; (*top part*) sommet m. ● v.t. couronner.

**crucial** a. crucial.

**crude** a. (*raw*) brut; (*rough, vulgar*) grossier.

**cruel** a. cruel. **~ty** n. cruauté f.

**cruet** n. huilier m.

**cruis|e** n. croisière f. ● v.i. (*ship*) croiser; (*tourists*) faire une croisière; (*vehicle*) rouler. **~er** n. croiseur m. **~ing speed,** vitesse de croisière f.

**crumb** n. miette f.

**crumble** v.t./i. (s')effriter; (*bread*) (s')émietter; (*collapse*) s'écrouler.

**crummy** a. (sl.) minable.

**crumpet** n. (*culin.*) petite crêpe (grillée) f.

**crumple** v.t./i. (se) froisser.

**crunch** v.t. croquer. ● n. (*event*) moment critique m.

**crusade** n. croisade f.

**crush** v.t. écraser; (clothes) froisser. ● n. (crowd) presse f. **a ~ on,** (sl.) le béguin pour.

**crust** n. croûte f. **~y** a. croustillant.

**crutch** n. béquille f.; (crotch) entre-jambes m. invar.

**cry** n. cri m. ● v.i. (weep) pleurer; (call out) crier. **~ off,** abandonner.

**crypt** n. crypte f.

**cryptic** a. énigmatique.

**crystal** n. cristal m. **~-clear** a. parfaitement clair. **~lize** v.t./i. (se) cristalliser.

**cub** n. petit m. **Cub (Scout),** louveteau m.

**Cuba** n. Cuba m. **~n** a. & n. cubain(e) (m. (f.)).

**cubby-hole** n. cagibi m.

**cub|e** n. cube m. **~ic** a. cubique; (metre etc.) cube.

**cubicle** n. (in room, hospital, etc.) box m.; (at swimming-pool) cabine f.

**cuckoo** n. coucou m.

**cucumber** n. concombre m.

**cuddl|e** v.t. câliner. ● v.i. (kiss and) **~e,** s'embrasser. ● n. caresse f. **~y** a. câlin.

**cue**[1] n. signal m.; (theatre) réplique f.

**cue**[2] n. (billiards) queue f.

**cuff** n. manchette f.; (Amer.) revers m. ● v.t. gifler. **~-link** n. bouton de manchette m.

**cul-de-sac** n. impasse f.

**culinary** a. culinaire.

**cull** v.t. (select) choisir; (kill) abattre sélectivement.

**culminat|e** v.i. **~e in,** se terminer par. **~ion** n. point culminant m.

**culprit** n. coupable m./f.

**cult** n. culte m.

**cultivat|e** v.t. cultiver. **~ion** n. culture f.

**cultural** a. culturel.

**culture** n. culture f.

**cunning** a. rusé. ● n. ruse f.

**cup** n. tasse f.; (prize) coupe f.

**cupboard** n. placard m.

**curator** n. (of museum) conservateur m.

**curb**[1] n. (restraint) frein m. ● v.t. (desires etc.) refréner; (price increase etc.) freiner.

**curb**[2] n. bord du trottoir m.

**curdle** v.t./i. (se) cailler.

**cure**[1] v.t. guérir; (fig.) éliminer. ● n. (recovery) guérison f.; (remedy) remède m.

**cure**[2] v.t. (culin.) fumer; (in brine) saler.

**curio** n. bibelot m.

**cur|ious** a. curieux. **~osity** n. curiosité f.

**curl** v.t./i. (hair) boucler. ● n. boucle f. **~ up,** se pelotonner; (shrivel) se racornir.

**curler** n. bigoudi m.

**curly** a. bouclé.

**currant** n. raisin de Corinthe m.; (berry) groseille f.

**currency** n. (money) monnaie f.; (acceptance) cours m. **foreign ~,** devises étrangères f. pl.

**current** a. (common) courant; (topical) actuel; (year etc.) en cours. ● n. courant m. **~ account,** compte courant m.

**curry** n. curry m., cari m.

**curse** n. malédiction f.; (oath) juron m. ● v.t. maudire. ● v.i. (swear) jurer.

**cursor** n. curseur m.

**curt** a. brusque.

**curtain** n. rideau m.

**curve** n. courbe f. ● v.t./i. (se) courber; (of road) tourner.

**cushion** n. coussin m. ● v.t. (a blow) amortir; (fig.) protéger.

**custard** n. crème anglaise f.; (set) crème renversée f.

**custody** n. garde f.; (jurid.) détention préventive f.

**custom** n. coutume f.; (patronage: comm.) clientèle f. **~-built,** **~-made** adjs. fait etc. sur commande. **~ary** a. d'usage.

**customer** n. client(e) m. (f.); (fam.) **an odd/a difficult ~,** un individu curieux/difficile.

**customize** v.t. personnaliser.

**customs** n. pl. douane f. **~ officer,** douanier m.

**cut** v.t./i. couper; (hedge, jewel) tailler; (prices etc.) réduire. ● n. coupure f.; (of clothes) coupe f.; (piece) morceau m.; réduction f. **~ back** or **down (on),** réduire. **~back** n. réduction f. **~ off,** couper; (fig.) isoler. **~ out,** découper; (leave out) supprimer. **~-price** a. à prix réduit.

**cute** a. (fam.) astucieux; (Amer.) mignon.

**cuticle** n. petites peaux f. pl. (de l'ongle).

**cutlery** n. couverts m. pl.

**cutlet** n. côtelette f.

**cutting** a. cinglant. ● n. (from newspaper) coupure f.; (plant) bouture f. **~ edge,** tranchant m.

**cycl|e** n. cycle m.; (bicycle) vélo m. ● v.i. aller à vélo. **~ing** n. cyclisme m. **~ist** n. cycliste m./f.

**cyclic(al)** a. cyclique.

**cyclone** n. cyclone m.

**cylinder** n. cylindre m.

**cymbal** n. cymbale f.

**cynic** n. cynique m./f. **~al** a. cynique. **~ism** n. cynisme m.

**cypress** n. cyprès m.

**Cypr|us** n. Chypre f. **~iot** a. & n. cypriote (m./f.).

**cyst** n. kyste m. **~ic fibrosis,** mucoviscidose f.

**cystitis** n. cystite f.

**Czech** a. & n. tchèque (m./f.).

# Dd

**dab** v.t. tamponner. ● n. **a ~ of,** un petit coup de; **~sth. on,** appliquer qch. à petits coups sur.

**dabble** v.i. **~ in,** se mêler un peu de.

**dad** n. (fam.) papa m. **~dy** n. (children's use) papa m.

**daffodil** n. jonquille f.

**daft** a. idiot.

**dagger** n. poignard m.

**dahlia** n. dahlia m.

**daily** a. quotidien. ● adv. tous les jours.

**dainty** a. délicat.

**dairy** n. (on farm) laiterie f.; (shop) crémerie f. ● a. laitier.

**daisy** n. pâquerette f. **~ wheel,** marguerite f.

**dale** n. vallée f.

**dam** n. barrage m. ● v.t. endiguer.

**damagｌe** n. dégâts m. pl., dommages m. pl.; (harm: fig.) préjudice m. **~es,** (jurid.) dommages et intérêts m. pl. ● v.t. abîmer; (fig.) nuire à.

**damn** v.t. (relig.) damner; (condemn: fig.) condamner. ● int. zut, merde. ● n. **not care a ~,** s'en foutre. ● a. sacré. ● adv. rudement.

**damp** n. humidité f. ● a. humide.

**dance** v.t./i. danser. ● n. danse f.; (gathering) bal m. **~r** n. danseu‖r, -se m., f.

**dandelion** n. pissenlit m.

**dandruff** n. pellicules f. pl.

**dandy** n. dandy m.

**Dane** n. Danois(e) m. (f.).

**danger** n. danger m.; (risk) risque m. **be in ~ of,** risquer de. **~ous** a. dangereux.

**dangle** v.t./i. (se) balancer, (laisser) pendre. **~ sth. in front of s.o.,** (fig.) faire miroiter qch. à qn.

**Danish** a. danois. ● n. (lang.) danois m.

**dare** v.t. **~ (to) do,** oser faire. **~ s.o. to do,** défier qn. de faire. ● n. défi m.

**daring** a. audacieux.

**dark** a. obscur, sombre, noir; (colour) foncé, sombre; (skin) brun, foncé; (gloomy) sombre. ● n. noir m.; (nightfall) tombée de la nuit f. **~ness** n. obscurité f.

**darken** v.t./i. (s')assombrir.

**darling** a. & n. chéri(e) (m. (f.)).

**darn** v.t. repriser.

**dart** n. fléchette f. **~s,** (game) fléchettes f. pl. ● v.i. s'élancer.

**dartboard** n. cible f.

**dash** v.i. (hurry) se dépêcher; (forward etc.) se précipiter. ● v.t. jeter (avec violence); (hopes) briser. ● n. ruée f.; (stroke) tiret m. **~ off,** (leave) partir en vitesse.

**dashboard** n. tableau de bord m.

**data** n. pl. données f. pl. **~ processing,** traitement des données m.

**database** n. base de données f.

**date**[1] n. date f.; (meeting: fam.) rendez-vous m. ● v.t./i. dater; (go out with: fam.) sortir avec. **out of ~,** (old-fashioned) démodé; (passport) périmé. **up to ~,** (modern) moderne; (list) à jour. **~d** a. démodé.

**date**[2] n. (fruit) datte f.

**daub** v.t. barbouiller.

**daughter** n. fille f. **~-in-law** n. belle-fille f.

**dawdle** v.i. lambiner.

**dawn** n. aube f. ● v.i. poindre; (fig.) naître. **it ~ed on me,** je m'en suis rendu compte.

**day** n. jour m.; (whole day) journée f.; (period) époque f. **~dream** n. rêverie f.; v.i. rêvasser. **the ~ before,** la veille. **the next ~,** le lendemain.

**daylight** n. jour m.

**daytime** n. jour m., journée f.

**daze** v.t. étourdir; (with drugs) hébéter. ● n. **in a ~,** étourdi; hébété.

**dazzle** v.t. éblouir.

**deacon** n. diacre m.

**dead** a. mort; (numb) engourdi. ● adv. complètement. ● n. **the ~,** les morts. **~ end,** impasse f. **~-end job,** travail sans avenir m. **stop ~,** s'arrêter net. **the race was a ~-heat,** ils ont été classés ex aequo.

**deaden** v.t. (sound, blow) amortir; (pain) calmer.

**deadline** n. date limite f.

**deadlock** n. impasse f.

**deadly** a. mortel; (weapon) meurtrier.

**deaf** a. sourd. **the ~ and dumb,** les sourds-muets. **~-aid** n. appareil acoustique m. **~ness** n. surdité f.

**deafen** v.t. assourdir.

**deal** v.t. donner; (a blow) porter. ● v.i. (trade) commercer. ● n. affaire f.; (cards) donne f. **a good ~,** beaucoup (of, de). **~ in,** faire le commerce de. **~ with,** (handle, manage) s'occuper de; (be about) traiter de. **~er** n. marchand(e) m. (f.); (agent) concessionnaire m./f.

**dealings** n. pl. relations f. pl.

**dean** n. doyen m.

**dear** a. cher. ● adv. cher. ● int. **oh ~!,** oh mon Dieu!

**death** n. mort f.

**debar** v.t. exclure.

**debase** v.t. avilir.

**debatｌe** n. discussion f., débat m. ● v.t. discuter. **~e whether,** se demander si. **~able** a. discutable.

**debilitate** v.t. débiliter.

**debility** n. débilité f.

**debit** n. débit m. **in ~,** débiteur. ● a. (balance) débiteur. ● v.t. débiter.

**debris** n. débris m. pl.

**debt** n. dette f. **in ~,** endetté. **~or** n. débi|teur,-trice m., f.

**debunk** v.t. (fam.) démythifier.

**decade** n. décennie f.

**decaden|t** a. décadent. **~ce** n. décadence f.

**decaffeinated** a. décaféiné.

**decanter** n. carafe f.

**decay** v.i. se gâter, pourrir; (fig.) décliner. ● n. pourriture f.; (of tooth) carie f.; (fig.) déclin m.

**deceased** a. décédé. ● n. défunt(e) m. (f.).

**deceit** n. tromperie f. **~ful** a. trompeur.

**deceive** v.t. tromper.

**December** n. décembre m.

**decen|t** a. décent, convenable; (good: fam.) (assez) bon; (kind: fam.) gentil. **~cy** n. décence f.

**decentralize** v.t. décentraliser.

**decept|ive** a. trompeur. **~ion** n. tromperie f.

**decide** v.t./i. décider; (question) régler. **~ on,** se décider pour. **~ to do,** décider de faire.

**deciduous** a. à feuillage caduc.

**decimal** a. décimal. ● n. décimale f. **~ point,** virgule f.

**decimate** v.t. décimer.

**decipher** v.t. déchiffrer.

**decision** n. décision f.

**decisive** a. (conclusive) décisif; (firm) décidé.

**deck** n. pont m.; (of cards: Amer.) jeu m. **~-chair** n. chaise longue f. **top ~,** (of bus) impériale f.

**declar|e** v.t. déclarer. **~ation** n. déclaration f.

**decline** v.t./i. refuser (poliment); (deteriorate) décliner; (fall) baisser. ● n. déclin m.; baisse f.

**decode** v.t. décoder.

**decompos|e** v.t./i. (se) décomposer. **~ition** n. décomposition f.

**décor** n. décor m.

**decorat|e** v.t. décorer; (room) peindre or tapisser. **~ion** n. décoration f. **~ive** a. décoratif.

**decorator** n. peintre en bâtiment m.

**decorum** n. décorum m.

**decoy**¹ n. (bird) appeau m.; (trap) piège m., leurre m.

**decoy**² v.t. attirer, appâter.

**decrease** v.t./i. diminuer. ● n. diminution f.

**decree** n. (pol., relig.) décret m.; (jurid.) jugement m. ● v.t. décréter.

**decrepit** a. (building) délabré; (person) décrépit.

**decry** v.t. dénigrer.

**dedicat|e** v.t. dédier. **~e o.s. to,** se consacrer à. **~ed** a. dévoué. **~ion** n. dévouement m.; (in book) dédicace f.

**deduce** v.t. déduire.

**deduct** v.t. déduire; (from wages) retenir. **~ion** n. déduction f.; retenue f.

**deed** n. acte m.

**deep** a. profond. ● adv. profondément. **~freeze** n. congélateur m.; v.t. congeler. **~fry,** frire. **~ly** adv. profondément.

**deepen** v.t. approfondir. ● v.i. devenir plus profond; (mystery, night) s'épaissir.

**deer** n. invar. cerf m.; (doe) biche f.

**deface** v.t. dégrader.

**defamation** n. diffamation f.

**default** v.i. (jurid.) faire défaut. ● n. **by ~,** (jurid.) par défaut. **win by ~,** gagner par forfait. ● a. (comput.) par défaut.

**defeat** v.t. vaincre; (thwart) faire échouer. ● n. défaite f.; (of plan etc.) échec m.

**defect**¹ n. défaut m. **~ive** a. défectueux.

**defect**² v.i. faire défection. **~ to,** passer à. **~or** n. transfuge m./f.

**defence** n. défense f.

**defend** v.t. défendre. **~ant** n. (jurid.) accusé(e) m. (f.).

**defensive** a. défensif.

**defer** v.t. remettre.

**deference** n. déférence f.

**defian|ce** n. défi m. **in ~ce of,** au mépris de. **~t** a. de défi.

**deficien|t** a. insuffisant. **be ~t in,** manquer de. **~cy** n. insuffisance f.; (fault) défaut m.

**deficit** n. déficit m.

**define** v.t. définir.

**definite** a. précis; (obvious) net; (firm) catégorique; (certain) certain. **~ly** adv. certainement; (clearly) nettement.

**definition** n. définition f.

**definitive** a. définitif.

**deflat|e** v.t. dégonfler. **~ion** n. dégonflement m.; (comm.) déflation f.

**deflect** v.t./i. (faire) dévier.

**deforestation** n. déforestation.

**deform** v.t. déformer. **~ed** a. difforme. **~ity** n. difformité f.

**defraud** v.t. (state, customs) frauder. **~ s.o. of sth.,** escroquer qch. à qn.

**defray** v.t. payer.

**defrost** v.t. dégivrer.

**deft** a. adroit.

**defuse** v.t. désamorcer.

**defy** v.t. défier; (attempts) résister à.

**degenerate**¹ v.i. dégénérer (into, en).

**degenerate**² a. & n. dégénéré(e) (m. (f.)).

**degrad|e** v.t. dégrader. **~ation** n. dégradation f.; (state) déchéance f.

**degree** *n.* degré *m.*; (*univ.*) diplôme universitaire *m.*; (*Bachelor's degree*) licence *f.*

**dehydrate** *v.t./i.* (se) déshydrater.

**de-ice** *v.t.* dégivrer.

**deign** *v.t.* ~ **to do,** daigner faire.

**deject|ed** *a.* abattu. ~**ion** *n.* abattement *m.*

**delay** *v.t.* retarder. ● *v.i.* tarder. ● *n.* (*lateness, time overdue*) retard *m.*; (*waiting*) délai *m.* ~ **doing,** attendre pour faire.

**delegate**[1] *n.* délégué(e) *m.* (*f.*).

**delegat|e**[2] *v.t.* déléguer. ~**ion** *n.* délégation *f.*

**delet|e** *v.t.* effacer; (*with line*) barrer. ~**ion** *n.* suppression *f.*

**deliberate**[1] *a.* délibéré. ~**ly** *adv.* exprès, délibérément.

**deliberat|e**[2] *v.i.* délibérer. ● *v.t.* considérer. ~**ion** *n.* délibération *f.*

**delica|te** *a.* délicat. ~**cy** *n.* délicatesse *f.*; (*food*) mets délicat *or* raffiné *m.*

**delicatessen** *n.* épicerie fine *f.*

**delicious** *a.* délicieux.

**delight** *n.* grand plaisir *m.*, joie *f.*; (*thing*) délice *m.* (*f. in pl.*). ● *v.t.* réjouir. ~**ed** *a.* ravi. ~**ful** *a.* charmant.

**delinquen|t** *a.* & *n.* délinquant(e) (*m.* (*f.*)) ~**cy** *n.* délinquance *f.*

**delirious** *a.* be ~**ous,** délirer.

**deliver** *v.t.* (*message*) remettre; (*goods*) livrer; (*letters*) distribuer; (*free*) délivrer; (*utter*) prononcer; (*med.*) accoucher; (*a blow*) porter. ~**y** *n.* livraison *f.*; distribution *f.*; accouchement *m.*

**delta** *n.* delta *m.*

**delu|de** *v.t.* tromper. ~**de o.s.,** se faire des illusions. ~**sion** *n.* illusion *f.*

**deluge** *n.* déluge *m.* ● *v.t.* inonder (**with,** de).

**de luxe** *a.* de luxe.

**demand** *v.t.* exiger; (*in negotiations*) réclamer. ● *n.* exigence *f.*; (*claim*) revendication *f.*; (*comm.*) demande *f.* ~**ing** *a.* exigeant.

**demarcation** *n.* démarcation *f.*

**demean** *v.t.* ~ **o.s.,** s'abaisser, s'avilir.

**demeanour** *n.* comportement *m.*

**demerara** *n.* (*brown sugar*) cassonade *f.*

**demobilize** *v.t.* démobiliser.

**democracy** *n.* démocratie *f.*

**democrat** *n.* démocrate *m./f.* ~**ic** *a.* démocratique.

**demoli|sh** *v.t.* démolir. ~**tion** *n.* démolition *f.*

**demon** *n.* démon *m.*

**demonstrat|e** *v.t.* démontrer. ● *v.i.* (*pol.*) manifester. ~**ion** *n.* démonstration *f.*; (*pol.*) manifestation *f.* ~**or** *n.* manifestant(e) *m.* (*f.*).

**demonstrative** *a.* démonstratif.

**demoralize** *v.t.* démoraliser.

**demote** *v.t.* rétrograder.

**demure** *a.* modeste.

**den** *n.* antre *m.*

**denial** *n.* dénégation *f.*; (*statement*) démenti *m.*

**denigrate** *v.t.* dénigrer.

**denim** *n.* toile de coton *f.* ~**s,** (*jeans*) blue-jeans *m. pl.*

**Denmark** *n.* Danemark *m.*

**denomination** *n.* (*relig.*) confession *f.*; (*money*) valeur *f.*

**denote** *v.t.* dénoter.

**denounce** *v.t.* dénoncer.

**dens|e** *a.* dense; (*person*) obtus. ~**ity** *n.* densité *f.*

**dent** *n.* bosse *f.* ● *v.t.* cabosser.

**dental** *a.* dentaire. ~ **floss,** fil dentaire *m.* ~ **surgeon,** dentiste *m./f.*

**dentist** *n.* dentiste *m./f.*

**dentures** *n. pl.* dentier *m.*

**denude** *v.t.* dénuder.

**denunciation** *n.* dénonciation *f.*

**deny** *v.t.* nier (**that,** que); (*rumour*) démentir; (*disown*) renier; (*refuse*) refuser.

**deodorant** *n.* & *a.* déodorant (*m.*).

**depart** *v.i.* partir. ~ **from,** (*deviate*) s'écarter de.

**department** *n.* département *m.*; (*in shop*) rayon *m.*; (*in office*) service *m.* ~ **store,** grand magasin *m.*

**departure** *n.* départ *m.*

**depend** *v.i.* dépendre (**on,** de). ~ **on,** (*rely on*) compter sur. ~**ing on the weather,** selon le temps qu'il fera. ~**able** *a.* sûr. ~**ence** *n.* dépendance *f.* ~**ent** *a.* dépendant.

**dependant** *n.* personne à charge *f.*

**depict** *v.t.* (*describe*) dépeindre; (*in picture*) représenter.

**deplor|e** *v.t.* déplorer. ~**able** *a.* déplorable.

**deploy** *v.t.* déployer.

**deport** *v.t.* expulser.

**deposit** *v.t.* déposer. ● *n.* dépôt *m.*; (*of payment*) acompte *m.*; (*to reserve*) arrhes *f. pl.*; (*against damage*) caution *f.*; (*on bottle etc.*) consigne *f.*; (*of mineral*) gisement *m.* ~ **account,** compte dépôt *m.* ~**or** *n.* (*comm.*) déposant(e) *m.* (*f.*), épargnant(e) *m.* (*f.*).

**depot** *n.* dépôt *m.*; (*Amer.*) gare (routière) *f.*

**depreciat|e** *v.t./i.* (se) déprécier. ~**ion** *n.* dépréciation *f.*

**depress** *v.t.* (*sadden*) déprimer; (*push down*) appuyer sur. **become** ~**ed,** déprimer. ~**ing** *a.* déprimant. ~**ion** *n.* dépression *f.*

**deprivation** *n.* privation *f.*

**deprive** *v.t.* ~ **of,** priver de. ~**d** *a.* (*child etc.*) déshérité.

**depth** *n.* profondeur *f.*

**deputation** *n.* députation *f.*

**deputize** *v.i.* assurer l'intérim (**for,** de).

**deputy** *n.* suppléant(e) *m.* (*f.*) ● *a.* adjoint.

**derail** v.t. faire dérailler. **be ~ed,** dérailler. **~ment** n. déraillement m.

**deranged** a. (mind) dérangé.

**derelict** a. abandonné.

**deri|de** v.t. railler. **~sion** n. dérision f.

**derisory** a. (scoffing) railleur; (offer etc.) dérisoire.

**derogatory** a. (word) péjoratif; (remark) désobligeant.

**derv** n. gas-oil m., gazole m.

**descend** v.t./i. descendre. **be ~ed from,** descendre de. **~ant** n. descendant(e) m. (f.).

**descent** n. descente f.; (lineage) origine f.

**descri|be** v.t. décrire. **~ption** n. description f. **~ptive** a. descriptif.

**desert**[1] n. désert m. **~ island,** île déserte f.

**desert**[2] v.t./i. déserter. **~ed** a. désert. **~er** n. déserteur m. **~ion** n. désertion f.

**deserve** v.t. mériter (**to,** de).

**design** n. (sketch) dessin m., plan m.; (construction) conception f.; (pattern) motif m.; (style of dress) modèle m.; (aim) dessein m. ● v.t. (sketch) dessiner; (devise, intend) concevoir. **~er** n. dessina|teur, -trice m., f.; (of fashion) styliste m./f.

**designat|e** v.t. désigner. **~ion** n. désignation f.

**desire** n. désir m. ● v.t. désirer. **~able** a. désirable.

**desk** n. bureau m.; (of pupil) pupitre m.; (in hotel) réception f.; (in bank) caisse f.

**desolat|e** a. (place) désolé; (bleak: fig.) morne. **~ion** n. désolation f.

**despair** n. désespoir m. ● v.i. désespérer (**of,** de).

**despatch** v.t. = dispatch.

**desperate** a. désespéré; (criminal) prêt à tout. **be ~ for,** avoir une envie folle de. **~ly** adv. désespérément; (worried) terriblement; (ill) gravement.

**desperation** n. désespoir m.

**despicable** a. méprisable.

**despise** v.t. mépriser.

**despite** prep. malgré.

**despondent** a. découragé.

**despot** n. despote m.

**dessert** n. dessert m. **~spoon** n. cuiller à dessert f.

**destination** n. destination f.

**destine** v.t. destiner.

**destiny** n. destin m.

**destitute** a. indigent.

**destr|oy** v.t. détruire; (animal) abattre. **~uction** n. destruction f. **~uctive** a. destructeur.

**destroyer** n. (warship) contre-torpilleur m.

**detach** v.t. détacher. **~able** a. détachable. **~ed** a. détaché. **~ed house,** maison individuelle f.

**detachment** n. détachement m.

**detail** n. détail m. ● v.t. exposer en détail; (troops) détacher. **go into ~,** entrer dans le détail. **~ed** a. détaillé.

**detain** v.t. retenir; (in prison) détenir. **~ee** n. détenu(e) m. (f.).

**detect** v.t. découvrir; (perceive) distinguer; (tumour) dépister; (mine) détecter. **~ion** n. découverte f.; dépistage m.; détection f. **~or** n. détecteur m.

**detective** n. policier m.; (private) détective m.

**detention** n. détention f.; (schol.) retenue f.

**deter** v.t. dissuader (**from,** de).

**detergent** a. & n. détergent (m.).

**deteriorat|e** v.i. se détériorer. **~ion** n. détérioration f.

**determin|e** v.t. déterminer. **~e to do,** décider de faire. **~ation** n. détermination f. **~ed** a. déterminé. **~ed to do,** décidé à faire.

**deterrent** n. force de dissuasion f.

**detest** v.t. détester.

**detonat|e** v.t./i. (faire) détoner. **~ion** n. détonation f.

**detour** n. détour m.

**detract** v.i. **~ from,** diminuer.

**detriment** n. détriment m. **~al** a. préjudiciable (**to,** à).

**devalu|e** v.t. dévaluer. **~ation** n. dévaluation f.

**devastat|e** v.t. dévaster; (overwhelm: fig.) accabler. **~ing** a. accablant.

**develop** v.t./i. (se) développer; (contract) contracter; (build on, transform) exploiter, aménager; (change) évoluer; (appear) se manifester. **~ into,** devenir. **~ing country,** pays en voie de développement m. **~ment** n. développement m. (**housing**) **~,** lotissement m.

**deviant** a. anormal. ● n. (psych.) déviant m.

**deviat|e** v.i. dévier. **~e from,** (norm) s'écarter de. **~ion** n. déviation f.

**device** n. appareil m.; (scheme) procédé m.

**devil** n. diable m.

**devious** a. tortueux. **he is ~,** il a l'esprit tortueux.

**devise** v.t. inventer; (plan, means) combiner, imaginer.

**devoid** a. **~ of,** dénué de.

**devolution** n. décentralisation f.; (of authority, power) délégation f. (**to,** à).

**devot|e** v.t. consacrer. **~ed** a. dévoué. **~ion** n. dévouement m.; (relig.) dévotion f.

**devotee** n. **~ of,** passionné(e) m. (f.).

**devour** v.t. dévorer.

**devout** a. fervent.

**dew** n. rosée f.

**dexterity** n. dextérité f.

**diabet|es** n. diabète m. **~ic** a. & n. diabétique (m./f.).

**diabolical** a. diabolique; (bad: fam.) atroce.

**diagnose** v.t. diagnostiquer.

**diagnosis** n. diagnostic m.

**diagonal** a. diagonal. ● n. diagonale f. ~ly adv. en diagonale.

**diagram** n. schéma m.

**dial** n. cadran m. ● v.t. (number) faire; (person) appeler. ~ling code, indicatif m. ~ling tone, tonalité f.

**dialect** n. dialecte m.

**dialogue** n. dialogue m.

**diameter** n. diamètre m.

**diamond** n. diamant m.; (shape) losange m.; (baseball) terrain m. ~s, (cards) carreau m.

**diaper** n. (Amer.) couche f.

**diaphragm** n. diaphragme m.

**diarrhoea** n. diarrhée f.

**diary** n. (for appointments etc.) agenda m.; (appointments) emploi du temps m. (for private thoughts) journal intime m.

**dice** n. invar. dé m. ● v.t. (food) couper en dés.

**dicey** a. (fam.) risqué.

**dictate** v.t./i. dicter. ~ion n. dictée f.

**dictator** n. dictateur m.

**dictatorial** a. dictatorial.

**diction** n. diction f.

**dictionary** n. dictionnaire m.

**diddle** v.t. (sl.) escroquer.

**die**[1] v.i. mourir. ~ out, disparaître. **be dying to do/for,** mourir d'envie de faire/de.

**die**[2] n. (metal mould) matrice f.

**diesel** n. diesel m.

**diet** n. (habitual food) alimentation f.; (restricted) régime m. ● v.i. suivre un régime.

**diet|etic** a. diététique. ~ician n. diététicien(ne) m. (f.).

**differ** v.i. différer (from, de); (disagree) ne pas être d'accord.

**differen|t** a. différent. ~ce n. différence f.; (disagreement) différend m.

**differentiate** v.t. différencier. ● v.i. faire la différence (between, entre).

**difficult** a. difficile. ~y n. difficulté f.

**diffiden|t** a. qui manque d'assurance. ~ce n. manque d'assurance m.

**diffuse**[1] a. diffus.

**diffus|e**[2] v.t. diffuser. ~ion n. diffusion f.

**dig** v.t./i. creuser; (thrust) enfoncer. ● n. (poke) coup de coude m.; (remark) coup de patte m.; (archaeol.) fouilles f. pl. ~s, (lodgings: fam.) chambre meublée f. ~ up, déterrer.

**digest**[1] v.t./i. digérer. ~ion n. digestion f.

**digest**[2] n. sommaire m.

**digestive** a. digestif.

**digger** n. (techn.) pelleteuse f.

**digit** n. chiffre m.

**digital** a. numérique.

**dignif|y** v.t. donner de la dignité à. ~ied a. digne.

**dignity** n. dignité f.

**digress** v.i. faire une digression. ~ from, s'écarter de. ~ion n. digression f.

**dike** n. digue f.

**dilapidated** a. délabré.

**dilat|e** v.t./i. (se) dilater. ~ion n. dilatation f.

**dilemma** n. dilemme m.

**dilettante** n. dilettante m./f.

**diligen|t** a. assidu. ~ce n. assiduité f.

**dilute** v.t. diluer.

**dim** a. (weak) faible; (dark) sombre; (indistinct) vague; (fam.) stupide. ● v.t./i. (light) (s')atténuer. ~mer n. ~ (switch), variateur d'intensité m.

**dime** n. pièce de dix cents f.

**dimension** n. dimension f.

**diminish** v.t./i. diminuer.

**diminutive** a. minuscule. ● n. diminutif m.

**dimple** n. fossette f.

**din** n. vacarme m.

**dine** v.i. dîner. ~r n. dîneu|r, -se m., f.; (rail.) wagon-restaurant m.; (Amer.) restaurant à service rapide m.

**dinghy** n. canot m.; (inflatable) canot pneumatique m.

**ding|y** a. minable.

**dining-room** n. salle à manger f.

**dinner** n. (evening meal) dîner m.; (lunch) déjeuner m. ~-jacket n. smoking m.

**dinosaur** n. dinosaure m.

**dint** n. **by ~ of,** à force de.

**diocese** n. diocèse m.

**dip** v.t./i. plonger. ● n. (slope) déclivité f.; (in sea) bain rapide m. ~ one's headlights, se mettre en code.

**diphtheria** n. diphtérie f.

**diphthong** n. diphtongue f.

**diploma** n. diplôme m.

**diplomacy** n. diplomatie f.

**diplomat** n. diplomate m./f. ~ic a. (pol.) diplomatique; (tactful) diplomate.

**dire** a. affreux; (need, poverty) extrême.

**direct** a. direct. ● adv. directement. ● v.t. diriger; (letter, remark) adresser; (a play) mettre en scène. ~ness n. franchise f.

**direction** n. direction f.; (theatre) mise en scène f. ~s, indications f. pl. **ask ~s,** demander le chemin. ~s for use, mode d'emploi m.

**directly** adv. directement; (at once) tout de suite. ● conj. dès que.

**director** n. direc|teur, -trice m., f.; (theatre) metteur en scène m.

**directory** n. (phone book) annuaire m.

**dirt** n. saleté f.; (earth) terre f.

**dirty** a. sale; (word) grossier. **get ~,** se salir.

**disability** n. handicap m.

**disabled** *a.* handicapé.

**disadvantage** *n.* désavantage *m.* ~d *a.* déshérité.

**disagree** *v.i.* ne pas être d'accord (**with,** avec). ~ **with s.o.,** (*food, climate*) ne pas convenir à qn. ~**ment** *n.* désaccord *m.*; (*quarrel*) différend *m.*

**disagreeable** *a.* désagréable.

**disappear** *v.i.* disparaître. ~**ance** *n.* disparition *f.*

**disappoint** *v.t.* décevoir. ~**ing** *a.* décevant. ~**ed** *a.* déçu. ~**ment** *n.* déception *f.*

**disapprov|e** *v.i.* ~**e (of),** désapprouver. ~**al** *n.* désapprobation *f.*

**disarm** *v.t./i.* désarmer. ~**ament** *n.* désarmement *m.*

**disarray** *n.* désordre *m.*

**disast|er** *n.* désastre *m.* ~**rous** *a.* désastreux.

**disband** *v.t./i.* (se) disperser.

**disbelief** *n.* incrédulité *f.*

**disc** *n.* disque *m.*; (*comput.*) = **disk.** ~ **brake,** frein à disque *m.* ~ **jockey,** disc-jockey *m.*

**discard** *v.t.* se débarrasser de; (*beliefs etc.*) abandonner.

**discern** *v.t.* discerner. ~**ible** *a.* perceptible. ~**ing** *a.* perspicace.

**discharge**[1] *v.t.* (*unload*) décharger; (*liquid*) déverser; (*duty*) remplir; (*dismiss*) renvoyer; (*prisoner*) libérer. ● *v.i.* (*of pus*) s'écouler.

**discharge**[2] *n.* (*med.*) écoulement *m.*; (*dismissal*) renvoi *m.*; (*electr.*) décharge *m.*

**disciple** *n.* disciple *m.*

**disciplin|e** *n.* discipline *f.* ● *v.t.* discipliner; (*punish*) punir. ~**ary** *a.* disciplinaire.

**disclaim** *v.t.* désavouer. ~**er** *n.* correctif *m.*

**disclos|e** *v.t.* révéler. ~**ure** *n.* révélation *f.*

**disco** *n.* disco *m.*

**discomfort** *n.* gêne *f.*

**disconcert** *v.t.* déconcerter.

**disconnect** *v.t.* détacher; (*unplug*) débrancher; (*cut off*) couper.

**discontent** *n.* mécontentement *m.* ~**ed** *a.* mécontent.

**discord** *n.* discorde *f.*; (*mus.*) dissonance *f.* ~**ant** *a.* discordant.

**discothèque** *n.* discothèque *f.*

**discount**[1] *n.* rabais *m.*

**discount**[2] *v.t.* ne pas tenir compte de.

**discourage** *v.t.* décourager.

**discourse** *n.* discours *m.*

**discover** *v.t.* découvrir. ~**y** *n.* découverte *f.*

**discredit** *v.t.* discréditer. ● *n.* discrédit *m.*

**discreet** *a.* discret. ~**ly** *adv.* discrètement.

**discrepancy** *n.* incohérence *f.*

**discretion** *n.* discrétion *f.*

**discriminat|e** *v.t./i.* distinguer. ~**e against,** faire de la discrimination contre. ~**ing** *a.* (*person*) qui a du discernement. ~**ion** *n.* discernement *m.*; (*bias*) discrimination *f.*

**discus** *n.* disque *m.*

**discuss** *v.t.* (*talk about*) discuter de; (*argue about, examine critically*) discuter. ~**ion** *n.* discussion *f.*

**disdain** *n.* dédain *m.*

**disease** *n.* maladie *f.* ~**d** *a.* malade.

**disembark** *v.t./i.* débarquer.

**disengage** *v.t.* dégager; (*mil.*) retirer. ● *v.i.* (*mil.*) retirer; (*auto.*) débrayer. ~**ment** *n.* dégagement *m.*

**disentangle** *v.t.* démêler.

**disfavour** *n.* défaveur *f.*

**disfigure** *v.t.* défigurer.

**disgrace** *n.* (*shame*) honte *f.*; (*disfavour*) disgrâce *f.* ● *v.t.* déshonorer. ~**ful** *a.* honteux.

**disgruntled** *a.* mécontent.

**disguise** *v.t.* déguiser. ● *n.* déguisement *m.* **in ~,** déguisé.

**disgust** *n.* dégoût *m.* ● *v.t.* dégoûter. ~**ing** *a.* dégoûtant.

**dish** *n.* plat *m.* ● *v.t.* ~ **out,** (*fam.*) distribuer. **the ~es,** (*crockery*) la vaisselle.

**dishcloth** *n.* lavette *f.*; (*for drying*) torchon *m.*

**dishonest** *a.* malhonnête. ~**y** *n.* malhonnêteté *f.*

**dishonour** *n.* déshonneur *m.* ● *v.t.* déshonorer. ~**able** *a.* déshonorant.

**dishwasher** *n.* lave-vaisselle *m. invar.*

**disillusion** *v.t.* désillusionner. ~**ment** *n.* désillusion *f.*

**disincentive** *n.* **be a ~ to,** décourager.

**disinclined** *a.* ~ **to,** peu disposé à.

**disinfect** *v.t.* désinfecter. ~**ant** *n.* désinfectant *m.*

**disinherit** *v.t.* déshériter.

**disintegrate** *v.t./i.* (se) désintégrer.

**disinterested** *a.* désintéressé.

**disjointed** *a.* (*talk*) décousu.

**disk** *n.* (*Amer.*) = **disc;** (*comput.*) disque *m.* ~ **drive,** drive *m.*, lecteur de disquettes *m.*

**diskette** *n.* disquette *f.*

**dislike** *n.* aversion *f.* ● *v.t.* ne pas aimer.

**dislocate** *v.t.* (*limb*) disloquer.

**dislodge** *v.t.* (*move*) déplacer; (*drive out*) déloger.

**disloyal** *a.* déloyal. ~**ty** *n.* déloyauté *f.*

**dismal** *a.* morne, triste.

**dismantle** *v.t.* démonter, défaire.

**dismay** *n.* consternation *f.* ● *v.t.* consterner.

**dismiss** *v.t.* renvoyer; (*appeal*) rejeter; (*from mind*) écarter. ~**al** *n.* renvoi *m.*

**dismount** *v.i.* descendre.

**disobedien|t** *a.* désobéissant. ~**ce** *n.* désobéissance *f.*

**disobey** *v.t.* désobéir à ● *v.i.* désobéir.

**disorder** *n.* désordre *m.*; (*ailment*) trouble(s) *m.* (*pl.*). ~**ly** *a.* désordonné.

**disorganize** *v.t.* désorganiser.

**disorientate** *v.t.* désorienter.

**disparaging** *a.* désobligeant.

**disparity** *n.* disparité *f.*, écart *m.*

**dispatch** *v.t.* (*send, complete*) expédier; (*troops*) envoyer. ● *n.* expédition *f.*; envoi *m.*; (*report*) dépêche *f.*

**dispel** *v.t.* dissiper.

**dispense** *v.t.* distribuer; (*medicine*) préparer. ● *v.i.* ~ **with**, se passer de. ~**r** *n.* (*container*) distributeur *m.*

**dispers|e** *v.t./i.* (se) disperser. ~**al** *n.* dispersion *f.*

**dispirited** *a.* abattu.

**displace** *v.t.* déplacer.

**display** *v.t.* montrer, exposer; (*feelings*) manifester. ● *n.* exposition *f.*; manifestation *f.*; (*comm.*) étalage *m.*; (*of computer*) visuel *m.*

**disposable** *a.* à jeter.

**dispos|e** *v.t.* disposer. ● *v.i.* ~**e of**, se débarrasser de. ~**al** *n.* (*of waste*) évacuation *f.* **at s.o.'s** ~**al**, à la disposition de qn.

**disposition** *n.* disposition *f.*; (*character*) naturel *m.*

**disprove** *v.t.* réfuter.

**dispute** *v.t.* contester. ● *n.* discussion *f.*; (*pol.*) conflit *m.* **in** ~, contesté.

**disqualif|y** *v.t.* rendre inapte; (*sport*) disqualifier. ~**y from driving,** retirer le permis à. ~**ication** *n.* disqualification *f.*

**disregard** *v.t.* ne pas tenir compte de. ● *n.* indifférence *f.* (**for**, à).

**disrepair** *n.* mauvais état *m.*

**disreputable** *a.* peu recommandable.

**disrespect** *n.* manque de respect *m.* ~**ful** *a.* irrespectueux.

**disrupt** *v.t.* (*disturb, break up*) perturber; (*plans*) déranger. ~**ion** *n.* perturbation *f.* ~**ive** *a.* perturbateur.

**dissatisf|ied** *a.* mécontent. ~**action** *n.* mécontentement *m.*

**dissect** *v.t.* disséquer.

**disseminate** *v.t.* disséminer.

**dissent** *v.i.* différer (**from**, de). ● *n.* dissentiment *m.*

**dissertation** *n.* (*univ.*) mémoire *m.*

**disservice** *n.* mauvais service *m.*

**dissident** *a. & n.* dissident(e) (*m.* (*f.*)).

**dissimilar** *a.* dissemblable, différent.

**dissipate** *v.t./i.* (se) dissiper; (*efforts*) gaspiller.

**dissociate** *v.t.* dissocier. ~ **o.s. from,** se désolidariser de.

**dissolute** *a.* dissolu.

**dissolve** *v.t./i.* (se) dissoudre.

**dissuade** *v.t.* dissuader.

**distance** *n.* distance *f.* **from a** ~, de loin. **in the** ~, au loin.

**distant** *a.* éloigné, lointain; (*relative*) éloigné; (*aloof*) distant.

**distaste** *n.* dégoût *m.* ~**ful** *a.* désagréable.

**distemper** *n.* (*paint*) badigeon *m.*; (*animal disease*) maladie *f.* ● *v.t.* badigeonner.

**distend** *v.t./i.* (se) distendre.

**distil** *v.t.* distiller. ~**lation** *n.* distillation *f.*

**distillery** *n.* distillerie *f.*

**distinct** *a.* distinct; (*marked*) net. **as** ~ **from,** par opposition à. ~**ion** *n.* distinction *f.* ~**ive** *a.* distinctif. ~**ly** *adv.* (*see*) distinctement; (*forbid*) expressément; (*markedly*) nettement.

**distinguish** *v.t./i.* distinguer. ~**ed** *a.* distingué.

**distort** *v.t.* déformer. ~**ion** *n.* distorsion *f.*; (*of facts*) déformation *f.*

**distract** *v.t.* distraire. ~**ed** *a.* (*distraught*) éperdu. ~**ing** *a.* gênant. ~**ion** *n.* distraction *f.*

**distraught** *a.* éperdu.

**distress** *n.* douleur *f.*; (*poverty, danger*) détresse *f.* ● *v.t.* peiner. ~**ing** *a.* pénible.

**distribut|e** *v.t.* distribuer. ~**ion** *n.* distribution *f.* ~**or** *n.* distributeur *m.*

**district** *n.* région *f.*; (*of town*) quartier *m.*

**distrust** *n.* méfiance *f.* ● *v.t.* se méfier de.

**disturb** *v.t.* déranger; (*alarm, worry*) troubler. ~**ance** *n.* dérangement *m.* (**of,** de); (*noise*) tapage *m.* ~**ed** *a.* troublé; (*psychologically*) perturbé. ~**ing** *a.* troublant.

**disused** *a.* désaffecté.

**ditch** *n.* fossé *m.* ● *v.t.* (*sl.*) abandonner.

**dither** *v.i.* hésiter.

**ditto** *adv.* idem.

**divan** *n.* divan *m.*

**div|e** *v.i.* plonger; (*rush*) se précipiter. ● *n.* plongeon *m.*; (*of plane*) piqué *m.*; (*place: sl.*) bouge *m.* ~**er** *n.* plongeu|r, -se *m.*, *f.* ~**ing-board** *n.* plongeoir *m.*

**diverge** *v.i.* diverger.

**diverse** *a.* divers.

**diversify** *v.t.* diversifier.

**diversity** *n.* diversité *f.*

**diver|t** *v.t.* détourner; (*traffic*) dévier. ~**sion** *n.* (*of traffic*) déviation *f.*

**divide** *v.t./i.* (se) diviser.

**dividend** *n.* dividende *m.*

**division** *n.* division *f.*

**divorce** *n.* divorce *m.* (**from,** d'avec). ● *v.t./i.* divorcer (d'avec). ~**d** *a.* divorcé.

**divorcee** *n.* divorcé(e) *n.* (*f.*).

**DIY** *abbr. see* **do-it-yourself.**

**dizz|y** *a.* (**-ier, -iest**) vertigineux. **be** *or* **feel** ~**y,** avoir le vertige. ~**iness** *n.* vertige *m.*

**do** *v.t./i.* faire; (*progress, be suitable*) aller; (*be enough*) suffire; (*swindle: sl.*) avoir. **do well/badly,** se débrouiller bien/mal. **do the house,** peindre *ou* nettoyer *etc.* la maison. **well done!** bravo! **well done,** (*culin.*) bien cuit. ● *v. aux.* **do you see?** voyez-vous? **do you live here?** ● I do, est-ce que vous habitez ici? ● oui. **I do live here,** si, j'habite ici. **I do**

**not smoke,** je ne fume pas. **don't you?, doesn't he?,** *etc.,* n'est-ce pas? ● *n.* (*pl.* **dos** *or* **do's**) soirée *f.*, fête *f.* **do-it-yourself** *n.* bricolage *m.* **do up,** (*fasten*) fermer; (*house*) refaire. **it's to ~ with the house,** c'est à propos de la maison. **it's nothing to do with me,** can'a rien à voir avec moi. **I could do with a holiday,** j'aurais bien besoin de vacances. **~ without,** se passer de.

**docile** *a.* docile.

**dock¹** *n.* dock *m.* ● *v.t./i.* (se) mettre à quai. **~er** *n.* docker *m.*

**dock²** *n.* (*jurid.*) banc des accusés *m.*

**dock³** *v.t.* (*money*) retrancher.

**doctor** *n.* médecin *m.*, docteur *m.*; (*univ.*) docteur *m.*

**doctrine** *n.* doctrine *f.*

**document** *n.* document *m.* **~ary** *a.* & *n.* documentaire (*m.*). **~ation** *n.* documentation *f.*

**dodge** *v.t.* esquiver. ● *v.i.* faire un saut de côté ● *n.* (*fam.*) truc *m.*

**dodgems** *n. pl.* autos tamponneuses *f. pl.*

**dodgy** *a.* (*fam.: difficult*) épineux, délicat; (*dangerous*) douteux.

**doe** *n.* (*deer*) biche *f.*

**dog** *n.* chien *m.* ● *v.t.* poursuivre.

**dogged** *a.* obstiné.

**doings** *n. pl.* (*fam.*) activités *f. pl.*, occupations *f. pl.*

**dole** *v.t.* **~ out,** distribuer. ● *n.* (*fam.*) indemnité de chômage *f.* **on the ~,** (*fam.*) au chômage.

**doll** *n.* poupée *f.* ● *v.t.* **~ up,** (*fam.*) bichonner.

**dollar** *n.* dollar *m.*

**dollop** *n.* (*of food etc.: fam.*) gros morceau *m.*

**dolphin** *n.* dauphin *m.*

**domain** *n.* domaine *m.*

**dome** *n.* dôme *m.*

**domestic** *a.* familial; (*trade, flights, etc.*) intérieur; (*animal*) domestique.

**dominant** *a.* dominant.

**dominat|e** *v.t./i.* dominer. **~ion** *n.* domination *f.*

**domineering** *a.* autoritaire.

**domino** *n. pl.* dominos *m. pl.*

**donat|e** *v.t.* faire don de. **~ion** *n.* don *m.*

**donkey** *n.* âne *m.*

**donor** *n.* dona|teur, -trice *m.*, *f.*; (*of blood*) donneu|r, -se *m.*, *f.*

**doodle** *v.i.* griffonner.

**doom** *n.* (*ruin*) ruine *f.*; (*fate*) destin *m.* ● *v.t.* **be ~ed to,** être destiné *or* condamné à. **~ed (to failure),** voué à l'échec.

**door** *n.* porte *f.*; (*of vehicle*) portière *f.*, porte *f.*

**doorbell** *n.* sonnette *f.*

**doorman** *n.* portier *m.*

**doormat** *n.* paillasson *m.*

**doorstep** *n.* seuil *m.*

**doorway** *n.* porte *f.*

**dope** *n.* (*fam.*) drogue *f.*; (*idiot: sl.*) imbécile *m./f.* ● *v.t.* doper. **~y** *a.* (*foolish: sl.*) imbécile.

**dormant** *a.* en sommeil.

**dormitory** *n.* dortoir *m.*; (*univ., Amer.*) résidence *f.*

**dormouse** *n.* loir *m.*

**dos|e** *n.* dose *f.* **~age** *n.* dose *f.*; (*on label*) posologie *f.*

**doss** *v.i.* (*sl.*) roupiller. **~-house** *n.* asile de nuit *m.*

**dossier** *n.* dossier *m.*

**dot** *n.* point *m.* **on the ~,** (*fam.*) à l'heure pile. **~-matrix** *a.* (*printer*) matriciel.

**dotted** *a.* (*fabric*) à pois. **~ line,** ligne en pointillés *f.* **~ with,** parsemé de.

**double** *a.* double; (*room, bed*) pour deux personnes. ● *adv.* deux fois. ● *n.* double *m.*; (*stuntman*) doublure *f.* **~s,** (*tennis*) double *m.* ● *v.t./i.* doubler; (*fold*) plier en deux. **~ the size,** deux fois plus grand: **pay ~,** payer le double. **~-bass** *n.* (*mus.*) contrebasse *f.* **~-breasted** *a.* croisé. **~-check** *v.t.* revérifier. **~-cross** *v.t.* tromper. **~-dealing** *n.* double jeu *m.* **~-decker** *n.* autobus à impériale *m.*

**doubly** *adv.* doublement.

**doubt** *n.* doute *m.* ● *v.t.* douter de. **~ if** *or* **that,** douter que. **~ful** *a.* incertain, douteux; (*person*) qui a des doutes.

**dough** *n.* pâte *f.*; (*money: sl.*) fric *m.*

**doughnut** *n.* beignet *m.*

**douse** *v.t.* arroser; (*light, fire*) éteindre.

**dove** *n.* colombe *f.*

**Dover** *n.* Douvres *m./f.*

**dovetail** *v.t./i.* (s')ajuster.

**dowdy** *a.* (*clothes*) sans chic, monotone.

**down¹** *n.* (*fluff*) duvet *m.*

**down²** *adv.* en bas; (*of sun*) couché; (*lower*) plus bas. ● *prep.* en bas de; (*along*) le long de. ● *v.t.* (*knock down, shoot down*) abattre; (*drink*) vider. **come** *or* **go ~,** descendre. **go ~ to the post office,** aller à la poste. **~ payment,** acompte *m.* **~-to-earth** *a.* terre-à-terre *invar.*

**downcast** *a.* démoralisé.

**downfall** *n.* chute *f.*

**downgrade** *v.t.* déclasser.

**downhill** *adv.* **go ~,** descendre; (*pej.*) baisser.

**downpour** *n.* grosse averse *f.*

**downright** *a.* (*utter*) véritable; (*honest*) franc. ● *adv.* carrément.

**downstairs** *adv.* en bas. ● *a.* d'en bas.

**downstream** *adv.* en aval.

**downtown** *a.* (*Amer.*) du centre de la ville. **~ Boston** /*etc.*, le centre de Boston/*etc.*

**downward** *a.* & *adv.*, **~s** *adv.* vers le bas.

**doze** *v.i.* sommeiller. **~ off,** s'assoupir. ● *n.* somme *m.*

**dozen** n. douzaine f. **a ~ eggs,** une douzaine d'œufs. **~s of,** (fam.) des dizaines de.

**drab** a. terne.

**draft**[1] n. (outline) brouillon m.; (comm.) traite f. ● v.t. faire le brouillon de; (draw up) rédiger. **the ~,** (mil., Amer.) la conscription. **a ~ treaty,** un projet de traité.

**draft**[2] n. (Amer.) = draught.

**drag** v.t./i. traîner; (river) draguer; (pull away) arracher. ● n. (task: fam.) corvée f.; (person: fam.) raseu|r, -se m., f.

**dragon** n. dragon m.

**dragon-fly** n. libellule f.

**drain** v.t. (land) drainer; (vegetables) égoutter; (tank, glass) vider; (use up) épuiser. **~ (off),** (liquid) faire écouler. ● v.i. **~ (off),** (of liquid) s'écouler. ● n. (sewer) égout m. **~ (-pipe),** tuyau d'écoulement m.

**drama** n. art dramatique m., théâtre m.; (play, event) drame m. **~tic** a. (situation) dramatique; (increase) spectaculaire.

**drape** v.t. draper. **~s** n. pl. (Amer.) rideaux m. pl.

**drastic** a. sévère.

**draught** n. courant d'air m. **~s,** (game) dames f. pl. **~ beer,** bière (à la) pression f. **~y** a. plein de courants d'air.

**draughtsman** n. dessina|teur, -trice industriel(le) m., f.

**draw** v.t. passer; (picture) dessiner; (line) tracer. ● v.i. dessiner; (sport) faire match nul; (come, move) venir. ● n. (sport) match nul m.; (in lottery) tirage au sort m. **~ up** v.i. (stop) s'arrêter; v.t. (document) dresser; (chair) approcher.

**drawback** n. inconvénient m.

**drawer** n. tiroir m.

**drawing** n. dessin m. **~-board** n. planche à dessin f. **~-pin** n. punaise f. **~-room** n. salon m.

**drawl** n. voix traînante f.

**dread** n. terreur f., crainte f. ● v.t. redouter.

**dreadful** a. épouvantable, affreux. **~ly** adv. terriblement.

**dream** n. rêve m. ● v.t./i. rêver. **~ up,** imaginer. **~er** n. rêveu|r, -se m., f.

**drear|y** a. triste; (boring) monotone. **~iness** n. tristesse f.; monotonie f.

**dredge** n. drague f. ● v.t./i. draguer. **~r** n. dragueur m.

**dregs** n. pl. lie f.

**drench** v.t. tremper.

**dress** n. robe f.; (clothing) tenue f. ● v.t./i. (s')habiller; (food) assaisonner; (wound) panser. **~ circle,** premier balcon m. **~ up as,** se déguiser en. **get ~ed,** s'habiller.

**dresser** n. buffet m.; (actor's) habilleu|r, -se m., f.

**dressing** n. (sauce) assaisonnement m.; (bandage) pansement m. **~-gown** n. robe de chambre f. **~-room** n. (sport) vestiaire m.; (theatre) loge f. **~-table** n. coiffeuse f.

**dressmaker** n. couturière f.

**dribble** v.i. couler goutte à goutte; (person) baver.

**dried** a. (fruit etc.) sec.

**drier** n. séchoir m.

**drift** v.i. aller à la dérive; (pile up) s'amonceler. ● n. dérive f.; amoncellement m.; (of events) tournure f.; (meaning) sens m. **~ towards,** glisser vers. **~er** n. personne sans but dans la vie f.

**drill** n. (tool) perceuse f.; (for teeth) roulette f.; (training) exercice m.; (procedure: fam.) marche à suivre f. **(pneumatic) ~,** marteau piqueur m. ● v.t. percer; (train) entraîner. ● v.i. être à l'exercice.

**drily** adv. sèchement.

**drink** v.t./i. boire. ● n. (liquid) boisson f.; (glass of alcohol) verre m. **a ~ of water,** un verre d'eau. **~er** n. buveu|r, -se m., f. **~ing water,** eau potable f.

**drip** v.i. (dé)goutter; (washing) s'égoutter. ● n. goutte f.; (person: sl.) lavette f. **~-dry** v.t. laisser égoutter; a. sans repassage.

**dripping** n. graisse de rôti f.

**drive** v.t. chasser, pousser; (vehicle) conduire; (machine) actionner. ● v.i. conduire. ● n. promenade en voiture f.; (private road) allée f.; (fig.) énergie f.; (psych.) instinct m.; (pol.) campagne f.; (auto.) traction f.; (golf, comput.) drive m. **~ at,** en venir à. **~ away,** (of car) partir. **~ mad,** rendre fou. **left-hand ~,** conduite à gauche f.

**drivel** n. radotage m.

**driver** n. conduc|teur, -trice m., f., chauffeur m.

**driving** n. conduite f. **~ licence,** permis de conduire m.

**drizzle** n. bruine f. ● v.i. bruiner.

**dromedary** n. dromadaire m.

**drone** n. (noise) bourdonnement m.; (bee) faux bourdon m. ● v.i. bourdonner; (fig.) parler d'une voix monotone.

**drool** v.i. baver (over, sur).

**droop** v.i. pencher, tomber.

**drop** n. goutte f.; (fall, lowering) chute f. ● v.t./i. (laisser) tomber; (decrease, lower) baisser. **~ (off),** (person from car) déposer. **~ in,** passer (on, chez). **~ off,** (doze) s'assoupir.

**droppings** n. pl. crottes f. pl.

**drought** n. sécheresse f.

**droves** n. pl. foule(s) f. (pl.).

**drown** v.t./i. (se) noyer.

**drowsy** a. somnolent. **be** or **feel ~,** avoir envie de dormir.

**drudge** n. esclave du travail m. **~ry** n. travail pénible et ingrat m.

**drug** *n.* drogue *f.*; (*med.*) médicament *m.* ● *v.t.* droguer. ~ **addict,** drogué(e) *m.* (*f.*).

**drugstore** *n.* (*Amer.*) drugstore *m.*

**drum** *n.* tambour *m.*; (*for oil*) bidon *m.* ~**s,** batterie *f.* ● *v.t.* ~ **into** s.o., répéter sans cesse à qn. ~ **up,** (*support*) susciter; (*business*) créer. ~**mer** *n.* tambour *m.*; (*in pop group*) batteur *m.*

**drumstick** *n.* baguette de tambour *f.*; (*of chicken*) pilon *m.*

**drunk** ● *a.* ivre. **get** ~, s'enivrer.

**dry** *a.* sec; (*day*) sans pluie. ● *v.t./i.* (faire) sécher. ~**-clean** *v.t.* nettoyer à sec. ~**-cleaner** *n.* teinturier *m.* ~ **up,** (*dry dishes*) essuyer la vaisselle; (*of supplies*) (se) tarir; (*be silent: fam.*) se taire. ~**ness** *n.* sécheresse *f.*

**dual** *a.* double. ~ **carriageway,** route à quatre voies *f.*

**dub** *v.t.* (*film*) doubler; (*nickname*) surnommer.

**dubious** *a.* (*pej.*) douteux. **be** ~ **about** sth., (*person*) avoir des doutes sur qch.

**duchess** *n.* duchesse *f.*

**duck** *n.* canard *m.* ● *v.i.* se baisser subitement. ● *v.t.* (*head*) baisser; (*person*) plonger dans l'eau.

**duct** *n.* conduit *m.*

**dud** *a.* (*tool etc.: sl.*) mal fichu; (*coin: sl.*) faux; (*cheque: sl.*) sans provision.

**due** *a.* (*owing*) dû; (*expected*) attendu; (*proper*) qui convient. ● *adv.* ~ **east**/*etc.*, droit vers l'est/*etc.* ● *n.* dû *m.* ~**s,** droits *m. pl.*; (*of club*) cotisation *f.* ~ **to,** à cause de; (*caused by*) dû à. **she's** ~ **to leave now,** c'est prévu qu'elle parte maintenant.

**duel** *n.* duel *m.*

**duet** *n.* duo *m.*

**duffle** *a.* ~ **bag,** sac de marin *m.* ~ **coat,** duffel-coat *m.*

**duke** *n.* duc *m.*

**dull** *a.* ennuyeux; (*colour*) terne; (*weather*) morne; (*sound*) sourd; (*stupid*) bête; (*blunt*) émoussé. ● *v.t.* (*pain*) amortir; (*mind*) engourdir.

**dumb** *a.* muet; (*stupid: fam.*) bête.

**dumbfound** *v.t.* sidérer.

**dummy** *n.* (*comm.*) article factice *m.*; (*of tailor*) mannequin *m.*; (*of baby*) sucette *f.* ● *a.* factice.

**dump** *v.t.* déposer; (*abandon: fam.*) se débarrasser de; (*comm.*) dumper. ● *n.* tas d'ordures *m.*; (*refuse tip*) décharge *f.*; (*mil.*) dépôt *m.*; (*dull place: fam.*) trou *m.*

**dumpling** *n.* boulette de pâte *f.*

**dumpy** *a.* boulot.

**dunce** *n.* cancre *m.*, âne *m.*

**dune** *n.* dune *f.*

**dung** *n.* (*excrement*) bouse *f.*, crotte *f.*; (*manure*) fumier *m.*

**dungarees** *n. pl.* salopette *f.*

**dungeon** *n.* cachot *m.*

**dunk** *v.t.* tremper.

**dupe** *v.t.* duper. ● *n.* dupe *f.*

**duplex** *n.* duplex *m.*

**duplicate**[^1] *n.* double *m.*

**duplicate**[^2] *v.t.* faire un double de; (*on machine*) polycopier. ~**or** *n.* duplicateur *m.*

**duplicity** *n.* duplicité *f.*

**durable** *a.* (*tough*) résistant; (*enduring*) durable.

**duration** *n.* durée *f.*

**during** *prep.* pendant.

**dusk** *n.* crépuscule *m.*

**dusky** *a.* foncé.

**dust** *n.* poussière *f.* ● *v.t.* épousseter; (*sprinkle*) saupoudrer (**with,** de).

**dustbin** *n.* poubelle *f.*

**duster** *n.* chiffon *m.*

**dustman** *n.* éboueur *m.*

**dustpan** *n.* pelle à poussière *f.*

**dusty** *a.* poussiéreux.

**Dutch** *a.* hollandais. ● *n.* (*lang.*) hollandais *m.* ~**man** *n.* Hollandais *m.* ~**woman** *n.* Hollandaise *f.*

**dutiful** *a.* obéissant.

**duty** *n.* devoir *m.*; (*tax*) droit *m.* ~**-free** *a.* hors-taxe. **on** ~, de service.

**duvet** *n.* couette *f.*

**dwarf** *n.* nain(e) *m.* (*f.*).

**dwell** *v.i.* demeurer. ~ **on,** s'étendre sur.

**dwindle** *v.i.* diminuer.

**dye** *v.t.* teindre. ● *n.* teinture *f.*

**dying** *a.* mourant; (*art*) qui se perd.

**dynamic** *a.* dynamique.

**dynamism** *n.* dynamisme *m.*

**dynamite** *n.* dynamite *f.*

**dynamo** *n.* dynamo *f.*

**dynasty** *n.* dynastie *f.*

**dysentery** *n.* dysenterie *f.*

**dyslexi|a** *n.* dyslexie *f.* ~**c** *a. & n.* dyslexique (*m./f.*).

●●●●●●●●●●●●●●●●●●●●●●●●●●●●

# Ee

●●●●●●●●●●●●●●●●●●●●●●●●●●●●

**each** *a.* chaque. ● *pron.* chacun(e). ~ **one,** chacun(e). ~ **other,** l'un(e) l'autre, les un(e)s les autres. **know** ~ **other,** se connaître. **love** ~ **other,** s'aimer.

**eager** *a.* impatient (**to,** de); (*supporter, desire*) ardent. **be** ~ **to,** (*want*) avoir envie de. ~**ly** *adv.* avec impatience *or* ardeur.

**eagle** *n.* aigle *m.*

**ear**¹ /ɪə(r)/ *n.* oreille *f.* **~-ring** *n.* boucle d'oreille *f.*

**ear**² *n.* (*of corn*) épi *m.*

**earache** *n.* mal à l'oreille *m.*, mal d'oreille *m.*

**earl** *n.* comte *m.*

**earlier** *a.* (*in series*) précédent; (*in history*) plus ancien, antérieur; (*in future*) plus avancé. ●*adv.* précédemment; antérieurement; avant.

**early** *adv.* tôt, de bonne heure; (*ahead of time*) en avance. ●*a.* premier; (*hour*) matinal; (*fruit*) précoce; (*retirement*) anticipé.

**earmark** *v.t.* destiner, réserver (**for**, à).

**earn** *v.t.* gagner; (*interest: comm.*) rapporter.

**earnest** *a.* sérieux. **in ~**, sérieusement.

**earnings** *n. pl.* salaire *m.*; (*profits*) bénéfices *m. pl.*

**earphone** *n.* écouteur *m.*

**earshot** *n.* **within ~**, à portée de voix.

**earth** *n.* terre *f.* ●*v.t.* (*electr.*) mettre à la terre.

**earthenware** *n.* faïence *f.*

**earthquake** *n.* tremblement de terre *m.*

**earthy** *a.* (*of earth*) terreux; (*coarse*) grossier.

**earwig** *n.* perce-oreille *m.*

**ease** *n.* aisance *f.*, facilité *f.*; (*comfort*) bienêtre *m.* ●*v.t./i.* (se) calmer; (*relax*) (se) détendre; (*slow down*) ralentir; (*slide*) glisser. **at ~**, à l'aise; (*mil.*) au repos.

**easel** *n.* chevalet *m.*

**east** *n.* est *m.* ●*a.* d'est. ●*adv.* vers l'est. **the E~**, (*Orient*) l'Orient *m.* **~erly** *a.* d'est. **~ern** *a.* de l'est, oriental.

**Easter** *n.* Pâques *f. pl.* (*or m. sing.*). **~ egg**, œuf de Pâques *m.*

**easy** *a.* facile; (*relaxed*) aisé. **~ chair**, fauteuil *m.* **easily** *adv.* facilement.

**easygoing** *a.* (*with people*) accommodant; (*relaxed*) décontracté.

**eat** *v.t./i.* manger. **~ into**, ronger.

**eau-de-Cologne** *n.* eau de Cologne *f.*

**eaves** *n. pl.* avant-toit *m.*

**eavesdrop** *v.i.* **~ (on)**, écouter en cachette.

**ebb** *n.* reflux *m.* ●*v.i.* refluer; (*fig.*) décliner.

**ebony** *n.* ébène *f.*

**EC** *abbr.* (*European Community*) CE.

**eccentric** *a. & n.* excentrique (*m./f.*). **~ity** *n.* excentricité *f.*

**ecclesiastical** *a.* ecclésiastique.

**echo** *n.* écho *m.* ●*v.t./i.* (se) répercuter; (*fig.*) répéter.

**eclipse** *n.* éclipse *f.* ●*v.t.* éclipser.

**ecolog|y** *n.* écologie *f.* **~ical** *a.* écologique.

**economic** *a.* économique; (*profitable*) rentable. **~al** *a.* économique; (*person*) économe. **~s** *n.* économie politique *f.*

**economist** *n.* économiste *m./f.*

**econom|y** *n.* économie *f.* **~ize** *v.i.* **~ (on)**, économiser.

**ECU** *n.* ÉCU *m.*

**eczema** *n.* eczéma *m.*

**eddy** *n.* tourbillon *m.*

**edge** *n.* bord *m.*; (*of town*) abords *m. pl.*; (*of knife*) tranchant *m.* ●*v.i.* (*move*) se glisser. **on ~**, énervé.

**edgeways** *adv.* de côte. **I can't get a word in ~**, je ne peux pas placer un mot.

**edgy** /'edʒɪ/ *a.* énervé.

**edible** *a.* mangeable; (*not poisonous*) comestible.

**edify** *v.t.* édifier.

**edit** *v.t.* (*newspaper*) diriger; (*prepare text of*) mettre au point, préparer; (*write*) rédiger; (*cut*) couper.

**edition** *n.* édition *f.*

**editor** *n.* (*writer*) rédac|teur, -trice *m.*, *f.*; (*annotator*) édi|teur, -trice *m.*, *f.* **the ~ (in chief)**, le rédacteur en chef.

**educat|e** *v.t.* instruire; (*mind, public*) éduquer. **~ed** *a.* instruit. **~ion** *n.* éducation *f.*; (*schooling*) enseignement *m.*

**EEC** *abbr.* (*European Economic Community*) CEE *f.*

**eel** *n.* anguille *f.*

**effect** *n.* effet *m.* ●*v.t.* effectuer.

**effective** *a.* efficace; (*striking*) frappant; (*actual*) effectif.

**effervescent** *a.* effervescent.

**efficien|t** *a.* efficace; (*person*) compétent. **~cy** *n.* efficacité *f.*; compétence *f.* **~tly** *adv.* efficacement.

**effort** *n.* effort *m.* **~less** *a.* facile.

**e.g.** *abbr.* par exemple.

**egalitarian** *a.* égalitaire.

**egg**¹ *n.* œuf *m.* **~-cup** *n.* coquetier *m.*

**egg**² *v.t.* **~ on**, (*fam.*) inciter.

**eggshell** *n.* coquille d'œuf *f.*

**ego** *n.* moi *m.*

**Egypt** *n.* Égypte *f.* **~ian** *a. & n.* égyptien(ne) (*m. (f.)*).

**eh** *int.* (*fam.*) hein.

**eiderdown** *n.* édredon *m.*

**eight** *a. & n.* huit (*m.*). **eighth** *a. & n.* huitième (*m./f.*).

**eighteen** *a. & n.* dix-huit (*m.*). **~th** *a. & n.* dix-huitième (*m./f.*).

**eight|y** *a. & n.* quatre-vingts (*m.*). **~ieth** *a. & n.* quatre-vingtième (*m./f.*).

**either** *a. & pron.* l'un(e) ou l'autre; (*with negative*) ni l'un(e) ni l'autre; (*each*) chaque. ●*adv.* non plus. ●*conj.* **~ ... or**, ou (bien) ... ou (bien); (*with negative*) ni ... ni.

**eject** *v.t.* éjecter.

**eke** *v.t.* **~ out**, faire durer; (*living*) gagner difficilement.

**elaborate**¹ *a.* compliqué

**elaborate**² *v.t.* élaborer.

**elapse** *v.i.* s'écouler.

**elastic** *a. & n.* élastique (*m.*). ∼ **band,** élastique *m.*

**elated** *a.* fou de joie.

**elbow** *n.* coude *m.*

**elder**[1] *a. & n.* aîné(e) (*m.* (*f.*)).

**elder**[2] *n.* (*tree*) sureau *m.*

**elderly** *a.* (assez) âgé.

**eldest** *a. & n.* aîné(e) (*m.* (*f.*)).

**elect** *v.t.* élire. ● *a.* (*president etc.*) futur. ∼**ion** *n.* élection *f.*

**elector** *n.* élec|teur, -trice *m., f.* ∼**al** *a.* électoral.

**electric** *a.* électrique. ∼ **blanket,** couverture chauffante *f.* ∼**al** *a.* électrique.

**electrician** *n.* électricien *m.*

**electricity** *n.* électricité *f.*

**electrify** *v.t.* électrifier; (*excite*) électriser.

**electron** *n.* électron *m.*

**electronic** *a.* électronique. ∼**s** *n.* électronique *f.*

**elegan|t** *a.* élégant. ∼**ce** *n.* élégance *f.*

**element** *n.* élément *m.*; (*of heater etc.*) résistance *f.* ∼**ary** *a.* élémentaire.

**elephant** *n.* éléphant *m.*

**elevator** *n.* (*Amer.*) ascenseur *m.*

**eleven** *a. & n.* onze (*m.*). ∼**th** *a. & n.* onzième (*m./f.*).

**elf** (*pl.* **elves**) lutin *m.*

**elicit** *v.t.* obtenir (**from,** de).

**eligible** *a.* be ∼ **for,** avoir droit à.

**eliminat|e** *v.t.* éliminer. ∼**ion** *n.* élimination *f.*

**ellipse** *n.* ellipse *f.*

**elm** *n.* orme *m.*

**elocution** *n.* élocution *f.*

**elongate** *v.t.* allonger.

**eloquen|t** *a.* éloquent. ∼**ce** *n.* éloquence *f.* ∼**tly** *adv.* avec éloquence.

**else** *adv.* d'autre. **everybody** ∼, tous les autres. **nobody** ∼, personne d'autre. **nothing** ∼, rien d'autre. **or** ∼, ou bien. **somewhere** ∼, autre part. ∼**where** *adv.* ailleurs.

**elucidate** *v.t.* élucider.

**elude** *v.t.* échapper à; (*question*) éluder.

**emaciated** *a.* émacié.

**emanate** *v.i.* émaner.

**emancipat|e** *v.t.* émanciper. ∼**ion** *n.* émancipation *f.*

**embalm** *v.t.* embaumer.

**embankment** *n.* (*of river*) quai *m.*; (*of railway*) remblai *m.*

**embark** *v.t./i.* (s')embarquer. ∼ **on,** (*business etc.*) se lancer dans; (*journey*) commencer.

**embarrass** *v.t.* embarrasser, gêner. ∼**ment** *n.* embarras *m.*

**embassy** *n.* ambassade *f.*

**embed** *v.t.* encastrer.

**embellish** *v.t.* embellir. ∼**ment** *n.* enjolivement *m.*

**embers** *n. pl.* braise *f.*

**embezzle** *v.t.* détourner. ∼**ment** *n.* détournement de fonds *m.* ∼**r** *n.* escroc *m.*

**embod|y** *v.t.* incarner, exprimer; (*include*) contenir. ∼**iment** *n.* incarnation *f.*

**emboss** *v.t.* (*metal*) repousser; (*paper*) gaufrer.

**embrace** *v.t./i.* (s')embrasser. ● *n.* étreinte *f.*

**embroider** *v.t.* broder. ∼**y** *n.* broderie *f.*

**embroil** *v.t.* mêler (**in,** à).

**embryo** *n.* embryon *m.*

**emerald** *n.* émeraude *f.*

**emerge** *v.i.* apparaître. ∼**nce** *n.* apparition *f.*

**emergency** *n.* (*crisis*) crise *f.*; (*urgent case: med.*) urgence *f.* ● *a.* d'urgence. ∼ **exit,** sortie de secours *f.*

**emigrant** *n.* émigrant(e) *m.* (*f.*).

**emigrat|e** *v.i.* émigrer. ∼**ion** *n.* émigration *f.*

**eminen|t** *a.* éminent. *f.* ∼**tly** *adv.* éminemment.

**emi|t** *v.t.* émettre. ∼**ssion** *n.* émission *f.*

**emotion** *n.* émotion *f.* ∼**al** *a.* (*person, shock*) émotif; (*speech, scene*) émouvant.

**emotive** *a.* émotif.

**emperor** *n.* empereur *m.*

**emphasis** *n.* (*on word*) accent *m.* **lay** ∼ **on,** mettre l'accent sur.

**emphasize** *v.t.* souligner; (*syllable*) insister sur.

**emphatic** *a.* catégorique; (*manner*) énergique.

**empire** *n.* empire *m.*

**employ** *v.t.* employer. ∼**er** *n.* employeu|r, -se *m., f.* ∼**ment** *n.* emploi *m.* ∼**ment agency,** agence de placement *f.*

**employee** *n.* employé(e) *m.* (*f.*).

**empower** *v.t.* autoriser (**to do,** à faire).

**empress** *n.* impératrice *f.*

**empt|y** *a.* vide; (*promise*) vain. ● *v.t./i.* (se) vider.

**emulate** *v.t.* imiter.

**emulsion** *n.* émulsion *f.* ∼ **(paint),** peinture-émulsion *f.*

**enable** *v.t.* ∼ **s.o. to,** permettre à qn. de.

**enact** *v.t.* (*law*) promulguer; (*scene*) représenter.

**enamel** *n.* émail *m.* ● *v.t.* émailler.

**encase** *v.t.* (*cover*) recouvrir (**in,** de); (*enclose*) enfermer (**in,** dans).

**enchant** *v.t.* enchanter. ∼**ing** *a.* enchanteur.

**encircle** *v.t.* encercler.

**enclave** *n.* enclave *f.*

**enclose** *v.t.* (*land*) clôturer; (*with letter*) joindre. ∼**d** *a.* (*space*) clos; (*market*) couvert; (*with letter*) ci-joint.

**enclosure** *n.* enceinte *f.*; (*comm.*) pièce jointe *f.*

**encore** *int. & n.* bis (*m.*).

**encounter** *v.t.* rencontrer. ● *n.* rencontre *f.*

**encourage** *v.t.* encourager. ~**ment** *n.* encouragement *m.*

**encroach** *v.i.* ~ **upon**, empiéter sur.

**encumber** *v.t.* encombrer.

**encyclopaed|ia, encyclopaed|ia** *n.* encyclopédie *f.* ~**ic** *a.* encyclopédique.

**end** *n.* fin *f.*; (*farthest part*) bout *m.* ● *v.t./i.* (se) terminer. ~**up doing**, finir par faire. **in the** ~, finalement. **put an** ~ **to**, mettre fin à.

**endanger** *v.t.* mettre en danger.

**endearing** *a.* attachant.

**endeavour** *n.* effort *m.* ● *v.i.* s'efforcer (**to**, de).

**ending** *n.* fin *f.*

**endive** *n.* chicorée *f.*

**endless** *a.* interminable; (*times*) innombrable; (*patience*) infini.

**endorse** *v.t.* (*document*) endosser; (*action*) approuver. ~**ment** *n.* (*auto.*) contravention *f.*

**endow** *v.t.* doter. ~**ed with**, doté de.

**endur|e** *v.t.* supporter. ● *v.i.* durer. ~**able** *a.* supportable. ~**ance** *n.* endurance *f.*

**enemy** *n. & a.* ennemi(e) (*m.* (*f.*)).

**energetic** *a.* énergique.

**energy** *n.* énergie *f.*

**enforce** *v.t.* appliquer, faire respecter; (*impose*) imposer (**on**, à). ~**d** *a.* forcé.

**engage** *v.t.* engager. ● *v.i.* ~ **in**, prendre part à. ~**d** *a.* fiancé; (*busy*) occupé. ~**ment** *n.* fiançailles *f. pl.*; (*meeting*) rendez-vous *m.*; (*undertaking*) engagement *m.*

**engender** *v.t.* engendrer.

**engine** *n.* moteur *m.*; (*of train*) locomotive *f.*; (*of ship*) machine *f.*

**engineer** *n.* ingénieur *m.*; (*appliance repairman*) dépanneur *m.* ● *v.t.* (*contrive: fam.*) machiner. ~**ing** *n.* (*mechanical*) mécanique *f.*; (*road-building etc.*) génie *m.*

**England** *n.* Angleterre *f.*

**English** *a.* anglais. ● *n.* (*lang.*) anglais *m.* ~**speaking** *a.* anglophone. **the** ~, les Anglais *m. pl.* ~**man** *n.* Anglais *m.* ~**woman** *n.* Anglaise *f.*

**engrav|e** *v.t.* graver. ~**ing** *n.* gravure *f.*

**enhance** *v.t.* rehausser; (*price, value*) augmenter.

**enigma** *n.* énigme *f.* ~**tic** *a.* énigmatique.

**enjoy** *v.t.* aimer (*doing*, faire); (*benefit from*) jouir de. ~ **o.s.**, s'amuser. ~**able** *a.* agréable. ~**ment** *n.* plaisir *m.*

**enlarge** *v.t./i.* (s')agrandir. ~**ment** *n.* agrandissement *m.*

**enlighten** *v.t.* éclairer. ~**ment** *n.* édification *f.*

**enlist** *v.t.* (*person*) recruter; (*fig.*) obtenir. ● *v.i.* s'engager.

**enliven** *v.t.* animer.

**enmity** *n.* inimitié *f.*

**enormity** *n.* énormité *f.*

**enormous** *a.* énorme. ~**ly** *adv.* énormément.

**enough** *adv. & n.* assez. ● *a.* assez de. ~ **glasses/time/***etc.*, assez de verres/de temps/*etc.* **have** ~ **of**, en avoir assez de.

**enquir|e** *v.t./i.* demander. ~**e about**, se renseigner sur. ~**y** *n.* demande de renseignements *f.*

**enrage** *v.t.* mettre en rage.

**enrol** *v.t./i.* (s')inscrire. ~**ment** *n.* inscription *f.*

**ensemble** *n.* (*clothing & mus.*) ensemble *m.*

**enslave** *v.t.* asservir.

**ensue** *v.i.* s'ensuivre.

**ensure** *v.t.* assurer. ~ **that**, (*ascertain*) s'assurer que.

**entail** *v.t.* entraîner.

**entangle** *v.t.* emmêler.

**enter** *v.t.* (*room, club, race, etc.*) entrer dans; (*note down, register*) inscrire; (*data*) entrer, saisir. ● *v.i.* entrer (**into**, dans). ~ **for**, s'inscrire à.

**enterprise** *n.* entreprise *f.*; (*boldness*) initiative *f.*

**enterprising** *a.* entreprenant.

**entertain** *v.t.* amuser, divertir; (*guests*) recevoir; (*ideas*) considérer. ~**er** *n.* artiste *m./f.* ~**ing** *a.* divertissant. ~**ment** *n.* amusement *m.*, divertissement *m.*; (*performance*) spectacle *m.*

**enthral** *v.t.* captiver.

**enthusiasm** *n.* enthousiasme *m.*

**enthusiast** *n.* fervent(e) *m.* (*f.*), passionné(e) *m.* (*f.*) (**for**, de). ~**ic** *a.* (*supporter*) enthousiaste. **be** ~**ic about**, être enthousiasmé par. ~**ically** *adv. adv.* avec enthousiasme.

**entice** *v.t.* attirer. ~ **to do**, entraîner à faire. ~**ment** *n.* (*attraction*) attrait *m.*

**entire** *a.* entier. ~**ly** *adv.* entièrement.

**entitle** *v.t.* donner droit à (**to sth.**, à qch.; **to do**, de faire). ~**d** *a.* (*book*) intitulé. **be** ~**d to sth.**, avoir droit à qch.

**entity** *n.* entité *f.*

**entrance**[1] *n.* (*entering, way in*) entrée *f.* (**to**, de); (*right to enter*) admission *f.* ● *a.* (*charge, exam*) d'entrée.

**entrance**[2] *v.t.* transporter.

**entrant** *n.* (*sport*) concurrent(e) *m.* (*f.*); (*in exam*) candidat(e) *m.* (*f.*).

**entrepreneur** *n.* entrepreneur *m.*

**entrust** *v.t.* confier.

**entry** *n.* (*entrance*) entrée *f.*; (*word on list*) mot inscrit *m.* ~ **form**, feuille d'inscription *f.*

**envelope** *n.* enveloppe *f.*

**enviable** *a.* enviable.

**envious** *a.* envieux (**of sth.**, de qch.). ~ **of s.o.**, jaloux de qn. ~**ly** *adv.* avec envie.

**environment** *n.* milieu *m.*; (*ecological*) environnement *m.* ∼**al** *a.* du milieu; de l'environnement. ∼**alist** *n.* spécialiste de l'environnement *m./f.*

**envisage** *v.t.* envisager.

**envoy** *n.* envoyé(e) *m.* (*f.*).

**envy** *n.* envie *f.* ● *v.t.* envier.

**enzyme** *n.* enzyme *m.*

**epidemic** *n.* épidémie *f.*

**epilep|sy** *n.* épilepsie *f.* ∼**tic** *a.* & *n.* épileptique (*m./f.*).

**episode** *n.* épisode *m.*

**epitom|e** *n.* (*embodiment*) modèle *m.*; (*summary*) résumé *m.* ∼**ize** *v.t.* incarner.

**epoch** *n.* époque *f.*

**equal** *a.* & *n.* égal(e) (*m.f.*). ● *v.t.* égaler. ∼ **to**, (*task*) à la hauteur de. ∼**ity** *n.* égalité *f.* ∼**ly** *adv.* également; (*just as*) tout aussi.

**equalize** *v.t./i.* égaliser. ∼**r** *n.* (*goal*) but égalisateur *m.*

**equanimity** *n.* égalité d'humeur *f.*, calme *m.*

**equate** *v.t.* assimiler, égaler (**with**, à).

**equation** *n.* équation *f.*

**equator** *n.* équateur *m.*

**equilibrium** *n.* équilibre *m.*

**equinox** *n.* équinoxe *m.*

**equip** *v.t.* équiper (**with**, de). ∼**ment** *n.* équipement *m.*

**equitable** *a.* équitable.

**equity** *n.* équité *f.*

**equivalent** *a.* & *n.* équivalent (*m.*).

**equivocal** *a.* équivoque.

**era** *n.* ère *f.*, époque *f.*

**eradicate** *v.t.* supprimer.

**erase** *v.t.* effacer. ∼**r** *n.* (*rubber*) gomme *f.*

**erect** *a.* droit. ● *v.t.* ériger. ∼**ion** *n.* érection *f.*

**ermine** *n.* hermine *f.*

**ero|de** *v.t.* ronger. ∼**sion** *n.* érosion *f.*

**erotic** *a.* érotique.

**err** *v.i.* (*be mistaken*) se tromper; (*sin*) pécher.

**errand** *n.* course *f.*

**erratic** *a.* (*uneven*) irrégulier; (*person*) capricieux.

**erroneous** *a.* erroné.

**error** *n.* erreur *f.*

**erudit|e** *a.* érudit. ∼**ion** *n.* érudition *f.*

**erupt** *v.i.* (*volcano*) entrer en éruption; (*fig.*) éclater. ∼**ion** *n.* éruption *f.*

**escalat|e** *v.t./i.* (s')intensifier; (*of prices*) monter en flèche. ∼**ion** *n.* escalade *f.*

**escalator** *n.* escalier mécanique *m.*, escalator *m.*

**escape** *v.i.* s'échapper (**from a place**, d'un lieu); (*prisoner*) s'évader. ● *v.t.* échapper à. ● *n.* fuite *f.*, évasion *f.*; (*of gas etc.*) fuite *f.* ∼ **from s.o.**, échapper à qn.

**escort**[1] *n.* (*guard*) escorte *f.*; (*of lady*) cavalier *m.*

**escort**[2] *v.t.* escorter.

**Eskimo** *n.* Esquimau(de) *m.* (*f.*).

**especial** *a.* particulier. ∼**ly** *adv.* particulièrement.

**espionage** *n.* espionnage *m.*

**espresso** *n.* (café) express *m.*

**essay** *n.* essai *m.*; (*schol.*) rédaction *f.*; (*univ.*) dissertation *f.*

**essence** *n.* essence *f.*; (*main point*) essentiel *m.*

**essential** *a.* essentiel. ● *n. pl.* **the** ∼**s**, l'essentiel *m.* ∼**ly** *adv.* essentiellement.

**establish** *v.t.* établir; (*business, state*) fonder. ∼**ment** *n.* établissement *m.*; fondation *f.*

**estate** *n.* (*land*) propriété *f.*; (*possessions*) biens *m. pl.*; (*inheritance*) succession *f.*; (*district*) cité *f.* ∼ **agent**, agent immobilier *m.* ∼ **car**, break *m.*

**esteem** *v.t.* estimer. ● *n.* estime *f.*

**estimate**[1] *n.* (*calculation*) estimation *f.*; (*comm.*) devis *m.*

**estimat|e**[2] *v.t.* estimer. ∼**ion** *n.* jugement *m.*; (*high regard*) estime *f.*

**estuary** *n.* estuaire *m.*

**etc.** *adv.* etc.

**etching** *n.* eau-forte *f.*

**eternal** *a.* éternel.

**eternity** *n.* éternité *f.*

**ether** *n.* éther *m.*

**ethic** *n.* éthique *f.* ∼**s**, moralité *f.* ∼**al** *a.* éthique.

**ethnic** *a.* ethnique.

**etiquette** *n.* étiquette *f.*

**etymology** *n.* étymologie *f.*

**eucalyptus** *n.* eucalyptus *m.*

**eurocheque** *n.* eurochèque *m.*

**Europe** *n.* Europe *f.* ∼**an** *a.* & *n.* européen(ne) (*m.* (*f.*)). **E∼an Community**, Communauté Européenne *f.*

**evacuat|e** *v.t.* évacuer. ∼**ion** *n.* évacuation *f.*

**evade** *v.t.* esquiver. ∼ **tax**, frauder le fisc.

**evaluate** *v.t.* évaluer.

**evangelist** *n.* évangéliste *m.*

**evaporat|e** *v.i.* s'évaporer. ∼**ion** *n.* évaporation *f.*

**evasion** *n.* fuite *f.* (**of**, devant); (*excuse*) subterfuge *m.* **tax** ∼, fraude fiscale *f.*

**eve** *n.* veille *f.* (**of**, de).

**even** *a.* régulier; (*surface*) uni; (*equal, unvarying*) égal; (*number*) pair. ● *v.t./i.* ∼ (**out** *or* **up**), (s')égaliser. ● *adv.* même. ∼ **better/etc.**, (*still*) encore mieux/*etc.* **get** ∼ **with**, se venger de.

**evening** *n.* soir *m.*; (*whole evening, event*) soirée *f.*

**event** *n.* événement *m.*; (*sport*) épreuve *f.*

**eventual** *a.* final, définitif. ∼**ly** *adv.* en fin de compte; (*in future*) un jour ou l'autre.

**ever** adv. jamais; (at all times) toujours. ~ **since** prep. & adv. depuis (ce moment-là); conj. depuis que.

**evergreen** n. arbre à feuilles persistantes m.

**everlasting** a. éternel.

**every** a. chaque. ~ **one,** chacun(e).

**everybody** pron. tout le monde.

**everyday** a. quotidien.

**everyone** pron. tout le monde.

**everything** pron. tout.

**everywhere** adv. partout.

**evict** v.t. expulser. ~**ion** n. expulsion f.

**evidence** n. (proof) preuve(s) f. (pl.); (certainty) évidence f.; (signs) signes m. pl.; (testimony) témoignage m. **give** ~, témoigner. **in** ~, en vue.

**evident** a. évident. ~**ly** adv. de toute évidence.

**evil** a. mauvais. ● n. mal m.

**evoke** v.t. évoquer.

**evolution** n. évolution f.

**evolve** v.i. se développer, évoluer. ● v.t. développer.

**ewe** n. brebis f.

**ex-** pref. ex-, ancien.

**exacerbate** v.t. exacerber.

**exact**[1] a. exact. ~**ly** adv. exactement.

**exact**[2] v.t. exiger (**from,** de). ~**ing** a. exigeant.

**exaggerat**|**e** v.t./i. exagérer. ~**ion** n. exagération f.

**exalted** a. (in rank) de haut rang; (ideal) élevé.

**exam** n. (fam.) examen m.

**examination** n. examen m.

**examine** v.t. examiner; (witness etc.) interroger.

**example** n. exemple m. **for** ~, par exemple.

**exasperat**|**e** v.t. exaspérer. ~**ion** n. exaspération f.

**excavat**|**e** v.t. creuser; (uncover) déterrer. ~**ions** n. pl. (archaeol.) fouilles f. pl.

**exceed** v.t. dépasser. ~**ingly** adv. extrêmement.

**excellen**|**t** a. excellent. ~**ce** n. excellence f.

**except** prep. sauf, excepté. ● v.t. excepter. ~ **for,** à part. ~**ing** prep. sauf, excepté.

**exception** n. exception f.

**exceptional** a. exceptionnel. ~**ly** adv. exceptionnellement.

**excerpt** n. extrait m.

**excess**[1] n. excès m.

**excess**[2] a. excédentaire. ~ **fare,** supplément m. ~ **luggage,** excédent de bagages m.

**excessive** a. excessif. ~**ly** adv. excessivement.

**exchange** v.t. échanger. ● n. échange m.; (between currencies) change m. ~ **rate,** taux d'échange m. (**telephone**) ~, central (téléphonique) m.

**excit**|**e** v.t. exciter; (enthuse) enthousiasmer. ~**able** a. excitable. ~**ed** a. excité. ~**ement** n. excitation f. ~**ing** a. passionnant.

**exclaim** v.t./i. s'écrier.

**exclamation** n. exclamation f. ~ **mark** or **point** (Amer.), point d'exclamation m.

**exclu**|**de** v.t. exclure. ~**sion** n. exclusion f.

**exclusive** a. (rights etc.) exclusif; (club etc.) sélect; (news item) en exclusivité. ~**ly** adv. exclusivement.

**excruciating** a. atroce.

**excursion** n. excursion f.

**excuse**[1] v.t. excuser. ~ **me!,** excusez-moi!, pardon!

**excuse**[2] n. excuse f.

**execute** v.t. exécuter.

**execution** n. exécution f. ~**er** n. bourreau m.

**executive** n. (pouvoir) exécutif m.; (person) cadre m. ● a. exécutif.

**exemplary** a. exemplaire.

**exemplify** v.t. illustrer.

**exempt** a. exempt (**from,** de). ● v.t. exempter. ~**ion** n. exemption f.

**exercise** n. exercice m. ● v.t. exercer; (restraint, patience) faire preuve de. ● v.i. prendre de l'exercice. ~ **book,** cahier m.

**exert** v.t. exercer. ~ **o.s.,** faire des efforts. ~**ion** n. effort m.

**exhaust** v.t. épuiser. ● n. (auto.) (pot d')échappement m. ~**ed** a. épuisé. ~**ion** n. épuisement m.

**exhibit** v.t. exposer; (fig.) faire preuve de. ● n. objet exposé m. ~**or** n. exposant(e) m. (f.).

**exhibition** n. exposition f.

**exhilarating** a. euphorisant.

**exile** n. exil m.; (person) exilé(e) m. (f.). ● v.t. exiler.

**exist** v.i. exister. ~**ence** n. existence f. **be in** ~**ence,** exister. ~**ing** a. actuel.

**exit** n. sortie f. ● v.t./i. (comput.) sortir (de).

**exodus** n. exode m.

**exonerate** v.t. disculper.

**exotic** a. exotique.

**expan**|**d** v.t./i. (develop) (se) développer; (extend) (s')étendre; (metal, liquid) (se) dilater. ~**sion** n. développement m.; dilatation f.

**expanse** n. étendue f.

**expatriate** a. & n. expatrié(e) (m. (f.)).

**expect** v.t. attendre, s'attendre à; (suppose) supposer; (demand) exiger; (baby) attendre. ~ **to do,** compter faire. ~**ation** n. attente f.

**expectant** a. ~ **look,** air d'attente m. ~ **mother,** future maman f.

**expedient** a. opportun. ● n. expédient m.

**expedition** n. expédition f.

**expel** v.t. expulser; (from school) renvoyer.

**expendable** a. remplaçable.

**expenditure** n. dépense(s) f. (pl.).

**expense** n. dépense f.; frais m. pl. **at s.o.'s ~,** aux dépens de qn.

**expensive** a. cher, coûteux; (*tastes, habits*) de luxe. **~ly** adv. coûteusement.

**experience** n. expérience f.; (*adventure*) aventure f. ● v.t. (*undergo*) connaître; (*feel*) éprouver. **~d** a. expérimenté.

**experiment** n. expérience f. ● v.i. faire une expérience. **~al** a. expérimental.

**expert** n. expert(e) m. (f.). ● a. expert. **~ly** adv. habilement.

**expertise** n. compétence f. (**in,** en).

**expir|e** v.i. expirer. **~ed** a. périmé. **~y** n. expiration f.

**expl|ain** v.t. expliquer. **~anation** n. explication f.

**explicit** a. explicite.

**explo|de** v.t./i. (faire) exploser. **~sion** n. explosion f. **~sive** a. & n. explosif (m.).

**exploit**[1] n. exploit m.

**exploit**[2] v.t. exploiter. **~ation** n. exploitation f.

**explor|e** v.t. explorer; (*fig.*) examiner. **~ation** n. exploration f. **~er** n. explora|teur, -trice m., f.

**export**[1] v.t. exporter. **~er** n. exportateur m.

**export**[2] n. exportation f.

**expos|e** /ɪk'spəʊz/ v.t. exposer; (*disclose*) dévoiler. **~ure** n. exposition f.; (*photo.*) pose f.

**express**[1] a. formel, exprès; (*letter*) exprès invar. ● adv. (*by express post*) (par) exprès. ● n. (*train*) rapide m.; (*less fast*) express m.

**express**[2] v.t. exprimer. **~ion** n. expression f.

**expressway** n. voie express f.

**expulsion** n. expulsion f.; (*from school*) renvoi m.

**exten|d** v.t. (*increase*) étendre, agrandir; (*arm, leg*) étendre; (*prolong*) prolonger; (*house*) agrandir; (*grant*) offrir. ● v.i. (*stretch*) s'étendre; (*in time*) se prolonger. **~sion** n. (*of line, road*) prolongement m.; (*in time*) prolongation f.; (*building*) annexe f.; (*of phone*) appareil supplémentaire m.; (*phone number*) poste m.; (*cable, hose, etc.*) rallonge f.

**extensive** a. vaste; (*study*) profond; (*damage etc.*) important. **~ly** adv. (*much*) beaucoup; (*very*) très.

**extent** n. (*size, scope*) étendue f.; (*degree*) mesure f. **to some ~,** dans une certaine mesure.

**exterior** a. & n. extérieur (m.).

**exterminate** v.t. exterminer.

**external** a. extérieur; (*cause, medical use*) externe. **~ly** adv. extérieurement.

**extinct** a. (*species*) disparu; (*volcano, passion*) éteint. **~ion** n. extinction f.

**extinguish** v.t. éteindre. **~er** n. extincteur m.

**extol** v.t. exalter, chanter les louanges de.

**extort** v.t. extorquer (**from,** à).

**extra** a. de plus, supplémentaire. ● adv. plus (que d'habitude). ● n. (*additional thing*) supplément m.; (*cinema*) figurant(e) m. (f.). **~ charge,** supplément m.

**extra-** pref. extra-.

**extract**[1] v.t. extraire; (*promise, tooth*) arracher; (*fig.*) obtenir. **~ion** n. extraction f.

**extract**[2] n. extrait m.

**extradite** v.t. extrader.

**extraordinary** a. extraordinaire.

**extravagan|t** a. extravagant; (*wasteful*) prodigue. **~ce** n. extravagance f.; prodigalité f.

**extrem|e** a. & n. extrême (m.). **~ely** adv. extrêmement. **~ist** n. extrémiste m./f.

**extremity** n. extrémité f.

**extricate** v.t. dégager.

**exuberan|t** a. exubérant. **~ce** n. exubérance f.

**exude** v.t. (*charm etc.*) dégager.

**exult** v.i. exulter.

**eye** n. œil m. (pl. yeux). ● v.t. regarder. **keep an ~ on,** surveiller. **~-shadow** n. ombre à paupières f.

**eyeball** n. globe oculaire m.

**eyebrow** n. sourcil m.

**eyeful** n. **get an ~,** (*fam.*) se rincer l'œil.

**eyelash** n. cil m.

**eyelid** n. paupière f.

**eyesight** n. vue f.

**eyesore** n. horreur f.

**eyewitness** n. témoin oculaire m.

••••••••••••••••••••••••••••••••••••••••

# Ff

••••••••••••••••••••••••••••••••••••••••

**fabric** n. (*cloth*) tissu m.

**fabrication** n. (*invention*) invention f.

**fabulous** a. fabuleux; (*marvellous: fam.*) formidable.

**façade** n. façade f.

**face** n. visage m., figure f.; (*aspect*) face f.; (*of clock*) cadran m. ● v.t. être en face de; (*risk*) devoir affronter; (*confront*) faire face à, affronter. ● v.i. se tourner; (*of house*) être exposé. **~ to face,** face à face. **~ up/down,** tourné vers le haut/bas. **~ up to,** faire face à. **in the ~ of, ~d with,** face à.

**facet** n. facette f.

**facetious** a. facétieux.

**facial** a. de la face, facial. ● n. soin du visage m.

**facile** a. facile, superficiel.

**facilitate** v.t. faciliter.

**facilit|y** n. facilité f. **~ies,** (equipment) équipements m. pl.

**facing** n. parement m. ● prep. en face de. ● a. en face.

**facsimile** n. facsimilé m. **~ transmission,** télécopiage m.

**fact** n. fait m. **in ~,** en fait.

**faction** n. faction f.

**factor** n. facteur m.

**factory** n. usine f.

**factual** a. basé sur les faits.

**faculty** n. faculté f.

**fad** n. manie f., folie f.

**fade** v.i. (sound) s'affaiblir; (memory) s'évanouir; (flower) se faner; (material) déteindre; (colour) passer.

**fag** n. (chore: fam.) corvée f.; (cigarette: sl.) sèche f.

**fail** v.i. échouer; (grow weak) (s'af)faiblir; (run short) manquer; (engine etc.) tomber en panne. ● v.t. (exam) échouer à; (candidate) refuser, recaler; (disappoint) décevoir. **~ to do,** (not do) ne pas faire; (not be able) ne pas réussir à faire. **without ~,** à coup sûr.

**failing** n. défaut m. ● prep. à défaut de.

**failure** n. échec m.; (person) raté(e) m. (f.); (breakdown) panne f.

**faint** a. léger, faible. ● v.i. s'évanouir. ● n. évanouissement m. **feel ~,** (ill) se trouver mal. **~ly** adv. (weakly) faiblement; (slightly) légèrement.

**fair**[1] n. foire f. **~-ground** n. champ de foire m.

**fair**[2] a. (hair, person) blond; (skin etc.) clair; (just) juste, équitable; (weather) beau; (amount, quality) raisonnable. ● adv. (play) loyalement. **~ly** adv. (justly) équitablement; (rather) assez. **~ness** n. justice f.

**fairy** n. fée f. **~ story, ~ tale** n. conte de fées m.

**faith** n. foi. f.

**faithful** a. fidèle. **~ly** adv. fidèlement.

**fake** n. (forgery) faux m.; (person) imposteur m. ● a. faux. ● v.t. (copy) faire un faux de; (alter) falsifier, truquer; (illness) simuler.

**falcon** n. faucon m.

**fall** v.i. tomber. ● n. chute f.; (autumn: Amer.) automne m. **~ back on,** se rabattre sur. **~ behind,** prendre du retard. **~ down or off,** tomber. **~ off,** (decrease) diminuer. **~ out,** se brouiller (with, avec). **~ out** n. retombées f. pl. **~ over,** tomber (par terre). **~ through,** (plans) tomber à l'eau.

**fallacy** n. erreur f.

**fallible** a. faillible.

**false** a. faux. **~ly** adv. faussement.

**falsetto** n. fausset m.

**falsify** v.t. falsifier.

**falter** v.i. vaciller; (nerve) faire défaut.

**fame** n. renommée f.

**familiar** a. familier. **be ~ with,** connaître. **~ity** n. familiarité f. **~ize** v.t. familiariser.

**family** n. famille f.

**famine** n. famine f.

**famished** a. affamé.

**famous** a. célèbre.

**fan**[1] n. ventilateur m.; (hand-held) éventail m. ● v.t. éventer; (fig.) attiser. **~ belt,** courroie de ventilateur f.

**fan**[2] n. (of person) fan m./f., admirateur, -trice m., f.; (enthusiast) fervent(e) m. (f.), passionné(e) m. (f.).

**fanatic** n. fanatique m./f. **~al** a. fanatique.

**fanciful** a. fantaisiste.

**fancy** n. (whim, fantasy) fantaisie f.; (liking) goût m. ● a. (buttons etc.) fantaisie invar.; (prices) extravagant; (impressive) impressionnant. ● v.t. s'imaginer; (want: fam.) avoir envie de; (like: fam.) aimer. **~ dress,** déguisement m.

**fanfare** n. fanfare f.

**fang** n. (of dog etc.) croc m.; (of snake) crochet m.

**fanlight** n. imposte f.

**fantastic** a. fantastique.

**fantasy** n. fantaisie f.; (day-dream) fantasme m.

**far** adv. loin; (much) beaucoup; (very) très. ● a. lointain; (end, side) autre. **~ away, ~ off,** au loin. **as ~ as,** (up to) jusqu'à. **~-away** a. lointain. **by ~,** de loin. **~ from,** loin de. **the Far East,** l'Extrême-Orient m. **~-fetched** a. bizarre, exagéré.

**farce** n. farce f.

**fare** n. (prix du) billet m.; (food) nourriture f. ● v.i. (progress) aller; (manage) se débrouiller.

**farewell** int. & n. adieu (m.).

**farm** n. ferme f. ● v.t. cultiver. ● v.i. être fermier. **~ worker,** ouvrier, -ère agricole m., f. **~er** n. fermier m. **~ing** n. agriculture f.

**farmhouse** n. ferme f.

**farmyard** n. basse-cour f.

**fart** v.i. péter. ● n. pet m.

**farth|er** adv. plus loin. ● a. plus éloigné. **~est** adv. le plus loin; a. le plus éloigné.

**fascinate** v.t. fasciner. **~ion** n. fascination f.

**Fascis|t** n. fasciste m./f. **~m** n. fascisme m.

**fashion** n. (current style) mode f.; (manner) façon f. **~ designer,** styliste m./f. **in ~,** à la mode. **out of ~,** démodé.

**fast**[1] a. rapide; (colour) grand teint invar., fixe; (firm) fixe, solide. ● adv. vite; (firmly) ferme. **be ~,** (clock etc.) avancer.

**fast**[2] v.i. (go without food) jeûner. ● n. jeûne m.

**fasten** v.t./i. (s')attacher. **~er** n. fermeture f.

**fastidious** a. difficile.

**fat** n. graisse f.; (on meat) gras m. ● a. gros, gras; (meat) gras; (sum, volume: fig.) gros.

**fatal** *a.* mortel; (*fateful, disastrous*) fatal. ~ity *n.* mort *m.* ~ly *adv.* mortellement.

**fate** *n.* (*controlling power*) destin *m.*, sort *m.*; (*one's lot*) sort *m.*

**father** *n.* père *m.* ~-in-law *n.* beau-père *m.*

**fathom** *n.* brasse *f.* ● *v.t.* ~ (out), comprendre.

**fatigue** *n.* fatigue *f.* ● *v.t.* fatiguer.

**fatten** *v.t./i.* engraisser. ~ing *a.* qui fait grossir.

**fatty** *a.* gras; (*tissue*) adipeux.

**fatuous** *a.* stupide.

**fault** *n.* (*defect, failing*) défaut *m.*; (*blame*) faute *f.*; (*geol.*) faille *f.* **at** ~, fautif. **find** ~ **with**, critiquer. ~y *a.* défectueux.

**fauna** *n.* faune *f.*

**favour** faveur *f.* ● *v.t.* favoriser; (*support*) être en faveur de; (*prefer*) préférer. **do s.o. a** ~, rendre service à qn. **in** ~ **of**, pour. ~able *a.* favorable. ~ably *adv.* favorablement.

**favourite** *a. & n.* favori(te) (*m.* (*f.*)).

**fawn**[1] *n.* faon *m.* ● *a.* fauve.

**fawn**[2] *v.i.* ~ **on**, flatter bassement, flagorner.

**fax** *n.* fax *m.*, télécopie *f.* ● *v.t.* faxer, envoyer par télécopie. ~ **machine**, télécopieur *m.*

**fear** *n.* crainte *f.*, peur *f.*; (*fig.*) risque *m.* ● *v.t.* craindre. ~ful *a.* (*terrible*) affreux; (*timid*) craintif. ~less *a.* intrépide.

**fearsome** *a.* redoutable.

**feasib|le** *a.* faisable; (*likely*) plausible. ~ility *n.* possibilité *f.*; plausibilité *f.*

**feast** *n.* festin *m.*; (*relig.*) fête *f.*

**feat** *n.* exploit *m.*

**feather** *n.* plume *f.*

**feature** *n.* caractéristique *f.*; (*of person, face*) trait *m.*; (*film*) long métrage *m.*; (*article*) article vedette *m.* ● *v.t.* représenter; (*give prominence to*) mettre en vedette. ● *v.i.* figurer (**in**, dans).

**February** *n.* février *m.*

**feckless** *a.* inepte.

**fed** *a.* **be** ~ **up**, (*fam.*) en avoir marre (**with**, de).

**federa|l** *a.* fédéral. ~tion *n.* fédération *f.*

**fee** *n.* (*for entrance*) prix *m.* ~(s), (*of doctor etc.*) honoraires *m. pl.*; (*of actor, artist*) cachet *m.*; (*for tuition*) frais *m. pl.*; (*for enrolment*) droits *m. pl.*

**feeble** *a.* faible.

**feed** *v.t.* (*p.t.* **fed**) nourrir, donner à manger à; (*suckle*) allaiter; (*supply*) alimenter. ● *v.i.* se nourrir (**on**, de). ● *n.* nourriture *f.*; (*of baby*) tétée *f.* ~ **in information**, rentrer des données. ~er *n.* alimentation *f.*

**feedback** *n.* réaction(s) *f.* (*pl.*); (*med., techn.*) feed-back *m.*

**feel** *v.t.* (*touch*) tâter; (*be conscious of*) sentir; (*emotion*) ressentir; (*experience*) éprouver; (*think*) estimer. ● *v.i.* (*tired, lonely, etc.*) se sentir. ~ **hot/thirsty/***etc.*, avoir chaud/soif/

*etc.* ~ **as if**, avoir l'impression que. ~ **awful**, (*ill*) se sentir malade. ~ **like**, (*want: fam.*) avoir envie de.

**feeler** *n.* antenne *f.* **put out a** ~, lancer un ballon d'essai.

**feeling** *n.* sentiment *m.*; (*physical*) sensation *f.*

**feign** *v.t.* feindre.

**feint** *n.* feinte *f.*

**feline** *a.* félin.

**fell** *v.t.* (*cut down*) abattre.

**fellow** *n.* compagnon *m.*, camarade *m.*; (*man: fam.*) type *m.* ~-**countryman** *n.* compatriote *m.* ~-**traveller** *n.* compagnon de voyage *m.*

**felony** *n.* crime *m.*

**felt** *n.* feutre *m.* ~-**tip** *n.* feutre *m.*

**female** *a.* (*animal etc.*) femelle; (*voice, sex, etc.*) féminin. ● *n.* femme *f.*; (*animal*) femelle *f.*

**feminine** *a. & n.* féminin (*m.*).

**feminist** *n.* féministe *m./f.*

**fenc|e** *n.* barrière *f.*; (*person: jurid.*) receleu|r, -se *m.*, *f.* ● *v.t.* ~ (**in**), clôturer. ● *v.i.* (*sport*) faire de l'escrime. ~er *n.* escrimeu|r, -se *m.*, *f.* ~ing *n.* escrime *f.*

**fend** *v.i.* ~ **for o.s.**, se débrouiller tout seul. ● *v.t.* ~ **off**, (*blow, attack*) parer.

**fender** *n.* (*for fireplace*) garde-feu *m. invar.*; (*mudguard: Amer.*) garde-boue *m. invar.*

**fennel** *n.* (*culin.*) fenouil *m.*

**ferment**[1] *v.t./i.* (faire) fermenter. ~ation *n.* fermentation *f.*

**ferment**[2] *n.* ferment *m.*; (*excitement: fig.*) agitation *f.*

**fern** *n.* fougère *f.*

**feroc|ious** *a.* féroce. ~ity *n.* férocité *f.*

**ferret** *n.* (*animal*) furet *m.* ● *v.i.* (*p.t.* **ferreted**) fureter. ● *v.t.* ~ **out**, dénicher.

**ferry** *n.* ferry *m.*, bac *m.* ● *v.t.* transporter.

**fertil|e** *a.* fertile; (*person, animal*) fécond. ~ity /fəˈtɪlətɪ/ *n.* fertilité *f.*; fécondité *f.*

**fertilizer** *n.* engrais *m.*

**fervent** *a.* fervent.

**fervour** *n.* ferveur *f.*

**festival** *n.* festival *m.*; (*relig.*) fête *f.*

**festiv|e** *a.* de fête, gai. ~ity *n.* réjouissances *f. pl.*

**fetch** *v.t.* (*go for*) aller chercher; (*bring person*) amener; (*bring thing*) apporter; (*be sold for*) rapporter.

**fête** *n.* fête *f.* ● *v.t.* fêter.

**fetid** *a.* fétide.

**fetish** *n.* (*object*) fétiche *m.*; (*psych.*) obsession *f.*

**feud** *n.* querelle *f.*

**feudal** *a.* féodal.

**fever** *n.* fièvre *f.* ~ish *a.* fiévreux.

**few** *a. & n.* peu (de). ~ **books,** peu de livres. **a ~** *a.* quelques; *n.* quelques-un(e)s. **quite a ~,** (*fam.*) bon nombre (de). ~**er** *a. & n.* moins (de). **be ~er,** être moins nombreux (**than,** que). ~**est** *a. & n.* le moins (de).

**fiancé** *n.* fiancé *m.*

**fiancée** *n.* fiancée *f.*

**fiasco** *n.* fiasco *m.*

**fib** *n.* mensonge *m.* ~**ber** *n.* menteu|r, -se *m.*, *f.*

**fibre** *n.* fibre *f.* ~ **optics,** fibres optiques.

**fibreglass,** *n.* fibre de verre *f.*

**fickle** *a.* inconstant.

**fiction** *n.* fiction *f.* **(works of) ~,** romans *m. pl.* ~**al** *a.* fictif.

**fictitious** *a.* fictif.

**fiddle** *n.* (*fam.*) violon *m.*; (*swindle: sl.*) combine *f.* ● *v.i.* (*sl.*) frauder. ● *v.t.* (*sl.*) falsifier. ~ **with,** (*fam.*) tripoter. ~**r** *n.* (*fam.*) violoniste *m./f.*

**fidelity** *n.* fidélité *f.*

**fidget** *v.i.* remuer sans cesse. ● *n.* **be a ~,** être remuant. ~ **with,** tripoter. ~**y** *a.* remuant.

**field** *n.* champ *m.*; (*sport*) terrain *m.*; (*fig.*) domaine *m.* ● *v.t.* (*ball: cricket*) bloquer.

**fieldwork** *n.* travaux pratiques *m. pl.*

**fiend** *n.* démon *m.*

**fierce** *a.* féroce; (*storm, attack*) violent. ~**ness** *n.* férocité *f.*; violence *f.*

**fiery** *a.* (*hot*) ardent; (*spirited*) fougueux.

**fiesta** *n.* fiesta *f.*

**fifteen** *a. & n.* quinze (*m.*). ~**th** *a. & n.* quinzième (*m./f.*).

**fifth** *a. & n.* cinquième (*m./f.*).

**fift|y** *a. & n.* cinquante (*m.*). ~**ieth** *a. & n.* cinquantième (*m./f.*). **a ~y-fifty chance,** (*equal*) une chance sur deux.

**fig** *n.* figue *f.*

**fight** *v.i.* se battre; (*struggle: fig.*) lutter; (*quarrel*) se disputer. ● *v.t.* se battre avec; (*evil etc.: fig.*) lutter contre. ● *n.* (*struggle*) lutte *f.*; (*quarrel*) dispute *f.*; (*brawl*) bagarre *f.*; (*mil.*) combat *m.* ~ **over sth.,** se disputer qch. ~**er** *n.* (*brawler, soldier*) combattant *m.*; (*fig.*) battant *m.*; (*aircraft*) chasseur *m.* ~**ing** *n.* combats *m. pl.*

**figment** *n.* invention *f.*

**figure** *n.* (*number*) chiffre *m.*; (*diagram*) figure *f.*; (*shape*) forme *f.*; (*body*) ligne *f.* ● *v.t.* s'imaginer. ● *v.i.* (*appear*) figurer. ~ **out,** comprendre.

**filament** *n.* filament *m.*

**filch** *v.t.* voler, piquer.

**file**[1] *n.* (*tool*) lime *f.* ● *v.t.* limer.

**file**[2] *n.* dossier *m.*, classeur *m.*; (*comput.*) fichier *m.*; (*row*) file *f.* ● *v.t.* (*papers*) classer; (*jurid.*) déposer. ● *v.i.* ~**e in,** entrer en file. ~**ing cabinet,** classeur *m.*

**fill** *v.t./i.* (se) remplir. ~ **in** *or* **up,** (*form*) remplir. ~ **out,** (*get fat*) grossir. ~ **up,** (*auto.*) faire le plein (d'essence).

**fillet** *n.* filet *m.* ● *v.t.* découper en filets.

**filling** *n.* (*of tooth*) plombage *m.*; (*of sandwich*) garniture *f.* ~ **station,** station-service *f.*

**filly** *n.* pouliche *f.*

**film** *n.* film *m.*; (*photo.*) pellicule *f.* ● *v.t.* filmer. ~ **star,** vedette de cinéma *f.*

**filter** *n.* filtre *m.*; (*traffic signal*) flèche *f.* ● *v.t./ i.* filtrer; (*of traffic*) suivre la flèche. ~ **coffee,** café-filtre *m.* ~**tip** *n.* bout filtre *m.*

**filth,** ~**iness** *n.* saleté *f.* ~**y** *a.* sale.

**fin** *n.* (*of fish, seal*) nageoire *f.*; (*of shark*) aileron *m.*

**final** *a.* dernier; (*conclusive*) définitif. ● *n.* (*sport*) finale *f.* ~**ist** *n.* finaliste *m./f.* ~**ly** *adv.* (*lastly, at last*) enfin, finalement; (*once and for all*) définitivement.

**finale** *n.* (*mus.*) final(e) *m.*

**finalize** *v.t.* mettre au point.

**finance** *n.* finance *f.* ● *a.* financier. ● *v.t.* financer.

**financial** *a.* financier. ~**ly** *adv.* financièrement.

**find** *v.t.* trouver; (*sth. lost*) retrouver. ● *n.* trouvaille *f.* ~ **out** *v.t.* découvrir; *v.i.* se renseigner (**about,** sur). ~**ings** *n. pl.* conclusions *f. pl.*

**fine**[1] *n.* amende *f.* ● *v.t.* condamner à une amende.

**fine**[2] *a.* fin; (*excellent*) beau. ● *adv.* (*très*) bien; (*small*) fin. ~**ly** *adv.* (*admirably*) magnifiquement; (*cut*) fin.

**finesse** *n.* finesse *f.*

**finger** *n.* doigt *m.* ● *v.t.* palper. ~**nail** *n.* ongle *m.*

**fingerprint** *n.* empreinte digitale *f.*

**fingertip** *n.* bout du doigt *m.*

**finish** *v.t./i.* finir. ● *n.* fin *f.*; (*of race*) arrivée *f.*; (*appearance*) finition *f.* ~ **doing,** finir de faire. ~ **up doing,** finir par faire. ~ **up in,** (*land up in*) se retrouver à.

**finite** *a.* fini.

**Fin|land** *n.* finlande *f.* ~**n** *n.* finlandais(e) *m.* (*f.*). ~**nish** *a.* finlandais; *n.* (*lang.*) finnois *m.*

**fir** *n.* sapin *m.*

**fire** *n.* feu *m.*; (*conflagration*) incendie *m.*; (*heater*) radiateur *m.* ● *v.t.* (*bullet etc.*) tirer; (*dismiss*) renvoyer. ● *v.i.* tirer (**at,** sur). ~ **a gun,** tirer un coup de revolver *or* de fusil. **set ~ to,** mettre le feu à. ~ **alarm,** avertisseur d'incendie *m.* ~ **brigade,** pompiers *m. pl.* ~ **engine** *n.* voiture de pompiers *f.* ~**escape** *n.* escalier de secours *m.* ~ **extinguisher,** extincteur d'incendie *m.*

**fireman** *n.* pompier *m.*

**fireplace** *n.* cheminée *f.*

**firewood** *n.* bois de chauffage *m.*

**firework** *n.* feu d'artifice *m.*

**firm**[1] *n.* firme *f.*, société *f.*

**firm**[2] *a.* ferme; (*belief*) solide. ~**ly** *adv.* fermement. ~**ness** *n.* fermeté *f.*

**first** *a.* premier. ● *n.* prem|ier, -ière *m.*, *f.*
● *adv.* d'abord, premièrement; (*arrive etc.*) le
premier, la première. **at ~**, d'abord. **~ aid**,
premiers soins *m. pl.* **~class** *a.* de première
classe. **~ (gear)**, première (vitesse) *f.* **~
name**, prénom *m.* **~ of all**, tout d'abord. **~-
rate** *a.* de premier ordre. **~ly** *adv.*
premièrement.

**fiscal** *a.* fiscal.

**fish** *n.* (*usually invar.*) poisson *m.* ● *v.i.*
pêcher. **~ for**, (*cod etc.*) pêcher. **~ out**, (*from
water*) repêcher; (*take out: fam.*) sortir. **~
shop**, poissonnerie *f.* **~ing** *n.* pêche *f.* **go
~ing**, aller à la pêche. **~ing rod**, canne à
pêche *f.*

**fisherman** *n. n.* pêcheur *m.*

**fishmonger** *n.* poissonn|ier, -ière *m.*, *f.*

**fission** *n.* fission *f.*

**fist** *n.* poing *m.*

**fit**[1] *n.* (*bout*) accès *m.*, crise *f.*

**fit**[2] *a.* en bonne santé; (*proper*) convenable;
(*good enough*) bon; (*able*) capable. ● *v.t./i.*
(*clothes*) aller (à); (*match*) s'accorder (avec);
(*put or go in or on*) (s')adapter (**to**, à); (*into
space*) aller; (*install*) poser. **~ in**, *v.t.* caser;
*v.i.* (*newcomer*) s'intégrer. **~ out**, **~ up**, équiper. **~ness** *n.* santé *f.*

**fitful** *a.* irrégulier.

**fitment** *n.* meuble fixe *m.*

**fitted** *a.* (*wardrobe*) encastré. **~ carpet**,
moquette *f.*

**fitting** *a.* approprié. **~ room**, cabine
d'essayage *f.*

**fittings** *n. pl.* (*in house*) installations *f. pl.*

**five** *a.* & *n.* cinq (*m.*).

**fiver** *n.* (*fam.*) billet de cinq livres *m.*

**fix** *v.t.* (*make firm, attach, decide*) fixer; (*mend*)
réparer; (*deal with*) arranger. **~ s.o. up with
sth.**, trouver qch. à qn. **~ed** *a.* fixe.

**fixation** *n.* fixation *f.*

**fixture** *n.* (*sport*) match *m.* **~s**, (*in house*)
installations *f. pl.*

**fizz** *v.i.* pétiller. ● *n.* pétillement *m.* **~y** *a.*
gazeux.

**fizzle** *v.i.* **~ out**, (*plan etc.*) finir en queue de
poisson.

**flab** *n.* (*fam.*) corpulence *f.* **~by** *a.* flasque.

**flabbergast** *v.t.* sidérer.

**flag**[1] *n.* drapeau *m.*; (*naut.*) pavillon *m.* **~-pole**
*n.* mât *m.*

**flag**[2] *v.i.* (*weaken*) faiblir; (*sick person*)
s'affaiblir; (*droop*) dépérir.

**flagrant** *a.* flagrant.

**flagstone** *n.* dalle *f.*

**flair** *n.* flair *m.*

**flak** *n.* (*fam.*) critiques *f. pl.*

**flak|e** *n.* flocon *m.*; (*of paint, metal*) écaille *f.*
● *v.i.* s'écailler. **~y** *a.* (*paint*) écailleux.

**flamboyant** *a.* (*colour*) éclatant; (*manner*)
extravagant.

**flame** *n.* flamme *f.* ● *v.i.* flamber.

**flamingo** *n.* flamant (rose) *m.*

**flammable** *a.* inflammable.

**flan** *n.* tarte *f.*; (*custard tart*) flan *m.*

**flank** *n.* flanc *m.* ● *v.t.* flanquer.

**flannel** *n.* flanelle *f.*; (*for face*) gant de toilette *m.*

**flannelette** *n.* pilou *m.*

**flap** *v.i.* battre. **~ its wings**, battre des
ailes. ● *n.* (*of pocket*) rabat *m.*; (*of table*)
abattant *m.*

**flare** *v.i.* **~ up**, s'enflammer, flamber;
(*fighting*) éclater; (*person*) s'emporter. ● *n.*
flamboiement *m.*; (*mil.*) fusée éclairante *f.*;
(*in skirt*) évasement *m.* **~d** *a.* (*skirt*) évasé.

**flash** *v.i.* briller; (*on and off*) clignoter. ● *v.t.*
faire briller; (*aim torch*) diriger (**at**, sur);
(*flaunt*) étaler. ● *n.* éclair *m.*, éclat *m.*; (*of news,
camera*) flash *m.* **in a ~**, en un éclair. **~ one's
headlights**, faire un appel de phares.

**flashback** *n.* retour en arrière *m.*

**flashlight** *n.* (*torch*) lampe électrique *f.*

**flashy** *a.* voyant.

**flask** *n.* flacon *m.*; (*vacuum flask*) thermos *m.*/
*f. invar.* (P.).

**flat** *a.* plat; (*tyre*) à plat; (*refusal*) catégorique;
(*fare, rate*) fixe. ● *adv.* (*say*) carrément. ● *n.*
(*rooms*) appartement *m.*; (*tyre: fam.*)
crevaison *f.*; (*mus.*) bémol *m.*

**flatten** *v.t./i.* (s')aplatir.

**flatter** *v.t.* flatter. **~er** *n.* flatteu|r, -se *m.*, *f.*
**~ing** *a.* flatteur. **~y** *n.* flatterie *f.*

**flatulence** *n.* flatulence *f.*

**flaunt** *v.t.* étaler, afficher.

**flavour** *n.* goût *m.*; (*of ice-cream etc.*) parfum
*m.* ● *v.t.* parfumer, assaisonner. **~ing** *n.*
arôme synthétique *m.*

**flaw** *n.* défaut *m.* **~ed** *a.* imparfait. **~less** *a.*
parfait.

**flax** *n.* lin *m.* **~en** *a.* de lin.

**flea** *n.* puce *f.*

**fleck** *n.* petite tache *f.*

**flee** *v.i.* s'enfuir. ● *v.t.* s'enfuir de; (*danger*)
fuir.

**fleece** *n.* toison *f.* ● *v.t.* voler.

**fleet** *n.* (*naut., aviat.*) flotte *f.* **a ~ of vehicles**,
un parc automobile.

**Flemish** *a.* flamand. ● *n.* (*lang.*) flamand *m.*

**flesh** *n.* chair *f.*

**flex**[1] *v.t.* (*knee etc.*) fléchir; (*muscle*) faire
jouer.

**flex**[2] *n.* (*electr.*) fil souple *m.*

**flexib|le** *a.* flexible. **~ility** *n.* flexibilité *f.*

**flick** *n.* petit coup *m.* ● *v.t.* donner un petit coup
à.

**flicker** *v.i.* vaciller. ● *n.* vacillement *m.*;
(*light*) lueur *f.*

**flies** *n. pl.* (*on trousers: fam.*) braguette *f.*

**flight** n. ( *of bird, plane, etc.* ) vol m. ∼ **of stairs,** escalier m.

**flimsy** a. ( *pej.* ) peu solide.

**flinch** v.i. ( *wince* ) broncher; ( *draw back* ) reculer.

**fling** v.t. jeter. ● n. **have a** ∼, faire la fête.

**flint** n. silex m.; ( *for lighter* ) pierre f.

**flip** v.t. donner un petit coup à. ● n. chiquenaude f. ∼ **through,** feuilleter. ∼ **flops** n. pl. tongs f. pl.

**flipper** n. ( *of seal etc.* ) nageoire f.; ( *of swimmer* ) palme f.

**flirt** v.i. flirter. ● n. flirteu|r, -se m., f. ∼**ation** n. flirt n.

**float** v.t./i. (faire) flotter. ● n. flotteur m.; ( *cart* ) char m.

**flock** n. ( *of sheep etc.* ) troupeau m.; ( *of people* ) foule f.

**flog** v.t. ( *beat* ) fouetter; ( *sell: sl.* ) vendre.

**flood** n. inondation f.; ( *fig.* ) flot m. ● v.t. inonder. ● v.i. ( *building etc.* ) être inondé; ( *river* ) déborder; ( *people: fig.* ) affluer.

**floodlight** n. projecteur m.

**floor** n. sol m., plancher m.; ( *storey* ) étage m. ● v.t. ( *knock down* ) terrasser.

**flop** v.i. ( *drop* ) s'affaler; ( *fail: sl.* ) échouer. ● n. ( *sl.* ) échec m., fiasco m. ∼**py** a. lâche, flasque. ∼**py (disk),** disquette f.

**flora** n. flore f.

**floral** a. floral.

**florist** n. fleuriste m./f.

**flounce** n. volant m.

**flounder** v.i. patauger (avec difficulté).

**flour** n. farine f. ∼**y** a. farineux.

**flourish** v.i. prospérer. ● v.t. brandir. ● n. geste élégant m.; ( *curve* ) fioriture f.

**flout** v.t. faire fi de.

**flow** v.i. couler; ( *circulate* ) circuler; ( *traffic* ) s'écouler; ( *hang loosely* ) flotter. ● n. ( *of liquid, traffic* ) écoulement m.; ( *of tide* ) flux m.; ( *of orders, words: fig.* ) flot m. ∼ **chart,** organigramme m.

**flower** n. fleur f. ● v.i. fleurir. ∼**-bed** n. plate-bande f. ∼**ed** a. à fleurs. ∼**y** a. fleuri.

**flu** n. ( *fam.* ) grippe f.

**fluctuat|e** v.i. varier. ∼**ion** n. variation f.

**flue** n. ( *duct* ) tuyau m.

**fluent** a. ( *style* ) aisé. **be** ∼ **(in a language),** parler (une langue) couramment. ∼**ly** adv. avec facilité; ( *lang.* ) couramment.

**fluff** n. peluche(s) f. ( *pl.* ); ( *down* ) duvet m. ∼**y** a. pelucheux.

**fluid** a. & n. fluide ( *m.* ).

**fluke** n. coup de chance m.

**fluorescent** a. fluorescent.

**fluoride** n. ( *in toothpaste, water* ) fluor m.

**flurry** n. ( *squall* ) rafale f.; ( *fig.* ) agitation f.

**flush**[1] v.i. rougir. ● v.t. nettoyer à grande eau. ● n. ( *blush* ) rougeur f.; ( *fig.* ) excitation f. ● a. ∼ **with,** ( *level with* ) au ras de. ∼ **the toilet,** tirer la chasse d'eau.

**flush**[2] v.t. ∼ **out,** chasser.

**fluster** v.t. énerver.

**flute** n. flûte f.

**flutter** v.i. voleter; ( *of wings* ) battre. ● n. ( *of wings* ) battement m.; ( *fig.* ) agitation f.; ( *bet: fam.* ) pari m.

**fly**[1] n. mouche f.

**fly**[2] v.i. voler; ( *of passengers* ) voyager en avion; ( *of flag* ) flotter; ( *rush* ) filer. ● v.t. ( *aircraft* ) piloter; ( *passengers, goods* ) transporter par avion; ( *flag* ) arborer. ● n. ( *of trousers* ) braguette f. ∼ **off,** s'envoler.

**flying** a. ( *saucer etc.* ) volant. ● n. ( *activity* ) aviation f.

**flyover** n. ( *road* ) toboggan m.

**foal** n. poulain m.

**foam** n. écume f., mousse f. ● v.i. écumer, mousser. ∼**(rubber)** n. caoutchouc mousse m.

**fob** v.t. ∼ **off on (to) s.o.,** ( *palm off* ) refiler à qn. ∼ **s.o. off with,** forcer qn. à se contenter de.

**focal** a. focal.

**focus** n. foyer m.; ( *fig.* ) centre m. ● v.t./i. (faire) converger; ( *instrument* ) mettre au point; ( *with camera* ) faire la mise au point ( **on,** sur); ( *fig.* ) (se) concentrer. **be in/out of** ∼, être/ne pas être au point.

**fodder** n. fourrage m.

**foe** n. ennemi(e) m.(f.).

**foetus** n. fœtus m.

**fog** n. brouillard m. ● v.t./i. ( *window etc.* ) (s')embuer. ∼**gy** a. brumeux. **it is** ∼**gy,** il fait du brouillard.

**foil** n. ( *tin foil* ) papier d'aluminium m.; ( *fig.* ) repoussoir m.

**foist** v.t. imposer ( **on,** à).

**fold** v.t./i. (se) plier; ( *arms* ) croiser; ( *fail* ) s'effondrer. ● n. pli m. ∼**er** n. ( *file* ) chemise f.; ( *leaflet* ) dépliant m. ∼**ing** a. pliant.

**foliage** n. feuillage m.

**folk** n. gens m. pl. ● a. folklorique.

**folklore** n. folklore m.

**follow** v.t./i. suivre. ∼**er** n. partisan m.

**folly** n. sottise f.

**fond** a. ( *loving* ) affectueux; ( *hope* ) cher. **be** ∼ **of,** aimer.

**fondle** v.t. caresser.

**food** n. nourriture f. ● a. alimentaire. **French** ∼, la cuisine française. ∼ **processor,** robot (ménager) m.

**fool** n. idiot(e) m. (f.). ● v.t. duper.

**foolish** a. idiot.

**foot** n. pied m.; ( *measure* ) pied m.; ( *of stairs, page* ) bas m. ● v.t. ( *bill* ) payer. **on** ∼, à pied.

**football** n. ( *ball* ) ballon m.; ( *game* ) football m. ∼ **pools,** paris sur les matchs de football m. pl. ∼**er** n. footballeur m.

**footing** n. prise (de pied) f., équilibre m. **on an equal ~,** sur un pied d'égalité.

**footpath** n. sentier m.; (at the side of the road) chemin m.

**footprint** n. empreinte (de pied) f.

**footstep** n. pas m.

**for** prep. pour; (during) pendant; (before) avant. ● conj. car. **he has been away ~,** il est absent depuis. **he stopped ~ ten minutes,** il s'est arrêté (pendant) dix minutes. **it continues ~ ten kilometres,** ça continue pendant dix kilomètres. **~ ever,** pour toujours. **~ good,** pour de bon.

**forbid** v.t. interdire, défendre (**s.o. to do,** à qn. de faire). **~ s.o. sth.,** interdire or défendre qch. à qn. **you are ~den to leave,** il vous est interdit de partir.

**force** n. force f. ● v.t. forcer. **~ into,** faire entrer de force. **~ on,** imposer à. **come into ~,** entrer en vigueur. **~ful** a. énergique.

**forcibl|e** a., **~y** adv. de force.

**ford** n. gué m. ● v.t. passer à gué.

**fore** a. antérieur. ● n. **to the ~,** en évidence.

**foreboding** n. pressentiment m.

**forecast** v.t. (p.t.) prévoir. ● n. prévision f.

**forecourt** n. (of garage) devant m.; (of station) cour f.

**forefinger** n. index m.

**forefront** n. premier rang m.

**foreground** n. premier plan m.

**forehead** n. front m.

**foreign** a. étranger; (trade) extérieur; (travel) à l'étranger. **~er** n. étranger, -ère m., f.

**foreman** n. contremaître m.

**forename** n. prénom m.

**foreplay** n. préliminaires m. pl.

**forerunner** n. précurseur m.

**foresee** v.t. prévoir. **~able** a. prévisible.

**foreshadow** v.t. présager.

**foresight** n. prévoyance f.

**forest** n. forêt f.

**forestall** v.t. devancer.

**forestry** n. sylviculture f.

**foretaste** n. avant-goût m.

**foretell** v.t. prédire.

**forever** adv. toujours.

**foreword** n. avant-propos m. invar.

**forfeit** n. (penalty) peine f.; (in game) gage m. ● v.t. perdre.

**forge¹** v.i. **~ ahead,** avancer.

**forge²** n. forge f. ● v.t. (metal, friendship) forger; (copy) contrefaire, falsifier. **~r** n. faussaire m. **~ry** n. faux m., contrefaçon f.

**forget** v.t./i. oublier. **~-me-not** n. myosotis m. **~ful** a. distrait.

**forgive** v.t. pardonner (**s.o. for sth.,** qch. à qn.). **~ness** n. pardon m.

**forgo** v.t. renoncer à.

**fork** n. fourchette f.; (for digging etc.) fourche f.; (in road) bifurcation f. ● v.i. (road) bifurquer. **~-lift truck,** chariot élévateur m. **~ out,** (sl.) payer.

**form** n. forme f.; (document) formulaire m.; (schol.) classe f. ● v.t./i. (se) former.

**formal** a. officiel, en bonne et due forme; (person) compassé, cérémonieux; (dress) de cérémonie; (denial, grammar) formel; (language) soutenu. **~ity** n. cérémonial m.; (requirement) formalité f. **~ly** adv. officiellement.

**format** n. format m. ● v.t. (disk) initialiser, formater.

**formation** n. formation f.

**formative** a. formateur.

**former** a. ancien; (first of two) premier. ● n. **the ~,** celui-là, celle-là. **~ly** adv. autrefois.

**formidable** a. redoutable.

**formula** n. formule f.

**formulate** v.t. formuler.

**fort** n. (mil.) fort m.

**forte** n. (talent) fort m.

**forth** adv. en avant. **and so ~,** et ainsi de suite. **go back and ~,** aller et venir.

**forthcoming** a. à venir, prochain; (sociable: fam.) communicatif.

**forthright** a. direct.

**fortify** v.t. fortifier.

**fortnight** n. quinze jours m. pl. **~ly** a. bimensuel; adv. tous les quinze jours.

**fortress** n. forteresse f.

**fortunate** a. heureux. **be ~,** avoir de la chance. **~ly** adv. heureusement.

**fortune** n. fortune f. **~-teller** n. diseuse de bonne aventure f.

**fort|y** a. & n. quarante (m.). **~ieth** a. & n. quarantième (m./f.).

**forum** n. forum m.

**forward** a. en avant; (advanced) précoce; (pert) effronté. ● n. (sport) avant m. ● adv. en avant. ● v.t. (letter) faire suivre; (goods) expédier; (fig.) favoriser. **come ~,** se présenter. **go ~,** avancer.

**forwards** adv. en avant.

**fossil** n. & a. fossile (m.).

**foster** v.t. (promote) encourager; (child) élever. **~-child** n. enfant adoptif m. **~-mother** n. mère adoptive f.

**foul** a. (smell, weather, etc.) infect; (place, action) immonde; (language) ordurier. ● n. (football) faute f. ● v.t. souiller, encrasser. **~ up,** (sl.) gâcher.

**found** v.t. fonder. **~ation** n. fondation f.; (basis) fondement m.; (make-up) fond de teint m. **~er¹** n. fonda|teur, -trice m., f.

**founder²** v.i. sombrer.

**foundry** n. fonderie f.

**fountain** n. fontaine f. **~-pen** n. stylo à encre m.

**four** _a. & n._ quatre (_m._). **~th** _a. & n._ quatrième (_m./f._). **~-wheel drive,** quatre roues motrices; (_car_) quatre-quatre _f._

**fourteen** _a. & n._ quatorze (_m._). **~th** _a. & n._ quatorzième (_m./f._).

**fowl** _n._ volaille _f._

**fox** _n._ renard _m._ ● _v.t._ (_baffle_) mystifier; (_deceive_) tromper.

**foyer** _n._ (_hall_) foyer _m._

**fraction** _n._ fraction _f._

**fracture** _n._ fracture _f._ ● _v.t./i._ (se) fracturer.

**fragile** _a._ fragile.

**fragment** _n._ fragment _m._

**fragran|t** _a._ parfumé. **~ce** _n._ parfum _m._

**frail** _a._ frêle.

**frame** _n._ charpente _f._; (_of picture_) cadre _m._; (_of window_) châssis _m._; (_of spectacles_) monture _f._ ● _v.t._ encadrer; (_fig._) formuler; (_jurid., sl._) monter un coup contre. **~ of mind,** humeur _f._

**framework** _n._ structure _f._; (_context_) cadre _m._

**franc** _n._ franc _m._

**France** _n._ France _f._

**franchise** _n._ (_pol._) droit de vote _m._; (_comm._) franchise _f._

**frank**[1] _a._ franc. **~ly** _adv._ franchement. **~ness** _n._ franchise _f._

**frank**[2] _v.t._ affranchir.

**frantic** _a._ frénétique.

**fraud** _n._ (_deception_) fraude _f._; (_person_) imposteur _m._ **~ulent** _a._ frauduleux.

**fraught** _a._ (_tense_) tendu. **~ with,** chargé de.

**fray**[1] _n._ rixe _f._

**fray**[2] _v.t./i._ (s')effilocher.

**freak** _n._ phénomène _m._ ● _a._ anormal. **~ish** _a._ anormal.

**freckle** _n._ tache de rousseur _f._ **~d** _a._ couvert de taches de rousseur.

**free** _a._ libre; (_gratis_) gratuit; (_lavish_) généreux. ● _v.t._ libérer; (_clear_) dégager. **~ enterprise,** la libre entreprise. **~ kick,** coup franc _m._ **~lance** _a. & n._ free-lance (_m./f._), indépendant(e) _m., f._ **~ (of charge),** gratuit(ement). **~ly** _adv._ librement.

**freedom** /ˈfriːdəm/ _n._ liberté _f._

**freeway** _n._ (_Amer._) autoroute _f._

**freez|e** _v.t./i._ geler; (_wages etc._) bloquer. ● _n._ gel _m._; blocage _m._ **~er** _n._ congélateur _m._ **~ing** _a._ glacial.

**freight** _n._ fret _m._

**French** _a._ français. ● _n._ (_lang._) français _m._ **~ bean,** haricot vert _m._ **~ fries,** frites _f. pl._ **~ window** _n._ porte-fenêtre _f._ **the ~,** les Français _m. pl._ **~man** _n._ Français _m._ **~woman** _n._ Française _f._

**frenz|y** _n._ frénésie _f._ **~ied** _a._ frénétique.

**frequen|t**[1] _a._ fréquent. **~cy** _n._ fréquence _f._ **~tly** _adv._ fréquemment.

**frequent**[2] _v.t._ fréquenter.

**fresco** _n._ fresque _f._

**fresh** _a._ frais; (_different, additional_) nouveau; (_cheeky: fam._) culotté. **~ly** _adv._ nouvellement. **~ness** _n._ fraîcheur _f._

**freshen** _v.i._ **~ up,** (_person_) se rafraîchir.

**fret** _v.i._ se tracasser. **~ful** _a._ insatisfait.

**friction** _n._ friction _f._

**Friday** _n._ vendredi _m._

**fridge** _n._ frigo _m._

**fried** _a._ frit. **~ eggs,** œufs sur le plat _m. pl._

**friend** _n._ ami(e) _m._ (_f._). **~ship** _n._ amitié _f._

**friendl|y** _a._ amical, gentil. **~iness** _n._ gentillesse _f._

**frieze** _n._ frise _f._

**frigate** _n._ frégate _f._

**fright** _n._ peur _f._; (_person, thing_) horreur _f._ **~ful** _a._ affreux. **~fully** _adv._ affreusement.

**frighten** _v.t._ effrayer. **~ off,** faire fuir. **~ed** _a._ effrayé. **be ~ed,** avoir peur (**of,** de). **~ing** _a._ effrayant.

**frill** _n._ (_trimming_) fanfreluche _f._

**fringe** _n._ (_edging, hair_) frange _f._; (_of area_) bordure _f._; (_of society_) marge _f._ **~ benefits,** avantages sociaux _m. pl._

**frisk** _v.t._ (_search_) fouiller.

**frisky** _a._ frétillant.

**fritter**[1] _n._ beignet _m._

**fritter**[2] _v.t._ **~ away,** gaspiller.

**frivol|ous** _a._ frivole. **~ity** _n._ frivolité _f._

**frock** _n._ robe _f._

**frog** _n._ grenouille _f._

**frogman** _n._ homme-grenouille _m._

**frolic** _v.i._ s'ébattre. ● _n._ ébats _m. pl._

**from** _prep._ de; (_with time, prices, etc._) à partir de, de; (_habit, conviction, etc._) par; (_according to_) d'après. **take ~ s.o.,** prendre à qn. **take ~ one's pocket,** prendre dans sa poche.

**front** _n._ (_of car, train, etc._) avant _m._; (_of garment, building_) devant _m._; (_mil., pol._) front _m._; (_of book, pamphlet, etc._) début _m._; (_appearance: fig._) façade _f._ ● _a._ de devant, avant _invar._; (_first_) premier. **~ door,** porte d'entrée _f._ **~-wheel drive,** traction avant _f._ **in ~ (of),** devant.

**frontier** _n._ frontière _f._

**frost** _n._ gel _m._, gelée _f._; (_on glass etc._) givre _m._ ● _v.t./i._ (se) givrer.

**froth** _n._ mousse _f._, écume _f._ ● _v.i._ mousser, écumer. **~y** _a._ mousseux.

**frown** _v.i._ froncer les sourcils. ● _n._ froncement de sourcils _m._

**frozen** _a._ congelé.

**frugal** _a._ (_person_) économe; (_meal, life_) frugal. **~ly** _adv._ (_live_) simplement.

**fruit** _n._ fruit _m._; (_collectively_) fruits _m. pl._ **~ machine,** machine à sous _f._ **~ salad,** salade de fruits _f._ **~y** _a._ (_taste_) fruité.

**fruit|ful** _a._ (_discussions_) fructueux. **~less** _a._ stérile.

**frustrat|e** v.t. (plan) faire échouer; (person: psych.) frustrer; (upset: fam.) exaspérer. ~**ion** n. (psych.) frustration f.; (disappointment) déception f.

**fry** v.t./i. (faire) frire. ~**ing-pan** n. poêle (à frire) f.

**fudge** n. (sorte de) caramel mou m. ● v.t. se dérober à.

**fuel** n. combustible m.; (for car engine) carburant m. ● v.t. alimenter en combustible.

**fugitive** n. & a. fugiti|f, -ve (m., f.).

**fugue** n. (mus.) fugue f.

**fulfil** v.t. accomplir, réaliser; (condition) remplir. ~ **o.s.,** s'épanouir. ~**ment** n. réalisation f.; épanouissement m.

**full** a. plein (**of,** de); (bus, hotel) complet; (name) complet; (skirt) ample. ● n. **in** ~, intégral(ement). ~**back,** (sport) arrière m. ~ **moon,** pleine lune f. ~**scale** a. (drawing etc.) grandeur nature invar.; (fig.) de grande envergure. **at** ~ **speed,** à toute vitesse. ~ **stop,** point m. ~**time** a. & adv. à plein temps. ~**y** adv. complètement.

**fumble** v.i. tâtonner, fouiller. ~ **with,** tripoter.

**fume** v.i. rager. ~**s** n. pl. exhalaisons f. pl., vapeurs f. pl.

**fumigate** v.t. désinfecter.

**fun** n. amusement m. **be** ~, être chouette. **for** ~, pour rire. ~**fair** n. fête foraine f. **make** ~ **of,** se moquer de.

**function** n. (purpose, duty) fonction f.; (event) réception f. ● v.i. fonctionner. ~**al** a. fonctionnel.

**fund** n. fonds m. ● v.t. fournir les fonds pour.

**fundamental** a. fondamental.

**funeral** n. enterrement m., funérailles f. pl. ● a. funèbre.

**fungus** n. (plant) champignon m.; (mould) moisissure f.

**funnel** n. (for pouring) entonnoir m.; (of ship) cheminée f.

**funny** a. drôle; (odd) bizarre.

**fur** n. fourrure f.; (in kettle) tartre m.

**furious** a. furieux. ~**ly** adv. furieusement.

**furnace** n. fourneau m.

**furnish** v.t. (with furniture) meubler; (supply) fournir. ~**ings** n. pl. ameublement m.

**furniture** n. meubles m. pl.

**furrow** n. sillon m.

**furry** a. (animal) à fourrure; (toy) en peluche.

**furth|er** a. plus éloigné; (additional) supplémentaire. ● adv. plus loin; (more) davantage. ● v.t. avancer. ~**er education,** formation continue f. ~**est** a. le plus éloigné; adv. le plus loin.

**furthermore** adv. de plus.

**furtive** a. furtif.

**fury** n. fureur f.

**fuse**[1] v.t./i. (melt) fondre; (unite: fig.) fusionner. ● n. fusible m., plomb m. ~ **the lights** etc., faire sauter les plombs.

**fuse**[2] n. (of bomb) amorce f.

**fuselage** n. fuselage m.

**fusion** n. fusion f.

**fuss** n. (when upset) histoire(s) f. (pl.); (when excited) agitation f. ● v.i. s'agiter. **make a** ~, faire des histoires; s'agiter; (about food) faire des chichis. **make a** ~ **of,** faire grand cas de. ~**y** a. (finicky) tatillon; (hard to please) difficile.

**futile** a. futile, vain.

**future** a. futur. ● n. avenir m.; (gram.) futur m. **in** ~, à l'avenir.

• • • • • • • • • • • • • • • • • • • • • • • • • • •

# Gg

• • • • • • • • • • • • • • • • • • • • • • • • • • •

**gabardine** n. gabardine f.

**gabble** v.t./i. bredouiller.

**gable** n. pignon m.

**gadget** n. gadget m.

**Gaelic** n. gaélique m.

**gaffe** n. (blunder) gaffe f.

**gag** n. bâillon m.; (joke) gag m. ● v.t. bâillonner.

**gaiety** n. gaieté f.

**gaily** adv. gaiement.

**gain** v.t. gagner; (speed, weight) prendre. ● v.i. (of clock) avancer. ● n. acquisition f.; (profit) gain m.

**gait** n. démarche f.

**gala** n. (festive occasion) gala m.; (sport) concours m.

**gale** n. tempête f.

**gall** n. bile f.; (fig.) fiel m.; (impudence: sl.) culot m. ~**bladder** n. vésicule biliaire f.

**gallant** a. (brave) courageux; (chivalrous) galant. ~**ry** n. courage m.

**gallery** n. galerie f.; (art) ~, (public) musée m.

**galley** n. (ship) galère f.; (kitchen) cambuse f.

**Gallic** a. français.

**gallon** n. gallon m.

**gallop** n. galop m. ● v.i. galoper.

**gallows** n. potence f.

**galvanize** v.t. galvaniser.

**gambit** n. (opening) ~, (move) première démarche f.; (ploy) stratagème m.

**gambl|e** v.t./i. jouer. ● n. (venture) entreprise risquée f.; (bet) pari m.; (risk) risque m. ~**e on,** miser sur. ~**er** n. joueu|r, -se m., f. ~**ing** n. le jeu.

**game**[1] *n.* jeu *m.*; (*football*) match *m.*; (*tennis*) partie *f.*; (*animals, birds*) gibier *m.* ● *a.* (*brave*) brave. ~ **for,** prêt à.

**game**[2] *a.* (*lame*) estropié.

**gammon** *n.* jambon fumé *m.*

**gamut** *n.* gamme *f.*

**gamy** *a.* faisandé.

**gang** *n.* bande *f.*; (*of workmen*) équipe *f.* ● *v.i.* ~ **up,** se liguer (**on, against,** contre).

**gangrene** *n.* gangrène *f.*

**gangster** *n.* gangster *m.*

**gangway** *n.* passage *m.*; (*aisle*) allée *f.*; (*of ship*) passerelle *f.*

**gap** *n.* trou *m.*, vide *m.*; (*in time*) intervalle *m.*; (*in education*) lacune *f.*; (*difference*) écart *m.*

**gap|e** *v.i.* rester bouche bée. ~**ing** *a.* béant.

**garage** *n.* garage *m.* ● *v.t.* mettre au garage.

**garb** *n.* costume *m.*

**garbage** *n.* ordures *f. pl.*

**garble** *v.t.* déformer.

**garden** *n.* jardin *m.* ● *v.i.* jardiner. ~**er** *n.* jardin|ier, -ière *m., f.* ~**ing** *n.* jardinage *m.*

**gargle** *v.i.* se gargariser. ● *n.* gargarisme *m.*

**garland** *n.* guirlande *f.*

**garlic** *n.* ail *m.*

**garment** *n.* vêtement *m.*

**garnish** *v.t.* garnir (**with,** de). ● *n.* garniture *f.*

**garter** *n.* jarretière *f.* ~**-belt** *n.* porte-jarretelles *m. invar.*

**gas** *n.* gaz *m.*; (*med.*) anesthésique *m.*; (*petrol: Amer., fam.*) essence *f.* ● *a.* (*mask, pipe*) à gaz. ● *v.t.* asphyxier; (*mil.*) gazer. ● *v.i.* (*fam.*) bavarder.

**gash** *n.* entaille *f.* ● *v.t.* entailler.

**gasket** *n.* (*auto.*) joint de culasse *m.*; (*for pressure cooker*) rondelle *f.*

**gasoline** *n.* (*petrol: Amer.*) essence *f.*

**gasp** *v.i.* haleter; (*in surprise: fig.*) avoir le souffle coupé. ● *n.* halètement *m.*

**gassy** *a.* gazeux.

**gastric** *a.* gastrique.

**gastronomy** *n.* gastronomie *f.*

**gate** *n.* porte *f.*; (*of metal*) grille *f.*; (*barrier*) barrière *f.*

**gather** *v.t.* (*people, objects*) rassembler; (*pick up*) ramasser; (*flowers*) cueillir; (*fig.*) comprendre; (*sewing*) froncer. ● *v.i.* (*people*) se rassembler; (*crowd*) se former; (*pile up*) s'accumuler. ~**ing** *n.* rassemblement *m.*

**gaudy** *a.* voyant, criard.

**gauge** *n.* jauge *f.*, indicateur *m.* ● *v.t.* jauger, évaluer.

**gaunt** *a.* (*lean*) émacié; (*grim*) lugubre.

**gauze** *n.* gaze *f.*

**gawky** *a.* gauche, maladroit.

**gawp** (*or* **gawk**) *v.i.* ~ (**at**), regarder bouche bée.

**gay** *a.* (*joyful*) gai; (*fam.*) gay *invar.* ● *n.* gay *m./f.*

**gaze** *v.i.* ~ (**at**), regarder (fixement). ● *n.* regard (fixe) *m.*

**gazelle** *n.* gazelle *f.*

**gazette** *n.* journal (officiel) *m.*

**gear** *n.* équipement *m.*; (*techn.*) engrenage *m.*; (*auto.*) vitesse *f.* ● *v.t.* adapter. ~**-lever,** (*Amer.*) ~**-shift** *ns.* levier de vitesse *m.* **in** ~, en prise.

**gearbox** *n.* (*auto.*) boîte de vitesses *f.*

**gel** *n.* gelée *f.*; (*for hair*) gel *m.*

**gelatine** *n.* gélatine *f.*

**gelignite** *n.* nitroglycérine *f.*

**gem** *n.* pierre précieuse *f.*

**Gemini** *n.* les Gémeaux *m. pl.*

**gender** *n.* genre *m.*

**gene** *n.* gène *m.*

**general** *a.* général. ● *n.* général *m.* ~ **practitioner,** (*med.*) généraliste *m.* **in** ~, en général. ~**ly** *adv.* généralement.

**generaliz|e** *v.t./i.* généraliser. ~**ation** *n.* généralisation *f.*

**generate** *v.t.* produire.

**generation** *n.* génération *f.*

**generator** *n.* (*electr.*) groupe électrogène *m.*

**gener|ous** *a.* généreux; (*plentiful*) copieux. ~**osity** *n.* générosité *f.*

**genetic** *a.* génétique. ~**s** *n.* génétique *f.*

**genial** *a.* affable, sympathique; (*climate*) doux.

**genital** *a.* génital. ~**s** *n. pl.* organes génitaux *m. pl.*

**genius** *n.* (*pl.* **-uses**) génie *m.*

**genteel** *a.* distingué.

**gentl|e** *a.* (*mild, kind*) doux; (*slight*) léger; (*hint*) discret. ~**eness** *n.* douceur *f.* ~**y** *adv.* doucement.

**gentleman** *n.* (*man*) monsieur *m.*; (*wellbred*) gentleman *m.*

**genuine** *a.* (*true*) véritable; (*person, belief*) sincère.

**geograph|y** *n.* géographie *f.* ~**ical** *a.* géographique.

**geolog|y** *n.* géologie *f.* ~**ical** *a.* géologique.

**geometr|y** *n.* géométrie *f.* ~**ic(al)** *a.* géométrique.

**geranium** *n.* géranium *m.*

**geriatric** *a.* gériatrique.

**germ** *n.* (*rudiment, seed*) germe *m.*; (*med.*) microbe *m.*

**German** *a. & n.* allemand(e) (*m.* (*f.*)); (*lang.*) allemand *m.* ~ **measles,** rubéole *f.* ~**y** *n.* Allemagne *f.*

**germinate** *v.t./i.* (faire) germer.

**gestation** *n.* gestation *f.*

**gesticulate** *v.i.* gesticuler.

**gesture** *n.* geste *m.*

**get** *v.t.* avoir, obtenir, recevoir; ( *catch* ) prendre; ( *buy* ) acheter, prendre; ( *find* ) trouver; ( *fetch* ) aller chercher; ( *understand: sl.* ) comprendre. ~ **s.o. to do sth.,** faire faire qch. à qn. ~ **sth. done,** faire faire qch. ● *v.i.* aller, arriver (**to,** à); ( *become* ) devenir; ( *start* ) se mettre (**to,** à); ( *manage* ) parvenir (**to,** à). ~ **married/ready/***etc.***,** se marier/se préparer/ *etc.* ~ **promoted/hurt/***etc.***,** être promu/ blessé/ *etc.* ~ **arrested/robbed/***etc.***,** se faire arrêter/voler/*etc.* ~ **across,** ( *cross* ) traverser. ~ **along** or **by,** ( *manage* ) se débrouiller. ~ **along** or **on,** ( *progress* ) avancer. ~ **along** or **on with,** s'entendre avec. ~ **at,** ( *reach* ) parvenir à. ~ **away,** partir; ( *escape* ) s'échapper. ~ **back** *v.i.* revenir; *v.t.* ( *recover* ) récupérer. ~ **by** or **through,** ( *pass* ) passer. ~ **down** *v.t./i.* descendre; ( *depress* ) déprimer. ~ **in,** entrer, arriver. ~ **into,** ( *car* ) monter dans; ( *dress* ) mettre. ~ **into trouble,** avoir des ennuis. ~ **off** *v.i.* ( *from bus etc.* ) descendre; ( *leave* ) partir; ( *jurid.* ) être acquitté; ( *remove* ) enlever. ~ **on,** ( *on train etc.* ) monter; ( *succeed* ) réussir. ~ **on with,** ( *job* ) attaquer; ( *person* ) s'entendre avec. ~ **out,** sortir. ~ **round,** ( *rule* ) contourner; ( *person* ) entortiller. ~ **through,** ( *finish* ) finir. ~ **up** *v.i.* se lever; *v.t.* ( *climb, bring* ) monter.

**Ghana** *n.* Ghana *m.*

**ghastly** *a.* affreux.

**gherkin** *n.* cornichon *m.*

**ghetto** *n.* ghetto *m.*

**ghost** *n.* fantôme *m.*

**giant** *n. & a.* géant ( *m.* ).

**gibe** *n.* raillerie *f.*

**giblets** *n. pl.* abattis *m. pl.*, abats *m. pl.*

**gidd|y** *a.* vertigineux. **be** or **feel ~y,** avoir le vertige. **~iness** *n.* vertige *m.*

**gift** *n.* cadeau *m.*; ( *ability* ) don *m.* **~-wrap** *v.t.* faire un paquet-cadeau de.

**gifted** *a.* doué.

**gig** *n.* ( *fam.* ) concert *m.*

**gigantic** *a.* gigantesque.

**giggle** *v.i.* ricaner (sottement), glousser. ● *n.* ricanement *m.*

**gild** *v.t.* dorer.

**gill** *n.* ( *approx.* ) décilitre.

**gills** *n. pl.* ouïes *f. pl.*

**gilt** *a.* doré. ● *n.* dorure *f.*

**gimmick** *n.* truc *m.*

**gin** *n.* gin *m.*

**ginger** *n.* gingembre *m.* ● *a.* roux. ~ **ale,** ~ **beer,** boisson gazeuse au gingembre *f.*

**gingerbread** *n.* pain d'épice *m.*

**gipsy** *n.* = **gypsy.**

**giraffe** *n.* girafe *f.*

**girder** *n.* poutre *f.*

**girdle** *n.* ( *belt* ) ceinture *f.*; ( *corset* ) gaine *f.*

**girl** *n.* (petite) fille *f.*; ( *young woman* ) (jeune) fille *f.* **~-friend** *n.* amie *f.*; ( *of boy* ) petite amie *f.*

**giro** *n.* virement bancaire *m.*; ( *cheque: fam.* ) mandat *m.*

**girth** *n.* circonférence *f.*

**gist** *n.* essentiel *m.*

**give** /gɪv/ *v.t.* donner; ( *gesture* ) faire; ( *laugh, sigh, etc.* ) pousser. ~ **s.o. sth.,** donner qch. à qn. ● *v.i.* donner; ( *yield* ) céder; ( *stretch* ) se détendre. ● *n.* élasticité *f.* ~ **away,** donner; ( *secret* ) trahir. ~ **back,** rendre. ~ **in,** ( *yield* ) se rendre. ~ **up** *v.t./i.* ( *renounce* ) renoncer (à); ( *yield* ) céder. ~ **o.s. up,** se rendre. ~ **way,** céder; ( *collapse* ) s'effondrer.

**glacier** *n.* glacier *m.*

**glad** *a.* content. **~ly** *adv.* avec plaisir.

**gladiolus** *n.* glaïeul *m.*

**glam|our** *n.* enchantement *m.*, séduction *f.* **~orous** *a.* séduisant, ensorcelant.

**glance** *n.* coup d'œil *m.* ● *v.i.* ~ **at,** jeter un coup d'œil à.

**gland** *n.* glande *f.*

**glare** *v.i.* briller très fort. ● *n.* éclat (aveuglant) *m.*; ( *stare: fig.* ) regard furieux *m.* ~ **at,** regarder d'un air furieux.

**glass** *n.* verre *m.*; ( *mirror* ) miroir *m.* **~es,** ( *spectacles* ) lunettes *f. pl.* **~y** *a.* vitreux.

**glaze** *v.t.* ( *door etc.* ) vitrer; ( *pottery* ) vernisser. ● *n.* vernis *m.*

**gleam** *n.* lueur *f.* ● *v.i.* luire.

**glen** *n.* vallon *m.*

**glib** *a.* ( *person: pej.* ) qui a la parole facile or du bagou; ( *reply, excuse* ) désinvolte, spécieux. **~ly** *adv.* avec désinvolture.

**glide** *v.i.* glisser; ( *of plane* ) planer. **~r** *n.* planeur *m.*

**glimmer** *n.* lueur *f.* ● *v.i.* luire.

**glimpse** *n.* aperçu *m.* **catch a ~ of,** entrevoir.

**glint** *n.* éclair *m.* ● *v.i.* étinceler.

**glitter** *v.i.* scintiller. ● *n.* scintillement *m.*

**gloat** *v.i.* jubiler (**over,** à l'idée de).

**global** *a.* ( *world-wide* ) mondial; ( *all-embracing* ) global.

**globe** *n.* globe *m.*

**gloom** *n.* obscurité *f.*; ( *sadness: fig.* ) tristesse *f.* **~y** *a.* triste; ( *pessimistic* ) pessimiste.

**glorious** *a.* splendide; ( *deed, hero, etc.* ) glorieux.

**glory** *n.* gloire *f.*

**gloss** *n.* lustre *m.*, brillant *m.* ● *a.* brillant. **~y** *a.* brillant.

**glove** *n.* gant *m.* ~ **compartment,** ( *auto.* ) vide-poches *m. invar.*

**glow** *v.i.* rougeoyer; ( *person, eyes* ) rayonner. ● *n.* rougeoiement *m.*, éclat *m.*

**glucose** *n.* glucose *m.*

**glue** *n.* colle *f.* ● *v.t.* coller.

**glum** *a.* triste, morne.

**glut** *n.* surabondance *f.*

**glutton** *n*. glouton(ne) *m.* (*f.*).

**glycerine** *n*. glycérine *f*.

**gnash** *v.t.* ~ one's teeth, grincer des dents.

**gnat** *n*. (*fly*) cousin *m*.

**gnaw** *v.t./i.* ronger.

**gnome** *n*. gnome *m*.

**go** *v.i.* aller; (*leave*) partir; (*work*) marcher; (*become*) devenir; (*be sold*) se vendre; (*vanish*) disparaître. ~ **by car/on foot**, aller en voiture/à pied. ~ **for a walk/ride**, aller se promener/faire un tour en voiture. **go red/dry/etc.**, rougir/tarir/ *etc.* ~ **riding/shopping**/ *etc.*, faire du cheval/les courses/ *etc.* ~ (*try*) coup *m.*; (*success*) réussite *f.*; (*turn*) tour *m.*; (*energy*) dynamisme *m.* **have a ~**, essayer. **be ~ing to do**, aller faire. ~ **across**, traverser. ~ **ahead!**, allez-y! ~ **away**, s'en aller. ~ **back**, retourner; (*go home*) rentrer. ~ **by**, (*pass*) passer. ~ **down**, descendre; (*sun*) se coucher. ~ **for**, aller chercher; (*like*) aimer; (*attack: sl.*) attaquer. ~ **in**, (r)entrer. ~ **in for**, (*exam*) se présenter à. ~ **into**, entrer dans; (*subject*) examiner. ~ **off**, partir; (*explode*) sauter; (*ring*) sonner; (*take place*) se dérouler; (*dislike*) revenir de. ~ **on**, continuer; (*happen*) se passer. ~ **out**, sortir; (*light, fire*) s'éteindre. ~ **over**, (*cross*) traverser; (*pass*) passer. ~ **over** or **through**, (*check*) vérifier; (*search*) fouiller. ~ **round**, (*be enough*) suffire. ~ **through**, (*suffer*) subir. ~ **up**, monter. ~ **without**, se passer de. **on the ~**, actif.

**goal** *n*. but *m*. ~**post** *n*. poteau de but *m*.

**goalkeeper** *n*. gardien de but *m*.

**goat** *n*. chèvre *f*.

**gobble** *v.t.* engouffrer.

**goblin** *n*. lutin *m*.

**God** *n*. Dieu *m*. ~**forsaken** *a*. perdu.

**god** *n*. dieu *m*. ~**dess** *n*. déesse *f*. ~**ly** *a*. dévot.

**god|child** *n*. filleul(e) *m.* (*f.*). ~**daughter** *n*. filleule *f.* ~**father** *n*. parrain *m.* ~**mother** *n*. marraine *f.* ~**son** *n*. filleul *m.*

**godsend** *n*. aubaine *f*.

**goggle** *v.i.* ~ (at), regarder avec de gros yeux.

**goggles** *n. pl.* lunettes (protectrices) *f. pl.*

**going** *n*. it **is slow/hard ~**, c'est lent/ difficile. ●*a.* (*price, rate*) actuel.

**gold** *n*. or *m.* ●*a.* en or, d'or.

**golden** *a.* d'or; (*in colour*) doré; (*opportunity*) unique.

**goldfish** *n. invar.* poisson rouge *m*.

**gold-plated** *a.* plaqué or.

**goldsmith** *n.* orfèvre *m*.

**golf** *n.* golf *m.* ~ **ball**, balle de golf *f.*; (*on typewriter*) boule *f.* ~**course** *n.* terrain de golf *m.* ~**er** *n.* joueur|r, -se de golf *m., f.*

**gong** *n.* gong *m*.

**good** *a.* bon; (*weather*) beau; (*well-behaved*) sage. ●*n.* bien *m.* **as ~ as**, (*almost*) pratiquement. **do ~**, faire du bien. **feel ~**, se sentir bien. ~**-for-nothing** *a. & n.* propre à

rien (*m./f.*). ~**afternoon**, ~**morning** *ints.* bonjour. ~**evening** *int.* bonsoir. ~**looking** *a.* beau. ~**night** *int.* bonsoir, bonne nuit. **it is ~ for you**, ça vous fait du bien. **is it any ~?**, est-ce que c'est bien? **it's no ~**, ça ne vaut rien. **it is no ~ shouting**/*etc.*, ça ne sert à rien de crier/*etc.* **for~**, pour toujours. ~**ness** *n.* bonté *f.* **my ~ness!**, mon Dieu!

**goodbye** *int. & n.* au revoir (*m. invar.*).

**goods** *n. pl.* marchandises *f. pl.*

**goose** *n.* oie *f.* ~ **pimples** *ns.* chair de poule *f.*

**gooseberry** *n.* groseille à maquereau *f.*

**gore** *n.* (*blood*) sang *m*.

**gorge** *n.* (*geog.*) gorge *f.* ●*v.t.* ~ **o.s.**, se gorger.

**gorgeous** *a.* magnifique.

**gorilla** *n.* gorille *m*.

**gorse** *n. invar.* ajonc(s) *m.* (*pl.*).

**gory** *a.* sanglant; (*horrific: fig.*) horrible.

**gosh** *int.* mince (alors).

**gospel** *n.* évangile *m*.

**gossip** *n.* commérage(s) *m.* (*pl.*); (*person*) bavard(e) *m.* (*f.*). ●*v.i.* bavarder.

**got** *in v.* have ~, avoir. **have ~ to do**, devoir faire.

**Gothic** *a.* gothique.

**gouge** *v.t.* ~ **out**, arracher.

**gourmet** *n.* gourmet *m*.

**gout** *n.* (*med.*) goutte *f*.

**govern** *v.t./i.* gouverner. ~**or** *n.* gouverneur *m*.

**government** *n.* gouvernement *m*.

**gown** *n.* robe *f.*; (*of judge, teacher*) toge *f*.

**GP** *abbr. see* **general practitioner**.

**grab** *v.t.* saisir.

**grace** *n.* grâce *f.* ●*v.t.* (*honour*) honorer; (*adorn*) orner. ~**ful** *a.* gracieux.

**gracious** *a.* (*kind*) bienveillant; (*elegant*) élégant.

**gradation** *n.* gradation *f*.

**grade** *n.* catégorie *f.*; (*of goods*) qualité *f.*; (*on scale*) grade *m.*; (*school mark*) note *f.*; (*class: Amer.*) classe *f.* ●*v.t.* classer; (*school work*) noter.

**gradient** *n.* (*slope*) inclinaison *f*.

**gradual** *a.* progressif, graduel. ~**ly** *adv.* progressivement.

**graduate**[1] *n.* (*univ.*) diplômé(e) *m.* (*f.*).

**graduate**[2] *v.i.* obtenir son diplôme. ●*v.t.* graduer. ~**ion** *n.* remise de diplômes *f*.

**graffiti** *n. pl.* graffiti *m. pl.*

**graft**[1] *n.* (*med., bot.*) greffe *f.* (*work*) boulot *m.* ●*v.t.* greffer; (*work*) trimer.

**graft**[2] *n.* (*bribery: fam.*) corruption *f*.

**grain** *n.* (*seed, quantity, texture*) grain *m.*; (*in wood*) fibre *f*.

**gram** *n.* gramme *m*.

**gramm|ar** *n.* grammaire *f.* ~**atical** *a.* grammatical.

**grand** *a.* magnifique; (*duke, chorus*) grand. **~ piano,** piano à queue *m.*

**grandad** *n.* (*fam.*) papy *m.*

**grand|child** *n.* petit(e)-enfant *m.* (*f.*). **~daughter** *n.* petite-fille *f.* **~father** *n.* grand-père *m.* **~mother** *n.* grand-mère *f.* **~parents** *n. pl.* grands-parents *m. pl.* **~son** *n.* petit-fils *m.*

**grandeur** *n.* grandeur *f.*

**grandiose** *a.* grandiose.

**grandma** *n.* = granny.

**grandstand** *n.* tribune *f.*

**granite** *n.* granit *m.*

**granny** *n.* mamie *f.*

**grant** *v.t.* (*give*) accorder; (*request*) accéder à; (*admit*) admettre (**that,** que). ● *n.* subvention *f.*; (*univ.*) bourse *f.* **take sth. for ~ed,** considérer qch. comme une chose acquise.

**granule** *n.* granule *m.*

**grape** *n.* grain de raisin *m.* **~s,** raisin(s) *m.* (*pl.*).

**grapefruit** *n. invar.* pamplemousse *m.*

**graph** *n.* graphique *m.*

**graphic** *a.* (*arts etc.*) graphique; (*fig.*) vivant, explicite. **~s** *n. pl.* (*comput.*) graphiques *m. pl.*

**grapple** *v.i.* **~ with,** affronter, être aux prises avec.

**grasp** *v.t.* saisir. ● *n.* (*hold*) prise *f.*; (*strength of hand*) poigne *f.*; (*reach*) portée *f.*; (*fig.*) compréhension *f.*

**grasping** *a.* rapace.

**grass** *n.* herbe *f.*

**grasshopper** *n.* sauterelle *f.*

**grate** [1] *n.* (*fireplace*) foyer *m.*; (*frame*) grille *f.*

**grate** [2] *v.t.* râper. ● *v.i.* grincer. **~r** *n.* râpe *f.*

**grateful** *a.* reconnaissant.

**gratitude** *n.* gratitude *f.*

**gratuitous** *a.* gratuit.

**grave** [1] *n.* tombe *f.* **~-digger** *n.* fossoyeur *m.*

**grave** [2] *a.* (*serious*) grave. **~ly** *adv.* gravement.

**grave** [3] *a.* **~ accent,** accent grave *m.*

**gravel** *n.* gravier *m.*

**gravestone** *n.* pierre tombale *f.*

**graveyard** *n.* cimetière *m.*

**gravity** *n.* (*seriousness*) gravité *f.*; (*force*) pesanteur *f.*

**gravy** *n.* jus (de viande) *m.*

**gray** *a. & n.* = grey.

**graze** [1] *v.t./i.* (*eat*) paître.

**graze** [2] *v.t.* (*touch*) frôler; (*scrape*) écorcher. ● *n.* écorchure *f.*

**greas|e** *n.* graisse *f.* ● *v.t.* graisser. **~e-proof paper,** papier sulfurisé *m.* **~y** *a.* graisseux.

**great** *a.* grand; (*very good*: *fam.*) magnifique. **~ Britain,** Grande-Bretagne *f.* **~ly** *adv.* (*very*) très; (*much*) beaucoup. **~ness** *n.* grandeur *f.*

**Greece** *n.* Grèce *f.*

**greed** *n.* avidité *f.*; (*for food*) gourmandise *f.* **~y** *a.* avide; gourmand.

**Greek** *a. & n.* grec(que) (*m.* (*f.*)); (*lang.*) grec *m.*

**green** *a.* vert; (*fig.*) naïf. ● *n.* vert *m.*; (*grass*) pelouse *f.*; (*golf*) green *m.*

**greengage** *n.* (*plum*) reine-claude *f.*

**greengrocer** *n.* marchand(e) de fruits et légumes *m.* (*f.*).

**greenhouse** *n.* serre *f.*

**greet** *v.t.* (*receive*) accueillir; (*address politely*) saluer. **~ing** *n.* accueil *m.* **~ings card,** carte de vœux *f.*

**grenade** *n.* grenade *f.*

**grey** *a.* gris; (*fig.*) triste. ● *n.* gris *m.*

**greyhound** *n.* lévrier *m.*

**grid** *n.* grille *f.*; (*network*: *electr.*) réseau *m.*; (*culin.*) gril *m.*

**grief** *n.* chagrin *m.*

**grievance** *n.* grief *m.*

**grieve** *v.t./i.* (s')affliger. **~ for,** pleurer.

**grill** *n.* (*cooking device*) gril *m.*; (*food*) grillade *f.*; (*auto.*) calandre *f.* ● *v.t./i.* griller; (*interrogate*) cuisiner.

**grille** *n.* grille *f.*

**grim** *a.* sinistre.

**grimace** *n.* grimace *f.* ● *v.i.* grimacer.

**grim|e** *n.* crasse *f.* **~y** *a.* crasseux.

**grin** *v.i.* sourire. ● *n.* (large) sourire *m.*

**grind** *v.t.* écraser; (*coffee*) moudre; (*sharpen*) aiguiser. ● *n.* corvée *f.*

**grip** *v.t.* saisir; (*interest*) passionner. ● *n.* prise *f.*; (*strength of hand*) poigne *f.*; (*bag*) sac de voyage *m.*

**grisly** *a.* horrible.

**gristle** *n.* cartilage *m.*

**grit** *n.* gravillon *m.*, sable *m.*; (*fig.*) courage *m.* ● *v.t.* (*road*) sabler; (*teeth*) serrer.

**grizzle** *v.i.* (*cry*) pleurnicher.

**groan** *v.i.* gémir. ● *n.* gémissement *m.*

**grocer** *n.* épic|ier, -ière *m.*, *f.* **~ies** *n. pl.* (*goods*) épicerie *f.* **~y** *n.* (*shop*) épicerie *f.*

**grog** *n.* grog *m.*

**groggy** *a.* (*weak*) faible; (*unsteady*) chancelant; (*ill*) mal fichu.

**groin** *n.* aine *f.*

**groom** *n.* marié *m.*; (*for horses*) valet d'écurie *m.* ● *v.t.* (*horse*) panser; (*fig.*) préparer.

**groove** *n.* (*for door etc.*) rainure *f.*; (*in record*) sillon *m.*

**grope** *v.i.* tâtonner. **~ for,** chercher à tâtons.

**gross** *a.* (*coarse*) grossier; (*comm.*) brut. ● *n. invar.* grosse *f.*

**grotesque** *a.* grotesque.

**grotto** *n.* grotte *f.*

**ground** *n.* terre *f.*, sol *m.*; (*area*) terrain *m.*; (*reason*) raison *f.* **~s,** terres *f. pl.*, parc *m.*; (*of coffee*) marc *m.* ● *v.t./i.* (*naut.*) échouer;

(*aircraft*) retenir au sol. **on the ~,** par terre. **lose ~,** perdre du terrain. **~ floor,** rez-de-chaussée *m. invar.* **~less** *a.* sans fondement.

**groundsheet** *n.* tapis de sol *m.*

**groundwork** *n.* travail préparatoire *m.*

**group** *n.* groupe *m.* ● *v.t./i.* (se) grouper.

**grouse**[1] *n. invar.* (*bird*) coq de bruyère *m.*, grouse *f.*

**grouse**[2] *v.i.* (*grumble: fam.*) rouspéter, râler.

**grove** *n.* bocage *m.*

**grovel** *v.i.* ramper.

**grow** *v.i.* grandir; (*of plant*) pousser; (*become*) devenir. ● *v.t.* cultiver. **~ up,** devenir adulte, grandir. **~er** *n.* cultiva|teur, -trice *m.*, *f.* **~ing** *a.* grandissant.

**growl** *v.i.* grogner. ● *n.* grognement *m.*

**grown-up** *a.* & *n.* adulte (*m./f.*).

**growth** *n.* croissance *f.*; (*in numbers*) accroissement *m.*; (*of hair, tooth*) pousse *f.*; (*med.*) tumeur *f.*

**grub** *n.* (*larva*) larve *f.*; (*food: sl.*) bouffe *f.*

**grubby** *a.* sale.

**grudge** *n.* rancune *f.* **have a ~ against,** en vouloir à. **grudgingly** *adv.* à contrecœur.

**gruesome** *a.* macabre.

**gruff** *a.* bourru.

**grumble** *v.i.* ronchonner, grogner (**at,** après).

**grumpy** *a.* grincheux.

**grunt** *v.i.* grogner. ● *n.* grognement *m.*

**guarantee** *n.* garantie *f.* ● *v.t.* garantir.

**guard** *v.t.* protéger; (*watch*) surveiller. ● *n.* (*vigilance, mil., group*) garde *f.*; (*person*) garde *m.*; (*on train*) chef de train *m.* **~ian** *n.* gardien(ne) (*f.*); (*of orphan*) tu|teur, -trice *m.*, *f.*

**guarded** *a.* prudent.

**guerrilla** *n.* guérillero *m.* **~ warfare,** guérilla *f.*

**guess** *v.t./i.* deviner; (*suppose*) penser. ● *n.* conjecture *f.*

**guesswork** *n.* conjectures *f. pl.*

**guest** *n.* invité(e) *m.* (*f.*); (*in hotel*) client(e) *m.* (*f.*).

**guffaw** *n.* gros rire *m.* ● *v.i.* s'esclaffer, rire bruyamment.

**guidance** *n.* (*advice*) conseils *m. pl.*; (*information*) information *f.*

**guide** *n.* (*person, book*) guide *m.* ● *v.t.* guider. **~d** *a.* **~d missile,** missile téléguidé *m.* **~lines** *n. pl.* grandes lignes *f. pl.*

**Guide** *n.* (*girl*) guide *f.*

**guidebook** *n.* guide *m.*

**guile** *n.* ruse *f.*

**guilt** *n.* culpabilité *f.* **~y** *a.* coupable.

**guinea-pig** *n.* cobaye *m.*

**guinea-fowl** *n.* pintade *f.*

**guitar** *n.* guitare *f.* **~ist** *n.* guitariste *m./f.*

**gulf** *n.* (*part of sea*) golfe *m.*; (*hollow*) gouffre *m.*

**gull** *n.* mouette *f.*, goéland *m.*

**gullet** *n.* gosier *m.*

**gullible** *a.* crédule.

**gully** *n.* (*ravine*) ravine *f.*; (*drain*) rigole *f.*

**gulp** *v.t.* **~ (down),** avaler en vitesse. ● *v.i.* (*from fear etc.*) avoir un serrement de gorge. ● *n.* gorgée *f.*

**gum**[1] *n.* (*anat.*) gencive *f.*

**gum**[2] *n.* (*from tree*) gomme *f.*; (*glue*) colle *f.*; (*for chewing*) chewing-gum *m.* ● *v.t.* gommer.

**gun** *n.* (*pistol*) revolver *m.*; (*rifle*) fusil *m.*; (*large*) canon *m.*

**gunpowder** *n.* poudre à canon *f.*

**gunshot** *n.* coup de feu *m.*

**gurgle** *n.* glouglou *m.* ● *v.i.* glouglouter.

**gush** *v.i.* **~ (out),** jaillir.

**gust** *n.* rafale *f.*; (*of smoke*) bouffée *f.* **~y** *a.* venteux.

**gusto** *n.* enthousiasme *m.*

**gut** *n.* boyau *m.* **~s,** boyaux *m. pl.*, ventre *m.*; (*courage: fam.*) cran *m.*

**gutter** *n.* (*on roof*) gouttière *f.*; (*in street*) caniveau *m.*

**guy** *n.* (*man: fam.*) type *m.*

**gym** *n.* (*fam.*) gymnase *m.*; (*fam.*) gym(nastique) *f.* **~-slip** *n.* tunique *f.* **~nasium** *n.* gymnase *m.*

**gymnast** *n.* gymnaste *m./f.* **~ics** *n. pl.* gymnastique *f.*

**gynaecolog|y** *n.* gynécologie *f.* **~ist** *n.* gynécologue *m./f.*

**gypsy** *n.* bohémien(ne) *m.* (*f.*).

**gyrate** *v.i.* tournoyer.

• • • • • • • • • • • • • • • • • • • • • • • • • • •

# Hh

• • • • • • • • • • • • • • • • • • • • • • • • • • •

**habit** *n.* habitude *f.*; (*costume: relig.*) habit *m.* **be in/get into the ~ of,** avoir/prendre l'habitude de.

**habitual** *a.* (*usual*) habituel; (*smoker, liar*) invétéré. **~ly** *adv.* habituellement.

**hack**[1] *n.* (*old horse*) haridelle *f.*; (*writer*) nègre *m.*, écrivailleu|r, -se *m.*, *f.*

**hack**[2] *v.t.* hacher, tailler.

**haddock** *n. invar.* églefin *m.* **smoked ~,** haddock *m.*

**haemorrhage** *n.* hémorragie *f.*

**haemorrhoids** *n. pl.* hémorroïdes *f. pl.*

**haggle** *v.i.* marchander. **~ over,** (*object*) marchander; (*price*) discuter.

**hail**[1] *v.t.* (*greet*) saluer; (*taxi*) héler. ● *v.i.* **~ from,** venir de.

**hail**[2] *n.* grêle *f.* ● *v.i.* grêler.

**hailstone** *n.* grêlon *m.*

**hair** n. (on head) cheveux m. pl.; (on body, of animal) poils m. pl.; (single strand on head) cheveu m.; (on body) poil n. ~**-do** n. (fam.) coiffure f. ~**-drier** n. séchoir (à cheveux) m. ~**-grip** n. pince à cheveux f. ~**-style** n. coiffure f.

**hairbrush** n. brosse à cheveux f.

**haircut** n. coupe de cheveux f. **have a** ~, se faire couper les cheveux.

**hairdresser** n. coiffeu|r, -se m., f.

**hairpin** n. épingle à cheveux f.

**hake** n. invar. colin m.

**half** n. moitié f., demi(e) m. (f.). ● a. demi. ● adv. à moitié. ~ **a dozen,** une demi-douzaine. ~ **an hour,** une demi-heure. **four and a** ~, quatre et demi (e). ~ **and half,** moitié moitié. **in** ~, en deux. ~**-back** n. (sport) demi m. ~ **price,** moitié prix. ~**-time** n. mi-temps f. ~**-way** adv. à mi-chemin.

**halibut** n. invar. (fish) flétan m.

**hall** n. (room) salle f.; (entrance) vestibule m.; (mansion) manoir m.; (corridor) couloir m.

**hallmark** n. (on gold etc.) poinçon m.; (fig.) sceau m.

**hallo** int. & n. bonjour (m.). ~**I,** (on telephone) allô!; (in surprise) tiens!

**hallucination** n. hallucination f.

**halo** n. auréole f.

**halt** n. halte f. ● v.t./i. (s')arrêter.

**halve** v.t. diviser en deux; (time etc.) réduire de moitié.

**ham** n. jambon m.; (theatre: sl.) cabotin(e) m. (f.).

**hamburger** n. hamburger m.

**hammer** n. marteau m. ● v.t./i. marteler, frapper; (defeat) battre à plate couture. ~ **out,** (differences) arranger; (agreement) arriver à.

**hammock** n. hamac m.

**hamper**[1] n. panier m.

**hamper**[2] v.t. gêner.

**hamster** n. hamster m.

**hand** n. main f.; (of clock) aiguille f.; (writing) écriture f.; (worker) ouvr|ier, -ière m., f.; (cards) jeu m. ● v.t. donner. **at** ~, proche. ~ **baggage** n. bagages à main m. pl. **give s.o. a** ~, donner un coup de main à qn. ~ **in** or **over,** remettre. ~ **out,** distribuer.

**handbag** n. sac à main m.

**handbook** n. manuel m.

**handbrake** n. frein à main m.

**handcuffs** n. pl. menottes f. pl.

**handful** n. poignée f.

**handicap** n. handicap m. ~**-ped** a. handicapé.

**handkerchief** n. mouchoir m.

**handle** n. (of door etc.) poignée f.; (of implement) manche m.; (of cup etc.) anse f.; (of pan etc.) queue f.; (for turning) manivelle f. ● v.t. manier; (deal with) s'occuper de; (touch) toucher à.

**handlebar** n. guidon m.

**handshake** n. poignée de main f.

**handsome** a. (goodlooking) beau; (generous) généreux; (large) considérable.

**handwriting** n. écriture f.

**handy** a. (useful) commode, utile; (person) adroit; (near) accessible.

**handyman** n. bricoleur m.; (servant) homme à tout faire m.

**hang** v.t. suspendre, accrocher; (criminal) pendre. ~ **about,** traîner. ~**-gliding** n. vol libre m. ~ **on,** (hold out) tenir bon; (wait: sl.) attendre. ~ **out** v.i. pendre; (live: sl.) crécher; (spend time: sl.) passer son temps; v.t. (washing) étendre. ~ **up,** (telephone) raccrocher. ~**-up** n. (sl.) complexe m.

**hangar** n. hangar m.

**hanger** n. (for clothes) cintre m.

**hangover** n. (after drinking) gueule de bois f.

**hanker** v.i. ~ **after,** avoir envie de.

**haphazard** a., ~**ly** adv. au petit bonheur, au hasard.

**happen** v.i. arriver, se passer. **it so** ~**s that,** il se trouve que. **he** ~**s to know that,** il se trouve qu'il sait que.

**happ**|**y** a. heureux. **I'm not** ~ **about the idea,** je n'aime pas trop l'idée. ~ **with sth.,** satisfait de qch. ~**ily** adv. joyeusement; (fortunately) heureusement. ~**iness** n. bonheur m.

**harass** v.t. harceler. ~**ment** n. harcèlement m.

**harbour,** n. port m. ● v.t. (shelter) héberger.

**hard** a. dur; (difficult) difficile, dur. ● adv. dur; (think) sérieusement; (pull) fort. ~**-boiled egg,** œuf dur m. ~ **disk,** disque dur m. ~**-headed** a. réaliste. **the** ~ **of hearing,** les malentendants m. pl. ~**-line** a. pur et dur. ~ **shoulder,** accotement stabilisé m. ~ **up,** (fam.) fauché. ~**ness** n. dureté f.

**hardboard** n. Isorel m. (P.).

**harden** v.t./i. durcir.

**hardly** adv. à peine. ~ **ever,** presque jamais.

**hardship** n. ~**(s),** épreuves f. pl.

**hardware** n. (metal goods) quincaillerie f.; (machinery, of computer) matériel m.

**hardy** a. résistant.

**hare** n. lièvre m.

**hark** v.i. écouter. ~ **back to,** revenir sur.

**harm** n. (hurt) mal m.; (wrong) tort m. ● v.t. (hurt) faire du mal à; (wrong) faire du tort à; (object) endommager. **there is no** ~ **in,** il n'y a pas de mal à. ~**ful** a. nuisible. ~**less** a. inoffensif.

**harmonica** n. harmonica m.

**harmony** n. harmonie f.

**harness** n. harnais m. ● v.t. (horse) harnacher; (control) maîtriser; (use) exploiter.

**harp** n. harpe f. ~**ist** n. harpiste m./f.

**harpoon** n. harpon m.

**harpsichord** n. clavecin m.

**harrowing** a. déchirant.

**harsh** *a.* dur, rude; (*taste*) âpre; (*sound*) rude, âpre. **~ly** *adv.* durement. **~ness** *n.* dureté *f.*

**harvest** *n.* moisson *f.*, récolte *f.* ● *v.t.* moissonner, récolter.

**hash** *n.* (*culin.*) hachis *m.*; (*fig.*) gâchis *m.* **make a ~ of**, (*bungle: sl.*) saboter.

**hashish** *n.* ha(s)chisch *m.*

**hassle** *n.* (*fam.*) difficulté(s) *f.* (*pl.*); (*bother, effort: fam.*) mal *m.*, peine *f.*; (*quarrel: fam.*) chamaillerie *f.* ● *v.t.* (*harass: fam.*) harceler.

**haste** *n.* hâte *f.* **in ~**, à la hâte.

**hast|y** *a.* précipité. **~ily** *adv.* à la hâte.

**hat** *n.* chapeau *m.*

**hatch**[1] *n.* (*for food*) passeplat *m.*; (*naut.*) écoutille *f.*

**hatch**[2] *v.t./i.* (faire) éclore.

**hatchback** *n.* voiture avec hayon arrière *f.*

**hatchet** *n.* hachette *f.*

**hate** *n.* haine *f.* ● *v.t.* haïr.

**hatred** *n.* haine *f.*

**haughty** *a.* hautain.

**haul** *v.t.* traîner, tirer. ● *n.* (*of thieves*) butin *m.*; (*catch*) prise *f.*; (*journey*) voyage *m.*

**haunch** *n.* **on one's ~es**, accroupi.

**haunt** *v.t.* hanter.

**have** *v.t.* avoir; (*meal, bath, etc.*) prendre; (*walk, dream, etc.*) faire. ● *v. aux.* avoir; (*with aller, partir, etc. & pronominal verbs*) être. ~ **just done**, venir de faire. ~ **sth. done**, faire faire qch. ~ **to do**, devoir faire.

**haven** *n.* havre *m.*, abri *m.*

**havoc** *n.* ravages *m. pl.*

**hawk**[1] *n.* faucon *m.*

**hawk**[2] *v.t.* colporter. **~er** *n.* colporteu|r, -se *m.*, *f.*

**hawthorn** *n.* aubépine *f.*

**hay** *n.* foin *m.* ~ **fever**, rhume des foins *m.*

**haywire** *a.* **go ~**, (*plans*) se désorganiser; (*machine*) se détraquer.

**hazard** *n.* risque *m.* ● *v.t.* risquer, hasarder. ~ **warning lights,** feux de détresse *m. pl.* **~ous** *a.* hasardeux, risqué.

**haze** *n.* brume *f.*

**hazel** *n.* (*bush*) noisetier *m.* **~-nut** *n.* noisette *f.*

**hazy** *a.* (*misty*) brumeux; (*fig.*) flou, vague.

**he** *pron.* il; (*emphatic*) lui. ● *n.* mâle *m.*

**head** *n.* tête *f.*; (*leader*) chef *m.*; (*of beer*) mousse *f.* ● *a.* principal. ● *v.t.* être à la tête de. ● *v.i.* ~ **for**, se diriger vers. **~s or tails?**, pile ou face? ~ **office,** siège *m.* ~ **rest,** appui-tête *m.* **~er** *n.* (*football*) tête *f.*

**headache** *n.* mal de tête *m.*

**heading** *n.* titre *m.*; (*subject category*) rubrique *f.*

**headlamp** *n.* phare *m.*

**headland** *n.* cap *m.*

**headlight** *n.* phare *m.*

**headline** *n.* titre *m.*

**headlong** *adv.* (*in a rush*) à toute allure.

**head|master** *n.* (*of school*) directeur *m.* **~mistress** *n.* directrice *f.*

**headphone** *n.* écouteur *m.* **~s,** casque (à écouteurs) *m.*

**headquarters** *n. pl.* siège *m.*, bureau central *m.*; (*mil.*) quartier général *m.*

**headstrong** *a.* têtu.

**headway** *n.* progrès *m.* (*pl.*) **make ~,** faire des progrès.

**heady** *a.* (*wine*) capiteux; (*exciting*) grisant.

**heal** *v.t./i.* guérir.

**health** *n.* santé *f.* ~ **centre,** dispensaire *m.* ~ **foods,** aliments diététiques *m. pl. f.* **~y** *a.* sain; (*person*) en bonne santé.

**heap** *n.* tas *m.* ● *v.t.* entasser. **~s of,** (*fam.*) des tas de.

**hear** *v.t./i.* entendre. ~ **about,** entendre parler de. **~ing** *n.* ouïe *f.*; (*of witness*) audition *f.*; (*of case*) audience *f.* **~ing-aid** *n.* appareil acoustique *m.*

**hearsay** *n.* ouï-dire *m. invar.* **from ~,** par ouï-dire.

**heart** *n.* cœur *m.* **~s,** (*cards*) cœur *m.* **by ~,** par cœur. ~ **attack,** crise cardiaque *f.* **be ~-broken,** avoir le cœur brisé.

**heartache** *n.* chagrin *m.*

**heartburn** *n.* brûlures d'estomac *f. pl.*

**hearten** *v.t.* encourager.

**hearth** *n.* foyer *m.*

**heartless** *a.* cruel.

**heart|y** *a.* (*sincere*) chaleureux; (*meal*) gros. **~ily** *adv.* (*eat*) avec appétit.

**heat** *n.* chaleur *f.*; (*excitement: fig.*) feu *m.*; (*contest*) éliminatoire *f.* ● *v.t./i.* chauffer. ~ **stroke,** insolation *f.* **~ up,** (*food*) réchauffer. ~ **wave,** vague de chaleur *f.* **~er** *n.* radiateur *m.* **~ing** *n.* chauffage *m.*

**heath** *n.* (*area*) lande *f.*

**heather** *n.* bruyère *f.*

**heave** *v.t./i.* (*lift*) (se) soulever; (*a sigh*) pousser; (*throw: fam.*) lancer; (*retch*) avoir des nausées.

**heaven** *n.* ciel *m.* **~ly** *a.* céleste; (*pleasing: fam.*) divin.

**heav|y** *a.* lourd; (*cold, work, etc.*) gros; (*traffic*) dense. **~y goods vehicle,** poids lourd *m.* **~ily** *adv.* lourdement; (*smoke, drink*) beaucoup.

**heavyweight** *n.* poids lourd *m.*

**Hebrew** *a.* hébreu (*m. only*), hébraïque. ● *n.* (*lang.*) hébreu *m.*

**heckle** *v.t.* interpeller.

**hectic** *a.* agité.

**hedge** *n.* haie *f.* ● *v.t.* entourer. ● *v.i.* (*in answering*) répondre évasivement.

**hedgehog** *n.* hérisson *m.*

**heed** *v.t.* faire attention à.

**heel** *n.* talon *m.*; (*man: sl.*) salaud *m.*

**hefty** *a.* gros, lourd.

**heifer** n. génisse f.

**height** n. hauteur f.; (of person) taille f.; (of plane, mountain) altitude f.; (of fame, glory) apogée m.; (of joy, folly, pain) comble m.

**heighten** v.t. (raise) rehausser; (fig.) augmenter.

**heir** n. héritier m. ~**ess** n. héritière f.

**heirloom** n. bijou (meuble, tableau, etc.) de famille m.

**helicopter** n. hélicoptère m.

**heliport** n. héliport m.

**hell** n. enfer m.

**hello** int. & n. = **hallo**.

**helm** n. (of ship) barre f.

**helmet** n. casque m.

**help** v.t./i. aider. ● n. aide f.; (employees) personnel m.; (charwoman) femme de ménage f. ~ **o.s. to**, se servir de. ~**er** n. aide m./f. c'est à elle or le sien. ~**ful** a. utile; (person) serviable. ~**less** a. impuissant.

**helping** n. portion f.

**hem** n. ourlet m. ● v.t. ourler. ~ **in**, enfermer.

**hemisphere** n. hémisphère m.

**hen** n. poule f.

**hence** adv. (for this reason) d'où; (from now) d'ici. ~**forth** adv. désormais.

**henchman** n. acolyte m., homme de main m.

**hepatitis** n. hépatite f.

**her** pron. la, l'*; (after prep.) elle. **(to)** ~, lùi. I know ~, je la connais. ● a. son, sa, pl. ses.

**herald** v.t. annoncer.

**herb** n. herbe f. ~**s**, (culin.) fines herbes f. pl.

**herd** n. troupeau m.

**here** adv. ici. ~**I**, (take this) tenez! ~ **is**, ~ **are**, voici.

**hereby** adv. par le présent acte; (in letter) par la présente.

**hereditary** a. héréditaire.

**heredity** n. hérédité f.

**here|sy** n. hérésie f. ~**tic** n. hérétique m./f.

**herewith** adv. (comm.), ci-joint.

**heritage** n. héritage m.

**hermit** n. ermite m.

**hernia** n. hernie f.

**hero** n. héros m. ~**ine** n. héroïne f. ~**ism** n. héroïsme m.

**heroic** a. héroïque.

**heroin** n. héroïne f.

**heron** n. héron m.

**herpes** n. herpès m.

**herring** n. hareng m.

**hers** poss. pron. le sien, la sienne, les sien(ne)s. **it is** ~, c'est à elle or le sien.

**herself** pron. elle-même; (reflexive) se; (after prep.) elle.

**hesitant** a. hésitant.

**hesitat|e** v.i. hésiter. ~**ion** n. hésitation f.

**heterosexual** a. & n. hétérosexuel(le) (m. (f.)).

**hexagon** n. hexagone m.

**hey** int. dites donc.

**heyday** n. apogée m.

**HGV** abbr. see **heavy goods vehicle**.

**hi** int. salut.

**hibernat|e** v.i. hiberner. ~**ion** n. hibernation f.

**hiccup** n. hoquet m. ● v.i. hoqueter. **(the)** ~**s**, le hoquet.

**hide**[1] v.t. cacher (**from**, à). ● v.i. se cacher (**from**, de). **go into hiding**, se cacher. ~**-out** n. (fam.) cachette f.

**hide**[2] n. (skin) peau f.

**hideous** a. (dreadful) atroce; (ugly) hideux.

**hiding** n. (thrashing: fam.) correction f.

**hierarchy** n. hiérarchie f.

**hi-fi** a. & n. hi-fi a. & f. invar.; (machine) chaîne hi-fi f.

**high** a. haut; (price, number) élevé; (priest, speed) grand; (voice) aigu. ● adv. haut. ~ **chair**, chaise haute f. ~**jump**, saut en hauteur m. ~**-level** a. de haut niveau. ~ **school**, lycée m. ~**-speed** a. ultra-rapide. ~ **spot**, (fam.) point culminant m. ~ **street**, grand-rue f.

**highbrow** a. & n. intellectuel(le) (m. (f.)).

**highlight** n. (vivid moment) moment fort m. ~**s**, (in hair) balayage m. **recorded** ~**s**, extraits enregistrés m. pl. ● v.t. (emphasize) souligner.

**highly** adv. extrêmement; (paid) très bien. ~**-strung** a. nerveux. **speak/think** ~ **of**, dire/penser du bien de.

**highway** n. route nationale f. ~ **code**, code de la route m.

**hijack** v.t. détourner. ● n. détournement m. ~**er** n. pirate (de l'air) m.

**hike** n. randonnée f. ● v.i. faire de la randonnée. **price** ~, hausse de prix f. ~**r** n. randonneu|r, -se m., f.

**hilarious** a. (funny) désopilant.

**hill** n. colline f.; (slope) côte f. ~**y** a. accidenté.

**hillside** n. coteau m.

**hilt** n. (of sword) garde f. **to the** ~, tout à fait, au maximum.

**him** pron. le, l'*; (after prep.) lui. **(to)** ~, lui.

**himself** pron. lui-même; (reflexive) se; (after prep.) lui.

**hinder** v.t. (hamper) gêner; (prevent) empêcher.

**hindsight** n. **with** ~, rétrospectivement.

**Hindu** a. & n. hindou(e) (m. (f.)). ~**ism** n. hindouisme m.

**hinge** n. charnière f. ● v.i. ~ **on**, (depend on) dépendre de.

**hint** n. allusion f.; (advice) conseil m. ● v.t. laisser entendre. ● v.i. ~ **at**, faire allusion à.

**hip** n. hanche f.

**hippopotamus** n. hippopotame m.

**hire** v.t. (thing) louer; (person) engager. ● n. location f. ~-car n. voiture de location f. ~-purchase n. achat à crédit m.

**his** a. son, sa, pl. ses. ● poss. pron. le sien, la sienne, les sien(ne)s. **it is** ~, c'est à lui or le sien.

**hiss** n. sifflement m. ● v.t./i. siffler.

**historian** n. historien(ne) m. (f.).

**histor|y** n. histoire f. ~**ic(al)** a. historique.

**hit** v.t. frapper; (knock against, collide with) heurter; (find) trouver; (affect, reach) toucher; (blow) coup m.; (fig.) succès m.; (song) tube m.

**hitch** v.t. (fasten) accrocher. ● n. (snag) anicroche f. ~ **a lift, ~-hike** v.i. faire de l'auto-stop. ~**-hiker** n. auto-stoppeu|r, -se m., f.

**hi-tech** a. & n. high-tech (m.) invar.

**HIV** abbr. HIV. ~**-positive** a. séropositif.

**hive** n. ruche f. ● v.t. ~**-off**, séparer; (industry) vendre.

**hoard** v.t. amasser. ● n. réserve(s) f. (pl.); (of money) magot m., trésor m.

**hoarding** n. panneau d'affichage m.

**hoarse** a. enroué.

**hoax** n. canular m.

**hob** n. plaque chauffante f.

**hobble** v.i. clopiner.

**hobby** n. passe-temps m. invar. ~**-horse** n. (fig.) dada m.

**hockey** n. hockey m.

**hoe** n. binette f. ● v.t. biner.

**hog** n. cochon m. ● v.t. (fam.) accaparer.

**hoist** v.t. hisser. ● n. palan m.

**hold**[1] v.t. (p.t. **held**) tenir; (contain) contenir; (interest, breath, etc.) retenir; (possess) avoir; (believe) maintenir. ● v.i. (of rope, weather, etc.) tenir. ● n. prise f. **get ~ of,** saisir; (fig.) trouver. ~ **down,** (job) garder; (in struggle) retenir. ~ **on,** (stand firm) tenir bon; (wait) attendre. ~ **on to,** (keep) garder; (cling to) se cramponner à. ~ **out** v.t. (offer) offrir; v.i. (resist) tenir le coup. ~ **(the line), please,** ne quittez pas. ~ **up,** (support) soutenir; (delay) retarder; (rob) attaquer. ~**-up** n. retard m.; (of traffic) bouchon m.; (robbery) hold-up m. invar.

**hold**[2] n. (of ship) cale f.

**holdall** n. (bag) fourre-tout m. invar.

**holding** n. (possession, land) possession f. ~ **company,** holding m.

**hole** n. trou m. ● v.t. trouer.

**holiday** n. vacances f. pl.; (public) jour férié m.; (day off) congé m. ● v.i. passer ses vacances. ● a. de vacances. ~**-maker** n. vacanc|ier, -ière m., f.

**holistic** a. holistique.

**Holland** n. Hollande f.

**hollow** a. creux; (fig.) faux. ● n. creux m. ● v.t. creuser.

**holly** n. houx m.

**holster** n. étui de revolver m.

**holy** a. saint, sacré; (water) bénit. **H~ Spirit,** Saint-Esprit m.

**homage** n. hommage m.

**home** n. maison f., foyer m.; (institution) maison f.; (for soldiers, workers) foyer m.; (country) pays natal m. ● a. de la maison, du foyer; (of family) de famille; (pol.) national, intérieur; (match, visit) à domicile. ● adv. **(at)** ~, à la maison, chez soi. **come** or **go** ~, rentrer; (from abroad) rentrer dans son pays. ~**-made** a. (food) fait maison; (clothes) fait à la maison. ~**less** a. sans abri.

**homeland** n. patrie f.

**homesick** a. be ~, avoir le mal du pays.

**homework** n. devoirs m. pl.

**homicide** n. homicide m.

**homœopath|y** n. homéopathie f. ~**ic** a. homéopathique.

**homogeneous** a. homogène.

**homosexual** a. & n. homosexuel(le) (m. (f.)).

**honest** a. honnête; (frank) franc. ~**ly** adv. honnêtement; franchement. ~**y** n. honnêteté f.

**honey** n. miel m.; (person: fam.) chéri(e) m. (f.).

**honeymoon** n. lune de miel f.

**honk** v.i. klaxonner.

**honorary** a. (person) honoraire; (duties) honorifique.

**honour** n. honneur m. ● v.t. honorer. ~**able** a. honorable.

**hood** n. capuchon m.; (car roof) capote f.

**hoof** n. sabot m.

**hook** n. crochet m.; (on garment) agrafe f.; (for fishing) hameçon m. ● v.t./i. (s')accrocher; (garment) (s')agrafer.

**hooligan** n. hooligan m.

**hoop** n. (toy etc.) cerceau m.

**hooray** int. & n. = **hurrah.**

**hoot** n. (h)ululement m.; coup de klaxon m.; huée f. ● v.i. (owl) (h)ululer; (of car) klaxonner; (jeer) huer. ~**er** n. klaxon m. (P.); (of factory) sirène f.

**Hoover** n. (P.) aspirateur m. ● v.t. passer à l'aspirateur.

**hop**[1] v.i. sauter (à cloche-pied). ● n. saut m.; (flight) étape f.

**hop**[2] n. ~**(s),** houblon m.

**hope** n. espoir m. ● v.t./i. espérer. ~ **for,** espérer (avoir). **I** ~ **so,** je l'espère. ~**ful** a. encourageant. **be** ~**ful (that),** avoir bon espoir (que). ~**fully** adv. avec espoir; (it is hoped) on l'espère. ~**less** a. sans espoir; (useless: fig.) nul.

**horde** n. horde f., foule f.

**horizon** n. horizon m.

**horizontal** a. horizontal.

**hormone** n. hormone f.

**horn** n. corne f.; (of car) klaxon m. (P.); (mus.) cor m.

**hornet** n. frelon m.

**horoscope** n. horoscope m.

**horrible** a. horrible.

**horrid** a. horrible.

**horrific** a. horrifiant.

**horr|or** n. horreur f. ● a. (film etc.) d'épouvante. ~**ify** v.t. horrifier.

**hors-d'œuvre** n. hors-d'œuvre m. invar.

**horse** n. cheval m.

**horsepower** n. (unit) cheval (vapeur) m.

**horseshoe** n. fer à cheval m.

**horticultur|e** n. horticulture f. ~**al** a. horticole.

**hose** n. (tube) tuyau m. ● v.t. arroser. ~**pipe** n. tuyau m.

**hosiery** n. bonneterie f.

**hospice** n. hospice m.

**hospit|able** a. hospitalier. ~**ably** adv. avec hospitalité. ~**ality** n. hospitalité f.

**hospital** n. hôpital m.

**host¹** n. (to guests) hôte m.; (on TV) animateur m. ~**ess** n. hôtesse f.

**host²** n. **a** ~ **of**, une foule de.

**host³** n. (relig.) hostie f.

**hostage** n. otage m.

**hostel** n. foyer m. (**youth**) ~, auberge (de jeunesse) f.

**hostil|e** a. hostile. ~**ity** n. hostilité f.

**hot** a. chaud; (culin.) épicé; (news) récent. **be** or **feel** ~, avoir chaud. **it is** ~, il fait chaud. ~ **dog**, hot-dog m. ~-**water bottle**, bouillotte f.

**hotchpotch** n. fatras m.

**hotel** n. hôtel m.

**hotplate** n. plaque chauffante f.

**hound** n. chien courant m. ● v.t. poursuivre.

**hour** n. heure f. ~**ly** a. & adv. toutes les heures. ~**ly rate**, tarif horaire m.

**house¹** n. maison f.; (theatre) salle f.; (pol.) chambre f.

**house²** v.t. loger; (of building) abriter; (keep) garder.

**housebreaking** n. cambriolage m.

**housecoat** n. blouse f., tablier m.

**household** n. (house, family) ménage m. ● a. ménager. ~**er** n. occupant(e) m. (f.); (owner) propriétaire m./f.

**housekeeper** n. gouvernante f.

**housewife** n. ménagère f.

**housework** n. ménage m. travaux de ménage m. pl.

**housing** n. logement m. ~ **development**, cité f.

**hover** v.i. (bird, threat, etc.) planer; (loiter) rôder.

**hovercraft** n. aéroglisseur m.

**how** adv. comment. ~ **long/tall is ...?**, quelle est la longueur/hauteur de ...? ~ **pretty!**, comme or que c'est joli! ~ **are you?**, comment allez-vous? ~ **do you do?**, (introduction) enchanté. ~ **many?**, ~ **much?**, combien?

**however** adv. de quelque manière que; (nevertheless) cependant. ~ **small/delicate/**etc. **it may be**, quelque petit/délicat/ etc. que ce soit.

**howl** n. hurlement m. ● v.i. hurler.

**HP** abbr. see **hire-purchase**.

**hp** abbr. see **horsepower**.

**HQ** abbr. see **headquarters**.

**hub** n. moyeu m.; (fig.) centre m. ~-**cap** n. enjoliveur m.

**huddle** /'hʌdl/ v.i. se blottir.

**hue** n. (colour) teinte f.

**hug** v.t. serrer dans ses bras; (keep close to) serrer. ● n. étreinte f.

**huge** a. énorme.

**hulk** n. (of ship) épave f.; (person) mastodonte m.

**hull** n. (of ship) coque f.

**hum** v.t./i. (person) fredonner; (insect) bourdonner; (engine) vrombir. ● n. bourdonnement m.; vrombissement m. ~ **and haw**, hésiter.

**human** a. humain. ● n. être humain m. ~**itarian** a. humanitaire.

**humane** a. humain.

**humanity** n. humanité f.

**humbl|e** a. humble. ● v.t. humilier. ~**y** adv. humblement.

**humid** a. humide. ~**ity** n. humidité f.

**humiliat|e** v.t. humilier. ~**ion** n. humiliation f.

**humility** n. humilité f.

**hum|our**, n. humour m.; (mood) humeur f. ● v.t. ménager. ~**orous** a. humoristique; (person) plein d'humour.

**hump** n. bosse f. ● v.t. voûter.

**hunch¹** v.t. voûter.

**hunch²** n. petite idée f.

**hundred** a. & n. cent (m.). ~**s of**, des centaines de. ~**fold** a. centuple; adv. au centuple. ~**th** a. & n. centième (m./f.).

**hundredweight** n. 50.8 kg.; (Amer.) 45.36 kg.

**Hungar|y** n. Hongrie f. ~**ian** a. & n. hongrois(e) (m. (f.)).

**hunger** n. faim f. ● v.i. ~ **for**, avoir faim de.

**hungr|y** a. affamé. **be** ~**y**, avoir faim.

**hunt** v.t./i. chasser. ● n. chasse f. ~ **for**, chercher. ~**er** n. chasseur m. ~**ing** n. chasse f.

**hurdle** n. (sport) haie f.; (fig.) obstacle m.

**hurl** v.t. lancer.

**hurrah, hurray** int. & n. hourra (m.).

**hurricane** n. ouragan m.

**hurried** a. précipité.

**hurry** *v.i.* se dépêcher, se presser. ● *v.t.* presser, activer. ● *n.* hâte *f.* **in a ~,** pressé.

**hurt** *v.t./i.* faire mal (à); (*injure,* offend) blesser. ● *a.* blessé. ● *n.* mal *m.*

**hurtle** *v.i.* **~ along,** avancer à toute vitesse.

**husband** *n.* mari *m.*

**hush** *v.t.* faire taire. ● *n.* silence *m.* **~up,** (*news etc.*) étouffer.

**husk** *n.* (*of grain*) enveloppe *f.*

**husky** *a.* (*hoarse*) rauque; (*burly*) costaud. ● *n.* chien de traîneau *m.*

**hustle** *v.t.* (*push, rush*) bousculer. ● *v.i.* (*work busily: Amer.*) se démener. ● *n.* bousculade *f.* **~ and bustle,** agitation *f.*

**hut** *n.* cabane *f.*

**hutch** *n.* clapier *m.*

**hyacinth** *n.* jacinthe *f.*

**hybrid** *a. & n.* hybride (*m.*).

**hydrangea** *n.* hortensia *m.*

**hydrant** *n.* **(fire) ~,** bouche d'incendie *f.*

**hydraulic** *a.* hydraulique.

**hydroelectric** *a.* hydro-électrique.

**hydrofoil** *n.* hydroptère *m.*

**hydrogen** *n.* hydrogène *m.*

**hyena** *n.* hyène *f.*

**hygiene** *n.* hygiène *f.*

**hygienic** *a.* hygiénique.

**hymn** *n.* cantique *m.*, hymne *m.*

**hype** *n.* tapage publicitaire *m.* ● *v.t.* faire du tapage autour de.

**hyper-** *pref.* hyper-.

**hypermarket** *n.* hypermarché *m.*

**hyphen** *n.* trait d'union *m.* **~ate** *v.t.* mettre un trait d'union à.

**hypno|sis** *n.* hypnose *f.* **~tic** *a.* hypnotique.

**hypnot|ize** *v.t.* hypnotiser. **~ism** *n.* hypnotisme *m.*

**hypochondriac** *n.* malade imaginaire *m./f.*

**hypocrisy** *n.* hypocrisie *f.*

**hypocrit|e** *n.* hypocrite *m./f.* **~ical** *a.* hypocrite.

**hypodermic** *a.* hypodermique. ● *n.* seringue hypodermique *f.*

**hypothe|sis** *n.* hypothèse *f.* **~tical** *a.* hypothétique.

**hyster|ia** *n.* hystérie *f.* **~ical** *a.* hystérique; (*person*) surexcité.

**hysterics** *n. pl.* crise de nerfs *or* de rire *f.*

**I** *pron.* je, j'*; (*stressed*) moi.

**ice** *n.* glace *f.*; (*on road*) verglas *m.* ● *v.t.* (*cake*) glacer. ● *v.i.* **~ (up),** (*window*) se givrer; (*river*) geler. **~-cream** *n.* glace *f.* **~-cube** *n.* glaçon *m.* **~ hockey,** hockey sur glace *m.* **~ lolly,** glace (*sur bâtonnet*) *f.* **~rink,** patinoire *f.* **~ skate,** patin à glace *m.*

**iceberg** *n.* iceberg *m.*

**Iceland** *n.* Islande *f.* **~er** *n.* Islandais(e) *m.* (*f.*). **~ic** *a.* islandais; *n.* (*lang.*) islandais *m.*

**icicle** *n.* glaçon *m.*

**icing** *n.* (*sugar*) glace *f.*

**icon** *n.* icône *f.*

**icy** *a.* (*hands, wind*) glacé; (*road*) verglacé; (*manner, welcome*) glacial.

**idea** *n.* idée *f.*

**ideal** *a.* idéal. ● *n.* idéal *m.* **~ly** *adv.* idéalement.

**idealis|t** *n.* idéaliste *m./f.* **~m** *n.* idéalisme *m.*

**identical** *a.* identique.

**identif|y** *v.t.* identifier. **~ication** *n.* identification *f.*; (*papers*) une pièce d'identité.

**identity** *n.* identité *f.*

**ideolog|y** *n.* idéologie *f.* **~ical** *a.* idéologique.

**idiom** *n.* expression idiomatique *f.*; (*language*) idiome *m.* **~atic** *a.* idiomatique.

**idiot** *n.* idiot(e) *m.* (*f.*). **~ic** *a.* idiot.

**idle** *a.* désœuvré, oisif; (*lazy*) paresseux; (*unemployed*) sans travail; (*machine*) au repos; (*fig.*) vain. ● *v.i.* (*engine*) tourner au ralenti. ● *v.t.* **~ away,** gaspiller. **~ness** *n.* oisiveté *f.*

**idol** *n.* idole *f.* **~ize** *v.t.* idolâtrer.

**idyllic** *a.* idyllique.

**i.e.** *abbr.* c'est-à-dire.

**if** *conj.* si.

**igloo** *n.* igloo *m.*

**ignite** *v.t./i.* (s')enflammer.

**ignition** *n.* (*auto.*) allumage *m.* **~ key,** clé de contact *f.* **~ (switch),** contact *m.*

**ignoran|t** *a.* ignorant (**of,** de). **~ce** *n.* ignorance *f.*

**ignore** *v.t.* ne faire *or* prêter aucune attention à; (*person in street etc.*) faire semblant de ne pas voir; (*facts*) ne pas tenir compte de.

**ill** *a.* malade; (*bad*) mauvais. ● *adv.* mal. ● *n.* mal *m.*

**illegal** *a.* illégal.

**illegible** *a.* illisible.

**illness** *n.* maladie *f.*

**illogical** *a.* illogique.

**illuminat|e** v.t. éclairer; (*decorate with lights*) illuminer. **~ion** n. éclairage m.; illumination f.

**illusion** n. illusion f.

**illusory** a. illusoire.

**illustrat|e** v.t. illustrer. **~ion** n. illustration f. **~ive** a. qui illustre.

**illustrious** a. illustre.

**image** n. image f. **(public) ~,** (*offirm, person*) image de marque f. **~ry** n. images f. pl.

**imaginary** a. imaginaire.

**imaginat|ion** n. imagination f. **~ive** a. plein d'imagination.

**imagin|e** v.t. (*picture to o.s.*) (s')imaginer; (*suppose*) imaginer. **~able** a. imaginable.

**imbalance** n. déséquilibre m.

**imbecile** n. & a. imbécile (m./f.).

**imitat|e** v.t. imiter. **~ion** n. imitation f. **~or** n. imita|teur, -trice m., f.

**immaterial** a. sans importance (**to,** pour; **that,** que).

**immature** a. pas mûr; (*person*) immature.

**immediate** a. immédiat. **~ly** adv. immédiatement; conj. dès que.

**immense** a. immense.

**immers|e** v.t. plonger, immerger. **~ion** n. immersion f. **~ion heater,** chauffe-eau (électrique) m. invar.

**immigr|ate** v.i. immigrer. **~ant** n. & a. immigré(e) (m. (f.)); (*newly-arrived*) immigrant(e) (m. (f.)). **~ation** n. immigration f.

**imminen|t** a. imminent. **~ce** n. imminence f.

**immobil|e** a. immobile. **~ize** v.t. immobiliser.

**immoral** a. immoral. **~ity** n. immoralité f.

**immortal** a. immortel. **~ity** n. immortalité f.

**immun|e** a. immunisé (**from, to,** contre). **~ity** n. immunité f.

**immuniz|e** v.t. immuniser. **~ation** n. immunisation f.

**imp** n. lutin m.

**impact** n. impact m.

**impair** v.t. détériorer.

**impartial** a. impartial.

**impassable** a. (*barrier etc.*) infranchissable; (*road*) impraticable.

**impasse** n. impasse f.

**impassive** a. impassible.

**impatien|t** a. impatient. **get ~t,** s'impatienter. **~ce** n. impatience f. **~tly** adv. impatiemment.

**impeccable** a. impeccable.

**impede** v.t. gêner.

**impel** v.t. pousser (**to do,** à faire).

**impending** a. imminent.

**impenetrable** a. impénétrable.

**imperative** a. nécessaire; (*need etc.*) impérieux. ● n. (*gram.*) impératif m.

**imperceptible** a. imperceptible.

**imperfect** a. imparfait; (*faulty*) défectueux.

**imperial** a. impérial; (*measure*) légal (au Royaume-Uni).

**imperil** v.t. mettre en péril.

**impersonal** a. impersonnel.

**impersonat|e** v.t. se faire passer pour; (*mimic*) imiter. **~ion** n. imitation f. **~or** n. imita|teur, -trice m., f.

**impertinen|t** a. impertinent. **~ce** n. impertinence f.

**impetuous** a. impétueux.

**impetus** n. impulsion f.

**impinge** v.i. **~ on,** affecter; (*encroach*) empiéter sur.

**implacable** a. implacable.

**implant** v.t. implanter. ● n. implant m.

**implement**[1] n. (*tool*) outil m.; (*utensil*) ustensile m.

**implement**[2] v.t. exécuter.

**implicat|e** v.t. impliquer. **~ion** n. implication f.

**implicit** a. (*implied*) implicite; (*unquestioning*) absolu.

**implore** v.t. implorer.

**impl|y** v.t. (*assume, mean*) impliquer; (*insinuate*) laisser entendre. **~ied** a. implicite.

**impolite** a. impoli.

**import**[1] v.t. importer. f. **~er** n. importa|teur, -trice m., f.

**import**[2] n. (*article*) importation f.; (*meaning*) sens m.

**importan|t** a. important. **~ce** n. importance f.

**impose** v.t. imposer.

**imposing** a. imposant.

**impossible** a. impossible.

**impostor** n. imposteur m.

**impoten|t** a. impuissant. **~ce** n. impuissance f.

**impound** v.t. confisquer.

**impoverish** v.t. appauvrir.

**impracticable** a. impraticable.

**impractical** a. peu pratique.

**impresario** n. impresario m.

**impress** v.t. impressionner; (*imprint*) imprimer.

**impression** n. impression f. **~able** a. impressionnable.

**impressive** a. impressionnant.

**imprint**[1] n. empreinte f.

**imprint**[2] v.t. imprimer.

**imprison** v.t. emprisonner. **~ment** n. emprisonnement m.

**improbable** a. (*not likely*) improbable; (*incredible*) invraisemblable.

**impromptu** a. & adv. impromptu.

**improper** *a.* inconvenant, indécent; (*wrong*) incorrect.

**improve** *v.t./i.* (s')améliorer. **~ment** *n.* amélioration *f.*

**improvis|e** *v.t./i.* improviser. **~ation** *n.* improvisation *f.*

**impuden|t** *a.* impudent. **~ce** *n.* impudence *f.*

**impulse** *n.* impulsion *f.* **on ~,** sur un coup de tête.

**impulsive** *a.* impulsif.

**impunity** *n.* impunité *f.* **with ~,** impunément.

**impur|e** *a.* impur. **~ity** *n.* impureté *f.*

**in** *prep.* dans, à, en. ● *adv.* (*inside*) dedans; (*at home*) là, à la maison; (*in fashion*) à la mode. **in the box/garden,** dans la boîte/le jardin. **in Paris/school,** à Paris/l'école. **in town,** en ville. **in the country,** à la campagne. **in winter/English,** en hiver/ anglais. **in India,** en Inde. **in Japan,** au Japon. **in blue,** en bleu. **in ink,** à l'encre. **in uniform,** en uniforme. **in a skirt,** en jupe. **in winter,** en hiver. **in spring,** au printemps. **in an hour,** au bout d'une heure. **in an hour('s time),** dans une heure. **in (the space of) an hour,** en une heure. **in the evening,** le soir. **in ten,** un sur dix. **in-laws** *n. pl.* (*fam.*) beaux-parents *m. pl.* **~patient** *n.* malade hospitalisé(e) *m.(f.)*.

**inability** *n.* incapacité *f.* (**to do,** de faire).

**inaccessible** *a.* inaccessible.

**inaccurate** *a.* inexact.

**inaction** *n.* inaction *f.*

**inactiv|e** *a.* inactif. **~ity** *n.* inaction *f.*

**inadequa|te** *a.* insuffisant. **~cy** *n.* insuffisance *f.*

**inadvertently** *adv.* par mégarde.

**inane** *a.* inepte.

**inanimate** *a.* inanimé.

**inappropriate** *a.* inopportun; (*term*) inapproprié.

**inarticulate** *a.* qui a du mal à s'exprimer.

**inaudible** *a.* inaudible.

**inaugural** *a.* inaugural.

**inaugurat|e** *v.t.* (*open, begin*) inaugurer; (*person*) investir. **~ion** *n.* inauguration *f.*; investiture *f.*

**inborn** *a.* inné.

**inbred** *a.* (*inborn*) inné.

**inc.** *abbr.* (*incorporated*) S.A.

**incalculable** *a.* incalculable.

**incapable** *a.* incapable.

**incapacit|y** *n.* incapacité *f.* **~ate** *v.t.* rendre incapable (*de travailler etc.*).

**incarnat|e** *a.* incarné. **~ion** *n.* incarnation *f.*

**incendiary** *a.* incendiaire. ● *n.* (*bomb*) bombe incendiaire *f.*

**incense**[1] *n.* encens *m.*

**incense**[2] *v.t.* mettre en fureur.

**incentive** *n.* motivation *f.*; (*payment*) prime (d'encouragement) *f.*

**inception** *n.* début *m.*

**incessant** *a.* incessant. **~ly** *adv.* sans cesse.

**incest** *n.* inceste *m.*

**inch** *n.* pouce *m.* (= 2.54 cm.).

**incidence** *n.* fréquence *f.*

**incident** *n.* incident *m.*; (*in play, film, etc.*) épisode *m.*

**incidental** *a.* accessoire. **~ly** *adv.* accessoirement; (*by the way*) à propos.

**incinerat|e** *v.t.* incinérer. **~or** *n.* incinérateur *m.*

**incision** *n.* incision *f.*

**incite** *v.t.* inciter, pousser. **~ment** *n.* incitation *f.*

**inclination** *n.* (*propensity, bowing*) inclination *f.*

**incline**[1] *v.t./i.* incliner. **be ~d to,** avoir tendance à.

**incline**[2] *n.* pente *f.*

**inclu|de** *v.t.* comprendre, inclure. **~ding** *prep.* (y) compris. **~sion** *n.* inclusion *f.*

**inclusive** *a. & adv.* inclus, compris. **be ~ of,** comprendre.

**incoherent** *a.* incohérent.

**income** *n.* revenu *m.* **~ tax,** impôt sur le revenu *m.*

**incoming** *a.* (*tide*) montant; (*tenant etc.*) nouveau.

**incomparable** *a.* incomparable.

**incompatible** *a.* incompatible.

**incompeten|t** *a.* incompétent. **~ce** *n.* incompétence *f.*

**incomplete** *a.* incomplet.

**incomprehensible** *a.* incompréhensible.

**inconceivable** *a.* inconcevable.

**incongruous** *a.* déplacé, incongru.

**inconsiderate** *a.* (*person*) qui ne se soucie pas des autres; (*act*) irréfléchi.

**inconsisten|t** *a.* (*treatment*) sans cohérence, inconséquent; (*argument*) contradictoire; (*performance*) irrégulier. **~t with,** incompatible avec. **~cy** *n.* inconséquence *f.*; contradiction *f.*; irrégularité *f.*

**inconspicuous** *a.* peu en évidence.

**inconvenien|t** *a.* incommode, peu pratique; (*time*) malchoisi. **be ~t for,** ne pas convenir à. **~ce** *n.* dérangement *m.*; (*drawback*) inconvénient *m.*; *v.t.* déranger.

**incorporate** *v.t.* incorporer; (*include*) contenir.

**incorrect** *a.* inexact.

**incorrigible** *a.* incorrigible.

**increas|e**[1] *v.t./i.* augmenter. **~ing** *a.* croissant. **~ingly** *adv.* de plus en plus.

**increase**[2] *n.* augmentation *f.* (**in, of,** de). **be on the ~,** augmenter.

**incredible** *a.* incroyable.

**increment** *n.* augmentation *f.*

**incriminat|e** *v.t.* incriminer. **∼ing** *a.* compromettant.

**incubat|e** *v.t.* (*eggs*) couver. **∼ion** *n.* incubation *f.* **∼or** *n.* couveuse *f.*

**inculcate** *v.t.* inculquer.

**incur** *v.t.* encourir; (*debts*) contracter; (*anger*) s'exposer à.

**incurable** *a.* incurable.

**incursion** *n.* incursion *f.*

**indebted** *a.* **∼ to s.o.**, redevable à qn. (**for**, de).

**indecen|t** *a.* indécent. **∼cy** *n.* indécence *f.*

**indecision** *n.* indécision *f.*

**indecisive** *a.* indécis; (*ending*) peu concluant.

**indeed** *adv.* en effet, vraiment.

**indefensible** *a.* indéfendable.

**indefinable** *a.* indéfinissable.

**indefinite** *a.* indéfini; (*time*) indéterminé. **∼ly** *adv.* indéfiniment.

**indelible** *a.* indélébile.

**indemnity** *n.* (*money*) indemnité *f.*; (*guarantee*) garantie *f.*

**indent** *v.t.* (*text*) renfoncer.

**independen|t** *a.* indépendant. **∼ce** *n.* indépendance *f.* **∼tly** *adv.* de façon indépendante. **∼tly of**, indépendamment de.

**indescribable** *a.* indescriptible.

**indestructible** *a.* indestructible.

**indeterminate** *a.* indéterminé.

**index** *n.* (*figure*) indice *m.*; (*in book*) index *m.*; (*in library*) catalogue *m.* ● *v.t.* classer. **∼ card**, fiche *f.* **∼ finger** index *m.* **∼-linked** *a.* indexé.

**India** *n.* Inde *f.* **∼n** *a.* & *n.* indien(ne) (*m.* (*f.*)).

**indicat|e** *v.t.* indiquer. **∼ion** *n.* indication *f.* **∼or** *n.* (*device*) indicateur *m.*; (*on vehicle*) clignotant *m.*; (*board*) tableau *m.*

**indict** *v.t.* accuser. **∼ment** *n.* accusation *f.*

**indifferen|t** *a.* indifférent; (*not good*) médiocre. **∼ce** *n.* indifférence *f.*

**indigenous** *a.* indigène.

**indigest|ion** *n.* indigestion *f.* **∼ible** *a.* indigeste.

**indign|ant** *a.* indigné. **∼ation** *n.* indignation *f.*

**indigo** *n.* indigo *m.*

**indirect** *a.* indirect. **∼ly** *adv.* indirectement.

**indiscr|eet** *a.* indiscret; (*not wary*) imprudent. **∼etion** *n.* indiscrétion *f.*

**indiscriminate** *a.* qui manque de discernement; (*random*) fait au hasard. **∼ly** *adv.* sans discernement; au hasard.

**indispensable** *a.* indispensable.

**indispos|ed** *a.* indisposé, souffrant. **∼ition** *n.* indisposition *f.*

**indisputable** *a.* incontestable.

**indistinguishable** *a.* indifférenciable.

**individual** *a.* individuel. ● *n.* individu *m.* **∼ity** *n.* individualité *f.* **∼ly** *adv.* individuellement.

**indivisible** *a.* indivisible.

**Indonesia** *n.* Indonésie *f.* **∼n** *a.* & *n.* indonésien(ne) (*m.* (*f.*)).

**indoor** *a.* (*clothes etc.*) d'intérieur; (*under cover*) couvert. **∼s** *adv.* à l'intérieur.

**induce** *v.t.* (*influence*) persuader; (*cause*) provoquer. **∼ment** *n.* encouragement *m.*

**indulge** *v.t.* (*desires*) satisfaire; (*person*) se montrer indulgent pour, gâter. ● *v.i.* **∼ in**, se livrer à, s'offrir.

**indulgen|t** *a.* indulgent. **∼ce** *n.* indulgence *f.*; (*treat*) gâterie *f.*

**industrial** *a.* industriel; (*unrest etc.*) ouvrier; (*action*) revendicatif; (*accident*) du travail. **∼ist** *n.* industriel(le) *m.*(*f.*). **∼ized** *a.* industrialisé.

**industrious** *a.* travailleur.

**industry** *n.* industrie *f.*; (*zeal*) application *f.*

**inedible** *a.* (*food*) immangeable.

**ineffective** *a.* inefficace; (*person*) incapable.

**ineffectual** *a.* inefficace; (*person*) incapable.

**inefficien|t** *a.* inefficace; (*person*) incompétent. **∼cy** *n.* inefficacité *f.*; incompétence *f.*

**ineligible** *a.* inéligible. **be ∼ for**, ne pas avoir droit à.

**inept** *a.* (*absurd*) inepte; (*out of place*) mal à propos.

**inequality** *n.* inégalité *f.*

**inert** *a.* inerte.

**inertia** *n.* inertie *f.*

**inescapable** *a.* inéluctable.

**inevitabl|e** *a.* inévitable. **∼y** *adv.* inévitablement.

**inexact** *a.* inexact.

**inexcusable** *a.* inexcusable.

**inexhaustible** *a.* inépuisable.

**inexpensive** *a.* bon marché *invar.*, pas cher.

**inexplicable** *a.* inexplicable.

**infallib|le** *a.* infaillible. **∼ility** *n.* infaillibilité *f.*

**infam|ous** *a.* infâme. **∼y** *n.* infamie *f.*

**infant** *n.* (*baby*) nourrisson *m.*; (*at school*) petit(e) enfant *m.*(*f.*).

**infantry** *n.* infanterie *f.*

**infatuat|ed** *a.* **∼ed with**, engoué de. **∼ion** *n.* engouement *m.*, béguin *m.*

**infect** *v.t.* infecter. **∼ s.o. with**, communiquer à qn. **∼ion** *n.* infection *f.*

**infectious** *a.* (*med.*) infectieux; (*fig.*) contagieux.

**infer** *v.t.* déduire. **∼ence** *n.* déduction *f.*

**inferior** *a.* inférieur (**to**, à); (*work, product*) de qualité inférieure. ● *n.* inférieur(e) *m.* (*f.*). **∼ity** *n.* infériorité *f.*

**infernal** *a.* infernal.

**inferno** *n.* (*hell*) enfer *m.*; (*blaze*) incendie *m.*

**infertil|e** *a.* infertile. ~**ity** *n.* infertilité *f.*

**infest** *v.t.* infester.

**infidelity** *n.* infidélité *f.*

**infiltrat|e** *v.t./i.* s'infiltrer (dans). ~**ion** *n.* infiltration *f.*

**infinite** *a.* infini. ~**ly** *adv.* infiniment.

**infinitive** *n.* infinitif *m.*

**infinity** *n.* infinité *f.*

**infirm** *a.* infirme. ~**ity** *n.* infirmité *f.*

**infirmary** *n.* hôpital *m.*; (*sick-bay*) infirmerie *f.*

**inflam|e** *v.t.* enflammer. ~**mable** *a.* inflammable. ~**mation** *n.* inflammation *f.*

**inflat|e** *v.t.* (*balloon, prices, etc.*) gonfler. ~**able** *a.* gonflable.

**inflation** *n.* inflation *f.*

**inflict** *v.t.* infliger (**on**, à).

**influence** *n.* influence *f.* ● *v.t.* influencer.

**influential** *a.* influent.

**influenza** *n.* grippe *f.*

**influx** *n.* afflux *m.*

**inform** *v.t.* informer (**of**, de). **keep** ~**ed**, tenir au courant. ~**er** *n.* indica|teur, -trice *m.*, *f.*

**informal** *a.* (*simple*) simple, sans cérémonie; (*unofficial*) officieux; (*colloquial*) familier. ~**ity** *n.* simplicité *f.* ~**ly** *adv.* sans cérémonie.

**information** *n.* renseignement(s) *m.* (*pl.*), information(s) *f.* (*pl.*). **some** ~, un renseignement. ~ **technology**, informatique *f.*

**informative** *a.* instructif.

**infra-red** *a.* infrarouge.

**infrastructure** *n.* infrastructure *f.*

**infringe** *v.t.* contrevenir à. ~ **on**, empiéter sur. ~**ment** *n.* infraction *f.*

**infuriate** *v.t.* rendre furieux.

**infus|e** *v.t.* infuser. ~**ion** *n.* infusion *f.*

**ingen|ious** *a.* ingénieux. ~**uity** *n.* ingéniosité *f.*

**ingenuous** *a.* ingénu.

**ingot** *n.* lingot *m.*

**ingrained** *a.* enraciné.

**ingratitude** *n.* ingratitude *f.*

**ingredient** *n.* ingrédient *m.*

**inhabit** *v.t.* habiter. ~**able** *a.* habitable. ~**ant** *n.* habitant(e) *m.* (*f.*).

**inhale** *v.t.* inhaler; (*tobacco smoke*) avaler. ~**r** *n.* spray *m.*

**inherent** *a.* inhérent. ~**ly** *adv.* en soi, intrinsèquement.

**inherit** *v.t.* hériter (de). ~**ance** *n.* héritage *m.*

**inhibit** *v.t.* (*hinder*) gêner; (*prevent*) empêcher. **be** ~**ed**, avoir des inhibitions. ~**ion** *n.* inhibition *f.*

**inhospitable** *a.* inhospitalier.

**inhuman** *a.* (*brutal, not human*) inhumain. ~**ity** *n.* inhumanité *f.*

**inhumane** *a.* inhumain.

**inimitable** *a.* inimitable.

**iniquit|ous** *a.* inique. ~**y** *n.* iniquité *f.*

**initial** *n.* initiale *f.* ● *v.t.* parapher. ● *a.* initial.

**initiat|e** *v.t.* (*begin*) amorcer; (*scheme*) lancer; (*person*) initier (**into**, à). ~**ion** *n.* initiation *f.*; (*start*) amorce *f.*

**initiative** *n.* initiative *f.*

**inject** *v.t.* injecter; (*new element:* *fig.*) insuffler. ~**ion** *n.* piqûre *f.*

**injunction** *n.* (*court order*) ordonnance *f.*

**injure** *v.t.* blesser; (*do wrong to*) nuire à.

**injury** *n.* (*physical*) blessure *f.*

**injustice** *n.* injustice *f.*

**ink** *n.* encre *f.*

**inkling** *n.* petite idée *f.*

**inland** *a.* l'intérieur. ● *adv.* à l'intérieur. **I**~ **Revenue**, fisc *m.*

**in-laws** *n. pl.* (*parents*) beaux-parents; (*family*) belle-famille *f.*

**inlay**[1] *v.t.* incruster.

**inlay**[2] *n.* incrustation *f.*

**inlet** *n.* bras de mer *m.*; (*techn.*) arrivée *f.*

**inmate** *n.* (*of asylum*) interné(e) *m.* (*f.*); (*of prison*) détenu(e) *m.* (*f.*).

**inn** *n.* auberge *f.*

**innate** *a.* inné.

**inner** *a.* intérieur, interne; (*fig.*) profond, intime. ~ **city**, quartiers défavorisés *m. pl.* ~ **tube**, chambre à air *f.*

**innings** *n. invar.* tour de batte *m.*; (*fig.*) tour *m.*

**innocen|t** *a. & n.* innocent(e) (*m.* (*f.*)). ~**ce** *n.* innocence *f.*

**innocuous** *a.* inoffensif.

**innovat|e** *v.i.* innover. ~**ion** *n.* innovation *f.* ~**or** *n.* innova|teur, -trice *m.*, *f.*

**innuendo** *n.* insinuation *f.*

**innumerable** *a.* innombrable.

**inoculat|e** *v.t.* inoculer. ~**ion** *n.* inoculation *f.*

**inoffensive** *a.* inoffensif.

**inoperative** *a.* inopérant.

**inopportune** *a.* inopportun.

**inordinate** *a.* excessif. ~**ly** *adv.* excessivement.

**input** *n.* (*data*) données *f. pl.*; (*computer process*) entrée *f.*; (*power: electr.*) énergie *f.*

**inquest** *n.* enquête *f.*

**inquire** *v.t./i.* = **enquire**.

**inquiry** *n.* enquête *f.*

**inquisition** *n.* inquisition *f.*

**inquisitive** *a.* curieux; (*prying*) indiscret.

**insan|e** *a.* fou. ~**ity** *n.* folie *f.*

**insatiable** *a.* insatiable.

**inscri|be** *v.t.* inscrire; (*book*) dédicacer. ~**ption** *n.* inscription *f.*; dédicace *f.*

**insect** *n.* insecte *m.*

**insecticide** *n.* insecticide *m.*

**insecur|e** *a.* (*not firm*) peu solide; (*unsafe*) peu sûr; (*worried*) anxieux. **~ity** *n.* insécurité *f.*

**insemination** *n.* insémination *f.*

**insensible** *a.* insensible; (*unconscious*) inconscient.

**insensitive** *a.* insensible.

**inseparable** *a.* inséparable.

**insert**[1] *v.t.* insérer. **~ion** *n.* insertion *f.*

**insert**[2] *n.* insertion *f.*; (*advertising*) encart *m.*

**in-service** (*training*) continu.

**inshore** *a.* côtier.

**inside** *n.* intérieur *m.* ● *a.* intérieur. ● *adv.* à l'intérieur, dedans. ● *prep.* à l'intérieur de; (*of time*) en moins de. **~ out,** à l'envers; (*thoroughly*) à fond.

**insidious** *a.* insidieux.

**insight** *n.* (*perception*) perspicacité *f.*; (*idea*) aperçu *m.*

**insignificant** *a.* insignifiant.

**insincer|e** *a.* peu sincère. **~ity** *n.* manque de sincérité *m.*

**insinuat|e** *v.t.* insinuer. **~ion** *n.* insinuation *f.*

**insipid** *a.* insipide.

**insist** *v.t./i.* insister. **~ on,** affirmer; (*demand*) exiger. **~ on doing,** insister pour faire.

**insisten|t** *a.* insistant. **~ce** *n.* insistance *f.* **~tly** *adv.* avec insistance.

**insole** *n.* (*separate*) semelle *f.*

**insolen|t** *a.* insolent. **~ce** *n.* insolence *f.*

**insoluble** *a.* insoluble.

**insolvent** *a.* insolvable.

**insomnia** *n.* insomnie *f.* **~c** *n.* insomniaque *m./f.*

**inspect** *v.t.* inspecter; (*tickets*) contrôler. **~ion** *n.* inspection *f.*; contrôle *m.* **~or** *n.* inspec|teur, -trice *m.*, *f.*; (*on train, bus*) contrôleu|r, -se *m.*, *f.*

**inspir|e** *v.t.* inspirer. **~ation** *n.* inspiration *f.*

**instability** *n.* instabilité *f.*

**install** *v.t.* installer. **~ation** *n.* installation *f.*

**instalment** *n.* (*payment*) acompte *m.*, versement *m.*; (*of serial*) épisode *m.*

**instance** *n.* exemple *m.*; (*case*) cas *m.* **for ~,** par exemple. **in the first ~,** en premier lieu.

**instant** *a.* immédiat; (*food*) instantané. ● *n.* instant *m.* **~ly** *adv.* immédiatement.

**instantaneous** *a.* instantané.

**instead** *adv.* plutôt. **~ of doing,** au lieu de faire. **~ of s.o.,** à la place de qn.

**instigat|e** *v.t.* provoquer. **~ion** *n.* instigation *f.*

**instil** *v.t.* inculquer; (*inspire*) insuffler.

**instinct** *n.* instinct *m.* **~ive** *a.* instinctif.

**institut|e** *n.* institut *m.* ● *v.t.* instituer; (*inquiry etc.*) entamer. **~ion** *n.* institution *f.*; (*school, hospital*) établissement *m.*

**instruct** *v.t.* instruire; (*order*) ordonner. **~ s.o. in sth.,** enseigner qch. à qn. **~ s.o. to do,** ordonner à qn. de faire. **~ion** *n.* instruction *f.* **~ions** *n. pl.* (*for use*) mode d'emploi *m.* **~ive** *a.* instructif. **~or** *n.* professeur *m.*; (*skiing, driving*) moni|teur, -trice *m.*, *f.*

**instrument** *n.* instrument *m.* **~ panel,** tableau de bord *m.*

**instrumental** *a.* instrumental. **be ~ in,** contribuer à. **~ist** *n.* instrumentaliste *m./f.*

**insufferable** *a.* intolérable.

**insufficient** *a.* insuffisant. **~ly** *adv.* insuffisamment.

**insular** *a.* insulaire; (*mind, person: fig.*) borné.

**insulat|e** *v.t.* (*room, wire, etc.*) isoler. **~ion** *n.* isolation *f.*

**insulin** *n.* insuline *f.*

**insult**[1] *v.t.* insulter.

**insult**[2] *n.* insulte *f.*

**insuperable** *a.* insurmontable.

**insur|e** *v.t.* assurer. **~ance** *n.* assurance *f.*

**insurmountable** *a.* insurmontable.

**insurrection** *n.* insurrection *f.*

**intact** *a.* intact.

**intake** *n.* admission(s) *f.* (*pl.*); (*techn.*) prise *f.*

**intangible** *a.* intangible.

**integral** *a.* intégral. **be an ~ part of,** faire partie intégrante de.

**integrat|e** *v.t./i.* (s')intégrer. **~ion** *n.* intégration *f.*

**integrity** *n.* intégrité *f.*

**intellect** *n.* intelligence *f.* **~ual** *a. & n.* intellectuel(le) (*m.* (*f.*)).

**intelligen|t** *a.* intelligent. **~ce** *n.* intelligence *f.*; (*mil.*) renseignements *m. pl.* **~tly** *adv.* intelligemment.

**intelligible** *a.* intelligible.

**intend** *v.t.* destiner. **~ to do,** avoir l'intention de faire. **~ed** *a.* (*deliberate*) intentionnel; (*planned*) prévu.

**intens|e** *a.* intense; (*person*) passionné. **~ely** *adv.* (*to live etc.*) intensément; (*very*) extrêmement. **~ity** *n.* intensité *f.*

**intensif|y** *v.t.* intensifier. **~ication** *n.* intensification *f.*

**intensive** *a.* intensif. **in ~ care,** en réanimation.

**intent** *n.* intention *f.* ● *a.* attentif. **~ on,** absorbé par. **~ on doing,** résolu à faire. **~ly** *adv.* attentivement.

**intention** *n.* intention *f.* **~al** *a.* intentionnel.

**inter** *v.t.* enterrer.

**inter-** *pref.* inter-.

**interact** *v.i.* avoir une action réciproque. **~ion** *n.* interaction *f.*

**intercede** *v.i.* intercéder.

**intercept** *v.t.* intercepter. **~ion** *n.* interception *f.*

**interchange** *n.* échangeur *m.*

**interchangeable** *a.* interchangeable.

**intercom** *n.* interphone *m.*

**interconnected** *a.* lié.

**intercourse** *n.* (*sexual, social*) rapports *m. pl.*

**interest** *n.* intérêt *m.*; (*stake*) intérêts *m. pl.* ● *v.t.* intéresser. **~ rates,** taux d'intérêt *m. pl.* **~ed** *a.* intéressé. **be ~ed in,** s'intéresser à. **~ing** *a.* intéressant.

**interface** *n.* (*comput.*) interface *f.*; (*fig.*) zone de rencontre *f.*

**interfer|e** *v.i.* se mêler des affaires des autres. **~e in,** s'ingérer dans. **~e with,** (*plans*) créer un contretemps avec; (*work*) s'immiscer dans; (*radio*) faire des interférences avec; (*lock*) toucher à. **~ence** *n.* ingérence *f.*; (*radio*) parasites *m. pl.*

**interim** *n.* intérim *m.* ● *a.* intérimaire.

**interior** *n.* intérieur *m.* ● *a.* intérieur.

**interjection** *n.* interjection *f.*

**interlinked** *a.* lié.

**interlock** *v.t./i.* (*techn.*) (s')emboîter, (s')enclencher.

**interlude** *n.* intervalle *m.*; (*theatre, mus.*) intermède *m.*

**intermediary** *a. & n.* intermédiaire (*m./f.*).

**intermediate** *a.* intermédiaire; (*exam etc.*) moyen.

**interminable** *a.* interminable.

**intermission** *n.* pause *f.*; (*theatre etc.*) entracte *m.*

**intern** *v.t.* interner. **~ment** *n.* internement *m.*

**internal** *a.* interne; (*domestic: pol.*) intérieur. **~ly** *adv.* intérieurement.

**international** *a. & n.* international (*m.*).

**interpolate** *v.t.* interpoler.

**interpret** *v.t.* interpréter. ● *v.i.* faire l'interprète. **~ation** *n.* interprétation *f.* **~er** *n.* interprète *m./f.*

**interrelated** *a.* lié.

**interrogat|e** *v.t.* interroger. **~ion** *n.* interrogation *f.* (*of,* de); (*session of questions*) interrogatoire *m.*

**interrogative** *a. & n.* interrogatif (*m.*).

**interrupt** *v.t.* interrompre. **~ion** *n.* interruption *f.*

**intersect** *v.t./i.* (*lines, roads*) (se) couper. **~ion** *n.* intersection *f.*; (*crossroads*) croisement *m.*

**interspersed** *a.* (*scattered*) dispersé.

**interval** *n.* intervalle *m.*; (*theatre*) entracte *m.* **at ~s,** par intervalles.

**interven|e** *v.i.* intervenir; (*of time*) s'écouler (**between,** entre); (*happen*) survenir. **~tion** *n.* intervention *f.*

**interview** *n.* (*with reporter*) interview *f.*; (*for job etc.*) entrevue *f.* ● *v.t.* interviewer. **~er** *n.* interviewer *m.*

**intestin|e** *n.* intestin *m.* **~al** *a.* intestinal.

**intima|te**[1] *a.* intime; (*detailed*) profond. **~cy** *n.* intimité *f.* **~tely** *adv.* intimement.

**intimate**[2] *v.t.* (*state*) annoncer; (*imply*) suggérer.

**intimidat|e** *v.t.* intimider. **~ion** *n.* intimidation *f.*

**into** *prep.* (*put, go, etc.*) dans; (*divide, translate, etc.*) en.

**intolerable** *a.* intolérable.

**intoleran|t** *a.* intolérant. **~ce** *n.* intolérance *f.*

**intonation** *n.* intonation *f.*

**intoxicat|e** *v.t.* enivrer. **~ed** *a.* ivre. **~ion** *n.* ivresse *f.*

**intra-** *pref.* intra-.

**intransigent** *a.* intransigeant.

**intransitive** *a.* (*verb*) intransitif.

**intravenous** *a.* (*med.*) intraveineux.

**intrepid** *a.* intrépide.

**intrica|te** *a.* complexe. **~cy** *n.* complexité *f.*

**intrigu|e** *v.t./i.* intriguer. ● *n.* intrigue *f.* **~ing** *a.* très intéressant; (*curious*) curieux.

**intrinsic** *a.* intrinsèque. **~ally** *adv.* intrinsèquement.

**introduce** *v.t.* (*bring in, insert*) introduire; (*programme, question*) présenter. **~ s.o. to,** (*person*) présenter qn. à; (*subject*) faire connaître à qn.

**introduct|ion** *n.* introduction *f.*; (*to person*) présentation *f.* **~ory** *a.* (*letter, words*) d'introduction.

**introspective** *a.* introspectif.

**intru|de** *v.i.* (*person*) s'imposer (**on s.o.,** à qn.), déranger. **~der** *n.* intrus(e) *m.* (*f.*). **~sion** *n.* intrusion *f.*

**intuit|ion** *n.* intuition *f.*

**inundat|e** *v.t.* inonder (**with,** de). **~ion** *n.* inondation *f.*

**invade** *v.t.* envahir. **~r** *n.* envahisseu|r, -se *m., f.*

**invalid**[1] *n.* malade *m./f.*; (*disabled*) infirme *m./f.*

**invalid**[2] *a.* non valable. **~ate** *v.t.* invalider.

**invaluable** *a.* inestimable.

**invariab|le** *a.* invariable. **~y** *adv.* invariablement.

**invasion** *n.* invasion *f.*

**invent** *v.t.* inventer. **~ion** *n.* invention *f.* **~ive** *a.* inventif. **~or** *n.* inven|teur, -trice *m., f.*

**inventory** *n.* inventaire *m.*

**inverse** *a. & n.* inverse (*m.*). **~ly** *adv.* inversement.

**inver|t** *v.t.* intervertir. **~ted commas,** guillemets *m. pl.* **~sion** *n.* inversion *f.*

**invest** *v.t.* investir; (*time, effort: fig.*) consacrer. ● *v.i.* faire un investissement. **~ in,** (*buy: fam.*) se payer. **~ment** *n.* investissement *m.* **~or** *n.* actionnaire *m./f.*; (*saver*) épargnant(e) *m.* (*f.*).

**investigat|e** *v.t.* étudier; (*crime etc.*) enquêter sur. **∼ion** *n.* investigation *f.* **∼or** *n.* (*police*) enquêteu|r, -se *m., f.*

**inveterate** *a.* invétéré.

**invigorate** *v.t.* vivifier; (*encourage*) stimuler.

**invincible** *a.* invincible.

**invisible** *a.* invisible.

**invit|e** *v.t.* inviter; (*ask for*) demander. **∼ation** *n.* invitation *f.* **∼ing** *a.* (*meal, smile, etc.*) engageant.

**invoice** *n.* facture *f.* ● *v.t.* facturer.

**invoke** *v.t.* invoquer.

**involuntary** *a.* involontaire.

**involve** *v.t.* entraîner; (*people*) faire participer. **∼d** *a.* (*complex*) compliqué; (*at stake*) en jeu. **be ∼d in**, (*work*) participer à; (*crime*) être mêlé à. **∼ment** *n.* participation *f.* (**in**, à).

**inward** *a. & adv.* vers l'intérieur; (*feeling etc.*) intérieur. **∼ly** *adv.* intérieurement. **∼s** *adv.* vers l'intérieur.

**iodine** *n.* iode *m.*; (*antiseptic*) teinture d'iode *f.*

**iota** *n.* (*amount*) brin *m.*

**IOU** *abbr.* (*I owe you*) reconnaissance de dette *f.*

**IQ** *abbr.* (*intelligence quotient*) QI *m.*

**Iran** *n.* Iran *m.* **∼ian** *a. & n.* iranien(ne) (*m. (f.)*).

**Iraq** *n.* Irak *m.* **∼i** *a. & n.* irakien(ne) (*m. (f.)*).

**irascible** *a.* irascible.

**irate** *a.* en colère, furieux.

**Ireland** *n.* Irlande *f.*

**iris** *n.* (*anat., bot.*) iris *m.*

**Irish** *a.* irlandais. ● *n.* (*lang.*) irlandais *m.* **∼man** *n.* Irlandais *m.* **∼woman** *n.* Irlandaise *f.*

**iron** *n.* fer *m.*; (*appliance*) fer (à repasser) *m.* ● *a.* de fer. ● *v.t.* repasser. **∼ing-board** *n.* planche à repasser *f.*

**ironic(al)** *a.* ironique.

**ironmonger** *n.* quincaillier *m.* **∼y** *n.* quincaillerie *f.*

**irony** *n.* ironie *f.*

**irrational** *a.* irrationnel; (*person*) pas rationnel.

**irreconcilable** *a.* irréconciliable; (*incompatible*) inconciliable.

**irregular** *a.* irrégulier. **∼ity** *n.* irrégularité *f.*

**irrelevan|t** *a.* sans rapport (**to**, avec). **∼ce** *n.* manque de rapport *m.*

**irreparable** *a.* irréparable.

**irreplaceable** *a.* irremplaçable.

**irrepressible** *a.* irrépressible.

**irresistible** *a.* irrésistible.

**irresolute** *a.* irrésolu.

**irrespective** *a.* **∼ of**, sans tenir compte de.

**irresponsible** *a.* irresponsable.

**irretrievable** *a.* irréparable.

**irreverent** *a.* irrévérencieux.

**irreversible** *a.* irréversible; (*decision*) irrévocable.

**irrigat|e** *v.t.* irriguer. **∼ion** *n.* irrigation *f.*

**irritable** *a.* irritable.

**irritat|e** *v.t.* irriter. **be ∼ed by**, être énervé par. **∼ing** *a.* énervant. **∼ion** *n.* irritation *f.*

**Islam** *n.* Islam *m.* **∼ic** *a.* islamique.

**island** *n.* île *f.*

**isle** *n.* île *f.*

**isolat|e** *v.t.* isoler. **∼ion** *n.* isolement *m.*

**Israel** *n.* Israël *m.* **∼i** *a. & n.* israélien(ne) (*m. (f.)*).

**issue** *n.* question *f.*; (*outcome*) résultat *m.*; (*of magazine etc.*) numéro *m.* ● *v.t.* distribuer, donner; (*stamps etc.*) émettre; (*book*) publier; (*order*) donner. **at ∼**, en cause. **take ∼**, engager une controverse.

**isthmus** *n.* isthme *m.*

**it** *pron.* (*subject*) il, elle; (*object*) le, la, l'*; (*impersonal subject*) il; (*non-specific*) ce, c'*, cela, ça. **it is**, (*quiet, my book, etc.*) c'est. **it is/ cold/warm/** *etc.*, il fait froid/chaud/*etc.* **that's it**, c'est ça. **who is it?**, qui est-ce? **of it, from it**, en. **in it, at it, to it**, y.

**IT** *abbr. see* **information technology**.

**italic** *a.* italique. **∼s** *n. pl.* italique *m.*

**Ital|y** *n.* Italie *f.* **∼ian** *a. & n.* italien(ne) (*m. (f.)*); (*lang.*) italien *m.*

**itch** *n.* démangeaison *f.* ● *v.i.* démanger. **my arm ∼es**, mon bras me démange. **∼y** *a.* qui démange.

**item** *n.* article *m.*, chose *f.*; (*on agenda*) question *f.* **news ∼**, nouvelle *f.* **∼ize** *v.t.* détailler.

**itinerant** *a.* itinérant; (*musician, actor*) ambulant.

**itinerary** *n.* itinéraire *m.*

**its** *a.* son, sa, *pl.* ses.

**itself** *pron.* lui-même, elle-même; (*reflexive*) se.

**IUD** *abbr.* (*intrauterine device*) stérilet *m.*

**ivory** *n.* ivoire *m.*

**ivy** *n.* lierre *m.*

••••••••••••••••••••••••••••••••••••

# Jj

••••••••••••••••••••••••••••••••••••

**jab** *v.t.* (*thrust*) enfoncer; (*prick*) piquer. ● *n.* coup *m.*; (*injection*) piqûre *f.*

**jack** *n.* (*techn.*) cric *m.*; (*cards*) valet *m.*; (*plug*) fiche *f.* ● *v.t.* **∼ up**, soulever (avec un cric).

**jackal** *n.* chacal *m.*

**jacket** *n.* veste *f.*, veston *m.*; (*of book*) jaquette *f.*

**jack-knife** n. couteau pliant m. ● v.i. (lorry) faire un tête-à-queue.

**jackpot** n. gros lot m. **hit the ~,** gagner le gros lot.

**jade** n. (stone) jade m.

**jaded** a. las; (appetite) blasé.

**jagged** a. dentelé.

**jail** n. prison f. ● v.t. mettre en prison. **~er** n. geôlier m.

**jam**¹ n. confiture f.

**jam**² v.t./i. (wedge, become wedged) (se) coincer; (cram) (s')entasser; (street etc.) encombrer; (thrust) enfoncer; (radio) brouiller. ● n. foule f.; (of traffic) embouteillage m.; (situation: fam.) pétrin m. **~-packed** a. (fam.) bourré.

**Jamaica** n. Jamaïque f.

**jangle** n. cliquetis m. ● v.t./i. (faire) cliqueter.

**janitor** n. concierge m.

**January** n. janvier m.

**Japan** n. Japon m. **~ese** a. & n. japonais(e) (m. (f.)); (lang.) japonais m.

**jar**¹ n. pot m., bocal m.

**jar**² v.i. grincer; (of colours etc.) détonner. ● v.t. ébranler. ● n. son discordant m.

**jargon** n. jargon m.

**jasmine** n. jasmin m.

**jaundice** n. jaunisse f.

**jaunt** n. (trip) balade f.

**jaunty** a. allègre.

**javelin** n. javelot m.

**jaw** n. mâchoire f.

**jay** n. geai m.

**jazz** n. jazz m.

**jealous** a. jaloux. **~y** n. jalousie f.

**jeans** n. pl. (blue-)jean m.

**jeep** n. jeep f.

**jeer** v.t./i. **~ (at),** railler; (boo) huer. ● n. raillerie f.; huée f.

**jelly** n. gelée f.

**jellyfish** n. méduse f.

**jeopard|y** n. péril m. **~ize** v.t. mettre en péril.

**jerk** n. secousse f.; (fool: sl.) idiot m.; (creep: sl.) salaud m. ● v.t. donner une secousse à.

**jersey** n. (garment) chandail m., tricot m.; (fabric) jersey m.

**jest** n. plaisanterie f. ● v.i. plaisanter. **~er** n. bouffon m.

**Jesus** n. Jésus m.

**jet**¹ n. (mineral) jais m.

**jet**² n. (stream) jet m.; (plane) avion à réaction m., jet m.

**jettison** v.t. jeter à la mer; (aviat.) larguer; (fig.) abandonner.

**jetty** n. (breakwater) jetée f.

**Jew** n. Juif m. **~ess** n. Juive f.

**jewel** n. bijou m. **~ler** n. bijout|ier, -ière m., f. **~lery** n. bijoux m. pl.

**Jewish** a. juif.

**jib** v.i. regimber (**at,** devant).

**jibe** n. = gibe.

**jig** n. (dance) gigue f.

**jigsaw** n. puzzle m.

**jingle** v.t./i. (faire) tinter. ● n. tintement m.; (advertising) jingle m., sonal m.

**jinx** n. (person: fam.) porte-malheur m. invar.; (spell: fig.) mauvais sort m.

**jitter|s** n. pl. **the ~s,** (fam.) la frousse f. **~y** a. **be ~y,** (fam.) avoir la frousse.

**job** n. travail m.; (post) poste m.

**jockey** n. jockey m. ● v.i. (manœuvre) manœuvrer.

**jocular** a. jovial.

**jog** v.t. pousser; (memory) rafraîchir. ● v.i. faire du jogging. **~ging** n. jogging m.

**join** v.t. joindre, unir; (club) devenir membre de; (political group) adhérer à; (army) s'engager dans. **~ s.o.,** (in activity) se joindre à qn.; (meet) rejoindre qn. ● v.i. (roads etc.) se rejoindre. ● n. joint m. **~ in,** participer (à).

**joiner** n. menuisier m.

**joint** a. (account, venture) commun. ● n. (join) joint m.; (anat.) articulation f.; (culin.) rôti m.

**joist** n. solive f.

**jok|e** n. plaisanterie f.; (trick) farce f. ● v.i. plaisanter. **~er** n. blagueu|r, -se m., f.; (pej.) petit malin m.; (cards) joker m.

**joll|y** a. gai. ● adv. (fam.) rudement.

**jolt** v.t./i. (vehicle, passenger) cahoter; (shake) secouer. ● n. cahot m.; secousse f.

**Jordan** n. Jordanie f.

**jostle** v.t./i. (push) bousculer; (push each other) se bousculer.

**jot** n. brin m. ● v.t. (p.t. **jotted**) **~ down,** noter. **~ter** n. (pad) bloc-notes m.

**journal** n. journal m. **~ism** n. journalisme m. **~ist** n. journaliste m./f.

**journey** n. voyage m.; (distance) trajet m. ● v.i. voyager.

**jovial** a. jovial.

**joy** n. joie f.

**joystick** n. (comput.) manette f.

**Judaism** n. judaïsme m.

**judder** v.i. vibrer. ● n. vibration f.

**judge** n. juge m. ● v.t. juger. **~ment** n. jugement m.

**judic|iary** n. magistrature f. **~ial** a. judiciaire.

**judicious** a. judicieux.

**judo** n. judo m.

**jug** n. cruche f., pichet m.

**juggernaut** n. (lorry) poids lourd m., mastodonte m.

**juggle** v.t./i. jongler (avec). **~r** n. jongleu|r, -se m., f.

**juic|e** *n.* jus *m.* **~y** *a.* juteux; (*details etc.*: *fam.*) croustillant.

**juke-box** *n.* juke-box *m.*

**July** *n.* juillet *m.*

**jumble** *v.t.* mélanger. ● *n.* (*muddle*) fouillis *m.* **~ sale,** vente (de charité) *f.*

**jumbo** *a.* **~ jet,** avion géant *m.*, jumbo-jet *m.*

**jump** *v.t./i.* sauter; (*start*) sursauter; (*of price etc.*) faire un bond. ● *n.* saut *m.*; sursaut *m.*; (*increase*) hausse *f.* **~ at,** sauter sur. **~-leads** *n. pl.* câbles de démarrage *m. pl.*

**jumper** *n.* pull(-over) *m.*

**junction** *n.* jonction *f.*; (*of roads etc.*) embranchement *m.*

**June** *n.* juin *m.*

**jungle** *n.* jungle *f.*

**junior** *a.* (*in age*) plus jeune (**to,** que); (*in rank*) subalterne; (*school*) élémentaire; (*executive, doctor*) jeune. ● *n.* cadet(te) *m.* (*f.*); (*schol.*) petit(e) élève *m.* (*f.*); (*sport*) junior *m./f.*

**junk** *n.* bric-à-brac *m. invar.*; (*poor material*) camelote *f.* ● *v.t.* (*Amer., sl.*) balancer.

**junkie** *n.* (*sl.*) drogué(e) *m.* (*f.*).

**junta** *n.* junte *f.*

**jurisdiction** *n.* juridiction *f.*

**juror** *n.* juré *m.*

**jury** *n.* jury *m.*

**just** *a.* (*fair*) juste. ● *adv.* juste, exactement; (*only, slightly*) juste; (*simply*) tout simplement. **he has/had ~ left**/*etc.*, il vient/venait de partir/*etc.* **have ~ missed,** avoir manqué de peu. **it's ~ a cold,** ce n'est qu'un rhume. **~ly** *adv.* avec justice.

**justice** *n.* justice *f.*

**justifiabl|e** *a.* justifiable.

**justif|y** *v.t.* justifier. **~ication** *n.* justification *f.*

**jut** *v.i.* **~ out,** dépasser.

**juvenile** *a.* (*youthful*) juvénile; (*childish*) puéril; (*delinquent*) jeune; (*court*) pour enfants. ● *n.* jeune *m./f.*

# Kk

**kangaroo** *n.* kangourou *m.*

**karate** *n.* karaté *m.*

**kebab** *n.* brochette *f.*

**keel** *n.* (*of ship*) quille *f.* ● *v.i.* **~ over,** chavirer.

**keen** *a.* (*interest, wind, feeling, etc.*) vif; (*mind, analysis*) pénétrant; (*edge, appetite*) aiguisé; (*eager*) enthousiaste. **be ~ on,** (*person, thing*: *fam.*) aimer beaucoup. **be ~ to do** *or* **on doing,** tenir beaucoup à faire.

**keep** *v.t.* garder; (*promise, shop, diary, etc.*) tenir; (*family*) entretenir; (*animals*) élever; (*rule etc.*) respecter; (*celebrate*) célébrer; (*delay*) retenir; (*prevent*) empêcher; (*conceal*) cacher. ● *v.i.* (*food*) se garder; (*remain*) rester. **~ (on),** continuer (**doing,** à faire). **~ back** *v.t.* retenir; *v.i.* ne pas s'approcher. **~ s.o. from doing,** empêcher qn. de faire. **~ in/out,** empêcher d'entrer/de sortir. **~ up,** (se) maintenir. **~ up (with),** suivre. **~-fit** *n.* exercices physiques *m. pl.*

**keg** *n.* tonnelet *m.*

**kennel** *n.* niche *f.*

**Kenya** *n.* Kenya *m.*

**kerb** *n.* bord du trottoir *m.*

**kernel** *n.* amande *f.*

**kerosene** *n.* (*aviation fuel*) kérosène *m.*; (*paraffin*) pétrole (lampant) *m.*

**ketchup** *n.* ketchup *m.*

**kettle** *n.* bouilloire *f.*

**key** *n.* clef *f.*; (*of piano etc.*) touche *f.* ● *a.* clef (*f. invar.*). **~-ring** *n.* porte-clefs *m. invar.* ● *v.t.* **~ in,** (*comput.*) saisir.

**keyboard** *n.* clavier *m.*

**keyhole** *n.* trou de la serrure *m.*

**khaki** *a.* kaki *invar.*

**kick** *v.t./i.* donner un coup de pied (à); (*of horse*) ruer. ● *n.* coup de pied *m.*; ruade *f.*; (*of gun*) recul *m.*; (*thrill*: *fam.*) (malin) plaisir *m.* **~-off** *n.* coup d'envoi *m.* **~ out,** (*fam.*) flanquer dehors.

**kid** *n.* (*goat, leather*) chevreau *m.*; (*child*: *sl.*) gosse *m./f.* ● *v.t./i.* blaguer.

**kidnap** *v.t.* enlever, kidnapper. **~ping** *n.* enlèvement *m.*

**kidney** *n.* rein *m.*; (*culin.*) rognon *m.*

**kill** *v.t.* tuer; (*fig.*) mettre fin à. ● *n.* mise à mort *f.* **~er** *n.* tueu|r, -se *m., f.* **~ing** *n.* massacre *m.*, meurtre *m.*; *a.* (*funny*: *fam.*) tordant; (*tiring*: *fam.*) tuant.

**kiln** *n.* four *m.*

**kilo** *n.* kilo *m.*

**kilobyte** /ˈkɪləbaɪt/ *n.* kilo-octet *m.*

**kilogram** *n.* kilogramme *m.*

**kilohertz** *n.* kilohertz *m.*

**kilometre** *n.* kilomètre *m.*

**kilowatt** *n.* kilowatt *m.*

**kilt** *n.* kilt *m.*

**kin** *n.* parents *m. pl.*

**kind**[1] *n.* genre *m.*, sorte *f.*, espèce *f.* **in ~,** en nature *f.*

**kind**[2] *a.* gentil, bon. **~ness** *n.* bonté *f.*

**kindle** *v.t./i.* (s')allumer.

**kindly** *a.* bienveillant. ● *adv.* avec bonté. **~ wait**/*etc.*, voulez-vous avoir la bonté d'attendre/*etc.*

**king** *n.* roi *m.* **~-size(d)** *a.* géant.

**kingdom** *n.* royaume *m.*; (*bot.*) règne *m.*

**kingfisher** *n.* martin-pêcheur *m.*

**kink** *n.* (*in rope*) entortillement *m.*, déformation *f.*; (*fig.*) perversion *f.*

**kiosk** *n.* kiosque *m.* **telephone ~,** cabine téléphonique *f.*

**kip** *n.* (*sl.*) roupillon *m.* ● *v.i.* (*sl.*) roupiller.

**kipper** *n.* hareng fumé *m.*

**kirby-grip** *n.* pince à cheveux *f.*

**kiss** *n.* baiser *m.* ● *v.t./i.* (s')embrasser.

**kit** *n.* équipement *m.*; (*clothing*) affaires *f. pl.*; (*set of tools etc.*) trousse *f.*; (*for assembly*) kit *m.* ● *v.t.* **~ out,** équiper.

**kitchen** *n.* cuisine *f.*

**kite** *n.* (*toy*) cerf-volant *m.*

**kitten** *n.* chaton *m.*

**kitty** *n.* (*fund*) cagnotte *f.*

**knack** *n.* truc *m.*, chic *m.*

**knead** *v.t.* pétrir.

**knee** *n.* genou *m.*

**kneecap** *n.* rotule *f.*

**kneel** *v.i.* **~ (down),** s'agenouiller.

**knickers** *n. pl.* (*woman's undergarment*) culotte *f.*, slip *m.*

**knife** *n.* couteau *m.* ● *v.t.* poignarder.

**knight** *n.* chevalier *m.*; (*chess*) cavalier *m.* ● *v.t.* faire *or* armer chevalier.

**knit** *v.t./i.* tricoter; (*bones etc.*) (se) souder. **~ting** *n.* tricot *m.*

**knitwear** *n.* tricots *m. pl.*

**knob** *n.* bouton *m.*

**knock** *v.t./i.* frapper, cogner; (*criticize: sl.*) critiquer. ● *n.* coup *m.* **~ down,** (*chair, pedestrian*) renverser; (*demolish*) abattre; (*reduce*) baisser. **~ off** *v.t.* faire tomber; (*fam.*) expédier; *v.i.* (*fam.*) s'arrêter de travailler. **~ out,** (*by blow*) assommer; (*tire*) épuiser. **~out** *n.* (*boxing*) knock-out *m.* **~ over,** renverser. **~ up,** (*meal etc.*) préparer en vitesse. **~er** *n.* heurtoir *m.*

**knot** *n.* nœud *m.* ● *v.t.* nouer.

**know** *v.t./i.* savoir (**that,** que); (*person, place*) connaître. **~ how to do,** savoir comment faire. **~ about,** (*cars etc.*) s'y connaître en.

**knowledge** *n.* connaissance *f.*; (*learning*) connaissances *f. pl.*

**knuckle** *n.* articulation du doigt *f.*

**Koran** *n.* Coran *m.*

**Korea** *n.* Corée *f.*

**kosher** *a.* kascher *invar.*

**Kurd** *a. & n.* kurde *m./f.*

**lab** *n.* (*fam.*) labo *m.*

**label** *n.* étiquette *f.* ● *v.t.* étiqueter.

**laboratory** *n.* laboratoire *m.*

**laborious** *a.* laborieux.

**labour** *n.* travail *m.*; (*workers*) main-d'œuvre *f.* ● *v.i.* peiner. ● *v.t.* trop insister sur. **in ~,** en train d'accoucher, en couches.

**Labour** *n.* le parti travailliste *m.* ● *a.* travailliste.

**labourer** *n.* manœuvre *m.*; (*on farm*) ouvrier agricole *m.*

**labyrinth** *n.* labyrinthe *m.*

**lace** *n.* dentelle *f.*; (*of shoe*) lacet *m.* ● *v.t.* (*fasten*) lacer; (*drink*) arroser. **~-ups** *n. pl.* chaussures à lacets *f. pl.*

**lack** *n.* manque *m.* ● *v.t.* manquer de. **be ~ing,** manquer (**in,** de). **for ~ of,** faute de.

**laconic** *a.* laconique.

**lacquer** *n.* laque *f.*

**lad** *n.* garçon *m.*, gars *m.*

**ladder** *n.* échelle *f.*; (*in stocking*) maille filée *f.* ● *v.t./i.* (*stocking*) filer.

**ladle** *n.* louche *f.*

**lady** *n.* dame *f.*

**ladybird** *n.* coccinelle *f.*

**lag¹** *v.i.* traîner. ● *n.* (*interval*) décalage *m.*

**lag²** *v.t.* (*pipes*) calorifuger.

**lager** *n.* bière blonde *f.*

**lagoon** *n.* lagune *f.*

**lake** *n.* lac *m.*

**lamb** *n.* agneau *m.*

**lambswool** *n.* laine d'agneau *f.*

**lame** *a.* boiteux; (*excuse*) faible.

**lament** *n.* lamentation *f.* ● *v.t./i.* se lamenter (sur).

**laminated** *a.* laminé.

**lamp** *n.* lampe *f.*

**lamppost** *n.* réverbère *m.*

**lampshade** *n.* abat-jour *m. invar.*

**lance** *n.* lance *f.* ● *v.t.* (*med.*) inciser.

**land** *n.* terre *f.*; (*plot*) terrain *m.*; (*country*) pays *m.* ● *a.* terrestre; (*policy, reform*) agraire. ● *v.t./i.* débarquer; (*aircraft*) (se) poser; (*fall*) atterrir; (*fall*) tomber; (*obtain*) décrocher; (*put*) mettre; (*a blow*) porter. **~ up,** se retrouver.

**landing** *n.* débarquement *m.*; (*aviat.*) atterrissage *m.*; (*top of stairs*) palier *m.* **~-stage** *n.* débarcadère *m.* **~-strip** *n.* piste d'atterrissage *f.*

**land|lady** n. propriétaire f.; (of inn) patronne f. ~**lord** n. propriétaire m.; patron m.

**landmark** n. (point de) repère m.

**landscape** n. paysage m.

**landslide** n. glissement de terrain m.; (pol.) raz-de-marée (électoral) m. invar.

**lane** n. (path, road) chemin m.; (strip of road) voie f.; (of traffic) file f.; (aviat.) couloir m.

**language** n. langue f.; (speech, style) langage m.

**languid** a. languissant.

**languish** v.i. languir.

**lank** a. grand et maigre.

**lanky** a. grand et maigre.

**lanolin** n. lanoline f.

**lantern** n. lanterne f.

**lap**[1] n. genoux m. pl.; (sport) tour (de piste) m.

**lap**[2] v.t. ~ **up,** laper. ● v.i. (waves) clapoter.

**lapel** n. revers m.

**lapse** v.i. (decline) se dégrader; (expire) se périmer. ● n. défaillance f., erreur f.; (of time) intervalle m. ~ **into,** retomber dans.

**lard** n. saindoux m.

**larder** n. garde-manger m. invar.

**large** a. grand, gros. **by and ~,** en général. ~**ly** adv. en grande mesure.

**lark**[1] n. (bird) alouette f.

**lark**[2] n. (bit of fun: fam.) rigolade f. ● v.i. (fam.) rigoler.

**larva** n. larve f.

**laryngitis** n. laryngite f.

**larynx** n. larynx m.

**laser** n. laser m. ~ **printer,** imprimante laser f.

**lash** v.t. fouetter. ● n. coup de fouet m.; (eyelash) cil m.

**lashings** n. pl. ~ **of,** (cream etc.: sl.) des masses de.

**lass** n. jeune fille f.

**lasso** n. lasso m.

**last**[1] a. dernier. ● adv. en dernier; (most recently) la dernière fois. ● n. dern|ier, -ière m., f.; (remainder) reste m. **at ~,** enfin. ~ **minute** a. de dernière minute. ~ **night,** hier soir. ~**ly** adv. en dernier lieu.

**last**[2] v.i. durer. ~**ing** a. durable.

**latch** n. loquet m.

**late** a. (not on time) en retard; (recent) récent; (former) ancien; (hour, fruit, etc.) tardif; (deceased) défunt. ~**st** (last) dernier. ● adv. (not early) tard; (not on time) en retard. **in ~ July,** fin juillet.

**latecomer** n. retardataire m./f.

**lately** adv. dernièrement.

**latent** a. latent.

**lateral** a. latéral.

**lathe** n. tour m.

**lather** n. mousse f. ● v.t. savonner. ● v.i. mousser.

**Latin** n. (lang.) latin m. ● a. latin. ~**America,** Amérique latine f.

**latitude** n. latitude f.

**latrine** n. latrines f. pl.

**latter** a. dernier. ● n. **the ~,** celui-ci, celle-ci.

**lattice** n. treillage m.

**laugh** v.i. rire (**at,** de). ● n. rire m. ~**able** a. ridicule.

**laughter** n. (act) rire m.; (sound of laughs) rires m. pl.

**launch**[1] v.t. lancer. ● n. lancement m. ~**ing pad,** aire de lancement f.

**launch**[2] n. (boat) vedette f.

**launderette** n. laverie automatique f.

**laundry** n. (place) blanchisserie f.; (clothes) linge m.

**laurel** n. laurier m.

**lava** n. lave f.

**lavatory** n. cabinets m. pl.

**lavender** n. lavande f.

**lavish** a. (person) prodigue; (plentiful) copieux; (lush) somptueux. ● v.t. prodiguer (**on,** à). ~**ly** adv. copieusement.

**law** n. loi f.; (profession, subject of study) droit m.

**lawcourt** n. tribunal m.

**lawn** n. pelouse f., gazon m. ~**-mower** n. tondeuse à gazon f. ~ **tennis,** tennis (sur gazon) m.

**lawsuit** n. procès m.

**lawyer** n. avocat m.

**lax** a. négligent; (morals etc.) relâché.

**laxative** n. laxatif m.

**lay**[1] a. (non-clerical) laïque; (opinion etc.) d'un profane.

**lay**[2] v.t. poser, mettre; (trap) tendre; (table) mettre; (plan) former; (eggs) pondre. ● v.i. pondre. ~ **down,** (dé)poser; (condition) (im)poser. ~ **off** v.t. (worker) licencier; v.i. (fam.) arrêter. ~**off** n. licenciement m. ~ **on,** (provide) fournir. ~ **out,** (design) dessiner; (display) disposer; (money) dépenser.

**lay-by** n. petite aire de stationnement f.

**layer** n. couche f.

**layman** n. profane m.

**layout** n. disposition f.

**laze** v.i. paresser.

**laz|y** a. paresseux. ~**iness** n. paresse f.

**lead**[1] v.t./i. (p.t. **led**) mener; (team etc.) diriger; (life) mener; (induce) amener. ~ **to,** conduire à, mener à. ~ **away,** emmener. ● n. avance f.; (clue) indice m.; (leash) laisse f.; (theatre) premier rôle m.; (wire) fil m.; (example) exemple m. ~ **up to,** (come to) en venir à; (precede) précéder.

**lead**[2] n. plomb m.; (of pencil) mine f.

**leader** n. chef m.; (of country, club, etc.) dirigeant(e) m. (f.); (leading article) éditorial m. ~**ship** n. direction f.

**leading** *a.* principal.

**leaf** *n.* feuille *f.*; (*of table*) rallonge *f.*

**leaflet** *n.* prospectus *m.*

**league** *n.* ligue *f.*; (*sport*) championnat *m.*

**leak** *n.* fuite *f.* ● *v.i.* fuir; (*news*: *fig.*) s'ébruiter. ● *v.t.* répandre; (*fig.*) divulguer. ~**age** *n.* fuite *f.* ~**y** *a.* qui a une fuite.

**lean**¹ *a.* maigre. ● *n.* (*of meat*) maigre *m.*

**lean**² *v.t./i.* (*rest*) (s')appuyer; (*slope*) pencher. ~ **out**, se pencher à l'extérieur.

**leaning** *a.* penché ● *n.* tendance *f.*

**leap** *v.i.* bondir. ● *n.* bond *m.* ~**frog** *n.* saute-mouton *m. invar.*

**learn** *v.t./i.* apprendre (**to do**, à faire). ~**er** *n.* débutant(e) *m. (f.).*

**learned** *a.* érudit.

**lease** *n.* bail *m.* ● *v.t.* louer à bail.

**leaseback** *n.* cession-bail *f.*

**leash** *n.* laisse *f.*

**least** *a.* **the** ~, (*smallest amount of*) le moins de; (*slightest*) le *or* la moindre. ● *n.* le moins. ● *adv.* le moins; (*with adjective*) le *or* la moins. **at** ~, au moins.

**leather** *n.* cuir *m.*

**leave** *v.t.* laisser; (*depart from*) quitter. ● *n.* (*holiday*) congé *m.*; (*consent*) permission *f.* **be left (over)**, rester. ~ **behind**, laisser. ~ **out**, omettre.

**Leban|on** *n.* Liban *m.* ~**ese** *a. &n.* libanais(e) (*m. (f.)*).

**lecture** *n.* cours *m.*, conférence *f.*; (*rebuke*) réprimande *f.* ● *v.t./i.* faire un cours *or* une conférence (à); (*rebuke*) réprimander. ~**r** *n.* conférenc|ier, -ière *m.*, *f.*, (*univ.*) enseignant(e) *m. (f.).*

**ledge** *n.* (*window*) rebord *m.*; (*rock*) saillie *f.*

**ledger** *n.* grand livre *m.*

**leek** *n.* poireau *m.*

**leer** *v.i.* ~ (**at**), lorgner. ● *n.* regard sournois *m.*

**leeway** *n.* (*naut.*) dérive *f.*; (*fig.*) liberté d'action *f.* **make up** ~, rattraper le retard.

**left**¹ ~ **luggage (office)**, consigne *f.* ~**overs** *n. pl.* restes *m. pl.*

**left**² *a.* gauche. ● *adv.* à gauche. ● *n.* gauche *f.* ~**hand** *a.* à *or* de gauche. ~**handed** *a.* gaucher. ~**wing** *a.* (*pol.*) de gauche.

**leg** *n.* jambe *f.*; (*of animal*) patte *f.*; (*of table*) pied *m.*; (*of chicken*) cuisse *f.*; (*of lamb*) gigot *m.*; (*of journey*) étape *f.*

**legacy** *n.* legs *m.*

**legal** *a.* légal; (*affairs etc.*) juridique. ~**ly** *adv.* légalement.

**legend** *n.* légende *f.* ~**ary** *a.* légendaire.

**leggings** *n. pl.* collant sans pieds *m.*

**legib|le** *a.* lisible. ~**ility** *n.* lisibilité *f.*

**legion** *n.* légion *f.*

**legislat|e** *v.i.* légiférer. ~**ion** *n.* (*body of laws*) législation *f.*; (*law*) loi *f.*

**legitimate** *a.* légitime.

**leisure** *n.* loisir(s) *m.* (*pl.*). ~ **centre**, centre de loisirs *m.* ~**ly** *a.* lent; *adv.* sans se presser.

**lemon** *n.* citron *m.*

**lemonade** *n.* (*fizzy*) limonade *f.*; (*still*) citronnade *f.*

**lend** *v.t.* prêter; (*contribute*) donner. ~**er** *n.* prêteu|r, -se *m.*, *f.*

**length** *n.* longueur *f.*; (*in time*) durée *f.*; (*section*) morceau *m.* **at** ~, (*at last*) enfin. **at (great)** ~, longuement. ~**y** *a.* long.

**lengthen** *v.t./i.* (s')allonger.

**lengthways** *adv.* dans le sens de la longueur.

**lenien|t** *a.* indulgent. ~**cy** *n.* indulgence *f.* ~**tly** *adv.* avec indulgence.

**lens** *n.* lentille *f.*; (*of spectacles*) verre *m.*; (*photo.*) objectif *m.*

**Lent** *n.* Carême *m.*

**lentil** *n.* (*bean*) lentille *f.*

**Leo** *n.* le Lion.

**leopard** *n.* léopard *m.*

**leotard** *n.* body *m.*

**leper** *n.* lépreu|x, -se *m.*, *f.*

**leprosy** *n.* lèpre *f.*

**lesbian** *n.* lesbienne *f.* ● *a.* lesbien.

**lesion** *n.* lésion *f.*

**less** *a.* (*in quantity etc.*) moins de (**than**, que). ● *adv.*, *n.* & *prep.* moins. ~ **than**, (*with numbers*) moins de. **work**/*etc.* ~ **than**, travailler/*etc.* moins que. **ten pounds**/*etc.* ~, dix livres/*etc.* de moins.

**lessen** *v.t./i.* diminuer.

**lesson** *n.* leçon *f.*

**lest** *conj.* de peur que *or* de.

**let** *v.t.* laisser; (*lease*) louer. ● *n.* location *f.* ~ **down**, baisser; (*deflate*) dégonfler; (*fig.*) décevoir. ~**down** *n.* déception *f.* ~ **go** *v.t.* lâcher; *v.i.* lâcher prise. ~ **sb. in**/**out**, laisser *or* faire entrer/sortir qn. ~ **off**, (*explode*, *fire*) faire éclater *or* partir; (*excuse*) dispenser; (*not punish*) ne pas punir.

**lethal** *a.* mortel; (*weapon*) meurtrier.

**letharg|y** *n.* léthargie *f.* ~**ic** *a.* léthargique.

**letter** *n.* lettre *f.* ~**box** *n.* boîte à *or* aux lettres *f.*

**lettuce** *n.* laitue *f.*, salade *f.*

**leukaemia** *n.* leucémie *f.*

**level** *a.* plat, uni; (*on surface*) horizontal; (*in height*) au même niveau (**with**, que); (*in score*) à égalité. ● *n.* niveau *m.* (**spirit**) ~, niveau à bulle *m.* ● *v.t.* niveler; (*aim*) diriger. ~ **crossing**, passage à niveau *m.*

**lever** *n.* levier *m.* ● *v.t.* soulever au moyen d'un levier.

**levy** *v.t.* (*tax*) (pré)lever. ● *n.* impôt *m.*

**liable** *a.* **be** ~ **to do**, avoir tendance à faire, pouvoir faire. ~ **to**, (*illness etc.*) sujet à; (*fine*) passible de. ~ **for**, responsable de.

**liability** *n.* responsabilité *f.*; (*fam.*) handicap *m.*

**liais|e** v.i. (fam.) faire la liaison. **~on** n. liaison f.

**liar** n. menteu|r, -se m., f.

**libel** n. diffamation f. ● v.t. diffamer.

**liberal** a. libéral; (generous) généreux, libéral.

**Liberal** a. & n. (pol.) libéral(e) (m. (f.)).

**liberat|e** v.t. libérer. **~ion** n. libération f.

**liberty** n. liberté f.

**Libra** n. la Balance.

**librar|y** n. bibliothèque f. **~ian** n. bibliothécaire m./f.

**libretto** n. (mus.) livret m.

**Libya|n** n. Libye f. **~a.** & n. libyen(ne) (m. (f.)).

**licence,** n. permis m.; (for television) redevance f.; (comm.) licence f.; (liberty: fig.) licence f.

**license** v.t. accorder un permis à, autoriser.

**lichen** n. lichen m.

**lick** v.t. lécher; (defeat: sl.) rosser. ● n. coup de langue m.

**lid** n. couvercle m.

**lie**[1] n. mensonge m. ● v.i. (tell lies) mentir.

**lie**[2] v.i. s'allonger; (remain) rester; (be) se trouver, être; (in grave) reposer. **be lying,** être allongé. **~ down,** s'allonger.

**lieutenant** n. lieutenant m.

**life** n. vie f. **~guard** n. sauveteur m. **~insurance,** assurance-vie f. **~jacket** n. gilet de sauvetage m. **~size(d)** a. grandeur nature invar. **~style** n. style de vie m.

**lifebelt** n. bouée de sauvetage f.

**lifeboat** n. canot de sauvetage m.

**lifebuoy** n. bouée de sauvetage f.

**lifelike** a. très ressemblant.

**lifetime** n. vie f.

**lift** v.t. lever; (steal: fam.) voler. ● v.i. (of fog) se lever. ● n. (in building) ascenseur m. **give a ~ to,** emmener (en voiture).

**ligament** n. ligament m.

**light**[1] n. lumière f.; (lamp) lampe f.; (for fire, on vehicle, etc.) feu m.; (headlight) phare m. ● a. (not dark) clair. ● v.t. allumer; (room etc.) éclairer; (match) frotter. **~ bulb,** ampoule f. **~ pen,** crayon optique m. **~ up** v.i. s'allumer; v.t. (room) éclairer. **~-year** n. année lumière f.

**light**[2] a. (not heavy) léger. **~-hearted** a. gai. **~ly** adv. légèrement. **~ness** n. légèreté f.

**lighten**[1] v.t. (give light to) éclairer; (make brighter) éclaircir.

**lighten**[2] v.t. (make less heavy) alléger.

**lighter** n. briquet m.

**lighthouse** n. phare m.

**lighting** n. éclairage m. **~ technician,** éclairagiste m./f.

**lightning** n. éclair(s) m. (pl.), foudre f. ● a. éclair invar.

**lightweight** a. léger. ● n. (boxing) poids léger m.

**like**[1] a. semblable, pareil. ● prep. comme. ● conj. (fam.) comme. ● n. pareil m.

**like**[2] v.t. aimer (bien). **~s** n. pl. goûts m. pl. **I should ~,** je voudrais, j'aimerais. **would you ~?,** voulez-vous? **~able** a. sympathique.

**likel|y** a. probable. ● adv. probablement. **he is ~y to do,** il fera probablement. **~ihood** n. probabilité f.

**liken** v.t. comparer.

**likewise** adv. de même.

**liking** n. (for thing) penchant m.; (for person) affection f.

**lilac** n. lilas m. ● a. lilas invar.

**lily** n. lis m., lys m. **~ of the valley,** muguet m.

**limb** n. membre m.

**limber** v.i. **~ up,** faire des exercices d'assouplissement.

**lime**[1] n. chaux f.

**lime**[2] n. (fruit) citron vert m.

**lime**[3] n. **~(-tree),** tilleul m.

**limit** n. limite f. ● v.t. limiter. **~ed company,** société anonyme f. **~ation** n. limitation f.

**limousine** n. (car) limousine f.

**limp**[1] v.i. boiter. ● n. **have a ~,** boiter.

**limp**[2] a. mou.

**limpid** a. limpide.

**line**[1] n. ligne f.; (track) voie f.; (wrinkle) ride f.; (row) rangée f., file f.; (of poem) vers m.; (rope) corde f.; (of goods) gamme f.; (queue: Amer.) queue f. ● v.t. (paper) régler; (streets etc.) border. **in ~ with,** en accord avec. **~ up,** (s')aligner; (in queue) faire la queue. **~ sth. up,** prévoir qch.

**line**[2] v.t. (garment) doubler; (fill) remplir, garnir.

**linear** a. linéaire.

**linen** n. (sheets etc.) linge m.; (material) lin m., toile de lin f.

**liner** n. paquebot m.

**linesman** n. (football) juge de touche m.

**linger** v.i. s'attarder; (smells etc.) persister.

**lingerie** n. lingerie f.

**linguist** n. linguiste m./f.

**linguistic** a. linguistique. **~s** n. linguistique f.

**lining** n. doublure f.

**link** n. lien m.; (of chain) maillon m. ● v.t. relier; (relate) (re)lier. **~ up,** (of roads) se rejoindre. **~age** n. lien m. **~-up** n. liaison f.

**lino** n. lino m.

**linoleum** n. linoléum m.

**lint** n. (med.) tissu ouaté m.; (fluff) peluche(s) f. (pl.).

**lion** n. lion m.>

**lip** n. lèvre f.; (edge) rebord m. **~-read** v.t./i. lire sur les lèvres.

**lipstick** n. rouge (à lèvres) m.

**liqueur** n. liqueur f.

**liquid** n. & a. liquide (m.). **~ize** v.t. passer au mixeur. **~izer** n. mixeur m.

**liquidat|e** v.t. liquider. **~ion** n. liquidation f. **go into ~ion,** déposer son bilan.

**liquor** n. alcool m.

**liquorice** n. réglisse f.

**lisp** n. zézaiement m. ● v.i. zézayer.

**list** n. liste f. ● v.t. dresser la liste de.

**listen** v.i. écouter. **~ to** écouter. **~er** n. audi|teur, -trice m., f.

**literal** a. littéral; (person) prosaïque. **~ly** adv. littéralement.

**literary** a. littéraire.

**litera|te** a. qui sait lire et écrire. **~cy** n. capacité de lire et écrire f.

**literature** n. littérature f.; (fig.) documentation f.

**litigation** n. litige m.

**litre** n. litre m.

**litter** n. détritus m. pl., papiers m. pl.; (animals) portée f. ● v.t. éparpiller; (make untidy) laisser des détritus dans. **~bin** n. poubelle f. **~ed with,** jonché de.

**little** a. petit; (not much) peu de. ● n. peu m. ● adv. peu. **a ~,** un peu (de).

**liturgy** n. liturgie f.

**live**[^1] a. vivant; (wire) sous tension; (broadcast) en direct.

**live**[^2] v.t./i. vivre; (reside) habiter, vivre. **~ on,** (feed o.s. on) vivre de; (continue) survivre.

**livelihood** n. moyens d'existence m. pl.

**lively** a. vif, vivant.

**liven** v.t./i. **~ up,** (s')animer; (cheer up) (s')égayer.

**liver** n. foie m.

**livestock** n. bétail m.

**livid** a. livide; (angry: fam.) furieux.

**living** a. vivant. ● n. vie f. **make a ~,** gagner sa vie. **~ conditions,** conditions de vie f. pl. **~-room** n. salle de séjour f.

**lizard** n. lézard m.

**llama** n. lama m.

**load** n. charge f.; (loaded goods) chargement m., charge f.; (weight, strain) poids m. **~s of,** (fam.) des masses de. ● v.t. charger.

**loaf**[^1] n. pain m.

**loaf**[^2] v.i. **~ (about),** fainéanter.

**loam** n. terreau m.

**loan** n. prêt m.; (money borrowed) emprunt m. ● v.t. (lend: fam.) prêter.

**loath|e** v.t. détester. **~ing** n. dégoût m.

**lobby** n. entrée f., vestibule m.; (pol.) lobby m., groupe de pression m. ● v.t. faire pression sur.

**lobe** n. lobe m.

**lobster** n. homard m.

**local** a. local; (shops etc.) du quartier. ● n. personne du coin f.; (pub: fam.) pub du coin m. **~ly** adv. localement; (nearby) dans les environs.

**locat|e** v.t. (situate) situer; (find) repérer. **~ion** n. emplacement m.

**lock**[^1] n. mèche (de cheveux) f.

**lock**[^2] n. (of door etc.) serrure f.; (on canal) écluse f. ● v.t./i. fermer à clef; (wheels: auto.) (se) bloquer. **~ in** or **up,** (person) enfermer. **~ out,** (by mistake) enfermer dehors. **~out** n. lockout m. invar.

**locker** n. casier m.

**locket** n. médaillon m.

**locomotion** n. locomotion f.

**locomotive** n. locomotive f.

**locum** n. (doctor etc.) remplaçant(e) m. (f.).

**locust** n. criquet m.

**lodge** n. (house) pavillon (de gardien or de chasse) m.; (of porter) loge f. ● v.t. loger; (money, complaint) déposer. ● v.i. être logé (with, chez); (become fixed) se loger. **~r** n. locataire m./f., pensionnaire m./f.

**lodgings** n. chambre (meublée) f.; (flat) logement m.

**loft** n. grenier m.

**lofty** a. (tall, noble) élevé; (haughty) hautain.

**log** n. (of wood) bûche f. **~(-book),** (naut.) journal de bord m.; (auto.) (équivalent de la) carte grise f. ● v.t. noter; (distance) parcourir. **~ on,** entrer. **~ off,** sortir.

**logarithm** n. logarithme m.

**logic** a. logique. **~al** a. logique. **~ally** adv. logiquement.

**logistics** n. logistique f.

**logo** n. (fam.) emblème m.

**loin** n. (culin.) filet m.

**loiter** v.i. traîner.

**loll** v.i. se prélasser.

**loll|ipop** n. sucette f. **~y** n. (fam.) sucette f.; (sl.) fric m.

**London** n. Londres m./f.

**lone** a. solitaire.

**lonely** a. solitaire; (person) seul, solitaire.

**long**[^1] a. long. ● adv. longtemps. **how ~ is?,** quelle est la longueur de?; (in time) quelle est la durée de? **how ~?,** combien de temps? **he will not be ~,** il n'en a pas pour longtemps. **a ~ time,** longtemps. **as ~ or so ~ as,** pourvu que. **before ~,** avant peu. **I no ~er do,** je ne fais plus. **~-distance** a. (flight) sur long parcours; (phone call) interurbain. **~ jump,** saut en longueur m. **~-term** a. à long terme. **~ wave,** grandes ondes f. pl. **~-winded** a. (speaker etc.) verbeux.

**long**[^2] v.i. avoir bien or très envie (for, to, de). **~ for s.o.,** (pine for) languir après qn. **~ing** n. envie f.; (nostalgia) nostalgie f.

**longevity** n. longévité f.

**longitude** n. longitude f.

**loo** n. (*fam.*) toilettes f. pl.

**look** v.t./i. regarder; (*seem*) avoir l'air. ● n. regard m.; (*appearance*) air m., aspect m. (*good*) ∼s, beauté f. ∼ **after**, s'occuper de, soigner. ∼ **at**, regarder. ∼ **for**, chercher. ∼ **forward to**, attendre avec impatience. ∼ **into**, examiner. ∼ **like**, ressembler à, avoir l'air de. ∼ **out**, faire attention. ∼ **out for**, chercher; (*watch*) guetter. ∼ **round**, se retourner. ∼ **up**, (*word*) chercher; (*visit*) passer voir. ∼ **up to**, respecter.

**loom**¹ n. métier à tisser m.

**loom**² v.i. surgir; (*event etc.: fig.*) paraître imminent.

**loop** n. boucle f. ● v.t. boucler.

**loophole** n. (*in rule*) échappatoire f.

**loose** a. (*knot etc.*) desserré; (*page etc.*) détaché; (*clothes*) ample, lâche; (*tooth*) qui bouge; (*lax*) relâché; (*not packed*) en vrac; (*inexact*) vague; (*pej.*) immoral. ∼**ly** adv. sans serrer; (*roughly*) vaguement.

**loosen** v.t. (*slacken*) desserrer; (*untie*) défaire.

**loot** n. butin m. ● v.t. piller.

**lop** v.t. ∼ **off**, couper.

**lop-sided** a. de travers.

**lord** n. seigneur m.; (*British title*) lord m. **the L∼**, le Seigneur.

**lore** n. traditions f. pl.

**lorry** n. camion m.

**lose** v.t./i. perdre. **get lost**, se perdre. ∼**r** n. perdant(e) m. (f.).

**loss** n. perte f. **be at a ∼**, être perplexe.

**lost** a. perdu. ∼ **property** objets trouvés m. pl.

**lot**¹ n. (*fate*) sort m.; (*at auction*) lot m.; (*land*) lotissement m.

**lot**² n. **the ∼**, (le) tout m.; (*people*) tous m. pl., toutes f. pl. **a ∼ (of)**, ∼**s (of)**, (*fam.*) beaucoup (de).

**lotion** n. lotion f.

**lottery** n. loterie f.

**loud** a. bruyant, fort. ● adv. fort. ∼**ly** adv. fort.

**loudspeaker** n. haut-parleur m.

**lounge** v.i. paresser. ● n. salon m.

**louse** n. pou m.

**lousy** a. pouilleux; (*bad: sl.*) infect.

**lout** n. rustre m.

**lovable** a. adorable.

**love** n. amour m.; (*tennis*) zéro m. ● v.t. aimer; (*like greatly*) aimer (beaucoup) (**to do**, faire). **in ∼**, amoureux (**with**, de). **make ∼**, faire l'amour.

**lovely** a. joli; (*delightful: fam.*) très agréable.

**lover** n. amant m.; (*devotee*) amateur m. (**of**, de).

**loving** a. affectueux.

**low** a. & adv. bas. ● n. (*low pressure*) dépression f. ∼ **in sth.**, à faible teneur en qch. ∼**-calorie** a. basses calories.

**lower** v.t. baisser. ∼ **o.s.**, s'abaisser.

**loyal** a. loyal. ∼**ly** adv. loyalement. ∼**ty** n. loyauté f.

**lozenge** n. (*shape*) losange m.; (*tablet*) pastille f.

**Ltd.** abbr. (*Limited*) SA.

**lubric|ate** v.t. graisser, lubrifier. ∼**ant** n. lubrifiant m. ∼**ation** n. graissage m.

**lucid** a. lucide.

**luck** n. chance f. **bad ∼**, malchance f. **good ∼!**, bonne chance!

**luck|y** a. qui a de la chance, heureux; (*event*) heureux; (*number*) qui porte bonheur. ∼**ily** adv. heureusement.

**lucrative** a. lucratif.

**ludicrous** a. ridicule.

**lug** v.t. traîner.

**luggage** n. bagages m. pl. ∼**-rack** n. porte-bagages m. invar.

**lukewarm** a. tiède.

**lull** v.t. (*soothe, send to sleep*) endormir. ● n. accalmie f.

**lullaby** n. berceuse f.

**lumbago** n. lumbago m.

**lumber** n. bric-à-brac m. invar.; (*wood*) bois de charpente m.

**lumberjack** n. (*Amer.*) bûcheron m.

**luminous** a. lumineux.

**lump** n. morceau m.; (*swelling on body*) grosseur f.; (*in liquid*) grumeau m. ∼**y** a. (*sauce*) grumeleux; (*bumpy*) bosselé.

**lunar** a. lunaire.

**lunatic** n. fou, folle m., f.

**lunch** n. déjeuner m. ● v.i. déjeuner. ∼ **box**, cantine f.

**lung** n. poumon m.

**lunge** n. mouvement brusque en avant m. ● v.i. s'élancer (**at**, sur).

**lurch**¹ n. **leave in the ∼**, planter là, laisser en plan.

**lurch**² v.i. (*person*) tituber.

**lure** v.t. appâter, attirer. ● n. (*attraction*) attrait m., appât m.

**lurid** a. choquant, affreux; (*gaudy*) voyant.

**lurk** v.i. se cacher; (*in ambush*) s'embusquer; (*prowl*) rôder.

**luscious** a. appétissant.

**lush** a. luxuriant.

**lust** n. luxure f.; (*fig.*) convoitise f. ● v.i. ∼ **after**, convoiter.

**lustre** n. lustre m.

**lusty** a. robuste.

**lute** n. (*mus.*) luth m.

**Luxemburg** n. Luxembourg m.

**luxuriant** a. luxuriant.

**luxurious** a. luxueux.

**luxury** n. luxe m. ● a. de luxe.

**lynch** v.t. lyncher.

**lynx** *n.* lynx *m.*

**lyric** *a.* lyrique. ~**s** *n. pl.* paroles *f. pl.* ~**al** *a.* lyrique.

# Mm

**mac** *n.* (*fam.*) imper *m.*

**macaroni** *n.* macaronis *m. pl.*

**macaroon** *n.* macaron *m.*

**machine** *n.* machine *f.* ● *v.t.* (*sew*) coudre à la machine; (*techn.*) usiner. ~**gun** *n.* mitrailleuse *f.* mitrailler. ~ **tool**, machine-outil *f.*

**machinery** *n.* machinerie *f.*; (*working parts & fig.*) mécanisme(s) *m.* (*pl.*).

**machinist** *n.* (*operator*) opéra|teur, -trice sur machine *m., f.*; (*on sewing-machine*) piqueu|r, -se *m., f.*

**macho** *n.* macho *m.* ● *a.* macho *invar.*

**mackerel** *n. invar.* (*fish*) maquereau *m.*

**mackintosh** *n.* imperméable *m.*

**macrobiotic** *a.* macrobiotique.

**mad** *a.* fou; (*foolish*) insensé; (*dog etc.*) enragé; (*angry: fam.*) furieux. **be ~ about,** se passionner pour; (*person*) être fou de. **drive s.o. ~,** exaspérer qn. ~**ly** *adv.* (*interested, in love, etc.*) follement; (*frantically*) comme un fou. ~**ness** *n.* folie *f.*

**madam** *n.* madame *f.*; (*unmarried*) mademoiselle *f.*

**madden** *v.t.* exaspérer.

**made ~ to measure,** fait sur mesure.

**madman** *n.* fou *m.*

**madrigal** *n.* madrigal *m.*

**magazine** *n.* revue *f.*, magazine *m.*; (*of gun*) magasin *m.*

**magenta** *a.* magenta (*invar.*).

**maggot** *n.* ver *m.*, asticot *m.* ~**y** *a.* véreux.

**magic** *n.* magie *f.* ● *a.* magique. ~**al** *a.* magique.

**magician** *n.* magicien(ne) *m.* (*f.*).

**magistrate** *n.* magistrat *m.*

**magnanim|ous** *a.* magnanime. ~**ity** *n.* magnanimité *f.*

**magnate** *n.* magnat *m.*

**magnesia** *n.* magnésie *f.*

**magnet** *n.* aimant *m.* ~**ic** *a.* magnétique. ~**ism** *n.* magnétisme *m.* ~**ize** *v.t.* magnétiser.

**magneto** *n.* magnéto *m.*

**magnificen|t** *a.* magnifique. ~**ce** *n.* magnificence *f.*

**magnif|y** *v.t.* grossir; (*sound*) amplifier; (*fig.*) exagérer. ~**ication** *n.* grossissement *m.*; amplification *f.* ~**ying glass**, loupe *f.*

**magnolia** *n.* magnolia *m.*

**magpie** *n.* pie *f.*

**mahogany** *n.* acajou *m.*

**maid** *n.* (*servant*) bonne *f.*

**maiden** *n.* (*old use*) jeune fille *f.* ● *a.* (*aunt*) célibataire; (*voyage*) premier. ~ **name,** nom de jeune fille *m.*

**mail**[1] *n.* poste *f.*; (*letters*) courrier *m.* ● *a.* (*bag, van*) postal. ● *v.t.* envoyer par la poste. **mail box,** boîte à lettres *f.* ~**ing list,** liste d'adresses *f.* ~ **order,** vente par correspondance *f.*

**mail**[2] /meɪl/ *n.* (*armour*) cotte de mailles *f.*

**maim** *v.t.* mutiler.

**main**[1] *a.* principal. ~ **line,** grande ligne *f.* **a ~ road,** une grande route. ~**ly** *adv.* principalement, surtout.

**main**[2] *n.* (*water/gas*) ~, conduite d'eau/de gaz *f.* **the ~s,** (*electr.*) le secteur.

**mainframe** *n.* unité centrale *f.*

**mainland** *n.* continent *m.*

**maintain** *v.t.* (*continue, keep, assert*) maintenir; (*house, machine, family*) entretenir; (*rights*) soutenir.

**maintenance** *n.* (*care*) entretien *m.*; (*continuation*) maintien *m.*; (*allowance*) pension alimentaire *f.*

**maisonette** *n.* duplex *m.*

**maize** *n.* maïs *m.*

**majestic** *a.* majestueux.

**majesty** *n.* majesté *f.*

**major** *a.* majeur. ● *n.* commandant *m.* ~**road,** route à priorité *f.*

**Majorca** *n.* Majorque *f.*

**majority** *n.* majorité *f.* ● *a.* majoritaire. **the ~ of people,** la plupart des gens.

**make** *v.t./i.* (*p.t.* **made**) faire; (*manufacture*) fabriquer; (*friends*) se faire; (*money*) gagner, se faire; (*decision*) prendre; (*destination*) arriver à; (*cause to be*) rendre. ~ **s.o. do sth.,** faire faire qch. à qn.; (*force*) obliger qn. à faire qch. ● *n.* fabrication *f.*; (*brand*) marque *f.* **be made of,** être fait de. ~ **s.o. happy,** rendre qn. heureux. **I cannot ~ anything of it,** je n'y comprends rien. ~ **believe,** faire semblant. ~**believe,** *a.* feint, illusoire; *n.* fantaisie *f.* ~ **do,** (*manage*) se débrouiller (**with,** avec). ~ **do with,** (*content o.s.*) se contenter de. ~ **off,** filer (**with,** avec). ~ **out** *v.t.* distinguer; (*understand*) comprendre; (*draw up*) faire; (*assert*) prétendre; *v.i.* (*fam.*) se débrouiller. ~ **over,** céder (**to,** à). ~ **up** *v.t.* faire, former; (*story*) inventer; (*deficit*) combler; *v.i.* se réconcilier. ~ **up (one's face),** se maquiller. ~**up** *n.* maquillage *m.*; (*of object*) constitution *f.*; (*psych.*) caractère *m.* ~ **up for,** compenser; (*time*) rattraper. ~ **up one's mind,** se décider.

**maker** *n.* fabricant *m.*

**makeshift** *n.* expédient *m.* ● *a.* provisoire.

**malaria** *n.* malaria *f.*

**Malay** *a. & n.* malais(e) (*m.* (*f.*)). ~**sia** *n.* Malaysia *f.*

**Malaya** *n.* Malaisie *f.*

**male** *a.* (*voice, sex*) masculin; (*bot., techn.*) mâle. ● *n.* mâle *m.*

**malform|ation** *n.* malformation *f.* ~**ed** *a.* difforme.

**malfunction** *n.* mauvais fonctionnement *m.* ● *v.i.* mal fonctionner.

**malice** *n.* méchanceté *f.*

**malicious** *a.* méchant. ~**ly** *adv.* méchamment.

**malign** *a.* pernicieux. ● *v.t.* calomnier.

**malignan|t** *a.* malveillant; (*tumour*) malin. ~**cy** *n.* malveillance *f.*; malignité *f.*

**mall** *n.* (**shopping**) ~, centre commercial *m.*

**malleable** *a.* malléable.

**mallet** *n.* maillet *m.*

**malnutrition** *n.* sous-alimentation *f.*

**malt** *n.* malt *m.*

**Malt|a** *n.* Malte *f.* ~**ese** *a. & n.* maltais(e) (*m.* (*f.*)).

**maltreat** *v.t.* maltraiter. ~**ment** *n.* mauvais traitement *m.*

**mammal** *n.* mammifère *m.*

**mammoth** *n.* mammouth *m.* ● *a.* monstre.

**man** *n.* homme *m.*; (*in sports team*) joueur *m.*; (*chess*) pièce *f.* ● *v.t.* pourvoir en hommes; (*ship*) armer; (*guns*) servir; (*be on duty at*) être de service à. ~**made** *a.* artificiel. ~**ned space flight**, vol spatial habité *m.*

**manage** *v.t.* diriger; (*shop, affairs*) gérer; (*handle*) manier. ● *v.i.* se débrouiller. ~**to do**, réussir à faire. ~**able** *a.* (*tool, size, person, etc.*) maniable; (*job*) faisable. ~**ment** *n.* direction *f.*; (*of shop*) gestion *f.* **managing director**, directeur général *m.*

**manager** *n.* direc|teur, -trice *m.,f.*; (*of shop*) gérant(e) *m.* (*f.*); (*of actor*) impresario *m.* ~**ess** *n.* directrice *f.*; gérante *f.* ~**ial** *a.* directorial.

**mandarin** *n.* mandarin *m.*; (*orange*) mandarine *f.*

**mandate** *n.* mandat *m.*

**mandatory** *a.* obligatoire.

**mane** *n.* crinière *f.*

**manganese** *n.* manganèse *m.*

**mangetout** *n.* mange-tout *m. invar.*

**mangle** *v.t.* mutiler.

**mango** *n.* mangue *f.*

**manhandle** *v.t.* maltraiter, malmener.

**manhole** *n.* trou d'homme *m.*

**mania** *n.* manie *f.* ~**c** *n.* maniaque *m./f.*, fou *m.*, folle *f.*

**manic-depressive** *a & n.* maniaco-dépressif(-ive) (*m.* (*f.*)).

**manicur|e** *n.* soin des mains *m.* ● *v.t.* soigner, manucurer. ~**ist** *n.* manucure *m./f.*

**manifest** *a.* manifeste. ● *v.t.* manifester. ~**ation** *n.* manifestation *f.*

**manifesto** *n.* manifeste *m.*

**manifold** *a.* multiple. ● *n.* (*auto.*) collecteur *m.*

**manipulat|e** *v.t.* (*tool, person*) manipuler. ~**ion** *n.* manipulation *f.*

**mankind** *n.* genre humain *m.*

**manly** *a.* viril.

**manner** *n.* manière *f.*; (*attitude*) attitude *f.*; (*kind*) sorte *f.* ~**s**, (*social behaviour*) manières *f. pl.* ~**ed** *a.* maniéré.

**manœuvre** *n.* manœuvre *f.* ● *v.t./i.* manœuvrer.

**manor** *n.* manoir *m.*

**manpower** *n.* main-d'œuvre *f.*

**mansion** *n.* château *m.*

**manslaughter** *n.* homicide involontaire *m.*

**mantelpiece** *n.* (*shelf*) cheminée *f.*

**manual** *a.* manuel. ● *n.* (*handbook*) manuel *m.*

**manufacture** *v.t.* fabriquer. ● *n.* fabrication *f.* ~**r** *n.* fabricant *m.*

**manure** *n.* fumier *m.*; (*artificial*) engrais *m.*

**manuscript** *n.* manuscrit *m.*

**many** *a. & n.* beaucoup (de). **a great** *or* **good** ~, un grand nombre (de). ~ **a**, bien des.

**Maori** *a.* maori. ● *n.* Maori(e) *m.* (*f.*).

**map** *n.* carte *f.*; (*of streets etc.*) plan *m.* ● *v.t.* faire la carte de. ~ **out**, (*route*) tracer; (*arrange*) organiser.

**maple** *n.* érable *m.*

**mar** *v.t.* gâter; (*spoil beauty of*) déparer.

**marathon** *n.* marathon *m.*

**marble** *n.* marbre *m.*; (*for game*) bille *f.*

**March** *n.* mars *m.*

**march** *v.i.* (*mil.*) marcher (au pas). ● *v.t.* ~ **off**, (*lead away*) emmener. ● *n.* marche *f.* ~ **past** *n.* défilé *m.*

**mare** *n.* jument *f.*

**margarine** *n.* margarine *f.*

**margin** *n.* marge *f.* ~**al** *a.* marginal; (*increase etc.*) léger, faible. ~**alize** *v.t.* marginaliser. ~**ally** *adv.* très légèrement.

**marigold** *n.* souci *m.*

**marijuana** *n.* marijuana *f.*

**marina** *n.* marina *f.*

**marinate** *v.t.* mariner.

**marine** *a.* marin. ● *n.* (*shipping*) marine *f.*; (*sailor*) fusilier marin *m.*

**marionette** *n.* marionnette *f.*

**marital** *a.* conjugal. ~ **status**, situation de famille *f.*

**maritime** *a.* maritime.

**marjoram** *n.* marjolaine *f.*

**mark**[1] *n.* (*currency*) mark *m.*

**mark**[2] *n.* marque *f.*; (*trace*) trace *f.*, marque *f.*; (*schol.*) note *f.*; (*target*) but *m.* ● *v.t.* marquer; (*exam*) corriger.

**marked** *a.* marqué.

**market** *n.* marché *m.* ● *v.t.* (*sell*) vendre; (*launch*) commercialiser. ~ **research**, étude de marché *f.* ~ **value**, valeur marchande *f.* **on the ~**, en vente. ~**ing** *n.* marketing *m.*

**marksman** *n.* tireur d'élite *m.*

**marmalade** *n.* confiture d'oranges *f.*

**maroon** *n.* bordeaux *m. invar.* ● *a.* bordeaux *invar.*

**marquee** *n.* grande tente *f.*; (*awning*: *Amer.*) marquise *f.*

**marriage** *n.* mariage *m.*

**marrow** *n.* (*of bone*) moelle *f.*; (*vegetable*) courge *f.*

**marr|y** *v.t.* épouser; (*give or unite in marriage*) marier. ● *v.i.* se marier. ~**ied** *a.* marié; (*life*) conjugal. **get ~ied**, se marier (**to**, avec).

**Mars** *n.* (*planet*) Mars *f.*

**marsh** *n.* marais *m.*

**marshal** *n.* maréchal *m.*; (*at event*) membre du service d'ordre *m.* ● *v.t.* rassembler.

**marshmallow** *n.* guimauve *f.*

**martial** *a.* martial. ~ **law**, loi martiale *f.*

**martyr** *n.* martyr(e) *m.* (*f.*). ● *v.t.* martyriser.

**marvel** *n.* merveille *f.* ● *v.i.* s'émerveiller (**at**, de).

**marvellous** *a.* merveilleux.

**Marxis|t** *a. & n.* marxiste (*m./f.*). ~**m** *n.* marxisme *m.*

**marzipan** *n.* pâte d'amandes *f.*

**mascara** *n.* mascara *m.*

**mascot** *n.* mascotte *f.*

**masculin|e** *a. & n.* masculin (*m.*). ~**ity** *n.* masculinité *f.*

**mash** *n.* pâtée *f.*; (*potatoes*: *fam.*) purée *f.* ● *v.t.* écraser. ~**ed potatoes**, purée (de pommes de terre) *f.*

**mask** *n.* masque *m.* ● *v.t.* masquer.

**masochis|t** *n.* masochiste *m./f.* ~**m** *n.* masochisme *m.*

**mason** *n.* (*builder*) maçon *m.* ~**ry** *n.* maçonnerie *f.*

**masquerade** *n.* mascarade *f.* ● *v.i.* ~ **as**, se faire passer pour.

**mass**¹ *n.* (*relig.*) messe *f.*

**mass**² *n.* masse *f.* ● *v.t./i.* (se) masser. ~ **produce** *v.t.* fabriquer en série. **the ~ media**, les média *m.pl.*

**massacre** *n.* massacre *m.* ● *v.t.* massacrer.

**massage** *n.* massage *m.* ● *v.t.* masser.

**masseu|r** *n.* masseur *m.* ~**se** *n.* masseuse *f.*

**massive** *a.* (*large*) énorme; (*heavy*) massif.

**mast** *n.* mât *m.*; (*for radio, TV*) pylône *m.*

**master** *n.* maître *m.*; (*in secondary school*) professeur *m.* ~**y** *n.* maîtrise *f.*

**masterpiece** *n.* chef-d'œuvre *m.*

**mastiff** *n.* dogue *m.*

**masturbat|e** *v.i.* se masturber. ~**ion** *n.* masturbation *f.*

**mat** *n.* (petit) tapis *m.*, natte *f.*; (*at door*) paillasson *m.*

**match**¹ *n.* allumette *f.*

**match**² *n.* (*sport*) match *m.*; (*equal*) égal(e) *m.* (*f.*); (*marriage*) mariage *m.*; (*s.o. to marry*) parti *m.* ● *v.t.* opposer; (*go with*) aller avec; (*cups etc.*) assortir; (*equal*) égaler. ● *v.i.* (*be alike*) être assorti. ~**ing** *a.* assorti.

**matchbox** *n.* boîte à allumettes *f.*

**mate**¹ *n.* camarade *m./f.*; (*of animal*) compagnon *m.*, compagne *f.*; (*assistant*) aide *m./f.* ● *v.t./i.* (s')accoupler (**with**, avec).

**mate**² *n.* (*chess*) mat *m.*

**material** *n.* matière *f.*; (*fabric*) tissu *m.*; (*documents, for building*) matériau(x) *m.* (*pl.*). ~**s**, (*equipment*) matériel *m.* ● *a.* matériel; (*fig.*) important.

**maternal** *a.* maternel.

**maternity** *n.* maternité *f.* ● *a.* (*clothes*) de grossesse. ~ **hospital**, maternité *f.* ~ **leave**, congé de maternité *m.*

**mathematic|s** *n. & n. pl.* mathématiques *f. pl.* ~**ian** *n.* mathématicien(ne) *m.* (*f.*). ~**al** *a.* mathématique.

**maths** *n. pl.* (*fam.*) maths *f. pl.*

**matinée** *n.* matinée *f.*

**mating** *n.* accouplement *m.* ~ **season**, saison des amours *f.*

**matrimon|y** *n.* mariage *m.* ~**ial** *a.* matrimonial.

**matrix** *n.* matrice *f.*

**matron** *n.* (*married, elderly*) dame âgée *f.*; (*in hospital*: *former use*) infirmière-major *f.*

**matt** *a.* mat.

**matted** *a.* (*hair*) emmêlé.

**matter** *n.* (*substance*) matière *f.*; (*affair*) affaire *f.*; (*pus*) pus *m.* ● *v.i.* importer. **as a ~ of fact**, en fait. **it does not ~**, ça ne fait rien. **no ~ what happens**, quoi qu'il arrive. **what is the ~?**, qu'est-ce qu'il y a?

**mattress** *n.* matelas *m.*

**matur|e** *a.* mûr. ● *v.t./i.* (se) mûrir. ~**ity** *n.* maturité *f.*

**mauve** *a. & n.* mauve (*m.*).

**maverick** *n.* non-conformiste.

**maxim** *n.* maxime *f.*

**maxim|um** *a. & n.* maximum (*m.*).

**may** *v. aux.* pouvoir. **he ~/might come**, il peut/pourrait venir. **you might have**, vous auriez pu. **you ~ leave**, vous pouvez partir. **~ I smoke?**, puis-je fumer? **I ~ or might as well stay**, je ferais aussi bien de rester.

**May** *n.* mai *m.* ~ **Day**, le Premier Mai.

**maybe** *adv.* peut-être.

**mayhem** *n.* (*havoc*) ravages *m. pl.*

**mayonnaise** *n.* mayonnaise *f.*

**mayor** *n.* maire *m.* ~**ess** *n.* (*wife*) femme du maire *f.*

**maze** *n.* labyrinthe *m.*

**me** *pron.* me, m'\*; (*after prep.*) moi. (**to**) ∼, me, m'\*. **he knows** ∼, il me connaît.

**meadow** *n.* pré *m.*

**meagre** *a.* maigre.

**meal**[1] *n.* repas *m.*

**meal**[2] *n.* (*grain*) farine *f.*

**mean**[1] *a.* (*poor*) misérable; (*miserly*) avare; (*unkind*) méchant. ∼**ness** *n.* avarice *f.*; méchanceté *f.*

**mean**[2] *a.* moyen. ● *n.* milieu *m.*; (*average*) moyenne *f.* **in the** ∼ **time**, en attendant.

**mean**[3] *v.t.* vouloir dire, signifier; (*involve*) entraîner. I ∼ **that!**, je suis sérieux. **be meant for**, être destiné à. ∼ **to do**, avoir l'intention de faire.

**meander** *v.i.* faire des méandres.

**meaning** *n.* sens *m.*, signification *f.* ∼**less** *a.* denué de sens.

**means** *n.* moyen(s) *m.* (*pl.*). **by** ∼ **of sth.**, au moyen de qch. ● *n. pl.* (*wealth*) moyens financiers *m. pl.*

**mean|time** ∼**while** *advs.* en attendant.

**measles** *n.* rougeole *f.*

**measly** *a.* (*sl.*) minable.

**measurable** *a.* mesurable.

**measure** *n.* mesure *f.*; (*ruler*) règle *f.* ● *v.t./i.* mesurer. ∼**d** *a.* mesuré. ∼**ment** *n.* mesure *f.*

**meat** *n.* viande *f.*

**mechanic** *a.* mécanicien(ne) *m.* (*f.*).

**mechanic|al** *d.* mécanique. ∼**s** *n.* (*science*) mécanique *f.*; *n. pl.* mécanisme *m.*

**mechan|ism** *n.* mécanisme *m.* ∼**ize** *v.t.* mécaniser.

**medal** *n.* médaille *f.* ∼**list** *n.* médaillé(e) *m.* (*f.*). **be a gold** ∼**list**, être médaille d'or.

**medallion** *n.* (*medal, portrait, etc.*) médaillon *m.*

**meddle** *v.i.* (*interfere*) se mêler (**in**, de); (*tinker*) toucher (**with**, à).

**media** *n. pl.* **the** ∼, les media *m. pl.* **talk to the** ∼, parler à la presse.

**median** *a.* médian. ● *n.* médiane *f.*

**mediat|e** *v.i.* servir d'intermédiaire. ∼**ion** *n.* médiation *f.* ∼**or** *n.* média|teur, -trice *m.*, *f.*

**medical** *a.* médical. ● *n.* (*fam.*) visite médicale *f.*

**medicat|ed** *a.* médical. ∼**ion** *n.* médicaments *m. pl.*

**medicine** *n.* (*science*) médecine *f.*; (*substance*) médicament *m.*

**medieval** *a.* médiéval.

**mediocr|e** *a.* médiocre. ∼**ity** *n.* médiocrité *f.*

**meditat|e** *v.t./i.* méditer. ∼**ion** *n.* méditation *f.*

**Mediterranean** *a.* méditerranéen. ● *n.* **the** ∼, la Méditerranée *f.*

**medium** *n.* milieu *m.*; (*for transmitting data etc.*) support *m.*; (*person*) médium *m.* ● *a.* moyen.

**medley** *n.* mélange *m.*; (*mus.*) pot-pourri *m.*

**meek** *a.* doux.

**meet** *v.t.* rencontrer; (*see again*) retrouver; (*fetch*) (aller) chercher; (*be introduced to*) faire la connaissance de; (*face*) faire face à; (*requirement*) satisfaire. ● *v.i.* se rencontrer; (*see each other again*) se retrouver; (*in session*) se réunir.

**meeting** *n.* réunion *f.*; (*between two people*) rencontre *f.*

**megaphone** *n.* portevoix *m. invar.*

**melamine** *n.* mélamine *f.*

**melanchol|y** *n.* mélancolie *f.* ● *a.* mélancolique. ∼**ic** *a.* mélancolique.

**mellow** *a.* (*fruit*) mûr; (*sound, colour*) moelleux, doux; (*person*) mûri. ● *v.t./i.* (*mature*) mûrir; (*soften*) (s')adoucir.

**melodious** *a.* mélodieux.

**melodrama** *n.* mélodrame *m.* ∼**tic** *a.* mélodramatique.

**melod|y** *n.* mélodie *f.* ∼**ic** *a.* mélodique.

**melon** *n.* melon *m.*

**melt** *v.t./i.* (faire) fondre.

**member** *n.* membre *m.* **M**∼ **of Parliament**, député *m.* ∼**ship** *n.* adhésion *f.*; (*members*) membres *m. pl.*; (*fee*) cotisation *f.*

**membrane** *n.* membrane *f.*

**memento** *n.* (*object*) souvenir *m.*

**memo** *n.* (*fam.*) note *f.*

**memoir** *n.* (*record, essay*) mémoire *m.*

**memorable** *a.* mémorable.

**memorandum** *n.* note *f.*

**memorial** *n.* monument *m.* ● *a.* commémoratif.

**memorize** *v.t.* apprendre par cœur.

**memory** *n.* (*mind, in computer*) mémoire *f.*; (*thing remembered*) souvenir *m.* **from** ∼, de mémoire. **in** ∼ **of**, à la mémoire de.

**menac|e** *n.* menace *f.*; (*nuisance*) peste *f.* ● *v.t.* menacer. ∼**ing** *a.* menaçant.

**mend** *v.t.* réparer; (*darn*) raccommoder.

**menial** *a.* servile.

**meningitis** *n.* méningite *f.*

**menopause** *n.* ménopause *f.*

**menstruation** *n.* menstruation *f.*

**mental** *a.* mental; (*hospital*) psychiatrique.

**mentality** *n.* mentalité *f.*

**menthol** *n.* menthol *m.* ● *a.* mentholé.

**mention** *v.t.* mentionner. ● *n.* mention *f.* **don't** ∼ **it!**, il n'y a pas de quoi!, je vous en prie!

**mentor** *n.* mentor *m.*

**menu** *n.* (*food, on computer*) menu *m.*; (*list*) carte *f.*

**MEP** (*abbr.*) (*member of the European Parliament*) député européen *m.*

**mercenary** *a.* & *n.* mercenaire (*m.*).

**merchandise** *n.* marchandises *f. pl.*

**merchant** *n.* marchand *m.* ● *a.* (*ship, navy*) marchand. ∼ **bank**, banque de commerce *f.*

**merciful** *a.* miséricordieux.

**merciless** *a.* impitoyable.

**mercury** *n.* mercure *m.*

**mercy** *n.* pitié *f.* **at the ~ of,** à la merci de.

**mere** *a.* simple. **~ly** *adv.* simplement.

**merest** *a.* moindre.

**merge** *v.t./i.* (se) mêler (**with,** à); (*companies*: *comm.*) fusionner. **~r** *n.* fusion *f.*

**meridian** *n.* méridien *m.*

**meringue** *n.* meringue *f.*

**merit** *n.* mérite *m.* ● *v.t.* mériter.

**mermaid** *n.* sirène *f.*

**merry** *a.* gai. **make ~,** faire la fête. **~-go-round** *n.* manège *m.* **merrily** *adv.* gaiement.

**mesh** *n.* maille *f.*; (*fabric*) tissu à mailles *m.*; (*network*) réseau *m.*

**mesmerize** *v.t.* hypnotiser.

**mess** *n.* désordre *m.*, gâchis *m.*; (*dirt*) saleté *f.*; (*mil.*) mess *m.* ● *v.t.* **~ up,** gâcher. ● *v.i.* **~ about,** s'amuser; (*dawdle*) traîner. **~ with,** (*tinker with*) tripoter. **make a ~ of,** gâcher.

**message** *n.* message *m.*

**messenger** *n.* messager *m.*

**messy** *a.* en désordre; (*dirty*) sale.

**metabolism** *n.* métabolisme *m.*

**metal** *n.* métal *m.* ● *a.* de métal. **~lic** *a.* métallique; (*paint, colour*) métallisé.

**metallurgy** *n.* métallurgie *f.*

**metamorphosis** *n.* métamorphose *f.*

**meteor** *n.* météore *m.*

**meteorite** *n.* météorite *m.*

**meteorolog|y** *n.* météorologie *f.* **~ical** *a.* météorologique.

**meter** *n.* compteur *m.*

**method** *n.* méthode *f.*

**methodical** *a.* méthodique.

**Methodist** *n.* & *a.* méthodiste (*m./f.*).

**methodology** *n.* méthodologie *f.*

**methylated** *a.* **~ spirit,** alcool à brûler *m.*

**meticulous** *a.* méticuleux.

**metre** *n.* mètre *m.*

**metric** *a.* métrique.

**metropolis** *n.* (*city*) métropole *f.*

**mew** *n.* miaulement *m.* ● *v.i.* miauler.

**mews** *n. pl.* (*dwellings*) appartements chic aménagés dans des anciennes écuries *m. pl.*

**Mexic|o** *n.* Mexique *m.* **~an** *a.* & *n.* mexicain(e) (*m.* (*f.*)).

**miaow** *n.* & *v.i.* = **mew.**

**micro-** *pref.* micro-.

**microbe** *n.* microbe *m.*

**microchip** *n.* microplaquette *f.*, puce *f.*

**microclimate** *n.* microclimat *n.*

**microcomputer** *n.* micro(-ordinateur) *m.*

**microcosm** *n.* microcosme *m.*

**microfilm** *n.* microfilm *n.*

**microlight** *n.* U.L.M. *m.*

**microphone** *n.* microphone *m.*

**microprocessor** *n.* microprocesseur *m.*

**microscop|e** *n.* microscope *m.* **~ic** *a.* microscopique.

**microwave** *n.* micro-onde *f.* **~ oven,** four à micro-ondes *m.*

**midday** *n.* midi *m.*

**middle** *a.* du milieu; (*quality*) moyen. ● *n.* milieu *m.* **in the ~ of,** au milieu de. **~-aged** *a.* d'un certain âge. **~ class,** classe moyenne *f.* **~-class** *a.* bourgeois. **M~ East,** Proche-Orient *m.*

**middleman** *n.* intermédiaire *m.*

**middling** *a.* moyen.

**midge** *n.* moucheron *m.*

**midget** *n.* nain(e) *m.* (*f.*). ● *a.* minuscule.

**Midlands** *n. pl.* région du centre de l'Angleterre *f.*

**midnight** *n.* minuit *m.*

**midriff** *n.* ventre *m.*

**midst** *n.* **in the ~ of,** au milieu de. **in our ~,** parmi nous.

**midway** *adv.* à mi-chemin.

**midwife** *n.* sage-femme *f.*

**mighty** *a.* puissant; (*very great: fam.*) très grand; *adv.* (*fam.*) rudement.

**migraine** *n.* migraine *f.*

**migrant** *a.* & *n.* (*bird*) migrateur (*m.*); (*worker*) migrant(e) (*m.* (*f.*)).

**migrat|e** *v.i.* émigrer. **~ion** *n.* migration *f.*

**mike** *n.* (*fam.*) micro *m.*

**mild** *a.* doux; (*illness*) bénin. **~ly** *adv.* doucement.

**mildew** *n.* moisissure *f.*

**mile** *n.* mille *m.* (= *1.6 km.*). **~age** *n.* (*loosely*) kilométrage *m.*

**milestone** *n.* borne *f.*; (*event, stage: fig.*) jalon *m.*

**military** *a.* militaire.

**milk** *n.* lait *m.* ● *a.* (*product*) laitier. ● *v.t.* (*cow etc.*) traire; (*fig.*) exploiter.

**milkman** *n.* laitier *m.*

**mill** *n.* moulin *m.*; (*factory*) usine *f.* ● *v.t.* moudre. ● *v.i.* **~ around,** tourner en rond; (*crowd*) grouiller.

**millennium** *n.* millénaire *m.*

**millet** *n.* millet *m.*

**milli-** *pref.* milli-.

**millimetre** *n.* millimètre *m.*

**milliner** *n.* modiste *f.*

**million** *n.* million *m.* **a ~ pounds,** un million de livres. **~aire** *n.* millionnaire *m.*

**milometer** *n.* compteur kilométrique *m.*

**mime** *n.* (*actor*) mime *m./f.*; (*art*) (art du) mime *m.* ● *v.t./i.* mimer.

**mimic** *v.t.* imiter. ● *n.* imita|teur, -trice *m.*; **~ry** *n.* imitation *f.*

**mince** *v.t.* hacher. ● *n.* viande hachée *f.* **~ pie,** tarte aux fruits confits *f.*

**mincemeat** *n.* hachis de fruits confits *m.*

**mind** *n*. esprit *m*.; (*sanity*) raison *f*.; (*opinion*) avis *m*. ● *v.t.* (*have charge of*) s'occuper de; (*heed*) faire attention à. **be on s.o.'s ~,** préoccuper qn. **change one's ~,** changer d'avis. **make up one's ~,** se décider (**to,** à). **I do not ~ the noise**/*etc.*, le bruit/*etc.* ne me dérange pas. **I do not ~,** ça m'est égal. **~less** *a*. irréfléchi.

**minder** *n*. (*for child*) gardien(ne) *m*. (*f*.); (*for protection*) ange gardien *m*.

**mine**[1] *poss. pron.* le mien, la mienne, les mien(ne)s. **it is ~,** c'est à moi *or* le mien.

**min|e**[2] *n*. mine *f*. ● *v.t.* extraire; (*mil.*) miner. **~er** *n*. mineur *m*. **~ing** *n*. exploitation minière *f*.; *a*. minier.

**minefield** *n*. champ de mines *m*.

**mineral** *n*. & *a*. minéral (*m*.). **~ (water),** (*fizzy soft drink*) boisson gazeuse *f*. **~ water,** (*natural*) eau minérale *f*.

**minesweeper** *n*. (*ship*) dragueur de mines *m*.

**mingle** *v.t./i.* (se) mêler (**with,** à).

**mini-** *pref.* mini-.

**miniatur|e** *a*. & *n*. miniature (*f*.). **~ize** *v.t.* miniaturiser.

**minibus** *n*. minibus *m*.

**minicab** *n*. taxi *m*.

**minim** *n*. blanche *f*.

**minim|um** *a*. & *n*. minimum (*m*.). **~al** *a*. minimal. **~ize** *v.t.* minimiser.

**minist|er** *n*. ministre *m*. **~ry** *n*. ministère *m*.

**mink** *n*. vison *m*.

**minor** *a*. petit, mineur *n*. ● *n*. (*jurid.*) mineur(e) *m*. (*f*.).

**minority** *n*. minorité *f*. ● *a*. minoritaire.

**mint**[1] *n*. **the M~,** l'Hôtel de la Monnaie *m*. **a ~,** une fortune. ● *v.t.* frapper.

**mint**[2] *n*. (*plant*) menthe *f*.; (*sweet*) pastille de menthe *f*.

**minus** *prep*. moins; (*without: fam.*) sans. ● *n*. (*sign*) moins *m*. **~ sign,** moins *m*.

**minute**[1] *n*. minute *f*. **~s,** (*of meeting*) procès-verbal *m*.

**minute**[2] *a*. (*tiny*) minuscule; (*detailed*) minutieux.

**mirac|le** *n*. miracle *m*. **~ulous** *a*. miraculeux.

**mirage** *n*. mirage *m*.

**mire** *n*. fange *f*.

**mirror** *n*. miroir *m*., glace *f*. ● *v.t.* refléter.

**misadventure** *n*. mésaventure *f*.

**misbehav|e** *v.i.* se conduire mal. **~iour** *n*. mauvaise conduite *f*.

**miscalculat|e** *v.t.* mal calculer. ● *v.i.* se tromper. **~ion** *n*. erreur de calcul *f*.

**miscarr|y** *v.i.* faire une fausse couche. **~iage** *n*. fausse couche *f*. **~iage of justice,** erreur judiciaire *f*.

**miscellaneous** *a*. divers.

**mischief** *n*. (*foolish conduct*) espièglerie *f*.; (*harm*) mal *m*. **get into ~,** faire des sottises.

**mischievous** *a*. espiègle; (*malicious*) méchant.

**misconception** *n*. idée fausse *f*.

**misconduct** *n*. mauvaise conduite *f*.

**misdemeanour** *n*. (*jurid.*) délit *m*.

**miser** *n*. avare *m./f.* **~ly** *a*. avare.

**miserable** *a*. (*sad*) malheureux; (*wretched*) misérable; (*unpleasant*) affreux.

**misery** *n*. (*unhappiness*) malheur *m*.; (*pain*) souffrances *f. pl.*; (*poverty*) misère *f*.; (*person: fam.*) grincheu|x, -se *m*., *f*.

**misfire** *v.i.* (*plan etc.*) rater; (*engine*) avoir des ratés.

**misfit** *n*. inadapté(e) *m*. (*f*.).

**misfortune** *n*. malheur *m*.

**misgiving** *n*. (*doubt*) doute *m*.; (*apprehension*) crainte *f*.

**misguided** *a*. (*foolish*) imprudent; (*mistaken*) erroné. **be ~,** (*person*) se tromper.

**mishap** *n*. mésaventure *f*., contretemps *m*.

**misinform** *v.t.* mal renseigner.

**misinterpret** *v.t.* mal interpréter.

**misjudge** *v.t.* mal juger.

**mislay** *v.t.* égarer.

**mislead** *v.t.* tromper. **~ing** *a*. trompeur.

**misplace** *v.t.* mal placer; (*lose*) égarer.

**misprint** *n*. coquille *f*.

**misread** *v.t.* mal lire; (*intentions*) mal comprendre.

**misrepresent** *v.t.* présenter sous un faux jour.

**miss**[1] *v.t./i.* manquer; (*deceased person etc.*) regretter. **he ~es her/Paris**/*etc.*, elle/Paris/*etc.* lui manque. **I ~ you,** tu me manques. ● *n*. coup manqué *m*. **it was a near ~,** on l'a échappé belle *or* de peu. **~ out,** omettre. **~ out on sth,** rater qch.

**miss**[2] *n*. mademoiselle *f*. (*pl.* mesdemoiselles).

**misshapen** *a*. difforme.

**missile** *n*. (*mil.*) missile *m*.; (*object thrown*) projectile *m*.

**missing** *a*. (*person*) disparu; (*thing*) qui manque. **something's ~,** il manque quelque chose.

**mission** *n*. mission *f*.

**missionary** *n*. missionnaire *m./f.*

**misspell** *v.t.* mal écrire.

**mist** *n*. brume *f*.; (*on window*) buée *f*. ● *v.t./i.* (s')embuer.

**mistake** *n*. erreur *f*. ● *v.t.* mal comprendre; (*choose wrongly*) se tromper de. **by ~,** par erreur. **make a ~,** faire une erreur. **~ for,** prendre pour. **~n** *a*. erroné. **be ~n,** se tromper.

**mistletoe** *n*. gui *m*.

**mistreat** *v.t.* maltraiter.

**mistress** *n*. maîtresse *f*.

**mistrust** v.t. se méfier de. ● n. méfiance f.

**misty** a. brumeux; (window) embué.

**misunderstand** v.t. mal comprendre. ~ing n. malentendu m.

**misuse**[1] v.t. mal employer; (power etc.) abuser de.

**misuse**[2] n. mauvais emploi m.; (unfair use) abus m.

**mitten** n. moufle f.

**mix** v.t./i. (se) mélanger. ● n. mélange m. ~ up, mélanger; (bewilder) embrouiller; (mistake, confuse) confondre (with, avec). ~-up n. confusion f. ~ with, (people) fréquenter. ~er n. (culin.) mélangeur m. **be a good ~er**, être sociable.

**mixed** a. (school etc.) mixte; (assorted) assorti.

**mixture** n. mélange m.

**moan** n. gémissement m. ● v.i. gémir; (complain) grogner. ~er n. (grumbler) grognon m.

**mob** n. (crowd) cohue f.; (gang: sl.) bande f. ● v.t. assiéger.

**mobil|e** a. mobile. ~e home, caravane f. ● n. mobile m. ~ity n. mobilité f.

**mobiliz|e** v.t./i. mobiliser. ~ation n. mobilisation f.

**moccasin** n. mocassin m.

**mock** v.t./i. se moquer (de). ● a. faux. ~-up n. maquette f.

**mockery** n. moquerie f.

**mode** n. (way, method) mode m.; (fashion) mode f.

**model** n. modèle m.; (of toy) modèle réduit m.; (artist's) modèle m.; (for fashion) mannequin m. ● a. modèle; (car etc.) modèle réduit invar. ● v.t. modeler; (clothes) présenter.

**modem** n. modem m.

**moderate**[2] a. & n. modéré(e) (m. (f.)). ~ly adv. (in moderation) modérément; (fairly) moyennement.

**moderat|e**[2] v.t./i. (se) modérer. ~ion n. modération f. **in ~ion**, avec modération.

**modern** a. moderne. pl. ~ize v.t. moderniser.

**modest** a. modeste. ~y n. modestie f.

**modif|y** v.t. modifier. ~ication n. modification f.

**modular** a. modulaire.

**modulat|e** v.t./i. moduler. ~ion n. modulation f.

**module** n. module m.

**mohair** n. mohair m.

**moist** a. humide, moite. ~ure n. humidité f. ~urizer n. produit hydratant m.

**moisten** v.t. humecter.

**molar** n. molaire f.

**molasses** n. mélasse f.

**mole**[1] /məʊl/ n. grain de beauté m.

**mole**[2] n. (animal) taupe f.

**molecule** n. molécule f.

**molest** v.t. (pester) importuner; (ill-treat) molester.

**mollusc** n. mollusque m.

**molten** a. en fusion.

**moment** n. moment m.

**momentar|y** a. momentané. ~ily adv. momentanément.

**momentous** a. important.

**momentum** n. élan m.

**Monaco** n. Monaco f.

**monarch** n. monarque m.

**monast|ery** n. monastère m. ~ic a. monastique.

**Monday** n. lundi m.

**monetary** a. monétaire.

**money** n. argent m. ~s, sommes d'argent f. pl. ~-box n. tirelire f. ~ order, mandat m.

**mongrel** n. (chien) bâtard m.

**monitor** n. (pupil) chef de classe m.; (techn.) moniteur m. ● v.t. contrôler; (a broadcast) écouter.

**monk** n. moine m.

**monkey** n. singe m. ~-nut n. cacahuète f. ~-wrench n. clef à molette f.

**mono** n. mono f. ● a. mono invar.

**monochrome** a. & n. (en) noir et blanc (m.).

**monogram** n. monogramme m.

**monologue** n. monologue m.

**monopol|y** n. monopole m. ~ize v.t. monopoliser.

**monoton|ous** a. monotone. ~y n. monotonie f.

**monsoon** n. mousson f.

**monst|er** n. monstre m. ~rous a. monstrueux.

**monstrosity** n. monstruosité f.

**month** n. mois m.

**monthly** a. mensuel. ● adv. mensuellement. ● n. (periodical) mensuel m.

**monument** n. monument m. ~al a. monumental.

**moo** n. meuglement m. ● v.i. meugler.

**mood** n. humeur f. **in a good/bad ~**, de bonne/mauvaise humeur. ~y a. d'humeur changeante; (sullen) maussade.

**moon** n. lune f.

**moon|light** n. clair de lune m. ~lit a. éclairé par la lune.

**moonlighting** n. (fam.) travail au noir m.

**moor**[1] n. lande f.

**moor**[2] v.t. amarrer. ~ings n. pl. (chains etc.) amarres f. pl.; (place) mouillage m.

**moose** n. invar. élan m.

**moot** a. discutable. ● v.t. (question) soulever.

**mop** n. balai à franges m. ● v.t. ~ (up), éponger.

**mope** v.i. se morfondre.

**moped** n. cyclomoteur m.

**moral** *a.* moral. ● *n.* morale *f.* **~s,** moralité *f.*
**~ize** *v.i.* moraliser. **~ly** *adv.* moralement.

**morale** *n.* moral *m.*

**morality** *n.* moralité *f.*

**morbid** *a.* morbide.

**more** *a.* (*a greater amount of*) plus de (**than,**
que). ● *n.* & *adv.* plus (**than,** que). (**some**) ~
**tea/pens**/*etc.*, (*additional*) encore du thé/
des stylos/*etc.* **no ~ bread**/*etc.*, plus de pain/
*etc.*

**moreover** *adv.* de plus.

**morgue** /mɔːg/ *n.* morgue *f.*

**morning** *n.* matin *m.*; (*whole morning*)
matinée *f.*

**Morocc|o** *n.* Maroc *m.* **~an** *a.* & *n.*
marocain(e) (*m.* (*f.*)).

**moron** *n.* crétin(e) *m.* (*f.*).

**morose** *a.* morose.

**morphine** *n.* morphine *f.*

**Morse** *n.* ~ (**code**), morse *m.*

**mortal** *a.* & *n.* mortel(le) (*m.*(*f.*)). **~ity** *n.*
mortalité *f.*

**mortar** *n.* mortier *m.*

**mortgage** *n.* crédit immobilier *m.* ● *v.t.*
hypothéquer.

**mortise** *n.* ~ **lock** serrure encastrée *f.*

**mortuary** *n.* morgue *f.*

**mosaic** *n.* mosaïque *f.*

**Moscow** *n.* Moscou *m.*/*f.*

**Moses** *a.* ~ **basket**, moïse *m.*

**mosque** *n.* mosquée *f.*

**mosquito** *n.* moustique *m.*

**moss** *n.* mousse *f.*

**most** *a.* (*the greatest amount of*) le plus de;
(*the majority of*) la plupart de. ● *n.* le plus.
● *adv.* (le) plus; (*very*) fort. ~ **of,** la plus
grande partie de; (*majority*) la plupart de. **at**
~, tout au plus. **~ly** *adv.* surtout.

**motel** *n.* motel *m.*

**moth** *n.* papillon de nuit *m.*; (*in cloth*) mite *f.*
**~-ball** *n.* boule de naphtaline *f.*

**mother** *n.* mère *f.* ● *v.t.* entourer de soins
maternels, materner. **~-in-law** *n.* belle-mère
*f.*

**motif** *n.* motif *m.*

**motion** *n.* mouvement *m.*; (*proposal*) motion
*f.*

**motivat|e** *v.t.* motiver. **~ion** *n.* motivation *f.*

**motive** *n.* motif *m.*

**motley** *a.* bigarré.

**motor** *n.* moteur *m.*; (*car*) auto *f.* ● *a.* (*anat.*)
moteur; (*boat*) à moteur. ● *v.i.* aller en auto. ~
**bike,** (*fam.*) moto *f.* ~ **car,** auto *f.* ~ **cycle,**
motocyclette *f.* **~cyclist** *n.* motocycliste *m.*/
*f.* **~ized** *a.* motorisé.

**motorist** *n.* automobiliste *m.*/*f.*

**motorway** *n.* autoroute *f.*

**mottled** *a.* tacheté.

**motto** *n.* devise *f.*

**mould¹** *n.* moule *m.* ● *v.t.* mouler; (*influence*)
former. **~ing** *n.* (*on wall etc.*) moulure *f.*

**mould²** *n.* (*fungus, rot*) moisissure *f.* **~y** *a.*
moisi.

**moult** *v.i.* muer.

**mound** *n.* monticule *m.*, tertre *m.*; (*pile: fig.*)
tas *m.*

**mount¹** *n.* (*hill*) mont *m.*

**mount²** *v.t.*/*i.* monter. ● *n.* monture *f.* ~ **up,**
s'accumuler; (*add up*) chiffrer (**to,** à).

**mountain** *n.* montagne *f.* ~ **bike,** (vélo) tout
terrain *m.*, vtt *m.* **~ous** *a.* montagneux.

**mountaineer** *n.* alpiniste *m.*/*f.* **~ing** *n.*
alpinisme *m.*

**mourn** *v.t.*/*i.* ~ (**for**), pleurer. **~er** *n.*
personne qui suit le cortège funèbre *f.* **~ing**
*n.* deuil *m.*

**mournful** *a.* triste.

**mouse** *n.* souris *f.*

**mousetrap** *n.* souricière *f.*

**mousse** *n.* mousse *f.*

**moustache** *n.* moustache *f.*

**mouth** *n.* bouche *f.*; (*of dog, cat, etc.*) gueule *f.*
**~-organ** *n.* harmonica *m.*

**mouthful** *n.* bouchée *f.*

**mouthpiece** *n.* (*mus.*) embouchure *f.*;
(*person: fig.*) porte-parole *m. invar.*

**mouthwash** *n.* eau dentifrice *f.*

**mouthwatering** *a.* qui fait venir l'eau à la
bouche.

**movable** *a.* mobile.

**move** *v.t.*/*i.* remuer, (se) déplacer, bouger;
(*incite*) pousser; (*emotionally*) émouvoir;
(*propose*) proposer; (*depart*) partir; (*act*) agir.
~ (**out**), déménager. ● *n.* mouvement *m.*; (*in
game*) coup *m.*; (*player's turn*) tour *m.*;
(*procedure: fig.*) démarche *f.*; (*house change*)
déménagement *m.* **~ back,** (faire) reculer. ~
**in,** emménager. ~ **over,** se pousser.

**movement** *n.* mouvement *m.*

**movie** *n.* film *m.* **the ~s,** le cinéma.

**moving** *a.* en mouvement; (*touching*)
émouvant.

**mow** *v.t.* (*corn etc.*) faucher; (*lawn*) tondre. ~
**down,** faucher. **~er** *n.* (*for lawn*) tondeuse *f.*

**MP** *abbr. see* **Member of Parliament**.

**Mr** *n.* ~ **Smith,** Monsieur *or* M. Smith.

**Mrs** *n.* ~ **Smith,** Madame *or* Mme Smith.

**Ms** *n.* ~ **Smith,** Madame *or* Mme Smith.

**much** *a.* beaucoup de. ● *adv.* & *n.* beaucoup.

**muck** *n.* fumier *m.*; (*dirt: fam.*) saleté *f.* ● *v.i.*
~ **about,** (*sl.*) s'amuser. ~ **about with,** (*sl.*)
tripoter. ● *v.t.* ~ **up,** (*sl.*) gâcher. **~y** *a.* sale.

**mucus** *n.* mucus *m.*

**mud** *n.* boue *f.* **~dy** *a.* couvert de boue.

**muddle** *v.t.* embrouiller. ● *v.i.* ~ **through,**
se débrouiller. ● *n.* désordre *m.*, confusion
*f.*; (*mix-up*) confusion *f.*

**mudguard** *n.* garde-boue *m. invar.*

**muff** n. manchon m.

**muffin** n. muffin m.

**muffle** v.t. emmitoufler; (sound) assourdir. ~r n. (scarf) cache-nez m. invar.

**mug** n. tasse f.; (in plastic, metal) gobelet m.; (for beer) chope f.; (face: sl.) gueule f.; (fool: sl.) idiot(e) m. (f.) ● v.t. agresser. ~ger n. agresseur m. ~ging n. agression f.

**mule** n. (male) mulet m.; (female) mule f.

**multi-** pref. multi-.

**multicoloured** a. multicolore.

**multinational** a. & n. multinational(e) (f.).

**multiple** a. & n. multiple (m.). ~ sclerosis, sclérose en plaques f.

**multipl|y** v.t./i. (se) multiplier. ~ication n. multiplication f.

**multistorey** a. (car park) à étages.

**multitude** n. multitude f.

**mum** n. (fam.) maman f.

**mumble** v.t./i. marmotter.

**mummy**¹ n. (embalmed body) momie f.

**mummy**² n. (mother: fam.) maman f.

**mumps** n. oreillons m. pl.

**munch** v.t./i. mastiquer.

**mundane** a. banal.

**municipal** a. municipal.

**munitions** n. pl. munitions f. pl.

**mural** a. mural. ● n. peinture murale f.

**murder** n. meurtre m. ● v.t. assassiner; (ruin: fam.) massacrer. ~er n. assassin m.

**murky** a. (night, plans, etc.) sombre, ténébreux; (liquid) épais, sale.

**murmur** n. murmure m. ● v.t./i. murmurer.

**muscle** n. muscle m.

**muscular** a. musculaire; (brawny) musclé.

**muse** v.i. méditer.

**museum** n. musée m.

**mush** n. (pulp, soft food) bouillie f. ~y a. mou.

**mushroom** n. champignon m.

**music** n. musique f. ~al a. musical; (instrument) de musique; (talented) doué pour la musique; n. comédie musicale f.

**musician** n. musicien(ne) m. (f.).

**musk** n. musc m.

**Muslim** a. & n. musulman(e) (m. (f.)).

**muslin** n. mousseline f.

**mussel** n. moule f.

**must** v. aux. devoir. **you ~ go**, vous devez partir, il faut que vous partiez. **he ~ be old**, il doit être vieux.

**mustard** n. moutarde f.

**muster** v.t./i. (se) rassembler.

**musty** a. (room, etc.) qui sent le moisi; (smell, taste) de moisi.

**mutation** n. mutation f.

**mute** a. & n. muet(te) (m. (f.)). ~d a. (colour, sound) sourd, atténué; (criticism) voilé.

**mutilat|e** v.t. mutiler. ~ion n. mutilation f.

**mutiny** n. mutinerie f. ● v.i. se mutiner.

**mutter** v.t./i. marmonner.

**mutton** n. mouton m.

**mutual** a. mutuel; (common to two or more: fam.) commun. ~ly adv. mutuellement.

**muzzle** n. (snout) museau m.; (device) muselière f.; (of gun) gueule f. ● v.t. museler.

**my** a. mon, ma, pl. mes.

**myopic** a. myope.

**myself** pron. moi-même; (reflexive) me, m'*; (after prep.) moi.

**mysterious** a. mystérieux.

**mystery** n. mystère m.

**mystify** v.t. laisser perplexe.

**myth** n. mythe m. ~ical a. mythique.

**mythology** n. mythologie f.

# Nn

**nab** v.t. (arrest: sl.) épingler, attraper.

**nag** v.t./i. critiquer; (pester) harceler.

**nail** n. clou m.; (of finger, toe) ongle m. ● v.t. clouer. ~brush n. brosse à ongles f. ~file n. lime à ongles f. ~ polish, vernis à ongles m.

**naïve** a. naïf.

**naked** a. nu.

**name** n. nom m.; (fig.) réputation f. ● v.t. nommer; (fix) fixer.

**namely** adv. à savoir.

**namesake** n. (person) homonyme m.

**nanny** n. nounou f. ~-goat n. chèvre f.

**nap** n. somme m.

**nape** n. nuque f.

**napkin** n. (at meals) serviette f.; (for baby) couche f.

**nappy** n. couche f.

**narcotic** a. & n. narcotique (m.).

**narrat|e** v.t. raconter. ~ion n. narration f. ~or n. narra|teur, -trice m., f.

**narrative** n. récit m.

**narrow** a. étroit. ● v.t./i. (se) rétrécir; (limit) (se) limiter. ~ **down the choices**, limiter les choix. ~ly adv. étroitement; (just) de justesse. ~-minded a. à l'esprit étroit; (ideas etc.) étroit.

**nasal** a. nasal.

**nasty** a. mauvais, désagréable; (malicious) méchant.

**nation** n. nation f. ~-wide a. dans l'ensemble du pays.

**national** a. national. ~ism n. nationalisme m. ~ize v.t. nationaliser.

**nationality** n. nationalité f.

**native** n. ( *local inhabitant* ) autochtone m./f.; ( *non-European* ) indigène m./f. ● a. indigène; ( *country* ) natal; ( *inborn* ) inné.

**natter** v.i. bavarder.

**natural** a. naturel. ~**ist** n. naturaliste m./f. ~**ly** adv. ( *normally, of course* ) naturellement; ( *by nature* ) de nature.

**naturaliz|e** v.t. naturaliser. ~**ation** n. naturalisation f.

**nature** n. nature f.

**naughty** a. vilain, méchant; ( *indecent* ) grivois.

**nause|a** n. nausée f. ~**ous** a. nauséabond.

**nauseate** v.t. écœurer.

**nautical** a. nautique.

**naval** a. ( *battle etc.* ) naval; ( *officer* ) de marine.

**nave** n. ( *of church* ) nef f.

**navel** n. nombril m.

**navigable** a. navigable.

**navigat|e** v.t. ( *sea etc.* ) naviguer sur; ( *ship* ) piloter. ● v.i. naviguer. ~**ion** n. navigation f. ~**or** n. navigateur m.

**navvy** n. terrassier m.

**navy** n. marine f. ~ **(blue),** bleu marine *invar.*

**near** adv. près. ● prep. près de. ● a. proche. ● v.t. approcher de. ~ **by** adv. tout près. ~ **to,** près de.

**nearby** a. proche.

**nearly** adv. presque. **I ~ forgot,** j'ai failli oublier.

**nearside** a. ( *auto.* ) du côté du passager.

**neat** a. soigné, net; ( *room etc.* ) bien rangé; ( *clever* ) habile; ( *whisky, brandy, etc.* ) sec.

**necessar|y** a. nécessaire. ~**ily** adv. nécessairement.

**necessitate** v.t. nécessiter.

**necessity** n. nécessité f.; ( *thing* ) chose indispensable f.

**neck** n. cou m.; ( *of dress* ) encolure f.

**necklace** n. collier m.

**neckline** n. encolure f.

**nectarine** n. nectarine f.

**need** n. besoin m. ● v.t. avoir besoin de; ( *demand* ) demander. **you ~ not come,** vous n'êtes pas obligé de venir. ~**less** a. inutile.

**needle** n. aiguille f. ● v.t. ( *annoy: fam.* ) asticoter, agacer.

**needlework** n. couture f.; ( *object* ) ouvrage (à l'aiguille) m.

**negation** n. négation f.

**negative** a. négatif. ● n. ( *of photograph* ) négatif m.; ( *word: gram.* ) négation f.

**neglect** v.t. négliger, laisser à l'abandon. ● n. manque de soins m. **(state of) ~,** abandon m.

**negligen|t** a. négligent. ~**ce** a. négligence f.

**negligible** a. négligeable.

**negotiable** a. négociable.

**negotiat|e** v.t./i. négocier. ~**ion** n. négociation f. ~**or** n. négocia|teur, -trice m., f.

**Negr|o** n. Noir m. ● a. noir; ( *art, music* ) nègre. ~**ess** n. Noire f.

**neigh** n. hennissement m. ● v.i. hennir.

**neighbour** n. voisin(e) m. (f.). ~**hood** n. voisinage m., quartier m. ~**ing** a. voisin.

**neither** a. & pron. aucun(e) des deux, ni l'un(e) ni l'autre. ● adv. ni. ● conj. (ne) non plus. ~ **big nor small,** ni grand ni petit.

**neon** n. néon m. ● a. ( *lamp etc.* ) au néon.

**nephew** n. neveu m.

**nerve** n. nerf m.; ( *courage* ) courage m.; ( *calm* ) sang-froid m.; ( *impudence: fam.* ) culot m. ~**s,** ( *before exams etc.* ) le trac m.

**nervous** a. nerveux. **be** or **feel ~,** ( *afraid* ) avoir peur. ~ **breakdown,** dépression nerveuse f. ~**ly** adv. ( *tensely* ) nerveusement; ( *timidly* ) craintivement. ~**ness** n. nervosité f.; ( *fear* ) crainte f.

**nest** n. nid m. ● v.i. nicher.

**nestle** v.i. se blottir.

**net**[1] n. filet m. ~**ting** n. ( *nets* ) filets m. pl.; ( *wire* ) treillis m.; ( *fabric* ) voile m.

**net**[2] a. ( *weight etc.* ) net.

**netball** n. netball m.

**Netherlands** n. pl. the ~, les Pays-Bas m. pl.

**nettle** n. ortie f.

**network** n. réseau m.

**neuralgia** n. névralgie f.

**neuro|sis** n. névrose f. ~**tic** a. & n. névrosé(e) (m. (f.)).

**neuter** a. & n. neutre (m.). ● v.t. ( *castrate* ) castrer.

**neutral** a. neutre. ~ **(gear),** ( *auto.* ) point mort m. ~**ity** n. neutralité f.

**never** adv. (ne) jamais; ( *not: fam.* ) (ne) pas. **I ~ saw him,** ( *fam.* ) je ne l'ai pas vu. ~ **again,** plus jamais. ~ **mind,** ( *don't worry* ) ne vous en faites pas; ( *it doesn't matter* ) peu importe.

**nevertheless** adv. toutefois.

**new** a. nouveau; ( *brand-new* ) neuf. ~-**laid egg,** œuf frais m. ~ **year,** nouvel an m. **New Year's Day,** le jour de l'an. **New Year's Eve,** la Saint-Sylvestre. **New Zealand,** Nouvelle-Zélande f. **New Zealander,** Néo-Zélandais(e) m. (f.).

**newcomer** n. nouveau venu m., nouvelle venue f.

**newly** adv. nouvellement. ~-**weds** n. pl. nouveaux mariés m. pl.

**news** n. nouvelle(s) f. (pl.); ( *radio, press* ) informations f. pl.; ( *TV* ) actualités f. pl., informations f. pl. ~ **agency,** agence de presse f.

**newsagent** n. marchand(e) de journaux m. (f.).

**newsletter** n. bulletin m.

**newspaper** n. journal m.

**newt** n. triton m.

**next** *a.* prochain; (*adjoining*) voisin; (*following*) suivant. ● *adv.* la prochaine fois; (*afterwards*) ensuite. ● *n.* suivant(e) *m.(f.).* ~**door,** à côté (**to,** de). ~**of kin,** parent le plus proche *m.* ~ **to,** à côté de.

**nib** *n.* bec *m.,* plume *f.*

**nibble** *v.t./i.* grignoter.

**nice** *a.* agréable, bon; (*kind*) gentil; (*pretty*) joli; (*respectable*) bien *invar.*; (*subtle*) délicat. *f.*

**niche** *n.* (*recess*) niche *f.*; (*fig.*) place *f.,* situation *f.*

**nick** *n.* petite entaille *f.* ● *v.t.* (*steal, arrest: sl.*) piquer.

**nickel** *n.* nickel *m.*

**nickname** *n.* surnom *m.*; (*short form*) diminutif *m.* ● *v.t.* surnommer.

**nicotine** *n.* nicotine *f.*

**niece** *n.* nièce *f.*

**Nigeria** *n.* Nigéria *m./f.* ~**n** *a.* & *n.* nigérian(e) (*m. (f.)*).

**niggardly** *a.* chiche.

**niggling** *a.* (*person*) tatillon; (*detail*) insignifiant.

**night** *n.* nuit *f.*; (*evening*) soir *m.* ● *a.* de nuit. ~**club** *n.* boîte de nuit *f.* ~**dress,** ~**ie** *ns.* chemise de nuit *f.* ~**time** *n.* nuit *f.*

**nightingale** *n.* rossignol *m.*

**nightly** *a.* & *adv.* (de) chaque nuit *or* soir.

**nightmare** *n.* cauchemar *m.*

**nil** *n.* rien *m.*; (*sport*) zéro *m.* ● *a.* (*chances, risk, etc.*) nul.

**nimble** *a.* agile.

**nin|e** *a.* & *n.* neuf (*m.*). ~**th** *a.* & *n.* neuvième (*m./f.*).

**nineteen** *a.* & *n.* dix-neuf (*m.*). ~**th** *a.* & *n.* dix-neuvième (*m./f.*).

**ninet|y** *a.* & *n.* quatre-vingt-dix (*m.*). ~**tieth** *a.* & *n.* quatre-vingt-dixième (*m./f.*).

**nip** *v.t./i.* (*pinch*) pincer; (*rush: sl.*) courir. ~ **out/back/***etc.,* sortir/rentrer/ *etc.* rapidement. ● *n.* pincement *m.*; (*cold*) fraîcheur *f.*

**nipple** *n.* bout de sein *m.*; (*of baby's bottle*) tétine *f.*

**nippy** *a.* (*fam.*) alerte; (*chilly: fam.*) frais.

**nitrogen** *n.* azote *m.*

**no** *a.* aucun(e); pas de. ● *adv.* non. ● *n.* non *m.* *invar.* **no man/***etc.,* aucun homme/*etc.* **no money/ time/***etc.,* pas d'argent/de temps/ *etc.* **no one = nobody. no smoking/entry,** défense de fumer/ d'entrer.

**noble** *a.* noble.

**nobody** *pron.* (ne) personne. ● *n.* nullité *f.* **he knows** ~, il ne connaît personne. ~ **is there,** personne n'est là.

**nocturnal** *a.* nocturne.

**nod** *v.t./i.* ~ (**one's head**), faire un signe de tête. ~ **off,** s'endormir. ● *n.* signe de tête *m.*

**noise** *n.* bruit *m.*

**nois|y** *a.* bruyant. ~**ily** *adv.* bruyamment.

**nomad** *n.* nomade *m./f.* ~**ic** *a.* nomade.

**nominal** *a.* symbolique, nominal; (*value*) nominal. ~**ly** *adv.* nominalement.

**nominat|e** *v.t.* nommer; (*put forward*) proposer. ~**ion** *n.* nomination *f.*

**non-** *pref.* non-. ~**iron** *a.* qui ne se repasse pas. ~**skid** *a.* antidérapant. ~**stick** *a.* à revêtement antiadhésif.

**nondescript** *a.* indéfinissable.

**none** *pron.* aucun(e). ~ **of us,** aucun de nous. **I have** ~, je n'en ai pas.

**non-existent** *a.* inexistant.

**nonsens|e** *n.* absurdités *f. pl.* ~**ical** *a.* absurde.

**non-smoker** *n.* non-fumeur *m.*

**non-stop** *a.* (*train, flight*) direct. ● *adv.* sans arrêt.

**noodles** *n. pl.* nouilles *f. pl.*

**nook** *n.* (re)coin *m.*

**noon** *n.* midi *m.*

**noose** *n.* nœud coulant *m.*

**nor** *adv.* ni. ● *conj.* (ne) non plus.

**norm** *n.* norme *f.*

**normal** *a.* normal. ~**ity** *n.* normalité *f.* ~**ly** *adv.* normalement.

**Norman** *a.* & *n.* normand(e) (*m.(f.)*). ~**dy** *n.* Normandie *f.*

**north** *n.* nord *m.* ● *a.* nord *invar.,* du nord. ● *adv.* vers le nord. **N~ America,** Amérique du Nord *f.* **N~ American** *a.* & *n.* nord-américain(e) (*m. (f.)*). ~**east** *n.* nord-est *m.* ~**wards** *adv.* vers le nord. ~**west** *n.* nord-ouest *m.*

**northern** *a.* du nord. ~**er** *n.* habitant(e) du nord *m. (f.).*

**Norw|ay** *n.* Norvège *f.* ~**egian** *a.* & *n.* norvégien(ne) (*m. (f.)*).

**nose** *n.* nez *m.* ● *v.i.* ~ **about,** fouiner.

**nosebleed** *n.* saignement de nez *m.*

**nosedive** *n.* piqué *m.* ● *v.i.* descendre en piqué.

**nostalg|ia** *n.* nostalgie *f.* ~**ic** *a.* nostalgique.

**nostril** *n.* narine *f.*

**nosy** *a.* (*fam.*) indiscret.

**not** *adv.* (ne) pas. **I do** ~ **know,** je ne sais pas. ~ **at all,** pas du tout. ~ **yet,** pas encore.

**notable** *a.* notable.

**notably** *adv.* notamment.

**notary** *n.* notaire *m.*

**notation** *n.* notation *f.*

**notch** *n.* entaille *f.*

**note** *n.* note *f.*; (*banknote*) billet *m.*; (*short letter*) mot *m.* ● *v.t.* noter; (*notice*) remarquer.

**notebook** *n.* carnet *m.*

**noted** *a.* connu (**for,** pour).

**notepaper** *n.* papier à lettres *m.*

**noteworthy** *a.* remarquable.

**nothing** *pron.* (ne) rien. ● *n.* rien *m.*; (*person*) nullité *f.* ● *adv.* nullement. ~ **much,** pas grand-chose. **for** ~, pour rien, gratis.

**notice** *n.* avis *m.*, annonce *f.*; (*poster*) affiche *f.* **at short ~,** dans des délais très brefs. ● *v.t.* remarquer, observer. **~-board** *n.* tableau d'affichage *m.* **take ~,** faire attention (**of,** à).

**noticeabl|e** *a.* visible. **~y** *adv.* visiblement.

**notif|y** *v.t.* (*inform*) aviser; (*make known*) notifier. **~ication** *n.* avis *m.*

**notion** *n.* idée, notion *f.*

**notor|ious** *a.* (tristement) célèbre. **~iety** *n.* notoriété *f.* **~iously** *adv.* notoirement.

**notwithstanding** *prep.* malgré. ● *adv.* néanmoins.

**nougat** *n.* nougat *m.*

**nought** *n.* zéro *m.*

**noun** *n.* nom *m.*

**nourish** *v.t.* nourrir. **~ing** *a.* nourrissant.

**novel** *n.* roman *m.* ● *a.* nouveau. **~ist** *n.* romanc|ier, -ière *m.*, *f.* **~ty** *n.* nouveauté *f.*

**November** *n.* novembre *m.*

**novice** *n.* novice *m./f.*

**now** *adv.* maintenant. ● *conj.* maintenant que. **~ and again, ~ and then,** de temps à autre.

**nowadays** *adv.* de nos jours.

**nowhere** *adv.* nulle part.

**nozzle** *n.* (*tip*) embout *m.*; (*of hose*) lance *f.*

**nuance** *n.* nuance *f.*

**nuclear** *a.* nucléaire.

**nucleus** *n.* noyau *m.*

**nud|e** *a.* nu. ● *n.* nu *m.* **in the ~e,** tout nu. **~ity** *n.* nudité *f.*

**nudge** *v.t.* pousser du coude. ● *n.* coup de coude *m.*

**nudist** *n.* nudiste *m./f.*

**nuisance** *n.* (*thing, event*) ennui *m.*; (*person*) peste *f.* **be a ~,** être embêtant.

**null** *a.* nul.

**numb** *a.* engourdi. ● *v.t.* engourdir.

**number** *n.* nombre *m.*; (*of ticket, house, page, etc.*) numéro *m.* ● *v.t.* numéroter; (*count, include*) compter. **a ~ of people,** plusieurs personnes. **~-plate** *n.* plaque d'immatriculation *f.*

**numeral** *n.* chiffre *m.*

**numerical** *a.* numérique.

**numerous** *a.* nombreux.

**nun** *n.* religieuse *f.*

**nurs|e** *n.* infirmière *f.*, infirmier *m.* ● *v.t.* soigner. **~ing home,** clinique *f.*

**nursery** *n.* chambre d'enfants *f.*; (*for plants*) pépinière *f.* **(day) ~,** crèche *f.* **~ school,** (école) maternelle *f.*

**nurture** *v.t.* élever.

**nut** *n.* (*walnut, Brazil nut, etc.*) noix *f.*; (*hazelnut*) noisette *f.*; (*peanut*) cacahuète *f.*; (*techn.*) écrou *m.*; (*sl.*) idiot(e) *m.* (*f.*).

**nutcrackers** *n. pl.* casse-noix *m. invar.*

**nutmeg** *n.* muscade *f.*

**nutrit|ion** *n.* nutrition *f.* **~ious** *a.* nutritif.

**nylon** *n.* nylon *m.* **~s,** bas nylon *m. pl.*

**Oo**

**oaf** *n.* lourdaud(e) *m.* (*f.*).

**oak** *n.* chêne *m.*

**OAP** *abbr.* (*old-age pensioner*) retraité(e) *m.* (*f.*), personne âgée *f.*

**oar** *n.* aviron *m.*, rame *f.*

**oasis** *n.* oasis *f.*

**oath** *n.* (*promise*) serment *m.*; (*swear-word*) juron *m.*

**oatmeal** *n.* farine d'avoine *f.*, flocons d'avoine *m. pl.*

**oats** *n. pl.* avoine *f.*

**obedien|t** *a.* obéissant. **~ce** *n.* obéissance *f.* **~tly** *adv.* docilement, avec soumission.

**obes|e** *a.* obèse. **~ity** *n.* obésité *f.*

**obey** *v.t./i.* obéir (à).

**obituary** *n.* nécrologie *f.*

**object**[1] *n.* (*thing*) objet *m.*; (*aim*) but *m.*, objet *m.*; (*gram.*) complément (d'objet) *m.* **money/etc. is no ~,** l'argent/*etc.* ne pose pas de problèmes.

**object**[2] *v.i.* protester. ● *v.t.* **~ that,** objecter que. **~ to,** (*behaviour*) désapprouver; (*plan*) protester contre. **~ion** *n.* objection *f.*; (*drawback*) inconvénient *m.*

**objective** *a.* objectif. ● *n.* objectif *m.*

**obligation** *n.* obligation *f.*

**obligatory** *a.* obligatoire.

**oblig|e** *v.t.* obliger. **~e to do,** obliger à faire. **~ed** *a.* obligé (**to,** de).

**oblique** *a.* oblique; (*reference etc.: fig.*) indirect.

**oblivious** *a.* (*unaware*) inconscient (**to, of,** de).

**oblong** *a.* oblong. ● *n.* rectangle *m.*

**obnoxious** *a.* odieux.

**oboe** *n.* hautbois *m.*

**obscen|e** *a.* obscène. **~ity** *n.* obscénité *f.*

**obscur|e** *a.* obscur. ● *v.t.* obscurcir; (*conceal*) cacher. **~ity** *n.* obscurité *f.*

**observan|t** *a.* observateur. **~ce** *n.* observance *f.*

**observatory** *n.* observatoire *m.*

**observ|e** *v.t.* observer; (*remark*) remarquer. **~ation** *n.* observation *f.* **~er** *n.* observa|teur, -trice *m.*, *f.*

**obsess** *v.t.* obséder. **~ion** *n.* obsession *f.*

**obsolete** *a.* dépassé.

**obstacle** *n.* obstacle *m.*

**obstetric|s** n. obstétrique f. **~ian** n. médecin accoucheur m.

**obstina|te** a. obstiné. **~cy** n. obstination f. **~tely** adv. obstinément.

**obstruct** v.t. (block) boucher; (congest) encombrer; (hinder) entraver. **~ion** n. (act) obstruction f.; (thing) obstacle m.; (traffic jam) encombrement m.

**obtain** v.t. obtenir. ● v.i. avoir cours.

**obtrusive** a. importun; (thing) trop en évidence.

**obvious** a. évident, manifeste. **~ly** adv. manifestement.

**occasion** n. occasion f.; (big event) événement m. ● v.t. occasionner. **on ~,** à l'occasion.

**occasional** a. fait, pris, etc. de temps en temps; (visitor etc.) qui vient de temps en temps. **~ly** adv. de temps en temps.

**occult** a. occulte.

**occupation** n. (activity, occupying) occupation f.; (job) métier m., profession f. **~al** a. professionnel, du métier.

**occup|y** v.i. occuper. **~ant, ~ier** ns. occupant(e) m. (f.).

**occur** v.i. se produire; (arise) se présenter. **~ to s.o.,** venir à l'esprit de qn.

**occurrence** n. événement m.

**ocean** n. océan m.

**o'clock** adv. **it is six ~**/etc., il est six heures/ etc.

**octagon** n. octogone m.

**octane** n. octane m.

**octave** n. octave f.

**October** n. octobre m.

**octopus** n. pieuvre f.

**odd** a. bizarre; (number) impair; (leftover) qui reste; (not of set) dépareillé; (occasional) fait, pris, etc. de temps en temps. **~ jobs,** menus travaux m. pl. **~ly** adv. bizarrement.

**oddment** n. fin de série f.

**odds** n. pl. chances f. pl.; (in betting) cote f. (**on,** de). **at ~,** en désaccord. **~ and ends,** des petites choses.

**ode** n. ode f.

**odious** a. odieux.

**odour** n. odeur f.

**of** prep. de. **of the,** du, de la, pl. des. **of it, of them,** en. **a friend of mine,** un de mes amis. **six of them,** six d'entre eux. **the fifth of June**/etc., le cinq juin/etc. **a litre of water,** un litre d'eau. **made of steel,** en acier.

**off** adv. parti, absent; (switched off) éteint; (tap) fermé; (taken off) enlevé, détaché; (cancelled) annulé. ● prep. de; (distant from) éloigné de. **go ~,** (leave) partir; (milk) tourner; (food) s'abîmer. **20% ~,** une réduction de 20%. **take sth. ~,** (a surface) prendre qch. sur. **~-licence** n. débit de vins m. **~-line** a. autonome; (switched off) déconnecté. **~-load** v.t. décharger. **~-peak** a.

(hours) creux; (rate) des heures creuses. **~-putting** a. (fam.) rebutant. **~-stage** a. & adv. dans les coulisses. **~-white** a. blanc cassé invar.

**offal** n. abats m. pl.

**offence** n. délit m. **give ~ to,** offenser. **take ~,** s'offenser (**at,** de).

**offend** v.t. offenser; (fig.) choquer. **be ~ed,** s'offenser (**at,** de). **~er** n. délinquant(e) m. (f.).

**offensive** a. offensant; (disgusting) dégoûtant; (weapon) offensif. ● n. offensive f.

**offer** v.t. offrir. ● n. offre f. **on ~,** en promotion.

**offhand** a. désinvolte. ● adv. à l'improviste.

**office** n. bureau m.; (duty) fonction f. ● a. de bureau. **in ~,** au pouvoir. **~ building,** immeuble de bureaux m.

**officer** n. (army etc.) officier m.; (policeman) agent m.

**official** a. officiel. ● n. officiel m.; (civil servant) fonctionnaire m./f. **~ly** adv. officiellement.

**officious** a. trop zélé.

**offset** v.t. compenser.

**offshoot** n. (bot.) rejeton m.; (fig.) ramification f.

**offshore** a. (waters) côtier; (exploration) en mer; (banking) dans les paradis fiscaux.

**offside** a. (sport) hors jeu invar.; (auto.) du côté du conducteur.

**offspring** n. invar. progéniture f.

**often** adv. souvent. **how ~?,** combien de fois? **every so ~,** de temps en temps.

**ogle** v.t. lorgner.

**oh** int. oh, ah.

**oil** n. huile f.; (petroleum) pétrole m.; (for heating) mazout m. ● v.t. graisser. **~-tanker** n. pétrolier m. **~y** a. graisseux.

**oilfield** n. gisement pétrolifère m.

**ointment** n. pommade f.

**OK** a. & adv. (fam.) bien.

**old** a. vieux; (person) vieux, âgé; (former) ancien. **how ~ is he?,** quel âge a-t-il? **he is eight years ~,** il a huit ans. **of ~,** jadis. **~ age,** vieillesse f. **old-age pensioner,** retraité(e) m. (f.). **~er, ~est,** (son etc.) aîné. **~-fashioned** a. démodé; (person) vieux jeu invar. **~ man,** vieillard m., vieux m. **~ woman,** vieille f.

**olive** n. olive f. ● a. olive invar. **~ oil,** huile d'olive f.

**Olympic** a. olympique. **~s** n. pl., **~ Games,** Jeux olympiques m. pl.

**omelette** n. omelette f.

**omen** n. augure m.

**ominous** a. de mauvais augure; (fig.) menaçant.

**omit** v.t. omettre. **~ssion** n. omission f.

**on** *prep.* sur. ● *adv.* en avant; (*switched on*) allumé; (*tap*) ouvert; (*machine*) en marche; (*put on*) mis. **on Tuesday,** mardi. **walk**/*etc.* **on,** continuer à marcher/*etc.* **be on,** (*of film*) passer. **on and off,** de temps en temps.

**once** *adv.* une fois; (*formerly*) autrefois. ● *conj.* une fois que. **all at ~,** tout à coup. **~ over** *n.* (*fam.*) coup d'œil rapide *m.*

**oncoming** *a.* (*vehicle etc.*) qui approche.

**one** *a. & n.* un(e) (*m.* (*f.*)). ● *pron.* un(e) *m.* (*f.*); (*impersonal*) on. **a big/red/***etc.* **~,** un(e) grand(e)/ rouge/*etc.* **this/that ~,** celui-ci/là, celle-ci/-là. **~ another,** l'un(e) l'autre. **~-sided** *a.* (*biased*) partial; (*unequal*) inégal. **~-way** *a.* (*street*) à sens unique; (*ticket*) simple.

**oneself** *pron.* soi-même; (*reflexive*) se.

**ongoing** *a.* qui continue à évoluer.

**onion** *n.* oignon *m.*

**onlooker** *n.* specta|teur, -trice *m., f.*

**only** *a.* seul. ● *adv. & conj.* seulement. **he ~ has six,** il n'en a que six, il en a six seulement.

**onset** *n.* début *m.*

**onslaught** *n.* attaque *f.*

**onward(s)** *adv.* en avant.

**ooze** *v.i.* suinter.

**opal** *n.* opale *f.*

**opaque** *a.* opaque.

**open** *a.* ouvert; (*view*) dégagé; (*free to all*) public; (*undisguised*) manifeste; (*question*) en attente. ● *v.t./i.* (s')ouvrir; (*of shop, play*) ouvrir. **in the ~ air,** en plein air. **~ out** *or* **up,** (s')ouvrir. **~-minded** *a.* à l'esprit ouvert.

**opener** *n.* ouvre-boîte(s) *m.*, ouvre-bouteille(s) *m.*

**opening** *n.* ouverture *f.*; (*job*) débouché *m.*, poste vacant *m.*

**openly** *adv.* ouvertement.

**opera** *n.* opéra *m.* **~tic** *a.* d'opéra.

**operat|e** *v.t./i.* opérer; (*techn.*) (faire) fonctionner. **~e on,** (*med.*) opérer. **~ing theatre,** salle d'opération *f.* **~ion** *n.* opération *f.* **have an ~ion,** se faire opérer. **in ~ion,** en vigueur; (*techn.*) en service. **~or** *n.* opéra|teur, -trice *m., f.*; (*telephonist*) standardiste *m./f.*

**operational** *a.* opérationnel.

**operetta** *n.* opérette *f.*

**opinion** *n.* opinion *f.*, avis *m.*

**opium** *n.* opium *m.*

**opponent** *n.* adversaire *m./f.*

**opportune** *a.* opportun.

**opportunist** *n.* opportuniste *m./f.*

**opportunity** *n.* occasion *f.* (**to do,** de faire).

**oppos|e** *v.t.* s'opposer à. **~ed to,** opposé à. **~ing** *a.* opposé.

**opposite** *a.* opposé. ● *n.* contraire *m.*, opposé *m.* ● *adv.* en face. ● *prep.* **~ (to),** en face de.

**opposition** *n.* opposition *f.*; (*mil.*) résistance *f.*

**oppress** *v.t.* opprimer. **~ion** *n.* oppression *f.* **~ive** *a.* (*cruel*) oppressif; (*heat*) oppressant. **~or** *n.* oppresseur *m.*

**opt** *v.i.* **~ for,** opter pour. **~ out,** refuser de participer (**of,** à).

**optical** *a.* optique.

**optician** *n.* opticien(ne) *m.* (*f.*).

**optimis|t** *n.* optimiste *m./f.* **~m** *n.* optimisme *m.* **~tic** *a.* optimiste. **~tically** *adv.* avec optimisme.

**optimum** *a. & n.* optimum (*m.*).

**option** *n.* choix *m.*, option *f.*

**optional** *a.* facultatif.

**opulent** *a.* opulent.

**or** *conj.* ou; (*with negative*) ni.

**oracle** *n.* oracle *m.*

**oral** *a.* oral. ● *n.* (*examination: fam.*) oral *m.*

**orange** *n.* (*fruit*) orange *f.* ● *a.* (*colour*) orange *invar.*

**oratorio** *n.* oratorio *m.*

**orbit** *n.* orbite *f.* ● *v.t.* graviter autour de, orbiter.

**orchard** *n.* verger *m.*

**orchestra** *n.* orchestre *m.*

**orchestrate** *v.t.* orchestrer.

**orchid** *n.* orchidée *f.*

**ordain** *v.t.* décréter (**that,** que); (*relig.*) ordonner.

**ordeal** *n.* épreuve *f.*

**order** *n.* ordre *m.*; (*comm.*) commande *f.* ● *v.t.* ordonner; (*goods etc.*) commander. **in ~,** (*tidy*) en ordre; (*document*) en règle; (*fitting*) de règle. **in ~ that,** pour que. **in ~ to,** pour. **~ s.o. to,** ordonner à qn. de.

**orderly** *a.* (*tidy*) ordonné; (*not unruly*) discipliné.

**ordinary** *a.* (*usual*) ordinaire; (*average*) moyen.

**ore** *n.* mineral *m.*

**organ** *n.* organe *m.*; (*mus.*) orgue *m.* **~ist** *n.* organiste *m./f.*

**organic** *a.* organique.

**organism** *n.* organisme *m.*

**organiz|e** *v.t.* organiser. **~ation** *n.* organisation *f.* **~er** *n.* organisa|teur, -trice *m., f.*

**orgasm** *n.* orgasme *m.*

**orgy** *n.* orgie *f.*

**oriental** *a.* oriental.

**orient(at|e)** *v.t.* orienter. **~ion** *n.* orientation *f.*

**orifice** *n.* orifice *m.*

**origin** *n.* origine *f.*

**original** *a.* (*first*) originel; (*not copied*) original. **~ity** *n.* originalité *f.* **~ly** *adv.* (*at the outset*) à l'origine; (*write etc.*) originalement.

**originat|e** *v.i.* (*plan*) prendre naissance. ● *v.t.* être l'auteur de. **~e from,** provenir de; (*person*) venir de. **~or** *n.* auteur *m.*

**ornament** n. (decoration) ornement m.; (object) objet décoratif m. ~**al** a. ornemental.

**ornate** a. richement orné.

**ornithology** n. ornithologie f.

**orphan** n. orphelin(e) m. (f.). ● v.t. rendre orphelin.

**orthodox** a. orthodoxe.

**orthopaedic** a. orthopédique.

**oscillate** v.i. osciller.

**ostentati|on** n. ostentation f. ~**ous** a. prétentieux.

**osteopath** n. ostéopathe m./f.

**ostrich** n. autruche f.

**other** a. autre. ● n. & pron. autre m./f. ● adv. ~ **than**, autrement que; (except) à part. **(some)** ~**s**, d'autres. **the** ~ **one**, l'autre m./f.

**otherwise** adv. autrement.

**otter** n. loutre f.

**ouch** int. aïe!

**ought** v. aux. devoir. **you** ~ **to stay**, vous devriez rester. **he** ~ **to succeed**, il devrait réussir. **I** ~ **to have done it**, j'aurais dû le faire.

**ounce** n. once f. (= 28.35 g.).

**our** a. notre, pl. nos.

**ours** poss. le or la nôtre, les nôtres.

**ourselves** pron. nous-mêmes; (reflexive & after prep.) nous.

**oust** v.t. évincer.

**out** adv. dehors; (sun) levé. **be** ~, (person, book) être sorti; (light) être éteint; (flower) être épanoui; (tide) être bas; (secret) se savoir; (wrong) se tromper. **be** ~ **to do**, être résolu à faire. **run**/etc. ~, sortir en courant/etc. ~ **of**, hors de; (without) sans, à court de. ~ **of pity**/etc., par pitié/etc. **made** ~ **of**, fait en or de. **take** ~ **of**, prendre dans. **5** ~ **of 6**, 5 sur 6. ~ **of date**, démodé; (not valid) périmé. ~ **of doors**, dehors. ~ **of order**, (broken) en panne. ~ **of place**, (object, remark) déplacé. **get** ~ **of the way!** écarte-toi! ~ **of work**, sans travail. ~-**patient** n. malade en consultation externe m./f.

**outboard** a. (motor) hors-bord invar.

**outbreak** n. (of war etc.) début m.; (of violence, boils) éruption f.

**outburst** n. explosion f.

**outcast** n. paria m.

**outclass** v.t. surclasser.

**outcome** n. résultat m.

**outcrop** n. affleurement m.

**outcry** n. tollé m.

**outdated** a. démodé.

**outdo** v.t. surpasser.

**outdoor** a. de or en plein air. ~**s** adv. dehors.

**outer** a. extérieur. ~ **space**, espace (cosmique) m.

**outfit** n. (articles) équipement m.; (clothes) tenue f.; (group: fam.) équipe f.

**outgoing** a. (minister, tenant) sortant; (sociable) ouvert. ~**s** n. pl. dépenses f. pl.

**outgrow** v.t. (clothes) devenir trop grand pour; (habit) dépasser.

**outhouse** n. appentis m.; (of mansion) dépendance f.

**outing** n. sortie f.

**outlandish** a. bizarre.

**outlaw** n. hors-la-loi m. invar. ● v.t. proscrire.

**outlay** n. dépenses f. pl.

**outlet** n. (for water, gases) sortie f.; (for goods) débouché m.; (for feelings) exutoire m.

**outline** n. contour m.; (summary) esquisse f. ● v.t. tracer le contour de; (summarize) exposer sommairement.

**outlook** n. perspective f.

**outlying** a. écarté.

**outmoded** a. démodé.

**outnumber** v.t. surpasser en nombre.

**outpost** n. avant-poste m.

**output** n. rendement m.; (comput.) sortie f. ● v.t./i. (comput.) sortir.

**outrage** n. atrocité f.; (scandal) scandale m. ● v.t. (morals) outrager; (person) scandaliser.

**outrageous** a. scandaleux.

**outright** adv. complètement; (at once) sur le coup; (frankly) carrément. ● a. complet; (refusal) net.

**outset** n. début m.

**outside**[1] n. extérieur m. ● adv. (au) dehors. ● prep. en dehors de; (in front of) devant.

**outside**[2] a. extérieur.

**outsider** n. étranger, -ère m., f.; (sport) outsider m.

**outsize** a. grande taille invar.

**outskirts** n. pl. banlieue f.

**outspoken** a. franc.

**outstanding** a. exceptionnel; (not settled) en suspens.

**outward** a. & adv. vers l'extérieur; (sign etc.) extérieur; (journey) d'aller. ~**ly** adv. extérieurement. ~**s** adv. vers l'extérieur.

**outweigh** v.t. (exceed in importance) l'emporter sur.

**outwit** v.t. duper.

**oval** n. & a. ovale (m.).

**ovary** n. ovaire m.

**oven** n. four m.

**over** prep. sur, au-dessus de; (across) de l'autre côté de; (during) pendant; (more than) plus de. ● adv. (par-)dessus; (ended) fini; (past) passé; (too) trop; (more) plus. **jump**/etc. ~, sauter/etc. par-dessus. ~ **the radio**, à la radio. **ask** ~, inviter chez soi. **he has some** ~, il lui en reste. **all** ~ **(the table)**, partout (sur la table). ~ **and above**, en plus de. ~ **here**, par ici. ~ **there**, là-bas.

**over-** pref. sur-, trop.

**overall**[1] *n.* blouse *f.* ~s, bleu(s) de travail *m.* (*pl.*).

**overall**[2] *a.* global, d'ensemble; (*length, width*) total. ● *adv.* globalement.

**overbalance** *v.t./i.* (faire) basculer.

**overbearing** *a.* autoritaire.

**overboard** *adv.* par-dessus bord.

**overcast** *a.* couvert.

**overcharge** *v.t.* ~ **s.o. (for),** faire payer trop cher à qn.

**overcoat** *n.* pardessus *m.*

**overcome** *v.t.* triompher de; (*difficulty*) surmonter, triompher de. ~ **by,** accablé de.

**overcrowded** *a.* bondé.

**overdo** *v.t.* exagérer; (*culin.*) trop cuire.

**overdose** *n.* overdose *f.*

**overdraft** *n.* découvert *m.*

**overdrawn** *a.* à découvert.

**overdrive** *n.* surmultipliée *f.*

**overdue** *a.* en retard; (*belated*) tardif; (*bill*) impayé.

**overestimate** *v.t.* surestimer.

**overexposed** *a.* surexposé.

**overflow**[1] *v.i.* déborder.

**overflow**[2] *n.* (*outlet*) trop-plein *m.*

**overgrown** *a.* (*garden etc.*) envahi par la végétation.

**overhaul**[1] *v.t.* réviser.

**overhaul**[2] *n.* révision *f.*

**overhead**[1] *adv.* au-dessus; (*in sky*) dans le ciel.

**overhead**[2] *a.* aérien. ~s *n. pl.* frais généraux *m. pl.* ~ **projector,** rétroprojecteur *m.*

**overhear** *v.t.* entendre.

**overjoyed** *a.* ravi.

**overland** *a. adv.* par voie de terre.

**overlap** *v.t./i.* (se) chevaucher.

**overleaf** *adv.* au verso.

**overload** *v.t.* surcharger.

**overlook** *v.t.* oublier, négliger; (*of window, house*) donner sur; (*of tower*) dominer.

**overnight** *adv.* (pendant) la nuit; (*instantly: fig.*) du jour au lendemain. ● *a.* (*train etc.*) de nuit; (*stay etc.*) d'une nuit; (*fig.*) soudain.

**overpower** *v.t.* subjuguer; (*opponent*) maîtriser; (*fig.*) accabler. ~ing *a.* irrésistible; (*heat, smell*) accablant.

**overreact** *v.i.* réagir excessivement.

**overrid|e** *v.t.* passer outre à. ~ing *a.* prépondérant; (*importance*) majeur.

**overrule** *v.t.* rejeter.

**overrun** *v.t.* envahir; (*a limit*) aller au-delà de. ● *v.i.* (*meeting*) durer plus longtemps que prévu.

**overseas** *a.* d'outre-mer, étranger. ● *adv.* outre-mer, à l'étranger.

**oversee** *v.t.* surveiller. ~r *n.* contremaître *m.*

**overshadow** *v.t.* (*darken*) assombrir; (*fig.*) éclipser.

**overshoot** *v.t.* dépasser.

**oversight** *n.* omission *f.*

**oversleep** *v.i.* se réveiller trop tard.

**overt** *a.* manifeste.

**overtake** *v.t./i.* dépasser; (*vehicle*) doubler, dépasser; (*surprise*) surprendre.

**overtax** *v.t.* (*strain*) fatiguer; (*taxpayer*) surimposer.

**overthrow** *v.t.* renverser.

**overtime** *n.* heures supplémentaires *f. pl.*

**overtone** *n.* nuance *f.*

**overture** *n.* ouverture *f.*

**overturn** *v.t./i.* renverser.

**overweight** *a.* be ~, peser trop.

**overwhelm** *v.t.* accabler; (*defeat*) écraser; (*amaze*) bouleverser. ~ing *a.* accablant; (*victory*) écrasant; (*urge*) irrésistible.

**overwork** *v.t./i.* (se) surmener. ● *n.* surmenage *m.*

**ow|e** *v.t.* devoir. ~ing *a.* dû. ~ing to, à cause de.

**owl** *n.* hibou *m.*

**own**[1] *a.* propre. **a house**/*etc.* **of one's** ~, sa propre maison/*etc.*, une maison/*etc.* à soi. **on one's** ~, tout seul.

**own**[2] *v.t.* posséder. ~ **up (to),** (*fam.*) avouer. ~**er** *n.* propriétaire *m./f.* ~**ership** *n.* possession *f.* (**of,** de); (*right*) propriété *f.*

**ox** *n.* bœuf *m.*

**oxygen** *n.* oxygène *m.*

**oyster** *n.* huître *f.*

**ozone** *n.* ozone *m.* ~ **layer,** couche d'ozone *f.*

**pace** *n.* pas *m.*; (*speed*) allure *f.* ● *v.i.* ~ (**up and down**), faire les cent pas. **keep** ~ **with,** suivre.

**pacemaker** *n.* (*med.*) stimulateur cardiaque *m.*

**Pacific** *a.* pacifique. ● *n.* ~ (**Ocean**), Pacifique *m.*

**pacifist** *n.* pacifiste *m./f.*

**pacify** *v.t.* (*country*) pacifier; (*person*) apaiser.

**pack** *n.* paquet *m.*; (*mil.*) sac *m.*; (*of hounds*) meute *f.* ● *v.t.* emballer; (*suitcase*) faire; (*box, room*) remplir; (*press down*) tasser. ● *v.i.* ~ (**one's bags**), faire ses valises. ~ **into,** (*cram*) (s')entasser dans. ~**ed** *a.* (*crowded*) bondé. ~**ed lunch,** repas froid *m.* ~**ing** *n.* (*action, material*) emballage *m.* ~**ing case,** caisse *f.*

**package** *n.* paquet *m.* ● *v.t.* empaqueter. ~ **deal,** forfait *m.* ~ **tour,** voyage organisé *m.*

**packet** *n.* paquet *m.*

**pact** *n.* pacte *m.*

**pad** *n.* bloc(-notes) *m.*; (*for ink*) tampon *m.*
● *v.t.* rembourrer. ~**ding** *n.* rembourrage *m.*

**paddle**¹ *n.* pagaie *f.* ● *v.t.* ~ **a canoe,**
pagayer.

**paddl|e**² *v.i.* barboter, se mouiller les pieds.
~**ing pool,** pataugeoire *f.*

**paddock** *n.* paddock *m.*

**padlock** *n.* cadenas *m.* ● *v.t.* cadenasser.

**paediatrician** *n.* pédiatre *m./f.*

**page**¹ *n.* (*of book etc.*) page *f.*

**page**² *n.* (*in hotel*) chasseur *m.* (*at wedding*)
page *m.* ● *v.t.* (faire) appeler.

**pageant** *n.* spectacle (historique) *m.* ~**ry** *n.*
pompe *f.*

**pail** *n.* seau *m.*

**pain** *n.* douleur *f.* ~**s,** efforts *m. pl.* ● *v.t.*
(*grieve*) peiner. **be in** ~, souffrir. ~**killer** *n.*
analgésique *m.* ~**less** *a.* indolore.

**painful** *a.* douloureux; (*laborious*) pénible.

**painstaking** *a.* appliqué.

**paint** *n.* peinture *f.* ~**s,** (*in tube, box*) couleurs
*f. pl.* ● *v.t./i.* peindre. ~**er** *n.* peintre *m.*
~**ing** *n.* peinture *f.*

**paintbrush** *n.* pinceau *m.*

**paintwork** *n.* peintures *f. pl.*

**pair** *n.* paire *f.*; (*of people*) couple *m.* **a** ~ **of
trousers,** un pantalon.

**Pakistan** *n.* Pakistan. *m.* ~**i** *a.* & *n.*
pakistanais(e) (*m.* (*f.*)).

**pal** *n.* (*fam.*) cop|ain, -ine *m.*, *f.*

**palace** *n.* palais *m.*

**palate** *n.* (*of mouth*) palais *m.*

**pale** *a.* pâle. ● *v.i.* pâlir. ~**ness** *n.* pâleur *f.*

**Palestin|e** *n.* Palestine *f.* ~**ian** *a.* & *n.*
palestinien(ne) (*m.* (*f.*)).

**palette** *n.* palette *f.*

**pallet** *n.* palette *f.*

**pallid** *a.* pâle.

**palm** *n.* (*of hand*) paume *f.*; (*tree*) palmier *m.*;
(*symbol*) palme *f.* ● *v.t.* ~ **off,** (*thing*) refiler,
coller (**on,** à); (*person*) coller.

**palpable** *a.* manifeste.

**palpitat|e** *v.i.* palpiter. ~**ion** *n.* palpitation *f.*

**paltry** *a.* dérisoire.

**pamper** *v.t.* dorloter.

**pamphlet** *n.* brochure *f.*

**pan** *n.* casserole *f.*; (*for frying*) poêle *f.*; (*of
lavatory*) cuvette *f.* ● *v.t.* (*fam.*) critiquer.

**pancake** *n.* crêpe *f.*

**pancreas** *n.* pancréas *m.*

**panda** *n.* panda *m.*

**pander** *v.i.* ~ **to,** (*person, taste*) flatter
bassement.

**pane** *n.* carreau *m.*, vitre *f.*

**panel** *n.* (*of door etc.*) panneau *m.*; (*jury*) jury
*m.*; (*speakers: TV*) invités *m. pl.* (**instrument**)
~, tableau de bord *m.* ~ **of experts,** groupe
d'experts *m.* ~**led** *a.* lambrissé. ~**ling** *n.*
lambrissage *m.*

**pang** *n.* pincement au cœur *m.* ~**s,** (*of hunger,
death*) affres *f. pl.*

**panic** *n.* panique *f.* ● *v.t./i.* paniquer. ~
**stricken** *a.* affolé.

**panorama** *n.* panorama *m.*

**pansy** *n.* (*bot.*) pensée *f.*

**pant** *v.i.* haleter.

**panther** *n.* panthère *f.*

**panties** *n. pl.* (*fam.*) slip *m.*, culotte *f.* (*de
femme*).

**pantomime** *n.* (*show*) spectacle de Noël *m.*;
(*mime*) pantomime *f.*

**pantry** *n.* office *m.*

**pants** *n. pl.* (*underwear: fam.*) slip *m.*;
(*trousers: fam. & Amer.*) pantalon *m.*

**paper** *n.* papier *m.*; (*newspaper*) journal *m.*;
(*exam*) épreuve *f.*; (*essay*) exposé *m.*;
(*wallpaper*) papier peint *m.* (*identity*) ~**s**
papiers (d'identité) *m. pl.* ● *v.t.* (*room*)
tapisser. **on** ~, par écrit. ~**-clip** *n.* trombone
*m.*

**paperback** *a. & n.* ~ (**book**), livre broché *m.*

**paperweight** *n.* presse-papiers *m. invar.*

**paperwork** *n.* paperasserie *f.*

**paprika** *n.* paprika *m.*

**par** *n.* **be below** ~, ne pas être en forme. **on
a** ~ **with,** à égalité avec.

**parable** *n.* parabole *f.*

**parachut|e** *n.* parachute *m.* ● *v.i.* descendre
en parachute. ~**ist** *n.* parachutiste *m./f.*

**parade** *n.* (*procession*) défilé *m.*; (*ceremony,
display*) parade *f.*; (*street*) avenue *f.* ● *v.i.*
défiler. ● *v.t.* faire parade de.

**paradise** *n.* paradis *m.*

**paradox** *n.* paradoxe *m.* ~**ical** *a.* paradoxal.

**paraffin** *n.* pétrole (lampant) *m.*; (*wax*)
paraffine *f.*

**paragon** *n.* modèle *m.*

**paragraph** *n.* paragraphe *m.*

**parallel** *a.* parallèle. ● *n.* (*line*) parallèle *f.*;
(*comparison & geog.*) parallèle *m.* ● *v.t.* être
semblable à; (*match*) égaler.

**paralyse** *v.t.* paralyser.

**paralysis** *n.* paralysie *f.*

**paramedic** *n.* auxiliaire médical(e) *m.* (*f.*).

**parameter** *n.* paramètre *m.*

**paramount** *a.* primordial.

**paranoi|a** *n.* paranoïa *f.* ~**d** *a.* paranoïaque;
(*fam.*) parano *invar.*

**parapet** *n.* parapet *m.*

**paraphernalia** *n.* attirail *m.*

**paraphrase** *n.* paraphrase *f.* ● *v.t.* para-
phraser.

**parasite** *n.* parasite *m.*

**parasol** n. ombrelle f.; (on table, at beach) parasol m.

**paratrooper** n. (mil.) parachutiste m/f.

**parcel** n. colis m., paquet m.

**parch** v.t. dessécher. **be ~ed**, (person) avoir très soif.

**parchment** n. parchemin m.

**pardon** n. pardon m.; (jurid.) grâce m. ● v.t. pardonner (**s.o. for sth.**), qch. à qn.); gracier. **I beg your ~**, pardon.

**pare** v.t. (clip) rogner; (peel) éplucher.

**parent** n. père m., mère f. **~s**, parents m. pl. **~al** a. des parents.

**parenthesis** n. parenthèse f.

**Paris** n. Paris m./f. **~ian** a. & n. parisien(ne) (m. (f.)).

**parish** n. (relig.) paroisse f.; (municipal) commune f. **~ioner** n. paroissien(ne) m. (f.).

**parity** n. parité f.

**park** n. parc m. ● v.t./i. (se) garer; (remain parked) stationner. **~ing-meter** n. parc-mètre m. **~ing ticket**, procès-verbal m.

**parka** n. parka m./f.

**parliament** n. parlement m. **~ary** a. parlementaire.

**parlour** n. salon m.

**parody** n. parodie f. ● v.t. parodier.

**parole** n. **on ~**, en liberté conditionnelle.

**parrot** n. perroquet m.

**parry** v.t. (sport) parer; (question etc.) esquiver. ● n. parade f.

**parsley** n. persil m.

**parsnip** n. panais m.

**parson** n. pasteur m.

**part** n. partie f.; (of serial) épisode m.; (of machine) pièce f.; (theatre) rôle m.; (side in dispute) parti m. ● a. partiel. ● adv. en partie. ● v.t./i. (separate) (se) séparer. **in ~**, en partie. **on the ~ of**, de la part de. **~-exchange** n. reprise f. **~-time** a. & adv. à temps partiel. **~ with**, se séparer de. **take ~ in**, participer à.

**partial** a. partiel; (biased) partial. **be ~ to**, avoir une prédilection pour.

**participate** v.i. participer (**in**, à). **~ant** n. participant(e) m. (f.). **~ation** n. participation f.

**participle** n. participe m.

**particle** n. particule f.

**particular** a. particulier; (fussy) difficile; (careful) méticuleux. **that ~ man**, cet homme-là en particulier. **~s** n. pl. détails m. pl. **in ~**, en particulier. **~ly** adv. particulièrement.

**parting** n. séparation f.; (in hair) raie f. ● a. d'adieu.

**partisan** n. partisan(e) m. (f.).

**partition** n. (of room) cloison f.; (pol.) partage m., partition f. ● v.t. (room) cloisonner; (country) partager.

**partly** adv. en partie.

**partner** n. associé(e) m. (f.); (sport) partenaire m./f. **~ship** n. association f.

**partridge** n. perdrix f.

**party** n. fête f.; (formal) réception f.; (for young people) boum f.; (group) groupe m., équipe f.; (pol.) parti m.

**pass** v.t./i. passer; (overtake) dépasser; (in exam) être reçu (à); (approve) accepter, autoriser; (law, bill) voter. **~ (by)**, (building) passer devant; (person) croiser. ● n. (permit) laissez-passer m. invar.; (ticket) carte (d'abonnement) f.; (geog.) col m.; (sport) passe f. **~ (mark)**, (in exam) moyenne f. **~ out** or **round**, distribuer. **~ up**, (forego: fam.) laisser passer.

**passable** a. (adequate) passable; (road) praticable.

**passage** n. (way through, text, etc.) passage m.; (voyage) traversée f.; (corridor) couloir m.

**passenger** n. passager, -ère m., f.; (in train) voyageur, -se m., f.

**passer-by** n. passant(e) m. (f.).

**passing** a. (fleeting) passager.

**passion** n. passion f. **~ate** a. passionné. **~ately** adv. passionnément.

**passive** a. passif.

**Passover** n. Pâque f.

**passport** n. passeport m.

**password** n. mot de passe m.

**past** a. passé; (former) ancien. ● n. passé m. ● prep. au-delà de; (in front of) devant. ● adv. devant. **~ midnight**, minuit passé. **10 ~ 6**, six heures dix.

**pasta** n. pâtes f. pl.

**paste** n. (glue) colle f.; (dough) pâte f.; (of fish, meat) pâté m.; (jewellery) strass m. ● v.t. coller.

**pastel** n. pastel m. ● a. pastel invar.

**pasteurize** v.t. pasteuriser.

**pastiche** n. pastiche m.

**pastime** n. passetemps m. invar.

**pastoral** a. pastoral.

**pastry** n. (dough) pâte f.; (tart) pâtisserie f.

**pasture** n. pâturage m.

**pat** v.t. tapoter. ● n. petite tape f. ● adv. & a. à propos; (ready) tout prêt.

**patch** n. pièce f.; (over eye) bandeau m.; (spot) tache f.; (of vegetables) carré m. ● v.t. **~ up**, rapiécer; (fig.) régler. **~y** a. inégal.

**patchwork** n. patchwork m.

**patent** a. patent. ● n. brevet (d'invention) m. ● v.t. breveter. **~ leather**, cuir verni m.

**paternal** a. paternel.

**path** n. sentier m., chemin m.; (in park) allée f.; (of rocket) trajectoire f.

**pathetic** a. pitoyable; (bad: fam.) minable.

**pathology** n. pathologie f.

**patience** n. patience f.

**patient** *a.* patient. ● *n.* malade *m./f.*, patient(e) *m.* (*f.*). ~**ly** *adv.* patiemment.

**patio** *n.* patio *m.*

**patriotic** *a.* patriotique; (*person*) patriote.

**patrol** *n.* patrouille *f.* ● *v.t./i.* patrouiller (dans). ~ **car,** voiture de police *f.*

**patron** *n.* (*of the arts*) mécène *m.* (*customer*) client(e) *m.* (*f.*) ~**ize** *v.t.* être client de; (*fig.*) traiter avec condescendance.

**patter**[1] *n.* (*of steps*) bruit *m.*; (*of rain*) crépitement *m.*

**patter**[2] *n.* (*speech*) baratin *m.*

**pattern** *n.* motif *m.*, dessin *m.*; (*for sewing*) patron *m.*; (*procedure, type*) schéma *m.*; (*example*) exemple *m.*

**paunch** *n.* panse *f.*

**pause** *n.* pause *f.* ● *v.i.* faire une pause; (*hesitate*) hésiter.

**pave** *v.t.* paver. ~**e the way,** ouvrir la voie (**for,** à).

**pavement** *n.* trottoir *m.*

**pavilion** *n.* pavillon *m.*

**paw** *n.* patte *f.*

**pawn**[1] *n.* (*chess & fig.*) pion *m.*

**pawn**[2] *v.t.* mettre en gage. ● *n.* **in ~,** en gage. ~**-shop** *n.* mont-de-piété *m.*

**pawnbroker** *n.* prêteur sur gages *m.*

**pay** *v.t./i.* payer; (*yield: comm.*) rapporter; (*compliment, visit*) faire. ● *n.* salaire *m.*, paie *f.* ~ **attention,** faire attention (**to,** à). ~ **back,** rembourser. ~ **for,** payer. ~ **out,** payer, verser.

**payable** *a.* payable.

**payment** *n.* paiement *m.*; (*regular*) versement *m.* (*reward*) récompense *f.*

**payroll** *n.* **be on the ~ of,** être membre du personnel de.

**pea** *n.* (petit) pois *m.*

**peace** *n.* paix *f.* ~ **of mind,** tranquillité d'esprit *f.*

**peaceful** *a.* paisible; (*intention, measure*) pacifique.

**peacemaker** *n.* conciliateur, -trice *m.*, *f.*

**peach** *n.* pêche *f.*

**peacock** *n.* paon *m.*

**peak** *n.* sommet *m.*; (*of mountain*) pic *m.*; (*maximum*) maximum *m.* ~ **hours,** heures de pointe *f. pl.*

**peal** *n.* (*of bells*) carillon *m.*; (*of laughter*) éclat *m.*

**peanut** *n.* cacahuète *f.*

**pear** *n.* poire *f.*

**pearl** *n.* perle *f.* ~**y** *a.* nacré.

**peasant** *n.* paysan(ne) *m.* (*f.*).

**peat** *n.* tourbe *f.*

**pebble** *n.* caillou *m.*; (*on beach*) galet *m.*

**peck** *v.t./i.* (*food etc.*) picorer; (*attack*) donner des coups de bec (à). ● *n.* coup de bec *m.*

**peculiar** *a.* (*odd*) bizarre; (*special*) particulier (**to,** à).

**pedal** *n.* pédale *f.* ● *v.i.* pédaler.

**peddle** *v.t.* colporter; (*drugs*) revendre.

**pedestal** *n.* piédestal *m.*

**pedestrian** *n.* piéton *m.* ● *a.* (*precinct, street*) piétonnier; (*fig.*) prosaïque. ~ **crossing,** passage piétons *m.*

**pedigree** *n.* (*of person*) ascendance *f.*; (*of animal*) pedigree *m.* ● *a.* (*cattle etc.*) de race.

**pee** *v.i.* (*fam.*) faire pipi.

**peek** *v.i. & n.* = **peep**[1].

**peel** *n.* épluchure(s) *f.* (*pl.*); (*of orange*) écorce *f.* ● *v.t.* éplucher; (*fruit, vegetables*) éplucher. ● *v.i.* (*of skin*) peler; (*of paint*) s'écailler. ~**ings** *n. pl.* épluchures *f. pl.*

**peep**[1] *v.i.* jeter un coup d'œil (furtif) (**at,** à). ● *n.* coup d'œil (furtif) *m.*

**peep**[2] *v.i.* (*chirp*) pépier.

**peer**[1] *v.i.* ~ (**at**), scruter.

**peer**[2] *n.* (*equal, noble*) pair *m.*

**peg** *n.* cheville *f.*; (*for clothes*) pince à linge *f.*; (*to hang coats etc.*) patère *f.*; (*for tent*) piquet *m.* ● *v.t.* (*prices*) stabiliser. **buy off the ~,** acheter en prêt-à-porter.

**pelican** *n.* pélican *m.*

**pellet** *n.* (*round mass*) boulette *f.*; (*for gun*) plomb *m.*

**pelt**[1] *n.* (*skin*) peau *f.*

**pelt**[2] *v.t.* bombarder (**with,** de). ● *v.i.* pleuvoir à torrents.

**pelvis** *n.* (*anat.*) bassin *m.*

**pen**[1] *n.* (*for sheep etc.*) enclos *m.*; (*for baby, cattle*) parc *m.*

**pen**[2] *n.* stylo *m.*; (*to be dipped in ink*) plume *f.* ● *v.t.* écrire. ~**-friend** *n.* correspondant(e) *m.* (*f.*).

**penal** *a.* pénal. ~**ize** *v.t.* pénaliser; (*fig.*) handicaper.

**penalty** *n.* peine *f.*; (*fine*) amende *f.*; (*sport*) pénalité *f.*

**penance** *n.* pénitence *f.*

**pencil** *n.* crayon *m.* ● *v.t.* ~ **in,** noter provisoirement. ~**-sharpener** *n.* taillecrayon(s) *m.*

**pendant** *n.* pendentif *m.*

**pending** *a.* en suspens. ● *prep.* (*until*) en attendant.

**pendulum** *n.* pendule *m.*; (*of clock*) balancier *m.*

**penetrat|e** *v.t.* (*enter*) pénétrer dans; (*understand, permeate*) pénétrer. ● *v.i.* pénétrer. ~**ing** *a.* pénétrant. ~**ion** *n.* pénétration *f.*

**penguin** *n.* manchot *m.*, pingouin *m.*

**penicillin** *n.* pénicilline *f.*

**peninsula** *n.* péninsule *f.*

**penis** *n.* pénis *m.*

**penknife** *n.* canif *m.*

**pennant** *n.* flamme *f.*

**penny** n. penny m.; (fig.) sou m.

**pension** n. pension f.; (for retirement) retraite f. ● v.t. ~ **off**, mettre à la retraite. ~ **scheme**, caisse de retraite f. ~**er** n. (**old-age**) ~**er**, retraité(e) m. (f.), personne âgée f.

**pensive** a. pensif.

**penthouse** n. appartement de luxe m.

**pent-up** a. refoulé.

**penultimate** a. avant-dernier.

**people** n. pl. gens m. pl., personnes f. pl. ● n. peuple m. ● v.t. peupler. **English**/etc. ~, les Anglais/ etc. m. (f.), personne âgée f.

**pep** n. entrain m. ● v.t. ~ **up**, donner de l'entrain à. ~ **talk**, discours d'encouragement m.

**pepper** n. poivre m.; (vegetable) poivron m. ● v.t. (culin.) poivrer. ~**y** a. poivré.

**peppermint** n. (plant) menthe poivrée f.; (sweet) bonbon à la menthe m.

**per** prep. par. ~ **annum**, par an. ~ **cent**, pour cent. ~ **kilo**/etc., le kilo/etc. **ten km.** ~ **hour**, dix km à l'heure.

**perceive** v.t. percevoir; (notice) s'apercevoir de.

**percentage** n. pourcentage m.

**perch** n. (of bird) perchoir m. ● v.i. (se) percher.

**percolator** n. cafetière f.

**percussion** n. percussion f.

**perfect**¹ a. parfait. ~**ly** adv. parfaitement.

**perfect**² v.t. parfaire, mettre au point. ~**ion** n. perfection f. **to** ~**ion**, à la perfection.

**perforat|e** v.t. perforer. ~**ion** n. perforation f.; (line of holes) pointillé m.

**perform** v.t. exécuter, faire; (a function) remplir; (mus., theatre) interpréter, jouer. ● v.i. jouer; (behave, function) se comporter. ~**ance** n. exécution f.; interprétation f.; (of car, team) performance f.; (show) représentation f.; séance f.; (fuss) histoire f. ~**er** n. artiste m./f.

**perfume** n. parfum m.

**perhaps** adv. peut-être.

**peril** n. péril m. ~**ous** a. périlleux.

**perimeter** n. périmètre m.

**period** n. période f.; époque f.; (era) époque f.; (lesson) cours m.; (gram.) point m.; (med.) règles f. pl. ● a. d'époque. ~**ic** a. périodique.

**periodical** n. périodique m.

**peripher|y** n. périphérie f. ~**al** a. périphérique; (of lesser importance: fig.) accessoire; n. (comput.) périphérique m.

**periscope** n. périscope m.

**perish** v.i. périr; (rot) se détériorer. ~**able** a. périssable.

**perjury** n. parjure m.

**perk**¹ v.t./i. ~ **up**, (fam.) (se) remonter. ~**y** a. (fam.) gai.

**perk**² n. (fam.) avantage m.

**perm** n. permanente f. ● v.t. **have one's hair** ~**ed**, se faire faire une permanente.

**permanen|t** a. permanent. ~**ce** n. permanence f. ~**tly** adv. à titre permanent.

**permissible** a. permis.

**permission** n. permission f.

**permit**¹ v.t. permettre (**s.o. to**, à qn. de), autoriser (**s.o. to**, qn. à).

**permit**² n. permis m.; (pass) laissez-passer m. invar.

**perpendicular** a. & n. perpendiculaire (f.).

**perpetrat|e** v.t. perpétrer. ~**or** n. auteur m.

**perpetual** a. perpétuel.

**perpetuate** v.t. perpétuer.

**perplex** v.t. rendre perplexe. ~**ed** a. perplexe. ~**ing** a. déroutant.

**persecut|e** v.t. persécuter. ~**ion** n. persécution f.

**persever|e** v.i. persévérer. ~**ance** n. persévérance f.

**Persian** a. & n. (lang.) persan (m.). ~ **Gulf**, golfe persique m.

**persist** v.i. persister (**in doing**, à faire). ~**ence** n. persistance f. ~**ent** a. (cough, snow, etc.) persistant; (obstinate) obstiné; (continual) continuel. ~**ently** adv. avec persistance.

**person** n. personne f.

**personal** a. personnel; (hygiene, habits) intime; (secretary) particulier. ~**ly** adv. personnellement. ~ **stereo**, baladeur m.

**personality** n. personnalité f.; (on TV) vedette f.

**personify** v.t. personnifier.

**personnel** n. personnel m.

**perspective** n. perspective f.

**Perspex** n. (P.) plexiglas m. (P.).

**perspir|e** v.i. transpirer. ~**ation** n. transpiration f.

**persua|de** v.t. persuader (**to**, de). ~**sion** n. persuasion f.

**persuasive** a. (person, speech, etc.) persuasif.

**Peru** n. Pérou m. ~**vian** a. & n. péruvien(ne) (m. (f.)).

**perva|de** v.t. imprégner, envahir. ~**sive** a. (mood, dust) envahissant.

**pervers|e** a. (stubborn) entêté; (wicked) pervers. ~**ity** n. perversité f.

**perver|t**¹ v.t. pervertir. ~**sion** n. perversion f.

**perver|t**² n. perverti(e) m. (f.)

**peseta** n. peseta f.

**pessimis|t** n. pessimiste m./f. ~**m** n. pessimisme m. ~**tic** a. pessimiste.

**pest** n. insecte or animal nuisible m.; (person: fam.) enquiquineu|r, -se m., f.

**pester** v.t. harceler.

**pesticide** n. pesticide m.

**pet** *n.* animal (domestique) *m.*; (*favourite*) chouchou(te) *m.* (*f.*). ● *a.* (*tame*) apprivoisé. ● *v.t.* caresser; (*sexually*) peloter.

**petal** *n.* pétale *m.*

**peter** *v.i.* ~ **out,** (*supplies*) s'épuiser; (*road*) finir.

**petite** *a.* (*woman*) menue.

**petition** *n.* pétition *f.* ● *v.t.* adresser une pétition à.

**petrify** *v.t.* pétrifier; (*scare: fig.*) pétrifier de peur.

**petrol** *n.* essence *f.* ~ **station,** station-service *f.* ~ **tank,** réservoir d'essence *m.*

**petroleum** *n.* pétrole *m.*

**petticoat** *n.* jupon *m.*

**petty** *a.* (*minor*) petit; (*mean*) mesquin. ~ **cash,** petite caisse *f.*

**petulan|t** *a.* irritable. ~**ce** *n.* irritabilité *f.*

**pew** *n.* banc (d'église) *m.*

**pewter** *n.* étain *m.*

**phantom** *n.* fantôme *m.*

**pharmaceutical** *a.* pharmaceutique.

**pharmac|y** *n.* pharmacie *f.* ~**ist** *n.* pharmacien(ne) *m.* (*f.*).

**pharyngitis** *n.* pharyngite *f.*

**phase** *n.* phase *f.* ● *v.t.* ~ **in/out,** introduire/retirer progressivement.

**pheasant** *n.* faisan *m.*

**phenomen|on** *n.* (*pl.* **-ena**) phénomène *m.* ~**al** *a.* phénoménal.

**Philippines** *n. pl.* **the** ~, les Philippines *f. pl.*

**philistine** *n.* philistin *m.*

**philosoph|y** *n.* philosophie *f.* ~**er** *n.* philosophe *m./f.* ~**ical** *a.* philosophique; (*resigned*) philosophe.

**phlegm** *n.* (*med.*) mucosité *f.*

**phlegmatic** *a.* flegmatique.

**phobia** *n.* phobie *f.*

**phone** *n.* téléphone *m.* ● *v.t.* (*person*) téléphoner à; (*message*) téléphoner. ● *v.i.* téléphoner. ~ **back,** rappeler. ~ **book,** annuaire *m.* ~ **box,** ~ **booth,** cabine téléphonique *f.* ~ **call,** coup de fil *m.*

**phonecard** *n.* télécarte *f.*

**phonetic** *a.* phonétique.

**phoney** *a.* (*sl.*) faux. ● *n.* (*person: sl.*) charlatan *m.*

**phosphate** *n.* phosphate *m.*

**phosphorus** *n.* phosphore *m.*

**photo** *a.* photo *f.*

**photocop|y** *n.* photocopie *f.* ● *v.t.* photocopier. ~**ier** *n.* photocopieuse *f.*

**photogenic** *a.* photogénique.

**photograph** *n.* photographie *f.* ● *v.t.* photographier. ~**er** *n.* photographe *m./f.* ~**ic** *a.* photographique. ~**y** *n.* (*activity*) photographie *f.*

**phrase** *n.* expression *f.*; (*idiom & gram.*) locution *f.* ● *v.t.* exprimer, formuler. ~**book** *n.* guide de conversation *m.*

**physical** *a.* physique. ~**ly** *adv.* physiquement.

**physicist** *n.* physicien(ne) *m.* (*f.*).

**physics** *n.* physique *f.*

**physiotherap|y** *n.* kinésithérapie *f.* ~**ist** *n.* kinésithérapeute *m./f.*

**physique** *n.* constitution *f.*; (*appearance*) physique *m.*

**pian|o** *n.* piano *m.* ~**ist** *n.* pianiste *m./f.*

**pick¹** (*tool*) *n.* pioche *f.*

**pick²** *v.t.* choisir; (*flower etc.*) cueillir; (*lock*) crocheter; (*nose*) se curer; (*pockets*) faire. ~ **(off),** enlever. ● *n.* choix *m.*; (*best*) meilleur(e) *m.* (*f.*). ~ **off,** (*mil.*) abattre un à un. ~ **on,** harceler. ~ **out,** choisir; (*identify*) distinguer. ~ **up** *v.t.* ramasser; (*sth. fallen*) relever; (*weight*) soulever; (*habit, passenger, speed, etc.*) prendre; (*learn*) apprendre; *v.i.* s'améliorer. ~**-up** *n.* partenaire de rencontre *m./f.*; (*truck, stylus-holder*) pick-up *m.*

**pickaxe** *n.* pioche *f.*

**picket** *n.* (*single striker*) gréviste *m./f.*; (*stake*) piquet *m.* ~ (**line),** piquet de grève *m.* ● *v.t.* mettre un piquet de grève devant.

**pickle** *n.* vinaigre *m.*; (*brine*) saumure *f.* ~**s,** pickles *m. pl.* ● *v.t.* conserver dans du vinaigre *or* de la saumure.

**pickpocket** *n.* (*thief*) pickpocket *m.*

**picnic** *n.* pique-nique *m.* ● *v.i.* pique-niquer.

**pictorial** *a.* illustré.

**picture** *n.* image *f.*; (*painting*) tableau *m.*; (*photograph*) photo *f.*; (*drawing*) dessin *m.*; (*film*) film *m.*; (*fig.*) description ; tableau *m.* ● *v.t.* s'imaginer; (*describe*) dépeindre. **the** ~**s,** (*cinema*) le cinéma.

**picturesque** *a.* pittoresque.

**pie** *n.* tarte *f.*; (*of meat*) pâté en croûte *m.* ~ **chart,** camembert *m.*

**piece** *n.* morceau *m.*; (*of currency, machine, etc.*) pièce *f.* **a** ~ **of advice/furniture/** *etc.,* un conseil/meuble/ *etc.*

**piecemeal** *a.* par bribes.

**pier** *n.* (*promenade*) jetée *f.*

**pierc|e** *v.t.* percer. ~**ing** *a.* perçant; (*cold*) glacial.

**pig** *n.* cochon *m.* ~**-headed** *a.* entêté.

**pigeon** *n.* pigeon *m.* ~**-hole** *n.* casier *m.*; *v.t.* classer.

**pigment** *n.* pigment *m.* ~**ation** *n.* pigmentation *f.*

**pigtail** *n.* natte *f.*

**pike** *n. invar.* (*fish*) brochet *m.*

**pilchard** *n.* pilchard *m.*

**pile** *n.* pile *f.*; tas *m.*; (*of carpet*) poils *m.pl.*
● *v.t.* ~ (**up**), (*stack*) empiler. ● *v.i.* ~
**into**, s'empiler dans. ~ **up**, (*accumulate*)
(s')accumuler. **a** ~ **of**, (*fam.*) un tas de. ~**-up**
*n.* (*auto.*) carambolage *m.*

**piles** *n. pl.* (*fam.*) hémorroïdes *f. pl.*

**pilfer** *v.t.* chaparder.

**pilgrim** *n.* pèlerin *m.* ~**age** *n.* pèlerinage *m.*

**pill** *n.* pilule *f.*

**pillar** *n.* pilier *m.* ~**-box** *n.* boîte à or aux
lettres *f.*

**pillion** *n.* siège arrière *m.* **ride** ~, monter
derrière.

**pillow** *n.* oreiller *m.*

**pillowcase** *n.* taie d'oreiller *f.*

**pilot** *n.* pilote *m.* ● *a.* pilote. ● *v.t.* piloter. ~
**light** *n.* veilleuse *f.*

**pimento** *n.* piment *m.*

**pimp** *n.* souteneur *m.*

**pimpl|e** *n.* bouton *m.* ~**y** *a.* boutonneux.

**pin** *n.* épingle *f.*; (*techn.*) goupille *f.* ● *v.t.*
épingler, attacher; (*hold down*) clouer. **have**
~**s and needles**, avoir des fourmis. ~**point**
*v.t.* repérer, définir.

**pinafore** *n.* tablier *m.*

**pincers** *n. pl.* tenailles *f. pl.*

**pinch** *v.t.* pincer; (*steal: sl.*) piquer. ● *v.i.* (*be
too tight*) serrer. ● *n.* (*mark*) pinçon *m.*; (*of
salt*) pincée *f.* **at a** ~, au besoin.

**pine**[1] *n.* (*tree*) pin *m.* ~**-cone** *n.* pomme de
pin *f.*

**pine**[2] *v.i.* ~ **away**, dépérir. ~ **for**, languir
après.

**pineapple** *n.* ananas *m.*

**ping** *n.* bruit métallique *m.*

**ping-pong** *n.* ping-pong *m.*

**pink** *a. & n.* rose (*m.*).

**pint** *n.* pinte *f.*

**pioneer** *n.* pionnier *m.* ● *v.t.* être le premier
à faire, utiliser, étudier, *etc.*

**pip**[1] *n.* (*seed*) pépin *m.*

**pip**[2] *n.* (*sound*) top *m.*

**pipe** *n.* tuyau *m.*; (*of smoker*) pipe *f.*; (*mus.*)
pipeau *m.* ● *v.t.* transporter par tuyau.

**pipeline** *n.* pipeline *m.* **in the** ~, en route.

**piping** *n.* tuyau(x) *m.* (*pl.*). ~ **hot**, très chaud.

**pirate** *n.* pirate *m.* ● *v.t.* pirater.

**Pisces** *n.* les Poissons *m. pl.*

**pistachio** *n.* pistache *f.*

**pistol** *n.* pistolet *m.*

**piston** *n.* piston *m.*

**pit** *n.* fosse *f.*, trou *m.*; (*mine*) puits *m.*; (*quarry*)
carrière *f.*; (*for orchestra*) fosse *f.*; (*of
stomach*) creux *m.* ● *v.t.* trouer; (*fig.*) opposer.
~ **o.s. against**, se mesurer à.

**pitch**[1] *n.* (*tar*) poix *f.* ~**-black** *a.* d'un noir
d'ébène.

**pitch**[2] *v.t.* lancer; (*tent*) dresser. ● *n.* degré *m.*;
(*of voice*) hauteur *f.*; (*mus.*) ton *m.*; (*sport*)
terrain *m.*

**pitcher** *n.* cruche *f.*

**pitfall** *n.* piège *m.*

**pith** *n.* (*of orange*) peau blanche *f.*; (*essence:
fig.*) moelle *f.*

**pithy** *a.* concis.

**pitiful** *a.* pitoyable.

**pittance** *n.* revenu or salaire dérisoire *m.*

**pity** *n.* pitié *f.*; (*regrettable fact*) dommage *m.*
● *v.t.* plaindre. **what a** ~, quel dommage.
**it's a** ~, c'est dommage.

**pivot** *n.* pivot *m.* ● *v.i.* pivoter.

**pizza** *n.* pizza *f.*

**placard** *n.* affiche *f.*

**placate** *v.t.* calmer.

**place** *n.* endroit *m.*, lieu *m.*; (*house*) maison *f.*;
(*seat, rank, etc.*) place *f.* ● *v.t.* placer; (*an
order*) passer; (*remember*) situer. **at** or **to my**
~, chez moi. **in the first** ~, d'abord. **out of** ~,
déplacé. **take** ~, avoir lieu. ~**-mat** *n.* set *m.*

**placenta** *n.* placenta *m.*

**placid** *a.* placide.

**plague** *n.* peste *f.*; (*nuisance: fam.*) fléau *m.*
● *v.t.* harceler.

**plaice** *n. invar.* carrelet *m.*

**plaid** *n.* tissu écossais *m.*

**plain** *a.* clair; (*candid*) franc; (*simple*) simple;
(*not pretty*) sans beauté; (*not patterned*) uni.
● *adv.* franchement. ● *n.* plaine *f.* ~
**chocolate**, chocolat noir *m.* **in** ~ **clothes**,
en civil.

**plaintiff** *n.* plaignant(e) *m.* (*f.*).

**plait** *v.t.* tresser. ● *n.* tresse *f.*

**plan** *n.* projet *m.*, plan *m.*; (*diagram*) plan *m.*
● *v.t.* prévoir, projeter; (*arrange*) organiser;
(*design*) concevoir; (*economy, work*) plani-
fier. ● *v.i.* faire des projets. ~ **to do**, avoir
l'intention de faire.

**plane**[1] *n.* (*tree*) platane *m.*

**plane**[2] *n.* (*level*) plan *m.*; (*aeroplane*) avion
*m.* ● *a.* plan.

**plane**[3] *n.* (*tool*) rabot *m.* ● *v.t.* raboter.

**planet** *n.* planète *f.*

**plank** *n.* planche *f.*

**planning** *n.* (*pol., comm.*) planification *f.*
**family** ~, planning familial *m.*

**plant** *n.* plante *f.*; (*techn.*) matériel *m.*;
(*factory*) usine *f.* ● *v.t.* planter; (*bomb*)
(dé)poser. ~**ation** *n.* plantation *f.*

**plaque** *n.* plaque *f.*

**plasma** *n.* plasma *m.*

**plaster** *n.* plâtre *m.*; (*adhesive*) sparadrap *m.*
● *v.t.* plâtrer; (*cover*) tapisser (**with**, de). **in**
~, dans le plâtre.

**plastic** *a.* en plastique; (*art, substance*)
plastique. ● *n.* plastique *m.* ~ **surgery**,
chirurgie esthétique *f.*

**Plasticine** *n.* (P.) pâte à modeler *f.*

**plate** n. assiette f.; (of metal) plaque f.

**plateau** n. plateau m.

**platform** n. (in classroom, hall, etc.) estrade f.; (for speaking) tribune f.; (rail.) quai m.

**platinum** n. platine m.

**platoon** n. (mil.) section f.

**plausible** a. plausible.

**play** v.t./i. jouer; (instrument) jouer de; (record) passer; (game) jouer à; (opponent) jouer contre; (match) disputer. ● n. jeu m.; (theatre) pièce f. ~ **down,** minimiser. ~ **group** n. garderie f. ~**off** n. (sport) belle f. ~ **on,** (take advantage of) jouer sur. ~**pen** n. parc m. ~**er** n. joueu|r, -se m., f.

**playful** a. enjoué; (child) joueur.

**playground** n. cour de récréation f.

**playing** n. jeu m. ~**-card** n. carte à jouer f. ~**field** n. terrain de sport.

**plc** abbr. (public limited company) SA.

**plea** n. (entreaty) supplication f.; (reason) excuse f.

**plead** v.t./i. (jurid.) plaider; (as excuse) alléguer. ~ **for,** (beg for) implorer. ~ **with,** (beg) implorer.

**pleasant** a. agréable.

**please** v.t./i. plaire (à), faire plaisir (à). ● adv. s'il vous or te plaît. ~**d** a. content (with, de).

**pleasure** n. plaisir m.

**pleat** n. pli m. ● v.t. plisser.

**pledge** n. (token) gage m.; (fig.) promesse f. ● v.t. promettre.

**plentiful** a. abondant.

**plenty** n. abondance f. ~ **(of),** (a great deal) beaucoup (de); (enough) assez (de).

**pliable** a. souple.

**pliers** n. pl. pince(s) f. (pl.).

**plight** n. triste situation f.

**plimsoll** n. chaussure de gym f.

**plinth** n. socle m.

**plod** v.i. avancer péniblement or d'un pas lent; (work) bûcher.

**plot** n. complot m.; (of novel etc.) intrigue f. ~ **(of land),** terrain m. ● v.t./i. comploter; (mark out) tracer.

**plough** n. charrue f. ● v.t./i. labourer. ~ **back,** réinvestir. ~ **into,** rentrer dans.

**ploy** n. (fam.) stratagème m.

**pluck** v.t. cueillir; (bird) plumer; (eyebrows) épiler; (strings: mus.) pincer. ● n. courage m.

**plug** n. (of cloth, paper, etc.) tampon m.; (for sink etc.) bonde f.; (electr.) fiche f., prise f. ● v.t. (hole) boucher; (publicize: fam.) faire du battage autour de. ~ **in,** brancher. ~**hole** n. vidange f.

**plum** n. prune f.

**plumb|er** n. plombier m. ~**ing** n. plomberie f.

**plum|e** n. plume(s) f. (pl.). ~**age** n. plumage m.

**plummet** v.i. plonger.

**plump** a. potelé, dodu. ● v.i. ~ **for,** choisir.

**plunder** v.t. piller. ● n. (act) pillage m.; (goods) butin m.

**plunge** v.t./i. (dive, thrust) plonger; (fall) tomber. ● n. plongeon m.; (fall) chute f.

**plunger** n. (for sink) ventouse f.

**plural** a. pluriel; (noun) au pluriel. ● n. pluriel m.

**plus** prep. plus. ● a. (electr. & fig.) positif. ● n. signe plus m.; (fig.) atout m. **ten ~,** plus de dix.

**plush(y)** a. somptueux.

**ply** v.t. (tool) manier; (trade) exercer. ● v.i. faire la navette.

**plywood** n. contreplaqué m.

**p.m.** adv. de l'après-midi or du soir.

**pneumatic** a. pneumatique. ~ **drill,** marteau-piqueur m.

**pneumonia** n. pneumonie f.

**PO** abbr. see **Post Office.**

**poach** v.t./i. (game) braconner; (staff) débaucher; (culin.) pocher. ~**er** n. braconnier m.

**pocket** n. poche f. ● a. de poche. ● v.t. empocher. ~**book** n. (notebook) carnet m. ~**money** n. argent de poche m.

**pod** n. (peas etc.) cosse f.; (vanilla) gousse f.

**poem** n. poème m.

**poet** n. poète m. ~**ic** a. poétique.

**poetry** n. poésie f.

**poignant** a. poignant.

**point** n. point m.; (tip) pointe f.; (decimal point) virgule f.; (meaning) sens m., intérêt m.; (remark) remarque f. ~**s,** (rail.) aiguillage m. ● v.t. (aim) braquer; (show) indiquer. ● v.i. indiquer du doigt (at or to s.o., qn.). ~ **out that,** faire remarquer que. **good ~s,** qualités f. pl. **on the ~ of,** sur le point de. ~**-blank** a. & adv. à bout portant. ~ **of view,** point de vue m. ~ **out,** signaler. **what is the ~?,** à quoi bon?

**pointed** a. pointu; (remark) lourd de sens.

**pointer** n. (indicator) index m.; (dog) chien d'arrêt m.; (advice: fam.) tuyau m.

**pointless** a. inutile.

**poise** n. équilibre m.; (carriage) maintien m.; (fig.) assurance f. ~**d** a. en équilibre; (confident) assuré. ~**d for,** prêt à.

**poison** n. poison m. ● v.t. empoisonner. ~**ous** a. (substance etc.) toxique; (plant) vénéneux; (snake) venimeux.

**poke** v.t./i. (push) pousser; (fire) tisonner; (thrust) fourrer. ● n. (petit) coup m. ~ **about,** fureter. ~ **fun at,** se moquer de.

**poker**¹ n. tisonnier m.

**poker**¹ n. (cards) poker m.

**poky** a. (small) exigu.

**Poland** n. Pologne f.

**polar** a. polaire. ~ **bear,** ours blanc m.

**polarize** v.t. polariser.

**Polaroid** n. (P.) polaroïd (P.) m.

**pole**[1] n. (*fixed*) poteau m.; (*rod*) perche f.; (*for flag*) mât m. ~-**vault** n. saut à la perche m.

**pole**[2] n. (*geog.*) pôle m.

**Pole** n. Polonais(e) m. (f.).

**police** n. police f. ● v.t. faire la police dans. ~ **station,** commissariat de police m.

**police|man** n. agent de police m. ~**woman** femme-agent f.

**policy**[1] n. politique f.

**policy**[2] n. (*insurance*) police (d'assurance) f.

**polio(myelitis)** n. polio(myélite) f.

**polish** v.t. polir; (*shoes, floor*) cirer. ● n. (*for shoes*) cirage m.; (*for floor*) encaustique f.; (*for nails*) vernis m.; (*shine*) poli m.; (*fig.*) raffinement m.

**Polish** a. polonais. ● n. (*lang.*) polonais m.

**polite** a. poli. ~**ly** adv. poliment. ~**ness** n. politesse f.

**political** a. politique.

**politician** n. homme politique m., femme politique f.

**politics** n. politique f.

**poll** n. scrutin m.; (*survey*) sondage m. ● v.t. (*votes*) obtenir. ~**ing-booth** n. isoloir m. ~**ing station,** bureau de vote m.

**pollen** n. pollen m.

**pollut|e** v.t. polluer. ~**ion** n. pollution f.

**polo** n. polo m. ~ **neck,** col roulé m. ~ **shirt,** polo m.

**polyester** n. polyester m.

**polytechnic** n. institut universitaire de technologie m.

**polythene** n. polythène m.

**pomegranate** n. grenade f.

**pomp** n. pompe f.

**pompon** n. pompon m.

**pomp|ous** a. pompeux. ~**osity** n. solennité f.

**pond** n. étang m.; (*artificial*) bassin m.; (*stagnant*) mare f.

**ponder** v.t./i. méditer (sur).

**pony** n. poney m. ~-**tail** n. queue de cheval f.

**poodle** n. caniche m.

**pool**[1] n. (*puddle*) flaque f.; (*pond*) étang m.; (*of blood*) mare f.; (*for swimming*) piscine f.

**pool**[2] n. (*fund*) fonds commun m., (*of ideas*) réservoir m.; (*of typists*) pool m.; (*snooker*) billard américain m. ~**s,** pari mutuel sur le football m. ● v.t. mettre en commun.

**poor** a. pauvre; (*not good*) médiocre, mauvais. ~**ly** adv. mal; a. malade.

**pop**[1] n. (*noise*) bruit sec m. ● v.t./i. (*burst*) crever; (*put*) mettre. ~ **in/out/ off,** entrer/sortir/partir. ~ **up,** surgir.

**pop**[2] n. (*mus.*) musique pop f. ● a. pop *invar.*

**popcorn** n. pop-corn m.

**pope** n. pape m.

**poplar** n. peuplier m.

**poppy** n. pavot m.; (*wild*) coquelicot m.

**popular** a. populaire; (*in fashion*) en vogue. **be ~ with,** plaire à. ~**ity** n. popularité f.

**population** n. population f.

**porcelain** n. porcelaine f.

**porch** n. porche m.

**porcupine** n. porc-épic m.

**pore**[1] n. pore m.

**pore**[2] v.i. ~ **over,** étudier minutieusement.

**pork** n. (*food*) porc m.

**pornography** n. pornographie f.

**porous** a. poreux.

**porpoise** n. marsouin m.

**porridge** n. porridge m.

**port**[1] n. (*harbour*) port m.

**port**[2] n. (*left: naut.*) bâbord m.

**port**[3] n. (*wine*) porto m.

**portable** a. portatif.

**portal** n. portail m.

**porter**[1] n. (*carrier*) porteur m.

**porter**[2] n. (*door-keeper*) portier m.

**portfolio** n. portefeuille m.

**porthole** n. hublot m.

**portion** n. (*share, helping*) portion f.; (*part*) partie f.

**portrait** n. portrait m.

**portray** v.t. représenter. ~**al** n. portrait m., peinture f.

**Portug|al** n. Portugal m. ~**uese** a. & n. *invar.* portugais(e) (m. (f.)).

**pose** v.t./i. poser. ● n. pose f. ~ **as,** (*expert etc.*) se poser en.

**poser** n. colle f.

**posh** a. (*sl.*) chic *invar.*

**position** n. position f.; (*job, state*) situation f. ● v.t. placer.

**positive** a. (*test, help, etc.*) positif; (*sure*) sûr, certain; (*real*) réel, vrai. ~**ly** adv. positivement; (*absolutely*) complètement.

**possess** v.t. posséder. ~**ion** n. possession f.

**possessive** a. possessif.

**possib|le** a. possible. ~**ility** n. possibilité f.

**possibly** adv. peut-être.

**post**[1] n. (*pole*) poteau m. ● v.t. ~ **(up),** (*a notice*) afficher.

**post**[2] n. (*station, job*) poste m. ● v.t. poster; (*appoint*) affecter.

**post**[3] n. (*mail service*) poste f.; (*letters*) courrier m. ● a. postal. ● v.t. (*put in box*) poster; (*send*) envoyer (par la poste). **keep ~ed,** tenir au courant. ~**box** n. boîte à or aux lettres f. ~ **code** n. code postal m. **P~ Office,** postes f. pl.; (*in France*) Postes et Télé-communications f. pl. ~ **office,** bureau de poste m., poste f.

**post-** *pref.* post-.

**postage** n. tarif postal m.

**postal** a. postal. ~ **order,** mandat m.

**postcard** n. carte postale f.

**poster** n. affiche f.; (*for decoration*) poster m.

**posterity** n. postérité f.

**postgraduate** n. étudiant(e) de troisième cycle m. (f.).

**postman** n. facteur m.

**postmark** n. cachet de la poste m.

**post-mortem** n. autopsie f.

**postpone** v.t. remettre. ~ment n. ajournement m.

**postscript** n. (to letter) post-scriptum m. invar.

**posture** n. posture f. ●v.i. (affectedly) prendre des poses.

**pot** n. pot m.; (for cooking) marmite f.; (drug: sl.) marie-jeanne f. ●v.t. (plants) mettre en pot.

**potato** n. pomme de terre f.

**potential** a. & n. potentiel (m.). ~ly adv. potentiellement.

**pot-hol|e** n. (in rock) caverne f.; (in road) nid de poule m. ~ing n. spéléologie f.

**potion** n. potion f.

**potted** a. (plant etc.) en pot; (preserved) en conserve; (abridged) condensé.

**potter**¹ n. potier m. ~y n. (art) poterie f.; (objects) poteries f.pl.

**potter**² v.i. bricoler.

**potty** n. pot m.

**pouch** n. poche f.; (for tobacco) blague f.

**pouffe** n. pouf m.

**poultry** n. volaille f.

**pounce** v.i. bondir (on, sur). ●n. bond m.

**pound**¹ n. (weight) livre f. (= 454 g.); (money) livre f.

**pound**² n. (for dogs, cars) fourrière f.

**pound**³ v.t. (crush) piler; (bombard) pilonner. ●v.i. frapper fort; (of heart) battre fort; (walk) marcher à pas lourds.

**pour** v.t. verser. ●v.i. couler, ruisseler (from, de); (rain) pleuvoir à torrents. ~ in/out, (people) arriver/sortir en masse. ~ off or out, vider.

**pout** v.t./i. ~ (one's lips), faire la moue. ●n. moue f.

**poverty** n. misère f., pauvreté f.

**powder** n. poudre f. ●v.t. poudrer. ~ed a. en poudre. ~y a. poudreux.

**power** n. puissance f.; (ability, authority) pouvoir m.; (energy) énergie f.; (electr.) courant m. ~ cut, coupure de courant f. ~ point, prise de courant f. ~-station n. centrale électrique f.

**powerful** a. puissant. ~ly adv. puissamment.

**practicable** a. praticable.

**practical** a. pratique. ~ity n. sens or aspect pratique m. ~ joke, farce f.

**practically** adv. pratiquement.

**practice** n. pratique f.; (of profession) exercice m.; (sport) entraînement m.; (clients) clientèle f. in ~, (in fact) en pratique. put into ~, mettre en pratique.

**practise** v.t./i. (musician, typist, etc.) s'exercer (à); (sport) s'entraîner (à); (put into practice) pratiquer; (profession) exercer. ~d a. expérimenté.

**practitioner** n. praticien(ne) m. (f.).

**pragmatic** a. pragmatique.

**prairie** n. prairie f.

**praise** v.t. louer. ●n. éloge(s) m. (pl.), louange(s) f. (pl.).

**pram** n. landau m.

**prance** v.i. caracoler.

**prank** n. farce f.

**prawn** n. crevette rose f.

**pray** v.i. prier.

**prayer** n. prière f.

**pre-** pref. pré-.

**preach** v.t./i. prêcher. ~ at or to, prêcher. ~er n. prédicateur m.

**preamble** n. préambule m.

**pre-arrange** v.t. fixer à l'avance.

**precarious** a. précaire.

**precaution** n. précaution f.

**preced|e** v.t. précéder. ~ing a. précédent.

**precedence** n. priorité f.; (in rank) préséance f.

**precedent** n. précédent m.

**precinct** n. enceinte f.; (pedestrian area) zone f.

**precious** a. précieux. ●adv. (very: fam.) très.

**precipice** n. (geog.) à-pic m. invar.; (fig.) précipice m.

**precipitat|e** v.t. (person, event, chemical) précipiter. ●a. précipité. ~ion n. précipitation f.

**précis** n. invar. précis m.

**precis|e** a. précis; (careful) méticuleux. ~ely adv. précisément. ~ion n. précision f.

**preclude** v.t. (prevent) empêcher; (rule out) exclure.

**precocious** a. précoce.

**preconc|eived** a. préconçu. ~eption n. préconception f.

**pre-condition** n. condition requise f.

**predator** n. prédateur m.

**predecessor** n. prédécesseur m.

**predicament** n. mauvaise situation or passe f.

**predict** v.t. prédire. ~able a. prévisible. ~ion n. prédiction f.

**predispose** v.t. prédisposer (to do, à faire).

**predominant** a. prédominant. ~ly adv. pour la plupart.

**predominate** v.i. prédominer.

**pre-empt** v.t. (buy) acquérir d'avance; (stop) prévenir. ~ive a. preventif.

**preen** v.t. (bird) lisser. ~ o.s., (person) se bichonner.

**prefab** n. (fam.) bâtiment préfabriqué m. **∼ricated** a. préfabriqué.

**preface** n. préface f.

**prefer** v.t. préférer (**to do**, faire). **∼able** /'prefrəbl/ a. préférable. **∼ably** adv. de préférence.

**preferen|ce** n. préférence f.

**prefix** n. préfixe m.

**pregnan|t** a. (woman) enceinte; (animal) pleine. **∼cy** n. (of woman) grossesse f.

**prehistoric** a. préhistorique.

**prejudice** n. préjugé(s) m. (pl.); (harm) préjudice m. ● v.t. (claim) porter préjudice à; (person) prévenir. **∼d** a. partial; (person) qui a des préjugés.

**preliminar|y** a. préliminaire. **∼ies** n. pl. préliminaires m. pl.

**prelude** n. prélude m.

**premature** a. prématuré.

**premeditated** a. prémédité.

**premier** a. premier. ● n. premier ministre m.

**première** n. première f.

**premises** n. pl. locaux m. pl. **on the ∼**, sur les lieux.

**premiss** n. prémisse f.

**premium** n. prime f. **be at a ∼**, faire prime.

**premonition** n. prémonition f., pressentiment m.

**preoccup|ation** n. préoccupation f. **∼ied** a. préoccupé.

**preparation** n. préparation f. **∼s**, préparatifs m. pl.

**preparatory** a. préparatoire.

**prepare** v.t./i. (se) préparer (**for**, à). **be ∼d for**, (expect) s'attendre à. **∼d to**, prêt à.

**preposition** n. préposition f.

**preposterous** a. ridicule.

**prerequisite** n. condition préalable f.

**prerogative** n. prérogative f.

**Presbyterian** a. & n. presbytérien(ne) (m. (f.)).

**prescri|be** v.t. prescrire. **∼ption** n. prescription f.; (med.) ordonnance f.

**presence** n. présence f.

**present**[1] a. présent. ● n. présent m. **at ∼**, à présent. **for the ∼**, pour le moment.

**present**[2] n. (gift) cadeau m.

**present**[3] v.t. présenter; (film, concert, etc.) donner. **∼ s.o. with**, offrir à qn. **∼ation** n. présentation f. **∼er** n. présenta|teur, -trice m., f.

**presently** adv. bientôt; (now: Amer.) en ce moment.

**preservative** n. (culin.) agent de conservation m.

**preserv|e** v.t. préserver; (maintain & culin.) conserver. ● n. réserve f.; (fig.) domaine m.; (jam) confiture f. **∼ation** n. conservation f.

**preside** v.i. présider. **∼ over**, présider.

**presiden|t** n. président(e) m. (f.). **∼cy** n. présidence f. **∼tial** a. présidentiel.

**press** v.t./i. (button etc.) appuyer (sur); (squeeze) presser; (iron) repasser; (pursue) poursuivre. ● n. (newspapers, machine) presse f.; (for wine) pressoir m. **∼ for sth.**, faire pression pour avoir qch. **∼ s.o. to do sth.**, pousser qn. à faire qch. **∼ conference** conférence de presse f. **∼ on**, continuer (**with sth.**, qch.). **∼-stud** n. bouton-pression m. **∼-up** n. traction f.

**pressure** n. pression f. ● v.t. faire pression sur. **∼-cooker** n. cocotte-minute f. **∼ group**, groupe de pression m.

**pressurize** v.t. (cabin etc.) pressuriser; (person) faire pression sur.

**prestige** n. prestige m.

**prestigious** a. prestigieux.

**presumably** adv. vraisemblablement.

**presum|e** v.t. (suppose) présumer. **∼ption** n. présomption f.

**presumptuous** a. présomptueux.

**pretence** n. feinte f., simulation f.; (claim) prétention f.; (pretext) prétexte m.

**pretend** v.t./i. faire semblant (**to do**, de faire).

**pretentious** a. prétentieux.

**pretext** n. prétexte m.

**pretty** a. joli. ● adv. assez. **∼ much**, presque.

**prevail** v.i. prédominer; (win) prévaloir. **∼ on**, persuader (**to do**, de faire). **∼ing** a. actuel; (wind) dominant.

**prevalent** a. répandu.

**prevent** v.t. empêcher (**from doing**, de faire). **∼ion** n. prévention f. **∼ive** a. préventif.

**preview** n. avant-première f.; (fig.) aperçu m.

**previous** a. précédent, antérieur. **∼ly** adv. auparavant.

**prey** n. proie f. ● v.i. **∼ on**, faire sa proie de; (worry) préoccuper. **bird of ∼**, rapace m.

**price** n. prix m. ● v.t. fixer le prix de. **∼less** a. inestimable; (amusing: sl.) impayable.

**prick** v.t. (with pin etc.) piquer. ● n. piqûre f.

**prickl|e** n. piquant m.; (sensation) picotement m. **∼y** a. piquant; (person) irritable.

**pride** n. orgueil m.; (satisfaction) fierté f.

**priest** n. prêtre m.

**primary** a. (school, elections, etc.) primaire; (chief, basic) premier, fondamental. ● n. (pol.: Amer.) primaire m.

**prime**[1] a. principal, premier; (first-rate) excellent. **P∼ Minister**, Premier Ministre m.

**prime**[2] v.t. (pump, gun) amorcer; (surface) apprêter. **∼r** n. (paint etc.) apprêt m.

**primeval** a. primitif.

**primitive** a. primitif.

**primrose** n. primevère (jaune) f.

**prince** n. prince m.

**princess** n. princesse f.

**principal** a. principal. ● n. (of school etc.) direc|teur, -trice m., f. ~**ly** adv. principalement.

**principle** n. principe m. **in/on ~,** en/par principe.

**print** /prmt/ v.t. imprimer; (write in capitals) écrire en majuscules. ● n. (of foot etc.) empreinte f.; (letters) caractères m. pl.; (photograph) épreuve f.; (engraving) gravure f. ~**out** n. listage m. ~**ed matter,** imprimés m. pl.

**print|er** n. (person) imprimeur m.; (comput.) imprimante f. ~**ing** n. impression f.

**prior** a. précédent. ~ **to,** prep. avant (de).

**priority** n. priorité f. **take ~,** avoir la priorité (**over,** sur).

**prise** v.t. forcer. ~ **open,** ouvrir en forçant.

**prism** n. prisme m.

**prison** n. prison f. ~**er** n. prisonn|ier, -ière m., f.

**pristine** a. primitif; (condition) parfait.

**privacy** n. intimité f., solitude f.

**private** a. privé; (confidential) personnel; (lessons, house, etc.) particulier; (ceremony) intime. ● n. (soldier) simple soldat m. **in ~,** en privé; (of ceremony) dans l'intimité.

**privation** n. privation f.

**privet** n. (bot.) troène m.

**privilege** n. privilège m. ~**d** a. privilégié. **be ~d to,** avoir le privilège de.

**prize** n. prix m. ● a. (entry etc.) primé; (fool etc.) parfait. ● v.t. (value) priser. ~-**winner** n. lauréat(e)n. (f.); (in lottery etc.) gagnant(e) m. (f.).

**pro** n. the ~**s and cons,** le pour et le contre.

**pro-** pref. pro-.

**probab|le** a. probable. ~**ility** n. probabilité f. ~**ly** adv. probablement.

**probation** n. (testing) essai m.; (jurid.) liberté surveillée f. ~**ary** a. d'essai.

**probe** n. (device) sonde f.; (fig.) enquête f. ● v.t. sonder. ● v.i. ~ **into,** sonder.

**problem** n. problème m. ● a. difficile. ~**atic** a. problématique.

**procedure** n. procédure f.; (way of doing sth.) démarche à suivre f.

**proceed** v.i. (go) aller, avancer; (pass) passer (**to,** à); (act) procéder. ~ (**with**), (continue) continuer. ~ **to do,** se mettre à faire.

**proceedings** n. pl. (jurid.) poursuites f. pl.

**proceeds** n. pl. bénéfices m. pl.

**process** n. processus m.; (method) procédé m. ● v.t. (material, data) traiter. **in the ~ of doing,** en train de faire.

**procession** n. défilé m.

**proclaim** v.t. proclamer.

**procure** v.t. obtenir.

**prod** v.t./i. pousser. ● n. poussée f., coup m.

**prodigious** a. prodigieux.

**prodigy** n. prodige m.

**produc|e**[1] v.t./i. produire; (bring out) sortir; (show) présenter; (cause) provoquer; (theatre, TV) mettre en scène; (radio) réaliser; (cinema) produire. ~**er** n. metteur en scène m.; réalisateur m.; producteur m. ~**tion** n. production f.; mise en scène f.; réalisation f.

**produce**[2] n. (food etc.) produits m. pl.

**product** n. produit m.

**productiv|e** a. productif. ~**ity** n. productivité f.

**profession** n. profession f. ~**al** a. professionnel; (of high quality) de professionnel; (person) qui exerce une profession libérale; n. professionnel(le) m. (f.).

**professor** n. professeur (titulaire d'une chaire) m.

**profile** n. profil m.

**profit** n. profit m., bénéfice m.

**profound** a. profond. ~**ly** adv. profondément.

**profuse** a. abondant.

**program** n. (computer) ~**,** programme m. ● v.t. programmer. ~**mer** n. programmeu|r, -se m., f. ~**ming** n. (on computer) programmation f.

**programme** n. programme m.; (broadcast) émission f.

**progress**[1] n. progrès m. (pl.). **in ~,** en cours. **make ~,** faire des progrès. ~ **report,** compterendu m.

**progress**[2] v.i. (advance, improve) progresser. ~**ion** n. progression f.

**progressive** a. progressif; (reforming) progressiste. ~**ly** adv. progressivement.

**prohibit** v.t. interdire (**s.o. from doing,** à qn. de faire).

**project**[1] v.t. projeter. ● v.i. (jut out) être en saillie. ~**ion** n. projection f.; saillie f.

**project**[2] n. (plan) projet m.; (undertaking) entreprise f.; (schol.) dossier m.

**projector** n. projecteur m.

**proliferat|e** v.i. proliférer. ~**ion** n. prolifération f.

**prolific** a. prolifique.

**prologue** n. prologue m.

**prolong** v.t. prolonger.

**promenade** n. promenade f.

**prominen|t** a. (projecting) proéminent; (conspicuous) bien en vue; (fig.) important. ~**ce** n. proéminence f.; importance f. ~**tly** adv. bien en vue.

**promiscu|ous** a. qui a plusieurs partenaires; (pej.) de mœurs faciles. ~**ity** n. les partenaires multiples; (pej.) liberté de mœurs f.

**promis|e** n. promesse f. ● v.t./i. promettre. ~**ing** a. prometteur; (person) qui promet.

**promot|e** v.t. promouvoir; (advertise) faire la promotion de. ~**ion** n. (of person, sales, etc.) promotion f.

**prompt** *a.* rapide; (*punctual*) à l'heure, ponctuel. ● *adv.* (*on the dot*) pile. ● *v.t.* inciter; (*cause*) provoquer; (*theatre*) souffler (son rôle) à. ~**er** *n.* souffleu|r, -se *m.*, *f.* ~**ly** *adv.* rapidement; ponctuellement.

**prone** *a.* ~ **to**, prédisposé à.

**prong** *n.* (*of fork*) dent *f.*

**pronoun** *n.* pronom *m.*

**pron|ounce** *v.t.* prononcer. ~**ouncement** *n.* déclaration *f.* ~**unciation** *n.* prononciation *f.*

**pronounced** *a.* (*noticeable*) prononcé.

**proof** *n.* (*evidence*) preuve *f.*; (*test, trial copy*) épreuve *f.*; (*of liquor*) teneur en alcool *f.* ● *a.* ~ **against**, à l'épreuve de.

**prop**[1] *n.* support *m.* ● *v.t.* ~ (**up**), (*support*) étayer; (*lean*) appuyer.

**prop**[2] *n.* (*theatre, fam.*) accessoire *m.*

**propaganda** *n.* propagande *f.*

**propagat|e** *v.t./i.* (se) propager. ~**ion** *n.* propagation *f.*

**propane** *n.* propane *m.*

**propel** *v.t.* propulser. ~**ling pencil**, porte-mine *m. invar.*

**propeller** *n.* hélice *f.*

**proper** *a.* correct, bon; (*seemly*) convenable; (*real*) vrai; (*thorough: fam.*) parfait. ~ **noun**, nom propre *m.* ~**ly** *adv.* correctement, comme il faut; (*rightly*) avec raison.

**property** *n.* propriété *f.*; (*things owned*) biens *m. pl.*, propriété *f.* ● *a.* immobilier, foncier.

**prophecy** *n.* prophétie *f.*

**prophet** *n.* prophète *m.* ~**ic** *a.* prophétique.

**proportion** *n.* (*ratio, dimension*) proportion *f.*; (*amount*) partie *f.* ~**al**, ~**ate** *adjs.* proportionnel.

**proposal** *n.* proposition *f.*; (*of marriage*) demande en mariage *f.*

**propos|e** *v.t.* proposer. ● *v.i.* ~**e to**, faire une demande en mariage à. ~**e to do**, se proposer de faire. ~**ition** *n.* proposition *f.*; (*matter: fam.*) affaire *f.*; *v.t.* (*fam.*) faire des propositions malhonnêtes à.

**proprietor** *n.* propriétaire *m./f.*

**propriety** *n.* (*correct behaviour*) bienséance *f.*

**propulsion** *n.* propulsion *f.*

**prosaic** *a.* prosaïque.

**prose** *n.* prose *f.*; (*translation*) thème *m.*

**prosecut|e** *v.t.* poursuivre. ~**ion** *n.* poursuites *f. pl.* ~**or** *n.* procureur *m.*

**prospect** *n.* perspective *f.*; (*chance*) espoir *m.*

**prospective** *a.* (*future*) futur; (*possible*) éventuel.

**prospectus** *n.* prospectus *m.*; (*univ.*) guide *m.*

**prosper** *v.i.* prospérer.

**prosper|ous** *a.* prospère. ~**ity** *n.* prospérité *f.*

**prostate** *n.* prostate *f.*

**prostitut|e** *n.* prostituée *f.* ~**ion** *n.* prostitution *f.*

**protect** *v.t.* protéger. ~**ion** *n.* protection *f.* ~**or** *n.* protec|teur, -trice *m.*, *f.*

**protective** *a.* protecteur; (*clothes*) de protection.

**protégé** *n.* protégé *m.* ~**e** *n.* protégée *f.*

**protein** *n.* protéine *f.*

**protest**[1] *n.* protestation *f.* **under** ~, en protestant.

**protest**[2] *v.t./i.* protester. ~**er** *n.* (*pol.*) manifestant(e) *m.* (*f.*).

**Protestant** *a. & n.* protestant(e) (*m.* (*f.*)).

**protocol** *n.* protocole *m.*

**prototype** *n.* prototype *m.*

**protract** *v.t.* prolonger, faire traîner. ~**ed** *a.* prolongé.

**protractor** *n.* (*for measuring*) rapporteur *m.*

**protrude** *v.i.* dépasser.

**proud** *a.* fier, orgueilleux. ~**ly** *adv.* fièrement.

**prove** *v.t.* prouver. ● *v.i.* ~ (**to be**) **easy**/*etc.*, se révéler facile/*etc.* ~ **o.s.**, faire ses preuves. ~**n** *a.* prouvé.

**proverb** *n.* proverbe *m.* ~**ial** *a.* proverbial.

**provide** *v.t.* fournir (**s.o. with sth.**, qch. à qn.). ● *v.i.* ~ **for**, (*allow for*) prévoir; (*guard against*) parer à; (*person*) pourvoir aux besoins de.

**provided** *conj.* ~ **that**, à condition que.

**providence** *n.* providence *f.*

**providing** *conj.* = **provided**.

**provinc|e** *n.* province *f.*; (*fig.*) compétence *f.* ~**ial** *a. & n.* provincial(e) (*m.* (*f.*)).

**provision** *n.* (*stock*) provision *f.*; (*supplying*) fourniture *f.*; (*stipulation*) disposition *f.* ~**s**, (*food*) provisions *f. pl.*

**provisional** *a.* provisoire. ~**ly** *adv.* provisoirement.

**proviso** *n.* condition *f.*

**provo|ke** *v.t.* provoquer. ~**cation** *n.* provocation *f.* ~**cative** *a.* provocant.

**prow** *n.* proue *f.*

**prowess** *n.* prouesse *f.*

**prowl** *v.i.* rôder. ~**er** *n.* rôdeu|r, -se *m.*, *f.*

**proxy** *n.* **by** ~, par procuration.

**prud|e** *n.* prude *f.* ~**ish** *a.* prude.

**pruden|t** *a.* prudent. ~**ce** *n.* prudence *f.* ~**tly** *adv.* prudemment.

**prune**[1] *n.* pruneau *m.*

**prune**[2] *v.t.* (*cut*) tailler.

**pry** *v.i.* être indiscret. ~ **into**, fourrer son nez dans.

**psalm** *n.* psaume *m.*

**pseudo-** *pref.* pseudo-.

**pseudonym** *n.* pseudonyme *m.*

**psoriasis** *n.* psoriasis *m.*

**psyche** *n.* psyché *f.*

**psychiatr|y** n. psychiatrie f. **~ic** a. psychiatrique. **~ist** n. psychiatre m./f.

**psychic** a. (phenomenon etc.) métapsychique; (person) doué de télépathie.

**psychoanalys|e** v.t. psychanalyser. **~t** n. psychanalyste m./f.

**psychoanalysis** n. psychanalyse f.

**psycholog|y** n. psychologie f. **~ical** a. psychologique. **~ist** n. psychologue m./f.

**psychosomatic** a. psychosomatique.

**psychotherap|y** n. psychothérapie f. **~ist** n. psychothérapeute m./f.

**pub** n. pub m.

**puberty** n. puberté f.

**public** a. public; (library etc.) municipal. **in ~,** en public. **~ address system,** sonorisation f. (dans un lieu public). **~ relations,** relations publiques f. pl. **~ transport,** transports en commun m. pl. **~ly** adv. publiquement.

**publication** n. publication f.

**publicity** n. publicité f.

**publicize** v.t. faire connaître au public.

**publish** v.t. publier. **~er** n. éditeur m. **~ing** n. édition f.

**puck** n. (ice hockey) palet m.

**pucker** v.t./i. (se) plisser.

**pudding** n. dessert m.; (steamed) pudding m. **black ~,** boudin m. **rice ~,** riz au lait m.

**puddle** n. flaque d'eau f.

**puff** n. bouffée f. ● v.t./i. souffler. **~ at,** (cigar) tirer sur. **~ out,** (swell) (se) gonfler.

**pull** v.t./i. tirer; (muscle) se froisser. ● n. traction f.; (fig.) attraction f.; (influence) influence f. **give a ~,** tirer. **~ apart,** mettre en morceaux. **~ away,** (auto.) démarrer. **~ back** or **out,** (withdraw) (se) retirer. **~ down,** baisser; (building) démolir. **~ in,** (enter) entrer; (stop) s'arrêter. **~ off,** enlever; (fig.) réussir. **~ out,** (from bag etc.) sortir; (extract) arracher; (auto.) déboîter. **~ over,** (auto.) se ranger. **~ up,** remonter; (uproot) déraciner; (auto.) (s')arrêter.

**pulley** n. poulie f.

**pullover** n. pull(-over) m.

**pulp** n. (of fruit) pulpe f.; (for paper) pâte à papier f.

**pulpit** n. chaire f.

**pulsate** v.i. battre.

**pulse** n. (med.) pouls m.

**pulverize** v.t. pulvériser.

**pump¹** n. pompe f. ● v.t./i. pomper; (person) soutirer des renseignements à. **~ up,** gonfler.

**pump²** n. (plimsoll) tennis m.

**pumpkin** n. potiron m.

**pun** n. jeu de mots m.

**punch¹** v.t. donner un coup de poing à; (perforate) poinçonner; (a hole) faire. ● n. coup de poing m.; (vigour: sl.) punch m.; (device) poinçonneuse f.

**punch²** n. (drink) punch m.

**punctual** a. à l'heure; (habitually) ponctuel. **~ity** n. ponctualité f. **~ly** adv. à l'heure; ponctuellement.

**punctuation** n. ponctuation f.

**puncture** n. (in tyre) crevaison f. ● v.t./i. crever.

**pundit** n. expert m.

**pungent** a. âcre.

**punish** v.t. punir (for sth., de qch.). **~ment** n. punition f.

**punk** n. (music, fan) punk m.

**puny** a. chétif.

**pup(py)** n. chiot m.

**pupil** n. (person) élève m./f.; (of eye) pupille f.

**puppet** n. marionnette f.

**purchase** v.t. acheter (from s.o., à qn.). ● n. achat m. **~r** n. acheteu|r, -se m., f.

**pur|e** a. pur. **~ely** adv. purement. **~ity** n. pureté f.

**purgatory** n. purgatoire m.

**purge** v.t. purger (of, de). ● n. purge f.

**purif|y** v.t. purifier. **~ication** n. purification f.

**purist** n. puriste m./f.

**puritan** n. puritain(e) m. (f.).

**purple** a. & n. violet (m.).

**purpose** n. but m.; (fig.) résolution f. **on ~,** exprès.

**purr** n. ronronnement m. ● v.i. ronronner.

**purse** n. porte-monnaie m. invar.; (handbag: Amer.) sac à main m. ● v.t. (lips) pincer.

**pursue** v.t. poursuivre. **~r** n. poursuivant(e) m. (f.).

**pursuit** n. poursuite f.; (fig.) activité f., occupation f.

**pus** n. pus m.

**push** v.t./i. pousser; (button) appuyer sur; (thrust) enfoncer; (recommend: fam.) proposer avec insistance. ● n. poussée f.; (effort) gros effort m.; (drive) dynamisme m. **~ back,** repousser. **~-chair** n. poussette f. **~ off,** (sl.) filer. **~ on,** continuer. **~over** n. jeu d'enfant m. **~ up,** (lift) relever; (prices) faire monter. **~y** a. (fam.) autoritaire.

**put** v.t./i. mettre, placer, poser; (question) poser. **~ sth. tactfully,** dire qch. avec tact. **~ across,** communiquer. **~ away,** ranger; (fig.) enfermer. **~ back,** remettre; (delay) retarder. **~ by,** mettre de côté. **~ down,** (dé)poser; (write) inscrire; (pay) verser; (suppress) réprimer. **~ forward,** (plan) soumettre. **~ in,** (insert) introduire; (fix) installer; (submit) soumettre. **~ off,** (postpone) renvoyer à plus tard; (disconcert) déconcerter; (displease) rebuter. **~ s.o. off sth.,** dégoûter qn. de qch. **~ on,** (clothes, radio) mettre; (light) allumer; (speed, accent, weight) prendre. **~ out,** sortir; (stretch) (é)tendre; (extinguish) éteindre; (disconcert) déconcerter; (inconvenience) déranger. **~ up,**

lever, remonter; (*building*) construire; (*notice*) mettre; (*price*) augmenter; (*guest*) héberger; (*offer*) offrir. ~**up with,** supporter.

**putt** n. (*golf*) putt m.

**putty** n. mastic m.

**puzzle** n. énigme f.; (*game*) casse-tête m. invar.; (*jigsaw*) puzzle m. ●v.t. rendre perplexe.

**pygmy** n. pygmée m.

**pyjamas** n. pl. pyjama m.

**pylon** n. pylône m.

**pyramid** n. pyramide f.

**python** n. python m.

# Qq

**quadruple** a. & n. quadruple (m.). ●v.t./i. quadrupler. ~**ts** n. pl. quadruplé(e)s m. (f.) pl.

**quail** n. (*bird*) caille f.

**quaint** a. pittoresque; (*old*) vieillot; (*odd*) bizarre. ~**ness** n. pittoresque m.

**quake** v.i. trembler. ●n. (*fam.*) tremblement de terre m.

**Quaker** n. quaker(esse) m. (f.).

**qualification** n. diplôme m.; (*ability*) compétence f.; (*fig.*) réserve f., restriction f.

**qualif|y** v.t. qualifier; (*modify: fig.*) mettre des réserves à; (*statement*) nuancer. ●v.i. obtenir son diplôme (**as,** de); (*sport*) se qualifier; (*fig.*) remplir les conditions requises. ~**ied** a. diplômé; (*able*) qualifié (**to do,** pour faire); (*fig.*) conditionnel; (*success*) modéré.

**quality** n. qualité f.

**qualm** n. scrupule m.

**quandary** n. dilemme m.

**quantity** n. quantité f.

**quarantine** n. quarantaine f.

**quarrel** n. dispute f., querelle f. ●v.i. se disputer. ~**some** a. querelleur.

**quarry**[1] n. (*prey*) proie f.

**quarry**[2] n. (*excavation*) carrière f. ●v.t. extraire.

**quart** n. (*approx.*) litre m.

**quarter** n. quart m.; (*of year*) trimestre m.; (25 *cents*: *Amer.*) quart de dollar m.; (*district*) quartier m. ~**s,** logement(s) m. (pl.) ●v.t. diviser en quatre; (*mil.*) cantonner.

**quartet** n. quatuor m.

**quartz** n. quartz m. ●a. (*watch etc.*) à quartz.

**quash** v.t. (*suppress*) étouffer; (*jurid.*) annuler.

**quasi-** pref. quasi-.

**quaver** v.i. trembler, chevroter. ●n. (*mus.*) croche f.

**quay** n. (*naut.*) quai m.

**queasy** a. (*stomach*) délicat. **feel** ~, avoir mal au cœur.

**queen** n. reine f.; (*cards*) dame f.

**queer** a. étrange; (*dubious*) louche; (*ill*) patraque. ●n. (*sl.*) homosexuel m.

**quell** v.t. réprimer.

**quench** v.t. éteindre; (*thirst*) étancher; (*desire*) étouffer.

**query** n. question f. ●v.t. mettre en question.

**quest** n. recherche f.

**question** n. question f. ●v.t. interroger; (*doubt*) mettre en question, douter de. **in** ~, en question. **out of the** ~, hors de question. ~ **mark,** point d'interrogation.

**questionable** a. discutable.

**questionnaire** n. questionnaire m.

**queue** n. queue f. ●v.i. faire la queue.

**quibble** v.i. ergoter.

**quick** a. rapide. ●adv. vite. **be** ~, (*hurry*) se dépêcher. ~**ly** adv. rapidement, vite. ~**witted** a. vif.

**quicken** v.t./i. (s')accélérer.

**quicksand** n. ~(s), sables mouvants m. pl.

**quid** n. invar. (*sl.*) livre f.

**quiet** a. (*calm, still*) tranquille; (*silent*) silencieux; (*gentle*) doux; (*discreet*) discret. ●n. tranquillité f. **keep** ~, se taire. ~**ly** adv. tranquillement; silencieusement; doucement; discrètement.

**quieten** v.t./i. (se) calmer.

**quilt** n. édredon m. **(continental)** ~, couette f. ●v.t. matelasser.

**quinine** n. quinine f.

**quintet** n. quintette m.

**quintuplets** n. pl. quintuplé(e)s m. (f.) pl.

**quip** n. mot piquant m.

**quirk** n. bizarrerie f.

**quit** v.t. quitter. ●v.i. abandonner; (*resign*) démissionner.

**quite** adv. tout à fait, vraiment; (*rather*) assez. ~ **a few,** un assez grand nombre (de).

**quits** a. quitte (**with,** envers). **call it** ~, en rester là.

**quiz** n. test m.; (*game*) jeu-concours m. ●v.t. questionner.

**quorum** n. quorum m.

**quota** n. quota m.

**quotation** n. citation f.; (*price*) devis m.; (*stock exchange*) cotation f. ~ **marks,** guillemets m. pl.

**quote** v.t. citer; (*reference: comm.*) rappeler; (*price*) indiquer; (*share price*) coter. ●v.i. ~ **for,** faire un devis pour. ~ **from,** citer. ●n. (*estimate*) devis m.; (*fam.*) = **quotation.**

**quotient** n. quotient m.

**rabbi** n. rabbin m.

**rabbit** n. lapin m.

**rabble** n. (*crowd*) cohue f.

**rabid** a. enragé.

**rabies** n. (*disease*) rage f.

**race**[1] n. course f. ● v.t. (*horse*) faire courir; (*engine*) emballer. ~ **(against),** faire la course à. ● v.i. courir; (*rush*) foncer.

**race**[2] n. (*group*) race f. ● a. racial; (*relations*) entre les races.

**racecourse** n. champ de courses m.

**racehorse** n. cheval de course m.

**racial** a. racial.

**racing** n. courses f. pl. ~ **car,** voiture de course f.

**racis|t** a. & n. raciste (m./f.). ~**m** n. racisme m.

**rack** n. (*shelf*) étagère f.; (*pigeon-holes*) casier m.; (*for luggage*) porte-bagages m. invar.; (*for dishes*) égouttoir m.; (*on car roof*) galerie f.

**racket**[1] n. raquette f.

**racket**[2] n. (*din*) tapage m.; (*dealings*) combine f.; (*crime*) racket m.

**radar** n. radar m. ● a. (*system etc.*) radar invar.

**radial** a. (*tyre*) à carcasse radiale.

**radiant** a. rayonnant.

**radiat|e** v.t. dégager. ● v.i. rayonner (**from,** de). ~**ion** n. (*radioactivity*) radiation f.

**radiator** n. radiateur m.

**radical** a. radical. ● n. (*person: pol.*) radical(e) m. (f.).

**radio** n. radio f. ● v.t. (*message*) envoyer par radio; (*person*) appeler par radio.

**radioactiv|e** a. radioactif. ~**ity** n. radioactivité f.

**radish** n. radis m.

**radius** n. rayon m.

**raffle** n. tombola f.

**raft** n. radeau m.

**rafter** n. chevron m.

**rag** n. lambeau m., loque f.; (*for wiping*) chiffon m.; (*newspaper*) torchon m. **in** ~**s,** (*person*) en haillons; (*clothes*) en lambeaux.

**rage** n. rage f., fureur f. ● v.i. rager; (*storm, battle*) faire rage.

**ragged** a. (*clothes, person*) loqueteux; (*edge*) déchiqueté.

**raging** a. (*storm etc.*) violent.

**raid** n. (*mil.*) raid m.; (*by police*) rafle f.; (*by criminals*) hold-up m. invar. ● v.t. faire un raid or une rafle or un hold-up dans. ~**er** n. (*person*) bandit m., pillard m. ~**ers** n. pl. (*mil.*) commando m.

**rail** n. (*on balcony*) balustrade f.; (*stairs*) main courante f., rampe f.; (*for train*) rail m.; (*for curtain*) tringle f.

**railing** n. ~**s,** grille f.

**railway** n. chemin de fer m. ~ **line,** voie ferrée f. ~**man** n. (*pl.* -**men**) cheminot m. ~ **station,** gare f.

**rain** n. pluie f. ● v.i. pleuvoir. ~ **forest,** forêt (humide) tropicale f.

**rainbow** n. arc-en-ciel m.

**raincoat** n. imperméable m.

**rainfall** n. précipitation f.

**rainy** a. pluvieux.

**raise** v.t. lever; (*breed, build*) élever; (*question etc.*) soulever; (*price etc.*) relever; (*money etc.*) obtenir; (*voice*) élever.

**raisin** n. raisin sec m.

**rake** n. râteau m. ● v.t. (*garden*) ratisser; (*search*) fouiller dans.

**rally** v.t./i. (se) rallier; (*strength*) reprendre; (*after illness*) aller mieux. ● n. rassemblement m.; (*auto.*) rallye m.; (*tennis*) échange m. ~ **round,** venir en aide.

**ram** n. bélier m. ● v.t. (*thrust*) enfoncer; (*crash into*) emboutir, percuter.

**RAM** abbr. (*random access memory*) mémoire vive f.

**rambl|e** n. randonnée f. ● v.i. faire une randonnée. ~**e on,** parler (sans cesse), divaguer. ~**er** n. randonneu|r, -se, m., f.

**ramp** n. (*slope*) rampe f.; (*in garage*) pont de graissage m.

**rampage** v.i. se déchaîner.

**rampant** a. **be** ~, (*disease etc.*) sévir, être répandu.

**rampart** n. rempart m.

**ramshackle** a. délabré.

**ranch** n. ranch m.

**rancid** a. rance.

**rancour** n. rancœur f.

**random** a. fait, pris, *etc.* au hasard, aléatoire (*techn.*). ● n. **at** ~, au hasard.

**randy** a. (*fam.*) excité.

**range** n. (*distance*) portée f.; (*of aircraft etc.*) rayon d'action m.; (*series*) gamme f.; (*scale*) échelle f.; (*choice*) choix m.; (*domain*) champ m.; (*of mountains*) chaîne f.; (*stove*) cuisinière f. ● v.i. s'étendre; (*vary*) varier.

**ranger** n. garde forestier m.

**rank** n. rang m.; (*grade: mil.*) grade m., rang m. ● v.t./i. ~ **among,** compter parmi. **the** ~ **and file,** les gens ordinaires.

**rankle** v.i. ~ **with s.o.,** rester sur le cœur à qn.

**ransack** v.t. (*search*) fouiller; (*pillage*) saccager.

**ransom** n. rançon f. ● v.t. rançonner; (redeem) racheter. **hold to ~,** rançonner.

**rant** v.i. tempêter.

**rap** n. petit coup sec m. ● v.t./i. frapper.

**rape** v.t. violer. ● n. viol m.

**rapid** a. rapide.

**rapist** n. violeur m.

**rapport** n. rapport m.

**raptur|e** n. extase f. **~ous** a. (person) en extase; (welcome etc.) frénétique.

**rar|e¹** a. rare. **~ely** adv. rarement. **~ity** n. rareté f.

**rare²** a. (culin.) saignant.

**rarefied** a. raréfié.

**raring** a. **~ to,** (fam.) impatient de.

**rascal** n. coquin(e) m. (f.).

**rash¹** n. (med.) éruption f.

**rash²** a. imprudent. **~ly** adv. imprudemment. **~ness** n. imprudence f.

**rasher** n. tranche (de lard) f.

**raspberry** n. framboise f.

**rasping** a. grinçant.

**rat** n. rat m.

**rate** n. (ratio, level) taux m.; (speed) allure f.; (price) tarif m. **~s,** (taxes) impôts locaux m. pl. ● v.t. évaluer; (consider) considérer ● v.i. **~ as,** être considéré comme. **at any ~,** en tout cas.

**ratepayer** n. contribuable m./f.

**rather** adv. (by preference) plutôt; (fairly) assez, plutôt; (a little) un peu. **I would ~ go,** j'aimerais mieux partir.

**ratif|y** v.t. ratifier. **~ication** n. ratification f.

**rating** n. classement m.; (sailor) matelot m.; (number) indice m. **the ~s,** (TV) l'audimat (P.).

**ratio** n. proportion f.

**ration** n. ration f. ● v.t. rationner.

**rational** a. rationnel; (person) raisonnable.

**rationalize** v.t. tenter de justifier; (organize) rationaliser.

**rattle** v.i. faire du bruit; (of bottles) cliqueter. ● v.t. secouer; (sl.) agacer. ● n. bruit (de ferraille) m.; (cliquetis m.; (toy) hochet m.

**raucous** a. rauque.

**ravage** v.t. ravager. **~s** n. pl. ravages m. pl.

**rave** v.i. divaguer; (in anger) tempêter. **~ about,** s'extasier sur.

**raven** n. corbeau m.

**ravine** n. ravin m.

**ravioli** n. ravioli m. pl.

**ravish** v.t. (rape) ravir. **~ing** a. (enchanting) ravissant.

**raw** a. cru; (not processed) brut; (wound) à vif; (immature) inexpérimenté. **~ materials,** matières premières f. pl.

**ray** n. (of light etc.) rayon m.

**raze** v.t. (destroy) raser.

**razor** n. rasoir m. **~-blade** n. lame de rasoir f.

**re** prep. concernant.

**re-** pref. re-, ré-, r-.

**reach** v.t. atteindre, arriver à; (contact) joindre; (hand over) passer. ● v.i. s'étendre. ● n. portée f. **~ for,** tendre la main pour prendre.

**react** v.i. réagir.

**reaction** n. réaction f. **~ary** a. & n. réactionnaire (m./f.).

**reactor** n. réacteur m.

**read** v.t./i. lire; (fig.) comprendre; (study) étudier; (of instrument) indiquer. ● n. (fam.) lecture f. **~ out,** lire à haute voix. **~able** a. agréable or facile à lire. **~ing** n. lecture f.; indication f. **~ing-glasses** pl. n. lunettes pour lire f. pl.

**reader** n. lec|teur, -trice m., f.

**readily** adv. (willingly) volontiers; (easily) facilement.

**readjust** v.t. rajuster. ● v.i. se réadapter (to, à).

**ready** a. prêt; (quick) prompt. **~-made** a. tout fait.

**real** a. vrai, véritable, réel. ● adv. (Amer., fam.) vraiment. **~ estate,** biens fonciers m. pl.

**realis|t** n. réaliste m./f. **~m** n. réalisme m. **~tic** a. réaliste.

**reality** n. réalité f.

**realiz|e** v.t. se rendre compte de, comprendre; (fulfil) réaliser. **~ation** n. prise de conscience f.; réalisation f.

**really** adv. vraiment.

**realm** n. royaume m.

**reap** v.t. (crop, field) moissonner; (fig.) récolter.

**reappear** v.i. réapparaître.

**reappraisal** n. réévaluation f.

**rear¹** n. arrière m., derrière m. ● a. arrière invar., de derrière. **~-view mirror,** rétroviseur m.

**rear²** v.t. (bring up, breed) élever. ● v.i. (horse) se cabrer. **~ one's head,** dresser la tête.

**rearguard** n. (mil.) arrière-garde f.

**rearm** v.t./i. réarmer.

**rearrange** v.t. réarranger.

**reason** n. raison f. ● v.i. raisonner. **~ with,** raisonner. **everything within ~,** tout dans les limites normales. **~ing** n. raisonnement m.

**reasonable** a. raisonnable.

**reassur|e** v.t. rassurer. **~ance** n. réconfort m.

**rebate** n. remboursement (partiel) m.; (discount) rabais m.

**rebel¹** n. & a. rebelle (m./f.).

**rebel²** v.i. se rebeller. **~lion** n. rébellion f. **~lious** a. rebelle.

**rebound** v.i. rebondir. **~ on,** (backfire) se retourner contre. ● n. rebond m.

**rebuff** v.t. repousser. ● n. rebuffade f.

**rebuild** v.t. reconstruire.

**rebuke** v.t. réprimander. ● n. réprimande f., reproche m.

**recall** v.t. (to s.o., call back) rappeler; (remember) se rappeler. ● n. rappel m.

**recap** v.t./i. (fam.) récapituler. ● n. (fam.) récapitulation f.

**recapture** v.t. reprendre; (recall) recréer.

**recede** v.i. s'éloigner.

**receipt** n. (written) reçu m.; (of letter) réception f. ~s, (money: comm.) recettes f. pl.

**receive** v.t. recevoir. ~r n. (of stolen goods) receleu|r, -se m., f.; (telephone) combiné m.

**recent** a. récent. ~ly adv. récemment.

**receptacle** n. récipient m.

**reception** n. réception f. **give s.o. a warm ~,** donner un accueil chaleureux à qn. ~ist n. réceptionniste m./f.

**receptive** a. réceptif.

**recess** n. (alcove) renfoncement m.; (nook) recoin m.; (holiday) vacances f. pl.

**recession** n. récession f.

**recharge** v.t. recharger.

**recipe** n. recette f.

**reciprocal** a. réciproque.

**reciprocate** v.t. offrir en retour. ● v.i. en faire autant.

**recital** n. récital m.

**recite** v.t. (poem, lesson, etc.) réciter; (list) énumérer.

**reckless** a. imprudent. ~ly adv. imprudemment.

**reckon** v.t./i. calculer; (judge) considérer; (think) penser. ~ **on/with,** compter sur/avec. ~ing n. calcul(s) m. (pl.).

**reclaim** v.t. (seek return of) réclamer; (land) défricher; (flooded land) assécher.

**reclin|e** v.i. être étendu. ~ing a. (person) étendu; (seat) à dossier réglable.

**recluse** n. reclus(e) m. (f.), ermite m.

**recognition** n. reconnaissance f. **beyond ~,** méconnaissable. **gain ~,** être reconnu.

**recognize** v.t. reconnaître.

**recoil** v.i. reculer (from, devant).

**recollect** v.t. se souvenir de, se rappeler. ~ion n. souvenir m.

**recommend** v.t. recommander. ~ation n. recommandation f.

**recompense** v.t. (ré)compenser. ● n. récompense f.

**reconcil|e** v.t. (people) réconcilier; (facts) concilier. ~iation n. réconciliation f.

**recondition** v.t. réviser.

**reconn|oitre** v.t. (mil.) reconnaître. ~aissance n. reconnaissance f.

**reconsider** v.t. reconsidérer. ● v.i. se déjuger.

**reconstruct** v.t. reconstruire; (crime) reconstituer.

**record¹** v.t./i. (in register, on tape, etc.) enregistrer; (in diary) noter. ~ **that,** rapporter que. ~ing n. enregistrement m.

**record²** n. (report) rapport m.; (register) registre m.; (mention) mention f.; (file) dossier m.; (fig.) résultats m. pl.; (mus.) disque m.; (sport) record m. **(criminal) ~,** casier judiciaire m. ● a. record invar.

**recorder** n. (mus.) flûte à bec f.

**recount** v.t. raconter.

**re-count** v.t. recompter.

**recoup** v.t. récupérer.

**recourse** n. recours m. **have ~ to,** avoir recours à.

**recover** v.t. récupérer. ● v.i. se remettre; (med.) se rétablir; (economy) se redresser. ~y n. récupération f.; (med.) rétablissement m.

**recreation** n. récréation f. ~al a. de récréation.

**recrimination** n. contre-accusation f.

**recruit** n. recrue f. ● v.t. recruter. ~ment n. recrutement m.

**rectang|le** n. rectangle m. ~ular a. rectangulaire.

**rectif|y** v.t. rectifier. ~ication n. rectification f.

**recuperate** v.i. (med.) se rétablir.

**recur** v.i. se répéter.

**recurren|t** a. fréquent. ~ce n. répétition f.

**recycle** v.t. recycler.

**red** a. rouge; (hair) roux. ● n. rouge m. **in the ~,** en déficit. ~-**handed** a. en flagrant délit. ~-**hot** a. brûlant. **the ~ light,** le feu rouge m.

**redcurrant** n. groseille f.

**redden** v.t./i. rougir.

**reddish** a. rougeâtre.

**redecorate** v.t. refaire.

**redeem** v.t. racheter.

**redemption** n. rachat m.

**redeploy** v.t. réorganiser; (troops) répartir.

**redirect** v.t. (letter) faire suivre.

**redness** n. rougeur f.

**redo** v.t. refaire.

**redolent** a. ~ **of,** qui évoque.

**redress** v.t. (wrong etc.) redresser. ● n. réparation f.

**reduc|e** v.t. réduire; (temperature etc.) faire baisser. ~tion n. réduction f.

**redundan|t** a. superflu; (worker) licencié. **make ~,** licencier. ~cy n. licenciement m.; (word, phrase) pléonasme m.

**reed** n. (plant) roseau m.; (mus.) anche f.

**reef** n. récif m., écueil m.

**reek** n. puanteur f. ● v.i. ~ **(of),** puer.

**reel** n. (of thread) bobine f.; (of film) bande f.; (winding device) dévidoir m. ● v.i. chanceler.

**refectory** n. réfectoire m.

**refer** v.t./i. ~ **to,** (allude to) faire allusion à; (concern) s'appliquer à; (consult) consulter; (submit) soumettre à; (direct) renvoyer à.

**referee** n. arbitre m. ● v.t. arbitrer.

**reference** n. référence f.; (mention) allusion f.; (person) répondant(e) m. (f.). **in** or **with ~ to,** en ce qui concerne; (comm.) suite à. ~ **book,** ouvrage de référence m.

**referendum** n. référendum m.

**refill**[1] v.t. remplir (à nouveau); (pen etc.) recharger.

**refill**[2] n. (of pen, lighter, lipstick) recharge f.

**refine** v.t. raffiner. ~**d** a. raffiné. ~**ment** n. raffinement m.; (techn.) raffinage m. ~**ry** n. raffinerie f.

**reflect** v.t. refléter; (of mirror) réfléchir, refléter. ● v.i. réfléchir (on, à). ~**ion** n. réflexion f.; (image) reflet m. ~**or** n. réflecteur m.

**reflective** a. réfléchissant.

**reflex** a. & n. réflexe (m.).

**reflexive** a. (gram.) réfléchi.

**reform** v.t. réformer. ● v.i. (person) s'amender. ● n. réforme f. ~**er** n. réforma|teur, -trice m., f.

**refrain**[1] n. refrain m.

**refrain**[2] v.i. s'abstenir (from, de).

**refresh** v.t. rafraîchir; (of rest etc.) ragaillardir, délasser. ~**ing** a. (drink) rafraîchissant; (sleep) réparateur. ~**ments** n. pl. rafraîchissements m. pl.

**refrigerator** n. réfrigérateur m.

**refuel** v.t./i. (se) ravitailler.

**refuge** n. refuge m. **take ~,** se réfugier.

**refugee** n. réfugié(e) m. (f.).

**refund** v.t. rembourser. ● n. remboursement m.

**refus|e**[1] v.t./i. refuser. ~**al** n. refus m.

**refuse**[2] n. ordures f. pl.

**refute** v.t. réfuter.

**regain** v.t. retrouver; (lost ground) regagner.

**regal** a. royal, majestueux.

**regard** v.t. considérer. ● n. considération f., estime f., amitiés f. pl. **as ~s, ~ing** prep. en ce qui concerne.

**regardless** adv. quand même. ~ **of,** sans tenir compte de.

**regatta** n. régates f. pl.

**regenerat|e** v.t. régénérer. ~**ion** n. régénération f.

**regime** n. régime m.

**regiment** n. régiment m.

**region** n. région f. **in the ~ of,** environ. ~**al** a. régional.

**regist|er** n. registre m. ● v.t. enregistrer; (vehicle) immatriculer; (birth) déclarer; (letter) recommander; (express) exprimer. ● v.i. (enrol) s'inscrire; (fig.) être compris. ~**er office,** bureau d'état civil m. ~**ration** n. enregistrement m.;

inscription f.; (vehicle document) carte grise f. ~**ration (number),** (auto.) numéro d'immatriculation m.

**regret** n. regret m. ● v.t. regretter (**to do,** de faire). ~**fully** adv. à regret.

**regroup** v.t./i. (se) regrouper.

**regular** a. régulier; (usual) habituel; (thorough: fam.) vrai. ● n. (fam.) habitué(e) m. (f.). ~**ity** n. régularité f. ~**ly** adv. régulièrement.

**regulat|e** v.t. régler. ~**ion** n. (rule) règlement m.

**rehabilitat|e** v.t. réadapter; (in public esteem) réhabiliter. ~**ion** n. réadaptation f.; réhabilitation f.

**rehash**[1] v.t. remanier.

**rehash**[2] n. réchauffé m.

**rehears|e** v.t./i. (theatre) répéter. ~**al** n. répétition f.

**re-heat** v.t. réchauffer.

**reign** n. règne m. ● v.i. régner (**over,** sur).

**reimburse** v.t. rembourser.

**rein** n. rêne f.

**reindeer** n. invar. renne m.

**reinforce** v.t. renforcer. ~**ment** n. renforcement m. ~**ments** n. pl. renforts m. pl. ~**d concrete,** béton armé m.

**reinstate** v.t. réintégrer.

**reiterate** v.t. réitérer.

**reject**[1] v.t. (offer, plea, etc.) rejeter; (book, goods, etc.) refuser. ~**ion** n. rejet m.; refus m.

**reject**[2] n. (article de) rebut m.

**rejoice** v.i. se réjouir.

**relapse** n. rechute f. ● v.i. rechuter. ~ **into,** retomber dans.

**relate** v.t. raconter; (associate) rapprocher. ● v.i. ~ **to,** se rapporter à; (get on with) s'entendre avec. ~**d** a. (ideas etc.) lié. ~**d to s.o.,** parent(e) de qn.

**relation** n. rapport m.; (person) parent(e) m. (f.). ~**ship** n. lien de parenté m.; (link) rapport m.; (affair) liaison f.

**relative** n. parent(e) m. (f.). ● a. relatif; (respective) respectif. ~**ly** adv. relativement.

**relax** v.t./i. (less tense) (se) relâcher; (for pleasure) (se) détendre. ~**ation** n. relâchement m.; détente f.

**relay**[1] n. relais m. ~ **race,** course de relais f.

**relay**[2] v.t. relayer.

**release** v.t. libérer; (bomb) lâcher; (film) sortir; (news) publier; (smoke) dégager; (spring) déclencher. ● n. libération f.; sortie f.; (record) nouveau disque m. (of pollution) émission f.

**relegate** v.t. reléguer.

**relent** v.i. se laisser fléchir. ~**less** a. impitoyable.

**relevan|t** a. pertinent. **be ~t to,** avoir rapport à. ~**ce** n. pertinence f., rapport m.

**reliab|le** *a.* sérieux, sûr; (*machine*) fiable. **~lity** *n.* sérieux *m.*; fiabilité *f.*

**reliance** *n.* dépendance *f.*; (*trust*) confiance *f.*

**relic** *n.* relique *f.*

**relief** *n.* soulagement *m.* (**from,** à); (*assistance*) secours *m.*; (*outline, design*) relief *m.*

**relieve** *v.t.* soulager; (*help*) secourir; (*take over from*) relayer.

**religion** *n.* religion *f.*

**religious** *a.* religieux.

**relinquish** *v.t.* abandonner.

**relish** *n.* plaisir *m.*, goût *m.*; (*culin.*) assaisonnement *m.* ● *v.t.* savourer; (*idea etc.*) aimer.

**relocate** *v.t.* (*company*) déplacer; (*employee*) muter. ● *v.i.* se déplacer, déménager.

**reluctan|t** *a.* fait, donné, *etc.* à contrecœur. **~t to,** peu disposé à. **~ce** *n.* répugnance *f.* **~tly** *adv.* à contrecœur.

**rely** *v.i.* **~ on,** compter sur; (*financially*) dépendre de.

**remain** *v.i.* rester. **~s** *n. pl.* restes *m. pl.*

**remainder** *n.* reste *m.*

**remand** *v.t.* mettre en détention préventive. ● *n.* **on ~,** en détention préventive.

**remark** *n.* remarque *f.* ● *v.t.* remarquer. ● *v.i.* **~ on,** faire des commentaires sur. **~able** *a.* remarquable.

**remarry** *v.i.* se remarier.

**remed|y** *n.* remède *m.* ● *v.t.* remédier à. **~ial** *a.* (*class etc.*) de rattrapage; (*treatment*: *med.*) curatif.

**remember** *v.t.* se souvenir de, se rappeler. **~ to do,** ne pas oublier de faire.

**remind** *v.t.* rappeler (**s.o. of sth.,** qch. à qn.). **~ s.o. to do,** rappeler à qn. qu'il doit faire. **~er** *n.* (*letter, signal*) rappel *m.*

**reminisce** *v.i.* évoquer ses souvenirs. **~nces** *n. pl.* réminiscences *f. pl.*

**reminiscent** *a.* **~ of,** qui évoque.

**remission** *n.* rémission *f.*; (*jurid.*) remise (de peine) *f.*

**remittance** *n.* paiement *m.*

**remnant** *n.* reste *m.*, débris *m.*; (*trace*) vestige *m.*; (*of cloth*) coupon *m.*

**remorse** *n.* remords *m.* (*pl.*). **~ful** *a.* plein de remords.

**remote** *a.* (*place, time*) lointain; (*person*) distant; (*slight*) vague. **~ control,** télécommande *f.*

**removable** *a.* amovible.

**remov|e** *v.t.* enlever; (*lead away*) emmener; (*dismiss*) renvoyer; (*do away with*) supprimer. **~al** *n.* enlèvement *m.*; renvoi *m.*; suppression *f.*; (*from house*) déménagement *m.* **~al men,** déménageurs *m. pl.*

**remuneration** *n.* rémunération *f.*

**rename** *v.t.* rebaptiser.

**render** *v.t.* (*give, make*) rendre.

**rendezvous** *n.* rendez-vous *m. invar.*

**renew** *v.t.* renouveler; (*resume*) reprendre. **~able** *a.* renouvelable. **~al** *n.* renouvellement *m.*; reprise *f.*

**renounce** *v.t.* renoncer à.

**renovat|e** *v.t.* rénover. **~ion** *n.* rénovation *f.*

**rent** *n.* loyer *m.* ● *v.t.* louer. **for ~,** à louer. **~al** *n.* prix de location *m.*

**renunciation** *n.* renonciation *f.*

**reopen** *v.t./i.* rouvrir. **~ing** *n.* réouverture *f.*

**reorganize** *v.t.* réorganiser.

**rep** *n.* (*comm., fam.*) représentant(e) *m.* (*f.*).

**repair** *v.t.* réparer. ● *n.* réparation *f.* **in good/ bad ~,** en bon/mauvais état. **~er** *n.* réparateur *m.*

**repartee** *n.* repartie *f.*

**repay** *v.t.* rembourser; (*reward*) récompenser. **~ment** *n.* remboursement *m.*; récompense *f.* **monthly ~ments,** mensualités *f. pl.*

**repeal** *v.t.* abroger, annuler. ● *n.* abrogation *f.*

**repeat** *v.t./i.* répéter; (*renew*) renouveler. ● *n.* répétition *f.*; (*broadcast*) reprise *f.*

**repel** *v.t.* repousser. **~lent** *a.* repoussant.

**repent** *v.i.* se repentir (*of,* de). **~ance** *n.* repentir *m.*

**repercussion** *n.* répercussion *f.*

**repertoire** *n.* répertoire *m.*

**repertory** *n.* répertoire *m.*

**repetit|ion** *n.* répétition *f.* **~ive** *adj.* plein de répétitions.

**replace** *v.t.* remettre; (*take the place of*) remplacer. **~ment** *n.* remplacement *m.* (**of,** de); (*person*) remplaçant(e) *m.* (*f.*); (*new part*) pièce de rechange *f.*

**replay** *n.* (*sport*) match rejoué *m.*; (*recording*) répétition immédiate *f.*

**replenish** *v.t.* (*refill*) remplir.

**replica** *n.* copie exacte *f.*

**reply** *v.t./i.* répondre. ● *n.* réponse *f.*

**report** *v.t.* rapporter, annoncer (**that,** que); (*notify*) signaler; (*denounce*) dénoncer. ● *v.i.* faire un rapport. **~ (on),** (*news item*) faire un reportage sur. ● *n.* rapport *m.*; (*in press*) reportage *m.*; (*schol.*) bulletin *m.*; (*sound*) détonation *f.*

**reporter** *n.* reporter *m.*

**repossess** *v.t.* reprendre.

**represent** *v.t.* représenter. **~ation** *n.* représentation *f.*

**representative** *a.* représentatif, typique (**of,** de). ● *n.* représentant(e) *m.* (*f.*).

**repress** *v.t.* réprimer. **~ion** *n.* répression *f.* *a.* répressif.

**reprieve** *n.* (*delay*) sursis *m.*; (*pardon*) grâce *f.* ● *v.t.* accorder un sursis à; gracier.

**reprimand** *v.t.* réprimander. ● *n.* réprimande *f.*

**reprisals** *n. pl.* représailles *f. pl.*

**reproach** *v.t.* reprocher (**s.o. for sth.,** qch. à qn.). ● *n.* reproche *m.*

**reproduc|e** *v.t./i.* (se) reproduire. ~**tion** *n.* reproduction *f.* ~**tive** *a.* reproducteur.

**reptile** *n.* reptile *m.*

**republic** *n.* république *f.* ~**an** *a.* & *n.* républicain(e) (*m.* (*f.*)).

**repugnan|t** *a.* répugnant. ~**ce** *n.* répugnance *f.*

**repuls|e** *v.t.* repousser. ~**ion** *n.* répulsion *f.* ~**ive** *a.* repoussant.

**reputable** *a.* honorable.

**reputation** *n.* réputation *f.*

**request** *n.* demande *f.* ● *v.t.* demander (**of, from,** à).

**requiem** *n.* requiem *m.*

**require** *v.t.* (*of thing*) demander; (*of person*) avoir besoin de; (*demand, order*) exiger. ~**d** *a.* requis. ~**ment** *n.* exigence *f.*; (*condition*) condition (requise) *f.*

**requisition** *v.t.* réquisitionner.

**resale** *n.* revente *f.*

**rescue** *v.t.* sauver. ● *n.* sauvetage *m.* (**of,** de); (*help*) secours *m.* ~**r** *n.* sauveteur *m.*

**research** *n.* recherche(s) *f.*(*pl.*). ● *v.t./i.* faire des recherches (sur). ~**er** *n.* chercheu|r, -se *m., f.*

**resembl|e** *v.t.* ressembler à. ~**ance** *f.* ressemblance *f.*

**resent** *v.t.* être indigné de, s'offenser de. ~**ment** *n.* ressentiment *m.*

**reservation** *n.* réserve *f.*; (*booking*) réservation *f.*

**reserve** *v.t.* réserver. ● *n.* (*reticence, stock, land*) réserve *f.*; (*sport*) remplaçant(e) *m.* (*f.*). **in** ~, en réserve. ~**d** *a.* (*person, room*) réservé.

**reservoir** *n.* réservoir *m.*

**reshape** *v.t.* remodeler.

**reshuffle** *v.t.* (*pol.*) remanier. ● *n.* (*pol.*) remaniement (ministériel) *m.*

**reside** *v.i.* résider.

**residen|t** *a.* résidant. ● *n.* habitant(e) *m.* (*f.*). ~**ce** *n.* résidence *f.*; (*of students*) foyer *m.*

**residential** *a.* résidentiel.

**residue** *n.* résidu *m.*

**resign** *v.t.* abandonner; (*job*) démissionner de. ● *v.i.* démissionner. ~**ation** *n.* résignation *f.*; (*from job*) démission *f.* ~**ed** *a.* résigné.

**resilient** *a.* (*person*) qui a du ressort.

**resin** *n.* résine *f.*

**resist** *v.t./i.* résister (à). ~**ance** *n.* résistance *f.* ~**ant** *a.* (*med.*) rebelle; (*metal*) résistant.

**resolut|e** *a.* résolu. ~**ion** *n.* résolution *f.*

**resolve** *v.t.* résoudre (**to do,** de faire). ● *n.* résolution *f.*

**resonan|t** *a.* résonnant. ~**ce** *n.* résonance *f.*

**resort** *v.i.* ~ **to,** avoir recours à. ● *n.* (*recourse*) recours *m.*; (*place*) station *f.* **in the last** ~, en dernier ressort.

**resounding** *a.* retentissant.

**resource** *n.* (*expedient*) ressource *f.* ~**s,** (*wealth etc.*) ressources *f. pl.* ~**ful** *a.* ingénieux. ~**fulness** *n.* ingéniosité *f.*

**respect** *n.* respect *m.*; (*aspect*) égard *m.* ● *v.t.* respecter. **with** ~ **to,** à l'égard de.

**respectab|le** *a.* respectable. ~**ility** *n.* respectabilité *f.*

**respective** *a.* respectif. ~**ly** *adv.* respectivement.

**respiration** *n.* respiration *f.*

**respite** *n.* répit *m.*

**respond** *v.i.* répondre (**to,** à) ~ **to,** (*react to*) réagir à.

**response** *n.* réponse *f.*

**responsib|le** *a.* responsable; (*job*) qui comporte des responsabilités. ~**ility** *n.* responsabilité *f.*

**rest**[1] *v.t./i.* (se) reposer; (*lean*) (s')appuyer (**on,** sur); (*be buried, lie*) reposer. ● *n.* (*repose*) repos *m.*; (*support*) support *m.* **have a** ~, se reposer; (*at work*) prendre une pause.

**rest**[2] *v.i.* (*remain*) demeurer. ● *n.* (*remainder*) reste *m.* (**of,** de). **the** ~ (**of the**), (*others, other*) les autres.

**restaurant** *n.* restaurant *m.*

**restful** *a.* reposant.

**restive** *a.* rétif.

**restless** *a.* agité. ~**ly** *adv.* avec agitation, fébrilement.

**restor|e** *v.t.* rétablir; (*building*) restaurer. ~**e sth. to s.o.,** restituer qch. à qn. ~**ation** *n.* rétablissement *m.*; restauration *f.* ~**er** *n.* (*art*) restaura|teur, -trice *m., f.*

**restrain** *v.t.* contenir. ~ **s.o. from,** retenir qn. de. ~**ed** *a.* (*moderate*) mesuré; (*in control of self*) maître de soi. ~**t** *n.* contrainte *f.*; (*moderation*) retenue *f.*

**restrict** *v.t.* restreindre. ~**ion** *n.* restriction *f.*

**result** *n.* résultat *m.* ● *v.i.* résulter. ~ **in,** aboutir à.

**resum|e** *v.t./i.* reprendre. ~**ption** *n.* reprise *f.*

**resurgence** *n.* réapparition *f.*

**resurrect** *v.t.* ressusciter. ~**ion** *n.* résurrection *f.*

**resuscitate** *v.t.* réanimer.

**retail** *n.* détail *m.* ● *a.* & *adv.* au détail. ● *v.t./i.* (se) vendre (au détail). ~**er** *n.* détaillant(e) *m.* (*f.*).

**retain** *v.t.* (*hold back, remember*) retenir; (*keep*) conserver.

**retaliat|e** *v.i.* riposter. ~**ion** *n.* représailles *f. pl.*

**retch** *v.i.* avoir un haut-le-cœur.

**reticen|t** *a.* réticent. ~**ce** *n.* réticence *f.*

**retina** *n.* rétine *f.*

**retire** *v.i.* (*from work*) prendre sa retraite; (*withdraw*) se retirer; (*go to bed*) se coucher. ● *v.t.* mettre à la retraite. ~**d** *a.* retraité. ~**ment** *n.* retraite *f.*

**retiring** *a.* réservé.

**retort** *v.t./i.* répliquer. ● *n.* réplique *f.*

**retract** *v.t./i.* (se) rétracter.

**retrain** *v.t./i.* (se) recycler.

**retread** *n.* pneu rechapé *m.*

**retreat** *v.i.* (*mil.*) battre en retraite. ● *n.* retraite *f.*

**retribution** *n.* châtiment *m.*; (*vengeance*) vengeance *f.*

**retriev|e** *v.t.* (*recover*) récupérer; (*restore*) rétablir; (*put right*) réparer. ~**er** *n.* (*dog*) chien d'arrêt *m.*

**retrospect** *n.* **in** ~, rétrospectivement.

**return** *v.i.* (*come back*) revenir; (*go back*) retourner; (*go home*) rentrer. ● *v.t.* (*give back*) rendre; (*bring back*) rapporter; (*send back*) renvoyer; (*put back*) remettre. ● *n.* retour *m.*; (*yield*) rapport *m.* **in** ~ **for,** en échange de. ~ **ticket,** aller-retour *m.*

**reunion** *n.* réunion *f.*

**reunite** *v.t.* réunir.

**rev** *n.* (*auto., fam.*) tour *m.* ● *v.t./i.* ~ **(up),** (*engine: fam.*) (s')emballer.

**revamp** *v.t.* rénover.

**reveal** *v.t.* révéler; (*allow to appear*) laisser voir. ~**ing** *a.* révélateur.

**revel** *v.i.* faire bombance. ~ **in,** se délecter de.

**revelation** *n.* révélation *f.*

**revenge** *n.* vengeance *f.*; (*sport*) revanche *f.* ● *v.t.* venger.

**revenue** *n.* revenu *m.*

**reverberate** *v.i.* se répercuter.

**revere** *v.t.* révérer. ~**nce** *n.* vénération *f.*

**reverend** *a.* révérend.

**revers|e** *a.* contraire, inverse. ● *n.* contraire *m.*; (*back*) revers *m.*, envers *m.*; (*gear*) marche arrière. ● *v.t.* (*situation*) renverser; (*order*) inverser; (*decision*) annuler. ● *v.i.* faire marche arrière. ~**al** *n.* renversement *m.*; (*of view*) revirement *m.*

**review** *n.* (*inspection, magazine*) revue *f.*; (*of book etc.*) critique *f.* ● *v.t.* passer en revue; (*situation*) réexaminer; faire la critique de. ~**er** *n.* critique *m.*

**revis|e** *v.t.* réviser; (*text*) revoir. ~**ion** *n.* révision *f.*

**revive** *v.t.* (*person, hopes*) ranimer; (*play*) reprendre; (*custom*) rétablir. ● *v.i.* se ranimer.

**revolt** *v.t./i.* (se) révolter. ● *n.* révolte *f.* ~**ing** *a.* dégoûtant.

**revolution** *n.* révolution *f.* ~**ary** *a.* & *n.* révolutionnaire (*m./f.*).

**revolve** *v.i.* tourner.

**revolver** *n.* revolver *m.*

**revulsion** *n.* dégoût *m.*

**reward** *n.* récompense *f.* ● *v.t.* récompenser (**for,** de).

**rewind** *v.t.* (*tape, film*) rembobiner.

**rheumatism** *n.* rhumatisme *m.*

**rhinoceros** *n.* rhinocéros *m.*

**rhubarb** *n.* rhubarbe *f.*

**rhyme** *n.* rime *f.*; (*poem*) vers *m. pl.* ● *v.t./i.* (faire) rimer.

**rhythm** *n.* rythme *m.*

**rib** *n.* côte *f.*

**ribbon** *n.* ruban *m.*

**rice** *n.* riz *m.*

**rich** *a.* riche.

**ricochet** *n.* ricochet *m.* ● *v.i.* ricocher.

**rid** *v.t.* débarrasser (**of,** de). **get** ~ **of,** se débarrasser de.

**riddle** *n.* énigme *f.*

**ride** *v.i.* aller (à bicyclette, à cheval, *etc.*); (*in car*) rouler. ~ **(a horse),** (*go riding as sport*) monter (à cheval). ● *v.t.* (*a particular horse*) monter; (*distance*) parcourir. ● *n.* promenade *f.*, tour *m.*; (*distance*) trajet *m.* ~**r** *n.* caval|ier, -ière *m., f.*; (*in horse race*) jockey *m.*; (*cyclist*) cycliste *m./f.*; (*motorcyclist*) motocycliste *m./f.*; (*in document*) annexe *f.*

**ridge** *n.* arête *f.*, crête *f.*

**ridicule** *v.t.* ridiculiser.

**ridiculous** *a.* ridicule.

**riding** *n.* équitation *f.*

**rifle** *n.* fusil *m.* ● *v.t.* (*rob*) dévaliser.

**rift** *n.* (*crack*) fissure *f.*; (*between people*) désaccord *m.*

**rig**[1] *v.t.* (*equip*) équiper. ● *n.* (*for oil*) derrick *m.*

**rig**[2] *v.t.* (*election*) truquer.

**right** *a.* (*morally*) bon; (*fair*) juste; (*best*) bon, qu'il faut; (*not left*) droit. **be** ~, (*person*) avoir raison (**to,** de); (*calculation, watch*) être exact. ● *n.* (*entitlement*) droit *m.*; (*not left*) droite *f.*; (*not evil*) le bien. ● *v.t.* (*a wrong, sth. fallen, etc.*) redresser. ● *adv.* (*not left*) à droite; (*directly*) tout droit; (*exactly*) bien, juste; (*completely*) tout (à fait). **on the** ~, à droite. **put** ~, arranger. ~ **away,** tout de suite. ~**hand** *a.* à or de droite. ~ **now,** (*at once*) tout de suite; (*at present*) en ce moment. ~**wing** *a.* (*pol.*) de droite.

**rightly** *adv.* correctement; (*with reason*) à juste titre.

**rigid** *a.* rigide. ~**ity** *n.* rigidité *f.*

**rig|our** *n.* rigueur *f.* ~**orous** *a.* rigoureux.

**rim** *n.* bord *m.*; (*of wheel*) jante *f.* ~**med** *a.* bordé.

**rind** *n.* (*on cheese*) croûte *f.*; (*on bacon*) couenne *f.*; (*on fruit*) écorce *f.*

**ring**[1] *n.* anneau *m.*; (*with stone*) bague *f.*; (*circle*) cercle *m.*; (*boxing*) ring *m.*; (*arena*) piste *f.* ● *v.t.* entourer; (*word in text etc.*) entourer d'un cercle. **(wedding)** ~, alliance *f.* ~ **road,** périphérique *m.*

**ring**[2] *v.t./i.* sonner; (*of words etc.*) retentir. ● *n.* sonnerie *f.* **give s.o. a** ~, donner un coup de fil à qn. ~ **back,** rappeler. ~ **up,** téléphoner (à).

**rink** *n.* patinoire *f.*

**rinse** *v.t.* rincer. **~ out,** rincer. ● *n.* rinçage *m.*

**riot** *n.* émeute *f.*; (*of colours*) orgie *f.* ● *v.i.* faire une émeute. **run ~,** se déchaîner. **~er** *n.* émeut|ier, -ière *m.*, *f.*

**rip** *v.t./i.* (se) déchirer. ● *n.* déchirure *f.* **~ off,** (*sl.*) rouler. **~-off** *n.* (*sl.*) vol *m.*

**ripe** *a.* mûr.

**ripen** *v.t./i.* mûrir.

**ripple** *n.* ride *f.*, ondulation *f.*; (*sound*) murmure *m.* ● *v.t./i.* (*water*) (se) rider.

**rise** *v.i.* (*go upwards, increase*) monter, s'élever; (*stand up, get up from bed*) se lever; (*rebel*) se soulever; (*sun, curtain*) se lever; (*water*) monter. ● *n.* (*slope*) pente *f.*; (*of curtain*) lever *m.*; (*increase*) hausse *f.*; (*in pay*) augmentation *f.*; (*progress, boom*) essor *m.* **give ~ to,** donner lieu à.

**rising** *n.* (*revolt*) soulèvement *m.* ● *a.* (*increasing*) croissant; (*price*) qui monte; (*tide*) montant; (*sun*) levant.

**risk** *n.* risque *m.* ● *v.t.* risquer. **at ~,** menacé. **~-doing,** (*venture*) se risquer à faire. **~y** *a.* risqué.

**rissole** *n.* croquette *f.*

**rite** *n.* rite *m.*

**ritual** *a.* & *n.* rituel (*m.*).

**rival** *n.* rival(e) *m.* (*f.*). ● *a.* rival; (*claim*) opposé. ● *v.t.* rivaliser avec. **~ry** *n.* rivalité *f.*

**river** *n.* rivière *f.*; (*flowing into sea & fig.*) fleuve *m.*.

**rivet** *n.* (*bolt*) rivet *m.* ● *v.t.* riveter. **~ing** *a.* fascinant.

**road** *n.* route *f.*; (*in town*) rue *f.*; (*small*) chemin *m.* ● *a.* (*sign, safety*) routier. **~-block** *n.* barrage routier *m.* **~-map** *n.* carte routière *f.* **~-works** *n. pl.* travaux *m. pl.*

**roadway** *n.* chaussée *f.*

**roam** *v.i.* errer. ● *v.t.* (*streets, seas, etc.*) parcourir.

**roar** *n.* hurlement *m.*; rugissement *m.*; grondement *m.* ● *v.t./i.* hurler; (*of lion, wind*) rugir; (*of lorry, thunder*) gronder.

**roast** *v.t./i.* rôtir. ● *n.* (*roast or roasting meat*) rôti *m.* ● *a.* rôti. **~ beef,** rôti de bœuf *m.*

**rob** *v.t.* voler (**s.o. of sth.**), qch. à qn.); (*bank, house*) dévaliser; (*deprive*) priver (**of,** de). **~ber** *n.* voleu|r, -se *m.*, *f.* **~bery** *n.* vol *m.*

**robe** *n.* (*of judge etc.*) robe *f.*; (*dressing-gown*) peignoir *m.*

**robin** *n.* rouge-gorge *m.*

**robot** *n.* robot *m.*

**robust** *a.* robuste.

**rock**¹ *n.* roche *f.*; (*rock face, boulder*) rocher *m.*; (*hurled stone*) pierre *f.*; (*sweet*) sucre d'orge *m.* **~-climbing** *n.* varappe *f.*

**rock**² *v.t./i.* (se) balancer; (*shake*) (faire) trembler; (*child*) bercer. ● *n.* (*mus.*) rock *m.* **~ing-chair** *n.* fauteuil à bascule *m.*

**rocket** *n.* fusée *f.*

**rocky** *a.* (*ground*) rocailleux; (*hill*) rocheux; (*shaky: fig.*) branlant.

**rod** *n.* (*metal*) tige *f.*; (*for curtain*) tringle *f.*; (*wooden*) baguette *f.*; (*for fishing*) canne à pêche *f.*

**rodent** *n.* rongeur *m.*

**roe**¹ *n.* œufs de poisson *m. pl.*

**roe**² *n.* (*deer*) chevreuil *m.*

**rogue** *n.* (*mischievous*) coquin(e) *m.* (*f.*).

**role** *n.* rôle *m.*

**roll** *v.t./i.* rouler. **~ (about),** (*child, dog*) se rouler. ● *n.* rouleau *m.*; (*list*) liste *f.*; (*bread*) petit pain *m.*; (*of drum, thunder*) roulement *m.*; (*of ship*) roulis *m.* **~-bar** *n.* arceau de sécurité *m.* **~ing-pin** *n.* rouleau à pâtisserie *m.* **~ over,** (*turn over*) se retourner.

**roller** *n.* rouleau *m.* **~-blind** *n.* store *m.* **~-skate** *n.* patin à roulettes *m.*

**ROM** (*abbr.*) (*read-only memory*) mémoire morte *f.*

**Roman** *a.* & *n.* romain(e) (*m.* (*f.*)). **~ Catholic** *a.* & *n.* catholique (*m./f.*). **~ numerals,** chiffres romains *m. pl.*

**romance** *n.* roman d'amour *m.*; (*love*) amour *m.*; (*affair*) idylle *f.*; (*fig.*) poésie *f.*

**Romania** *n.* Roumanie *f.* **~n** *a.* & *n.* roumain(e) (*m.* (*f.*)).

**romantic** *a.* (*of love etc.*) romantique; (*of the imagination*) romanesque.

**romp** *v.i.* s'ébattre; (*fig.*) réussir. ● *n.* **have a ~,** s'ébattre.

**roof** *n.* toit *m.*; (*of tunnel*) plafond *m.*; (*of mouth*) palais *m.* ● *v.t.* recouvrir. **~-rack** *n.* galerie *f.*

**rook**¹ *n.* (*bird*) corneille *f.*

**rook**² *n.* (*chess*) tour *f.*

**room** *n.* pièce *f.*; (*bedroom*) chambre *f.*; (*large hall*) salle *f.*; (*space*) place *f.*

**roost** *n.* perchoir *m.* ● *v.i.* percher. **~er** *n.* coq *m.*

**root**¹ *n.* racine *f.*; (*source*) origine *f.* ● *v.t./i.* (s')enraciner. **~out,** extirper.

**root**² *v.i.* **~ about,** fouiller. **~ for,** (*Amer., fam.*) encourager.

**rope** *n.* corde *f.*

**rosary** *n.* chapelet *m.*

**rose**¹ *n.* (*flower*) rose *f.*; (*colour*) rose *m.*; (*nozzle*) pomme *f.*

**roster** *n.* liste (de service) *f.*

**rostrum** *n.* tribune *f.*; (*sport*) podium *m.*

**rosy** *a.* rose; (*hopeful*) plein d'espoir.

**rot** *v.t./i.* pourrir. ● *n.* pourriture *f.*

**rota** *n.* liste (de service) *f.*

**rotary** *a.* rotatif.

**rotat|e** *v.t./i.* (faire) tourner; (*change round*) alterner. **~ing** *a.* tournant. **~ion** *n.* rotation *f.*

**rotten** *a.* pourri; (*tooth*) gâté; (*bad: fam.*) mauvais, sale.

**rouge** *n.* rouge (à joues) *m.*

**rough** a. (*manners*) rude; (*to touch*) rugueux; (*ground*) accidenté; (*violent*) brutal; (*bad*) mauvais; (*estimate etc.*) approximatif; (*diamond*) brut. ● v.t. ~ **it,** vivre à la dure. ~**-and-ready** a. (*solution etc.*) grossier (mais efficace). ~**and-tumble** a. mêlée f. ~ **out,** ébaucher. ~**ly** adv. rudement; (*approximately*) à peu près. ~**ness** n. rudesse f.; brutalité f.

**roughage** n. fibres (alimentaires) f. pl.

**roulette** n. roulette f.

**round** a. rond. ● n. (*circle*) rond m.; (*slice*) tranche f.; (*of visits, drinks*) tournée f.; (*mil.*) ronde f.; (*competition*) partie f., manche f.; (*boxing*) round m.; (*of talks*) série f. ● prep. autour de. ● adv. autour. ● v.t. (*object*) arrondir; (*corner*) tourner. ~ **about,** (*near by*) par ici; (*fig.*) à peu près. ~ **off,** terminer. ~ **trip,** voyage aller-retour m. ~ **up,** rassembler. ~**up** n. rassemblement m.; (*of suspects*) rafle f.

**roundabout** n. manège m.; (*for traffic*) rond-point (à sens giratoire) m. ● a. indirect.

**rous|e** v.t. éveiller; (*wake up*) réveiller. **be** ~**ed,** (*angry*) être en colère. ~**ing** a. (*speech, music*) excitant; (*cheers*) frénétique.

**rout** n. (*defeat*) déroute f. ● v.t. mettre en déroute.

**route** n. itinéraire m., parcours m.; (*naut., aviat.*) route f.

**routine** n. routine f. ● a. de routine.

**rov|e** v.t./i. errer (dans). ~**ing** a. (*life*) vagabond.

**row**[1] n. rangée f., rang m. **in a** ~, (*consecutive*) consécutif.

**row**[2] v.i. ramer; (*sport*) faire de l'aviron. ● v.t. faire aller à la rame. ~**ing** n. aviron m. ~**(ing)-boat** n. bateau à rames m.

**row**[3] n. (*noise: fam.*) tapage m.; (*quarrel: fam.*) engueulade f.

**rowdy** a. tapageur.

**royal** a. royal.

**royalt|y** n. famille royale f. ~**ies,** droits d'auteur m. pl.

**rub** v.t./i. frotter. ● n. friction f. ~ **out,** (s')effacer.

**rubber** n. caoutchouc m.; (*eraser*) gomme f. ~**band,** élastique m. ~ **stamp,** tampon m. ~ **stamp** v.t. approuver. ~**y** a. caoutchouteux.

**rubbish** n. (*refuse*) ordures f. pl.; (*junk*) saletés f. pl.; (*fig.*) bêtises f. pl. ~**y** a. sans valeur.

**rubble** n. décombres m. pl.

**ruby** n. rubis m.

**rucksack** n. sac à dos m.

**rudder** n. gouvernail m.

**ruddy** a. coloré, rougeâtre; (*damned: sl.*) fichu.

**rude** a. impoli, grossier; (*improper*) indécent; (*shock, blow*) brutal. ~**ly** adv. impoliment. ~**ness** n. impolitesse f.; indécence f.; brutalité f.

**ruffian** n. voyou m.

**ruffle** v.t. (*hair*) ébouriffer; (*clothes*) froisser; (*person*) contrarier. ● n. (*frill*) ruche f.

**rug** n. petit tapis m.

**Rugby** n. ~ **(football),** rugby m.

**rugged** a. (*surface*) rude, rugueux; (*ground*) accidenté; (*character, features*) rude.

**ruin** n. ruine f. ● v.t. (*destroy*) ruiner; (*damage*) abîmer; (*spoil*) gâter.

**rule** n. règle f.; (*regulation*) règlement m.; (*pol.*) gouvernement m. ● v.t. gouverner; (*master*) dominer; (*decide*) décider. ● v.i. régner. **as a** ~, en règle générale. ~ **out,** exclure. ~**r** n. dirigeant(e) m. (f.), gouvernant m.; (*measure*) règle f.

**ruling** a. (*class*) dirigeant; (*party*) au pouvoir. ● n. décision f.

**rum** n. rhum m.

**rumble** v.i. gronder; (*stomach*) gargouiller. ● n. grondement m.; gargouillement m.

**rummage** v.i. fouiller.

**rumour** n. bruit m., rumeur f.

**rump** n. (*of horse etc.*) croupe f.; (*of fowl*) croupion m.; (*steak*) romsteck m.

**run** v.i. courir; (*flow*) couler; (*pass*) passer; (*function*) marcher; (*melt*) fondre; (*extend*) s'étendre; (*of bus etc.*) circuler; (*of play*) se jouer; (*last*) durer; (*of colour in washing*) déteindre; (*in election*) être candidat. ● v.t. (*manage*) diriger; (*organize*) organiser; (*risk, race*) courir; (*house*) tenir; (*blockade*) forcer; (*temperature, errand*) faire; (*comput.*) exécuter. ● n. course f.; (*journey*) parcours m.; (*outing*) promenade f.; (*rush*) ruée f.; (*series*) série f.; (*in cricket*) point m. ~ **across,** rencontrer par hasard. ~ **away,** s'enfuir. ~ **down,** descendre en courant; (*of vehicle*) renverser; (*production*) réduire progressivement; (*belittle*) dénigrer. ~ **in,** (*vehicle*) roder. ~ **into,** (*hit*) heurter. ~ **out,** (*be used up*) s'épuiser; (*of lease*) expirer. ~ **out of,** manquer de. ~ **over,** (*of vehicle*) écraser; (*details*) revoir. ~ **through sth.,** regarder qch. rapidement. ~ **up,** (*bill*) accumuler. **the** ~**up to,** la période qui précède.

**runaway** n. fugitif f, -ve m., f. ● a. fugitif; (*horse, vehicle*) fou; (*inflation*) galopant.

**rung** n. (*of ladder*) barreau m.

**runner** n. coureu|r, -se m., f. ~ **bean,** haricot (grimpant) m. ~**up** n. second(e) m. (f.).

**running** n. course f.; (*of business*) gestion f.; (*of machine*) marche f. ● a. (*commentary*) suivi; (*water*) courant. **four days/etc.** ~, quatre jours/etc. de suite.

**runny** a. (*nose*) qui coule.

**runt** n. avorton m.

**runway** n. piste f.

**rupture** n. (*breaking, breach*) rupture f.; (*med.*) hernie f.

**rural** a. rural.

**ruse** n. (*trick*) ruse f.

**rush**[1] *n.* (*plant*) jonc *m.*

**rush**[2] *v.i.* (*move*) se précipiter; (*be in a hurry*) se dépêcher. ● *v.t.* faire, envoyer, *etc.* en vitesse; (*person*) bousculer; (*mil.*) prendre d'assaut. ● *n.* ruée *f.*; (*haste*) bousculade *f.* **in a ~**, pressé. **~-hour** *n.* heure de pointe *f.*

**rusk** *n.* biscotte *f.*

**Russia** *n.* Russie *f.* **~n** *a.* & *n.* russe (*m./f.*); (*lang.*) russe *m.*

**rust** *n.* rouille *f.* ● *v.t./i.* rouiller. **~-proof** *a.* inoxydable. **~y** *a.* (*tool, person, etc.*) rouillé.

**rustic** *a.* rustique.

**rustle** *v.t./i.* (*leaves*) (faire) bruire. **~ up**, (*food etc.: fam.*) préparer.

**rut** *n.* ornière *f.* **be in a ~**, rester dans l'ornière.

**ruthless** *a.* impitoyable. **~ness** *n.* cruauté *f.*

**rye** *n.* seigle *m.*

# Ss

**sabbath** *n.* (*Jewish*) sabbat *m.*; (*Christian*) dimanche *m.*

**sabot|age** *n.* sabotage *m.* ● *v.t.* saboter. **~eur** *n.* saboteu|r, -se *m., f.*

**saccharin** *n.* saccharine *f.*

**sachet** *n.* sachet *m.*

**sack**[1] *n.* (*bag*) sac *m.* ● *v.t.* (*fam.*) renvoyer. **get the ~**, (*fam.*) être renvoyé.

**sack**[2] *v.t.* (*plunder*) saccager.

**sacrament** *n.* sacrement *m.*

**sacred** *a.* sacré.

**sacrifice** *n.* sacrifice *m.* ● *v.t.* sacrifier.

**sad** *a.* triste. **~ly** *adv.* tristement; (*unfortunately*) malheureusement.

**sadden** *v.t.* attrister.

**saddle** *n.* selle *f.* ● *v.t.* (*horse*) seller. **~ s.o. with**, (*task, person*) coller à qn.

**sadis|t** *n.* sadique *m./f.* **~m** *n.* sadisme *m.* **~tic** *a.* sadique.

**safari** *n.* safari *m.*

**safe** *a.* (*not dangerous*) sans danger; (*reliable*) sûr; (*out of danger*) en sécurité; (*after accident*) sain et sauf; (*wise: fig.*) prudent. ● *n.* coffre-fort *m.* **to be on the ~ side**, pour être sûr. **~ from**, à l'abri de. **~ly** *adv.* sans danger; (*in safe place*) en sûreté.

**safeguard** *n.* sauvegarde *f.* ● *v.t.* sauvegarder.

**safety** *n.* sécurité *f.* **~-belt** *n.* ceinture de sécurité *f.* **~-pin** *n.* épingle de sûreté *f.* **~-valve** *n.* soupape de sûreté *f.*

**saffron** *n.* safran *m.*

**sag** *v.i.* s'affaisser.

**saga** *n.* saga *f.*

**sage** *n.* (*herb*) sauge *f.*

**Sagittarius** *n.* le Sagittaire.

**sail** *n.* voile *f.*; (*journey*) tour en bateau *m.* ● *v.i.* naviguer; (*leave*) partir; (*sport*) faire de la voile; (*glide*) glisser. ● *v.t.* (*boat*) piloter.

**sailor** *n.* marin *m.*

**saint** *n.* saint(e) *m.* (*f.*).

**sake** *n.* **for the ~ of**, pour, pour l'amour de.

**salad** *n.* salade *f.* **~-dressing** *n.* vinaigrette *f.*

**salami** *n.* salami *m.*

**salary** *n.* salaire *m.*

**sale** *n.* vente *f.* **~s**, (*at reduced prices*) soldes *m. pl.* **~s assistant**, vendeu|r, -se *m., f.* **for ~**, à vendre.

**sales|man** *n.* (*in shop*) vendeur *m.*; (*traveller*) représentant *m.* **~woman** *n.* vendeuse *f.*

**saline** *a.* salin. ● *n.* sérum physiologique *m.*

**saliva** *n.* salive *f.*

**sallow** *a.* jaunâtre.

**salmon** *n. invar.* saumon *m.*

**salon** *n.* salon *m.*

**saloon** *n.* (*on ship*) salon *m.*; (*bar: Amer.*) bar *m.*, saloon *m.* **~ (car)**, berline *f.*

**salt** *n.* sel *m.* ● *a.* (*culin.*) salé; (*water*) de mer. ● *v.t.* saler. **~-cellar** *n.* salière *f.* **~y** *a.* salé.

**salute** *n.* (*mil.*) salut *m.* ● *v.t.* saluer. ● *v.i.* faire un salut.

**salvage** *n.* sauvetage *m.*; (*of waste*) récupération *f.*; (*goods*) objets sauvés *m. pl.* ● *v.t.* sauver; (*for re-use*) récupérer.

**salvation** *n.* salut *m.*

**same** *a.* même (**as**, que). ● *pron.* **the ~**, le *or* la même, les mêmes. **at the ~ time**, en même temps. **the ~ (thing)**, la même chose.

**sample** *n.* échantillon *m.*; (*of blood*) prélèvement *m.* ● *v.t.* essayer; (*food*) goûter.

**sanction** *n.* sanction *f.* ● *v.t.* sanctionner.

**sanctuary** *n.* (*relig.*) sanctuaire *m.*; (*for animals*) réserve *f.*; (*refuge*) asile *m.*

**sand** *n.* sable *m.* **~s**, (*beach*) plage *f.* ● *v.t.* sabler. **~-castle** *n.* château de sable *m.* **~-pit** *n.* bac à sable *m.*

**sandal** *n.* sandale *f.*

**sandpaper** *n.* papier de verre *m.* ● *v.t.* poncer.

**sandstone** *n.* grès *m.*

**sandwich** *n.* sandwich *m.* ● *v.t.* **~ed between**, pris en sandwich entre. **~ course**, stage de formation continue à mi-temps *m.*

**sandy** *a.* sablonneux, de sable; (*hair*) blond roux *invar.*

**sane** *a.* (*view etc.*) sain; (*person*) sain d'esprit.

**sanitary** *a.* (*clean*) hygiénique; (*system etc.*) sanitaire. **~ towel**, serviette hygiénique *f.*

**sanitation** *n.* hygiène (publique) *f.*; (*drainage etc.*) système sanitaire *m.*

**sanity** *n.* santé mentale *f.*; (*good sense: fig.*) bon sens *m.*

**sap** n. (*of plants*) sève f. ● v.t. (*undermine*) saper.

**sapphire** n. saphir m.

**sarcas|m** n. sarcasme m. **~tic** a. sarcastique.

**sardine** n. sardine f.

**Sardinia** n. Sardaigne f.

**sash** n. (*on uniform*) écharpe f.; (*on dress*) ceinture f. **~-window** n. fenêtre à guillotine f.

**satchel** n. cartable m.

**satellite** n. & a. satellite (m.). **~ dish,** antenne parabolique f.

**satin** n. satin m.

**satir|e** n. satire f. **~ical** a. satirique.

**satisfactor|y** a. satisfaisant.

**satisf|y** v.t. satisfaire; (*convince*) convaincre. **~action** n. satisfaction f. **~ying** a. satisfaisant.

**satsuma** n. mandarine f.

**saturat|e** v.t. saturer. **~ed** a. (*wet*) trempé. **~ion** n. saturation f.

**Saturday** n. samedi m.

**sauce** n. sauce f.

**saucepan** n. casserole f.

**saucer** n. soucoupe f.

**saucy** a. impertinent; (*boldly smart*) coquin.

**Saudi Arabia** n. Arabie Séoudite f.

**sauna** n. sauna m.

**saunter** v.i. flâner.

**sausage** n. saucisse f.; (*pre-cooked*) saucisson m.

**savage** a. (*fierce*) féroce; (*wild*) sauvage. ● n. sauvage m./f.

**sav|e** v.t. sauver; (*money*) économiser; (*time*) (faire) gagner; (*keep*) garder; (*prevent*) éviter (**from**, de). ● n. (*football*) arrêt m. **~ings** n. pl. économies f. pl.

**saviour** n. sauveur m.

**savour,** n. saveur f. ● v.t. savourer. **~y** a. (*tasty*) savoureux; (*culin.*) salé.

**saw** n. scie f. ● v.t. scier.

**sawdust** n. sciure f.

**saxophone** n. saxophone m.

**say** v.t./i. dire; (*prayer*) faire.

**saying** n. proverbe m.

**scab** n. (*on sore*) croûte f.; (*blackleg: fam.*) jaune m.

**scaffold** n. (*gallows*) échafaud m. **~ing** n. (*for workmen*) échafaudage m.

**scald** v.t. (*injure, cleanse*) ébouillanter. ● n. brûlure f.

**scale**[1] n. (*of fish*) écaille f.

**scale**[2] n. (*for measuring, size, etc.*) échelle f.; (*mus.*) gamme f.; (*of salaries, charges*) barème m. **on a small/*etc.* ~,** sur une petite *etc.* échelle. ● v.t. (*climb*) escalader. **~ down,** réduire (proportionnellement).

**scales** n. pl. balance f.

**scallop** n. coquille Saint-Jacques f.

**scalp** n. cuir chevelu m.

**scalpel** n. scalpel m.

**scamper** v.i. trotter.

**scampi** n. pl. gambas f. pl.

**scan** v.t. scruter; (*quickly*) parcourir; (*poetry*) scander; (*of radar*) balayer. ● n. (*ultrasound*) échographie f.

**scandal** n. (*disgrace, outrage*) scandale m.; (*gossip*) cancans m. pl. **~ous** a. scandaleux.

**scandalize** v.t. scandaliser.

**Scandinavia** n. Scandinavie f. **~n** a. & n. scandinave (m./f.).

**scant** a. insuffisant.

**scant|y** a. insuffisant; (*clothing*) sommaire. **~ily dressed,** à peine vêtu.

**scapegoat** n. bouc émissaire m.

**scar** n. cicatrice f. ● v.t. marquer d'une cicatrice; (*fig.*) marquer.

**scarc|e** a. rare. **~ity** n. rareté f., pénurie f.

**scarcely** adv. à peine.

**scare** v.t. faire peur à. ● n. peur f. **be ~d,** avoir peur.

**scarecrow** n. épouvantail m.

**scarf** n. écharpe f.; (*over head*) foulard m.

**scarlet** a. écarlate. **~ fever,** scarlatine f.

**scary** a. (*fam.*) effrayant.

**scathing** a. cinglant.

**scatter** v.t. (*throw*) éparpiller, répandre; (*disperse*) disperser. ● v.i. se disperser.

**scavenge** v.i. fouiller (dans les ordures).

**scenario** n. scénario m.

**scene** n. scène f.; (*of accident, crime*) lieu(x) m. (pl.); (*sight*) spectacle m.; (*incident*) incident m.

**scenery** n. paysage m.; (*theatre*) décor(s) m. pl.

**scenic** a. pittoresque.

**scent** n. (*perfume*) parfum m.; (*trail*) piste f. ● v.t. flairer; (*make fragrant*) parfumer.

**sceptic** n. sceptique m./f. **~al** a. sceptique. **~ism** n. scepticisme m.

**schedule** n. horaire m.; (*for job*) planning m. ● v.t. prévoir. **behind ~,** en retard. **on ~,** (*train*) à l'heure; (*work*) dans les temps. **~d flight,** vol régulier m.

**scheme** n. plan m.; (*dishonest*) combine f.; (*fig.*) arrangement m. ● v.i. intriguer. **pension ~,** caisse de retraite f.

**schizophrenic** a. & n. schizophrène (m./f.).

**scholar** n. érudit(e) m. (f.). **~ship** n. érudition f.; (*grant*) bourse f.

**school** n. école f.; (*secondary*) lycée m. ● a. (*age, year, holidays*) scolaire.

**school|boy** n. écolier m. **~girl** n. écolière f.

**school|master ~mistress, ~teacher** ns. (*primary*) institu|teur, -trice m., f.; (*secondary*) professeur m.

**sciatica** n. sciatique f.

**scien|ce** n. science f. **~ce fiction,** science-fiction f. **~tific** a. scientifique.

**scientist** n. scientifique m./f.

**scissors** n. pl. ciseaux m. pl.

**scold** v.t. réprimander. **~ing** n. réprimande f.

**scoop** n. (for grain, sugar) pelle (à main) f.; (for food) cuiller f.; (icecream) boule f.; (news) exclusivité f. **~ out,** creuser. **~ up,** ramasser.

**scooter** n. (child's) trottinette f.; (motor cycle) scooter m.

**scope** n. étendue f.; (competence) compétence f.; (opportunity) possibilité(s) f. (pl.).

**scorch** v.t. brûler, roussir. **~ing** a. brûlant, très chaud.

**score** n. score m.; (mus.) partition f. ● v.t. marquer; (success) remporter. ● v.i. marquer un point; (football) marquer un but; (keep score) compter les points. **a ~ (of),** (twenty) vingt. **~board** n. tableau m.

**scorn** n. mépris m. ● v.t. mépriser. **~ful** a. méprisant.

**Scorpio** n. le Scorpion.

**scorpion** n. scorpion m.

**Scot** n. Écossais(e) m. (f.). **~tish** a. écossais.

**Scotch** a. écossais. ● n. whisky m., scotch m.

**scotch** v.t. mettre fin à.

**Scotland** n. Écosse f.

**Scots** a. écossais. **~man** n. Écossais m. **~woman** n. Écossaise f.

**scour**[1] v.t. (pan) récurer. **~er** n. tampon à récurer m.

**scour**[2] v.t. (search) parcourir.

**scourge** n. fléau m.

**scout** n. (mil.) éclaireur m. ● v.i. **~ around (for),** chercher.

**Scout** n. (boy) scout m.

**scowl** n. air renfrogné m. ● v.i. faire la tête (**at,** à).

**scraggy** a. efflanqué.

**scram** v.i. (sl.) se tirer.

**scramble** v.i. (clamber) grimper. ● v.t. (eggs) brouiller. ● n. bousculade f., ruée f. **~ for,** se bousculer pour avoir.

**scrap**[1] n. petit morceau m. **~s,** (of metal, fabric, etc.) déchets m. pl.; (of food) restes m. pl. ● v.t. mettre au rebut; (plan etc.) abandonner. **~paper** n. brouillon m. **~py** a. fragmentaire.

**scrap**[2] n. (fight: fam.) bagarre f.

**scrape** v.t. racler, gratter; (graze) érafler. ● v.i. (rub) frotter. ● n. raclement m.; éraflure f. **~ through,** réussir de justesse.

**scratch** v.t./i. (se) gratter; (with claw, nail) griffer; (graze) érafler; (mark) rayer. ● n. éraflure f. **start from ~,** partir de zéro.

**scrawl** n. gribouillage m. ● v.t./i. gribouiller.

**scrawny** a. décharné.

**scream** v.t./i. crier, hurler. ● n. cri (perçant) m.

**scree** n. éboulis m.

**screech** v.i. (scream) hurler; (of brakes) grincer. ● n. hurlement m.; grincement m.

**screen** n. écran m.; (folding) paravent m. ● v.t. masquer; (protect) protéger; (film) projeter; (candidates) filtrer; (med.) faire subir un test de dépistage. **~ing** n. projection f.

**screw** n. vis f. ● v.t. visser.

**screwdriver** n. tournevis m.

**scribble** v.t./i. griffonner.

**scribe** n. scribe m.

**script** n. écriture f.; (of film) scénario m.; (of play) texte m. **~-writer** n. scénariste m./f.

**Scriptures** n. pl. **the ~,** l'Écriture (sainte) f.

**scroll** n. rouleau m. ● v.t./i. (comput.) (faire) défiler.

**scrounge** v.t. (meal) se faire payer; (steal) chiper. ● v.i. (beg) quémander. **~ money from,** taper. **~r** n. parasite m.; (of money) tapeu|r, -se m., f.

**scrub**[1] n. (land) broussailles f. pl.

**scrub**[2] v.t./i. nettoyer (à la brosse)

**scruffy** a. (fam.) sale.

**scrum** n. (Rugby) mêlée f.

**scruple** n. scrupule m.

**scrupulous** a. scrupuleux. **~ly clean,** impeccable.

**scrutin|y** n. examen minutieux m. **~ize** v.t. scruter.

**scuba-diving** n. plongée sous-marine f.

**scuffle** n. bagarre f.

**sculpt** v.t./i. sculpter. **~or** n. sculpteur m. **~ure** n. sculpture f.; v.t./i. sculpter.

**scum** n. (on liquid) écume f.; (people: pej.) racaille f.

**scurf** n. pellicules f. pl.

**scythe** n. faux f.

**sea** n. mer f. ● a. de (la) mer, marin. **at ~,** en mer. **by ~,** par mer. **~-level** n. niveau de la mer m. **~shore** n. rivage m.

**seafood** n. fruits de mer m. pl.

**seagull** n. mouette f.

**seal**[1] n. (animal) phoque m.

**seal**[2] n. sceau m.; (with wax) cachet m. ● v.t. sceller; cacheter; (stick down) coller. **~ing-wax** n. cire à cacheter f. **~ off,** (area) boucler.

**seam** n. (in cloth etc.) couture f.; (of coal) veine f.

**seaman** n. marin m.

**seance** n. séance de spiritisme f.

**search** v.t./i. fouiller; (study) examiner. ● n. fouille f.; (quest) recherche(s) f. (pl.). **in ~ of,** à la recherche de. **~ for,** chercher. **~ing** a. (piercing) pénétrant.

**searchlight** n. projecteur m.

**seasick** a. **be ~,** avoir le mal de mer.

**seaside** n. bord de la mer m.

**season** n. saison f. ● v.t. assaisonner. **in ~,** de saison. **~ing** n. assaisonnement m. **~-ticket** n. carte d'abonnement f.

**seasoned** *a.* expérimenté.

**seat** *n.* siège *m.*; (*place*) place *f.*; (*of trousers*) fond *m.* ● *v.t.* (*put*) placer; (*have seats for*) avoir des places assises pour. **take a ~,** s'asseoir. **~belt** *n.* ceinture de sécurité *f.*

**seaweed** *n.* algues *f. pl.*

**secateurs** *n. pl.* sécateur *m.*

**seclu|de** *v.t.* isoler. **~ded** *a.* isolé. **~sion** *n.* solitude *f.*

**second¹** *a.* deuxième, second. ● *n.* deuxième *m./f.*; (*unit of time*) seconde *f.* **~-class** *a.* de deuxième classe. **at ~ hand,** de seconde main. **~-hand** *a. & adv.* d'occasion; *n.* (*on clock*) trotteuse *f.* **~-rate** *a.* médiocre.

**second²** *v.t.* (*transfer*) détacher (**to,** à).

**secondary** *a.* secondaire. **~ school,** lycée *m.*

**secrecy** *n.* secret *m.*

**secret** *a.* secret. ● *n.* secret *m.* **in ~,** en secret. **~ly** *adv.* en secret, secrètement.

**secretary** *n.* secrétaire *m./f.* **S~y of State,** ministre *m.*; (*Amer.*) ministre des Affaires étrangères *m.*

**secret|e²** *v.t.* (*med.*) sécréter. **~ion** *n.* sécrétion *f.*

**secretive** *a.* cachottier.

**sect** *n.* secte *f.* **~arian** *a.* sectaire.

**section** *n.* section *f.*; (*of country, town*) partie *f.*; (*in store*) rayon *m.*; (*newspaper column*) rubrique *f.*

**sector** *n.* secteur *m.*

**secular** *a.* (*school etc.*) laïque; (*art, music, etc.*) profane.

**secure** *a.* (*safe*) en sûreté; (*in mind*) tranquille; (*psychologically*) sécurisé; (*firm*) solide; (*against attack*) sûr; (*window etc.*) bien fermé. ● *v.t.* attacher; (*obtain*) s'assurer; (*ensure*) assurer. **~ly** *adv.* solidement; (*safely*) en sûreté.

**security** *f.* (*safety*) sécurité *f.*; (*for loan*) caution *f.* **~ guard,** vigile *m.*

**sedate¹** *a.* calme.

**sedat|e²** *v.t.* donner un sédatif à. **~ion** *n.* sédation *f.*

**sedative** *n.* sédatif *m.*

**sediment** *n.* sédiment *m.*

**seduce** *v.t.* séduire. **~r** *n.* séduc|teur, -trice *m., f.*

**seduct|ion** *n.* séduction *f.* **~ive** *a.* séduisant.

**see** *v.t./i.* voir; (*escort*) (r)accompagner. **~ about** *or* **to,** s'occuper de. **see you (soon)!,** à bientôt! **~ing that,** vu que.

**seed** *n.* graine *f.*; (*collectively*) graines *f. pl.*; (*origin: fig.*) germe *m.*; (*tennis*) tête de série *f.*

**seedy** *a.* miteux.

**seek** *v.t.* chercher. **~ out,** aller chercher.

**seem** *v.i.* sembler.

**seep** *v.i.* (*ooze*) suinter. **~ into,** s'infiltrer dans.

**see-saw** *n.* balançoire *f.*, tape-cul *m.* ● *v.t.* osciller.

**seethe** *v.i.* **~ with,** (*anger*) bouillir de; (*people*) grouiller de.

**segment** *n.* segment *m.*; (*of orange*) quartier *m.*

**segregat|e** *v.t.* séparer. **~ion** *n.* ségréga-tion *f.*

**seize** *v.t.* saisir; (*take possession of*) s'emparer de. ● *v.i.* **~ on,** (*chance etc.*) saisir.

**seizure** *n.* (*med.*) crise *f.*

**seldom** *adv.* rarement.

**select** *v.t.* choisir, sélectionner. ● *a.* choisi; (*exclusive*) sélect. **~ion** *n.* sélection *f.*

**selective** *a.* sélectif.

**self** *n.* (*on cheque*) moi-même. **the ~,** le moi *m. invar.*

**self-** *pref.* **~assurance** *n.* assurance *f.* **~assured** *a.* sûr de soi. **~catering** *a.* où l'on fait la cuisine soi-même. **~centred** *a.* égocentrique. **~coloured** *a.* uni. **~confidence** *f.* confiance en soi *f.* **~confident** *a.* sûr de soi. **~conscious** *a.* gêné, timide. **~contained** *a.* (*flat*) indépendant. **~control** *n.* maîtrise de soi *f.* **~defence** *n.* autodéfense *f.*; (*jurid.*) légitime défense *f.* **~respect** *n.* respect de soi *m.*, dignité *f.* **~service** *n. & a.* libre-service (*m.*). **~sufficient** *a.* indépendant.

**selfish** *a.* égoïste; (*motive*) intéressé. **~ness** *n.* égoïsme *m.*

**sell** *v.t./i.* (*se*) vendre. **~-by date,** date limite de vente *f.* **be sold out of,** n'avoir plus de. **~er** *n.* vendeu|r, -se *m., f.*

**Sellotape** *n.* (P.) scotch *m.* (P.).

**semantic** *a.* sémantique. **~s** *n.* sémantique *f.*

**semen** *n.* sperme *m.*

**semi-** *pref.* semi-, demi-.

**semibreve** *n.* (*mus.*) ronde *f.*

**semicirc|le** *n.* demi-cercle *m.* **~ular** *a.* en demi-cercle.

**semicolon** *n.* point-virgule *m.*

**semiconductor** *n.* semi-conducteur *n.*

**semi-detached** *a.* **~ house,** maison jumelle *f.*

**semifinal** *n.* demi-finale *f.*

**seminar** *n.* séminaire *m.*

**seminary** *n.* séminaire *m.*

**semiquaver** *n.* (*mus.*) double croche *f.*

**semolina** *n.* semoule *f.*

**senat|e** *n.* sénat *m.* **~or** *n.* sénateur *m.*

**send** *v.t./i.* envoyer. **~ away,** (*dismiss*) renvoyer. **~ back,** renvoyer. **~ for,** (*person, help*) envoyer chercher. **~er** *n.* expédi|teur, -trice *m., f.*

**senil|e** *a.* sénile. **~ity** *n.* sénilité *f.*

**senior** *a.* plus âgé (**to,** que); (*in rank*) supérieur; (*teacher, partner*) principal. ● *n.* aîné(e) *m.* (*f.*); (*schol.*) grand(e) *m.* (*f.*). **~ citizen,** personne âgée *f.*

**sensation** *n.* sensation *f.* **~al** *a.* (*event*) qui fait sensation; (*wonderful*) sensationnel.

**sense** *n.* sens *m.*; (*sensation*) sensation *f.*; (*mental impression*) sentiment *m.*; (*common sense*) bon sens *m.* **~s,** (*mind*) raison *f.* ● *v.t.* (*pres*)sentir. **make ~,** avoir du sens.

**sensibilit|y** *n.* sensibilité *f.* **~ies,** suscepti-bilité *f.*

**sensible** *a.* raisonnable, sensé; (*clothing*) fonctionnel.

**sensitiv|e** *a.* sensible (**to,** à); (*touchy*) susceptible. **~ity** *n.* sensibilité *f.*

**sensual** *a.* sensuel. **~ity** *n.* sensualité *f.*

**sensuous** *a.* sensuel.

**sentence** *n.* phrase *f.*; (*decision: jurid.*) jugement *m.*, condamnation *f.*; (*punishment*) peine *f.* ● *v.t.* **~ to,** condamner à.

**sentiment** *n.* sentiment *m.*

**sentimental** *a.* sentimental.

**sentry** *n.* sentinelle *f.*

**separate¹** *a.* séparé, différent; (*independent*) indépendant. **~s** *n. pl.* coordonnés *m. pl.* **~ly** *adv.* séparément.

**separat|e²** *v.t./i.* (se) séparer. **~ion** *n.* séparation *f.*

**September** *n.* septembre *m.*

**septic** *a.* (*wound*) infecté. **~ tank,** fosse septique *f.*

**sequel** *n.* suite *f.*

**sequence** *n.* (*order*) ordre *m.*; (*series*) suite *f.*; (*of film*) séquence *f.*

**sequin** *n.* paillette *f.*

**serene** *a.* serein.

**sergeant** *n.* (*mil.*) sergent *m.*; (*policeman*) brigadier *m.*

**serial** *n.* (*story*) feuilleton *m.* ● *a.* (*number*) de série.

**series** *n. invar.* série *f.*

**serious** *a.* sérieux; (*very bad, critical*) grave, sérieux. **~ly** *adv.* sérieusement, gravement.

**sermon** *n.* sermon *m.*

**serpent** *n.* serpent *m.*

**serrated** *a.* (*edge*) en dents de scie.

**serum** *n.* sérum *m.*

**servant** *n.* domestique *m./f.*; (*of God etc.*) serviteur *m.*

**serve** *v.t./i.* servir; (*undergo, carry out*) faire; (*of transport*) desservir. ● *n.* (*tennis*) service *m.*

**service** *n.* service *m.*; (*maintenance*) révi-sion *f.*; (*relig.*) office *m.* **~s,** (*mil.*) forces armées *f. pl.* ● *v.t.* (*car etc.*) réviser. **of ~ to,** utile à. **~ area,** (*auto.*) aire de services *f.* **~ charge,** service *m.* **~ station,** station-service *f.*

**serviceable** *a.* (*usable*) utilisable; (*useful*) commode; (*durable*) solide.

**serviceman** *n.* militaire *m.*

**serviette** *n.* serviette *f.*

**servile** *a.* servile.

**session** *n.* séance *f.*; (*univ.*) année (universitaire) *f.*

**set** *v.t.* mettre; (*put down*) poser, mettre; (*limit etc.*) fixer; (*watch, clock*) régler; (*example, task*) donner; (*for printing*) composer; (*in plaster*) plâtrer. ● *v.i.* (*of sun*) se coucher; (*of jelly*) prendre. ● *n.* (*of chairs, stamps, etc.*) série *f.*; (*of knives, keys, etc.*) jeu *m.*; (*of people*) groupe *m.*; (*TV, radio*) poste *m.*; (*style of hair*) mise en plis *f.*; (*theatre*) décor *m.*; (*tennis*) set *m.*; (*mathematics*) ensemble *m.* ● *a.* fixe; (*in habits*) régulier; (*meal*) à prix fixe; (*book*) au programme. **~ against sth.,** opposé à. **~ about or to,** se mettre à. **~back** *n.* revers *m.* **~in,** (*take hold*) s'installer, commencer. **~off or out,** partir. **~ off,** (*mechanism, activity*) déclencher; (*bomb*) faire éclater. **~ out,** (*state*) exposer; (*arrange*) disposer. **~ out to do sth.,** entreprendre de faire qch. **~ up,** (*establih*) lancer. **~up** *n.* (*fam.*) affaire *f.*

**settee** *n.* canapé *m.*

**setting** *n.* cadre *m.*

**settle** *v.t.* (*arrange, pay*) régler; (*date*) fixer; (*nerves*) calmer. ● *v.i.* (*come to rest*) se poser; (*live*) s'installer. **~ down,** se calmer; (*become orderly*) se ranger. **~ for,** accepter. **~ in,** s'installer. **~ up (with),** régler. **~r** *n.* colon *m.*

**settlement** *n.* règlement *m.* (**of,** de); (*agreement*) accord *m.*; (*place*) colonie *f.*

**seven** *a. & n.* sept (*m.*). **~th** *a. & n.* septième (*m./f.*).

**seventeen** *a. & n.* dix-sept (*m.*). **~th** *a. & n.* dix-septième (*m./f.*).

**sevent|y** *a. & n.* soixante-dix (*m.*). **~ieth** *a. & n.* soixante-dixième (*m./f.*).

**sever** *v.t.* (*cut*) couper; (*relations*) rompre.

**several** *a. & pron.* plusieurs.

**severe** *a.* sévère; (*violent*) violent; (*serious*) grave. **~ly** *adv.* sévèrement; gravement.

**sew** *v.t./i.* coudre. **~ing-machine** *n.* machine à coudre *f.*

**sewage** *n.* eaux d'égout *f. pl.*

**sewer** *n.* égout *m.*

**sex** *n.* sexe *m.* ● *a.* sexuel. **have ~,** avoir des rapports (sexuels). **~y** *a.* sexy *invar.*

**sexist** *a. & n.* sexiste (*m./f.*).

**sexual** *a.* sexuel. **~ intercourse,** rapports sexuels *m. pl.*

**shabb|y** *a.* (*place, object*) minable, miteux; (*person*) pauvrement vêtu; (*mean*) mesquin.

**shack** *n.* cabane *f.*

**shade** *n.* ombre *f.*; (*of colour, opinion*) nuance *f.*; (*for lamp*) abat-jour *m.* ● *v.t.* (*of person etc.*) abriter; (*of tree*) ombrager.

**shadow** *n.* ombre *f.* ● *v.t.* (*follow*) filer.

**shady** *a.* ombragé; (*dubious: fig.*) louche.

**shaft** n. (of arrow) hampe f.; (axle) arbre m.; (of mine) puits m.; (of light) rayon m.

**shaggy** a. (beard) hirsute; (hair) broussailleux; (animal) à longs poils.

**shake** v.t. secouer; (bottle) agiter; (house, belief, etc.) ébranler. ● v.i. trembler. ● n. secousse f. ~ **hands with,** serrer la main à. ~ **one's head,** (in refusal) dire non de la tête.

**shaky** a. (hand, voice) tremblant; (table etc.) branlant; (weak: fig.) faible.

**shall** v. aux. **I ~ do,** je ferai.

**shallot** n. échalote f.

**shallow** a. peu profond; (fig.) superficiel.

**sham** n. comédie f.; (person) imposteur m.; (jewel) imitation f. ● a. faux. ● v.t. feindre.

**shambles** n. pl. (mess: fam.) désordre m., pagaille f.

**shame** n. honte f. ● v.t. faire honte à. **it's a ~,** c'est dommage.

**shampoo** n. shampooing m. ● v.t. shampooiner.

**shandy** n. panaché m.

**shanty** n. (shack) baraque f. ~ **town,** bidonville m.

**shape** n. forme f. ● v.t. (fashion, mould) façonner; (future etc.: fig.) déterminer. ~**less** a. informe.

**shapely** a. bien tourné.

**share** n. part f.; (comm.) action f. ● v.t./i. partager; (feature) avoir en commun.

**shareholder** n. actionnaire m./f.

**shark** n. requin m.

**sharp** a. (knife etc.) tranchant; (pin etc.) pointu; (point) aigu; (acute) vif; (sudden) brusque; (dishonest) peu scrupuleux. ● adv. (stop) net.

**sharpen** v.t. aiguiser; (pencil) tailler.

**shatter** v.t./i. (glass etc.) (faire) voler en éclats, (se) briser; (upset, ruin) anéantir.

**shav|e** v.t./i. (se) raser. ● n. **have a ~e,** se raser. ~**er** n. rasoir électrique m. ~**ing-brush** n. blaireau m. ~**ing-cream** n. crème à raser f.

**shaving** n. copeau m.

**shawl** n. châle m.

**she** pron. elle. ● n. femelle f.

**sheaf** n. gerbe f.

**shears** n. pl. cisaille(s) f. (pl.).

**sheath** n. gaine f., fourreau m.; (contraceptive) préservatif m.

**sheathe** v.t. rengainer.

**shed**¹ n. remise f.

**shed**² v.t. perdre; (light, tears) répandre.

**sheen** n. lustre m.

**sheep** n. invar. mouton m. ~**-dog** n. chien de berger m.

**sheepskin** n. peau de mouton f.

**sheer** a. pur (et simple); (steep) à pic; (fabric) très fin. ● adv. à pic, verticalement.

**sheet** n. drap m.; (of paper) feuille f.; (of glass, ice) plaque f.

**shelf** n. (pl. **shelves**) rayon m., étagère f.

**shell** n. coquille f.; (on beach) coquillage m.; (of building) carcasse f.; (explosive) obus m. ● v.t. (nut etc.) décortiquer; (peas) écosser; (mil.) bombarder.

**shellfish** n. invar. (lobster etc.) crustacé(s) m. (pl.); (mollusc) coquillage(s) m. (pl.).

**shelter** n. abri m. ● v.t./i. (s')abriter; (give lodging to) donner asile à. ~**ed** a. (life etc.) protégé.

**shelve** v.t. (plan etc.) laisser en suspens, remettre à plus tard.

**shepherd** n. berger m. ● v.t. (people) guider. ~**'s pie,** hachis Parmentier m.

**sheriff** n. shérif m.

**sherry** n. xérès m.

**shield** n. bouclier m.; (screen) écran m. ● v.t. protéger.

**shift** v.t./i. (se) déplacer, bouger; (exchange, alter) changer de. ● n. changement m.; (workers) équipe f.; (work) poste m.

**shilling** n. shilling m.

**shimmer** v.i. chatoyer. ● n. chatoiement m.

**shin** n. tibia m.

**shine** v.t./i. (faire) briller. ● n. éclat m., brillant m. ~ **one's torch** or **the light (on),** éclairer.

**shingle** n. (pebbles) galets m. pl.; (on roof) bardeau m.

**shingles** n. pl. (med.) zona m.

**shiny** a. brillant.

**ship** n. bateau m., navire m. ● v.t. transporter; (send) expédier; (load) embarquer. ~**ping** n. (ships) navigation f.

**shipyard** n. chantier naval m.

**shirk** v.t. esquiver. ~**er** n. tire-au-flanc m. invar.

**shirt** n. chemise f.; (of woman) chemisier m. **in ~-sleeves,** en bras de chemise.

**shiver** v.i. frissonner. ● n. frisson m.

**shoal** n. (of fish) banc m.

**shock** n. choc m., secousse f.; (electr.) décharge f.; (med.) choc m. ● a. (result) choc invar.; (tactics) de choc. ● v.t. choquer. ~ **absorber,** amortisseur m. ~**ing** a. choquant; (bad: fam.) affreux.

**shoddy** a. mauvais.

**shoe** n. chaussure f., soulier m.; (of horse) fer (à cheval) m.; (in vehicle) sabot (de frein) m. ● v.t. (horse) ferrer. ~ **repairer,** cordonnier m.

**shoehorn** n. chausse-pied m.

**shoelace** n. lacet m.

**shoot** v.t. (gun) tirer un coup de; (missile, glance) lancer; (kill, wound) tuer, blesser (d'un coup de fusil, de pistolet, etc.); (execute) fusiller; (hunt) chasser; (film) tourner. ● v.i.

tirer (**at,** sur). ● *n.* (*bot.*) pousse *f.* ~ **down,** abattre. ~ **out,** (*rush*) sortir en vitesse. ~ **up,** (*spurt*) jaillir; (*grow*) pousser vite.

**shop** *n.* magasin *m.,* boutique *f.;* (*workshop*) atelier *m.* ● *v.i.* faire ses courses. ~ **assistant,** vendeu|r, -se *m.,* *f.* ~**per** *n.* acheteu|r, -se *m.,* *f.* ~**soiled** *adjs.* abîmé. ~ **window,** vitrine *f.*

**shopkeeper** *n.* commerçant(e) *m.* (*f.*).

**shoplift|er** *n.* voleu|r, -se à l'étalage *m.,* *f.* ~**ing** *n.* vol à l'étalage *m.*

**shopping** *n.* (*goods*) achats *m. pl.* go ~, faire ses courses. ~ **centre,** centre commercial *m.*

**shore** *n.* rivage *m.*

**short** *a.* court; (*person*) petit; (*brief*) court, bref; (*curt*) brusque. be ~ (**of**), (*lack*) manquer (de). ● *adv.* (*stop*) net. ● *n.* (*electr.*) court-circuit *m.;* (*film*) court-métrage *m.* ~**s,** (*trousers*) short *m.* ~ **of money,** à court d'argent. ~ **of doing sth,** à moins de faire qch. **cut** ~, écourter. **in** ~, en bref. ~ **circuit,** court-circuit *m.* ~**circuit** *v.t.* court-circuiter. ~ **cut,** raccourci *m.* ~**lived** *a.* éphémère. ~**sighted** *a.* myope. ~**staffed** *a.* à court de personnel. ~ **story,** nouvelle *f.* ~**term** *a.* à court terme. ~ **wave,** ondes courtes *f. pl.*

**shortage** *n.* manque *m.*

**shortbread** *n.* sablé *m.*

**shortcoming** *n.* défaut *m.*

**shorten** *v.t.* raccourcir.

**shortfall** *n.* déficit *m.*

**shorthand** *n.* sténo(-graphie) *f.* ~ **typist,** sténodactylo *f.*

**shortly** *adv.* bientôt.

**shot** *n.* (*firing, attempt, etc.*) coup de feu *m.;* (*person*) tireur *m.;* (*bullet*) balle *f.;* (*photograph*) photo *f.;* (*injection*) piqûre *f.* **like a** ~, comme une flèche. ~**gun** *n.* fusil de chasse *m.*

**should** *v.aux.* devoir. **you** ~ **help me,** vous devriez m'aider. **I** ~ **have stayed,** j'aurais dû rester. **I** ~ **like to,** j'aimerais bien.

**shoulder** *n.* épaule *f.* ● *v.t.* (*responsibility*) endosser; (*burden*) se charger de. ~**bag** *n.* sac à bandoulière *m.* ~**blade** *n.* omoplate *f.* ~**pad** *n.* épaulette *f.*

**shout** *n.* cri *m.* ● *v.t./i.* crier.

**shove** *n.* poussée *f.* ● *v.t./i.* pousser; (*put: fam.*) ficher.

**shovel** *n.* pelle *f.* ● *v.t.* pelleter.

**show** *v.t.* montrer; (*of dial, needle*) indiquer; (*put on display*) exposer; (*film*) donner; (*conduct*) conduire. ● *v.i.* (*be visible*) se voir. ● *n.* démonstration *f.;* (*ostentation*) parade *f.;* (*exhibition*) exposition *f.,* salon *m.;* (*theatre*) spectacle *m.;* (*cinema*) séance *f.* **for** ~, pour l'effet. **on** ~, exposé. ~**down** *n.* épreuve de force *f.* ~**jumping** *n.* concours hippique *m.* ~**ing** *n.* performance *f.;* (*cinema*) séance *f.*

**shower** *n.* (*of rain*) averse *f.;* (*for washing*) douche *f.* ● *v.t.* ~ **with,** couvrir de. ● *v.i.* se doucher. ~**y** *a.* pluvieux.

**showerproof** *a.* imperméable.

**showroom** *n.* salle d'exposition *f.*

**showy** *a.* voyant; (*manner*) prétentieux.

**shrapnel** *n.* éclats d'obus *m. pl.*

**shred** *n.* lambeau *m.;* (*least amount: fig.*) parcelle *f.* ● *v.t.* déchiqueter; (*culin.*) râper. ~**der** *n.* destructeur de documents *m.*

**shrewd** *a.* astucieux.

**shriek** *n.* hurlement *m.* ● *v.t./i.* hurler.

**shrill** *a.* strident, aigu.

**shrimp** *n.* crevette *f.*

**shrine** *n.* (*place*) lieu saint *m.;* (*tomb*) châsse *f.*

**shrink** *v.t./i.* rétrécir; (*lessen*) diminuer.

**shrivel** *v.t./i.* (se) ratatiner.

**shroud** *n.* linceul *m.* ● *v.t.* (*veil*) envelopper.

**shrub** *n.* arbuste *m.*

**shrug** *v.t.* ~ **one's shoulders,** hausser les épaules. ● *n.* haussement d'épaules *m.*

**shudder** *v.i.* frémir. ● *n.* frémissement *m.*

**shuffle** *v.t.* (*feet*) traîner; (*cards*) battre. ● *v.i.* traîner les pieds. ● *n.* démarche traînante *f.*

**shun** *v.t.* éviter, fuir.

**shunt** *v.t.* (*train*) aiguiller.

**shut** *v.t.* fermer. ● *v.i.* se fermer; (*of shop, bank, etc.*) fermer. ~ **down** *or* **up,** fermer. ~ **up** *v.i.* (*fam.*) se taire; *v.t.* (*fam.*) faire taire.

**shutter** *n.* volet *m.;* (*photo.*) obturateur *m.*

**shuttle** *n.* (*bus etc.*) navette *f.* ● *v.i.* faire la navette. ● *v.t.* transporter. ~ **service,** navette *f.*

**shuttlecock** *n.* (*badminton*) volant *m.*

**shy** *a.* timide. ● *v.i.* reculer. ~**ness** *n.* timidité *f.*

**sibling** *n.* frère *m.,* sœur *f.*

**Sicily** *n.* Sicile *f.*

**sick** *a.* malade; (*humour*) macabre. **be** ~, (*vomit*) vomir. **be** ~ **of,** en avoir assez or marre de. **feel** ~, avoir mal au cœur.

**sickle** *n.* faucille *f.*

**sickly** *a.* (*person*) maladif; (*taste, smell, etc.*) écœurant.

**sickness** *n.* maladie *f.*

**side** *n.* côté *m.;* (*of road, river*) bord *m.;* (*of hill*) flanc *m.;* (*sport*) équipe *f.* ● *a.* latéral. ~**effect** *n.* effet secondaire *m.* ~**step** *v.t.* éviter. ~**street** *n.* rue latérale *f.* ~**track** *v.t.* faire dévier de son sujet.

**sideboard** *n.* buffet *m.* ~**s,** (*whiskers: sl.*) pattes *f. pl.*

**sidelight** *n.* (*auto.*) veilleuse *f.*

**sideline** *n.* activité secondaire *f.*

**side|ways,** ~**long** *adv. & a.* de côté.

**siding** *n.* voie de garage *f.*

**siege** *n.* siège *m.*

**siesta** *n.* sieste *f.*

**sieve** *n.* tamis *m.;* (*for liquids*) passoire *f.* ● *v.t.* tamiser.

**sift** *v.t.* tamiser. ● *v.i.* ~ **through,** examiner.

**sigh** *n.* soupir *m.* ● *v.t./i.* soupirer.

**sight** *n.* vue *f.*; (*scene*) spectacle *m.* ● *v.t.* apercevoir.

**sightsee|ing** *n.* tourisme *m.* ~**r** *n.* touriste *m./f.*

**sign** *n.* signe *m.*; (*notice*) panneau *m.* ● *v.t./i.* signer.

**signal** *n.* signal *m.* ● *v.t.* communiquer (par signaux); (*person*) faire signe à. ~**box** *n.* poste d'aiguillage *m.*

**signalman** *n.* aiguilleur *m.*

**signature** *n.* signature *f.*

**significan|t** *a.* important; (*meaningful*) significatif. ~**ce** *n.* importance *f.*; (*meaning*) signification *f.* ~**tly** *adv.* (*much*) sensiblement.

**signify** *v.t.* signifier.

**signpost** *n.* poteau indicateur *m.*

**silence** *n.* silence *m.* ● *v.t.* faire taire. ~**r** *n.* (*on car*) silencieux *m.*

**silent** *a.* silencieux; (*film*) muet. ~**ly** *adv.* silencieusement.

**silhouette** *n.* silhouette *f.*

**silicon** *n.* silicium *m.* ~ **chip,** microplaquette *f.*

**silk** *n.* soie *f.*

**sill** *n.* rebord *m.*

**silly** *a.* bête, idiot.

**silo** *n.* silo *m.*

**silt** *n.* vase *f.*

**silver** *n.* argent *m.*; (*silverware*) argenterie *f.* ● *a.* en argent, d'argent.

**similar** *a.* semblable (**to,** à). ~**ity** *n.* ressemblance *f.* ~**ly** *adv.* de même.

**simile** *n.* comparaison *f.*

**simmer** *v.t./i.* (*soup etc.*) mijoter; (*water*) (laisser) frémir; (*smoulder: fig.*) couver. ~ **down,** se calmer.

**simpl|e** *a.* simple. ~**e-minded** *a.* simple d'esprit. ~**icity** *n.* simplicité *f.* ~**y** *adv.* simplement; (*absolutely*) absolument.

**simplif|y** *v.t.* simplifier. ~**ication** *n.* simplification *f.*

**simplistic** *a.* simpliste.

**simulat|e** *v.t.* simuler. ~**ion** *n.* simulation *f.*

**simultaneous** *a.* simultané. ~**ly** *adv.* simultanément.

**sin** *n.* péché *m.* ● *v.i.* pécher.

**since** *prep. & adv.* depuis. ● *conj.* depuis que; (*because*) puisque. ~ **then,** depuis.

**sincer|e** *a.* sincère. ~**ely** *adv.* sincèrement. ~**ity** *n.* sincérité *f.*

**sinew** *n.* tendon *m.* ~**s,** muscles *m. pl.*

**sinful** *a.* (*act*) coupable; (*shocking*) scandaleux.

**sing** *v.t./i.* chanter. ~**er** *n.* chanteu|r, -se *m., f.*

**singe** *v.t.* roussir.

**single** *a.* seul; (*not double*) simple; (*unmarried*) célibataire; (*room, bed*) pour une personne; (*ticket*) simple. ● *n.* (*ticket*) aller simple *m.*; (*record*) 45 tours *m. invar.* ~**s,** (*tennis*) simple *m.* ● *v.t.* ~ **out,** choisir. **in** ~ **file,** en file indienne. ~**-handed** *a.* sans aide. ~ **parent,** parent seul *m.*

**singly** *adv.* un à un.

**singlet** *n.* maillot de corps *m.*

**singular** *n.* singulier *m.* ● *a.* (*uncommon & gram.*) singulier; (*noun*) au singulier. ~**ly** *adv.* singulièrement.

**sinister** *a.* sinistre.

**sink** *v.t./i.* (faire) couler; (*of ground, person*) s'affaisser; (*well*) creuser; (*money*) investir. ● *n.* (*in kitchen*) évier *m.*; (*wash-basin*) lavabo *m.* ~ **in,** (*fig.*) être compris. ~ **unit,** bloc-évier *m.*

**sinner** *n.* péch|eur, -eresse *m., f.*

**sinus** *n.* (*anat.*) sinus *m.*

**sip** *n.* petite gorgée *f.* ● *v.t.* boire à petites gorgées.

**siphon** *n.* siphon *m.* ● *v.t.* ~ **off,** siphonner.

**sir** *n.* monsieur *m.*

**siren** *n.* sirène *f.*

**sirloin** *n.* faux-filet *m.*

**sister** *n.* sœur *f.*; (*nurse*) infirmière en chef *f.* ~**-in-law** belle-sœur *f.* ~**ly** *a.* fraternel.

**sit** *v.t./i.* (s')asseoir; (*of committee etc.*) siéger. **be** ~**ting,** être assis. ~ **down,** s'asseoir. ~**ting** *n.* séance *f.*; (*in restaurant*) service *m.* ~**ting-room** *n.* salon *m.*

**site** *n.* emplacement *m.* **(building)** ~, chantier *m.* ● *v.t.* placer, construire, situer.

**situat|e** *v.t.* situer. **be** ~**ed,** être situé. ~**ion** *n.* situation *f.*

**six** *a. & n.* six (*m.*). ~**th** *a. & n.* sixième (*m./f.*).

**sixteen** *a. & n.* seize (*m.*). ~**th** *a. & n.* seizième (*m./f.*).

**sixt|y** *a. & n.* soixante (*m.*). ~**ieth** *a. & n.* soixantième (*m./f.*).

**size** *n.* dimension *f.*; (*of person, garment, etc.*) taille *f.*; (*of shoes*) pointure *f.*; (*of sum, salary*) montant *m.*; (*extent*) ampleur *f.* ~**able** *a.* assez grand.

**sizzle** *v.i.* grésiller.

**skate¹** *n. invar.* (*fish*) raie *f.*

**skat|e²** *n.* patin *m.* ● *v.i.* patiner. ~**er** *n.* patineu|r, -se *m., f.* ~**ing-rink** *n.* patinoire *f.*

**skateboard** *n.* skateboard *m.*, planche à roulettes *f.*

**skeleton** *n.* squelette *m.*

**sketch** *n.* esquisse *f.*, croquis *m.*; (*theatre*) sketch *m.* ● *v.t.* faire un croquis de, esquisser. ● *v.i.* faire des esquisses. ~ **out,** esquisser. ~ **pad,** bloc à dessins.

**sketchy** *a.* sommaire.

**skewer** *n.* brochette *f.*

**ski** n. ski m. ● a. de ski. ● v.i. skier; (*go ski-ing*) faire du ski. ~ **jump,** saut à skis m. ~ **lift,** remonte-pente m. ~**er** n. skieu|r, -se m., f. ~**ing** n. ski m.

**skid** v.i. déraper. ● n. dérapage m.

**skilful** a. habile.

**skill** n. habileté f.; (*craft*) métier m. ~**s,** aptitudes f. pl. ~**ed** a. habile; (*worker*) qualifié.

**skim** v.t. écumer; (*milk*) écrémer; (*pass or glide over*) effleurer. ● v.i. ~ **through,** parcourir.

**skimp** v.t./i. ~ **(on),** lésiner (sur).

**skimpy** a. (*clothes*) étriqué; (*meal*) chiche.

**skin** n. peau f. ● v.t. (*animal*) écorcher; (*fruit*) éplucher. ~-**diving** n. plongée sous-marine f.

**skinny** a. maigrichon.

**skint** a. (*sl.*) fauché.

**skip**[1] v.i. sautiller; (*with rope*) sauter à la corde. ● v.t. (*page, class, etc.*) sauter. ● n. petit saut m.

**skip**[2] n. (*container*) benne f.

**skipper** n. capitaine m.

**skirt** n. jupe f. ● v.t. contourner. ~**ing-board** n. plinthe f.

**skit** n. sketch satirique m.

**skittle** n. quille f.

**skulk** v.i. (*move*) rôder furtivement; (*hide*) se cacher.

**skull** n. crâne m.

**skunk** n. (*animal*) mouffette f.; (*person: sl.*) salaud m.

**sky** n. ciel m. ~-**blue** a. & n. bleu ciel a. & m. invar.

**skylight** n. lucarne f.

**skyscraper** n. gratte-ciel m. invar.

**slab** n. plaque f., bloc m.; (*of paving-stone*) dalle f.

**slack** a. (*rope*) lâche; (*person*) négligent; (*business*) stagnant; (*period*) creux. ● v.t./i. (se) relâcher.

**slacken** v.t./i. (se) relâcher; (*slow*) (se) ralentir.

**slacks** n. pl. pantalon m.

**slag** n. scories f. pl. ~-**heap** n. crassier m.

**slake** v.t. étancher.

**slalom** n. slalom m.

**slam** v.t./i. (*door etc.*) claquer; (*throw*) flanquer; (*criticize: sl.*) critiquer. ● n. (*noise*) claquement m.

**slander** n. diffamation f., calomnie f. ● v.t. diffamer, calomnier. ~**ous** a. diffamatoire.

**slang** n. argot m.

**slant** v.t./i. (faire) pencher; (*news*) présenter sous un certain jour. ● n. inclinaison f.; (*bias*) angle m. **be** ~**ing,** être penché.

**slap** v.t. (*strike*) donner une claque à; (*face*) gifler; (*put*) flanquer. ● n. claque f.; gifle f. ● adv. tout droit.

**slash** v.t. (*cut*) taillader; (*sever*) trancher; (*fig.*) réduire (radicalement). ● n. taillade f.

**slat** n. (*in blind*) lamelle f.; (*on bed*) latte f.

**slate** n. ardoise f. ● v.t. (*fam.*) critiquer, éreinter.

**slaughter** v.t. massacrer; (*animals*) abattre. ● n. massacre m.; abattage m.

**slaughterhouse** n. abattoir m.

**Slav** a. & n. slave (*m./f.*). ~**onic** a. (*lang.*) slave.

**slave** n. esclave m./f. ● v.i. trimer. ~**ry** n. esclavage m.

**slay** v.t. tuer.

**sleazy** a. (*fam.*) sordide.

**sledge** n. luge f.; (*horse-drawn*) traîneau m. ~-**hammer** n. marteau de forgeron m.

**sleek** a. lisse, brillant; (*manner*) onctueux.

**sleep** n. sommeil m. ● v.i. dormir; (*spend the night*) coucher. ● v.t. loger. **go to** ~, s'endormir. ~**er** n. dormeu|r, -se m., f.; (*beam: rail*) traverse f.; (*berth*) couchette f. ~**ing-bag** n. sac de couchage m. ~**ing pill,** somnifère m.

**sleep|y** a. somnolent. **be** ~**y,** avoir sommeil. ~**ily** adv. à moitié endormi.

**sleet** n. neige fondue f.

**sleeve** n. manche f.; (*of record*) pochette f.

**sleigh** n. traîneau m.

**sleight** n. ~ **of hand,** prestidigitation f.

**slender** a. mince, svelte; (*scanty: fig.*) faible.

**sleuth** n. limier m.

**slew** v.i. (*turn*) virer.

**slice** n. tranche f. ● v.t. couper (en tranches).

**slick** a. (*unctuous*) mielleux; (*cunning*) astucieux. ● n. (*oil*) ~, nappe de pétrole f., marée noire f.

**slide** v.t./i. glisser. ● n. glissade f.; (*fall: fig.*) baisse f.; (*in playground*) toboggan m.; (*for hair*) barrette f.; (*photo.*) diapositive f. ~-**rule** n. règle à calcul f.

**slight** a. petit, léger; (*slender*) mince; (*frail*) frêle. ● v.t. (*insult*) offenser. ● n. affront m. ~**est** a. moindre. ~**ly** adv. légèrement, un peu.

**slim** a. mince. ● v.i. maigrir. ~**ness** n. minceur f.

**slim|e** n. boue (visqueuse) f.; (*on river-bed*) vase f. ~**y** a. boueux; vaseux; (*sticky, servile*) visqueux.

**sling** n. (*weapon, toy*) fronde f.; (*bandage*) écharpe f. ● v.t. jeter, lancer.

**slip** v.t./i. glisser. ● n. faux pas m.; (*mistake*) erreur f.; (*petticoat*) combinaison f.; (*paper*) fiche f. ~ **away,** s'esquiver. ~**ped disc,** hernie discale f. ~-**road** n. bretelle f. ~ **s.o.'s mind,** échapper à qn. ~ **up,** (*fam.*) gaffer. ~-**up** n. (*fam.*) gaffe f.

**slipper** n. pantoufle f.

**slippery** a. glissant.

**slipshod** a. (*person*) négligent; (*work*) négligé.

**slit** *n.* fente *f.* ● *v.t.* couper.

**slither** *v.i.* glisser.

**sliver** *n.* (*of cheese etc.*) lamelle *f.*; (*splinter*) éclat *m.*

**slob** *n.* (*fam.*) rustre *m.*

**slobber** *v.i.* baver.

**slog** *v.t.* (*hit*) frapper dur. ● *v.i.* (*work*) trimer. ● *n.* (*work*) travail dur *m.*; (*effort*) gros effort *m.*

**slogan** *n.* slogan *m.*

**slop** *v.t./i.* (se) répandre. **~s** *n. pl.* eaux sales *f. pl.*

**slop|e** *v.i.* être en pente; (*of handwriting*) pencher. ● *n.* pente *f.*; (*of mountain*) flanc *m.* **~ing** *a.* en pente.

**sloppy** *a.* (*ground*) détrempé; (*food*) liquide; (*work*) négligé; (*person*) négligent; (*fig.*) sentimental.

**slosh** *v.t.* (*fam.*) répandre; (*hit*: *sl.*) frapper. ● *v.i.* patauger.

**slot** *n.* fente *f.* ● *v.t./i.* (s')insérer. **~-machine** *n.* distributeur automatique *m.*; (*for gambling*) machine à sous *f.*

**sloth** *n.* paresse *f.*

**slouch** *v.i.* avoir le dos voûté; (*move*) marcher le dos voûté.

**slow** *a.* lent. ● *adv.* lentement. ● *v.t./i.* ralentir. **be ~,** (*clock etc.*) retarder. **~ly** *adv.* lentement. **~ness** *n.* lenteur *f.*

**sludge** *n.* gadoue *f.*, boue *f.*

**slug** *n.* (*mollusc*) limace *f.*; (*bullet*) balle *f.*; (*blow*) coup *m.*

**sluggish** *a.* lent, mou.

**sluice** *n.* (*gate*) vanne *f.*

**slum** *n.* taudis *m.*

**slumber** *n.* sommeil. *m.* ● *v.i.* dormir.

**slump** *n.* effondrement *m.*; baisse *f.*; (*in business*) marasme *m.* ● *v.i.* (*collapse, fall limply*) s'effondrer; (*decrease*) baisser.

**slur** *v.t./i.* (*spoken words*) mal articuler. ● *n.* bredouillement *m.*; (*discredit*) atteinte *f.* (**on,** à).

**slush** *n.* (*snow*) neige fondue *f.*

**slut** *n.* (*dirty*) souillon *f.*; (*immoral*) dévergondée *f.*

**sly** *a.* (*crafty*) rusé; (*secretive*) sournois. ● *n.* **on the ~,** en cachette. **~ly** *adv.* sournoisement.

**smack**[1] *n.* tape *f.*; (*on face*) gifle *f.* ● *v.t.* donner une tape à; gifler. ● *adv.* (*fam.*) tout droit.

**smack**[2] *v.i.* **~ of sth.,** (*have flavour*) sentir qch.

**small** *a.* petit. ● *n.* **~ of the back,** creux des reins *m.* ● *adv.* (*cut etc.*) menu. **~ ads,** petites annonces *f. pl.* **~ businesses,** les petites entreprises. **~ change,** petite monnaie *f.* **~ talk,** menus propos *m. pl.*

**smallpox** *n.* variole *f.*

**smart** *a.* élégant; (*clever*) astucieux, intelligent; (*brisk*) rapide. ● *v.i.* (*of wound etc.*) brûler. **~ly** *adv.* élégamment.

**smarten** *v.t./i.* **~ (up),** embellir. **~ (o.s.) up,** se faire beau; (*tidy*) s'arranger.

**smash** *v.t./i.* (se) briser, (se) fracasser; (*opponent, record*) pulvériser. ● *n.* (*noise*) fracas *m.*; (*blow*) coup *m.*; (*fig.*) collision *f.*

**smashing** *a.* (*fam.*) épatant.

**smattering** *n.* **a ~ of,** des notions de.

**smear** *v.t.* (*stain*) tacher; (*coat*) enduire; (*discredit*: *fig.*) entacher. ● *n.* tache *f.* **~ test,** frottis *m.*

**smell** *n.* odeur *f.*; (*sense*) odorat *m.* ● *v.t./i.* sentir. **~ of,** sentir. **~y** *a.* malodorant, qui pue.

**smelt** *v.t.* (*ore*) fondre.

**smil|e** *n.* sourire. ● *v.i.* sourire. **~ing** *a.* souriant.

**smirk** *n.* sourire affecté *m.*

**smith** *n.* forgeron *m.*

**smock** *n.* blouse *f.*

**smog** *n.* brouillard mélangé de fumée *m.*, smog *m.*

**smoke** *n.* fumée *f.* ● *v.t./i.* fumer. **have a ~,** fumer. **~d** *a.* fumé. **~less** *a.* (*fuel*) non polluant. **~r** *n.* fumeu|r, -se *m.*, *f.* **~-screen** *n.* écran de fumée *m.*; (*fig.*) manœuvre de diversion *f.* **smoky** *a.* (*air*) enfumé.

**smooth** *a.* lisse; (*movement*) régulier; (*manners, cream*) onctueux; (*flight*) sans turbulence; (*changes*) sans heurt. ● *v.t.* lisser. **~ly** *adv.* doucement.

**smother** *v.t.* (*stifle*) étouffer; (*cover*) couvrir.

**smoulder** *v.i.* couver.

**smudge** *n.* tache *f.* ● *v.t./i.* (se) salir, (se) tacher.

**smug** *a.* suffisant. **~ly** *adv.* avec suffisance. **~ness** *n.* suffisance *f.*

**smuggl|e** *v.t.* passer (en contrebande). **~er** *n.* contreband|ier, -ière *m.*, *f.* **~ing** *n.* contrebande *f.*

**smut** *n.* saleté *f.*

**snack** *n.* casse-croûte *m. invar.* **~-bar** *n.* snack(-bar) *m.*

**snag** *n.* difficulté *f.*, inconvénient *m.*; (*in cloth*) accroc *m.*

**snail** *n.* escargot *m.* **at a ~'s pace,** à un pas de tortue.

**snake** *n.* serpent *m.*

**snap** *v.t./i.* (*whip, fingers, etc.*) (faire) claquer; (*break*) (se) casser net; (*say*) dire sèchement. ● *n.* claquement *m.*; (*photograph*) instantané *m.* ● *a.* soudain.

**snappy** *a.* (*brisk*: *fam.*) prompt, rapide. **make it ~,** (*fam.*) se dépêcher.

**snapshot** *n.* instantané *m.*

**snare** *n.* piège *m.*

**snarl** *v.i.* gronder (en montrant les dents). ● *n.* grondement *m.* **~-up,** *n.* embouteillage *m.*

**snatch** *v.t.* (*grab*) saisir; (*steal*) voler. **~ from s.o.,** arracher à qn. ● *n.* (*theft*) vol *m.*; (*short part*) fragment *m.*

**sneak** *v.i.* aller furtivement. ● *n.* (*schol., sl.*) rapporteu|r, -se *m.*, *f.* ~**y** *a.* sournois.

**sneer** *n.* ricanement *m.* ● *v.i.* ricaner.

**sneeze** *n.* éternuement *m.* ● *v.i.* éternuer.

**sniff** *v.t./i.* renifler. ● *n.* reniflement *m.*

**snigger** *n.* ricanement *m.* ● *v.i.* ricaner.

**snip** *v.t.* couper. ● *n.* morceau coupé *m.*; (*bargain: sl.*) bonne affaire *f.*

**snipe** *v.i.* canarder. ~**r** *n.* tireur embusqué *m.*

**snippet** *n.* bribe *f.*

**snivel** *v.i.* pleurnicher.

**snob** *n.* snob *m./f.* ~**bery** *n.* snobisme *m.* ~**bish** *a.* snob *invar.*

**snooker** *n.* (*sorte de*) jeu de billard *m.*

**snooze** *n.* petit somme *m.* ● *v.i.* faire un petit somme.

**snore** *n.* ronflement *m.* ● *v.i.* ronfler.

**snorkel** *n.* tuba *m.*

**snort** *n.* grognement *m.* ● *v.i.* (*person*) grogner.

**snout** *n.* museau *m.*

**snow** *n.* neige *f.* ● *v.i.* neiger. ~**y** *a.* neigeux.

**snowball** *n.* boule de neige *f.* ● *v.i.* faire boule de neige.

**snowdrop** *n.* perce-neige *m./f. invar.*

**snowflake** *n.* flocon de neige *m.*

**snowman** *n.* bonhomme de neige *m.*

**snowstorm** *n.* tempête de neige *f.*

**snub** *v.t.* (*person*) snober; (*offer*) repousser. ● *n.* rebuffade *f.*

**snub-nosed** *a.* au nez retroussé.

**snuffle** *v.i.* renifler.

**snug** *a.* (*cosy*) confortable; (*tight*) bien ajusté; (*safe*) sûr.

**snuggle** *v.i.* se pelotonner.

**so** *adv.* si, tellement; (*thus*) ainsi. ● *conj.* donc, alors. **so am I,** moi aussi. **so good**/*etc.* **as,** aussi bon/*etc.* que. **so does he,** lui aussi. **I think so,** je pense que oui. **so as to,** de manière à. **so long!,** (*fam.*) à bientôt! **so many, so much,** tant (de). **so that,** pour que.

**soak** *v.t./i.* (faire) tremper (**in,** dans). ~ **in** or **up,** absorber. ~**ing** *a.* trempé.

**soap** *n.* savon *m.* ● *v.t.* savonner. ~ **powder,** lessive *f.* ~**y** *a.* savonneux.

**soar** *v.i.* monter (en flèche).

**sob** *n.* sanglot *m.* ● *v.i.* sangloter.

**sober** *a.* qui n'est pas ivre; (*serious*) sérieux.

**soccer** *n.* (*fam.*) football *m.*

**sociable** *a.* sociable.

**social** *a.* social; (*gathering, life*) mondain. ● *n.* réunion (amicale) *f.*, fête *f.* ~ **security,** aide sociale *f.* ~ **worker,** assistant(e) social(e) *m.* (*f.*).

**socialis|t** *n.* socialiste *m./f.* ~**m** *n.* socialisme *m.*

**society** *n.* société *f.*

**sociolog|y** *n.* sociologie *f.* ~**ical** *a.* sociologique. ~**ist** *n.* sociologue *m./f.*

**sock** *n.* chaussette *f.*

**socket** *n.* cavité *f.*; (*for lamp*) douille *f.*; (*electr.*) prise (de courant) *f.*; (*of tooth*) alvéole *f.*

**soda** *n.* soude *f.* ~**(-water),** soda *m.*, eau de Seltz *f.*

**sodden** *a.* détrempé.

**sodium** *n.* sodium *m.*

**sofa** *n.* canapé *m.*, sofa *m.*

**soft** *a.* (*gentle, lenient*) doux; (*not hard*) doux, mou; (*heart, wood*) tendre; (*silly*) ramolli; (*easy: sl.*) facile. ~ **drink,** boisson non alcoolisée *f.* ~**ly** *adv.* doucement. ~**ness** *n.* douceur *f.*

**soften** *v.t./i.* (se) ramollir; (*tone down, lessen*) (s')adoucir.

**software** *n.* logiciel *m.*

**softwood** *n.* bois tendre *m.*

**soggy** *a.* détrempé; (*bread etc.*) ramolli.

**soil**[1] *n.* sol *m.*, terre *f.*

**soil**[2] *v.t./i.* (se) salir.

**solar** *a.* solaire.

**sold** *a.* ~ **out,** épuisé.

**solder** *n.* soudure *f.* ● *v.t.* souder. ~**ing iron,** fer à souder *m.*

**soldier** *n.* soldat *m.* ● *v.i.* ~ **on,** (*fam.*) persévérer.

**sole**[1] *n.* (*of foot*) plante *f.*; (*of shoe*) semelle *f.*

**sole**[2] *n.* (*fish*) sole *f.*

**sole**[3] *a.* unique, seul. ~**ly** *adv.* uniquement.

**solemn** *a.* (*formal*) solennel; (*not cheerful*) grave. ~**ly** *adv.* solennellement; gravement.

**solicit** *v.t.* (*seek*) solliciter. ● *v.i.* (*of prostitute*) racoler.

**solicitor** *n.* avoué *m.*

**solid** *a.* solide; (*not hollow*) plein; (*gold*) massif; (*mass*) compact; (*meal*) substantiel. ● *n.* solide *m.* ~**ly** *adv.* solidement.

**solidarity** *n.* solidarité *f.*

**solidify** *v.t./i.* (se) solidifier.

**solitary** *a.* (*alone, lonely*) solitaire; (*only, single*) seul.

**solitude** *n.* solitude *f.*

**solo** *n.* solo *m.* ● *a.* (*mus.*) solo *invar.*; (*flight*) en solitaire. ~**ist** *n.* soliste *m./f.*

**solstice** *n.* solstice *m.*

**soluble** *a.* soluble.

**solution** *n.* solution *f.*

**solve** *v.t.* résoudre.

**solvent** *a.* (*comm.*) solvable. ● *n.* (dis)solvant *m.*

**sombre** *a.* sombre.

**some** *a.* (*quantity, number*) du, de l'*, de la, des; (*unspecified, some or other*) un(e), quelque; (*a little*) un peu de; (*a certain*) un(e) certain(e), quelque; (*contrasted with others*) quelques, certain.e(s). ● *pron.* quelquesun(e)s; (*certain quantity of it or them*) en; (*a little*) un peu. ● *adv.* (*approximately*) quelque.

~ **of my friends,** quelques amis à moi. **he wants** ~, il en veut. ~ **time ago,** il y a un certain temps.

**somebody** *pron.* quelqu'un.

**somehow** *adv.* d'une manière ou d'une autre; (*for some reason*) je ne sais pas pourquoi.

**someone** *pron. & n.* = somebody.

**somersault** *n.* culbute *f.* ● *v.i.* faire la culbute.

**something** *pron. & n.* quelque chose (*m.*). ~ **good/etc.** quelque chose de bon/*etc.* ● **like,** un peu comme.

**sometime** *adv.* un jour. ● *a.* (*former*) ancien.

**sometimes** *adv.* parfois.

**somewhat** *adv.* un peu.

**somewhere** *adv.* quelque part.

**son** *n.* fils *m.* ~-**in-law** *n.* beau-fils *m.*, gendre *m.*

**sonar** *n.* sonar *m.*

**sonata** *n.* sonate *f.*

**song** *n.* chanson *f.*

**sonic** *a.* ~ **boom,** bang supersonique *m.*

**sonnet** *n.* sonnet *m.*

**sonny** *n.* (*fam.*) fiston *m.*

**soon** *adv.* bientôt; (*early*) tôt. ~ **after,** peu après. ~-**er or later,** tôt ou tard.

**soot** *n.* suie *f.* ~**y** *a.* couvert de suie.

**sooth|e** *v.t.* calmer. ~**ing** *a.* (*remedy, words, etc.*) calmant.

**sophisticated** *a.* raffiné; (*machine etc.*) sophistiqué.

**soprano** *n.* (*voice*) soprano *m.*; (*singer*) soprano *m./f.*

**sordid** *a.* sordide.

**sore** *a.* douloureux. ● *n.* plaie *f.*

**sorrow** *n.* chagrin *m.*

**sorry** *a.* (*regretful*) désolé (**to,** de; **that,** que); (*wretched*) triste.

**sort** *n.* genre *m.*, sorte *f.*, espèce *f.*; (*person: fam.*) type *m.* ● *v.t.* ~ (**out**), (*classify*) trier. ~ **out,** (*tidy*) ranger; (*arrange*) arranger; (*problem*) régler.

**SOS** *n.* SOS *m.*

**soufflé** *n.* soufflé *m.*

**soul** *n.* âme *f.* ~-**destroying** *a.* démoralisant.

**sound**[1] *n.* son *m.*, bruit *m.* ● *v.t./i.* sonner; (*seem*) sembler (**as if,** que). ~ **like,** sembler être. ~-**proof** *a.* insonorisé; *v.t.* insonoriser. ~-**track** *n.* bande sonore *f.*

**sound**[2] *a.* solide; (*healthy*) sain; (*sensible*) sensé. ~ **asleep,** profondément endormi.

**sound**[3] *v.t.* (*test*) sonder. ~ **out,** sonder.

**soup** *n.* soupe *f.*, potage *m.*

**sour** *a.* aigre.

**source** *n.* source *f.*

**south** *n.* sud *m.* ● *a.* sud *invar.*, du sud. ● *adv.* vers le sud. ~-**east** *n.* sud-est *m.* ~-**erly** *a.* du sud. ~-**wards** *adv.* vers le sud. ~-**west** *n.* sud-ouest *m.*

**southern** *a.* du sud. ~-**er** *n.* habitant(e) du sud *m.* (*f.*).

**souvenir** *n.* (*thing*) souvenir *m.*

**sovereign** *n. & a.* souverain(e) (*m.* (*f.*)). ~**ty** *n.* souveraineté *f.*

**Soviet** *a.* soviétique. **the ~ Union,** l'Union soviétique *f.*

**sow**[1] *v.t.* (*seed etc.*) semer; (*land*) ensemencer.

**sow**[2] *n.* (*pig*) truie *f.*

**soya, soy** *n.* ~ **bean,** graine de soja *f.* ~ **sauce,** sauce soja *f.*

**spa** *n.* station thermale *f.*

**space** *n.* espace *m.*; (*room*) place *f.*; (*period*) période *f.* ● *a.* (*research etc.*) spatial. ● *v.t.* ~ (**out**), espacer.

**spacious** *a.* spacieux.

**spade**[1] *n.* (*large, for garden*) bêche *f.*; (*child's*) pelle *f.*

**spade**[2] *n.* (*cards*) pique *m.*

**spaghetti** *n.* spaghetti *m. pl.*

**Spa|in** *n.* Espagne *f.* ~**niard** *n.* Espagnol(e) *m.* (*f.*). ~**nish** *a.* espagnol; *n.* (*lang.*) espagnol *m.*

**span** *n.* (*of arch*) portée *f.*; (*of wings*) envergure *f.*; (*of time*) durée *f.* ● *v.t.* enjamber; (*in time*) embrasser.

**spaniel** *n.* épagneul *m.*

**spank** *v.t.* donner une fessée à. ~**ing** *n.* fessée *f.*

**spanner** *n.* (*tool*) clé (plate) *f.*; (*adjustable*) clé à molette *f.*

**spar** *v.i.* s'entraîner (à la boxe).

**spare** *v.t.* épargner; (*do without*) se passer de; (*afford to give*) donner, accorder; (*use with restraint*) ménager. ● *a.* en réserve; (*surplus*) de trop; (*tyre, shoes, etc.*) de rechange; (*room, bed*) d'ami. ● *n.* ~ (**part**), pièce de rechange *f.* ~ **time,** loisirs *m. pl.*

**spark** *n.* étincelle *f.* ● *v.t.* ~ **off,** (*initiate*) provoquer. ~(**ing**)-**plug** *n.* bougie *f.*

**sparkle** *v.i.* étinceler. ● *n.* étincellement *m.*

**sparkling** *a.* (*wine*) mousseux, pétillant; (*eyes*) pétillant.

**sparrow** *n.* moineau *m.*

**sparse** *a.* clairsemé. ~**ly** *adv.* (*furnished etc.*) peu.

**spartan** *a.* spartiate.

**spasm** *n.* (*of muscle*) spasme *m.*; (*of coughing, anger, etc.*) accès *m.*

**spasmodic** *a.* intermittent.

**spastic** *n.* handicapé(e) moteur *m.* (*f.*).

**spate** *n.* **a** ~ **of,** (*letters etc.*) une avalanche de.

**spatter** *v.t.* éclabousser (**with,** de).

**spatula** *n.* spatule *f.*

**spawn** *n.* frai *m.*, œufs *m. pl.* ● *v.t.* pondre. ● *v.i.* frayer.

**speak** *v.i.* parler. ● *v.t.* (*say*) dire; (*language*) parler. ~ **up,** parler plus fort.

**speaker** *n.* (*in public*) orateur *m.*; (*pol.*) président *m.*; (*loudspeaker*) baffle *m.*

**spear** n. lance f.

**spearhead** n. fer de lance m. ● v.t. (lead) mener.

**spearmint** n. menthe verte f. ● a. à la menthe.

**special** a. spécial; (exceptional) exceptionnel. ~ity n. spécialité f. ~ly adv. spécialement.

**specialist** n. spécialiste m./f.

**specialize** v.i. se spécialiser (in, en). ~d a. spécialisé.

**species** n. invar. espèce f.

**specific** a. précis, explicite. ~ally adv. explicitement; (exactly) précisément.

**specif|y** v.t. spécifier. ~ication n. spécification f.; (details) prescriptions f. pl.

**specimen** n. spécimen m.

**speck** n. (stain) (petite) tache f.; (particle) grain m.

**speckled** a. tacheté.

**specs** n. pl. (fam.) lunettes f. pl.

**spectacle** n. spectacle m. ~s, lunettes f. pl.

**spectacular** a. spectaculaire.

**spectator** n. specta|teur, -trice m., f.

**spectre** n. spectre m.

**spectrum** n. spectre m.; (of ideas etc.) gamme f.

**speculat|e** v.i. s'interroger (about, sur); (comm.) spéculer. ~ion n. conjectures f. pl.; (comm.) spéculation f. ~or n. spécula|teur, -trice m., f.

**speech** n. (faculty) parole f.; (diction) élocution f.; (dialect) langage m.; (address) discours m.

**speed** n. (of movement) vitesse f.; (swiftness) rapidité f. ● v.i. aller vite; (drive too fast) aller trop vite. ~ limit, limitation de vitesse f. ~ up, accélérer; (of pace) s'accélérer. ~ing n. excès de vitesse m.

**speedboat** n. vedette f.

**speedometer** n. compteur (de vitesse) m.

**speed|y** a. rapide. ~ily adv. rapidement.

**spell**[1] n. (magic) charme m., sortilège m.; (curse) sort m.

**spell**[2] v.t./i. écrire; (mean) signifier. ~ out, épeler; (explain) expliquer. ~ing n. orthographe f. ~ing mistake, faute d'orthographe f.

**spell**[3] n. (courte) période f.

**spend** v.t. (money) dépenser (on, pour); (time, holiday) passer; (energy) consacrer (on, à). ● v.i. dépenser.

**spendthrift** n. dépens|ier, -ière m., f.

**spent** a. (used) utilisé; (person) épuisé.

**sperm** n. (semen) sperme m.; (cell) spermatozoïde m. ~icide n. spermicide m.

**spew** v.t./i. vomir.

**sphere** n. sphère f.

**spherical** a. sphérique.

**spic|e** n. épice f.; (fig.) piquant m. ~y a. épicé; piquant.

**spider** n. araignée f.

**spik|e** n. (of metal etc.) pointe f. ~y a. garni de pointes.

**spill** v.t. renverser, répandre. ● v.i. se répandre. ~ over, déborder.

**spin** v.t./i. (wool, web, of spinner) filer; (turn) (faire) tourner; (story) débiter. ● n. (movement, excursion) tour m. ~ out, faire durer. ~drier n. essoreuse f. ~off n. avantage accessoire m.; (by-product) dérivé m.

**spinach** n. (plant) épinard m.; (as food) épinards m. pl.

**spinal** a. vertébral. ~ cord, moelle épinière f.

**spindle** n. fuseau m.

**spine** n. colonne vertébrale f.; (prickle) piquant m.

**spiral** a. en spirale; (staircase) en colimaçon. ● n. spirale f. ● v.i. (prices) monter (en flèche).

**spire** n. flèche f.

**spirit** n. esprit m.; (boldness) courage m. ~s, (morale) moral m.; (drink) spiritueux m. pl. ~level n. niveau à bulle m.

**spirited** a. fougueux.

**spiritual** a. spirituel. ● n. (song) (negro-) spiritual m.

**spit**[1] v.t./i. cracher; (of rain) crachiner. ● n. crachat(s) m. (pl.). ~ out, cracher.

**spit**[2] n. (for meat) broche f.

**spite** n. rancune f. ● v.t. contrarier. in ~ of, malgré. ~ful a. méchant, rancunier.

**spittle** n. crachat(s) m. (pl.).

**splash** v.t. éclabousser. ● v.i. faire des éclaboussures. ● n. (act, mark) éclaboussure f.; (sound) plouf m.; (of colour) tache f.

**spleen** n. (anat.) rate f.

**splendid** a. magnifique.

**splendour** n. splendeur f.

**splint** n. (med.) attelle f.

**splinter** n. éclat m.; (in finger) écharde f. ~ group, groupe dissident m.

**split** v.t./i. (se) fendre; (tear) (se) déchirer; (divide) (se) diviser; (share) partager. ● n. fente f.; déchirure f.; (share: fam.) part f., partage m.; (quarrel) rupture f.; (pol.) scission f. ~ up, (couple) rompre.

**splutter** v.i. crachoter; (stammer) bafouiller; (engine) tousser; (fat) crépiter.

**spoil** v.t. (pamper) gâter; (ruin) abîmer; (mar) gâcher, gâter. ● n. ~(s), (plunder) butin m. ~sport n. trouble-fête m./f. invar.

**spoke** n. rayon m.

**spokesman** n. porte-parole m. invar.

**sponge** n. éponge f. ● v.t. éponger. ● v.i. ~ on, vivre aux crochets de. ~bag n. trousse de toilette f. ~cake n. génoise f. ~r n. parasite m.

**spongy** a. spongieux.

**sponsor** n. (of concert) parrain m., sponsor m.; (surety) garant m.; (for membership) parrain m., marraine f. ● v.t. parrainer, sponsoriser; (member) parrainer. ~**ship** n. patronage m.; parrainage m.

**spontane|ous** a. spontané. ~**ity** n. spontanéité f. ~**ously** adv. spontanément.

**spool** n. bobine f.

**spoon** n. cuiller f. ~**ful** n. cuillerée f.

**sporadic** a. sporadique.

**sport** n. sport m. ● v.t. (display) exhiber, arborer. ~**s car/coat,** voiture/veste de sport f. ~**y** a. (fam.) sportif.

**sports|man** n. (pl. -**men**) sportif m. ~**woman** n. (pl. -**women**) sportive f.

**spot** n. (mark, stain) tache f.; (dot) point m.; (in pattern) pois m.; (drop) goutte f.; (place) endroit m.; (pimple) bouton m. ● v.t. (p.t. **spotted**) (fam.) apercevoir. **a** ~ **of,** (fam.) un peu de. **on the** ~, sur place; (without delay) sur le coup. ~ **check,** contrôle à l'improviste m. ~**ted** a. tacheté; (fabric) à pois.

**spotless** a. impeccable.

**spotlight** n. (lamp) projecteur m., spot m.

**spouse** n. époux m., épouse f.

**spout** n. (of vessel) bec m.; (of liquid) jet m. ● v.i. jaillir.

**sprain** n. entorse f., foulure f. ● v.t. ~ **one's wrist/** etc., se fouler le poignet/etc.

**sprawl** v.i. (town, person, etc.) s'étaler. ● n. étalement m.

**spray**[1] n. (of flowers) gerbe f.

**spray**[2] n. (water) gerbe d'eau f.; (from sea) embruns m. pl.; (device) bombe f., atomiseur m. ● v.t. (surface, insecticide) vaporiser; (plant etc.) arroser; (crops) traiter.

**spread** v.t./i. (stretch, extend) (s')étendre; (news, fear, etc.) (se) répandre; (illness) (se) propager; (butter etc.) (s')étaler. ● n. propagation f.; (of population) distribution f.; (paste) pâte à tartiner f.; (food) belle table f.

**spreadsheet** n. tableur m.

**spree** n. **go on a** ~, (have fun: fam.) faire la noce.

**sprig** n. (shoot) brin m.; (twig) brindille f.

**sprightly** a. alerte, vif.

**spring** v.i. bondir. ● v.t. faire, annoncer, etc. à l'improviste (**on,** à). ● n. bond m.; (device) ressort m.; (season) printemps m.; (of water) source f. ~ **onion,** oignon blanc m. ~ **up,** surgir.

**springboard** n. tremplin m.

**sprinkle** v.t. (with liquid) arroser (**with,** de); (with salt, flour) saupoudrer (**with,** de). ~ **sand/** etc., répandre du sable/etc. ~**r** n. (in garden) arroseur m.; (for fires) extincteur (à déclenchement) automatique m.

**sprint** v.i. (sport) sprinter. ● n. sprint m. ~**er** n. sprinteu|r, -se m., f.

**sprout** v.t./i. pousser. ● n. (on plant etc.) pousse f. **(Brussels)** ~**s,** choux de Bruxelles m. pl.

**spruce**[1] a. pimpant. ● v.t. ~ **o.s. up,** se faire beau.

**spruce**[2] n. (tree) épicéa m.

**spry** a. alerte, vif.

**spud** n. (sl.) patate f.

**spur** n. (of rider, cock, etc.) éperon m.; (stimulus) aiguillon m. ● v.t. éperonner. **on the** ~ **of the moment,** sous l'impulsion du moment.

**spurious** a. faux.

**spurt** v.i. jaillir; (fig.) accélérer. ● n. jet m.; (at work) coup de collier m.

**spy** n. espion(ne) m. (f.). ● v.i. espionner. ● v.t. apercevoir. ~ **on,** espionner.

**squabble** v.i. se chamailler. ● n. chamaillerie f.

**squad** n. (of soldiers etc.) escouade f.; (sport) équipe f.

**squal|id** a. sordide. ~**or** n. conditions sordides f. pl.

**squall** n. rafale f.

**squander** v.t. (money, time, etc.) gaspiller.

**square** n. carré m.; (open space in town) place f.; (instrument) équerre f. ● a. carré; (honest) honnête; (meal) solide; (fam.) ringard. **(all)** ~, (quits) quitte. ● v.t. (settle) régler. ● v.i. (agree) cadrer (**with,** avec). ~ **metre,** mètre carré m.

**squash** v.t. écraser; (crowd) serrer. ● n. (game) squash m. **orange** ~, orangeade f.

**squat** v.i. s'accroupir. ● a. (dumpy) trapu. ~**ter** n. squatter m.

**squawk** n. cri rauque m. ● v.i. pousser un cri rauque.

**squeak** n. petit cri m.; (of door etc.) grincement m. ● v.i. crier; grincer. ~**y** a. grinçant.

**squeal** n. cri aigu m. ● v.i. pousser un cri aigu. ~ **on,** (inform on: sl.) dénoncer.

**squeamish** a. (trop) délicat.

**squeeze** v.t. presser; (hand, arm) serrer; (extract) exprimer (**from,** de); (extort) soutirer (**from,** à). ● v.i. (force one's way) se glisser.

**squid** n. calmar m.

**squiggle** n. ligne onduleuse f.

**squint** v.i. loucher; (with half-shut eyes) plisser les yeux. ● n. (med.) strabisme m.

**squirm** v.i. se tortiller.

**squirrel** n. écureuil m.

**squirt** v.t./i. (faire) jaillir. ● n. jet m.

**stab** v.t. (with knife etc.) poignarder. ● n. coup (de couteau) m. **have a** ~ **at sth.,** essayer de faire qch.

**stabilize** v.t. stabiliser.

**stab|le**[1] a. stable. ~**ility** n. stabilité f.

**stable**[2] n. écurie f. ~**boy** n. lad m.

**stack** n. tas m. ● v.t. ~ **(up),** entasser, empiler.

**stadium** n. stade m.

**staff** n. personnel m.; (in school) professeurs m. pl.; (mil.) état-major m.; (stick) bâton m.

**stag** n. cerf m.

**stage** n. (theatre) scène f.; (phase) stade m., étape f.; (platform in hall) estrade f. ● v.t. mettre en scène; (fig.) organiser. **~-manage** v.t. monter, organiser. **~-manager** n. régisseur m.

**stagger** v.i. chanceler. ● v.t. (shock) stupéfier; (holidays etc.) étaler. **~ing** a. stupéfiant.

**stagnant** a. stagnant.

**stagnat|e** v.i. stagner. **~ion** n. stagnation f.

**staid** a. sérieux.

**stain** v.t. tacher; (wood etc.) colorer. ● n. tache f.; (colouring) colorant m. **~ed glass window**, vitrail m. **~less steel**, acier inoxydable m. **~ remover**, détachant m.

**stair** n. marche f. **the ~s**, l'escalier m.

**staircase** n. escalier m.

**stake** n. (post) pieu m.; (wager) enjeu m. ● v.t. (area) jalonner; (wager) jouer. **at ~**, en jeu.

**stale** a. pas frais; (bread) rassis; (smell) de renfermé; (news) vieux.

**stalemate** n. (chess) pat m.; (fig.) impasse f.

**stalk**[1] n. (of plant) tige f.

**stalk**[2] v.i. marcher de façon guindée. ● v.t. (prey) traquer.

**stall** n. (in stable) stalle f.; (in market) éventaire m. **~s**, (theatre) orchestre m. ● v.t./ i. (auto.) caler.

**stallion** n. étalon m.

**stamina** n. résistance f.

**stammer** v.t./i. bégayer. ● n. bégaiement m.

**stamp** n. (for postage, marking) timbre m.; (mark: fig.) sceau m. **~ out**, supprimer.

**stampede** n. fuite désordonnée f.; (rush: fig.) ruée f. ● v.i. s'enfuir en désordre; se ruer.

**stance** n. position f.

**stand** v.i. être or se tenir (debout); (rise) se lever; (be situated) se trouver; (rest) reposer; (pol.) être candidat (**for**, à). ● v.t. mettre (debout); (tolerate) supporter. ● n. position f.; (mil.) résistance f.; (for lamp etc.) support m.; (at fair) stand m.; (in street) kiosque m.; (for spectators) tribune f.; (jurid., Amer.) barre f. **make a ~**, prendre position. **~ back**, reculer. **~ by**, (be ready) se tenir prêt; (promise, person) rester fidèle à. **~-by** a. de réserve; **be a ~-by**, être de réserve. **~ for**, représenter; (fam.) supporter. **~ in for**, remplacer. **~-in** n. remplaçant(e) m. (f.). **~ up**, se lever. **~ up to**, résister à.

**standard** n. norme f.; (level) niveau (voulu) m.; (flag) étendard m. **~s**, (morals) principes m. pl. ● a. ordinaire. **~ lamp**, lampadaire m. **~ of living**, niveau de vie m.

**standardize** v.t. standardiser.

**standing** a. debout invar.; (army, offer) permanent. ● n. position f., réputation f.; (duration) durée f. **~ order**, prélèvement bancaire m.

**standpoint** n. point de vue m.

**standstill** n. **at a ~**, immobile. **bring/come to a ~**, (s')immobiliser.

**staple**[1] n. agrafe f. ● v.t. agrafer. **~r** n. agrafeuse f.

**staple**[2] a. de base.

**star** n. étoile f.; (famous person) vedette f. ● v.t. (of film) avoir pour vedette. ● v.i. **~ in**, être la vedette de.

**starboard** n. tribord m.

**starch** n. amidon m.; (in food) fécule f. ● v.t. amidonner.

**stare** v.i. **~ at**, regarder fixement. ● n. regard fixe m.

**starfish** n. étoile de mer f.

**start** v.t./i. commencer; (machine) (se) mettre en marche; (fashion etc.) lancer; (cause) provoquer; (jump) sursauter; (of vehicle) démarrer. ● n. commencement m., début m.; (of race) départ m.; (lead) avance f.; (jump) sursaut m. **~ to do**, commencer or se mettre à faire. **~ out**, partir. **~er** n. (auto.) démarreur m.; (runner) partant m.; (culin.) entrée f. **~ing point**, point de départ m.

**startle** v.t. (make jump) faire tressaillir; (shock) alarmer.

**starv|e** v.i. mourir de faim. ● v.t. affamer; (deprive) priver.

**stash** v.t. (hide: sl.) cacher.

**state** n. état m. ● a. d'État, de l'État; (school) public. ● v.t. affirmer (**that**, que); (views) exprimer; (fix) fixer. **the S~s**, les États-Unis.

**statement** n. déclaration f.; (of account) relevé m.

**statesman** n. homme d'État m.

**static** a. statique. ● n. (radio, TV) parasites m. pl.

**station** n. station f.; (rail.) gare f.; (mil.) poste m.; (rank) condition f. ● v.t. poster, placer.

**stationary** a. immobile, stationnaire; (vehicle) à l'arrêt.

**stationery** n. papeterie f.

**statistic** n. statistique f. **~s**, statistique f. **~al** a. statistique.

**statue** n. statue f.

**stature** n. stature f.

**status** n. situation f., statut m.; (prestige) standing m. **~ quo**, statu quo m.

**statut|e** n. loi f. **~es**, (rules) statuts m. pl. **~ory** a. statutaire; (holiday) légal.

**stave** n. (mus.) portée f. ● v.t. **~ off**, éviter, conjurer.

**stay** v.i. rester; (spend time) séjourner; (reside) loger. ● v.t. (hunger) tromper. ● n. séjour m. **~ behind/on/late/etc.**, rester. **~ in/out**, rester à la maison/dehors.

**steadfast** a. ferme.

**stead|y** a. stable; (*hand, voice*) ferme; (*regular*) régulier; (*staid*) sérieux. ● v.t. maintenir, assurer; (*calm*) calmer. ~**ily** adv. fermement; régulièrement.

**steak** n. steak m., bifteck m.; (*of fish*) darne f.

**steal** v.t./i. voler (**from s.o.**, à qn.).

**stealth** n. by ~, furtivement. ~**y** a. furtif.

**steam** n. vapeur f.; (*on glass*) buée f. ● v.t. (*cook*) cuire à la vapeur; (*window*) embuer. ● v.i. fumer. ~ **iron**, fer à vapeur m. ~**y** a. humide.

**steam|er** n. (*culin.*) cuit-vapeur m.; (*also* ~**ship**) bateau à vapeur m.

**steamroller** n. rouleau compresseur m.

**steel** n. acier m.

**steep¹** v.t. (*soak*) tremper. ~**ed in**, (*fig.*) imprégné de.

**steep²** a. raide, rapide; (*price: fam.*) excessif.

**steeple** n. clocher m.

**steer¹** n. (*ox*) bouvillon m.

**steer²** v.t. diriger; (*ship*) gouverner; (*fig.*) guider. ● v.i. (*in ship*) gouverner. ~**ing** n. (*auto.*) direction f. ~**ing-wheel** n. volant m.

**stem¹** n. tige f.; (*of glass*) pied m. ● v.i. ~ **from**, provenir de.

**stem²** v.t. (*stop*) contenir.

**stench** n. puanteur f.

**stencil** n. pochoir m.; (*for typing*) stencil m.

**step** v.i. marcher, aller. ● v.t. ~ **up**, augmenter. ● n. pas m.; (*stair*) marche f.; (*of train*) marchepied m.; (*action*) mesure f. ~**s**, (*ladder*) escabeau m. ~ **down**, (*resign*) démissionner; (*from ladder*) descendre. ~ **forward**, (faire un) pas en avant. ~ **up**, (*pressure*) augmenter. ~ **in**, (*intervene*) intervenir. ~**ladder** n. escabeau m.

**step|brother** n. demi-frère m. ~**daughter** n. belle-fille f. ~**father** n. beau-père m. ~**mother** n. belle-mère f. ~**sister** n. demi-sœur f. ~**son** n. beau-fils m.

**stereo** n. stéréo f.; (*record-player*) chaîne stéréo f. ● a. stéréo *invar*.

**stereotype** n. stéréotype m. ~**d** a. stéréotypé.

**steril|e** a. stérile. ~**ity** n. stérilité f.

**steriliz|e** v.t. stériliser. ~**ation** n. stérilisation f.

**sterling** n. livre(s) sterling f. (*pl.*). ● a. sterling *invar*.; (*silver*) fin; (*fig.*) excellent.

**stern¹** a. sévère.

**stern²** n. (*of ship*) arrière m.

**steroid** n. stéroïde m.

**stethoscope** n. stéthoscope m.

**stew** v.t./i. cuire à la casserole. ● n. ragoût m.

**steward** n. (*of club etc.*) intendant m.; (*on ship etc.*) steward m. ~**ess** n. hôtesse f.

**stick¹** n. bâton m.; (*for walking*) canne f.

**stick²** v.t. (*glue*) coller; (*thrust*) enfoncer; (*put: fam.*) mettre; (*endure: sl.*) supporter. ● v.i. (*adhere*) coller, adhérer; (*to pan*) attacher; (*remain: fam.*) rester; (*be jammed*) être coincé. ~ **at**, persévérer dans. ~ **out** v.t. (*head etc.*) sortir; (*tongue*) tirer; v.i. (*protrude*) dépasser. ~ **to**, (*promise etc.*) rester fidèle à. ~**ing-plaster** n. sparadrap m.

**sticker** n. autocollant m.

**sticky** a. poisseux; (*label, tape*) adhésif.

**stiff** a. raide; (*limb, joint*) ankylosé; (*tough*) dur; (*drink*) fort; (*price*) élevé; (*manner*) guindé.

**stifle** v.t./i. étouffer.

**stile** n. échalier m.

**stiletto** a. & n. ~**s**, ~ **heels** talons aiguille.

**still** a. immobile; (*quiet*) calme, tranquille. ● n. silence m. ● adv. encore, toujours; (*even*) encore; (*nevertheless*) tout de même.

**stilted** a. guindé.

**stilts** n. pl. échasses f. pl.

**stimul|ate** v.t. stimuler. ~**ant** n. stimulant m. ~**ation** n. stimulation f.

**stimulus** n. stimulant m.

**sting** n. piqûre f.; (*organ*) dard m. ● v.t./i. piquer.

**stingy** a. avare (**with**, de).

**stink** n. puanteur f. ● v.i. ~ (**of**), puer.

**stint** v.i. ~ **on**, lésiner sur. ● n. (*work*) tour m.

**stipulat|e** v.t. stipuler. ~**ion** n. stipulation f.

**stir** v.t./i. (*move*) remuer; (*excite*) exciter. ● n. agitation f. ~ **up**, (*trouble etc.*) provoquer.

**stirrup** n. étrier m.

**stitch** n. point m.; (*in knitting*) maille f.; (*med.*) point de suture m.; (*muscle pain*) point de côté m. ● v.t. coudre.

**stock** n. réserve f.; (*comm.*) stock m.; (*financial*) valeurs f. pl.; (*family*) souche f.; (*soup*) bouillon m. ● a. (*goods*) courant. ● v.t. (*shop etc.*) approvisionner; (*sell*) vendre. ● v.i. ~ **up**, s'approvisionner (**with**, de). ~**taking** n. (*comm.*) inventaire m. **in** ~, en stock.

**stockbroker** n. agent de change m.

**stocking** n. bas m.

**stockist** n. stockiste m.

**stockpile** n. stock m. ● v.t. stocker; (*arms*) amasser.

**stocky** a. trapu.

**stoic** n. stoïque m./f. ~**al** a. stoïque.

**stoke** v.t. (*boiler, fire*) alimenter.

**stole** n. (*garment*) étole f.

**stomach** n. estomac m.; (*abdomen*) ventre m. ● v.t. (*put up with*) supporter. ~**ache** n. mal à l'estomac or au ventre m.

**stone** n. pierre f.; (*pebble*) caillou m.; (*in fruit*) noyau m.; (*weight*) 6.350 kg. ● a. de pierre. ● v.t. lapider; (*fruit*) dénoyauter.

**stool** n. tabouret m.

**stoop** v.i. (*bend*) se baisser; (*condescend*) s'abaisser. ● n. **have a** ~, être voûté.

**stop** *v.t./i.* arrêter (**doing,** de faire); (*moving, talking*) s'arrêter; (*prevent*) empêcher (**from,** de); (*hole, leak, etc.*) boucher; (*of pain, noise, etc.*) cesser; (*stay: fam.*) rester. ● *n.* arrêt *m.*; (*full stop*) point *m.* ~ **off,** s'arrêter. ~ **up,** boucher. ~**watch** *n.* chronomètre *m.*

**stopgap** *n.* bouche-trou *m.* ● *a.* intérimaire.

**stoppage** *n.* arrêt *m.*; (*of work*) arrêt de travail *m.*; (*of pay*) retenue *f.*

**stopper** *n.* bouchon *m.*

**storage** *n.* (*of goods, food, etc.*) emmagasinage *m.* ~ **heater,** radiateur électrique à accumulation *m.*

**store** *n.* réserve *f.*; (*warehouse*) entrepôt *m.*; (*shop*) grand magasin *m.*; (*Amer.*) magasin *m.* ● *v.t.* (*for future*) mettre en réserve; (*in warehouse, mind*) emmagasiner. ~**room** *n.* réserve *f.*

**storey** *n.* étage *m.*

**stork** *n.* cigogne *f.*

**storm** *n.* tempête *f.*, orage *m.* ● *v.t.* prendre d'assaut. ● *v.i.* (*rage*) tempêter. ~**y** *a.* orageux.

**story** *n.* histoire *f.*; (*in press*) article *m.*

**stout** *a.* corpulent; (*strong*) solide. ● *n.* bière brune *f.*

**stove** *n.* (*for cooking*) cuisinière *f.*; (*heater*) poêle *m.*

**stow** *v.t.* ~ **away,** (*put away*) ranger; (*hide*) cacher. ● *v.i.* voyager clandestinement.

**stowaway** *n.* passager, ère clandestin(e) *m.*, *f.*

**straddle** *v.t.* être à cheval sur.

**straggle** *v.i.* (*lag behind*) traîner en désordre. ~**r** *n.* traînard(e) *m.* (*f.*).

**straight** *a.* droit; (*tidy*) en ordre; (*frank*) franc. ● *adv.* (*in straight line*) droit; (*direct*) tout droit. ● *n.* ligne droite *f.* ~ **ahead** *or* **on,** tout droit. ~ **away,** tout de suite.

**straighten** *v.t.* (*nail, situation, etc.*) redresser; (*tidy*) arranger.

**straightforward** *a.* honnête; (*easy*) simple.

**strain**¹ *n.* (*breed*) race *f.*; (*streak*) tendance *f.*

**strain**² *v.t.* (*rope, ears*) tendre; (*limb*) fouler; (*eyes*) fatiguer; (*muscle*) froisser; (*filter*) passer; (*vegetables*) égoutter. ● *n.* tension *f.*; (*fig.*) effort *m.* ~**ed** *a.* forcé; (*relations*) tendu. ~**er** *n.* passoire *f.*

**strait** *n.* détroit *m.* ~**s,** détroit *m.*; (*fig.*) embarras *m.*

**strand** *n.* (*thread*) fil *m.*, brin *m.*; (*lock of hair*) mèche *f.*

**stranded** *a.* (*person*) en rade; (*ship*) échoué.

**strange** *a.* étrange; (*unknown*) inconnu. ~**ly** *adv.* étrangement.

**stranger** *n.* inconnu(e) *m.* (*f.*).

**strangle** *v.t.* étrangler.

**strap** *n.* (*of leather etc.*) courroie *f.*; (*of dress*) bretelle *f.*; (*of watch*) bracelet *m.* ● *v.t.* attacher.

**strategic** *a.* stratégique.

**strategy** *n.* stratégie *f.*

**stratum** *n.* couche *f.*

**straw** *n.* paille *f.*

**strawberry** *n.* fraise *f.*

**stray** *v.i.* s'égarer; (*deviate*) s'écarter. ● *a.* perdu; (*isolated*) isolé. ● *n.* animal perdu *m.*

**streak** *n.* raie *f.*, bande *f.*; (*trace*) trace *f.*; (*period*) période *f.*; (*tendency*) tendance *f.* ● *v.t.* (*mark*) strier. ● *v.i.* filer à toute allure. ~**y** *a.* strié.

**stream** *n.* ruisseau *m.*; (*current*) courant *m.*; (*flow*) flot *m.*; (*in schools*) classe (de niveau) *f.* ● *v.i.* ruisseler (**with,** de); (*eyes, nose*) couler.

**streamer** *n.* (*of paper*) serpentin *m.*; (*flag*) banderole *f.*

**streamline** *v.t.* rationaliser. ~**d** *a.* (*shape*) aérodynamique.

**street** *n.* rue *f.* ~ **map,** plan des rues *m.*

**strength** *n.* force *f.*; (*of wall, fabric, etc.*) solidité *f.*

**strengthen** *v.t.* renforcer.

**strenuous** *a.* énergique; (*arduous*) ardu; (*tiring*) fatigant.

**stress** *n.* accent *m.*; (*pressure*) pression *f.*; (*med.*) stress *m.* ● *v.t.* souligner, insister sur.

**stretch** *v.t.* (*pull taut*) tendre; (*arm, leg*) étendre; (*neck*) tendre; (*clothes*) étirer; (*truth etc.*) forcer. ● *v.i.* s'étendre; (*person, clothes*) s'étirer. ● *n.* étendue *f.*; (*period*) période *f.*; (*of road*) tronçon *m.* ● *a.* (*fabric*) extensible.

**stretcher** *n.* brancard *m.*

**strew** *v.t.* (*scatter*) répandre; (*cover*) joncher.

**stricken** *a.* ~ **with,** frappé *or* atteint de.

**strict** *a.* strict. ~**ly** *adv.* strictement.

**stride** *v.i.* faire de grands pas. ● *n.* grand pas *m.*

**strident** *a.* strident.

**strife** *n.* conflit(s) *m.* (*pl.*).

**strike** *v.t.* frapper; (*blow*) donner; (*match*) frotter; (*gold etc.*) trouver. ● *v.i.* faire grève; (*attack*) attaquer; (*clock*) sonner. ● *n.* (*of workers*) grève *f.*; (*mil.*) attaque *f.*; (*find*) découverte *f.* **on** ~**,** en grève.

**striker** *n.* gréviste *m.* / *f.*; (*football*) buteur *m.*

**striking** *a.* frappant.

**string** *n.* ficelle *f.*; (*of violin, racket, etc.*) corde *f.*; (*of pearls*) collier *m.*; (*of lies etc.*) chapelet *m.* ● *v.t.* (*thread*) enfiler. ~ **bean,** haricot vert *m.*

**stringent** *a.* rigoureux.

**strip**¹ *v.t./i.* (*undress*) (se) déshabiller; (*machine*) démonter; (*deprive*) dépouiller. ~**per** *n.* strip-teaseuse *f.*; (*solvent*) décapant *m.* ~**tease** *n.* strip-tease *m.*

**strip**² *n.* bande *f.* ~ **light,** néon *m.*

**stripe** *n.* rayure *f.*, raie *f.* ~**d** *a.* rayé.

**strive** *v.i.* s'efforcer (**to,** de).

**stroke**¹ *n.* coup *m.*; (*of pen*) trait *m.*; (*swimming*) nage *f.*; (*med.*) attaque *f.*, congestion *f.*

**stroke**² *v.t.* (*with hand*) caresser. ● *n.* caresse *f.*

**stroll** v.i. flâner. ● n. petit tour m. ~ **in**/etc., entrer/etc. tranquillement.

**strong** a. fort; (shoes, fabric, etc.) solide. ~**box** n. coffre-fort m. ~**ly** adv. (greatly) fortement; (with energy) avec force; (deeply) profondément.

**stronghold** n. bastion m.

**structur|e** n. (of cell, poem, etc.) structure f.; (building) construction f. ~**al** a. structurel; de (la) construction.

**struggle** v.i. lutter, se battre. ● n. lutte f.; (effort) effort m. **have a ~ to,** avoir du mal à.

**strum** v.t. gratter de.

**strut** n. (support) étai m. ● v.i. se pavaner.

**stub** n. bout m.; (of tree) souche f.; (counterfoil) talon m. ● v.t. ~**one's toe,** se cogner le doigt de pied. ~ **out,** écraser.

**stubble** n. (on chin) barbe de plusieurs jours f.; (remains of wheat) chaume m.

**stubborn** a. opiniâtre, obstiné. ~**ly** adv. obstinément. ~**ness** n. opiniâtreté f.

**stubby** a. (finger) épais; (person) trapu.

**stuck** a. (jammed) coincé. **I'm ~,** (for answer) je sèche.

**stud**[1] n. clou m.; (for collar) bouton m. ● v.t. clouter. ~**ded with,** parsemé de.

**stud**[2] n. (horses) écurie f.

**student** n. (univ.) étudiant(e) m. (f.); (schol.) élève m./f. ● a. (restaurant, life, residence) universitaire.

**studio** n. studio m. ~ **flat,** studio m.

**studious** a. (person) studieux; (deliberate) étudié.

**study** n. étude f.; (office) bureau m. ● v.t./i. étudier.

**stuff** n. substance f.; (sl.) chose(s) f. (pl.). ● v.t. rembourrer; (animal) empailler; (cram) bourrer; (culin.) farcir; (block up) boucher; (put) fourrer. ~**ing** n. bourre f.; (culin.) farce f.

**stuffy** a. mal aéré; (dull: fam.) vieux jeu invar.

**stumble** v.i. trébucher. ~ **across** or **on,** tomber sur.

**stump** n. (of tree) souche f.; (of limb) moignon m.; (of pencil) bout m.

**stun** v.t. étourdir; (bewilder) stupéfier.

**stunning** a. (delightful: fam.) sensationnel.

**stunt**[1] v.t. (growth) retarder. ~**ed** a. (person) rabougri.

**stunt**[2] n. (feat: fam.) tour de force m.; (dangerous) cascade f. ~**man** n. cascadeur m.

**stupefy** v.t. abrutir; (amaze) stupéfier.

**stupid** a. stupide, bête. ~**ity** n. stupidité f. ~**ly** adv. bêtement.

**sturdy** a. robuste.

**stutter** v.i. bégayer. ● n. bégaiement m.

**sty**[1] n. (pigsty) porcherie f.

**sty**[2] n. (on eye) orgelet m.

**styl|e** n. style m.; (fashion) mode f.; (sort) genre m.; (pattern) modèle m. ● v.t. (design) créer. ~**ist** n. (of hair) coiffeu|r, -se m., f.

**stylish** a. élégant.

**stylized** a. stylisé.

**stylus** n. saphir m.

**suave** a. (urbane) courtois; (smooth: pej.) doucereux.

**sub-** pref. sous-, sub-.

**subconscious** a. & n. inconscient (m.), subconscient (m.). ~**ly** adv. inconsciemment.

**subcontract** v.t. sous-traiter.

**subdivide** v.t. subdiviser.

**subdue** v.t. (feeling) maîtriser; (country) subjuguer. ~**d** a. (weak) faible; (light) tamisé; (person, criticism) retenu.

**subject**[1] a. (state etc.) soumis. ● n. sujet m.; (schol., univ.) matière f.; (citizen) ressortissant(e) m. (f.), sujet(te) m. (f.). ~ **to,** soumis à; (liable to, dependent on) sujet à.

**subject**[2] v.t. soumettre. ~**ion** /-kʃn/ n. soumission f.

**subjective** a. subjectif.

**subjunctive** a. & n. subjonctif (m.).

**sublet** v.t. sous-louer.

**sublime** a. sublime.

**submarine** n. sousmarin m.

**submerge** v.t. submerger. ● v.i. plonger.

**submi|t** v.t./i. (se) soumettre (**to,** à). ~**ssion** n. soumission f.

**subordinate**[1] a. subalterne; (gram.) subordonné. ● n. subordonné(e) m. (f.).

**subordinate**[2] v.t. subordonner (**to,** à).

**subroutine** n. sous-programme m.

**subscribe** v.t./i. verser (de l'argent) (**to,** à). ~ **to,** (loan, theory) souscrire à; (newspaper) s'abonner à, être abonné à. ~**r** n. abonné(e) m. (f.).

**subscription** n. souscription f.; abonnement m.; (membership dues) cotisation f.

**subsequent** a. (later) ultérieur; (next) suivant. ~**ly** adv. par la suite.

**subside** v.i. (land etc.) s'affaisser; (flood, wind) baisser. ~**nce** /-əns/ n. affaissement m.

**subsidiary** a. accessoire. ● n. (comm.) filiale f.

**subsid|y** n. subvention f. ~**ize** v.t. subventionner.

**subsist** v.i. subsister. ~**ence** n. subsistance f.

**substance** n. substance f.

**substandard** a. de qualité inférieure.

**substantial** a. considérable; (meal) substantiel.

**substantiate** v.t. prouver.

**substitut|e** n. succédané m.; (person) remplaçant(e) m. (f.). ● v.t. substituer (**for,** à). ~**ion** n. substitution f.

**subterfuge** n. subterfuge m.

**subtitle** n. sous-titre m.

**subtle** a. subtil. ~**ty** n. subtilité f.

**subtract** v.t. soustraire. ~**ion** n. soustraction f.

**suburb** n. faubourg m., banlieue f. ~**s**, banlieue f. ~**an** a. de banlieue.

**subversive** a. subversif.

**subway** n. passage souterrain m.; (*Amer.*) métro m.

**succeed** v.i. réussir (**in doing**, à faire). ● v.t. (*follow*) succéder à. ~**ing** a. suivant.

**success** n. succès m.

**successful** a. réussi, couronné de succès; (*favourable*) heureux; (*in exam*) reçu.

**succession** n. succession f. **in** ~, de suite.

**successive** a. successif. **six** ~ **days,** six jours consécutifs.

**successor** n. successeur m.

**succinct** a. succinct.

**succulent** a. succulent.

**succumb** v.i. succomber.

**such** a. & pron. tel(le), tel(le)s; (*so much*) tant (de). ● adv. si. ~ **a book**/etc., un tel livre/etc. ~ **books**/etc., de tels livres/etc. ~ **courage**/etc., tant de courage/ etc. ~ **a big house,** une si grande maison. ~ **as,** comme, tel que. **as** ~, en tant que tel.

**suck** v.t. sucer. ~ **in** or **up,** aspirer.

**sudden** a. soudain, subit. **all of a** ~, tout à coup. ~**ly** adv. subitement, brusquement. ~**ness** n. soudaineté f.

**suds** n. pl. (*froth*) mousse de savon f.

**sue** v.t. poursuivre (en justice).

**suede** n. daim m.

**suet** n. graisse de rognon f.

**suffer** v.t./i. souffrir; (*loss, attack, etc.*) subir.

**sufficient** a. (*enough*) suffisamment de; (*big enough*) suffisant. ~**ly** adv. suffisamment.

**suffix** n. suffixe m.

**suffocat|e** v.t./i. suffoquer. ~**ion** n. suffocation f.; (*med.*) asphyxie f.

**sugar** n. sucre m. ● v.t. sucrer. ~**y** a. sucré.

**suggest** v.t. suggérer. ~**ion** n. suggestion f.

**suggestive** a. suggestif. **be** ~ **of,** suggérer.

**suicide** n. suicide m. **commit** ~, se suicider.

**suit** n. costume m.; (*woman's*) tailleur m.; (*cards*) couleur f. ● v.t. convenir à; (*of garment, style, etc.*) aller à; (*adapt*) adapter. ~**able** a. qui convient (**for,** à), convenable. ~**ably** adv. convenablement.

**suitcase** n. valise f.

**suite** n. (*rooms, retinue*) suite f.; (*furniture*) mobilier m.

**sulk** v.i. bouder. ~**y** a. boudeur.

**sullen** a. maussade. ~**ly** adv. d'un air maussade.

**sulphur** n. soufre m. ~**ic** a. ~**ic acid,** acide sulfurique m.

**sultana** n. raisin de Smyrne m.

**sultry** a. étouffant, lourd; (*fig.*) sensuel.

**sum** n. somme f.; (*in arithmetic*) calcul m. ● v.t./i. ~ **up,** résumer, récapituler; (*assess*) évaluer.

**summar|y** n. résumé m. ● a. sommaire. ~**ize** v.t. résumer.

**summer** n. été m. ● a. d'été.

**summit** n. sommet m.

**summon** v.t. appeler; (*meeting, s.o. to meeting*) convoquer.

**summons** n. (*jurid.*) assignation f. ● v.t. assigner.

**sump** n. (*auto.*) carter m.

**sumptuous** a. somptueux.

**sun** n. soleil m. ~**glasses** n. pl. lunettes de soleil f. pl. ~**roof** n. toit ouvrant m. ~**tan** n. bronzage m. ~**tanned** a. bronzé.

**sunbathe** v.i. prendre un bain de soleil.

**sunburn** n. coup de soleil m. ~**t** a. brûlé par le soleil.

**Sunday** n. dimanche m.

**sundial** n. cadran solaire m.

**sundr|y** a. divers. ~**ies** n. pl. articles divers m. pl.

**sunflower** n. tournesol m.

**sunlight** n. soleil m.

**sunny** a. ensoleillé.

**sunrise** n. lever du soleil m.

**sunset** n. coucher du soleil m.

**sunshade** n. (*lady's*) ombrelle f.; (*awning*) parasol m.

**sunshine** n. soleil m.

**sunstroke** n. insolation f.

**super** a. (*sl.*) formidable.

**superb** a. superbe.

**superficial** a. superficiel.

**superfluous** a. superflu.

**superimpose** v.t. superposer (**on,** à).

**superintendent** n. direc|teur, -trice m., f.; (*of police*) commissaire m.

**superior** a. & n. supérieur(e) (m. (f.)). ~**ity** n. supériorité f.

**superlative** a. suprême. ● n. (*gram.*) superlatif m.

**supermarket** n. supermarché m.

**supernatural** a. surnaturel.

**superpower** n. superpuissance f.

**supersede** v.t. supplanter.

**supersonic** a. supersonique.

**superstiti|on** n. superstition f. ~**ous** a. superstitieux.

**superstore** n. hypermarché m.

**supertanker** n. pétrolier géant m.

**supervis|e** v.t. surveiller, diriger. ~**ion** n. surveillance f. ~**or** n. surveillant(e) m. (f.); (*shop*) chef de rayon m.; (*firm*) chef de service m.

**supper** n. dîner m.; (*late at night*) souper m.

**supple** a. souple.

**supplement¹** n. supplément m. **~ary** a. supplémentaire.

**supplement²** v.t. compléter.

**supplier** n. fournisseur m.

**suppl|y** v.t. fournir; (equip) pourvoir; (feed) alimenter (with, en). ● n. provision f.; (of gas etc.) alimentation f. **~ies,** (food) vivres m. pl.; (material) fournitures f. pl.

**support** v.t. soutenir; (family) assurer la subsistance de; (endure) supporter. ● n. soutien m., appui m.; (techn.) support m. **~er** n. partisan(e)m. (f.); (sport) supporter m.

**suppos|e** v.t./i. supposer. **be ~ed to do,** être censé faire, devoir faire. **~ing he comes,** supposons qu'il vienne.

**supposedly** adv. soi-disant.

**suppress** v.t. (put an end to) supprimer; (restrain) réprimer; (stifle) étouffer. **~ion** n. suppression f.; répression f.

**supreme** a. suprême.

**surcharge** n. prix supplémentaire m.; (tax) surtaxe f.; (on stamp) surcharge f.

**sure** a. sûr. ● adv. (Amer., fam.) pour sûr. **make ~ of,** s'assurer de. **make ~ that,** vérifier que. **~ly** adv. sûrement.

**surety** n. caution f.

**surf** n. (waves) ressac m. **~ing** n. surf m.

**surface** n. surface f. ● a. superficiel. ● v.t. revêtir. ● v.i. faire surface; (fig.) réapparaître.

**surfboard** n. planche de surf f.

**surfeit** n. excès m. (of, de).

**surge** v.i. (of crowd) déferler; (of waves) s'enfler; (increase) monter. ● n. (wave) vague f.; (rise) montée f.

**surgeon** n. chirurgien m.

**surg|ery** n. chirurgie f.; (office) cabinet m.; (session) consultation f. **~ical** a. chirurgical. **~ical spirit,** alcool à 90 degrés m.

**surly** a. bourru.

**surmount** v.t. surmonter.

**surname** n. nom de famille m.

**surpass** v.t. surpasser.

**surplus** n. surplus m. ● a. en surplus.

**surpris|e** n. surprise f. ● v.t. surprendre. **~ed** a. surpris (at, de). **~ing** a. surprenant.

**surrender** v.i. se rendre. ● v.t. (hand over) remettre; (mil.) rendre. ● n. (mil.) reddition f.

**surround** v.t. entourer; (mil.) encercler. **~ing** a. environnant. **~ings** n. pl. environs m. pl.; (setting) cadre m.

**surveillance** n. surveillance f.

**survey¹** v.t. (review) passer en revue; (inquire into) enquêter sur; (building) inspecter. **~or** n. expert (géomètre) m.

**survey²** n. (inquiry) enquête f.; inspection f.; (general view) vue d'ensemble f.

**survival** n. survie f.

**surviv|e** v.t./i. survivre (à). **~or** n. survivant(e) m. (f.).

**susceptible** a. sensible (to, à). **~ to,** (prone to) prédisposé à.

**suspect¹** v.t. soupçonner; (doubt) douter de.

**suspect²** n. & a. suspect(e) (m. (f.)).

**suspen|d** v.t. (hang, stop) suspendre; (licence) retirer provisoirement. **~ded sentence,** condamnation avec sursis f. **~sion** n. suspension f.; retrait provisoire m.

**suspender** n. jarretelle f. **~ belt,** porte-jarretelles m.

**suspense** n. attente f.; (in book etc.) suspense m.

**suspicion** n. soupçon m.; (distrust) méfiance f.

**suspicious** a. soupçonneux; (causing suspicion) suspect. **be ~ of,** (distrust) se méfier de. **~ly** adv. de façon suspecte.

**sustain** v.t. supporter; (effort etc.) soutenir; (suffer) subir.

**swab** n. (pad) tampon m.

**swallow¹** v.t./i. avaler. **~ up,** (absorb, engulf) engloutir.

**swallow²** n. hirondelle f.

**swamp** n. marais m. ● v.t. (flood, overwhelm) submerger. **~y** a. marécageux.

**swan** n. cygne m.

**swank** n. (behaviour: fam.) épate f., esbroufe f.; (person: fam.) crâneu|r, -se m., f. ● v.i. (show off: fam.) crâner.

**swap** v.t./i. (fam.) échanger. ● n. (fam.) échange m.

**swarm** n. (of insects, people) essaim m. ● v.i. fourmiller. **~ into** or **round,** (crowd) envahir.

**swat** v.t. (fly etc.) écraser.

**sway** v.t./i. (se) balancer; (influence) influencer. ● n. balancement m.; (rule) empire m.

**swear** v.t./i. jurer (to sth., de qch.). **~ at,** injurier.

**sweat** n. sueur f. ● v.i. suer. **~-shirt** n. sweat-shirt m. **~y** a. en sueur.

**sweater** n. pull-over m.

**swede** n. rutabaga m.

**Swed|e** n. Suédois(e) m. (f.). **~en** n. Suède f. **~ish** a. suédois; n. (lang.) suédois m.

**sweep** v.t./i. balayer; (carry away) emporter, entraîner; (chimney) ramonner. ● n. coup de balai m.; (curve) courbe f.; (movement) geste m., mouvement m.; (for chimneys) ramoneur m. **~ out,** balayer. **~er** n. (for carpet) balai mécanique m.; (football) arrière volant m.

**sweet** a. (not sour, pleasant) doux; (not savoury) sucré; (charming) gentil. ● n. bonbon m.; (dish) dessert m.; (person) chéri(e) m. (f.). **~ corn,** maïs m. **~ pea,** pois de senteur m. **~ shop,** confiserie f. **~ly** adv. gentiment. **~ness** n. douceur f.; goût sucré m.

**sweeten** v.t. sucrer; (fig.) adoucir. **~er** n. édulcorant m.

**swell** v.t./i. (increase) grossir; (expand) (se) gonfler; (of hand, face) enfler. ● n. (of sea) houle f. ● a. (fam.) formidable. ~ing n. (med.) enflure f.

**swerve** v.i. faire un écart.

**swift** a. rapide. ● n. (bird) martinet m. ~ly adv. rapidement. ~ness n. rapidité f.

**swill** v.t. rincer; (drink) lamper. ● n. (pig-food) pâtée f.

**swim** v.i. nager; (be dizzy) tourner. ● v.t. traverser à la nage; (distance) nager. ● n. baignade f. **go for a ~,** aller se baigner. ~mer n. nageu|r, -se m., f. ~ming n. natation f. ~ming-pool n. piscine f. ~suit n. maillot (de bain) m.

**swindle** v.t. escroquer. ● n. escroquerie f. ~r n. escroc m.

**swine** n. pl. (pigs) pourceaux m. pl. ● n. invar. (person: fam.) salaud m.

**swing** v.t./i. (se) balancer; (turn round) tourner; (of pendulum) osciller. ● n. balancement m.; (seat) balançoire f.; (of opinion) revirement m. (**towards,** en faveur de); (mus.) rythme m. ~ **round,** (of person) se retourner.

**swirl** v.i. tourbillonner. ● n. tourbillon m.

**Swiss** a. suisse. ● n. invar. Suisse(sse) m. (f.).

**switch** n. bouton (électrique) m., interrupteur m.; (shift) changement m., revirement m. ● v.t. (transfer) transférer; (exchange) échanger (**for,** contre); (reverse positions of) changer de place. ~ **trains**/etc., (change) changer de train/etc. ● v.i. (go over) passer. ~ **off,** éteindre. ~ **on,** mettre, allumer.

**switchboard** n. (telephone) standard m.

**Switzerland** n. Suisse f.

**swivel** v.t./i. (faire) pivoter.

**swoon** v.i. se pâmer.

**swoop** v.i. (bird) fondre; (police) faire une descente, foncer. ● n. (police raid) descente f.

**sword** n. épée f.

**swot** v.t./i. (study: sl.) bûcher. ● n. (sl.) bûcheu|r, -se m., f.

**sycamore** n. sycomore m.

**syllable** n. syllabe f.

**syllabus** n. programme m.

**symbol** n. symbole m. ~ic(al) a. symbolique. ~ism n. symbolisme m.

**symbolize** v.t. symboliser.

**symmetr|y** n. symétrie f. ~ical a. symétrique.

**sympathize** v.i. ~ **with,** (pity) plaindre; (fig.) comprendre les sentiments de. ~r n. sympathisant(e) m. (f.).

**sympath|y** n. (pity) compassion f.; (fig.) compréhension f.; (solidarity) solidarité f.; (condolences) condoléances f. pl. **be in ~y with,** comprendre, être en accord avec. ~etic a. compatissant; (fig.) compréhensif.

**symphon|y** n. symphonie f. ● a. symphonique. ~ic a. symphonique.

**symptom** n. symptôme m.

**synagogue** n. synagogue f.

**synchronize** v.t. synchroniser.

**syndicate** n. syndicat m.

**syndrome** n. syndrome m.

**synonym** n. synonyme m. ~ous a. synonyme.

**synopsis** n. résumé m.

**syntax** n. syntaxe f.

**synthesis** n. synthèse f.

**synthetic** a. synthétique.

**syphilis** n. syphilis f.

**Syria** n. Syrie f. ~n a. & n. syrien(ne) (m. (f.)).

**syringe** n. seringue f.

**syrup** n. (liquid) sirop m.; (treacle) mélasse raffinée f. ~y a. sirupeux.

**system** n. système m.; (body) organisme m.; (order) méthode f. ~s **analyst,** analyste-programmeu|r, -se m., f. ~s **disk,** disque système m.

**systematic** a. systématique.

# Tt

**tab** n. (flap) languette f., patte f.; (loop) attache f.; (label) étiquette f.

**table** n. table f. ● v.t. présenter; (postpone) ajourner. ● a. (lamp, wine) de table. **at ~,** à table. **lay** or **set the ~,** mettre la table. ~-cloth n. nappe f. ~-mat n. dessous-de-plat m. invar.; (cloth) set m. ~ **tennis,** ping-pong m.

**tablespoon** n. cuiller à soupe f. ~ful n. cuillerée à soupe f.

**tablet** n. (of stone) plaque f.; (drug) comprimé m.

**taboo** n. & a. tabou (m.).

**tabulator** n. tabulateur m.

**tacit** a. tacite.

**taciturn** a. taciturne.

**tack** n. (nail) broquette f.; (stitch) point de bâti m.; (course of action) voie f. ● v.t. (nail) clouer; (stitch) bâtir; (add) ajouter. ● v.i. (naut.) louvoyer.

**tackle** n. équipement m., matériel m.; (football) plaquage m. ● v.t. (problem etc.) s'attaquer à; (football player) plaquer.

**tacky** a. poisseux, pas sec; (shabby, mean: Amer.) moche.

**tact** n. tact m. ~ful a. plein de tact. ~fully adv. avec tact. ~less a. qui manque de tact.

**tactic** n. tactique f. ~s n. & n. pl. tactique f. ~al a. tactique.

**tadpole** n. têtard m.

**tag** n. (*label*) étiquette f.; (*end piece*) bout m.; (*phrase*) cliché m. ● v.t. étiqueter; (*join*) ajouter. ● v.i. ~ **along,** (*fam.*) suivre.

**tail** n. queue f.; (*of shirt*) pan m. ● v.t. (*follow*) filer. ● v.i. ~ **away** or **off,** diminuer. ~**-back** n. (*traffic*) bouchon m. ~**gate** n. hayon arrière m.

**tailor** n. tailleur m. ● v.t. (*garment*) façonner; (*fig.*) adapter. ~**-made for,** (*fig.*) fait pour.

**take** v.t./i. prendre; (*carry*) (ap)porter (**to,** à); (*escort*) accompagner, amener; (*contain*) contenir; (*tolerate*) supporter; (*prize*) remporter; (*exam*) passer; (*choice*) faire; (*precedence*) avoir. ~ **sth. from s.o.,** prendre qch. à qn. ~ **sth. from a place,** prendre qch. d'un endroit. ~ **s.o. home,** ramener qn. chez lui. **it ~s time/courage/**etc. **to,** il faut du temps/du courage/etc. pour. ~ **apart,** démonter. ~ **away,** (*object*) emporter; (*person*) emmener; (*remove*) enlever (**from,** à). ~**away** n. (*meal*) plat à emporter m.; (*shop*) restaurant qui fait des plats à emporter m. ~ **back,** reprendre; (*return*) rendre; (*accompany*) raccompagner; (*statement*) retirer. ~ **down,** (*object*) descendre; (*notes*) prendre. ~ **in,** (*object*) rentrer; (*include*) inclure; (*cheat*) tromper; (*grasp*) saisir. ~ **on,** (*task, staff, passenger, etc.*) prendre. ~ **out,** sortir; (*stain etc.*) enlever. ~ **over** v.t. (*factory, country, etc.*) prendre la direction de; (*firm: comm.*) racheter; v.i. (*of dictator*) prendre le pouvoir. ~**over** n. (*pol.*) prise de pouvoir f.; (*comm.*) rachat m. ~ **part,** participer (**in,** à). ~ **place,** avoir lieu. ~ **to doing,** se mettre à faire. ~ **up,** (*object*) monter; (*hobby*) se mettre à; (*occupy*) prendre; (*resume*) reprendre.

**takings** n. pl. recette f.

**talcum** n. ~ (**powder**), talc m.

**tale** n. conte m.; (*report*) récit m.; (*lie*) histoire f.

**talent** n. talent m. ~**ed** a. doué.

**talk** v.t./i. parler; (*say*) dire; (*chat*) bavarder. ● n. conversation f., entretien m.; (*words*) propos m. pl.; (*lecture*) exposé m.

**talkative** a. bavard.

**tall** a. (*high*) haut; (*person*) grand.

**tally** v.i. correspondre (**with,** avec).

**tambourine** n. tambourin m.

**tame** a. apprivoisé; (*dull*) insipide. ● v.t. apprivoiser; (*lion*) dompter.

**tamper** v.i. ~ **with,** toucher à, tripoter; (*text*) altérer.

**tampon** n. (*med.*) tampon hygiénique m.

**tan** v.t./i. bronzer; (*hide*) tanner. ● n. bronzage m. ● a. marron clair invar.

**tang** n. (*taste*) saveur forte f.; (*smell*) odeur forte f.

**tangent** n. tangente f.

**tangerine** n. mandarine f.

**tangible** a. tangible.

**tangle** v.t. enchevêtrer. ● n. enchevêtrement m. **become ~d,** s'enchevêtrer.

**tank** n. réservoir m.; (*vat*) cuve f.; (*for fish*) aquarium m.; (*mil.*) char m., tank m.

**tankard** n. chope f.

**tanker** n. camion-citerne m.; (*ship*) pétrolier m.

**tantaliz|e** v.t. tourmenter. ~**ing** a. tentant.

**tantamount** a. **be ~ to,** équivaloir à.

**tantrum** n. crise de rage f.

**tap**[1] n. (*for water etc.*) robinet m. ● v.t. (*resources*) exploiter; (*telephone*) mettre sur table d'écoute.

**tap**[2] v.t./i. frapper (doucement). ● n. petit coup m.

**tape** n. ruban m.; (*sticky*) ruban adhésif m. (**magnetic**) ~, bande (magnétique) f. ● v.t. (*tie*) attacher; (*stick*) coller; (*record*) enregistrer. ~**-measure** n. mètre (à) ruban m. ~ **recorder,** magnétophone m.

**taper** n. (*for lighting*) bougie f. ● v.t./i. (s')effiler. ~ **off,** (*diminish*) diminuer.

**tapestry** n. tapisserie f.

**tar** n. goudron m. ● v.t. goudronner.

**target** n. cible f.; (*objective*) objectif m. ● v.t. prendre pour cible.

**tariff** n. (*charges*) tarif m.; (*on imports*) tarif douanier m.

**Tarmac** n. (P.) macadam (goudronné) m.; (*runway*) piste f.

**tarnish** v.t./i. (se) ternir.

**tarpaulin** n. bâche goudronnée f.

**tarragon** n. estragon m.

**tart**[1] a. acide.

**tart**[2] n. tarte f.; (*prostitute: sl.*) poule f. ● v.t. ~ **up,** (*pej., sl.*) embellir (sans le moindre goût).

**tartan** n. tartan m. ● a. écossais.

**tartar** n. tartre m. ~ **sauce,** sauce tartare f.

**task** n. tâche f., travail m. ~ **force,** détachement spécial m.

**taste** n. goût m. ● v.t. (*eat, enjoy*) goûter; (*try*) goûter à; (*perceive taste of*) sentir le goût de. ● v.i. ~ **of** or **like,** avoir un goût de. ~**less** a. sans goût; (*fig.*) de mauvais goût.

**tasteful** a. de bon goût. ~**ly** adv. avec goût.

**tasty** a. savoureux.

**tattoo** v.t. tatouer. ● n. tatouage m.

**tatty** a. (*fam.*) minable.

**taunt** v.t. railler. ● n. raillerie f. ~**ing** a. railleur.

**Taurus** n. le Taureau.

**taut** a. tendu.

**tavern** n. taverne f.

**tawdry** a. (*showy*) tape-à-l'œil invar.

**tax** n. taxe f., impôt m.; (*on income*) impôts m. pl. ● v.t. imposer; (*put to test: fig.*) mettre à l'épreuve. ~**able** a. imposable. ~**ation** n. imposition f.; (*taxes*) impôts m. pl. ~**-free** a.

exempt d'impôts. ~ **inspector,** inspecteur des impôts *m.* ~ **relief,** dégrèvement fiscal *m.* ~ **return,** déclaration d'impôts *f.*

**taxi** *n.* taxi *m.* ● *v.i.* ~ **rank,** station de taxi *f.*

**taxpayer** *n.* contribuable *m./f.*

**tea** *n.* thé *m.*; (*snack*) goûter *m.* ~**towel** *n.* torchon *m.*

**teach** *v.t.* apprendre (**s.o. sth.,** qch. à qn.); (*in school*) enseigner (**s.o. sth.,** qch. à qn.). ● *v.i.* enseigner. ~**er** *n.* professeur *m.*; (*primary*) institu|teur, -trice *m., f.*

**teacup** *n.* tasse à thé *f.*

**teak** *n.* (*wood*) teck *m.*

**team** *n.* équipe *f.*; (*of animals*) attelage *m.* ● *v.i.* ~ **up,** faire équipe (**with,** avec).

**teapot** *n.* théière *f.*

**tear**[1] *v.t./i.* (se) déchirer; (*snatch*) arracher (**from,** à); (*rush*) aller à toute vitesse. ● *n.* déchirure *f.*

**tear**[2] *n.* larme *f.*

**tease** *v.t.* taquiner. ● *n.* (*person: fam.*) taquin(e) *m.* (*f.*).

**teaspoon** *n.* petite cuiller *f.* ~**ful** *n.* cuillerée à café *f.*

**teat** *n.* tétine *f.*

**technical** *a.* technique. ~**ity** *n.* détail technique *m.* ~**ly** *adv.* techniquement.

**technician** *n.* technicien(ne) *m.* (*f.*).

**technique** *n.* technique *f.*

**technolog|y** *n.* technologie *f.* ~**ical** *a.* technologique.

**teddy** *a.* ~ **bear,** nounours *m.*

**tedious** *a.* fastidieux.

**tee** *n.* (*golf*) tee *m.*

**teem**[1] *v.i.* (*swarm*) grouiller (**with,** de).

**teem**[2] *v.i.* ~ (**with rain**), pleuvoir à torrents.

**teenage** *a.* (d')adolescent. ~**d** *a.* adolescent. ~**r** *n.* adolescent(e) *m.* (*f.*).

**teeter** *v.i.* chanceler.

**teeth|e** *v.i.* faire ses dents. ~**ing troubles,** (*fig.*) difficultés initiales *f. pl.*

**telecommunications** *n. pl.* télécommunications *f. pl.*

**telegram** *n.* télégramme *m.*

**telegraph** *n.* télégraphe *m.*

**telepath|y** *n.* télépathie *f.* ~**ic** *a.* télépathique.

**telephone** *n.* téléphone *m.* ● *v.t.* (*person*) téléphoner à; (*message*) téléphoner. ● *v.i.* téléphoner. ~ **book,** annuaire *m.* ~ **booth,** cabine téléphonique *f.* ~ **call,** coup de téléphone *m.* ~**number,** numéro de téléphone *m.*

**telephoto** *a.* ~ **lens,** téléobjectif *m.*

**telescop|e** *n.* télescope *m.* ● *v.t./i.* (se) télescoper. ~**ic** *a.* télescopique.

**teletext** *n.* télétexte *m.*

**televise** *v.t.* téléviser.

**television** *n.* télévision *f.*

**telex** *n.* télex *m.* ● *v.t.* envoyer par télex.

**tell** *v.t.* dire (**s.o. sth.,** qch. à qn.); (*story*) raconter; (*distinguish*) distinguer. ● *v.i.* avoir un effet; (*know*) savoir. ~ **of,** parler de. ~ **off,** (*fam.*) gronder.

**teller** *n.* (*in bank*) caiss|ier, -ière *m., f.*

**telling** *a.* révélateur.

**telly** *n.* (*fam.*) télé *f.*

**temerity** *n.* témérité *f.*

**temp** *n.* (*temporary employee: fam.*) intérimaire *m./f.* ● *v.i.* faire de l'intérim.

**temper** *n.* humeur *f.*; (*anger*) colère *f.* ● *v.t.* (*metal*) tremper; (*fig.*) tempérer. **lose one's** ~, se mettre en colère.

**temperament** *n.* tempérament *m.* ~**al** *a.* capricieux; (*innate*) inné.

**temperate** *a.* tempéré.

**temperature** *n.* température *f.* **have a** ~, avoir (de) la fièvre *or* de la température.

**template** *n.* patron *m.*

**temple**[1] *n.* temple *m.*

**temple**[2] *n.* (*of head*) tempe *f.*

**tempo** *n.* tempo *m.*

**temporal** *a.* temporel.

**temporar|y** *a.* temporaire, provisoire. ~**ily** *adv.* temporairement, provisoirement.

**tempt** *v.t.* tenter. ~ **s.o. to do,** donner envie à qn. de faire. ~**ation** *n.* tentation *f.* ~**ing** *a.* tentant.

**ten** *a. & n.* dix (*m.*).

**tenable** *a.* défendable.

**tenac|ious** *a.* tenace. ~**ity** *n.* ténacité *f.*

**tenant** /'tenənt/ *n.* locataire *m./f.*

**tend**[1] *v.t.* s'occuper de.

**tend**[2] *v.i.* ~ **to,** (*be apt to*) avoir tendance à.

**tendency** *n.* tendance *f.*

**tender**[1] *a.* tendre; (*sore, painful*) sensible. ~**ly** *adv.* tendrement. ~**ness** *n.* tendresse *f.*

**tender**[2] *v.t.* offrir, donner. ● *v.i.* faire une soumission. ● *n.* (*comm.*) soumission *f.* **put sth. out to** ~, faire un appel d'offres pour qch.

**tendon** *n.* tendon *m.*

**tenement** *n.* maison de rapport *f.*, H.L.M. *m./f.*

**tenet** *n.* principe *m.*

**tennis** *n.* tennis *m.* ● *a.* de tennis ~ **shoes,** tennis *m. pl.*

**tenor** *n.* (*meaning*) sens général *m.*; (*mus.*) ténor *m.*

**tense**[1] *n.* (*gram.*) temps *m.*

**tense**[2] *a.* tendu. ● *v.t.* (*muscles*) tendre, raidir. ● *v.i.* (*of face*) se crisper.

**tension** *n.* tension *f.*

**tent** *n.* tente *f.*

**tentacle** *n.* tentacule *m.*

**tentative** *a.* provisoire; (*hesitant*) timide.

**tenth** *a. & n.* dixième (*m./f.*).

**tenuous** *a.* ténu.

**tepid** *a.* tiède.

**term** *n.* (*word, limit*) terme *m.*; (*of imprisonment*) temps; (*in school etc.*) trimestre *m.*; (*Amer.*) semestre *m.* ~s, conditions *f. pl.* ● *v.t.* appeler, **on good/bad** ~s, en bons/mauvais termes. **in the short/ long** ~, à court/long terme. **come to** ~s **with sth.,** accepter qch.

**terminal** *a.* terminal, final; (*med.*) en phase terminale. ● *n.* (*oil, computer*) terminal *m.*; (*rail.*) terminus *m.*; (*electr.*) borne *f.* (**air**) ~, aérogare *f.*

**terminat|e** *v.t.* mettre fin à. ● *v.i.* prendre fin. ~**ion** *n.* fin *f.*

**terminology** *n.* terminologie *f.*

**terminus** *n.* terminus *m.*

**terrace** *n.* terrasse *f.*; (*houses*) rangée de maisons contiguës *f.*

**terracotta** *n.* terre cuite *f.*

**terrain** *n.* terrain *m.*

**terribl|e** *a.* affreux, atroce. ~**y** *adv.* (*very*) terriblement.

**terrier** *n.* (*dog*) terrier *m.*

**terrific** *a.* (*fam.*) terrible. ~**ally** *adv.* (*very: fam.*) terriblement; (*very well: fam.*) terriblement bien.

**terrif|y** *v.t.* terrifier. **be** ~**ied of,** avoir très peur de.

**territorial** *a.* territorial.

**territory** *n.* territoire *m.*

**terror** *n.* terreur *f.*

**terroris|t** *n.* terroriste *m./f.* ~**m** *n.* terrorisme *m.*

**terrorize** *v.t.* terroriser.

**terse** *a.* concis, laconique.

**test** *n.* examen *m.*, analyse *f.*; (*of goods*) contrôle *m.*; (*of machine etc.*) essai *m.*; (*in school*) interrogation *f.*; (*of strength etc.: fig.*) épreuve *f.* ● *v.t.* examiner, analyser; (*check*) contrôler; (*try*) essayer; (*pupil*) donner une interrogation à; (*fig.*) éprouver. **driving** ~, (épreuve *f.* du) permis de conduire *m.* ~**tube** *n.* éprouvette *f.*

**testament** *n.* testament *m.* **Old/New T**~, Ancien/Nouveau Testament *m.*

**testicle** *n.* testicule *m.*

**testify** *v.t./i.* témoigner (**to**, de). ~ **that,** témoigner que.

**testimony** *n.* témoignage *m.*

**testy** *a.* grincheux.

**tetanus** *n.* tétanos *m.*

**tetchy** *a.* grincheux.

**tether** *v.t.* attacher.

**text** *n.* texte *m.*

**textbook** *n.* manuel *m.*

**textile** *n.* & *a.* textile (*m.*).

**texture** *n.* (*of paper etc.*) grain *m.*; (*of fabric*) texture *f.*

**Thai** *a.* & *n.* thaïlandais(e) (*m.* (*f.*)). ~**land** *n.* Thaïlande *f.*

**Thames** *n.* Tamise *f.*

**than** *conj.* que, qu'*; (*with numbers*) de. **more/less** ~ **ten,** plus/moins de dix.

**thank** *v.t.* remercier. ~**s** *n. pl.* remerciements *m. pl.* ~ **you!,** merci! ~**s!,** (*fam.*) merci! ~**s to,** grâce à.

**thankful** *a.* reconnaissant (**for**, de). ~**ly** *adv.* (*happily*) heureusement.

**that** *a.* ce or cet*, cette. **those,** ces. ● *pron.* ce or c'*, cela, ça. ~ (**one**), celui-là, celle-là. **those** (**ones**), ceux-là, celles-là. ● *adv.* si, aussi. ● *rel. pron.* (*subject*) qui; (*object*) que, qu'*. ● *conj.* que, qu'*. ~ **boy,** ce garçon (*with emphasis*) ce garçon-là. ~ **is,** c'est. ~ **is** (**to say**), c'est-à-dire. **after** ~, après ça or cela. ~ **big,** grand comme ça. ~ **many,** ~ **much,** tant que ça.

**thatch** *n.* chaume *m.* ~**ed** *a.* en chaume. ~**ed cottage,** chaumière *f.*

**thaw** *v.t./i.* (faire) dégeler; (*snow*) (faire) fondre. ● *n.* dégel *m.*

**the** *a.* le or l'*, la or l'*, *pl.* les. **of** ~, **from** ~, du, de l'*, de la, *pl.* des. **to** ~, **at** ~, au, à l'*, à la, *pl.* aux.

**theatre** *n.* théâtre *m.*

**theatrical** *a.* théâtral.

**theft** *n.* vol *m.*

**their** *a.* leur, *pl.* leurs.

**theirs** *poss. pron.* le or la leur, les leurs.

**them** *pron.* les; (*after prep.*) eux, elles. (**to**) ~, leur. **I know** ~, je les connais.

**theme** *n.* thème *m.*

**themselves** *pron.* eux-mêmes, elles-mêmes; (*reflexive*) se; (*after prep.*) eux, elles.

**then** *adv.* alors; (*next*) ensuite, puis; (*therefore*) alors, donc. ● *a.* d'alors. **from** ~ **on,** dès lors.

**theolog|y** *n.* théologie *f.* ~**ian** *n.* théologien(ne) *m.* (*f.*).

**theorem** *n.* théorème *m.*

**theor|y** *n.* théorie *f.* ~**etical** *a.* théorique.

**therapy** *n.* thérapie *f.*

**there** *adv.* là; (*with verb*) y; (*over there*) là-bas. ● *int.* allez. **he goes** ~, il y va. **on** ~, là-dessus. ~ **is,** ~ **are,** il y a; (*pointing*) voilà. ~, ~**!,** allons, allons! ~**by** *adv.* de cette manière.

**therefore** *adv.* donc.

**thermal** *a.* thermique.

**thermometer** *n.* thermomètre *m.*

**Thermos** *n.* (P.) thermos *m./f. invar.* (P.).

**thermostat** *n.* thermostat *m.*

**thesis** *n.* thèse *f.*

**they** *pron.* ils, elles; (*emphatic*) eux, elles; (*people in general*) on.

**thick** *a.* épais; (*stupid*) bête; (*friends: fam.*) très lié. ~**ly** *adv.* (*grow*) dru; (*spread*) en couche épaisse. ~**ness** *n.* épaisseur *f.*

**thicken** *v.t./i.* (s')épaissir.

**thief** *n.* voleu|r, -se *m.*, *f.*

**thigh** *n.* cuisse *f.*

**thimble** *n.* dé (à coudre) *m.*

**thin** *a.* mince; (*person*) maigre, mince; (*sparse*) clairsemé; (*fine*) fin. ● *v.t./i.* (*p.t.* **thinned**) (*liquid*) (s')éclaircir. ~ **out**, (*in quantity*) (s')éclaircir. ~**ly** *adv.* (*slightly*) légèrement. ~**ner** *n.* diluant *m.*

**thing** *n.* chose *f.* ~**s**, (*belongings*) affaires *f.pl.*

**think** *v.t./i.* penser (**about, of,** à); (*carefully*) réfléchir (**about, of,** à); (*believe*) croire. **I** ~ **so,** je crois que oui. ~ **better of it,** se raviser. ~ **nothing of,** trouver naturel de. ~ **of,** (*hold opinion of*) penser de. ~ **over,** bien réfléchir à. ~**er** *n.* penseu|r, -se *m., f.*

**third** *a.* troisième. ● *n.* troisième *m./f.*; (*fraction*) tiers *m.* **T**~ **World,** Tiers-Monde *m.*

**thirst** *n.* soif *f.* ~**y** *a.* **be** ~**y**, avoir soif.

**thirteen** *a. & n.* treize (*m.*). ~**th** *a. & n.* treizième (*m./f.*).

**thirt|y** *a. & n.* trente (*m.*). ~**ieth** *a. & n.* trentième (*m./f.*).

**this** *a.* ce *or* cet*, cette. **these,** ces. ● *pron.* ce *or* c'*, ceci. ~ (**one**), celui-ci, celle-ci. **these (ones),** ceux-ci, celles-ci. ~ **boy,** ce garçon; (*with emphasis*) ce garçon-ci. ~ **is a mistake,** c'est une erreur. ~ **is the book,** voici le livre. ~ **is my son,** je vous présente mon fils. **after** ~, après ceci.

**thistle** *n.* chardon *m.*

**thorn** *n.* épine *f.*

**thorough** *a.* consciencieux; (*deep*) profond; (*cleaning, washing*) à fond. ~**ly** *adv.* (*clean, study, etc.*) à fond; (*very*) tout à fait.

**though** *conj.* bien que. ● *adv.* (*fam.*) cependant.

**thought** *n.* pensée *f.*; (*idea*) idée *f.*

**thoughtful** *a.* pensif; (*considerate*) attentionné.

**thoughtless** *a.* étourdi.

**thousand** *a. & n.* mille (*m. invar.*). ~**s of,** des milliers de.

**thrash** *v.t.* rosser; (*defeat*) écraser.

**thread** *n.* (*yarn & fig.*) fil *m.*; (*of screw*) pas *m.* ● *v.t.* enfiler.

**threadbare** *a.* râpé.

**threat** *n.* menace *f.*

**threaten** *v.t./i.* menacer (**with,** de).

**three** *a. & n.* trois (*m.*). ~**-dimensional** *a.* en trois dimensions.

**thresh** *v.t.* (*corn etc.*) battre.

**threshold** *n.* seuil *m.*

**thrift** *n.* économie *f.* ~**y** *a.* économe.

**thrill** *n.* émotion *f.*, frisson *m.* ● *v.t.* transporter (de joie). ● *v.i.* frissonner (de joie). **be** ~**ed,** être ravi. ~**er** *n.* livre *or* film à suspense *m.* ~**ing** *a.* excitant.

**thriv|e** *v.i.* prospérer. **he** ~**es on it,** cela lui réussit. ~**ing** *a.* prospère.

**throat** *n.* gorge *f.* **have a sore** ~, avoir mal à la gorge.

**throb** *v.i.* (*wound*) causer des élancements; (*heart*) palpiter; (*fig.*) vibrer. ● *n.* (*pain*) élancement *m.*; palpitation *f.* ~**bing** *a.* (*pain*) lancinant.

**thrombosis** *n.* thrombose *f.*

**throne** *n.* trône *m.*

**throng** *n.* foule *f.* ● *v.t.* (*streets etc.*) se presser dans. ● *v.i.* (*arrive*) affluer.

**throttle** *n.* (*auto.*) accélérateur *m.* ● *v.t.* étrangler.

**through** *prep.* à travers; (*during*) pendant; (*by means or way of, out of*) par; (*by reason of*) grâce à, à cause de. ● *adv.* à travers; (*entirely*) jusqu'au bout. ● *a.* (*train etc.*) direct. **be** ~, (*finished*) avoir fini. **come** *or* **go** ~, (*cross, pierce*) traverser.

**throughout** *prep.* ~ **the country**/*etc.*, dans tout le pays/*etc.* ~ **the day**/*etc.*, pendant toute la journée/*etc.* ● *adv.* (*place*) partout; (*time*) tout le temps.

**throw** *v.t.* jeter, lancer; (*baffle: fam.*) déconcerter. ● *n.* jet *m.*; (*of dice*) coup *m.* ~ **away,** jeter. ~**-away** *a.* à jeter. ~ **off,** (*get rid of*) se débarrasser de. ~ **out,** jeter; (*person*) expulser; (*reject*) rejeter.

**thrush** *n.* (*bird*) grive *f.*

**thrust** *v.t.* pousser. ● *n.* poussée *f.* ~ **into,** (*put*) enforcer dans, mettre dans.

**thud** *n.* bruit sourd *m.*

**thug** *n.* voyou *m.*, bandit *m.*

**thumb** *n.* pouce *m.* ● *v.t.* (*book*) feuilleter.

**thump** *v.t./i.* cogner (sur); (*of heart*) battre fort. ● *n.* grand coup *m.* ~**ing** *a.* (*fam.*) énorme.

**thunder** *n.* tonnerre *m.* ● *v.i.* (*weather, person, etc.*) tonner.

**thunderstorm** *n.* orage *m.*

**Thursday** *n.* jeudi *m.*

**thus** *adv.* ainsi.

**thwart** *v.t.* contrecarrer.

**thyme** *n.* thym *m.*

**thyroid** *n.* thyroïde *f.*

**tiara** *n.* diadème *m.*

**tic** *n.* tic (nerveux) *m.*

**tick¹** *n.* (*sound*) tic-tac *m.*; (*mark*) coche *f.*; (*moment: fam.*) instant *m.* ● *v.i.* faire tic-tac. ● *v.t.* ~ (**off**), cocher. ~ **off,** (*fam.*) réprimander. ~ **over,** (*engine, factory*) tourner au ralenti.

**tick²** *n.* (*insect*) tique *f.*

**ticket** *n.* billet *m.*; (*for bus, cloakroom, etc.*) ticket *m.*; (*label*) étiquette *f.* ~**-office** *n.* guichet *m.*

**tickle** *v.t.* chatouiller; (*amuse: fig.*) amuser. ● *n.* chatouillement *m.*

**tidal** *a.* qui a des marées. ~ **wave,** raz-de-marée *m. invar.*

**tide** *n.* marée *f.*; (*of events*) cours *m.* ● *v.t.* ~ **over,** dépanner.

**tid|y** a. ( room ) bien rangé; ( appearance, work ) soigné; ( methodical ) ordonné; ( amount: fam. ) joli. ● v.t./i. ranger. **~ily** adv. avec soin. **~iness** n. ordre m.

**tie** v.t. attacher, nouer; ( a knot ) faire; ( link ) lier. ● v.i. ( football ) faire match nul; ( in race ) être ex aequo. ● n. attache f.; ( necktie ) cravate f.; ( link ) lien m.; égalité (de points) f.; match nul m. **~ up**, attacher; ( money ) immobiliser; ( occupy ) occuper.

**tier** n. étage m., niveau m.; ( in stadium etc. ) gradin m.

**tiger** n. tigre m.

**tight** a. ( clothes ) étroit, juste; ( rope ) tendu; ( lid ) solidement fixé; ( control ) strict; ( knot, collar, schedule ) serré; ( drunk: fam. ) ivre. ● adv. ( hold, sleep, etc. ) bien; ( squeeze ) fort.

**tighten** v.t./i. (se) tendre; ( bolt etc. ) resserrer; ( control etc. ) renforcer. **~ up on**, se montrer plus strict à l'égard de.

**tightrope** n. corde raide f.

**tights** n. pl. collant m.

**tile** n. ( on wall, floor ) carreau m.; ( on roof ) tuile f. ● v.t. carreler; couvrir de tuiles.

**till**[1] v.t. ( land ) cultiver.

**till**[2] prep. & conj. = **until**.

**till**[3] n. caisse (enregistreuse) f.

**tilt** v.i./i. pencher. ● n. ( slope ) inclinaison f.

**timber** n. bois (de construction) m.; ( trees ) arbres m. pl.

**time** n. temps m.; ( moment ) moment m.; ( epoch ) époque f.; ( by clock ) heure f.; ( occasion ) fois f.; ( rhythm ) mesure f. **~s**, ( multiplying ) fois f. pl. ● v.t. choisir le moment de; ( measure ) minuter; ( sport ) chronométrer. **have a good ~**, s'amuser. **in ~**, à temps; ( eventually ) avec le temps. **a long ~**, longtemps. **on ~**, à l'heure. **what's the ~?**, quelle heure est-il? **~-bomb**, bombe à retardement f. **~-lag** n. décalage m. **~-limit** n. délai m. **~-scale** n. délais fixés m. pl.

**timeless** a. éternel.

**timely** a. à propos.

**timer** n. ( for cooker etc. ) minuteur m.; ( on video ) programmateur m.; ( culin. ) compte-minutes m. invar.; ( with sand ) sablier m.

**timetable** n. horaire m.

**timid** a. timide; ( fearful ) peureux. **~ly** adv. timidement.

**timing** n. ( measuring ) minutage m.; ( moment ) moment m.; ( of artist ) rythme m.

**tin** n. étain m.; ( container ) boîte f. **~(plate)**, fer-blanc m. **~-opener** n. ouvre-boîte(s) m.

**tinge** v.t. teinter ( **with**, de). ● n. teinte f.

**tingle** v.i. ( prickle ) picoter. ● n. picotement m.

**tinker** v.i. **~ (with)**, bricoler.

**tinkle** n. tintement m.; ( fam. ) coup de téléphone m.

**tinsel** n. cheveux d'ange m. pl.

**tint** n. teinte f.; ( for hair ) shampooing colorant m. ● v.t. ( glass, paper ) teinter.

**tiny** a. tout petit.

**tip**[1] n. bout m.; ( cover ) embout m. **~ped** **cigarette**, cigarette (à bout) filtre f.

**tip**[2] v.t./i. ( tilt ) pencher; ( overturn ) (faire) basculer; ( pour ) verser; ( empty ) déverser; ( give money ) donner un pourboire à. ● n. ( money ) pourboire m.; ( advice ) tuyau m.; ( for rubbish ) décharge f. **~ off**, prévenir. **~-off** n. tuyau m. ( pour prévenir ).

**tire** v.t./i. (se) fatiguer. **~ing** a. fatigant.

**tired** a. fatigué. **be ~ of**, en avoir assez de.

**tiresome** a. ennuyeux.

**tissue** n. tissu m.; ( handkerchief ) mouchoir en papier m. **~-paper** n. papier de soie m.

**tit** n. ( bird ) mésange f.

**titbit** n. friandise f.

**titillate** v.t. exciter.

**title** n. titre m.

**titter** v.i. rigoler.

**to** prep. à; ( towards ) vers; ( of attitude ) envers. ● adv. **to France**/etc., en France/etc. **to town**, en ville. **to Canada**/etc., au Canada/etc. **to the baker's**/ etc., chez le boulanger/etc. **the road**/**door**/ etc. **to**, la route/ porte/etc. de. **to me**/**her**/etc., me/lui/etc. **to do**/ **sit**/etc., faire/s'asseoir/etc. **I wrote to tell her**, j'ai écrit pour lui dire. **ten to six**, ( by clock ) six heures moins dix. **go to and fro**, aller et venir.

**toad** n. crapaud m.

**toadstool** n. champignon (vénéneux) m.

**toast** n. pain grillé m., toast m.; ( drink ) toast m. ● v.t. ( bread ) faire griller; ( drink to ) porter un toast à; ( event ) arroser. **~er** n. grille-pain m. invar.

**tobacco** n. tabac m.

**toboggan** n. toboggan m.

**today** n. & adv. aujourd'hui ( m. ).

**toddler** n. tout(e) petit(e) enfant m.(f.).

**toe** n. orteil m.; ( of shoe ) bout m.

**toffee** n. caramel m. **~-apple** n. pomme caramélisée f.

**together** adv. ensemble; ( at same time ) en même temps. **~ with**, avec.

**toil** v.i. peiner. ● n. labeur m.

**toilet** n. toilettes f. pl.; ( grooming ) toilette f. **~-paper** n. papier hygiénique m. **~-roll** n. rouleau de papier hygiénique m. **~ water**, eau de toilette f.

**toiletries** n. pl. articles de toilette m. pl.

**token** n. témoignage m., marque f.; ( voucher ) bon m.; ( coin ) jeton m. ● a. symbolique.

**tolerabl|e** a. tolérable; ( not bad ) passable. **~y** adv. ( work, play, etc. ) passablement.

**toleran|t** a. tolérant ( of, à l'égard de). **~ce** n. tolérance f.

**tolerate** v.t. tolérer.

**toll**[1] n. péage m.

**toll**[2] v.i. ( of bell ) sonner.

**tom, ~-cat** ns. matou m.

**tomato** n. tomate f.

**tomb** n. tombeau m.

**tombola** n. tombola f.

**tomboy** n. garçon manqué m.

**tombstone** n. pierre tombale f.

**tomorrow** n. & adv. demain (m.). ~ **morning/night,** demain matin/soir.

**ton** n. tonne f. ( = 1016 kg.). **(metric) ~,** tonne f. ( = 1000 kg.). **~s of,** (fam.) des masses de.

**tone** n. ton m.; (of radio, telephone, etc.) tonalité f. ● v.t. ~ **down,** atténuer. ● v.i. ~ **in,** s'harmoniser **(with,** avec).

**tongs** n. pl. pinces f. pl.; (for sugar) pince f.; (for hair) fer m.

**tongue** n. langue f.

**tonic** n. (med.) tonique m ● a. (effect, accent) tonique. ~ **(water),** tonic m.

**tonight** n. & adv. cette nuit (f.); (evening) ce soir (m.).

**tonne** n. (metric) tonne f.

**tonsil** n. amygdale f.

**tonsillitis** n. amygdalite f.

**too** adv. trop; (also) aussi. ~ **many** a. trop de; n. trop. ~ **much** a. trop de; adv. & n. trop.

**tool** n. outil m. **~-bag** n. trousse à outils f.

**toot** n. coup de klaxon m. ● v.t./i. ~ **(the horn),** klaxonner.

**tooth** n. dent f.

**toothache** n. mal de dents m.

**toothbrush** n. brosse à dents f.

**toothpaste** n. dentifrice m.

**toothpick** n. cure-dent m.

**top** n. (highest point) sommet m.; (upper part) haut m.; (upper surface) dessus m.; (lid) couvercle m.; (of bottle, tube) bouchon m.; (of beer bottle) capsule f.; (of list) tête f. ● a. (shelf etc.) du haut; (floor) dernier; (in rank) premier; (best) meilleur; (distinguished) éminent; (maximum) maximum. ● v.t. (exceed) dépasser; (list) venir en tête de. **on ~ of,** sur; (fig.) en plus de. **~ secret,** ultra-secret. **~ up,** remplir. **~ped with,** surmonté de; (cream etc.: culin.) nappé de.

**topic** n. sujet m.

**topical** a. d'actualité.

**topple** v.t./i. (faire) basculer.

**topsy-turvy** adv. & a. sens dessus dessous.

**torch** n. (electric) lampe de poche f.; (flaming) torche f.

**torment**[1] n. tourment m.

**torment**[2] v.t. tourmenter; (annoy) agacer.

**tornado** n. tornade f.

**torpedo** n. torpille f. ● v.t. torpiller.

**torrent** n. torrent m.

**torrid** a. (climate etc.) torride; (fig.) passionné.

**torso** n. torse m.

**tortoise** n. tortue f.

**tortoiseshell** n. écaille f.

**tortuous** a. tortueux.

**torture** n. torture f., supplice m. ● v.t. torturer.

**Tory** n. tory m. ● a. tory (f. invar.).

**toss** v.t. jeter, lancer; (shake) agiter. ● v.i. s'agiter. **~ a coin** tirer à pile ou face **(for,** pour).

**tot**[1] n. petit(e) enfant m.(f.); (glass: fam.) petit verre m.

**tot**[2] v.t. ~ **up,** (fam.) additionner.

**total** a. total. ● n. total m. ● v.t. (find total of) totaliser; (amount to) s'élever à. **~ly** adv. totalement.

**totalitarian** a. totalitaire.

**totter** v.i. chanceler.

**touch** v.t./i. toucher; (of ends, gardens, etc.) se toucher; (tamper with) toucher à. ● n. (sense) toucher m.; (contact) contact m.; (of colour) touche f.; (football) touche f. **a ~ of,** (small amount) un peu de. **get in ~ with,** contacter. ~ **down,** (aviat.) atterrir. **~-line** n. (ligne de) touche f. ~ **on,** (mention) aborder. ~ **up,** retoucher.

**touchdown** n. atterrissage m.

**touching** a. touchant.

**touchy** a. susceptible.

**tough** a. (hard, difficult) dur; (strong) solide; (relentless) acharné. **~ness** n. dureté f.; solidité f.

**toughen** v.t. (strengthen) renforcer; (person) endurcir.

**toupee** n. postiche m.

**tour** n. voyage m.; (visit) visite f.; (by team etc.) tournée f. ● v.t. visiter. **on ~,** en tournée. ~ **operator,** voyagiste m.

**tourism** n. tourisme m.

**tourist** n. touriste m./f. ● a. touristique. ~ **office,** syndicat d'initiative m.

**tournament** n. tournoi m.

**tousle** v.t. ébouriffer.

**tout** v.i. ~ **(for),** racoler. ● v.t. (sell) revendre. ● n. racoleu|r, -se m., f.; revendeu|r, -se m., f.

**tow** v.t. remorquer. ● n. remorque f. **on ~,** en remorque. ~ **away,** (vehicle) (faire) enlever. ~ **truck,** dépanneuse f.

**toward(s)** prep. vers; (of attitude) envers.

**towel** n. serviette f.; (teatowel) torchon f. **~ling** n. tissu-éponge m.

**tower** n. tour f. ● v.i. ~ **above,** dominer. ~ **block,** tour f., immeuble m.

**town** n. ville f. ~ **hall,** hôtel de ville m.

**toxic** a. toxique.

**toxin** n. toxine f.

**toy** n. jouet m. ● v.i. ~ **with,** (object) jouer avec; (idea) caresser.

**trace** n. trace f. ● v.t. suivre or retrouver la trace de; (draw) tracer; (with tracing-paper) décalquer; (relate) retracer.

**tracing** n. calque m. ~**-paper** n. papier-calque m. invar.

**track** n. ( of person etc. ) trace f., piste f.; ( path, race-track & of tape ) piste f.; ( on disc ) plage f.; ( of rocket etc. ) trajectoire f.; ( rail. ) voie f. ● v.t. suivre la trace or la trajectoire de. **keep ~ of,** suivre. ~ **down,** ( find ) retrouver; ( hunt ) traquer. ~ **suit,** survêtement m.; ( with sweatshirt ) jogging m.

**tract**[1] n. ( land ) étendue f.; ( anat. ) appareil m.

**tract**[2] n. ( pamphlet ) tract m.

**tractor** n. tracteur m.

**trade** n. commerce m.; ( job ) métier m.; ( swap ) échange m. ● v.i. faire du commerce. ● v.t. échanger. ~ **deficit,** déficit commercial m. ~ **in,** ( used article ) faire reprendre. ~**-in** n. reprise f. ~ **mark,** marque de fabrique f.; ( name ) marque déposée f. ~ **union,** syndicat m. ~**-unionist** n. syndicaliste m./f. ~**r** n. négociant(e) m. ( f. ), commerçant(e) m. ( f. ).

**trading** n. commerce m. ~ **estate,** zone industrielle f.

**tradition** n. tradition f. ~**al** a. traditionnel.

**traffic** n. trafic m.; ( on road ) circulation f. ● v.i. trafiquer ( **in,** de ). ~ **jam,** embouteillage m. ~**-lights** n. pl. feux (de circulation) m. pl. ~ **warden,** contractuel(le) m. ( f. ).

**tragedy** n. tragédie f.

**tragic** a. tragique.

**trail** v.t./i. trainer; ( of plant ) ramper; ( track ) suivre. ● n. ( of powder etc. ) trainée f.; ( track ) piste f.; ( beaten path ) sentier m. ~ **behind,** trainer.

**trailer** n. remorque f.; ( film ) bande-annonce f.

**train** n. ( rail. ) train m.; ( underground ) rame f. ● v.t. ( instruct, develop ) former; ( sportsman ) entrainer; ( animal ) dresser; ( aim ) braquer. ● v.i. recevoir une formation; s'entrainer. ~**ed** a. ( skilled ) qualifié; ( doctor etc. ) diplômé. ~**er** n. ( sport ) entraineu|r, -se m., f. ~**ers,** ( shoes ) chaussures de sport f. pl. ~**ing** n. formation f.; entrainement m.; dressage m.

**trainee** n. stagiaire m./f.

**trait** n. trait m.

**traitor** n. traitre m.

**tram** n. tram(way) m.

**tramp** v.i. marcher (d'un pas lourd). ● v.t. parcourir. ● n. pas lourds m. pl.; ( vagrant ) clochard(e) m. ( f. ); ( hike ) randonnée f.

**trample** v.t./i. ~ (**on**), piétiner; ( fig. ) fouler aux pieds.

**trampoline** n. trampoline m.

**trance** n. transe f.

**tranquil** a. tranquille. ~**lity** n. tranquillité f.

**tranquillizer** n. ( drug ) tranquillisant m.

**transaction** n. transaction f.

**transatlantic** a. transatlantique.

**transcript** n. transcription f.

**transfer**[1] v.t. transférer; ( power ) faire passer. ● v.i. être transféré.

**transfer**[2] n. transfert m.; ( of power ) passation f.; ( image ) décalcomanie f.; ( sticker ) autocollant m.

**transform** v.t. transformer. ~**ation** n. transformation f. ~**er** n. ( electr. ) transformateur m.

**transfusion** n. transfusion f.

**transient** a. transitoire.

**transistor** n. transistor m.

**transit** n. transit m.

**transition** n. transition f.

**transitive** a. transitif.

**transitory** a. transitoire.

**translat|e** v.t. traduire. ~**ion** n. traduction f. ~**or** n. traduc|teur, -trice m., f.

**transmi|t** v.t. ( pass on etc. ) transmettre; ( broadcast ) émettre. ~**ssion** n. transmission f.; émission f. ~**tter** n. émetteur m.

**transparen|t** a. transparent. ~**cy** n. transparence f.; ( photo. ) diapositive f.

**transplant**[1] v.t. transplanter; ( med. ) greffer.

**transplant**[2] n. transplantation f.; greffe f.

**transport**[1] v.t. ( carry, delight ) transporter. ~**ation** n. transport m.

**transport**[2] n. ( of goods, delight, etc. ) transport m.

**transvestite** n. travesti(e) m. ( f. ).

**trap** n. piège m. ● v.t. ( jam, pin down ) coincer; ( cut off ) bloquer; ( snare ) prendre au piège.

**trapdoor** n. trappe f.

**trapeze** n. trapèze m.

**trash** n. ( junk ) saleté(s) f. ( pl. ); ( refuse ) ordures f. pl.; ( nonsense ) idioties f. pl.

**trauma** n. traumatisme m. ~**tic** a. traumatisant.

**travel** v.i. voyager; ( of vehicle, bullet, etc. ) aller. ● v.t. parcourir. ● n. voyage(s) m. ( pl. ). ~ **agent,** agent de voyage m. ~**ler** n. voyageu|r, -se m., f. ~**ler's cheque,** chèque de voyage m. ~ **sickness,** mal des transports m.

**travesty** n. parodie f.

**trawler** n. chalutier m.

**tray** n. plateau m.; ( on office desk ) corbeille f.

**treacherous** a. traitre.

**treachery** n. traitrise f.

**treacle** n. mélasse f.

**tread** v.i. marcher ( **on,** sur). ● n. démarche f.; ( sound ) (bruit m. de) pas m. pl.; ( of tyre ) chape f. ~ **sth. into,** ( carpet ) étaler qch. sur (avec les pieds).

**treason** n. trahison f.

**treasure** n. trésor m. ● v.t. attacher une grande valeur à; ( store ) conserver. ~**r** n. trésor|ier, -ière m., f.

**treasury** n. trésorerie f. **the T~,** le ministère des Finances.

**treat** *v.t.* traiter; (*consider*) considérer. ● *n.* (*pleasure*) plaisir *m.*, régal *m.*; (*present*) gâterie *f.*; (*food*) régal *m.* ∼ **s.o. to sth.,** offrir qch. à qn.

**treatment** *n.* traitement *m.*

**treaty** *n.* (*pact*) traité *m.*

**treble** *a.* triple. ● *v.t./i.* tripler. ● *n.* (*voice*: *mus.*) soprano *m.*

**tree** *n.* arbre *m.*

**trek** *n.* voyage pénible *m.*; (*sport*) randonnée *f.* ● *v.i.* voyager (péniblement); (*sport*) faire de la randonnée.

**trellis** *n.* treillage *m.*

**tremble** *v.i.* trembler.

**tremendous** *a.* énorme; (*excellent*: *fam.*) fantastique. ∼**ly** *adv.* fantastiquement.

**tremor** *n.* tremblement *m.*

**trench** *n.* tranchée *f.*

**trend** *n.* tendance *f.*; (*fashion*) mode *f.* ∼**y** *a.* (*fam.*) dans le vent.

**trespass** *v.i.* s'introduire sans autorisation (**on**, dans). ∼**er** *n.* intrus(e) *m.* (*f.*).

**tresses** *n. pl.* chevelure *f.*

**trestle** *n.* tréteau *m.* ∼**-table** *n.* table à tréteaux *f.*

**trial** *n.* (*jurid.*) procès *m.*; (*test*) essai *m.*; (*ordeal*) épreuve *f.* **go on** ∼, passer en jugement. ∼ **run,** galop d'essai *m.*

**triang|le** *n.* triangle *m.* ∼**ular** *a.* triangulaire.

**trib|e** *n.* tribu *f.* ∼**al** *a.* tribal.

**tribunal** *n.* tribunal *m.*; (*mil.*) commission *f.*

**tributary** *n.* affluent *m.*

**tribute** *n.* tribut *m.* **pay** ∼ **to,** rendre hommage à.

**trick** *n.* astuce *f.*, ruse *f.*; (*joke, feat of skill*) tour *m.*; (*habit*) manie *f.* ● *v.t.* tromper.

**trickery** *n.* ruse *f.*

**trickle** *v.i.* dégouliner. ● *n.* filet *m.*; (*fig.*) petit nombre *m.*

**tricky** *a.* (*crafty*) rusé; (*problem*) délicat, difficile.

**tricycle** *n.* tricycle *m.*

**trifle** *n.* bagatelle *f.*; (*cake*) diplomate *m.* **a** ∼, (*small amount*) un peu.

**trigger** *n.* (*of gun*) gâchette *f.*, détente *f.* ● *v.t.* ∼ (**off**), (*initiate*) déclencher.

**trim** *a.* net, soigné; (*figure*) svelte. ● *v.t.* (*cut*) couper légèrement; (*hair*) rafraîchir; (*budget*) réduire. ● *n.* (*cut*) coupe légère *f.*; (*decoration*) garniture *f.* ∼**ming(s)** *n.* (*pl.*) garniture(s) *f.* (*pl.*).

**Trinity** *n.* Trinité *f.*

**trinket** *n.* colifichet *m.*

**trio** *n.* trio *m.*

**trip** *v.t./i.* (faire) trébucher ● *n.* (*journey*) voyage *m.*; (*outing*) excursion *f.*; (*stumble*) faux pas *m.*

**tripe** *n.* (*food*) tripes *f. pl.*; (*nonsense*: *sl.*) bêtises *f. pl.*

**triple** *a.* triple. ● *v.t./i.* tripler. ∼**ts** *n. pl.* triplé(e)s *m.* (*f.*) *pl.*

**tripod** *n.* trépied *m.*

**trite** *a.* banal.

**triumph** *n.* triomphe *m.* ● *v.i.* triompher (**over**, de). ∼**ant** *a.* triomphant, triomphal.

**trivial** *a.* insignifiant.

**trolley** *n.* chariot *m.* (**tea-**)∼, table roulante *f.*

**trombone** *n.* (*mus.*) trombone *m.*

**troop** *n.* bande *f.* ∼**s,** (*mil.*) troupes *f. pl.* ● *v.i.* ∼ **in/out,** entrer/sortir en bande.

**trophy** *n.* trophée *m.*

**tropic** *n.* tropique *m.* ∼**s,** tropiques *m. pl.* ∼**al** *a.* tropical.

**trot** *n.* trot *m.* ● *v.i.* trotter. ∼ **out,** (*produce*: *fam.*) sortir; (*state*: *fam.*) formuler.

**trouble** *n.* ennui(s) *m.* (*pl.*), difficulté(s) *f.* (*pl.*); (*pains, effort*) mal *m.*, peine *f.* ∼**(s),** ennuis *m. pl.*; (*unrest*) conflits *m. pl.* ● *v.t./i.* (*bother*) (se) déranger; (*worry*) ennuyer. **be in** ∼, avoir des ennuis. **what's the** ∼**?,** quel est le problème? ∼**-maker** *n.* provoca|teur, -trice *m.*, *f.*

**troublesome** *a.* pénible.

**trough** *n.* (*drinking*) abreuvoir *m.*; (*feeding*) auge *f.* ∼ (**of low pressure**), dépression *f.*

**troupe** *n.* (*theatre*) troupe *f.*

**trousers** *n. pl.* pantalon *m.* **short** ∼, culotte courte *f.*

**trout** *n. invar.* truite *f.*

**trowel** *n.* (*garden*) déplantoir *m.*; (*for mortar*) truelle *f.*

**truan|t** *n.* absentéiste *m./f.*; (*schol.*) élève absent(e) sans permission *m.(f.).* **play** ∼**t,** sécher les cours.

**truce** *n.* trêve *f.*

**truck** *n.* (*lorry*) camion *m.*; (*cart*) chariot *m.*; (*rail.*) wagon *m.*, plateforme *f.* ∼**-driver** *n.* camionneur *m.*

**trudge** *v.i.* se traîner.

**true** *a.* vrai; (*accurate*) exact; (*faithful*) fidèle.

**truffle** *n.* truffe *f.*

**truly** *adv.* vraiment; (*faithfully*) fidèlement; (*truthfully*) sincèrement.

**trump** *n.* atout *m.* ● *v.t.* ∼ **up,** inventer. ∼ **card,** atout *m.*

**trumpet** *n.* trompette *f.*

**trundle** *v.t./i.* rouler bruyamment.

**trunk** *n.* (*of tree, body*) tronc *m.*; (*of elephant*) trompe *f.*; (*box*) malle *f.* ∼**s,** (*for swimming*) slip de bain *m.*

**truss** *n.* (*med.*) bandage herniaire *m.* ● *v.t.* (*fowl*) trousser.

**trust** *n.* confiance *f.*; (*association*) trust *m.* ● *v.t.* avoir confiance en. ● *v.i.* ∼ **in** *or* **to,** s'en remettre à. **on** ∼, de confiance. ∼ **s.o. with,** confier à qn.

**trustee** *n.* administra|teur, -trice *m.*, *f.*

**truth** *n.* vérité *f.* ∼**ful** *a.* (*account etc.*) véridique; (*person*) qui dit la vérité.

**try** v.t./i. essayer; (*be a strain on*) éprouver; (*jurid.*)juger. ● n.(*attempt*)essai m.;(*Rugby*) essai m. ~ **on,** essayer. ~ **to do,** essayer de faire.

**T-shirt** n. tee-shirt m.

**tub** n. baquet m., cuve f.; (*bath: fam.*) baignoire f.

**tuba** n. tuba m.

**tubby** a. dodu.

**tube** n. tube m.; (*railway: fam.*) métro m.; (*in tyre*) chambre à air f.

**tuberculosis** n. tuberculose f.

**tubular** a. tubulaire.

**tuck** n. (*fold*) rempli m., (re)pli m. ● v.t. (*put away, place*) ranger; (*hide*) cacher. ● v.i. ~ **in** or **into,** (*eat: sl.*) attaquer. ~ **in,** (*shirt*) rentrer; (*person*) border.

**Tuesday** n. mardi m.

**tuft** n. (*of hair etc.*) touffe f.

**tug** v.t. tirer fort (sur). ● v.i. tirer fort. ● n. (*boat*) remorqueur m. ~ **of war,** jeu de la corde tirée m.

**tuition** n. cours m. pl.

**tulip** n. tulipe f.

**tumble** v.i. (*fall*) dégringoler. ● n. chute f. ~**drier** n. séchoir à linge (à air chaud) m.

**tumbler** n. gobelet m.

**tummy** n. (*fam.*) ventre m.

**tumour** n. tumeur f.

**tumult** n. tumulte m. ~**uous** a. tumultueux.

**tuna** n. invar. thon m.

**tune** n. air m. ● v.t. (*engine*) régler; (*mus.*) accorder. ● v.i. ~ **in (to),** (*radio, TV*) écouter. **be in ~/out of ~,** (*instrument*)être accordé/ désaccordé; (*singer*) chanter juste/faux.

**tunic** n. tunique f.

**Tunisia** n. Tunisie f. ~**n** a. & n. tunisien(ne) (m. (f.)).

**tunnel** n. tunnel m.; (*in mine*) galerie f.

**turban** n. turban m.

**turbine** n. turbine f.

**turbo** n. turbo m.

**turbulen|t** a. turbulent. ~**ce** n. turbulence f.

**turf** n. gazon m. ● v.t. ~ **out,** (*sl.*) jeter dehors.

**Turk** n. Turc m., Turque f. ~**ey** n. Turquie f. ~**ish** a. turc m. (*lang.*) turc m.

**turkey** n. dinde f.

**turn** v.t./i. tourner; (*of person*) se tourner; (*to other side*) retourner; (*change*) (se) transfor-mer (**into,** en); (*become*) devenir; (*deflect*) détourner; (*milk*) tourner. ● n. tour m.; (*in road*) tournant m.; (*of mind, events*) tournure f.; (*illness: fam.*) crise f. **in ~,** à tour de rôle. **take ~s,** se relayer. ~ **away** v.i. se détourner; v.t. (*avert*) détourner; (*refuse*) refuser; (*send back*) renvoyer. ~ **back** v.i. (*return*) retourner; (*vehicle*) faire demi-tour; v.t. (*fold*) rabattre. ~ **down,** refuser; (*fold*) rabattre; (*reduce*) baisser. ~ **off,** (*light etc.*) éteindre; (*engine*) arrêter; (*tap*) fermer; (*of*

**driver*) tourner. ~**off** n. (*auto.*) embranche-ment m. ~ **on,** (*light etc.*) allumer; (*engine*) allumer; (*tap*) ouvrir. ~ **out** v.t. (*light*) éteindre; (*empty*) vider; (*produce*) produire; v.i. (*transpire*) s'avérer; (*come: fam.*) venir. ~ **over,** (se) retourner. ~ **round,** (*person*) se retourner. ~**round** n. revirement m. ~ **up** v.i. arriver; (*be found*) se retrouver; v.t. (*find*) déterrer; (*collar*) remonter. ~**up** n. (*of trousers*) revers m.

**turning** n. rue (latérale) f.; (*bend*) tournant m. ~**point** n. tournant m.

**turnip** n. navet m.

**turnover** n. (*comm.*) chiffre d'affaires m.

**turnstile** n. (*gate*) tourniquet m.

**turntable** n. (*for record*) platine f.

**turpentine** n. térébenthine f.

**turquoise** a. turquoise invar.

**turret** n. tourelle f.

**turtle** n. tortue (de mer) f. ~**neck** a. à col montant, roulé.

**tusk** n. (*tooth*) défense f.

**tussle** n. bagarre f., lutte f.

**tutor** n. précep|teur, -trice m., f.; (*univ.*) direc|teur, -trice d'études m., f.

**TV** n. télé f.

**twang** n. (*son: mus.*) pincement m.; (*in voice*) nasillement m. ● v.t./i. (faire) vibrer.

**tweed** n. tweed m.

**tweezers** n. pl. pince (à épiler) f.

**twel|ve** a. & n. douze (m.). ~**fth** a. & n. douzième (m./f.). ~**ve (o'clock),** midi m. or minuit m.

**twent|y** a. & n. vingt (m.). ~**ieth** a. & n. vingtième (m./f.).

**twice** adv. deux fois.

**twiddle** v.t./i. ~ **(with),** (*fiddle with*) tripoter.

**twig**[1] n. brindille f.

**twig**[2] v.t./i. (*fam.*) piger.

**twilight** n. crépuscule m.

**twin** n. & a. jum|eau, -elle (m., f.).

**twine** n. ficelle f.

**twinge** n. élancement m.; (*remorse*) remords m.

**twinkle** v.i. (*star etc.*) scintiller; (*eye*) pétiller. ● n. scintillement m.; pétillement m.

**twirl** v.t./i. (faire) tournoyer.

**twist** v.t. tordre; (*weave together*) entortiller; (*roll*)enrouler; (*distort*)déformer. ● v.i. (*rope etc.*) s'entortiller; (*road*) zigzaguer. ● n. torsion f.; (*in rope*) tortillon m.; (*in road*) tournant m.; (*of events*) tournure f.

**twit** n. (*fam.*) idiot(e) m. (f.).

**twitch** v.t./i. (se) contracter nerveusement. ● n. (*tic*) tic m.; (*jerk*) secousse f.

**two** a. & n. deux (m.).

**tycoon** n. magnat m.

**type** n. (*example*) type m.; (*kind*) genre m., sorte f.; (*person: fam.*) type m.; (*print*) caractères m. pl. ● v.t./i. (*write*) taper (à la machine).

**typewriter** n. machine à écrire f.

**typhoid** n. ~ (**fever**), typhoïde f.

**typhoon** n. typhon m.

**typical** a. typique. ~**ly** adv. typiquement.

**typing** n. dactylo(graphie) f.

**typist** n. dactylo f.

**tyrann|y** n. tyrannie f. ~**ical** a. tyrannique.

**tyrant** n. tyran m.

**tyre** n. pneu m.

••••••••••••••••••••••••••••••••••

# Uu

••••••••••••••••••••••••••••••••••

**udder** n. pis m., mamelle f.

**UFO** n. OVNI m.

**Uganda** n. Ouganda m.

**ugly** a. laid.

**UK** abbr. see **United Kingdom**.

**ulcer** n. ulcère m.

**ultimate** a. dernier, ultime; (*definitive*) définitif; (*basic*) fondamental. ~**ly** adv. à la fin; (*in the last analysis*) en fin de compte.

**ultimatum** n. ultimatum m.

**ultrasound** n. ultrason m.

**ultraviolet** a. ultraviolet.

**umbilical** a. ~ **cord**, cordon ombilical m.

**umbrella** n. parapluie m.

**umpire** n. (*sport*) arbitre m. ● v.t. arbitrer.

**umpteen** a. (*many: sl.*) un tas de. ~**th** a. (*fam.*) énième.

**UN** abbr. (*United Nations*) ONU f.

**un-** pref. in-, dé(s)-, non, peu, mal, sans.

**unable** a. incapable; (*through circumstances*) dans l'impossibilité (**to do**, de faire).

**unacceptable** a. inacceptable.

**unaccustomed** a. inaccoutumé. ~ **to**, peu habitué à.

**unadulterated** a. (*sheer*) pur.

**unaided** a. sans aide.

**unanim|ous** a. unanime. ~**ity** n. unanimité f. ~**ously** adv. à l'unanimité.

**unarmed** a. non armé.

**unattainable** a. inaccessible.

**unattended** a. (laissé) sans surveillance.

**unattractive** a. peu séduisant, laid; (*offer*) peu intéressant.

**unauthorized** a. non autorisé.

**unavailable** a. pas disponible.

**unavoidabl|e** a. inévitable. ~**y** adv. inévitablement.

**unaware** a. **be** ~ **of**, ignorer. ~**s** adv. au dépourvu.

**unbalanced** a. déséquilibré.

**unbearable** a. insupportable.

**unbeat|able** a. imbattable. ~**en** a. non battu.

**unbelievable** a. incroyable.

**unbiased** a. impartial.

**unblock** v.t. déboucher.

**unborn** a. futur, à venir.

**unbounded** a. illimité.

**unbreakable** a. incassable.

**unbroken** a. (*intact*) intact; (*continuous*) continu.

**unbutton** v.t. déboutonner.

**uncanny** a. étrange.

**uncertain** a. incertain. **be** ~ **whether**, ne pas savoir exactement si (**to do**, on doit faire). ~**ty** n. incertitude f.

**unchanged** a. inchangé.

**uncivilized** a. barbare.

**uncle** n. oncle m.

**uncomfortable** a. (*thing*) peu confortable; (*unpleasant*) désagréable. **feel** or **be** ~, (*person*) être mal à l'aise.

**uncommon** a. rare.

**uncompromising** a. intransigeant.

**unconcerned** a. (*indifferent*) indifférent (**by**, à).

**unconditional** a. inconditionnel.

**unconscious** a. sans connaissance, in-animé; (*not aware*) inconscient (**of**, de) ● n. inconscient m. ~**ly** adv. inconsciemment.

**unconventional** a. peu conventionnel.

**uncooperative** a. peu coopératif.

**uncork** v.t. déboucher.

**uncouth** a. grossier.

**uncover** v.t. découvrir.

**undecided** a. indécis.

**undeniable** a. incontestable.

**under** prep. sous; (*less than*) moins de; (*according to*) selon. ● adv. au-dessous. ~ **age**, mineur. ~ **it/there**, là-dessous. ~**side** n. dessous m.

**undercarriage** n. (*aviat.*) train d'atterrissage m.

**underclothes** n. pl. sous-vêtements m. pl.

**undercoat** n. (*of paint*) couche de fond f.

**undercover** a. secret.

**undercut** v.t. (*comm.*) vendre moins cher que.

**underdeveloped** a. sous-développé.

**underdog** n. (*pol.*) opprimé(e) m. (f.); (*socially*) déshérité(e) m. (f.).

**underdone** a. pas assez cuit; (*steak*) saignant.

**underestimate** v.t. sous-estimer.

**underfed** a. sous-alimenté.

**undergo** v.t. subir.

**undergraduate** n. étudiant(e) m. (f.).
**underground**[1] adv. sous terre.
**underground**[2] a. souterrain; (secret) clandestin. ● n. (rail.) métro m.
**undergrowth** n. sous-bois m. invar.
**underhand** a. sournois.
**underlying** a. fondamental.
**underline** v.t. souligner.
**undermine** v.t. miner.
**underneath** prep. sous. ● adv. (en) dessous.
**underpaid** a. sous-payé.
**underpants** n. pl. slip m.
**underpass** n. (for cars, people) passage souterrain m.
**underprivileged** a. défavorisé.
**underrate** v.t. sous-estimer.
**underskirt** n. jupon m.
**understand** v.t./i. comprendre. ~able a. compréhensible. ~ing a. compréhensif; n. compréhension f.; (agreement) entente f.
**understatement** n. litote f.
**understudy** n. doublure f.
**undertak|e** v.t. entreprendre; (responsibility) assumer. ~e to, s'engager à. ~ing n. (task) entreprise f.; (promise) promesse f.
**undertaker** n. entrepreneur de pompes funèbres m.
**undervalue** v.t. sous-évaluer.
**underwater** a. sous-marin. ● adv. sous l'eau.
**underwear** n. sous-vêtements m. pl.
**underworld** n. milieu m.
**undeserved** a. immérité.
**undies** n. pl. (female underwear: fam.) dessous m. pl.
**undignified** a. sans dignité.
**undisputed** a. incontesté.
**undo** v.t. défaire, détacher; (a wrong) réparer.
**undoubted** a. indubitable. ~ly adv. indubitablement.
**undress** v.t./i. (se) déshabiller. **get ~ed**, se déshabiller.
**undu|e** a. excessif. ~ly adv. excessivement.
**undulate** v.i. onduler.
**unearth** v.t. déterrer.
**unearthly** a. mystérieux. ~ **hour,** (fam.) heure indue f.
**uneasy** a. (ill at ease) mal à l'aise; (worried) inquiet; (situation) difficile.
**uneducated** a. (person) inculte; (speech) populaire.
**unemploy|ed** a. en chômage. ~ment n. chômage m. ~ment **benefit,** allocations de chômage f. pl.
**unending** a. sans fin.
**unequal** a. inégal. ~led a. inégalé.
**uneven** a. inégal.
**uneventful** a. sans incident.

**unexpected** a. inattendu, imprévu. ~ly adv. subitement; (arrive) à l'improviste.
**unfailing** a. constant, continuel; (loyal) fidèle.
**unfair** a. injuste. ~ness n. injustice f.
**unfaithful** a. infidèle.
**unfamiliar** a. inconnu. **be ~ with,** ne pas connaître.
**unfashionable** a. (clothes) démodé. **it's ~ to,** ce n'est pas à la mode de.
**unfasten** v.t. défaire.
**unfavourable** a. défavorable.
**unfeeling** a. insensible.
**unfinished** a. inachevé.
**unfit** a. (med.) peu en forme; (unsuitable) impropre (for, à). ~ **to,** (unable) pas en état de.
**unfold** v.t. déplier; (expose) exposer. ● v.i. se dérouler.
**unforeseen** a. imprévu.
**unforgettable** a. inoubliable.
**unforgivable** a. inexcusable.
**unfortunate** a. malheureux; (event) fâcheux. ~ly adv. malheureusement.
**unfounded** a. sans fondement.
**unfriendly** a. peu amical.
**ungainly** a. gauche.
**ungrateful** a. ingrat.
**unhapp|y** a. malheureux, triste; (not pleased) mécontent (with, de). ~iness n. tristesse f.
**unharmed** a. sain et sauf.
**unhealthy** a. (climate etc.) malsain; (person) en mauvaise santé.
**unhook** v.t. décrocher; (dress) dégrafer.
**unhoped** a. ~ **for,** inespéré.
**unhurt** a. indemne.
**unicorn** n. licorne f.
**uniform** n. uniforme m. ● a. uniforme. ~ity n. uniformité f. ~ly adv. uniformément.
**unif|y** v.t. unifier. ~ication n. unification f.
**unilateral** a. unilatéral.
**unimaginable** a. inimaginable.
**unimportant** a. peu important.
**uninhabited** a. inhabité.
**unintentional** a. involontaire.
**uninterest|ed** a. indifférent (in, à). ~ing a. peu intéressant.
**union** n. union f.; (trade union) syndicat m. ~ist n. syndiqué(e) m. (f.). **U~ Jack,** drapeau britannique m.
**unique** a. unique. ~ly adv. exceptionnellement.
**unisex** a. unisexe.
**unison** n. **in ~,** à l'unisson.
**unit** n. unité f.; (of furniture etc.) élément m., bloc m. ~ **trust,** (équivalent d'une) SICAV f.
**unite** v.t./i. (s')unir. **U~d Kingdom,** Royaume-Uni m. **U~d Nations,** Nations Unies f. pl. **U~d States (of America),** États-Unis (d'Amérique) m. pl.

**unity** n. unité f.; (harmony: fig.) harmonie f.

**universal** a. universel.

**universe** n. univers m.

**university** n. université f.

**unjust** a. injuste.

**unkempt** a. négligé.

**unkind** a. pas gentil, méchant. ∼ly adv. méchamment.

**unknowingly** adv. sans le savoir, inconsciemment.

**unknown** a. inconnu. ● n. the ∼, l'inconnu m.

**unleash** v.t. déchaîner.

**unless** conj. à moins que.

**unlike** a. (brothers etc.) différents. ● prep. à la différence de; (different from) très différent de.

**unlikel|y** a. improbable. ∼ihood n. improbabilité f.

**unlimited** a. illimité.

**unload** v.t. décharger.

**unlock** v.t. ouvrir.

**unlucky** a. malheureux; (number) qui porte malheur.

**unmarried** a. célibataire.

**unmask** v.t. démasquer.

**unmistakable** a. (voice etc.) facilement reconnaissable; (clear) très net.

**unmoved** a. indifférent (by, à), insensible (by, à).

**unnatural** a. pas naturel.

**unnecessary** a. inutile; (superfluous) superflu.

**unnerve** v.t. troubler.

**unnoticed** a. inaperçu.

**unobtainable** n. impossible à obtenir.

**unobtrusive** a. discret.

**unofficial** a. officieux.

**unorthodox** a. peu orthodoxe.

**unpack** v.t. (suitcase etc.) défaire; (contents) déballer. ● v.i. défaire sa valise.

**unpalatable** a. (food, fact, etc.) désagréable.

**unparalleled** a. incomparable.

**unpleasant** a. désagréable (to, avec).

**unplug** v.t. (electr.) débrancher; (unblock) déboucher.

**unpopular** a. impopulaire. ∼ with, mal vu de.

**unprecedented** a. sans précédent.

**unpredictable** a. imprévisible.

**unprepared** a. non préparé; (person) qui n'a rien préparé. be ∼ for, (not expect) ne pas s'attendre à.

**unpretentious** a. sans prétention(s).

**unprofessional** a. (work) d'amateur; (conduct) contraire au code professionel.

**unqualified** a. non diplômé; (success etc.) total.

**unquestionabl|e** a. incontestable. ∼y adv. incontestablement.

**unravel** v.t. démêler, débrouiller.

**unreal** a. irréel.

**unreasonable** a. déraisonnable.

**unrecognizable** a. méconnaissable.

**unrelated** a. (facts) sans rapport (to, avec).

**unreliable** a. peu sérieux; (machine) peu fiable.

**unreservedly** adv. sans réserve.

**unrest** n. troubles m. pl.

**unrivalled** a. incomparable.

**unroll** v.t. dérouler.

**unruly** a. indiscipliné.

**unsafe** a. (dangerous) dangereux; (person) en danger.

**unsatisfactory** a. peu satisfaisant.

**unsavoury** a. répugnant.

**unscathed** a. indemne.

**unscheduled** a. pas prévu.

**unscrew** v.t. dévisser.

**unscrupulous** a. sans scrupules.

**unseen** a. inaperçu. ● n. (translation) version f.

**unsettle** v.t. troubler. ∼d a. (weather) instable.

**unshakeable** a. inébranlable.

**unshaven** a. pas rasé.

**unsightly** a. laid.

**unskilled** a. inexpert; (worker) non qualifié.

**unsociable** a. insociable.

**unsophisticated** a. simple.

**unsound** a. peu solide. of ∼ mind, fou.

**unspecified** a. indéterminé.

**unstable** a. instable.

**unsteady** a. (step) chancelant; (ladder) instable; (hand) mal assuré.

**unsuccessful** a. (result, candidate) malheureux; (attempt) infructueux. be ∼, ne pas réussir (in doing, à faire).

**unsuitable** a. qui ne convient pas (for, à), peu approprié.

**unsure** a. incertain.

**unsuspecting** a. qui ne se doute de rien.

**unsympathetic** a. (unhelpful) peu compréhensif; (unpleasant) antipathique.

**untangle** v.t. démêler.

**untenable** a. intenable.

**unthinkable** a. impensable.

**untidy** a. (person) désordonné; (clothes, hair, room) en désordre; (work) mal soigné.

**untie** v.t. (knot, parcel) défaire; (person) détacher.

**until** prep. jusqu'à. not ∼, pas avant. ● conj. jusqu'à ce que; (before) avant que.

**untimely** a. inopportun; (death) prématuré.

**untold** a. incalculable.

**untrue** a. faux.

**unused**[1] a. (new) neuf; (not in use) inutilisé.

**unused**[2] a. ∼ to, peu habitué à.

**unusual** *a.* exceptionnel; (*strange*) insolite, étrange. **~ly** *adv.* exceptionnellement.

**unveil** *v.t.* dévoiler.

**unwanted** *a.* (*useless*) superflu; (*child*) non désirée.

**unwelcome** *a.* fâcheux; (*guest*) importun.

**unwell** *a.* indisposé.

**unwieldy** *a.* difficile à manier.

**unwilling** *a.* peu disposé (**to,** à); (*victim*) récalcitrant. **~ly** *adv.* à contrecœur.

**unwind** *v.t./i.* (se) dérouler; (*relax: fam.*) se détendre.

**unwise** *a.* imprudent.

**unwittingly** *adv.* involontairement.

**unworthy** *a.* indigne.

**unwrap** *v.t.* ouvrir.

**unwritten** *a.* (*agreement*) tacite.

**up** *adv.* en haut, en l'air; (*sun, curtain*) levé; (*out of bed*) levé, debout; (*finished*) fini. **be up,** (*level, price*) avoir monté. ● *prep.* (*a hill*) en haut de; (*a tree*) dans; (*a ladder*) sur. ● *v.t.* augmenter. **come** or **go up,** monter. **up there,** là-haut. **up to,** jusqu'à; (*task*) à la hauteur de. **it is up to you,** ça dépend de vous (**to,** de). **be up to sth.,** (*able*) être capable de qch.; (*do*) faire qch.; (*plot*) préparer qch. **feel up to doing,** (*able*) être de taille à faire. **up-and-coming** *a.* prometteur. **up-market** *a.* haut-de-gamme. **up to date,** moderne; (*news*) récent.

**upbringing** *n.* éducation *f.*

**update** *v.t.* mettre à jour.

**upgrade** *v.t.* (*person*) promouvoir; (*job*) revaloriser.

**upheaval** *n.* bouleversement *m.*

**uphill** *a.* qui monte; (*fig.*) difficile. ● *adv.* **go ~,** monter.

**uphold** *v.t.* maintenir.

**upholster** *v.t.* (*pad*) rembourrer; (*cover*) recouvrir. **~y** *n.* (*in vehicle*) garniture *f.*

**upkeep** *n.* entretien *m.*

**upon** *prep.* sur.

**upper** *a.* supérieur. ● *n.* (*of shoe*) empeigne *f.*

**upright** *a.* droit. ● *n.* (*post*) montant *m.*

**uprising** *n.* soulèvement *m.*

**uproar** *n.* tumulte *m.*

**uproot** *v.t.* déraciner.

**upset**[1] *v.t.* (*overturn*) renverser; (*plan, stomach*) déranger; (*person*) contrarier, affliger. ● *a.* peiné.

**upset**[2] *n.* dérangement *m.*; (*distress*) chagrin *m.*

**upshot** *n.* résultat *m.*

**upside-down** *adv.* (*in position, in disorder*) à l'envers, sens dessus dessous.

**upstairs** *adv.* en haut. ● *a.* (*flat etc.*) d'en haut.

**upstart** *n.* (*pej.*) parvenu(e) *m.* (*f.*).

**upstream** *adv.* en amont.

**upsurge** *n.* recrudescence *f.*; (*of anger*) accès *m.*

**uptight** *a.* (*tense: fam.*) crispé; (*angry: fam.*) en colère.

**upturn** *n.* amélioration *f.*

**upward** *a.* & *adv.,* **~s** *adv.* vers le haut.

**uranium** *n.* uranium *m.*

**urban** *a.* urbain.

**urbane** *a.* courtois.

**urchin** *n.* garnement *m.*

**urge** *v.t.* conseiller vivement (**to do,** de faire). ● *n.* forte envie *f.*

**urgen|t** *a.* urgent; (*request*) pressant. **~cy** *n.* urgence *f.*; (*of request, tone*) insistance *f.* **~tly** *adv.* d'urgence.

**urinal** *n.* urinoir *m.*

**urin|e** *n.* urine *f.* **~ate** *v.i.* uriner.

**urn** *n.* urne *f.*; (*for tea, coffee*) fontaine *f.*

**us** *pron.* nous. (**to) us,** nous.

**US** *abbr. see* **United States.**

**USA** *abbr. see* **United States of America.**

**usable** *a.* utilisable.

**usage** *n.* usage *m.*

**use**[1] *v.t.* se servir de, utiliser; (*consume*) consommer. **~ up,** épuiser. **~r** *n.* usager *m.* **~r-friendly** *a.* facile d'emploi.

**use**[2] *n.* usage *m.*, emploi *m.* **it is no ~ shouting**/*etc.*, ça ne sert à rien de crier/*etc.* **make ~ of,** se servir de.

**used**[1] *a.* (*second-hand*) d'occasion.

**used**[2] *p.t.* **he ~ to do,** il faisait (autrefois), il avait l'habitude de faire. ● *a.* **~ to,** habitué à.

**use|ful** *a.* utile. **~fully** *adv.* utilement. **~less** *a.* inutile; (*person*) incompétent.

**usher** *n.* (*in theatre, hall*) placeur *m.* ● *v.t.* **~ in,** faire entrer. **~ette** *n.* ouvreuse *f.*

**USSR** *abbr.* (*Union of Soviet Socialist Republics*) URSS *f.*

**usual** *a.* habituel, normal. **as ~,** comme d'habitude. **~ly** *adv.* d'habitude.

**usurp** *v.t.* usurper.

**utensil** *n.* ustensile *m.*

**uterus** *n.* utérus *m.*

**utility** *n.* utilité *f.* (**public**) **~,** service public *m.*

**utilize** *v.t.* utiliser.

**utmost** *a.* (*furthest, most intense*) extrême. **the ~ care**/*etc.*, (*greatest*) le plus grand soin/ *etc.* ● *n.* **do one's ~,** faire tout son possible.

**utter**[1] *a.* complet, absolu. **~ly** *adv.* complètement.

**utter**[2] *v.t.* proférer; (*sigh, shout*) pousser. **~ance** *n.* déclaration *f.*

**U-turn** *n.* demi-tour *m.*

**vacan|t** a. (*post*) vacant; (*seat etc.*) libre; (*look*) vague. **~cy** n. (*post*) poste vacant m.; (*room*) chambre disponible f.

**vacate** v.t. quitter.

**vacation** n. vacances f. pl.

**vaccinat|e** v.t. vacciner. **~ion** n. vaccination f.

**vaccine** n. vaccin m.

**vacuum** n. vide m. **~ cleaner,** aspirateur m. **~ flask,** bouteille thermos f. (P.). **~-packed** a. emballé sous vide.

**vagina** n. vagin m.

**vagrant** n. clochard(e) m. (f.).

**vague** a. vague; (*outline*) flou. **be ~ about,** ne pas préciser. **~ly** adv. vaguement.

**vain** a. (*conceited*) vaniteux; (*useless*) vain. **in ~,** en vain. **~ly** adv. en vain.

**valid** a. valable.

**validate** v.t. valider.

**valley** n. vallée f.

**valour** n. courage m.

**valuable** a. (*object*) de valeur; (*help etc.*) précieux. **~s** n. pl. objets de valeur m. pl.

**valuation** n. expertise f.; (*of house*) évaluation f.

**value** n. valeur f. ● v.t. (*appraise*) évaluer; (*cherish*) attacher de la valeur à.

**valve** n. (*techn.*) soupape f.; (*of tyre*) valve f.

**vampire** n. vampire m.

**van** n. (*vehicle*) camionnette f.; (*rail.*) fourgon m.

**vandal** n. vandale m./f. **~ism** n. vandalisme m.

**vandalize** v.t. abîmer.

**vanilla** n. vanille f.

**vanish** v.i. disparaître.

**vanity** n. vanité f. **~ case,** mallette de toilette f.

**vapour** n. vapeur f.

**vari|able** a. variable. **~ation** n. variation f. **~ed** a. varié.

**variance** n. **at ~,** en désaccord (**with,** avec).

**varicose** a. **~ veins,** varices f. pl.

**variety** n. variété f.

**various** a. divers.

**varnish** n. vernis m. ● v.t. vernir.

**vary** v.t./i. varier.

**vase** n. vase m.

**vast** a. vaste, immense.

**vat** n. cuve f.

**VAT** abbr. (*value added tax*) TVA f.

**vault**[1] n. (*roof*) voûte f.; (*in bank*) chambre forte f.; (*tomb*) caveau m.; (*cellar*) cave f.

**vault**[2] v.t./i. sauter. ● n. saut m.

**vaunt** v.t. vanter.

**VCR** abbr. see **video cassette recorder**.

**VDU** abbr. see **visual display unit**.

**veal** n. (*meat*) veau m.

**veer** v.i. tourner, virer.

**vegan** a. & n. végétalien(-ne) (m. (f.)).

**vegetable** n. légume m. ● a. végétal.

**vegetarian** a. & n. végétarien(ne) (m. (f.)).

**vegetate** v.i. végéter.

**vegetation** n. végétation f.

**vehement** a. véhément.

**vehicle** n. véhicule m.

**veil** n. voile m. ● v.t. voiler.

**vein** n. (*in body, rock*) veine f. (*mood*) esprit m.

**velocity** n. vélocité f.

**velvet** n. velours m.

**veneer** n. placage m.; (*appearance*: fig.) vernis m.

**venerable** a. vénérable.

**venereal** a. vénérien.

**venetian** a. **~ blind,** store vénitien m.

**vengeance** n. vengeance f.

**venison** n. venaison f.

**venom** n. venin m. **~ous** a. venimeux.

**vent**[1] n. (*in coat*) fente f.

**vent**[2] n. (*hole*) orifice m.; (*for air*) bouche d'aération f. ● v.t. (*anger*) décharger (**on,** sur). **give ~ to,** donner libre cours à.

**ventilat|e** v.t. ventiler. **~ion** n. ventilation f.

**ventriloquist** n. ventriloque m./f.

**venture** n. entreprise f. ● v.t./i. (se) risquer.

**veranda** n. véranda f.

**verb** n. verbe m.

**verbal** a. verbal.

**verbatim** adv. mot pour mot.

**verdict** n. verdict m.

**verge** n. bord m. ● v.i. **~ on,** friser, frôler.

**verif|y** v.t. vérifier. **~ication** n. vérification f.

**vermicelli** n. vermicelle(s) m. (pl.).

**vermin** n. vermine f.

**vermouth** n. vermouth m.

**versatil|e** a. (*person*) aux talents variés; (*mind*) souple. **~ity** n. souplesse f.

**verse** n. strophe f.; (*of Bible*) verset m.; (*poetry*) vers m. pl.

**versed** a. **~ in,** versé dans.

**version** n. version f.

**versus** prep. contre.

**vertebra** n. vertèbre f.

**vertical** a. vertical. **~ly** adv. verticalement.

**vertigo** n. vertige m.

**verve** n. fougue f.

**very** adv. très. ● a. (*actual*) même. **the ~ first,** le tout premier. **~ much,** beaucoup.

**vessel** n. (*duct, ship*) vaisseau m.

**vest** n. maillot de corps m.

**vet** n. (*fam.*) vétérinaire m./f. ● v.t. examiner (de près).

**veteran** n. vétéran m.

**veterinary** a. vétérinaire. ~ **surgeon**, vétérinaire m./f.

**veto** n. veto m.; (*right*) droit de veto m. ● v.t. mettre son veto à.

**vex** v.t. contrarier, irriter.

**via** prep. via, par.

**viable** a. viable.

**viaduct** n. viaduc m.

**vibrat|e** v.t./i. (faire) vibrer. ~**ion** n. vibration f.

**vicar** n. pasteur m.

**vice¹** n. (*depravity*) vice m.

**vice²** n. (*techn.*) étau m.

**vice-** pref. vice-.

**vice versa** adv. vice versa.

**vicious** a. (*spiteful*) méchant; (*violent*) brutal. ~ **circle**, cercle vicieux m. ~**ly** adv. méchamment; brutalement.

**victim** n. victime f.

**victimiz|e** v.t. persécuter. ~**ation** n. persécution f.

**victor** n. vainqueur m.

**Victorian** a. & n. victorien(ne) (m. (f.)).

**victor|y** n. victoire f. ~**ious** a. victorieux.

**video** a. (*game, camera*) vidéo invar. ● n. (*recorder*) magnétoscope m.; (*film*) vidéo f. ~ **cassette**, vidéocassette f. ~ (**cassette**) **recorder**, magnétoscope m. ● v.t. (*programme*) enregistrer.

**videotape** n. bande vidéo f. ● v.t. (*programme*) enregistrer.

**vie** v.i. rivaliser (**with**, avec).

**view** n. vue f. ● v.t. (*watch*) regarder; (*consider*) considérer (**as**, comme); (*house*) visiter. **in ~ of**, compte tenu de. ~**er** n. (*TV*) téléspecta|teur, -trice m., f.; (*for slides*) visionneuse f.

**viewfinder** n. viseur m.

**viewpoint** n. point de vue m.

**vigilan|t** a. vigilant. ~**ce** n. vigilance f.

**vig|our** /'vɪgə(r)/ n. vigueur f. ~**orous** a. vigoureux.

**vile** a. exécrable.

**villa** n. pavillon m.

**village** n. village m.

**villain** n. scélérat m., bandit m.; (*in story etc.*) méchant m.

**vindicat|e** v.t. justifier. ~**ion** n. justification f.

**vindictive** a. vindicatif.

**vine** n. vigne f.

**vinegar** n. vinaigre m.

**vineyard** n. vignoble m.

**vintage** n. (*year*) année f., millésime m. ● a. (*wine*) de grand cru; (*car*) d'époque.

**vinyl** n. vinyle m.

**viola** n. (*mus.*) alto m.

**violat|e** v.t. violer. ~**ion** n. violation f.

**violen|t** a. violent. ~**ce** n. violence f.

**violet** n. (*bot.*) violette f.; (*colour*) violet m. ● a. violet.

**violin** n. violon m. ~**ist** n. violoniste m./f.

**VIP** abbr. (*very important person*) personnage de marque m.

**viper** n. vipère f.

**virgin** n. (*woman*) vierge f. ● a. vierge.

**Virgo** n. la Vierge.

**viril|e** a. viril. ~**ity** n. virilité f.

**virtual** a. vrai. a ~ **failure**/*etc.*, pratiquement un échec/*etc.* ~**ly** adv. pratiquement.

**virtue** n. (*goodness, chastity*) vertu f.; (*merit*) mérite m.

**virtuous** a. vertueux.

**virus** n. virus m.

**visa** n. visa m.

**viscount** n. vicomte m.

**viscous** a. visqueux.

**visib|le** a. (*discernible, obvious*) visible. ~**ility** n. visibilité f.

**vision** n. vision f.

**visit** v.t. (*person*) rendre visite à; (*place*) visiter. ● v.i. être en visite. ● n. (*tour, call*) visite f.; (*stay*) séjour m. ~**or** n. visiteu|r, -se m., f.; (*guest*) invité(e) m. (f.); (*in hotel*) client(e) m. (f.).

**visor** n. visière f.

**vista** n. perspective f.

**visual** a. visuel. ~ **display unit**, visuel m., console de visualisation f.

**visualize** v.t. se représenter; (*foresee*) envisager.

**vital** a. vital.

**vitality** n. vitalité f.

**vitamin** n. vitamine f.

**vivac|ious** a. plein d'entrain, animé. ~**ity** n. vivacité f.

**vivid** a. vif; (*graphic*) vivant. ~**ly** adv. vivement; (*describe*) de façon vivante.

**vivisection** n. vivisection f.

**vocabulary** n. vocabulaire m.

**vocal** a. vocal; (*person: fig.*) qui s'exprime franchement. ~**ist** n. chanteu|r, -se m., f.

**vocation** n. vocation f.

**vodka** n. vodka f.

**vogue** n. (*fashion, popularity*) vogue f. **in ~,** en vogue.

**voice** n. voix f. ● v.t. (*express*) formuler.

**void** a. vide (**of**, de); (*not valid*) nul. ● n. vide m.

**volatile** a. (*person*) versatile; (*situation*) variable.

**volcan|o** n. volcan m. ~**ic** a. volcanique.

**volley** *n.* (*of blows etc., in tennis*) volée *f.*; (*of gunfire*) salve *f.* ~**ball** *n.* volley(-ball) *m.*

**volt** *n.* (*electr.*) volt *m.* ~**age** *n.* voltage *m.*

**volume** *n.* volume *m.*

**voluntar|y** *a.* volontaire; (*unpaid*) bénévole. ~**ily** *adv.* volontairement.

**volunteer** *n.* volontaire *m./f.* ● *v.i.* s'offrir (**to do,** pour faire); (*mil.*) s'engager comme volontaire. ● *v.t.* offrir.

**vomit** *v.t./i.* vomir. ● *n.* vomi(ssement) *m.*

**voracious** *a.* vorace.

**vot|e** *n.* vote *m.*; (*right*) droit de vote *m.* ● *v.t./i.* voter. ~**er** *n.* élec|teur, -trice *m., f.* ~**ing** *n.* vote *m.* (**of,** de); (*poll*) scrutin *m.*

**vouch** *v.i.* ~ **for,** répondre de.

**voucher** *n.* bon *m.*

**vow** *n.* vœu *m.* ● *v.t.* (*loyalty etc.*) jurer (**to,** à). ~ **to do,** jurer de faire.

**vowel** *n.* voyelle *f.*

**voyage** *n.* voyage (par mer) *m.*

**vulgar** *a.* vulgaire. ~**ity** *n.* vulgarité *f.*

**vulnerab|le** *a.* vulnérable. ~**ility** *n.* vulnérabilité *f.*

**vulture** *n.* vautour *m.*

·············································

# Ww

·············································

**wad** *n.* (*pad*) tampon *m.*; (*bundle*) liasse *f.*

**wadding** *n.* rembourrage *m.*

**waddle** *v.i.* se dandiner.

**wade** *v.i.* ~ **through,** (*mud etc.*) patauger dans.

**wafer** *n.* (*biscuit*) gaufrette *f.*

**waffle**[1] *n.* (*talk: fam.*) verbiage *m.* ● *v.i.* (*fam.*) divaguer.

**waffle**[2] *n.* (*cake*) gaufre *f.*

**waft** *v.i.* flotter. ● *v.t.* porter.

**wag** *v.t./i.* (*tail*) remuer.

**wage**[1] *v.t.* (*campaign*) mener. ~ **war,** faire la guerre.

**wage**[2] *n.* (*weekly, daily*) salaire *m.* ~**s,** salaire *m.*

**wager** *n.* (*bet*) pari *m.* ● *v.t.* parier (**that,** que).

**waggle** *v.t./i.* remuer.

**wagon** *n.* (*horse-drawn*) chariot *m.*; (*rail.*) wagon (de marchandises) *m.*

**wail** *v.i.* gémir. ● *n.* gémissement *m.*

**waist** *n.* taille *f.*

**waistcoat** *n.* gilet *m.*

**wait** *v.t./i.* attendre. ● *n.* attente *f.* **while you** ~, sur place. ~ **for,** attendre. ~ **on,** servir. ~**ing-list** *n.* liste d'attente *f.*

**wait|er** *n.* garçon *m.*, serveur *m.* ~**ress** *n.* serveuse *f.*

**waive** *v.t.* renoncer à

**wake**[1] *v.t./i.* ~ (**up**), (se) réveiller.

**wake**[2] *n.* (*track*) sillage *m.*

**waken** *v.t./i.* (se) réveiller.

**Wales** *n.* pays de Galles *m.*

**walk** *v.i.* marcher; (*not ride*) aller à pied; (*stroll*) se promener. ● *v.t.* (*streets*) parcourir; (*distance*) faire à pied; (*dog*) promener. ● *n.* promenade *f.*, tour *m.*; (*gait*) (dé)marche *f.*; (*pace*) marche *f.*, pas *m.*; (*path*) allée *f.*

**walker** *n.* (*person*) marcheu|r, -se *m., f.*

**walkie-talkie** *n.* talkie-walkie *m.*

**walking** *n.* marche (à pied) *f.* ● *a.* (*corpse, dictionary: fig.*) vivant. ~**-stick** *n.* canne *f.*

**Walkman** *n.* (P.) Walkman (P.) *m.*, baladeur *m.*

**wall** *n.* mur *m.*; (*of tunnel, stomach, etc.*) paroi *f.* ● *a.* mural.

**wallet** *n.* portefeuille *m.*

**wallflower** *n.* (*bot.*) giroflée *f.*

**wallop** *v.t.* (*hit: sl.*) taper sur. ● *n.* (*blow: sl.*) grand coup *m.*

**wallow** *v.i.* se vautrer.

**wallpaper** *n.* papier peint *m.* ● *v.t.* tapisser.

**walnut** *n.* (*nut*) noix *f.*; (*tree*) noyer *m.*

**walrus** *n.* morse *m.*

**waltz** *n.* valse *f.* ● *v.i.* valser.

**wand** *n.* baguette (magique) *f.*

**wander** *v.i.* errer; (*stroll*) flâner; (*digress*) s'écarter du sujet; (*in mind*) divaguer. ~**er** *n.* vagabond(e) *m.* (*f.*).

**wane** *v.i.* décroître. ● *n.* **on the** ~, (*strength, fame, etc.*) en déclin; (*person*) sur son déclin.

**wangle** *v.t.* (*obtain: sl.*) se débrouiller pour avoir.

**want** *v.t.* vouloir (**to do,** faire); (*need*) avoir besoin de (**doing,** d'être fait); (*ask for*) demander. ● *v.i.* ~ **for,** manquer de. ● *n.* (*need, poverty*) besoin *m.*; (*desire*) désir *m.*; (*lack*) manque *m.* **I** ~ **you to do it,** je veux que vous le fassiez.

**war** *n.* guerre *f.* **at** ~, en guerre.

**ward** *n.* (*in hospital*) salle *f.*; (*minor: jurid.*) pupille *m./f.*; (*pol.*) division électorale *f.* ● *v.t.* ~ **off,** (*danger*) prévenir; (*blow, anger*) détourner.

**warden** *n.* direc|teur, -trice *n., f.*; (*of park*) gardien(ne) *m.* (*f.*). (**traffic**) ~, contractuel(le) *m.* (*f.*).

**warder** *n.* gardien (de prison) *m.*

**wardrobe** *n.* (*place*) armoire *f.*; (*clothes*) garde-robe *f.*

**warehouse** *n.* entrepôt *m.*

**warm** a. chaud; (*hearty*) chaleureux. **be** or **feel ~**, avoir chaud. **it is ~**, il fait chaud. ● *v.t./i.* **~ (up)**, (se) réchauffer; (*food*) chauffer; (*liven up*) (s')animer; (*exercise*) s'échauffer. **~th** n. chaleur f.

**warn** v.t. avertir, prévenir. **~ing** n. avertissement m.; (*notice*) avis m. **without ~ing**, sans prévenir. **~ing light**, voyant m.

**warp** v.t./i. (*wood etc.*) (se) voiler; (*pervert*) pervertir.

**warrant** n. (*for arrest*) mandat (d'arrêt) m.; (*comm.*) autorisation f. ● v.t. justifier.

**warranty** n. garantie f.

**warrior** n. guerr|ier, -ière m., f.

**warship** n. navire de guerre m.

**wart** n. verrue f.

**wary** a. prudent.

**wash** v.t./i. (se) laver; (*flow over*) baigner. ● n. lavage m.; (*clothes*) lessive f.; (*of ship*) sillage m. **have a ~**, se laver. **~basin** n. lavabo m. **~ out**, (*cup etc.*) laver; (*stain*) (faire) partir. **~ out**. n. (*sl.*) fiasco m. **~ up**, faire la vaisselle. **~able** a. lavable. **~ing** n. lessive f. **~ing-machine** n. machine à laver f. **~ing-powder** n. lessive f. **~ing-up** n. vaisselle f.; **~ing-up liquid**, produit pour la vaisselle m.

**washer** n. rondelle f.

**wasp** n. guêpe f.

**wastage** n. gaspillage m. **some ~**, (*in goods, among candidates, etc.*) du déchet.

**waste** v.t. gaspiller; (*time*) perdre. ● v.i. **~ away**, dépérir. ● a. superflu; (*product*) de rebut. ● n. gaspillage m.; (*of time*) perte f.; (*rubbish*) déchets m. pl. **~ paper**, vieux papiers m. pl. **~-paper basket**, corbeille (à papier) f.

**wasteful** a. peu économique; (*person*) gaspilleur.

**watch** v.t./i. (*television*) regarder; (*observe*) observer; (*guard, spy on*) surveiller; (*be careful about*) faire attention à. ● n. (*for telling time*) montre f.; (*naut.*) quart. **~ out**, (*take care*) faire attention (**for**, à). **~ out for**, guetter.

**water** n. eau f. ● v.t. arroser. ● v.i. (*of eyes*) larmoyer. **~-bottle** n. bouillotte f. **~-colour** n. couleur pour aquarelle f.; (*painting*) aquarelle f. **~ down**, couper (d'eau); (*tone down*) édulcorer. **~ heater**, chauffe-eau m. **~-ice** n. sorbet m. **~-main** n. canalisation d'eau f. **~-melon** n. pastèque f. **~-skiing** n. ski nautique m.

**watercress** n. cresson (de fontaine) m.

**waterfall** n. cascade f.

**watering-can** n. arrosoir m.

**waterlogged** a. imprégné d'eau; (*land*) détrempé.

**watermark** n. filigrane m.

**waterproof** a. imperméable.

**watershed** n. (*in affairs*) tournant décisif m.

**watertight** a. étanche.

**waterway** n. voie navigable f.

**watery** a. (*colour*) délavé; (*eyes*) humide; (*soup*) trop liquide; (*tea*) faible.

**watt** n. watt m.

**wav|e** n. vague f.; (*in hair*) ondulation f.; (*radio*) onde f.; (*sign*) signe m. ● v.t. agiter. ● v.i. faire signe (de la main); (*move in wind*) flotter. **~y of**, (*line*) onduleux; (*hair*) ondulé.

**wavelength** n. (*radio & fig.*) longueur d'ondes f.

**waver** v.i. vaciller.

**wax¹** n. cire f.; (*for skis*) fart m. ● v.t. cirer; farter; (*car*) astiquer. **~en**, **~y** adjs. cireux.

**wax²** v.i. (*of moon*) croître.

**way** n. (*road, path*) chemin m. (**to**, de); (*distance*) distance f.; (*direction*) direction f.; (*manner*) façon f.; (*means*) moyen m.; (*particular*) égard m. **~s**, (*habits*) habitudes f. pl. ● adv. (*fam.*) loin. **be in the ~**, bloquer le passage; (*hindrance: fig.*) gêner (qn.). **be on one's** or **the ~**, être sur son or le chemin. **by the ~**, à propos. **in a ~**, dans un sens. **make one's ~ somewhere**, se rendre quelque part. **that ~**, par là. **this ~**, par ici. **~ in**, entrée f. **~ out**, sortie f.

**wayward** a. capricieux.

**WC** n. w.-c. m. pl.

**we** pron. nous.

**weak** a. faible; (*delicate*) fragile. **~ly** adv. faiblement; a. faible. **~ness** n. faiblesse f.; (*fault*) point faible m. **a ~ness for**, (*liking*) un faible pour.

**weaken** v.t. affaiblir ● v.i. s'affaiblir, faiblir.

**weakling** n. gringalet m.

**wealth** n. richesse f.; (*riches, resources*) richesses f. pl.; (*quantity*) profusion f.

**wealthy** a. riche.

**wean** v.t. (*baby*) sevrer.

**weapon** n. arme f.

**wear** v.t. porter; (*put on*) mettre; (*expression etc.*) avoir. ● v.i. (*last*) durer. **~ (out)**, (s')user. ● n. usage m.; (*damage*) usure f.; (*clothing*) vêtements m. pl. **~ off**, (*colour, pain*) passer. **~ on**, (*time*) passer. **~ out**, (*exhaust*) épuiser.

**wear|y** a. fatigué, las; (*tiring*) fatigant. ● v.i. **~y of**, se lasser de. **~ily** adv. avec lassitude.

**weasel** n. belette f.

**weather** n. temps m. ● v.t. (*survive*) réchapper de or à. **~ forecast**, météo f.

**weave** v.t./i. tisser; (*basket etc.*) tresser; (*move*) se faufiler. ● n. (*style*) tissage m.

**web** n. (*of spider*) toile f.; (*fabric*) tissu m.; (*on foot*) palmure f. **~bed** a. (*foot*) palmé.

**wed** v.t. épouser. ● v.i. se marier.

**wedding** n. mariage m. **~-ring** n. alliance f.

**wedge** n. coin m.; (*under wheel etc.*) cale f. ● v.t. caler; (*push*) enfoncer; (*crowd*) coincer.

**Wednesday** n. mercredi m.

**wee** a. (*fam.*) tout petit.

**weed** *n.* mauvaise herbe *f.* ● *v.t./i.* désherber. **~killer** *n.* désherbant *m.* **~ out,** extirper.

**week** *n.* semaine *f.* **a ~ today/tomorrow,** aujourd'hui/ demain en huit. **~ly** *adv.* toutes les semaines; *a. & n. (periodical)* hebdomadaire (*m.*).

**weekday** *n.* jour de semaine *m.*

**weekend** *n.* week-end *m.*

**weep** *v.t./i.* pleurer (**for s.o.,** qn.). **~ing willow,** saule pleureur *m.*

**weigh** *v.t./i.* peser. **~ down,** lester (avec un poids); (*bend*) faire plier; (*fig.*) accabler. **~ up,** (*examine: fam.*) calculer.

**weight** *n.* poids *m.* **lose/put on ~,** perdre/ prendre du poids. **~-lifting** *n.* haltérophilie *f.*

**weighting** *n.* indemnité *f.*

**weir** *n.* barrage *m.*

**weird** *a.* mystérieux; (*strange*) bizarre.

**welcome** *a.* agréable; (*timely*) opportun. **be ~,** être le *or* la bienvenu(e), être les bienvenu(e)s. **you're ~!,** (*after thank you*) il n'y a pas de quoi! **~ to do,** libre de faire. ● *int.* soyez le *or* la bienvenu(e), soyez les bienvenu(e)s. ● *n.* accueil *m.* ● *v.t.* accueillir; (*as greeting*) souhaiter la bienvenue à; (*fig.*) se réjouir de.

**weld** *v.t.* souder. ● *n.* soudure *f.* **~er** *n.* soudeur *m.*

**welfare** *n.* bien-être *m.*; (*aid*) aide sociale *f.*

**well**[1] *n.* (*for water, oil*) puits *m.*; (*of stairs*) cage *f.*

**well**[2] *adv.* bien. ● *a.* bien *invar.* **as ~,** aussi. **be ~,** (*healthy*) aller bien. ● *int.* eh bien; (*surprise*) tiens. **do ~,** (*succeed*) réussir. **~-behaved** *a.* sage. **~-being** *n.* bien-être *m.* **~-built** *a.* bien bâti. **~ done!,** bravo! **~-dressed** *a.* bien habillé. **~-known** *a.* (bien) connu. **~-off,** aisé, riche. **~-to-do** *a.* riche.

**wellington** *n.* (*boot*) botte de caoutchouc *f.*

**Welsh** *a.* gallois. ● *n.* (*lang.*) gallois *m.* **~man** *n.* Gallois *m.* **~woman** *n.* Galloise *f.*

**welsh** *v.i.* **~ on,** (*debt, promise*) ne pas honorer.

**wend** *v.t.* **~ one's way,** se diriger, aller son chemin.

**west** *n.* ouest *m.* **the W~,** (*pol.*) l'Occident *m.* ● *a.* d'ouest. ● *adv.* vers l'ouest. **W~ Indian** *a. & n.* antillais(e) (*m.* (*f.*)). **the W~ Indies,** les Antilles *f. pl.* **~ern** *a.* de l'ouest; (*pol.*) occidental; *n.* (*film*) western *m.* **~ward** *a.* à l'ouest. **~wards** *adv.* vers l'ouest.

**wet** *a.* mouillé; (*damp, rainy*) humide; (*paint*) frais. ● *v.t.* mouiller. **get ~,** se mouiller. **~ suit,** combinaison de plongée *f.*

**whack** *n.* (*fam.*) grand coup *m.* ● *v.t.* (*fam.*) taper sur.

**whale** *n.* baleine *f.*

**wharf** *n.* quai *m.*

**what** *a.* (*in questions*) quel(le), quel(le)s. ● *pron.* (*in questions*) qu'est-ce qui; (*object*) (qu'est-ce) que *or* qu'*; (*after prep.*) quoi; (*that which*) ce qui; (*object*) ce que, ce qu'*. ● *int.* quoi, comment. **~ time?,** à quelle heure? **~ he said,** ce qu'il a dit. **~ is it?,** qu'est-ce que c'est? **~ you need,** ce dont vous avez besoin. **~ a fool/etc.,** quel idiot/etc. **~ about me/him/ etc.?,** et moi/lui/etc.? **~ about doing?,** si on faisait? **~ for?,** pourquoi?

**whatever** *a.* **~ book/etc.,** quel que soit le livre/etc. ● *pron.* (*no matter what*) quoi que, quoi qu'*; (*anything that*) tout ce qui; (*object*) tout ce que *or* qu'*. **~ happens,** quoi qu'il arrive. **~ you want,** tout ce que vous voulez. **nothing ~,** rien du tout.

**whatsoever** *a. & pron.* = **whatever.**

**wheat** *n.* blé *m.*, froment *m.*

**wheedle** *v.t.* cajoler.

**wheel** *n.* roue *f.* ● *v.t.* pousser. ● *v.i.* tourner. **at the ~,** (*of vehicle*) au volant; (*helm*) au gouvernail.

**wheelbarrow** *n.* brouette *f.*

**wheelchair** *n.* fauteuil roulant *m.*

**wheeze** *v.i.* siffler (en respirant). ● *n.* sifflement *m.*

**when** *adv. & pron.* quand. ● *conj.* quand, lorsque. **the day/ moment ~,** le jour/ moment où.

**whenever** *conj. & adv.* (*at whatever time*) quand; (*every time that*) chaque fois que.

**where** *adv., conj., & pron.* où; (*whereas*) alors que; (*the place that*) là où.

**whereas** *conj.* alors que.

**wherever** *conj. & adv.* où que; (*everywhere*) partout où; (*anywhere*) (là) où; (*emphatic where*) où donc.

**whet** *v.t.* (*appetite*) aiguiser.

**whether** *conj.* si. **not know ~,** ne pas savoir si. **~ I go or not,** que j'aille ou non.

**which** *a.* (*in questions*) quel(le), quel(le)s. ● *pron.* (*in questions*) lequel, laquelle, lesquel(le)s; (*the one or ones that*) celui (celle, ceux, celles) qui; (*object*) celui (celle, ceux, celles) que *or* qu'*; (*referring to whole sentence: = and that*) ce qui; (*object*) ce que, ce qu'*; (*after prep.*) lequel/etc. ● *rel. pron.* qui; (*object*) que, qu'*. **~ house?,** quelle maison? **~ (one) do you want?,** lequel voulez-vous? **of ~, from ~,** duquel/etc. **to ~, at ~,** auquel/ etc. **the book of ~,** le livre dont *or* duquel. **after ~,** après quoi.

**whichever** *a.* **~ book/etc.,** quel que soit le livre/etc. que *or* qui. **take ~ book you wish,** prenez le livre que vous voulez. ● *pron.* celui (celle, ceux, celles) qui *or* que.

**whiff** *n.* (*puff*) bouffée *f.*

**while** *n.* moment *m.* ● *conj.* (*when*) pendant que; (*although*) bien que; (*as long as*) tant que. ● *v.t.* **~ away,** (*time*) passer.

**whilst** *conj.* = **while.**

**whim** n. caprice m.

**whimper** v.i. geindre, pleurnicher. ● n. pleurnichement m.

**whimsical** a. (person) capricieux; (odd) bizarre.

**whine** v.i. gémir, se plaindre. ● n. gémissement m.

**whip** n. fouet m. ● v.t. fouetter; (culin.) fouetter, battre; (seize) enlever brusquement. ~-round n. (fam.) collecte f. ~ out, (gun etc.) sortir. ~ up, exciter; (cause) provoquer; (meal: fam.) préparer.

**whirl** v.t./i. (faire) tourbillonner. ● n. tourbillon m.

**whirlpool** n. (in sea etc.) tourbillon m.

**whirlwind** n. tourbillon (de vent) m.

**whirr** v.i. vrombir.

**whisk** v.t. (snatch) enlever or emmener brusquement; (culin.) fouetter. ● n. (culin.) fouet m.; (broom, brush) petit balai m.

**whisker** n. poil m. ~s, (man's) barbe f., moustache f.; (sideboards) favoris m. pl.

**whisky** n. whisky m.

**whisper** v.t./i. chuchoter. ● n. chuchotement m.

**whistle** n. sifflement m.; (instrument) sifflet m. ● v.t./i. siffler. ~ at or for, siffler.

**Whit** a. ~ Sunday, dimanche de Pentecôte m.

**white** a. blanc. ● n. blanc m.; (person) blanc(he) m. (f.). ~ coffee, café au lait m. ~-collar worker, employé(e) de bureau m. (f.).

**whitewash** n. blanc de chaux m. ● v.t. blanchir à la chaux; (person: fig.) blanchir.

**whiting** n. invar. (fish) merlan m.

**Whitsun** n. la Pentecôte f.

**whittle** v.t. ~ down, tailler (au couteau); (fig.) réduire.

**whiz** v.i. (through air) fendre l'air; (hiss) siffler; (rush) aller à toute vitesse. ~-kid n. jeune prodige m.

**who** pron. qui.

**whoever** pron. (no matter who) qui que ce soit qui or que; (the one who) quiconque.

**whole** a. entier; (intact) intact. the ~ house/etc., toute la maison/etc. ● n. totalité f.; (unit) tout m. on the ~, dans l'ensemble. ~-hearted a., ~-heartedly adv. sans réserve.

**wholefoods** n. pl. aliments naturels et diététiques m. pl.

**wholemeal** a. ~ bread, pain complet m.

**wholesale** n. gros m. ● a. (firm) de gros; (fig.) systématique. ● adv. (in large quantities) en gros; (buy or sell one item) au prix de gros; (fig.) en masse. ~r n. grossiste m./f.

**wholesome** a. sain.

**wholewheat** a. = wholemeal.

**whom** pron. (that) que, qu'*; (after prep. & in questions) qui. of ~, dont. with ~, avec qui.

**whooping cough** n. coqueluche f.

**whore** n. putain f.

**whose** pron. & a. à qui, de qui. ~ hat is this?, ~ is this hat?, à qui est ce chapeau? ~ son are you?, de qui êtes-vous le fils?

**why** adv. pourquoi. the reason ~, la raison pour laquelle.

**wick** n. (of lamp etc.) mèche f.

**wicked** a. méchant, mauvais, vilain.

**wicker** n. osier m. ~work n. vannerie f.

**wicket** n. guichet m.

**wide** a. large; (ocean etc.) vaste. ● adv. (fall etc.) loin du but. open ~, ouvrir tout grand. ~ open, grand ouvert. ~ angle lens grand-angle m. ~ awake, éveillé. ~ly adv. (spread, space) largement; (travel) beaucoup; (generally) généralement; (extremely) extrêmement.

**widen** v.t./i. (s')élargir.

**widespread** a. très répandu.

**widow** n. veuve f. ~er n. veuf m.

**width** n. largeur f.

**wield** v.t. (axe etc.) manier; (power: fig.) exercer.

**wife** n. femme f., épouse f.

**wig** n. perruque f.

**wiggle** v.t./i. remuer; (hips) tortiller; (of worm) se tortiller.

**wild** a. sauvage; (sea, enthusiasm) déchaîné; (mad) fou; (angry) furieux. ● adv. (grow) à l'état sauvage. ~s n. pl. régions sauvages f. pl. ~-goose chase, fausse piste f. ~ly adv. violemment; (madly) follement.

**wildcat** a. ~ strike, grève sauvage f.

**wilderness** n. désert m.

**wildlife** n. faune f.

**wile** n. ruse f., artifice m.

**wilful** a. volontaire.

**will**[1] v. aux. he ~ do/you ~ sing/etc., (future tense) il fera/tu chanteras/etc. ~ you have a coffee?, voulez-vous prendre un café?

**will**[2] n. volonté f.; (document) testament m. ● v.t. (wish) vouloir. at ~, quand or comme on veut. ~power n. volonté f.

**willing** a. (help, offer) spontané; (helper) bien disposé. ~ to, disposé à. ~ly adv. (with pleasure) volontiers; (not forced) volontairement.

**willow** n. saule m.

**wilt** v.i. (plant etc.) dépérir.

**wily** a. rusé.

**win** v.t./i. gagner; (victory, prize) remporter; (fame, fortune) acquérir, trouver. ● n. victoire f. ~ round, convaincre.

**wince** v.i. se crisper, tressaillir.

**winch** n. treuil m. ● v.t. hisser au treuil.

**wind**[1] n. vent m.; (breath) souffle m. ● v.t. essouffler. ~cheater n. blouson m. ~ instrument, instrument à vent m.

**wind**[1] *v.t./i.* (s')enrouler; ( *of path, river* ) serpenter. ~ **(up),** ( *clock etc.* ) remonter. ~ **up,** ( *end* ) (se) terminer. ~ **up in hospital,** finir à l'hôpital. ~**ing** *a.* ( *path* ) sinueux.

**windfall** *n.* fruit tombé *m.*; ( *money: fig.* ) aubaine *f.*

**windmill** *n.* moulin à vent *m.*

**window** *n.* fenêtre *f.*; ( *glass pane* ) vitre *f.*; ( *in vehicle, train* ) vitre *f.*; ( *in shop* ) vitrine *f.*; ( *counter* ) guichet *m.* ~**cleaner** *n.* laveur de carreaux *m.* ~**shopping** *n.* lèche-vitrines *m.* ~**sill** *n.* ( *inside* ) appui de (la) fenêtre *m.*; ( *outside* ) rebord de (la) fenêtre *m.*

**windscreen** *n.* pare-brise *m. invar.* ~ **washer,** lave-glace *m.* ~ **wiper,** essuie-glace *m.*

**windsurf|ing** *n.* planche à voile *f.* ~**er** *n.* véliplanchiste *m./f.*

**windy** *a.* venteux. **it is** ~, il y a du vent.

**wine** *n.* vin *m.* ~ **list,** carte des vins *f.*

**wineglass** *n.* verre à vin *m.*

**wing** *n.* aile *f.* ~**s,** ( *theatre* ) coulisses *f. pl.* ~ **mirror,** rétroviseur extérieur *m.* ~**er** *n.* ( *sport* ) ailier *m.*

**wink** *v.i.* faire un clin d'œil; ( *light, star* ) clignoter. ● *n.* clin d'œil *m.*; clignotement *m.*

**winner** *n.* ( *of game* ) gagnant(e) *m.* (*f.*); ( *of fight* ) vainqueur *m.*

**winning** *a.* ( *number, horse* ) gagnant; ( *team* ) victorieux; ( *smile* ) engageant. ~**s** *n. pl.* gains *m. pl.*

**winter** *n.* hiver *m.*

**wipe** *v.t.* essuyer. ● *v.i.* ~ **up,** essuyer la vaisselle. ● *n.* coup de torchon *or* d'éponge *m.* ~ **out,** ( *destroy* ) anéantir; ( *remove* ) effacer.

**wir|e** *n.* fil *m.* ~**ing** *n.* ( *electr.* ) installation électrique *f.*

**wireless** *n.* radio *f.*

**wiry** *a.* ( *person* ) nerveux et maigre.

**wisdom** *n.* sagesse *f.*

**wise** *a.* prudent, sage; ( *look* ) averti. ~**ly** *adv.* prudemment.

**wish** *n.* ( *specific* ) souhait *m.*, vœu *m.*; ( *general* ) désir *m.* ● *v.t.* souhaiter, vouloir, désirer ( **to do,** faire); ( *bid* ) souhaiter. ● *v.i.* ~ **for,** souhaiter. **I** ~ **he'd leave,** je voudrais bien qu'il parte.

**wisp** *n.* ( *of smoke* ) volute *f.*

**wit** *n.* intelligence *f.*; ( *humour* ) esprit *m.*; ( *person* ) homme d'esprit *m.*, femme d'esprit *f.*

**witch** *n.* sorcière *f.*

**with** *prep.* avec; ( *having* ) à; ( *because of* ) de; ( *at house of* ) chez. **the man** ~ **the beard,** l'homme à la barbe. **fill** /*etc.* ~, remplir/ *etc.* de.

**withdraw** *v.t./i.* (se) retirer. ~**al** *n.* retrait *m.* ~**n** *a.* ( *person* ) renfermé.

**wither** *v.t./i.* (se) flétrir.

**withhold** *v.t.* refuser (de donner); ( *retain* ) retenir; ( *conceal, not tell* ) cacher ( **from,** à).

**within** *prep. & adv.* à l'intérieur (de); ( *in distances* ) à moins de. ~ **a month,** ( *before* ) avant un mois. ~ **sight,** en vue.

**without** *prep.* sans. ~ **my knowing,** sans que je sache.

**withstand** *v.t.* résister à.

**witness** *n.* témoin *m.*; ( *evidence* ) témoignage *m.* ● *v.t.* être le témoin de, voir; ( *document* ) signer.

**witty** *a.* spirituel.

**wizard** *n.* magicien *m.*; ( *genius: fig.* ) génie *m.*

**wobbl|e** *v.i.* ( *of jelly, voice, hand* ) trembler; ( *stagger* ) chanceler; ( *of table, chair* ) branler. ~**y** *a.* tremblant; branlant.

**wolf** *n.* loup *m.* ● *v.t.* ( *food* ) engloutir. ~ **whistle** *n.* sifflement admiratif *m.*

**woman** *n.* femme *f.* ~ **doctor,** femme médecin *f.* ~ **friend,** amie *f.*

**womb** *n.* utérus *m.*

**wonder** *n.* émerveillement *m.*; ( *thing* ) merveille *f.* ● *v.t.* se demander ( **if,** si). ● *v.i.* s'étonner ( **at,** de); ( *reflect* ) songer ( **about,** à). **it is no** ~, ce *or* il n'est pas étonnant ( **that,** que).

**wonderful** *a.* merveilleux.

**wood** *n.* bois *m.* ~**en** *a.* en *or* de bois; ( *stiff: fig.* ) raide.

**woodland** *n.* région boisée *f.*

**woodpecker** *n.* pivert *m.*

**woodwind** *n.* ( *mus.* ) bois *m. pl.*

**woodwork** *n.* menuiserie *f.*

**woodworm** *n.* ( *larvae* ) vers (de bois) *m. pl.*

**woody** *a.* ( *wooded* ) boisé; ( *like wood* ) ligneux.

**wool** *n.* laine *f.* ~**len** *a.* de laine. ~**lens** *n. pl.* lainages *m. pl.* ~**ly** *a.* laineux; ( *vague* ) nébuleux; *n.* ( *garment: fam.* ) lainage *m.*

**word** *n.* mot *m.*; ( *spoken* ) parole *f.*, mot *m.*; ( *promise* ) parole *f.*; ( *news* ) nouvelles *f. pl.* ● *v.t.* rédiger. **give/keep one's** ~, donner/ tenir sa parole. **have a** ~ **with,** parler à. ~ **processor,** machine de traitement de texte *f.*

**work** *n.* travail *m.*; ( *product, book, etc.* ) œuvre *f.*, ouvrage *m.*; ( *building etc. work* ) travaux *m. pl.* ~**s,** ( *techn.* ) mécanisme *m.*; ( *factory* ) usine *f.* ● *v.t./i.* ( *of person* ) travailler; ( *shape, hammer, etc.* ) travailler; ( *techn.* ) (faire) fonctionner, (faire) marcher; ( *land, mine* ) exploiter; ( *of drug etc.* ) agir. ~**force** *n.* main-d'œuvre *f.* ~ **out** *v.t.* ( *solve* ) résoudre; ( *calculate* ) calculer; ( *elaborate* ) élaborer; *v.i.* ( *succeed* ) marcher; ( *sport* ) s'entraîner. ~ **station** *n.* poste de travail *m.* ~**to-rule** *n.* grève du zèle *f.* ~ **up** *v.t.* développer; *v.i.* ( *to climax* ) monter vers. ~**ed up,** ( *person* ) énervé.

**worker** *n.* travailleu|r, -se *m.*, *f.*; ( *manual* ) ouvri|er, -ère *m.*, *f.*

**working** *a.* ( *day, lunch, etc.* ) de travail. ~**s** *n. pl.* mécanisme *m.* ~ **class,** classe ouvrière *f.* ~**class** *a.* ouvrier.

**workman** *n.* ouvrier *m.*

**workshop** n. atelier m.
**world** n. monde m. ● a. (*power etc.*) mondial; (*record etc.*) du monde. **~-wide** a. universel.
**worldly** a. de ce monde, terrestre.
**worm** n. ver m.
**worn** a. usé. **~-out** a. (*thing*) complètement usé; (*person*) épuisé.
**worr|y** v.t./i. (s')inquiéter. ● n. souci m. **~ied** a. inquiet.
**worse** a. pire, plus mauvais. ● adv. plus mal. ● n. pire m. **be ~ off**, perdre.
**worsen** v.t./i. empirer.
**worship** n. (*adoration*) culte m. ● v.t. adorer. ● v.i. faire ses dévotions.
**worst** a. pire, plus mauvais. ● adv. **(the) ~**, (*sing etc.*) le plus mal. ● n. **the ~ (one)**, (*person, object*) le or la pire.
**worsted** n. worsted m.
**worth** a. **be ~**, valoir. **it is ~ waiting**/*etc.*, ça vaut la peine d'attendre/*etc.* ● n. valeur f. **it is ~ (one's) while**, ça (en) vaut la peine. **~less** a. qui ne vaut rien.
**worthwhile** a. qui (en) vaut la peine.
**worthy** a. digne (**of**, de); (*laudable*) louable.
**would** v. aux. **he ~ do**/**you ~ sing**/*etc.*, (*conditional tense*) il ferait/tu chanterais/*etc.* **he ~ have done**, il aurait fait. **I ~ come every day,** (*used to*) je venais chaque jour. **I ~ like some tea,** je voudrais du thé. **~ you come here?**, voulez-vous venir ici? **he ~n't come,** il a refusé de venir. **~-be** a. soi-disant.
**wound** n. blessure f. ● v.t. blesser.
**wrangle** v.i. se disputer. ● n. dispute f.
**wrap** v.t. **~ (up)**, envelopper. ● v.i. **~ up**, (*dress warmly*) se couvrir. ● n. châle m. **~per** n. (*of book*) jaquette f.; (*of sweet*) papier m. **~ping** n. emballage m.; **~ping paper,** papier d'emballage m.
**wreath** n. couronne f.
**wreck** n. (*sinking*) naufrage m.; (*ship, remains, person*) épave f.; (*vehicle*) voiture accidentée f. ● v.t. détruire; (*ship*) provoquer le naufrage de. **~age** n. (*pieces*) débris m. pl.; (*wrecked building*) décombres m. pl.
**wren** n. roitelet m.
**wrench** v.t. (*pull*) tirer sur; (*twist*) tordre; (*snatch*) arracher (**from**, à). ● n. (*tool*) clé f.
**wrestl|e** v.i. lutter, se débattre (**with,** contre). **~er** n. lutteu|r, -se m./f.; catcheu|r, -se m., f. **~ing** n. lutte f. **(all-in) ~ing,** catch m.
**wretch** n. malheureu|x, -se m., f.; (*rascal*) misérable m./f.
**wretched** a. (*pitiful, poor*) misérable; (*bad*) affreux.
**wriggle** v.t./i. (se) tortiller.
**wring** v.t. (*twist*) tordre; (*clothes*) essorer.
**wrinkle** n. (*crease*) pli m.; (*on skin*) ride f. ● v.t./i. (se) rider.
**wrist** n. poignet m. **~-watch** n. montre-bracelet f.

**writ** n. acte judiciaire m.
**write** v.t./i. écrire. **~ down**, noter. **~ off**, (*debt*) passer aux profits et pertes; (*vehicle*) considérer bon pour la casse. **~-off** n. perte totale f.
**writer** n. écrivain m.
**writhe** v.i. se tordre.
**writing** n. écriture f. **in ~**, par écrit. **~-paper** n. papier à lettres m.
**wrong** a. (*incorrect, mistaken*) faux, mauvais; (*unfair*) injuste; (*amiss*) qui ne va pas; (*clock*) pas à l'heure. **be ~**, (*person*) avoir tort (**to,** de); (*be mistaken*) se tromper. ● adv. mal. ● n. injustice f.; (*evil*) mal m. ● v.t. faire (du) tort à. **what's ~?**, qu'est-ce qui ne va pas?
**wrought** a. **~ iron,** fer forgé m..
**wry** a. (*smile*) désabusé.

· · · · · · · · · · · · · · · · · · · · ·

· · · · · · · · · · · · · · · · · · · · ·

**xerox** v.t. photocopier.
**Xmas** n. Noël m.
**X-ray** n. rayon X m.; (*photograph*) radio (graphie) f. ● v.t. radiographier.
**xylophone** n. xylophone m.

· · · · · · · · · · · · · · · · · · · · ·

· · · · · · · · · · · · · · · · · · · · ·

**yacht** n. yacht m. **~ing** n. yachting m.
**yank** v.t. tirer brusquement. ● n. coup brusque m.
**Yank** n. (*fam.*) Américain(e) m. (f.), Amerloque m./f.
**yap** v.i. japper.
**yard**[1] n. (*measure*) yard m. (= 0.9144 metre).
**yard**[2] n. (*of house etc.*) cour f.; (*for storage*) dépôt m.
**yarn** n. (*thread*) fil m.; (*tale: fam.*) (longue) histoire f.
**yawn** v.i. bâiller. ● n. bâillement m.
**year** n. an m., année f. **be ten**/*etc.* **~s old,** avoir dix/*etc.* ans. **~ly** a. annuel; adv. annuellement.
**yearn** v.i. avoir bien or très envie (**for, to,** de). **~ing** n. envie f.
**yeast** n. levure f.
**yell** v.t./i. hurler. ● n. hurlement m.
**yellow** a. jaune ● n. jaune m.
**yelp** n. (*of dog etc.*) jappement m. ● v.i. japper.

**yen** *n.* (*desire*) grande envie *f.*

**yes** *adv.* oui; (*as answer to negative question*) si. ● *n.* oui *m. invar.*

**yesterday** *n. & adv.* hier (*m.*).

**yet** *adv.* encore; (*already*) déjà. ● *conj.* pourtant.

**yew** *n.* (*tree, wood*) if *m.*

**Yiddish** *n.* yiddish *m.*

**yield** *v.t.* (*produce*) produire, rendre; (*profit*) rapporter; (*surrender*) céder. ● *v.i.* (*give way*) céder. ● *n.* rendement *m.*

**yoga** *n.* yoga *m.*

**yoghurt** *n.* yaourt *m.*

**yolk** *n.* jaune (d'œuf) *m.*

**yonder** *adv.* là-bas.

**you** *pron.* (*familiar form*) tu, *pl.* vous; (*polite form*) vous; (*object*) te, t'*, *pl.* vous; (*polite*) vous; (*after prep.*) toi, *pl.* vous; (*polite*) vous; (*indefinite*) on; (*object*) vous. (**to**) ~, te, t'*, *pl.* vous; (*polite*) vous. **I gave ~ a pen,** je vous ai donné un stylo. **I know ~,** je te connais; je vous connais.

**young** *a.* jeune. ● *n.* (*people*) jeunes *m. pl.*; (*of animals*) petits *m. pl.*

**youngster** *n.* jeune *m./f.*

**your** *a.* (*familiar form*) ton, ta, *pl.* tes; (*polite form, & familiar form pl.*) votre, *pl.* vos.

**yours** *poss. pron.* (*familiar form*) le tien, la tienne, les tien(ne)s; (*polite form, & familiar form pl.*) le or la vôtre, les vôtres. **~s faithfully/sincerely,** je vous prie d'agréer/ de croire en l'expression de mes sentiments les meilleurs.

**yourself** *pron.* (*familiar form*) toi-même; (*polite form*) vous-même; (*reflexive & after prep.*) te, t'*; vous. **~ves** *pron. pl.* vous-mêmes; (*reflexive*) vous.

**youth** *n.* jeunesse *f.*; (*young man*) jeune *m.* **~ club,** centre de jeunes *m.* **~ hostel,** auberge de jeunesse *f.*

**Yugoslav** *a. & n.* Yougoslave (*m./f.*). **~ia** *n.* Yougoslavie *f.*

# Zz

**zany** *a.* farfelu.

**zeal** *n.* zèle *m.*

**zebra** *n.* zèbre *m.* **~ crossing,** passage pour piétons *m.*

**zenith** *n.* zénith *m.*

**zero** *n.* zéro *m.* **~ hour,** l'heure H *f.*

**zest** *n.* (*gusto*) entrain *m.*; (*spice: fig.*) piment *m.*; (*of orange or lemon peel*) zeste *m.*

**zigzag** *n.* zigzag *m.* ● *a. & adv.* en zigzag. ● *v.i.* zigzaguer.

**zinc** *n.* zinc *m.*

**Zionism** *n.* sionisme *m.*

**zip** *n.* (*vigour*) allant *m.* **~(-fastener),** fermeture éclair *f.* (P.). ● *v.t.* fermer avec une fermeture éclair (P.). ● *v.i.* aller à toute vitesse.

**zodiac** *n.* zodiaque *m.*

**zone** *n.* zone *f.*

**zoo** *n.* zoo *m.*

**zoology** *n.* zoologie *f.* **~ical** *a.* zoologique. **~ist** *n.* zoologiste *m./f.*

**zoom** *v.i.* (*rush*) se précipiter. **~ lens,** zoom *m.* **~ off** *or* **past,** filer (comme une flèche).

# French Verb Tables

## Notes

The conditional may be formed by substituting the following endings for those of the future: *ais* for *ai* and *as*, *ait* for *a*, *ions* for *ons*, *iez* for *ez*, *aient* for *ont*. The present participle is formed (unless otherwise indicated) by substituting *ant* for *ons* in the first person plural of the present tense (e.g. *finissant* and *donnant* may be derived from *finissons* and *donnons*). The imperative forms are (unless otherwise indicated) the same as the second persons singular and plural and the first person plural of the present tense. The second person singular does not take *s* after *e* or *a* (e.g. *donne, va*), except when followed by *y* or *en* (e.g. *vas-y*).

●●●●●●●　**Regular verbs**　●●●●●●●

**1. in -er (e.g. donn|er)**

| | |
|---|---|
| *Present* | ~e, ~es, ~e, ~ons, ~ez, ~ent. |
| *Imperfect* | ~ais, ~ais, ~ait, ~ions, ~iez, ~aient. |
| *Past historic* | ~ai, ~as, ~a, ~âmes, ~âtes, ~èrent. |
| *Future* | ~erai, ~eras, ~era, ~erons, ~erez, ~eront. |
| *Present subjunctive* | ~e, ~es, ~e, ~ions, ~iez, ~ent. |
| *Past participle* | ~é. |

**2. in -ir (e.g. fin|ir)**

| | |
|---|---|
| *Present* | ~is, ~is, ~it, ~issons, ~issez, ~issent. |
| *Imperfect* | ~issais, ~issais, ~issait, ~issions, ~issiez, ~issaient. |
| *Past historic* | ~is, ~is, ~it, ~îmes, ~îtes, ~irent. |
| *Future* | ~irai, ~iras, ~ira, ~irons, ~irez, ~iront. |
| *Present subjunctive* | ~isse, ~isses, ~isse, ~issions, ~issiez, ~issent. |
| *Past participle* | ~i. |

**3. in -re (e.g. vend|re)**

| | |
|---|---|
| *Present* | ~s, ~s, ~, ~ons, ~ez, ~ent. |
| *Imperfect* | ~ais, ~ais, ~ait, ~ions, ~iez, ~aient. |
| *Past historic* | ~is, ~is, ~it, ~îmes, ~îtes, ~irent. |
| *Future* | ~rai, ~ras, ~ra, ~rons, ~rez, ~ront. |
| *Present subjunctive* | ~e, ~es, ~e, ~ions, ~iez, ~ent. |
| *Past participle* | ~u. |

## Peculiarities of -er verbs

In verbs in -cer (e.g. **commencer**) and -ger (e.g. **manger**), c becomes ç and g becomes ge before a and o (e.g. **commença, commençons, mangea, mangeons**).

In verbs in -yer (e.g. **nettoyer**), y becomes i before mute e (e.g. **nettoie, nettoierai**). Verbs in -ayer (e.g. **payer**) may retain y before mute e (e.g. **paye** or **paie, payerai** or **paierai**).

In verbs in -eler (e.g. **appeler**) and in -eter (e.g. **jeter**), l becomes ll and t becomes tt before a syllable containing mute e (e.g. **appelle, appellerai; jette, jetterai**). In the verbs **celer, ciseler, congeler, déceler, démanteler, écarteler, geler, marteler, modeler**, and **peler**, and in the verbs **acheter, crocheter, fureter, haleter**, and **racheter**, e becomes è before a syllable containing mute e (e.g. **cèle, cèlerai; achète, achèterai**).

In verbs in which the penultimate syllable contains mute e (e.g. **semer**) or é (e.g. **révéler**), both e and é become è before a syllable containing mute e (e.g. **sème, sèmerai; révèle**). However, in the verbs in which the penultimate syllable contains é, é remains unchanged in the future and conditional (e.g. **révélerai**).

●●●●●●● **Irregular verbs** ●●●●●●●

At least the first persons singular and plural of the present tense are shown. Forms not listed may be derived from these. Though the base form of the imperfect, future, and present subjunctive may be irregular, the endings of these tenses are as shown in the regular verb section. Only the first person singular of these tenses is given in most cases. The base form of the past historic may also be irregular but the endings of this tense shown in the verbs below fall (with few exceptions) into the 'u' category, listed under **être** and **avoir**, and the 'i' category shown under **finir** and **vendre** in the regular verb section. Only the first person singular of the past historic is listed in most cases.

Additional forms appear throughout when these cannot be derived from the forms given or when it is considered helpful to list them. Only those irregular verbs judged to be the most useful are shown in the tables.

| | |
|---|---|
| **abattre** | *as* BATTRE. |
| **accueillir** | *as* CUEILLIR. |
| **acquérir** | •*Pres.* acquiers, acquérons, acquièrent. •*Impf.* acquérais. •*Past hist.* acquis. •*Fut.* acquerrai. •*Pres. sub.* acquière. •*Past part.* acquis. |
| **admettre** | *as* METTRE. |
| **aller** | •*Pres.* vais, vas, va, allons, allez, vont. •*Fut.* irai. •*Pres. sub.* aille, allions. |
| **apercevoir** | *as* RECEVOIR. |
| **apparaître** | *as* CONNAÎTRE. |
| **appartenir** | *as* TENIR. |
| **apprendre** | *as* PRENDRE. |
| **asseoir** | •*Pres.* assieds, asseyons, asseyent. •*Impf.* asseyais. •*Past hist.* assis. •*Fut.* assiérai. •*Pres. sub.* asseye. •*Past part.* assis. |
| **atteindre** | •*Pres.* atteins, atteignons, atteignent. •*Impf.* atteignais. •*Past hist.* atteignis. •*Fut.* atteindrai. •*Pres. sub.* atteigne. •*Past part.* atteint. |
| **avoir** | •*Pres.* ai, as, a, avons, avez, ont. •*Impf.* avais. •*Past hist.* eus, eut, eûmes, eûtes, eurent. •*Fut.* aurai. •*Pres. sub.* aie, aies, ait, ayons, ayez, aient. •*Pres. part.* ayant. •*Past part.* eu. •*Imp.* aie, ayons, ayez. |
| **battre** | •*Pres.* bats, bat, battons, battez, battent. |
| **boire** | •*Pres.* bois, buvons, boivent. •*Impf.* buvais. •*Past hist.* bus. •*Pres. sub.* boive, buvions. •*Past part.* bu. |
| **bouillir** | •*Pres.* bous, bouillons, bouillent. •*Impf.* bouillais. •*Pres. sub.* bouille. |
| **combattre** | *as* BATTRE. |
| **commettre** | *as* METTRE. |
| **comprendre** | *as* PRENDRE. |
| **concevoir** | *as* RECEVOIR. |
| **conclure** | •*Pres.* conclus, concluons, concluent. •*Past hist.* conclus. •*Past part.* conclu. |
| **conduire** | •*Pres.* conduis, conduisons, conduisent. •*Impf.* conduisais. •*Past hist.* conduisis. •*Pres. sub.* conduise. •*Past part.* conduit. |
| **connaître** | •*Pres.* connais, connaît, connaissons. •*Impf.* connaissais. •*Past hist.* connus. •*Pres. sub.* connaisse. •*Past part.* connu. |
| **construire** | *as* CONDUIRE. |
| **contenir** | *as* TENIR. |
| **contraindre** | *as* ATTEINDRE (except *ai* replaces *ei*). |
| **contredire** | *as* DIRE except •*Pres.* vous contredisez. |
| **convaincre** | *as* VAINCRE. |
| **convenir** | *as* TENIR. |

| | |
|---|---|
| **corrompre** | *as* ROMPRE. |
| **coudre** | •*Pres.* couds, cousons, cousent. •*Impf.* cousais. •*Past hist.* cousis. •*Pres. sub.* couse. •*Past part.* cousu. |
| **courir** | •*Pres.* cours, courons, courent. •*Impf.* courais. •*Past hist.* courus. •*Fut.* courrai. •*Pres. sub.* coure. •*Past part.* couru. |
| **couvrir** | •*Pres.* couvre, couvrons. •*Impf.* couvrais. •*Pres. sub.* couvre. •*Past part.* couvert. |
| **craindre** | *as* ATTEINDRE (except *ai* replaces *ei*). |
| **croire** | •*Pres.* crois, croit, croyons, croyez, croient. •*Impf.* croyais. •*Past hist.* crus. •*Pres. sub.* croie, croyions. •*Past part.* cru. |
| **croître** | •*Pres.* crois, croît, croissons. •*Impf.* croissais. •*Past hist.* croîs. •*Pres. sub.* croisse. •*Past part.* crû, crue. |
| **cueillir** | •*Pres.* cueille, cueillons. •*Impf.* cueillais. •*Fut.* cueillerai. •*Pres. sub.* cueille. |
| **débattre** | *as* BATTRE. |
| **décevoir** | *as* RECEVOIR. |
| **découvrir** | *as* COUVRIR. |
| **décrire** | *as* ÉCRIRE. |
| **déduire** | *as* CONDUIRE. |
| **défaire** | *as* FAIRE. |
| **détenir** | *as* TENIR. |
| **détruire** | *as* CONDUIRE. |
| **devenir** | *as* TENIR. |
| **devoir** | •*Pres.* dois, devons, doivent. •*Impf.* devais. •*Past hist.* dus. •*Fut.* devrai. •*Pres. sub.* doive. •*Past part.* dû, due. |
| **dire** | •*Pres.* dis, dit, disons, dites, disent. •*Impf.* disais. •*Past hist.* dis. •*Past part.* dit. |
| **disparaître** | *as* CONNAÎTRE. |
| **dissoudre** | •*Pres.* dissous, dissolvons. •*Impf.* dissolvais. •*Pres. sub.* dissolve. •*Past part.* dissous, dissoute. |
| **distraire** | *as* EXTRAIRE. |
| **dormir** | •*Pres.* dors, dormons. •*Impf.* dormais. •*Pres. sub* dorme. |
| **écrire** | •*Pres.* écris, écrivons. •*Impf.* écrivais. •*Past hist.* écrivis. •*Pres. sub.* écrive. •*Past part.* écrit. |
| **élire** | *as* LIRE. |
| **émettre** | *as* METTRE. |
| **s'enfuir** | *as* FUIR. |
| **entreprendre** | *as* PRENDRE. |
| **entretenir** | *as* TENIR. |

| | |
|---|---|
| **envoyer** | •*Fut.* enverrai. |
| **éteindre** | *as* ATTEINDRE. |
| **être** | •*Pres.* suis, es, est, sommes, êtes, sont. •*Impf.* étais. •*Past hist.* fus, fut, fûmes, fûtes, furent. •*Fut.* serai. •*Pres. sub.* sois, soit, soyons, soyez, soient. •*Pres. part.* étant. •*Past part.* été. •*Imp.* sois, soyons, soyez. |
| **exclure** | *as* CONCLURE. |
| **extraire** | •*Pres.* extrais, extrayons. •*Impf.* extrayais. •*Pres. sub.* extraie. •*Past part.* extrait. |
| **faire** | •*Pres.* fais, fait, faisons, faites, font. •*Impf.* faisais. •*Past hist.* fis. *Fut.* ferai. •*Pres. sub.* fasse. •*Past part.* fait. |
| **falloir** | (impersonal) •*Pres.* faut. •*Impf.* fallait. •*Past hist.* fallut. •*Fut.* faudra. •*Pres. sub.* faille. •*Past part.* fallu. |
| **feindre** | *as* ATTEINDRE. |
| **fuir** | •*Pres.* fuis, fuyons, fuient. •*Impf.* fuyais. •*Past hist.* fuis. •*Pres sub.* fuie. •*Past part.* fui. |
| **inscrire** | *as* ÉCRIRE. |
| **instruire** | *as* CONDUIRE. |
| **interdire** | *as* DIRE except •*Pres.* vous interdisez. |
| **interrompre** | *as* ROMPRE. |
| **intervenir** | *as* TENIR. |
| **introduire** | *as* CONDUIRE. |
| **joindre** | *as* ATTEINDRE (except *oi* replaces *ei*). |
| **lire** | •*Pres.* lis, lit, lisons, lisez, lisent. •*Impf.* lisais. •*Past hist.* lus. •*Pres. sub.* lise. •*Past part.* lu. |
| **luire** | •*Pres.* luis, luisons. •*Impf.* luisais. •*Past hist.* luisis. •*Pres. sub.* luise. •*Past part.* lui. |
| **maintenir** | *as* TENIR. |
| **maudire** | •*Pres.* maudis, maudissons. •*Impf.* maudissais. •*Past hist.* maudis. •*Pres. sub.* maudisse. •*Past part.* maudit. |
| **mentir** | *as* SORTIR (except *en* replaces *or*). |
| **mettre** | •*Pres.* mets, met, mettons, mettez, mettent. •*Past hist.* mis. •*Past part.* mis. |
| **mourir** | •*Pres.* meurs, mourons, meurent. •*Impf.* mourais. •*Past hist.* mourus. •*Fut.* mourrai. •*Pres sub.* meure, mourions. •*Past part.* mort. |
| **mouvoir** | •*Pres.* meus, mouvons, meuvent. •*Impf.* mouvais. •*Fut.* mouvrai. •*Pres. sub.* meuve, mouvions. •*Past part.* mû, mue. |
| **naître** | •*Pres.* nais, naît, naissons. •*Impf.* naissais. •*Past hist.* naquis. •*Pres. sub.* naisse. •*Past part.* né. |
| **nuire** | *as* LUIRE. |
| **obtenir** | *as* TENIR. |

| | |
|---|---|
| **offrir, ouvrir** | *as* COUVRIR. |
| **omettre** | *as* METTRE. |
| **paraître** | *as* CONNAÎTRE. |
| **parcourir** | *as* COURIR. |
| **partir** | *as* SORTIR (except *ar* replaces *or*). |
| **parvenir** | *as* TENIR. |
| **peindre** | *as* ATTEINDRE. |
| **percevoir** | *as* RECEVOIR. |
| **permettre** | *as* METTRE. |
| **plaindre** | *as* ATTEINDRE (except *ai* replaces *ei*). |
| **plaire** | •*Pres.* plais, plaît, plaisons. •*Impf.* plaisais. •*Past hist.* plus. •*Pres. sub.* plaise. •*Past part.* plu. |
| **pleuvoir** | (impersonal) •*Pres.* pleut. •*Impf.* pleuvait. •*Past hist.* plut. •*Fut.* pleuvra. •*Pres. sub.* pleuve. •*Past part.* plu. |
| **poursuivre** | *as* SUIVRE. |
| **pourvoir** | *as* VOIR, except •*Fut.* pourvoirai. |
| **pouvoir** | •*Pres.* peux, peut, pouvons, pouvez, peuvent. •*Impf.* pouvais. •*Past hist.* pus. •*Fut.* pourrai. •*Pres. sub.* puisse. •*Past part.* pu. |
| **prédire** | *as* DIRE, except •*Pres.* vous prédisez. |
| **prendre** | •*Pres.* prends, prenons, prennent. •*Impf.* prenais. •*Past hist.* pris. •*Pres. sub.* prenne, prenions. •*Past part.* pris. |
| **prescrire** | *as* ÉCRIRE. |
| **prévenir** | *as* TENIR. |
| **prévoir** | *as* VOIR, except •*Fut.* prévoirai. |
| **produire** | *as* CONDUIRE. |
| **promettre** | *as* METTRE. |
| **provenir** | *as* TENIR. |
| **recevoir** | •*Pres.* reçois, recevons, reçoivent. •*Impf.* recevais. •*Past hist.* reçus. •*Fut.* recevrai. •*Pres. sub.* reçoive, recevions. •*Past part.* reçu. |
| **reconduire** | *as* CONDUIRE. |
| **reconnaître** | *as* CONNAÎTRE. |
| **reconstruire** | *as* CONDUIRE. |
| **recouvrir** | *as* COUVRIR. |
| **recueillir** | *as* CUEILLIR. |
| **redire** | *as* DIRE. |
| **réduire** | *as* CONDUIRE. |
| **refaire** | *as* FAIRE. |
| **rejoindre** | *as* ATTEINDRE (except *oi* replaces *ei*). |

**remettre** *as* METTRE.

**renvoyer** *as* ENVOYER.

**repartir** *as* SORTIR (except *ar* replaces *or*).

**reprendre** *as* PRENDRE.

**reproduire** *as* CONDUIRE.

**résoudre** •*Pres.* résous, résolvons. •*Impf.* résolvais.
•*Past hist.* résolus. •*Pres. sub.* résolve.
•*Past part.* résolu.

**ressortir** *as* SORTIR.

**restreindre** *as* ATTEINDRE.

**retenir** *as* TENIR.

**revenir** *as* TENIR.

**revivre** *as* VIVRE.

**revoir** *as* VOIR.

**rire** •*Pres.* ris, rit, rions, riez, rient. •*Impf.* riais.
•*Past hist.* ris. •*Pres. sub.* rie, riions. •*Past part.* ri.

**rompre** *as* VENDRE (regular), except •*Pres.* il rompt.

**satisfaire** *as* FAIRE.

**savoir** •*Pres.* sais, sait, savons, savez, savent. •*Impf.* savais.
•*Past hist.* sus. •*Fut.* saurai. •*Pres. sub.* sache, sachions.
•*Pres. part.* sachant. •*Past part.* su. •*Imp.* sache,
sachons, sachez.

**séduire** *as* CONDUIRE.

**sentir** *as* SORTIR (except *en* replaces *or*).

**servir** •*Pres.* sers, servons. •*Impf.* servais. •*Pres. sub.* serve.

**sortir** •*Pres.* sors, sortons. •*Impf.* sortais. •*Pres. sub.* sorte.

**souffrir** *as* COUVRIR.

**soumettre** *as* METTRE.

**soustraire** *as* EXTRAIRE.

**soutenir** *as* TENIR.

**suffire** •*Pres.* suffis, suffisons. •*Impf.* suffisais.
•*Past hist.* suffis. •*Pres. sub.* suffise. •*Past part.* suffi.

**suivre** •*Pres.* suis, suivons. •*Impf.* suivais. •*Past hist.* suivis.
•*Pres. sub.* suive. •*Past part.* suivi.

**surprendre** *as* PRENDRE.

**survivre** *as* VIVRE.

**taire** •*Pres.* tais, taisons. •*Impf.* taisais. •*Past hist.* tus.
•*Pres. sub.* taise. •*Past part.* tu.

**teindre** *as* ATTEINDRE.

**tenir** •*Pres.* tiens, tenons, tiennent. •*Impf.* tenais.
•*Past hist.* tins, tint, tînmes, tîntes, tinrent.
•*Fut.* tiendrai. •*Pres. sub.* tienne. •*Past part.* tenu.

**traduire** *as* CONDUIRE.

| | |
|---|---|
| **traire** | *as* EXTRAIRE. |
| **transmettre** | *as* METTRE. |
| **vaincre** | •*Pres.* vaincs, vainc, vainquons. •*Impf.* vainquais. •*Past hist.* vainquis. •*Pres. sub.* vainque. •*Past part.* vaincu. |
| **valoir** | •*Pres.* vaux, vaut, valons, valez, valent. •*Impf.* valais. •*Past hist.* valus. •*Fut.* vaudrai. •*Pres. sub.* vaille. •*Past part.* valu. |
| **venir** | *as* TENIR. |
| **vivre** | •*Pres.* vis, vit, vivons, vivez, vivent. •*Impf.* vivais. •*Past hist.* vécus. •*Pres. sub.* vive. •*Past part.* vécu. |
| **voir** | •*Pres.* vois, voyons, voient. •*Impf.* voyais. •*Past hist.* vis. •*Fut.* verrai. •*Pres. sub.* voie, voyions. •*Past part.* vu. |
| **vouloir** | •*Pres.* veux, veut, voulons, voulez, veulent. •*Impf.* voulais. •*Past hist.* voulus. •*Fut.* voudrai. •*Pres. sub.* veuille, voulions. •*Past part.* voulu. •*Imp.* veuille, veuillons, veuillez. |